America's
Top-Rated Cities:
A Statistical Handbook

Volume 3

2019
Twenty-sixth Edition

America's
Top-Rated Cities:
A Statistical Handbook

Volume 3: Central Region

A UNIVERSAL REFERENCE BOOK

Grey House
Publishing

Cover image – Des Moines, Iowa

PRESIDENT:	Richard Gottlieb
PUBLISHER:	Leslie Mackenzie
EDITORIAL DIRECTOR:	Laura Mars
SENIOR EDITOR:	David Garoogian

RESEARCHER & WRITER:	Jael Bridgemahon
PRODUCTION MANAGER:	Kristen Hayes
MARKETING DIRECTOR:	Jessica Moody

A Universal Reference Book
Grey House Publishing, Inc.
4919 Route 22
Amenia, NY 12501
518.789.8700 • Fax 845.373.6390
www.greyhouse.com
books@greyhouse.com

Twenty-sixth Edition
Printed in Canada

Publisher's Cataloging-in-Publication Data
(Prepared by The Donohue Group, Inc.)

America's top-rated cities. Vol. III, Central region : a statistical handbook. — 1992-

v. : ill. ; cm.
Annual, 1995-
Irregular, 1992-1993
ISSN: 1082-7102

1. Cities and towns--Ratings--Central States--Statistics--Periodicals. 2. Cities and towns--Central States--Statistics--Periodicals. 3. Social indicators--Central States--Periodicals. 4. Quality of life--Central States--Statistics--Periodicals. 5. Central States--Social conditions--Statistics--Periodicals. I. Title: America's top rated cities. II. Title: Central region

HT123.5.S6 A44
307.76/0973/05   95644648

4-Volume Set	ISBN: 978-1-64265-079-2
Volume 1	ISBN: 978-1-64265-080-8
Volume 2	ISBN: 978-1-64265-081-5
Volume 3	**ISBN: 978-1-64265-082-2**
Volume 4	ISBN: 978-1-64265-083-9

Des Moines, Iowa

Evansville, Indiana

Fargo, North Dakota

Fort Wayne, Indiana

Grand Rapids, Michigan

Green Bay, Wisconsin

Indianapolis, Indiana

Kansas City, Missouri

Lincoln, Nebraska

Little Rock, Arkansas

Madison, Wisconsin

Minneapolis, Minnesota

Oklahoma City, Oklahoma

Omaha, Nebraska

Peoria, Illinois

Rochester, Minnesota

Introduction

This twenty-sixth edition of *America's Top-Rated Cities* is a concise, statistical, 4-volume work identifying America's top-rated cities with estimated populations of approximately 100,000 or more. It profiles 100 cities that have received high marks for business and living from prominent sources such as *Forbes, Fortune, U.S. News & World Report, The Brookings Institution, U.S. Conference of Mayors, The Wall Street Journal,* and *CNNMoney.*

Each volume covers a different region of the country—Southern, Western, Central and Eastern—and includes a detailed Table of Contents, City Chapters, Appendices, and Maps. Each city chapter incorporates information from hundreds of resources to create the following major sections:

- **Background**—lively narrative of significant, up-to-date news for both businesses and residents. These combine historical facts with current developments, "known-for" annual events, and climate data.
- **Rankings**—fun-to-read, bulleted survey results from over 250 books, magazines, and online articles, ranging from general (Great Places to Live), to specific (Friendliest Cities), and everything in between.
- **Statistical Tables**—126 tables and detailed topics that offer an unparalleled view of each city's Business and Living Environments. They are carefully organized with data that is easy to read and understand.
- **Appendices**—five in all, appearing at the end of each volume. These range from listings of Metropolitan Statistical Areas to Comparative Statistics for all 100 cities.

This new edition of *America's Top-Rated Cities* includes cities that not only surveyed well, but ranked highest using our unique weighting system. We looked at violent crime, property crime, population growth, median household income, housing affordability, poverty, educational attainment, and unemployment. You'll find that a number of American cities remain "top-rated" despite less-than-stellar numbers. New York, Los Angeles, and Miami remain world-class cities despite challenges faced by many large urban centers. A final consideration is location—we strive to include as many states in the country as possible.

Part of this year's city criteria is that it be the "primary" city in a given metropolitan area. For example, if the metro area is Raleigh-Cary, NC, we would consider Raleigh, not Cary. This allows for a more equitable core city comparison. In general, the core city of a metro area is defined as having substantial influence on neighboring cities.

New to this edition are: Evansville, IN; Tyler, TX; and Visalia, CA.

Praise for previous editions:

> "...[ATRC] has...proven its worth to a wide audience...from businesspeople and corporations planning to launch, relocate, or expand their operations to market researchers, real estate professionals, urban planners, job-seekers, students...interested in...reliable, attractively presented statistical information about larger U.S. cities."
> —ARBA

> "...For individuals or businesses looking to relocate, this resource conveniently reports rankings from more than 300 sources for the top 100 US cities. Recommended..."
> —Choice

> "...While patrons are becoming increasingly comfortable locating statistical data online, there is still something to be said for the ease associated with such a compendium of otherwise scattered data. A well-organized and appropriate update..."
> —Library Journal

BACKGROUND

Each city begins with an informative Background that combines history with current events. These narratives often reflect changes that have occurred during the past year, and touch on the city's environment, politics, employment, cultural offerings, and climate, and include interesting trivia. For example: Peregrine Falcons were rehabilitated and released into the wild from Boise City's World Center for Birds of Prey; Gainesville is home to a 6,800 square-foot living Butterfly Rainforest; Grand Rapids was the first city to introduce fluoride into its drinking water in 1945; and Thomas Alva Edison discovered the phonograph and the light bulb in the city whose name was changed in 1954 from Raritan Township to Edison in his honor.

RANKINGS

This section has rankings from a possible 263 books, articles, and reports. For easy reference, these Rankings are categorized into 16 topics including Business/Finance, Dating/Romance, and Health/Fitness.

The Rankings are presented in an easy-to-read, bulleted format and include results from both annual surveys and one-shot studies. **Fastest-Growing Economies** . . . **Best Drivers** . . . **Most Well-Read** . . . **Most Wired** . . . **Healthiest for Women** . . . **Best for Minority Entrepreneurs** . . . **Safest** . . . **Best to Retire** . . . **Most Polite** . . . **Best for Moviemakers** . . . **Most Frugal** . . . **Best for Bikes** . . . **Most Cultured** . . . **Least Stressful** . . . **Best for Families** . . . **Most Romantic** . . . **Most Charitable** . . . **Most Attractive** . . . **Best for Telecommuters** . . . **Best for Singles** . . . **Nerdiest** . . . **Fittest** . . . **Best for Dogs** . . . **Most Tattooed** . . . **Best for Wheelchair Users**, and more.

Sources for these Rankings include both well-known magazines and other media, including *Forbes, Fortune, USA Today, Condé Nast Traveler, Gallup, Kiplinger's Personal Finance, Men's Journal,* and *Travel + Leisure,* as well as *Asthma & Allergy Foundation of America, American Lung Association, League of American Bicyclists, The Advocate, National Civic League, National Alliance to End Homelessness, MovieMaker Magazine, National Insurance Crime Bureau, Center for Digital Government, National Association of Home Builders,* and the *Milken Institute.*

Rankings cover a variety of geographic areas; see Appendix B for full geographic definitions.

STATISTICAL TABLES

Each city chapter includes a possible 126 tables and detailed topics—69 in BUSINESS and 57 in LIVING. Over 95% of statistical data has been updated. In addition to more detailed data on individual income tax rates, the Health Risk section now includes four tables: Health Risk Factors; Health Screening and Vaccination Rates; Disability Status; and Acute and Chronic Health Conditions. New subcategories include shingles vaccination and high blood pressure rates. The table on Disability Status is brand new and includes the following subcategories: adults who reported being deaf or blind; adults who reported having difficulty doing errands alone; adults who reported difficulty dressing or bathing; adults who reported having serious difficulty concentrating/remembering/making decisions; adults who reported having serious difficulty walking or climbing stairs; and adults who reported being limited in their usual daily activities due to arthritis.

Business Environment includes hard facts and figures on 10 major categories, including City Finances, Demographics, Income, Economy, Employment, and Taxes. *Living Environment* includes 11 major categories, such as Cost of Living, Housing, Health, Education, Safety, Recreation, and Climate.

To compile the Statistical Tables, editors have again turned to a wide range of sources, some well known, such as the *U.S. Census Bureau, U.S. Environmental Protection Agency, Bureau of Labor Statistics, Centers for Disease Control and Prevention,* and the *Federal Bureau of Investigation,* plus others like *The Council for Community and Economic Research, Texas Transportation Institute,* and *Federation of Tax Administrators.*

APPENDICES: Data for all cities appear in all volumes.
- **Appendix A**—*Comparative Statistics*
- **Appendix B**—*Metropolitan Area Definitions*
- **Appendix C**—*Government Type and County*
- **Appendix D**—*Chambers of Commerce and Economic Development Organizations*
- **Appendix E**—*State Departments of Labor and Employment*

Material provided by public and private agencies and organizations was supplemented by original research, numerous library sources and Internet sites. *America's Top-Rated Cities, 2019,* is designed for a wide range of readers: private individuals considering relocating a residence or business; professionals considering expanding their businesses or changing careers; corporations considering relocating, opening up additional offices or creating new divisions; government agencies; general and market researchers; real estate consultants; human resource personnel; urban planners; investors; and urban government students.

Customers who purchase the four-volume set receive free online access to *America's Top-Rated Cities* allowing them to download city reports and sort and rank by 50-plus data points.

AMERICA'S TOP-RATED CITIES

Seattle
Seattle-Tacoma-Bellevue, WA

WASHINGTON

MONTANA

NORTH DAKOTA

Portland
Portland-Vancouver-Hillsboro, OR-WA

Salem
Salem, OR

Eugene
Eugene, OR

OREGON

IDAHO

Boise City
Boise City-Nampa, ID

Billings
Billings, MT

WYOMING

SOUTH DAKOTA

NEBRASKA

CALIFORNIA

Santa Rosa
Santa Rosa, CA

Reno
Reno, NV

NEVADA

Salt Lake City
Salt Lake City, UT

Provo
Provo-Orem, UT

Fort Collins
Fort Collins-Loveland, CO

Greeley
Greeley, CO

Boulder
Boulder, CO

Denver
Denver-Aurora-Lakewood, CO

Colorado Springs
Colorado Springs, CO

San Francisco
San Francisco-Oakland-Hayward, CA

San Jose
San Jose-Sunnyvale-Santa Clara, CA

Visalia
Visalia-Porterville, CA

UTAH

COLORADO

KS

Las Vegas
Las Vegas-Henderson-Paradise, NV

Los Angeles
Los Angeles-Long Beach-Anaheim, CA

San Diego
San Diego-Carlsbad, CA

ARIZONA

Phoenix
Phoenix-Mesa-Scottsdale, AZ

Albuquerque
Albuquerque, NM

NEW MEXICO

TEXAS

Las Cruces
Las Cruces, NM

ALASKA

Anchorage, AK

Anchorage

Urban Honolulu, HI

Honolulu

HAWAII

AMERICA'S TOP-RATED CITIES

CBSA: Core Based Statistical Area

STATE

○ Top Rated City

Western Region

©Larry Mandelin 2019

N
W E
S

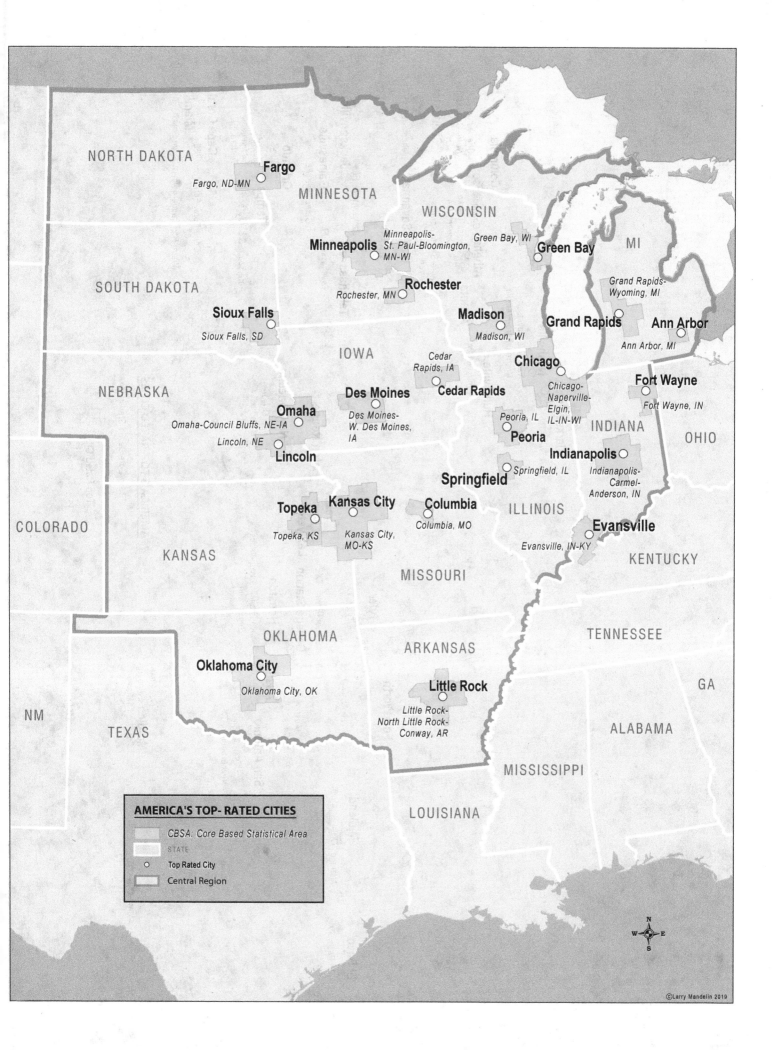

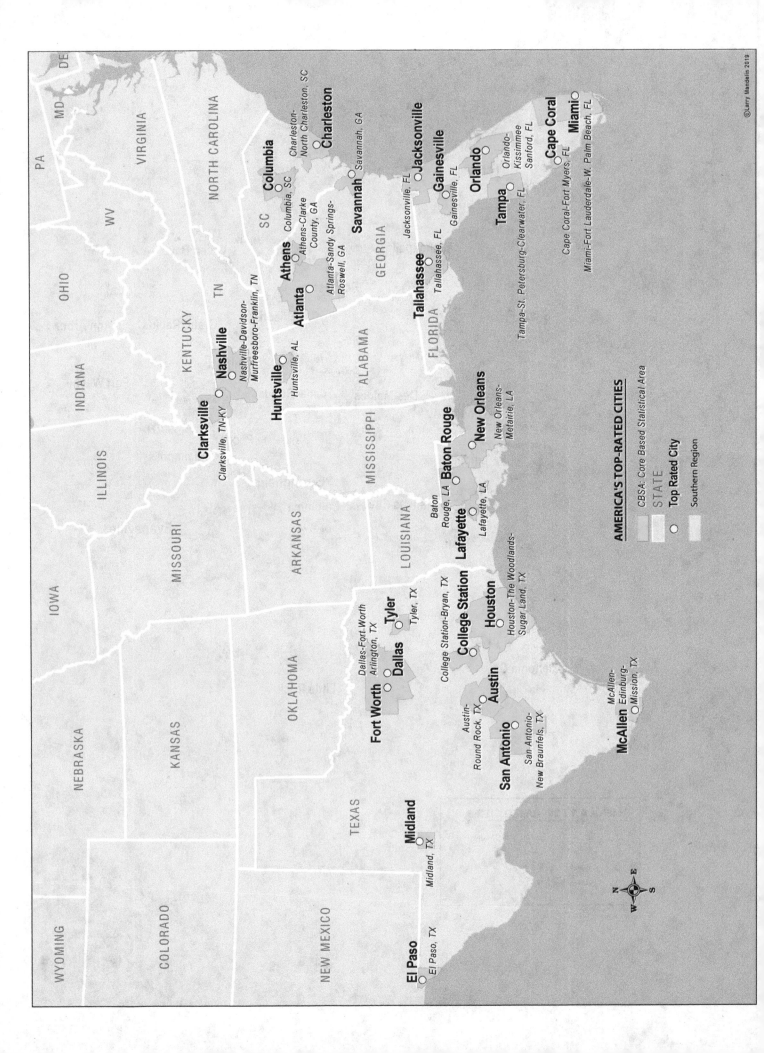

AMERICA'S TOP-RATED CITIES

CBSA: Core Based Statistical Area
STATE
○ Top Rated City
Southern Region

©Larry Mandelin 2019

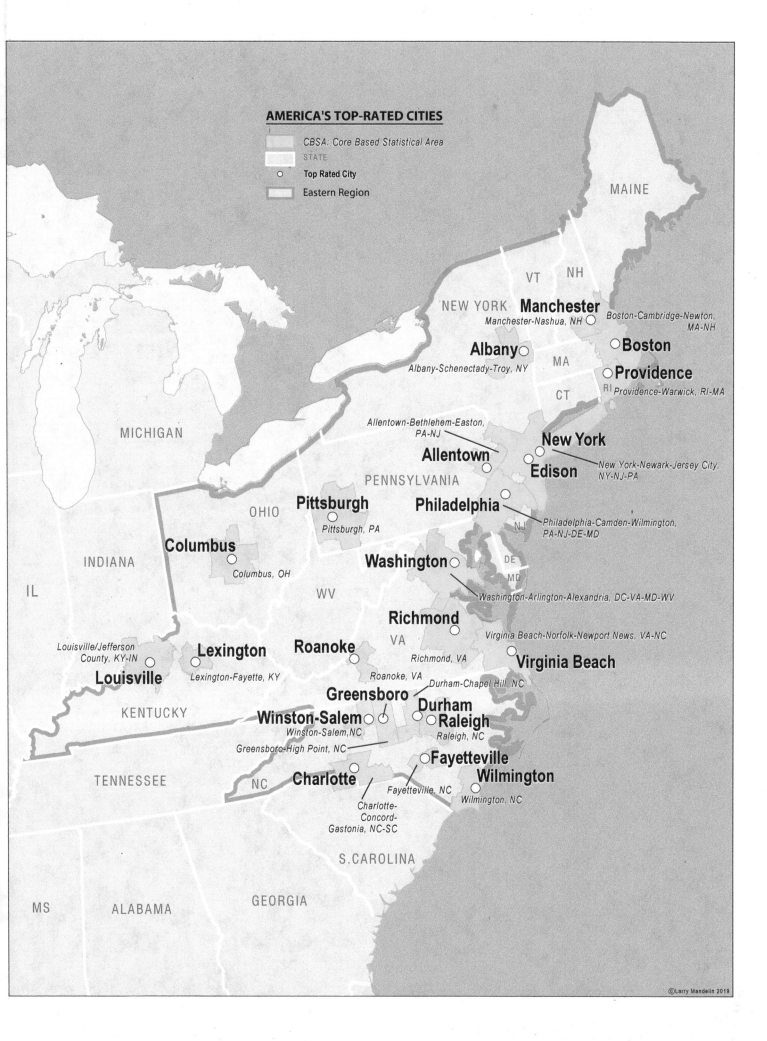

AMERICA'S TOP-RATED CITIES

CBSA: Core Based Statistical Area
STATE
○ Top Rated City
Eastern Region

MAINE

VT   NH

NEW YORK   **Manchester**
Manchester-Nashua, NH ○   Boston-Cambridge-Newton,
MA-NH

Albany ○   MA   ○ **Boston**

Providence ○ **Providence**
RI Providence-Warwick, RI-MA
CT

Allentown-Bethlehem-Easton,
PA-NJ   **New York**

Allentown ○○ **Edison**   New York-Newark-Jersey City,
NY-NJ-PA

PENNSYLVANIA

OHIO   **Pittsburgh** ○   **Philadelphia** ○
Pittsburgh, PA   NJ   Philadelphia-Camden-Wilmington,
PA-NJ-DE-MD

Columbus ○   DE
Columbus, OH   MD

INDIANA   **Washington** ○
WV   Washington-Arlington-Alexandria, DC-VA-MD-WV

IL   **Richmond** ○
VA   Virginia Beach-Norfolk-Newport News, VA-NC

Louisville/Jefferson   **Roanoke** ○   Richmond, VA
County, KY-IN   **Lexington** ○   **Virginia Beach** ○
Louisville ○   Lexington-Fayette, KY   Roanoke, VA
Durham-Chapel Hill, NC
Greensboro ○○ **Durham**
KENTUCKY   **Winston-Salem** ○○   ○ **Raleigh**
Winston-Salem, NC   Raleigh, NC
Greensboro-High Point, NC
Fayetteville ○
TENNESSEE   NC   **Charlotte** ○   **Wilmington**
Charlotte ○   Fayetteville, NC
Charlotte-   Wilmington, NC
Concord-
Gastonia, NC-SC

S.CAROLINA

MS   ALABAMA   GEORGIA

©Larry Mandelin 2019

Ann Arbor, Michigan

Background

Ann Arbor is located on the Huron River, 36 miles west of Detroit. It was founded in 1824 by John Allen and Elisha W. Rumsey, two East Coast entrepreneurs who named the settlement for their wives—both Ann—and for the community's location within natural groves. In 1851, Ann Arbor was chartered as a city.

After the arrival of the Michigan Central Railroad in 1839, the settlement developed as an agricultural center, and it continues to be such for the rich agricultural area surrounding it.

Before the arrival of settlers, the Ojibwa tribe roamed the area, which they called Washtenaw—the land beyond—which now serves as the county for which Ann Arbor is the seat.

The city manufactures machinery, tools, steel ball bearings, scientific instruments, doors and blinds, cameras, and coil springs. Lasers, computers, hospital and laboratory equipment, automotive parts, and high-tech/software products are also vibrant industries. Major opportunities exist in health care, with the University of Michigan Medical Center and St. Joseph Mercy Hospital employing over 11,000. The region is also strong in book printing and manufacturing.

Ann Arbor's population is about one-third college or university students. The University of Michigan, the town's largest employer, played a prominent role in Ann Arbor's development as a major Midwest center for aeronautical, space, nuclear, chemical, and metallurgical research. The university also houses fascinating exhibits within its Museum of Natural History, known for an outstanding collection of dinosaur and mastodon skeletons and fossils, detailed dioramas of prehistoric life and Native American cultures, exhibits on Michigan wildlife, anthropology, and geology, and even its planetarium. Also located at the university is a 250-acre botanical garden with a conservatory featuring tropical, temperate, and arid houses, over six miles of nature trails, and a variety of outdoor display gardens. The University of Michigan Museum of Art (UMMA), with more than 18,000 works of art from all over the world, and the university's Detroit Observatory, a historic scientific laboratory built in 1854, make this a truly unique, world-class institution. UMMA expanded 2009, more than doubling its space.

The university is also home to the Gerald R. Ford School of Policy, named in honor of the former President, who graduated from the university in 1935. The 85,000 square-foot Joan and Sanford Weill Hall, designed by the noted firm of Robert A. M. Stern Architects, opened in 2006. The University of Michigan is also the site of the Ford Presidential Library.

Other cultural attractions in the city include: the African-American Cultural and Historical Museum; the Ann Arbor Art Center, including two contemporary art galleries, and art classes for all ages; the Ann Arbor Hands-On Museum, offering interactive exhibits in physics, mathematics, biology, physiology, botany and geology; and Gallery Von Glahn, specializing in serigraphs, lithographs, and original bronze and porcelain art. The Detroit Institute of Arts displays Diego Rivera's spectacular "Detroit Industry" frescoes. In addition, Ann Arbor offers dozens more artists' guilds, museums, top-rated art fairs, music and film festivals, plus its share of fine restaurants with cuisine ranging from Italian to Ethiopian.

In nearby Dearborn are the Henry Ford Estate and Museum and the Automotive Hall of Fame. Historic Ypsilanti hosts the annual Orphan Car Show, which pays homage to elegant vehicles of a bygone era such as the Kaiser, Triumph and Packard.

With its high-tech industries and great university, Ann Arbor is an exceptionally livable city and full of cultural events, including an annual arts fair, and jazz, film, and summer festivals. The city boasts 157 city parks, seven golf courses and endless trails.

Located in the humid continental climate zone, Ann Arbor's summers are hot, winters are cold, and there is an above-average occurrence of snow and rain. Proximity to the Great Lakes causes extreme temperatures to be moderated, but also results in high humidity and cloud cover two-thirds of the year.

Rankings

General Rankings

- Ann Arbor was selected as one of the best places to live in the United States by *Money* magazine. The city ranked #47 out of 50. This year's list focused on cities with populations of 50,000 or greater. Beginning with a pool of 583 candidates, editors looked at 70 separate types of data, from local economy and housing market to schools, diversity and amenities—and then sent reporters to interview residents, search neighborhoods and look for other intangibles. *Money, "Best Places to Live, 2018" September 17, 2018*

Business/Finance Rankings

- The personal finance site NerdWallet analyzed 183 American metropolitan areas with populations over 250,000 and more than 15,000 businesses to rank where entrepreneurs find the most success. Criteria included area economy, annual income, housing cost, unemployment rate, and the success rate of area businesses. Ann Arbor ranked #76. *www.nerdwallet.com, "Best Places to Start a Business," April 27, 2015*

- Using data from the Council for Community and Economic Research's 2014 cost of living index, NerdWallet ranked the 100 most affordable cities in America. Median income was compared with cost of living to find truly affordable places. Ann Arbor ranked #34. *NerdWallet.com, "America's Most Affordable Places," May 18, 2015*

- The Ann Arbor metro area appeared on the Milken Institute "2018 Best Performing Cities" list. Rank: #87 out of 200 large metro areas. Criteria: job growth; wage and salary growth; high-tech output growth. *Milken Institute, "Best-Performing Cities 2018," January 24, 2019*

- *Forbes* ranked the 200 most populous metro areas to determine the nation's "Best Places for Business and Careers." The Ann Arbor metro area was ranked #51. Criteria: costs (business and living); job growth (past and projected); income growth; quality of life; educational attainment (college and high school); projected economic growth; cultural and recreational opportunities; net migration patterns; number of highly ranked colleges. *Forbes, "The Best Places for Business and Careers 2018: Seattle Leads the Way," October 24, 2018*

Dating/Romance Rankings

- Ann Arbor was selected as one of America's best cities for singles by the readers of *Travel + Leisure* in their annual "America's Favorite Cities" survey. Criteria included good-looking locals, cool shopping, an active bar scene and hipster-magnet coffee bars. *Travel + Leisure, "Best Cities in America for Singles," July 21, 2017*

- Ann Arbor was selected as one of the nation's most romantic cities with 100,000 or more residents by Amazon.com. The city ranked #10 of 20. Criteria: per capita sales of romance novels, relationship books, romantic comedy movies, romantic music, and sexual wellness products. *Amazon.com, "Top 20 Most Romantic Cities in the U.S.," February 1, 2017*

Education Rankings

- Personal finance website *WalletHub* analyzed the 150 largest U.S. metropolitan statistical areas to determine where the most educated Americans are choosing to settle. Criteria: education quality and attainment gap; education levels; percentage of workers with degrees; public school quality rankings; quality and size of each metro area's universities. Ann Arbor was ranked #1 (#1 = most educated city). *www.WalletHub.com, "2018's Most and Least Educated Cities in America," July 24, 2018*

Environmental Rankings

- Niche compiled a list of the nation's snowiest cities, based on the National Oceanic and Atmospheric Administration's 30-year average snowfall data. Among cities with a population of at least 50,000, Ann Arbor ranked #19. *Niche.com, Top 25 Snowiest Cities in America, December 10, 2018*

Food/Drink Rankings

- Ann Arbor was identified as one of the cities in America most likely to order vegetarian menu options by GrubHub.com, the nation's largest food ordering service. The city ranked #9 out of 10. Criteria: percentage of vegetarian restaurants. *GrubHub.com, "Top U.S. Cities for Vegans and Vegetarians," November 17, 2015*

Health/Fitness Rankings

- The Ann Arbor metro area ranked #12 out of 189 in The Gallup-Healthways Well-Being Index. Criteria: purpose; social well being; financial health; community and physical health. Results are based on telephone interviews with adults, aged 18 and older, living in metropolitan areas in the 50 U.S. states and the District of Columbia. *Gallup-Healthways, "State of American Well-Being, 2017 Community Well-Being Rankings" March 2018*

Real Estate Rankings

- Ann Arbor was ranked #115 out of 237 metro areas in terms of housing affordability in 2018 by the National Association of Home Builders (#1 = most affordable). Criteria: the share of homes sold in that area affordable to a family earning the local median income, based on standard mortgage underwriting criteria. *National Association of Home Builders®, NAHB-Wells Fargo Housing Opportunity Index, 4th Quarter 2018*

Safety Rankings

- The National Insurance Crime Bureau ranked 382 metro areas in the U.S. in terms of per capita rates of vehicle theft. The Ann Arbor metro area ranked #297 (#1 = highest rate). Criteria: number of vehicle theft offenses per 100,000 inhabitants in 2017. *National Insurance Crime Bureau, "Hot Spots 2017," July 12, 2018*

Seniors/Retirement Rankings

- From its Best Cities for Successful Aging indexes, the Milken Institute generated rankings for metropolitan areas, weighing data in nine categories—health care, wellness, living arrangements, transportation and convenience, financial characteristics, education, employment, community engagement, and overall livability. The Ann Arbor metro area was ranked #6 overall in the small metro area category. *Milken Institute, "Best Cities for Successful Aging, 2017" March 14, 2017*

Women/Minorities Rankings

- NerdWallet examined data for 529 U.S. cities and ranked them based on the environment for working women. Ann Arbor ranked #7. Criteria: women's earnings; labor force participation rate; cost of living; unemployment rate. *www.nerdwallet.com, "Best Cities for Women in the Workforce 2016," April 4, 2016*

Business Environment

CITY FINANCES

City Government Finances

Component	2016 ($000)	2016 ($ per capita)
Total Revenues	253,793	2,168
Total Expenditures	281,265	2,403
Debt Outstanding	313,838	2,681
Cash and Securities[1]	669,364	5,718

Note: (1) Cash and security holdings of a government at the close of its fiscal year, including those of its dependent agencies, utilities, and liquor stores.
Source: U.S. Census Bureau, State & Local Government Finances 2016

City Government Revenue by Source

Source	2016 ($000)	2016 ($ per capita)	2016 (%)
General Revenue			
From Federal Government	17,668	151	7.0
From State Government	21,859	187	8.6
From Local Governments	3,178	27	1.3
Taxes			
Property	91,519	782	36.1
Sales and Gross Receipts	2,255	19	0.9
Personal Income	0	0	0.0
Corporate Income	0	0	0.0
Motor Vehicle License	0	0	0.0
Other Taxes	5,115	44	2.0
Current Charges	67,732	579	26.7
Liquor Store	0	0	0.0
Utility	24,054	205	9.5
Employee Retirement	6,282	54	2.5

Source: U.S. Census Bureau, State & Local Government Finances 2016

City Government Expenditures by Function

Function	2016 ($000)	2016 ($ per capita)	2016 (%)
General Direct Expenditures			
Air Transportation	579	4	0.2
Corrections	0	0	0.0
Education	0	0	0.0
Employment Security Administration	0	0	0.0
Financial Administration	3,319	28	1.2
Fire Protection	15,790	134	5.6
General Public Buildings	0	0	0.0
Governmental Administration, Other	2,223	19	0.8
Health	0	0	0.0
Highways	34,035	290	12.1
Hospitals	0	0	0.0
Housing and Community Development	19,148	163	6.8
Interest on General Debt	7,863	67	2.8
Judicial and Legal	4,260	36	1.5
Libraries	0	0	0.0
Parking	21,789	186	7.7
Parks and Recreation	13,331	113	4.7
Police Protection	26,665	227	9.5
Public Welfare	0	0	0.0
Sewerage	39,576	338	14.1
Solid Waste Management	19,033	162	6.8
Veterans' Services	0	0	0.0
Liquor Store	0	0	0.0
Utility	21,907	187	7.8
Employee Retirement	33,960	290	12.1

Source: U.S. Census Bureau, State & Local Government Finances 2016

DEMOGRAPHICS

Population Growth

Area	1990 Census	2000 Census	2010 Census	2017* Estimate	Population Growth (%)	
					1990-2017	2010-2017
City	111,018	114,024	113,934	119,303	7.5	4.7
MSA[1]	282,937	322,895	344,791	361,509	27.8	4.8
U.S.	248,709,873	281,421,906	308,745,538	321,004,407	29.1	4.0

Note: (1) Figures cover the Ann Arbor, MI Metropolitan Statistical Area—see Appendix B for areas included;
(*) 2013-2017 5-year estimated population
Source: U.S. Census Bureau, 1990 Census, Census 2000, Census 2010, 2013-2017 American Community
Survey 5-Year Estimates

Household Size

Area	Persons in Household (%)							Average Household Size
	One	Two	Three	Four	Five	Six	Seven or More	
City	35.8	35.8	12.3	10.7	3.2	1.4	0.9	2.30
MSA[1]	30.2	35.8	13.8	12.5	4.9	1.7	1.1	2.50
U.S.	27.7	33.8	15.7	13.0	6.0	2.3	1.4	2.60

Note: (1) Figures cover the Ann Arbor, MI Metropolitan Statistical Area—see Appendix B for areas included
Source: U.S. Census Bureau, 2013-2017 American Community Survey 5-Year Estimates

Race

Area	White Alone[2] (%)	Black Alone[2] (%)	Asian Alone[2] (%)	AIAN[3] Alone[2] (%)	NHOPI[4] Alone[2] (%)	Other Race Alone[2] (%)	Two or More Races (%)
City	72.0	7.0	15.9	0.4	0.0	0.5	4.2
MSA[1]	73.9	11.9	8.7	0.3	0.0	0.7	4.4
U.S.	73.0	12.7	5.4	0.8	0.2	4.8	3.1

Note: (1) Figures cover the Ann Arbor, MI Metropolitan Statistical Area—see Appendix B for areas included;
(2) Alone is defined as not being in combination with one or more other races; (3) American Indian and Alaska
Native; (4) Native Hawaiian and Other Pacific Islander
Source: U.S. Census Bureau, 2013-2017 American Community Survey 5-Year Estimates

Hispanic or Latino Origin

Area	Total (%)	Mexican (%)	Puerto Rican (%)	Cuban (%)	Other (%)
City	4.4	1.9	0.3	0.2	1.9
MSA[1]	4.5	2.4	0.3	0.2	1.7
U.S.	17.6	11.1	1.7	0.7	4.1

Note: Persons of Hispanic or Latino origin can be of any race; (1) Figures cover the Ann Arbor, MI
Metropolitan Statistical Area—see Appendix B for areas included
Source: U.S. Census Bureau, 2013-2017 American Community Survey 5-Year Estimates

Segregation

Type	Segregation Indices[1]				Percent Change		
	1990	2000	2010	2010 Rank[2]	1990-2000	1990-2010	2000-2010
Black/White	n/a	n/a	n/a	n/a	n/a	n/a	n/a
Asian/White	n/a	n/a	n/a	n/a	n/a	n/a	n/a
Hispanic/White	n/a	n/a	n/a	n/a	n/a	n/a	n/a

Note: All figures cover the Metropolitan Statistical Area—see Appendix B for areas included; Figures are based
on an analysis of 1990, 2000, and 2010 Census Decennial Census tract data by William H. Frey, Brookings
Institution and the University of Michigan Social Science Data Analysis Network. In this analysis all racial
groups (whites, blacks, and asians) are non-Hispanic members of those races. Hispanics are shown as a
separate category; (1) Segregation Indices are Dissimilarity Indices that measure the degree to which the
minority group is distributed differently than whites across census tracts. They range from 0 (complete
integration) to 100 (complete segregation) where the value indicates the percentage of the minority group that
needs to move to be distributed exactly like whites; (2) Ranges from 1 (most segregated) to 102 (least
segregated); n/a not available.
Source: www.CensusScope.org

Ancestry

Area	German	Irish	English	American	Italian	Polish	French[2]	Scottish	Dutch
City	17.6	9.4	9.8	4.9	5.0	6.6	3.2	2.6	2.2
MSA[1]	20.1	10.5	10.3	7.2	4.7	6.8	3.2	2.6	2.2
U.S.	14.1	10.1	7.5	6.6	5.3	2.9	2.5	1.7	1.3

Note: Figures are the percentage of the total population reporting a particular ancestry. The nine most commonly reported ancestries in the U.S. are shown. Figures include multiple ancestries (e.g. if a person reported being Irish and Italian, they were included in both columns); (1) Figures cover the Ann Arbor, MI Metropolitan Statistical Area—see Appendix B for areas included; (2) Excludes Basque
Source: U.S. Census Bureau, 2013-2017 American Community Survey 5-Year Estimates

Foreign-Born Population

Area	Percent of Population Born in								
	Any Foreign Country	Asia	Mexico	Europe	Carribean	Central America[2]	South America	Africa	Canada
City	18.6	11.9	0.4	3.3	0.2	0.2	0.8	0.8	0.8
MSA[1]	12.0	7.0	0.4	2.1	0.2	0.4	0.5	0.7	0.6
U.S.	13.4	4.1	3.6	1.5	1.3	1.0	0.9	0.6	0.3

Note: (1) Figures cover the Ann Arbor, MI Metropolitan Statistical Area—see Appendix B for areas included; (2) Excludes Mexico.
Source: U.S. Census Bureau, 2013-2017 American Community Survey 5-Year Estimates

Marital Status

Area	Never Married	Now Married[2]	Separated	Widowed	Divorced
City	55.3	34.0	0.7	2.7	7.3
MSA[1]	42.7	43.7	0.9	3.8	8.9
U.S.	33.1	48.2	2.0	5.8	10.9

Note: Figures are percentages and cover the population 15 years of age and older; (1) Figures cover the Ann Arbor, MI Metropolitan Statistical Area—see Appendix B for areas included; (2) Excludes separated
Source: U.S. Census Bureau, 2013-2017 American Community Survey 5-Year Estimates

Disability by Age

Area	All Ages	Under 18 Years Old	18 to 64 Years Old	65 Years and Over
City	6.9	1.7	4.8	26.9
MSA[1]	8.8	2.9	6.8	29.0
U.S.	12.6	4.2	10.3	35.5

Note: Figures show percent of the civilian noninstitutionalized population that reported having a disability. Disability status is determined from six types of difficulty: vision, hearing, cognitive, ambulatory, self-care, and independent living. For children under 5 years old, hearing and vision difficulty are used to determine disability status. For children between the ages of 5 and 14, disability status is determined from hearing, vision, cognitive, ambulatory, and self-care difficulties. For people aged 15 years and older, they are considered to have a disability if they have difficulty with any one of the six difficulty types; Note: (1) Figures cover the Ann Arbor, MI Metropolitan Statistical Area—see Appendix B for areas included
Source: U.S. Census Bureau, 2013-2017 American Community Survey 5-Year Estimates

Age

Area	Percent of Population									Median Age
	Under Age 5	Age 5–19	Age 20–34	Age 35–44	Age 45–54	Age 55–64	Age 65–74	Age 75–84	Age 85+	
City	4.1	18.9	38.7	9.5	8.7	8.9	6.5	3.2	1.6	27.5
MSA[1]	5.1	19.8	27.3	11.5	12.3	11.6	7.6	3.4	1.5	33.4
U.S.	6.2	19.5	20.7	12.7	13.4	12.7	8.6	4.4	1.9	37.8

Note: (1) Figures cover the Ann Arbor, MI Metropolitan Statistical Area—see Appendix B for areas included
Source: U.S. Census Bureau, 2013-2017 American Community Survey 5-Year Estimates

Gender

Area	Males	Females	Males per 100 Females
City	59,344	59,959	99.0
MSA[1]	178,949	182,560	98.0
U.S.	158,018,753	162,985,654	97.0

Note: (1) Figures cover the Ann Arbor, MI Metropolitan Statistical Area—see Appendix B for areas included
Source: U.S. Census Bureau, 2013-2017 American Community Survey 5-Year Estimates

Religious Groups by Family

Area	Catholic	Baptist	Non-Den.	Methodist[2]	Lutheran	LDS[3]	Pente-costal	Presby-terian[4]	Muslim[5]	Judaism
MSA[1]	12.4	2.2	1.6	3.1	2.9	0.9	1.9	3.0	1.3	0.9
U.S.	19.1	9.3	4.0	4.0	2.3	2.0	1.9	1.6	0.8	0.7

Note: Figures are the number of adherents as a percentage of the total population; (1) Figures cover the Ann Arbor, MI Metropolitan Statistical Area—see Appendix B for areas included; (2) Methodist/Pietist; (3) Latter Day Saints; (4) Reformed; (5) Figures are estimates
Source: Association of Statisticians of American Religious Bodies, 2010 U.S. Religion Census: Religious Congregations & Membership Study

Religious Groups by Tradition

Area	Catholic	Evangelical Protestant	Mainline Protestant	Other Tradition	Black Protestant	Orthodox
MSA[1]	12.4	7.3	7.5	3.8	1.6	0.3
U.S.	19.1	16.2	7.3	4.3	1.6	0.3

Note: Figures are the number of adherents as a percentage of the total population; (1) Figures cover the Ann Arbor, MI Metropolitan Statistical Area—see Appendix B for areas included
Source: Association of Statisticians of American Religious Bodies, 2010 U.S. Religion Census: Religious Congregations & Membership Study

ECONOMY

Gross Metropolitan Product

Area	2016	2017	2018	2019	Rank[2]
MSA[1]	22.0	22.8	23.7	25.0	114

Note: Figures are in billions of dollars; (1) Figures cover the Ann Arbor, MI Metropolitan Statistical Area—see Appendix B for areas included; (2) Rank is based on 2017 data and ranges from 1 to 381
Source: U.S. Conference of Mayors, U.S. Metro Economies: Economic Growth & Full Employment, June 2018

Economic Growth

Area	2017-2018 (%)	2019-2020 (%)	2021-2022 (%)
MSA[1]	2.8	2.4	1.5

Note: Figures are real gross metropolitan product (GMP) growth rates and represent average annual percent change; (1) Figures cover the Ann Arbor, MI Metropolitan Statistical Area—see Appendix B for areas included
Source: U.S. Conference of Mayors, U.S. Metro Economies: Economic Growth & Full Employment, June 2018

Metropolitan Area Exports

Area	2012	2013	2014	2015	2016	2017	Rank[2]
MSA[1]	1,053.4	1,156.2	1,213.6	1,053.0	1,207.9	1,447.4	120

Note: Figures are in millions of dollars; (1) Figures cover the Ann Arbor, MI Metropolitan Statistical Area—see Appendix B for areas included; (2) Rank is based on 2017 data and ranges from 1 to 387
Source: U.S. Department of Commerce, International Trade Administration, Office of Trade and Economic Analysis, Industry and Analysis, Exports by Metropolitan Area, extracted March 25, 2019

Building Permits

Area	Single-Family 2016	2017	Pct. Chg.	Multi-Family 2016	2017	Pct. Chg.	Total 2016	2017	Pct. Chg.
City	25	105	320.0	0	7	–	25	112	348.0
MSA[1]	438	583	33.1	0	74	–	438	657	50.0
U.S.	750,800	820,000	9.2	455,800	462,000	1.4	1,206,600	1,282,000	6.2

Note: (1) Figures cover the Ann Arbor, MI Metropolitan Statistical Area—see Appendix B for areas included; Figures represent new, privately-owned housing units authorized (unadjusted data); All permit data are based on estimates with imputation
Source: U.S. Census Bureau, Manufacturing, Mining, and Construction Statistics, Building Permits, 2016, 2017

Bankruptcy Filings

Area	Business Filings			Nonbusiness Filings		
	2017	2018	% Chg.	2017	2018	% Chg.
Washtenaw County	18	12	-33.3	645	583	-9.6
U.S.	23,157	22,232	-4.0	765,863	751,186	-1.9

Note: Business filings include Chapter 7, Chapter 11, Chapter 12, and Chapter 13; Nonbusiness filings include Chapter 7, Chapter 11, and Chapter 13
Source: Administrative Office of the U.S. Courts, Business and Nonbusiness Bankruptcy, County Cases Commenced by Chapter of the Bankruptcy Code, During the 12-Month Period Ending December 31, 2017 and Business and Nonbusiness Bankruptcy, County Cases Commenced by Chapter of the Bankruptcy Code, During the 12-Month Period Ending December 31, 2018

Housing Vacancy Rates

Area	Gross Vacancy Rate[2] (%)			Year-Round Vacancy Rate[3] (%)			Rental Vacancy Rate[4] (%)			Homeowner Vacancy Rate[5] (%)		
	2016	2017	2018	2016	2017	2018	2016	2017	2018	2016	2017	2018
MSA[1]	n/a	n/a	n/a	n/a	n/a	n/a	n/a	n/a	n/a	n/a	n/a	n/a
U.S.	12.8	12.7	12.3	9.9	9.9	9.7	6.9	7.2	6.9	1.7	1.6	1.5

Note: (1) Figures cover the Ann Arbor, MI Metropolitan Statistical Area—see Appendix B for areas included; (2) The percentage of the total housing inventory that is vacant; (3) The percentage of the housing inventory (excluding seasonal units) that is year-round vacant; (4) The percentage of rental inventory that is vacant for rent; (5) The percentage of homeowner inventory that is vacant for sale; n/a not available
Source: U.S. Census Bureau, Housing Vacancies and Homeownership Annual Statistics: 2016, 2017, 2018

INCOME

Income

Area	Per Capita ($)	Median Household ($)	Average Household ($)
City	39,253	61,247	89,295
MSA[1]	37,455	65,618	92,429
U.S.	31,177	57,652	81,283

Note: (1) Figures cover the Ann Arbor, MI Metropolitan Statistical Area—see Appendix B for areas included
Source: U.S. Census Bureau, 2013-2017 American Community Survey 5-Year Estimates

Household Income Distribution

Area	Percent of Households Earning							
	Under $15,000	$15,000 -$24,999	$25,000 -$34,999	$35,000 -$49,999	$50,000 -$74,999	$75,000 -$99,999	$100,000 -$149,999	$150,000 and up
City	14.0	8.0	8.2	11.2	15.6	11.4	14.9	16.6
MSA[1]	10.7	8.0	7.9	12.1	16.7	11.5	16.4	16.7
U.S.	11.6	9.8	9.5	13.0	17.7	12.3	14.1	12.1

Note: (1) Figures cover the Ann Arbor, MI Metropolitan Statistical Area—see Appendix B for areas included
Source: U.S. Census Bureau, 2013-2017 American Community Survey 5-Year Estimates

Poverty Rate

Area	All Ages	Under 18 Years Old	18 to 64 Years Old	65 Years and Over
City	22.1	10.8	26.9	7.2
MSA[1]	14.5	12.7	16.7	6.1
U.S.	14.6	20.3	13.7	9.3

Note: Figures are percentage of people whose income during the past 12 months was below the poverty level; (1) Figures cover the Ann Arbor, MI Metropolitan Statistical Area—see Appendix B for areas included
Source: U.S. Census Bureau, 2013-2017 American Community Survey 5-Year Estimates

EMPLOYMENT

Labor Force and Employment

Area	Civilian Labor Force			Workers Employed		
	Dec. 2017	Dec. 2018	% Chg.	Dec. 2017	Dec. 2018	% Chg.
City	65,171	65,503	0.5	63,515	64,041	0.8
MSA[1]	194,270	195,123	0.4	188,260	189,818	0.8
U.S.	159,880,000	162,510,000	1.6	153,602,000	156,481,000	1.9

Note: Data is not seasonally adjusted and covers workers 16 years of age and older; (1) Figures cover the Ann Arbor, MI Metropolitan Statistical Area—see Appendix B for areas included
Source: Bureau of Labor Statistics, Local Area Unemployment Statistics

Unemployment Rate

Area	\multicolumn{12}{c}{2018}

Area	Jan.	Feb.	Mar.	Apr.	May	Jun.	Jul.	Aug.	Sep.	Oct.	Nov.	Dec.
City	3.0	3.0	2.5	2.3	2.5	2.9	3.3	2.5	2.3	2.4	2.2	2.2
MSA[1]	3.6	3.6	3.1	2.8	3.1	3.6	4.0	3.0	2.8	2.9	2.6	2.7
U.S.	4.5	4.4	4.1	3.7	3.6	4.2	4.1	3.9	3.6	3.5	3.5	3.7

Note: Data is not seasonally adjusted and covers workers 16 years of age and older; (1) Figures cover the Ann Arbor, MI Metropolitan Statistical Area—see Appendix B for areas included
Source: Bureau of Labor Statistics, Local Area Unemployment Statistics

Average Wages

Occupation	$/Hr.	Occupation	$/Hr.
Accountants and Auditors	36.00	Maids and Housekeeping Cleaners	12.30
Automotive Mechanics	25.60	Maintenance and Repair Workers	17.80
Bookkeepers	19.80	Marketing Managers	65.80
Carpenters	31.10	Nuclear Medicine Technologists	36.30
Cashiers	11.10	Nurses, Licensed Practical	24.40
Clerks, General Office	16.50	Nurses, Registered	35.40
Clerks, Receptionists/Information	15.00	Nursing Assistants	15.70
Clerks, Shipping/Receiving	18.40	Packers and Packagers, Hand	12.20
Computer Programmers	37.30	Physical Therapists	41.10
Computer Systems Analysts	39.10	Postal Service Mail Carriers	24.20
Computer User Support Specialists	22.60	Real Estate Brokers	n/a
Cooks, Restaurant	13.30	Retail Salespersons	13.80
Dentists	91.60	Sales Reps., Exc. Tech./Scientific	37.30
Electrical Engineers	42.70	Sales Reps., Tech./Scientific	41.50
Electricians	33.10	Secretaries, Exc. Legal/Med./Exec.	20.40
Financial Managers	64.00	Security Guards	13.30
First-Line Supervisors/Managers, Sales	22.10	Surgeons	n/a
Food Preparation Workers	13.30	Teacher Assistants*	14.60
General and Operations Managers	64.90	Teachers, Elementary School*	31.20
Hairdressers/Cosmetologists	12.60	Teachers, Secondary School*	28.90
Internists, General	n/a	Telemarketers	n/a
Janitors and Cleaners	14.90	Truck Drivers, Heavy/Tractor-Trailer	23.10
Landscaping/Groundskeeping Workers	14.20	Truck Drivers, Light/Delivery Svcs.	18.60
Lawyers	57.30	Waiters and Waitresses	11.40

Note: Wage data covers the Ann Arbor, MI Metropolitan Statistical Area—see Appendix B for areas included; (*) Hourly wages for elementary/secondary school teachers and teacher assistants were calculated by the editors from annual wage data based on a 40 hour work week; n/a not available.
Source: Bureau of Labor Statistics, Metro Area Occupational Employment & Wage Estimates, May 2018

Employment by Occupation

Occupation Classification	City (%)	MSA[1] (%)	U.S. (%)
Management, Business, Science, and Arts	64.9	52.6	37.4
Natural Resources, Construction, and Maintenance	2.2	4.4	8.9
Production, Transportation, and Material Moving	4.8	8.8	12.2
Sales and Office	15.1	18.4	23.5
Service	13.0	15.7	18.0

Note: Figures cover employed civilians 16 years of age and older; (1) Figures cover the Ann Arbor, MI Metropolitan Statistical Area—see Appendix B for areas included
Source: U.S. Census Bureau, 2013-2017 American Community Survey 5-Year Estimates

Employment by Industry

Sector	MSA[1]		U.S.
	Number of Employees	Percent of Total	Percent of Total
Construction, Mining, and Logging	4,400	1.9	5.3
Education and Health Services	27,900	12.3	15.9
Financial Activities	6,900	3.0	5.7
Government	86,700	38.1	15.1
Information	5,300	2.3	1.9
Leisure and Hospitality	17,700	7.8	10.7
Manufacturing	15,300	6.7	8.5
Other Services	6,400	2.8	3.9
Professional and Business Services	30,400	13.4	14.1
Retail Trade	16,500	7.2	10.8
Transportation, Warehousing, and Utilities	4,000	1.8	4.2
Wholesale Trade	6,200	2.7	3.9

Note: Figures are non-farm employment as of December 2018. Figures are not seasonally adjusted and include workers 16 years of age and older; (1) Figures cover the Ann Arbor, MI Metropolitan Statistical Area—see Appendix B for areas included
Source: Bureau of Labor Statistics, Current Employment Statistics, Employment, Hours, and Earnings

Occupations with Greatest Projected Employment Growth: 2018 – 2020

Occupation[1]	2018 Employment	2020 Projected Employment	Numeric Employment Change	Percent Employment Change
Combined Food Preparation and Serving Workers, Including Fast Food	121,730	124,870	3,140	2.6
Registered Nurses	99,430	102,150	2,720	2.7
Personal Care Aides	43,960	46,370	2,410	5.5
Laborers and Freight, Stock, and Material Movers, Hand	71,260	73,160	1,900	2.7
Home Health Aides	28,090	29,900	1,810	6.4
Heavy and Tractor-Trailer Truck Drivers	58,310	59,830	1,520	2.6
General and Operations Managers	60,330	61,750	1,420	2.4
Customer Service Representatives	93,100	94,460	1,360	1.5
Mechanical Engineers	43,910	45,230	1,320	3.0
Light Truck or Delivery Services Drivers	31,300	32,510	1,210	3.9

Note: Projections cover Michigan; (1) Sorted by numeric employment change
Source: www.projectionscentral.com, State Occupational Projections, 2018–2020 Short-Term Projections

Fastest Growing Occupations: 2018 – 2020

Occupation[1]	2018 Employment	2020 Projected Employment	Numeric Employment Change	Percent Employment Change
Veterinary Assistants and Laboratory Animal Caretakers	3,200	3,750	550	17.2
Veterinarians	2,870	3,340	470	16.4
Veterinary Technologists and Technicians	3,160	3,670	510	16.1
Dental Laboratory Technicians	1,400	1,610	210	15.0
Credit Counselors	1,080	1,220	140	13.0
Airline Pilots, Copilots, and Flight Engineers	2,930	3,220	290	9.9
Orthotists and Prosthetists	620	680	60	9.7
Reservation and Transportation Ticket Agents and Travel Clerks	4,340	4,710	370	8.5
Nonfarm Animal Caretakers	7,830	8,410	580	7.4
Interpreters and Translators	1,280	1,370	90	7.0

Note: Projections cover Michigan; (1) Sorted by percent employment change and excludes occupations with numeric employment change less than 50
Source: www.projectionscentral.com, State Occupational Projections, 2018–2020 Short-Term Projections

TAXES

State Corporate Income Tax Rates

State	Tax Rate (%)	Income Brackets ($)	Num. of Brackets	Financial Institution Tax Rate (%)[a]	Federal Income Tax Ded.
Michigan	6.0	Flat rate	1	(a)	No

Note: Tax rates as of January 1, 2019; (a) Rates listed are the corporate income tax rate applied to financial institutions or excise taxes based on income. Some states have other taxes based upon the value of deposits or shares.
Source: Federation of Tax Administrators, Range of State Corporate Income Tax Rates, January 1, 2019

State Individual Income Tax Rates

State	Tax Rate (%)	Income Brackets ($)	Personal Exemptions ($)			Standard Ded. ($)	
			Single	Married	Depend.	Single	Married
Michigan (a)	4.25	Flat rate	4,050	8,100	4,050	–	–

Note: Tax rates as of January 1, 2019; Local- and county-level taxes are not included; n/a not applicable; Federal income tax is not deductible on state income tax returns; (a) 19 states have statutory provision for automatically adjusting to the rate of inflation the dollar values of the income tax brackets, standard deductions, and/or personal exemptions. Michigan indexes the personal exemption only. Oregon does not index the income brackets for $125,000 and over.
Source: Federation of Tax Administrators, State Individual Income Tax Rates, January 1, 2019

Various State Sales and Excise Tax Rates

State	State Sales Tax (%)	Gasoline[1] (¢/gal.)	Cigarette[2] ($/pack)	Spirits[3] ($/gal.)	Wine[4] ($/gal.)	Beer[5] ($/gal.)	Recreational Marijuana (%)
Michigan	6	38.41	2.00	11.99 (g)	0.51 (l)	0.2	10.0 (bb)

Note: All tax rates as of January 1, 2019; (1) The American Petroleum Institute has developed a methodology for determining the average tax rate on a gallon of fuel. Rates may include any of the following: excise taxes, environmental fees, storage tank fees, other fees or taxes, general sales tax, and local taxes. In states where gasoline is subject to the general sales tax, or where the fuel tax is based on the average sale price, the average rate determined by API is sensitive to changes in the price of gasoline. States that fully or partially apply general sales taxes to gasoline: CA, CO, GA, IL, IN, MI, NY; (2) The federal excise tax of $1.0066 per pack and local taxes are not included; (3) Rates are those applicable to off-premise sales of 40% alcohol by volume (a.b.v.) distilled spirits in 750ml containers. Local excise taxes are excluded; (4) Rates are those applicable to off-premise sales of 11% a.b.v. non-carbonated wine in 750ml containers; (5) Rates are those applicable to off-premise sales of 4.7% a.b.v. beer in 12 ounce containers; (g) Control states, where the government controls all sales. Products can be subject to ad valorem mark-up as well as excise taxes; (l) Different rates also applicable to alcohol content, place of production, size of container, place purchased (on- or off-premise or on board airlines) or type of wine (carbonated, vermouth, etc.); (bb) 10% excise tax (retail price)
Source: Tax Foundation, 2019 Facts & Figures: How Does Your State Compare?

State Business Tax Climate Index Rankings

State	Overall Rank	Corporate Tax Rank	Individual Income Tax Rank	Sales Tax Rank	Unemployment Insurance Tax Rank	Property Tax Rank
Michigan	13	11	12	11	49	22

Note: The index is a measure of how each state's tax laws affect economic performance. The lower the rank, the more favorable a state's tax system is for business. States without a given tax are given a ranking of 1. The scores/rankings for the District of Columbia do not affect other states. The 2019 index represents the tax climate as of July 1, 2018.
Source: Tax Foundation, State Business Tax Climate Index 2019

COMMERCIAL UTILITIES

Typical Monthly Electric Bills

Area	Commercial Service ($/month)		Industrial Service ($/month)	
	1,500 kWh	40 kW demand 14,000 kWh	1,000 kW demand 200,000 kWh	50,000 kW demand 32,500,000 kWh
City	n/a	n/a	n/a	n/a
Average[1]	203	1,619	25,886	2,540,077

Note: Figures are based on annualized rates; (1) Average based on 187 utilities surveyed; n/a not available
Source: Edison Electric Institute, Typical Bills and Average Rates Report, Summer 2018

TRANSPORTATION

Means of Transportation to Work

Area	Car/Truck/Van		Public Transportation			Bicycle	Walked	Other Means	Worked at Home
	Drove Alone	Car-pooled	Bus	Subway	Railroad				
City	54.2	6.7	10.9	0.1	0.0	4.4	15.3	0.9	7.4
MSA[1]	72.2	7.7	5.1	0.0	0.0	1.7	6.5	0.7	5.9
U.S.	76.4	9.2	2.5	1.9	0.6	0.6	2.7	1.3	4.7

Note: Figures are percentages and cover workers 16 years of age and older; (1) Figures cover the Ann Arbor, MI Metropolitan Statistical Area—see Appendix B for areas included
Source: U.S. Census Bureau, 2013-2017 American Community Survey 5-Year Estimates

Travel Time to Work

Area	Less Than 10 Minutes	10 to 19 Minutes	20 to 29 Minutes	30 to 44 Minutes	45 to 59 Minutes	60 to 89 Minutes	90 Minutes or More
City	13.8	44.1	19.7	13.8	4.8	2.9	0.9
MSA[1]	11.2	33.5	24.1	19.0	6.9	4.1	1.2
U.S.	12.7	28.9	20.9	20.5	8.1	6.2	2.7

Note: Note: Figures are percentages and include workers 16 years old and over; (1) Figures cover the Ann Arbor, MI Metropolitan Statistical Area—see Appendix B for areas included
Source: U.S. Census Bureau, 2013-2017 American Community Survey 5-Year Estimates

Freeway Travel Time Index

Area	1985	1990	1995	2000	2005	2010	2014
Urban Area Rank[1,2]	n/a	n/a	n/a	n/a	n/a	n/a	n/a
Urban Area Index[1]	n/a	n/a	n/a	n/a	n/a	n/a	n/a
Average Index[3]	1.09	1.11	1.14	1.17	1.20	1.19	1.20

Note: Freeway Travel Time Index—the ratio of travel time in the peak period to the travel time at free-flow conditions. For example, a value of 1.30 indicates a 20-minute free-flow trip takes 26 minutes in the peak (20 minutes x 1.30 = 26 minutes); (1) Data for the Ann Arbor, MI urban area was not available; (2) Rank is based on 101 urban areas (#1 = highest travel time index); (3) Average of 101 urban areas
Source: Texas Transportation Institute, 2015 Urban Mobility Scorecard, August 2015

Freeway Commuter Stress Index

Area	1985	1990	1995	2000	2005	2010	2014
Urban Area Rank[1,2]	n/a	n/a	n/a	n/a	n/a	n/a	n/a
Urban Area Index[1]	n/a	n/a	n/a	n/a	n/a	n/a	n/a
Average Index[3]	1.13	1.16	1.19	1.22	1.25	1.24	1.25

Note: The Freeway Commuter Stress Index is the same as the Freeway Travel Time Index (see table above) except that it includes only the travel in the peak directions during the peak periods; the TTI includes travel in all directions during the peak period. Thus, the CSI is more indicative of the work trip experienced by each commuter on a daily basis; (1) Data for the Ann Arbor, MI urban area was not available; (2) Rank is based on 101 urban areas (#1 = highest travel time index); (3) Average of 101 urban areas
Source: Texas Transportation Institute, 2015 Urban Mobility Scorecard, August 2015

Public Transportation

Agency Name / Mode of Transportation	Vehicles Operated in Maximum Service[1]	Annual Unlinked Passenger Trips[2] (in thous.)	Annual Passenger Miles[3] (in thous.)
Ann Arbor Transportation Authority (AATA)			
Bus (directly operated)	84	6,596.9	23,183.9
Commuter Bus (directly operated)	2	26.2	445.3
Commuter Bus (purchased transportation)	2	84.8	2,247.6
Demand Response (purchased transportation)	54	212.6	1,427.5
Demand Response Taxi (purchased transportation)	11	28.5	291.5

Note: (1) The number of revenue vehicles operated by the given mode and type of service to meet the annual maximum service requirement. This is the revenue vehicle count during the peak season of the year; on the week and day that maximum service is provided. Vehicles operated in maximum service (VOMS) exclude atypical days and one-time special events; (2) The number of passengers who boarded public transportation vehicles. Passengers are counted each time they board a vehicle no matter how many vehicles they use to travel from their origin to their destination. (3) The sum of the distances ridden by all passengers during the entire fiscal year.
Source: Federal Transit Administration, National Transit Database, 2017

Air Transportation

Airport Name and Code / Type of Service	Passenger Airlines[1]	Passenger Enplanements	Freight Carriers[2]	Freight (lbs)
Detroit Metro Wayne County (25 miles) (DTW)				
Domestic service (U.S. carriers - 2018)	31	15,567,138	18	145,729,509
International service (U.S. carriers - 2017)	13	1,501,185	3	29,372,023

Note: (1) Includes all U.S.-based major, minor and commuter airlines that carried at least one passenger during the year; (2) Includes all U.S.-based airlines and freight carriers that transported at least one pound of freight during the year.
Source: Bureau of Transportation Statistics, The Intermodal Transportation Database, Air Carriers: T-100 Domestic Market (U.S. Carriers), 2018; Bureau of Transportation Statistics, The Intermodal Transportation Database, Air Carriers: T-100 International Market (U.S. Carriers), 2017

Other Transportation Statistics

Major Highways:	I-94
Amtrak Service:	Yes
Major Waterways/Ports:	None

Source: Amtrak.com; Google Maps

BUSINESSES

Major Business Headquarters

Company Name	Industry	Rankings	
		Fortune[1]	Forbes[2]
No companies listed	-	-	-

Note: (1) Companies that produce a 10-K are ranked 1 to 500 based on 2017 revenue; (2) All private companies with at least $2 billion in annual revenue through the end of their most current fiscal year are ranked 1 to 229; companies listed are headquartered in the city; dashes indicate no ranking
Source: Fortune, "Fortune 500," June 2018; Forbes, "America's Largest Private Companies," 2018 Rankings

Minority Business Opportunity

Ann Arbor is home to one company which is on the *Black Enterprise* Industrial/Service list (100 largest companies based on gross sales): **Boersma Travel Services** (#67). Criteria: operational in previous calendar year; at least 51% black-owned and manufactures/owns the product it sells or provides industrial or consumer services. Brokerages, real estate firms and firms that provide professional services are not eligible. *Black Enterprise, B.E. 100s, 2018*

Minority- and Women-Owned Businesses

Group	All Firms		Firms with Paid Employees			
	Firms	Sales ($000)	Firms	Sales ($000)	Employees	Payroll ($000)
AIAN[1]	86	1,866	6	528	17	315
Asian	709	234,063	153	220,708	2,000	83,027
Black	657	49,598	26	33,952	329	12,062
Hispanic	335	21,494	28	13,195	143	6,737
NHOPI[2]	n/a	n/a	n/a	n/a	n/a	n/a
Women	3,885	337,383	345	249,277	3,290	86,638
All Firms	11,982	9,905,332	2,455	8,098,875	48,259	2,231,617

Note: Figures cover firms located in the city; minority- and women-owned business are defined as firms in which the corresponding group own 51% or more of the stock or equity of the company; (1) American Indian and Alaska Native; (2) Native Hawaiian and Other Pacific Islander; n/a not available
Source: U.S. Census Bureau, 2012 Economic Census, Survey of Business Owners

HOTELS & CONVENTION CENTERS

Hotels, Motels and Vacation Rentals

Area	5 Star		4 Star		3 Star		2 Star		1 Star		Not Rated	
	Num.	Pct.[3]	Num.	Pct.[3]	Num.	Pct.[3]	Num.	Pct.[3]	Num.	Pct.[3]	Num.	Pct.[3]
City[1]	0	0.0	3	1.6	46	25.3	54	29.7	2	1.1	77	42.3
Total[2]	286	0.4	5,236	7.1	16,715	22.6	10,259	13.9	293	0.4	41,056	55.6

Note: (1) Figures cover Ann Arbor and vicinity; (2) Figures cover all 100 cities in this book; (3) Percentage of hotels which have a given star rating; Star ratings are determined by expedia.com and offer an indication of the general quality of a particular hotel.
Source: www.expedia.com, April 3, 2019

Major Convention Centers

Name	Overall Space (sq. ft.)	Exhibit Space (sq. ft.)	Meeting Space (sq. ft.)	Meeting Rooms

There are no major convention centers located in the metro area
Source: Original research

Living Environment

COST OF LIVING

Cost of Living Index

Composite Index	Groceries	Housing	Utilities	Trans-portation	Health Care	Misc. Goods/ Services
n/a	n/a	n/a	n/a	n/a	n/a	n/a

Note: The Cost of Living Index measures regional differences in the cost of consumer goods and services, excluding taxes and non-consumer expenditures, for professional and managerial households in the top income quintile. It is based on more than 50,000 prices covering almost 60 different items for which prices are collected three times a year by chambers of commerce, economic development organizations or university applied economic centers in each participating urban area. The numbers shown should be read as a percentage above or below the national average of 100. For example, a value of 115.4 in the groceries column indicates that grocery prices are 15.4% higher than the national average. Small differences in the index numbers should not be interpreted as significant; n/a not available.
Source: The Council for Community and Economic Research, ACCRA Cost of Living Index, 2018

Grocery Prices

Area[1]	T-Bone Steak ($/pound)	Frying Chicken ($/pound)	Whole Milk ($/half gal.)	Eggs ($/dozen)	Orange Juice ($/64 oz.)	Coffee ($/11.5 oz.)
City[2]	n/a	n/a	n/a	n/a	n/a	n/a
Avg.	11.35	1.42	1.94	1.81	3.52	4.35
Min.	7.45	0.92	0.80	0.75	2.72	3.06
Max.	15.05	2.76	4.18	4.00	5.36	8.20

Note: (1) Values for the local area are compared with the average, minimum and maximum values for all 291 areas in the Cost of Living Index; (2) Figures cover the Ann Arbor MI urban area; n/a not available; T-Bone Steak (price per pound); Frying Chicken (price per pound, whole fryer); Whole Milk (half gallon carton); Eggs (price per dozen, Grade A, large); Orange Juice (64 oz. Tropicana or Florida Natural); Coffee (11.5 oz. can, vacuum-packed, Maxwell House, Hills Bros, or Folgers).
Source: The Council for Community and Economic Research, ACCRA Cost of Living Index, 2018

Housing and Utility Costs

Area[1]	New Home Price ($)	Apartment Rent ($/month)	All Electric ($/month)	Part Electric ($/month)	Other Energy ($/month)	Telephone ($/month)
City[2]	n/a	n/a	n/a	n/a	n/a	n/a
Avg.	347,000	1,087	165.93	100.16	67.73	178.70
Min.	200,468	500	93.58	25.64	26.78	163.10
Max.	1,901,222	4,888	388.65	246.86	332.81	197.70

Note: (1) Values for the local area are compared with the average, minimum and maximum values for all 291 areas in the Cost of Living Index; (2) Figures cover the Ann Arbor MI urban area; n/a not available; New Home Price (2,400 sf living area, 8,000 sf lot, in urban area with full utilities); Apartment Rent (950 sf 2 bedroom/1.5 or 2 bath, unfurnished, excluding all utilities except water); All Electric (average monthly cost for an all-electric home); Part Electric (average monthly cost for a part-electric home); Other Energy (average monthly cost for natural gas, fuel oil, coal, wood, and any other forms of energy except electricity); Telephone (price includes the base monthly rate plus taxes and fees for three lines of mobile phone service).
Source: The Council for Community and Economic Research, ACCRA Cost of Living Index, 2018

Health Care, Transportation, and Other Costs

Area[1]	Doctor ($/visit)	Dentist ($/visit)	Optometrist ($/visit)	Gasoline ($/gallon)	Beauty Salon ($/visit)	Men's Shirt ($)
City[2]	n/a	n/a	n/a	n/a	n/a	n/a
Avg.	110.71	95.11	103.74	2.61	37.48	32.03
Min.	33.60	62.55	54.63	1.89	17.00	11.44
Max.	195.97	153.93	225.79	3.59	71.88	58.64

Note: (1) Values for the local area are compared with the average, minimum and maximum values for all 291 areas in the Cost of Living Index; (2) Figures cover the Ann Arbor MI urban area; n/a not available; Doctor (general practitioners routine exam of an established patient); Dentist (adult teeth cleaning and periodic oral examination); Optometrist (full vision eye exam for established adult patient); Gasoline (one gallon regular unleaded, national brand, including all taxes, cash price at self-service pump if available); Beauty Salon (woman's shampoo, trim, and blow-dry); Men's Shirt (cotton/polyester dress shirt, pinpoint weave, long sleeves).
Source: The Council for Community and Economic Research, ACCRA Cost of Living Index, 2018

HOUSING

House Price Index (HPI)

Area	National Ranking[2]	Quarterly Change (%)	One-Year Change (%)	Five-Year Change (%)
MSA[1]	38	-0.05	9.08	40.94
U.S.[3]	–	1.12	5.73	32.81

Note: The HPI is a weighted repeat sales index. It measures average price changes in repeat sales or refinancings on the same properties. This information is obtained by reviewing repeat mortgage transactions on single-family properties whose mortgages have been purchased or securitized by Fannie Mae or Freddie Mac in January 1975; (1) Figures cover the Ann Arbor, MI Metropolitan Statistical Area—see Appendix B for areas included; (2) Rankings are based on annual percentage change for all metro areas containing at least 15,000 transactions over the last 10 years and ranges from 1 to 245; (3) figures based on a weighted average of Census Division estimates using a seasonally adjusted, purchase-only index; all figures are for the period ending December 31, 2018
Source: Federal Housing Finance Agency, House Price Index, February 26, 2019

Median Single-Family Home Prices

Area	2016	2017	2018p	Percent Change 2017 to 2018
MSA[1]	243.4	263.7	281.0	6.6
U.S. Average	235.5	248.8	261.6	5.1

Note: Figures are median sales prices of existing single-family homes in thousands of dollars; (p) preliminary; (1) Figures cover the Ann Arbor, MI Metropolitan Statistical Area—see Appendix B for areas included
Source: National Association of Realtors, Median Sales Price of Existing Single-Family Homes for Metropolitan Areas, 4th Quarter 2018

Qualifying Income Based on Median Sales Price of Existing Single-Family Homes

Area	With 5% Down ($)	With 10% Down ($)	With 20% Down ($)
MSA[1]	66,497	62,997	55,998
U.S. Average	62,954	59,640	53,013

Note: Figures are preliminary; Qualifying income is based on a mortgage rate of 4.9%. Monthly principal and interest payment is limited to 25% of income; (1) Figures cover the Ann Arbor, MI Metropolitan Statistical Area—see Appendix B for areas included
Source: National Association of Realtors, Qualifying Income Based on Median Sales Price of Existing Single-Family Homes for Metropolitan Areas, 4th Quarter 2018

Median Apartment Condo-Coop Home Prices

Area	2016	2017	2018p	Percent Change 2017 to 2018
MSA[1]	n/a	n/a	n/a	n/a
U.S. Average	220.7	234.3	241.0	2.9

Note: Figures are median sales prices of existing apartment condo-coop homes in thousands of dollars; (p) preliminary; n/a not available; (1) Figures cover the Ann Arbor, MI Metropolitan Statistical Area—see Appendix B for areas included
Source: National Association of Realtors, Median Sales Price of Existing Apartment Condo-Coop Homes for Metropolitan Areas, 4th Quarter 2018

Home Value Distribution

Area	Under $50,000	$50,000 -$99,999	$100,000 -$149,999	$150,000 -$199,999	$200,000 -$299,999	$300,000 -$499,999	$500,000 -$999,999	$1,000,000 or more
City	3.1	4.9	7.3	12.1	30.3	29.2	11.8	1.4
MSA[1]	7.2	7.7	10.5	15.9	25.1	23.7	8.6	1.4
U.S.	8.3	13.9	14.7	14.6	18.7	17.3	9.7	2.7

Note: Figures are percentages and cover owner-occupied housing units; (1) Figures cover the Ann Arbor, MI Metropolitan Statistical Area—see Appendix B for areas included
Source: U.S. Census Bureau, 2013-2017 American Community Survey 5-Year Estimates

Homeownership Rate

Area	2010 (%)	2011 (%)	2012 (%)	2013 (%)	2014 (%)	2015 (%)	2016 (%)	2017 (%)	2018 (%)
MSA[1]	n/a	n/a	n/a	n/a	n/a	n/a	n/a	n/a	n/a
U.S.	66.9	66.1	65.4	65.1	64.5	63.7	63.4	63.9	64.4

Note: (1) Figures cover the Ann Arbor, MI Metropolitan Statistical Area—see Appendix B for areas included; n/a not available
Source: U.S. Census Bureau, Housing Vacancies and Homeownership Annual Statistics: 2010-2018

Year Housing Structure Built

Area	2010 or Later	2000 -2009	1990 -1999	1980 -1989	1970 -1979	1960 -1969	1950 -1959	1940 -1949	Before 1940	Median Year
City	2.2	6.7	10.4	10.4	16.8	17.7	14.0	5.8	16.0	1968
MSA[1]	2.2	13.5	17.3	11.1	16.4	12.3	10.9	4.5	11.9	1976
U.S.	3.2	14.5	14.0	13.6	15.5	10.8	10.5	5.1	12.9	1977

Note: Figures are percentages except for Median Year; Note: (1) Figures cover the Ann Arbor, MI Metropolitan Statistical Area—see Appendix B for areas included
Source: U.S. Census Bureau, 2013-2017 American Community Survey 5-Year Estimates

Gross Monthly Rent

Area	Under $500	$500 -$999	$1,000 -$1,499	$1,500 -$1,999	$2,000 -$2,499	$2,500 -$2,999	$3,000 and up	Median ($)
City	5.3	30.6	38.6	14.9	6.2	2.0	2.3	1,166
MSA[1]	5.9	42.1	34.1	11.3	3.6	1.4	1.6	1,025
U.S.	10.5	41.1	28.7	11.7	4.5	1.8	1.7	982

Note: Figures are percentages except for Median; Gross rent is the contract rent plus the estimated average monthly cost of utilities (electricity, gas, and water and sewer) and fuels (oil, coal, kerosene, wood, etc.) if these are paid by the renter (or paid for the renter by someone else); (1) Figures cover the Ann Arbor, MI Metropolitan Statistical Area—see Appendix B for areas included
Source: U.S. Census Bureau, 2013-2017 American Community Survey 5-Year Estimates

HEALTH

Health Risk Factors

Category	MSA[1] (%)	U.S. (%)
Adults aged 18–64 who have any kind of health care coverage	n/a	87.3
Adults who reported being in good or better health	n/a	82.4
Adults who have been told they have high blood cholesterol	n/a	33.0
Adults who have been told they have high blood pressure	n/a	32.3
Adults who are current smokers	n/a	17.1
Adults who currently use E-cigarettes	n/a	4.6
Adults who currently use chewing tobacco, snuff, or snus	n/a	4.0
Adults who are heavy drinkers[2]	n/a	6.3
Adults who are binge drinkers[3]	n/a	17.4
Adults who are overweight (BMI 25.0 - 29.9)	n/a	35.3
Adults who are obese (BMI 30.0 - 99.8)	n/a	31.3
Adults who participated in any physical activities in the past month	n/a	74.4
Adults who always or nearly always wears a seat belt	n/a	94.3

Note: n/a not available; (1) Figures cover the Ann Arbor, MI Metropolitan Statistical Area—see Appendix B for areas included; (2) Heavy drinkers are classified as adult men having more than 14 drinks per week and adult women having more than 7 drinks per week; (3) Binge drinkers are classified as males having five or more drinks on one occasion or females having four or more drinks on one occasion
Source: Centers for Disease Control and Prevention, Behaviorial Risk Factor Surveillance System, SMART: Selected Metropolitan Area Risk Trends, 2017

Acute and Chronic Health Conditions

Category	MSA[1] (%)	U.S. (%)
Adults who have ever been told they had a heart attack	n/a	4.2
Adults who have ever been told they have angina or coronary heart disease	n/a	3.9
Adults who have ever been told they had a stroke	n/a	3.0
Adults who have ever been told they have asthma	n/a	14.2
Adults who have ever been told they have arthritis	n/a	24.9
Adults who have ever been told they have diabetes[2]	n/a	10.5
Adults who have ever been told they had skin cancer	n/a	6.2
Adults who have ever been told they had any other types of cancer	n/a	7.1
Adults who have ever been told they have COPD	n/a	6.5
Adults who have ever been told they have kidney disease	n/a	3.0
Adults who have ever been told they have a form of depression	n/a	20.5

Note: n/a not available; (1) Figures cover the Ann Arbor, MI Metropolitan Statistical Area—see Appendix B for areas included; (2) Figures do not include pregnancy-related, borderline, or pre-diabetes
Source: Centers for Disease Control and Prevention, Behaviorial Risk Factor Surveillance System, SMART: Selected Metropolitan Area Risk Trends, 2017

Health Screening and Vaccination Rates

Category	MSA[1] (%)	U.S. (%)
Adults aged 65+ who have had flu shot within the past year	n/a	60.7
Adults aged 65+ who have ever had a pneumonia vaccination	n/a	75.4
Adults who have ever been tested for HIV	n/a	36.1
Adults who have ever had the shingles or zoster vaccine?	n/a	28.9
Adults who have had their blood cholesterol checked within the last five years	n/a	85.9

Note: n/a not available; (1) Figures cover the Ann Arbor, MI Metropolitan Statistical Area—see Appendix B for areas included.
Source: Centers for Disease Control and Prevention, Behaviorial Risk Factor Surveillance System, SMART: Selected Metropolitan Area Risk Trends, 2017

Disability Status

Category	MSA[1] (%)	U.S. (%)
Adults who reported being deaf	n/a	6.7
Are you blind or have serious difficulty seeing, even when wearing glasses?	n/a	4.5
Are you limited in any way in any of your usual activities due of arthritis?	n/a	12.9
Do you have difficulty doing errands alone?	n/a	6.8
Do you have difficulty dressing or bathing?	n/a	3.6
Do you have serious difficulty concentrating/remembering/making decisions?	n/a	10.7
Do you have serious difficulty walking or climbing stairs?	n/a	13.6

Note: n/a not available; (1) Figures cover the Ann Arbor, MI Metropolitan Statistical Area—see Appendix B for areas included.
Source: Centers for Disease Control and Prevention, Behaviorial Risk Factor Surveillance System, SMART: Selected Metropolitan Area Risk Trends, 2017

Mortality Rates for the Top 10 Causes of Death in the U.S.

ICD-10[a] Sub-Chapter	ICD-10[a] Code	Age-Adjusted Mortality Rate[1] per 100,000 population	
		County[2]	U.S.
Malignant neoplasms	C00-C97	141.4	155.5
Ischaemic heart diseases	I20-I25	81.4	94.8
Other forms of heart disease	I30-I51	44.2	52.9
Chronic lower respiratory diseases	J40-J47	26.5	41.0
Cerebrovascular diseases	I60-I69	34.4	37.5
Other degenerative diseases of the nervous system	G30-G31	35.8	35.0
Other external causes of accidental injury	W00-X59	32.2	33.7
Organic, including symptomatic, mental disorders	F01-F09	22.6	31.0
Hypertensive diseases	I10-I15	25.7	21.9
Diabetes mellitus	E10-E14	14.9	21.2

Note: (a) ICD-10 = International Classification of Diseases 10th Revision; (1) Mortality rates are a three year average covering 2015-2017; (2) Figures cover Washtenaw County.
Source: Centers for Disease Control and Prevention, National Center for Health Statistics. Underlying Cause of Death 1999-2017 on CDC WONDER Online Database

Mortality Rates for Selected Causes of Death

ICD-10[a] Sub-Chapter	ICD-10[a] Code	Age-Adjusted Mortality Rate[1] per 100,000 population	
		County[2]	U.S.
Assault	X85-Y09	2.8	5.9
Diseases of the liver	K70-K76	9.0	14.1
Human immunodeficiency virus (HIV) disease	B20-B24	Suppressed	1.8
Influenza and pneumonia	J09-J18	11.0	14.3
Intentional self-harm	X60-X84	11.1	13.6
Malnutrition	E40-E46	2.1	1.6
Obesity and other hyperalimentation	E65-E68	Suppressed	2.1
Renal failure	N17-N19	8.4	13.0
Transport accidents	V01-V99	6.7	12.4
Viral hepatitis	B15-B19	Suppressed	1.6

Note: (a) ICD-10 = International Classification of Diseases 10th Revision; (1) Mortality rates are a three year average covering 2015-2017; (2) Figures cover Washtenaw County; Data are suppressed when the data meet the criteria for confidentiality constraints; Mortality rates are flagged as unreliable when the rate would be calculated with a numerator of 20 or less.
Source: Centers for Disease Control and Prevention, National Center for Health Statistics. Underlying Cause of Death 1999-2017 on CDC WONDER Online Database

Health Insurance Coverage

Area	With Health Insurance	With Private Health Insurance	With Public Health Insurance	Without Health Insurance	Population Under Age 18 Without Health Insurance
City	96.5	87.9	18.8	3.5	1.5
MSA[1]	95.3	83.3	24.4	4.7	2.2
U.S.	89.5	67.2	33.8	10.5	5.7

Note: Figures are percentages that cover the civilian noninstitutionalized population; (1) Figures cover the Ann Arbor, MI Metropolitan Statistical Area—see Appendix B for areas included
Source: U.S. Census Bureau, 2013-2017 American Community Survey 5-Year Estimates

Number of Medical Professionals

Area	MDs[3]	DOs[3,4]	Dentists	Podiatrists	Chiropractors	Optometrists
County[1] (number)	4,457	150	638	25	91	62
County[1] (rate[2])	1,221.9	41.1	173.5	6.8	24.8	16.9
U.S. (rate[2])	279.3	23.0	68.4	6.0	27.1	16.2

Note: Data as of 2017 unless noted; (1) Data covers Washtenaw County; (2) Rate per 100,000 population; (3) Data as of 2016 and includes all active, non-federal physicians; (4) Doctor of Osteopathic Medicine
Source: U.S. Department of Health and Human Services, Health Resources and Services Administration, Bureau of Health Professions, Area Resource File (ARF) 2017-2018

Best Hospitals

According to *U.S. News,* the Ann Arbor, MI metro area is home to one of the best hospitals in the U.S.: **University of Michigan Hospitals-Michigan Medicine** (Honor Roll/14 adult specialties and 10 pediatric specialties). The hospital listed was nationally ranked in at least one of 16 adult or 10 pediatric specialties. Only 170 hospitals nationwide were nationally ranked in one or more adult or pediatric specialty. Twenty hospitals in the U.S. made the Honor Roll. The Best Hospitals Honor Roll takes both the national rankings and the procedure and condition ratings into account. Hospitals received points if they were nationally ranked in one of the 16 adult specialties—the higher they ranked, the more points they got—and how many ratings of "high performing" they earned in the nine procedures and conditions. *U.S. News Online, "America's Best Hospitals 2018-19"*

According to *U.S. News,* the Ann Arbor, MI metro area is home to one of the best children's hospitals in the U.S.: **C.S. Mott Children's Hospital-Michigan Medicine** (10 pediatric specialties). The hospital listed was highly ranked in at least one of 10 pediatric specialties. Eighty-six children's hospitals in the U.S. were nationally ranked in at least one specialty. Hospitals received points for being ranked in a specialty, and the 10 hospitals with the most points across the 10 specialties make up the Honor Roll. *U.S. News Online, "America's Best Children's Hospitals 2018-19"*

EDUCATION

Public School District Statistics

District Name	Schls	Pupils	Pupil/ Teacher Ratio	Minority Pupils[1] (%)	Free Lunch Eligible[2] (%)	IEP[3] (%)
Ann Arbor Public Schools	31	17,565	18.0	47.2	19.0	11.2

Note: Table includes school districts with 2,000 or more students; (1) Percentage of students that are not non-Hispanic white; (2) Percentage of students that are eligible for the free lunch program; (3) Percentage of students that have an Individualized Education Program.
Source: U.S. Department of Education, National Center for Education Statistics, Common Core of Data, Local Education Agency (School District) Universe Survey: School Year 2016-2017; U.S. Department of Education, National Center for Education Statistics, Common Core of Data, Public Elementary/Secondary School Universe Survey: School Year 2016-2017

Highest Level of Education

Area	Less than H.S.	H.S. Diploma	Some College, No Deg.	Associate Degree	Bachelor's Degree	Master's Degree	Prof. School Degree	Doctorate Degree
City	3.2	7.4	11.3	4.0	29.5	26.8	7.2	10.7
MSA[1]	4.9	15.3	18.4	7.0	25.7	18.6	4.4	5.7
U.S.	12.7	27.3	20.8	8.3	19.1	8.4	2.0	1.4

Note: Figures cover persons age 25 and over; (1) Figures cover the Ann Arbor, MI Metropolitan Statistical Area—see Appendix B for areas included
Source: U.S. Census Bureau, 2013-2017 American Community Survey 5-Year Estimates

Educational Attainment by Race

Area	High School Graduate or Higher (%)					Bachelor's Degree or Higher (%)				
	Total	White	Black	Asian	Hisp.[2]	Total	White	Black	Asian	Hisp.[2]
City	96.8	98.3	85.0	96.1	92.5	74.2	76.4	35.6	84.7	69.5
MSA[1]	95.1	96.2	88.1	95.7	85.2	54.3	56.2	25.4	81.5	39.7
U.S.	87.3	89.3	84.9	86.5	66.7	30.9	32.2	20.6	52.7	15.2

Note: Figures shown cover persons 25 years old and over; (1) Figures cover the Ann Arbor, MI Metropolitan Statistical Area—see Appendix B for areas included; (2) People of Hispanic origin can be of any race
Source: U.S. Census Bureau, 2013-2017 American Community Survey 5-Year Estimates

School Enrollment by Grade and Control

Area	Preschool (%)		Kindergarten (%)		Grades 1 - 4 (%)		Grades 5 - 8 (%)		Grades 9 - 12 (%)	
	Public	Private	Public	Private	Public	Private	Public	Private	Public	Private
City	24.8	75.2	91.7	8.3	91.4	8.6	84.4	15.6	93.8	6.2
MSA[1]	46.3	53.7	88.5	11.5	87.7	12.3	87.3	12.7	91.3	8.7
U.S.	58.8	41.2	87.7	12.3	89.7	10.3	89.6	10.4	90.3	9.7

Note: Figures shown cover persons 3 years old and over; (1) Figures cover the Ann Arbor, MI Metropolitan Statistical Area—see Appendix B for areas included
Source: U.S. Census Bureau, 2013-2017 American Community Survey 5-Year Estimates

Average Salaries of Public School Classroom Teachers

Area	2016		2017		Change from 2016 to 2017	
	Dollars	Rank[1]	Dollars	Rank[1]	Percent	Rank[2]
Michigan	61,875	12	62,287	12	0.7	39
U.S. Average	58,479	–	59,660	–	2.0	–

Note: (1) Rank ranges from 1 to 51 where 1 indicates highest salary; (2) Rank ranges from 1 to 51 where 1 indicates highest percent change.
Source: National Education Association, Rankings & Estimates: Rankings of the States 2017 and Estimates of School Statistics 2018

Higher Education

Four-Year Colleges			Two-Year Colleges			Medical Schools[1]	Law Schools[2]	Voc/ Tech[3]
Public	Private Non-profit	Private For-profit	Public	Private Non-profit	Private For-profit			
1	1	0	1	0	0	1	1	1

Note: Figures cover institutions located within the city limits and include main campuses only; (1) includes schools accredited by the Liaison Committee on Medical Education and the American Osteopathic Association's Commission on Osteopathic College Accreditation; (2) includes ABA-accredited schools, schools with provisional ABA accreditation, and state accredited schools; (3) includes all schools with programs that are less than 2 years.
Source: National Center for Education Statistics, Integrated Postsecondary Education System (IPEDS), 2017-18; Wikipedia, List of Medical Schools in the United States, accessed April 3, 2019; Wikipedia, List of Law Schools in the United States, accessed April 3, 2019

According to *U.S. News & World Report,* the Ann Arbor, MI metro area is home to one of the best national universities in the U.S.: **University of Michigan—Ann Arbor** (#27 tie). The indicators used to capture academic quality fall into a number of categories: assessment by administrators at peer institutions; retention of students; faculty resources; student selectivity; financial resources; alumni giving; high school counselor ratings of colleges; and graduation rate. *U.S. News & World Report, "America's Best Colleges 2019"*

According to *U.S. News & World Report,* the Ann Arbor, MI metro area is home to one of the top 100 law schools in the U.S.: **University of Michigan—Ann Arbor** (#9). The rankings are based on a weighted average of 12 measures of quality: peer assessment score; assessment score by lawyers/judges; median LSAT scores; median undergrad GPA; acceptance rate; employment rates for graduates; placement success; bar passage rate; faculty resources; expenditures per student; student/faculty ratio; and library resources. *U.S. News & World Report, "America's Best Graduate Schools, Law, 2020"*

According to *U.S. News & World Report,* the Ann Arbor, MI metro area is home to one of the top 75 medical schools for research in the U.S.: **University of Michigan—Ann Arbor** (#16 tie). The rankings are based on a weighted average of 11 measures of quality: quality assessment; peer assessment score; assessment score by residency directors; research activity; total research activity; average research activity per faculty member; student selectivity; median MCAT total score; median undergraduate GPA; acceptance rate; and faculty resources. *U.S. News & World Report, "America's Best Graduate Schools, Medical, 2020"*

According to *U.S. News & World Report,* the Ann Arbor, MI metro area is home to one of the top 75 business schools in the U.S.: **University of Michigan—Ann Arbor (Ross)** (#10 tie). The rankings are based on a weighted average of the following nine measures: quality assessment; peer assessment; recruiter assessment; placement success; mean starting salary and bonus; student selectivity; mean GMAT and GRE scores; mean undergraduate GPA; and acceptance rate. *U.S. News & World Report, "America's Best Graduate Schools, Business, 2020"*

PRESIDENTIAL ELECTION

2016 Presidential Election Results

Area	Clinton	Trump	Johnson	Stein	Other
Washtenaw County	67.6	26.6	3.1	1.3	1.4
U.S.	48.0	45.9	3.3	1.1	1.7

Note: Results are percentages and may not add to 100% due to rounding
Source: Dave Leip's Atlas of U.S. Presidential Elections

EMPLOYERS

Major Employers

Company Name	Industry
Ann Arbor Public Schools	Education
Citizens Insurance Company of America	FInance & insurance
City of Ann Arbor	Government
Domino's Pizza	Food services
Eastern Michigan University	Education
Faurecia Interior Systems	Automotive component mfg.
Ford Motor Company	Automotive component mfg.
General Motors Milford Proving Grounds	OEM research
Grupo Antolin	Automotive component mfg.
Integrated Health Associates (IHA)	Medical center
JAC Products	Auto component mfg.
ProQuest	Data & information
Terumo Carviocascular Systems	Medical device manufacturer
Thai Summit America	Automotive component mfg.
Thomson Reuters	Software/IT
Toyota Technical Center	Automotive research & development
Trinity Health	Medical center
Truven Health Analytics	Data & information
University of Michigan	Education
University of Michigan Medical Center	Medical center
VA Ann Arbor Healthcare System	Medical center
Washtenaw Community College	Education
Washtenaw County Government	Government
Ypsilanti Public Schools	Education
Zingerman's	Food processing

Note: Companies shown are located within the Ann Arbor, MI Metropolitan Statistical Area.
Source: Hoovers.com; Wikipedia

PUBLIC SAFETY

Crime Rate

Area	All Crimes	Violent Crimes				Property Crimes		
		Murder	Rape[3]	Robbery	Aggrav. Assault	Burglary	Larceny -Theft	Motor Vehicle Theft
City	1,941.3	0.0	46.7	43.5	122.2	228.0	1,419.7	81.2
Suburbs[1]	1,971.1	4.5	71.3	51.0	256.7	237.3	1,223.6	126.7
Metro[2]	1,961.2	3.0	63.2	48.5	212.3	234.2	1,288.4	111.7
U.S.	2,756.1	5.3	41.7	98.0	248.9	430.4	1,694.4	237.4

Note: Figures are crimes per 100,000 population; (1) All areas within the metro area that are located outside the city limits; (2) Figures cover the Ann Arbor, MI Metropolitan Statistical Area—see Appendix B for areas included; (3) The city and U.S. figures shown were reported using the revised Uniform Crime Reporting (UCR) definition of rape. The suburban and metro area figures shown are an aggregate total of the data submitted using both the revised and legacy UCR definitions.
Source: FBI Uniform Crime Reports, 2017

Hate Crimes

Area	Number of Quarters Reported	Number of Incidents per Bias Motivation					
		Race/Ethnicity/Ancestry	Religion	Sexual Orientation	Disability	Gender	Gender Identity
City	4	3	13	3	0	0	0
U.S.	4	4,131	1,564	1,130	116	46	119

Source: Federal Bureau of Investigation, Hate Crime Statistics 2017

Identity Theft Consumer Reports

Area	Reports	Reports per 100,000 Population	Rank[2]
MSA[1]	650	178	18
U.S.	444,602	135	-

Note: (1) Figures cover the Ann Arbor, MI Metropolitan Statistical Area—see Appendix B for areas included;
(2) Rank ranges from 1 to 389 where 1 indicates greatest number of identity theft reports per 100,000
population
Source: Federal Trade Commission, Consumer Sentinel Network Data Book for January–December 2018

Fraud and Other Consumer Reports

Area	Reports	Reports per 100,000 Population	Rank[2]
MSA[1]	1,835	503	173
U.S.	2,552,917	776	-

Note: (1) Figures cover the Ann Arbor, MI Metropolitan Statistical Area—see Appendix B for areas included;
(2) Rank ranges from 1 to 389 where 1 indicates greatest number of fraud and other consumer reports per
100,000 population
Source: Federal Trade Commission, Consumer Sentinel Network Data Book for January–December 2018

SPORTS

Professional Sports Teams

Team Name	League	Year Established
No teams are located in the metro area		

Source: Wikipedia, Major Professional Sports Teams of the United States and Canada, April 5, 2019

CLIMATE

Average and Extreme Temperatures

Temperature	Jan	Feb	Mar	Apr	May	Jun	Jul	Aug	Sep	Oct	Nov	Dec	Yr.
Extreme High (°F)	62	65	81	89	93	104	102	100	98	91	77	68	104
Average High (°F)	30	33	44	58	70	79	83	81	74	61	48	35	58
Average Temp. (°F)	23	26	36	48	59	68	72	71	64	52	40	29	49
Average Low (°F)	16	18	27	37	47	56	61	60	53	41	32	21	39
Extreme Low (°F)	-21	-15	-4	10	25	36	41	38	29	17	9	-10	-21

Note: Figures cover the years 1958-1990
Source: National Climatic Data Center, International Station Meteorological Climate Summary, 9/96

Average Precipitation/Snowfall/Humidity

Precip./Humidity	Jan	Feb	Mar	Apr	May	Jun	Jul	Aug	Sep	Oct	Nov	Dec	Yr.
Avg. Precip. (in.)	1.8	1.8	2.5	3.0	2.9	3.6	3.1	3.4	2.8	2.2	2.6	2.7	32.4
Avg. Snowfall (in.)	10	9	7	2	Tr	0	0	0	0	Tr	3	11	41
Avg. Rel. Hum. 7am (%)	80	79	79	78	78	79	82	86	87	84	82	81	81
Avg. Rel. Hum. 4pm (%)	67	63	59	53	51	52	52	54	55	55	64	70	58

Note: Figures cover the years 1958-1990; Tr = Trace amounts (<0.05 in. of rain; <0.5 in. of snow)
Source: National Climatic Data Center, International Station Meteorological Climate Summary, 9/96

Weather Conditions

Temperature			Daytime Sky			Precipitation		
5°F & below	32°F & below	90°F & above	Clear	Partly cloudy	Cloudy	0.01 inch or more precip.	0.1 inch or more snow/ice	Thunder-storms
15	136	12	74	134	157	135	38	32

Note: Figures are average number of days per year and cover the years 1958-1990
Source: National Climatic Data Center, International Station Meteorological Climate Summary, 9/96

**HAZARDOUS
WASTE**

Superfund Sites

The Ann Arbor, MI metro area has no sites on the EPA's Superfund Final National Priorities List. There are a total of 1,390 Superfund sites with a status of proposed or final on the list in the U.S.
U.S. Environmental Protection Agency, National Priorities List, April 5, 2019

**AIR & WATER
QUALITY**

Air Quality Trends: Ozone

	1990	1995	2000	2005	2010	2012	2014	2015	2016	2017
MSA[1]	n/a	n/a	n/a	n/a	n/a	n/a	n/a	n/a	n/a	n/a
U.S.	0.088	0.089	0.082	0.080	0.073	0.075	0.067	0.068	0.069	0.068

Note: (1) Data covers the Ann Arbor, MI Metropolitan Statistical Area—see Appendix B for areas included; n/a not available. The values shown are the composite ozone concentration averages among trend sites based on the highest fourth daily maximum 8-hour concentration in parts per million. These trends are based on sites having an adequate record of monitoring data during the trend period. Data from exceptional events are included.
Source: U.S. Environmental Protection Agency, Air Quality Monitoring Information, "Air Quality Trends by City, 1990-2017"

Air Quality Index

Area	Percent of Days when Air Quality was...[2]					AQI Statistics[2]	
	Good	Moderate	Unhealthy for Sensitive Groups	Unhealthy	Very Unhealthy	Maximum	Median
MSA[1]	77.8	21.4	0.8	0.0	0.0	119	40

Note: (1) Data covers the Ann Arbor, MI Metropolitan Statistical Area—see Appendix B for areas included; (2) Based on 365 days with AQI data in 2017. Air Quality Index (AQI) is an index for reporting daily air quality. EPA calculates the AQI for five major air pollutants regulated by the Clean Air Act: ground-level ozone, particle pollution (aka particulate matter), carbon monoxide, sulfur dioxide, and nitrogen dioxide. The AQI runs from 0 to 500. The higher the AQI value, the greater the level of air pollution and the greater the health concern. There are six AQI categories: "Good" AQI is between 0 and 50. Air quality is considered satisfactory; "Moderate" AQI is between 51 and 100. Air quality is acceptable; "Unhealthy for Sensitive Groups" When AQI values are between 101 and 150, members of sensitive groups may experience health effects; "Unhealthy" When AQI values are between 151 and 200 everyone may begin to experience health effects; "Very Unhealthy" AQI values between 201 and 300 trigger a health alert; "Hazardous" AQI values over 300 trigger warnings of emergency conditions (not shown).
Source: U.S. Environmental Protection Agency, Air Quality Index Report, 2017

Air Quality Index Pollutants

Area	Percent of Days when AQI Pollutant was...[2]					
	Carbon Monoxide	Nitrogen Dioxide	Ozone	Sulfur Dioxide	Particulate Matter 2.5	Particulate Matter 10
MSA[1]	0.0	0.0	65.8	0.0	34.2	0.0

Note: (1) Data covers the Ann Arbor, MI Metropolitan Statistical Area—see Appendix B for areas included; (2) Based on 365 days with AQI data in 2017. The Air Quality Index (AQI) is an index for reporting daily air quality. EPA calculates the AQI for five major air pollutants regulated by the Clean Air Act: ground-level ozone, particle pollution (also known as particulate matter), carbon monoxide, sulfur dioxide, and nitrogen dioxide. The AQI runs from 0 to 500. The higher the AQI value, the greater the level of air pollution and the greater the health concern.
Source: U.S. Environmental Protection Agency, Air Quality Index Report, 2017

Maximum Air Pollutant Concentrations: Particulate Matter, Ozone, CO and Lead

	Particulate Matter 10 (ug/m^3)	Particulate Matter 2.5 Wtd AM (ug/m^3)	Particulate Matter 2.5 24-Hr (ug/m^3)	Ozone (ppm)	Carbon Monoxide (ppm)	Lead (ug/m^3)
MSA[1] Level	n/a	8	19	0.069	n/a	n/a
NAAQS[2]	150	15	35	0.075	9	0.15
Met NAAQS[2]	n/a	Yes	Yes	Yes	n/a	n/a

Note: (1) Data covers the Ann Arbor, MI Metropolitan Statistical Area—see Appendix B for areas included; Data from exceptional events are included; (2) National Ambient Air Quality Standards; ppm = parts per million; ug/m^3 = micrograms per cubic meter; n/a not available.
Concentrations: Particulate Matter 10 (coarse particulate)—highest second maximum 24-hour concentration; Particulate Matter 2.5 Wtd AM (fine particulate)—highest weighted annual mean concentration; Particulate Matter 2.5 24-Hour (fine particulate)—highest 98th percentile 24-hour concentration; Ozone—highest fourth daily maximum 8-hour concentration; Carbon Monoxide—highest second maximum non-overlapping 8-hour concentration; Lead—maximum running 3-month average
Source: U.S. Environmental Protection Agency, Air Quality Monitoring Information, "Air Quality Statistics by City, 2017"

Maximum Air Pollutant Concentrations: Nitrogen Dioxide and Sulfur Dioxide

	Nitrogen Dioxide AM (ppb)	Nitrogen Dioxide 1-Hr (ppb)	Sulfur Dioxide AM (ppb)	Sulfur Dioxide 1-Hr (ppb)	Sulfur Dioxide 24-Hr (ppb)
MSA[1] Level	n/a	n/a	n/a	n/a	n/a
NAAQS[2]	53	100	30	75	140
Met NAAQS[2]	n/a	n/a	n/a	n/a	n/a

Note: (1) Data covers the Ann Arbor, MI Metropolitan Statistical Area—see Appendix B for areas included; Data from exceptional events are included; (2) National Ambient Air Quality Standards; ppm = parts per million; ug/m^3 = micrograms per cubic meter; n/a not available.
Concentrations: Nitrogen Dioxide AM—highest arithmetic mean concentration; Nitrogen Dioxide 1-Hr—highest 98th percentile 1-hour daily maximum concentration; Sulfur Dioxide AM—highest annual mean concentration; Sulfur Dioxide 1-Hr—highest 99th percentile 1-hour daily maximum concentration; Sulfur Dioxide 24-Hr—highest second maximum 24-hour concentration
Source: U.S. Environmental Protection Agency, Air Quality Monitoring Information, "Air Quality Statistics by City, 2017"

Drinking Water

Water System Name	Pop. Served	Primary Water Source Type	Violations[1] Health Based	Violations[1] Monitoring/ Reporting
Ann Arbor	118,017	Surface	0	0

Note: (1) Based on violation data from January 1, 2018 to December 31, 2018
Source: U.S. Environmental Protection Agency, Office of Ground Water and Drinking Water, Safe Drinking Water Information System (based on data extracted April 5, 2019)

Cedar Rapids, Iowa

Background

Cedar Rapids, on the Cedar River that gave it its name, is the principal city in eastern Iowa, located some 100 miles northeast of Des Moines. The Cedar Rapids of today is one of the Midwest's most diversified and modern cities.

Prior to European expansion, the site was intermittently home to nomadic bands of Fox, Meskwaki, and Winnebago Indians. Its first western settler was Osgood Shephard, a hunter, trapper, and horse trader who lived in a cabin on the river at a site, which is now the corner of First Avenue and First Street SE. A stainless-steel sculpture, The Tree of Five Seasons, commemorates Shephard's first settlement, and is a common point of reference for the city's citizens.

Cedar Rapids, first called Rapids City, was incorporated as a town in 1849 and as a city in 1856. By 1858 the city boasted a population of 1,400. Both in the city itself and in the immediate environs, one is exposed to rich ethnic traditions and a pride in the preservation of local performing and visual arts.

Cedar Rapids, distinctively, was the first home of the North Star Oatmeal Mill, which eventually became Quaker Oats, long a giant in the cereals industry. The Cedar Rapids-based company still operates, under one roof, the largest cereal mill in the world.

The city has extensively diversified, however, from its original agricultural focus. Many industries, both locally and internationally owned, provide stability and dynamism to the local economy, which is increasingly tied into a larger global framework. Cedar Rapids also hosts industries specializing in food processing, construction machinery, pharmaceuticals, financial services, and biotechnology, and is one of the largest exporter per capita in the United States, with the nearby Eastern Iowa Airport designated as a foreign trade zone. The city has also become a major telecommunications hub.

Cedar Rapids is home to Coe College, founded in 1851, and Mount Mercy College, founded in 1928. The National Capital Language Resource Center (NCLRC) in Washington DC maintains 93 schools that teach Arabic, one of which is in Cedar Rapids. The town also benefits from the presence of the Cedar Rapids Museum of Art, the Cedar Rapids Symphony Orchestra, the Science Station, which boasts the first IMAX Theater in Iowa, the History Center, and the National Czech and Slovak Museum and Library. Other area attractions include Duffy's Collectible Cars, Brucemore Mansion, the Iowa Children's Museum, the Indian Creek Nature Center, and the Czech Village. Government buildings are located on Municipal Island in the main channel of the Cedar River. Within a half-hour's drive are 75 public parks and seven public golf courses.

Nearby are several points of historical interest, including the Herbert Hoover Birthplace and Library, and the Amana Colonies, founded in the 1850s as a utopian society by members of a German religious sect. At the Amana villages, visitors can still view the operations of working farms, wool mills, and bakeries. Cedar Rapids is also the home to a large number of American Muslims. The oldest exclusively Muslim cemetery in the United States is located in Cedar Rapids, along with the historic Mother Mosque of America.

Grant Wood—the famous painter of *American Gothic* and other icons of the Great Plains—was a resident of the city and taught there for many years. Many of his canvases are on display and others are owned by private citizens. The Cedar Rapids Museum houses 7,200 works of art, including the world's largest collections of works by Wood, Marvin D. Cone, and Mauricio Lasansky. The Museum also operates the Grant Wood Studio and Visitor Center.

In June 2008, the Cedar River flooded its banks, leaving 1,300 city blocks under water. The city was almost entirely evacuated and hundreds of homes were destroyed. Rebuilding efforts have been strong and a restored City Hall and Paramount Theater opened in 2012, with many other facilities opening in 2013, including fire stations, the library, and the ground transportation center. In September 2016, when Hurricane Paine threatened to flood Cedar Rapids again, the residents were prepared as hundreds of thousands of volunteers, as well as over 400 National Guard troops, filled more than 250,000 sand bags which effectively prevented major flooding of the city.

There are four distinct seasons in Cedar Rapids. Winters are cold and dry, with winds out of the northwest. Some summer days bring rain from the Gulf of Mexico, but on other days hot dry air from the southwest can cause unusually high temperatures. Fall and spring can be mild, tempered by air from the Pacific. Precipitation throughout the year is moderate.

Rankings

General Rankings

- In their sixth annual survey, Livability.com looked at data for more than 1,000 U.S. cities to determine the rankings for Livability's "Top 100 Best Places to Live" in 2019. Cedar Rapids ranked #50. Criteria: median home value capped at $250,000; affordable living; vibrant economy; education, demographics, health care options. transportation & infrastructure; abundant lifestyle amenities. *Livability.com, "Top 100 Best Places to Live 2019" March 2019*

Business/Finance Rankings

- The personal finance site NerdWallet analyzed 183 American metropolitan areas with populations over 250,000 and more than 15,000 businesses to rank where entrepreneurs find the most success. Criteria included area economy, annual income, housing cost, unemployment rate, and the success rate of area businesses. Cedar Rapids ranked #6. *www.nerdwallet.com, "Best Places to Start a Business," April 27, 2015*

- Using data from the Council for Community and Economic Research's 2014 cost of living index, NerdWallet ranked the 100 most affordable cities in America. Median income was compared with cost of living to find truly affordable places. Cedar Rapids ranked #19. *NerdWallet.com, "America's Most Affordable Places," May 18, 2015*

- The Cedar Rapids metro area appeared on the Milken Institute "2018 Best Performing Cities" list. Rank: #149 out of 200 large metro areas. Criteria: job growth; wage and salary growth; high-tech output growth. *Milken Institute, "Best-Performing Cities 2018," January 24, 2019*

- *Forbes* ranked the 200 most populous metro areas to determine the nation's "Best Places for Business and Careers." The Cedar Rapids metro area was ranked #116. Criteria: costs (business and living); job growth (past and projected); income growth; quality of life; educational attainment (college and high school); projected economic growth; cultural and recreational opportunities; net migration patterns; number of highly ranked colleges. *Forbes, "The Best Places for Business and Careers 2018: Seattle Leads the Way," October 24, 2018*

Environmental Rankings

- Cedar Rapids was highlighted as one of the cleanest metro areas for ozone air pollution in the U.S. during 2014 through 2016. The list represents cities with no monitored ozone air pollution in unhealthful ranges. *American Lung Association, State of the Air 2018*

Health/Fitness Rankings

- The Cedar Rapids metro area was identified as one of the worst cities for bed bugs in America by pest control company Orkin. The area ranked #44 out of 50 based on the number of bed bug treatments Orkin performed from December 2017 to November 2018. *Orkin, "Baltimore Remains Front Runner, Atlanta and Philadelphia Break Into Top 10," January 14, 2019*

- The Cedar Rapids metro area ranked #135 out of 189 in The Gallup-Healthways Well-Being Index. Criteria: purpose; social well being; financial health; community and physical health. Results are based on telephone interviews with adults, aged 18 and older, living in metropolitan areas in the 50 U.S. states and the District of Columbia. *Gallup-Healthways, "State of American Well-Being, 2017 Community Well-Being Rankings" March 2018*

Real Estate Rankings

- *WalletHub* compared the most populated U.S. cities, as well as at least two of the most populated cities in each state, for a total of 179, to determine which had the best markets for real estate agents. Cedar Rapids ranked #96 where demand was high and pay was the best. Criteria: sales per agent; annual median wage for real-estate agents; monthly average starting salary for real estate agents; real estate job density and competition; unemployment rate; housing-market health index; and other relevant metrics. *www.WalletHub.com, "2018's Best Places to Be a Real Estate Agent," April 25, 2018*

Safety Rankings

- The National Insurance Crime Bureau ranked 382 metro areas in the U.S. in terms of per capita rates of vehicle theft. The Cedar Rapids metro area ranked #166 (#1 = highest rate). Criteria: number of vehicle theft offenses per 100,000 inhabitants in 2017. *National Insurance Crime Bureau, "Hot Spots 2017," July 12, 2018*

Seniors/Retirement Rankings

- From its Best Cities for Successful Aging indexes, the Milken Institute generated rankings for metropolitan areas, weighing data in nine categories—health care, wellness, living arrangements, transportation and convenience, financial characteristics, education, employment, community engagement, and overall livability. The Cedar Rapids metro area was ranked #82 overall in the small metro area category. *Milken Institute, "Best Cities for Successful Aging, 2017" March 14, 2017*

Women/Minorities Rankings

- Personal finance website *WalletHub* compared more than 180 U.S. cities—including the 150 most populated U.S. cities, plus at least two of the most populated cities in each state—across two key dimensions, "Hispanic Business-Friendliness" and "Hispanic Purchasing Power", to arrive at the most favorable conditions for Hispanic entrepreneurs. Cedar Rapids was ranked #89 out of 182. Criteria includes: share of Hispanic-Owned Businesses; Hispanic entrepreneurship rate to median annual income of Hispanics; Small Business-Friendliness score; cost of living; and number of Hispanics with at least a bachelor's degree. *WalletHub.com, "2018's Best Cities for Hispanic Entrepreneurs," April 26, 2018*

Miscellaneous Rankings

- *WalletHub* compared the 150 most populated U.S. cities to determine their operating efficiency. A "Quality of Services" score was constructed for each city and then divided by the total budget per capita to reveal which were managed the best. Cedar Rapids ranked #13. Criteria: financial stability; economy; education; safety; health; infrastructure and pollution. *www.WalletHub.com, "2018's Best- & Worst-Run Cities in America," July 9, 2018*

Business Environment

CITY FINANCES

City Government Finances

Component	2016 ($000)	2016 ($ per capita)
Total Revenues	423,039	3,244
Total Expenditures	391,920	3,005
Debt Outstanding	502,737	3,855
Cash and Securities[1]	468,290	3,591

Note: (1) Cash and security holdings of a government at the close of its fiscal year, including those of its dependent agencies, utilities, and liquor stores.
Source: U.S. Census Bureau, State & Local Government Finances 2016

City Government Revenue by Source

Source	2016 ($000)	2016 ($ per capita)	2016 (%)
General Revenue			
From Federal Government	74,516	571	17.6
From State Government	39,142	300	9.3
From Local Governments	1,722	13	0.4
Taxes			
Property	97,845	750	23.1
Sales and Gross Receipts	33,578	257	7.9
Personal Income	0	0	0.0
Corporate Income	0	0	0.0
Motor Vehicle License	0	0	0.0
Other Taxes	2,616	20	0.6
Current Charges	109,345	839	25.8
Liquor Store	0	0	0.0
Utility	33,283	255	7.9
Employee Retirement	0	0	0.0

Source: U.S. Census Bureau, State & Local Government Finances 2016

City Government Expenditures by Function

Function	2016 ($000)	2016 ($ per capita)	2016 (%)
General Direct Expenditures			
Air Transportation	21,070	161	5.4
Corrections	0	0	0.0
Education	0	0	0.0
Employment Security Administration	0	0	0.0
Financial Administration	4,981	38	1.3
Fire Protection	20,352	156	5.2
General Public Buildings	1,122	8	0.3
Governmental Administration, Other	2,766	21	0.7
Health	1,116	8	0.3
Highways	17,620	135	4.5
Hospitals	0	0	0.0
Housing and Community Development	6,409	49	1.6
Interest on General Debt	15,388	118	3.9
Judicial and Legal	861	6	0.2
Libraries	6,205	47	1.6
Parking	1,571	12	0.4
Parks and Recreation	10,123	77	2.6
Police Protection	43,010	329	11.0
Public Welfare	0	0	0.0
Sewerage	34,878	267	8.9
Solid Waste Management	9,640	73	2.5
Veterans' Services	0	0	0.0
Liquor Store	0	0	0.0
Utility	42,757	327	10.9
Employee Retirement	0	0	0.0

Source: U.S. Census Bureau, State & Local Government Finances 2016

DEMOGRAPHICS

Population Growth

Area	1990 Census	2000 Census	2010 Census	2017* Estimate	Population Growth (%)	
					1990-2017	2010-2017
City	110,829	120,758	126,326	130,330	17.6	3.2
MSA[1]	210,640	237,230	257,940	266,122	26.3	3.2
U.S.	248,709,873	281,421,906	308,745,538	321,004,407	29.1	4.0

Note: (1) Figures cover the Cedar Rapids, IA Metropolitan Statistical Area—see Appendix B for areas included; (*) 2013-2017 5-year estimated population
Source: U.S. Census Bureau, 1990 Census, Census 2000, Census 2010, 2013-2017 American Community Survey 5-Year Estimates

Household Size

Area	Persons in Household (%)							Average Household Size
	One	Two	Three	Four	Five	Six	Seven or More	
City	33.5	34.3	14.1	11.4	3.7	2.1	0.9	2.30
MSA[1]	28.7	36.8	14.1	12.6	4.7	2.1	0.9	2.40
U.S.	27.7	33.8	15.7	13.0	6.0	2.3	1.4	2.60

Note: (1) Figures cover the Cedar Rapids, IA Metropolitan Statistical Area—see Appendix B for areas included
Source: U.S. Census Bureau, 2013-2017 American Community Survey 5-Year Estimates

Race

Area	White Alone[2] (%)	Black Alone[2] (%)	Asian Alone[2] (%)	AIAN[3] Alone[2] (%)	NHOPI[4] Alone[2] (%)	Other Race Alone[2] (%)	Two or More Races (%)
City	85.8	6.4	3.0	0.2	0.1	1.2	3.2
MSA[1]	90.2	4.3	1.9	0.2	0.1	0.8	2.5
U.S.	73.0	12.7	5.4	0.8	0.2	4.8	3.1

Note: (1) Figures cover the Cedar Rapids, IA Metropolitan Statistical Area—see Appendix B for areas included; (2) Alone is defined as not being in combination with one or more other races; (3) American Indian and Alaska Native; (4) Native Hawaiian and Other Pacific Islander
Source: U.S. Census Bureau, 2013-2017 American Community Survey 5-Year Estimates

Hispanic or Latino Origin

Area	Total (%)	Mexican (%)	Puerto Rican (%)	Cuban (%)	Other (%)
City	3.8	2.9	0.1	0.0	0.8
MSA[1]	2.8	2.1	0.1	0.0	0.6
U.S.	17.6	11.1	1.7	0.7	4.1

Note: Persons of Hispanic or Latino origin can be of any race; (1) Figures cover the Cedar Rapids, IA Metropolitan Statistical Area—see Appendix B for areas included
Source: U.S. Census Bureau, 2013-2017 American Community Survey 5-Year Estimates

Segregation

Type	Segregation Indices[1]				Percent Change		
	1990	2000	2010	2010 Rank[2]	1990-2000	1990-2010	2000-2010
Black/White	n/a	n/a	n/a	n/a	n/a	n/a	n/a
Asian/White	n/a	n/a	n/a	n/a	n/a	n/a	n/a
Hispanic/White	n/a	n/a	n/a	n/a	n/a	n/a	n/a

Note: All figures cover the Metropolitan Statistical Area—see Appendix B for areas included; Figures are based on an analysis of 1990, 2000, and 2010 Census Decennial Census tract data by William H. Frey, Brookings Institution and the University of Michigan Social Science Data Analysis Network. In this analysis all racial groups (whites, blacks, and asians) are non-Hispanic members of those races. Hispanics are shown as a separate category; (1) Segregation Indices are Dissimilarity Indices that measure the degree to which the minority group is distributed differently than whites across census tracts. They range from 0 (complete integration) to 100 (complete segregation) where the value indicates the percentage of the minority group that needs to move to be distributed exactly like whites; (2) Ranges from 1 (most segregated) to 102 (least segregated); n/a not available.
Source: www.CensusScope.org

Ancestry

Area	German	Irish	English	American	Italian	Polish	French[2]	Scottish	Dutch
City	33.8	14.7	8.5	4.8	1.7	1.5	2.4	1.5	2.2
MSA[1]	37.0	15.3	8.1	5.5	1.7	1.3	2.4	1.6	2.1
U.S.	14.1	10.1	7.5	6.6	5.3	2.9	2.5	1.7	1.3

Note: Figures are the percentage of the total population reporting a particular ancestry. The nine most commonly reported ancestries in the U.S. are shown. Figures include multiple ancestries (e.g. if a person reported being Irish and Italian, they were included in both columns); (1) Figures cover the Cedar Rapids, IA Metropolitan Statistical Area—see Appendix B for areas included; (2) Excludes Basque
Source: U.S. Census Bureau, 2013-2017 American Community Survey 5-Year Estimates

Foreign-Born Population

Area	Percent of Population Born in								
	Any Foreign Country	Asia	Mexico	Europe	Carribean	Central America[2]	South America	Africa	Canada
City	5.0	2.5	0.9	0.4	0.2	0.1	0.1	0.7	0.1
MSA[1]	3.5	1.6	0.6	0.4	0.1	0.0	0.1	0.5	0.2
U.S.	13.4	4.1	3.6	1.5	1.3	1.0	0.9	0.6	0.3

Note: (1) Figures cover the Cedar Rapids, IA Metropolitan Statistical Area—see Appendix B for areas included; (2) Excludes Mexico.
Source: U.S. Census Bureau, 2013-2017 American Community Survey 5-Year Estimates

Marital Status

Area	Never Married	Now Married[2]	Separated	Widowed	Divorced
City	34.2	47.0	1.3	6.0	11.5
MSA[1]	28.9	53.2	1.2	5.8	10.9
U.S.	33.1	48.2	2.0	5.8	10.9

Note: Figures are percentages and cover the population 15 years of age and older; (1) Figures cover the Cedar Rapids, IA Metropolitan Statistical Area—see Appendix B for areas included; (2) Excludes separated
Source: U.S. Census Bureau, 2013-2017 American Community Survey 5-Year Estimates

Disability by Age

Area	All Ages	Under 18 Years Old	18 to 64 Years Old	65 Years and Over
City	10.4	3.9	8.4	30.0
MSA[1]	10.3	4.0	8.1	29.3
U.S.	12.6	4.2	10.3	35.5

Note: Figures show percent of the civilian noninstitutionalized population that reported having a disability. Disability status is determined from six types of difficulty: vision, hearing, cognitive, ambulatory, self-care, and independent living. For children under 5 years old, hearing and vision difficulty are used to determine disability status. For children between the ages of 5 and 14, disability status is determined from hearing, vision, cognitive, ambulatory, and self-care difficulties. For people aged 15 years and older, they are considered to have a disability if they have difficulty with any one of the six difficulty types; Note: (1) Figures cover the Cedar Rapids, IA Metropolitan Statistical Area—see Appendix B for areas included
Source: U.S. Census Bureau, 2013-2017 American Community Survey 5-Year Estimates

Age

Area	Percent of Population									Median Age
	Under Age 5	Age 5–19	Age 20–34	Age 35–44	Age 45–54	Age 55–64	Age 65–74	Age 75–84	Age 85+	
City	6.9	19.0	22.9	12.7	12.2	12.1	7.6	4.4	2.3	36.0
MSA[1]	6.2	19.9	19.8	12.6	13.5	12.8	8.4	4.6	2.3	38.1
U.S.	6.2	19.5	20.7	12.7	13.4	12.7	8.6	4.4	1.9	37.8

Note: (1) Figures cover the Cedar Rapids, IA Metropolitan Statistical Area—see Appendix B for areas included
Source: U.S. Census Bureau, 2013-2017 American Community Survey 5-Year Estimates

Gender

Area	Males	Females	Males per 100 Females
City	63,400	66,930	94.7
MSA[1]	131,848	134,274	98.2
U.S.	158,018,753	162,985,654	97.0

Note: (1) Figures cover the Cedar Rapids, IA Metropolitan Statistical Area—see Appendix B for areas included
Source: U.S. Census Bureau, 2013-2017 American Community Survey 5-Year Estimates

Religious Groups by Family

Area	Catholic	Baptist	Non-Den.	Methodist[2]	Lutheran	LDS[3]	Pentecostal	Presbyterian[4]	Muslim[5]	Judaism
MSA[1]	18.8	2.4	3.0	7.3	11.3	0.9	1.8	3.3	0.5	0.1
U.S.	19.1	9.3	4.0	4.0	2.3	2.0	1.9	1.6	0.8	0.7

Note: Figures are the number of adherents as a percentage of the total population; (1) Figures cover the Cedar Rapids, IA Metropolitan Statistical Area—see Appendix B for areas included; (2) Methodist/Pietist; (3) Latter Day Saints; (4) Reformed; (5) Figures are estimates
Source: Association of Statisticians of American Religious Bodies, 2010 U.S. Religion Census: Religious Congregations & Membership Study

Religious Groups by Tradition

Area	Catholic	Evangelical Protestant	Mainline Protestant	Other Tradition	Black Protestant	Orthodox
MSA[1]	18.8	13.7	17.5	2.0	0.2	0.2
U.S.	19.1	16.2	7.3	4.3	1.6	0.3

Note: Figures are the number of adherents as a percentage of the total population; (1) Figures cover the Cedar Rapids, IA Metropolitan Statistical Area—see Appendix B for areas included
Source: Association of Statisticians of American Religious Bodies, 2010 U.S. Religion Census: Religious Congregations & Membership Study

ECONOMY

Gross Metropolitan Product

Area	2016	2017	2018	2019	Rank[2]
MSA[1]	18.3	18.6	19.1	19.9	134

Note: Figures are in billions of dollars; (1) Figures cover the Cedar Rapids, IA Metropolitan Statistical Area—see Appendix B for areas included; (2) Rank is based on 2017 data and ranges from 1 to 381
Source: U.S. Conference of Mayors, U.S. Metro Economies: Economic Growth & Full Employment, June 2018

Economic Growth

Area	2017-2018 (%)	2019-2020 (%)	2021-2022 (%)
MSA[1]	0.7	1.8	1.5

Note: Figures are real gross metropolitan product (GMP) growth rates and represent average annual percent change; (1) Figures cover the Cedar Rapids, IA Metropolitan Statistical Area—see Appendix B for areas included
Source: U.S. Conference of Mayors, U.S. Metro Economies: Economic Growth & Full Employment, June 2018

Metropolitan Area Exports

Area	2012	2013	2014	2015	2016	2017	Rank[2]
MSA[1]	889.1	930.2	879.0	873.5	945.0	1,071.6	149

Note: Figures are in millions of dollars; (1) Figures cover the Cedar Rapids, IA Metropolitan Statistical Area—see Appendix B for areas included; (2) Rank is based on 2017 data and ranges from 1 to 387
Source: U.S. Department of Commerce, International Trade Administration, Office of Trade and Economic Analysis, Industry and Analysis, Exports by Metropolitan Area, extracted March 25, 2019

Building Permits

Area	Single-Family			Multi-Family			Total		
	2016	2017	Pct. Chg.	2016	2017	Pct. Chg.	2016	2017	Pct. Chg.
City	268	219	-18.3	127	313	146.5	395	532	34.7
MSA[1]	555	537	-3.2	232	455	96.1	787	992	26.0
U.S.	750,800	820,000	9.2	455,800	462,000	1.4	1,206,600	1,282,000	6.2

Note: (1) Figures cover the Cedar Rapids, IA Metropolitan Statistical Area—see Appendix B for areas included; Figures represent new, privately-owned housing units authorized (unadjusted data); All permit data are based on estimates with imputation
Source: U.S. Census Bureau, Manufacturing, Mining, and Construction Statistics, Building Permits, 2016, 2017

Bankruptcy Filings

Area	Business Filings			Nonbusiness Filings		
	2017	2018	% Chg.	2017	2018	% Chg.
Linn County	9	8	-11.1	289	351	21.5
U.S.	23,157	22,232	-4.0	765,863	751,186	-1.9

Note: Business filings include Chapter 7, Chapter 11, Chapter 12, and Chapter 13; Nonbusiness filings include Chapter 7, Chapter 11, and Chapter 13
Source: Administrative Office of the U.S. Courts, Business and Nonbusiness Bankruptcy, County Cases Commenced by Chapter of the Bankruptcy Code, During the 12-Month Period Ending December 31, 2017 and Business and Nonbusiness Bankruptcy, County Cases Commenced by Chapter of the Bankruptcy Code, During the 12-Month Period Ending December 31, 2018

Housing Vacancy Rates

Area	Gross Vacancy Rate[2] (%)			Year-Round Vacancy Rate[3] (%)			Rental Vacancy Rate[4] (%)			Homeowner Vacancy Rate[5] (%)		
	2016	2017	2018	2016	2017	2018	2016	2017	2018	2016	2017	2018
MSA[1]	n/a	n/a	n/a	n/a	n/a	n/a	n/a	n/a	n/a	n/a	n/a	n/a
U.S.	12.8	12.7	12.3	9.9	9.9	9.7	6.9	7.2	6.9	1.7	1.6	1.5

Note: (1) Figures cover the Cedar Rapids, IA Metropolitan Statistical Area—see Appendix B for areas included; (2) The percentage of the total housing inventory that is vacant; (3) The percentage of the housing inventory (excluding seasonal units) that is year-round vacant; (4) The percentage of rental inventory that is vacant for rent; (5) The percentage of homeowner inventory that is vacant for sale; n/a not available
Source: U.S. Census Bureau, Housing Vacancies and Homeownership Annual Statistics: 2016, 2017, 2018

INCOME

Income

Area	Per Capita ($)	Median Household ($)	Average Household ($)
City	31,585	56,828	73,859
MSA[1]	32,504	62,399	79,045
U.S.	31,177	57,652	81,283

Note: (1) Figures cover the Cedar Rapids, IA Metropolitan Statistical Area—see Appendix B for areas included
Source: U.S. Census Bureau, 2013-2017 American Community Survey 5-Year Estimates

Household Income Distribution

Area	Percent of Households Earning							
	Under $15,000	$15,000 -$24,999	$25,000 -$34,999	$35,000 -$49,999	$50,000 -$74,999	$75,000 -$99,999	$100,000 -$149,999	$150,000 and up
City	9.8	9.2	10.4	14.3	19.6	13.7	14.8	8.1
MSA[1]	8.4	8.6	9.6	13.5	18.8	15.0	16.2	9.9
U.S.	11.6	9.8	9.5	13.0	17.7	12.3	14.1	12.1

Note: (1) Figures cover the Cedar Rapids, IA Metropolitan Statistical Area—see Appendix B for areas included
Source: U.S. Census Bureau, 2013-2017 American Community Survey 5-Year Estimates

Poverty Rate

Area	All Ages	Under 18 Years Old	18 to 64 Years Old	65 Years and Over
City	11.4	13.6	11.8	6.2
MSA[1]	9.4	11.3	9.4	6.0
U.S.	14.6	20.3	13.7	9.3

Note: Figures are percentage of people whose income during the past 12 months was below the poverty level; (1) Figures cover the Cedar Rapids, IA Metropolitan Statistical Area—see Appendix B for areas included
Source: U.S. Census Bureau, 2013-2017 American Community Survey 5-Year Estimates

EMPLOYMENT

Labor Force and Employment

Area	Civilian Labor Force			Workers Employed		
	Dec. 2017	Dec. 2018	% Chg.	Dec. 2017	Dec. 2018	% Chg.
City	70,152	70,700	0.8	67,761	68,658	1.3
MSA[1]	141,463	142,627	0.8	136,902	138,776	1.4
U.S.	159,880,000	162,510,000	1.6	153,602,000	156,481,000	1.9

Note: Data is not seasonally adjusted and covers workers 16 years of age and older; (1) Figures cover the Cedar Rapids, IA Metropolitan Statistical Area—see Appendix B for areas included
Source: Bureau of Labor Statistics, Local Area Unemployment Statistics

Unemployment Rate

Area	2018											
	Jan.	Feb.	Mar.	Apr.	May	Jun.	Jul.	Aug.	Sep.	Oct.	Nov.	Dec.
City	3.9	3.8	3.3	2.9	2.7	3.1	3.0	2.9	2.6	2.4	2.5	2.9
MSA[1]	4.0	3.8	3.3	2.8	2.4	2.7	2.7	2.6	2.4	2.1	2.2	2.7
U.S.	4.5	4.4	4.1	3.7	3.6	4.2	4.1	3.9	3.6	3.5	3.5	3.7

Note: Data is not seasonally adjusted and covers workers 16 years of age and older; (1) Figures cover the
Cedar Rapids, IA Metropolitan Statistical Area—see Appendix B for areas included
Source: Bureau of Labor Statistics, Local Area Unemployment Statistics

Average Wages

Occupation	$/Hr.	Occupation	$/Hr.
Accountants and Auditors	34.20	Maids and Housekeeping Cleaners	11.20
Automotive Mechanics	21.20	Maintenance and Repair Workers	22.30
Bookkeepers	19.30	Marketing Managers	54.10
Carpenters	22.00	Nuclear Medicine Technologists	n/a
Cashiers	10.60	Nurses, Licensed Practical	20.40
Clerks, General Office	17.30	Nurses, Registered	27.90
Clerks, Receptionists/Information	13.60	Nursing Assistants	13.90
Clerks, Shipping/Receiving	18.60	Packers and Packagers, Hand	14.00
Computer Programmers	39.50	Physical Therapists	37.20
Computer Systems Analysts	40.90	Postal Service Mail Carriers	24.70
Computer User Support Specialists	22.50	Real Estate Brokers	n/a
Cooks, Restaurant	11.40	Retail Salespersons	13.60
Dentists	n/a	Sales Reps., Exc. Tech./Scientific	31.60
Electrical Engineers	44.20	Sales Reps., Tech./Scientific	42.00
Electricians	25.50	Secretaries, Exc. Legal/Med./Exec.	17.90
Financial Managers	59.30	Security Guards	13.30
First-Line Supervisors/Managers, Sales	20.00	Surgeons	n/a
Food Preparation Workers	11.80	Teacher Assistants*	13.40
General and Operations Managers	53.10	Teachers, Elementary School*	26.70
Hairdressers/Cosmetologists	12.10	Teachers, Secondary School*	26.20
Internists, General	n/a	Telemarketers	13.10
Janitors and Cleaners	14.60	Truck Drivers, Heavy/Tractor-Trailer	20.80
Landscaping/Groundskeeping Workers	15.60	Truck Drivers, Light/Delivery Svcs.	16.30
Lawyers	56.70	Waiters and Waitresses	10.40

Note: Wage data covers the Cedar Rapids, IA Metropolitan Statistical Area—see Appendix B for areas
included; (*) Hourly wages for elementary/secondary school teachers and teacher assistants were calculated
by the editors from annual wage data based on a 40 hour work week; n/a not available.
Source: Bureau of Labor Statistics, Metro Area Occupational Employment & Wage Estimates, May 2018

Employment by Occupation

Occupation Classification	City (%)	MSA[1] (%)	U.S. (%)
Management, Business, Science, and Arts	36.4	37.5	37.4
Natural Resources, Construction, and Maintenance	8.1	9.1	8.9
Production, Transportation, and Material Moving	13.9	14.1	12.2
Sales and Office	25.8	24.1	23.5
Service	15.8	15.2	18.0

Note: Figures cover employed civilians 16 years of age and older; (1) Figures cover the Cedar Rapids, IA
Metropolitan Statistical Area—see Appendix B for areas included
Source: U.S. Census Bureau, 2013-2017 American Community Survey 5-Year Estimates

Employment by Industry

Sector	MSA[1]		U.S.
	Number of Employees	Percent of Total	Percent of Total
Construction, Mining, and Logging	7,800	5.4	5.3
Education and Health Services	21,200	14.6	15.9
Financial Activities	10,800	7.4	5.7
Government	17,000	11.7	15.1
Information	3,700	2.5	1.9
Leisure and Hospitality	11,800	8.1	10.7
Manufacturing	19,800	13.6	8.5
Other Services	5,100	3.5	3.9
Professional and Business Services	15,300	10.5	14.1
Retail Trade	15,100	10.4	10.8
Transportation, Warehousing, and Utilities	11,600	8.0	4.2
Wholesale Trade	6,000	4.1	3.9

Note: Figures are non-farm employment as of December 2018. Figures are not seasonally adjusted and include workers 16 years of age and older; (1) Figures cover the Cedar Rapids, IA Metropolitan Statistical Area—see Appendix B for areas included
Source: Bureau of Labor Statistics, Current Employment Statistics, Employment, Hours, and Earnings

Occupations with Greatest Projected Employment Growth: 2018 – 2020

Occupation[1]	2018 Employment	2020 Projected Employment	Numeric Employment Change	Percent Employment Change
Combined Food Preparation and Serving Workers, Including Fast Food	36,450	37,630	1,180	3.2
Heavy and Tractor-Trailer Truck Drivers	44,890	46,070	1,180	2.6
Registered Nurses	33,850	34,820	970	2.9
Laborers and Freight, Stock, and Material Movers, Hand	28,350	28,870	520	1.8
Home Health Aides	8,280	8,790	510	6.2
Janitors and Cleaners, Except Maids and Housekeeping Cleaners	26,490	26,940	450	1.7
Waiters and Waitresses	24,260	24,660	400	1.6
Personal Care Aides	9,050	9,440	390	4.3
Slaughterers and Meat Packers	7,780	8,130	350	4.5
Nursing Assistants	21,370	21,710	340	1.6

Note: Projections cover Iowa; (1) Sorted by numeric employment change
Source: www.projectionscentral.com, State Occupational Projections, 2018–2020 Short-Term Projections

Fastest Growing Occupations: 2018 – 2020

Occupation[1]	2018 Employment	2020 Projected Employment	Numeric Employment Change	Percent Employment Change
Wind Turbine Service Technicians	340	390	50	14.7
Information Security Analysts	1,520	1,640	120	7.9
Operations Research Analysts	720	770	50	6.9
Home Health Aides	8,280	8,790	510	6.2
Respiratory Therapists	960	1,010	50	5.2
Nurse Practitioners	1,150	1,210	60	5.2
Woodworking Machine Setters, Operators, and Tenders, Except Sawing	1,420	1,490	70	4.9
Heating, Air Conditioning, and Refrigeration Mechanics and Installers	3,730	3,910	180	4.8
Food Batchmakers	2,690	2,820	130	4.8
Personal Financial Advisors	1,750	1,830	80	4.6

Note: Projections cover Iowa; (1) Sorted by percent employment change and excludes occupations with numeric employment change less than 50
Source: www.projectionscentral.com, State Occupational Projections, 2018–2020 Short-Term Projections

TAXES

State Corporate Income Tax Rates

State	Tax Rate (%)	Income Brackets ($)	Num. of Brackets	Financial Institution Tax Rate (%)[a]	Federal Income Tax Ded.
Iowa	6.0 - 12.0	25,000 - 250,001	4	5.0	Yes (j)

Note: Tax rates as of January 1, 2019; (a) Rates listed are the corporate income tax rate applied to financial institutions or excise taxes based on income. Some states have other taxes based upon the value of deposits or shares; (j) 50% of the federal income tax is deductible.
Source: Federation of Tax Administrators, Range of State Corporate Income Tax Rates, January 1, 2019

State Individual Income Tax Rates

State	Tax Rate (%)	Income Brackets ($)	Personal Exemptions ($)			Standard Ded. ($)	
			Single	Married	Depend.	Single	Married
Iowa (a)	0.33 - 8.53	1,598 - 71,910	40 (c)	80 (c)	40 (c)	2,080	5,120 (a)

Note: Tax rates as of January 1, 2019; Local- and county-level taxes are not included; n/a not applicable; Federal income tax is deductible on state income tax returns; (a) 19 states have statutory provision for automatically adjusting to the rate of inflation the dollar values of the income tax brackets, standard deductions, and/or personal exemptions. Michigan indexes the personal exemption only. Oregon does not index the income brackets for $125,000 and over; (c) The personal exemption takes the form of a tax credit instead of a deduction
Source: Federation of Tax Administrators, State Individual Income Tax Rates, January 1, 2019

Various State Sales and Excise Tax Rates

State	State Sales Tax (%)	Gasoline[1] (¢/gal.)	Cigarette[2] ($/pack)	Spirits[3] ($/gal.)	Wine[4] ($/gal.)	Beer[5] ($/gal.)	Recreational Marijuana (%)
Iowa	6	30.7	1.36	13.07 (g)	1.75 (l)	0.19 (q)	Not legal

Note: All tax rates as of January 1, 2019; (1) The American Petroleum Institute has developed a methodology for determining the average tax rate on a gallon of fuel. Rates may include any of the following: excise taxes, environmental fees, storage tank fees, other fees or taxes, general sales tax, and local taxes. In states where gasoline is subject to the general sales tax, or where the fuel tax is based on the average sale price, the average rate determined by API is sensitive to changes in the price of gasoline. States that fully or partially apply general sales taxes to gasoline: CA, CO, GA, IL, IN, MI, NY; (2) The federal excise tax of $1.0066 per pack and local taxes are not included; (3) Rates are those applicable to off-premise sales of 40% alcohol by volume (a.b.v.) distilled spirits in 750ml containers. Local excise taxes are excluded; (4) Rates are those applicable to off-premise sales of 11% a.b.v. non-carbonated wine in 750ml containers; (5) Rates are those applicable to off-premise sales of 4.7% a.b.v. beer in 12 ounce containers; (g) Control states, where the government controls all sales. Products can be subject to ad valorem mark-up as well as excise taxes; (l) Different rates also applicable to alcohol content, place of production, size of container, place purchased (on- or off-premise or on board airlines) or type of wine (carbonated, vermouth, etc.); (q) Different rates also applicable according to alcohol content, place of production, size of container, or place purchased (on- or off-premise or onboard airlines).
Source: Tax Foundation, 2019 Facts & Figures: How Does Your State Compare?

State Business Tax Climate Index Rankings

State	Overall Rank	Corporate Tax Rank	Individual Income Tax Rank	Sales Tax Rank	Unemployment Insurance Tax Rank	Property Tax Rank
Iowa	45	48	42	19	33	39

Note: The index is a measure of how each state's tax laws affect economic performance. The lower the rank, the more favorable a state's tax system is for business. States without a given tax are given a ranking of 1. The scores/rankings for the District of Columbia do not affect other states. The 2019 index represents the tax climate as of July 1, 2018.
Source: Tax Foundation, State Business Tax Climate Index 2019

COMMERCIAL UTILITIES

Typical Monthly Electric Bills

Area	Commercial Service ($/month)		Industrial Service ($/month)	
	1,500 kWh	40 kW demand 14,000 kWh	1,000 kW demand 200,000 kWh	50,000 kW demand 32,500,000 kWh
City	n/a	n/a	n/a	n/a
Average[1]	203	1,619	25,886	2,540,077

Note: Figures are based on annualized rates; (1) Average based on 187 utilities surveyed; n/a not available
Source: Edison Electric Institute, Typical Bills and Average Rates Report, Summer 2018

TRANSPORTATION

Means of Transportation to Work

Area	Car/Truck/Van		Public Transportation			Bicycle	Walked	Other Means	Worked at Home
	Drove Alone	Car-pooled	Bus	Subway	Railroad				
City	83.8	9.0	1.1	0.0	0.0	0.5	2.0	0.9	2.7
MSA[1]	84.4	8.3	0.6	0.0	0.0	0.3	2.1	0.7	3.6
U.S.	76.4	9.2	2.5	1.9	0.6	0.6	2.7	1.3	4.7

Note: Figures are percentages and cover workers 16 years of age and older; (1) Figures cover the Cedar Rapids, IA Metropolitan Statistical Area—see Appendix B for areas included
Source: U.S. Census Bureau, 2013-2017 American Community Survey 5-Year Estimates

Travel Time to Work

Area	Less Than 10 Minutes	10 to 19 Minutes	20 to 29 Minutes	30 to 44 Minutes	45 to 59 Minutes	60 to 89 Minutes	90 Minutes or More
City	17.9	49.3	18.1	9.7	2.1	1.9	1.0
MSA[1]	17.9	40.3	21.7	13.3	3.5	2.0	1.2
U.S.	12.7	28.9	20.9	20.5	8.1	6.2	2.7

Note: Note: Figures are percentages and include workers 16 years old and over; (1) Figures cover the Cedar Rapids, IA Metropolitan Statistical Area—see Appendix B for areas included
Source: U.S. Census Bureau, 2013-2017 American Community Survey 5-Year Estimates

Freeway Travel Time Index

Area	1985	1990	1995	2000	2005	2010	2014
Urban Area Rank[1,2]	n/a	n/a	n/a	n/a	n/a	n/a	n/a
Urban Area Index[1]	n/a	n/a	n/a	n/a	n/a	n/a	n/a
Average Index[3]	1.09	1.11	1.14	1.17	1.20	1.19	1.20

Note: Freeway Travel Time Index—the ratio of travel time in the peak period to the travel time at free-flow conditions. For example, a value of 1.30 indicates a 20-minute free-flow trip takes 26 minutes in the peak (20 minutes x 1.30 = 26 minutes); (1) Data for the Cedar Rapids, IA urban area was not available; (2) Rank is based on 101 urban areas (#1 = highest travel time index); (3) Average of 101 urban areas
Source: Texas Transportation Institute, 2015 Urban Mobility Scorecard, August 2015

Freeway Commuter Stress Index

Area	1985	1990	1995	2000	2005	2010	2014
Urban Area Rank[1,2]	n/a	n/a	n/a	n/a	n/a	n/a	n/a
Urban Area Index[1]	n/a	n/a	n/a	n/a	n/a	n/a	n/a
Average Index[3]	1.13	1.16	1.19	1.22	1.25	1.24	1.25

Note: The Freeway Commuter Stress Index is the same as the Freeway Travel Time Index (see table above) except that it includes only the travel in the peak directions during the peak periods; the TTI includes travel in all directions during the peak period. Thus, the CSI is more indicative of the work trip experienced by each commuter on a daily basis; (1) Data for the Cedar Rapids, IA urban area was not available; (2) Rank is based on 101 urban areas (#1 = highest travel time index); (3) Average of 101 urban areas
Source: Texas Transportation Institute, 2015 Urban Mobility Scorecard, August 2015

Public Transportation

Agency Name / Mode of Transportation	Vehicles Operated in Maximum Service[1]	Annual Unlinked Passenger Trips[2] (in thous.)	Annual Passenger Miles[3] (in thous.)
Five Seasons Transportation and Parking (FSTP)			
Bus (directly operated)	22	1,185.7	5,677.9
Demand Response (purchased transportation)	13	85.9	532.4

Note: (1) The number of revenue vehicles operated by the given mode and type of service to meet the annual maximum service requirement. This is the revenue vehicle count during the peak season of the year; on the week and day that maximum service is provided. Vehicles operated in maximum service (VOMS) exclude atypical days and one-time special events; (2) The number of passengers who boarded public transportation vehicles. Passengers are counted each time they board a vehicle no matter how many vehicles they use to travel from their origin to their destination. (3) The sum of the distances ridden by all passengers during the entire fiscal year.
Source: Federal Transit Administration, National Transit Database, 2017

Air Transportation

Airport Name and Code / Type of Service	Passenger Airlines[1]	Passenger Enplanements	Freight Carriers[2]	Freight (lbs)
The Eastern Iowa (CID)				
Domestic service (U.S. carriers - 2018)	23	601,682	10	49,676,160
International service (U.S. carriers - 2017)	2	57	0	0

Note: (1) Includes all U.S.-based major, minor and commuter airlines that carried at least one passenger during the year; (2) Includes all U.S.-based airlines and freight carriers that transported at least one pound of freight during the year.
Source: Bureau of Transportation Statistics, The Intermodal Transportation Database, Air Carriers: T-100 Domestic Market (U.S. Carriers), 2018; Bureau of Transportation Statistics, The Intermodal Transportation Database, Air Carriers: T-100 International Market (U.S. Carriers), 2017

Other Transportation Statistics

Major Highways:	I-380
Amtrak Service:	No
Major Waterways/Ports:	Cedar River

Source: Amtrak.com; Google Maps

BUSINESSES

Major Business Headquarters

Company Name	Industry	Rankings	
		Fortune[1]	Forbes[2]
Rockwell Collins	Aerospace and Defense	415	-

Note: (1) Companies that produce a 10-K are ranked 1 to 500 based on 2017 revenue; (2) All private companies with at least $2 billion in annual revenue through the end of their most current fiscal year are ranked 1 to 229; companies listed are headquartered in the city; dashes indicate no ranking
Source: Fortune, "Fortune 500," June 2018; Forbes, "America's Largest Private Companies," 2018 Rankings

Minority- and Women-Owned Businesses

Group	All Firms		Firms with Paid Employees			
	Firms	Sales ($000)	Firms	Sales ($000)	Employees	Payroll ($000)
AIAN[1]	34	574	0	0	0	0
Asian	288	71,587	86	64,737	515	16,645
Black	351	14,021	7	8,445	129	2,669
Hispanic	139	(s)	7	(s)	250 - 499	(s)
NHOPI[2]	n/a	n/a	n/a	n/a	n/a	n/a
Women	3,513	1,807,700	431	1,744,169	9,337	277,821
All Firms	9,807	27,778,483	2,763	27,473,339	88,551	4,137,794

Note: Figures cover firms located in the city; minority- and women-owned business are defined as firms in which the corresponding group own 51% or more of the stock or equity of the company; (1) American Indian and Alaska Native; (2) Native Hawaiian and Other Pacific Islander; (s) estimates are suppressed when publication standards are not met; n/a not available
Source: U.S. Census Bureau, 2012 Economic Census, Survey of Business Owners

HOTELS & CONVENTION CENTERS

Hotels, Motels and Vacation Rentals

Area	5 Star		4 Star		3 Star		2 Star		1 Star		Not Rated	
	Num.	Pct.[3]	Num.	Pct.[3]	Num.	Pct.[3]	Num.	Pct.[3]	Num.	Pct.[3]	Num.	Pct.[3]
City[1]	0	0.0	1	0.9	26	24.3	53	49.5	1	0.9	26	24.3
Total[2]	286	0.4	5,236	7.1	16,715	22.6	10,259	13.9	293	0.4	41,056	55.6

Note: (1) Figures cover Cedar Rapids and vicinity; (2) Figures cover all 100 cities in this book; (3) Percentage of hotels which have a given star rating; Star ratings are determined by expedia.com and offer an indication of the general quality of a particular hotel.
Source: www.expedia.com, April 3, 2019

Major Convention Centers

Name	Overall Space (sq. ft.)	Exhibit Space (sq. ft.)	Meeting Space (sq. ft.)	Meeting Rooms
Cedar Rapids Convention Complex	104,000	72,300	21,500	n/a

Note: Table includes convention centers located in the Cedar Rapids, IA metro area; n/a not available
Source: Original research

Living Environment

COST OF LIVING

Cost of Living Index

Composite Index	Groceries	Housing	Utilities	Trans-portation	Health Care	Misc. Goods/ Services
93.9	95.6	84.9	109.0	97.1	95.4	95.9

Note: The Cost of Living Index measures regional differences in the cost of consumer goods and services, excluding taxes and non-consumer expenditures, for professional and managerial households in the top income quintile. It is based on more than 50,000 prices covering almost 60 different items for which prices are collected three times a year by chambers of commerce, economic development organizations or university applied economic centers in each participating urban area. The numbers shown should be read as a percentage above or below the national average of 100. For example, a value of 115.4 in the groceries column indicates that grocery prices are 15.4% higher than the national average. Small differences in the index numbers should not be interpreted as significant; Figures cover the Cedar Rapids IA urban area.
Source: The Council for Community and Economic Research, ACCRA Cost of Living Index, 2018

Grocery Prices

Area[1]	T-Bone Steak ($/pound)	Frying Chicken ($/pound)	Whole Milk ($/half gal.)	Eggs ($/dozen)	Orange Juice ($/64 oz.)	Coffee ($/11.5 oz.)
City[2]	10.86	1.42	1.98	1.32	3.00	4.20
Avg.	11.35	1.42	1.94	1.81	3.52	4.35
Min.	7.45	0.92	0.80	0.75	2.72	3.06
Max.	15.05	2.76	4.18	4.00	5.36	8.20

Note: (1) Values for the local area are compared with the average, minimum and maximum values for all 291 areas in the Cost of Living Index; (2) Figures cover the Cedar Rapids IA urban area; T-Bone Steak (price per pound); Frying Chicken (price per pound, whole fryer); Whole Milk (half gallon carton); Eggs (price per dozen, Grade A, large); Orange Juice (64 oz. Tropicana or Florida Natural); Coffee (11.5 oz. can, vacuum-packed, Maxwell House, Hills Bros, or Folgers).
Source: The Council for Community and Economic Research, ACCRA Cost of Living Index, 2018

Housing and Utility Costs

Area[1]	New Home Price ($)	Apartment Rent ($/month)	All Electric ($/month)	Part Electric ($/month)	Other Energy ($/month)	Telephone ($/month)
City[2]	326,278	731	-	138.07	59.23	175.20
Avg.	347,000	1,087	165.93	100.16	67.73	178.70
Min.	200,468	500	93.58	25.64	26.78	163.10
Max.	1,901,222	4,888	388.65	246.86	332.81	197.70

Note: (1) Values for the local area are compared with the average, minimum and maximum values for all 291 areas in the Cost of Living Index; (2) Figures cover the Cedar Rapids IA urban area; New Home Price (2,400 sf living area, 8,000 sf lot, in urban area with full utilities); Apartment Rent (950 sf 2 bedroom/1.5 or 2 bath, unfurnished, excluding all utilities except water); All Electric (average monthly cost for an all-electric home); Part Electric (average monthly cost for a part-electric home); Other Energy (average monthly cost for natural gas, fuel oil, coal, wood, and any other forms of energy except electricity); Telephone (price includes the base monthly rate plus taxes and fees for three lines of mobile phone service).
Source: The Council for Community and Economic Research, ACCRA Cost of Living Index, 2018

Health Care, Transportation, and Other Costs

Area[1]	Doctor ($/visit)	Dentist ($/visit)	Optometrist ($/visit)	Gasoline ($/gallon)	Beauty Salon ($/visit)	Men's Shirt ($)
City[2]	112.26	79.30	104.10	2.52	32.49	40.60
Avg.	110.71	95.11	103.74	2.61	37.48	32.03
Min.	33.60	62.55	54.63	1.89	17.00	11.44
Max.	195.97	153.93	225.79	3.59	71.88	58.64

Note: (1) Values for the local area are compared with the average, minimum and maximum values for all 291 areas in the Cost of Living Index; (2) Figures cover the Cedar Rapids IA urban area; Doctor (general practitioners routine exam of an established patient); Dentist (adult teeth cleaning and periodic oral examination); Optometrist (full vision eye exam for established adult patient); Gasoline (one gallon regular unleaded, national brand, including all taxes, cash price at self-service pump if available); Beauty Salon (woman's shampoo, trim, and blow-dry); Men's Shirt (cotton/polyester dress shirt, pinpoint weave, long sleeves).
Source: The Council for Community and Economic Research, ACCRA Cost of Living Index, 2018

HOUSING

House Price Index (HPI)

Area	National Ranking[2]	Quarterly Change (%)	One-Year Change (%)	Five-Year Change (%)
MSA[1]	196	-0.95	3.59	13.75
U.S.[3]	–	1.12	5.73	32.81

Note: The HPI is a weighted repeat sales index. It measures average price changes in repeat sales or refinancings on the same properties. This information is obtained by reviewing repeat mortgage transactions on single-family properties whose mortgages have been purchased or securitized by Fannie Mae or Freddie Mac in January 1975; (1) Figures cover the Cedar Rapids, IA Metropolitan Statistical Area—see Appendix B for areas included; (2) Rankings are based on annual percentage change for all metro areas containing at least 15,000 transactions over the last 10 years and ranges from 1 to 245; (3) figures based on a weighted average of Census Division estimates using a seasonally adjusted, purchase-only index; all figures are for the period ending December 31, 2018
Source: Federal Housing Finance Agency, House Price Index, February 26, 2019

Median Single-Family Home Prices

Area	2016	2017	2018p	Percent Change 2017 to 2018
MSA[1]	151.0	152.6	159.2	4.3
U.S. Average	235.5	248.8	261.6	5.1

Note: Figures are median sales prices of existing single-family homes in thousands of dollars; (p) preliminary; (1) Figures cover the Cedar Rapids, IA Metropolitan Statistical Area—see Appendix B for areas included
Source: National Association of Realtors, Median Sales Price of Existing Single-Family Homes for Metropolitan Areas, 4th Quarter 2018

Qualifying Income Based on Median Sales Price of Existing Single-Family Homes

Area	With 5% Down ($)	With 10% Down ($)	With 20% Down ($)
MSA[1]	37,831	35,840	31,857
U.S. Average	62,954	59,640	53,013

Note: Figures are preliminary; Qualifying income is based on a mortgage rate of 4.9%. Monthly principal and interest payment is limited to 25% of income; (1) Figures cover the Cedar Rapids, IA Metropolitan Statistical Area—see Appendix B for areas included
Source: National Association of Realtors, Qualifying Income Based on Median Sales Price of Existing Single-Family Homes for Metropolitan Areas, 4th Quarter 2018

Median Apartment Condo-Coop Home Prices

Area	2016	2017	2018p	Percent Change 2017 to 2018
MSA[1]	n/a	n/a	n/a	n/a
U.S. Average	220.7	234.3	241.0	2.9

Note: Figures are median sales prices of existing apartment condo-coop homes in thousands of dollars; (p) preliminary; n/a not available; (1) Figures cover the Cedar Rapids, IA Metropolitan Statistical Area—see Appendix B for areas included
Source: National Association of Realtors, Median Sales Price of Existing Apartment Condo-Coop Homes for Metropolitan Areas, 4th Quarter 2018

Home Value Distribution

Area	Under $50,000	$50,000 -$99,999	$100,000 -$149,999	$150,000 -$199,999	$200,000 -$299,999	$300,000 -$499,999	$500,000 -$999,999	$1,000,000 or more
City	5.3	18.1	34.8	21.2	14.6	4.6	1.2	0.2
MSA[1]	6.8	15.7	27.8	20.1	19.2	7.6	2.3	0.5
U.S.	8.3	13.9	14.7	14.6	18.7	17.3	9.7	2.7

Note: Figures are percentages and cover owner-occupied housing units; (1) Figures cover the Cedar Rapids, IA Metropolitan Statistical Area—see Appendix B for areas included
Source: U.S. Census Bureau, 2013-2017 American Community Survey 5-Year Estimates

Homeownership Rate

Area	2010 (%)	2011 (%)	2012 (%)	2013 (%)	2014 (%)	2015 (%)	2016 (%)	2017 (%)	2018 (%)
MSA[1]	n/a	n/a	n/a	n/a	n/a	n/a	n/a	n/a	n/a
U.S.	66.9	66.1	65.4	65.1	64.5	63.7	63.4	63.9	64.4

Note: (1) Figures cover the Cedar Rapids, IA Metropolitan Statistical Area—see Appendix B for areas included; n/a not available
Source: U.S. Census Bureau, Housing Vacancies and Homeownership Annual Statistics: 2010-2018

Year Housing Structure Built

Area	2010 or Later	2000 -2009	1990 -1999	1980 -1989	1970 -1979	1960 -1969	1950 -1959	1940 -1949	Before 1940	Median Year
City	4.2	12.2	14.0	8.1	14.8	14.4	12.2	4.4	15.7	1972
MSA[1]	4.4	14.7	15.3	7.3	13.7	12.7	10.0	3.9	17.9	1974
U.S.	3.2	14.5	14.0	13.6	15.5	10.8	10.5	5.1	12.9	1977

Note: Figures are percentages except for Median Year; Note: (1) Figures cover the Cedar Rapids, IA Metropolitan Statistical Area—see Appendix B for areas included
Source: U.S. Census Bureau, 2013-2017 American Community Survey 5-Year Estimates

Gross Monthly Rent

Area	Under $500	$500 -$999	$1,000 -$1,499	$1,500 -$1,999	$2,000 -$2,499	$2,500 -$2,999	$3,000 and up	Median ($)
City	19.6	63.9	13.8	1.4	0.8	0.2	0.4	729
MSA[1]	20.2	63.1	14.0	1.5	0.7	0.1	0.4	714
U.S.	10.5	41.1	28.7	11.7	4.5	1.8	1.7	982

Note: Figures are percentages except for Median; Gross rent is the contract rent plus the estimated average monthly cost of utilities (electricity, gas, and water and sewer) and fuels (oil, coal, kerosene, wood, etc.) if these are paid by the renter (or paid for the renter by someone else); (1) Figures cover the Cedar Rapids, IA Metropolitan Statistical Area—see Appendix B for areas included
Source: U.S. Census Bureau, 2013-2017 American Community Survey 5-Year Estimates

HEALTH

Health Risk Factors

Category	MSA[1] (%)	U.S. (%)
Adults aged 18–64 who have any kind of health care coverage	93.7	87.3
Adults who reported being in good or better health	86.4	82.4
Adults who have been told they have high blood cholesterol	36.1	33.0
Adults who have been told they have high blood pressure	28.4	32.3
Adults who are current smokers	18.1	17.1
Adults who currently use E-cigarettes	3.5	4.6
Adults who currently use chewing tobacco, snuff, or snus	6.7	4.0
Adults who are heavy drinkers[2]	5.9	6.3
Adults who are binge drinkers[3]	22.9	17.4
Adults who are overweight (BMI 25.0 - 29.9)	35.3	35.3
Adults who are obese (BMI 30.0 - 99.8)	34.2	31.3
Adults who participated in any physical activities in the past month	75.4	74.4
Adults who always or nearly always wears a seat belt	96.4	94.3

Note: (1) Figures cover the Cedar Rapids, IA Metropolitan Statistical Area—see Appendix B for areas included; (2) Heavy drinkers are classified as adult men having more than 14 drinks per week and adult women having more than 7 drinks per week; (3) Binge drinkers are classified as males having five or more drinks on one occasion or females having four or more drinks on one occasion
Source: Centers for Disease Control and Prevention, Behaviorial Risk Factor Surveillance System, SMART: Selected Metropolitan Area Risk Trends, 2017

Acute and Chronic Health Conditions

Category	MSA[1] (%)	U.S. (%)
Adults who have ever been told they had a heart attack	3.4	4.2
Adults who have ever been told they have angina or coronary heart disease	3.7	3.9
Adults who have ever been told they had a stroke	2.8	3.0
Adults who have ever been told they have asthma	11.5	14.2
Adults who have ever been told they have arthritis	20.6	24.9
Adults who have ever been told they have diabetes[2]	8.4	10.5
Adults who have ever been told they had skin cancer	6.7	6.2
Adults who have ever been told they had any other types of cancer	9.3	7.1
Adults who have ever been told they have COPD	5.3	6.5
Adults who have ever been told they have kidney disease	2.3	3.0
Adults who have ever been told they have a form of depression	20.8	20.5

Note: (1) Figures cover the Cedar Rapids, IA Metropolitan Statistical Area—see Appendix B for areas included; (2) Figures do not include pregnancy-related, borderline, or pre-diabetes
Source: Centers for Disease Control and Prevention, Behaviorial Risk Factor Surveillance System, SMART: Selected Metropolitan Area Risk Trends, 2017

Health Screening and Vaccination Rates

Category	MSA[1] (%)	U.S. (%)
Adults aged 65+ who have had flu shot within the past year	71.4	60.7
Adults aged 65+ who have ever had a pneumonia vaccination	86.7	75.4
Adults who have ever been tested for HIV	27.8	36.1
Adults who have ever had the shingles or zoster vaccine?	38.8	28.9
Adults who have had their blood cholesterol checked within the last five years	85.3	85.9

Note: n/a not available; (1) Figures cover the Cedar Rapids, IA Metropolitan Statistical Area—see Appendix B for areas included.
Source: Centers for Disease Control and Prevention, Behaviorial Risk Factor Surveillance System, SMART: Selected Metropolitan Area Risk Trends, 2017

Disability Status

Category	MSA[1] (%)	U.S. (%)
Adults who reported being deaf	6.7	6.7
Are you blind or have serious difficulty seeing, even when wearing glasses?	4.2	4.5
Are you limited in any way in any of your usual activities due of arthritis?	9.8	12.9
Do you have difficulty doing errands alone?	5.2	6.8
Do you have difficulty dressing or bathing?	2.4	3.6
Do you have serious difficulty concentrating/remembering/making decisions?	8.6	10.7
Do you have serious difficulty walking or climbing stairs?	9.0	13.6

Note: (1) Figures cover the Cedar Rapids, IA Metropolitan Statistical Area—see Appendix B for areas included.
Source: Centers for Disease Control and Prevention, Behaviorial Risk Factor Surveillance System, SMART: Selected Metropolitan Area Risk Trends, 2017

Mortality Rates for the Top 10 Causes of Death in the U.S.

ICD-10[a] Sub-Chapter	ICD-10[a] Code	Age-Adjusted Mortality Rate[1] per 100,000 population	
		County[2]	U.S.
Malignant neoplasms	C00-C97	156.6	155.5
Ischaemic heart diseases	I20-I25	101.9	94.8
Other forms of heart disease	I30-I51	35.4	52.9
Chronic lower respiratory diseases	J40-J47	44.3	41.0
Cerebrovascular diseases	I60-I69	24.9	37.5
Other degenerative diseases of the nervous system	G30-G31	44.6	35.0
Other external causes of accidental injury	W00-X59	30.7	33.7
Organic, including symptomatic, mental disorders	F01-F09	28.0	31.0
Hypertensive diseases	I10-I15	12.8	21.9
Diabetes mellitus	E10-E14	21.9	21.2

Note: (a) ICD-10 = International Classification of Diseases 10th Revision; (1) Mortality rates are a three year average covering 2015-2017; (2) Figures cover Linn County.
Source: Centers for Disease Control and Prevention, National Center for Health Statistics. Underlying Cause of Death 1999-2017 on CDC WONDER Online Database

Mortality Rates for Selected Causes of Death

ICD-10[a] Sub-Chapter	ICD-10[a] Code	Age-Adjusted Mortality Rate[1] per 100,000 population	
		County[2]	U.S.
Assault	X85-Y09	3.7	5.9
Diseases of the liver	K70-K76	13.1	14.1
Human immunodeficiency virus (HIV) disease	B20-B24	Suppressed	1.8
Influenza and pneumonia	J09-J18	13.4	14.3
Intentional self-harm	X60-X84	15.3	13.6
Malnutrition	E40-E46	Unreliable	1.6
Obesity and other hyperalimentation	E65-E68	Suppressed	2.1
Renal failure	N17-N19	6.5	13.0
Transport accidents	V01-V99	9.4	12.4
Viral hepatitis	B15-B19	Suppressed	1.6

Note: (a) ICD-10 = International Classification of Diseases 10th Revision; (1) Mortality rates are a three year average covering 2015-2017; (2) Figures cover Linn County; Data are suppressed when the data meet the criteria for confidentiality constraints; Mortality rates are flagged as unreliable when the rate would be calculated with a numerator of 20 or less.
Source: Centers for Disease Control and Prevention, National Center for Health Statistics. Underlying Cause of Death 1999-2017 on CDC WONDER Online Database

Health Insurance Coverage

Area	With Health Insurance	With Private Health Insurance	With Public Health Insurance	Without Health Insurance	Population Under Age 18 Without Health Insurance
City	95.0	76.4	31.7	5.0	3.2
MSA[1]	95.6	77.9	31.3	4.4	2.7
U.S.	89.5	67.2	33.8	10.5	5.7

Note: Figures are percentages that cover the civilian noninstitutionalized population; (1) Figures cover the Cedar Rapids, IA Metropolitan Statistical Area—see Appendix B for areas included
Source: U.S. Census Bureau, 2013-2017 American Community Survey 5-Year Estimates

Number of Medical Professionals

Area	MDs[3]	DOs[3,4]	Dentists	Podiatrists	Chiropractors	Optometrists
County[1] (number)	393	49	164	19	126	38
County[1] (rate[2])	177.1	22.1	73.2	8.5	56.2	17.0
U.S. (rate[2])	279.3	23.0	68.4	6.0	27.1	16.2

Note: Data as of 2017 unless noted; (1) Data covers Linn County; (2) Rate per 100,000 population; (3) Data as of 2016 and includes all active, non-federal physicians; (4) Doctor of Osteopathic Medicine
Source: U.S. Department of Health and Human Services, Health Resources and Services Administration, Bureau of Health Professions, Area Resource File (ARF) 2017-2018

EDUCATION

Public School District Statistics

District Name	Schls	Pupils	Pupil/ Teacher Ratio	Minority Pupils[1] (%)	Free Lunch Eligible[2] (%)	IEP[3] (%)
Cedar Rapids Community SD	31	17,627	16.2	33.5	44.3	14.2
College Comm School District	9	5,322	14.7	18.7	25.7	10.1

Note: Table includes school districts with 2,000 or more students; (1) Percentage of students that are not non-Hispanic white; (2) Percentage of students that are eligible for the free lunch program; (3) Percentage of students that have an Individualized Education Program.
Source: U.S. Department of Education, National Center for Education Statistics, Common Core of Data, Local Education Agency (School District) Universe Survey: School Year 2016-2017; U.S. Department of Education, National Center for Education Statistics, Common Core of Data, Public Elementary/Secondary School Universe Survey: School Year 2016-2017

Highest Level of Education

Area	Less than H.S.	H.S. Diploma	Some College, No Deg.	Associate Degree	Bachelor's Degree	Master's Degree	Prof. School Degree	Doctorate Degree
City	6.1	26.6	23.4	12.1	22.4	6.7	1.6	1.2
MSA[1]	5.7	29.2	22.5	12.5	21.0	6.7	1.3	1.0
U.S.	12.7	27.3	20.8	8.3	19.1	8.4	2.0	1.4

Note: Figures cover persons age 25 and over; (1) Figures cover the Cedar Rapids, IA Metropolitan Statistical Area—see Appendix B for areas included
Source: U.S. Census Bureau, 2013-2017 American Community Survey 5-Year Estimates

Educational Attainment by Race

Area	High School Graduate or Higher (%)					Bachelor's Degree or Higher (%)				
	Total	White	Black	Asian	Hisp.[2]	Total	White	Black	Asian	Hisp.[2]
City	93.9	95.0	80.4	95.5	74.3	31.9	32.1	14.5	64.8	19.1
MSA[1]	94.3	95.0	81.4	94.1	77.8	30.1	30.1	15.3	62.7	23.4
U.S.	87.3	89.3	84.9	86.5	66.7	30.9	32.2	20.6	52.7	15.2

Note: Figures shown cover persons 25 years old and over; (1) Figures cover the Cedar Rapids, IA Metropolitan Statistical Area—see Appendix B for areas included; (2) People of Hispanic origin can be of any race
Source: U.S. Census Bureau, 2013-2017 American Community Survey 5-Year Estimates

School Enrollment by Grade and Control

Area	Preschool (%)		Kindergarten (%)		Grades 1 - 4 (%)		Grades 5 - 8 (%)		Grades 9 - 12 (%)	
	Public	Private	Public	Private	Public	Private	Public	Private	Public	Private
City	64.6	35.4	82.2	17.8	88.5	11.5	91.0	9.0	92.6	7.4
MSA[1]	68.6	31.4	85.0	15.0	89.4	10.6	91.7	8.3	93.4	6.6
U.S.	58.8	41.2	87.7	12.3	89.7	10.3	89.6	10.4	90.3	9.7

Note: Figures shown cover persons 3 years old and over; (1) Figures cover the Cedar Rapids, IA Metropolitan Statistical Area—see Appendix B for areas included
Source: U.S. Census Bureau, 2013-2017 American Community Survey 5-Year Estimates

Average Salaries of Public School Classroom Teachers

Area	2016		2017		Change from 2016 to 2017	
	Dollars	Rank[1]	Dollars	Rank[1]	Percent	Rank[2]
Iowa	54,386	22	55,647	22	2.3	17
U.S. Average	58,479	–	59,660	–	2.0	–

Note: (1) Rank ranges from 1 to 51 where 1 indicates highest salary; (2) Rank ranges from 1 to 51 where 1 indicates highest percent change.
Source: National Education Association, Rankings & Estimates: Rankings of the States 2017 and Estimates of School Statistics 2018

Higher Education

Four-Year Colleges			Two-Year Colleges			Medical Schools[1]	Law Schools[2]	Voc/ Tech[3]
Public	Private Non-profit	Private For-profit	Public	Private Non-profit	Private For-profit			
0	2	1	1	1	1	0	0	0

Note: Figures cover institutions located within the city limits and include main campuses only; (1) includes schools accredited by the Liaison Committee on Medical Education and the American Osteopathic Association's Commission on Osteopathic College Accreditation; (2) includes ABA-accredited schools, schools with provisional ABA accreditation, and state accredited schools; (3) includes all schools with programs that are less than 2 years.
Source: National Center for Education Statistics, Integrated Postsecondary Education System (IPEDS), 2017-18; Wikipedia, List of Medical Schools in the United States, accessed April 3, 2019; Wikipedia, List of Law Schools in the United States, accessed April 3, 2019

According to *U.S. News & World Report,* the Cedar Rapids, IA metro area is home to two of the best liberal arts colleges in the U.S.: **Cornell College** (#81 tie); **Coe College** (#124 tie). The indicators used to capture academic quality fall into a number of categories: assessment by administrators at peer institutions; retention of students; faculty resources; student selectivity; financial resources; alumni giving; high school counselor ratings of colleges; and graduation rate. *U.S. News & World Report, "America's Best Colleges 2019"*

PRESIDENTIAL ELECTION

2016 Presidential Election Results

Area	Clinton	Trump	Johnson	Stein	Other
Linn County	50.3	41.3	4.7	0.9	2.7
U.S.	48.0	45.9	3.3	1.1	1.7

Note: Results are percentages and may not add to 100% due to rounding
Source: Dave Leip's Atlas of U.S. Presidential Elections

EMPLOYERS

Major Employers

Company Name	Industry
AEGON USA	Insurance
Alliant Energy	Energy
Amana Refrigeration Products	Appliances
Cedar Rapids Community School District	Education
City of Cedar Rapids	Government
Gazette Communications	Publishing
General Mills	Food products
Hy-Vee Food Stores	Grocery stores
Kirkwood Community College	Education
Linn County Offices	Government
Linn-Mar Community Schools	Education
Maytag Appliances	Appliances
MCI	Communications
McLeodUSA Incorporated	Communications
Mercy Medical Center	Healthcare
Nash Finch Company	Retail
Rockwell Collins	Aerospace/defense
St. Luke's Hospital	Education
Wal-Mart Stores	Retail
Yellowbook USA	Publisher

Note: Companies shown are located within the Cedar Rapids, IA Metropolitan Statistical Area.
Source: Hoovers.com; Wikipedia

PUBLIC SAFETY

Crime Rate

Area	All Crimes	Violent Crimes				Property Crimes		
		Murder	Rape[3]	Robbery	Aggrav. Assault	Burglary	Larceny -Theft	Motor Vehicle Theft
City	4,035.5	4.5	25.8	91.8	158.5	704.4	2,791.2	259.3
Suburbs[1]	1,273.6	1.5	27.0	12.4	115.9	313.5	720.3	83.1
Metro[2]	2,627.4	3.0	26.4	51.3	136.8	505.1	1,735.4	169.5
U.S.	2,756.1	5.3	41.7	98.0	248.9	430.4	1,694.4	237.4

Note: Figures are crimes per 100,000 population; (1) All areas within the metro area that are located outside the city limits; (2) Figures cover the Cedar Rapids, IA Metropolitan Statistical Area—see Appendix B for areas included; (3) The city and U.S. figures shown were reported using the revised Uniform Crime Reporting (UCR) definition of rape. The suburban and metro area figures shown are an aggregate total of the data submitted using both the revised and legacy UCR definitions.
Source: FBI Uniform Crime Reports, 2017

Hate Crimes

Area	Number of Quarters Reported	Number of Incidents per Bias Motivation					
		Race/Ethnicity/ Ancestry	Religion	Sexual Orientation	Disability	Gender	Gender Identity
City	4	0	0	0	0	0	0
U.S.	4	4,131	1,564	1,130	116	46	119

Source: Federal Bureau of Investigation, Hate Crime Statistics 2017

Identity Theft Consumer Reports

Area	Reports	Reports per 100,000 Population	Rank[2]
MSA[1]	154	58	324
U.S.	444,602	135	-

Note: (1) Figures cover the Cedar Rapids, IA Metropolitan Statistical Area—see Appendix B for areas included; (2) Rank ranges from 1 to 389 where 1 indicates greatest number of identity theft reports per 100,000 population
Source: Federal Trade Commission, Consumer Sentinel Network Data Book for January–December 2018

Fraud and Other Consumer Reports

Area	Reports	Reports per 100,000 Population	Rank[2]
MSA[1]	1,253	468	221
U.S.	2,552,917	776	-

Note: (1) Figures cover the Cedar Rapids, IA Metropolitan Statistical Area—see Appendix B for areas included; (2) Rank ranges from 1 to 389 where 1 indicates greatest number of fraud and other consumer reports per 100,000 population
Source: Federal Trade Commission, Consumer Sentinel Network Data Book for January–December 2018

SPORTS

Professional Sports Teams

Team Name	League	Year Established

No teams are located in the metro area
Source: Wikipedia, Major Professional Sports Teams of the United States and Canada, April 5, 2019

CLIMATE

Average and Extreme Temperatures

Temperature	Jan	Feb	Mar	Apr	May	Jun	Jul	Aug	Sep	Oct	Nov	Dec	Yr.
Extreme High (°F)	58	66	87	100	94	103	105	105	97	95	76	65	105
Average High (°F)	24	30	43	59	71	81	84	82	73	62	45	29	57
Average Temp. (°F)	15	21	34	48	60	69	73	71	62	50	36	21	47
Average Low (°F)	6	11	24	36	48	58	62	59	50	39	26	12	36
Extreme Low (°F)	-33	-29	-34	-4	25	38	42	38	22	11	-17	-27	-34

Note: Figures cover the years 1960-1995
Source: National Climatic Data Center, International Station Meteorological Climate Summary, 9/96

Average Precipitation/Snowfall/Humidity

Precip./Humidity	Jan	Feb	Mar	Apr	May	Jun	Jul	Aug	Sep	Oct	Nov	Dec	Yr.
Avg. Precip. (in.)	0.8	1.0	2.3	3.6	4.1	4.5	4.8	4.0	3.5	2.5	1.9	1.3	34.4
Avg. Snowfall (in.)	7	7	6	2	Tr	0	0	0	0	Tr	4	8	33
Avg. Rel. Hum. 6am (%)	77	80	82	81	81	83	87	90	89	84	83	82	83
Avg. Rel. Hum. 3pm (%)	68	66	62	52	51	51	55	55	55	52	62	70	58

Note: Figures cover the years 1960-1995; Tr = Trace amounts (<0.05 in. of rain; <0.5 in. of snow)
Source: National Climatic Data Center, International Station Meteorological Climate Summary, 9/96

Weather Conditions

Temperature			Daytime Sky			Precipitation		
5°F & below	32°F & below	90°F & above	Clear	Partly cloudy	Cloudy	0.01 inch or more precip.	0.1 inch or more snow/ice	Thunder-storms
38	156	16	89	132	144	109	28	42

Note: Figures are average number of days per year and cover the years 1960-1995
Source: National Climatic Data Center, International Station Meteorological Climate Summary, 9/96

HAZARDOUS WASTE

Superfund Sites

The Cedar Rapids, IA metro area is home to one site on the EPA's Superfund National Priorities List: **Electro-Coatings, Inc.** (final). There are a total of 1,390 Superfund sites with a status of proposed or final on the list in the U.S. *U.S. Environmental Protection Agency, National Priorities List, April 5, 2019*

AIR & WATER QUALITY

Air Quality Trends: Ozone

	1990	1995	2000	2005	2010	2012	2014	2015	2016	2017
MSA[1]	n/a	n/a	n/a	n/a	n/a	n/a	n/a	n/a	n/a	n/a
U.S.	0.088	0.089	0.082	0.080	0.073	0.075	0.067	0.068	0.069	0.068

Note: (1) Data covers the Cedar Rapids, IA Metropolitan Statistical Area—see Appendix B for areas included; n/a not available. The values shown are the composite ozone concentration averages among trend sites based on the highest fourth daily maximum 8-hour concentration in parts per million. These trends are based on sites having an adequate record of monitoring data during the trend period. Data from exceptional events are included.
Source: U.S. Environmental Protection Agency, Air Quality Monitoring Information, "Air Quality Trends by City, 1990-2017"

Air Quality Index

Area	Percent of Days when Air Quality was...[2]					AQI Statistics[2]	
	Good	Moderate	Unhealthy for Sensitive Groups	Unhealthy	Very Unhealthy	Maximum	Median
MSA[1]	76.7	23.3	0.0	0.0	0.0	100	40

Note: (1) Data covers the Cedar Rapids, IA Metropolitan Statistical Area—see Appendix B for areas included; (2) Based on 365 days with AQI data in 2017. Air Quality Index (AQI) is an index for reporting daily air quality. EPA calculates the AQI for five major air pollutants regulated by the Clean Air Act: ground-level ozone, particle pollution (aka particulate matter), carbon monoxide, sulfur dioxide, and nitrogen dioxide. The AQI runs from 0 to 500. The higher the AQI value, the greater the level of air pollution and the greater the health concern. There are six AQI categories: "Good" AQI is between 0 and 50. Air quality is considered satisfactory; "Moderate" AQI is between 51 and 100. Air quality is acceptable; "Unhealthy for Sensitive Groups" When AQI values are between 101 and 150, members of sensitive groups may experience health effects; "Unhealthy" When AQI values are between 151 and 200 everyone may begin to experience health effects; "Very Unhealthy" AQI values between 201 and 300 trigger a health alert; "Hazardous" AQI values over 300 trigger warnings of emergency conditions (not shown).
Source: U.S. Environmental Protection Agency, Air Quality Index Report, 2017

Air Quality Index Pollutants

| Area | Percent of Days when AQI Pollutant was...[2] | | | | | |
	Carbon Monoxide	Nitrogen Dioxide	Ozone	Sulfur Dioxide	Particulate Matter 2.5	Particulate Matter 10
MSA[1]	0.0	0.0	44.7	5.2	49.6	0.5

*Note: (1) Data covers the Cedar Rapids, IA Metropolitan Statistical Area—see Appendix B for areas included;
(2) Based on 365 days with AQI data in 2017. The Air Quality Index (AQI) is an index for reporting daily air
quality. EPA calculates the AQI for five major air pollutants regulated by the Clean Air Act: ground-level
ozone, particle pollution (also known as particulate matter), carbon monoxide, sulfur dioxide, and nitrogen
dioxide. The AQI runs from 0 to 500. The higher the AQI value, the greater the level of air pollution and the
greater the health concern.
Source: U.S. Environmental Protection Agency, Air Quality Index Report, 2017*

Maximum Air Pollutant Concentrations: Particulate Matter, Ozone, CO and Lead

	Particulate Matter 10 (ug/m^3)	Particulate Matter 2.5 Wtd AM (ug/m^3)	Particulate Matter 2.5 24-Hr (ug/m^3)	Ozone (ppm)	Carbon Monoxide (ppm)	Lead (ug/m^3)
MSA[1] Level	57	7.8	20	0.062	1	n/a
NAAQS[2]	150	15	35	0.075	9	0.15
Met NAAQS[2]	Yes	Yes	Yes	Yes	Yes	n/a

*Note: (1) Data covers the Cedar Rapids, IA Metropolitan Statistical Area—see Appendix B for areas included;
Data from exceptional events are included; (2) National Ambient Air Quality Standards; ppm = parts per
million; ug/m³ = micrograms per cubic meter; n/a not available.
Concentrations: Particulate Matter 10 (coarse particulate)—highest second maximum 24-hour concentration;
Particulate Matter 2.5 Wtd AM (fine particulate)—highest weighted annual mean concentration; Particulate
Matter 2.5 24-Hour (fine particulate)—highest 98th percentile 24-hour concentration; Ozone—highest fourth
daily maximum 8-hour concentration; Carbon Monoxide—highest second maximum non-overlapping 8-hour
concentration; Lead—maximum running 3-month average
Source: U.S. Environmental Protection Agency, Air Quality Monitoring Information, "Air Quality Statistics by
City, 2017"*

Maximum Air Pollutant Concentrations: Nitrogen Dioxide and Sulfur Dioxide

	Nitrogen Dioxide AM (ppb)	Nitrogen Dioxide 1-Hr (ppb)	Sulfur Dioxide AM (ppb)	Sulfur Dioxide 1-Hr (ppb)	Sulfur Dioxide 24-Hr (ppb)
MSA[1] Level	n/a	n/a	n/a	53	n/a
NAAQS[2]	53	100	30	75	140
Met NAAQS[2]	n/a	n/a	n/a	Yes	n/a

*Note: (1) Data covers the Cedar Rapids, IA Metropolitan Statistical Area—see Appendix B for areas included;
Data from exceptional events are included; (2) National Ambient Air Quality Standards; ppm = parts per
million; ug/m³ = micrograms per cubic meter; n/a not available.
Concentrations: Nitrogen Dioxide AM—highest arithmetic mean concentration; Nitrogen Dioxide
1-Hr—highest 98th percentile 1-hour daily maximum concentration; Sulfur Dioxide AM—highest annual mean
concentration; Sulfur Dioxide 1-Hr—highest 99th percentile 1-hour daily maximum concentration; Sulfur
Dioxide 24-Hr—highest second maximum 24-hour concentration
Source: U.S. Environmental Protection Agency, Air Quality Monitoring Information, "Air Quality Statistics by
City, 2017"*

Drinking Water

| Water System Name | Pop. Served | Primary Water Source Type | Violations[1] | |
			Health Based	Monitoring/ Reporting
Cedar Rapids Water Dept.	128,576	(2)	0	0

*Note: (1) Based on violation data from January 1, 2018 to December 31, 2018; (2) Ground water under direct
influence of surface water
Source: U.S. Environmental Protection Agency, Office of Ground Water and Drinking Water, Safe Drinking
Water Information System (based on data extracted April 5, 2019).*

Chicago, Illinois

Background

City of Big Shoulders, The Windy City, That Toddling Town, and The Second City, are some of Chicago's nicknames. Whatever one calls Chicago, it has always exemplified a great American city, from a bustling downtown with towering skyscrapers to a quaint collection of closely packed urban neighborhoods stretching into the suburban landscape, then into the fields of the Illinois prairie.

Innovation has been part of Chicago's history from the very start. Cyrus McCormick invented his McCormick Reaper in 1831 and put Chicago on the map, revolutionizing harvesting across the world. The first mail-order business, Montgomery Ward, was established in Chicago in 1872. The world's first skyscraper was built in Chicago in 1885 for the Home Insurance Company. In 1907, University of Chicago's Albert Michelson, received the first American Nobel Prize for science. In 1931, Enrico Fermi split the atom underneath the University of Chicago football field. In 1983, Motorola set up the first modern portable cellular phone system in Chicago. All of this is part of the same history that has given Chicago 78 Nobel Prize Winners, more than any city in the world.

Present-day Chicago is "greener" than ever before. It has 300 square miles of protected lands and is home to 131 plant species of global importance. The city is the nation's largest municipal marina with over 5,000 boat slips. Bicycling, walking trails, beaches and golf are all abundant and top notch. The Oceanarium is the world's largest indoor marine mammal pavilion.

Chicago, with the third largest gross metropolitan product in the nation, has been rated the most balanced economy in the United States, due to its high level of diversification. The Boeing Company relocated its corporate headquarters from Seattle to Chicago in 2001. The city is also a major convention destination. Chicago is first in the country and third worldwide, in number of conventions hosted annually. In addition, Chicago and its metro area are home to dozens of Fortune 500 companies.

When the Willis (formerly Sears) Tower was completed in 1973, it was the tallest building in North America. Chicago is also home to the tenth and twenty-second tallest buildings in the world, and the work of homegrown architects Frank Lloyd Wright, Louis Sullivan, and Helmut Jahn. In addition, Mies van der Rohe immigrated here and became one of the most influential architects of the post-World War II era.

Chicago boasts the Art Institute of Chicago, the Adler Planetarium, the Chicago Architecture Foundation, and the Hellenic Museum and Cultural Center. Classical musical offerings include the Chicago Symphony Orchestra, its Chamber Music Series, the Chicago Opera Theater, and the Lyric Opera of Chicago. The city is famous for its eclectic nightlife. You can hear music at dozens of clubs, and comedy at Second City, where such comics as John Belushi, John Candy, Chris Farley, and Stephen Colbert had their start.

Chicago professional sports have long been in the national spotlight. Chicago is home to two major league baseball teams, the Chicago Cubs who play at Wrigley Field in the city's North Side and the Chicago White Sox who play in the city's South Side at U.S. Cellular Field. The Cubs won the 2016 World Series, ending a 108-year record World Series Champion drought. The Chicago Bears, the city's NFL team, won thirteen NFL championships, and Chicago's professional basketball team, the Chicago Bulls, is one of the world's most recognized teams. The NHL's Chicago Blackhawks, who share the United Center on the Near West Side with the Bulls, hosted the 2008-2009 Winter Classic.

The Chicago Marathon, one of five world marathon events, has been held every October since 1977. Chicago is also the starting point for the Chicago Yacht Club Race to Mackinac—the longest annual freshwater sailboat race in the world. Considering Chicago's athletic legacy, it's not surprising that the city was selected by the International Olympic Committee as one of four candidates for the 2016 games, but lost the bid to Rio de Janeiro.

Outstanding educational institutions in Chicago include the University of Chicago (1891); Northwestern University (1851); DePaul University; Loyola University; and the School of the Art Institute of Chicago.

Located along the southwest shore of Lake Michigan, Chicago has four true seasons, with a white Christmas, spring flowers, a steamy summer, and the beautiful colors of fall. Summers can be very hot and winters are often quite cold.

Rankings

General Rankings

- *Insider* listed 33 places in the U.S. that were a must see vacation destination. Whether it is the great beaches, exploring a new city or experiencing the great outdoors, according to the website thisisinsider.com Chicago is a place to visit in 2018. *Insider, "33 Trips Everyone Should Take in the U.S. in 2018,"November 27, 2017*

- In its eighth annual survey, *Travel + Leisure* readers nominated their favorite small cities and towns in America—those with 100,000 or fewer residents—voting on numerous attractive features in categories including culture, food and drink, quality of life, style, and people. After 50,000 votes, Chicago was ranked #6 among the proposed favorites. *www.travelandleisure.com, "America's Favorite Cities," October 20, 2017*

- The human resources consulting firm Mercer ranked 231 major cities worldwide in terms of overall quality of life. Chicago ranked #49. Criteria: political, social, economic, and socio-cultural factors; medical and health considerations; schools and education; public services and transportation; recreation; consumer goods; housing; and natural environment. *Mercer, "Mercer 2019 Quality of Living Survey," March 13, 2019*

- Chicago appeared on *Travel + Leisure's* list of the fifteen best cities in the United States. The city was ranked #6. Criteria: sights/landmarks; culture/arts; cuisine; people/friendliness; shopping; and value. *Travel + Leisure, "The World's Best Awards 2018" July 10, 2018*

- Based on more than 425,000 responses, *Condé Nast Traveler* ranked its readers' favorite cities in the U.S. The list was broken into cities over 1 million and cities under 1 million. Chicago ranked #1 in the big city category. *Condé Nast Traveler, Readers' Choice Awards 2018, "Best Big Cities in the U.S." October 9, 2018*

Business/Finance Rankings

- The personal finance site NerdWallet analyzed 183 American metropolitan areas with populations over 250,000 and more than 15,000 businesses to rank where entrepreneurs find the most success. Criteria included area economy, annual income, housing cost, unemployment rate, and the success rate of area businesses. Chicago ranked #71. *www.nerdwallet.com, "Best Places to Start a Business," April 27, 2015*

- Recognizing the sizeable percentage of American workers who are self-employed, NerdWallet editors assessed the country's cities according to percentage of freelancers, median rental costs, cell phone plans/taxes, and healthcare affordability and access. By these criteria, Chicago placed #16 among the best cities for independent workers. *www.nerdwallet.com, "Best Places for Freelance Workers," August 30, 2016*

- Based on metro area social media reviews, the employment opinion group Glassdoor surveyed 50 of the largest U.S. metro areas and equally weighed cost of living, hiring opportunity, and job satisfaction to compose a list of "25 Best Cities for Jobs." Median pay and home value, in-demand jobs and number of current job openings was also factored in. The Chicago metro area was ranked #14 in overall job satisfaction. *www.glassdoor.com, "Best Cities for Jobs," October 16, 2018*

- In a survey of economic confidence in the nation's 50 largest metropolitan areas conducted January–December 2014, the Chicago metro area placed #16, according to Gallup's 2014 Economic Confidence Index. *Gallup, "San Jose and San Francisco Lead in Economic Confidence," March 19, 2015*

- NerdWallet.com identified the 10 most promising cities for job seekers of the nation's 100 largest cities. Chicago was ranked #69. Criteria: job availability; annual salary; workforce growth; affordability. *NerdWallet.com, "Best Cities for Job Seekers in 2017," December 19, 2016*

- The Brookings Institution ranked the nation's largest cities based on income inequality. Chicago was ranked #22 (#1 = greatest inequality). Criteria: the "95/20 ratio," a figure representing the income at which a household earns more than 95 percent of all other households, divided by the income at which a household earns more than only 20 percent of all other households. *Brookings Institution, "Household Income Inequality, Largest Cities of 97 Large U.S. Metro Areas, 2014-2016," February 5, 2018*

- The Brookings Institution ranked the 100 largest metro areas in the U.S. based on income inequality. Chicago was ranked #15 (#1 = greatest inequality). Criteria: the "95/20 ratio," a figure representing the income at which a household earns more than 95 percent of all other households, divided by the income at which a household earns more than only 20 percent of all other households. *Brookings Institution, "Household Income Inequality, 100 Largest U.S. Metro Areas, 2014-2016," February 5, 2018*

- Payscale.com ranked the 32 largest metro areas in terms of wage growth. The Chicago metro area ranked #10. Criteria: private-sector wage growth between the 4th quarter of 2017 and the 4th quarter of 2018. *PayScale, "Wage Trends by Metro Area-4th Quarter," January 8, 2019*

- The Chicago metro area was identified as one of the most debt-ridden places in America by the finance site Credit.com. The metro area was ranked #12. Criteria: residents' average credit card debt as well as median income. *Credit.com, "25 Cities With the Most Credit Card Debt," February 28, 2018*

- Chicago was cited as one of America's top metros for new and expanded facility projects in 2018. The area ranked #1 in the large metro area category (population over 1 million). *Site Selection, "Top Metros of 2018," March 2019*

- Chicago was identified as one of the happiest cities to work in by CareerBliss.com, an online community for career advancement. The city ranked #2 out of 10. Criteria: an employee's relationship with his or her boss and co-workers; daily tasks; general work environment; compensation; opportunities for advancement; company culture and job reputation; and resources. *Businesswire.com, "CareerBliss Happiest Cities to Work 2019," February 12, 2019*

- The Chicago metro area appeared on the Milken Institute "2018 Best Performing Cities" list. Rank: #132 out of 200 large metro areas. Criteria: job growth; wage and salary growth; high-tech output growth. *Milken Institute, "Best-Performing Cities 2018," January 24, 2019*

- *Forbes* ranked the 200 most populous metro areas to determine the nation's "Best Places for Business and Careers." The Chicago metro area was ranked #66. Criteria: costs (business and living); job growth (past and projected); income growth; quality of life; educational attainment (college and high school); projected economic growth; cultural and recreational opportunities; net migration patterns; number of highly ranked colleges. *Forbes, "The Best Places for Business and Careers 2018: Seattle Leads the Way," October 24, 2018*

- Mercer Human Resources Consulting ranked 209 cities worldwide in terms of cost-of-living. Chicago ranked #51 (the lower the ranking, the higher the cost-of-living). The survey measured the comparative cost of over 200 items (such as housing, food, clothing, household goods, transportation, and entertainment) in each location. *Mercer, "2018 Cost of Living Survey," June 26, 2018*

Children/Family Rankings

- Chicago was selected as one of the most playful cities in the U.S. by KaBOOM! The organization's Playful City USA initiative honors cities and towns across the nation that have made their communities more playable. Criteria: pledging to integrate play as a solution to challenges in their communities; making it easy for children to get active and balanced play; creating more family-friendly and innovative communities as a result. *KaBOOM! National Campaign for Play, "2017 Playful City USA Communities"*

Culture/Performing Arts Rankings

- Chicago was selected as one of the twenty best large U.S. cities for moviemakers. Of cities with a population over 400,000, the city was ranked #6. Criteria: film community and culture; access to equipment and facilities; film activity in 2018; number of film schools; tax incentives. ease of movement and traffic. *MovieMaker Magazine, "Best Places to Live and Work as a Moviemaker: 2019," January 16, 2019*

- Chicago was selected as one of "America's Favorite Cities." The city ranked #10 in the "Culture" category. Respondents to an online survey were asked to rate 38 top urban destinations in the U.S. from a visitor's perspective. Criteria: theater scene and community; number of bookstores; live music; and sense of history. *Travelandleisure.com, "These Are America's 20 Most Cultured Cities," October 2016*

- Chicago was selected as one of "America's Favorite Cities." The city ranked #11 in the "Culture: Music Scene " category. Respondents to an online survey were asked to rate 38 top urban destinations in the U.S. from a visitor's perspective. *Travelandleisure.com, "From the Honkytonk Capital to Jazz's Birthplace: America's Best Music Scenes," October 2016*

- Chicago was selected as one of "America's Favorite Cities." The city ranked #3 in the "Architecture " category. Respondents to an online survey were asked to rate their favorite place (population over 100,000) in over 65 categories. *Travelandleisure.com, "America's Favorite Cities for Architecture 2016," March 2, 2017*

Education Rankings

- Personal finance website *WalletHub* analyzed the 150 largest U.S. metropolitan statistical areas to determine where the most educated Americans are choosing to settle. Criteria: education quality and attainment gap; education levels; percentage of workers with degrees; public school quality rankings; quality and size of each metro area's universities. Chicago was ranked #33 (#1 = most educated city). *www.WalletHub.com, "2018's Most and Least Educated Cities in America, " July 24, 2018*

- Chicago was selected as one of the most well-read cities in America by Amazon.com. The city ranked #17 among the top 20. Cities with populations greater than 500,000 were evaluated based on per capita sales of books, magazines and newspapers (both print and Kindle format). *Amazon.com, "The 20 Most Well-Read Cities in America," May 24, 2016*

- Chicago was selected as one of America's most literate cities. The city ranked #22 out of the 82 largest U.S. cities. Criteria: number of booksellers; library resources; Internet resources; educational attainment; periodical publishing resources; newspaper circulation. *Central Connecticut State University, "America's Most Literate Cities, 2016," March 31, 2017*

Environmental Rankings

- The U.S. Environmental Protection Agency (EPA) released a list of U.S. metropolitan areas with the most ENERGY STAR certified buildings in 2017. The Chicago metro area was ranked #7 out of 25. *U.S. Environmental Protection Agency, "2018 Energy Star Top Cities," April 11, 2018*

- Chicago was highlighted as one of the 25 most ozone-polluted metro areas in the U.S. during 2014 through 2016. The area ranked #22. *American Lung Association, State of the Air 2018*

Food/Drink Rankings

- The U.S. Chamber of Commerce Foundation conducted an in-depth study on local food truck regulations, surveyed 288 food truck owners, and ranked 20 major American cities based on how friendly they are for operating a food truck. The compiled index assessed the following: procedures for obtaining permits and licenses; complying with restrictions; and financial obligations associated with operating a food truck. Chicago ranked #13 overall (1 being the best) for ease in operating a food truck. *www.foodtrucknation.us, "Food Truck Nation," March 20, 2018*

- According to Fodor's Travel, Chicago placed among the 14 best U.S. cities for food-truck cuisine. *www.fodors.com, "America's Best Food Truck Cities," August 23, 2016*

- *Men's Health* ranked 100 major U.S. cities in terms of alcohol intoxication. Chicago ranked #85 (#1 = most sober).Criteria: binge drinking; alcohol-related traffic accidents, arrests, and fatalities. *Men's Health, "America's Drunkest Cities," March 9, 2015*

Health/Fitness Rankings

- For each of the 100 largest cities in the United States, the American College of Sports Medicine's American Fitness Index evaluated infrastructure, community assets, and policies that encourage healthy and fit lifestyles, including preventive health behaviors, levels of chronic disease conditions, health care access, and community resources and policies that support physical activity. Chicago ranked #32 for "community fitness." *www.americanfitnessindex.org, "ACSM American Fitness Index Health and Community Fitness Status of the 100 Largest U.S. Cities," May 2018*

- Chicago was identified as one of the 10 most walkable cities in the U.S. by Walk Score, a Seattle-based service that rates the convenience and transit access of 10,000 neighborhoods in 3,000 cities. The area ranked #8 out of the 50 largest U.S. cities. Walk Score measures walkability by analyzing hundreds of walking routes to nearby amenities, and also measures pedestrian friendliness by analyzing population density and road metrics such as block length and intersection density. *WalkScore.com, May 31, 2017*

- The Chicago metro area was identified as one of the worst cities for bed bugs in America by pest control company Orkin. The area ranked #3 out of 50 based on the number of bed bug treatments Orkin performed from December 2017 to November 2018. *Orkin, "Baltimore Remains Front Runner, Atlanta and Philadelphia Break Into Top 10," January 14, 2019*

- Chicago was identified as a "2018 Spring Allergy Capital." The area ranked #65 out of 100. Three groups of factors were used to identify the most challenging cities for people with allergies during the spring season: annual pollen levels; medicine utilization; access to board-certified allergists. *Asthma and Allergy Foundation of America, "Spring Allergy Capitals 2018"*

- Chicago was identified as a "2018 Fall Allergy Capital." The area ranked #58 out of 100. Three groups of factors were used to identify the most challenging cities for people with allergies during the fall season: annual pollen levels; medicine utilization; access to board-certified allergists. *Asthma and Allergy Foundation of America, "Fall Allergy Capitals 2018"*

- Chicago was identified as a "2018 Asthma Capital." The area ranked #43 out of the nation's 100 largest metropolitan areas. Criteria: estimated prevalence; self-reported prevalence; crude death rate for asthma; annual pollen score; annual air quality; public smoking laws; number of board-certified asthma specialists; school inhaler access laws; rescue medication use; controller medication use; ER visits for asthma; uninsured rate; poverty rate. *Asthma and Allergy Foundation of America, "Asthma Capitals 2018: The Most Challenging Places to Live With Asthma"*

- *Men's Health* ranked 100 major U.S. cities in terms of the best cities for men. Chicago ranked #55. Criteria: health; fitness; quality of life. *Men's Health, "The Best & Worst Cities for Men Who Want to Be Fit and Happy," January 1, 2016*

- The Chicago metro area ranked #95 out of 189 in The Gallup-Healthways Well-Being Index. Criteria: purpose; social well being; financial health; community and physical health. Results are based on telephone interviews with adults, aged 18 and older, living in metropolitan areas in the 50 U.S. states and the District of Columbia. *Gallup-Healthways, "State of American Well-Being, 2017 Community Well-Being Rankings" March 2018*

Real Estate Rankings

- FitSmallBusiness looked at 50 of the largest metropolitan areas in the U.S. to determine which metro was the best to start a real estate business. Data was compiled from such sources as: Zillow, Trulia, U.S. Census Bureau, and the Bureau of Labor Statistics. Criteria: location; inventory; annual wages; median sales price of homes; days on the market; median price cut percentage; and other factors that would influence real estate professional growth. The Chicago metro area ranked #4. *fitsmallbusiness.com, "The Best Cities to Become a Real Estate Agent in 2018," January 30, 2018*

- *WalletHub* compared the most populated U.S. cities, as well as at least two of the most populated cities in each state, for a total of 179, to determine which had the best markets for real estate agents. Chicago ranked #110 where demand was high and pay was the best. Criteria: sales per agent; annual median wage for real-estate agents; monthly average starting salary for real estate agents; real estate job density and competition; unemployment rate; housing-market health index; and other relevant metrics. *www.WalletHub.com, "2018's Best Places to Be a Real Estate Agent," April 25, 2018*

- Chicago was ranked #126 out of 237 metro areas in terms of housing affordability in 2018 by the National Association of Home Builders (#1 = most affordable). Criteria: the share of homes sold in that area affordable to a family earning the local median income, based on standard mortgage underwriting criteria. *National Association of Home Builders®, NAHB-Wells Fargo Housing Opportunity Index, 4th Quarter 2018*

Safety Rankings

- To identify the most dangerous cities in America, 24/7 Wall Street focused on violent crime categories—murder, rape, robbery, and aggravated assault—and property crime as reported in the FBI's 2017 annual Uniform Crime Report. Criteria also included median income from American Community Survey and unemployment figures from Bureau of Labor Statistics. For cities with populations over 100,000, Chicago was ranked #21. *247wallst.com, "25 Most Dangerous Cities in America" October 17, 2018*

- Allstate ranked the 200 largest cities in America in terms of driver safety. Chicago ranked #129. Criteria: internal property damage claims over a two-year period from January 2015 to December 2016. The report helps increase the importance of safety awareness behind the wheel. *Allstate, "Allstate America's Best Drivers Report, 2018" August 28, 2018*

- Chicago was identified as one of the most dangerous cities in America by NeighborhoodScout. The city ranked #57 out of 100. Criteria: number of violent crimes per 1,000 residents. The editors only considered cities with 25,000 or more residents. *NeighborhoodScout.com, "Top 100 Most Dangerous Cities in the U.S. 2019" January 2, 2019*

- The National Insurance Crime Bureau ranked 382 metro areas in the U.S. in terms of per capita rates of vehicle theft. The Chicago metro area ranked #118 (#1 = highest rate). Criteria: number of vehicle theft offenses per 100,000 inhabitants in 2017. *National Insurance Crime Bureau, "Hot Spots 2017," July 12, 2018*

Seniors/Retirement Rankings

- From its Best Cities for Successful Aging indexes, the Milken Institute generated rankings for metropolitan areas, weighing data in nine categories—health care, wellness, living arrangements, transportation and convenience, financial characteristics, education, employment, community engagement, and overall livability. The Chicago metro area was ranked #48 overall in the large metro area category. *Milken Institute, "Best Cities for Successful Aging, 2017" March 14, 2017*

Sports/Recreation Rankings

- Chicago was chosen as one of America's best cities for bicycling. The city ranked #6 out of 50. Criteria: cycling infrastructure that is safe and friendly for all ages; energy and bike culture. The editors only considered cities with populations of 100,000 or more. *Bicycling, "The 50 Best Bike Cities in America," October 10, 2018*

Transportation Rankings

- Business Insider presented an AllTransit Performance Score ranking of public transportation in major U.S. cities and towns, with populations over 250,000, in which Chicago earned the #6-ranked "Transit Score," awarded for frequency of service, access to jobs, quality and number of stops, and affordability. *www.businessinsider.com, "The 17 Major U.S. Cities with the Best Public Transportation," April 17, 2018*

- NerdWallet surveyed average annual car insurance premiums in 125 U.S. cities to identify the least expensive U.S. cities in which to insure a car. Locations with no-fault insurance laws was a strong determinant. Chicago came in at #12 for the most expensive rates. *www.nerdwallet.com, "Best Cities for Cheap Car Insurance," February 3, 2014*

- Chicago was identified as one of the most congested metro areas in the U.S. The area ranked #8 out of 10. Criteria: yearly delay per auto commuter in hours. *Texas A&M Transportation Institute, "2015 Urban Mobility Scorecard," August 2015*

- According to the INRIX "2018 Global Traffic Scorecard," Chicago was identified as one of the most congested metro areas in the U.S. The area ranked #3 out of 10. Criteria: average annual time spent in traffic and average cost of congestion per motorist. *Forbes.com, "Do You Live in the City With the Worst Traffic?," February 11, 2019*

Women/Minorities Rankings

- The *Houston Chronicle* listed the Chicago metro area as #8 in top places for young Latinos to live in the U.S. Research was largely based on housing and occupational data from the largest metropolitan areas performed by *Forbes* and NBC Universo. Criteria: percentage of 18-34 year-olds; Latino college grad rates; and diversity. *blog.chron.com, "The 15 Best Big Cities for Latino Millenials," January 26, 2016*

- Personal finance website *WalletHub* compared more than 180 U.S. cities—including the 150 most populated U.S. cities, plus at least two of the most populated cities in each state—across two key dimensions, "Hispanic Business-Friendliness" and "Hispanic Purchasing Power", to arrive at the most favorable conditions for Hispanic entrepreneurs. Chicago was ranked #138 out of 182. Criteria includes: share of Hispanic-Owned Businesses; Hispanic entrepreneurship rate to median annual income of Hispanics; Small Business-Friendliness score; cost of living; and number of Hispanics with at least a bachelor's degree. *WalletHub.com, "2018's Best Cities for Hispanic Entrepreneurs," April 26, 2018*

Miscellaneous Rankings

- Chicago was selected as a 2018 Digital Cities Survey winner. The city ranked #9 in the large city (500,000 or more population) category. The survey examined and assessed how city governments are utilizing technology to improve transparency, enhance cybersecurity, and solve social challenges. Survey questions focused on ten characteristics: engaged, mobile, open, secure, staffed/supported, efficient, connected, resilient, best practices, and use of innovation. *Center for Digital Government, "2018 Digital Cities Survey," November 2, 2018*

- In its roundup of St. Patrick's Day parades "Gayot" listed the best festivals and parades of all things Irish. The festivities in Chicago as among the best. *www.gayot.com, "Best St. Patrick's Day Parades," March 17, 2018*

- The watchdog site Charity Navigator conducts an annual study of charities in the nation's major markets both to analyze statistical differences in their financial, accountability, and transparency practices and to track year-to-year variations in individual philanthropic communities. Charity Navigator's analysis demonstrated that the financial, accountability and transparency behaviors of America's largest charities can be influenced by the metropolitan market within which the charity operates. The Chicago metro area was ranked #11 among the 30 metro markets in the rating category of Overall Score. *www.charitynavigator.org, "2017 Metro Market Study," May 1, 2017*

- The real estate site Zillow has compiled the 2016 Trick-or-Treat Index, which used its own Home Value Index and Walk Score along with population density, age of residents, and local crime stats to determine that Chicago ranked #13 for "getting the best candy in the least amount of time." Zillow also zeroes in on the best neighborhoods in its top 20 cities. *www.zillow.com, "20 Best Cities for Trick or Treating in 2017," October 13, 2017*

- *WalletHub* compared the 150 most populated U.S. cities to determine their operating efficiency. A "Quality of Services" score was constructed for each city and then divided by the total budget per capita to reveal which were managed the best. Chicago ranked #140. Criteria: financial stability; economy; education; safety; health; infrastructure and pollution. *www.WalletHub.com, "2018's Best- & Worst-Run Cities in America," July 9, 2018*

- Chicago was selected as one of the 20 memorable places in the world during Thanksgiving by *Fodor's Travel*. Criteria: attractions; history; events. *Fodors.com, "Where to Go for Thanksgiving 2016," November 4, 2016*

- The National Alliance to End Homelessness listed the 25 most populous metro areas with the highest rate of homelessness. The Chicago metro area had a high rate of homelessness. Criteria: number of homeless people per 10,000 population in 2016. *National Alliance to End Homelessness, "Homelessness in the 25 Most Populous U.S. Metro Areas," September 1, 2017*

Business Environment

CITY FINANCES

City Government Finances

Component	2016 ($000)	2016 ($ per capita)
Total Revenues	8,533,344	3,137
Total Expenditures	10,187,796	3,745
Debt Outstanding	23,696,546	8,710
Cash and Securities[1]	15,941,402	5,860

Note: (1) Cash and security holdings of a government at the close of its fiscal year, including those of its dependent agencies, utilities, and liquor stores.
Source: U.S. Census Bureau, State & Local Government Finances 2016

City Government Revenue by Source

Source	2016 ($000)	2016 ($ per capita)	2016 (%)
General Revenue			
From Federal Government	550,668	202	6.5
From State Government	1,216,880	447	14.3
From Local Governments	0	0	0.0
Taxes			
Property	836,598	308	9.8
Sales and Gross Receipts	1,651,839	607	19.4
Personal Income	0	0	0.0
Corporate Income	0	0	0.0
Motor Vehicle License	24,071	9	0.3
Other Taxes	413,428	152	4.8
Current Charges	1,744,120	641	20.4
Liquor Store	0	0	0.0
Utility	793,001	291	9.3
Employee Retirement	337,417	124	4.0

Source: U.S. Census Bureau, State & Local Government Finances 2016

City Government Expenditures by Function

Function	2016 ($000)	2016 ($ per capita)	2016 (%)
General Direct Expenditures			
Air Transportation	1,059,558	389	10.4
Corrections	0	0	0.0
Education	0	0	0.0
Employment Security Administration	0	0	0.0
Financial Administration	139,687	51	1.4
Fire Protection	562,866	206	5.5
General Public Buildings	188,024	69	1.8
Governmental Administration, Other	60,167	22	0.6
Health	132,652	48	1.3
Highways	751,822	276	7.4
Hospitals	0	0	0.0
Housing and Community Development	229,848	84	2.3
Interest on General Debt	1,306,875	480	12.8
Judicial and Legal	30,169	11	0.3
Libraries	93,430	34	0.9
Parking	6,511	2	0.1
Parks and Recreation	30,801	11	0.3
Police Protection	1,397,790	513	13.7
Public Welfare	296,680	109	2.9
Sewerage	374,502	137	3.7
Solid Waste Management	168,282	61	1.7
Veterans' Services	0	0	0.0
Liquor Store	0	0	0.0
Utility	309,316	113	3.0
Employee Retirement	1,947,324	715	19.1

Source: U.S. Census Bureau, State & Local Government Finances 2016

DEMOGRAPHICS

Population Growth

Area	1990 Census	2000 Census	2010 Census	2017* Estimate	Population Growth (%) 1990-2017	2010-2017
City	2,783,726	2,896,016	2,695,598	2,722,586	-2.2	1.0
MSA[1]	8,182,076	9,098,316	9,461,105	9,549,229	16.7	0.9
U.S.	248,709,873	281,421,906	308,745,538	321,004,407	29.1	4.0

Note: (1) Figures cover the Chicago-Naperville-Elgin, IL-IN-WI Metropolitan Statistical Area—see Appendix B for areas included; (*) 2013-2017 5-year estimated population
Source: U.S. Census Bureau, 1990 Census, Census 2000, Census 2010, 2013-2017 American Community Survey 5-Year Estimates

Household Size

Area	One	Two	Three	Four	Five	Six	Seven or More	Average Household Size
City	36.7	29.1	13.9	10.4	5.6	2.4	1.9	2.50
MSA[1]	28.6	30.7	15.7	14.0	6.9	2.6	1.6	2.70
U.S.	27.7	33.8	15.7	13.0	6.0	2.3	1.4	2.60

Note: (1) Figures cover the Chicago-Naperville-Elgin, IL-IN-WI Metropolitan Statistical Area—see Appendix B for areas included
Source: U.S. Census Bureau, 2013-2017 American Community Survey 5-Year Estimates

Race

Area	White Alone[2] (%)	Black Alone[2] (%)	Asian Alone[2] (%)	AIAN[3] Alone[2] (%)	NHOPI[4] Alone[2] (%)	Other Race Alone[2] (%)	Two or More Races (%)
City	49.1	30.5	6.2	0.3	0.0	11.2	2.6
MSA[1]	66.0	16.7	6.3	0.2	0.0	8.1	2.5
U.S.	73.0	12.7	5.4	0.8	0.2	4.8	3.1

Note: (1) Figures cover the Chicago-Naperville-Elgin, IL-IN-WI Metropolitan Statistical Area—see Appendix B for areas included; (2) Alone is defined as not being in combination with one or more other races; (3) American Indian and Alaska Native; (4) Native Hawaiian and Other Pacific Islander
Source: U.S. Census Bureau, 2013-2017 American Community Survey 5-Year Estimates

Hispanic or Latino Origin

Area	Total (%)	Mexican (%)	Puerto Rican (%)	Cuban (%)	Other (%)
City	29.0	21.7	3.8	0.3	3.2
MSA[1]	21.8	17.2	2.1	0.2	2.2
U.S.	17.6	11.1	1.7	0.7	4.1

Note: Persons of Hispanic or Latino origin can be of any race; (1) Figures cover the Chicago-Naperville-Elgin, IL-IN-WI Metropolitan Statistical Area—see Appendix B for areas included
Source: U.S. Census Bureau, 2013-2017 American Community Survey 5-Year Estimates

Segregation

Type	1990	2000	2010	2010 Rank[2]	1990-2000	1990-2010	2000-2010
Black/White	84.4	81.2	76.4	3	-3.2	-8.0	-4.8
Asian/White	46.5	46.8	44.9	26	0.3	-1.6	-1.8
Hispanic/White	61.4	60.7	56.3	10	-0.8	-5.1	-4.3

Note: All figures cover the Metropolitan Statistical Area—see Appendix B for areas included; Figures are based on an analysis of 1990, 2000, and 2010 Census Decennial Census tract data by William H. Frey, Brookings Institution and the University of Michigan Social Science Data Analysis Network. In this analysis all racial groups (whites, blacks, and asians) are non-Hispanic members of those races. Hispanics are shown as a separate category; (1) Segregation Indices are Dissimilarity Indices that measure the degree to which the minority group is distributed differently than whites across census tracts. They range from 0 (complete integration) to 100 (complete segregation) where the value indicates the percentage of the minority group that needs to move to be distributed exactly like whites; (2) Ranges from 1 (most segregated) to 102 (least segregated); n/a not available.
Source: www.CensusScope.org

Ancestry

Area	German	Irish	English	American	Italian	Polish	French[2]	Scottish	Dutch
City	7.4	7.5	2.4	2.0	3.9	5.9	1.0	0.6	0.5
MSA[1]	14.9	11.0	4.2	2.8	6.8	9.0	1.5	1.0	1.2
U.S.	14.1	10.1	7.5	6.6	5.3	2.9	2.5	1.7	1.3

Note: Figures are the percentage of the total population reporting a particular ancestry. The nine most commonly reported ancestries in the U.S. are shown. Figures include multiple ancestries (e.g. if a person reported being Irish and Italian, they were included in both columns); (1) Figures cover the Chicago-Naperville-Elgin, IL-IN-WI Metropolitan Statistical Area—see Appendix B for areas included; (2) Excludes Basque
Source: U.S. Census Bureau, 2013-2017 American Community Survey 5-Year Estimates

Foreign-Born Population

Area	Percent of Population Born in								
	Any Foreign Country	Asia	Mexico	Europe	Carribean	Central America[2]	South America	Africa	Canada
City	20.7	4.9	8.9	3.5	0.4	0.9	1.0	0.9	0.2
MSA[1]	17.7	5.0	6.7	3.8	0.3	0.5	0.6	0.6	0.2
U.S.	13.4	4.1	3.6	1.5	1.3	1.0	0.9	0.6	0.3

Note: (1) Figures cover the Chicago-Naperville-Elgin, IL-IN-WI Metropolitan Statistical Area—see Appendix B for areas included; (2) Excludes Mexico.
Source: U.S. Census Bureau, 2013-2017 American Community Survey 5-Year Estimates

Marital Status

Area	Never Married	Now Married[2]	Separated	Widowed	Divorced
City	49.0	35.1	2.3	5.2	8.4
MSA[1]	36.9	47.0	1.7	5.5	8.9
U.S.	33.1	48.2	2.0	5.8	10.9

Note: Figures are percentages and cover the population 15 years of age and older; (1) Figures cover the Chicago-Naperville-Elgin, IL-IN-WI Metropolitan Statistical Area—see Appendix B for areas included; (2) Excludes separated
Source: U.S. Census Bureau, 2013-2017 American Community Survey 5-Year Estimates

Disability by Age

Area	All Ages	Under 18 Years Old	18 to 64 Years Old	65 Years and Over
City	10.6	3.0	8.4	37.8
MSA[1]	9.9	3.0	7.7	33.6
U.S.	12.6	4.2	10.3	35.5

Note: Figures show percent of the civilian noninstitutionalized population that reported having a disability. Disability status is determined from six types of difficulty: vision, hearing, cognitive, ambulatory, self-care, and independent living. For children under 5 years old, hearing and vision difficulty are used to determine disability status. For children between the ages of 5 and 14, disability status is determined from hearing, vision, cognitive, ambulatory, and self-care difficulties. For people aged 15 years and older, they are considered to have a disability if they have difficulty with any one of the six difficulty types; Note: (1) Figures cover the Chicago-Naperville-Elgin, IL-IN-WI Metropolitan Statistical Area—see Appendix B for areas included
Source: U.S. Census Bureau, 2013-2017 American Community Survey 5-Year Estimates

Age

Area	Percent of Population									Median Age
	Under Age 5	Age 5–19	Age 20–34	Age 35–44	Age 45–54	Age 55–64	Age 65–74	Age 75–84	Age 85+	
City	6.6	17.6	27.4	14.0	12.1	10.7	6.7	3.5	1.4	34.1
MSA[1]	6.2	19.9	21.2	13.4	13.7	12.5	7.7	3.9	1.8	37.0
U.S.	6.2	19.5	20.7	12.7	13.4	12.7	8.6	4.4	1.9	37.8

Note: (1) Figures cover the Chicago-Naperville-Elgin, IL-IN-WI Metropolitan Statistical Area—see Appendix B for areas included
Source: U.S. Census Bureau, 2013-2017 American Community Survey 5-Year Estimates

Gender

Area	Males	Females	Males per 100 Females
City	1,321,621	1,400,965	94.3
MSA[1]	4,671,861	4,877,368	95.8
U.S.	158,018,753	162,985,654	97.0

Note: (1) Figures cover the Chicago-Naperville-Elgin, IL-IN-WI Metropolitan Statistical Area—see Appendix B for areas included
Source: U.S. Census Bureau, 2013-2017 American Community Survey 5-Year Estimates

Religious Groups by Family

Area	Catholic	Baptist	Non-Den.	Methodist[2]	Lutheran	LDS[3]	Pente-costal	Presby-terian[4]	Muslim[5]	Judaism
MSA[1]	34.2	3.2	4.5	1.9	3.0	0.4	1.2	1.9	3.3	0.8
U.S.	19.1	9.3	4.0	4.0	2.3	2.0	1.9	1.6	0.8	0.7

Note: Figures are the number of adherents as a percentage of the total population; (1) Figures cover the Chicago-Naperville-Elgin, IL-IN-WI Metropolitan Statistical Area—see Appendix B for areas included; (2) Methodist/Pietist; (3) Latter Day Saints; (4) Reformed; (5) Figures are estimates
Source: Association of Statisticians of American Religious Bodies, 2010 U.S. Religion Census: Religious Congregations & Membership Study

Religious Groups by Tradition

Area	Catholic	Evangelical Protestant	Mainline Protestant	Other Tradition	Black Protestant	Orthodox
MSA[1]	34.2	9.8	5.1	5.1	2.1	0.9
U.S.	19.1	16.2	7.3	4.3	1.6	0.3

Note: Figures are the number of adherents as a percentage of the total population; (1) Figures cover the Chicago-Naperville-Elgin, IL-IN-WI Metropolitan Statistical Area—see Appendix B for areas included
Source: Association of Statisticians of American Religious Bodies, 2010 U.S. Religion Census: Religious Congregations & Membership Study

ECONOMY

Gross Metropolitan Product

Area	2016	2017	2018	2019	Rank[2]
MSA[1]	655.7	675.8	703.9	737.3	3

Note: Figures are in billions of dollars; (1) Figures cover the Chicago-Naperville-Elgin, IL-IN-WI Metropolitan Statistical Area—see Appendix B for areas included; (2) Rank is based on 2017 data and ranges from 1 to 381
Source: U.S. Conference of Mayors, U.S. Metro Economies: Economic Growth & Full Employment, June 2018

Economic Growth

Area	2017-2018 (%)	2019-2020 (%)	2021-2022 (%)
MSA[1]	1.6	1.9	1.0

Note: Figures are real gross metropolitan product (GMP) growth rates and represent average annual percent change; (1) Figures cover the Chicago-Naperville-Elgin, IL-IN-WI Metropolitan Statistical Area—see Appendix B for areas included
Source: U.S. Conference of Mayors, U.S. Metro Economies: Economic Growth & Full Employment, June 2018

Metropolitan Area Exports

Area	2012	2013	2014	2015	2016	2017	Rank[2]
MSA[1]	40,568.0	44,910.6	47,340.1	44,820.9	43,932.7	46,140.2	5

Note: Figures are in millions of dollars; (1) Figures cover the Chicago-Naperville-Elgin, IL-IN-WI Metropolitan Statistical Area—see Appendix B for areas included; (2) Rank is based on 2017 data and ranges from 1 to 387
Source: U.S. Department of Commerce, International Trade Administration, Office of Trade and Economic Analysis, Industry and Analysis, Exports by Metropolitan Area, extracted March 25, 2019

Building Permits

Area	Single-Family			Multi-Family			Total		
	2016	2017	Pct. Chg.	2016	2017	Pct. Chg.	2016	2017	Pct. Chg.
City	613	525	-14.4	8,491	8,414	-0.9	9,104	8,939	-1.8
MSA[1]	8,032	8,416	4.8	11,909	13,716	15.2	19,941	22,132	11.0
U.S.	750,800	820,000	9.2	455,800	462,000	1.4	1,206,600	1,282,000	6.2

Note: (1) Figures cover the Chicago-Naperville-Elgin, IL-IN-WI Metropolitan Statistical Area—see Appendix B for areas included; Figures represent new, privately-owned housing units authorized (unadjusted data); All permit data are based on estimates with imputation
Source: U.S. Census Bureau, Manufacturing, Mining, and Construction Statistics, Building Permits, 2016, 2017

Bankruptcy Filings

Area	Business Filings			Nonbusiness Filings		
	2017	2018	% Chg.	2017	2018	% Chg.
Cook County	435	441	1.4	29,321	27,072	-7.7
U.S.	23,157	22,232	-4.0	765,863	751,186	-1.9

Note: Business filings include Chapter 7, Chapter 11, Chapter 12, and Chapter 13; Nonbusiness filings include Chapter 7, Chapter 11, and Chapter 13
Source: Administrative Office of the U.S. Courts, Business and Nonbusiness Bankruptcy, County Cases Commenced by Chapter of the Bankruptcy Code, During the 12-Month Period Ending December 31, 2017 and Business and Nonbusiness Bankruptcy, County Cases Commenced by Chapter of the Bankruptcy Code, During the 12-Month Period Ending December 31, 2018

Housing Vacancy Rates

Area	Gross Vacancy Rate[2] (%)			Year-Round Vacancy Rate[3] (%)			Rental Vacancy Rate[4] (%)			Homeowner Vacancy Rate[5] (%)		
	2016	2017	2018	2016	2017	2018	2016	2017	2018	2016	2017	2018
MSA[1]	8.6	8.4	7.5	8.5	8.3	7.4	6.4	7.0	7.0	2.3	1.8	1.6
U.S.	12.8	12.7	12.3	9.9	9.9	9.7	6.9	7.2	6.9	1.7	1.6	1.5

Note: (1) Figures cover the Chicago-Naperville-Elgin, IL-IN-WI Metropolitan Statistical Area—see Appendix B for areas included; (2) The percentage of the total housing inventory that is vacant; (3) The percentage of the housing inventory (excluding seasonal units) that is year-round vacant; (4) The percentage of rental inventory that is vacant for rent; (5) The percentage of homeowner inventory that is vacant for sale
Source: U.S. Census Bureau, Housing Vacancies and Homeownership Annual Statistics: 2016, 2017, 2018

INCOME

Income

Area	Per Capita ($)	Median Household ($)	Average Household ($)
City	32,560	52,497	81,061
MSA[1]	34,624	65,757	91,944
U.S.	31,177	57,652	81,283

Note: (1) Figures cover the Chicago-Naperville-Elgin, IL-IN-WI Metropolitan Statistical Area—see Appendix B for areas included
Source: U.S. Census Bureau, 2013-2017 American Community Survey 5-Year Estimates

Household Income Distribution

Area	Percent of Households Earning							
	Under $15,000	$15,000 -$24,999	$25,000 -$34,999	$35,000 -$49,999	$50,000 -$74,999	$75,000 -$99,999	$100,000 -$149,999	$150,000 and up
City	15.8	10.9	9.2	11.9	15.8	10.9	12.7	12.9
MSA[1]	10.4	8.6	8.2	11.6	16.8	12.8	16.0	15.7
U.S.	11.6	9.8	9.5	13.0	17.7	12.3	14.1	12.1

Note: (1) Figures cover the Chicago-Naperville-Elgin, IL-IN-WI Metropolitan Statistical Area—see Appendix B for areas included
Source: U.S. Census Bureau, 2013-2017 American Community Survey 5-Year Estimates

Poverty Rate

Area	All Ages	Under 18 Years Old	18 to 64 Years Old	65 Years and Over
City	20.6	30.7	18.1	16.2
MSA[1]	13.1	18.6	11.8	9.3
U.S.	14.6	20.3	13.7	9.3

Note: Figures are percentage of people whose income during the past 12 months was below the poverty level; (1) Figures cover the Chicago-Naperville-Elgin, IL-IN-WI Metropolitan Statistical Area—see Appendix B for areas included
Source: U.S. Census Bureau, 2013-2017 American Community Survey 5-Year Estimates

EMPLOYMENT

Labor Force and Employment

Area	Civilian Labor Force			Workers Employed		
	Dec. 2017	Dec. 2018	% Chg.	Dec. 2017	Dec. 2018	% Chg.
City	1,361,078	1,335,474	-1.9	1,288,701	1,283,431	-0.4
MD[1]	3,739,557	3,718,529	-0.6	3,578,093	3,586,035	0.2
U.S.	159,880,000	162,510,000	1.6	153,602,000	156,481,000	1.9

Note: Data is not seasonally adjusted and covers workers 16 years of age and older; (1) Figures cover the
Chicago-Naperville-Arlington Heights, IL Metropolitan Division—see Appendix B for areas included
Source: Bureau of Labor Statistics, Local Area Unemployment Statistics

Unemployment Rate

Area	2018											
	Jan.	Feb.	Mar.	Apr.	May	Jun.	Jul.	Aug.	Sep.	Oct.	Nov.	Dec.
City	5.9	5.6	4.5	3.9	3.6	4.7	4.5	4.3	4.0	4.4	4.0	3.9
MD[1]	4.9	4.6	3.9	3.6	3.3	4.4	4.1	3.9	3.5	3.6	3.3	3.6
U.S.	4.5	4.4	4.1	3.7	3.6	4.2	4.1	3.9	3.6	3.5	3.5	3.7

Note: Data is not seasonally adjusted and covers workers 16 years of age and older; (1) Figures cover the
Chicago-Naperville-Arlington Heights, IL Metropolitan Division—see Appendix B for areas included
Source: Bureau of Labor Statistics, Local Area Unemployment Statistics

Average Wages

Occupation	$/Hr.	Occupation	$/Hr.
Accountants and Auditors	40.30	Maids and Housekeeping Cleaners	13.60
Automotive Mechanics	23.10	Maintenance and Repair Workers	22.20
Bookkeepers	21.40	Marketing Managers	63.60
Carpenters	33.90	Nuclear Medicine Technologists	42.00
Cashiers	11.40	Nurses, Licensed Practical	26.50
Clerks, General Office	18.40	Nurses, Registered	37.40
Clerks, Receptionists/Information	14.90	Nursing Assistants	14.40
Clerks, Shipping/Receiving	17.30	Packers and Packagers, Hand	12.70
Computer Programmers	45.20	Physical Therapists	44.50
Computer Systems Analysts	43.30	Postal Service Mail Carriers	25.20
Computer User Support Specialists	25.90	Real Estate Brokers	49.70
Cooks, Restaurant	13.60	Retail Salespersons	13.60
Dentists	81.80	Sales Reps., Exc. Tech./Scientific	34.20
Electrical Engineers	45.60	Sales Reps., Tech./Scientific	41.60
Electricians	38.40	Secretaries, Exc. Legal/Med./Exec.	19.10
Financial Managers	73.00	Security Guards	16.10
First-Line Supervisors/Managers, Sales	21.20	Surgeons	107.90
Food Preparation Workers	12.30	Teacher Assistants*	13.80
General and Operations Managers	64.40	Teachers, Elementary School*	31.60
Hairdressers/Cosmetologists	14.20	Teachers, Secondary School*	37.40
Internists, General	88.20	Telemarketers	14.20
Janitors and Cleaners	14.70	Truck Drivers, Heavy/Tractor-Trailer	24.20
Landscaping/Groundskeeping Workers	15.40	Truck Drivers, Light/Delivery Svcs.	19.80
Lawyers	76.90	Waiters and Waitresses	11.20

Note: Wage data covers the Chicago-Naperville-Elgin, IL-IN-WI Metropolitan Statistical Area—see Appendix B
for areas included; (*) Hourly wages for elementary/secondary school teachers and teacher assistants were
calculated by the editors from annual wage data based on a 40 hour work week; n/a not available.
Source: Bureau of Labor Statistics, Metro Area Occupational Employment & Wage Estimates, May 2018

Employment by Occupation

Occupation Classification	City (%)	MSA[1] (%)	U.S. (%)
Management, Business, Science, and Arts	40.1	38.8	37.4
Natural Resources, Construction, and Maintenance	5.2	6.7	8.9
Production, Transportation, and Material Moving	12.5	13.3	12.2
Sales and Office	22.3	24.2	23.5
Service	19.8	16.9	18.0

Note: Figures cover employed civilians 16 years of age and older; (1) Figures cover the
Chicago-Naperville-Elgin, IL-IN-WI Metropolitan Statistical Area—see Appendix B for areas included
Source: U.S. Census Bureau, 2013-2017 American Community Survey 5-Year Estimates

Employment by Industry

| Sector | MD[1] | | U.S. |
	Number of Employees	Percent of Total	Percent of Total
Construction	125,100	3.3	4.8
Education and Health Services	610,800	16.0	15.9
Financial Activities	271,500	7.1	5.7
Government	421,500	11.0	15.1
Information	67,700	1.8	1.9
Leisure and Hospitality	381,200	10.0	10.7
Manufacturing	288,400	7.5	8.5
Mining and Logging	1,100	<0.1	0.5
Other Services	162,000	4.2	3.9
Professional and Business Services	716,200	18.7	14.1
Retail Trade	362,200	9.5	10.8
Transportation, Warehousing, and Utilities	224,200	5.9	4.2
Wholesale Trade	194,900	5.1	3.9

Note: Figures are non-farm employment as of December 2018. Figures are not seasonally adjusted and include workers 16 years of age and older; (1) Figures cover the Chicago-Naperville-Arlington Heights, IL Metropolitan Division—see Appendix B for areas included
Source: Bureau of Labor Statistics, Current Employment Statistics, Employment, Hours, and Earnings

Occupations with Greatest Projected Employment Growth: 2018 – 2020

Occupation[1]	2018 Employment	2020 Projected Employment	Numeric Employment Change	Percent Employment Change
Combined Food Preparation and Serving Workers, Including Fast Food	139,870	145,560	5,690	4.1
Laborers and Freight, Stock, and Material Movers, Hand	153,200	158,690	5,490	3.6
Registered Nurses	126,530	130,420	3,890	3.1
General and Operations Managers	122,420	125,420	3,000	2.5
Waiters and Waitresses	91,610	93,810	2,200	2.4
Heavy and Tractor-Trailer Truck Drivers	71,040	73,220	2,180	3.1
Personal Care Aides	50,390	52,470	2,080	4.1
Light Truck or Delivery Services Drivers	50,560	52,420	1,860	3.7
Software Developers, Applications	27,370	29,190	1,820	6.6
Management Analysts	41,280	42,960	1,680	4.1

Note: Projections cover Illinois; (1) Sorted by numeric employment change
Source: www.projectionscentral.com, State Occupational Projections, 2018–2020 Short-Term Projections

Fastest Growing Occupations: 2018 – 2020

Occupation[1]	2018 Employment	2020 Projected Employment	Numeric Employment Change	Percent Employment Change
Statisticians	1,340	1,440	100	7.5
Nurse Practitioners	7,960	8,530	570	7.2
Computer Numerically Controlled Machine Tool Programmers, Metal and Plastic	1,320	1,410	90	6.8
Software Developers, Applications	27,370	29,190	1,820	6.6
Operations Research Analysts	6,770	7,200	430	6.4
Computer and Information Research Scientists	970	1,030	60	6.2
Physician Assistants	3,700	3,930	230	6.2
Locker Room, Coatroom, and Dressing Room Attendants	850	900	50	5.9
Occupational Therapy Aides	1,780	1,880	100	5.6
Market Research Analysts and Marketing Specialists	23,210	24,420	1,210	5.2

Note: Projections cover Illinois; (1) Sorted by percent employment change and excludes occupations with numeric employment change less than 50
Source: www.projectionscentral.com, State Occupational Projections, 2018–2020 Short-Term Projections

TAXES

State Corporate Income Tax Rates

State	Tax Rate (%)	Income Brackets ($)	Num. of Brackets	Financial Institution Tax Rate (%)[a]	Federal Income Tax Ded.
Illinois	9.5 (h)	Flat rate	1	9.5 (h)	No

Note: Tax rates as of January 1, 2019; (a) Rates listed are the corporate income tax rate applied to financial institutions or excise taxes based on income. Some states have other taxes based upon the value of deposits or shares; (h) The Illinois rate of 9.5% is the sum of a corporate income tax rate of 7.0% plus a replacement tax of 2.5%.
Source: Federation of Tax Administrators, Range of State Corporate Income Tax Rates, January 1, 2019

State Individual Income Tax Rates

State	Tax Rate (%)	Income Brackets ($)	Personal Exemptions ($)			Standard Ded. ($)	
			Single	Married	Depend.	Single	Married
Illinois (a)	4.95	Flat rate	2,225	4,450	2,225	–	–

Note: Tax rates as of January 1, 2019; Local- and county-level taxes are not included; n/a not applicable; Federal income tax is not deductible on state income tax returns; (a) 19 states have statutory provision for automatically adjusting to the rate of inflation the dollar values of the income tax brackets, standard deductions, and/or personal exemptions. Michigan indexes the personal exemption only. Oregon does not index the income brackets for $125,000 and over.
Source: Federation of Tax Administrators, State Individual Income Tax Rates, January 1, 2019

Various State Sales and Excise Tax Rates

State	State Sales Tax (%)	Gasoline[1] (¢/gal.)	Cigarette[2] ($/pack)	Spirits[3] ($/gal.)	Wine[4] ($/gal.)	Beer[5] ($/gal.)	Recreational Marijuana (%)
Illinois	6.25	31.98	1.98	8.55 (f)	1.39 (l)	0.23	Not legal

Note: All tax rates as of January 1, 2019; (1) The American Petroleum Institute has developed a methodology for determining the average tax rate on a gallon of fuel. Rates may include any of the following: excise taxes, environmental fees, storage tank fees, other fees or taxes, general sales tax, and local taxes. In states where gasoline is subject to the general sales tax, or where the fuel tax is based on the average sale price, the average rate determined by API is sensitive to changes in the price of gasoline. States that fully or partially apply general sales taxes to gasoline: CA, CO, GA, IL, IN, MI, NY; (2) The federal excise tax of $1.0066 per pack and local taxes are not included; (3) Rates are those applicable to off-premise sales of 40% alcohol by volume (a.b.v.) distilled spirits in 750ml containers. Local excise taxes are excluded; (4) Rates are those applicable to off-premise sales of 11% a.b.v. non-carbonated wine in 750ml containers; (5) Rates are those applicable to off-premise sales of 4.7% a.b.v. beer in 12 ounce containers; (f) Different rates also applicable according to alcohol content, place of production, size of container, or place purchased (on- or off-premise or onboard airlines); (l) Different rates also applicable to alcohol content, place of production, size of container, place purchased (on- or off-premise or on board airlines) or type of wine (carbonated, vermouth, etc.).
Source: Tax Foundation, 2019 Facts & Figures: How Does Your State Compare?

State Business Tax Climate Index Rankings

State	Overall Rank	Corporate Tax Rank	Individual Income Tax Rank	Sales Tax Rank	Unemployment Insurance Tax Rank	Property Tax Rank
Illinois	36	39	13	36	42	45

Note: The index is a measure of how each state's tax laws affect economic performance. The lower the rank, the more favorable a state's tax system is for business. States without a given tax are given a ranking of 1. The scores/rankings for the District of Columbia do not affect other states. The 2019 index represents the tax climate as of July 1, 2018.
Source: Tax Foundation, State Business Tax Climate Index 2019

COMMERCIAL REAL ESTATE

Office Market

Market Area	Inventory (sq. ft.)	Vacancy Rate (%)	Under Construction (sq. ft.)	YTD Net Absorption (sq. ft.)	Total Average Asking Rent ($/sq. ft./year)
Chicago	235,820,022	16.4	5,027,128	2,449,204	29.64
National	4,905,867,938	13.1	83,553,714	45,846,470	28.46

Source: Newmark Grubb Knight Frank, National Office Market Report, 4th Quarter 2018

Industrial/Warehouse/R&D Market

Market Area	Inventory (sq. ft.)	Vacancy Rate (%)	Under Construction (sq. ft.)	YTD Net Absorption (sq. ft.)	Total Average Asking Rent ($/sq. ft./year)
Chicago	1,138,298,840	7.7	15,461,596	13,822,281	5.50
National	14,796,839,085	5.0	262,662,294	238,014,726	7.16

Source: Newmark Grubb Knight Frank, National Industrial Market Report, 4th Quarter 2018

COMMERCIAL UTILITIES

Typical Monthly Electric Bills

Area	Commercial Service ($/month)		Industrial Service ($/month)	
	1,500 kWh	40 kW demand 14,000 kWh	1,000 kW demand 200,000 kWh	50,000 kW demand 32,500,000 kWh
City	n/a	n/a	n/a	n/a
Average[1]	203	1,619	25,886	2,540,077

Note: Figures are based on annualized rates; (1) Average based on 187 utilities surveyed; n/a not available
Source: Edison Electric Institute, Typical Bills and Average Rates Report, Summer 2018

TRANSPORTATION

Means of Transportation to Work

Area	Car/Truck/Van		Public Transportation			Bicycle	Walked	Other Means	Worked at Home
	Drove Alone	Car-pooled	Bus	Subway	Railroad				
City	49.2	7.9	13.7	12.5	1.8	1.7	6.7	1.9	4.6
MSA[1]	70.5	7.8	4.5	4.1	3.2	0.7	3.1	1.3	4.7
U.S.	76.4	9.2	2.5	1.9	0.6	0.6	2.7	1.3	4.7

Note: Figures are percentages and cover workers 16 years of age and older; (1) Figures cover the Chicago-Naperville-Elgin, IL-IN-WI Metropolitan Statistical Area—see Appendix B for areas included
Source: U.S. Census Bureau, 2013-2017 American Community Survey 5-Year Estimates

Travel Time to Work

Area	Less Than 10 Minutes	10 to 19 Minutes	20 to 29 Minutes	30 to 44 Minutes	45 to 59 Minutes	60 to 89 Minutes	90 Minutes or More
City	4.8	16.4	17.9	30.1	14.7	12.6	3.6
MSA[1]	8.5	21.9	18.5	24.9	12.3	10.6	3.3
U.S.	12.7	28.9	20.9	20.5	8.1	6.2	2.7

Note: Note: Figures are percentages and include workers 16 years old and over; (1) Figures cover the Chicago-Naperville-Elgin, IL-IN-WI Metropolitan Statistical Area—see Appendix B for areas included
Source: U.S. Census Bureau, 2013-2017 American Community Survey 5-Year Estimates

Freeway Travel Time Index

Area	1985	1990	1995	2000	2005	2010	2014
Urban Area Rank[1,2]	9	9	8	11	13	14	14
Urban Area Index[1]	1.17	1.20	1.24	1.27	1.29	1.28	1.31
Average Index[3]	1.09	1.11	1.14	1.17	1.20	1.19	1.20

Note: Freeway Travel Time Index—the ratio of travel time in the peak period to the travel time at free-flow conditions. For example, a value of 1.30 indicates a 20-minute free-flow trip takes 26 minutes in the peak (20 minutes x 1.30 = 26 minutes); (1) Covers the Chicago IL-IN urban area; (2) Rank is based on 101 urban areas (#1 = highest travel time index); (3) Average of 101 urban areas
Source: Texas Transportation Institute, 2015 Urban Mobility Scorecard, August 2015

Freeway Commuter Stress Index

Area	1985	1990	1995	2000	2005	2010	2014
Urban Area Rank[1,2]	19	19	19	20	18	19	19
Urban Area Index[1]	1.21	1.24	1.27	1.30	1.33	1.32	1.34
Average Index[3]	1.13	1.16	1.19	1.22	1.25	1.24	1.25

Note: The Freeway Commuter Stress Index is the same as the Freeway Travel Time Index (see table above) except that it includes only the travel in the peak directions during the peak periods; the TTI includes travel in all directions during the peak period. Thus, the CSI is more indicative of the work trip experienced by each commuter on a daily basis; (1) Covers the Chicago IL-IN urban area; (2) Rank is based on 101 urban areas (#1 = highest travel time index); (3) Average of 101 urban areas
Source: Texas Transportation Institute, 2015 Urban Mobility Scorecard, August 2015

Public Transportation

Agency Name / Mode of Transportation	Vehicles Operated in Maximum Service[1]	Annual Unlinked Passenger Trips[2] (in thous.)	Annual Passenger Miles[3] (in thous.)
Chicago Transit Authority (CTA)			
Bus (directly operated)	1,579	249,231.2	613,043.9
Heavy Rail (directly operated)	1,140	230,204.0	1,359,029.7
Northeast Illinois Regional Commuter Railroad (Metra)			
Commuter Rail (directly operated)	1,064	70,592.2	1,577,342.9

Note: (1) The number of revenue vehicles operated by the given mode and type of service to meet the annual maximum service requirement. This is the revenue vehicle count during the peak season of the year; on the week and day that maximum service is provided. Vehicles operated in maximum service (VOMS) exclude atypical days and one-time special events; (2) The number of passengers who boarded public transportation vehicles. Passengers are counted each time they board a vehicle no matter how many vehicles they use to travel from their origin to their destination. (3) The sum of the distances ridden by all passengers during the entire fiscal year.
Source: Federal Transit Administration, National Transit Database, 2017

Air Transportation

Airport Name and Code / Type of Service	Passenger Airlines[1]	Passenger Enplanements	Freight Carriers[2]	Freight (lbs)
O'Hare International (ORD)				
Domestic service (U.S. carriers - 2018)	32	33,152,311	17	433,598,554
International service (U.S. carriers - 2017)	14	3,097,738	9	141,337,597
Midway International (MDW)				
Domestic service (U.S. carriers - 2018)	21	10,278,307	3	21,708,658
International service (U.S. carriers - 2017)	7	169,983	1	8,951

Note: (1) Includes all U.S.-based major, minor and commuter airlines that carried at least one passenger during the year; (2) Includes all U.S.-based airlines and freight carriers that transported at least one pound of freight during the year.
Source: Bureau of Transportation Statistics, The Intermodal Transportation Database, Air Carriers: T-100 Domestic Market (U.S. Carriers), 2018; Bureau of Transportation Statistics, The Intermodal Transportation Database, Air Carriers: T-100 International Market (U.S. Carriers), 2017

Other Transportation Statistics

Major Highways:	I-55; I-57; I-80; I-88; I-90
Amtrak Service:	Yes
Major Waterways/Ports:	Port of Chicago (St. Lawrence Seaway)

Source: Amtrak.com; Google Maps

BUSINESSES

Major Business Headquarters

Company Name	Industry	Rankings Fortune[1]	Rankings Forbes[2]
Amsted Industries	Capital Goods	-	150
Archer Daniels Midland	Food Production	48	-
Boeing	Aerospace and Defense	27	-
Conagra Brands	Food Consumer Products	321	-
Exelon	Utilities: Gas and Electric	92	-
Heico Cos	Capital Goods	-	183
Jones Lang LaSalle	Real estate	356	-
Kirkland & Ellis	Services	-	134
LKQ	Wholesalers: Diversified	300	-
Northern Trust	Commercial Banks	486	-
Old Republic International	Insurance: Property and Casualty (Stock)	450	-
R.R. Donnelley & Sons	Publishing, Printing	406	-
Sidley Austin	Services	-	228
United Continental Holdings	Airlines	81	-
Walsh Group	Construction	-	87

Note: (1) Companies that produce a 10-K are ranked 1 to 500 based on 2017 revenue; (2) All private companies with at least $2 billion in annual revenue through the end of their most current fiscal year are ranked 1 to 229; companies listed are headquartered in the city; dashes indicate no ranking
Source: Fortune, "Fortune 500," June 2018; Forbes, "America's Largest Private Companies," 2018 Rankings

Fast-Growing Businesses

According to *Inc.*, Chicago is home to 16 of America's 500 fastest-growing private companies: **Home Chef** (#3); **GForce Life Sciences** (#8); **Edge Logistics** (#46); **RedShelf** (#121); **Pinnacle Furnished Suites** (#159); **Strike Social** (#165); **G2 Crowd** (#179); **SEI-Chicago** (#193); **Meridian Appraisal Management** (#220); **First Stop Health** (#276); **Era Transport** (#277); **Novatio Solutions** (#280); **OppLoans** (#340); **Home Invest** (#352); **Reverb.com** (#382); **Shiftgig** (#487). Criteria: must be an independent, privately-held, for-profit, U.S. corporation, proprietorship or partnership as of December 31, 2017; revenues must be at least $100,000 in 2014 and $2 million in 2017; must have four-year operating/sales history. Holding companies, regulated banks, and utilities were excluded. *Inc., "America's 500 Fastest-Growing Private Companies," 2018*

According to *Fortune*, Chicago is home to two of the 100 fastest-growing companies in the world: **GrubHub** (#13); **John Bean Technologies** (#89). Companies were ranked by their revenue growth rate; their EPS growth rate; and their three-year annualized total return to investors for the period ending June 30, 2018. Criteria for inclusion: a company, foreign or domestic, must trade on a major U.S. stock exchange; must file quarterly reports with the SEC; must have a minimum market capitalization of $250 million; must have a stock price of at least $5 on June 30, 2018; must have been trading continuously since June 30, 2015; must have revenue and net income for the four quarters ended on or before April 30, 2018, of at least $50 million and $10 million, respectively; and must have posted a compound annual growth in revenue and earnings per share of at least 15% annually over the three years ending on or before April 30, 2018. Real estate investment trusts, limited-liability companies, limited parterships, business development companies, closed-end investment firms, companies about to be acquired, and companies that lost money in the quarter ending April 30, 2018 were excluded. *Fortune, "100 Fastest-Growing Companies," 2018*

According to *Initiative for a Competitive Inner City (ICIC)*, Chicago is home to 11 of America's 100 fastest-growing "inner city" companies: **Bowa Construction** (#9); **Rowboat Creative** (#12); **Cloudbakers** (#16); **Transportation One** (#25); **Studio ARQ** (#31); **LEEP Forward** (#37); **Gorilla Group** (#41); **PACO Collective** (#58); **Nova Driving School** (#72); **Sandstorm Design** (#88); **LaSalle Network** (#97). Criteria for inclusion: company must be headquartered in or have 51 percent or more of its physical operations in an economically distressed urban area; must be an independent, for-profit corporation, partnership or proprietorship; must have 10 or more employees and have a five-year sales history that includes sales of at least $200,000 in the base year and at least $1 million in the current year with no decrease in sales over the two most recent years. Companies were ranked overall by revenue growth over the five-year period between 2013 and 2017. *Initiative for a Competitive Inner City (ICIC), "Inner City 100 Companies," 2018*

According to Deloitte, Chicago is home to seven of North America's 500 fastest-growing high-technology companies: **OppLoans** (#86); **PowerReviews** (#104); **Hireology** (#133); **Snapsheet** (#147); **Avant** (#249); **Cision** (#301); **Liquidus** (#439). Companies are ranked by percentage growth in revenue over a four-year period. Criteria for inclusion: company must be headquartered within North America; must own proprietary intellectual property or technology that is sold to customers in products that contributes to a significant portion of the company's operating revenue; must have been in business for a minumum of four years with 2014 operating revenues of at least $50,000 USD/CD and 2017 operating revenues of at least $5 million USD/CD. *Deloitte, 2018 Technology Fast 500*™

Minority Business Opportunity

Chicago is home to two companies which are on the *Black Enterprise* Industrial/Service list (100 largest companies based on gross sales): **Harpo** (#51); **UJAMAA Construction** (#55). Criteria: operational in previous calendar year; at least 51% black-owned and manufactures/owns the product it sells or provides industrial or consumer services. Brokerages, real estate firms and firms that provide professional services are not eligible. *Black Enterprise, B.E. 100s, 2018*

Chicago is home to one company which is on the *Black Enterprise* Bank list (15 largest banks based on total assets, capital, deposits and loans, including mortgage-backed securities for the calendar year): **Illinois Service Federal (ISF Bank)** (#11). Only commercial banks or savings and loans that are classified by the Federal Reserve as black institutions and have been fully operational for the previous calendar year were considered. *Black Enterprise, B.E. 100s, 2018*

Chicago is home to three companies which are on the *Black Enterprise* Asset Manager list (10 largest asset management firms based on assets under management): **Ariel Investments** (#1); **Capri Investment Group** (#8); **Channing Capital Management** (#9). Criteria: company must have been operational in previous calendar year and be at least 51% black-owned. *Black Enterprise, B.E. 100s, 2018*

Chicago is home to one company which is on the *Black Enterprise* Private Equity list (10 largest private equity firms based on capital under management): **Muller & Monroe Asset Management** (#7). Criteria: company must be operational in previous calendar year and be at least 51% black-owned. *Black Enterprise, B.E. 100s, 2018*

Chicago is home to 10 companies which are on the *Hispanic Business* 500 list (500 largest U.S. Hispanic-owned companies based on revenue): **Cardenas Marketing Network** (#93); **Primera Engineers Ltd.** (#212); **MZI Group** (#213); **Cristina Foods** (#227); **Monterrey Security** (#277); **Sanchez Daniels & Hoffman** (#299); **The San Jose Group Co.** (#333); **American Surveying & Engineering P.C.** (#356); **CivCon Services** (#392); **HCM Banners and Graphics** (#496). Companies included must show at least 51 percent ownership by Hispanic U.S. citizens, and must maintain headquarters in one of the 50 states or Washington, D.C. *Hispanic Business, "Hispanic Business 500," June 20, 2013*

Minority- and Women-Owned Businesses

Group	All Firms		Firms with Paid Employees			
	Firms	Sales ($000)	Firms	Sales ($000)	Employees	Payroll ($000)
AIAN[1]	1,655	(s)	112	(s)	250 - 499	(s)
Asian	23,333	6,696,989	5,069	6,105,786	37,844	1,155,038
Black	78,010	3,685,698	2,056	2,539,943	19,420	709,676
Hispanic	39,124	5,995,530	4,449	5,215,672	35,433	967,229
NHOPI[2]	334	44,951	50	40,051	389	8,984
Women	123,632	11,717,510	9,561	9,392,195	74,642	2,553,554
All Firms	291,007	395,746,404	48,499	387,004,804	1,183,301	71,043,548

Note: Figures cover firms located in the city; minority- and women-owned business are defined as firms in which the corresponding group own 51% or more of the stock or equity of the company; (1) American Indian and Alaska Native; (2) Native Hawaiian and Other Pacific Islander; (s) estimates are suppressed when publication standards are not met
Source: U.S. Census Bureau, 2012 Economic Census, Survey of Business Owners

HOTELS & CONVENTION CENTERS

Hotels, Motels and Vacation Rentals

Area	5 Star		4 Star		3 Star		2 Star		1 Star		Not Rated	
	Num.	Pct.[3]	Num.	Pct.[3]	Num.	Pct.[3]	Num.	Pct.[3]	Num.	Pct.[3]	Num.	Pct.[3]
City[1]	7	0.5	98	6.4	278	18.2	291	19.1	11	0.7	840	55.1
Total[2]	286	0.4	5,236	7.1	16,715	22.6	10,259	13.9	293	0.4	41,056	55.6

Note: (1) Figures cover Chicago and vicinity; (2) Figures cover all 100 cities in this book; (3) Percentage of hotels which have a given star rating; Star ratings are determined by expedia.com and offer an indication of the general quality of a particular hotel.
Source: www.expedia.com, April 3, 2019

The Chicago-Naperville-Arlington Heights, IL metro area is home to one of the best city hotels in the continental U.S. according to *Travel & Leisure*: **The Langham**. Magazine readers were surveyed and asked to rate hotels on the following criteria: rooms/facilities; location; service; food; and value. The list includes the top 15 city hotels in the continental U.S. *Travel & Leisure, "The World's Best Awards 2018"*

The Chicago-Naperville-Arlington Heights, IL metro area is home to two of the best hotels in the world according to *Condé Nast Traveler*: **The Peninsula Chicago**; **The Robey**. The selections are based on editors' picks. The list includes the top 13 hotels in the U.S. *Condé Nast Traveler, "The 78 Best Hotels in the World: The Gold List 2019"*

Major Convention Centers

Name	Overall Space (sq. ft.)	Exhibit Space (sq. ft.)	Meeting Space (sq. ft.)	Meeting Rooms
McCormick Place	n/a	2,670,000	600,000	173
Navy Pier-Festival Hall	n/a	170,100	44,000	36

Note: Table includes convention centers located in the Chicago-Naperville-Elgin, IL-IN-WI metro area; n/a not available
Source: Original research

Living Environment

COST OF LIVING

Cost of Living Index

Composite Index	Groceries	Housing	Utilities	Trans-portation	Health Care	Misc. Goods/Services
123.3	102.6	157.5	93.0	125.2	101.6	112.5

Note: The Cost of Living Index measures regional differences in the cost of consumer goods and services, excluding taxes and non-consumer expenditures, for professional and managerial households in the top income quintile. It is based on more than 50,000 prices covering almost 60 different items for which prices are collected three times a year by chambers of commerce, economic development organizations or university applied economic centers in each participating urban area. The numbers shown should be read as a percentage above or below the national average of 100. For example, a value of 115.4 in the groceries column indicates that grocery prices are 15.4% higher than the national average. Small differences in the index numbers should not be interpreted as significant; Figures cover the Chicago IL urban area.
Source: The Council for Community and Economic Research, ACCRA Cost of Living Index, 2018

Grocery Prices

Area[1]	T-Bone Steak ($/pound)	Frying Chicken ($/pound)	Whole Milk ($/half gal.)	Eggs ($/dozen)	Orange Juice ($/64 oz.)	Coffee ($/11.5 oz.)
City[2]	12.25	1.36	2.09	1.82	4.40	4.59
Avg.	11.35	1.42	1.94	1.81	3.52	4.35
Min.	7.45	0.92	0.80	0.75	2.72	3.06
Max.	15.05	2.76	4.18	4.00	5.36	8.20

Note: (1) Values for the local area are compared with the average, minimum and maximum values for all 291 areas in the Cost of Living Index; (2) Figures cover the Chicago IL urban area; T-Bone Steak (price per pound); Frying Chicken (price per pound, whole fryer); Whole Milk (half gallon carton); Eggs (price per dozen, Grade A, large); Orange Juice (64 oz. Tropicana or Florida Natural); Coffee (11.5 oz. can, vacuum-packed, Maxwell House, Hills Bros, or Folgers).
Source: The Council for Community and Economic Research, ACCRA Cost of Living Index, 2018

Housing and Utility Costs

Area[1]	New Home Price ($)	Apartment Rent ($/month)	All Electric ($/month)	Part Electric ($/month)	Other Energy ($/month)	Telephone ($/month)
City[2]	500,332	2,051	-	83.93	48.57	197.70
Avg.	347,000	1,087	165.93	100.16	67.73	178.70
Min.	200,468	500	93.58	25.64	26.78	163.10
Max.	1,901,222	4,888	388.65	246.86	332.81	197.70

Note: (1) Values for the local area are compared with the average, minimum and maximum values for all 291 areas in the Cost of Living Index; (2) Figures cover the Chicago IL urban area; New Home Price (2,400 sf living area, 8,000 sf lot, in urban area with full utilities); Apartment Rent (950 sf 2 bedroom/1.5 or 2 bath, unfurnished, excluding all utilities except water); All Electric (average monthly cost for an all-electric home); Part Electric (average monthly cost for a part-electric home); Other Energy (average monthly cost for natural gas, fuel oil, coal, wood, and any other forms of energy except electricity); Telephone (price includes the base monthly rate plus taxes and fees for three lines of mobile phone service).
Source: The Council for Community and Economic Research, ACCRA Cost of Living Index, 2018

Health Care, Transportation, and Other Costs

Area[1]	Doctor ($/visit)	Dentist ($/visit)	Optometrist ($/visit)	Gasoline ($/gallon)	Beauty Salon ($/visit)	Men's Shirt ($)
City[2]	105.00	102.00	97.00	3.34	69.90	32.00
Avg.	110.71	95.11	103.74	2.61	37.48	32.03
Min.	33.60	62.55	54.63	1.89	17.00	11.44
Max.	195.97	153.93	225.79	3.59	71.88	58.64

Note: (1) Values for the local area are compared with the average, minimum and maximum values for all 291 areas in the Cost of Living Index; (2) Figures cover the Chicago IL urban area; Doctor (general practitioners routine exam of an established patient); Dentist (adult teeth cleaning and periodic oral examination); Optometrist (full vision eye exam for established adult patient); Gasoline (one gallon regular unleaded, national brand, including all taxes, cash price at self-service pump if available); Beauty Salon (woman's shampoo, trim, and blow-dry); Men's Shirt (cotton/polyester dress shirt, pinpoint weave, long sleeves).
Source: The Council for Community and Economic Research, ACCRA Cost of Living Index, 2018

HOUSING

House Price Index (HPI)

Area	National Ranking[2]	Quarterly Change (%)	One-Year Change (%)	Five-Year Change (%)
MD[1]	194	0.05	3.62	22.76
U.S.[3]	–	1.12	5.73	32.81

Note: The HPI is a weighted repeat sales index. It measures average price changes in repeat sales or refinancings on the same properties. This information is obtained by reviewing repeat mortgage transactions on single-family properties whose mortgages have been purchased or securitized by Fannie Mae or Freddie Mac in January 1975; (1) Figures cover the Chicago-Naperville-Arlington Heights, IL Metropolitan Division—see Appendix B for areas included; (2) Rankings are based on annual percentage change for all metro areas containing at least 15,000 transactions over the last 10 years and ranges from 1 to 245; (3) figures based on a weighted average of Census Division estimates using a seasonally adjusted, purchase-only index; all figures are for the period ending December 31, 2018
Source: Federal Housing Finance Agency, House Price Index, February 26, 2019

Median Single-Family Home Prices

Area	2016	2017	2018[p]	Percent Change 2017 to 2018
MSA[1]	234.9	248.5	259.4	4.4
U.S. Average	235.5	248.8	261.6	5.1

Note: Figures are median sales prices of existing single-family homes in thousands of dollars; (p) preliminary; (1) Figures cover the Chicago-Naperville-Elgin, IL-IN-WI Metropolitan Statistical Area—see Appendix B for areas included
Source: National Association of Realtors, Median Sales Price of Existing Single-Family Homes for Metropolitan Areas, 4th Quarter 2018

Qualifying Income Based on Median Sales Price of Existing Single-Family Homes

Area	With 5% Down ($)	With 10% Down ($)	With 20% Down ($)
MSA[1]	59,459	56,329	50,071
U.S. Average	62,954	59,640	53,013

Note: Figures are preliminary; Qualifying income is based on a mortgage rate of 4.9%. Monthly principal and interest payment is limited to 25% of income; (1) Figures cover the Chicago-Naperville-Elgin, IL-IN-WI Metropolitan Statistical Area—see Appendix B for areas included
Source: National Association of Realtors, Qualifying Income Based on Median Sales Price of Existing Single-Family Homes for Metropolitan Areas, 4th Quarter 2018

Median Apartment Condo-Coop Home Prices

Area	2016	2017	2018[p]	Percent Change 2017 to 2018
MSA[1]	186.6	195.8	200.9	2.6
U.S. Average	220.7	234.3	241.0	2.9

Note: Figures are median sales prices of existing apartment condo-coop homes in thousands of dollars; (p) preliminary; (1) Figures cover the Chicago-Naperville-Elgin, IL-IN-WI Metropolitan Statistical Area—see Appendix B for areas included
Source: National Association of Realtors, Median Sales Price of Existing Apartment Condo-Coop Homes for Metropolitan Areas, 4th Quarter 2018

Home Value Distribution

Area	Under $50,000	$50,000 -$99,999	$100,000 -$149,999	$150,000 -$199,999	$200,000 -$299,999	$300,000 -$499,999	$500,000 -$999,999	$1,000,000 or more
City	3.6	8.7	13.2	15.7	23.3	21.6	10.5	3.3
MSA[1]	4.1	8.8	14.1	16.9	24.3	20.6	8.9	2.1
U.S.	8.3	13.9	14.7	14.6	18.7	17.3	9.7	2.7

Note: Figures are percentages and cover owner-occupied housing units; (1) Figures cover the Chicago-Naperville-Elgin, IL-IN-WI Metropolitan Statistical Area—see Appendix B for areas included
Source: U.S. Census Bureau, 2013-2017 American Community Survey 5-Year Estimates

Homeownership Rate

Area	2010 (%)	2011 (%)	2012 (%)	2013 (%)	2014 (%)	2015 (%)	2016 (%)	2017 (%)	2018 (%)
MSA[1]	68.2	67.7	67.1	68.2	66.3	64.3	64.5	64.1	64.6
U.S.	66.9	66.1	65.4	65.1	64.5	63.7	63.4	63.9	64.4

Note: (1) Figures cover the Chicago-Naperville-Elgin, IL-IN-WI Metropolitan Statistical Area—see Appendix B for areas included
Source: U.S. Census Bureau, Housing Vacancies and Homeownership Annual Statistics: 2010-2018

Year Housing Structure Built

Area	2010 or Later	2000 -2009	1990 -1999	1980 -1989	1970 -1979	1960 -1969	1950 -1959	1940 -1949	Before 1940	Median Year
City	1.5	8.1	4.7	4.2	7.4	9.8	12.2	9.1	43.1	1948
MSA[1]	1.4	11.7	11.1	8.9	14.1	11.9	13.3	6.2	21.4	1968
U.S.	3.2	14.5	14.0	13.6	15.5	10.8	10.5	5.1	12.9	1977

Note: Figures are percentages except for Median Year; Note: (1) Figures cover the Chicago-Naperville-Elgin, IL-IN-WI Metropolitan Statistical Area—see Appendix B for areas included
Source: U.S. Census Bureau, 2013-2017 American Community Survey 5-Year Estimates

Gross Monthly Rent

Area	Under $500	$500 -$999	$1,000 -$1,499	$1,500 -$1,999	$2,000 -$2,499	$2,500 -$2,999	$3,000 and up	Median ($)
City	9.9	37.9	29.9	13.5	5.1	2.1	1.6	1,029
MSA[1]	8.0	38.1	33.0	13.4	4.6	1.6	1.3	1,048
U.S.	10.5	41.1	28.7	11.7	4.5	1.8	1.7	982

Note: Figures are percentages except for Median; Gross rent is the contract rent plus the estimated average monthly cost of utilities (electricity, gas, and water and sewer) and fuels (oil, coal, kerosene, wood, etc.) if these are paid by the renter (or paid for the renter by someone else); (1) Figures cover the Chicago-Naperville-Elgin, IL-IN-WI Metropolitan Statistical Area—see Appendix B for areas included
Source: U.S. Census Bureau, 2013-2017 American Community Survey 5-Year Estimates

HEALTH

Health Risk Factors

Category	MSA[1] (%)	U.S. (%)
Adults aged 18–64 who have any kind of health care coverage	86.1	87.3
Adults who reported being in good or better health	82.6	82.4
Adults who have been told they have high blood cholesterol	31.6	33.0
Adults who have been told they have high blood pressure	31.5	32.3
Adults who are current smokers	13.6	17.1
Adults who currently use E-cigarettes	3.9	4.6
Adults who currently use chewing tobacco, snuff, or snus	2.1	4.0
Adults who are heavy drinkers[2]	6.3	6.3
Adults who are binge drinkers[3]	19.9	17.4
Adults who are overweight (BMI 25.0 - 29.9)	34.4	35.3
Adults who are obese (BMI 30.0 - 99.8)	30.1	31.3
Adults who participated in any physical activities in the past month	77.3	74.4
Adults who always or nearly always wears a seat belt	95.7	94.3

Note: (1) Figures cover the Chicago-Naperville-Elgin, IL-IN-WI Metropolitan Statistical Area—see Appendix B for areas included; (2) Heavy drinkers are classified as adult men having more than 14 drinks per week and adult women having more than 7 drinks per week; (3) Binge drinkers are classified as males having five or more drinks on one occasion or females having four or more drinks on one occasion
Source: Centers for Disease Control and Prevention, Behaviorial Risk Factor Surveillance System, SMART: Selected Metropolitan Area Risk Trends, 2017

Acute and Chronic Health Conditions

Category	MSA[1] (%)	U.S. (%)
Adults who have ever been told they had a heart attack	3.3	4.2
Adults who have ever been told they have angina or coronary heart disease	3.5	3.9
Adults who have ever been told they had a stroke	2.8	3.0
Adults who have ever been told they have asthma	13.1	14.2
Adults who have ever been told they have arthritis	22.5	24.9
Adults who have ever been told they have diabetes[2]	10.3	10.5
Adults who have ever been told they had skin cancer	3.9	6.2
Adults who have ever been told they had any other types of cancer	5.6	7.1
Adults who have ever been told they have COPD	6.1	6.5
Adults who have ever been told they have kidney disease	2.9	3.0
Adults who have ever been told they have a form of depression	16.3	20.5

Note: (1) Figures cover the Chicago-Naperville-Elgin, IL-IN-WI Metropolitan Statistical Area—see Appendix B for areas included; (2) Figures do not include pregnancy-related, borderline, or pre-diabetes
Source: Centers for Disease Control and Prevention, Behaviorial Risk Factor Surveillance System, SMART: Selected Metropolitan Area Risk Trends, 2017

Health Screening and Vaccination Rates

Category	MSA[1] (%)	U.S. (%)
Adults aged 65+ who have had flu shot within the past year	55.4	60.7
Adults aged 65+ who have ever had a pneumonia vaccination	71.8	75.4
Adults who have ever been tested for HIV	37.8	36.1
Adults who have ever had the shingles or zoster vaccine?	25.3	28.9
Adults who have had their blood cholesterol checked within the last five years	88.4	85.9

Note: n/a not available; (1) Figures cover the Chicago-Naperville-Elgin, IL-IN-WI Metropolitan Statistical Area—see Appendix B for areas included.
Source: Centers for Disease Control and Prevention, Behavioral Risk Factor Surveillance System, SMART: Selected Metropolitan Area Risk Trends, 2017

Disability Status

Category	MSA[1] (%)	U.S. (%)
Adults who reported being deaf	3.2	6.7
Are you blind or have serious difficulty seeing, even when wearing glasses?	4.0	4.5
Are you limited in any way in any of your usual activities due of arthritis?	10.8	12.9
Do you have difficulty doing errands alone?	6.0	6.8
Do you have difficulty dressing or bathing?	3.2	3.6
Do you have serious difficulty concentrating/remembering/making decisions?	8.1	10.7
Do you have serious difficulty walking or climbing stairs?	11.8	13.6

Note: (1) Figures cover the Chicago-Naperville-Elgin, IL-IN-WI Metropolitan Statistical Area—see Appendix B for areas included.
Source: Centers for Disease Control and Prevention, Behavioral Risk Factor Surveillance System, SMART: Selected Metropolitan Area Risk Trends, 2017

Mortality Rates for the Top 10 Causes of Death in the U.S.

ICD-10[a] Sub-Chapter	ICD-10[a] Code	Age-Adjusted Mortality Rate[1] per 100,000 population	
		County[2]	U.S.
Malignant neoplasms	C00-C97	162.8	155.5
Ischaemic heart diseases	I20-I25	88.9	94.8
Other forms of heart disease	I30-I51	56.5	52.9
Chronic lower respiratory diseases	J40-J47	28.9	41.0
Cerebrovascular diseases	I60-I69	40.2	37.5
Other degenerative diseases of the nervous system	G30-G31	26.1	35.0
Other external causes of accidental injury	W00-X59	29.1	33.7
Organic, including symptomatic, mental disorders	F01-F09	32.3	31.0
Hypertensive diseases	I10-I15	28.4	21.9
Diabetes mellitus	E10-E14	20.4	21.2

Note: (a) ICD-10 = International Classification of Diseases 10th Revision; (1) Mortality rates are a three year average covering 2015-2017; (2) Figures cover Cook County.
Source: Centers for Disease Control and Prevention, National Center for Health Statistics. Underlying Cause of Death 1999-2017 on CDC WONDER Online Database

Mortality Rates for Selected Causes of Death

ICD-10[a] Sub-Chapter	ICD-10[a] Code	Age-Adjusted Mortality Rate[1] per 100,000 population	
		County[2]	U.S.
Assault	X85-Y09	14.5	5.9
Diseases of the liver	K70-K76	11.4	14.1
Human immunodeficiency virus (HIV) disease	B20-B24	2.3	1.8
Influenza and pneumonia	J09-J18	15.3	14.3
Intentional self-harm	X60-X84	8.2	13.6
Malnutrition	E40-E46	1.4	1.6
Obesity and other hyperalimentation	E65-E68	2.2	2.1
Renal failure	N17-N19	16.2	13.0
Transport accidents	V01-V99	6.6	12.4
Viral hepatitis	B15-B19	1.1	1.6

Note: (a) ICD-10 = International Classification of Diseases 10th Revision; (1) Mortality rates are a three year average covering 2015-2017; (2) Figures cover Cook County; Data are suppressed when the data meet the criteria for confidentiality constraints; Mortality rates are flagged as unreliable when the rate would be calculated with a numerator of 20 or less.
Source: Centers for Disease Control and Prevention, National Center for Health Statistics. Underlying Cause of Death 1999-2017 on CDC WONDER Online Database

Health Insurance Coverage

Area	With Health Insurance	With Private Health Insurance	With Public Health Insurance	Without Health Insurance	Population Under Age 18 Without Health Insurance
City	87.2	57.2	36.6	12.8	3.8
MSA[1]	90.5	68.8	31.0	9.5	3.5
U.S.	89.5	67.2	33.8	10.5	5.7

Note: Figures are percentages that cover the civilian noninstitutionalized population; (1) Figures cover the Chicago-Naperville-Elgin, IL-IN-WI Metropolitan Statistical Area—see Appendix B for areas included
Source: U.S. Census Bureau, 2013-2017 American Community Survey 5-Year Estimates

Number of Medical Professionals

Area	MDs[3]	DOs[3,4]	Dentists	Podiatrists	Chiropractors	Optometrists
County[1] (number)	22,714	1,191	4,666	650	1,411	1,030
County[1] (rate[2])	434.2	22.8	89.5	12.5	27.1	19.8
U.S. (rate[2])	279.3	23.0	68.4	6.0	27.1	16.2

Note: Data as of 2017 unless noted; (1) Data covers Cook County; (2) Rate per 100,000 population; (3) Data as of 2016 and includes all active, non-federal physicians; (4) Doctor of Osteopathic Medicine
Source: U.S. Department of Health and Human Services, Health Resources and Services Administration, Bureau of Health Professions, Area Resource File (ARF) 2017-2018

Best Hospitals

According to *U.S. News,* the Chicago-Naperville-Arlington Heights, IL metro area is home to nine of the best hospitals in the U.S.: **Advocate Christ Medical Center** (1 pediatric specialty); **Advocate Good Samaritan Hospital** (2 adult specialties); **Advocate Lutheran General Hospital** (2 pediatric specialties); **Loyola University Medical Center** (6 adult specialties); **Northwestern Medicine Central DuPage Hospital** (1 adult specialty); **Northwestern Memorial Hospital** (Honor Roll/11 adult specialties); **Rush University Medical Center** (7 adult specialties); **Shirley Ryan AbilityLab (formerly Rehabilitation Institute of Chicago)** (1 adult specialty); **University of Chicago Medical Center** (3 adult specialties and 4 pediatric specialties). The hospitals listed were nationally ranked in at least one of 16 adult or 10 pediatric specialties. Only 170 hospitals nationwide were nationally ranked in one or more adult or pediatric specialty. Twenty hospitals in the U.S. made the Honor Roll. The Best Hospitals Honor Roll takes both the national rankings and the procedure and condition ratings into account. Hospitals received points if they were nationally ranked in one of the 16 adult specialties—the higher they ranked, the more points they got—and how many ratings of "high performing" they earned in the nine procedures and conditions. *U.S. News Online, "America's Best Hospitals 2018-19"*

According to *U.S. News,* the Chicago-Naperville-Arlington Heights, IL metro area is home to four of the best children's hospitals in the U.S.: **Advocate Children's Hospital-Oak Lawn** (1 pediatric specialty); **Advocate Children's Hospital-Park Ridge** (2 pediatric specialties); **Ann and Robert H. Lurie Children's Hospital of Chicago** (Honor Roll/10 pediatric specialties); **University of Chicago Comer Children's Hospital** (4 pediatric specialties). The hospitals listed were highly ranked in at least one of 10 pediatric specialties. Eighty-six children's hospitals in the U.S. were nationally ranked in at least one specialty. Hospitals received points for being ranked in a specialty, and the 10 hospitals with the most points across the 10 specialties make up the Honor Roll. *U.S. News Online, "America's Best Children's Hospitals 2018-19"*

EDUCATION

Public School District Statistics

District Name	Schls	Pupils	Pupil/ Teacher Ratio	Minority Pupils[1] (%)	Free Lunch Eligible[2] (%)	IEP[3] (%)
City of Chicago SD 299	585	378,199	19.9	90.0	83.6	13.7

Note: Table includes school districts with 2,000 or more students; (1) Percentage of students that are not non-Hispanic white; (2) Percentage of students that are eligible for the free lunch program; (3) Percentage of students that have an Individualized Education Program.
Source: U.S. Department of Education, National Center for Education Statistics, Common Core of Data, Local Education Agency (School District) Universe Survey: School Year 2016-2017; U.S. Department of Education, National Center for Education Statistics, Common Core of Data, Public Elementary/Secondary School Universe Survey: School Year 2016-2017

Best High Schools

According to *U.S. News,* Chicago is home to nine of the best high schools in the U.S.: **Payton College Preparatory High School** (#52); **Northside College Preparatory High School** (#82);

Lane Technical High School (#112); **Phoenix Military Academy High School** (#122); **Jones College Prep High School** (#124); **Young Magnet High School** (#140); **Lincoln Park High School** (#324); **Brooks College Prep Academy High School** (#345); **Lindblom Math and Science Academy** (#395). More than 20,000 public, magnet and charter schools were ranked based on their performance on state assessments and how well they prepare students for college. Schools with the highest unrounded College Readiness Index values were numerically ranked from 1 to 500 and were classified as gold medal winners. *U.S. News & World Report, "Best High Schools 2018"*

Highest Level of Education

Area	Less than H.S.	H.S. Diploma	Some College, No Deg.	Associate Degree	Bachelor's Degree	Master's Degree	Prof. School Degree	Doctorate Degree
City	16.2	22.9	17.7	5.7	22.3	10.5	3.0	1.6
MSA[1]	12.1	24.2	19.9	7.1	22.3	10.5	2.5	1.4
U.S.	12.7	27.3	20.8	8.3	19.1	8.4	2.0	1.4

Note: Figures cover persons age 25 and over; (1) Figures cover the Chicago-Naperville-Elgin, IL-IN-WI Metropolitan Statistical Area—see Appendix B for areas included
Source: U.S. Census Bureau, 2013-2017 American Community Survey 5-Year Estimates

Educational Attainment by Race

Area	High School Graduate or Higher (%)					Bachelor's Degree or Higher (%)				
	Total	White	Black	Asian	Hisp.[2]	Total	White	Black	Asian	Hisp.[2]
City	83.8	87.5	84.1	87.8	65.0	37.5	48.9	20.2	59.4	14.9
MSA[1]	87.9	90.7	87.0	90.9	65.2	36.7	40.1	21.8	63.9	13.9
U.S.	87.3	89.3	84.9	86.5	66.7	30.9	32.2	20.6	52.7	15.2

Note: Figures shown cover persons 25 years old and over; (1) Figures cover the Chicago-Naperville-Elgin, IL-IN-WI Metropolitan Statistical Area—see Appendix B for areas included; (2) People of Hispanic origin can be of any race
Source: U.S. Census Bureau, 2013-2017 American Community Survey 5-Year Estimates

School Enrollment by Grade and Control

Area	Preschool (%)		Kindergarten (%)		Grades 1 - 4 (%)		Grades 5 - 8 (%)		Grades 9 - 12 (%)	
	Public	Private	Public	Private	Public	Private	Public	Private	Public	Private
City	61.9	38.1	81.5	18.5	86.2	13.8	86.7	13.3	87.0	13.0
MSA[1]	58.6	41.4	84.8	15.2	88.8	11.2	89.1	10.9	90.4	9.6
U.S.	58.8	41.2	87.7	12.3	89.7	10.3	89.6	10.4	90.3	9.7

Note: Figures shown cover persons 3 years old and over; (1) Figures cover the Chicago-Naperville-Elgin, IL-IN-WI Metropolitan Statistical Area—see Appendix B for areas included
Source: U.S. Census Bureau, 2013-2017 American Community Survey 5-Year Estimates

Average Salaries of Public School Classroom Teachers

Area	2016		2017		Change from 2016 to 2017	
	Dollars	Rank[1]	Dollars	Rank[1]	Percent	Rank[2]
Illinois	63,475	11	64,933	11	2.3	19
U.S. Average	58,479	–	59,660	–	2.0	–

Note: (1) Rank ranges from 1 to 51 where 1 indicates highest salary; (2) Rank ranges from 1 to 51 where 1 indicates highest percent change.
Source: National Education Association, Rankings & Estimates: Rankings of the States 2017 and Estimates of School Statistics 2018

Higher Education

Four-Year Colleges			Two-Year Colleges			Medical Schools[1]	Law Schools[2]	Voc/ Tech[3]
Public	Private Non-profit	Private For-profit	Public	Private Non-profit	Private For-profit			
3	34	7	7	1	6	4	6	16

Note: Figures cover institutions located within the city limits and include main campuses only; (1) includes schools accredited by the Liaison Committee on Medical Education and the American Osteopathic Association's Commission on Osteopathic College Accreditation; (2) includes ABA-accredited schools, schools with provisional ABA accreditation, and state accredited schools; (3) includes all schools with programs that are less than 2 years.
Source: National Center for Education Statistics, Integrated Postsecondary Education System (IPEDS), 2017-18; Wikipedia, List of Medical Schools in the United States, accessed April 3, 2019; Wikipedia, List of Law Schools in the United States, accessed April 3, 2019

According to *U.S. News & World Report,* the Chicago-Naperville-Arlington Heights, IL metro division is home to seven of the best national universities in the U.S.: **University of Chicago** (#3 tie); **Northwestern University** (#10 tie); **Loyola University Chicago** (#89 tie); **Illinois Institute of Technology** (#96 tie); **DePaul University** (#119 tie); **University of Illinois—Chicago** (#129 tie); **Benedictine University** (#221 tie). The indicators used to capture academic quality fall into a number of categories: assessment by administrators at peer institutions; retention of students; faculty resources; student selectivity; financial resources; alumni giving; high school counselor ratings of colleges; and graduation rate. *U.S. News & World Report, "America's Best Colleges 2019"*

According to *U.S. News & World Report,* the Chicago-Naperville-Arlington Heights, IL metro division is home to one of the best liberal arts colleges in the U.S.: **Wheaton College** (#61 tie). The indicators used to capture academic quality fall into a number of categories: assessment by administrators at peer institutions; retention of students; faculty resources; student selectivity; financial resources; alumni giving; high school counselor ratings of colleges; and graduation rate. *U.S. News & World Report, "America's Best Colleges 2019"*

According to *U.S. News & World Report,* the Chicago-Naperville-Arlington Heights, IL metro division is home to four of the top 100 law schools in the U.S.: **University of Chicago** (#4); **Northwestern University (Pritzker)** (#10 tie); **Loyola University Chicago** (#77 tie); **Illinois Institute of Technology (Chicago-Kent)** (#87 tie). The rankings are based on a weighted average of 12 measures of quality: peer assessment score; assessment score by lawyers/judges; median LSAT scores; median undergrad GPA; acceptance rate; employment rates for graduates; placement success; bar passage rate; faculty resources; expenditures per student; student/faculty ratio; and library resources. *U.S. News & World Report, "America's Best Graduate Schools, Law, 2020"*

According to *U.S. News & World Report,* the Chicago-Naperville-Arlington Heights, IL metro division is home to four of the top 75 medical schools for research in the U.S.: **University of Chicago (Pritzker)** (#16 tie); **Northwestern University (Feinberg)** (#19 tie); **University of Illinois** (#50 tie); **Rush University** (#70 tie). The rankings are based on a weighted average of 11 measures of quality: quality assessment; peer assessment score; assessment score by residency directors; research activity; total research activity; average research activity per faculty member; student selectivity; median MCAT total score; median undergraduate GPA; acceptance rate; and faculty resources. *U.S. News & World Report, "America's Best Graduate Schools, Medical, 2020"*

According to *U.S. News & World Report,* the Chicago-Naperville-Arlington Heights, IL metro division is home to two of the top 75 business schools in the U.S.: **University of Chicago (Booth)** (#3 tie); **Northwestern University (Kellogg)** (#6 tie). The rankings are based on a weighted average of the following nine measures: quality assessment; peer assessment; recruiter assessment; placement success; mean starting salary and bonus; student selectivity; mean GMAT and GRE scores; mean undergraduate GPA; and acceptance rate. *U.S. News & World Report, "America's Best Graduate Schools, Business, 2020"*

PRESIDENTIAL ELECTION

2016 Presidential Election Results

Area	Clinton	Trump	Johnson	Stein	Other
Cook County	73.9	20.8	2.7	1.5	1.1
U.S.	48.0	45.9	3.3	1.1	1.7

Note: Results are percentages and may not add to 100% due to rounding
Source: Dave Leip's Atlas of U.S. Presidential Elections

EMPLOYERS

Major Employers

Company Name	Industry
Abbott Laboratories	Pharmaceutical preparations
Addus HomeCare Corporation	Home health care services
Advocate Lutheran General Hospital	General medical & surgical hospitals
BMO Bankcorp	National commercial banks
City of Chicago	General government
Cook County Bureau of Health Services	Administration of public health programs, county govt
Graphic Packaging International	Folding boxboard
Loyola University Health System	General medical & surgical hospitals
Northshore University Healthsystem	General medical & surgical hospitals
Northwestern Memorial Hospital	General medical & surgical hospitals
SCC Holding Co.	Cups, plastics, except foam
Schneider Electric Holdings	Air transportation, scheduled
SOLO Cup Company	Cups, plastics, except foam
The Allstate Corporation	Fire, marine, & casualty insurance
The University of Chicago Medical Center	General medical & surgical hospitals
United Parcel Service	Mailing & messenger services
United States Steel Corporation	Steel foundries
WM Recycle America	Material recovery

Note: Companies shown are located within the Chicago-Naperville-Elgin, IL-IN-WI Metropolitan Statistical Area.
Source: Hoovers.com; Wikipedia

Best Companies to Work For

Crowe; Hyatt Hotels, headquartered in Chicago, are among "The 100 Best Companies to Work For." To pick the best companies, *Fortune* partnered with the Great Place to Work Institute. Two-thirds of a company's score is based on the results of the Institute's Trust Index survey, which is sent to a random sample of employees from each company. The questions related to attitudes about management's credibility, job satisfaction, and camaraderie. The other third of the scoring is based on the company's responses to the Institute's Culture Audit, which includes detailed questions about pay and benefit programs, and a series of open-ended questions about hiring practices, internal communication, training, recognition programs, and diversity efforts. Any company that is at least five years old with more than 1,000 U.S. employees is eligible. *Fortune, "The 100 Best Companies to Work For," 2019*

BDO USA; Federal Reserve Bank of Chicago; Grant Thornton; JLL; Katten Muchin Rosenman; Leo Burnett; Northwestern Memorial HealthCare; RSM; Starcom USA, headquartered in Chicago, are among the "100 Best Companies for Working Mothers." Criteria: paid time off and leaves; workforce profile; benefits; women's issues and advancement; flexible work; company culture and work life programs. *Working Mother, "100 Best Companies 2018"*

CME Group; Enova International; Motorola Solutions; RSM US, headquartered in Chicago, are among the "100 Best Places to Work in IT." To qualify, companies had to be U.S.-based organizations or be non-U.S.- based employers that met the following criteria: have a minimum of 300 total employees at a U.S. headquarters and a minimum of 30 IT employees in the U.S., with at least 50% of their IT employees based in the U.S. The best places to work were selected based on compensation, benefits, work/life balance, employee morale, and satisfaction with training and development programs. In addition, *Computerworld* looked at retention efforts, programs for recognizing and rewarding outstanding performances, and benefits such as flextime, elder care and child care, and reimbursement for college tuition and the cost of pursuing technology certifications. *Computerworld, "100 Best Places to Work in IT 2018"*

BDO USA; Federal Reserve Bank of Chicago; Grant Thornton; JLL; Katten Muchin Rosenman, headquartered in Chicago, are among the "Top Companies for Executive Women." The 2019 National Association for Female Executives (NAFE) Top Companies for Executive Women application included more than 200 questions on female representation at all levels, but especially the corporate officer and profit-and-loss leadership ranks. The application tracked how many employees have access to programs and policies that promote the advancement of women, and how many employees take advantage of them. The application also examined how companies train managers to help women advance, and how managers are held accountable for the advancement of female employees they oversee. *National Association for Female Executives, "2019 NAFE Top 70 Companies for Executive Women"*

PUBLIC SAFETY

Crime Rate

Area	All Crimes	Violent Crimes				Property Crimes		
		Murder	Rape[3]	Robbery	Aggrav. Assault	Burglary	Larceny -Theft	Motor Vehicle Theft
City	4,362.7	24.1	65.1	439.3	570.4	477.1	2,358.8	427.8
Suburbs[1]	n/a	3.5	26.6	58.5	n/a	217.8	1,218.6	96.5
Metro[2]	n/a	9.4	37.5	166.7	n/a	291.5	1,542.5	190.6
U.S.	2,756.1	5.3	41.7	98.0	248.9	430.4	1,694.4	237.4

Note: Figures are crimes per 100,000 population; (1) All areas within the metro area that are located outside the city limits; (2) Figures cover the Chicago-Naperville-Arlington Heights, IL Metropolitan Division—see Appendix B for areas included; (3) The city and U.S. figures shown were reported using the revised Uniform Crime Reporting (UCR) definition of rape. The suburban and metro area figures shown are an aggregate total of the data submitted using both the revised and legacy UCR definitions.
Source: FBI Uniform Crime Reports, 2017

Hate Crimes

Area	Number of Quarters Reported	Number of Incidents per Bias Motivation					
		Race/Ethnicity/ Ancestry	Religion	Sexual Orientation	Disability	Gender	Gender Identity
City	4	16	17	7	0	0	1
U.S.	4	4,131	1,564	1,130	116	46	119

Source: Federal Bureau of Investigation, Hate Crime Statistics 2017

Identity Theft Consumer Reports

Area	Reports	Reports per 100,000 Population	Rank[2]
MSA[1]	13,949	147	38
U.S.	444,602	135	-

Note: (1) Figures cover the Chicago-Naperville-Elgin, IL-IN-WI Metropolitan Statistical Area—see Appendix B for areas included; (2) Rank ranges from 1 to 389 where 1 indicates greatest number of identity theft reports per 100,000 population
Source: Federal Trade Commission, Consumer Sentinel Network Data Book for January–December 2018

Fraud and Other Consumer Reports

Area	Reports	Reports per 100,000 Population	Rank[2]
MSA[1]	51,170	538	123
U.S.	2,552,917	776	-

Note: (1) Figures cover the Chicago-Naperville-Elgin, IL-IN-WI Metropolitan Statistical Area—see Appendix B for areas included; (2) Rank ranges from 1 to 389 where 1 indicates greatest number of fraud and other consumer reports per 100,000 population
Source: Federal Trade Commission, Consumer Sentinel Network Data Book for January–December 2018

SPORTS

Professional Sports Teams

Team Name	League	Year Established
Chicago Bears	National Football League (NFL)	1921
Chicago Blackhawks	National Hockey League (NHL)	1926
Chicago Bulls	National Basketball Association (NBA)	1966
Chicago Cubs	Major League Baseball (MLB)	1874
Chicago Fire	Major League Soccer (MLS)	1997
Chicago White Sox	Major League Baseball (MLB)	1900

Note: Includes teams located in the Chicago-Naperville-Elgin, IL-IN-WI Metropolitan Statistical Area.
Source: Wikipedia, Major Professional Sports Teams of the United States and Canada, April 5, 2019

CLIMATE

Average and Extreme Temperatures

Temperature	Jan	Feb	Mar	Apr	May	Jun	Jul	Aug	Sep	Oct	Nov	Dec	Yr.
Extreme High (°F)	65	71	88	91	93	104	102	100	99	91	78	71	104
Average High (°F)	29	33	45	59	70	79	84	82	75	63	48	34	59
Average Temp. (°F)	21	26	37	49	59	69	73	72	65	53	40	27	49
Average Low (°F)	13	17	28	39	48	57	63	62	54	42	32	19	40
Extreme Low (°F)	-27	-17	-8	7	24	36	40	41	28	17	1	-25	-27

Note: Figures cover the years 1958-1990
Source: National Climatic Data Center, International Station Meteorological Climate Summary, 9/96

Average Precipitation/Snowfall/Humidity

Precip./Humidity	Jan	Feb	Mar	Apr	May	Jun	Jul	Aug	Sep	Oct	Nov	Dec	Yr.
Avg. Precip. (in.)	1.6	1.4	2.7	3.6	3.3	3.7	3.7	4.1	3.7	2.4	2.8	2.3	35.4
Avg. Snowfall (in.)	11	8	7	2	Tr	0	0	0	0	1	2	9	39
Avg. Rel. Hum. 6am (%)	76	77	79	77	77	78	82	85	85	82	80	80	80
Avg. Rel. Hum. 3pm (%)	65	63	59	53	51	52	54	55	55	53	61	68	57

Note: Figures cover the years 1958-1990; Tr = Trace amounts (<0.05 in. of rain; <0.5 in. of snow)
Source: National Climatic Data Center, International Station Meteorological Climate Summary, 9/96

Weather Conditions

Temperature			Daytime Sky			Precipitation		
5°F & below	32°F & below	90°F & above	Clear	Partly cloudy	Cloudy	0.01 inch or more precip.	0.1 inch or more snow/ice	Thunder-storms
21	132	17	84	135	146	125	31	38

Note: Figures are average number of days per year and cover the years 1958-1990
Source: National Climatic Data Center, International Station Meteorological Climate Summary, 9/96

HAZARDOUS WASTE

Superfund Sites

The Chicago-Naperville-Arlington Heights, IL metro division is home to 10 sites on the EPA's Superfund National Priorities List: **Amoco Chemicals (Joliet Landfill)** (final); **Dupage County Landfill/Blackwell Forest Preserve** (final); **Estech General Chemical Company** (final); **Joliet Army Ammunition Plant (Load-Assembly-Packing Area)** (final); **Joliet Army Ammunition Plant (Manufacturing Area)** (final); **Kerr-Mcgee (Kress Creek/West Branch Of Dupage River)** (final); **Kerr-Mcgee (Residential Areas)** (final); **Lake Calumet Cluster** (final); **Lenz Oil Service, Inc.** (final); **Woodstock Municipal Landfill** (final). There are a total of 1,390 Superfund sites with a status of proposed or final on the list in the U.S. *U.S. Environmental Protection Agency, National Priorities List, April 5, 2019*

AIR & WATER QUALITY

Air Quality Trends: Ozone

	1990	1995	2000	2005	2010	2012	2014	2015	2016	2017
MSA[1]	0.074	0.094	0.073	0.084	0.070	0.082	0.068	0.066	0.074	0.071
U.S.	0.088	0.089	0.082	0.080	0.073	0.075	0.067	0.068	0.069	0.068

Note: (1) Data covers the Chicago-Naperville-Elgin, IL-IN-WI Metropolitan Statistical Area—see Appendix B for areas included. The values shown are the composite ozone concentration averages among trend sites based on the highest fourth daily maximum 8-hour concentration in parts per million. These trends are based on sites having an adequate record of monitoring data during the trend period. Data from exceptional events are included.
Source: U.S. Environmental Protection Agency, Air Quality Monitoring Information, "Air Quality Trends by City, 1990-2017"

Air Quality Index

Area	Percent of Days when Air Quality was...[2]					AQI Statistics[2]	
	Good	Moderate	Unhealthy for Sensitive Groups	Unhealthy	Very Unhealthy	Maximum	Median
MSA[1]	43.0	50.1	6.3	0.5	0.0	177	53

Note: (1) Data covers the Chicago-Naperville-Elgin, IL-IN-WI Metropolitan Statistical Area—see Appendix B for areas included; (2) Based on 365 days with AQI data in 2017. Air Quality Index (AQI) is an index for reporting daily air quality. EPA calculates the AQI for five major air pollutants regulated by the Clean Air Act: ground-level ozone, particle pollution (aka particulate matter), carbon monoxide, sulfur dioxide, and nitrogen dioxide. The AQI runs from 0 to 500. The higher the AQI value, the greater the level of air pollution and the greater the health concern. There are six AQI categories: "Good" AQI is between 0 and 50. Air quality is considered satisfactory; "Moderate" AQI is between 51 and 100. Air quality is acceptable; "Unhealthy for Sensitive Groups" When AQI values are between 101 and 150, members of sensitive groups may experience health effects; "Unhealthy" When AQI values are between 151 and 200 everyone may begin to experience health effects; "Very Unhealthy" AQI values between 201 and 300 trigger a health alert; "Hazardous" AQI values over 300 trigger warnings of emergency conditions (not shown).
Source: U.S. Environmental Protection Agency, Air Quality Index Report, 2017

Air Quality Index Pollutants

Area	Percent of Days when AQI Pollutant was...[2]					
	Carbon Monoxide	Nitrogen Dioxide	Ozone	Sulfur Dioxide	Particulate Matter 2.5	Particulate Matter 10
MSA[1]	0.0	5.8	41.6	3.0	44.9	4.7

Note: (1) Data covers the Chicago-Naperville-Elgin, IL-IN-WI Metropolitan Statistical Area—see Appendix B for areas included; (2) Based on 365 days with AQI data in 2017. The Air Quality Index (AQI) is an index for reporting daily air quality. EPA calculates the AQI for five major air pollutants regulated by the Clean Air Act: ground-level ozone, particle pollution (also known as particulate matter), carbon monoxide, sulfur dioxide, and nitrogen dioxide. The AQI runs from 0 to 500. The higher the AQI value, the greater the level of air pollution and the greater the health concern.
Source: U.S. Environmental Protection Agency, Air Quality Index Report, 2017

Maximum Air Pollutant Concentrations: Particulate Matter, Ozone, CO and Lead

	Particulate Matter 10 (ug/m^3)	Particulate Matter 2.5 Wtd AM (ug/m^3)	Particulate Matter 2.5 24-Hr (ug/m^3)	Ozone (ppm)	Carbon Monoxide (ppm)	Lead (ug/m^3)
MSA[1] Level	108	10.3	24	0.079	1	0.02
NAAQS[2]	150	15	35	0.075	9	0.15
Met NAAQS[2]	Yes	Yes	Yes	No	Yes	Yes

Note: (1) Data covers the Chicago-Naperville-Elgin, IL-IN-WI Metropolitan Statistical Area—see Appendix B for areas included; Data from exceptional events are included; (2) National Ambient Air Quality Standards; ppm = parts per million; ug/m^3 = micrograms per cubic meter; n/a not available.
Concentrations: Particulate Matter 10 (coarse particulate)—highest second maximum 24-hour concentration; Particulate Matter 2.5 Wtd AM (fine particulate)—highest weighted annual mean concentration; Particulate Matter 2.5 24-Hour (fine particulate)—highest 98th percentile 24-hour concentration; Ozone—highest fourth daily maximum 8-hour concentration; Carbon Monoxide—highest second maximum non-overlapping 8-hour concentration; Lead—maximum running 3-month average
Source: U.S. Environmental Protection Agency, Air Quality Monitoring Information, "Air Quality Statistics by City, 2017"

Maximum Air Pollutant Concentrations: Nitrogen Dioxide and Sulfur Dioxide

	Nitrogen Dioxide AM (ppb)	Nitrogen Dioxide 1-Hr (ppb)	Sulfur Dioxide AM (ppb)	Sulfur Dioxide 1-Hr (ppb)	Sulfur Dioxide 24-Hr (ppb)
MSA[1] Level	16	55	n/a	36	n/a
NAAQS[2]	53	100	30	75	140
Met NAAQS[2]	Yes	Yes	n/a	Yes	n/a

Note: (1) Data covers the Chicago-Naperville-Elgin, IL-IN-WI Metropolitan Statistical Area—see Appendix B for areas included; Data from exceptional events are included; (2) National Ambient Air Quality Standards; ppm = parts per million; ug/m^3 = micrograms per cubic meter; n/a not available.
Concentrations: Nitrogen Dioxide AM—highest arithmetic mean concentration; Nitrogen Dioxide 1-Hr—highest 98th percentile 1-hour daily maximum concentration; Sulfur Dioxide AM—highest annual mean concentration; Sulfur Dioxide 1-Hr—highest 99th percentile 1-hour daily maximum concentration; Sulfur Dioxide 24-Hr—highest second maximum 24-hour concentration
Source: U.S. Environmental Protection Agency, Air Quality Monitoring Information, "Air Quality Statistics by City, 2017"

Drinking Water

Water System Name	Pop. Served	Primary Water Source Type	Violations[1]	
			Health Based	Monitoring/ Reporting
Chicago	2,700,000	Surface	0	0

Note: (1) Based on violation data from January 1, 2018 to December 31, 2018
Source: U.S. Environmental Protection Agency, Office of Ground Water and Drinking Water, Safe Drinking Water Information System (based on data extracted April 5, 2019)

Columbia, Missouri

Background

In the middle of the state, along its namesake river, Columbia is a college town teeming with the bright young minds and technological breakthroughs.

The city, located in Boone County, has ridden out the economic downturn with less trauma than the rest of Missouri. Recent surveys give the city high marks in general and for retirees.

The founding of its colleges and university dovetails with the growth and founding of the city itself. A settlement called Smithton grew from the Smithton Land Company's 2,000-acre land purchase on the other side of Flat Branch, not far from where Lewis and Clark passed by during their 1803 explorations. In 1821 the settlement moved across the river and Columbia was established. Daniel Boone and sons ran a salt lick about forty miles away.

Six counties competed for the right to host Missouri's university when it was founded in 1838, the first public university west of the Mississippi River. Boone County responded by raising more than $118,000 in land, cash and buildings. It was forced to repeat its largess decades later, when the academic hall burned down and talked turned to moving the university. The city responded by raising $50,000 to build Jesse Hall, now a local landmark.

Two other institutions of higher learning contributed to Columbia's focus on education. Stephens College, a private women's college, was founded in 1833, and Columbia College, now grown to 30,000 students, was founded as the Christian Female College in 1851. This school arrived as the first women's college west of the Mississippi chartered by a state legislature, and it went co-ed in 1970.

Although these three institutions help to define the historic downtown area, it is the state's massive flagship university—with a rare combination of law school, medical school, and veterinary school all on the same campus—that is Boone County's largest employer. As a major research institution, "Mizzou" conducts $435 million in research and even has a nuclear research reactor on campus. It is the nation's largest supplier of radioisotopes for diagnosing and treating cancer, and hosts interdisciplinary research in a range of scientific enterprises: biofuels, energy logistics, energy policy, wind, biomass and solar. The licensing of products invented by MU products by various companies is a huge market.

The MU Life Science Business Incubator, which opened in 2008, encourages and supports business based on these technologies. For instance, the Indian pharma company Shasun collaborated to create Shasun-NBI based in the incubator and to develop a cancer treatment. Another research park, Discovery Ridge, recently opened. Columbia is also home to several more state-certified sites under development.

The campus also houses a well-regarded journalism school and IRE, Investigative Reporters and Editors, Inc. The 1,250-acre campus is also home to a botanic garden and a number of cultural opportunities enjoyed by the community at large including the Missouri Theatre Center for the Arts, the Jesse Auditorium, and the university's Museum of Art and Architecture. The State Historical Society of Missouri also operates a research center at the university.

The county's other large employers include University Hospital and Clinics, Columbia Public Schools, Boone Hospital Center, the City of Columbia, and the U.S. Dept. of Veterans Affairs.

The city operates a regional airport, a short line railroad, and utilities for both water and electricity. It also has its own Office of Cultural Affairs, which distributes art guides and a cultural newsletter, funds local arts organizations, and underwrites advertising for local arts opportunities. Columbia offers a "percent for art" program that allows one percent of the cost of new city construction or renovation to be used for site-specific public art. The town is also full of galleries and various arts organizations.

Columbia has four distinct seasons, with highs in the upper 80s in July and August, lows below 20 degrees in January, and rainfall peaking in May.

Rankings

General Rankings

- In their sixth annual survey, Livability.com looked at data for more than 1,000 U.S. cities to determine the rankings for Livability's "Top 100 Best Places to Live" in 2019. Columbia ranked #6. Criteria: median home value capped at $250,000; affordable living; vibrant economy; education, demographics, health care options. transportation & infrastructure; abundant lifestyle amenities. *Livability.com, "Top 100 Best Places to Live 2019" March 2019*

Business/Finance Rankings

- Using data from the Council for Community and Economic Research's 2014 cost of living index, NerdWallet ranked the 100 most affordable cities in America. Median income was compared with cost of living to find truly affordable places. Columbia ranked #87. *NerdWallet.com, "America's Most Affordable Places," May 18, 2015*

- The Columbia metro area appeared on the Milken Institute "2018 Best Performing Cities" list. Rank: #50 out of 201 small metro areas. Criteria: job growth; wage and salary growth; high-tech output growth. *Milken Institute, "Best-Performing Cities 2018," January 24, 2019*

- *Forbes* ranked 200 smaller metro areas (population under 265,400) to determine the nation's "Best Small Places for Business and Careers." The Columbia metro area was ranked #24. Criteria: costs (business and living); job growth (past and projected); income growth; quality of life; educational attainment (college and high school); projected economic growth; cultural and recreational opportunities; net migration patterns; number of highly ranked colleges. *Forbes, "The Best Small Cities for Business and Careers 2018," October, 24 2018*

Dating/Romance Rankings

- Columbia was selected as one of the most romantic cities in the U.S. by video-rental kiosk company Redbox. The city ranked #6 out of 20. Criteria: number of romance-related rentals in 2016. *Redbox, "20 Most Romantic Cities," February 6, 2017*

Environmental Rankings

- Columbia was highlighted as one of the cleanest metro areas for ozone air pollution in the U.S. during 2014 through 2016. The list represents cities with no monitored ozone air pollution in unhealthful ranges. *American Lung Association, State of the Air 2018*

Safety Rankings

- The National Insurance Crime Bureau ranked 382 metro areas in the U.S. in terms of per capita rates of vehicle theft. The Columbia metro area ranked #163 (#1 = highest rate). Criteria: number of vehicle theft offenses per 100,000 inhabitants in 2017. *National Insurance Crime Bureau, "Hot Spots 2017," July 12, 2018*

Seniors/Retirement Rankings

- From its Best Cities for Successful Aging indexes, the Milken Institute generated rankings for metropolitan areas, weighing data in nine categories—health care, wellness, living arrangements, transportation and convenience, financial characteristics, education, employment, community engagement, and overall livability. The Columbia metro area was ranked #4 overall in the small metro area category. *Milken Institute, "Best Cities for Successful Aging, 2017" March 14, 2017*

- Columbia made the 2018 *Forbes* list of "25 Best Places to Retire." Criteria, focused on a high-quality retirement living an affordable price, include: housing/living costs compared to the national average and state taxes; weather and air quality; crime rates; vibrant economy and low unemployment; doctor availability; bikability; walkability; healthy living and volunteering. *Forbes.com, "The Best Places to Retire in 2018," April 23, 2018*

Sports/Recreation Rankings

- Columbia was chosen as a bicycle friendly community by the League of American Bicyclists. A "Bicycle Friendly Community" welcomes cyclists by providing safe and supportive accommodation for cycling and encouraging people to bike for transportation and recreation. There are five award levels: Diamond; Platinum; Gold; Silver; and Bronze. The community achieved an award level of Silver. *League of American Bicyclists, "Fall 2018 Awards-Bicycle Friendly Community Master List," December 6, 2018*

- Columbia was chosen as one of America's best cities for bicycling. The city ranked #46 out of 50. Criteria: cycling infrastructure that is safe and friendly for all ages; energy and bike culture. The editors only considered cities with populations of 100,000 or more. *Bicycling, "The 50 Best Bike Cities in America," October 10, 2018*

Miscellaneous Rankings

- Columbia was selected as a 2018 Digital Cities Survey winner. The city ranked #10 in the small city (75,000 to 124,999 population) category. The survey examined and assessed how city governments are utilizing technology to improve transparency, enhance cybersecurity, and solve social challenges. Survey questions focused on ten characteristics: engaged, mobile, open, secure, staffed/supported, efficient, connected, resilient, best practices, and use of innovation. *Center for Digital Government, "2018 Digital Cities Survey," November 2, 2018*

Business Environment

CITY FINANCES

City Government Finances

Component	2016 ($000)	2016 ($ per capita)
Total Revenues	325,178	2,730
Total Expenditures	348,900	2,929
Debt Outstanding	388,577	3,262
Cash and Securities[1]	510,532	4,286

Note: (1) Cash and security holdings of a government at the close of its fiscal year, including those of its dependent agencies, utilities, and liquor stores.
Source: U.S. Census Bureau, State & Local Government Finances 2016

City Government Revenue by Source

Source	2016 ($000)	2016 ($ per capita)	2016 (%)
General Revenue			
From Federal Government	11,931	100	3.7
From State Government	4,707	40	1.4
From Local Governments	20,445	172	6.3
Taxes			
Property	11,716	98	3.6
Sales and Gross Receipts	58,638	492	18.0
Personal Income	0	0	0.0
Corporate Income	0	0	0.0
Motor Vehicle License	0	0	0.0
Other Taxes	1,906	16	0.6
Current Charges	50,016	420	15.4
Liquor Store	0	0	0.0
Utility	150,090	1,260	46.2
Employee Retirement	0	0	0.0

Source: U.S. Census Bureau, State & Local Government Finances 2016

City Government Expenditures by Function

Function	2016 ($000)	2016 ($ per capita)	2016 (%)
General Direct Expenditures			
Air Transportation	7,335	61	2.1
Corrections	0	0	0.0
Education	0	0	0.0
Employment Security Administration	0	0	0.0
Financial Administration	3,264	27	0.9
Fire Protection	13,744	115	3.9
General Public Buildings	1,796	15	0.5
Governmental Administration, Other	6,818	57	2.0
Health	5,388	45	1.5
Highways	14,009	117	4.0
Hospitals	0	0	0.0
Housing and Community Development	1,295	10	0.4
Interest on General Debt	5,734	48	1.6
Judicial and Legal	2,586	21	0.7
Libraries	0	0	0.0
Parking	2,598	21	0.7
Parks and Recreation	18,064	151	5.2
Police Protection	17,213	144	4.9
Public Welfare	891	7	0.3
Sewerage	12,059	101	3.5
Solid Waste Management	16,116	135	4.6
Veterans' Services	0	0	0.0
Liquor Store	0	0	0.0
Utility	170,013	1,427	48.7
Employee Retirement	0	0	0.0

Source: U.S. Census Bureau, State & Local Government Finances 2016

DEMOGRAPHICS

Population Growth

Area	1990 Census	2000 Census	2010 Census	2017* Estimate	Population Growth (%) 1990-2017	2010-2017
City	71,069	84,531	108,500	118,620	66.9	9.3
MSA[1]	122,010	145,666	172,786	174,589	43.1	1.0
U.S.	248,709,873	281,421,906	308,745,538	321,004,407	29.1	4.0

Note: (1) Figures cover the Columbia, MO Metropolitan Statistical Area—see Appendix B for areas included; (*) 2013-2017 5-year estimated population
Source: U.S. Census Bureau, 1990 Census, Census 2000, Census 2010, 2013-2017 American Community Survey 5-Year Estimates

Household Size

Area	One	Two	Three	Four	Five	Six	Seven or More	Average Household Size
City	33.0	33.4	14.5	12.7	4.9	1.1	0.4	2.30
MSA[1]	29.9	34.7	14.9	13.3	5.2	1.2	0.8	2.40
U.S.	27.7	33.8	15.7	13.0	6.0	2.3	1.4	2.60

Note: (1) Figures cover the Columbia, MO Metropolitan Statistical Area—see Appendix B for areas included
Source: U.S. Census Bureau, 2013-2017 American Community Survey 5-Year Estimates

Race

Area	White Alone[2] (%)	Black Alone[2] (%)	Asian Alone[2] (%)	AIAN[3] Alone[2] (%)	NHOPI[4] Alone[2] (%)	Other Race Alone[2] (%)	Two or More Races (%)
City	77.4	10.4	6.0	0.3	0.1	1.0	4.8
MSA[1]	81.4	8.5	4.2	0.3	0.1	1.0	4.4
U.S.	73.0	12.7	5.4	0.8	0.2	4.8	3.1

Note: (1) Figures cover the Columbia, MO Metropolitan Statistical Area—see Appendix B for areas included; (2) Alone is defined as not being in combination with one or more other races; (3) American Indian and Alaska Native; (4) Native Hawaiian and Other Pacific Islander
Source: U.S. Census Bureau, 2013-2017 American Community Survey 5-Year Estimates

Hispanic or Latino Origin

Area	Total (%)	Mexican (%)	Puerto Rican (%)	Cuban (%)	Other (%)
City	3.2	2.0	0.1	0.1	1.0
MSA[1]	3.3	2.2	0.1	0.2	0.8
U.S.	17.6	11.1	1.7	0.7	4.1

Note: Persons of Hispanic or Latino origin can be of any race; (1) Figures cover the Columbia, MO Metropolitan Statistical Area—see Appendix B for areas included
Source: U.S. Census Bureau, 2013-2017 American Community Survey 5-Year Estimates

Segregation

Type	1990	2000	2010	2010 Rank[2]	1990-2000	1990-2010	2000-2010
Black/White	n/a	n/a	n/a	n/a	n/a	n/a	n/a
Asian/White	n/a	n/a	n/a	n/a	n/a	n/a	n/a
Hispanic/White	n/a	n/a	n/a	n/a	n/a	n/a	n/a

Note: All figures cover the Metropolitan Statistical Area—see Appendix B for areas included; Figures are based on an analysis of 1990, 2000, and 2010 Census Decennial Census tract data by William H. Frey, Brookings Institution and the University of Michigan Social Science Data Analysis Network. In this analysis all racial groups (whites, blacks, and asians) are non-Hispanic members of those races. Hispanics are shown as a separate category; (1) Segregation Indices are Dissimilarity Indices that measure the degree to which the minority group is distributed differently than whites across census tracts. They range from 0 (complete integration) to 100 (complete segregation) where the value indicates the percentage of the minority group that needs to move to be distributed exactly like whites; (2) Ranges from 1 (most segregated) to 102 (least segregated); n/a not available.
Source: www.CensusScope.org

Ancestry

Area	German	Irish	English	American	Italian	Polish	French[2]	Scottish	Dutch
City	25.1	12.6	9.7	5.4	3.5	2.3	2.7	2.1	1.3
MSA[1]	25.2	12.5	10.4	6.5	3.5	1.9	2.6	2.1	1.4
U.S.	14.1	10.1	7.5	6.6	5.3	2.9	2.5	1.7	1.3

Note: Figures are the percentage of the total population reporting a particular ancestry. The nine most commonly reported ancestries in the U.S. are shown. Figures include multiple ancestries (e.g. if a person reported being Irish and Italian, they were included in both columns); (1) Figures cover the Columbia, MO Metropolitan Statistical Area—see Appendix B for areas included; (2) Excludes Basque
Source: U.S. Census Bureau, 2013-2017 American Community Survey 5-Year Estimates

Foreign-Born Population

Area	Any Foreign Country	Asia	Mexico	Europe	Carribean	Central America[2]	South America	Africa	Canada
City	7.8	4.8	0.3	1.0	0.1	0.1	0.4	0.7	0.3
MSA[1]	6.0	3.4	0.4	0.9	0.1	0.1	0.3	0.5	0.3
U.S.	13.4	4.1	3.6	1.5	1.3	1.0	0.9	0.6	0.3

Note: (1) Figures cover the Columbia, MO Metropolitan Statistical Area—see Appendix B for areas included; (2) Excludes Mexico.
Source: U.S. Census Bureau, 2013-2017 American Community Survey 5-Year Estimates

Marital Status

Area	Never Married	Now Married[2]	Separated	Widowed	Divorced
City	49.1	37.6	1.1	3.3	8.9
MSA[1]	41.8	43.5	1.3	3.8	9.7
U.S.	33.1	48.2	2.0	5.8	10.9

Note: Figures are percentages and cover the population 15 years of age and older; (1) Figures cover the Columbia, MO Metropolitan Statistical Area—see Appendix B for areas included; (2) Excludes separated
Source: U.S. Census Bureau, 2013-2017 American Community Survey 5-Year Estimates

Disability by Age

Area	All Ages	Under 18 Years Old	18 to 64 Years Old	65 Years and Over
City	9.6	3.2	7.8	36.3
MSA[1]	11.3	4.1	9.6	35.7
U.S.	12.6	4.2	10.3	35.5

Note: Figures show percent of the civilian noninstitutionalized population that reported having a disability. Disability status is determined from six types of difficulty: vision, hearing, cognitive, ambulatory, self-care, and independent living. For children under 5 years old, hearing and vision difficulty are used to determine disability status. For children between the ages of 5 and 14, disability status is determined from hearing, vision, cognitive, ambulatory, and self-care difficulties. For people aged 15 years and older, they are considered to have a disability if they have difficulty with any one of the six difficulty types; Note: (1) Figures cover the Columbia, MO Metropolitan Statistical Area—see Appendix B for areas included
Source: U.S. Census Bureau, 2013-2017 American Community Survey 5-Year Estimates

Age

Area	Under Age 5	Age 5–19	Age 20–34	Age 35–44	Age 45–54	Age 55–64	Age 65–74	Age 75–84	Age 85+	Median Age
City	5.9	18.7	36.0	10.8	9.6	9.2	5.5	3.0	1.3	27.6
MSA[1]	6.0	19.5	30.6	11.4	11.0	10.7	6.5	3.3	1.2	30.6
U.S.	6.2	19.5	20.7	12.7	13.4	12.7	8.6	4.4	1.9	37.8

Note: (1) Figures cover the Columbia, MO Metropolitan Statistical Area—see Appendix B for areas included
Source: U.S. Census Bureau, 2013-2017 American Community Survey 5-Year Estimates

Gender

Area	Males	Females	Males per 100 Females
City	56,935	61,685	92.3
MSA[1]	84,812	89,777	94.5
U.S.	158,018,753	162,985,654	97.0

Note: (1) Figures cover the Columbia, MO Metropolitan Statistical Area—see Appendix B for areas included
Source: U.S. Census Bureau, 2013-2017 American Community Survey 5-Year Estimates

Religious Groups by Family

Area	Catholic	Baptist	Non-Den.	Methodist[2]	Lutheran	LDS[3]	Pente-costal	Presby-terian[4]	Muslim[5]	Judaism
MSA[1]	6.6	14.7	5.4	4.3	1.7	1.4	1.1	2.3	0.3	0.3
U.S.	19.1	9.3	4.0	4.0	2.3	2.0	1.9	1.6	0.8	0.7

Note: Figures are the number of adherents as a percentage of the total population; (1) Figures cover the Columbia, MO Metropolitan Statistical Area—see Appendix B for areas included; (2) Methodist/Pietist; (3) Latter Day Saints; (4) Reformed; (5) Figures are estimates
Source: Association of Statisticians of American Religious Bodies, 2010 U.S. Religion Census: Religious Congregations & Membership Study

Religious Groups by Tradition

Area	Catholic	Evangelical Protestant	Mainline Protestant	Other Tradition	Black Protestant	Orthodox
MSA[1]	6.6	19.9	10.5	2.3	0.5	0.1
U.S.	19.1	16.2	7.3	4.3	1.6	0.3

Note: Figures are the number of adherents as a percentage of the total population; (1) Figures cover the Columbia, MO Metropolitan Statistical Area—see Appendix B for areas included
Source: Association of Statisticians of American Religious Bodies, 2010 U.S. Religion Census: Religious Congregations & Membership Study

ECONOMY

Gross Metropolitan Product

Area	2016	2017	2018	2019	Rank[2]
MSA[1]	8.9	9.2	9.4	9.9	220

Note: Figures are in billions of dollars; (1) Figures cover the Columbia, MO Metropolitan Statistical Area—see Appendix B for areas included; (2) Rank is based on 2017 data and ranges from 1 to 381
Source: U.S. Conference of Mayors, U.S. Metro Economies: Economic Growth & Full Employment, June 2018

Economic Growth

Area	2017-2018 (%)	2019-2020 (%)	2021-2022 (%)
MSA[1]	1.4	2.4	2.2

Note: Figures are real gross metropolitan product (GMP) growth rates and represent average annual percent change; (1) Figures cover the Columbia, MO Metropolitan Statistical Area—see Appendix B for areas included
Source: U.S. Conference of Mayors, U.S. Metro Economies: Economic Growth & Full Employment, June 2018

Metropolitan Area Exports

Area	2012	2013	2014	2015	2016	2017	Rank[2]
MSA[1]	296.6	423.9	237.7	214.0	213.7	224.0	294

Note: Figures are in millions of dollars; (1) Figures cover the Columbia, MO Metropolitan Statistical Area—see Appendix B for areas included; (2) Rank is based on 2017 data and ranges from 1 to 387
Source: U.S. Department of Commerce, International Trade Administration, Office of Trade and Economic Analysis, Industry and Analysis, Exports by Metropolitan Area, extracted March 25, 2019

Building Permits

Area	Single-Family			Multi-Family			Total		
	2016	2017	Pct. Chg.	2016	2017	Pct. Chg.	2016	2017	Pct. Chg.
City	568	403	-29.0	405	861	112.6	973	1,264	29.9
MSA[1]	863	769	-10.9	441	865	96.1	1,304	1,634	25.3
U.S.	750,800	820,000	9.2	455,800	462,000	1.4	1,206,600	1,282,000	6.2

Note: (1) Figures cover the Columbia, MO Metropolitan Statistical Area—see Appendix B for areas included; Figures represent new, privately-owned housing units authorized (unadjusted data); All permit data are based on estimates with imputation
Source: U.S. Census Bureau, Manufacturing, Mining, and Construction Statistics, Building Permits, 2016, 2017

Bankruptcy Filings

Area	Business Filings			Nonbusiness Filings		
	2017	2018	% Chg.	2017	2018	% Chg.
Boone County	6	7	16.7	427	368	-13.8
U.S.	23,157	22,232	-4.0	765,863	751,186	-1.9

Note: Business filings include Chapter 7, Chapter 11, Chapter 12, and Chapter 13; Nonbusiness filings include Chapter 7, Chapter 11, and Chapter 13
Source: Administrative Office of the U.S. Courts, Business and Nonbusiness Bankruptcy, County Cases Commenced by Chapter of the Bankruptcy Code, During the 12-Month Period Ending December 31, 2017 and Business and Nonbusiness Bankruptcy, County Cases Commenced by Chapter of the Bankruptcy Code, During the 12-Month Period Ending December 31, 2018

Housing Vacancy Rates

Area	Gross Vacancy Rate[2] (%)			Year-Round Vacancy Rate[3] (%)			Rental Vacancy Rate[4] (%)			Homeowner Vacancy Rate[5] (%)		
	2016	2017	2018	2016	2017	2018	2016	2017	2018	2016	2017	2018
MSA[1]	n/a	n/a	n/a	n/a	n/a	n/a	n/a	n/a	n/a	n/a	n/a	n/a
U.S.	12.8	12.7	12.3	9.9	9.9	9.7	6.9	7.2	6.9	1.7	1.6	1.5

Note: (1) Figures cover the Columbia, MO Metropolitan Statistical Area—see Appendix B for areas included; (2) The percentage of the total housing inventory that is vacant; (3) The percentage of the housing inventory (excluding seasonal units) that is year-round vacant; (4) The percentage of rental inventory that is vacant for rent; (5) The percentage of homeowner inventory that is vacant for sale; n/a not available
Source: U.S. Census Bureau, Housing Vacancies and Homeownership Annual Statistics: 2016, 2017, 2018

INCOME

Income

Area	Per Capita ($)	Median Household ($)	Average Household ($)
City	28,253	47,236	69,694
MSA[1]	28,495	52,005	70,887
U.S.	31,177	57,652	81,283

Note: (1) Figures cover the Columbia, MO Metropolitan Statistical Area—see Appendix B for areas included
Source: U.S. Census Bureau, 2013-2017 American Community Survey 5-Year Estimates

Household Income Distribution

Area	Percent of Households Earning							
	Under $15,000	$15,000 -$24,999	$25,000 -$34,999	$35,000 -$49,999	$50,000 -$74,999	$75,000 -$99,999	$100,000 -$149,999	$150,000 and up
City	18.3	10.6	9.5	13.2	15.5	10.9	12.4	9.7
MSA[1]	15.0	9.8	9.7	13.3	17.7	12.1	13.1	9.2
U.S.	11.6	9.8	9.5	13.0	17.7	12.3	14.1	12.1

Note: (1) Figures cover the Columbia, MO Metropolitan Statistical Area—see Appendix B for areas included
Source: U.S. Census Bureau, 2013-2017 American Community Survey 5-Year Estimates

Poverty Rate

Area	All Ages	Under 18 Years Old	18 to 64 Years Old	65 Years and Over
City	22.9	15.9	27.4	4.9
MSA[1]	18.7	15.2	21.8	6.9
U.S.	14.6	20.3	13.7	9.3

Note: Figures are percentage of people whose income during the past 12 months was below the poverty level; (1) Figures cover the Columbia, MO Metropolitan Statistical Area—see Appendix B for areas included
Source: U.S. Census Bureau, 2013-2017 American Community Survey 5-Year Estimates

EMPLOYMENT

Labor Force and Employment

Area	Civilian Labor Force			Workers Employed		
	Dec. 2017	Dec. 2018	% Chg.	Dec. 2017	Dec. 2018	% Chg.
City	66,863	67,317	0.7	65,375	65,918	0.8
MSA[1]	97,854	98,566	0.7	95,671	96,465	0.8
U.S.	159,880,000	162,510,000	1.6	153,602,000	156,481,000	1.9

Note: Data is not seasonally adjusted and covers workers 16 years of age and older; (1) Figures cover the Columbia, MO Metropolitan Statistical Area—see Appendix B for areas included
Source: Bureau of Labor Statistics, Local Area Unemployment Statistics

Unemployment Rate

Area	2018											
	Jan.	Feb.	Mar.	Apr.	May	Jun.	Jul.	Aug.	Sep.	Oct.	Nov.	Dec.
City	2.8	2.5	2.5	2.3	2.4	2.5	2.9	2.6	1.9	1.5	1.8	2.1
MSA[1]	2.9	2.6	2.6	2.3	2.3	2.6	2.9	2.6	1.9	1.6	1.8	2.1
U.S.	4.5	4.4	4.1	3.7	3.6	4.2	4.1	3.9	3.6	3.5	3.5	3.7

Note: Data is not seasonally adjusted and covers workers 16 years of age and older; (1) Figures cover the Columbia, MO Metropolitan Statistical Area—see Appendix B for areas included
Source: Bureau of Labor Statistics, Local Area Unemployment Statistics

Average Wages

Occupation	$/Hr.	Occupation	$/Hr.
Accountants and Auditors	28.90	Maids and Housekeeping Cleaners	11.00
Automotive Mechanics	21.40	Maintenance and Repair Workers	16.40
Bookkeepers	16.80	Marketing Managers	42.20
Carpenters	25.00	Nuclear Medicine Technologists	n/a
Cashiers	10.20	Nurses, Licensed Practical	20.20
Clerks, General Office	15.80	Nurses, Registered	32.80
Clerks, Receptionists/Information	12.70	Nursing Assistants	11.60
Clerks, Shipping/Receiving	15.50	Packers and Packagers, Hand	11.90
Computer Programmers	32.60	Physical Therapists	39.70
Computer Systems Analysts	28.40	Postal Service Mail Carriers	24.90
Computer User Support Specialists	20.90	Real Estate Brokers	n/a
Cooks, Restaurant	11.90	Retail Salespersons	14.90
Dentists	112.80	Sales Reps., Exc. Tech./Scientific	30.50
Electrical Engineers	38.60	Sales Reps., Tech./Scientific	39.40
Electricians	25.00	Secretaries, Exc. Legal/Med./Exec.	16.60
Financial Managers	64.40	Security Guards	14.00
First-Line Supervisors/Managers, Sales	22.00	Surgeons	n/a
Food Preparation Workers	11.70	Teacher Assistants*	13.10
General and Operations Managers	38.50	Teachers, Elementary School*	n/a
Hairdressers/Cosmetologists	13.90	Teachers, Secondary School*	n/a
Internists, General	n/a	Telemarketers	13.10
Janitors and Cleaners	13.70	Truck Drivers, Heavy/Tractor-Trailer	19.90
Landscaping/Groundskeeping Workers	14.00	Truck Drivers, Light/Delivery Svcs.	17.30
Lawyers	46.10	Waiters and Waitresses	9.40

Note: Wage data covers the Columbia, MO Metropolitan Statistical Area—see Appendix B for areas included; (*) Hourly wages for elementary/secondary school teachers and teacher assistants were calculated by the editors from annual wage data based on a 40 hour work week; n/a not available.
Source: Bureau of Labor Statistics, Metro Area Occupational Employment & Wage Estimates, May 2018

Employment by Occupation

Occupation Classification	City (%)	MSA[1] (%)	U.S. (%)
Management, Business, Science, and Arts	46.2	44.8	37.4
Natural Resources, Construction, and Maintenance	4.9	6.3	8.9
Production, Transportation, and Material Moving	6.9	7.9	12.2
Sales and Office	22.6	23.1	23.5
Service	19.5	17.9	18.0

Note: Figures cover employed civilians 16 years of age and older; (1) Figures cover the Columbia, MO Metropolitan Statistical Area—see Appendix B for areas included
Source: U.S. Census Bureau, 2013-2017 American Community Survey 5-Year Estimates

Employment by Industry

Sector	MSA[1]		U.S.
	Number of Employees	Percent of Total	Percent of Total
Construction, Mining, and Logging	n/a	n/a	5.3
Education and Health Services	n/a	n/a	15.9
Financial Activities	n/a	n/a	5.7
Government	30,800	30.3	15.1
Information	n/a	n/a	1.9
Leisure and Hospitality	n/a	n/a	10.7
Manufacturing	n/a	n/a	8.5
Other Services	n/a	n/a	3.9
Professional and Business Services	n/a	n/a	14.1
Retail Trade	11,100	10.9	10.8
Transportation, Warehousing, and Utilities	n/a	n/a	4.2
Wholesale Trade	n/a	n/a	3.9

Note: Figures are non-farm employment as of December 2018. Figures are not seasonally adjusted and include workers 16 years of age and older; (1) Figures cover the Columbia, MO Metropolitan Statistical Area—see Appendix B for areas included; n/a not available
Source: Bureau of Labor Statistics, Current Employment Statistics, Employment, Hours, and Earnings

Occupations with Greatest Projected Employment Growth: 2018 – 2020

Occupation[1]	2018 Employment	2020 Projected Employment	Numeric Employment Change	Percent Employment Change
Personal Care Aides	53,690	56,960	3,270	6.1
Combined Food Preparation and Serving Workers, Including Fast Food	74,280	77,040	2,760	3.7
Registered Nurses	76,570	78,150	1,580	2.1
Laborers and Freight, Stock, and Material Movers, Hand	51,110	52,350	1,240	2.4
General and Operations Managers	46,620	47,750	1,130	2.4
Janitors and Cleaners, Except Maids and Housekeeping Cleaners	47,160	48,290	1,130	2.4
Software Developers, Applications	14,740	15,690	950	6.4
Waiters and Waitresses	52,130	53,070	940	1.8
Customer Service Representatives	61,300	62,210	910	1.5
Construction Laborers	26,060	26,900	840	3.2

Note: Projections cover Missouri; (1) Sorted by numeric employment change
Source: www.projectionscentral.com, State Occupational Projections, 2018–2020 Short-Term Projections

Fastest Growing Occupations: 2018 – 2020

Occupation[1]	2018 Employment	2020 Projected Employment	Numeric Employment Change	Percent Employment Change
Helpers—Pipelayers, Plumbers, Pipefitters, and Steamfitters	700	750	50	7.1
Information Security Analysts	2,910	3,110	200	6.9
Software Developers, Applications	14,740	15,690	950	6.4
Statisticians	970	1,030	60	6.2
Personal Care Aides	53,690	56,960	3,270	6.1
Home Health Aides	12,570	13,310	740	5.9
Dental Laboratory Technicians	870	920	50	5.7
Market Research Analysts and Marketing Specialists	10,590	11,130	540	5.1
Nurse Practitioners	4,210	4,420	210	5.0
Helpers—Carpenters	1,030	1,080	50	4.9

Note: Projections cover Missouri; (1) Sorted by percent employment change and excludes occupations with numeric employment change less than 50
Source: www.projectionscentral.com, State Occupational Projections, 2018–2020 Short-Term Projections

TAXES

State Corporate Income Tax Rates

State	Tax Rate (%)	Income Brackets ($)	Num. of Brackets	Financial Institution Tax Rate (%)[a]	Federal Income Tax Ded.
Missouri	6.25	Flat rate	1	7.0	Yes (j)

Note: Tax rates as of January 1, 2019; (a) Rates listed are the corporate income tax rate applied to financial institutions or excise taxes based on income. Some states have other taxes based upon the value of deposits or shares; (j) 50% of the federal income tax is deductible.
Source: Federation of Tax Administrators, Range of State Corporate Income Tax Rates, January 1, 2019

State Individual Income Tax Rates

State	Tax Rate (%)	Income Brackets ($)	Personal Exemptions ($)			Standard Ded. ($)	
			Single	Married	Depend.	Single	Married
Missouri (a)	1.5 - 5.4	1,053 - 8,424	(d)	(d)	(d)	12,200	24,400 (d)

Note: Tax rates as of January 1, 2019; Local- and county-level taxes are not included; n/a not applicable; The deduction for federal income tax is limited to $5,000 for individuals and $10,000 for joint returns in Missouri and Montana, and to $6,500 for all filers in Oregon; (a) 19 states have statutory provision for automatically adjusting to the rate of inflation the dollar values of the income tax brackets, standard deductions, and/or personal exemptions. Michigan indexes the personal exemption only. Oregon does not index the income brackets for $125,000 and over; (d) These states use the personal exemption/standard deduction amounts provided in the federal Internal Revenue Code. Note, the Tax Cut and Reform Act of 2017 has eliminated personal exemptions from the IRC. CO, ID, NM, ND, SC, and DC have adopted the new exemptions and standard deduction amounts. MN conforms to a previous IRC year, while ME adopts the higher standard deduction but retains the exemption amounts.
Source: Federation of Tax Administrators, State Individual Income Tax Rates, January 1, 2019

Various State Sales and Excise Tax Rates

State	State Sales Tax (%)	Gasoline[1] (¢/gal.)	Cigarette[2] ($/pack)	Spirits[3] ($/gal.)	Wine[4] ($/gal.)	Beer[5] ($/gal.)	Recreational Marijuana (%)
Missouri	4.225	17.35	0.17	2	0.42	0.06	Not legal

Note: All tax rates as of January 1, 2019; (1) The American Petroleum Institute has developed a methodology for determining the average tax rate on a gallon of fuel. Rates may include any of the following: excise taxes, environmental fees, storage tank fees, other fees or taxes, general sales tax, and local taxes. In states where gasoline is subject to the general sales tax, or where the fuel tax is based on the average sale price, the average rate determined by API is sensitive to changes in the price of gasoline. States that fully or partially apply general sales taxes to gasoline: CA, CO, GA, IL, IN, MI, NY; (2) The federal excise tax of $1.0066 per pack and local taxes are not included; (3) Rates are those applicable to off-premise sales of 40% alcohol by volume (a.b.v.) distilled spirits in 750ml containers. Local excise taxes are excluded; (4) Rates are those applicable to off-premise sales of 11% a.b.v. non-carbonated wine in 750ml containers; (5) Rates are those applicable to off-premise sales of 4.7% a.b.v. beer in 12 ounce containers.
Source: Tax Foundation, 2019 Facts & Figures: How Does Your State Compare?

State Business Tax Climate Index Rankings

State	Overall Rank	Corporate Tax Rank	Individual Income Tax Rank	Sales Tax Rank	Unemployment Insurance Tax Rank	Property Tax Rank
Missouri	14	4	25	25	8	7

Note: The index is a measure of how each state's tax laws affect economic performance. The lower the rank, the more favorable a state's tax system is for business. States without a given tax are given a ranking of 1. The scores/rankings for the District of Columbia do not affect other states. The 2019 index represents the tax climate as of July 1, 2018.
Source: Tax Foundation, State Business Tax Climate Index 2019

COMMERCIAL UTILITIES

Typical Monthly Electric Bills

Area	Commercial Service ($/month)		Industrial Service ($/month)	
	1,500 kWh	40 kW demand 14,000 kWh	1,000 kW demand 200,000 kWh	50,000 kW demand 32,500,000 kWh
City	n/a	n/a	n/a	n/a
Average[1]	203	1,619	25,886	2,540,077

Note: Figures are based on annualized rates; (1) Average based on 187 utilities surveyed; n/a not available
Source: Edison Electric Institute, Typical Bills and Average Rates Report, Summer 2018

TRANSPORTATION

Means of Transportation to Work

Area	Car/Truck/Van		Public Transportation			Bicycle	Walked	Other Means	Worked at Home
	Drove Alone	Car-pooled	Bus	Subway	Railroad				
City	76.4	10.2	1.6	0.0	0.0	1.3	5.2	1.2	4.1
MSA[1]	77.7	11.0	1.1	0.0	0.0	0.9	3.9	1.2	4.2
U.S.	76.4	9.2	2.5	1.9	0.6	0.6	2.7	1.3	4.7

Note: Figures are percentages and cover workers 16 years of age and older; (1) Figures cover the Columbia, MO Metropolitan Statistical Area—see Appendix B for areas included
Source: U.S. Census Bureau, 2013-2017 American Community Survey 5-Year Estimates

Travel Time to Work

Area	Less Than 10 Minutes	10 to 19 Minutes	20 to 29 Minutes	30 to 44 Minutes	45 to 59 Minutes	60 to 89 Minutes	90 Minutes or More
City	20.6	53.8	12.9	7.6	2.9	1.1	1.0
MSA[1]	17.2	48.6	18.4	10.2	3.5	1.2	0.9
U.S.	12.7	28.9	20.9	20.5	8.1	6.2	2.7

Note: Note: Figures are percentages and include workers 16 years old and over; (1) Figures cover the Columbia, MO Metropolitan Statistical Area—see Appendix B for areas included
Source: U.S. Census Bureau, 2013-2017 American Community Survey 5-Year Estimates

Freeway Travel Time Index

Area	1985	1990	1995	2000	2005	2010	2014
Urban Area Rank[1,2]	n/a	n/a	n/a	n/a	n/a	n/a	n/a
Urban Area Index[1]	n/a	n/a	n/a	n/a	n/a	n/a	n/a
Average Index[3]	1.09	1.11	1.14	1.17	1.20	1.19	1.20

Note: Freeway Travel Time Index—the ratio of travel time in the peak period to the travel time at free-flow conditions. For example, a value of 1.30 indicates a 20-minute free-flow trip takes 26 minutes in the peak (20 minutes x 1.30 = 26 minutes); (1) Data for the Columbia, MO urban area was not available; (2) Rank is based on 101 urban areas (#1 = highest travel time index); (3) Average of 101 urban areas
Source: Texas Transportation Institute, 2015 Urban Mobility Scorecard, August 2015

Freeway Commuter Stress Index

Area	1985	1990	1995	2000	2005	2010	2014
Urban Area Rank[1,2]	n/a	n/a	n/a	n/a	n/a	n/a	n/a
Urban Area Index[1]	n/a	n/a	n/a	n/a	n/a	n/a	n/a
Average Index[3]	1.13	1.16	1.19	1.22	1.25	1.24	1.25

Note: The Freeway Commuter Stress Index is the same as the Freeway Travel Time Index (see table above) except that it includes only the travel in the peak directions during the peak periods; the TTI includes travel in all directions during the peak period. Thus, the CSI is more indicative of the work trip experienced by each commuter on a daily basis; (1) Data for the Columbia, MO urban area was not available; (2) Rank is based on 101 urban areas (#1 = highest travel time index); (3) Average of 101 urban areas
Source: Texas Transportation Institute, 2015 Urban Mobility Scorecard, August 2015

Public Transportation

Agency Name / Mode of Transportation	Vehicles Operated in Maximum Service[1]	Annual Unlinked Passenger Trips[2] (in thous.)	Annual Passenger Miles[3] (in thous.)
Columbia Transit (CT)			
Bus (directly operated)	27	1,516.4	3,728.7
Demand Response (directly operated)	9	53.8	286.7

Note: (1) The number of revenue vehicles operated by the given mode and type of service to meet the annual maximum service requirement. This is the revenue vehicle count during the peak season of the year; on the week and day that maximum service is provided. Vehicles operated in maximum service (VOMS) exclude atypical days and one-time special events; (2) The number of passengers who boarded public transportation vehicles. Passengers are counted each time they board a vehicle no matter how many vehicles they use to travel from their origin to their destination. (3) The sum of the distances ridden by all passengers during the entire fiscal year.
Source: Federal Transit Administration, National Transit Database, 2017

Air Transportation

Airport Name and Code / Type of Service	Passenger Airlines[1]	Passenger Enplanements	Freight Carriers[2]	Freight (lbs)
Columbia Regional (COU)				
Domestic service (U.S. carriers - 2018)	15	120,183	1	986
International service (U.S. carriers - 2017)	0	0	0	0

Note: (1) Includes all U.S.-based major, minor and commuter airlines that carried at least one passenger during the year; (2) Includes all U.S.-based airlines and freight carriers that transported at least one pound of freight during the year.
Source: Bureau of Transportation Statistics, The Intermodal Transportation Database, Air Carriers: T-100 Domestic Market (U.S. Carriers), 2018; Bureau of Transportation Statistics, The Intermodal Transportation Database, Air Carriers: T-100 International Market (U.S. Carriers), 2017

Other Transportation Statistics

Major Highways:	I-70; SR-63
Amtrak Service:	No
Major Waterways/Ports:	Near the Missouri River (15 miles)

Source: Amtrak.com; Google Maps

BUSINESSES

Major Business Headquarters

Company Name	Industry	Rankings	
		Fortune[1]	Forbes[2]
No companies listed	-	-	-

Note: (1) Companies that produce a 10-K are ranked 1 to 500 based on 2017 revenue; (2) All private companies with at least $2 billion in annual revenue through the end of their most current fiscal year are ranked 1 to 229; companies listed are headquartered in the city; dashes indicate no ranking
Source: Fortune, "Fortune 500," June 2018; Forbes, "America's Largest Private Companies," 2018 Rankings

Fast-Growing Businesses

According to *Inc.*, Columbia is home to one of America's 500 fastest-growing private companies: **Precision SEM** (#315). Criteria: must be an independent, privately-held, for-profit, U.S. corporation, proprietorship or partnership as of December 31, 2017; revenues must be at least $100,000 in 2014 and $2 million in 2017; must have four-year operating/sales history. Holding companies, regulated banks, and utilities were excluded. *Inc., "America's 500 Fastest-Growing Private Companies," 2018*

Minority- and Women-Owned Businesses

Group	All Firms		Firms with Paid Employees			
	Firms	Sales ($000)	Firms	Sales ($000)	Employees	Payroll ($000)
AIAN[1]	47	24,456	16	23,452	109	9,444
Asian	395	90,432	92	76,643	715	10,907
Black	427	16,695	42	8,907	235	4,118
Hispanic	224	(s)	47	(s)	100 - 249	(s)
NHOPI[2]	n/a	n/a	n/a	n/a	n/a	n/a
Women	3,340	(s)	525	(s)	2,500 - 4,999	(s)
All Firms	10,543	12,132,769	3,219	11,714,258	53,511	1,918,079

Note: Figures cover firms located in the city; minority- and women-owned business are defined as firms in which the corresponding group own 51% or more of the stock or equity of the company; (1) American Indian and Alaska Native; (2) Native Hawaiian and Other Pacific Islander; (s) estimates are suppressed when publication standards are not met; n/a not available
Source: U.S. Census Bureau, 2012 Economic Census, Survey of Business Owners

**HOTELS &
CONVENTION
CENTERS**

Hotels, Motels and Vacation Rentals

Area	5 Star		4 Star		3 Star		2 Star		1 Star		Not Rated	
	Num.	Pct.[3]	Num.	Pct.[3]	Num.	Pct.[3]	Num.	Pct.[3]	Num.	Pct.[3]	Num.	Pct.[3]
City[1]	0	0.0	3	1.6	24	12.5	62	32.3	1	0.5	102	53.1
Total[2]	286	0.4	5,236	7.1	16,715	22.6	10,259	13.9	293	0.4	41,056	55.6

Note: (1) Figures cover Columbia and vicinity; (2) Figures cover all 100 cities in this book; (3) Percentage of hotels which have a given star rating; Star ratings are determined by expedia.com and offer an indication of the general quality of a particular hotel.
Source: www.expedia.com, April 3, 2019

Major Convention Centers

Name	Overall Space (sq. ft.)	Exhibit Space (sq. ft.)	Meeting Space (sq. ft.)	Meeting Rooms

There are no major convention centers located in the metro area
Source: Original research

Living Environment

COST OF LIVING

Cost of Living Index

Composite Index	Groceries	Housing	Utilities	Trans-portation	Health Care	Misc. Goods/ Services
93.0	96.6	81.8	99.7	91.1	101.3	98.8

Note: The Cost of Living Index measures regional differences in the cost of consumer goods and services, excluding taxes and non-consumer expenditures, for professional and managerial households in the top income quintile. It is based on more than 50,000 prices covering almost 60 different items for which prices are collected three times a year by chambers of commerce, economic development organizations or university applied economic centers in each participating urban area. The numbers shown should be read as a percentage above or below the national average of 100. For example, a value of 115.4 in the groceries column indicates that grocery prices are 15.4% higher than the national average. Small differences in the index numbers should not be interpreted as significant; Figures cover the Columbia MO urban area.
Source: The Council for Community and Economic Research, ACCRA Cost of Living Index, 2018

Grocery Prices

Area[1]	T-Bone Steak ($/pound)	Frying Chicken ($/pound)	Whole Milk ($/half gal.)	Eggs ($/dozen)	Orange Juice ($/64 oz.)	Coffee ($/11.5 oz.)
City[2]	11.04	1.53	1.93	1.38	3.39	4.27
Avg.	11.35	1.42	1.94	1.81	3.52	4.35
Min.	7.45	0.92	0.80	0.75	2.72	3.06
Max.	15.05	2.76	4.18	4.00	5.36	8.20

Note: (1) Values for the local area are compared with the average, minimum and maximum values for all 291 areas in the Cost of Living Index; (2) Figures cover the Columbia MO urban area; T-Bone Steak (price per pound); Frying Chicken (price per pound, whole fryer); Whole Milk (half gallon carton); Eggs (price per dozen, Grade A, large); Orange Juice (64 oz. Tropicana or Florida Natural); Coffee (11.5 oz. can, vacuum-packed, Maxwell House, Hills Bros, or Folgers).
Source: The Council for Community and Economic Research, ACCRA Cost of Living Index, 2018

Housing and Utility Costs

Area[1]	New Home Price ($)	Apartment Rent ($/month)	All Electric ($/month)	Part Electric ($/month)	Other Energy ($/month)	Telephone ($/month)
City[2]	301,682	756	-	95.13	66.53	185.40
Avg.	347,000	1,087	165.93	100.16	67.73	178.70
Min.	200,468	500	93.58	25.64	26.78	163.10
Max.	1,901,222	4,888	388.65	246.86	332.81	197.70

Note: (1) Values for the local area are compared with the average, minimum and maximum values for all 291 areas in the Cost of Living Index; (2) Figures cover the Columbia MO urban area; New Home Price (2,400 sf living area, 8,000 sf lot, in urban area with full utilities); Apartment Rent (950 sf 2 bedroom/1.5 or 2 bath, unfurnished, excluding all utilities except water); All Electric (average monthly cost for an all-electric home); Part Electric (average monthly cost for a part-electric home); Other Energy (average monthly cost for natural gas, fuel oil, coal, wood, and any other forms of energy except electricity); Telephone (price includes the base monthly rate plus taxes and fees for three lines of mobile phone service).
Source: The Council for Community and Economic Research, ACCRA Cost of Living Index, 2018

Health Care, Transportation, and Other Costs

Area[1]	Doctor ($/visit)	Dentist ($/visit)	Optometrist ($/visit)	Gasoline ($/gallon)	Beauty Salon ($/visit)	Men's Shirt ($)
City[2]	138.83	84.03	89.20	2.45	36.42	37.78
Avg.	110.71	95.11	103.74	2.61	37.48	32.03
Min.	33.60	62.55	54.63	1.89	17.00	11.44
Max.	195.97	153.93	225.79	3.59	71.88	58.64

Note: (1) Values for the local area are compared with the average, minimum and maximum values for all 291 areas in the Cost of Living Index; (2) Figures cover the Columbia MO urban area; Doctor (general practitioners routine exam of an established patient); Dentist (adult teeth cleaning and periodic oral examination); Optometrist (full vision eye exam for established adult patient); Gasoline (one gallon regular unleaded, national brand, including all taxes, cash price at self-service pump if available); Beauty Salon (woman's shampoo, trim, and blow-dry); Men's Shirt (cotton/polyester dress shirt, pinpoint weave, long sleeves).
Source: The Council for Community and Economic Research, ACCRA Cost of Living Index, 2018

HOUSING

House Price Index (HPI)

Area	National Ranking[2]	Quarterly Change (%)	One-Year Change (%)	Five-Year Change (%)
MSA[1]	185	0.56	4.16	17.20
U.S.[3]	–	1.12	5.73	32.81

Note: The HPI is a weighted repeat sales index. It measures average price changes in repeat sales or refinancings on the same properties. This information is obtained by reviewing repeat mortgage transactions on single-family properties whose mortgages have been purchased or securitized by Fannie Mae or Freddie Mac in January 1975; (1) Figures cover the Columbia, MO Metropolitan Statistical Area—see Appendix B for areas included; (2) Rankings are based on annual percentage change for all metro areas containing at least 15,000 transactions over the last 10 years and ranges from 1 to 245; (3) figures based on a weighted average of Census Division estimates using a seasonally adjusted, purchase-only index; all figures are for the period ending December 31, 2018
Source: Federal Housing Finance Agency, House Price Index, February 26, 2019

Median Single-Family Home Prices

Area	2016	2017	2018p	Percent Change 2017 to 2018
MSA[1]	172.8	179.7	189.3	5.3
U.S. Average	235.5	248.8	261.6	5.1

Note: Figures are median sales prices of existing single-family homes in thousands of dollars; (p) preliminary; (1) Figures cover the Columbia, MO Metropolitan Statistical Area—see Appendix B for areas included
Source: National Association of Realtors, Median Sales Price of Existing Single-Family Homes for Metropolitan Areas, 4th Quarter 2018

Qualifying Income Based on Median Sales Price of Existing Single-Family Homes

Area	With 5% Down ($)	With 10% Down ($)	With 20% Down ($)
MSA[1]	45,456	43,063	38,278
U.S. Average	62,954	59,640	53,013

Note: Figures are preliminary; Qualifying income is based on a mortgage rate of 4.9%. Monthly principal and interest payment is limited to 25% of income; (1) Figures cover the Columbia, MO Metropolitan Statistical Area—see Appendix B for areas included
Source: National Association of Realtors, Qualifying Income Based on Median Sales Price of Existing Single-Family Homes for Metropolitan Areas, 4th Quarter 2018

Median Apartment Condo-Coop Home Prices

Area	2016	2017	2018p	Percent Change 2017 to 2018
MSA[1]	n/a	n/a	n/a	n/a
U.S. Average	220.7	234.3	241.0	2.9

Note: Figures are median sales prices of existing apartment condo-coop homes in thousands of dollars; (p) preliminary; n/a not available; (1) Figures cover the Columbia, MO Metropolitan Statistical Area—see Appendix B for areas included
Source: National Association of Realtors, Median Sales Price of Existing Apartment Condo-Coop Homes for Metropolitan Areas, 4th Quarter 2018

Home Value Distribution

Area	Under $50,000	$50,000 -$99,999	$100,000 -$149,999	$150,000 -$199,999	$200,000 -$299,999	$300,000 -$499,999	$500,000 -$999,999	$1,000,000 or more
City	3.7	8.7	21.7	21.8	24.4	16.1	3.3	0.3
MSA[1]	5.4	10.3	21.2	20.8	22.8	15.3	3.6	0.6
U.S.	8.3	13.9	14.7	14.6	18.7	17.3	9.7	2.7

Note: Figures are percentages and cover owner-occupied housing units; (1) Figures cover the Columbia, MO Metropolitan Statistical Area—see Appendix B for areas included
Source: U.S. Census Bureau, 2013-2017 American Community Survey 5-Year Estimates

Homeownership Rate

Area	2010 (%)	2011 (%)	2012 (%)	2013 (%)	2014 (%)	2015 (%)	2016 (%)	2017 (%)	2018 (%)
MSA[1]	n/a	n/a	n/a	n/a	n/a	n/a	n/a	n/a	n/a
U.S.	66.9	66.1	65.4	65.1	64.5	63.7	63.4	63.9	64.4

Note: (1) Figures cover the Columbia, MO Metropolitan Statistical Area—see Appendix B for areas included; n/a not available
Source: U.S. Census Bureau, Housing Vacancies and Homeownership Annual Statistics: 2010-2018

Year Housing Structure Built

Area	2010 or Later	2000 -2009	1990 -1999	1980 -1989	1970 -1979	1960 -1969	1950 -1959	1940 -1949	Before 1940	Median Year
City	6.9	23.7	17.4	14.0	12.7	11.3	5.6	2.7	5.8	1989
MSA[1]	5.7	21.9	18.5	14.1	16.2	10.4	5.2	2.4	5.6	1987
U.S.	3.2	14.5	14.0	13.6	15.5	10.8	10.5	5.1	12.9	1977

Note: Figures are percentages except for Median Year; Note: (1) Figures cover the Columbia, MO Metropolitan Statistical Area—see Appendix B for areas included
Source: U.S. Census Bureau, 2013-2017 American Community Survey 5-Year Estimates

Gross Monthly Rent

Area	Under $500	$500 -$999	$1,000 -$1,499	$1,500 -$1,999	$2,000 -$2,499	$2,500 -$2,999	$3,000 and up	Median ($)
City	8.3	60.8	22.1	4.9	2.9	0.6	0.2	825
MSA[1]	8.8	61.1	22.4	4.3	2.7	0.5	0.2	826
U.S.	10.5	41.1	28.7	11.7	4.5	1.8	1.7	982

Note: Figures are percentages except for Median; Gross rent is the contract rent plus the estimated average monthly cost of utilities (electricity, gas, and water and sewer) and fuels (oil, coal, kerosene, wood, etc.) if these are paid by the renter (or paid for the renter by someone else); (1) Figures cover the Columbia, MO Metropolitan Statistical Area—see Appendix B for areas included
Source: U.S. Census Bureau, 2013-2017 American Community Survey 5-Year Estimates

HEALTH

Health Risk Factors

Category	MSA[1] (%)	U.S. (%)
Adults aged 18–64 who have any kind of health care coverage	n/a	87.3
Adults who reported being in good or better health	n/a	82.4
Adults who have been told they have high blood cholesterol	n/a	33.0
Adults who have been told they have high blood pressure	n/a	32.3
Adults who are current smokers	n/a	17.1
Adults who currently use E-cigarettes	n/a	4.6
Adults who currently use chewing tobacco, snuff, or snus	n/a	4.0
Adults who are heavy drinkers[2]	n/a	6.3
Adults who are binge drinkers[3]	n/a	17.4
Adults who are overweight (BMI 25.0 - 29.9)	n/a	35.3
Adults who are obese (BMI 30.0 - 99.8)	n/a	31.3
Adults who participated in any physical activities in the past month	n/a	74.4
Adults who always or nearly always wears a seat belt	n/a	94.3

Note: n/a not available; (1) Figures cover the Columbia, MO Metropolitan Statistical Area—see Appendix B for areas included; (2) Heavy drinkers are classified as adult men having more than 14 drinks per week and adult women having more than 7 drinks per week; (3) Binge drinkers are classified as males having five or more drinks on one occasion or females having four or more drinks on one occasion
Source: Centers for Disease Control and Prevention, Behaviorial Risk Factor Surveillance System, SMART: Selected Metropolitan Area Risk Trends, 2017

Acute and Chronic Health Conditions

Category	MSA[1] (%)	U.S. (%)
Adults who have ever been told they had a heart attack	n/a	4.2
Adults who have ever been told they have angina or coronary heart disease	n/a	3.9
Adults who have ever been told they had a stroke	n/a	3.0
Adults who have ever been told they have asthma	n/a	14.2
Adults who have ever been told they have arthritis	n/a	24.9
Adults who have ever been told they have diabetes[2]	n/a	10.5
Adults who have ever been told they had skin cancer	n/a	6.2
Adults who have ever been told they had any other types of cancer	n/a	7.1
Adults who have ever been told they have COPD	n/a	6.5
Adults who have ever been told they have kidney disease	n/a	3.0
Adults who have ever been told they have a form of depression	n/a	20.5

Note: n/a not available; (1) Figures cover the Columbia, MO Metropolitan Statistical Area—see Appendix B for areas included; (2) Figures do not include pregnancy-related, borderline, or pre-diabetes
Source: Centers for Disease Control and Prevention, Behaviorial Risk Factor Surveillance System, SMART: Selected Metropolitan Area Risk Trends, 2017

Health Screening and Vaccination Rates

Category	MSA[1] (%)	U.S. (%)
Adults aged 65+ who have had flu shot within the past year	n/a	60.7
Adults aged 65+ who have ever had a pneumonia vaccination	n/a	75.4
Adults who have ever been tested for HIV	n/a	36.1
Adults who have ever had the shingles or zoster vaccine?	n/a	28.9
Adults who have had their blood cholesterol checked within the last five years	n/a	85.9

Note: n/a not available; (1) Figures cover the Columbia, MO Metropolitan Statistical Area—see Appendix B for areas included.
Source: Centers for Disease Control and Prevention, Behaviorial Risk Factor Surveillance System, SMART: Selected Metropolitan Area Risk Trends, 2017

Disability Status

Category	MSA[1] (%)	U.S. (%)
Adults who reported being deaf	n/a	6.7
Are you blind or have serious difficulty seeing, even when wearing glasses?	n/a	4.5
Are you limited in any way in any of your usual activities due of arthritis?	n/a	12.9
Do you have difficulty doing errands alone?	n/a	6.8
Do you have difficulty dressing or bathing?	n/a	3.6
Do you have serious difficulty concentrating/remembering/making decisions?	n/a	10.7
Do you have serious difficulty walking or climbing stairs?	n/a	13.6

Note: n/a not available; (1) Figures cover the Columbia, MO Metropolitan Statistical Area—see Appendix B for areas included.
Source: Centers for Disease Control and Prevention, Behaviorial Risk Factor Surveillance System, SMART: Selected Metropolitan Area Risk Trends, 2017

Mortality Rates for the Top 10 Causes of Death in the U.S.

ICD-10[a] Sub-Chapter	ICD-10[a] Code	Age-Adjusted Mortality Rate[1] per 100,000 population	
		County[2]	U.S.
Malignant neoplasms	C00-C97	139.8	155.5
Ischaemic heart diseases	I20-I25	71.5	94.8
Other forms of heart disease	I30-I51	58.5	52.9
Chronic lower respiratory diseases	J40-J47	34.6	41.0
Cerebrovascular diseases	I60-I69	39.6	37.5
Other degenerative diseases of the nervous system	G30-G31	29.4	35.0
Other external causes of accidental injury	W00-X59	24.7	33.7
Organic, including symptomatic, mental disorders	F01-F09	32.0	31.0
Hypertensive diseases	I10-I15	17.5	21.9
Diabetes mellitus	E10-E14	23.3	21.2

Note: (a) ICD-10 = International Classification of Diseases 10th Revision; (1) Mortality rates are a three year average covering 2015-2017; (2) Figures cover Boone County.
Source: Centers for Disease Control and Prevention, National Center for Health Statistics. Underlying Cause of Death 1999-2017 on CDC WONDER Online Database

Mortality Rates for Selected Causes of Death

ICD-10[a] Sub-Chapter	ICD-10[a] Code	Age-Adjusted Mortality Rate[1] per 100,000 population	
		County[2]	U.S.
Assault	X85-Y09	Unreliable	5.9
Diseases of the liver	K70-K76	11.4	14.1
Human immunodeficiency virus (HIV) disease	B20-B24	Suppressed	1.8
Influenza and pneumonia	J09-J18	10.6	14.3
Intentional self-harm	X60-X84	10.7	13.6
Malnutrition	E40-E46	Suppressed	1.6
Obesity and other hyperalimentation	E65-E68	Suppressed	2.1
Renal failure	N17-N19	12.0	13.0
Transport accidents	V01-V99	7.7	12.4
Viral hepatitis	B15-B19	Suppressed	1.6

Note: (a) ICD-10 = International Classification of Diseases 10th Revision; (1) Mortality rates are a three year average covering 2015-2017; (2) Figures cover Boone County; Data are suppressed when the data meet the criteria for confidentiality constraints; Mortality rates are flagged as unreliable when the rate would be calculated with a numerator of 20 or less.
Source: Centers for Disease Control and Prevention, National Center for Health Statistics. Underlying Cause of Death 1999-2017 on CDC WONDER Online Database

Health Insurance Coverage

Area	With Health Insurance	With Private Health Insurance	With Public Health Insurance	Without Health Insurance	Population Under Age 18 Without Health Insurance
City	93.2	83.0	18.9	6.8	3.8
MSA[1]	92.6	80.8	21.5	7.4	4.0
U.S.	89.5	67.2	33.8	10.5	5.7

Note: Figures are percentages that cover the civilian noninstitutionalized population; (1) Figures cover the Columbia, MO Metropolitan Statistical Area—see Appendix B for areas included
Source: U.S. Census Bureau, 2013-2017 American Community Survey 5-Year Estimates

Number of Medical Professionals

Area	MDs[3]	DOs[3,4]	Dentists	Podiatrists	Chiropractors	Optometrists
County[1] (number)	1,393	118	116	9	60	48
County[1] (rate[2])	789.0	66.8	65.1	5.0	33.7	26.9
U.S. (rate[2])	279.3	23.0	68.4	6.0	27.1	16.2

Note: Data as of 2017 unless noted; (1) Data covers Boone County; (2) Rate per 100,000 population; (3) Data as of 2016 and includes all active, non-federal physicians; (4) Doctor of Osteopathic Medicine
Source: U.S. Department of Health and Human Services, Health Resources and Services Administration, Bureau of Health Professions, Area Resource File (ARF) 2017-2018

EDUCATION

Public School District Statistics

District Name	Schls	Pupils	Pupil/ Teacher Ratio	Minority Pupils[1] (%)	Free Lunch Eligible[2] (%)	IEP[3] (%)
Columbia 93	35	18,171	13.3	39.2	40.6	10.3

Note: Table includes school districts with 2,000 or more students; (1) Percentage of students that are not non-Hispanic white; (2) Percentage of students that are eligible for the free lunch program; (3) Percentage of students that have an Individualized Education Program.
Source: U.S. Department of Education, National Center for Education Statistics, Common Core of Data, Local Education Agency (School District) Universe Survey: School Year 2016-2017; U.S. Department of Education, National Center for Education Statistics, Common Core of Data, Public Elementary/Secondary School Universe Survey: School Year 2016-2017

Highest Level of Education

Area	Less than H.S.	H.S. Diploma	Some College, No Deg.	Associate Degree	Bachelor's Degree	Master's Degree	Prof. School Degree	Doctorate Degree
City	5.8	16.9	17.8	6.1	28.3	15.1	4.5	5.5
MSA[1]	6.5	21.0	19.5	7.1	25.9	12.3	3.6	4.1
U.S.	12.7	27.3	20.8	8.3	19.1	8.4	2.0	1.4

Note: Figures cover persons age 25 and over; (1) Figures cover the Columbia, MO Metropolitan Statistical Area—see Appendix B for areas included
Source: U.S. Census Bureau, 2013-2017 American Community Survey 5-Year Estimates

Educational Attainment by Race

Area	High School Graduate or Higher (%)					Bachelor's Degree or Higher (%)				
	Total	White	Black	Asian	Hisp.[2]	Total	White	Black	Asian	Hisp.[2]
City	94.2	95.4	88.4	91.6	88.3	53.4	56.7	18.6	71.5	41.3
MSA[1]	93.5	94.5	87.9	91.5	79.1	45.9	47.6	17.6	70.2	35.8
U.S.	87.3	89.3	84.9	86.5	66.7	30.9	32.2	20.6	52.7	15.2

Note: Figures shown cover persons 25 years old and over; (1) Figures cover the Columbia, MO Metropolitan Statistical Area—see Appendix B for areas included; (2) People of Hispanic origin can be of any race
Source: U.S. Census Bureau, 2013-2017 American Community Survey 5-Year Estimates

School Enrollment by Grade and Control

Area	Preschool (%)		Kindergarten (%)		Grades 1 - 4 (%)		Grades 5 - 8 (%)		Grades 9 - 12 (%)	
	Public	Private	Public	Private	Public	Private	Public	Private	Public	Private
City	39.7	60.3	71.2	28.8	77.5	22.5	87.7	12.3	88.7	11.3
MSA[1]	45.3	54.7	76.4	23.6	82.0	18.0	90.0	10.0	90.8	9.2
U.S.	58.8	41.2	87.7	12.3	89.7	10.3	89.6	10.4	90.3	9.7

Note: Figures shown cover persons 3 years old and over; (1) Figures cover the Columbia, MO Metropolitan Statistical Area—see Appendix B for areas included
Source: U.S. Census Bureau, 2013-2017 American Community Survey 5-Year Estimates

Average Salaries of Public School Classroom Teachers

Area	2016		2017		Change from 2016 to 2017	
	Dollars	Rank[1]	Dollars	Rank[1]	Percent	Rank[2]
Missouri	47,959	40	48,618	41	1.4	27
U.S. Average	58,479	–	59,660	–	2.0	–

Note: (1) Rank ranges from 1 to 51 where 1 indicates highest salary; (2) Rank ranges from 1 to 51 where 1 indicates highest percent change.
Source: National Education Association, Rankings & Estimates: Rankings of the States 2017 and Estimates of School Statistics 2018

Higher Education

Four-Year Colleges			Two-Year Colleges			Medical Schools[1]	Law Schools[2]	Voc/ Tech[3]
Public	Private Non-profit	Private For-profit	Public	Private Non-profit	Private For-profit			
1	2	0	0	0	1	1	1	2

Note: Figures cover institutions located within the city limits and include main campuses only; (1) includes schools accredited by the Liaison Committee on Medical Education and the American Osteopathic Association's Commission on Osteopathic College Accreditation; (2) includes ABA-accredited schools, schools with provisional ABA accreditation, and state accredited schools; (3) includes all schools with programs that are less than 2 years.
Source: National Center for Education Statistics, Integrated Postsecondary Education System (IPEDS), 2017-18; Wikipedia, List of Medical Schools in the United States, accessed April 3, 2019; Wikipedia, List of Law Schools in the United States, accessed April 3, 2019

According to *U.S. News & World Report,* the Columbia, MO metro area is home to one of the best national universities in the U.S.: **University of Missouri** (#129 tie). The indicators used to capture academic quality fall into a number of categories: assessment by administrators at peer institutions; retention of students; faculty resources; student selectivity; financial resources; alumni giving; high school counselor ratings of colleges; and graduation rate. *U.S. News & World Report, "America's Best Colleges 2019"*

According to *U.S. News & World Report,* the Columbia, MO metro area is home to one of the top 100 law schools in the U.S.: **University of Missouri** (#64 tie). The rankings are based on a weighted average of 12 measures of quality: peer assessment score; assessment score by lawyers/judges; median LSAT scores; median undergrad GPA; acceptance rate; employment rates for graduates; placement success; bar passage rate; faculty resources; expenditures per student; student/faculty ratio; and library resources. *U.S. News & World Report, "America's Best Graduate Schools, Law, 2020"*

According to *U.S. News & World Report,* the Columbia, MO metro area is home to one of the top 75 business schools in the U.S.: **University of Missouri (Trulaske)** (#69 tie). The rankings are based on a weighted average of the following nine measures: quality assessment; peer assessment; recruiter assessment; placement success; mean starting salary and bonus; student selectivity; mean GMAT and GRE scores; mean undergraduate GPA; and acceptance rate. *U.S. News & World Report, "America's Best Graduate Schools, Business, 2020"*

PRESIDENTIAL ELECTION

2016 Presidential Election Results

Area	Clinton	Trump	Johnson	Stein	Other
Boone County	49.0	43.2	5.1	1.5	1.2
U.S.	48.0	45.9	3.3	1.1	1.7

Note: Results are percentages and may not add to 100% due to rounding
Source: Dave Leip's Atlas of U.S. Presidential Elections

EMPLOYERS

Major Employers

Company Name	Industry
BJC Health System	Hospital management
City of Columbia	Courts
Columbia College	Colleges & universities
Kraft Foods Global	Frankfurters, from purchased meat
MBS Textbook Exchange	Books, periodicals, & newspapers
MCI Worldcom Communications	Telephone communication, except radio
Regional Medical Pharmacy	Home health care services
Schneider Electric USA	Switchgear & switchboard apparatus
Shelter Insurance Companies	Fire, marine, & casualty insurance
State Farm Mutual Automobile Insurance	Insurance agents & brokers
University of Missouri Hospital	General medical & surgical hospitals
University of Missouri System	Colleges & universities
University Physicians Hospital	Gynecologist
Veterans Health Administration	Administration of veterans' affairs

Note: Companies shown are located within the Columbia, MO Metropolitan Statistical Area.
Source: Hoovers.com; Wikipedia

Best Companies to Work For

Veterans United Home Loans, headquartered in Columbia, is among "The 100 Best Companies to Work For." To pick the best companies, *Fortune* partnered with the Great Place to Work Institute. Two-thirds of a company's score is based on the results of the Institute's Trust Index survey, which is sent to a random sample of employees from each company. The questions related to attitudes about management's credibility, job satisfaction, and camaraderie. The other third of the scoring is based on the company's responses to the Institute's Culture Audit, which includes detailed questions about pay and benefit programs, and a series of open-ended questions about hiring practices, internal communication, training, recognition programs, and diversity efforts. Any company that is at least five years old with more than 1,000 U.S. employees is eligible. *Fortune, "The 100 Best Companies to Work For," 2019*

PUBLIC SAFETY

Crime Rate

Area	All Crimes	Violent Crimes				Property Crimes		
		Murder	Rape[3]	Robbery	Aggrav. Assault	Burglary	Larceny -Theft	Motor Vehicle Theft
City	3,431.9	7.3	93.8	95.4	301.0	412.0	2,305.3	217.0
Suburbs[1]	2,125.9	1.8	23.0	21.3	175.4	240.9	1,500.5	163.0
Metro[2]	3,020.1	5.6	71.5	72.1	261.4	358.0	2,051.6	200.0
U.S.	2,756.1	5.3	41.7	98.0	248.9	430.4	1,694.4	237.4

Note: Figures are crimes per 100,000 population; (1) All areas within the metro area that are located outside the city limits; (2) Figures cover the Columbia, MO Metropolitan Statistical Area—see Appendix B for areas included; (3) The city and U.S. figures shown were reported using the revised Uniform Crime Reporting (UCR) definition of rape. The suburban and metro area figures shown are an aggregate total of the data submitted using both the revised and legacy UCR definitions.
Source: FBI Uniform Crime Reports, 2017

Hate Crimes

Area	Number of Quarters Reported	Number of Incidents per Bias Motivation					
		Race/Ethnicity/ Ancestry	Religion	Sexual Orientation	Disability	Gender	Gender Identity
City	4	1	0	0	0	0	0
U.S.	4	4,131	1,564	1,130	116	46	119

Source: Federal Bureau of Investigation, Hate Crime Statistics 2017

Identity Theft Consumer Reports

Area	Reports	Reports per 100,000 Population	Rank[2]
MSA[1]	136	77	235
U.S.	444,602	135	-

Note: (1) Figures cover the Columbia, MO Metropolitan Statistical Area—see Appendix B for areas included;
(2) Rank ranges from 1 to 389 where 1 indicates greatest number of identity theft reports per 100,000 population
Source: Federal Trade Commission, Consumer Sentinel Network Data Book for January–December 2018

Fraud and Other Consumer Reports

Area	Reports	Reports per 100,000 Population	Rank[2]
MSA[1]	812	460	234
U.S.	2,552,917	776	-

Note: (1) Figures cover the Columbia, MO Metropolitan Statistical Area—see Appendix B for areas included;
(2) Rank ranges from 1 to 389 where 1 indicates greatest number of fraud and other consumer reports per 100,000 population
Source: Federal Trade Commission, Consumer Sentinel Network Data Book for January–December 2018

SPORTS

Professional Sports Teams

Team Name	League	Year Established
No teams are located in the metro area		

Source: Wikipedia, Major Professional Sports Teams of the United States and Canada, April 5, 2019

CLIMATE

Average and Extreme Temperatures

Temperature	Jan	Feb	Mar	Apr	May	Jun	Jul	Aug	Sep	Oct	Nov	Dec	Yr.
Extreme High (°F)	74	76	85	90	90	103	111	110	101	93	83	76	111
Average High (°F)	36	42	54	66	74	83	89	87	79	67	53	41	64
Average Temp. (°F)	28	33	44	55	64	73	78	76	68	56	44	33	54
Average Low (°F)	19	23	34	44	53	62	67	65	57	45	34	24	44
Extreme Low (°F)	-19	-15	-5	19	29	40	48	42	32	22	0	-20	-20

Note: Figures cover the years 1969-1995
Source: National Climatic Data Center, International Station Meteorological Climate Summary, 9/96

Average Precipitation/Snowfall/Humidity

Precip./Humidity	Jan	Feb	Mar	Apr	May	Jun	Jul	Aug	Sep	Oct	Nov	Dec	Yr.
Avg. Precip. (in.)	1.6	2.0	3.2	4.3	5.1	3.9	3.9	3.8	3.7	3.1	3.5	2.6	40.6
Avg. Snowfall (in.)	7	7	4	1	0	0	0	0	0	Tr	2	5	25
Avg. Rel. Hum. 6am (%)	80	80	79	79	85	86	87	89	88	84	82	81	83
Avg. Rel. Hum. 3pm (%)	62	59	53	52	57	56	53	52	54	53	59	64	56

Note: Figures cover the years 1969-1995; Tr = Trace amounts (<0.05 in. of rain; <0.5 in. of snow)
Source: National Climatic Data Center, International Station Meteorological Climate Summary, 9/96

Weather Conditions

Temperature			Daytime Sky			Precipitation		
10°F & below	32°F & below	90°F & above	Clear	Partly cloudy	Cloudy	0.01 inch or more precip.	0.1 inch or more snow/ice	Thunderstorms
17	108	36	99	127	139	110	17	52

Note: Figures are average number of days per year and cover the years 1969-1995
Source: National Climatic Data Center, International Station Meteorological Climate Summary, 9/96

HAZARDOUS WASTE

Superfund Sites

The Columbia, MO metro area has no sites on the EPA's Superfund Final National Priorities List.
There are a total of 1,390 Superfund sites with a status of proposed or final on the list in the U.S.
U.S. Environmental Protection Agency, National Priorities List, April 5, 2019

**AIR & WATER
QUALITY**

Air Quality Trends: Ozone

	1990	1995	2000	2005	2010	2012	2014	2015	2016	2017
MSA[1]	n/a	n/a	n/a	n/a	n/a	n/a	n/a	n/a	n/a	n/a
U.S.	0.088	0.089	0.082	0.080	0.073	0.075	0.067	0.068	0.069	0.068

Note: (1) Data covers the Columbia, MO Metropolitan Statistical Area—see Appendix B for areas included; n/a not available. The values shown are the composite ozone concentration averages among trend sites based on the highest fourth daily maximum 8-hour concentration in parts per million. These trends are based on sites having an adequate record of monitoring data during the trend period. Data from exceptional events are included.
Source: U.S. Environmental Protection Agency, Air Quality Monitoring Information, "Air Quality Trends by City, 1990-2017"

Air Quality Index

Area	Percent of Days when Air Quality was...[2]					AQI Statistics[2]	
	Good	Moderate	Unhealthy for Sensitive Groups	Unhealthy	Very Unhealthy	Maximum	Median
MSA[1]	89.4	10.6	0.0	0.0	0.0	77	41

Note: (1) Data covers the Columbia, MO Metropolitan Statistical Area—see Appendix B for areas included; (2) Based on 245 days with AQI data in 2017. Air Quality Index (AQI) is an index for reporting daily air quality. EPA calculates the AQI for five major air pollutants regulated by the Clean Air Act: ground-level ozone, particle pollution (aka particulate matter), carbon monoxide, sulfur dioxide, and nitrogen dioxide. The AQI runs from 0 to 500. The higher the AQI value, the greater the level of air pollution and the greater the health concern. There are six AQI categories: "Good" AQI is between 0 and 50. Air quality is considered satisfactory; "Moderate" AQI is between 51 and 100. Air quality is acceptable; "Unhealthy for Sensitive Groups" When AQI values are between 101 and 150, members of sensitive groups may experience health effects; "Unhealthy" When AQI values are between 151 and 200 everyone may begin to experience health effects; "Very Unhealthy" AQI values between 201 and 300 trigger a health alert; "Hazardous" AQI values over 300 trigger warnings of emergency conditions (not shown).
Source: U.S. Environmental Protection Agency, Air Quality Index Report, 2017

Air Quality Index Pollutants

Area	Percent of Days when AQI Pollutant was...[2]					
	Carbon Monoxide	Nitrogen Dioxide	Ozone	Sulfur Dioxide	Particulate Matter 2.5	Particulate Matter 10
MSA[1]	0.0	0.0	100.0	0.0	0.0	0.0

Note: (1) Data covers the Columbia, MO Metropolitan Statistical Area—see Appendix B for areas included; (2) Based on 245 days with AQI data in 2017. The Air Quality Index (AQI) is an index for reporting daily air quality. EPA calculates the AQI for five major air pollutants regulated by the Clean Air Act: ground-level ozone, particle pollution (also known as particulate matter), carbon monoxide, sulfur dioxide, and nitrogen dioxide. The AQI runs from 0 to 500. The higher the AQI value, the greater the level of air pollution and the greater the health concern.
Source: U.S. Environmental Protection Agency, Air Quality Index Report, 2017

Maximum Air Pollutant Concentrations: Particulate Matter, Ozone, CO and Lead

	Particulate Matter 10 (ug/m^3)	Particulate Matter 2.5 Wtd AM (ug/m^3)	Particulate Matter 2.5 24-Hr (ug/m^3)	Ozone (ppm)	Carbon Monoxide (ppm)	Lead (ug/m^3)
MSA[1] Level	n/a	n/a	n/a	0.061	n/a	n/a
NAAQS[2]	150	15	35	0.075	9	0.15
Met NAAQS[2]	n/a	n/a	n/a	Yes	n/a	n/a

Note: (1) Data covers the Columbia, MO Metropolitan Statistical Area—see Appendix B for areas included; Data from exceptional events are included; (2) National Ambient Air Quality Standards; ppm = parts per million; ug/m^3 = micrograms per cubic meter; n/a not available.
Concentrations: Particulate Matter 10 (coarse particulate)—highest second maximum 24-hour concentration; Particulate Matter 2.5 Wtd AM (fine particulate)—highest weighted annual mean concentration; Particulate Matter 2.5 24-Hour (fine particulate)—highest 98th percentile 24-hour concentration; Ozone—highest fourth daily maximum 8-hour concentration; Carbon Monoxide—highest second maximum non-overlapping 8-hour concentration; Lead—maximum running 3-month average
Source: U.S. Environmental Protection Agency, Air Quality Monitoring Information, "Air Quality Statistics by City, 2017"

Maximum Air Pollutant Concentrations: Nitrogen Dioxide and Sulfur Dioxide

	Nitrogen Dioxide AM (ppb)	Nitrogen Dioxide 1-Hr (ppb)	Sulfur Dioxide AM (ppb)	Sulfur Dioxide 1-Hr (ppb)	Sulfur Dioxide 24-Hr (ppb)
MSA[1] Level	n/a	n/a	n/a	n/a	n/a
NAAQS[2]	53	100	30	75	140
Met NAAQS[2]	n/a	n/a	n/a	n/a	n/a

Note: (1) Data covers the Columbia, MO Metropolitan Statistical Area—see Appendix B for areas included; Data from exceptional events are included; (2) National Ambient Air Quality Standards; ppm = parts per million; ug/m³ = micrograms per cubic meter; n/a not available.
Concentrations: Nitrogen Dioxide AM—highest arithmetic mean concentration; Nitrogen Dioxide 1-Hr—highest 98th percentile 1-hour daily maximum concentration; Sulfur Dioxide AM—highest annual mean concentration; Sulfur Dioxide 1-Hr—highest 99th percentile 1-hour daily maximum concentration; Sulfur Dioxide 24-Hr—highest second maximum 24-hour concentration
Source: U.S. Environmental Protection Agency, Air Quality Monitoring Information, "Air Quality Statistics by City, 2017"

Drinking Water

Water System Name	Pop. Served	Primary Water Source Type	Violations[1] Health Based	Violations[1] Monitoring/ Reporting
Columbia PWS	100,733	Ground	0	0

Note: (1) Based on violation data from January 1, 2018 to December 31, 2018
Source: U.S. Environmental Protection Agency, Office of Ground Water and Drinking Water, Safe Drinking Water Information System (based on data extracted April 5, 2019)

Des Moines, Iowa

Background

In 1843, Fort Des Moines was founded at the confluence of the Des Moines and Raccoon rivers. Though the fort was initially established to protect local Native American populations, within two years the area was opened to white settlers. By 1857, the state capital was moved from Iowa City to Des Moines. Today, Des Moines remains the capital of Iowa and is its largest city.

The city frequently finds itself near the top of best-of lists extolling its reasonable cost of living, quality of life, or job opportunities. It has taken an active role in acquiring properties in its downtown for redevelopment, and also takes a progressive approach to planning, most recently joining with other counties and regional partners to plan for transportation and other future needs. The Capital Corridor encourages the development of creative high-value growth and development for industry, including animal science.

Des Moines's significant industries include the financial services industry; Greater Des Moines has the nation's highest concentration of employment in this sector. Additionally, logistics, bioscience, and data centers are significant economic sectors. Major employers include Wells Fargo & Co., Principal Financial Group, Nationwide/Allied Insurance, DuPont Pioneer, the John Deere companies, and Firestone Agricultural Tire Company, which houses its global distribution center for agricultural tires.

Greater Des Moines is home to the first statewide fiber optics network in the country. The city proper also boasts world-class architecture. The Des Moines Art Center was designed in 1944 by Eliel Saarinen, a Finnish architect and then-president of the renowned Cranbrook Academy of Art in Detroit. In 1968, I.M. Pei, architect of the Pyramid du Louvre and the East Wing of the National Gallery of Art in Washington, D.C., designed a gallery addition to the main Art Center structure. In 1985, Richard Meier, who had designed the Museum of Modern Art in Florence, Italy, designed an addition to the Art Center's north wing and went on to design the famed Getty Center in Los Angeles. The city's Home Federal Savings and Loan Building was designed by Mies van der Rohe, of the famous German Bauhaus School of Design, and a sculpture called The Crusoe Umbrella, designed by pop artist Claes Oldenberg, stands in the middle of Nollen Plaza, a wooded park and popular gathering place.

The Greater Des Moines Botanical Center has been renovated to include Iowa's first "living wall," a new office suite and lobby, and improvements to the center's gardens.

Des Moines Civic Center offers ballet, symphony and other performances. The Science Center of Iowa features hands-on science and technology exhibits, an IMAX theater, and a planetarium with an interactive program and laser light show.

Every four years, Des Moines becomes the center of national attention as correspondents from all over the U.S. and abroad arrive to cover the Iowa political caucuses in January, which has become a financial boon for the state.

Located in the heart of North America, Des Moines has a continental climate, resulting in a seasonal contrast in both temperature and precipitation. Exceptionally high summer rains have caused the nearby Des Moines River and Raccoon River to breach the city's levees on two occasions, in 1993 and again in 2008. The winter is a season of cold, dry air, interrupted by occasional storms of short duration. The autumn is characteristically sunny with diminishing precipitation.

Rankings

General Rankings

- *US News & World Report* conducted a survey of more than 2,000 people and analyzed the 125 largest metropolitan areas to determine what matters the most when selecting the next place to live. Des Moines ranked #4 out of the top 25 as having the best combination of desirable factors. Criteria: cost of living; quality of education; job market, crime rates; and other factors. *realestate.usnews.com, "The 25 Best Places to Live in the U.S. in 2018," April 10, 2018*

- The Des Moines metro area was identified as one of America's fastest-growing areas in terms of population and business growth by *MagnifyMoney*. The area ranked #15 out of 35. The 100 most populous metro areas in the U.S. were evaluated on their change from 2011-2016 in the following categories: people and housing; workforce and employment opportunities; growing industry. *www.businessinsider.com, "The 35 Cities in the US with the Biggest Influx of People, the Most Work Opportunities, and the Hottest Business Growth," August 12, 2018*

- In their sixth annual survey, Livability.com looked at data for more than 1,000 U.S. cities to determine the rankings for Livability's "Top 100 Best Places to Live" in 2019. Des Moines ranked #96. Criteria: median home value capped at $250,000; affordable living; vibrant economy; education, demographics, health care options. transportation & infrastructure; abundant lifestyle amenities. *Livability.com, "Top 100 Best Places to Live 2019" March 2019*

Business/Finance Rankings

- The personal finance site NerdWallet analyzed 183 American metropolitan areas with populations over 250,000 and more than 15,000 businesses to rank where entrepreneurs find the most success. Criteria included area economy, annual income, housing cost, unemployment rate, and the success rate of area businesses. Des Moines ranked #11. *www.nerdwallet.com, "Best Places to Start a Business," April 27, 2015*

- Using data from the Council for Community and Economic Research's 2014 cost of living index, NerdWallet ranked the 100 most affordable cities in America. Median income was compared with cost of living to find truly affordable places. Des Moines ranked #53. *NerdWallet.com, "America's Most Affordable Places," May 18, 2015*

- The Brookings Institution ranked the nation's largest cities based on income inequality. Des Moines was ranked #88 (#1 = greatest inequality). Criteria: the "95/20 ratio," a figure representing the income at which a household earns more than 95 percent of all other households, divided by the income at which a household earns more than only 20 percent of all other households. *Brookings Institution, "Household Income Inequality, Largest Cities of 97 Large U.S. Metro Areas, 2014-2016," February 5, 2018*

- The Brookings Institution ranked the 100 largest metro areas in the U.S. based on income inequality. Des Moines was ranked #93 (#1 = greatest inequality). Criteria: the "95/20 ratio," a figure representing the income at which a household earns more than 95 percent of all other households, divided by the income at which a household earns more than only 20 percent of all other households. *Brookings Institution, "Household Income Inequality, 100 Largest U.S. Metro Areas, 2014-2016," February 5, 2018*

- Des Moines was cited as one of America's top metros for new and expanded facility projects in 2018. The area ranked #3 in the mid-sized metro area category (population 200,000 to 1 million). *Site Selection, "Top Metros of 2018," March 2019*

- The Des Moines metro area appeared on the Milken Institute "2018 Best Performing Cities" list. Rank: #69 out of 200 large metro areas. Criteria: job growth; wage and salary growth; high-tech output growth. *Milken Institute, "Best-Performing Cities 2018," January 24, 2019*

- *Forbes* ranked the 200 most populous metro areas to determine the nation's "Best Places for Business and Careers." The Des Moines metro area was ranked #7. Criteria: costs (business and living); job growth (past and projected); income growth; quality of life; educational attainment (college and high school); projected economic growth; cultural and recreational opportunities; net migration patterns; number of highly ranked colleges. *Forbes, "The Best Places for Business and Careers 2018: Seattle Leads the Way," October 24, 2018*

Children/Family Rankings

- *Forbes* analyzed data on the 100 largest metropolitan areas in the United States to compile its 2016 ranking of the best cities for raising a family. The Des Moines metro area was ranked #11. Criteria: median income; childcare costs; percent of population under 18; commuting delays; crime rate; percentage of families owning homes; education quality (mainly test scores). Overall cost of living and housing affordability was also unofficially considered. *Forbes, "America's Best Cities for Raising a Family 2016," August 30, 2016*

Dating/Romance Rankings

- *Apartment List* conducted its annual survey of renters to compile a list of cities that have the best opportunities for dating. More than 9,000 respondents, from February 2018 through the end of December 2018, rated their current city or neighborhood for opportunities to date and make friends. Des Moines ranked #60 out of 66 where single residents were very satisfied or somewhat satisfied, making it among the ten worst metros for dating opportunities. Other criteria analyzed included gender and education levels of renters. *Apartment List, "The Best & Worst Cities for Dating 2019," February 8, 2019*

- Des Moines was ranked #6 out of 25 cities that stood out for inspiring romance and attracting diners on the website OpenTable.com. Criteria: percentage of people who dined out on Valentine's Day in 2018; percentage of romantic restaurants as rated by OpenTable diner reviews; and percentage of tables seated for two. *OpenTable, "25 Most Romantic Cities in America for 2019," February 7, 2019*

Education Rankings

- Personal finance website *WalletHub* analyzed the 150 largest U.S. metropolitan statistical areas to determine where the most educated Americans are choosing to settle. Criteria: education quality and attainment gap; education levels; percentage of workers with degrees; public school quality rankings; quality and size of each metro area's universities. Des Moines was ranked #35 (#1 = most educated city). *www.WalletHub.com, "2018's Most and Least Educated Cities in America," July 24, 2018*

Environmental Rankings

- The U.S. Environmental Protection Agency (EPA) released a list of mid-size U.S. metropolitan areas with the most ENERGY STAR certified buildings in 2017. The Des Moines metro area was ranked #7 out of 10. *U.S. Environmental Protection Agency, "2018 Energy Star Top Cities," April 11, 2018*

- Des Moines was highlighted as one of the cleanest metro areas for ozone air pollution in the U.S. during 2014 through 2016. The list represents cities with no monitored ozone air pollution in unhealthful ranges. *American Lung Association, State of the Air 2018*

Food/Drink Rankings

- *Men's Health* ranked 100 major U.S. cities in terms of alcohol intoxication. Des Moines ranked #54 (#1 = most sober).Criteria: binge drinking; alcohol-related traffic accidents, arrests, and fatalities. *Men's Health, "America's Drunkest Cities," March 9, 2015*

Health/Fitness Rankings

- Des Moines was identified as a "2018 Spring Allergy Capital." The area ranked #75 out of 100. Three groups of factors were used to identify the most challenging cities for people with allergies during the spring season: annual pollen levels; medicine utilization; access to board-certified allergists. *Asthma and Allergy Foundation of America, "Spring Allergy Capitals 2018"*

- Des Moines was identified as a "2018 Fall Allergy Capital." The area ranked #64 out of 100. Three groups of factors were used to identify the most challenging cities for people with allergies during the fall season: annual pollen levels; medicine utilization; access to board-certified allergists. *Asthma and Allergy Foundation of America, "Fall Allergy Capitals 2018"*

- Des Moines was identified as a "2018 Asthma Capital." The area ranked #84 out of the nation's 100 largest metropolitan areas. Criteria: estimated prevalence; self-reported prevalence; crude death rate for asthma; annual pollen score; annual air quality; public smoking laws; number of board-certified asthma specialists; school inhaler access laws; rescue medication use; controller medication use; ER visits for asthma; uninsured rate; poverty rate. *Asthma and Allergy Foundation of America, "Asthma Capitals 2018: The Most Challenging Places to Live With Asthma"*

- *Men's Health* ranked 100 major U.S. cities in terms of the best cities for men. Des Moines ranked #41. Criteria: health; fitness; quality of life. *Men's Health, "The Best & Worst Cities for Men Who Want to Be Fit and Happy," January 1, 2016*

- The Des Moines metro area ranked #52 out of 189 in The Gallup-Healthways Well-Being Index. Criteria: purpose; social well being; financial health; community and physical health. Results are based on telephone interviews with adults, aged 18 and older, living in metropolitan areas in the 50 U.S. states and the District of Columbia. *Gallup-Healthways, "State of American Well-Being, 2017 Community Well-Being Rankings" March 2018*

Real Estate Rankings

- *WalletHub* compared the most populated U.S. cities, as well as at least two of the most populated cities in each state, for a total of 179, to determine which had the best markets for real estate agents. Des Moines ranked #126 where demand was high and pay was the best. Criteria: sales per agent; annual median wage for real-estate agents; monthly average starting salary for real estate agents; real estate job density and competition; unemployment rate; housing-market health index; and other relevant metrics. *www.WalletHub.com, "2018's Best Places to Be a Real Estate Agent," April 25, 2018*

- The Des Moines metro area was identified as one of the 20 worst housing markets in the U.S. in 2018. The area ranked #161 out of 178 markets. Criteria: year-over-year change of median sales price of existing single-family homes between the 4th quarter of 2017 and the 4th quarter of 2018. *National Association of Realtors®, Median Sales Price of Existing Single-Family Homes for Metropolitan Areas, 4th Quarter 2018*

Safety Rankings

- Allstate ranked the 200 largest cities in America in terms of driver safety. Des Moines ranked #34. Criteria: internal property damage claims over a two-year period from January 2015 to December 2016. The report helps increase the importance of safety awareness behind the wheel. *Allstate, "Allstate America's Best Drivers Report, 2018" August 28, 2018*

- The National Insurance Crime Bureau ranked 382 metro areas in the U.S. in terms of per capita rates of vehicle theft. The Des Moines metro area ranked #120 (#1 = highest rate). Criteria: number of vehicle theft offenses per 100,000 inhabitants in 2017. *National Insurance Crime Bureau, "Hot Spots 2017," July 12, 2018*

Seniors/Retirement Rankings

- From its Best Cities for Successful Aging indexes, the Milken Institute generated rankings for metropolitan areas, weighing data in nine categories—health care, wellness, living arrangements, transportation and convenience, financial characteristics, education, employment, community engagement, and overall livability. The Des Moines metro area was ranked #5 overall in the large metro area category. *Milken Institute, "Best Cities for Successful Aging, 2017" March 14, 2017*

Sports/Recreation Rankings

■ Des Moines was chosen as one of America's best cities for bicycling. The city ranked #38 out of 50. Criteria: cycling infrastructure that is safe and friendly for all ages; energy and bike culture. The editors only considered cities with populations of 100,000 or more. *Bicycling, "The 50 Best Bike Cities in America," October 10, 2018*

Women/Minorities Rankings

■ Personal finance website *WalletHub* compared more than 180 U.S. cities—including the 150 most populated U.S. cities, plus at least two of the most populated cities in each state—across two key dimensions, "Hispanic Business-Friendliness" and "Hispanic Purchasing Power", to arrive at the most favorable conditions for Hispanic entrepreneurs. Des Moines was ranked #127 out of 182. Criteria includes: share of Hispanic-Owned Businesses; Hispanic entrepreneurship rate to median annual income of Hispanics; Small Business-Friendliness score; cost of living; and number of Hispanics with at least a bachelor's degree. *WalletHub.com, "2018's Best Cities for Hispanic Entrepreneurs," April 26, 2018*

Miscellaneous Rankings

■ *WalletHub* compared the 150 most populated U.S. cities to determine their operating efficiency. A "Quality of Services" score was constructed for each city and then divided by the total budget per capita to reveal which were managed the best. Des Moines ranked #54. Criteria: financial stability; economy; education; safety; health; infrastructure and pollution. *www.WalletHub.com, "2018's Best- & Worst-Run Cities in America," July 9, 2018*

Business Environment

CITY FINANCES

City Government Finances

Component	2016 ($000)	2016 ($ per capita)
Total Revenues	501,802	2,386
Total Expenditures	456,940	2,172
Debt Outstanding	513,513	2,441
Cash and Securities[1]	264,444	1,257

Note: (1) Cash and security holdings of a government at the close of its fiscal year, including those of its dependent agencies, utilities, and liquor stores.
Source: U.S. Census Bureau, State & Local Government Finances 2016

City Government Revenue by Source

Source	2016 ($000)	2016 ($ per capita)	2016 (%)
General Revenue			
From Federal Government	54,626	260	10.9
From State Government	44,877	213	8.9
From Local Governments	10,600	50	2.1
Taxes			
Property	138,123	657	27.5
Sales and Gross Receipts	27,862	132	5.6
Personal Income	0	0	0.0
Corporate Income	0	0	0.0
Motor Vehicle License	0	0	0.0
Other Taxes	6,056	29	1.2
Current Charges	144,540	687	28.8
Liquor Store	0	0	0.0
Utility	54,003	257	10.8
Employee Retirement	303	1	0.1

Source: U.S. Census Bureau, State & Local Government Finances 2016

City Government Expenditures by Function

Function	2016 ($000)	2016 ($ per capita)	2016 (%)
General Direct Expenditures			
Air Transportation	41,185	195	9.0
Corrections	0	0	0.0
Education	0	0	0.0
Employment Security Administration	0	0	0.0
Financial Administration	3,292	15	0.7
Fire Protection	36,440	173	8.0
General Public Buildings	3,344	15	0.7
Governmental Administration, Other	3,050	14	0.7
Health	954	4	0.2
Highways	58,559	278	12.8
Hospitals	0	0	0.0
Housing and Community Development	19,619	93	4.3
Interest on General Debt	22,753	108	5.0
Judicial and Legal	1,723	8	0.4
Libraries	9,704	46	2.1
Parking	8,644	41	1.9
Parks and Recreation	19,829	94	4.3
Police Protection	62,323	296	13.6
Public Welfare	5,684	27	1.2
Sewerage	40,088	190	8.8
Solid Waste Management	11,445	54	2.5
Veterans' Services	0	0	0.0
Liquor Store	0	0	0.0
Utility	60,110	285	13.2
Employee Retirement	2,827	13	0.6

Source: U.S. Census Bureau, State & Local Government Finances 2016

DEMOGRAPHICS

Population Growth

Area	1990 Census	2000 Census	2010 Census	2017* Estimate	Population Growth (%)	
					1990-2017	2010-2017
City	193,569	198,682	203,433	214,778	11.0	5.6
MSA[1]	416,346	481,394	569,633	623,113	49.7	9.4
U.S.	248,709,873	281,421,906	308,745,538	321,004,407	29.1	4.0

Note: (1) Figures cover the Des Moines-West Des Moines, IA Metropolitan Statistical Area—see Appendix B for areas included; (*) 2013-2017 5-year estimated population
Source: U.S. Census Bureau, 1990 Census, Census 2000, Census 2010, 2013-2017 American Community Survey 5-Year Estimates

Household Size

Area	Persons in Household (%)							Average Household Size
	One	Two	Three	Four	Five	Six	Seven or More	
City	33.1	30.7	15.3	11.2	5.8	2.4	1.6	2.50
MSA[1]	27.6	34.2	15.0	13.6	6.4	2.2	1.0	2.50
U.S.	27.7	33.8	15.7	13.0	6.0	2.3	1.4	2.60

Note: (1) Figures cover the Des Moines-West Des Moines, IA Metropolitan Statistical Area—see Appendix B for areas included
Source: U.S. Census Bureau, 2013-2017 American Community Survey 5-Year Estimates

Race

Area	White Alone[2] (%)	Black Alone[2] (%)	Asian Alone[2] (%)	AIAN[3] Alone[2] (%)	NHOPI[4] Alone[2] (%)	Other Race Alone[2] (%)	Two or More Races (%)
City	76.1	11.0	6.0	0.5	0.1	2.5	3.9
MSA[1]	87.0	5.1	3.9	0.2	0.1	1.2	2.5
U.S.	73.0	12.7	5.4	0.8	0.2	4.8	3.1

Note: (1) Figures cover the Des Moines-West Des Moines, IA Metropolitan Statistical Area—see Appendix B for areas included; (2) Alone is defined as not being in combination with one or more other races; (3) American Indian and Alaska Native; (4) Native Hawaiian and Other Pacific Islander
Source: U.S. Census Bureau, 2013-2017 American Community Survey 5-Year Estimates

Hispanic or Latino Origin

Area	Total (%)	Mexican (%)	Puerto Rican (%)	Cuban (%)	Other (%)
City	13.1	10.2	0.3	0.2	2.4
MSA[1]	7.2	5.4	0.2	0.1	1.4
U.S.	17.6	11.1	1.7	0.7	4.1

Note: Persons of Hispanic or Latino origin can be of any race; (1) Figures cover the Des Moines-West Des Moines, IA Metropolitan Statistical Area—see Appendix B for areas included
Source: U.S. Census Bureau, 2013-2017 American Community Survey 5-Year Estimates

Segregation

Type	Segregation Indices[1]				Percent Change		
	1990	2000	2010	2010 Rank[2]	1990-2000	1990-2010	2000-2010
Black/White	65.2	58.6	51.6	66	-6.7	-13.7	-7.0
Asian/White	40.7	39.2	35.5	76	-1.5	-5.2	-3.8
Hispanic/White	32.6	47.5	46.7	40	14.9	14.1	-0.8

Note: All figures cover the Metropolitan Statistical Area—see Appendix B for areas included; Figures are based on an analysis of 1990, 2000, and 2010 Census Decennial Census tract data by William H. Frey, Brookings Institution and the University of Michigan Social Science Data Analysis Network. In this analysis all racial groups (whites, blacks, and asians) are non-Hispanic members of those races. Hispanics are shown as a separate category; (1) Segregation Indices are Dissimilarity Indices that measure the degree to which the minority group is distributed differently than whites across census tracts. They range from 0 (complete integration) to 100 (complete segregation) where the value indicates the percentage of the minority group that needs to be distributed exactly like whites; (2) Ranges from 1 (most segregated) to 102 (least segregated); n/a not available.
Source: www.CensusScope.org

Ancestry

Area	German	Irish	English	American	Italian	Polish	French[2]	Scottish	Dutch
City	20.3	11.5	6.9	4.5	3.9	1.1	2.1	1.5	2.8
MSA[1]	27.7	13.2	8.7	4.7	3.4	1.4	2.0	1.8	3.4
U.S.	14.1	10.1	7.5	6.6	5.3	2.9	2.5	1.7	1.3

Note: Figures are the percentage of the total population reporting a particular ancestry. The nine most commonly reported ancestries in the U.S. are shown. Figures include multiple ancestries (e.g. if a person reported being Irish and Italian, they were included in both columns); (1) Figures cover the Des Moines-West Des Moines, IA Metropolitan Statistical Area—see Appendix B for areas included; (2) Excludes Basque
Source: U.S. Census Bureau, 2013-2017 American Community Survey 5-Year Estimates

Foreign-Born Population

Area	Any Foreign Country	Asia	Mexico	Europe	Carribean	Central America[2]	South America	Africa	Canada
City	12.3	4.1	3.5	1.0	0.1	1.1	0.1	2.2	0.1
MSA[1]	7.8	2.9	1.7	1.3	0.1	0.6	0.2	1.1	0.1
U.S.	13.4	4.1	3.6	1.5	1.3	1.0	0.9	0.6	0.3

Note: (1) Figures cover the Des Moines-West Des Moines, IA Metropolitan Statistical Area—see Appendix B for areas included; (2) Excludes Mexico.
Source: U.S. Census Bureau, 2013-2017 American Community Survey 5-Year Estimates

Marital Status

Area	Never Married	Now Married[2]	Separated	Widowed	Divorced
City	37.0	41.2	2.0	5.5	14.2
MSA[1]	29.5	52.4	1.3	5.0	11.7
U.S.	33.1	48.2	2.0	5.8	10.9

Note: Figures are percentages and cover the population 15 years of age and older; (1) Figures cover the Des Moines-West Des Moines, IA Metropolitan Statistical Area—see Appendix B for areas included; (2) Excludes separated
Source: U.S. Census Bureau, 2013-2017 American Community Survey 5-Year Estimates

Disability by Age

Area	All Ages	Under 18 Years Old	18 to 64 Years Old	65 Years and Over
City	13.7	5.1	13.0	36.2
MSA[1]	10.5	3.9	9.2	31.3
U.S.	12.6	4.2	10.3	35.5

Note: Figures show percent of the civilian noninstitutionalized population that reported having a disability. Disability status is determined from six types of difficulty: vision, hearing, cognitive, ambulatory, self-care, and independent living. For children under 5 years old, hearing and vision difficulty are used to determine disability status. For children between the ages of 5 and 14, disability status is determined from hearing, vision, cognitive, ambulatory, and self-care difficulties. For people aged 15 years and older, they are considered to have a disability if they have difficulty with any one of the six difficulty types; Note: (1) Figures cover the Des Moines-West Des Moines, IA Metropolitan Statistical Area—see Appendix B for areas included
Source: U.S. Census Bureau, 2013-2017 American Community Survey 5-Year Estimates

Age

Area	Under Age 5	Age 5–19	Age 20–34	Age 35–44	Age 45–54	Age 55–64	Age 65–74	Age 75–84	Age 85+	Median Age
City	7.3	20.1	24.1	13.0	12.2	11.6	6.7	3.3	1.6	33.9
MSA[1]	7.2	20.7	21.1	13.6	13.2	11.6	7.2	3.6	1.7	35.7
U.S.	6.2	19.5	20.7	12.7	13.4	12.7	8.6	4.4	1.9	37.8

Note: (1) Figures cover the Des Moines-West Des Moines, IA Metropolitan Statistical Area—see Appendix B for areas included
Source: U.S. Census Bureau, 2013-2017 American Community Survey 5-Year Estimates

Gender

Area	Males	Females	Males per 100 Females
City	105,981	108,797	97.4
MSA[1]	306,668	316,445	96.9
U.S.	158,018,753	162,985,654	97.0

Note: (1) Figures cover the Des Moines-West Des Moines, IA Metropolitan Statistical Area—see Appendix B for areas included
Source: U.S. Census Bureau, 2013-2017 American Community Survey 5-Year Estimates

Religious Groups by Family

Area	Catholic	Baptist	Non-Den.	Methodist[2]	Lutheran	LDS[3]	Pente-costal	Presby-terian[4]	Muslim[5]	Judaism
MSA[1]	13.6	4.8	3.3	7.0	8.2	1.0	2.4	3.0	0.3	0.3
U.S.	19.1	9.3	4.0	4.0	2.3	2.0	1.9	1.6	0.8	0.7

Note: Figures are the number of adherents as a percentage of the total population; (1) Figures cover the Des Moines-West Des Moines, IA Metropolitan Statistical Area—see Appendix B for areas included; (2) Methodist/Pietist; (3) Latter Day Saints; (4) Reformed; (5) Figures are estimates
Source: Association of Statisticians of American Religious Bodies, 2010 U.S. Religion Census: Religious Congregations & Membership Study

Religious Groups by Tradition

Area	Catholic	Evangelical Protestant	Mainline Protestant	Other Tradition	Black Protestant	Orthodox
MSA[1]	13.6	12.4	16.8	1.9	0.9	0.1
U.S.	19.1	16.2	7.3	4.3	1.6	0.3

Note: Figures are the number of adherents as a percentage of the total population; (1) Figures cover the Des Moines-West Des Moines, IA Metropolitan Statistical Area—see Appendix B for areas included
Source: Association of Statisticians of American Religious Bodies, 2010 U.S. Religion Census: Religious Congregations & Membership Study

ECONOMY

Gross Metropolitan Product

Area	2016	2017	2018	2019	Rank[2]
MSA[1]	52.3	54.4	55.9	58.9	58

Note: Figures are in billions of dollars; (1) Figures cover the Des Moines-West Des Moines, IA Metropolitan Statistical Area—see Appendix B for areas included; (2) Rank is based on 2017 data and ranges from 1 to 381
Source: U.S. Conference of Mayors, U.S. Metro Economies: Economic Growth & Full Employment, June 2018

Economic Growth

Area	2017-2018 (%)	2019-2020 (%)	2021-2022 (%)
MSA[1]	2.3	2.5	2.3

Note: Figures are real gross metropolitan product (GMP) growth rates and represent average annual percent change; (1) Figures cover the Des Moines-West Des Moines, IA Metropolitan Statistical Area—see Appendix B for areas included
Source: U.S. Conference of Mayors, U.S. Metro Economies: Economic Growth & Full Employment, June 2018

Metropolitan Area Exports

Area	2012	2013	2014	2015	2016	2017	Rank[2]
MSA[1]	1,183.2	1,279.4	1,361.8	1,047.8	1,052.2	1,141.2	142

Note: Figures are in millions of dollars; (1) Figures cover the Des Moines-West Des Moines, IA Metropolitan Statistical Area—see Appendix B for areas included; (2) Rank is based on 2017 data and ranges from 1 to 387
Source: U.S. Department of Commerce, International Trade Administration, Office of Trade and Economic Analysis, Industry and Analysis, Exports by Metropolitan Area, extracted March 25, 2019

Building Permits

Area	Single-Family			Multi-Family			Total		
	2016	2017	Pct. Chg.	2016	2017	Pct. Chg.	2016	2017	Pct. Chg.
City	236	173	-26.7	1,209	1,124	-7.0	1,445	1,297	-10.2
MSA[1]	3,760	3,697	-1.7	2,937	2,670	-9.1	6,697	6,367	-4.9
U.S.	750,800	820,000	9.2	455,800	462,000	1.4	1,206,600	1,282,000	6.2

Note: (1) Figures cover the Des Moines-West Des Moines, IA Metropolitan Statistical Area—see Appendix B for areas included; Figures represent new, privately-owned housing units authorized (unadjusted data); All permit data are based on estimates with imputation
Source: U.S. Census Bureau, Manufacturing, Mining, and Construction Statistics, Building Permits, 2016, 2017

Bankruptcy Filings

Area	Business Filings			Nonbusiness Filings		
	2017	2018	% Chg.	2017	2018	% Chg.
Polk County	20	22	10.0	820	848	3.4
U.S.	23,157	22,232	-4.0	765,863	751,186	-1.9

Note: Business filings include Chapter 7, Chapter 11, Chapter 12, and Chapter 13; Nonbusiness filings include Chapter 7, Chapter 11, and Chapter 13
Source: Administrative Office of the U.S. Courts, Business and Nonbusiness Bankruptcy, County Cases Commenced by Chapter of the Bankruptcy Code, During the 12-Month Period Ending December 31, 2017 and Business and Nonbusiness Bankruptcy, County Cases Commenced by Chapter of the Bankruptcy Code, During the 12-Month Period Ending December 31, 2018

Housing Vacancy Rates

Area	Gross Vacancy Rate[2] (%)			Year-Round Vacancy Rate[3] (%)			Rental Vacancy Rate[4] (%)			Homeowner Vacancy Rate[5] (%)		
	2016	2017	2018	2016	2017	2018	2016	2017	2018	2016	2017	2018
MSA[1]	n/a	n/a	n/a	n/a	n/a	n/a	n/a	n/a	n/a	n/a	n/a	n/a
U.S.	12.8	12.7	12.3	9.9	9.9	9.7	6.9	7.2	6.9	1.7	1.6	1.5

Note: (1) Figures cover the Des Moines-West Des Moines, IA Metropolitan Statistical Area—see Appendix B for areas included; (2) The percentage of the total housing inventory that is vacant; (3) The percentage of the housing inventory (excluding seasonal units) that is year-round vacant; (4) The percentage of rental inventory that is vacant for rent; (5) The percentage of homeowner inventory that is vacant for sale; n/a not available
Source: U.S. Census Bureau, Housing Vacancies and Homeownership Annual Statistics: 2016, 2017, 2018

INCOME

Income

Area	Per Capita ($)	Median Household ($)	Average Household ($)
City	26,494	49,999	64,820
MSA[1]	34,537	65,971	86,866
U.S.	31,177	57,652	81,283

Note: (1) Figures cover the Des Moines-West Des Moines, IA Metropolitan Statistical Area—see Appendix B for areas included
Source: U.S. Census Bureau, 2013-2017 American Community Survey 5-Year Estimates

Household Income Distribution

Area	Percent of Households Earning							
	Under $15,000	$15,000 -$24,999	$25,000 -$34,999	$35,000 -$49,999	$50,000 -$74,999	$75,000 -$99,999	$100,000 -$149,999	$150,000 and up
City	13.6	10.9	10.3	15.1	20.8	12.7	10.5	5.9
MSA[1]	8.3	7.8	8.4	12.5	19.4	14.6	16.2	12.8
U.S.	11.6	9.8	9.5	13.0	17.7	12.3	14.1	12.1

Note: (1) Figures cover the Des Moines-West Des Moines, IA Metropolitan Statistical Area—see Appendix B for areas included
Source: U.S. Census Bureau, 2013-2017 American Community Survey 5-Year Estimates

Poverty Rate

Area	All Ages	Under 18 Years Old	18 to 64 Years Old	65 Years and Over
City	18.1	27.5	15.8	11.0
MSA[1]	10.3	13.6	9.5	7.3
U.S.	14.6	20.3	13.7	9.3

Note: Figures are percentage of people whose income during the past 12 months was below the poverty level; (1) Figures cover the Des Moines-West Des Moines, IA Metropolitan Statistical Area—see Appendix B for areas included
Source: U.S. Census Bureau, 2013-2017 American Community Survey 5-Year Estimates

EMPLOYMENT

Labor Force and Employment

Area	Civilian Labor Force			Workers Employed		
	Dec. 2017	Dec. 2018	% Chg.	Dec. 2017	Dec. 2018	% Chg.
City	111,536	115,184	3.3	107,681	111,687	3.7
MSA[1]	344,073	355,975	3.5	335,149	347,559	3.7
U.S.	159,880,000	162,510,000	1.6	153,602,000	156,481,000	1.9

Note: Data is not seasonally adjusted and covers workers 16 years of age and older; (1) Figures cover the Des Moines-West Des Moines, IA Metropolitan Statistical Area—see Appendix B for areas included
Source: Bureau of Labor Statistics, Local Area Unemployment Statistics

Unemployment Rate

Area	2018											
	Jan.	Feb.	Mar.	Apr.	May	Jun.	Jul.	Aug.	Sep.	Oct.	Nov.	Dec.
City	4.4	4.3	3.7	2.9	2.6	2.8	2.7	2.6	2.4	2.3	2.4	3.0
MSA[1]	3.4	3.3	2.9	2.3	2.1	2.4	2.3	2.2	2.1	1.9	1.9	2.4
U.S.	4.5	4.4	4.1	3.7	3.6	4.2	4.1	3.9	3.6	3.5	3.5	3.7

Note: Data is not seasonally adjusted and covers workers 16 years of age and older; (1) Figures cover the Des Moines-West Des Moines, IA Metropolitan Statistical Area—see Appendix B for areas included
Source: Bureau of Labor Statistics, Local Area Unemployment Statistics

Average Wages

Occupation	$/Hr.	Occupation	$/Hr.
Accountants and Auditors	34.30	Maids and Housekeeping Cleaners	11.80
Automotive Mechanics	21.40	Maintenance and Repair Workers	19.60
Bookkeepers	20.80	Marketing Managers	60.80
Carpenters	20.70	Nuclear Medicine Technologists	n/a
Cashiers	10.90	Nurses, Licensed Practical	21.50
Clerks, General Office	18.00	Nurses, Registered	29.90
Clerks, Receptionists/Information	15.30	Nursing Assistants	14.60
Clerks, Shipping/Receiving	18.40	Packers and Packagers, Hand	14.50
Computer Programmers	39.20	Physical Therapists	41.30
Computer Systems Analysts	41.20	Postal Service Mail Carriers	24.60
Computer User Support Specialists	25.00	Real Estate Brokers	25.10
Cooks, Restaurant	13.30	Retail Salespersons	13.40
Dentists	113.40	Sales Reps., Exc. Tech./Scientific	36.00
Electrical Engineers	40.60	Sales Reps., Tech./Scientific	42.50
Electricians	26.30	Secretaries, Exc. Legal/Med./Exec.	18.80
Financial Managers	62.50	Security Guards	14.80
First-Line Supervisors/Managers, Sales	20.40	Surgeons	85.50
Food Preparation Workers	12.00	Teacher Assistants*	12.90
General and Operations Managers	53.90	Teachers, Elementary School*	28.60
Hairdressers/Cosmetologists	16.40	Teachers, Secondary School*	30.50
Internists, General	n/a	Telemarketers	n/a
Janitors and Cleaners	13.50	Truck Drivers, Heavy/Tractor-Trailer	23.60
Landscaping/Groundskeeping Workers	14.60	Truck Drivers, Light/Delivery Svcs.	17.30
Lawyers	59.70	Waiters and Waitresses	12.20

Note: Wage data covers the Des Moines-West Des Moines, IA Metropolitan Statistical Area—see Appendix B for areas included; (*) Hourly wages for elementary/secondary school teachers and teacher assistants were calculated by the editors from annual wage data based on a 40 hour work week; n/a not available.
Source: Bureau of Labor Statistics, Metro Area Occupational Employment & Wage Estimates, May 2018

Employment by Occupation

Occupation Classification	City (%)	MSA[1] (%)	U.S. (%)
Management, Business, Science, and Arts	30.7	40.6	37.4
Natural Resources, Construction, and Maintenance	8.4	7.9	8.9
Production, Transportation, and Material Moving	14.6	10.7	12.2
Sales and Office	25.5	25.1	23.5
Service	20.8	15.7	18.0

Note: Figures cover employed civilians 16 years of age and older; (1) Figures cover the Des Moines-West Des Moines, IA Metropolitan Statistical Area—see Appendix B for areas included
Source: U.S. Census Bureau, 2013-2017 American Community Survey 5-Year Estimates

Employment by Industry

Sector	MSA[1]		U.S.
	Number of Employees	Percent of Total	Percent of Total
Construction, Mining, and Logging	20,800	5.5	5.3
Education and Health Services	54,100	14.4	15.9
Financial Activities	56,300	15.0	5.7
Government	45,700	12.2	15.1
Information	6,900	1.8	1.9
Leisure and Hospitality	34,800	9.3	10.7
Manufacturing	21,100	5.6	8.5
Other Services	12,900	3.4	3.9
Professional and Business Services	51,100	13.6	14.1
Retail Trade	41,600	11.1	10.8
Transportation, Warehousing, and Utilities	11,900	3.2	4.2
Wholesale Trade	18,200	4.8	3.9

Note: Figures are non-farm employment as of December 2018. Figures are not seasonally adjusted and include workers 16 years of age and older; (1) Figures cover the Des Moines-West Des Moines, IA Metropolitan Statistical Area—see Appendix B for areas included
Source: Bureau of Labor Statistics, Current Employment Statistics, Employment, Hours, and Earnings

Occupations with Greatest Projected Employment Growth: 2018 – 2020

Occupation[1]	2018 Employment	2020 Projected Employment	Numeric Employment Change	Percent Employment Change
Combined Food Preparation and Serving Workers, Including Fast Food	36,450	37,630	1,180	3.2
Heavy and Tractor-Trailer Truck Drivers	44,890	46,070	1,180	2.6
Registered Nurses	33,850	34,820	970	2.9
Laborers and Freight, Stock, and Material Movers, Hand	28,350	28,870	520	1.8
Home Health Aides	8,280	8,790	510	6.2
Janitors and Cleaners, Except Maids and Housekeeping Cleaners	26,490	26,940	450	1.7
Waiters and Waitresses	24,260	24,660	400	1.6
Personal Care Aides	9,050	9,440	390	4.3
Slaughterers and Meat Packers	7,780	8,130	350	4.5
Nursing Assistants	21,370	21,710	340	1.6

Note: Projections cover Iowa; (1) Sorted by numeric employment change
Source: www.projectionscentral.com, State Occupational Projections, 2018–2020 Short-Term Projections

Fastest Growing Occupations: 2018 – 2020

Occupation[1]	2018 Employment	2020 Projected Employment	Numeric Employment Change	Percent Employment Change
Wind Turbine Service Technicians	340	390	50	14.7
Information Security Analysts	1,520	1,640	120	7.9
Operations Research Analysts	720	770	50	6.9
Home Health Aides	8,280	8,790	510	6.2
Respiratory Therapists	960	1,010	50	5.2
Nurse Practitioners	1,150	1,210	60	5.2
Woodworking Machine Setters, Operators, and Tenders, Except Sawing	1,420	1,490	70	4.9
Heating, Air Conditioning, and Refrigeration Mechanics and Installers	3,730	3,910	180	4.8
Food Batchmakers	2,690	2,820	130	4.8
Personal Financial Advisors	1,750	1,830	80	4.6

Note: Projections cover Iowa; (1) Sorted by percent employment change and excludes occupations with numeric employment change less than 50
Source: www.projectionscentral.com, State Occupational Projections, 2018–2020 Short-Term Projections

TAXES

State Corporate Income Tax Rates

State	Tax Rate (%)	Income Brackets ($)	Num. of Brackets	Financial Institution Tax Rate (%)[a]	Federal Income Tax Ded.
Iowa	6.0 - 12.0	25,000 - 250,001	4	5.0	Yes (j)

Note: Tax rates as of January 1, 2019; (a) Rates listed are the corporate income tax rate applied to financial institutions or excise taxes based on income. Some states have other taxes based upon the value of deposits or shares; (j) 50% of the federal income tax is deductible.
Source: Federation of Tax Administrators, Range of State Corporate Income Tax Rates, January 1, 2019

State Individual Income Tax Rates

State	Tax Rate (%)	Income Brackets ($)	Personal Exemptions ($)			Standard Ded. ($)	
			Single	Married	Depend.	Single	Married
Iowa (a)	0.33 - 8.53	1,598 - 71,910	40 (c)	80 (c)	40 (c)	2,080	5,120 (a)

Note: Tax rates as of January 1, 2019; Local- and county-level taxes are not included; n/a not applicable; Federal income tax is deductible on state income tax returns; (a) 19 states have statutory provision for automatically adjusting to the rate of inflation the dollar values of the income tax brackets, standard deductions, and/or personal exemptions. Michigan indexes the personal exemption only. Oregon does not index the income brackets for $125,000 and over; (c) The personal exemption takes the form of a tax credit instead of a deduction
Source: Federation of Tax Administrators, State Individual Income Tax Rates, January 1, 2019

Various State Sales and Excise Tax Rates

State	State Sales Tax (%)	Gasoline[1] (¢/gal.)	Cigarette[2] ($/pack)	Spirits[3] ($/gal.)	Wine[4] ($/gal.)	Beer[5] ($/gal.)	Recreational Marijuana (%)
Iowa	6	30.7	1.36	13.07 (g)	1.75 (l)	0.19 (q)	Not legal

Note: All tax rates as of January 1, 2019; (1) The American Petroleum Institute has developed a methodology for determining the average tax rate on a gallon of fuel. Rates may include any of the following: excise taxes, environmental fees, storage tank fees, other fees or taxes, general sales tax, and local taxes. In states where gasoline is subject to the general sales tax, or where the fuel tax is based on the average sale price, the average rate determined by API is sensitive to changes in the price of gasoline. States that fully or partially apply general sales taxes to gasoline: CA, CO, GA, IL, IN, MI, NY; (2) The federal excise tax of $1.0066 per pack and local taxes are not included; (3) Rates are those applicable to off-premise sales of 40% alcohol by volume (a.b.v.) distilled spirits in 750ml containers. Local excise taxes are excluded; (4) Rates are those applicable to off-premise sales of 11% a.b.v. non-carbonated wine in 750ml containers; (5) Rates are those applicable to off-premise sales of 4.7% a.b.v. beer in 12 ounce containers; (g) Control states, where the government controls all sales. Products can be subject to ad valorem mark-up as well as excise taxes; (l) Different rates also applicable to alcohol content, place of production, size of container, place purchased (on- or off-premise or on board airlines) or type of wine (carbonated, vermouth, etc.); (q) Different rates also applicable according to alcohol content, place of production, size of container, or place purchased (on- or off-premise or onboard airlines).
Source: Tax Foundation, 2019 Facts & Figures: How Does Your State Compare?

State Business Tax Climate Index Rankings

State	Overall Rank	Corporate Tax Rank	Individual Income Tax Rank	Sales Tax Rank	Unemployment Insurance Tax Rank	Property Tax Rank
Iowa	45	48	42	19	33	39

Note: The index is a measure of how each state's tax laws affect economic performance. The lower the rank, the more favorable a state's tax system is for business. States without a given tax are given a ranking of 1. The scores/rankings for the District of Columbia do not affect other states. The 2019 index represents the tax climate as of July 1, 2018.
Source: Tax Foundation, State Business Tax Climate Index 2019

COMMERCIAL UTILITIES

Typical Monthly Electric Bills

Area	Commercial Service ($/month)		Industrial Service ($/month)	
	1,500 kWh	40 kW demand 14,000 kWh	1,000 kW demand 200,000 kWh	50,000 kW demand 32,500,000 kWh
City	n/a	n/a	n/a	n/a
Average[1]	203	1,619	25,886	2,540,077

Note: Figures are based on annualized rates; (1) Average based on 187 utilities surveyed; n/a not available
Source: Edison Electric Institute, Typical Bills and Average Rates Report, Summer 2018

TRANSPORTATION

Means of Transportation to Work

Area	Car/Truck/Van		Public Transportation			Bicycle	Walked	Other Means	Worked at Home
	Drove Alone	Car-pooled	Bus	Subway	Railroad				
City	80.6	9.8	2.1	0.0	0.0	0.4	2.9	1.0	3.1
MSA[1]	83.9	8.0	1.1	0.0	0.0	0.2	1.9	0.7	4.2
U.S.	76.4	9.2	2.5	1.9	0.6	0.6	2.7	1.3	4.7

Note: Figures are percentages and cover workers 16 years of age and older; (1) Figures cover the Des Moines-West Des Moines, IA Metropolitan Statistical Area—see Appendix B for areas included
Source: U.S. Census Bureau, 2013-2017 American Community Survey 5-Year Estimates

Travel Time to Work

Area	Less Than 10 Minutes	10 to 19 Minutes	20 to 29 Minutes	30 to 44 Minutes	45 to 59 Minutes	60 to 89 Minutes	90 Minutes or More
City	14.0	43.8	25.7	11.8	2.2	1.4	1.0
MSA[1]	15.4	36.3	27.0	15.5	3.1	1.5	1.2
U.S.	12.7	28.9	20.9	20.5	8.1	6.2	2.7

Note: Note: Figures are percentages and include workers 16 years old and over; (1) Figures cover the Des Moines-West Des Moines, IA Metropolitan Statistical Area—see Appendix B for areas included
Source: U.S. Census Bureau, 2013-2017 American Community Survey 5-Year Estimates

Freeway Travel Time Index

Area	1985	1990	1995	2000	2005	2010	2014
Urban Area Rank[1,2]	n/a	n/a	n/a	n/a	n/a	n/a	n/a
Urban Area Index[1]	n/a	n/a	n/a	n/a	n/a	n/a	n/a
Average Index[3]	1.09	1.11	1.14	1.17	1.20	1.19	1.20

Note: Freeway Travel Time Index—the ratio of travel time in the peak period to the travel time at free-flow conditions. For example, a value of 1.30 indicates a 20-minute free-flow trip takes 26 minutes in the peak (20 minutes x 1.30 = 26 minutes); (1) Data for the Des Moines-West Des Moines, IA urban area was not available; (2) Rank is based on 101 urban areas (#1 = highest travel time index); (3) Average of 101 urban areas
Source: Texas Transportation Institute, 2015 Urban Mobility Scorecard, August 2015

Freeway Commuter Stress Index

Area	1985	1990	1995	2000	2005	2010	2014
Urban Area Rank[1,2]	n/a	n/a	n/a	n/a	n/a	n/a	n/a
Urban Area Index[1]	n/a	n/a	n/a	n/a	n/a	n/a	n/a
Average Index[3]	1.13	1.16	1.19	1.22	1.25	1.24	1.25

Note: The Freeway Commuter Stress Index is the same as the Freeway Travel Time Index (see table above) except that it includes only the travel in the peak directions during the peak periods; the TTI includes travel in all directions during the peak period. Thus, the CSI is more indicative of the work trip experienced by each commuter on a daily basis; (1) Data for the Des Moines-West Des Moines, IA urban area was not available; (2) Rank is based on 101 urban areas (#1 = highest travel time index); (3) Average of 101 urban areas
Source: Texas Transportation Institute, 2015 Urban Mobility Scorecard, August 2015

Public Transportation

Agency Name / Mode of Transportation	Vehicles Operated in Maximum Service[1]	Annual Unlinked Passenger Trips[2] (in thous.)	Annual Passenger Miles[3] (in thous.)
Des Moines Metropolitan Transit Authority (MTA)			
Bus (directly operated)	112	4,267.8	18,635.0
Demand Response (directly operated)	21	106.8	937.9
Demand Response Taxi (purchased transportation)	2	10.4	95.8
Vanpool (directly operated)	94	195.7	7,763.6

Note: (1) The number of revenue vehicles operated by the given mode and type of service to meet the annual maximum service requirement. This is the revenue vehicle count during the peak season of the year; on the week and day that maximum service is provided. Vehicles operated in maximum service (VOMS) exclude atypical days and one-time special events; (2) The number of passengers who boarded public transportation vehicles. Passengers are counted each time they board a vehicle no matter how many vehicles they use to travel from their origin to their destination. (3) The sum of the distances ridden by all passengers during the entire fiscal year.
Source: Federal Transit Administration, National Transit Database, 2017

Air Transportation

Airport Name and Code / Type of Service	Passenger Airlines[1]	Passenger Enplanements	Freight Carriers[2]	Freight (lbs)
Des Moines International (DSM)				
Domestic service (U.S. carriers - 2018)	26	1,346,150	12	30,206,462
International service (U.S. carriers - 2017)	1	12	0	0

Note: (1) Includes all U.S.-based major, minor and commuter airlines that carried at least one passenger during the year; (2) Includes all U.S.-based airlines and freight carriers that transported at least one pound of freight during the year.
Source: Bureau of Transportation Statistics, The Intermodal Transportation Database, Air Carriers: T-100 Domestic Market (U.S. Carriers), 2018; Bureau of Transportation Statistics, The Intermodal Transportation Database, Air Carriers: T-100 International Market (U.S. Carriers), 2017

Other Transportation Statistics

Major Highways:	I-35; I-80
Amtrak Service:	No
Major Waterways/Ports:	None

Source: Amtrak.com; Google Maps

BUSINESSES

Major Business Headquarters

Company Name	Industry	Rankings Fortune[1]	Rankings Forbes[2]
Principal Financial	Insurance: Life, Health (Stock)	210	-

Note: (1) Companies that produce a 10-K are ranked 1 to 500 based on 2017 revenue; (2) All private companies with at least $2 billion in annual revenue through the end of their most current fiscal year are ranked 1 to 229; companies listed are headquartered in the city; dashes indicate no ranking
Source: Fortune, "Fortune 500," June 2018; Forbes, "America's Largest Private Companies," 2018 Rankings

Minority Business Opportunity

Des Moines is home to one company which is on the *Black Enterprise* Industrial/Service list (100 largest companies based on gross sales): **Keystone Electrical Manufacturing Co.** (#78). Criteria: operational in previous calendar year; at least 51% black-owned and manufactures/owns the product it sells or provides industrial or consumer services. Brokerages, real estate firms and firms that provide professional services are not eligible. *Black Enterprise, B.E. 100s, 2018*

Minority- and Women-Owned Businesses

Group	All Firms Firms	All Firms Sales ($000)	Firms with Paid Employees Firms	Firms with Paid Employees Sales ($000)	Firms with Paid Employees Employees	Firms with Paid Employees Payroll ($000)
AIAN[1]	107	(s)	23	(s)	100 - 249	(s)
Asian	857	156,781	99	125,716	556	17,991
Black	1,197	82,259	22	60,836	920	14,023
Hispanic	931	70,008	65	39,733	450	8,919
NHOPI[2]	n/a	n/a	n/a	n/a	n/a	n/a
Women	5,681	708,100	428	597,154	4,000	121,008
All Firms	16,543	40,200,054	3,725	39,655,646	115,109	5,550,235

Note: Figures cover firms located in the city; minority- and women-owned business are defined as firms in which the corresponding group own 51% or more of the stock or equity of the company; (1) American Indian and Alaska Native; (2) Native Hawaiian and Other Pacific Islander; (s) estimates are suppressed when publication standards are not met; n/a not available
Source: U.S. Census Bureau, 2012 Economic Census, Survey of Business Owners

HOTELS & CONVENTION CENTERS

Hotels, Motels and Vacation Rentals

Area	5 Star Num.	5 Star Pct.[3]	4 Star Num.	4 Star Pct.[3]	3 Star Num.	3 Star Pct.[3]	2 Star Num.	2 Star Pct.[3]	1 Star Num.	1 Star Pct.[3]	Not Rated Num.	Not Rated Pct.[3]
City[1]	0	0.0	1	0.6	53	29.6	77	43.0	2	1.1	46	25.7
Total[2]	286	0.4	5,236	7.1	16,715	22.6	10,259	13.9	293	0.4	41,056	55.6

Note: (1) Figures cover Des Moines and vicinity; (2) Figures cover all 100 cities in this book; (3) Percentage of hotels which have a given star rating; Star ratings are determined by expedia.com and offer an indication of the general quality of a particular hotel.
Source: www.expedia.com, April 3, 2019

Major Convention Centers

Name	Overall Space (sq. ft.)	Exhibit Space (sq. ft.)	Meeting Space (sq. ft.)	Meeting Rooms
The Iowa Events Center	234,505	n/a	n/a	n/a

Note: Table includes convention centers located in the Des Moines-West Des Moines, IA metro area; n/a not available
Source: Original research

Living Environment

COST OF LIVING

Cost of Living Index

Composite Index	Groceries	Housing	Utilities	Trans-portation	Health Care	Misc. Goods/ Services
90.6	95.9	82.1	89.5	102.2	98.5	92.0

Note: The Cost of Living Index measures regional differences in the cost of consumer goods and services, excluding taxes and non-consumer expenditures, for professional and managerial households in the top income quintile. It is based on more than 50,000 prices covering almost 60 different items for which prices are collected three times a year by chambers of commerce, economic development organizations or university applied economic centers in each participating urban area. The numbers shown should be read as a percentage above or below the national average of 100. For example, a value of 115.4 in the groceries column indicates that grocery prices are 15.4% higher than the national average. Small differences in the index numbers should not be interpreted as significant; Figures cover the Des Moines IA urban area.
Source: The Council for Community and Economic Research, ACCRA Cost of Living Index, 2018

Grocery Prices

Area[1]	T-Bone Steak ($/pound)	Frying Chicken ($/pound)	Whole Milk ($/half gal.)	Eggs ($/dozen)	Orange Juice ($/64 oz.)	Coffee ($/11.5 oz.)
City[2]	10.79	1.85	1.89	2.22	3.06	4.07
Avg.	11.35	1.42	1.94	1.81	3.52	4.35
Min.	7.45	0.92	0.80	0.75	2.72	3.06
Max.	15.05	2.76	4.18	4.00	5.36	8.20

*Note: (1) Values for the local area are compared with the average, minimum and maximum values for all 291 areas in the Cost of Living Index; (2) Figures cover the Des Moines IA urban area; **T-Bone Steak** (price per pound); **Frying Chicken** (price per pound, whole fryer); **Whole Milk** (half gallon carton); **Eggs** (price per dozen, Grade A, large); **Orange Juice** (64 oz. Tropicana or Florida Natural); **Coffee** (11.5 oz. can, vacuum-packed, Maxwell House, Hills Bros, or Folgers).*
Source: The Council for Community and Economic Research, ACCRA Cost of Living Index, 2018

Housing and Utility Costs

Area[1]	New Home Price ($)	Apartment Rent ($/month)	All Electric ($/month)	Part Electric ($/month)	Other Energy ($/month)	Telephone ($/month)
City[2]	312,876	673	-	79.68	59.16	175.10
Avg.	347,000	1,087	165.93	100.16	67.73	178.70
Min.	200,468	500	93.58	25.64	26.78	163.10
Max.	1,901,222	4,888	388.65	246.86	332.81	197.70

*Note: (1) Values for the local area are compared with the average, minimum and maximum values for all 291 areas in the Cost of Living Index; (2) Figures cover the Des Moines IA urban area; **New Home Price** (2,400 sf living area, 8,000 sf lot, in urban area with full utilities); **Apartment Rent** (950 sf 2 bedroom/1.5 or 2 bath, unfurnished, excluding all utilities except water); **All Electric** (average monthly cost for an all-electric home); **Part Electric** (average monthly cost for a part-electric home); **Other Energy** (average monthly cost for natural gas, fuel oil, coal, wood, and any other forms of energy except electricity); **Telephone** (price includes the base monthly rate plus taxes and fees for three lines of mobile phone service).*
Source: The Council for Community and Economic Research, ACCRA Cost of Living Index, 2018

Health Care, Transportation, and Other Costs

Area[1]	Doctor ($/visit)	Dentist ($/visit)	Optometrist ($/visit)	Gasoline ($/gallon)	Beauty Salon ($/visit)	Men's Shirt ($)
City[2]	128.15	82.71	100.87	2.61	32.24	21.60
Avg.	110.71	95.11	103.74	2.61	37.48	32.03
Min.	33.60	62.55	54.63	1.89	17.00	11.44
Max.	195.97	153.93	225.79	3.59	71.88	58.64

*Note: (1) Values for the local area are compared with the average, minimum and maximum values for all 291 areas in the Cost of Living Index; (2) Figures cover the Des Moines IA urban area; **Doctor** (general practitioners routine exam of an established patient); **Dentist** (adult teeth cleaning and periodic oral examination); **Optometrist** (full vision eye exam for established adult patient); **Gasoline** (one gallon regular unleaded, national brand, including all taxes, cash price at self-service pump if available); **Beauty Salon** (woman's shampoo, trim, and blow-dry); **Men's Shirt** (cotton/polyester dress shirt, pinpoint weave, long sleeves).*
Source: The Council for Community and Economic Research, ACCRA Cost of Living Index, 2018

HOUSING

House Price Index (HPI)

Area	National Ranking[2]	Quarterly Change (%)	One-Year Change (%)	Five-Year Change (%)
MSA[1]	160	0.68	5.16	25.14
U.S.[3]	—	1.12	5.73	32.81

Note: The HPI is a weighted repeat sales index. It measures average price changes in repeat sales or refinancings on the same properties. This information is obtained by reviewing repeat mortgage transactions on single-family properties whose mortgages have been purchased or securitized by Fannie Mae or Freddie Mac in January 1975; (1) Figures cover the Des Moines-West Des Moines, IA Metropolitan Statistical Area—see Appendix B for areas included; (2) Rankings are based on annual percentage change for all metro areas containing at least 15,000 transactions over the last 10 years and ranges from 1 to 245; (3) figures based on a weighted average of Census Division estimates using a seasonally adjusted, purchase-only index; all figures are for the period ending December 31, 2018
Source: Federal Housing Finance Agency, House Price Index, February 26, 2019

Median Single-Family Home Prices

Area	2016	2017	2018[p]	Percent Change 2017 to 2018
MSA[1]	185.2	194.0	204.8	5.6
U.S. Average	235.5	248.8	261.6	5.1

Note: Figures are median sales prices of existing single-family homes in thousands of dollars; (p) preliminary; (1) Figures cover the Des Moines-West Des Moines, IA Metropolitan Statistical Area—see Appendix B for areas included
Source: National Association of Realtors, Median Sales Price of Existing Single-Family Homes for Metropolitan Areas, 4th Quarter 2018

Qualifying Income Based on Median Sales Price of Existing Single-Family Homes

Area	With 5% Down ($)	With 10% Down ($)	With 20% Down ($)
MSA[1]	48,217	45,679	40,604
U.S. Average	62,954	59,640	53,013

Note: Figures are preliminary; Qualifying income is based on a mortgage rate of 4.9%. Monthly principal and interest payment is limited to 25% of income; (1) Figures cover the Des Moines-West Des Moines, IA Metropolitan Statistical Area—see Appendix B for areas included
Source: National Association of Realtors, Qualifying Income Based on Median Sales Price of Existing Single-Family Homes for Metropolitan Areas, 4th Quarter 2018

Median Apartment Condo-Coop Home Prices

Area	2016	2017	2018[p]	Percent Change 2017 to 2018
MSA[1]	n/a	n/a	n/a	n/a
U.S. Average	220.7	234.3	241.0	2.9

Note: Figures are median sales prices of existing apartment condo-coop homes in thousands of dollars; (p) preliminary; n/a not available; (1) Figures cover the Des Moines-West Des Moines, IA Metropolitan Statistical Area—see Appendix B for areas included
Source: National Association of Realtors, Median Sales Price of Existing Apartment Condo-Coop Homes for Metropolitan Areas, 4th Quarter 2018

Home Value Distribution

Area	Under $50,000	$50,000 -$99,999	$100,000 -$149,999	$150,000 -$199,999	$200,000 -$299,999	$300,000 -$499,999	$500,000 -$999,999	$1,000,000 or more
City	6.9	26.1	34.0	19.1	8.6	3.9	1.4	0.1
MSA[1]	5.2	13.4	21.7	21.2	22.5	12.0	3.5	0.4
U.S.	8.3	13.9	14.7	14.6	18.7	17.3	9.7	2.7

Note: Figures are percentages and cover owner-occupied housing units; (1) Figures cover the Des Moines-West Des Moines, IA Metropolitan Statistical Area—see Appendix B for areas included
Source: U.S. Census Bureau, 2013-2017 American Community Survey 5-Year Estimates

Homeownership Rate

Area	2010 (%)	2011 (%)	2012 (%)	2013 (%)	2014 (%)	2015 (%)	2016 (%)	2017 (%)	2018 (%)
MSA[1]	n/a	n/a	n/a	n/a	n/a	n/a	n/a	n/a	n/a
U.S.	66.9	66.1	65.4	65.1	64.5	63.7	63.4	63.9	64.4

Note: (1) Figures cover the Des Moines-West Des Moines, IA Metropolitan Statistical Area—see Appendix B for areas included; n/a not available
Source: U.S. Census Bureau, Housing Vacancies and Homeownership Annual Statistics: 2010-2018

Year Housing Structure Built

Area	2010 or Later	2000 -2009	1990 -1999	1980 -1989	1970 -1979	1960 -1969	1950 -1959	1940 -1949	Before 1940	Median Year
City	2.1	7.7	7.0	6.3	12.8	10.6	16.7	8.5	28.3	1958
MSA[1]	7.1	18.0	13.5	8.7	13.8	9.0	9.7	4.5	15.7	1978
U.S.	3.2	14.5	14.0	13.6	15.5	10.8	10.5	5.1	12.9	1977

Note: Figures are percentages except for Median Year; Note: (1) Figures cover the Des Moines-West Des Moines, IA Metropolitan Statistical Area—see Appendix B for areas included
Source: U.S. Census Bureau, 2013-2017 American Community Survey 5-Year Estimates

Gross Monthly Rent

Area	Under $500	$500 -$999	$1,000 -$1,499	$1,500 -$1,999	$2,000 -$2,499	$2,500 -$2,999	$3,000 and up	Median ($)
City	11.5	64.3	20.0	3.2	0.7	0.2	0.1	797
MSA[1]	8.8	58.4	26.0	4.6	1.1	0.5	0.5	857
U.S.	10.5	41.1	28.7	11.7	4.5	1.8	1.7	982

Note: Figures are percentages except for Median; Gross rent is the contract rent plus the estimated average monthly cost of utilities (electricity, gas, and water and sewer) and fuels (oil, coal, kerosene, wood, etc.) if these are paid by the renter (or paid for the renter by someone else); (1) Figures cover the Des Moines-West Des Moines, IA Metropolitan Statistical Area—see Appendix B for areas included
Source: U.S. Census Bureau, 2013-2017 American Community Survey 5-Year Estimates

HEALTH

Health Risk Factors

Category	MSA[1] (%)	U.S. (%)
Adults aged 18–64 who have any kind of health care coverage	91.6	87.3
Adults who reported being in good or better health	86.3	82.4
Adults who have been told they have high blood cholesterol	33.4	33.0
Adults who have been told they have high blood pressure	29.4	32.3
Adults who are current smokers	14.4	17.1
Adults who currently use E-cigarettes	5.5	4.6
Adults who currently use chewing tobacco, snuff, or snus	4.0	4.0
Adults who are heavy drinkers[2]	7.2	6.3
Adults who are binge drinkers[3]	21.5	17.4
Adults who are overweight (BMI 25.0 - 29.9)	34.4	35.3
Adults who are obese (BMI 30.0 - 99.8)	34.4	31.3
Adults who participated in any physical activities in the past month	79.4	74.4
Adults who always or nearly always wears a seat belt	95.6	94.3

Note: (1) Figures cover the Des Moines-West Des Moines, IA Metropolitan Statistical Area—see Appendix B for areas included; (2) Heavy drinkers are classified as adult men having more than 14 drinks per week and adult women having more than 7 drinks per week; (3) Binge drinkers are classified as males having five or more drinks on one occasion or females having four or more drinks on one occasion
Source: Centers for Disease Control and Prevention, Behavioral Risk Factor Surveillance System, SMART: Selected Metropolitan Area Risk Trends, 2017

Acute and Chronic Health Conditions

Category	MSA[1] (%)	U.S. (%)
Adults who have ever been told they had a heart attack	3.4	4.2
Adults who have ever been told they have angina or coronary heart disease	2.9	3.9
Adults who have ever been told they had a stroke	2.9	3.0
Adults who have ever been told they have asthma	12.9	14.2
Adults who have ever been told they have arthritis	22.8	24.9
Adults who have ever been told they have diabetes[2]	8.4	10.5
Adults who have ever been told they had skin cancer	6.3	6.2
Adults who have ever been told they had any other types of cancer	5.0	7.1
Adults who have ever been told they have COPD	5.6	6.5
Adults who have ever been told they have kidney disease	1.9	3.0
Adults who have ever been told they have a form of depression	20.1	20.5

Note: (1) Figures cover the Des Moines-West Des Moines, IA Metropolitan Statistical Area—see Appendix B for areas included; (2) Figures do not include pregnancy-related, borderline, or pre-diabetes
Source: Centers for Disease Control and Prevention, Behavioral Risk Factor Surveillance System, SMART: Selected Metropolitan Area Risk Trends, 2017

Health Screening and Vaccination Rates

Category	MSA[1] (%)	U.S. (%)
Adults aged 65+ who have had flu shot within the past year	70.6	60.7
Adults aged 65+ who have ever had a pneumonia vaccination	83.0	75.4
Adults who have ever been tested for HIV	34.1	36.1
Adults who have ever had the shingles or zoster vaccine?	38.4	28.9
Adults who have had their blood cholesterol checked within the last five years	85.6	85.9

Note: n/a not available; (1) Figures cover the Des Moines-West Des Moines, IA Metropolitan Statistical Area—see Appendix B for areas included.
Source: Centers for Disease Control and Prevention, Behaviorial Risk Factor Surveillance System, SMART: Selected Metropolitan Area Risk Trends, 2017

Disability Status

Category	MSA[1] (%)	U.S. (%)
Adults who reported being deaf	5.4	6.7
Are you blind or have serious difficulty seeing, even when wearing glasses?	3.7	4.5
Are you limited in any way in any of your usual activities due of arthritis?	10.5	12.9
Do you have difficulty doing errands alone?	6.2	6.8
Do you have difficulty dressing or bathing?	2.5	3.6
Do you have serious difficulty concentrating/remembering/making decisions?	9.1	10.7
Do you have serious difficulty walking or climbing stairs?	10.1	13.6

Note: (1) Figures cover the Des Moines-West Des Moines, IA Metropolitan Statistical Area—see Appendix B for areas included.
Source: Centers for Disease Control and Prevention, Behaviorial Risk Factor Surveillance System, SMART: Selected Metropolitan Area Risk Trends, 2017

Mortality Rates for the Top 10 Causes of Death in the U.S.

ICD-10[a] Sub-Chapter	ICD-10[a] Code	Age-Adjusted Mortality Rate[1] per 100,000 population	
		County[2]	U.S.
Malignant neoplasms	C00-C97	164.1	155.5
Ischaemic heart diseases	I20-I25	93.1	94.8
Other forms of heart disease	I30-I51	44.3	52.9
Chronic lower respiratory diseases	J40-J47	54.7	41.0
Cerebrovascular diseases	I60-I69	33.3	37.5
Other degenerative diseases of the nervous system	G30-G31	41.8	35.0
Other external causes of accidental injury	W00-X59	38.4	33.7
Organic, including symptomatic, mental disorders	F01-F09	33.2	31.0
Hypertensive diseases	I10-I15	19.4	21.9
Diabetes mellitus	E10-E14	23.0	21.2

Note: (a) ICD-10 = International Classification of Diseases 10th Revision; (1) Mortality rates are a three year average covering 2015-2017; (2) Figures cover Polk County.
Source: Centers for Disease Control and Prevention, National Center for Health Statistics. Underlying Cause of Death 1999-2017 on CDC WONDER Online Database

Mortality Rates for Selected Causes of Death

ICD-10[a] Sub-Chapter	ICD-10[a] Code	Age-Adjusted Mortality Rate[1] per 100,000 population	
		County[2]	U.S.
Assault	X85-Y09	5.1	5.9
Diseases of the liver	K70-K76	14.4	14.1
Human immunodeficiency virus (HIV) disease	B20-B24	Unreliable	1.8
Influenza and pneumonia	J09-J18	14.3	14.3
Intentional self-harm	X60-X84	15.4	13.6
Malnutrition	E40-E46	3.6	1.6
Obesity and other hyperalimentation	E65-E68	2.7	2.1
Renal failure	N17-N19	8.3	13.0
Transport accidents	V01-V99	8.2	12.4
Viral hepatitis	B15-B19	Unreliable	1.6

Note: (a) ICD-10 = International Classification of Diseases 10th Revision; (1) Mortality rates are a three year average covering 2015-2017; (2) Figures cover Polk County; Data are suppressed when the data meet the criteria for confidentiality constraints; Mortality rates are flagged as unreliable when the rate would be calculated with a numerator of 20 or less.
Source: Centers for Disease Control and Prevention, National Center for Health Statistics. Underlying Cause of Death 1999-2017 on CDC WONDER Online Database

Health Insurance Coverage

Area	With Health Insurance	With Private Health Insurance	With Public Health Insurance	Without Health Insurance	Population Under Age 18 Without Health Insurance
City	91.8	63.4	40.0	8.2	3.8
MSA[1]	94.8	77.1	29.7	5.2	2.6
U.S.	89.5	67.2	33.8	10.5	5.7

Note: Figures are percentages that cover the civilian noninstitutionalized population; (1) Figures cover the Des Moines-West Des Moines, IA Metropolitan Statistical Area—see Appendix B for areas included
Source: U.S. Census Bureau, 2013-2017 American Community Survey 5-Year Estimates

Number of Medical Professionals

Area	MDs[3]	DOs[3,4]	Dentists	Podiatrists	Chiropractors	Optometrists
County[1] (number)	955	525	336	44	246	106
County[1] (rate[2])	201.2	110.6	69.7	9.1	51.1	22.0
U.S. (rate[2])	279.3	23.0	68.4	6.0	27.1	16.2

Note: Data as of 2017 unless noted; (1) Data covers Polk County; (2) Rate per 100,000 population; (3) Data as of 2016 and includes all active, non-federal physicians; (4) Doctor of Osteopathic Medicine
Source: U.S. Department of Health and Human Services, Health Resources and Services Administration, Bureau of Health Professions, Area Resource File (ARF) 2017-2018

EDUCATION

Public School District Statistics

District Name	Schls	Pupils	Pupil/ Teacher Ratio	Minority Pupils[1] (%)	Free Lunch Eligible[2] (%)	IEP[3] (%)
Des Moines Independent CSD	61	34,656	14.3	59.2	61.0	16.2

Note: Table includes school districts with 2,000 or more students; (1) Percentage of students that are not non-Hispanic white; (2) Percentage of students that are eligible for the free lunch program; (3) Percentage of students that have an Individualized Education Program.
Source: U.S. Department of Education, National Center for Education Statistics, Common Core of Data, Local Education Agency (School District) Universe Survey: School Year 2016-2017; U.S. Department of Education, National Center for Education Statistics, Common Core of Data, Public Elementary/Secondary School Universe Survey: School Year 2016-2017

Highest Level of Education

Area	Less than H.S.	H.S. Diploma	Some College, No Deg.	Associate Degree	Bachelor's Degree	Master's Degree	Prof. School Degree	Doctorate Degree
City	13.6	30.5	21.4	9.2	17.6	5.2	1.6	0.8
MSA[1]	7.6	25.3	20.8	10.2	25.2	7.6	2.3	1.0
U.S.	12.7	27.3	20.8	8.3	19.1	8.4	2.0	1.4

Note: Figures cover persons age 25 and over; (1) Figures cover the Des Moines-West Des Moines, IA Metropolitan Statistical Area—see Appendix B for areas included
Source: U.S. Census Bureau, 2013-2017 American Community Survey 5-Year Estimates

Educational Attainment by Race

Area	High School Graduate or Higher (%)					Bachelor's Degree or Higher (%)				
	Total	White	Black	Asian	Hisp.[2]	Total	White	Black	Asian	Hisp.[2]
City	86.4	89.3	82.9	63.6	57.1	25.2	27.6	13.6	18.9	8.5
MSA[1]	92.4	93.8	85.0	77.5	61.3	36.1	37.3	18.9	40.7	13.2
U.S.	87.3	89.3	84.9	86.5	66.7	30.9	32.2	20.6	52.7	15.2

Note: Figures shown cover persons 25 years old and over; (1) Figures cover the Des Moines-West Des Moines, IA Metropolitan Statistical Area—see Appendix B for areas included; (2) People of Hispanic origin can be of any race
Source: U.S. Census Bureau, 2013-2017 American Community Survey 5-Year Estimates

School Enrollment by Grade and Control

Area	Preschool (%)		Kindergarten (%)		Grades 1 - 4 (%)		Grades 5 - 8 (%)		Grades 9 - 12 (%)	
	Public	Private	Public	Private	Public	Private	Public	Private	Public	Private
City	77.7	22.3	91.0	9.0	89.0	11.0	89.6	10.4	90.4	9.6
MSA[1]	64.7	35.3	89.6	10.4	90.9	9.1	90.5	9.5	91.1	8.9
U.S.	58.8	41.2	87.7	12.3	89.7	10.3	89.6	10.4	90.3	9.7

Note: Figures shown cover persons 3 years old and over; (1) Figures cover the Des Moines-West Des Moines, IA Metropolitan Statistical Area—see Appendix B for areas included
Source: U.S. Census Bureau, 2013-2017 American Community Survey 5-Year Estimates

Average Salaries of Public School Classroom Teachers

Area	2016		2017		Change from 2016 to 2017	
	Dollars	Rank[1]	Dollars	Rank[1]	Percent	Rank[2]
Iowa	54,386	22	55,647	22	2.3	17
U.S. Average	58,479	–	59,660	–	2.0	–

Note: (1) Rank ranges from 1 to 51 where 1 indicates highest salary; (2) Rank ranges from 1 to 51 where 1 indicates highest percent change.
Source: National Education Association, Rankings & Estimates: Rankings of the States 2017 and Estimates of School Statistics 2018

Higher Education

Four-Year Colleges			Two-Year Colleges			Medical Schools[1]	Law Schools[2]	Voc/ Tech[3]
Public	Private Non-profit	Private For-profit	Public	Private Non-profit	Private For-profit			
0	4	0	0	1	3	1	1	0

Note: Figures cover institutions located within the city limits and include main campuses only; (1) includes schools accredited by the Liaison Committee on Medical Education and the American Osteopathic Association's Commission on Osteopathic College Accreditation; (2) includes ABA-accredited schools, schools with provisional ABA accreditation, and state accredited schools; (3) includes all schools with programs that are less than 2 years.
Source: National Center for Education Statistics, Integrated Postsecondary Education System (IPEDS), 2017-18; Wikipedia, List of Medical Schools in the United States, accessed April 3, 2019; Wikipedia, List of Law Schools in the United States, accessed April 3, 2019

According to *U.S. News & World Report*, the Des Moines-West Des Moines, IA metro area is home to one of the best liberal arts colleges in the U.S.: **Simpson College** (#135 tie). The indicators used to capture academic quality fall into a number of categories: assessment by administrators at peer institutions; retention of students; faculty resources; student selectivity; financial resources; alumni giving; high school counselor ratings of colleges; and graduation rate. *U.S. News & World Report, "America's Best Colleges 2019"*

PRESIDENTIAL ELECTION

2016 Presidential Election Results

Area	Clinton	Trump	Johnson	Stein	Other
Polk County	51.7	40.4	4.3	0.8	2.8
U.S.	48.0	45.9	3.3	1.1	1.7

Note: Results are percentages and may not add to 100% due to rounding
Source: Dave Leip's Atlas of U.S. Presidential Elections

EMPLOYERS

Major Employers

Company Name	Industry
Bridgestone Americas Tire Operations	Global distribution center for tires
DuPont Pioneer	Crop inputs for worldwide agribusiness
Emerson Process Management Fisher Div	Control valves & systems, divisional headquarters
Grinnell Mutual Reinsurance Company	Reinsurance
Hy-Vee Food Stores	Retail grocery & drugstore chain
JBS USA	Pork processing & packaging
John Deere companies	Agricultural machinery, consumer financial services
Lennox Manufacturing	Heating & air conditioners
Mercer	Insurance
Mercy Medical Center	Healthcare
Meredith Corporation	Magazine, book publishing, tv, integrated marketing
Nationwide	Insurance
Principal Financial Group	Financial services
United Parcel Service	Logistics, distribution, transportation, freight
UnityPoint Health	Healthcare
Vermeer Manufacturing Company	Manufacturing
Wellmark	Health insurance
Wells Fargo	Financial services & home mortgage

Note: Companies shown are located within the Des Moines-West Des Moines, IA Metropolitan Statistical Area.
Source: Hoovers.com; Wikipedia

Best Companies to Work For

Principal, headquartered in Des Moines, is among the "100 Best Companies for Working Mothers." Criteria: paid time off and leaves; workforce profile; benefits; women's issues and advancement; flexible work; company culture and work life programs. *Working Mother, "100 Best Companies 2018"*

Principal Financial Group, headquartered in Des Moines, is among the "100 Best Places to Work in IT." To qualify, companies had to be U.S.-based organizations or be non-U.S.- based employers that met the following criteria: have a minimum of 300 total employees at a U.S. headquarters and a minimum of 30 IT employees in the U.S., with at least 50% of their IT employees based in the U.S. The best places to work were selected based on compensation, benefits, work/life balance, employee morale, and satisfaction with training and development programs. In addition, *Computerworld* looked at retention efforts, programs for recognizing and rewarding outstanding performances, and benefits such as flextime, elder care and child care, and reimbursement for college tuition and the cost of pursuing technology certifications. *Computerworld, "100 Best Places to Work in IT 2018"*

Principal, headquartered in Des Moines, is among the "Top Companies for Executive Women." The 2019 National Association for Female Executives (NAFE) Top Companies for Executive Women application included more than 200 questions on female representation at all levels, but especially the corporate officer and profit-and-loss leadership ranks. The application tracked how many employees have access to programs and policies that promote the advancement of women, and how many employees take advantage of them. The application also examined how companies train managers to help women advance, and how managers are held accountable for the advancement of female employees they oversee. *National Association for Female Executives, "2019 NAFE Top 70 Companies for Executive Women"*

PUBLIC SAFETY

Crime Rate

Area	All Crimes	Violent Crimes				Property Crimes		
		Murder	Rape[3]	Robbery	Aggrav. Assault	Burglary	Larceny-Theft	Motor Vehicle Theft
City	5,083.4	12.9	33.6	167.5	456.1	1,099.1	2,734.3	579.9
Suburbs[1]	n/a	n/a	n/a	n/a	n/a	n/a	n/a	n/a
Metro[2]	n/a	n/a	n/a	n/a	n/a	n/a	n/a	n/a
U.S.	2,756.1	5.3	41.7	98.0	248.9	430.4	1,694.4	237.4

Note: Figures are crimes per 100,000 population; (1) All areas within the metro area that are located outside the city limits; (2) Figures cover the Des Moines-West Des Moines, IA Metropolitan Statistical Area—see Appendix B for areas included; n/a not available; (3) The city and U.S. figures shown were reported using the revised Uniform Crime Reporting (UCR) definition of rape. The suburban and metro area figures shown are an aggregate total of the data submitted using both the revised and legacy UCR definitions.
Source: FBI Uniform Crime Reports, 2017

Hate Crimes

Area	Number of Quarters Reported	Number of Incidents per Bias Motivation					
		Race/Ethnicity/ Ancestry	Religion	Sexual Orientation	Disability	Gender	Gender Identity
City	4	0	0	0	0	0	0
U.S.	4	4,131	1,564	1,130	116	46	119

Source: Federal Bureau of Investigation, Hate Crime Statistics 2017

Identity Theft Consumer Reports

Area	Reports	Reports per 100,000 Population	Rank[2]
MSA[1]	457	72	257
U.S.	444,602	135	-

Note: (1) Figures cover the Des Moines-West Des Moines, IA Metropolitan Statistical Area—see Appendix B for areas included; (2) Rank ranges from 1 to 389 where 1 indicates greatest number of identity theft reports per 100,000 population
Source: Federal Trade Commission, Consumer Sentinel Network Data Book for January–December 2018

Fraud and Other Consumer Reports

Area	Reports	Reports per 100,000 Population	Rank[2]
MSA[1]	3,213	506	166
U.S.	2,552,917	776	-

Note: (1) Figures cover the Des Moines-West Des Moines, IA Metropolitan Statistical Area—see Appendix B for areas included; (2) Rank ranges from 1 to 389 where 1 indicates greatest number of fraud and other consumer reports per 100,000 population
Source: Federal Trade Commission, Consumer Sentinel Network Data Book for January–December 2018

Professional Sports Teams

Team Name	League	Year Established
No teams are located in the metro area		

Source: Wikipedia, Major Professional Sports Teams of the United States and Canada, April 5, 2019

Average and Extreme Temperatures

Temperature	Jan	Feb	Mar	Apr	May	Jun	Jul	Aug	Sep	Oct	Nov	Dec	Yr.
Extreme High (°F)	65	70	91	93	98	103	105	108	99	95	76	69	108
Average High (°F)	29	34	45	61	72	82	86	84	76	65	48	33	60
Average Temp. (°F)	20	25	36	51	62	72	76	74	65	54	39	25	50
Average Low (°F)	11	16	27	40	51	61	66	64	54	43	29	17	40
Extreme Low (°F)	-24	-20	-22	9	28	42	47	40	28	14	-3	-22	-24

Note: Figures cover the years 1945-1990
Source: National Climatic Data Center, International Station Meteorological Climate Summary, 9/96

Average Precipitation/Snowfall/Humidity

Precip./Humidity	Jan	Feb	Mar	Apr	May	Jun	Jul	Aug	Sep	Oct	Nov	Dec	Yr.
Avg. Precip. (in.)	1.1	1.1	2.3	3.1	3.8	4.4	3.5	3.9	3.1	2.4	1.7	1.2	31.8
Avg. Snowfall (in.)	8	7	7	2	Tr	0	0	0	Tr	Tr	3	7	33
Avg. Rel. Hum. 6am (%)	77	79	79	78	78	81	83	86	85	80	79	80	80
Avg. Rel. Hum. 3pm (%)	65	63	57	50	51	52	52	54	52	50	58	66	56

Note: Figures cover the years 1945-1990; Tr = Trace amounts (<0.05 in. of rain; <0.5 in. of snow)
Source: National Climatic Data Center, International Station Meteorological Climate Summary, 9/96

Weather Conditions

Temperature			Daytime Sky			Precipitation		
5°F & below	32°F & below	90°F & above	Clear	Partly cloudy	Cloudy	0.01 inch or more precip.	0.1 inch or more snow/ice	Thunder-storms
25	137	26	99	128	138	106	25	46

Note: Figures are average number of days per year and cover the years 1945-1990
Source: National Climatic Data Center, International Station Meteorological Climate Summary, 9/96

Superfund Sites

The Des Moines-West Des Moines, IA metro area is home to two sites on the EPA's Superfund National Priorities List: **Des Moines Tce** (final); **Railroad Avenue Groundwater Contamination** (final). There are a total of 1,390 Superfund sites with a status of proposed or final on the list in the U.S. *U.S. Environmental Protection Agency, National Priorities List, April 5, 2019*

AIR & WATER
QUALITY

Air Quality Trends: Ozone

	1990	1995	2000	2005	2010	2012	2014	2015	2016	2017
MSA[1]	n/a	n/a	n/a	n/a	n/a	n/a	n/a	n/a	n/a	n/a
U.S.	0.088	0.089	0.082	0.080	0.073	0.075	0.067	0.068	0.069	0.068

Note: (1) Data covers the Des Moines-West Des Moines, IA Metropolitan Statistical Area—see Appendix B for areas included; n/a not available. The values shown are the composite ozone concentration averages among trend sites based on the highest fourth daily maximum 8-hour concentration in parts per million. These trends are based on sites having an adequate record of monitoring data during the trend period. Data from exceptional events are included.
Source: U.S. Environmental Protection Agency, Air Quality Monitoring Information, "Air Quality Trends by City, 1990-2017"

Air Quality Index

Area	Percent of Days when Air Quality was...[2]					AQI Statistics[2]	
	Good	Moderate	Unhealthy for Sensitive Groups	Unhealthy	Very Unhealthy	Maximum	Median
MSA[1]	80.0	19.7	0.3	0.0	0.0	135	40

Note: (1) Data covers the Des Moines-West Des Moines, IA Metropolitan Statistical Area—see Appendix B for areas included; (2) Based on 365 days with AQI data in 2017. Air Quality Index (AQI) is an index for reporting daily air quality. EPA calculates the AQI for five major air pollutants regulated by the Clean Air Act: ground-level ozone, particle pollution (aka particulate matter), carbon monoxide, sulfur dioxide, and nitrogen dioxide. The AQI runs from 0 to 500. The higher the AQI value, the greater the level of air pollution and the greater the health concern. There are six AQI categories: "Good" AQI is between 0 and 50. Air quality is considered satisfactory; "Moderate" AQI is between 51 and 100. Air quality is acceptable; "Unhealthy for Sensitive Groups" When AQI values are between 101 and 150, members of sensitive groups may experience health effects; "Unhealthy" When AQI values are between 151 and 200 everyone may begin to experience health effects; "Very Unhealthy" AQI values between 201 and 300 trigger a health alert; "Hazardous" AQI values over 300 trigger warnings of emergency conditions (not shown).
Source: U.S. Environmental Protection Agency, Air Quality Index Report, 2017

Air Quality Index Pollutants

Area	Percent of Days when AQI Pollutant was...[2]					
	Carbon Monoxide	Nitrogen Dioxide	Ozone	Sulfur Dioxide	Particulate Matter 2.5	Particulate Matter 10
MSA[1]	0.0	1.1	59.2	0.0	39.7	0.0

Note: (1) Data covers the Des Moines-West Des Moines, IA Metropolitan Statistical Area—see Appendix B for areas included; (2) Based on 365 days with AQI data in 2017. The Air Quality Index (AQI) is an index for reporting daily air quality. EPA calculates the AQI for five major air pollutants regulated by the Clean Air Act: ground-level ozone, particle pollution (also known as particulate matter), carbon monoxide, sulfur dioxide, and nitrogen dioxide. The AQI runs from 0 to 500. The higher the AQI value, the greater the level of air pollution and the greater the health concern.
Source: U.S. Environmental Protection Agency, Air Quality Index Report, 2017

Maximum Air Pollutant Concentrations: Particulate Matter, Ozone, CO and Lead

	Particulate Matter 10 (ug/m^3)	Particulate Matter 2.5 Wtd AM (ug/m^3)	Particulate Matter 2.5 24-Hr (ug/m^3)	Ozone (ppm)	Carbon Monoxide (ppm)	Lead (ug/m^3)
MSA[1] Level	47	7.3	17	0.06	1	n/a
NAAQS[2]	150	15	35	0.075	9	0.15
Met NAAQS[2]	Yes	Yes	Yes	Yes	Yes	n/a

Note: (1) Data covers the Des Moines-West Des Moines, IA Metropolitan Statistical Area—see Appendix B for areas included; Data from exceptional events are included; (2) National Ambient Air Quality Standards; ppm = parts per million; ug/m³ = micrograms per cubic meter; n/a not available.
Concentrations: Particulate Matter 10 (coarse particulate)—highest second maximum 24-hour concentration; Particulate Matter 2.5 Wtd AM (fine particulate)—highest weighted annual mean concentration; Particulate Matter 2.5 24-Hour (fine particulate)—highest 98th percentile 24-hour concentration; Ozone—highest fourth daily maximum 8-hour concentration; Carbon Monoxide—highest second maximum non-overlapping 8-hour concentration; Lead—maximum running 3-month average
Source: U.S. Environmental Protection Agency, Air Quality Monitoring Information, "Air Quality Statistics by City, 2017"

Maximum Air Pollutant Concentrations: Nitrogen Dioxide and Sulfur Dioxide

	Nitrogen Dioxide AM (ppb)	Nitrogen Dioxide 1-Hr (ppb)	Sulfur Dioxide AM (ppb)	Sulfur Dioxide 1-Hr (ppb)	Sulfur Dioxide 24-Hr (ppb)
MSA[1] Level	6	38	n/a	1	n/a
NAAQS[2]	53	100	30	75	140
Met NAAQS[2]	Yes	Yes	n/a	Yes	n/a

Note: (1) Data covers the Des Moines-West Des Moines, IA Metropolitan Statistical Area—see Appendix B for areas included; Data from exceptional events are included; (2) National Ambient Air Quality Standards; ppm = parts per million; ug/m³ = micrograms per cubic meter; n/a not available.
Concentrations: Nitrogen Dioxide AM—highest arithmetic mean concentration; Nitrogen Dioxide 1-Hr—highest 98th percentile 1-hour daily maximum concentration; Sulfur Dioxide AM—highest annual mean concentration; Sulfur Dioxide 1-Hr—highest 99th percentile 1-hour daily maximum concentration; Sulfur Dioxide 24-Hr—highest second maximum 24-hour concentration
Source: U.S. Environmental Protection Agency, Air Quality Monitoring Information, "Air Quality Statistics by City, 2017"

Drinking Water

Water System Name	Pop. Served	Primary Water Source Type	Violations[1]	
			Health Based	Monitoring/ Reporting
Des Moines Water Works	233,020	Surface	0	0

Note: (1) Based on violation data from January 1, 2018 to December 31, 2018
Source: U.S. Environmental Protection Agency, Office of Ground Water and Drinking Water, Safe Drinking Water Information System (based on data extracted April 5, 2019)

Evansville, Indiana

Background

Evansville is located at the southwestern tip of Indiana at the heart of the Indiana-Kentucky-Illinois tri-state area. Its location on the Ohio River has helped it to become a major hub for a wide variety of industries including commercial trade, manufacturing and higher education.

The area that is now Evansville was inhabited by many European and Native American groups before its founding by American settlers. French explorers had called it "La belle riviere" or "the beautiful river." The city was incorporated in 1819 and named in honor of Robert Morgan Evans, who was an officer in the War of 1812. The town thrived as a commercial trading hub, and grew quickly after the construction of the Wabash and Erie Canal in 1853. The canal linked the Great Lakes to the Ohio River and greatly increased trade to the region. Further infrastructure improvements continued the expansion of trade and commercial activity. The Evansville & Crawfordsville Railroad was established there in 1850. In 1932, a bridge was built to span the Ohio River and connect Evansville to Henderson, Kentucky.

During World War II, Evansville produced tank landing ships and P-47 aircraft. After the war, industry and commercial trading continued to thrive and many residents migrated further away from the downtown area. Encouraging this migration was the construction in 1963 of Indiana's first indoor mall, Washington Square.

The later part of the twentieth century has seen Evansville develop into a modern center for manufacturing and commercial trade, known for its diversified industry and economic stability. Thousands of new jobs were created during the 1990s with the opening of Toyota automobile and AK Steel plants, as well as by the growth of the University of Southern Indiana. Today, the city's largest industry sectors are healthcare, finance, education and manufacturing.

Evansville is home to The University of Evansville, a small private university, and the University of Southern Indiana, with its School of Medicine, is located just outside the city.

The city has an excellent transportation infrastructure served by road, rail, water and air systems. The Metropolitan Evansville Transit System (METS) provides bus service throughout the city and the Evansville Regional Airport provides over 50 domestic flights daily. Interstate highway systems are crucial to the city's manufacturing, warehousing and shipping industries. Interstate 64 connects the city to St. Louis, Missouri and Louisville, Kentucky and a new highway also connects Evansville to Interstate 69, an important artery with access to both Mexico and Canada.

Evansville has thirteen distinct neighborhoods with historic districts that are listed on the National Register of Historic Places.

Major attractions in the city include the Evansville Museum of Arts, History and Science, the Reitz Home Museum, and the Children's Museum of Evansville. In addition, the USS *LST-325*, is now permanently docked at Evansville, a museum to commemorate the city's contribution to the shipbuilding effort during World War II. Performing arts venues in Evansville include the Victory Theatre, which is the home of the Evansville Philharmonic Orchestra, The Centre, the Evansville Civic Theatre and the Mesker Amphitheater. Casino Aztar is the first riverboat casino in Indiana. In addition being a popular tourist attraction, the 2,700-passenger floating entertainment complex is also a major employer in the city.

Evansville has a humid seasonal climate typical of inland regions of the country. Summers can be very hot and often feel even hotter due to high humidity. Winters are cold with moderate snowfall. The majority of rain falls between March and May.

Rankings

Business/Finance Rankings

- The personal finance site NerdWallet analyzed 183 American metropolitan areas with populations over 250,000 and more than 15,000 businesses to rank where entrepreneurs find the most success. Criteria included area economy, annual income, housing cost, unemployment rate, and the success rate of area businesses. Evansville ranked #4. *www.nerdwallet.com, "Best Places to Start a Business," April 27, 2015*

- The Evansville metro area appeared on the Milken Institute "2018 Best Performing Cities" list. Rank: #164 out of 200 large metro areas. Criteria: job growth; wage and salary growth; high-tech output growth. *Milken Institute, "Best-Performing Cities 2018," January 24, 2019*

- *Forbes* ranked the 200 most populous metro areas to determine the nation's "Best Places for Business and Careers." The Evansville metro area was ranked #139. Criteria: costs (business and living); job growth (past and projected); income growth; quality of life; educational attainment (college and high school); projected economic growth; cultural and recreational opportunities; net migration patterns; number of highly ranked colleges. *Forbes, "The Best Places for Business and Careers 2018: Seattle Leads the Way," October 24, 2018*

Environmental Rankings

- Evansville was highlighted as one of the top 90 cleanest metro areas for short-term particle pollution (24-hour PM 2.5) in the U.S. during 2014 through 2016. Monitors in these cities reported no days with unhealthful PM 2.5 levels. *American Lung Association, State of the Air 2018*

Health/Fitness Rankings

- The Evansville metro area ranked #126 out of 189 in The Gallup-Healthways Well-Being Index. Criteria: purpose; social well being; financial health; community and physical health. Results are based on telephone interviews with adults, aged 18 and older, living in metropolitan areas in the 50 U.S. states and the District of Columbia. *Gallup-Healthways, "State of American Well-Being, 2017 Community Well-Being Rankings" March 2018*

Safety Rankings

- The National Insurance Crime Bureau ranked 382 metro areas in the U.S. in terms of per capita rates of vehicle theft. The Evansville metro area ranked #149 (#1 = highest rate). Criteria: number of vehicle theft offenses per 100,000 inhabitants in 2017. *National Insurance Crime Bureau, "Hot Spots 2017," July 12, 2018*

Seniors/Retirement Rankings

- From its Best Cities for Successful Aging indexes, the Milken Institute generated rankings for metropolitan areas, weighing data in nine categories—health care, wellness, living arrangements, transportation and convenience, financial characteristics, education, employment, community engagement, and overall livability. The Evansville metro area was ranked #113 overall in the small metro area category. *Milken Institute, "Best Cities for Successful Aging, 2017" March 14, 2017*

Business Environment

CITY FINANCES

City Government Finances

Component	2016 ($000)	2016 ($ per capita)
Total Revenues	252,819	2,108
Total Expenditures	248,979	2,076
Debt Outstanding	510,948	4,260
Cash and Securities[1]	210,693	1,757

Note: (1) Cash and security holdings of a government at the close of its fiscal year,
including those of its dependent agencies, utilities, and liquor stores.
Source: U.S. Census Bureau, State & Local Government Finances 2016

City Government Revenue by Source

Source	2016 ($000)	2016 ($ per capita)	2016 (%)
General Revenue			
From Federal Government	2,265	19	0.9
From State Government	18,269	152	7.2
From Local Governments	3,312	28	1.3
Taxes			
Property	68,281	569	27.0
Sales and Gross Receipts	3,225	27	1.3
Personal Income	15,019	125	5.9
Corporate Income	0	0	0.0
Motor Vehicle License	0	0	0.0
Other Taxes	1,061	9	0.4
Current Charges	63,190	527	25.0
Liquor Store	0	0	0.0
Utility	32,237	269	12.8
Employee Retirement	174	1	0.1

Source: U.S. Census Bureau, State & Local Government Finances 2016

City Government Expenditures by Function

Function	2016 ($000)	2016 ($ per capita)	2016 (%)
General Direct Expenditures			
Air Transportation	9,449	78	3.8
Corrections	0	0	0.0
Education	0	0	0.0
Employment Security Administration	0	0	0.0
Financial Administration	2,303	19	0.9
Fire Protection	27,019	225	10.9
General Public Buildings	0	0	0.0
Governmental Administration, Other	2,345	19	0.9
Health	1,105	9	0.4
Highways	20,002	166	8.0
Hospitals	0	0	0.0
Housing and Community Development	2,197	18	0.9
Interest on General Debt	17,985	149	7.2
Judicial and Legal	0	0	0.0
Libraries	0	0	0.0
Parking	68	< 1	< 0.1
Parks and Recreation	11,233	93	4.5
Police Protection	32,902	274	13.2
Public Welfare	0	0	0.0
Sewerage	65,854	549	26.4
Solid Waste Management	0	0	0.0
Veterans' Services	0	0	0.0
Liquor Store	0	0	0.0
Utility	25,121	209	10.1
Employee Retirement	938	7	0.4

Source: U.S. Census Bureau, State & Local Government Finances 2016

DEMOGRAPHICS

Population Growth

Area	1990 Census	2000 Census	2010 Census	2017* Estimate	Population Growth (%)	
					1990-2017	2010-2017
City	126,272	121,582	117,429	119,806	-5.1	2.0
MSA[1]	324,858	342,815	358,676	315,263	-3.0	-12.1
U.S.	248,709,873	281,421,906	308,745,538	321,004,407	29.1	4.0

Note: (1) Figures cover the Evansville, IN-KY Metropolitan Statistical Area—see Appendix B for areas included; (*) 2013-2017 5-year estimated population
Source: U.S. Census Bureau, 1990 Census, Census 2000, Census 2010, 2013-2017 American Community Survey 5-Year Estimates

Household Size

Area	Persons in Household (%)							Average Household Size
	One	Two	Three	Four	Five	Six	Seven or More	
City	37.9	33.1	13.2	9.2	4.0	1.2	1.3	2.20
MSA[1]	30.0	36.4	14.4	11.6	5.0	1.6	1.1	2.40
U.S.	27.7	33.8	15.7	13.0	6.0	2.3	1.4	2.60

Note: (1) Figures cover the Evansville, IN-KY Metropolitan Statistical Area—see Appendix B for areas included
Source: U.S. Census Bureau, 2013-2017 American Community Survey 5-Year Estimates

Race

Area	White Alone[2] (%)	Black Alone[2] (%)	Asian Alone[2] (%)	AIAN[3] Alone[2] (%)	NHOPI[4] Alone[2] (%)	Other Race Alone[2] (%)	Two or More Races (%)
City	81.7	12.6	0.7	0.3	0.2	1.2	3.3
MSA[1]	88.6	6.8	1.3	0.2	0.1	0.8	2.3
U.S.	73.0	12.7	5.4	0.8	0.2	4.8	3.1

Note: (1) Figures cover the Evansville, IN-KY Metropolitan Statistical Area—see Appendix B for areas included; (2) Alone is defined as not being in combination with one or more other races; (3) American Indian and Alaska Native; (4) Native Hawaiian and Other Pacific Islander
Source: U.S. Census Bureau, 2013-2017 American Community Survey 5-Year Estimates

Hispanic or Latino Origin

Area	Total (%)	Mexican (%)	Puerto Rican (%)	Cuban (%)	Other (%)
City	3.0	2.5	0.2	0.0	0.2
MSA[1]	2.2	1.6	0.2	0.1	0.4
U.S.	17.6	11.1	1.7	0.7	4.1

Note: Persons of Hispanic or Latino origin can be of any race; (1) Figures cover the Evansville, IN-KY Metropolitan Statistical Area—see Appendix B for areas included
Source: U.S. Census Bureau, 2013-2017 American Community Survey 5-Year Estimates

Segregation

Type	Segregation Indices[1]				Percent Change		
	1990	2000	2010	2010 Rank[2]	1990-2000	1990-2010	2000-2010
Black/White	n/a	n/a	n/a	n/a	n/a	n/a	n/a
Asian/White	n/a	n/a	n/a	n/a	n/a	n/a	n/a
Hispanic/White	n/a	n/a	n/a	n/a	n/a	n/a	n/a

Note: All figures cover the Metropolitan Statistical Area—see Appendix B for areas included; Figures are based on an analysis of 1990, 2000, and 2010 Census Decennial Census tract data by William H. Frey, Brookings Institution and the University of Michigan Social Science Data Analysis Network. In this analysis all racial groups (whites, blacks, and asians) are non-Hispanic members of those races. Hispanics are shown as a separate category; (1) Segregation Indices are Dissimilarity Indices that measure the degree to which the minority group is distributed differently than whites across census tracts. They range from 0 (complete integration) to 100 (complete segregation) where the value indicates the percentage of the minority group that needs to move to be distributed exactly like whites; (2) Ranges from 1 (most segregated) to 102 (least segregated); n/a not available.
Source: www.CensusScope.org

Ancestry

Area	German	Irish	English	American	Italian	Polish	French[2]	Scottish	Dutch
City	25.7	11.6	11.3	7.1	1.5	1.2	1.7	1.5	1.1
MSA[1]	28.2	11.6	11.4	10.4	1.9	1.1	1.9	1.8	1.2
U.S.	14.1	10.1	7.5	6.6	5.3	2.9	2.5	1.7	1.3

Note: Figures are the percentage of the total population reporting a particular ancestry. The nine most commonly reported ancestries in the U.S. are shown. Figures include multiple ancestries (e.g. if a person reported being Irish and Italian, they were included in both columns); (1) Figures cover the Evansville, IN-KY Metropolitan Statistical Area—see Appendix B for areas included; (2) Excludes Basque
Source: U.S. Census Bureau, 2013-2017 American Community Survey 5-Year Estimates

Foreign-Born Population

Area	Percent of Population Born in								
	Any Foreign Country	Asia	Mexico	Europe	Carribean	Central America[2]	South America	Africa	Canada
City	2.7	0.7	0.9	0.5	0.1	0.1	0.0	0.2	0.1
MSA[1]	2.6	1.2	0.5	0.5	0.1	0.2	0.1	0.1	0.1
U.S.	13.4	4.1	3.6	1.5	1.3	1.0	0.9	0.6	0.3

Note: (1) Figures cover the Evansville, IN-KY Metropolitan Statistical Area—see Appendix B for areas included; (2) Excludes Mexico.
Source: U.S. Census Bureau, 2013-2017 American Community Survey 5-Year Estimates

Marital Status

Area	Never Married	Now Married[2]	Separated	Widowed	Divorced
City	34.3	39.4	1.6	7.0	17.7
MSA[1]	27.9	50.7	1.2	6.3	13.9
U.S.	33.1	48.2	2.0	5.8	10.9

Note: Figures are percentages and cover the population 15 years of age and older; (1) Figures cover the Evansville, IN-KY Metropolitan Statistical Area—see Appendix B for areas included; (2) Excludes separated
Source: U.S. Census Bureau, 2013-2017 American Community Survey 5-Year Estimates

Disability by Age

Area	All Ages	Under 18 Years Old	18 to 64 Years Old	65 Years and Over
City	17.9	6.1	16.5	41.2
MSA[1]	15.2	5.5	13.4	36.6
U.S.	12.6	4.2	10.3	35.5

Note: Figures show percent of the civilian noninstitutionalized population that reported having a disability. Disability status is determined from six types of difficulty: vision, hearing, cognitive, ambulatory, self-care, and independent living. For children under 5 years old, hearing and vision difficulty are used to determine disability status. For children between the ages of 5 and 14, disability status is determined from hearing, vision, cognitive, ambulatory, and self-care difficulties. For people aged 15 years and older, they are considered to have a disability if they have difficulty with any one of the six difficulty types; Note: (1) Figures cover the Evansville, IN-KY Metropolitan Statistical Area—see Appendix B for areas included
Source: U.S. Census Bureau, 2013-2017 American Community Survey 5-Year Estimates

Age

Area	Percent of Population									Median Age
	Under Age 5	Age 5–19	Age 20–34	Age 35–44	Age 45–54	Age 55–64	Age 65–74	Age 75–84	Age 85+	
City	6.4	17.6	23.2	11.8	12.6	12.9	8.2	4.5	2.8	37.2
MSA[1]	6.1	19.2	19.7	11.9	13.2	14.0	9.0	4.7	2.2	39.3
U.S.	6.2	19.5	20.7	12.7	13.4	12.7	8.6	4.4	1.9	37.8

Note: (1) Figures cover the Evansville, IN-KY Metropolitan Statistical Area—see Appendix B for areas included
Source: U.S. Census Bureau, 2013-2017 American Community Survey 5-Year Estimates

Gender

Area	Males	Females	Males per 100 Females
City	57,153	62,653	91.2
MSA[1]	153,544	161,719	94.9
U.S.	158,018,753	162,985,654	97.0

Note: (1) Figures cover the Evansville, IN-KY Metropolitan Statistical Area—see Appendix B for areas included
Source: U.S. Census Bureau, 2013-2017 American Community Survey 5-Year Estimates

Religious Groups by Family

Area	Catholic	Baptist	Non-Den.	Methodist[2]	Lutheran	LDS[3]	Pente-costal	Presby-terian[4]	Muslim[5]	Judaism
MSA[1]	14.7	16.7	5.6	5.7	1.5	0.6	1.9	3.1	0.1	0.1
U.S.	19.1	9.3	4.0	4.0	2.3	2.0	1.9	1.6	0.8	0.7

Note: Figures are the number of adherents as a percentage of the total population; (1) Figures cover the Evansville, IN-KY Metropolitan Statistical Area—see Appendix B for areas included; (2) Methodist/Pietist; (3) Latter Day Saints; (4) Reformed; (5) Figures are estimates
Source: Association of Statisticians of American Religious Bodies, 2010 U.S. Religion Census: Religious Congregations & Membership Study

Religious Groups by Tradition

Area	Catholic	Evangelical Protestant	Mainline Protestant	Other Tradition	Black Protestant	Orthodox
MSA[1]	14.7	24.1	10.0	0.8	1.9	<0.1
U.S.	19.1	16.2	7.3	4.3	1.6	0.3

Note: Figures are the number of adherents as a percentage of the total population; (1) Figures cover the Evansville, IN-KY Metropolitan Statistical Area—see Appendix B for areas included
Source: Association of Statisticians of American Religious Bodies, 2010 U.S. Religion Census: Religious Congregations & Membership Study

ECONOMY

Gross Metropolitan Product

Area	2016	2017	2018	2019	Rank[2]
MSA[1]	17.1	17.8	18.6	19.5	143

Note: Figures are in billions of dollars; (1) Figures cover the Evansville, IN-KY Metropolitan Statistical Area—see Appendix B for areas included; (2) Rank is based on 2017 data and ranges from 1 to 381
Source: U.S. Conference of Mayors, U.S. Metro Economies: Economic Growth & Full Employment, June 2018

Economic Growth

Area	2017-2018 (%)	2019-2020 (%)	2021-2022 (%)
MSA[1]	2.4	1.9	1.0

Note: Figures are real gross metropolitan product (GMP) growth rates and represent average annual percent change; (1) Figures cover the Evansville, IN-KY Metropolitan Statistical Area—see Appendix B for areas included
Source: U.S. Conference of Mayors, U.S. Metro Economies: Economic Growth & Full Employment, June 2018

Metropolitan Area Exports

Area	2012	2013	2014	2015	2016	2017	Rank[2]
MSA[1]	4,025.3	3,865.6	3,756.5	4,483.7	3,022.4	4,001.9	62

Note: Figures are in millions of dollars; (1) Figures cover the Evansville, IN-KY Metropolitan Statistical Area—see Appendix B for areas included; (2) Rank is based on 2017 data and ranges from 1 to 387
Source: U.S. Department of Commerce, International Trade Administration, Office of Trade and Economic Analysis, Industry and Analysis, Exports by Metropolitan Area, extracted March 25, 2019

Building Permits

Area	Single-Family			Multi-Family			Total		
	2016	2017	Pct. Chg.	2016	2017	Pct. Chg.	2016	2017	Pct. Chg.
City	96	72	-25.0	80	6	-92.5	176	78	-55.7
MSA[1]	633	618	-2.4	314	303	-3.5	947	921	-2.7
U.S.	750,800	820,000	9.2	455,800	462,000	1.4	1,206,600	1,282,000	6.2

Note: (1) Figures cover the Evansville, IN-KY Metropolitan Statistical Area—see Appendix B for areas included; Figures represent new, privately-owned housing units authorized (unadjusted data); All permit data are based on estimates with imputation
Source: U.S. Census Bureau, Manufacturing, Mining, and Construction Statistics, Building Permits, 2016, 2017

Bankruptcy Filings

Area	Business Filings			Nonbusiness Filings		
	2017	2018	% Chg.	2017	2018	% Chg.
Vanderburgh County	10	4	-60.0	648	729	12.5
U.S.	23,157	22,232	-4.0	765,863	751,186	-1.9

Note: Business filings include Chapter 7, Chapter 11, Chapter 12, and Chapter 13; Nonbusiness filings include Chapter 7, Chapter 11, and Chapter 13
Source: Administrative Office of the U.S. Courts, Business and Nonbusiness Bankruptcy, County Cases Commenced by Chapter of the Bankruptcy Code, During the 12-Month Period Ending December 31, 2017 and Business and Nonbusiness Bankruptcy, County Cases Commenced by Chapter of the Bankruptcy Code, During the 12-Month Period Ending December 31, 2018

Housing Vacancy Rates

Area	Gross Vacancy Rate[2] (%)			Year-Round Vacancy Rate[3] (%)			Rental Vacancy Rate[4] (%)			Homeowner Vacancy Rate[5] (%)		
	2016	2017	2018	2016	2017	2018	2016	2017	2018	2016	2017	2018
MSA[1]	n/a	n/a	n/a	n/a	n/a	n/a	n/a	n/a	n/a	n/a	n/a	n/a
U.S.	12.8	12.7	12.3	9.9	9.9	9.7	6.9	7.2	6.9	1.7	1.6	1.5

Note: (1) Figures cover the Evansville, IN-KY Metropolitan Statistical Area—see Appendix B for areas included; (2) The percentage of the total housing inventory that is vacant; (3) The percentage of the housing inventory (excluding seasonal units) that is year-round vacant; (4) The percentage of rental inventory that is vacant for rent; (5) The percentage of homeowner inventory that is vacant for sale; n/a not available
Source: U.S. Census Bureau, Housing Vacancies and Homeownership Annual Statistics: 2016, 2017, 2018

INCOME

Income

Area	Per Capita ($)	Median Household ($)	Average Household ($)
City	22,375	36,956	50,350
MSA[1]	28,086	49,873	67,860
U.S.	31,177	57,652	81,283

Note: (1) Figures cover the Evansville, IN-KY Metropolitan Statistical Area—see Appendix B for areas included
Source: U.S. Census Bureau, 2013-2017 American Community Survey 5-Year Estimates

Household Income Distribution

Area	Percent of Households Earning							
	Under $15,000	$15,000 -$24,999	$25,000 -$34,999	$35,000 -$49,999	$50,000 -$74,999	$75,000 -$99,999	$100,000 -$149,999	$150,000 and up
City	17.5	15.0	14.9	15.8	18.0	8.9	6.5	3.4
MSA[1]	12.7	11.3	11.7	14.3	18.1	12.2	12.3	7.2
U.S.	11.6	9.8	9.5	13.0	17.7	12.3	14.1	12.1

Note: (1) Figures cover the Evansville, IN-KY Metropolitan Statistical Area—see Appendix B for areas included
Source: U.S. Census Bureau, 2013-2017 American Community Survey 5-Year Estimates

Poverty Rate

Area	All Ages	Under 18 Years Old	18 to 64 Years Old	65 Years and Over
City	23.3	37.3	21.5	10.8
MSA[1]	15.4	22.4	14.5	9.0
U.S.	14.6	20.3	13.7	9.3

Note: Figures are percentage of people whose income during the past 12 months was below the poverty level; (1) Figures cover the Evansville, IN-KY Metropolitan Statistical Area—see Appendix B for areas included
Source: U.S. Census Bureau, 2013-2017 American Community Survey 5-Year Estimates

EMPLOYMENT

Labor Force and Employment

Area	Civilian Labor Force			Workers Employed		
	Dec. 2017	Dec. 2018	% Chg.	Dec. 2017	Dec. 2018	% Chg.
City	58,960	59,887	1.6	57,218	57,922	1.2
MSA[1]	160,568	162,866	1.4	156,131	157,860	1.1
U.S.	159,880,000	162,510,000	1.6	153,602,000	156,481,000	1.9

Note: Data is not seasonally adjusted and covers workers 16 years of age and older; (1) Figures cover the Evansville, IN-KY Metropolitan Statistical Area—see Appendix B for areas included
Source: Bureau of Labor Statistics, Local Area Unemployment Statistics

Unemployment Rate

Area	2018											
	Jan.	Feb.	Mar.	Apr.	May	Jun.	Jul.	Aug.	Sep.	Oct.	Nov.	Dec.
City	3.3	3.6	3.1	2.9	3.2	3.6	3.5	3.8	3.2	3.6	3.5	3.3
MSA[1]	3.2	3.4	3.0	2.8	3.1	3.5	3.3	3.5	2.9	3.4	3.3	3.1
U.S.	4.5	4.4	4.1	3.7	3.6	4.2	4.1	3.9	3.6	3.5	3.5	3.7

Note: Data is not seasonally adjusted and covers workers 16 years of age and older; (1) Figures cover the Evansville, IN-KY Metropolitan Statistical Area—see Appendix B for areas included
Source: Bureau of Labor Statistics, Local Area Unemployment Statistics

Average Wages

Occupation	$/Hr.	Occupation	$/Hr.
Accountants and Auditors	29.80	Maids and Housekeeping Cleaners	10.80
Automotive Mechanics	19.70	Maintenance and Repair Workers	19.30
Bookkeepers	17.00	Marketing Managers	53.90
Carpenters	23.70	Nuclear Medicine Technologists	n/a
Cashiers	9.90	Nurses, Licensed Practical	21.30
Clerks, General Office	15.40	Nurses, Registered	29.30
Clerks, Receptionists/Information	12.80	Nursing Assistants	13.30
Clerks, Shipping/Receiving	16.50	Packers and Packagers, Hand	13.50
Computer Programmers	41.80	Physical Therapists	37.70
Computer Systems Analysts	37.60	Postal Service Mail Carriers	24.40
Computer User Support Specialists	21.90	Real Estate Brokers	n/a
Cooks, Restaurant	12.40	Retail Salespersons	12.80
Dentists	77.30	Sales Reps., Exc. Tech./Scientific	32.10
Electrical Engineers	40.10	Sales Reps., Tech./Scientific	36.60
Electricians	27.80	Secretaries, Exc. Legal/Med./Exec.	15.00
Financial Managers	53.90	Security Guards	14.60
First-Line Supervisors/Managers, Sales	19.40	Surgeons	136.30
Food Preparation Workers	10.10	Teacher Assistants*	11.80
General and Operations Managers	43.50	Teachers, Elementary School*	23.10
Hairdressers/Cosmetologists	14.10	Teachers, Secondary School*	26.20
Internists, General	n/a	Telemarketers	n/a
Janitors and Cleaners	14.30	Truck Drivers, Heavy/Tractor-Trailer	21.00
Landscaping/Groundskeeping Workers	12.20	Truck Drivers, Light/Delivery Svcs.	16.10
Lawyers	52.70	Waiters and Waitresses	9.80

Note: Wage data covers the Evansville, IN-KY Metropolitan Statistical Area—see Appendix B for areas included; (*) Hourly wages for elementary/secondary school teachers and teacher assistants were calculated by the editors from annual wage data based on a 40 hour work week; n/a not available.
Source: Bureau of Labor Statistics, Metro Area Occupational Employment & Wage Estimates, May 2018

Employment by Occupation

Occupation Classification	City (%)	MSA[1] (%)	U.S. (%)
Management, Business, Science, and Arts	28.4	33.7	37.4
Natural Resources, Construction, and Maintenance	7.5	8.8	8.9
Production, Transportation, and Material Moving	19.8	17.6	12.2
Sales and Office	24.4	22.7	23.5
Service	19.9	17.2	18.0

Note: Figures cover employed civilians 16 years of age and older; (1) Figures cover the Evansville, IN-KY Metropolitan Statistical Area—see Appendix B for areas included
Source: U.S. Census Bureau, 2013-2017 American Community Survey 5-Year Estimates

Employment by Industry

Sector	MSA[1]		U.S.
	Number of Employees	Percent of Total	Percent of Total
Construction, Mining, and Logging	10,000	6.1	5.3
Education and Health Services	29,100	17.6	15.9
Financial Activities	5,500	3.3	5.7
Government	17,800	10.8	15.1
Information	1,500	0.9	1.9
Leisure and Hospitality	16,000	9.7	10.7
Manufacturing	24,000	14.6	8.5
Other Services	8,500	5.2	3.9
Professional and Business Services	20,300	12.3	14.1
Retail Trade	17,700	10.7	10.8
Transportation, Warehousing, and Utilities	8,100	4.9	4.2
Wholesale Trade	6,400	3.9	3.9

Note: Figures are non-farm employment as of December 2018. Figures are not seasonally adjusted and include workers 16 years of age and older; (1) Figures cover the Evansville, IN-KY Metropolitan Statistical Area—see Appendix B for areas included
Source: Bureau of Labor Statistics, Current Employment Statistics, Employment, Hours, and Earnings

Occupations with Greatest Projected Employment Growth: 2018 – 2020

Occupation[1]	2018 Employment	2020 Projected Employment	Numeric Employment Change	Percent Employment Change
Laborers and Freight, Stock, and Material Movers, Hand	76,430	78,940	2,510	3.3
Combined Food Preparation and Serving Workers, Including Fast Food	84,030	86,500	2,470	2.9
Registered Nurses	67,010	69,350	2,340	3.5
Personal Care Aides	29,290	30,960	1,670	5.7
Janitors and Cleaners, Except Maids and Housekeeping Cleaners	48,510	49,760	1,250	2.6
Home Health Aides	13,830	14,930	1,100	8.0
Heavy and Tractor-Trailer Truck Drivers	56,570	57,630	1,060	1.9
Industrial Truck and Tractor Operators	21,430	22,480	1,050	4.9
General and Operations Managers	49,870	50,850	980	2.0
Helpers—Production Workers	17,700	18,520	820	4.6

Note: Projections cover Indiana; (1) Sorted by numeric employment change
Source: www.projectionscentral.com, State Occupational Projections, 2018–2020 Short-Term Projections

Fastest Growing Occupations: 2018 – 2020

Occupation[1]	2018 Employment	2020 Projected Employment	Numeric Employment Change	Percent Employment Change
Flight Attendants	620	680	60	9.7
Home Health Aides	13,830	14,930	1,100	8.0
Airline Pilots, Copilots, and Flight Engineers	670	720	50	7.5
Physician Assistants	1,160	1,240	80	6.9
Software Developers, Applications	8,720	9,300	580	6.7
Nurse Practitioners	4,170	4,440	270	6.5
Computer Numerically Controlled Machine Tool Programmers, Metal and Plastic	960	1,020	60	6.3
Physical Therapist Assistants	2,260	2,390	130	5.8
Personal Care Aides	29,290	30,960	1,670	5.7
Health Specialties Teachers, Postsecondary	3,020	3,190	170	5.6

Note: Projections cover Indiana; (1) Sorted by percent employment change and excludes occupations with numeric employment change less than 50
Source: www.projectionscentral.com, State Occupational Projections, 2018–2020 Short-Term Projections

TAXES

State Corporate Income Tax Rates

State	Tax Rate (%)	Income Brackets ($)	Num. of Brackets	Financial Institution Tax Rate (%)[a]	Federal Income Tax Ded.
Indiana	5.75 (i)	Flat rate	1	6.25	No

Note: Tax rates as of January 1, 2019; (a) Rates listed are the corporate income tax rate applied to financial institutions or excise taxes based on income. Some states have other taxes based upon the value of deposits or shares; (i) The Indiana Corporate tax rate is scheduled to decrease to 5.5% on July 1, 2019. Bank tax rate is scheduled to decrease to 6.0% on 1/1/20.
Source: Federation of Tax Administrators, Range of State Corporate Income Tax Rates, January 1, 2019

State Individual Income Tax Rates

State	Tax Rate (%)	Income Brackets ($)	Personal Exemptions ($) Single	Married	Depend.	Standard Ded. ($) Single	Married
Indiana	3.23	Flat rate	1,000	2,000	2,500 (j)	–	–

Note: Tax rates as of January 1, 2019; Local- and county-level taxes are not included; n/a not applicable; Federal income tax is not deductible on state income tax returns; (j) In Indiana, includes an additional exemption of $1,500 for each dependent child.
Source: Federation of Tax Administrators, State Individual Income Tax Rates, January 1, 2019

Various State Sales and Excise Tax Rates

State	State Sales Tax (%)	Gasoline[1] (¢/gal.)	Cigarette[2] ($/pack)	Spirits[3] ($/gal.)	Wine[4] ($/gal.)	Beer[5] ($/gal.)	Recreational Marijuana (%)
Indiana	7	42.9	0.995	2.68 (f)	0.47 (l)	0.12	Not legal

Note: All tax rates as of January 1, 2019; (1) The American Petroleum Institute has developed a methodology for determining the average tax rate on a gallon of fuel. Rates may include any of the following: excise taxes, environmental fees, storage tank fees, other fees or taxes, general sales tax, and local taxes. In states where gasoline is subject to the general sales tax, or where the fuel tax is based on the average sale price, the average rate determined by API is sensitive to changes in the price of gasoline. States that fully or partially apply general sales taxes to gasoline: CA, CO, GA, IL, IN, MI, NY; (2) The federal excise tax of $1.0066 per pack and local taxes are not included; (3) Rates are those applicable to off-premise sales of 40% alcohol by volume (a.b.v.) distilled spirits in 750ml containers. Local excise taxes are excluded; (4) Rates are those applicable to off-premise sales of 11% a.b.v. non-carbonated wine in 750ml containers; (5) Rates are those applicable to off-premise sales of 4.7% a.b.v. beer in 12 ounce containers; (f) Different rates also applicable according to alcohol content, place of production, size of container, or place purchased (on- or off-premise or onboard airlines); (l) Different rates also applicable to alcohol content, place of production, size of container, place purchased (on- or off-premise or on board airlines) or type of wine (carbonated, vermouth, etc.).
Source: Tax Foundation, 2019 Facts & Figures: How Does Your State Compare?

State Business Tax Climate Index Rankings

State	Overall Rank	Corporate Tax Rank	Individual Income Tax Rank	Sales Tax Rank	Unemployment Insurance Tax Rank	Property Tax Rank
Indiana	10	18	15	12	11	2

Note: The index is a measure of how each state's tax laws affect economic performance. The lower the rank, the more favorable a state's tax system is for business. States without a given tax are given a ranking of 1. The scores/rankings for the District of Columbia do not affect other states. The 2019 index represents the tax climate as of July 1, 2018.
Source: Tax Foundation, State Business Tax Climate Index 2019

COMMERCIAL UTILITIES

Typical Monthly Electric Bills

Area	Commercial Service ($/month) 1,500 kWh	40 kW demand 14,000 kWh	Industrial Service ($/month) 1,000 kW demand 200,000 kWh	50,000 kW demand 32,500,000 kWh
City	201	1,647	21,680	2,437,293
Average[1]	203	1,619	25,886	2,540,077

Note: Figures are based on annualized rates; (1) Average based on 187 utilities surveyed
Source: Edison Electric Institute, Typical Bills and Average Rates Report, Summer 2018

TRANSPORTATION

Means of Transportation to Work

| Area | Car/Truck/Van | | Public Transportation | | | Bicycle | Walked | Other Means | Worked at Home |
	Drove Alone	Car-pooled	Bus	Subway	Railroad				
City	82.9	9.0	2.3	0.0	0.0	0.3	2.5	1.3	1.7
MSA[1]	86.4	7.3	1.0	0.0	0.0	0.1	1.7	1.0	2.5
U.S.	76.4	9.2	2.5	1.9	0.6	0.6	2.7	1.3	4.7

Note: Figures are percentages and cover workers 16 years of age and older; (1) Figures cover the Evansville, IN-KY Metropolitan Statistical Area—see Appendix B for areas included
Source: U.S. Census Bureau, 2013-2017 American Community Survey 5-Year Estimates

Travel Time to Work

Area	Less Than 10 Minutes	10 to 19 Minutes	20 to 29 Minutes	30 to 44 Minutes	45 to 59 Minutes	60 to 89 Minutes	90 Minutes or More
City	17.5	46.7	17.7	11.8	3.2	2.0	1.1
MSA[1]	15.5	37.5	23.8	15.3	4.2	2.4	1.3
U.S.	12.7	28.9	20.9	20.5	8.1	6.2	2.7

Note: Note: Figures are percentages and include workers 16 years old and over; (1) Figures cover the Evansville, IN-KY Metropolitan Statistical Area—see Appendix B for areas included
Source: U.S. Census Bureau, 2013-2017 American Community Survey 5-Year Estimates

Freeway Travel Time Index

Area	1985	1990	1995	2000	2005	2010	2014
Urban Area Rank[1,2]	n/a	n/a	n/a	n/a	n/a	n/a	n/a
Urban Area Index[1]	n/a	n/a	n/a	n/a	n/a	n/a	n/a
Average Index[3]	1.09	1.11	1.14	1.17	1.20	1.19	1.20

Note: Freeway Travel Time Index—the ratio of travel time in the peak period to the travel time at free-flow conditions. For example, a value of 1.30 indicates a 20-minute free-flow trip takes 26 minutes in the peak (20 minutes x 1.30 = 26 minutes); (1) Data for the Evansville, IN-KY urban area was not available; (2) Rank is based on 101 urban areas (#1 = highest travel time index); (3) Average of 101 urban areas
Source: Texas Transportation Institute, 2015 Urban Mobility Scorecard, August 2015

Freeway Commuter Stress Index

Area	1985	1990	1995	2000	2005	2010	2014
Urban Area Rank[1,2]	n/a	n/a	n/a	n/a	n/a	n/a	n/a
Urban Area Index[1]	n/a	n/a	n/a	n/a	n/a	n/a	n/a
Average Index[3]	1.13	1.16	1.19	1.22	1.25	1.24	1.25

Note: The Freeway Commuter Stress Index is the same as the Freeway Travel Time Index (see table above) except that it includes only the travel in the peak directions during the peak periods; the TTI includes travel in all directions during the peak period. Thus, the CSI is more indicative of the work trip experienced by each commuter on a daily basis; (1) Data for the Evansville, IN-KY urban area was not available; (2) Rank is based on 101 urban areas (#1 = highest travel time index); (3) Average of 101 urban areas
Source: Texas Transportation Institute, 2015 Urban Mobility Scorecard, August 2015

Public Transportation

Agency Name / Mode of Transportation	Vehicles Operated in Maximum Service[1]	Annual Unlinked Passenger Trips[2] (in thous.)	Annual Passenger Miles[3] (in thous.)
Metropolitan Evansville Transit System (METS)			
Bus (directly operated)	22	1,494.2	5,462.2
Demand Response (directly operated)	14	67.4	421.7

Note: (1) The number of revenue vehicles operated by the given mode and type of service to meet the annual maximum service requirement. This is the revenue vehicle count during the peak season of the year; on the week and day that maximum service is provided. Vehicles operated in maximum service (VOMS) exclude atypical days and one-time special events; (2) The number of passengers who boarded public transportation vehicles. Passengers are counted each time they board a vehicle no matter how many vehicles they use to travel from their origin to their destination. (3) The sum of the distances ridden by all passengers during the entire fiscal year.
Source: Federal Transit Administration, National Transit Database, 2017

Air Transportation

Airport Name and Code / Type of Service	Passenger Airlines[1]	Passenger Enplanements	Freight Carriers[2]	Freight (lbs)
Evansville Regional (EVV)				
Domestic service (U.S. carriers - 2018)	14	228,548	9	127,561
International service (U.S. carriers - 2017)	1	106	1	1,500

Note: (1) Includes all U.S.-based major, minor and commuter airlines that carried at least one passenger during the year; (2) Includes all U.S.-based airlines and freight carriers that transported at least one pound of freight during the year.
Source: Bureau of Transportation Statistics, The Intermodal Transportation Database, Air Carriers: T-100 Domestic Market (U.S. Carriers), 2018; Bureau of Transportation Statistics, The Intermodal Transportation Database, Air Carriers: T-100 International Market (U.S. Carriers), 2017

Other Transportation Statistics

Major Highways:	I-64
Amtrak Service:	No
Major Waterways/Ports:	Ohio River

Source: Amtrak.com; Google Maps

BUSINESSES

Major Business Headquarters

Company Name	Industry	Rankings Fortune[1]	Rankings Forbes[2]
Berry Global Group	Packaging, Containers	399	-

Note: (1) Companies that produce a 10-K are ranked 1 to 500 based on 2017 revenue; (2) All private companies with at least $2 billion in annual revenue through the end of their most current fiscal year are ranked 1 to 229; companies listed are headquartered in the city; dashes indicate no ranking
Source: Fortune, "Fortune 500," June 2018; Forbes, "America's Largest Private Companies," 2018 Rankings

Minority- and Women-Owned Businesses

Group	All Firms Firms	All Firms Sales ($000)	Firms with Paid Employees Firms	Firms with Paid Employees Sales ($000)	Firms with Paid Employees Employees	Firms with Paid Employees Payroll ($000)
AIAN[1]	46	2,502	2	(s)	0 - 19	(s)
Asian	268	63,906	104	48,977	842	8,691
Black	497	(s)	18	(s)	100 - 249	(s)
Hispanic	120	8,893	25	7,161	168	1,934
NHOPI[2]	n/a	n/a	n/a	n/a	n/a	n/a
Women	2,902	851,873	388	790,608	14,952	220,685
All Firms	9,082	18,569,035	3,011	18,166,291	92,382	3,512,434

Note: Figures cover firms located in the city; minority- and women-owned business are defined as firms in which the corresponding group own 51% or more of the stock or equity of the company; (1) American Indian and Alaska Native; (2) Native Hawaiian and Other Pacific Islander; (s) estimates are suppressed when publication standards are not met; n/a not available
Source: U.S. Census Bureau, 2012 Economic Census, Survey of Business Owners

HOTELS & CONVENTION CENTERS

Hotels, Motels and Vacation Rentals

Area	5 Star Num.	5 Star Pct.[3]	4 Star Num.	4 Star Pct.[3]	3 Star Num.	3 Star Pct.[3]	2 Star Num.	2 Star Pct.[3]	1 Star Num.	1 Star Pct.[3]	Not Rated Num.	Not Rated Pct.[3]
City[1]	0	0.0	2	2.7	9	12.0	54	72.0	0	0.0	10	13.3
Total[2]	286	0.4	5,236	7.1	16,715	22.6	10,259	13.9	293	0.4	41,056	55.6

Note: (1) Figures cover Evansville and vicinity; (2) Figures cover all 100 cities in this book; (3) Percentage of hotels which have a given star rating; Star ratings are determined by expedia.com and offer an indication of the general quality of a particular hotel.
Source: www.expedia.com, April 3, 2019

Major Convention Centers

Name	Overall Space (sq. ft.)	Exhibit Space (sq. ft.)	Meeting Space (sq. ft.)	Meeting Rooms
Old National Events Plaza	280,000	38,000	12,000	12

Note: Table includes convention centers located in the Evansville, IN-KY metro area
Source: Original research

Living Environment

COST OF LIVING

Cost of Living Index

Composite Index	Groceries	Housing	Utilities	Trans-portation	Health Care	Misc. Goods/ Services
92.3	89.4	82.2	109.3	92.8	98.4	96.8

Note: The Cost of Living Index measures regional differences in the cost of consumer goods and services, excluding taxes and non-consumer expenditures, for professional and managerial households in the top income quintile. It is based on more than 50,000 prices covering almost 60 different items for which prices are collected three times a year by chambers of commerce, economic development organizations or university applied economic centers in each participating urban area. The numbers shown should be read as a percentage above or below the national average of 100. For example, a value of 115.4 in the groceries column indicates that grocery prices are 15.4% higher than the national average. Small differences in the index numbers should not be interpreted as significant; Figures cover the Evansville IN urban area.
Source: The Council for Community and Economic Research, ACCRA Cost of Living Index, 2018

Grocery Prices

Area[1]	T-Bone Steak ($/pound)	Frying Chicken ($/pound)	Whole Milk ($/half gal.)	Eggs ($/dozen)	Orange Juice ($/64 oz.)	Coffee ($/11.5 oz.)
City[2]	11.68	1.25	0.96	1.21	3.36	3.27
Avg.	11.35	1.42	1.94	1.81	3.52	4.35
Min.	7.45	0.92	0.80	0.75	2.72	3.06
Max.	15.05	2.76	4.18	4.00	5.36	8.20

Note: (1) Values for the local area are compared with the average, minimum and maximum values for all 291 areas in the Cost of Living Index; (2) Figures cover the Evansville IN urban area; T-Bone Steak (price per pound); Frying Chicken (price per pound, whole fryer); Whole Milk (half gallon carton); Eggs (price per dozen, Grade A, large); Orange Juice (64 oz. Tropicana or Florida Natural); Coffee (11.5 oz. can, vacuum-packed, Maxwell House, Hills Bros, or Folgers).
Source: The Council for Community and Economic Research, ACCRA Cost of Living Index, 2018

Housing and Utility Costs

Area[1]	New Home Price ($)	Apartment Rent ($/month)	All Electric ($/month)	Part Electric ($/month)	Other Energy ($/month)	Telephone ($/month)
City[2]	287,646	861	-	121.89	73.70	178.60
Avg.	347,000	1,087	165.93	100.16	67.73	178.70
Min.	200,468	500	93.58	25.64	26.78	163.10
Max.	1,901,222	4,888	388.65	246.86	332.81	197.70

Note: (1) Values for the local area are compared with the average, minimum and maximum values for all 291 areas in the Cost of Living Index; (2) Figures cover the Evansville IN urban area; New Home Price (2,400 sf living area, 8,000 sf lot, in urban area with full utilities); Apartment Rent (950 sf 2 bedroom/1.5 or 2 bath, unfurnished, excluding all utilities except water); All Electric (average monthly cost for an all-electric home); Part Electric (average monthly cost for a part-electric home); Other Energy (average monthly cost for natural gas, fuel oil, coal, wood, and any other forms of energy except electricity); Telephone (price includes the base monthly rate plus taxes and fees for three lines of mobile phone service).
Source: The Council for Community and Economic Research, ACCRA Cost of Living Index, 2018

Health Care, Transportation, and Other Costs

Area[1]	Doctor ($/visit)	Dentist ($/visit)	Optometrist ($/visit)	Gasoline ($/gallon)	Beauty Salon ($/visit)	Men's Shirt ($)
City[2]	106.38	92.08	119.53	2.59	33.29	28.61
Avg.	110.71	95.11	103.74	2.61	37.48	32.03
Min.	33.60	62.55	54.63	1.89	17.00	11.44
Max.	195.97	153.93	225.79	3.59	71.88	58.64

Note: (1) Values for the local area are compared with the average, minimum and maximum values for all 291 areas in the Cost of Living Index; (2) Figures cover the Evansville IN urban area; Doctor (general practitioners routine exam of an established patient); Dentist (adult teeth cleaning and periodic oral examination); Optometrist (full vision eye exam for established adult patient); Gasoline (one gallon regular unleaded, national brand, including all taxes, cash price at self-service pump if available); Beauty Salon (woman's shampoo, trim, and blow-dry); Men's Shirt (cotton/polyester dress shirt, pinpoint weave, long sleeves).
Source: The Council for Community and Economic Research, ACCRA Cost of Living Index, 2018

HOUSING

House Price Index (HPI)

Area	National Ranking[2]	Quarterly Change (%)	One-Year Change (%)	Five-Year Change (%)
MSA[1]	109	3.54	6.54	21.71
U.S.[3]	–	1.12	5.73	32.81

Note: The HPI is a weighted repeat sales index. It measures average price changes in repeat sales or refinancings on the same properties. This information is obtained by reviewing repeat mortgage transactions on single-family properties whose mortgages have been purchased or securitized by Fannie Mae or Freddie Mac in January 1975; (1) Figures cover the Evansville, IN-KY Metropolitan Statistical Area—see Appendix B for areas included; (2) Rankings are based on annual percentage change for all metro areas containing at least 15,000 transactions over the last 10 years and ranges from 1 to 245; (3) figures based on a weighted average of Census Division estimates using a seasonally adjusted, purchase-only index; all figures are for the period ending December 31, 2018
Source: Federal Housing Finance Agency, House Price Index, February 26, 2019

Median Single-Family Home Prices

Area	2016	2017	2018[p]	Percent Change 2017 to 2018
MSA[1]	n/a	n/a	n/a	n/a
U.S. Average	235.5	248.8	261.6	5.1

Note: Figures are median sales prices of existing single-family homes in thousands of dollars; (p) preliminary; n/a not available; (1) Figures cover the Evansville, IN-KY Metropolitan Statistical Area—see Appendix B for areas included
Source: National Association of Realtors, Median Sales Price of Existing Single-Family Homes for Metropolitan Areas, 4th Quarter 2018

Qualifying Income Based on Median Sales Price of Existing Single-Family Homes

Area	With 5% Down ($)	With 10% Down ($)	With 20% Down ($)
MSA[1]	n/a	n/a	n/a
U.S. Average	62,954	59,640	53,013

Note: Figures are preliminary; Qualifying income is based on a mortgage rate of 4.9%. Monthly principal and interest payment is limited to 25% of income; n/a not available; (1) Figures cover the Evansville, IN-KY Metropolitan Statistical Area—see Appendix B for areas included
Source: National Association of Realtors, Qualifying Income Based on Median Sales Price of Existing Single-Family Homes for Metropolitan Areas, 4th Quarter 2018

Median Apartment Condo-Coop Home Prices

Area	2016	2017	2018[p]	Percent Change 2017 to 2018
MSA[1]	n/a	n/a	n/a	n/a
U.S. Average	220.7	234.3	241.0	2.9

Note: Figures are median sales prices of existing apartment condo-coop homes in thousands of dollars; (p) preliminary; n/a not available; (1) Figures cover the Evansville, IN-KY Metropolitan Statistical Area—see Appendix B for areas included
Source: National Association of Realtors, Median Sales Price of Existing Apartment Condo-Coop Homes for Metropolitan Areas, 4th Quarter 2018

Home Value Distribution

Area	Under $50,000	$50,000 -$99,999	$100,000 -$149,999	$150,000 -$199,999	$200,000 -$299,999	$300,000 -$499,999	$500,000 -$999,999	$1,000,000 or more
City	12.5	47.0	22.7	9.2	5.8	1.9	0.8	0.2
MSA[1]	8.9	26.4	23.4	18.6	13.8	6.6	2.0	0.3
U.S.	8.3	13.9	14.7	14.6	18.7	17.3	9.7	2.7

Note: Figures are percentages and cover owner-occupied housing units; (1) Figures cover the Evansville, IN-KY Metropolitan Statistical Area—see Appendix B for areas included
Source: U.S. Census Bureau, 2013-2017 American Community Survey 5-Year Estimates

Homeownership Rate

Area	2010 (%)	2011 (%)	2012 (%)	2013 (%)	2014 (%)	2015 (%)	2016 (%)	2017 (%)	2018 (%)
MSA[1]	n/a	n/a	n/a	n/a	n/a	n/a	n/a	n/a	n/a
U.S.	66.9	66.1	65.4	65.1	64.5	63.7	63.4	63.9	64.4

Note: (1) Figures cover the Evansville, IN-KY Metropolitan Statistical Area—see Appendix B for areas included; n/a not available
Source: U.S. Census Bureau, Housing Vacancies and Homeownership Annual Statistics: 2010-2018

Year Housing Structure Built

Area	2010 or Later	2000 -2009	1990 -1999	1980 -1989	1970 -1979	1960 -1969	1950 -1959	1940 -1949	Before 1940	Median Year
City	0.9	6.0	7.1	8.6	12.9	10.5	17.7	12.1	24.1	1958
MSA[1]	2.3	11.7	13.0	11.0	15.6	9.6	13.0	7.7	16.1	1972
U.S.	3.2	14.5	14.0	13.6	15.5	10.8	10.5	5.1	12.9	1977

Note: Figures are percentages except for Median Year; Note: (1) Figures cover the Evansville, IN-KY Metropolitan Statistical Area—see Appendix B for areas included
Source: U.S. Census Bureau, 2013-2017 American Community Survey 5-Year Estimates

Gross Monthly Rent

Area	Under $500	$500 -$999	$1,000 -$1,499	$1,500 -$1,999	$2,000 -$2,499	$2,500 -$2,999	$3,000 and up	Median ($)
City	15.1	69.4	14.4	0.7	0.2	0.0	0.1	738
MSA[1]	15.9	66.6	15.4	1.1	0.2	0.2	0.5	732
U.S.	10.5	41.1	28.7	11.7	4.5	1.8	1.7	982

Note: Figures are percentages except for Median; Gross rent is the contract rent plus the estimated average monthly cost of utilities (electricity, gas, and water and sewer) and fuels (oil, coal, kerosene, wood, etc.) if these are paid by the renter (or paid for the renter by someone else); (1) Figures cover the Evansville, IN-KY Metropolitan Statistical Area—see Appendix B for areas included
Source: U.S. Census Bureau, 2013-2017 American Community Survey 5-Year Estimates

HEALTH

Health Risk Factors

Category	MSA[1] (%)	U.S. (%)
Adults aged 18–64 who have any kind of health care coverage	90.0	87.3
Adults who reported being in good or better health	77.9	82.4
Adults who have been told they have high blood cholesterol	35.5	33.0
Adults who have been told they have high blood pressure	35.0	32.3
Adults who are current smokers	23.0	17.1
Adults who currently use E-cigarettes	8.9	4.6
Adults who currently use chewing tobacco, snuff, or snus	6.4	4.0
Adults who are heavy drinkers[2]	8.9	6.3
Adults who are binge drinkers[3]	17.6	17.4
Adults who are overweight (BMI 25.0 - 29.9)	34.1	35.3
Adults who are obese (BMI 30.0 - 99.8)	31.5	31.3
Adults who participated in any physical activities in the past month	68.0	74.4
Adults who always or nearly always wears a seat belt	92.5	94.3

Note: (1) Figures cover the Evansville, IN-KY Metropolitan Statistical Area—see Appendix B for areas included; (2) Heavy drinkers are classified as adult men having more than 14 drinks per week and adult women having more than 7 drinks per week; (3) Binge drinkers are classified as males having five or more drinks on one occasion or females having four or more drinks on one occasion
Source: Centers for Disease Control and Prevention, Behaviorial Risk Factor Surveillance System, SMART: Selected Metropolitan Area Risk Trends, 2017

Acute and Chronic Health Conditions

Category	MSA[1] (%)	U.S. (%)
Adults who have ever been told they had a heart attack	6.1	4.2
Adults who have ever been told they have angina or coronary heart disease	3.9	3.9
Adults who have ever been told they had a stroke	3.0	3.0
Adults who have ever been told they have asthma	16.9	14.2
Adults who have ever been told they have arthritis	34.5	24.9
Adults who have ever been told they have diabetes[2]	12.8	10.5
Adults who have ever been told they had skin cancer	6.9	6.2
Adults who have ever been told they had any other types of cancer	7.0	7.1
Adults who have ever been told they have COPD	8.9	6.5
Adults who have ever been told they have kidney disease	3.0	3.0
Adults who have ever been told they have a form of depression	29.8	20.5

Note: (1) Figures cover the Evansville, IN-KY Metropolitan Statistical Area—see Appendix B for areas included; (2) Figures do not include pregnancy-related, borderline, or pre-diabetes
Source: Centers for Disease Control and Prevention, Behaviorial Risk Factor Surveillance System, SMART: Selected Metropolitan Area Risk Trends, 2017

Health Screening and Vaccination Rates

Category	MSA[1] (%)	U.S. (%)
Adults aged 65+ who have had flu shot within the past year	61.8	60.7
Adults aged 65+ who have ever had a pneumonia vaccination	80.0	75.4
Adults who have ever been tested for HIV	33.8	36.1
Adults who have ever had the shingles or zoster vaccine?	30.9	28.9
Adults who have had their blood cholesterol checked within the last five years	89.2	85.9

Note: n/a not available; (1) Figures cover the Evansville, IN-KY Metropolitan Statistical Area—see Appendix B for areas included.
Source: Centers for Disease Control and Prevention, Behaviorial Risk Factor Surveillance System, SMART: Selected Metropolitan Area Risk Trends, 2017

Disability Status

Category	MSA[1] (%)	U.S. (%)
Adults who reported being deaf	7.5	6.7
Are you blind or have serious difficulty seeing, even when wearing glasses?	5.3	4.5
Are you limited in any way in any of your usual activities due of arthritis?	19.3	12.9
Do you have difficulty doing errands alone?	11.0	6.8
Do you have difficulty dressing or bathing?	5.0	3.6
Do you have serious difficulty concentrating/remembering/making decisions?	13.8	10.7
Do you have serious difficulty walking or climbing stairs?	17.9	13.6

Note: (1) Figures cover the Evansville, IN-KY Metropolitan Statistical Area—see Appendix B for areas included.
Source: Centers for Disease Control and Prevention, Behaviorial Risk Factor Surveillance System, SMART: Selected Metropolitan Area Risk Trends, 2017

Mortality Rates for the Top 10 Causes of Death in the U.S.

ICD-10[a] Sub-Chapter	ICD-10[a] Code	Age-Adjusted Mortality Rate[1] per 100,000 population	
		County[2]	U.S.
Malignant neoplasms	C00-C97	176.8	155.5
Ischaemic heart diseases	I20-I25	93.7	94.8
Other forms of heart disease	I30-I51	54.4	52.9
Chronic lower respiratory diseases	J40-J47	64.7	41.0
Cerebrovascular diseases	I60-I69	33.1	37.5
Other degenerative diseases of the nervous system	G30-G31	45.4	35.0
Other external causes of accidental injury	W00-X59	51.8	33.7
Organic, including symptomatic, mental disorders	F01-F09	42.2	31.0
Hypertensive diseases	I10-I15	18.4	21.9
Diabetes mellitus	E10-E14	26.9	21.2

Note: (a) ICD-10 = International Classification of Diseases 10th Revision; (1) Mortality rates are a three year average covering 2015-2017; (2) Figures cover Vanderburgh County.
Source: Centers for Disease Control and Prevention, National Center for Health Statistics. Underlying Cause of Death 1999-2017 on CDC WONDER Online Database

Mortality Rates for Selected Causes of Death

ICD-10[a] Sub-Chapter	ICD-10[a] Code	Age-Adjusted Mortality Rate[1] per 100,000 population	
		County[2]	U.S.
Assault	X85-Y09	6.0	5.9
Diseases of the liver	K70-K76	22.2	14.1
Human immunodeficiency virus (HIV) disease	B20-B24	Suppressed	1.8
Influenza and pneumonia	J09-J18	14.3	14.3
Intentional self-harm	X60-X84	18.2	13.6
Malnutrition	E40-E46	Suppressed	1.6
Obesity and other hyperalimentation	E65-E68	4.0	2.1
Renal failure	N17-N19	19.2	13.0
Transport accidents	V01-V99	10.0	12.4
Viral hepatitis	B15-B19	Unreliable	1.6

Note: (a) ICD-10 = International Classification of Diseases 10th Revision; (1) Mortality rates are a three year average covering 2015-2017; (2) Figures cover Vanderburgh County; Data are suppressed when the data meet the criteria for confidentiality constraints; Mortality rates are flagged as unreliable when the rate would be calculated with a numerator of 20 or less.
Source: Centers for Disease Control and Prevention, National Center for Health Statistics. Underlying Cause of Death 1999-2017 on CDC WONDER Online Database

Health Insurance Coverage

Area	With Health Insurance	With Private Health Insurance	With Public Health Insurance	Without Health Insurance	Population Under Age 18 Without Health Insurance
City	88.3	61.1	39.9	11.7	4.9
MSA[1]	92.0	71.8	33.6	8.0	3.9
U.S.	89.5	67.2	33.8	10.5	5.7

Note: Figures are percentages that cover the civilian noninstitutionalized population; (1) Figures cover the Evansville, IN-KY Metropolitan Statistical Area—see Appendix B for areas included
Source: U.S. Census Bureau, 2013-2017 American Community Survey 5-Year Estimates

Number of Medical Professionals

Area	MDs[3]	DOs[3,4]	Dentists	Podiatrists	Chiropractors	Optometrists
County[1] (number)	489	42	130	23	41	62
County[1] (rate[2])	269.0	23.1	71.6	12.7	22.6	34.1
U.S. (rate[2])	279.3	23.0	68.4	6.0	27.1	16.2

Note: Data as of 2017 unless noted; (1) Data covers Vanderburgh County; (2) Rate per 100,000 population; (3) Data as of 2016 and includes all active, non-federal physicians; (4) Doctor of Osteopathic Medicine
Source: U.S. Department of Health and Human Services, Health Resources and Services Administration, Bureau of Health Professions, Area Resource File (ARF) 2017-2018

EDUCATION

Public School District Statistics

District Name	Schls	Pupils	Pupil/ Teacher Ratio	Minority Pupils[1] (%)	Free Lunch Eligible[2] (%)	IEP[3] (%)
Evansville Vanderburgh School Corp	37	22,879	13.2	30.3	47.2	17.4

Note: Table includes school districts with 2,000 or more students; (1) Percentage of students that are not non-Hispanic white; (2) Percentage of students that are eligible for the free lunch program; (3) Percentage of students that have an Individualized Education Program.
Source: U.S. Department of Education, National Center for Education Statistics, Common Core of Data, Local Education Agency (School District) Universe Survey: School Year 2016-2017; U.S. Department of Education, National Center for Education Statistics, Common Core of Data, Public Elementary/Secondary School Universe Survey: School Year 2016-2017

Best High Schools

According to *U.S. News,* Evansville is home to one of the best high schools in the U.S.: **Signature School** (#17). More than 20,000 public, magnet and charter schools were ranked based on their performance on state assessments and how well they prepare students for college. Schools with the highest unrounded College Readiness Index values were numerically ranked from 1 to 500 and were classified as gold medal winners. *U.S. News & World Report, "Best High Schools 2018"*

Highest Level of Education

Area	Less than H.S.	H.S. Diploma	Some College, No Deg.	Associate Degree	Bachelor's Degree	Master's Degree	Prof. School Degree	Doctorate Degree
City	13.1	34.8	23.2	8.2	13.7	5.3	1.0	0.7
MSA[1]	10.0	33.4	22.3	9.4	15.7	6.9	1.5	0.8
U.S.	12.7	27.3	20.8	8.3	19.1	8.4	2.0	1.4

Note: Figures cover persons age 25 and over; (1) Figures cover the Evansville, IN-KY Metropolitan Statistical Area—see Appendix B for areas included
Source: U.S. Census Bureau, 2013-2017 American Community Survey 5-Year Estimates

Educational Attainment by Race

Area	High School Graduate or Higher (%)					Bachelor's Degree or Higher (%)				
	Total	White	Black	Asian	Hisp.[2]	Total	White	Black	Asian	Hisp.[2]
City	86.9	87.6	83.3	94.0	53.4	20.7	21.9	11.9	40.0	10.6
MSA[1]	90.0	90.5	84.8	93.6	61.8	24.9	25.5	12.6	53.1	18.0
U.S.	87.3	89.3	84.9	86.5	66.7	30.9	32.2	20.6	52.7	15.2

Note: Figures shown cover persons 25 years old and over; (1) Figures cover the Evansville, IN-KY Metropolitan Statistical Area—see Appendix B for areas included; (2) People of Hispanic origin can be of any race
Source: U.S. Census Bureau, 2013-2017 American Community Survey 5-Year Estimates

School Enrollment by Grade and Control

Area	Preschool (%)		Kindergarten (%)		Grades 1 - 4 (%)		Grades 5 - 8 (%)		Grades 9 - 12 (%)	
	Public	Private	Public	Private	Public	Private	Public	Private	Public	Private
City	60.2	39.8	83.0	17.0	87.0	13.0	82.7	17.3	90.8	9.2
MSA[1]	50.2	49.8	81.4	18.6	82.5	17.5	81.3	18.7	87.9	12.1
U.S.	58.8	41.2	87.7	12.3	89.7	10.3	89.6	10.4	90.3	9.7

Note: Figures shown cover persons 3 years old and over; (1) Figures cover the Evansville, IN-KY Metropolitan Statistical Area—see Appendix B for areas included
Source: U.S. Census Bureau, 2013-2017 American Community Survey 5-Year Estimates

Average Salaries of Public School Classroom Teachers

Area	2016		2017		Change from 2016 to 2017	
	Dollars	Rank[1]	Dollars	Rank[1]	Percent	Rank[2]
Indiana	53,645	26	54,308	26	1.2	30
U.S. Average	58,479	–	59,660	–	2.0	–

Note: (1) Rank ranges from 1 to 51 where 1 indicates highest salary; (2) Rank ranges from 1 to 51 where 1 indicates highest percent change.
Source: National Education Association, Rankings & Estimates: Rankings of the States 2017 and Estimates of School Statistics 2018

Higher Education

Four-Year Colleges			Two-Year Colleges			Medical Schools[1]	Law Schools[2]	Voc/ Tech[3]
Public	Private Non-profit	Private For-profit	Public	Private Non-profit	Private For-profit			
1	1	0	0	0	1	1	0	2

Note: Figures cover institutions located within the city limits and include main campuses only; (1) includes schools accredited by the Liaison Committee on Medical Education and the American Osteopathic Association's Commission on Osteopathic College Accreditation; (2) includes ABA-accredited schools, schools with provisional ABA accreditation, and state accredited schools; (3) includes all schools with programs that are less than 2 years.
Source: National Center for Education Statistics, Integrated Postsecondary Education System (IPEDS), 2017-18; Wikipedia, List of Medical Schools in the United States, accessed April 3, 2019; Wikipedia, List of Law Schools in the United States, accessed April 3, 2019

PRESIDENTIAL ELECTION

2016 Presidential Election Results

Area	Clinton	Trump	Johnson	Stein	Other
Vanderburgh County	38.9	55.2	4.4	0.3	1.2
U.S.	48.0	45.9	3.3	1.1	1.7

Note: Results are percentages and may not add to 100% due to rounding
Source: Dave Leip's Atlas of U.S. Presidential Elections

EMPLOYERS

Major Employers

Company Name	Industry
Alcoa Warrick Operations	Aluminum sheet and ingot manufacturing
AstraZeneca Pharmaceuticals	Pharmaceutical manufacturing
AT&T	Wireless and wireline communications
Berry Global	Injection-molded plastics
Deaconess Hospital	General medical & surgical hospitals
Evansville Vanderburgh School Corp.	School districts
Koch Enterprises	Industrial and auto parts manufacturing
Mead Johnson Nutrition	Pediatric nutrition
Old National Bancorp.	Banking and financial services
One Main Financial	Financial services
SABIC	Engineering thermoplastics
SKANSKA	Construction and engineering
St. Vincent's-Evansville	General medical & surgical hospitals
T.J. Maxx	Clothing and household goods, distribution
Toyota Boshoku Indiana	Automotive supplier
Toyota Motor Manufacturing, Indiana	SUV and van manufacturing
Tropicana Evansville	Gaming and entertainment
University of Southern Indiana	Post-secondary education
Vectren Corp.	Gas and electric utility
Vuteq Corporation	Automotive interior parts

Note: Companies shown are located within the Evansville, IN-KY Metropolitan Statistical Area.
Source: Hoovers.com; Wikipedia

PUBLIC SAFETY

Crime Rate

Area	All Crimes	Violent Crimes				Property Crimes		
		Murder	Rape[3]	Robbery	Aggrav. Assault	Burglary	Larceny -Theft	Motor Vehicle Theft
City	5,699.9	16.8	62.8	155.0	456.6	723.0	3,887.9	397.9
Suburbs[1]	1,625.2	3.0	22.3	25.3	131.6	302.1	1,040.8	100.2
Metro[2]	3,159.5	8.2	37.5	74.1	253.9	460.6	2,112.9	212.3
U.S.	2,756.1	5.3	41.7	98.0	248.9	430.4	1,694.4	237.4

Note: Figures are crimes per 100,000 population; (1) All areas within the metro area that are located outside the city limits; (2) Figures cover the Evansville, IN-KY Metropolitan Statistical Area—see Appendix B for areas included; (3) The city and U.S. figures shown were reported using the revised Uniform Crime Reporting (UCR) definition of rape. The suburban and metro area figures shown are an aggregate total of the data submitted using both the revised and legacy UCR definitions.
Source: FBI Uniform Crime Reports, 2017

Hate Crimes

Area	Number of Quarters Reported	Number of Incidents per Bias Motivation					
		Race/Ethnicity/ Ancestry	Religion	Sexual Orientation	Disability	Gender	Gender Identity
City	n/a	n/a	n/a	n/a	n/a	n/a	n/a
U.S.	4	4,131	1,564	1,130	116	46	119

Note: n/a not available.
Source: Federal Bureau of Investigation, Hate Crime Statistics 2017

Identity Theft Consumer Reports

Area	Reports	Reports per 100,000 Population	Rank[2]
MSA[1]	154	49	360
U.S.	444,602	135	-

Note: (1) Figures cover the Evansville, IN-KY Metropolitan Statistical Area—see Appendix B for areas included; (2) Rank ranges from 1 to 389 where 1 indicates greatest number of identity theft reports per 100,000 population
Source: Federal Trade Commission, Consumer Sentinel Network Data Book for January–December 2018

Fraud and Other Consumer Reports

Area	Reports	Reports per 100,000 Population	Rank[2]
MSA[1]	1,407	445	255
U.S.	2,552,917	776	-

Note: (1) Figures cover the Evansville, IN-KY Metropolitan Statistical Area—see Appendix B for areas included; (2) Rank ranges from 1 to 389 where 1 indicates greatest number of fraud and other consumer reports per 100,000 population
Source: Federal Trade Commission, Consumer Sentinel Network Data Book for January–December 2018

SPORTS

Professional Sports Teams

Team Name	League	Year Established
No teams are located in the metro area		

Source: Wikipedia, Major Professional Sports Teams of the United States and Canada, April 5, 2019

CLIMATE

Average and Extreme Temperatures

Temperature	Jan	Feb	Mar	Apr	May	Jun	Jul	Aug	Sep	Oct	Nov	Dec	Yr.
Extreme High (°F)	71	72	85	89	93	102	104	102	100	90	81	74	104
Average High (°F)	35	39	50	63	73	82	85	84	78	66	51	39	62
Average Temp. (°F)	27	31	41	52	63	72	76	73	67	55	43	31	53
Average Low (°F)	18	22	31	41	52	61	65	63	55	44	33	23	42
Extreme Low (°F)	-22	-21	-7	18	28	39	48	41	34	20	-2	-23	-23

Note: Figures cover the years 1948-1990
Source: National Climatic Data Center, International Station Meteorological Climate Summary, 9/96

Average Precipitation/Snowfall/Humidity

Precip./Humidity	Jan	Feb	Mar	Apr	May	Jun	Jul	Aug	Sep	Oct	Nov	Dec	Yr.
Avg. Precip. (in.)	2.8	2.5	3.6	3.6	4.0	3.9	4.3	3.4	2.9	2.6	3.3	3.3	40.2
Avg. Snowfall (in.)	7	6	4	1	Tr	0	0	0	0	Tr	2	5	25
Avg. Rel. Hum. 7am (%)	81	81	79	77	79	80	84	87	87	85	83	83	82
Avg. Rel. Hum. 4pm (%)	68	64	59	53	53	53	56	56	53	53	63	70	59

Note: Figures cover the years 1948-1990; Tr = Trace amounts (<0.05 in. of rain; <0.5 in. of snow)
Source: National Climatic Data Center, International Station Meteorological Climate Summary, 9/96

Weather Conditions

Temperature			Daytime Sky			Precipitation		
10°F & below	32°F & below	90°F & above	Clear	Partly cloudy	Cloudy	0.01 inch or more precip.	0.1 inch or more snow/ice	Thunder-storms
19	119	19	83	128	154	127	24	43

Note: Figures are average number of days per year and cover the years 1948-1990
Source: National Climatic Data Center, International Station Meteorological Climate Summary, 9/96

HAZARDOUS WASTE

Superfund Sites

The Evansville, IN-KY metro area is home to one site on the EPA's Superfund National Priorities List: **Jacobsville Neighborhood Soil Contamination** (final). There are a total of 1,390 Superfund sites with a status of proposed or final on the list in the U.S. *U.S. Environmental Protection Agency, National Priorities List, April 5, 2019*

**AIR & WATER
QUALITY**

Air Quality Trends: Ozone

	1990	1995	2000	2005	2010	2012	2014	2015	2016	2017
MSA[1]	0.088	0.092	0.076	0.072	0.072	0.078	0.067	0.067	0.071	0.067
U.S.	0.088	0.089	0.082	0.080	0.073	0.075	0.067	0.068	0.069	0.068

Note: (1) Data covers the Evansville, IN-KY Metropolitan Statistical Area—see Appendix B for areas included. The values shown are the composite ozone concentration averages among trend sites based on the highest fourth daily maximum 8-hour concentration in parts per million. These trends are based on sites having an adequate record of monitoring data during the trend period. Data from exceptional events are included.
Source: U.S. Environmental Protection Agency, Air Quality Monitoring Information, "Air Quality Trends by City, 1990-2017"

Air Quality Index

Area	Percent of Days when Air Quality was...[2]					AQI Statistics[2]	
	Good	Moderate	Unhealthy for Sensitive Groups	Unhealthy	Very Unhealthy	Maximum	Median
MSA[1]	57.5	39.7	2.7	0.0	0.0	126	48

Note: (1) Data covers the Evansville, IN-KY Metropolitan Statistical Area—see Appendix B for areas included; (2) Based on 365 days with AQI data in 2017. Air Quality Index (AQI) is an index for reporting daily air quality. EPA calculates the AQI for five major air pollutants regulated by the Clean Air Act: ground-level ozone, particle pollution (aka particulate matter), carbon monoxide, sulfur dioxide, and nitrogen dioxide. The AQI runs from 0 to 500. The higher the AQI value, the greater the level of air pollution and the greater the health concern. There are six AQI categories: "Good" AQI is between 0 and 50. Air quality is considered satisfactory; "Moderate" AQI is between 51 and 100. Air quality is acceptable; "Unhealthy for Sensitive Groups" When AQI values are between 101 and 150, members of sensitive groups may experience health effects; "Unhealthy" When AQI values are between 151 and 200 everyone may begin to experience health effects; "Very Unhealthy" AQI values between 201 and 300 trigger a health alert; "Hazardous" AQI values over 300 trigger warnings of emergency conditions (not shown).
Source: U.S. Environmental Protection Agency, Air Quality Index Report, 2017

Air Quality Index Pollutants

Area	Percent of Days when AQI Pollutant was...[2]					
	Carbon Monoxide	Nitrogen Dioxide	Ozone	Sulfur Dioxide	Particulate Matter 2.5	Particulate Matter 10
MSA[1]	0.0	0.0	37.8	15.3	46.8	0.0

Note: (1) Data covers the Evansville, IN-KY Metropolitan Statistical Area—see Appendix B for areas included; (2) Based on 365 days with AQI data in 2017. The Air Quality Index (AQI) is an index for reporting daily air quality. EPA calculates the AQI for five major air pollutants regulated by the Clean Air Act: ground-level ozone, particle pollution (also known as particulate matter), carbon monoxide, sulfur dioxide, and nitrogen dioxide. The AQI runs from 0 to 500. The higher the AQI value, the greater the level of air pollution and the greater the health concern.
Source: U.S. Environmental Protection Agency, Air Quality Index Report, 2017

Maximum Air Pollutant Concentrations: Particulate Matter, Ozone, CO and Lead

	Particulate Matter 10 (ug/m^3)	Particulate Matter 2.5 Wtd AM (ug/m^3)	Particulate Matter 2.5 24-Hr (ug/m^3)	Ozone (ppm)	Carbon Monoxide (ppm)	Lead (ug/m^3)
MSA[1] Level	26	8.9	19	0.068	1	n/a
NAAQS[2]	150	15	35	0.075	9	0.15
Met NAAQS[2]	Yes	Yes	Yes	Yes	Yes	n/a

Note: (1) Data covers the Evansville, IN-KY Metropolitan Statistical Area—see Appendix B for areas included; Data from exceptional events are included; (2) National Ambient Air Quality Standards; ppm = parts per million; ug/m^3 = micrograms per cubic meter; n/a not available.
Concentrations: Particulate Matter 10 (coarse particulate)—highest second maximum 24-hour concentration; Particulate Matter 2.5 Wtd AM (fine particulate)—highest weighted annual mean concentration; Particulate Matter 2.5 24-Hour (fine particulate)—highest 98th percentile 24-hour concentration; Ozone—highest fourth daily maximum 8-hour concentration; Carbon Monoxide—highest second maximum non-overlapping 8-hour concentration; Lead—maximum running 3-month average
Source: U.S. Environmental Protection Agency, Air Quality Monitoring Information, "Air Quality Statistics by City, 2017"

Maximum Air Pollutant Concentrations: Nitrogen Dioxide and Sulfur Dioxide

	Nitrogen Dioxide AM (ppb)	Nitrogen Dioxide 1-Hr (ppb)	Sulfur Dioxide AM (ppb)	Sulfur Dioxide 1-Hr (ppb)	Sulfur Dioxide 24-Hr (ppb)
MSA[1] Level	8	29	n/a	94	n/a
NAAQS[2]	53	100	30	75	140
Met NAAQS[2]	Yes	Yes	n/a	No	n/a

Note: (1) Data covers the Evansville, IN-KY Metropolitan Statistical Area—see Appendix B for areas included; Data from exceptional events are included; (2) National Ambient Air Quality Standards; ppm = parts per million; ug/m³ = micrograms per cubic meter; n/a not available.
Concentrations: Nitrogen Dioxide AM—highest arithmetic mean concentration; Nitrogen Dioxide 1-Hr—highest 98th percentile 1-hour daily maximum concentration; Sulfur Dioxide AM—highest annual mean concentration; Sulfur Dioxide 1-Hr—highest 99th percentile 1-hour daily maximum concentration; Sulfur Dioxide 24-Hr—highest second maximum 24-hour concentration
Source: U.S. Environmental Protection Agency, Air Quality Monitoring Information, "Air Quality Statistics by City, 2017"

Drinking Water

Water System Name	Pop. Served	Primary Water Source Type	Violations[1] Health Based	Violations[1] Monitoring/ Reporting
Evansville Water Utility	173,000	Surface	0	0

Note: (1) Based on violation data from January 1, 2018 to December 31, 2018
Source: U.S. Environmental Protection Agency, Office of Ground Water and Drinking Water, Safe Drinking Water Information System (based on data extracted April 5, 2019)

Fargo, North Dakota

Background

Fargo sits on the western bank of the Red River in the Red River Valley in the southeastern part of the state. The city is in Cass County and about 300 miles northwest of Minneapolis.

Fargo was originally a stopping point for steamboats on the Red River in the later part of the 19th century. Founded in 1871, the city was originally named Centralia, but renamed Fargo in honor of the Northern Pacific Railway director Wells Fargo. It began to flourish after the arrival of the railroad and became known as the Gateway to the West. During the 1880s, Fargo was also known for its lenient divorce laws.

A major fire in 1893 destroyed hundreds of homes and businesses but the city was quickly rebuilt with new brick buildings, new streets and a water system. The North Dakota State Agricultural College was founded in 1890 as the state's land-grant university, and was accredited by the North Central Association in 1915. The school eventually became known as North Dakota State University during the 1960s.

Fargo grew rapidly after World War II as the connection of two interstates, I-29 and I-94, revolutionized travel in the region and allowed for further expansion in the southern and western parts of the city. In 1972, the West Acres Shopping Center was constructed near the intersection of the two interstates and served as a catalyst for retail growth in the area.

Fargo is the crossroads and economic center of eastern North Dakota and western Minnesota. Though the economy of the region was historically dependent on agriculture, other sectors have become increasingly prevalent in recent years. Today, the city's growing economy is based on food processing, manufacturing, technology, retail trade, higher education, and healthcare. The University is the city's largest public sector employer.

A significant landmark in Fargo is the main campus of North Dakota State University, which has a full-time enrollment of nearly 9,000. The city also features a large number of public parks including Percy Godwin Park, Lindenwood Park, Mickelson Field, Island Park, Roosevelt Playground, and Oak Grove Park.

As the city continues to energize the downtown area, the Renaissance Zone and Storefront Rehab programs encourage new business, renovate deteriorating buildings, and increase the availability of housing in the downtown area. The renovated Fargo Public Library's main downtown branch is popular with the city's residents.

Fargo, an Academy Award-winning 1996 film named after the city, shows the city briefly at the film's opening scene set in a bar, and is mentioned twice in the film. *Fargo* the TV series based on the film, debuted on FX in 2014. The city was featured in its seventh episode of season 1, "Who Shaves the Barber?" and more prominently in season 2. The series was filmed in Calgary, Alberta, Canada.

Fargo has a moderate northern climate. Summer temperatures average 65 degrees, while winter averages fall to 10 degrees during of December and January. The city averages 2.5 inches of rainfall per month from April to October and 8 inches of snowfall per month from December to March. Natural disaster struck in 2009, when heavy snowfall caused the Red River to flood the area, followed by extended periods of freezing temperatures.

Rankings

General Rankings

- In their sixth annual survey, Livability.com looked at data for more than 1,000 U.S. cities to determine the rankings for Livability's "Top 100 Best Places to Live" in 2019. Fargo ranked #11. Criteria: median home value capped at $250,000; affordable living; vibrant economy; education, demographics, health care options. transportation & infrastructure; abundant lifestyle amenities. *Livability.com, "Top 100 Best Places to Live 2019" March 2019*

Business/Finance Rankings

- The Fargo metro area appeared on the Milken Institute "2018 Best Performing Cities" list. Rank: #68 out of 201 small metro areas. Criteria: job growth; wage and salary growth; high-tech output growth. *Milken Institute, "Best-Performing Cities 2018," January 24, 2019*

- *Forbes* ranked 200 smaller metro areas (population under 265,400) to determine the nation's "Best Small Places for Business and Careers." The Fargo metro area was ranked #23. Criteria: costs (business and living); job growth (past and projected); income growth; quality of life; educational attainment (college and high school); projected economic growth; cultural and recreational opportunities; net migration patterns; number of highly ranked colleges. *Forbes, "The Best Small Cities for Business and Careers 2018," October, 24 2018*

Dating/Romance Rankings

- Fargo was selected as one of the most romantic cities in the U.S. by video-rental kiosk company Redbox. The city ranked #10 out of 20. Criteria: number of romance-related rentals in 2016. *Redbox, "20 Most Romantic Cities," February 6, 2017*

Environmental Rankings

- Niche compiled a list of the nation's snowiest cities, based on the National Oceanic and Atmospheric Administration's 30-year average snowfall data. Among cities with a population of at least 50,000, Fargo ranked #18. *Niche.com, Top 25 Snowiest Cities in America, December 10, 2018*

- Fargo was highlighted as one of the cleanest metro areas for ozone air pollution in the U.S. during 2014 through 2016. The list represents cities with no monitored ozone air pollution in unhealthful ranges. *American Lung Association, State of the Air 2018*

Food/Drink Rankings

- *Men's Health* ranked 100 major U.S. cities in terms of alcohol intoxication. Fargo ranked #26 (#1 = most sober).Criteria: binge drinking; alcohol-related traffic accidents, arrests, and fatalities. *Men's Health, "America's Drunkest Cities," March 9, 2015*

Health/Fitness Rankings

- *Men's Health* ranked 100 major U.S. cities in terms of the best cities for men. Fargo ranked #20. Criteria: health; fitness; quality of life. *Men's Health, "The Best & Worst Cities for Men Who Want to Be Fit and Happy," January 1, 2016*

Real Estate Rankings

- *WalletHub* compared the most populated U.S. cities, as well as at least two of the most populated cities in each state, for a total of 179, to determine which had the best markets for real estate agents. Fargo ranked #18 where demand was high and pay was the best. Criteria: sales per agent; annual median wage for real-estate agents; monthly average starting salary for real estate agents; real estate job density and competition; unemployment rate; housing-market health index; and other relevant metrics. *www.WalletHub.com, "2018's Best Places to Be a Real Estate Agent,"April 25, 2018*

Safety Rankings

- The National Insurance Crime Bureau ranked 382 metro areas in the U.S. in terms of per capita rates of vehicle theft. The Fargo metro area ranked #204 (#1 = highest rate). Criteria: number of vehicle theft offenses per 100,000 inhabitants in 2017. *National Insurance Crime Bureau, "Hot Spots 2017," July 12, 2018*

Seniors/Retirement Rankings

- From its Best Cities for Successful Aging indexes, the Milken Institute generated rankings for metropolitan areas, weighing data in nine categories—health care, wellness, living arrangements, transportation and convenience, financial characteristics, education, employment, community engagement, and overall livability. The Fargo metro area was ranked #14 overall in the small metro area category. *Milken Institute, "Best Cities for Successful Aging, 2017" March 14, 2017*

- Fargo made the 2018 *Forbes* list of "25 Best Places to Retire." Criteria, focused on a high-quality retirement living an affordable price, include: housing/living costs compared to the national average and state taxes; weather and air quality; crime rates; vibrant economy and low unemployment; doctor availability; bikability; walkability; healthy living and volunteering. *Forbes.com, "The Best Places to Retire in 2018," April 23, 2018*

Sports/Recreation Rankings

- Fargo was chosen as a bicycle friendly community by the League of American Bicyclists. A "Bicycle Friendly Community" welcomes cyclists by providing safe and supportive accommodation for cycling and encouraging people to bike for transportation and recreation. There are five award levels: Diamond; Platinum; Gold; Silver; and Bronze. The community achieved an award level of Bronze. *League of American Bicyclists, "Fall 2018 Awards-Bicycle Friendly Community Master List," December 6, 2018*

Women/Minorities Rankings

- Personal finance website *WalletHub* compared more than 180 U.S. cities—including the 150 most populated U.S. cities, plus at least two of the most populated cities in each state—across two key dimensions, "Hispanic Business-Friendliness" and "Hispanic Purchasing Power", to arrive at the most favorable conditions for Hispanic entrepreneurs. Fargo was ranked #59 out of 182. Criteria includes: share of Hispanic-Owned Businesses; Hispanic entrepreneurship rate to median annual income of Hispanics; Small Business-Friendliness score; cost of living; and number of Hispanics with at least a bachelor's degree. *WalletHub.com, "2018's Best Cities for Hispanic Entrepreneurs," April 26, 2018*

Miscellaneous Rankings

- *WalletHub* compared the 150 most populated U.S. cities to determine their operating efficiency. A "Quality of Services" score was constructed for each city and then divided by the total budget per capita to reveal which were managed the best. Fargo ranked #19. Criteria: financial stability; economy; education; safety; health; infrastructure and pollution. *www.WalletHub.com, "2018's Best- & Worst-Run Cities in America," July 9, 2018*

Business Environment

CITY FINANCES

City Government Finances

Component	2016 ($000)	2016 ($ per capita)
Total Revenues	271,968	2,295
Total Expenditures	236,988	2,000
Debt Outstanding	599,569	5,059
Cash and Securities[1]	433,171	3,655

Note: (1) Cash and security holdings of a government at the close of its fiscal year, including those of its dependent agencies, utilities, and liquor stores.
Source: U.S. Census Bureau, State & Local Government Finances 2016

City Government Revenue by Source

Source	2016 ($000)	2016 ($ per capita)	2016 (%)
General Revenue			
From Federal Government	1,042	9	0.4
From State Government	57,016	481	21.0
From Local Governments	0	0	0.0
Taxes			
Property	24,820	209	9.1
Sales and Gross Receipts	58,340	492	21.5
Personal Income	0	0	0.0
Corporate Income	0	0	0.0
Motor Vehicle License	0	0	0.0
Other Taxes	6,866	58	2.5
Current Charges	57,478	485	21.1
Liquor Store	0	0	0.0
Utility	22,135	187	8.1
Employee Retirement	4,366	37	1.6

Source: U.S. Census Bureau, State & Local Government Finances 2016

City Government Expenditures by Function

Function	2016 ($000)	2016 ($ per capita)	2016 (%)
General Direct Expenditures			
Air Transportation	0	0	0.0
Corrections	0	0	0.0
Education	0	0	0.0
Employment Security Administration	0	0	0.0
Financial Administration	5,850	49	2.5
Fire Protection	0	0	0.0
General Public Buildings	1,200	10	0.5
Governmental Administration, Other	9,237	77	3.9
Health	0	0	0.0
Highways	98,583	831	41.6
Hospitals	0	0	0.0
Housing and Community Development	1,662	14	0.7
Interest on General Debt	23,008	194	9.7
Judicial and Legal	42	< 1	< 0.1
Libraries	0	0	0.0
Parking	985	8	0.4
Parks and Recreation	7,996	67	3.4
Police Protection	33,326	281	14.1
Public Welfare	10,413	87	4.4
Sewerage	6,585	55	2.8
Solid Waste Management	9,262	78	3.9
Veterans' Services	0	0	0.0
Liquor Store	0	0	0.0
Utility	17,445	147	7.4
Employee Retirement	8,242	69	3.5

Source: U.S. Census Bureau, State & Local Government Finances 2016

DEMOGRAPHICS

Population Growth

Area	1990 Census	2000 Census	2010 Census	2017* Estimate	Population Growth (%)	
					1990-2017	2010-2017
City	74,372	90,599	105,549	118,099	58.8	11.9
MSA[1]	153,296	174,367	208,777	232,660	51.8	11.4
U.S.	248,709,873	281,421,906	308,745,538	321,004,407	29.1	4.0

Note: (1) Figures cover the Fargo, ND-MN Metropolitan Statistical Area—see Appendix B for areas included;
(*) 2013-2017 5-year estimated population
Source: U.S. Census Bureau, 1990 Census, Census 2000, Census 2010, 2013-2017 American Community
Survey 5-Year Estimates

Household Size

Area	Persons in Household (%)							Average Household Size
	One	Two	Three	Four	Five	Six	Seven or More	
City	36.7	33.3	15.1	8.9	4.4	1.2	0.4	2.10
MSA[1]	31.0	34.8	14.9	12.0	5.0	1.5	0.7	2.30
U.S.	27.7	33.8	15.7	13.0	6.0	2.3	1.4	2.60

Note: (1) Figures cover the Fargo, ND-MN Metropolitan Statistical Area—see Appendix B for areas included
Source: U.S. Census Bureau, 2013-2017 American Community Survey 5-Year Estimates

Race

Area	White Alone[2] (%)	Black Alone[2] (%)	Asian Alone[2] (%)	AIAN[3] Alone[2] (%)	NHOPI[4] Alone[2] (%)	Other Race Alone[2] (%)	Two or More Races (%)
City	86.2	5.5	3.6	1.1	0.0	0.6	2.9
MSA[1]	89.3	3.9	2.5	1.1	0.0	0.6	2.6
U.S.	73.0	12.7	5.4	0.8	0.2	4.8	3.1

Note: (1) Figures cover the Fargo, ND-MN Metropolitan Statistical Area—see Appendix B for areas included;
(2) Alone is defined as not being in combination with one or more other races; (3) American Indian and Alaska
Native; (4) Native Hawaiian and Other Pacific Islander
Source: U.S. Census Bureau, 2013-2017 American Community Survey 5-Year Estimates

Hispanic or Latino Origin

Area	Total (%)	Mexican (%)	Puerto Rican (%)	Cuban (%)	Other (%)
City	2.8	1.8	0.3	0.0	0.7
MSA[1]	3.0	2.1	0.2	0.0	0.6
U.S.	17.6	11.1	1.7	0.7	4.1

Note: Persons of Hispanic or Latino origin can be of any race; (1) Figures cover the Fargo, ND-MN
Metropolitan Statistical Area—see Appendix B for areas included
Source: U.S. Census Bureau, 2013-2017 American Community Survey 5-Year Estimates

Segregation

Type	Segregation Indices[1]				Percent Change		
	1990	2000	2010	2010 Rank[2]	1990-2000	1990-2010	2000-2010
Black/White	n/a	n/a	n/a	n/a	n/a	n/a	n/a
Asian/White	n/a	n/a	n/a	n/a	n/a	n/a	n/a
Hispanic/White	n/a	n/a	n/a	n/a	n/a	n/a	n/a

Note: All figures cover the Metropolitan Statistical Area—see Appendix B for areas included; Figures are based
on an analysis of 1990, 2000, and 2010 Census Decennial Census tract data by William H. Frey, Brookings
Institution and the University of Michigan Social Science Data Analysis Network. In this analysis all racial
groups (whites, blacks, and asians) are non-Hispanic members of those races. Hispanics are shown as a
separate category; (1) Segregation Indices are Dissimilarity Indices that measure the degree to which the
minority group is distributed differently than whites across census tracts. They range from 0 (complete
integration) to 100 (complete segregation) where the value indicates the percentage of the minority group that
needs to move to be distributed exactly like whites; (2) Ranges from 1 (most segregated) to 102 (least
segregated); n/a not available.
Source: www.CensusScope.org

Ancestry

Area	German	Irish	English	American	Italian	Polish	French[2]	Scottish	Dutch
City	38.7	8.8	4.1	2.1	1.2	2.9	3.8	1.4	1.1
MSA[1]	39.4	8.0	4.1	2.0	1.2	2.8	3.4	1.3	1.2
U.S.	14.1	10.1	7.5	6.6	5.3	2.9	2.5	1.7	1.3

Note: Figures are the percentage of the total population reporting a particular ancestry. The nine most commonly reported ancestries in the U.S. are shown. Figures include multiple ancestries (e.g. if a person reported being Irish and Italian, they were included in both columns); (1) Figures cover the Fargo, ND-MN Metropolitan Statistical Area—see Appendix B for areas included; (2) Excludes Basque
Source: U.S. Census Bureau, 2013-2017 American Community Survey 5-Year Estimates

Foreign-Born Population

Area	Percent of Population Born in								
	Any Foreign Country	Asia	Mexico	Europe	Carribean	Central America[2]	South America	Africa	Canada
City	8.2	3.5	0.2	1.1	0.1	0.1	0.3	2.8	0.2
MSA[1]	5.9	2.6	0.2	0.7	0.1	0.1	0.2	1.8	0.3
U.S.	13.4	4.1	3.6	1.5	1.3	1.0	0.9	0.6	0.3

Note: (1) Figures cover the Fargo, ND-MN Metropolitan Statistical Area—see Appendix B for areas included; (2) Excludes Mexico.
Source: U.S. Census Bureau, 2013-2017 American Community Survey 5-Year Estimates

Marital Status

Area	Never Married	Now Married[2]	Separated	Widowed	Divorced
City	43.9	41.4	1.1	4.5	9.1
MSA[1]	37.5	48.6	0.9	4.3	8.7
U.S.	33.1	48.2	2.0	5.8	10.9

Note: Figures are percentages and cover the population 15 years of age and older; (1) Figures cover the Fargo, ND-MN Metropolitan Statistical Area—see Appendix B for areas included; (2) Excludes separated
Source: U.S. Census Bureau, 2013-2017 American Community Survey 5-Year Estimates

Disability by Age

Area	All Ages	Under 18 Years Old	18 to 64 Years Old	65 Years and Over
City	10.4	3.0	8.6	36.2
MSA[1]	9.9	3.2	8.1	34.7
U.S.	12.6	4.2	10.3	35.5

Note: Figures show percent of the civilian noninstitutionalized population that reported having a disability. Disability status is determined from six types of difficulty: vision, hearing, cognitive, ambulatory, self-care, and independent living. For children under 5 years old, hearing and vision difficulty are used to determine disability status. For children between the ages of 5 and 14, disability status is determined from hearing, vision, cognitive, ambulatory, and self-care difficulties. For people aged 15 years and older, they are considered to have a disability if they have difficulty with any one of the six difficulty types; Note: (1) Figures cover the Fargo, ND-MN Metropolitan Statistical Area—see Appendix B for areas included
Source: U.S. Census Bureau, 2013-2017 American Community Survey 5-Year Estimates

Age

Area	Percent of Population									Median Age
	Under Age 5	Age 5–19	Age 20–34	Age 35–44	Age 45–54	Age 55–64	Age 65–74	Age 75–84	Age 85+	
City	6.9	17.8	32.7	11.2	10.1	10.2	5.7	3.4	2.0	30.3
MSA[1]	7.1	19.5	27.7	12.2	11.2	10.8	6.1	3.4	1.8	32.3
U.S.	6.2	19.5	20.7	12.7	13.4	12.7	8.6	4.4	1.9	37.8

Note: (1) Figures cover the Fargo, ND-MN Metropolitan Statistical Area—see Appendix B for areas included
Source: U.S. Census Bureau, 2013-2017 American Community Survey 5-Year Estimates

Gender

Area	Males	Females	Males per 100 Females
City	59,777	58,322	102.5
MSA[1]	116,897	115,763	101.0
U.S.	158,018,753	162,985,654	97.0

Note: (1) Figures cover the Fargo, ND-MN Metropolitan Statistical Area—see Appendix B for areas included
Source: U.S. Census Bureau, 2013-2017 American Community Survey 5-Year Estimates

Religious Groups by Family

Area	Catholic	Baptist	Non-Den.	Methodist[2]	Lutheran	LDS[3]	Pente-costal	Presby-terian[4]	Muslim[5]	Judaism
MSA[1]	17.4	0.4	0.5	3.3	32.5	0.6	1.5	1.9	0.1	<0.1
U.S.	19.1	9.3	4.0	4.0	2.3	2.0	1.9	1.6	0.8	0.7

Note: Figures are the number of adherents as a percentage of the total population; (1) Figures cover the Fargo, ND-MN Metropolitan Statistical Area—see Appendix B for areas included; (2) Methodist/Pietist; (3) Latter Day Saints; (4) Reformed; (5) Figures are estimates
Source: Association of Statisticians of American Religious Bodies, 2010 U.S. Religion Census: Religious Congregations & Membership Study

Religious Groups by Tradition

Area	Catholic	Evangelical Protestant	Mainline Protestant	Other Tradition	Black Protestant	Orthodox
MSA[1]	17.4	10.7	30.8	0.9	<0.1	<0.1
U.S.	19.1	16.2	7.3	4.3	1.6	0.3

Note: Figures are the number of adherents as a percentage of the total population; (1) Figures cover the Fargo, ND-MN Metropolitan Statistical Area—see Appendix B for areas included
Source: Association of Statisticians of American Religious Bodies, 2010 U.S. Religion Census: Religious Congregations & Membership Study

ECONOMY

Gross Metropolitan Product

Area	2016	2017	2018	2019	Rank[2]
MSA[1]	15.8	16.5	17.2	18.1	154

Note: Figures are in billions of dollars; (1) Figures cover the Fargo, ND-MN Metropolitan Statistical Area—see Appendix B for areas included; (2) Rank is based on 2017 data and ranges from 1 to 381
Source: U.S. Conference of Mayors, U.S. Metro Economies: Economic Growth & Full Employment, June 2018

Economic Growth

Area	2017-2018 (%)	2019-2020 (%)	2021-2022 (%)
MSA[1]	0.4	1.6	1.5

Note: Figures are real gross metropolitan product (GMP) growth rates and represent average annual percent change; (1) Figures cover the Fargo, ND-MN Metropolitan Statistical Area—see Appendix B for areas included
Source: U.S. Conference of Mayors, U.S. Metro Economies: Economic Growth & Full Employment, June 2018

Metropolitan Area Exports

Area	2012	2013	2014	2015	2016	2017	Rank[2]
MSA[1]	785.9	817.9	782.8	543.2	474.5	519.5	205

Note: Figures are in millions of dollars; (1) Figures cover the Fargo, ND-MN Metropolitan Statistical Area—see Appendix B for areas included; (2) Rank is based on 2017 data and ranges from 1 to 387
Source: U.S. Department of Commerce, International Trade Administration, Office of Trade and Economic Analysis, Industry and Analysis, Exports by Metropolitan Area, extracted March 25, 2019

Building Permits

Area	Single-Family			Multi-Family			Total		
	2016	2017	Pct. Chg.	2016	2017	Pct. Chg.	2016	2017	Pct. Chg.
City	474	444	-6.3	859	781	-9.1	1,333	1,225	-8.1
MSA[1]	1,192	1,065	-10.7	1,287	826	-35.8	2,479	1,891	-23.7
U.S.	750,800	820,000	9.2	455,800	462,000	1.4	1,206,600	1,282,000	6.2

Note: (1) Figures cover the Fargo, ND-MN Metropolitan Statistical Area—see Appendix B for areas included; Figures represent new, privately-owned housing units authorized (unadjusted data); All permit data are based on estimates with imputation
Source: U.S. Census Bureau, Manufacturing, Mining, and Construction Statistics, Building Permits, 2016, 2017

Bankruptcy Filings

Area	Business Filings			Nonbusiness Filings		
	2017	2018	% Chg.	2017	2018	% Chg.
Cass County	14	6	-57.1	177	187	5.6
U.S.	23,157	22,232	-4.0	765,863	751,186	-1.9

Note: Business filings include Chapter 7, Chapter 11, Chapter 12, and Chapter 13; Nonbusiness filings include Chapter 7, Chapter 11, and Chapter 13
Source: Administrative Office of the U.S. Courts, Business and Nonbusiness Bankruptcy, County Cases Commenced by Chapter of the Bankruptcy Code, During the 12-Month Period Ending December 31, 2017 and Business and Nonbusiness Bankruptcy, County Cases Commenced by Chapter of the Bankruptcy Code, During the 12-Month Period Ending December 31, 2018

Housing Vacancy Rates

Area	Gross Vacancy Rate[2] (%)			Year-Round Vacancy Rate[3] (%)			Rental Vacancy Rate[4] (%)			Homeowner Vacancy Rate[5] (%)		
	2016	2017	2018	2016	2017	2018	2016	2017	2018	2016	2017	2018
MSA[1]	n/a	n/a	n/a	n/a	n/a	n/a	n/a	n/a	n/a	n/a	n/a	n/a
U.S.	12.8	12.7	12.3	9.9	9.9	9.7	6.9	7.2	6.9	1.7	1.6	1.5

Note: (1) Figures cover the Fargo, ND-MN Metropolitan Statistical Area—see Appendix B for areas included; (2) The percentage of the total housing inventory that is vacant; (3) The percentage of the housing inventory (excluding seasonal units) that is year-round vacant; (4) The percentage of rental inventory that is vacant for rent; (5) The percentage of homeowner inventory that is vacant for sale; n/a not available
Source: U.S. Census Bureau, Housing Vacancies and Homeownership Annual Statistics: 2016, 2017, 2018

INCOME

Income

Area	Per Capita ($)	Median Household ($)	Average Household ($)
City	31,866	50,561	71,030
MSA[1]	32,574	59,074	78,102
U.S.	31,177	57,652	81,283

Note: (1) Figures cover the Fargo, ND-MN Metropolitan Statistical Area—see Appendix B for areas included
Source: U.S. Census Bureau, 2013-2017 American Community Survey 5-Year Estimates

Household Income Distribution

Area	Percent of Households Earning							
	Under $15,000	$15,000 -$24,999	$25,000 -$34,999	$35,000 -$49,999	$50,000 -$74,999	$75,000 -$99,999	$100,000 -$149,999	$150,000 and up
City	11.9	11.1	11.6	14.8	18.2	12.7	11.8	8.0
MSA[1]	9.9	9.5	9.8	13.3	18.7	14.5	14.3	9.9
U.S.	11.6	9.8	9.5	13.0	17.7	12.3	14.1	12.1

Note: (1) Figures cover the Fargo, ND-MN Metropolitan Statistical Area—see Appendix B for areas included
Source: U.S. Census Bureau, 2013-2017 American Community Survey 5-Year Estimates

Poverty Rate

Area	All Ages	Under 18 Years Old	18 to 64 Years Old	65 Years and Over
City	13.9	13.4	15.1	7.1
MSA[1]	11.5	11.4	12.5	6.3
U.S.	14.6	20.3	13.7	9.3

Note: Figures are percentage of people whose income during the past 12 months was below the poverty level; (1) Figures cover the Fargo, ND-MN Metropolitan Statistical Area—see Appendix B for areas included
Source: U.S. Census Bureau, 2013-2017 American Community Survey 5-Year Estimates

EMPLOYMENT

Labor Force and Employment

Area	Civilian Labor Force			Workers Employed		
	Dec. 2017	Dec. 2018	% Chg.	Dec. 2017	Dec. 2018	% Chg.
City	69,596	68,580	-1.5	68,045	67,103	-1.4
MSA[1]	137,092	135,806	-0.9	133,678	132,655	-0.8
U.S.	159,880,000	162,510,000	1.6	153,602,000	156,481,000	1.9

Note: Data is not seasonally adjusted and covers workers 16 years of age and older; (1) Figures cover the Fargo, ND-MN Metropolitan Statistical Area—see Appendix B for areas included
Source: Bureau of Labor Statistics, Local Area Unemployment Statistics

Unemployment Rate

Area	2018											
	Jan.	Feb.	Mar.	Apr.	May	Jun.	Jul.	Aug.	Sep.	Oct.	Nov.	Dec.
City	2.9	2.8	2.8	2.5	2.0	2.5	2.1	2.2	2.1	1.8	2.0	2.2
MSA[1]	3.2	3.2	3.1	2.7	2.1	2.6	2.2	2.2	2.1	1.8	1.9	2.3
U.S.	4.5	4.4	4.1	3.7	3.6	4.2	4.1	3.9	3.6	3.5	3.5	3.7

Note: Data is not seasonally adjusted and covers workers 16 years of age and older; (1) Figures cover the Fargo, ND-MN Metropolitan Statistical Area—see Appendix B for areas included
Source: Bureau of Labor Statistics, Local Area Unemployment Statistics

Average Wages

Occupation	$/Hr.	Occupation	$/Hr.
Accountants and Auditors	30.80	Maids and Housekeeping Cleaners	11.50
Automotive Mechanics	20.90	Maintenance and Repair Workers	18.90
Bookkeepers	18.70	Marketing Managers	56.00
Carpenters	20.10	Nuclear Medicine Technologists	n/a
Cashiers	11.50	Nurses, Licensed Practical	21.90
Clerks, General Office	18.50	Nurses, Registered	32.30
Clerks, Receptionists/Information	13.70	Nursing Assistants	16.10
Clerks, Shipping/Receiving	16.80	Packers and Packagers, Hand	12.70
Computer Programmers	36.80	Physical Therapists	37.30
Computer Systems Analysts	40.70	Postal Service Mail Carriers	24.20
Computer User Support Specialists	27.60	Real Estate Brokers	n/a
Cooks, Restaurant	14.50	Retail Salespersons	15.00
Dentists	81.10	Sales Reps., Exc. Tech./Scientific	31.30
Electrical Engineers	39.70	Sales Reps., Tech./Scientific	30.70
Electricians	25.80	Secretaries, Exc. Legal/Med./Exec.	18.30
Financial Managers	65.30	Security Guards	16.60
First-Line Supervisors/Managers, Sales	21.60	Surgeons	n/a
Food Preparation Workers	12.30	Teacher Assistants*	15.30
General and Operations Managers	53.40	Teachers, Elementary School*	33.00
Hairdressers/Cosmetologists	15.90	Teachers, Secondary School*	30.60
Internists, General	n/a	Telemarketers	15.60
Janitors and Cleaners	13.40	Truck Drivers, Heavy/Tractor-Trailer	22.20
Landscaping/Groundskeeping Workers	16.90	Truck Drivers, Light/Delivery Svcs.	17.70
Lawyers	57.60	Waiters and Waitresses	9.60

Note: Wage data covers the Fargo, ND-MN Metropolitan Statistical Area—see Appendix B for areas included; (*) Hourly wages for elementary/secondary school teachers and teacher assistants were calculated by the editors from annual wage data based on a 40 hour work week; n/a not available.
Source: Bureau of Labor Statistics, Metro Area Occupational Employment & Wage Estimates, May 2018

Employment by Occupation

Occupation Classification	City (%)	MSA[1] (%)	U.S. (%)
Management, Business, Science, and Arts	37.6	38.1	37.4
Natural Resources, Construction, and Maintenance	7.9	8.7	8.9
Production, Transportation, and Material Moving	11.5	11.9	12.2
Sales and Office	23.4	23.9	23.5
Service	19.5	17.3	18.0

Note: Figures cover employed civilians 16 years of age and older; (1) Figures cover the Fargo, ND-MN Metropolitan Statistical Area—see Appendix B for areas included
Source: U.S. Census Bureau, 2013-2017 American Community Survey 5-Year Estimates

Employment by Industry

Sector	MSA[1]		U.S.
	Number of Employees	Percent of Total	Percent of Total
Construction, Mining, and Logging	8,000	5.6	5.3
Education and Health Services	25,100	17.6	15.9
Financial Activities	11,100	7.8	5.7
Government	20,500	14.4	15.1
Information	3,000	2.1	1.9
Leisure and Hospitality	13,700	9.6	10.7
Manufacturing	10,300	7.2	8.5
Other Services	5,000	3.5	3.9
Professional and Business Services	15,600	10.9	14.1
Retail Trade	15,600	10.9	10.8
Transportation, Warehousing, and Utilities	6,000	4.2	4.2
Wholesale Trade	8,900	6.2	3.9

Note: Figures are non-farm employment as of December 2018. Figures are not seasonally adjusted and include workers 16 years of age and older; (1) Figures cover the Fargo, ND-MN Metropolitan Statistical Area—see Appendix B for areas included
Source: Bureau of Labor Statistics, Current Employment Statistics, Employment, Hours, and Earnings

Occupations with Greatest Projected Employment Growth: 2018 – 2020

Occupation[1]	2018 Employment	2020 Projected Employment	Numeric Employment Change	Percent Employment Change
Roustabouts, Oil and Gas	3,590	4,030	440	12.3
Heavy and Tractor-Trailer Truck Drivers	12,540	12,970	430	3.4
Combined Food Preparation and Serving Workers, Including Fast Food	7,320	7,630	310	4.2
Personal Care Aides	5,700	5,940	240	4.2
Registered Nurses	8,880	9,110	230	2.6
First-Line Supervisors of Construction Trades and Extraction Workers	3,630	3,840	210	5.8
Waiters and Waitresses	7,360	7,550	190	2.6
General and Operations Managers	6,880	7,050	170	2.5
Janitors and Cleaners, Except Maids and Housekeeping Cleaners	7,360	7,510	150	2.0
Construction Laborers	4,990	5,120	130	2.6

Note: Projections cover North Dakota; (1) Sorted by numeric employment change
Source: www.projectionscentral.com, State Occupational Projections, 2018–2020 Short-Term Projections

Fastest Growing Occupations: 2018 – 2020

Occupation[1]	2018 Employment	2020 Projected Employment	Numeric Employment Change	Percent Employment Change
Extraction Workers, All Other	750	850	100	13.3
Derrick Operators, Oil and Gas	860	970	110	12.8
Roustabouts, Oil and Gas	3,590	4,030	440	12.3
Rotary Drill Operators, Oil and Gas	1,130	1,260	130	11.5
Service Unit Operators, Oil, Gas, and Mining	930	1,030	100	10.8
Wellhead Pumpers	750	820	70	9.3
Petroleum Pump System Operators, Refinery Operators, and Gaugers	760	820	60	7.9
First-Line Supervisors of Construction Trades and Extraction Workers	3,630	3,840	210	5.8
Mobile Heavy Equipment Mechanics, Except Engines	1,140	1,200	60	5.3
Bus and Truck Mechanics and Diesel Engine Specialists	1,850	1,940	90	4.9

Note: Projections cover North Dakota; (1) Sorted by percent employment change and excludes occupations with numeric employment change less than 50
Source: www.projectionscentral.com, State Occupational Projections, 2018–2020 Short-Term Projections

TAXES

State Corporate Income Tax Rates

State	Tax Rate (%)	Income Brackets ($)	Num. of Brackets	Financial Institution Tax Rate (%)[a]	Federal Income Tax Ded.
North Dakota	1.41 - 4.31 (s)	25,000 - 50,001	3	1.41 - 4.31 (s)	No

Note: Tax rates as of January 1, 2019; (a) Rates listed are the corporate income tax rate applied to financial institutions or excise taxes based on income. Some states have other taxes based upon the value of deposits or shares; (s) North Dakota imposes a 3.5% surtax for filers electing to use the water's edge method to apportion income.
Source: Federation of Tax Administrators, Range of State Corporate Income Tax Rates, January 1, 2019

State Individual Income Tax Rates

State	Tax Rate (%)	Income Brackets ($)	Personal Exemptions ($)			Standard Ded. ($)	
			Single	Married	Depend.	Single	Married
North Dakota (a)	1.1 - 2.9	39,450 - 433,200 (r)	(d)	(d)	(d)	12,200	24,400 (d)

Note: Tax rates as of January 1, 2019; Local- and county-level taxes are not included; n/a not applicable; Federal income tax is not deductible on state income tax returns; (a) 19 states have statutory provision for automatically adjusting to the rate of inflation the dollar values of the income tax brackets, standard deductions, and/or personal exemptions. Michigan indexes the personal exemption only. Oregon does not index the income brackets for $125,000 and over; (d) These states use the personal exemption/standard deduction amounts provided in the federal Internal Revenue Code. Note, the Tax Cut and Reform Act of 2017 has eliminated personal exemptions from the IRC. CO, ID, NM, ND, SC, and DC have adopted the new exemptions and standard deduction amounts. MN conforms to a previous IRC year, while ME adopts the higher standard deduction but retains the exemption amounts; (r) The income brackets reported for North Dakota are for single individuals. For married couples filing jointly, the same tax rates apply to income brackets ranging from $65,900 to $433,200.
Source: Federation of Tax Administrators, State Individual Income Tax Rates, January 1, 2019

Various State Sales and Excise Tax Rates

State	State Sales Tax (%)	Gasoline[1] (¢/gal.)	Cigarette[2] ($/pack)	Spirits[3] ($/gal.)	Wine[4] ($/gal.)	Beer[5] ($/gal.)	Recreational Marijuana (%)
North Dakota	5	23	0.44	4.92 (f)(j)	0.98 (l)	0.42 (q)	Not legal

Note: All tax rates as of January 1, 2019; (1) The American Petroleum Institute has developed a methodology for determining the average tax rate on a gallon of fuel. Rates may include any of the following: excise taxes, environmental fees, storage tank fees, other fees or taxes, general sales tax, and local taxes. In states where gasoline is subject to the general sales tax, or where the fuel tax is based on the average sale price, the average rate determined by API is sensitive to changes in the price of gasoline. States that fully or partially apply general sales taxes to gasoline: CA, CO, GA, IL, IN, MI, NY; (2) The federal excise tax of $1.0066 per pack and local taxes are not included; (3) Rates are those applicable to off-premise sales of 40% alcohol by volume (a.b.v.) distilled spirits in 750ml containers. Local excise taxes are excluded; (4) Rates are those applicable to off-premise sales of 11% a.b.v. non-carbonated wine in 750ml containers; (5) Rates are those applicable to off-premise sales of 4.7% a.b.v. beer in 12 ounce containers; (f) Different rates also applicable according to alcohol content, place of production, size of container, or place purchased (on- or off-premise or onboard airlines); (j) Includes sales taxes specific to alcoholic beverages; (l) Different rates also applicable to alcohol content, place of production, size of container, place purchased (on- or off-premise or on board airlines) or type of wine (carbonated, vermouth, etc.); (q) Different rates also applicable according to alcohol content, place of production, size of container, or place purchased (on- or off-premise or onboard airlines).
Source: Tax Foundation, 2019 Facts & Figures: How Does Your State Compare?

State Business Tax Climate Index Rankings

State	Overall Rank	Corporate Tax Rank	Individual Income Tax Rank	Sales Tax Rank	Unemployment Insurance Tax Rank	Property Tax Rank
North Dakota	17	23	20	32	14	6

Note: The index is a measure of how each state's tax laws affect economic performance. The lower the rank, the more favorable a state's tax system is for business. States without a given tax are given a ranking of 1. The scores/rankings for the District of Columbia do not affect other states. The 2019 index represents the tax climate as of July 1, 2018.
Source: Tax Foundation, State Business Tax Climate Index 2019

COMMERCIAL UTILITIES

Typical Monthly Electric Bills

Area	Commercial Service ($/month)		Industrial Service ($/month)	
	1,500 kWh	40 kW demand 14,000 kWh	1,000 kW demand 200,000 kWh	50,000 kW demand 32,500,000 kWh
City	154	1,296	22,211	2,264,463
Average[1]	203	1,619	25,886	2,540,077

Note: Figures are based on annualized rates; (1) Average based on 187 utilities surveyed
Source: Edison Electric Institute, Typical Bills and Average Rates Report, Summer 2018

TRANSPORTATION

Means of Transportation to Work

Area	Car/Truck/Van		Public Transportation			Bicycle	Walked	Other Means	Worked at Home
	Drove Alone	Car-pooled	Bus	Subway	Railroad				
City	82.8	8.0	1.2	0.0	0.0	0.9	3.4	0.8	2.9
MSA[1]	82.0	8.4	0.9	0.0	0.0	0.6	3.0	0.9	4.1
U.S.	76.4	9.2	2.5	1.9	0.6	0.6	2.7	1.3	4.7

Note: Figures are percentages and cover workers 16 years of age and older; (1) Figures cover the Fargo, ND-MN Metropolitan Statistical Area—see Appendix B for areas included
Source: U.S. Census Bureau, 2013-2017 American Community Survey 5-Year Estimates

Travel Time to Work

Area	Less Than 10 Minutes	10 to 19 Minutes	20 to 29 Minutes	30 to 44 Minutes	45 to 59 Minutes	60 to 89 Minutes	90 Minutes or More
City	20.8	55.7	16.9	3.6	0.9	1.3	0.7
MSA[1]	19.5	50.3	18.7	7.4	1.7	1.5	0.9
U.S.	12.7	28.9	20.9	20.5	8.1	6.2	2.7

Note: Note: Figures are percentages and include workers 16 years old and over; (1) Figures cover the Fargo, ND-MN Metropolitan Statistical Area—see Appendix B for areas included
Source: U.S. Census Bureau, 2013-2017 American Community Survey 5-Year Estimates

Freeway Travel Time Index

Area	1985	1990	1995	2000	2005	2010	2014
Urban Area Rank[1,2]	n/a	n/a	n/a	n/a	n/a	n/a	n/a
Urban Area Index[1]	n/a	n/a	n/a	n/a	n/a	n/a	n/a
Average Index[3]	1.09	1.11	1.14	1.17	1.20	1.19	1.20

Note: Freeway Travel Time Index—the ratio of travel time in the peak period to the travel time at free-flow conditions. For example, a value of 1.30 indicates a 20-minute free-flow trip takes 26 minutes in the peak (20 minutes x 1.30 = 26 minutes); (1) Data for the Fargo, ND-MN urban area was not available; (2) Rank is based on 101 urban areas (#1 = highest travel time index); (3) Average of 101 urban areas
Source: Texas Transportation Institute, 2015 Urban Mobility Scorecard, August 2015

Freeway Commuter Stress Index

Area	1985	1990	1995	2000	2005	2010	2014
Urban Area Rank[1,2]	n/a	n/a	n/a	n/a	n/a	n/a	n/a
Urban Area Index[1]	n/a	n/a	n/a	n/a	n/a	n/a	n/a
Average Index[3]	1.13	1.16	1.19	1.22	1.25	1.24	1.25

Note: The Freeway Commuter Stress Index is the same as the Freeway Travel Time Index (see table above) except that it includes only the travel in the peak directions during the peak periods; the TTI includes travel in all directions during the peak period. Thus, the CSI is more indicative of the work trip experienced by each commuter on a daily basis; (1) Data for the Fargo, ND-MN urban area was not available; (2) Rank is based on 101 urban areas (#1 = highest travel time index); (3) Average of 101 urban areas
Source: Texas Transportation Institute, 2015 Urban Mobility Scorecard, August 2015

Public Transportation

Agency Name / Mode of Transportation	Vehicles Operated in Maximum Service[1]	Annual Unlinked Passenger Trips[2] (in thous.)	Annual Passenger Miles[3] (in thous.)
Fargo Metropolitan Area Transit (MAT)			
Bus (purchased transportation)	24	1,421.3	5,814.3
Demand Response (purchased transportation)	13	52.5	290.0

Note: (1) The number of revenue vehicles operated by the given mode and type of service to meet the annual maximum service requirement. This is the revenue vehicle count during the peak season of the year; on the week and day that maximum service is provided. Vehicles operated in maximum service (VOMS) exclude atypical days and one-time special events; (2) The number of passengers who boarded public transportation vehicles. Passengers are counted each time they board a vehicle no matter how many vehicles they use to travel from their origin to their destination. (3) The sum of the distances ridden by all passengers during the entire fiscal year.
Source: Federal Transit Administration, National Transit Database, 2017

Air Transportation

Airport Name and Code / Type of Service	Passenger Airlines[1]	Passenger Enplanements	Freight Carriers[2]	Freight (lbs)
Hector International (FAR)				
Domestic service (U.S. carriers - 2018)	16	427,144	6	28,357,511
International service (U.S. carriers - 2017)	3	552	1	38,420

Note: (1) Includes all U.S.-based major, minor and commuter airlines that carried at least one passenger during the year; (2) Includes all U.S.-based airlines and freight carriers that transported at least one pound of freight during the year.
Source: Bureau of Transportation Statistics, The Intermodal Transportation Database, Air Carriers: T-100 Domestic Market (U.S. Carriers), 2018; Bureau of Transportation Statistics, The Intermodal Transportation Database, Air Carriers: T-100 International Market (U.S. Carriers), 2017

Other Transportation Statistics

Major Highways:	I-29; I-94
Amtrak Service:	Yes
Major Waterways/Ports:	North River

Source: Amtrak.com; Google Maps

BUSINESSES

Major Business Headquarters

Company Name	Industry	Rankings	
		Fortune[1]	Forbes[2]
No companies listed	-	-	-

Note: (1) Companies that produce a 10-K are ranked 1 to 500 based on 2017 revenue; (2) All private companies with at least $2 billion in annual revenue through the end of their most current fiscal year are ranked 1 to 229; companies listed are headquartered in the city; dashes indicate no ranking
Source: Fortune, "Fortune 500," June 2018; Forbes, "America's Largest Private Companies," 2018 Rankings

Fast-Growing Businesses

According to *Inc.*, Fargo is home to one of America's 500 fastest-growing private companies: **Haga Kommer,** (#333). Criteria: must be an independent, privately-held, for-profit, U.S. corporation, proprietorship or partnership as of December 31, 2017; revenues must be at least $100,000 in 2014 and $2 million in 2017; must have four-year operating/sales history. Holding companies, regulated banks, and utilities were excluded. *Inc., "America's 500 Fastest-Growing Private Companies," 2018*

Minority- and Women-Owned Businesses

Group	All Firms		Firms with Paid Employees			
	Firms	Sales ($000)	Firms	Sales ($000)	Employees	Payroll ($000)
AIAN[1]	73	(s)	29	(s)	100 - 249	(s)
Asian	251	128,405	80	116,765	948	23,616
Black	156	7,305	6	3,478	119	1,537
Hispanic	82	(s)	12	(s)	250 - 499	(s)
NHOPI[2]	n/a	n/a	n/a	n/a	n/a	n/a
Women	3,404	813,664	548	741,150	5,645	160,769
All Firms	11,347	21,269,902	3,362	20,817,554	84,294	3,584,192

Note: Figures cover firms located in the city; minority- and women-owned business are defined as firms in which the corresponding group own 51% or more of the stock or equity of the company; (1) American Indian and Alaska Native; (2) Native Hawaiian and Other Pacific Islander; (s) estimates are suppressed when publication standards are not met; n/a not available
Source: U.S. Census Bureau, 2012 Economic Census, Survey of Business Owners

HOTELS & CONVENTION CENTERS

Hotels, Motels and Vacation Rentals

Area	5 Star		4 Star		3 Star		2 Star		1 Star		Not Rated	
	Num.	Pct.[3]	Num.	Pct.[3]	Num.	Pct.[3]	Num.	Pct.[3]	Num.	Pct.[3]	Num.	Pct.[3]
City[1]	0	0.0	0	0.0	22	32.4	39	57.4	2	2.9	5	7.4
Total[2]	286	0.4	5,236	7.1	16,715	22.6	10,259	13.9	293	0.4	41,056	55.6

Note: (1) Figures cover Fargo and vicinity; (2) Figures cover all 100 cities in this book; (3) Percentage of hotels which have a given star-rating; Star ratings are determined by expedia.com and offer an indication of the general quality of a particular hotel.
Source: www.expedia.com, April 3, 2019

Major Convention Centers

Name	Overall Space (sq. ft.)	Exhibit Space (sq. ft.)	Meeting Space (sq. ft.)	Meeting Rooms
Fargo Civic Center	n/a	n/a	40,000	4

Note: Table includes convention centers located in the Fargo, ND-MN metro area; n/a not available
Source: Original research

Living Environment

COST OF LIVING

Cost of Living Index

Composite Index	Groceries	Housing	Utilities	Trans-portation	Health Care	Misc. Goods/ Services
99.3	110.4	89.2	89.9	99.8	115.4	103.9

Note: The Cost of Living Index measures regional differences in the cost of consumer goods and services, excluding taxes and non-consumer expenditures, for professional and managerial households in the top income quintile. It is based on more than 50,000 prices covering almost 60 different items for which prices are collected three times a year by chambers of commerce, economic development organizations or university applied economic centers in each participating urban area. The numbers shown should be read as a percentage above or below the national average of 100. For example, a value of 115.4 in the groceries column indicates that grocery prices are 15.4% higher than the national average. Small differences in the index numbers should not be interpreted as significant; Figures cover the Fargo-Moorhead ND-MN urban area.
Source: The Council for Community and Economic Research, ACCRA Cost of Living Index, 2018

Grocery Prices

Area[1]	T-Bone Steak ($/pound)	Frying Chicken ($/pound)	Whole Milk ($/half gal.)	Eggs ($/dozen)	Orange Juice ($/64 oz.)	Coffee ($/11.5 oz.)
City[2]	13.91	1.70	2.79	2.00	3.80	4.43
Avg.	11.35	1.42	1.94	1.81	3.52	4.35
Min.	7.45	0.92	0.80	0.75	2.72	3.06
Max.	15.05	2.76	4.18	4.00	5.36	8.20

Note: (1) Values for the local area are compared with the average, minimum and maximum values for all 291 areas in the Cost of Living Index; (2) Figures cover the Fargo-Moorhead ND-MN urban area; T-Bone Steak (price per pound); Frying Chicken (price per pound, whole fryer); Whole Milk (half gallon carton); Eggs (price per dozen, Grade A, large); Orange Juice (64 oz. Tropicana or Florida Natural); Coffee (11.5 oz. can, vacuum-packed, Maxwell House, Hills Bros, or Folgers).
Source: The Council for Community and Economic Research, ACCRA Cost of Living Index, 2018

Housing and Utility Costs

Area[1]	New Home Price ($)	Apartment Rent ($/month)	All Electric ($/month)	Part Electric ($/month)	Other Energy ($/month)	Telephone ($/month)
City[2]	323,100	909	-	76.53	57.71	182.70
Avg.	347,000	1,087	165.93	100.16	67.73	178.70
Min.	200,468	500	93.58	25.64	26.78	163.10
Max.	1,901,222	4,888	388.65	246.86	332.81	197.70

Note: (1) Values for the local area are compared with the average, minimum and maximum values for all 291 areas in the Cost of Living Index; (2) Figures cover the Fargo-Moorhead ND-MN urban area; New Home Price (2,400 sf living area, 8,000 sf lot, in urban area with full utilities); Apartment Rent (950 sf 2 bedroom/1.5 or 2 bath, unfurnished, excluding all utilities except water); All Electric (average monthly cost for an all-electric home); Part Electric (average monthly cost for a part-electric home); Other Energy (average monthly cost for natural gas, fuel oil, coal, wood, and any other forms of energy except electricity); Telephone (price includes the base monthly rate plus taxes and fees for three lines of mobile phone service).
Source: The Council for Community and Economic Research, ACCRA Cost of Living Index, 2018

Health Care, Transportation, and Other Costs

Area[1]	Doctor ($/visit)	Dentist ($/visit)	Optometrist ($/visit)	Gasoline ($/gallon)	Beauty Salon ($/visit)	Men's Shirt ($)
City[2]	167.97	98.00	102.20	2.47	35.60	28.20
Avg.	110.71	95.11	103.74	2.61	37.48	32.03
Min.	33.60	62.55	54.63	1.89	17.00	11.44
Max.	195.97	153.93	225.79	3.59	71.88	58.64

Note: (1) Values for the local area are compared with the average, minimum and maximum values for all 291 areas in the Cost of Living Index; (2) Figures cover the Fargo-Moorhead ND-MN urban area; Doctor (general practitioners routine exam of an established patient); Dentist (adult teeth cleaning and periodic oral examination); Optometrist (full vision eye exam for established adult patient); Gasoline (one gallon regular unleaded, national brand, including all taxes, cash price at self-service pump if available); Beauty Salon (woman's shampoo, trim, and blow-dry); Men's Shirt (cotton/polyester dress shirt, pinpoint weave, long sleeves).
Source: The Council for Community and Economic Research, ACCRA Cost of Living Index, 2018

HOUSING

House Price Index (HPI)

Area	National Ranking[2]	Quarterly Change (%)	One-Year Change (%)	Five-Year Change (%)
MSA[1]	230	0.01	1.38	26.29
U.S.[3]	–	1.12	5.73	32.81

Note: The HPI is a weighted repeat sales index. It measures average price changes in repeat sales or refinancings on the same properties. This information is obtained by reviewing repeat mortgage transactions on single-family properties whose mortgages have been purchased or securitized by Fannie Mae or Freddie Mac in January 1975; (1) Figures cover the Fargo, ND-MN Metropolitan Statistical Area—see Appendix B for areas included; (2) Rankings are based on annual percentage change for all metro areas containing at least 15,000 transactions over the last 10 years and ranges from 1 to 245; (3) figures based on a weighted average of Census Division estimates using a seasonally adjusted, purchase-only index; all figures are for the period ending December 31, 2018
Source: Federal Housing Finance Agency, House Price Index, February 26, 2019

Median Single-Family Home Prices

Area	2016	2017	2018[p]	Percent Change 2017 to 2018
MSA[1]	203.2	208.5	217.5	4.3
U.S. Average	235.5	248.8	261.6	5.1

Note: Figures are median sales prices of existing single-family homes in thousands of dollars; (p) preliminary; (1) Figures cover the Fargo, ND-MN Metropolitan Statistical Area—see Appendix B for areas included
Source: National Association of Realtors, Median Sales Price of Existing Single-Family Homes for Metropolitan Areas, 4th Quarter 2018

Qualifying Income Based on Median Sales Price of Existing Single-Family Homes

Area	With 5% Down ($)	With 10% Down ($)	With 20% Down ($)
MSA[1]	53,838	51,004	45,337
U.S. Average	62,954	59,640	53,013

Note: Figures are preliminary; Qualifying income is based on a mortgage rate of 4.9%. Monthly principal and interest payment is limited to 25% of income; (1) Figures cover the Fargo, ND-MN Metropolitan Statistical Area—see Appendix B for areas included
Source: National Association of Realtors, Qualifying Income Based on Median Sales Price of Existing Single-Family Homes for Metropolitan Areas, 4th Quarter 2018

Median Apartment Condo-Coop Home Prices

Area	2016	2017	2018[p]	Percent Change 2017 to 2018
MSA[1]	n/a	n/a	n/a	n/a
U.S. Average	220.7	234.3	241.0	2.9

Note: Figures are median sales prices of existing apartment condo-coop homes in thousands of dollars; (p) preliminary; n/a not available; (1) Figures cover the Fargo, ND-MN Metropolitan Statistical Area—see Appendix B for areas included
Source: National Association of Realtors, Median Sales Price of Existing Apartment Condo-Coop Homes for Metropolitan Areas, 4th Quarter 2018

Home Value Distribution

Area	Under $50,000	$50,000 -$99,999	$100,000 -$149,999	$150,000 -$199,999	$200,000 -$299,999	$300,000 -$499,999	$500,000 -$999,999	$1,000,000 or more
City	3.7	6.9	20.0	23.9	28.0	14.5	2.5	0.5
MSA[1]	4.5	7.4	18.8	23.1	27.1	14.8	3.7	0.4
U.S.	8.3	13.9	14.7	14.6	18.7	17.3	9.7	2.7

Note: Figures are percentages and cover owner-occupied housing units; (1) Figures cover the Fargo, ND-MN Metropolitan Statistical Area—see Appendix B for areas included
Source: U.S. Census Bureau, 2013-2017 American Community Survey 5-Year Estimates

Homeownership Rate

Area	2010 (%)	2011 (%)	2012 (%)	2013 (%)	2014 (%)	2015 (%)	2016 (%)	2017 (%)	2018 (%)
MSA[1]	n/a	n/a	n/a	n/a	n/a	n/a	n/a	n/a	n/a
U.S.	66.9	66.1	65.4	65.1	64.5	63.7	63.4	63.9	64.4

Note: (1) Figures cover the Fargo, ND-MN Metropolitan Statistical Area—see Appendix B for areas included; n/a not available
Source: U.S. Census Bureau, Housing Vacancies and Homeownership Annual Statistics: 2010-2018

Year Housing Structure Built

Area	2010 or Later	2000 -2009	1990 -1999	1980 -1989	1970 -1979	1960 -1969	1950 -1959	1940 -1949	Before 1940	Median Year
City	10.3	15.9	18.9	13.9	15.1	6.8	6.7	2.8	9.5	1986
MSA[1]	9.8	18.7	15.9	11.3	16.0	7.7	8.0	2.9	9.8	1985
U.S.	3.2	14.5	14.0	13.6	15.5	10.8	10.5	5.1	12.9	1977

Note: Figures are percentages except for Median Year; Note: (1) Figures cover the Fargo, ND-MN Metropolitan Statistical Area—see Appendix B for areas included
Source: U.S. Census Bureau, 2013-2017 American Community Survey 5-Year Estimates

Gross Monthly Rent

Area	Under $500	$500 -$999	$1,000 -$1,499	$1,500 -$1,999	$2,000 -$2,499	$2,500 -$2,999	$3,000 and up	Median ($)
City	9.6	69.6	15.7	3.6	1.3	0.2	0.0	765
MSA[1]	10.6	66.9	16.4	4.3	1.3	0.3	0.1	770
U.S.	10.5	41.1	28.7	11.7	4.5	1.8	1.7	982

Note: Figures are percentages except for Median; Gross rent is the contract rent plus the estimated average monthly cost of utilities (electricity, gas, and water and sewer) and fuels (oil, coal, kerosene, wood, etc.) if these are paid by the renter (or paid for the renter by someone else); (1) Figures cover the Fargo, ND-MN Metropolitan Statistical Area—see Appendix B for areas included
Source: U.S. Census Bureau, 2013-2017 American Community Survey 5-Year Estimates

HEALTH

Health Risk Factors

Category	MSA[1] (%)	U.S. (%)
Adults aged 18–64 who have any kind of health care coverage	90.5	87.3
Adults who reported being in good or better health	86.1	82.4
Adults who have been told they have high blood cholesterol	29.8	33.0
Adults who have been told they have high blood pressure	25.4	32.3
Adults who are current smokers	16.7	17.1
Adults who currently use E-cigarettes	3.8	4.6
Adults who currently use chewing tobacco, snuff, or snus	5.9	4.0
Adults who are heavy drinkers[2]	8.4	6.3
Adults who are binge drinkers[3]	26.2	17.4
Adults who are overweight (BMI 25.0 - 29.9)	39.6	35.3
Adults who are obese (BMI 30.0 - 99.8)	29.0	31.3
Adults who participated in any physical activities in the past month	76.3	74.4
Adults who always or nearly always wears a seat belt	94.0	94.3

Note: (1) Figures cover the Fargo, ND-MN Metropolitan Statistical Area—see Appendix B for areas included; (2) Heavy drinkers are classified as adult men having more than 14 drinks per week and adult women having more than 7 drinks per week; (3) Binge drinkers are classified as males having five or more drinks on one occasion or females having four or more drinks on one occasion
Source: Centers for Disease Control and Prevention, Behaviorial Risk Factor Surveillance System, SMART: Selected Metropolitan Area Risk Trends, 2017

Acute and Chronic Health Conditions

Category	MSA[1] (%)	U.S. (%)
Adults who have ever been told they had a heart attack	2.8	4.2
Adults who have ever been told they have angina or coronary heart disease	3.2	3.9
Adults who have ever been told they had a stroke	1.6	3.0
Adults who have ever been told they have asthma	11.1	14.2
Adults who have ever been told they have arthritis	20.7	24.9
Adults who have ever been told they have diabetes[2]	7.4	10.5
Adults who have ever been told they had skin cancer	4.9	6.2
Adults who have ever been told they had any other types of cancer	5.7	7.1
Adults who have ever been told they have COPD	4.4	6.5
Adults who have ever been told they have kidney disease	2.4	3.0
Adults who have ever been told they have a form of depression	22.4	20.5

Note: (1) Figures cover the Fargo, ND-MN Metropolitan Statistical Area—see Appendix B for areas included; (2) Figures do not include pregnancy-related, borderline, or pre-diabetes
Source: Centers for Disease Control and Prevention, Behaviorial Risk Factor Surveillance System, SMART: Selected Metropolitan Area Risk Trends, 2017

Health Screening and Vaccination Rates

Category	MSA[1] (%)	U.S. (%)
Adults aged 65+ who have had flu shot within the past year	62.8	60.7
Adults aged 65+ who have ever had a pneumonia vaccination	78.5	75.4
Adults who have ever been tested for HIV	27.5	36.1
Adults who have ever had the shingles or zoster vaccine?	38.5	28.9
Adults who have had their blood cholesterol checked within the last five years	81.0	85.9

Note: n/a not available; (1) Figures cover the Fargo, ND-MN Metropolitan Statistical Area—see Appendix B for areas included.
Source: Centers for Disease Control and Prevention, Behaviorial Risk Factor Surveillance System, SMART: Selected Metropolitan Area Risk Trends, 2017

Disability Status

Category	MSA[1] (%)	U.S. (%)
Adults who reported being deaf	5.0	6.7
Are you blind or have serious difficulty seeing, even when wearing glasses?	2.1	4.5
Are you limited in any way in any of your usual activities due of arthritis?	9.6	12.9
Do you have difficulty doing errands alone?	4.3	6.8
Do you have difficulty dressing or bathing?	n/a	3.6
Do you have serious difficulty concentrating/remembering/making decisions?	8.1	10.7
Do you have serious difficulty walking or climbing stairs?	8.6	13.6

Note: n/a not available; (1) Figures cover the Fargo, ND-MN Metropolitan Statistical Area—see Appendix B for areas included.
Source: Centers for Disease Control and Prevention, Behaviorial Risk Factor Surveillance System, SMART: Selected Metropolitan Area Risk Trends, 2017

Mortality Rates for the Top 10 Causes of Death in the U.S.

ICD-10[a] Sub-Chapter	ICD-10[a] Code	Age-Adjusted Mortality Rate[1] per 100,000 population	
		County[2]	U.S.
Malignant neoplasms	C00-C97	146.7	155.5
Ischaemic heart diseases	I20-I25	60.4	94.8
Other forms of heart disease	I30-I51	43.1	52.9
Chronic lower respiratory diseases	J40-J47	36.4	41.0
Cerebrovascular diseases	I60-I69	26.9	37.5
Other degenerative diseases of the nervous system	G30-G31	41.1	35.0
Other external causes of accidental injury	W00-X59	24.7	33.7
Organic, including symptomatic, mental disorders	F01-F09	24.3	31.0
Hypertensive diseases	I10-I15	17.3	21.9
Diabetes mellitus	E10-E14	20.0	21.2

Note: (a) ICD-10 = International Classification of Diseases 10th Revision; (1) Mortality rates are a three year average covering 2015-2017; (2) Figures cover Cass County.
Source: Centers for Disease Control and Prevention, National Center for Health Statistics. Underlying Cause of Death 1999-2017 on CDC WONDER Online Database

Mortality Rates for Selected Causes of Death

ICD-10[a] Sub-Chapter	ICD-10[a] Code	Age-Adjusted Mortality Rate[1] per 100,000 population	
		County[2]	U.S.
Assault	X85-Y09	Unreliable	5.9
Diseases of the liver	K70-K76	17.5	14.1
Human immunodeficiency virus (HIV) disease	B20-B24	Suppressed	1.8
Influenza and pneumonia	J09-J18	14.0	14.3
Intentional self-harm	X60-X84	15.7	13.6
Malnutrition	E40-E46	Suppressed	1.6
Obesity and other hyperalimentation	E65-E68	Unreliable	2.1
Renal failure	N17-N19	11.1	13.0
Transport accidents	V01-V99	6.9	12.4
Viral hepatitis	B15-B19	Suppressed	1.6

Note: (a) ICD-10 = International Classification of Diseases 10th Revision; (1) Mortality rates are a three year average covering 2015-2017; (2) Figures cover Cass County; Data are suppressed when the data meet the criteria for confidentiality constraints; Mortality rates are flagged as unreliable when the rate would be calculated with a numerator of 20 or less.
Source: Centers for Disease Control and Prevention, National Center for Health Statistics. Underlying Cause of Death 1999-2017 on CDC WONDER Online Database

Health Insurance Coverage

Area	With Health Insurance	With Private Health Insurance	With Public Health Insurance	Without Health Insurance	Population Under Age 18 Without Health Insurance
City	92.4	79.6	24.1	7.6	5.2
MSA[1]	93.6	81.4	24.1	6.4	5.1
U.S.	89.5	67.2	33.8	10.5	5.7

Note: Figures are percentages that cover the civilian noninstitutionalized population; (1) Figures cover the Fargo, ND-MN Metropolitan Statistical Area—see Appendix B for areas included
Source: U.S. Census Bureau, 2013-2017 American Community Survey 5-Year Estimates

Number of Medical Professionals

Area	MDs[3]	DOs[3,4]	Dentists	Podiatrists	Chiropractors	Optometrists
County[1] (number)	678	29	140	6	114	52
County[1] (rate[2])	388.3	16.6	78.7	3.4	64.1	29.2
U.S. (rate[2])	279.3	23.0	68.4	6.0	27.1	16.2

Note: Data as of 2017 unless noted; (1) Data covers Cass County; (2) Rate per 100,000 population; (3) Data as of 2016 and includes all active, non-federal physicians; (4) Doctor of Osteopathic Medicine
Source: U.S. Department of Health and Human Services, Health Resources and Services Administration, Bureau of Health Professions, Area Resource File (ARF) 2017-2018

EDUCATION

Public School District Statistics

District Name	Schls	Pupils	Pupil/ Teacher Ratio	Minority Pupils[1] (%)	Free Lunch Eligible[2] (%)	IEP[3] (%)
Fargo 1	22	11,263	13.3	25.6	26.3	12.8

Note: Table includes school districts with 2,000 or more students; (1) Percentage of students that are not non-Hispanic white; (2) Percentage of students that are eligible for the free lunch program; (3) Percentage of students that have an Individualized Education Program.
Source: U.S. Department of Education, National Center for Education Statistics, Common Core of Data, Local Education Agency (School District) Universe Survey: School Year 2016-2017; U.S. Department of Education, National Center for Education Statistics, Common Core of Data, Public Elementary/Secondary School Universe Survey: School Year 2016-2017

Highest Level of Education

Area	Less than H.S.	H.S. Diploma	Some College, No Deg.	Associate Degree	Bachelor's Degree	Master's Degree	Prof. School Degree	Doctorate Degree
City	6.2	20.3	20.4	14.3	27.4	7.4	2.0	2.0
MSA[1]	5.6	21.6	21.4	14.4	26.4	7.4	1.5	1.7
U.S.	12.7	27.3	20.8	8.3	19.1	8.4	2.0	1.4

Note: Figures cover persons age 25 and over; (1) Figures cover the Fargo, ND-MN Metropolitan Statistical Area—see Appendix B for areas included
Source: U.S. Census Bureau, 2013-2017 American Community Survey 5-Year Estimates

Educational Attainment by Race

Area	High School Graduate or Higher (%)					Bachelor's Degree or Higher (%)				
	Total	White	Black	Asian	Hisp.[2]	Total	White	Black	Asian	Hisp.[2]
City	93.8	95.5	79.4	74.1	78.5	38.8	40.0	18.5	50.3	19.9
MSA[1]	94.4	95.7	80.0	77.6	77.3	37.0	37.8	21.3	46.7	20.3
U.S.	87.3	89.3	84.9	86.5	66.7	30.9	32.2	20.6	52.7	15.2

Note: Figures shown cover persons 25 years old and over; (1) Figures cover the Fargo, ND-MN Metropolitan Statistical Area—see Appendix B for areas included; (2) People of Hispanic origin can be of any race
Source: U.S. Census Bureau, 2013-2017 American Community Survey 5-Year Estimates

School Enrollment by Grade and Control

Area	Preschool (%)		Kindergarten (%)		Grades 1 - 4 (%)		Grades 5 - 8 (%)		Grades 9 - 12 (%)	
	Public	Private	Public	Private	Public	Private	Public	Private	Public	Private
City	57.8	42.2	92.9	7.1	90.1	9.9	90.0	10.0	89.3	10.7
MSA[1]	65.7	34.3	92.5	7.5	89.9	10.1	89.1	10.9	90.7	9.3
U.S.	58.8	41.2	87.7	12.3	89.7	10.3	89.6	10.4	90.3	9.7

Note: Figures shown cover persons 3 years old and over; (1) Figures cover the Fargo, ND-MN Metropolitan Statistical Area—see Appendix B for areas included
Source: U.S. Census Bureau, 2013-2017 American Community Survey 5-Year Estimates

Average Salaries of Public School Classroom Teachers

Area	2016		2017		Change from 2016 to 2017	
	Dollars	Rank[1]	Dollars	Rank[1]	Percent	Rank[2]
North Dakota	51,223	31	52,968	27	3.4	6
U.S. Average	58,479	–	59,660	–	2.0	–

Note: (1) Rank ranges from 1 to 51 where 1 indicates highest salary; (2) Rank ranges from 1 to 51 where 1 indicates highest percent change.
Source: National Education Association, Rankings & Estimates: Rankings of the States 2017 and Estimates of School Statistics 2018

Higher Education

Four-Year Colleges			Two-Year Colleges			Medical Schools[1]	Law Schools[2]	Voc/ Tech[3]
Public	Private Non-profit	Private For-profit	Public	Private Non-profit	Private For-profit			
1	0	1	0	0	3	0	0	2

Note: Figures cover institutions located within the city limits and include main campuses only; (1) includes schools accredited by the Liaison Committee on Medical Education and the American Osteopathic Association's Commission on Osteopathic College Accreditation; (2) includes ABA-accredited schools, schools with provisional ABA accreditation, and state accredited schools; (3) includes all schools with programs that are less than 2 years.
Source: National Center for Education Statistics, Integrated Postsecondary Education System (IPEDS), 2017-18; Wikipedia, List of Medical Schools in the United States, accessed April 3, 2019; Wikipedia, List of Law Schools in the United States, accessed April 3, 2019

According to *U.S. News & World Report,* the Fargo, ND-MN metro area is home to one of the best national universities in the U.S.: **North Dakota State University** (#215 tie). The indicators used to capture academic quality fall into a number of categories: assessment by administrators at peer institutions; retention of students; faculty resources; student selectivity; financial resources; alumni giving; high school counselor ratings of colleges; and graduation rate. *U.S. News & World Report, "America's Best Colleges 2019"*

According to *U.S. News & World Report,* the Fargo, ND-MN metro area is home to one of the best liberal arts colleges in the U.S.: **Concordia College—Moorhead** (#127 tie). The indicators used to capture academic quality fall into a number of categories: assessment by administrators at peer institutions; retention of students; faculty resources; student selectivity; financial resources; alumni giving; high school counselor ratings of colleges; and graduation rate. *U.S. News & World Report, "America's Best Colleges 2019"*

PRESIDENTIAL ELECTION

2016 Presidential Election Results

Area	Clinton	Trump	Johnson	Stein	Other
Cass County	38.8	49.3	7.5	1.5	2.9
U.S.	48.0	45.9	3.3	1.1	1.7

Note: Results are percentages and may not add to 100% due to rounding
Source: Dave Leip's Atlas of U.S. Presidential Elections

EMPLOYERS

Major Employers

Company Name	Industry
BlueCross BlueShield of North Dakota	Insurance
City of Fargo	Government
CNH Industrial America	Agriculture equipment
Concordia College	Education
Essentia Health	General medical & surgical hospitals
Fargo Public School District	Education
John Deere Electronic Solutions	Manufacturers
Microsoft	Computer software
Minnesota State University Moorhead	Education
Moorhead Area Public Schools	Education
Noridian Heathcare Solutions	Insurance
North Dakota State University	Education
Sanford Fargo Medical Center	Healthcare services
U.S. Bank	Financial services
Veterans Affairs	General medical & surgical hospitals
West Fargo Public School	Education

Note: Companies shown are located within the Fargo, ND-MN Metropolitan Statistical Area.
Source: Hoovers.com; Wikipedia

PUBLIC SAFETY

Crime Rate

Area	All Crimes	Violent Crimes				Property Crimes		
		Murder	Rape[3]	Robbery	Aggrav. Assault	Burglary	Larceny -Theft	Motor Vehicle Theft
City	3,538.0	2.4	67.2	55.1	277.9	480.4	2,410.3	244.7
Suburbs[1]	1,777.2	0.9	43.2	14.7	90.7	266.8	1,204.7	156.3
Metro[2]	2,685.7	1.7	55.6	35.5	187.3	377.0	1,826.7	201.9
U.S.	2,756.1	5.3	41.7	98.0	248.9	430.4	1,694.4	237.4

Note: Figures are crimes per 100,000 population; (1) All areas within the metro area that are located outside the city limits; (2) Figures cover the Fargo, ND-MN Metropolitan Statistical Area—see Appendix B for areas included; (3) The city and U.S. figures shown were reported using the revised Uniform Crime Reporting (UCR) definition of rape. The suburban and metro area figures shown are an aggregate total of the data submitted using both the revised and legacy UCR definitions.
Source: FBI Uniform Crime Reports, 2017

Hate Crimes

Area	Number of Quarters Reported	Number of Incidents per Bias Motivation					
		Race/Ethnicity/ Ancestry	Religion	Sexual Orientation	Disability	Gender	Gender Identity
City	4	1	2	0	0	0	0
U.S.	4	4,131	1,564	1,130	116	46	119

Source: Federal Bureau of Investigation, Hate Crime Statistics 2017

Identity Theft Consumer Reports

Area	Reports	Reports per 100,000 Population	Rank[2]
MSA[1]	170	71	262
U.S.	444,602	135	-

Note: (1) Figures cover the Fargo, ND-MN Metropolitan Statistical Area—see Appendix B for areas included; (2) Rank ranges from 1 to 389 where 1 indicates greatest number of identity theft reports per 100,000 population
Source: Federal Trade Commission, Consumer Sentinel Network Data Book for January–December 2018

Fraud and Other Consumer Reports

Area	Reports	Reports per 100,000 Population	Rank[2]
MSA[1]	855	359	350
U.S.	2,552,917	776	-

Note: (1) Figures cover the Fargo, ND-MN Metropolitan Statistical Area—see Appendix B for areas included; (2) Rank ranges from 1 to 389 where 1 indicates greatest number of fraud and other consumer reports per 100,000 population

Source: Federal Trade Commission, Consumer Sentinel Network Data Book for January–December 2018

SPORTS

Professional Sports Teams

Team Name	League	Year Established
No teams are located in the metro area		

Source: Wikipedia, Major Professional Sports Teams of the United States and Canada, April 5, 2019

CLIMATE

Average and Extreme Temperatures

Temperature	Jan	Feb	Mar	Apr	May	Jun	Jul	Aug	Sep	Oct	Nov	Dec	Yr.
Extreme High (°F)	52	66	78	100	98	100	106	106	102	93	74	57	106
Average High (°F)	15	21	34	54	69	77	83	81	70	57	36	21	52
Average Temp. (°F)	6	12	26	43	56	66	71	69	58	46	28	13	41
Average Low (°F)	-3	3	17	32	44	54	59	57	46	35	19	4	31
Extreme Low (°F)	-36	-34	-34	-7	20	30	36	33	19	5	-24	-32	-36

Note: Figures cover the years 1948-1995

Source: National Climatic Data Center, International Station Meteorological Climate Summary, 9/96

Average Precipitation/Snowfall/Humidity

Precip./Humidity	Jan	Feb	Mar	Apr	May	Jun	Jul	Aug	Sep	Oct	Nov	Dec	Yr.
Avg. Precip. (in.)	0.6	0.5	1.0	1.7	2.3	3.1	3.2	2.4	1.8	1.5	0.8	0.6	19.6
Avg. Snowfall (in.)	9	6	7	3	Tr	0	0	0	Tr	1	6	7	40
Avg. Rel. Hum. 6am (%)	75	77	82	79	77	82	86	86	85	80	81	78	81
Avg. Rel. Hum. 3pm (%)	70	71	67	51	45	50	50	47	49	51	65	73	57

Note: Figures cover the years 1948-1995; Tr = Trace amounts (<0.05 in. of rain; <0.5 in. of snow)

Source: National Climatic Data Center, International Station Meteorological Climate Summary, 9/96

Weather Conditions

Temperature			Daytime Sky			Precipitation		
5°F & below	32°F & below	90°F & above	Clear	Partly cloudy	Cloudy	0.01 inch or more precip.	0.1 inch or more snow/ice	Thunder-storms
65	180	15	81	145	139	100	38	31

Note: Figures are average number of days per year and cover the years 1948-1995

Source: National Climatic Data Center, International Station Meteorological Climate Summary, 9/96

HAZARDOUS WASTE

Superfund Sites

The Fargo, ND-MN metro area has no sites on the EPA's Superfund Final National Priorities List. There are a total of 1,390 Superfund sites with a status of proposed or final on the list in the U.S.

U.S. Environmental Protection Agency, National Priorities List, April 5, 2019

**AIR & WATER
QUALITY**

Air Quality Trends: Ozone

	1990	1995	2000	2005	2010	2012	2014	2015	2016	2017
MSA[1]	n/a	n/a	n/a	n/a	n/a	n/a	n/a	n/a	n/a	n/a
U.S.	0.088	0.089	0.082	0.080	0.073	0.075	0.067	0.068	0.069	0.068

Note: (1) Data covers the Fargo, ND-MN Metropolitan Statistical Area—see Appendix B for areas included; n/a not available. The values shown are the composite ozone concentration averages among trend sites based on the highest fourth daily maximum 8-hour concentration in parts per million. These trends are based on sites having an adequate record of monitoring data during the trend period. Data from exceptional events are included.
Source: U.S. Environmental Protection Agency, Air Quality Monitoring Information, "Air Quality Trends by City, 1990-2017"

Air Quality Index

Area	Percent of Days when Air Quality was...[2]					AQI Statistics[2]	
	Good	Moderate	Unhealthy for Sensitive Groups	Unhealthy	Very Unhealthy	Maximum	Median
MSA[1]	84.5	15.5	0.0	0.0	0.0	77	38

Note: (1) Data covers the Fargo, ND-MN Metropolitan Statistical Area—see Appendix B for areas included; (2) Based on 362 days with AQI data in 2017. Air Quality Index (AQI) is an index for reporting daily air quality. EPA calculates the AQI for five major air pollutants regulated by the Clean Air Act: ground-level ozone, particle pollution (aka particulate matter), carbon monoxide, sulfur dioxide, and nitrogen dioxide. The AQI runs from 0 to 500. The higher the AQI value, the greater the level of air pollution and the greater the health concern. There are six AQI categories: "Good" AQI is between 0 and 50. Air quality is considered satisfactory; "Moderate" AQI is between 51 and 100. Air quality is acceptable; "Unhealthy for Sensitive Groups" When AQI values are between 101 and 150, members of sensitive groups may experience health effects; "Unhealthy" When AQI values are between 151 and 200 everyone may begin to experience health effects; "Very Unhealthy" AQI values between 201 and 300 trigger a health alert; "Hazardous" AQI values over 300 trigger warnings of emergency conditions (not shown).
Source: U.S. Environmental Protection Agency, Air Quality Index Report, 2017

Air Quality Index Pollutants

Area	Percent of Days when AQI Pollutant was...[2]					
	Carbon Monoxide	Nitrogen Dioxide	Ozone	Sulfur Dioxide	Particulate Matter 2.5	Particulate Matter 10
MSA[1]	0.0	0.3	48.1	0.0	47.5	4.1

Note: (1) Data covers the Fargo, ND-MN Metropolitan Statistical Area—see Appendix B for areas included; (2) Based on 362 days with AQI data in 2017. The Air Quality Index (AQI) is an index for reporting daily air quality. EPA calculates the AQI for five major air pollutants regulated by the Clean Air Act: ground-level ozone, particle pollution (also known as particulate matter), carbon monoxide, sulfur dioxide, and nitrogen dioxide. The AQI runs from 0 to 500. The higher the AQI value, the greater the level of air pollution and the greater the health concern.
Source: U.S. Environmental Protection Agency, Air Quality Index Report, 2017

Maximum Air Pollutant Concentrations: Particulate Matter, Ozone, CO and Lead

	Particulate Matter 10 (ug/m³)	Particulate Matter 2.5 Wtd AM (ug/m³)	Particulate Matter 2.5 24-Hr (ug/m³)	Ozone (ppm)	Carbon Monoxide (ppm)	Lead (ug/m³)
MSA[1] Level	71	n/a	n/a	0.061	n/a	n/a
NAAQS[2]	150	15	35	0.075	9	0.15
Met NAAQS[2]	Yes	n/a	n/a	Yes	n/a	n/a

Note: (1) Data covers the Fargo, ND-MN Metropolitan Statistical Area—see Appendix B for areas included; Data from exceptional events are included; (2) National Ambient Air Quality Standards; ppm = parts per million; ug/m³ = micrograms per cubic meter; n/a not available.
Concentrations: Particulate Matter 10 (coarse particulate)—highest second maximum 24-hour concentration; Particulate Matter 2.5 Wtd AM (fine particulate)—highest weighted annual mean concentration; Particulate Matter 2.5 24-Hour (fine particulate)—highest 98th percentile 24-hour concentration; Ozone—highest fourth daily maximum 8-hour concentration; Carbon Monoxide—highest second maximum non-overlapping 8-hour concentration; Lead—maximum running 3-month average
Source: U.S. Environmental Protection Agency, Air Quality Monitoring Information, "Air Quality Statistics by City, 2017"

Maximum Air Pollutant Concentrations: Nitrogen Dioxide and Sulfur Dioxide

	Nitrogen Dioxide AM (ppb)	Nitrogen Dioxide 1-Hr (ppb)	Sulfur Dioxide AM (ppb)	Sulfur Dioxide 1-Hr (ppb)	Sulfur Dioxide 24-Hr (ppb)
MSA[1] Level	4	34	n/a	4	n/a
NAAQS[2]	53	100	30	75	140
Met NAAQS[2]	Yes	Yes	n/a	Yes	n/a

Note: (1) Data covers the Fargo, ND-MN Metropolitan Statistical Area—see Appendix B for areas included; Data from exceptional events are included; (2) National Ambient Air Quality Standards; ppm = parts per million; ug/m³ = micrograms per cubic meter; n/a not available.
Concentrations: Nitrogen Dioxide AM—highest arithmetic mean concentration; Nitrogen Dioxide 1-Hr—highest 98th percentile 1-hour daily maximum concentration; Sulfur Dioxide AM—highest annual mean concentration; Sulfur Dioxide 1-Hr—highest 99th percentile 1-hour daily maximum concentration; Sulfur Dioxide 24-Hr—highest second maximum 24-hour concentration
Source: U.S. Environmental Protection Agency, Air Quality Monitoring Information, "Air Quality Statistics by City, 2017"

Drinking Water

Water System Name	Pop. Served	Primary Water Source Type	Violations[1] Health Based	Violations[1] Monitoring/ Reporting
City of Fargo	120,762	Surface	1	0

Note: (1) Based on violation data from January 1, 2018 to December 31, 2018
Source: U.S. Environmental Protection Agency, Office of Ground Water and Drinking Water, Safe Drinking Water Information System (based on data extracted April 5, 2019)

Fort Wayne, Indiana

Background

Fort Wayne lies 100 miles northeast of Indianapolis, at the confluence of the St. Mary and St. Joseph rivers, which form the Maumee River. The waters, spanned by 21 bridges, divide the town into three parts.

Once the stronghold of the Miami tribe, the area was prominent in frontier history. The Miami Native Americans ruled the lower peninsula region, fighting against the Iroquois who had been armed by the English colonists. Later, the Miami tribe established itself in the Wabash Valley and built a village at the Lakeside district in Fort Wayne. They continued to side with the British during the American Revolution, after which President Washington ordered armies into the center of the Miami Territory to stop the Miami war parties, which had been encouraged to attack the new nation by the British. After Chief Little Turtle, one of the most feared and respected tribal leaders, defeated the army of General Arthur St. Clair, Washington sought the help of General "Mad" Anthony Wayne, who succeeded in defeating the rebellious tribes. Wayne marched on Miamitown and built the first American fort there. When the fort was turned over to Colonel John Hamtramck on October 21, 1794, the colonel immediately changed the name to Fort Wayne.

Fort Wayne's industrial growth began with the building of the Wabash and Erie Canal in the 1830s and was further stimulated in the 1850s when the railway came.

Nearly equidistant from Chicago, Cincinnati, and Detroit, the city is a regional transportation and communications center. Although the city is in an area rich in dairy, livestock, and vegetable farming, it is primarily a diversified industrial center, with several strong clusters of industry including advanced manufacturing, defense engineering, automotive-related development and production (home to the world's first full-size hybrid pickup truck), life science, higher education, aerospace/avionics-related, logistics and finance. Fort Wayne also enjoys additional prosperity due to its proximity to Warsaw, Indiana, termed the Orthopedic Capitol of the World due to its many orthopedic-implant manufacturers.

The city's Northeast Indiana Innovation Center is designed to attract high-tech businesses and to provide community outreach to local entrepreneurs and schools. Ongoing projects include the Core Incubation System, which specializes in biomedical, information systems, and advanced manufacturing plans, and the Digital Kids Initiative, which promotes early mastery of digital skills. The city has developed a blueprint for preservation and restoration of various downtown districts, including the Landing District, the Old Canal District, and the Barr Street District, which features an "International Marketplace," a cluster of businesses owned and operated by ethnic groups and supplemented by cultural centers serving them.

Fort Wayne is sometimes referred to as the "City of Churches," an unofficial moniker dating to the late-19th century when the city was the regional hub of Catholic, Lutheran, and Episcopal faiths. Today, there are nearly 400 churches in the city.

Parkview Field is home to baseball's TinCaps, nearby to a parking garage, condominiums, shops and a centrally located Courtyard Marriott hotel. Fort Wayne's renovated Grand Wayne Convention Center encompasses 225,000 square feet.

Fort Wayne's varied cultural and educational attractions combined with a low cost of living have earned Fort Wayne awards over the years, such as All-American City, Best Place to Live, and City Livability Outstanding Achievement. Arts events are held at the Allen County War Memorial Coliseum, Foellinger Outdoor Theater, and IPFW Performing Arts Center. Additional attractions include: the Foellinger-Freimann Botanical Conservatory with a Tropical House and cascading waterfall, Sonoran Desert House, Woody the talking tree, and hands-on exhibits; the Fort Wayne Museum of Art; the nationally acclaimed Fort Wayne Children's Zoo; and the Lincoln Museum with its award-winning permanent exhibit honoring the life and legacy of our 16th president.

The land surrounding the city is generally level to the south and east, rolling to the west and southwest, and quite hilly to the north and northwest. The climate is influenced by the Great Lakes, with rain fairly constant throughout the warmer months. Damaging hailstorms occur approximately twice a year, and severe flooding is possible. While snow generally covers the ground for about a month during the winter, heavy snowstorms are infrequent. With the exception of considerable cloudiness during the winter, Fort Wayne enjoys a good Midwestern average for sunshine.

Rankings

General Rankings

- In their sixth annual survey, Livability.com looked at data for more than 1,000 U.S. cities to determine the rankings for Livability's "Top 100 Best Places to Live" in 2019. Fort Wayne ranked #93. Criteria: median home value capped at $250,000; affordable living; vibrant economy; education, demographics, health care options. transportation & infrastructure; abundant lifestyle amenities. *Livability.com, "Top 100 Best Places to Live 2019" March 2019*

Business/Finance Rankings

- The personal finance site NerdWallet analyzed 183 American metropolitan areas with populations over 250,000 and more than 15,000 businesses to rank where entrepreneurs find the most success. Criteria included area economy, annual income, housing cost, unemployment rate, and the success rate of area businesses. Fort Wayne ranked #9. *www.nerdwallet.com, "Best Places to Start a Business," April 27, 2015*

- NerdWallet.com identified the 10 most promising cities for job seekers of the nation's 100 largest cities. Fort Wayne was ranked #46. Criteria: job availability; annual salary; workforce growth; affordability. *NerdWallet.com, "Best Cities for Job Seekers in 2017," December 19, 2016*

- The Fort Wayne metro area appeared on the Milken Institute "2018 Best Performing Cities" list. Rank: #118 out of 200 large metro areas. Criteria: job growth; wage and salary growth; high-tech output growth. *Milken Institute, "Best-Performing Cities 2018," January 24, 2019*

- *Forbes* ranked the 200 most populous metro areas to determine the nation's "Best Places for Business and Careers." The Fort Wayne metro area was ranked #103. Criteria: costs (business and living); job growth (past and projected); income growth; quality of life; educational attainment (college and high school); projected economic growth; cultural and recreational opportunities; net migration patterns; number of highly ranked colleges. *Forbes, "The Best Places for Business and Careers 2018: Seattle Leads the Way," October 24, 2018*

Children/Family Rankings

- Fort Wayne was selected as one of the most playful cities in the U.S. by KaBOOM! The organization's Playful City USA initiative honors cities and towns across the nation that have made their communities more playable. Criteria: pledging to integrate play as a solution to challenges in their communities; making it easy for children to get active and balanced play; creating more family-friendly and innovative communities as a result. *KaBOOM! National Campaign for Play, "2017 Playful City USA Communities"*

Education Rankings

- Personal finance website *WalletHub* analyzed the 150 largest U.S. metropolitan statistical areas to determine where the most educated Americans are choosing to settle. Criteria: education quality and attainment gap; education levels; percentage of workers with degrees; public school quality rankings; quality and size of each metro area's universities. Fort Wayne was ranked #93 (#1 = most educated city). *www.WalletHub.com, "2018's Most and Least Educated Cities in America," July 24, 2018*

- Fort Wayne was selected as one of America's most literate cities. The city ranked #49 out of the 82 largest U.S. cities. Criteria: number of booksellers; library resources; Internet resources; educational attainment; periodical publishing resources; newspaper circulation. *Central Connecticut State University, "America's Most Literate Cities, 2016," March 31, 2017*

Food/Drink Rankings

- *Men's Health* ranked 100 major U.S. cities in terms of alcohol intoxication. Fort Wayne ranked #92 (#1 = most sober).Criteria: binge drinking; alcohol-related traffic accidents, arrests, and fatalities. *Men's Health, "America's Drunkest Cities," March 9, 2015*

Health/Fitness Rankings

- For each of the 100 largest cities in the United States, the American College of Sports Medicine's American Fitness Index evaluated infrastructure, community assets, and policies that encourage healthy and fit lifestyles, including preventive health behaviors, levels of chronic disease conditions, health care access, and community resources and policies that support physical activity. Fort Wayne ranked #84 for "community fitness." *www.americanfitnessindex.org, "ACSM American Fitness Index Health and Community Fitness Status of the 100 Largest U.S. Cities," May 2018*

- *Men's Health* ranked 100 major U.S. cities in terms of the best cities for men. Fort Wayne ranked #66. Criteria: health; fitness; quality of life. *Men's Health, "The Best & Worst Cities for Men Who Want to Be Fit and Happy," January 1, 2016*

- The Fort Wayne metro area ranked #153 out of 189 in The Gallup-Healthways Well-Being Index. Criteria: purpose; social well being; financial health; community and physical health. Results are based on telephone interviews with adults, aged 18 and older, living in metropolitan areas in the 50 U.S. states and the District of Columbia. *Gallup-Healthways, "State of American Well-Being, 2017 Community Well-Being Rankings" March 2018*

Real Estate Rankings

- *WalletHub* compared the most populated U.S. cities, as well as at least two of the most populated cities in each state, for a total of 179, to determine which had the best markets for real estate agents. Fort Wayne ranked #132 where demand was high and pay was the best. Criteria: sales per agent; annual median wage for real-estate agents; monthly average starting salary for real estate agents; real estate job density and competition; unemployment rate; housing-market health index; and other relevant metrics. *www.WalletHub.com, "2018's Best Places to Be a Real Estate Agent,"April 25, 2018*

- The Fort Wayne metro area was identified as one of the nations's 20 hottest housing markets in 2019. Criteria: listing views as an indicator of demand and median days on the market as an indicator of supply. The area ranked #4. *Realtor.com, "January Top 20 Hottest Housing Markets," February 11, 2019*

Safety Rankings

- Allstate ranked the 200 largest cities in America in terms of driver safety. Fort Wayne ranked #30. Criteria: internal property damage claims over a two-year period from January 2015 to December 2016. The report helps increase the importance of safety awareness behind the wheel. *Allstate, "Allstate America's Best Drivers Report, 2018" August 28, 2018*

- The National Insurance Crime Bureau ranked 382 metro areas in the U.S. in terms of per capita rates of vehicle theft. The Fort Wayne metro area ranked #226 (#1 = highest rate). Criteria: number of vehicle theft offenses per 100,000 inhabitants in 2017. *National Insurance Crime Bureau, "Hot Spots 2017," July 12, 2018*

Seniors/Retirement Rankings

- From its Best Cities for Successful Aging indexes, the Milken Institute generated rankings for metropolitan areas, weighing data in nine categories—health care, wellness, living arrangements, transportation and convenience, financial characteristics, education, employment, community engagement, and overall livability. The Fort Wayne metro area was ranked #115 overall in the small metro area category. *Milken Institute, "Best Cities for Successful Aging, 2017" March 14, 2017*

Women/Minorities Rankings

- Personal finance website *WalletHub* compared more than 180 U.S. cities—including the 150 most populated U.S. cities, plus at least two of the most populated cities in each state—across two key dimensions, "Hispanic Business-Friendliness" and "Hispanic Purchasing Power", to arrive at the most favorable conditions for Hispanic entrepreneurs. Fort Wayne was ranked #86 out of 182. Criteria includes: share of Hispanic-Owned Businesses; Hispanic entrepreneurship rate to median annual income of Hispanics; Small Business-Friendliness score; cost of living; and number of Hispanics with at least a bachelor's degree. *WalletHub.com, "2018's Best Cities for Hispanic Entrepreneurs," April 26, 2018*

Miscellaneous Rankings

- *WalletHub* compared the 150 most populated U.S. cities to determine their operating efficiency. A "Quality of Services" score was constructed for each city and then divided by the total budget per capita to reveal which were managed the best. Fort Wayne ranked #18. Criteria: financial stability; economy; education; safety; health; infrastructure and pollution. *www.WalletHub.com, "2018's Best- & Worst-Run Cities in America," July 9, 2018*

Business Environment

CITY FINANCES

City Government Finances

Component	2016 ($000)	2016 ($ per capita)
Total Revenues	370,446	1,423
Total Expenditures	470,137	1,806
Debt Outstanding	638,240	2,452
Cash and Securities[1]	279,498	1,074

Note: (1) Cash and security holdings of a government at the close of its fiscal year, including those of its dependent agencies, utilities, and liquor stores.
Source: U.S. Census Bureau, State & Local Government Finances 2016

City Government Revenue by Source

Source	2016 ($000)	2016 ($ per capita)	2016 (%)
General Revenue			
From Federal Government	9,385	36	2.5
From State Government	36,354	140	9.8
From Local Governments	13,491	52	3.6
Taxes			
Property	124,817	479	33.7
Sales and Gross Receipts	3,221	12	0.9
Personal Income	38,746	149	10.5
Corporate Income	0	0	0.0
Motor Vehicle License	0	0	0.0
Other Taxes	787	3	0.2
Current Charges	87,269	335	23.6
Liquor Store	0	0	0.0
Utility	47,599	183	12.8
Employee Retirement	0	0	0.0

Source: U.S. Census Bureau, State & Local Government Finances 2016

City Government Expenditures by Function

Function	2016 ($000)	2016 ($ per capita)	2016 (%)
General Direct Expenditures			
Air Transportation	0	0	0.0
Corrections	0	0	0.0
Education	0	0	0.0
Employment Security Administration	0	0	0.0
Financial Administration	9,234	35	2.0
Fire Protection	37,004	142	7.9
General Public Buildings	0	0	0.0
Governmental Administration, Other	2,812	10	0.6
Health[1]	2,833	10	0.6
Highways	35,010	134	7.4
Hospitals	0	0	0.0
Housing and Community Development	35,893	137	7.6
Interest on General Debt	25,557	98	5.4
Judicial and Legal	1	< 1	< 0.1
Libraries	0	0	0.0
Parking	10,784	41	2.3
Parks and Recreation	19,292	74	4.1
Police Protection	72,656	279	15.5
Public Welfare	0	0	0.0
Sewerage	83,242	319	17.7
Solid Waste Management	9,244	35	2.0
Veterans' Services	0	0	0.0
Liquor Store	0	0	0.0
Utility	59,487	228	12.7
Employee Retirement	0	0	0.0

Source: U.S. Census Bureau, State & Local Government Finances 2016

DEMOGRAPHICS

Population Growth

Area	1990 Census	2000 Census	2010 Census	2017* Estimate	Population Growth (%) 1990-2017	Population Growth (%) 2010-2017
City	205,671	205,727	253,691	262,450	27.6	3.5
MSA[1]	354,435	390,156	416,257	429,060	21.1	3.1
U.S.	248,709,873	281,421,906	308,745,538	321,004,407	29.1	4.0

Note: (1) Figures cover the Fort Wayne, IN Metropolitan Statistical Area—see Appendix B for areas included;
(*) 2013-2017 5-year estimated population
Source: U.S. Census Bureau, 1990 Census, Census 2000, Census 2010, 2013-2017 American Community
Survey 5-Year Estimates

Household Size

Area	Persons in Household (%) One	Two	Three	Four	Five	Six	Seven or More	Average Household Size
City	32.4	31.8	15.2	11.3	5.9	2.2	1.2	2.50
MSA[1]	28.8	34.0	14.8	12.6	6.1	2.4	1.4	2.50
U.S.	27.7	33.8	15.7	13.0	6.0	2.3	1.4	2.60

Note: (1) Figures cover the Fort Wayne, IN Metropolitan Statistical Area—see Appendix B for areas included
Source: U.S. Census Bureau, 2013-2017 American Community Survey 5-Year Estimates

Race

Area	White Alone[2] (%)	Black Alone[2] (%)	Asian Alone[2] (%)	AIAN[3] Alone[2] (%)	NHOPI[4] Alone[2] (%)	Other Race Alone[2] (%)	Two or More Races (%)
City	74.2	15.0	4.3	0.2	0.1	2.1	4.2
MSA[1]	81.9	9.9	3.1	0.2	0.0	1.6	3.2
U.S.	73.0	12.7	5.4	0.8	0.2	4.8	3.1

Note: (1) Figures cover the Fort Wayne, IN Metropolitan Statistical Area—see Appendix B for areas included;
(2) Alone is defined as not being in combination with one or more other races; (3) American Indian and Alaska
Native; (4) Native Hawaiian and Other Pacific Islander
Source: U.S. Census Bureau, 2013-2017 American Community Survey 5-Year Estimates

Hispanic or Latino Origin

Area	Total (%)	Mexican (%)	Puerto Rican (%)	Cuban (%)	Other (%)
City	8.7	6.2	0.6	0.1	1.8
MSA[1]	6.5	4.6	0.5	0.1	1.3
U.S.	17.6	11.1	1.7	0.7	4.1

Note: Persons of Hispanic or Latino origin can be of any race; (1) Figures cover the Fort Wayne, IN
Metropolitan Statistical Area—see Appendix B for areas included
Source: U.S. Census Bureau, 2013-2017 American Community Survey 5-Year Estimates

Segregation

Type	Segregation Indices[1] 1990	2000	2010	2010 Rank[2]	Percent Change 1990-2000	1990-2010	2000-2010
Black/White	n/a	n/a	n/a	n/a	n/a	n/a	n/a
Asian/White	n/a	n/a	n/a	n/a	n/a	n/a	n/a
Hispanic/White	n/a	n/a	n/a	n/a	n/a	n/a	n/a

Note: All figures cover the Metropolitan Statistical Area—see Appendix B for areas included; Figures are based
on an analysis of 1990, 2000, and 2010 Census Decennial Census tract data by William H. Frey, Brookings
Institution and the University of Michigan Social Science Data Analysis Network. In this analysis all racial
groups (whites, blacks, and asians) are non-Hispanic members of those races. Hispanics are shown as a
separate category; (1) Segregation Indices are Dissimilarity Indices that measure the degree to which the
minority group is distributed differently than whites across census tracts. They range from 0 (complete
integration) to 100 (complete segregation) where the value indicates the percentage of the minority group that
needs to move to be distributed exactly like whites; (2) Ranges from 1 (most segregated) to 102 (least
segregated); n/a not available.
Source: www.CensusScope.org

Ancestry

Area	German	Irish	English	American	Italian	Polish	French[2]	Scottish	Dutch
City	26.1	9.5	6.5	6.4	2.7	1.9	3.2	1.8	1.4
MSA[1]	28.8	9.4	7.1	7.8	2.8	2.0	3.5	1.8	1.5
U.S.	14.1	10.1	7.5	6.6	5.3	2.9	2.5	1.7	1.3

Note: Figures are the percentage of the total population reporting a particular ancestry. The nine most commonly reported ancestries in the U.S. are shown. Figures include multiple ancestries (e.g. if a person reported being Irish and Italian, they were included in both columns); (1) Figures cover the Fort Wayne, IN Metropolitan Statistical Area—see Appendix B for areas included; (2) Excludes Basque
Source: U.S. Census Bureau, 2013-2017 American Community Survey 5-Year Estimates

Foreign-Born Population

Area	Percent of Population Born in								
	Any Foreign Country	Asia	Mexico	Europe	Carribean	Central America[2]	South America	Africa	Canada
City	7.8	3.5	1.9	0.9	0.1	0.7	0.3	0.2	0.1
MSA[1]	5.7	2.6	1.3	0.7	0.1	0.5	0.2	0.2	0.1
U.S.	13.4	4.1	3.6	1.5	1.3	1.0	0.9	0.6	0.3

Note: (1) Figures cover the Fort Wayne, IN Metropolitan Statistical Area—see Appendix B for areas included; (2) Excludes Mexico.
Source: U.S. Census Bureau, 2013-2017 American Community Survey 5-Year Estimates

Marital Status

Area	Never Married	Now Married[2]	Separated	Widowed	Divorced
City	34.8	44.7	1.4	5.9	13.2
MSA[1]	30.4	50.6	1.2	5.8	12.0
U.S.	33.1	48.2	2.0	5.8	10.9

Note: Figures are percentages and cover the population 15 years of age and older; (1) Figures cover the Fort Wayne, IN Metropolitan Statistical Area—see Appendix B for areas included; (2) Excludes separated
Source: U.S. Census Bureau, 2013-2017 American Community Survey 5-Year Estimates

Disability by Age

Area	All Ages	Under 18 Years Old	18 to 64 Years Old	65 Years and Over
City	13.3	5.7	12.3	33.4
MSA[1]	12.7	4.7	11.5	33.4
U.S.	12.6	4.2	10.3	35.5

Note: Figures show percent of the civilian noninstitutionalized population that reported having a disability. Disability status is determined from six types of difficulty: vision, hearing, cognitive, ambulatory, self-care, and independent living. For children under 5 years old, hearing and vision difficulty are used to determine disability status. For children between the ages of 5 and 14, disability status is determined from hearing, vision, cognitive, ambulatory, and self-care difficulties. For people aged 15 years and older, they are considered to have a disability if they have difficulty with any one of the six difficulty types; Note: (1) Figures cover the Fort Wayne, IN Metropolitan Statistical Area—see Appendix B for areas included
Source: U.S. Census Bureau, 2013-2017 American Community Survey 5-Year Estimates

Age

Area	Percent of Population									Median Age
	Under Age 5	Age 5–19	Age 20–34	Age 35–44	Age 45–54	Age 55–64	Age 65–74	Age 75–84	Age 85+	
City	7.2	21.1	22.0	12.3	12.2	11.9	7.9	3.6	1.9	34.9
MSA[1]	7.0	21.3	19.8	12.3	12.9	12.7	8.1	3.9	2.0	36.4
U.S.	6.2	19.5	20.7	12.7	13.4	12.7	8.6	4.4	1.9	37.8

Note: (1) Figures cover the Fort Wayne, IN Metropolitan Statistical Area—see Appendix B for areas included
Source: U.S. Census Bureau, 2013-2017 American Community Survey 5-Year Estimates

Gender

Area	Males	Females	Males per 100 Females
City	126,804	135,646	93.5
MSA[1]	209,819	219,241	95.7
U.S.	158,018,753	162,985,654	97.0

Note: (1) Figures cover the Fort Wayne, IN Metropolitan Statistical Area—see Appendix B for areas included
Source: U.S. Census Bureau, 2013-2017 American Community Survey 5-Year Estimates

Religious Groups by Family

Area	Catholic	Baptist	Non-Den.	Methodist[2]	Lutheran	LDS[3]	Pente-costal	Presby-terian[4]	Muslim[5]	Judaism
MSA[1]	14.2	6.1	6.8	5.1	8.5	0.4	1.5	1.7	0.3	0.1
U.S.	19.1	9.3	4.0	4.0	2.3	2.0	1.9	1.6	0.8	0.7

Note: Figures are the number of adherents as a percentage of the total population; (1) Figures cover the Fort Wayne, IN Metropolitan Statistical Area—see Appendix B for areas included; (2) Methodist/Pietist; (3) Latter Day Saints; (4) Reformed; (5) Figures are estimates
Source: Association of Statisticians of American Religious Bodies, 2010 U.S. Religion Census: Religious Congregations & Membership Study

Religious Groups by Tradition

Area	Catholic	Evangelical Protestant	Mainline Protestant	Other Tradition	Black Protestant	Orthodox
MSA[1]	14.2	24.6	9.2	1.0	2.4	0.2
U.S.	19.1	16.2	7.3	4.3	1.6	0.3

Note: Figures are the number of adherents as a percentage of the total population; (1) Figures cover the Fort Wayne, IN Metropolitan Statistical Area—see Appendix B for areas included
Source: Association of Statisticians of American Religious Bodies, 2010 U.S. Religion Census: Religious Congregations & Membership Study

ECONOMY

Gross Metropolitan Product

Area	2016	2017	2018	2019	Rank[2]
MSA[1]	21.1	21.9	22.7	23.8	115

Note: Figures are in billions of dollars; (1) Figures cover the Fort Wayne, IN Metropolitan Statistical Area—see Appendix B for areas included; (2) Rank is based on 2017 data and ranges from 1 to 381
Source: U.S. Conference of Mayors, U.S. Metro Economies: Economic Growth & Full Employment, June 2018

Economic Growth

Area	2017-2018 (%)	2019-2020 (%)	2021-2022 (%)
MSA[1]	2.0	1.9	1.1

Note: Figures are real gross metropolitan product (GMP) growth rates and represent average annual percent change; (1) Figures cover the Fort Wayne, IN Metropolitan Statistical Area—see Appendix B for areas included
Source: U.S. Conference of Mayors, U.S. Metro Economies: Economic Growth & Full Employment, June 2018

Metropolitan Area Exports

Area	2012	2013	2014	2015	2016	2017	Rank[2]
MSA[1]	1,353.5	1,441.8	1,581.1	1,529.0	1,322.2	1,422.8	121

Note: Figures are in millions of dollars; (1) Figures cover the Fort Wayne, IN Metropolitan Statistical Area—see Appendix B for areas included; (2) Rank is based on 2017 data and ranges from 1 to 387
Source: U.S. Department of Commerce, International Trade Administration, Office of Trade and Economic Analysis, Industry and Analysis, Exports by Metropolitan Area, extracted March 25, 2019

Building Permits

Area	Single-Family			Multi-Family			Total		
	2016	2017	Pct. Chg.	2016	2017	Pct. Chg.	2016	2017	Pct. Chg.
City	n/a	n/a	n/a	n/a	n/a	n/a	n/a	n/a	n/a
MSA[1]	1,076	1,222	13.6	460	500	8.7	1,536	1,722	12.1
U.S.	750,800	820,000	9.2	455,800	462,000	1.4	1,206,600	1,282,000	6.2

Note: (1) Figures cover the Fort Wayne, IN Metropolitan Statistical Area—see Appendix B for areas included; Figures represent new, privately-owned housing units authorized (unadjusted data); All permit data are based on estimates with imputation
Source: U.S. Census Bureau, Manufacturing, Mining, and Construction Statistics, Building Permits, 2016, 2017

Bankruptcy Filings

Area	Business Filings			Nonbusiness Filings		
	2017	2018	% Chg.	2017	2018	% Chg.
Allen County	16	16	0.0	1,386	1,398	0.9
U.S.	23,157	22,232	-4.0	765,863	751,186	-1.9

Note: Business filings include Chapter 7, Chapter 11, Chapter 12, and Chapter 13; Nonbusiness filings include Chapter 7, Chapter 11, and Chapter 13
Source: Administrative Office of the U.S. Courts, Business and Nonbusiness Bankruptcy, County Cases Commenced by Chapter of the Bankruptcy Code, During the 12-Month Period Ending December 31, 2017 and Business and Nonbusiness Bankruptcy, County Cases Commenced by Chapter of the Bankruptcy Code, During the 12-Month Period Ending December 31, 2018

Housing Vacancy Rates

Area	Gross Vacancy Rate[2] (%)			Year-Round Vacancy Rate[3] (%)			Rental Vacancy Rate[4] (%)			Homeowner Vacancy Rate[5] (%)		
	2016	2017	2018	2016	2017	2018	2016	2017	2018	2016	2017	2018
MSA[1]	n/a	n/a	n/a	n/a	n/a	n/a	n/a	n/a	n/a	n/a	n/a	n/a
U.S.	12.8	12.7	12.3	9.9	9.9	9.7	6.9	7.2	6.9	1.7	1.6	1.5

Note: (1) Figures cover the Fort Wayne, IN Metropolitan Statistical Area—see Appendix B for areas included; (2) The percentage of the total housing inventory that is vacant; (3) The percentage of the housing inventory (excluding seasonal units) that is year-round vacant; (4) The percentage of rental inventory that is vacant for rent; (5) The percentage of homeowner inventory that is vacant for sale; n/a not available
Source: U.S. Census Bureau, Housing Vacancies and Homeownership Annual Statistics: 2016, 2017, 2018

INCOME

Income

Area	Per Capita ($)	Median Household ($)	Average Household ($)
City	25,066	45,853	60,942
MSA[1]	26,951	51,642	67,688
U.S.	31,177	57,652	81,283

Note: (1) Figures cover the Fort Wayne, IN Metropolitan Statistical Area—see Appendix B for areas included
Source: U.S. Census Bureau, 2013-2017 American Community Survey 5-Year Estimates

Household Income Distribution

Area	Percent of Households Earning							
	Under $15,000	$15,000 -$24,999	$25,000 -$34,999	$35,000 -$49,999	$50,000 -$74,999	$75,000 -$99,999	$100,000 -$149,999	$150,000 and up
City	13.4	12.1	12.5	15.8	19.7	11.9	9.3	5.3
MSA[1]	10.7	10.5	11.3	15.4	20.6	13.2	11.8	6.4
U.S.	11.6	9.8	9.5	13.0	17.7	12.3	14.1	12.1

Note: (1) Figures cover the Fort Wayne, IN Metropolitan Statistical Area—see Appendix B for areas included
Source: U.S. Census Bureau, 2013-2017 American Community Survey 5-Year Estimates

Poverty Rate

Area	All Ages	Under 18 Years Old	18 to 64 Years Old	65 Years and Over
City	17.8	27.1	16.2	7.3
MSA[1]	14.1	21.1	12.9	6.2
U.S.	14.6	20.3	13.7	9.3

Note: Figures are percentage of people whose income during the past 12 months was below the poverty level; (1) Figures cover the Fort Wayne, IN Metropolitan Statistical Area—see Appendix B for areas included
Source: U.S. Census Bureau, 2013-2017 American Community Survey 5-Year Estimates

EMPLOYMENT

Labor Force and Employment

Area	Civilian Labor Force			Workers Employed		
	Dec. 2017	Dec. 2018	% Chg.	Dec. 2017	Dec. 2018	% Chg.
City	124,295	128,942	3.7	120,667	124,877	3.5
MSA[1]	209,676	217,559	3.8	203,947	211,085	3.5
U.S.	159,880,000	162,510,000	1.6	153,602,000	156,481,000	1.9

Note: Data is not seasonally adjusted and covers workers 16 years of age and older; (1) Figures cover the Fort Wayne, IN Metropolitan Statistical Area—see Appendix B for areas included
Source: Bureau of Labor Statistics, Local Area Unemployment Statistics

Unemployment Rate

Area	2018											
	Jan.	Feb.	Mar.	Apr.	May	Jun.	Jul.	Aug.	Sep.	Oct.	Nov.	Dec.
City	3.4	3.6	3.1	2.8	3.2	3.5	3.4	3.6	2.8	3.4	3.4	3.2
MSA[1]	3.2	3.3	2.9	2.6	3.0	3.3	3.2	3.4	2.7	3.2	3.2	3.0
U.S.	4.5	4.4	4.1	3.7	3.6	4.2	4.1	3.9	3.6	3.5	3.5	3.7

Note: Data is not seasonally adjusted and covers workers 16 years of age and older; (1) Figures cover the Fort Wayne, IN Metropolitan Statistical Area—see Appendix B for areas included
Source: Bureau of Labor Statistics, Local Area Unemployment Statistics

Average Wages

Occupation	$/Hr.	Occupation	$/Hr.
Accountants and Auditors	31.70	Maids and Housekeeping Cleaners	10.00
Automotive Mechanics	17.00	Maintenance and Repair Workers	19.70
Bookkeepers	18.50	Marketing Managers	59.50
Carpenters	20.70	Nuclear Medicine Technologists	n/a
Cashiers	10.20	Nurses, Licensed Practical	21.20
Clerks, General Office	16.60	Nurses, Registered	27.70
Clerks, Receptionists/Information	13.60	Nursing Assistants	12.90
Clerks, Shipping/Receiving	15.10	Packers and Packagers, Hand	13.60
Computer Programmers	36.40	Physical Therapists	41.80
Computer Systems Analysts	34.50	Postal Service Mail Carriers	24.80
Computer User Support Specialists	21.30	Real Estate Brokers	n/a
Cooks, Restaurant	11.50	Retail Salespersons	12.30
Dentists	120.30	Sales Reps., Exc. Tech./Scientific	33.20
Electrical Engineers	42.30	Sales Reps., Tech./Scientific	44.90
Electricians	27.20	Secretaries, Exc. Legal/Med./Exec.	16.10
Financial Managers	59.30	Security Guards	16.20
First-Line Supervisors/Managers, Sales	19.70	Surgeons	n/a
Food Preparation Workers	10.80	Teacher Assistants*	12.30
General and Operations Managers	49.40	Teachers, Elementary School*	24.10
Hairdressers/Cosmetologists	13.00	Teachers, Secondary School*	25.70
Internists, General	n/a	Telemarketers	12.50
Janitors and Cleaners	11.40	Truck Drivers, Heavy/Tractor-Trailer	21.10
Landscaping/Groundskeeping Workers	13.00	Truck Drivers, Light/Delivery Svcs.	15.80
Lawyers	62.50	Waiters and Waitresses	10.50

Note: Wage data covers the Fort Wayne, IN Metropolitan Statistical Area—see Appendix B for areas included; (*) Hourly wages for elementary/secondary school teachers and teacher assistants were calculated by the editors from annual wage data based on a 40 hour work week; n/a not available.
Source: Bureau of Labor Statistics, Metro Area Occupational Employment & Wage Estimates, May 2018

Employment by Occupation

Occupation Classification	City (%)	MSA[1] (%)	U.S. (%)
Management, Business, Science, and Arts	32.5	32.7	37.4
Natural Resources, Construction, and Maintenance	7.0	8.0	8.9
Production, Transportation, and Material Moving	18.2	19.0	12.2
Sales and Office	24.7	24.1	23.5
Service	17.6	16.2	18.0

Note: Figures cover employed civilians 16 years of age and older; (1) Figures cover the Fort Wayne, IN Metropolitan Statistical Area—see Appendix B for areas included
Source: U.S. Census Bureau, 2013-2017 American Community Survey 5-Year Estimates

Employment by Industry

| Sector | MSA[1] | | U.S. |
	Number of Employees	Percent of Total	Percent of Total
Construction, Mining, and Logging	11,000	4.8	5.3
Education and Health Services	43,500	19.1	15.9
Financial Activities	12,200	5.3	5.7
Government	22,000	9.6	15.1
Information	2,500	1.1	1.9
Leisure and Hospitality	20,600	9.0	10.7
Manufacturing	37,500	16.4	8.5
Other Services	11,600	5.1	3.9
Professional and Business Services	22,700	10.0	14.1
Retail Trade	24,700	10.8	10.8
Transportation, Warehousing, and Utilities	8,900	3.9	4.2
Wholesale Trade	10,900	4.8	3.9

Note: Figures are non-farm employment as of December 2018. Figures are not seasonally adjusted and include workers 16 years of age and older; (1) Figures cover the Fort Wayne, IN Metropolitan Statistical Area—see Appendix B for areas included
Source: Bureau of Labor Statistics, Current Employment Statistics, Employment, Hours, and Earnings

Occupations with Greatest Projected Employment Growth: 2018 – 2020

Occupation[1]	2018 Employment	2020 Projected Employment	Numeric Employment Change	Percent Employment Change
Laborers and Freight, Stock, and Material Movers, Hand	76,430	78,940	2,510	3.3
Combined Food Preparation and Serving Workers, Including Fast Food	84,030	86,500	2,470	2.9
Registered Nurses	67,010	69,350	2,340	3.5
Personal Care Aides	29,290	30,960	1,670	5.7
Janitors and Cleaners, Except Maids and Housekeeping Cleaners	48,510	49,760	1,250	2.6
Home Health Aides	13,830	14,930	1,100	8.0
Heavy and Tractor-Trailer Truck Drivers	56,570	57,630	1,060	1.9
Industrial Truck and Tractor Operators	21,430	22,480	1,050	4.9
General and Operations Managers	49,870	50,850	980	2.0
Helpers—Production Workers	17,700	18,520	820	4.6

Note: Projections cover Indiana; (1) Sorted by numeric employment change
Source: www.projectionscentral.com, State Occupational Projections, 2018–2020 Short-Term Projections

Fastest Growing Occupations: 2018 – 2020

Occupation[1]	2018 Employment	2020 Projected Employment	Numeric Employment Change	Percent Employment Change
Flight Attendants	620	680	60	9.7
Home Health Aides	13,830	14,930	1,100	8.0
Airline Pilots, Copilots, and Flight Engineers	670	720	50	7.5
Physician Assistants	1,160	1,240	80	6.9
Software Developers, Applications	8,720	9,300	580	6.7
Nurse Practitioners	4,170	4,440	270	6.5
Computer Numerically Controlled Machine Tool Programmers, Metal and Plastic	960	1,020	60	6.3
Physical Therapist Assistants	2,260	2,390	130	5.8
Personal Care Aides	29,290	30,960	1,670	5.7
Health Specialties Teachers, Postsecondary	3,020	3,190	170	5.6

Note: Projections cover Indiana; (1) Sorted by percent employment change and excludes occupations with numeric employment change less than 50
Source: www.projectionscentral.com, State Occupational Projections, 2018–2020 Short-Term Projections

TAXES

State Corporate Income Tax Rates

State	Tax Rate (%)	Income Brackets ($)	Num. of Brackets	Financial Institution Tax Rate (%)[a]	Federal Income Tax Ded.
Indiana	5.75 (i)	Flat rate	1	6.25	No

Note: Tax rates as of January 1, 2019; (a) Rates listed are the corporate income tax rate applied to financial institutions or excise taxes based on income. Some states have other taxes based upon the value of deposits or shares; (i) The Indiana Corporate tax rate is scheduled to decrease to 5.5% on July 1, 2019. Bank tax rate is scheduled to decrease to 6.0% on 1/1/20.
Source: Federation of Tax Administrators, Range of State Corporate Income Tax Rates, January 1, 2019

State Individual Income Tax Rates

State	Tax Rate (%)	Income Brackets ($)	Personal Exemptions ($)			Standard Ded. ($)	
			Single	Married	Depend.	Single	Married
Indiana	3.23	Flat rate	1,000	2,000	2,500 (j)	–	–

Note: Tax rates as of January 1, 2019; Local- and county-level taxes are not included; n/a not applicable; Federal income tax is not deductible on state income tax returns; (j) In Indiana, includes an additional exemption of $1,500 for each dependent child.
Source: Federation of Tax Administrators, State Individual Income Tax Rates, January 1, 2019

Various State Sales and Excise Tax Rates

State	State Sales Tax (%)	Gasoline[1] (¢/gal.)	Cigarette[2] ($/pack)	Spirits[3] ($/gal.)	Wine[4] ($/gal.)	Beer[5] ($/gal.)	Recreational Marijuana (%)
Indiana	7	42.9	0.995	2.68 (f)	0.47 (l)	0.12	Not legal

Note: All tax rates as of January 1, 2019; (1) The American Petroleum Institute has developed a methodology for determining the average tax rate on a gallon of fuel. Rates may include any of the following: excise taxes, environmental fees, storage tank fees, other fees or taxes, general sales tax, and local taxes. In states where gasoline is subject to the general sales tax, or where the fuel tax is based on the average sale price, the average rate determined by API is sensitive to changes in the price of gasoline. States that fully or partially apply general sales taxes to gasoline: CA, CO, GA, IL, IN, MI, NY; (2) The federal excise tax of $1.0066 per pack and local taxes are not included; (3) Rates are those applicable to off-premise sales of 40% alcohol by volume (a.b.v.) distilled spirits in 750ml containers. Local excise taxes are excluded; (4) Rates are those applicable to off-premise sales of 11% a.b.v. non-carbonated wine in 750ml containers; (5) Rates are those applicable to off-premise sales of 4.7% a.b.v. beer in 12 ounce containers; (f) Different rates also applicable according to alcohol content, place of production, size of container, or place purchased (on- or off-premise or onboard airlines); (l) Different rates also applicable to alcohol content, place of production, size of container, place purchased (on- or off-premise or on board airlines) or type of wine (carbonated, vermouth, etc.).
Source: Tax Foundation, 2019 Facts & Figures: How Does Your State Compare?

State Business Tax Climate Index Rankings

State	Overall Rank	Corporate Tax Rank	Individual Income Tax Rank	Sales Tax Rank	Unemployment Insurance Tax Rank	Property Tax Rank
Indiana	10	18	15	12	11	2

Note: The index is a measure of how each state's tax laws affect economic performance. The lower the rank, the more favorable a state's tax system is for business. States without a given tax are given a ranking of 1. The scores/rankings for the District of Columbia do not affect other states. The 2019 index represents the tax climate as of July 1, 2018.
Source: Tax Foundation, State Business Tax Climate Index 2019

COMMERCIAL UTILITIES

Typical Monthly Electric Bills

Area	Commercial Service ($/month)		Industrial Service ($/month)	
	1,500 kWh	40 kW demand 14,000 kWh	1,000 kW demand 200,000 kWh	50,000 kW demand 32,500,000 kWh
City	202	1,628	27,271	2,058,340
Average[1]	203	1,619	25,886	2,540,077

Note: Figures are based on annualized rates; (1) Average based on 187 utilities surveyed
Source: Edison Electric Institute, Typical Bills and Average Rates Report, Summer 2018

TRANSPORTATION

Means of Transportation to Work

| Area | Car/Truck/Van | | Public Transportation | | | Bicycle | Walked | Other Means | Worked at Home |
	Drove Alone	Carpooled	Bus	Subway	Railroad				
City	83.9	9.0	1.0	0.0	0.0	0.3	1.2	0.9	3.7
MSA[1]	84.8	8.4	0.7	0.0	0.0	0.3	1.2	0.7	3.9
U.S.	76.4	9.2	2.5	1.9	0.6	0.6	2.7	1.3	4.7

Note: Figures are percentages and cover workers 16 years of age and older; (1) Figures cover the Fort Wayne, IN Metropolitan Statistical Area—see Appendix B for areas included
Source: U.S. Census Bureau, 2013-2017 American Community Survey 5-Year Estimates

Travel Time to Work

Area	Less Than 10 Minutes	10 to 19 Minutes	20 to 29 Minutes	30 to 44 Minutes	45 to 59 Minutes	60 to 89 Minutes	90 Minutes or More
City	13.2	39.9	27.5	12.3	3.3	2.0	1.7
MSA[1]	13.8	35.6	27.9	15.3	3.9	1.9	1.7
U.S.	12.7	28.9	20.9	20.5	8.1	6.2	2.7

Note: Note: Figures are percentages and include workers 16 years old and over; (1) Figures cover the Fort Wayne, IN Metropolitan Statistical Area—see Appendix B for areas included
Source: U.S. Census Bureau, 2013-2017 American Community Survey 5-Year Estimates

Freeway Travel Time Index

Area	1985	1990	1995	2000	2005	2010	2014
Urban Area Rank[1,2]	n/a	n/a	n/a	n/a	n/a	n/a	n/a
Urban Area Index[1]	n/a	n/a	n/a	n/a	n/a	n/a	n/a
Average Index[3]	1.09	1.11	1.14	1.17	1.20	1.19	1.20

Note: Freeway Travel Time Index—the ratio of travel time in the peak period to the travel time at free-flow conditions. For example, a value of 1.30 indicates a 20-minute free-flow trip takes 26 minutes in the peak (20 minutes x 1.30 = 26 minutes); (1) Data for the Fort Wayne, IN urban area was not available; (2) Rank is based on 101 urban areas (#1 = highest travel time index); (3) Average of 101 urban areas
Source: Texas Transportation Institute, 2015 Urban Mobility Scorecard, August 2015

Freeway Commuter Stress Index

Area	1985	1990	1995	2000	2005	2010	2014
Urban Area Rank[1,2]	n/a	n/a	n/a	n/a	n/a	n/a	n/a
Urban Area Index[1]	n/a	n/a	n/a	n/a	n/a	n/a	n/a
Average Index[3]	1.13	1.16	1.19	1.22	1.25	1.24	1.25

Note: The Freeway Commuter Stress Index is the same as the Freeway Travel Time Index (see table above) except that it includes only the travel in the peak directions during the peak periods; the TTI includes travel in all directions during the peak period. Thus, the CSI is more indicative of the work trip experienced by each commuter on a daily basis; (1) Data for the Fort Wayne, IN urban area was not available; (2) Rank is based on 101 urban areas (#1 = highest travel time index); (3) Average of 101 urban areas
Source: Texas Transportation Institute, 2015 Urban Mobility Scorecard, August 2015

Public Transportation

Agency Name / Mode of Transportation	Vehicles Operated in Maximum Service[1]	Annual Unlinked Passenger Trips[2] (in thous.)	Annual Passenger Miles[3] (in thous.)
Fort Wayne Public Transportation Corp. (Citilink)			
Bus (directly operated)	28	1,696.8	5,352.7
Demand Response (directly operated)	15	83.8	751.9

Note: (1) The number of revenue vehicles operated by the given mode and type of service to meet the annual maximum service requirement. This is the revenue vehicle count during the peak season of the year; on the week and day that maximum service is provided. Vehicles operated in maximum service (VOMS) exclude atypical days and one-time special events; (2) The number of passengers who boarded public transportation vehicles. Passengers are counted each time they board a vehicle no matter how many vehicles they use to travel from their origin to their destination. (3) The sum of the distances ridden by all passengers during the entire fiscal year.
Source: Federal Transit Administration, National Transit Database, 2017

Air Transportation

Airport Name and Code / Type of Service	Passenger Airlines[1]	Passenger Enplanements	Freight Carriers[2]	Freight (lbs)
Fort Wayne International (FWA)				
Domestic service (U.S. carriers - 2018)	11	371,594	11	26,079,519
International service (U.S. carriers - 2017)	0	0	2	35,950

Note: (1) Includes all U.S.-based major, minor and commuter airlines that carried at least one passenger during the year; (2) Includes all U.S.-based airlines and freight carriers that transported at least one pound of freight during the year.
Source: Bureau of Transportation Statistics, The Intermodal Transportation Database, Air Carriers: T-100 Domestic Market (U.S. Carriers), 2018; Bureau of Transportation Statistics, The Intermodal Transportation Database, Air Carriers: T-100 International Market (U.S. Carriers), 2017

Other Transportation Statistics

Major Highways:	I-69
Amtrak Service:	No
Major Waterways/Ports:	None

Source: Amtrak.com; Google Maps

BUSINESSES

Major Business Headquarters

Company Name	Industry	Rankings Fortune[1]	Rankings Forbes[2]
Steel Dynamics	Metals	312	-

Note: (1) Companies that produce a 10-K are ranked 1 to 500 based on 2017 revenue; (2) All private companies with at least $2 billion in annual revenue through the end of their most current fiscal year are ranked 1 to 229; companies listed are headquartered in the city; dashes indicate no ranking
Source: Fortune, "Fortune 500," June 2018; Forbes, "America's Largest Private Companies," 2018 Rankings

Minority- and Women-Owned Businesses

Group	All Firms Firms	All Firms Sales ($000)	Firms with Paid Employees Firms	Firms with Paid Employees Sales ($000)	Firms with Paid Employees Employees	Firms with Paid Employees Payroll ($000)
AIAN[1]	178	(s)	62	(s)	100 - 249	(s)
Asian	848	346,698	277	315,177	2,330	65,979
Black	2,432	102,162	85	69,491	954	16,097
Hispanic	740	81,514	83	(s)	500 - 999	(s)
NHOPI[2]	31	5,314	21	5,115	51	1,057
Women	7,313	1,215,206	847	1,090,664	7,378	251,535
All Firms	20,502	33,229,404	5,545	32,720,966	126,993	4,909,699

Note: Figures cover firms located in the city; minority- and women-owned business are defined as firms in which the corresponding group own 51% or more of the stock or equity of the company; (1) American Indian and Alaska Native; (2) Native Hawaiian and Other Pacific Islander; (s) estimates are suppressed when publication standards are not met
Source: U.S. Census Bureau, 2012 Economic Census, Survey of Business Owners

HOTELS & CONVENTION CENTERS

Hotels, Motels and Vacation Rentals

Area	5 Star Num.	5 Star Pct.[3]	4 Star Num.	4 Star Pct.[3]	3 Star Num.	3 Star Pct.[3]	2 Star Num.	2 Star Pct.[3]	1 Star Num.	1 Star Pct.[3]	Not Rated Num.	Not Rated Pct.[3]
City[1]	0	0.0	3	2.1	20	14.3	63	45.0	0	0.0	54	38.6
Total[2]	286	0.4	5,236	7.1	16,715	22.6	10,259	13.9	293	0.4	41,056	55.6

Note: (1) Figures cover Fort Wayne and vicinity; (2) Figures cover all 100 cities in this book; (3) Percentage of hotels which have a given star rating; Star ratings are determined by expedia.com and offer an indication of the general quality of a particular hotel.
Source: www.expedia.com, April 3, 2019

Major Convention Centers

Name	Overall Space (sq. ft.)	Exhibit Space (sq. ft.)	Meeting Space (sq. ft.)	Meeting Rooms
Grand Wayne Center	225,000	n/a	n/a	n/a

Note: Table includes convention centers located in the Fort Wayne, IN metro area; n/a not available
Source: Original research

Living Environment

COST OF LIVING

Cost of Living Index

Composite Index	Groceries	Housing	Utilities	Trans-portation	Health Care	Misc. Goods/ Services
88.1	87.4	67.0	91.1	101.7	100.6	100.1

Note: The Cost of Living Index measures regional differences in the cost of consumer goods and services, excluding taxes and non-consumer expenditures, for professional and managerial households in the top income quintile. It is based on more than 50,000 prices covering almost 60 different items for which prices are collected three times a year by chambers of commerce, economic development organizations or university applied economic centers in each participating urban area. The numbers shown should be read as a percentage above or below the national average of 100. For example, a value of 115.4 in the groceries column indicates that grocery prices are 15.4% higher than the national average. Small differences in the index numbers should not be interpreted as significant; Figures cover the Fort Wayne-Allen County IN urban area.
Source: The Council for Community and Economic Research, ACCRA Cost of Living Index, 2018

Grocery Prices

Area[1]	T-Bone Steak ($/pound)	Frying Chicken ($/pound)	Whole Milk ($/half gal.)	Eggs ($/dozen)	Orange Juice ($/64 oz.)	Coffee ($/11.5 oz.)
City[2]	11.93	1.03	1.47	1.02	3.28	4.29
Avg.	11.35	1.42	1.94	1.81	3.52	4.35
Min.	7.45	0.92	0.80	0.75	2.72	3.06
Max.	15.05	2.76	4.18	4.00	5.36	8.20

Note: (1) Values for the local area are compared with the average, minimum and maximum values for all 291 areas in the Cost of Living Index; (2) Figures cover the Fort Wayne-Allen County IN urban area; T-Bone Steak (price per pound); Frying Chicken (price per pound, whole fryer); Whole Milk (half gallon carton); Eggs (price per dozen, Grade A, large); Orange Juice (64 oz. Tropicana or Florida Natural); Coffee (11.5 oz. can, vacuum-packed, Maxwell House, Hills Bros, or Folgers).
Source: The Council for Community and Economic Research, ACCRA Cost of Living Index, 2018

Housing and Utility Costs

Area[1]	New Home Price ($)	Apartment Rent ($/month)	All Electric ($/month)	Part Electric ($/month)	Other Energy ($/month)	Telephone ($/month)
City[2]	237,439	674	-	87.68	53.38	178.60
Avg.	347,000	1,087	165.93	100.16	67.73	178.70
Min.	200,468	500	93.58	25.64	26.78	163.10
Max.	1,901,222	4,888	388.65	246.86	332.81	197.70

Note: (1) Values for the local area are compared with the average, minimum and maximum values for all 291 areas in the Cost of Living Index; (2) Figures cover the Fort Wayne-Allen County IN urban area; New Home Price (2,400 sf living area, 8,000 sf lot, in urban area with full utilities); Apartment Rent (950 sf 2 bedroom/1.5 or 2 bath, unfurnished, excluding all utilities except water); All Electric (average monthly cost for an all-electric home); Part Electric (average monthly cost for a part-electric home); Other Energy (average monthly cost for natural gas, fuel oil, coal, wood, and any other forms of energy except electricity); Telephone (price includes the base monthly rate plus taxes and fees for three lines of mobile phone service).
Source: The Council for Community and Economic Research, ACCRA Cost of Living Index, 2018

Health Care, Transportation, and Other Costs

Area[1]	Doctor ($/visit)	Dentist ($/visit)	Optometrist ($/visit)	Gasoline ($/gallon)	Beauty Salon ($/visit)	Men's Shirt ($)
City[2]	126.33	90.67	94.17	2.64	31.50	49.31
Avg.	110.71	95.11	103.74	2.61	37.48	32.03
Min.	33.60	62.55	54.63	1.89	17.00	11.44
Max.	195.97	153.93	225.79	3.59	71.88	58.64

Note: (1) Values for the local area are compared with the average, minimum and maximum values for all 291 areas in the Cost of Living Index; (2) Figures cover the Fort Wayne-Allen County IN urban area; Doctor (general practitioners routine exam of an established patient); Dentist (adult teeth cleaning and periodic oral examination); Optometrist (full vision eye exam for established adult patient); Gasoline (one gallon regular unleaded, national brand, including all taxes, cash price at self-service pump if available); Beauty Salon (woman's shampoo, trim, and blow-dry); Men's Shirt (cotton/polyester dress shirt, pinpoint weave, long sleeves).
Source: The Council for Community and Economic Research, ACCRA Cost of Living Index, 2018

HOUSING

House Price Index (HPI)

Area	National Ranking[2]	Quarterly Change (%)	One-Year Change (%)	Five-Year Change (%)
MSA[1]	33	1.27	9.35	29.51
U.S.[3]	–	1.12	5.73	32.81

Note: The HPI is a weighted repeat sales index. It measures average price changes in repeat sales or refinancings on the same properties. This information is obtained by reviewing repeat mortgage transactions on single-family properties whose mortgages have been purchased or securitized by Fannie Mae or Freddie Mac in January 1975; (1) Figures cover the Fort Wayne, IN Metropolitan Statistical Area—see Appendix B for areas included; (2) Rankings are based on annual percentage change for all metro areas containing at least 15,000 transactions over the last 10 years and ranges from 1 to 245; (3) figures based on a weighted average of Census Division estimates using a seasonally adjusted, purchase-only index; all figures are for the period ending December 31, 2018
Source: Federal Housing Finance Agency, House Price Index, February 26, 2019

Median Single-Family Home Prices

Area	2016	2017	2018[p]	Percent Change 2017 to 2018
MSA[1]	125.6	132.9	143.3	7.8
U.S. Average	235.5	248.8	261.6	5.1

Note: Figures are median sales prices of existing single-family homes in thousands of dollars; (p) preliminary; (1) Figures cover the Fort Wayne, IN Metropolitan Statistical Area—see Appendix B for areas included
Source: National Association of Realtors, Median Sales Price of Existing Single-Family Homes for Metropolitan Areas, 4th Quarter 2018

Qualifying Income Based on Median Sales Price of Existing Single-Family Homes

Area	With 5% Down ($)	With 10% Down ($)	With 20% Down ($)
MSA[1]	35,216	33,362	29,655
U.S. Average	62,954	59,640	53,013

Note: Figures are preliminary; Qualifying income is based on a mortgage rate of 4.9%. Monthly principal and interest payment is limited to 25% of income; (1) Figures cover the Fort Wayne, IN Metropolitan Statistical Area—see Appendix B for areas included
Source: National Association of Realtors, Qualifying Income Based on Median Sales Price of Existing Single-Family Homes for Metropolitan Areas, 4th Quarter 2018

Median Apartment Condo-Coop Home Prices

Area	2016	2017	2018[p]	Percent Change 2017 to 2018
MSA[1]	n/a	n/a	n/a	n/a
U.S. Average	220.7	234.3	241.0	2.9

Note: Figures are median sales prices of existing apartment condo-coop homes in thousands of dollars; (p) preliminary; n/a not available; (1) Figures cover the Fort Wayne, IN Metropolitan Statistical Area—see Appendix B for areas included
Source: National Association of Realtors, Median Sales Price of Existing Apartment Condo-Coop Homes for Metropolitan Areas, 4th Quarter 2018

Home Value Distribution

Area	Under $50,000	$50,000 -$99,999	$100,000 -$149,999	$150,000 -$199,999	$200,000 -$299,999	$300,000 -$499,999	$500,000 -$999,999	$1,000,000 or more
City	12.3	33.6	28.8	13.8	7.8	2.8	0.8	0.1
MSA[1]	10.1	27.6	27.0	15.6	12.1	5.9	1.5	0.3
U.S.	8.3	13.9	14.7	14.6	18.7	17.3	9.7	2.7

Note: Figures are percentages and cover owner-occupied housing units; (1) Figures cover the Fort Wayne, IN Metropolitan Statistical Area—see Appendix B for areas included
Source: U.S. Census Bureau, 2013-2017 American Community Survey 5-Year Estimates

Homeownership Rate

Area	2010 (%)	2011 (%)	2012 (%)	2013 (%)	2014 (%)	2015 (%)	2016 (%)	2017 (%)	2018 (%)
MSA[1]	n/a	n/a	n/a	n/a	n/a	n/a	n/a	n/a	n/a
U.S.	66.9	66.1	65.4	65.1	64.5	63.7	63.4	63.9	64.4

Note: (1) Figures cover the Fort Wayne, IN Metropolitan Statistical Area—see Appendix B for areas included; n/a not available
Source: U.S. Census Bureau, Housing Vacancies and Homeownership Annual Statistics: 2010-2018

Year Housing Structure Built

Area	2010 or Later	2000 -2009	1990 -1999	1980 -1989	1970 -1979	1960 -1969	1950 -1959	1940 -1949	Before 1940	Median Year
City	0.8	6.6	14.1	11.7	16.7	15.6	12.2	6.9	15.3	1970
MSA[1]	2.5	11.0	15.2	11.0	15.1	13.3	10.5	5.7	15.6	1973
U.S.	3.2	14.5	14.0	13.6	15.5	10.8	10.5	5.1	12.9	1977

Note: Figures are percentages except for Median Year; Note: (1) Figures cover the Fort Wayne, IN Metropolitan Statistical Area—see Appendix B for areas included
Source: U.S. Census Bureau, 2013-2017 American Community Survey 5-Year Estimates

Gross Monthly Rent

Area	Under $500	$500 -$999	$1,000 -$1,499	$1,500 -$1,999	$2,000 -$2,499	$2,500 -$2,999	$3,000 and up	Median ($)
City	16.0	70.7	10.8	1.6	0.7	0.1	0.1	708
MSA[1]	16.8	68.4	12.1	1.7	0.8	0.1	0.1	714
U.S.	10.5	41.1	28.7	11.7	4.5	1.8	1.7	982

Note: Figures are percentages except for Median; Gross rent is the contract rent plus the estimated average monthly cost of utilities (electricity, gas, and water and sewer) and fuels (oil, coal, kerosene, wood, etc.) if these are paid by the renter (or paid for the renter by someone else); (1) Figures cover the Fort Wayne, IN Metropolitan Statistical Area—see Appendix B for areas included
Source: U.S. Census Bureau, 2013-2017 American Community Survey 5-Year Estimates

HEALTH

Health Risk Factors

Category	MSA[1] (%)	U.S. (%)
Adults aged 18–64 who have any kind of health care coverage	85.9	87.3
Adults who reported being in good or better health	78.3	82.4
Adults who have been told they have high blood cholesterol	32.3	33.0
Adults who have been told they have high blood pressure	35.0	32.3
Adults who are current smokers	21.1	17.1
Adults who currently use E-cigarettes	3.9	4.6
Adults who currently use chewing tobacco, snuff, or snus	3.9	4.0
Adults who are heavy drinkers[2]	4.3	6.3
Adults who are binge drinkers[3]	15.5	17.4
Adults who are overweight (BMI 25.0 - 29.9)	30.4	35.3
Adults who are obese (BMI 30.0 - 99.8)	33.9	31.3
Adults who participated in any physical activities in the past month	72.6	74.4
Adults who always or nearly always wears a seat belt	94.7	94.3

Note: (1) Figures cover the Fort Wayne, IN Metropolitan Statistical Area—see Appendix B for areas included; (2) Heavy drinkers are classified as adult men having more than 14 drinks per week and adult women having more than 7 drinks per week; (3) Binge drinkers are classified as males having five or more drinks on one occasion or females having four or more drinks on one occasion
Source: Centers for Disease Control and Prevention, Behaviorial Risk Factor Surveillance System, SMART: Selected Metropolitan Area Risk Trends, 2017

Acute and Chronic Health Conditions

Category	MSA[1] (%)	U.S. (%)
Adults who have ever been told they had a heart attack	5.3	4.2
Adults who have ever been told they have angina or coronary heart disease	5.8	3.9
Adults who have ever been told they had a stroke	3.3	3.0
Adults who have ever been told they have asthma	14.7	14.2
Adults who have ever been told they have arthritis	29.3	24.9
Adults who have ever been told they have diabetes[2]	10.9	10.5
Adults who have ever been told they had skin cancer	3.9	6.2
Adults who have ever been told they had any other types of cancer	6.5	7.1
Adults who have ever been told they have COPD	7.8	6.5
Adults who have ever been told they have kidney disease	2.2	3.0
Adults who have ever been told they have a form of depression	24.7	20.5

Note: (1) Figures cover the Fort Wayne, IN Metropolitan Statistical Area—see Appendix B for areas included; (2) Figures do not include pregnancy-related, borderline, or pre-diabetes
Source: Centers for Disease Control and Prevention, Behaviorial Risk Factor Surveillance System, SMART: Selected Metropolitan Area Risk Trends, 2017

Health Screening and Vaccination Rates

Category	MSA[1] (%)	U.S. (%)
Adults aged 65+ who have had flu shot within the past year	46.3	60.7
Adults aged 65+ who have ever had a pneumonia vaccination	69.2	75.4
Adults who have ever been tested for HIV	31.9	36.1
Adults who have ever had the shingles or zoster vaccine?	22.5	28.9
Adults who have had their blood cholesterol checked within the last five years	83.5	85.9

Note: n/a not available; (1) Figures cover the Fort Wayne, IN Metropolitan Statistical Area—see Appendix B for areas included.
Source: Centers for Disease Control and Prevention, Behaviorial Risk Factor Surveillance System, SMART: Selected Metropolitan Area Risk Trends, 2017

Disability Status

Category	MSA[1] (%)	U.S. (%)
Adults who reported being deaf	4.4	6.7
Are you blind or have serious difficulty seeing, even when wearing glasses?	3.2	4.5
Are you limited in any way in any of your usual activities due of arthritis?	16.0	12.9
Do you have difficulty doing errands alone?	7.5	6.8
Do you have difficulty dressing or bathing?	3.8	3.6
Do you have serious difficulty concentrating/remembering/making decisions?	11.1	10.7
Do you have serious difficulty walking or climbing stairs?	14.7	13.6

Note: (1) Figures cover the Fort Wayne, IN Metropolitan Statistical Area—see Appendix B for areas included.
Source: Centers for Disease Control and Prevention, Behaviorial Risk Factor Surveillance System, SMART: Selected Metropolitan Area Risk Trends, 2017

Mortality Rates for the Top 10 Causes of Death in the U.S.

ICD-10[a] Sub-Chapter	ICD-10[a] Code	Age-Adjusted Mortality Rate[1] per 100,000 population	
		County[2]	U.S.
Malignant neoplasms	C00-C97	171.6	155.5
Ischaemic heart diseases	I20-I25	85.1	94.8
Other forms of heart disease	I30-I51	54.5	52.9
Chronic lower respiratory diseases	J40-J47	50.3	41.0
Cerebrovascular diseases	I60-I69	36.5	37.5
Other degenerative diseases of the nervous system	G30-G31	40.8	35.0
Other external causes of accidental injury	W00-X59	38.2	33.7
Organic, including symptomatic, mental disorders	F01-F09	43.1	31.0
Hypertensive diseases	I10-I15	35.8	21.9
Diabetes mellitus	E10-E14	27.2	21.2

Note: (a) ICD-10 = International Classification of Diseases 10th Revision; (1) Mortality rates are a three year average covering 2015-2017; (2) Figures cover Allen County.
Source: Centers for Disease Control and Prevention, National Center for Health Statistics. Underlying Cause of Death 1999-2017 on CDC WONDER Online Database

Mortality Rates for Selected Causes of Death

ICD-10[a] Sub-Chapter	ICD-10[a] Code	Age-Adjusted Mortality Rate[1] per 100,000 population	
		County[2]	U.S.
Assault	X85-Y09	10.8	5.9
Diseases of the liver	K70-K76	14.6	14.1
Human immunodeficiency virus (HIV) disease	B20-B24	Unreliable	1.8
Influenza and pneumonia	J09-J18	9.3	14.3
Intentional self-harm	X60-X84	13.6	13.6
Malnutrition	E40-E46	3.0	1.6
Obesity and other hyperalimentation	E65-E68	2.1	2.1
Renal failure	N17-N19	21.5	13.0
Transport accidents	V01-V99	11.6	12.4
Viral hepatitis	B15-B19	Unreliable	1.6

Note: (a) ICD-10 = International Classification of Diseases 10th Revision; (1) Mortality rates are a three year average covering 2015-2017; (2) Figures cover Allen County; Data are suppressed when the data meet the criteria for confidentiality constraints; Mortality rates are flagged as unreliable when the rate would be calculated with a numerator of 20 or less.
Source: Centers for Disease Control and Prevention, National Center for Health Statistics. Underlying Cause of Death 1999-2017 on CDC WONDER Online Database

Health Insurance Coverage

Area	With Health Insurance	With Private Health Insurance	With Public Health Insurance	Without Health Insurance	Population Under Age 18 Without Health Insurance
City	88.3	63.5	34.7	11.7	7.0
MSA[1]	89.6	68.6	31.6	10.4	7.4
U.S.	89.5	67.2	33.8	10.5	5.7

Note: Figures are percentages that cover the civilian noninstitutionalized population; (1) Figures cover the Fort Wayne, IN Metropolitan Statistical Area—see Appendix B for areas included
Source: U.S. Census Bureau, 2013-2017 American Community Survey 5-Year Estimates

Number of Medical Professionals

Area	MDs[3]	DOs[3,4]	Dentists	Podiatrists	Chiropractors	Optometrists
County[1] (number)	960	80	237	20	77	90
County[1] (rate[2])	259.5	21.6	63.6	5.4	20.7	24.1
U.S. (rate[2])	279.3	23.0	68.4	6.0	27.1	16.2

Note: Data as of 2017 unless noted; (1) Data covers Allen County; (2) Rate per 100,000 population; (3) Data as of 2016 and includes all active, non-federal physicians; (4) Doctor of Osteopathic Medicine
Source: U.S. Department of Health and Human Services, Health Resources and Services Administration, Bureau of Health Professions, Area Resource File (ARF) 2017-2018

EDUCATION

Public School District Statistics

District Name	Schls	Pupils	Pupil/ Teacher Ratio	Minority Pupils[1] (%)	Free Lunch Eligible[2] (%)	IEP[3] (%)
Fort Wayne Community Schools	49	30,150	19.7	55.3	54.1	17.7
M S D Southwest Allen County Schls	9	7,193	17.5	19.3	10.4	9.6
Northwest Allen County Schools	11	7,459	18.0	14.3	9.7	13.6

Note: Table includes school districts with 2,000 or more students; (1) Percentage of students that are not non-Hispanic white; (2) Percentage of students that are eligible for the free lunch program; (3) Percentage of students that have an Individualized Education Program.
Source: U.S. Department of Education, National Center for Education Statistics, Common Core of Data, Local Education Agency (School District) Universe Survey: School Year 2016-2017; U.S. Department of Education, National Center for Education Statistics, Common Core of Data, Public Elementary/Secondary School Universe Survey: School Year 2016-2017

Highest Level of Education

Area	Less than H.S.	H.S. Diploma	Some College, No Deg.	Associate Degree	Bachelor's Degree	Master's Degree	Prof. School Degree	Doctorate Degree
City	11.4	29.0	23.0	9.8	17.6	7.0	1.5	0.7
MSA[1]	10.4	30.8	22.3	10.4	17.2	6.8	1.5	0.7
U.S.	12.7	27.3	20.8	8.3	19.1	8.4	2.0	1.4

Note: Figures cover persons age 25 and over; (1) Figures cover the Fort Wayne, IN Metropolitan Statistical Area—see Appendix B for areas included
Source: U.S. Census Bureau, 2013-2017 American Community Survey 5-Year Estimates

Educational Attainment by Race

Area	High School Graduate or Higher (%)					Bachelor's Degree or Higher (%)				
	Total	White	Black	Asian	Hisp.[2]	Total	White	Black	Asian	Hisp.[2]
City	88.6	91.4	83.3	63.2	58.4	26.8	29.5	13.3	32.6	9.9
MSA[1]	89.6	91.5	84.0	66.5	61.0	26.2	27.5	14.3	35.5	10.4
U.S.	87.3	89.3	84.9	86.5	66.7	30.9	32.2	20.6	52.7	15.2

Note: Figures shown cover persons 25 years old and over; (1) Figures cover the Fort Wayne, IN Metropolitan Statistical Area—see Appendix B for areas included; (2) People of Hispanic origin can be of any race
Source: U.S. Census Bureau, 2013-2017 American Community Survey 5-Year Estimates

School Enrollment by Grade and Control

Area	Preschool (%)		Kindergarten (%)		Grades 1 - 4 (%)		Grades 5 - 8 (%)		Grades 9 - 12 (%)	
	Public	Private	Public	Private	Public	Private	Public	Private	Public	Private
City	50.5	49.5	84.8	15.2	83.3	16.7	82.5	17.5	82.9	17.1
MSA[1]	46.6	53.4	78.1	21.9	79.9	20.1	79.5	20.5	82.9	17.1
U.S.	58.8	41.2	87.7	12.3	89.7	10.3	89.6	10.4	90.3	9.7

Note: Figures shown cover persons 3 years old and over; (1) Figures cover the Fort Wayne, IN Metropolitan Statistical Area—see Appendix B for areas included
Source: U.S. Census Bureau, 2013-2017 American Community Survey 5-Year Estimates

Average Salaries of Public School Classroom Teachers

Area	2016		2017		Change from 2016 to 2017	
	Dollars	Rank[1]	Dollars	Rank[1]	Percent	Rank[2]
Indiana	53,645	26	54,308	26	1.2	30
U.S. Average	58,479	–	59,660	–	2.0	–

Note: (1) Rank ranges from 1 to 51 where 1 indicates highest salary; (2) Rank ranges from 1 to 51 where 1 indicates highest percent change.
Source: National Education Association, Rankings & Estimates: Rankings of the States 2017 and Estimates of School Statistics 2018

Higher Education

Four-Year Colleges			Two-Year Colleges			Medical Schools[1]	Law Schools[2]	Voc/ Tech[3]
Public	Private Non-profit	Private For-profit	Public	Private Non-profit	Private For-profit			
1	4	2	0	0	1	0	1	2

Note: Figures cover institutions located within the city limits and include main campuses only; (1) includes schools accredited by the Liaison Committee on Medical Education and the American Osteopathic Association's Commission on Osteopathic College Accreditation; (2) includes ABA-accredited schools, schools with provisional ABA accreditation, and state accredited schools; (3) includes all schools with programs that are less than 2 years.
Source: National Center for Education Statistics, Integrated Postsecondary Education System (IPEDS), 2017-18; Wikipedia, List of Medical Schools in the United States, accessed April 3, 2019; Wikipedia, List of Law Schools in the United States, accessed April 3, 2019

PRESIDENTIAL ELECTION

2016 Presidential Election Results

Area	Clinton	Trump	Johnson	Stein	Other
Allen County	37.3	56.5	4.6	0.5	1.2
U.S.	48.0	45.9	3.3	1.1	1.7

Note: Results are percentages and may not add to 100% due to rounding
Source: Dave Leip's Atlas of U.S. Presidential Elections

EMPLOYERS

Major Employers

Company Name	Industry
Allen County Government	Government
BAE Systems Platform Solutions	Aircraft electronics
Benchmark Human Services	Services for people with disabilities
BFGoodrich	Rubber tire manufacturing
City of Fort Wayne	Government
Dana Corp.	Motor vehicle parts manufacturing
Edy's Grand Ice Cream	Ice cream & other frozen treats
Fort Wayne Community Schools	Elementary & secondary schools
Fort Wayne Metals Research Products Corp.	Wire for medical devices
Frontier Communications Corp.	Wired telecommunications carriers
General Motors	Motor vehicle manufacturing
Harris Corporation	Wireless networking systems & satellite imaging systems
IPFW	University
Ivy Tech Community College- Northeast	Community college
Lincoln Financial Group	Insurance carriers
Lutheran Health Network	General medical & surgical hospitals
Norfolk Southern Corp2	Rail transportation
Northwest Allen County Schools	Elementary & secondary schools
Parker Hannifin Corporation	Metal product manufacturing for a/c systems
Parkview Health Systems	General medical & surgical hospitals
Raytheon Systems Co.	Mission solutions for aerospace industry
Shambaugh & Son	Commercial building construction
Steel Dynamics1	Corporate headquarters & scrap metal processing
Sweetwater Sound	Sound recording studio & equipment distribution
Vera Bradley	Handbags, luggage, & accessories

Note: Companies shown are located within the Fort Wayne, IN Metropolitan Statistical Area.
Source: Hoovers.com; Wikipedia

PUBLIC SAFETY

Crime Rate

Area	All Crimes	Violent Crimes				Property Crimes		
		Murder	Rape[3]	Robbery	Aggrav. Assault	Burglary	Larceny -Theft	Motor Vehicle Theft
City	3,537.2	13.9	51.1	112.3	180.3	491.3	2,488.6	199.8
Suburbs[1]	n/a	1.2	30.2	28.5	106.7	201.6	n/a	91.9
Metro[2]	n/a	9.0	43.0	79.8	151.8	378.9	n/a	158.0
U.S.	2,756.1	5.3	41.7	98.0	248.9	430.4	1,694.4	237.4

Note: Figures are crimes per 100,000 population; (1) All areas within the metro area that are located outside the city limits; (2) Figures cover the Fort Wayne, IN Metropolitan Statistical Area—see Appendix B for areas included; (3) The city and U.S. figures shown were reported using the revised Uniform Crime Reporting (UCR) definition of rape. The suburban and metro area figures shown are an aggregate total of the data submitted using both the revised and legacy UCR definitions.
Source: FBI Uniform Crime Reports, 2017

Hate Crimes

Area	Number of Quarters Reported	Number of Incidents per Bias Motivation					
		Race/Ethnicity/ Ancestry	Religion	Sexual Orientation	Disability	Gender	Gender Identity
City	4	2	0	2	0	0	0
U.S.	4	4,131	1,564	1,130	116	46	119

Source: Federal Bureau of Investigation, Hate Crime Statistics 2017

Identity Theft Consumer Reports

Area	Reports	Reports per 100,000 Population	Rank[2]
MSA[1]	394	91	166
U.S.	444,602	135	-

Note: (1) Figures cover the Fort Wayne, IN Metropolitan Statistical Area—see Appendix B for areas included; (2) Rank ranges from 1 to 389 where 1 indicates greatest number of identity theft reports per 100,000 population
Source: Federal Trade Commission, Consumer Sentinel Network Data Book for January–December 2018

Fraud and Other Consumer Reports

Area	Reports	Reports per 100,000 Population	Rank[2]
MSA[1]	2,161	500	182
U.S.	2,552,917	776	-

Note: (1) Figures cover the Fort Wayne, IN Metropolitan Statistical Area—see Appendix B for areas included; (2) Rank ranges from 1 to 389 where 1 indicates greatest number of fraud and other consumer reports per 100,000 population
Source: Federal Trade Commission, Consumer Sentinel Network Data Book for January–December 2018

SPORTS

Professional Sports Teams

Team Name	League	Year Established
No teams are located in the metro area		

Source: Wikipedia, Major Professional Sports Teams of the United States and Canada, April 5, 2019

CLIMATE

Average and Extreme Temperatures

Temperature	Jan	Feb	Mar	Apr	May	Jun	Jul	Aug	Sep	Oct	Nov	Dec	Yr.
Extreme High (°F)	69	69	82	88	94	106	103	101	100	90	79	71	106
Average High (°F)	31	35	46	60	71	81	84	82	76	64	49	36	60
Average Temp. (°F)	24	27	37	49	60	70	74	72	65	53	41	29	50
Average Low (°F)	16	19	28	39	49	59	63	61	53	42	32	22	40
Extreme Low (°F)	-22	-18	-10	7	27	38	44	38	29	19	-1	-18	-22

Note: Figures cover the years 1948-1990
Source: National Climatic Data Center, International Station Meteorological Climate Summary, 9/96

Average Precipitation/Snowfall/Humidity

Precip./Humidity	Jan	Feb	Mar	Apr	May	Jun	Jul	Aug	Sep	Oct	Nov	Dec	Yr.
Avg. Precip. (in.)	2.3	2.1	2.9	3.4	3.6	3.8	3.6	3.4	2.6	2.7	2.8	2.7	35.9
Avg. Snowfall (in.)	8	8	5	2	Tr	0	0	0	0	Tr	3	7	33
Avg. Rel. Hum. 7am (%)	81	81	80	77	76	78	81	86	86	84	83	83	81
Avg. Rel. Hum. 4pm (%)	71	68	62	54	52	52	53	55	53	55	67	74	59

Note: Figures cover the years 1948-1990; Tr = Trace amounts (<0.05 in. of rain; <0.5 in. of snow)
Source: National Climatic Data Center, International Station Meteorological Climate Summary, 9/96

Weather Conditions

Temperature			Daytime Sky			Precipitation		
5°F & below	32°F & below	90°F & above	Clear	Partly cloudy	Cloudy	0.01 inch or more precip.	0.1 inch or more snow/ice	Thunder-storms
16	131	16	75	140	150	131	31	39

Note: Figures are average number of days per year and cover the years 1948-1990
Source: National Climatic Data Center, International Station Meteorological Climate Summary, 9/96

HAZARDOUS WASTE

Superfund Sites

The Fort Wayne, IN metro area is home to two sites on the EPA's Superfund National Priorities List: **Fort Wayne Reduction Dump** (final); **Wayne Waste Oil** (final). There are a total of 1,390 Superfund sites with a status of proposed or final on the list in the U.S. *U.S. Environmental Protection Agency, National Priorities List, April 5, 2019*

AIR & WATER
QUALITY

Air Quality Trends: Ozone

	1990	1995	2000	2005	2010	2012	2014	2015	2016	2017
MSA[1]	0.086	0.094	0.086	0.081	0.067	0.076	0.063	0.061	0.068	0.063
U.S.	0.088	0.089	0.082	0.080	0.073	0.075	0.067	0.068	0.069	0.068

Note: (1) Data covers the Fort Wayne, IN Metropolitan Statistical Area—see Appendix B for areas included. The values shown are the composite ozone concentration averages among trend sites based on the highest fourth daily maximum 8-hour concentration in parts per million. These trends are based on sites having an adequate record of monitoring data during the trend period. Data from exceptional events are included.
Source: U.S. Environmental Protection Agency, Air Quality Monitoring Information, "Air Quality Trends by City, 1990-2017"

Air Quality Index

Area	Percent of Days when Air Quality was...[2]					AQI Statistics[2]	
	Good	Moderate	Unhealthy for Sensitive Groups	Unhealthy	Very Unhealthy	Maximum	Median
MSA[1]	70.7	29.0	0.3	0.0	0.0	105	44

Note: (1) Data covers the Fort Wayne, IN Metropolitan Statistical Area—see Appendix B for areas included; (2) Based on 365 days with AQI data in 2017. Air Quality Index (AQI) is an index for reporting daily air quality. EPA calculates the AQI for five major air pollutants regulated by the Clean Air Act: ground-level ozone, particle pollution (aka particulate matter), carbon monoxide, sulfur dioxide, and nitrogen dioxide. The AQI runs from 0 to 500. The higher the AQI value, the greater the level of air pollution and the greater the health concern. There are six AQI categories: "Good" AQI is between 0 and 50. Air quality is considered satisfactory; "Moderate" AQI is between 51 and 100. Air quality is acceptable; "Unhealthy for Sensitive Groups" When AQI values are between 101 and 150, members of sensitive groups may experience health effects; "Unhealthy" When AQI values are between 151 and 200 everyone may begin to experience health effects; "Very Unhealthy" AQI values between 201 and 300 trigger a health alert; "Hazardous" AQI values over 300 trigger warnings of emergency conditions (not shown).
Source: U.S. Environmental Protection Agency, Air Quality Index Report, 2017

Air Quality Index Pollutants

Area	Percent of Days when AQI Pollutant was...[2]					
	Carbon Monoxide	Nitrogen Dioxide	Ozone	Sulfur Dioxide	Particulate Matter 2.5	Particulate Matter 10
MSA[1]	0.0	0.0	49.6	0.0	50.4	0.0

Note: (1) Data covers the Fort Wayne, IN Metropolitan Statistical Area—see Appendix B for areas included; (2) Based on 365 days with AQI data in 2017. The Air Quality Index (AQI) is an index for reporting daily air quality. EPA calculates the AQI for five major air pollutants regulated by the Clean Air Act: ground-level ozone, particle pollution (also known as particulate matter), carbon monoxide, sulfur dioxide, and nitrogen dioxide. The AQI runs from 0 to 500. The higher the AQI value, the greater the level of air pollution and the greater the health concern.
Source: U.S. Environmental Protection Agency, Air Quality Index Report, 2017

Maximum Air Pollutant Concentrations: Particulate Matter, Ozone, CO and Lead

	Particulate Matter 10 (ug/m^3)	Particulate Matter 2.5 Wtd AM (ug/m^3)	Particulate Matter 2.5 24-Hr (ug/m^3)	Ozone (ppm)	Carbon Monoxide (ppm)	Lead (ug/m^3)
MSA[1] Level	n/a	8.2	20	0.064	n/a	n/a
NAAQS[2]	150	15	35	0.075	9	0.15
Met NAAQS[2]	n/a	Yes	Yes	Yes	n/a	n/a

Note: (1) Data covers the Fort Wayne, IN Metropolitan Statistical Area—see Appendix B for areas included; Data from exceptional events are included; (2) National Ambient Air Quality Standards; ppm = parts per million; ug/m^3 = micrograms per cubic meter; n/a not available.
Concentrations: Particulate Matter 10 (coarse particulate)—highest second maximum 24-hour concentration; Particulate Matter 2.5 Wtd AM (fine particulate)—highest weighted annual mean concentration; Particulate Matter 2.5 24-Hour (fine particulate)—highest 98th percentile 24-hour concentration; Ozone—highest fourth daily maximum 8-hour concentration; Carbon Monoxide—highest second maximum non-overlapping 8-hour concentration; Lead—maximum running 3-month average
Source: U.S. Environmental Protection Agency, Air Quality Monitoring Information, "Air Quality Statistics by City, 2017"

Maximum Air Pollutant Concentrations: Nitrogen Dioxide and Sulfur Dioxide

	Nitrogen Dioxide AM (ppb)	Nitrogen Dioxide 1-Hr (ppb)	Sulfur Dioxide AM (ppb)	Sulfur Dioxide 1-Hr (ppb)	Sulfur Dioxide 24-Hr (ppb)
MSA[1] Level	n/a	n/a	n/a	n/a	n/a
NAAQS[2]	53	100	30	75	140
Met NAAQS[2]	n/a	n/a	n/a	n/a	n/a

Note: (1) Data covers the Fort Wayne, IN Metropolitan Statistical Area—see Appendix B for areas included; Data from exceptional events are included; (2) National Ambient Air Quality Standards; ppm = parts per million; ug/m³ = micrograms per cubic meter; n/a not available.
Concentrations: Nitrogen Dioxide AM—highest arithmetic mean concentration; Nitrogen Dioxide 1-Hr—highest 98th percentile 1-hour daily maximum concentration; Sulfur Dioxide AM—highest annual mean concentration; Sulfur Dioxide 1-Hr—highest 99th percentile 1-hour daily maximum concentration; Sulfur Dioxide 24-Hr—highest second maximum 24-hour concentration
Source: U.S. Environmental Protection Agency, Air Quality Monitoring Information, "Air Quality Statistics by City, 2017"

Drinking Water

Water System Name	Pop. Served	Primary Water Source Type	Violations[1] Health Based	Violations[1] Monitoring/ Reporting
Ft. Wayne-3 Rivers Filtration Plant	250,000	Surface	0	0

Note: (1) Based on violation data from January 1, 2018 to December 31, 2018
Source: U.S. Environmental Protection Agency, Office of Ground Water and Drinking Water, Safe Drinking Water Information System (based on data extracted April 5, 2019)

Grand Rapids, Michigan

Background

The city of Grand Rapids is located in the west-central part of Kent County in the picturesque Grand River Valley, about 30 miles east of Lake Michigan. It is known for its fine furniture making.

The presence of an abundant forest, as well as the hydropower and trade afforded by a powerful river, contributed to the reputation of an industry that is known worldwide. Today Grand Rapids' manufacturing industry produces not only office furniture, but industrial machinery, metal, paper, plastics, printing products, food and information technology. There are 14 universities and colleges in Grand Rapids.

However, before Grand Rapids became involved in making seating for churches, buses, and schools, among other furniture, the site was a Native American settlement of the Ottawa, Chippewa, and Potawatomi tribes. The earliest white settlers in the area were fur traders who bought pelts from the Native American tribes in the early nineteenth century. One by one, more white settlers found their way into the area on the rapids of the Grand River. A Baptist mission was established in 1825, and a year after that, Louis Campau erected a trading post. In 1833, the area's first permanent white settlement appeared, led by Samuel Dexter of Herkimer County, New York. In 1945, Grand Rapids became the first city in the United States to add fluoride to its drinking water.

Revitalization efforts have resulted in a thriving downtown district that includes restaurants, hotels, clubs, four museums, and the 12,000-square foot Van Andel Arena. Also here is the DeVos Place Convention Center, with its 162,000 square foot, column-free exhibit hall, 40,000 square foot ballroom, 26 individual meeting rooms, and a 2,404-seat performing arts theater that is home to the Grand Rapids Symphony, the Grand Rapids Ballet Company, Opera Grand Rapids, and Broadway Grand Rapids.

The city's other attractions include museums, entertainment and cultural events. A yearly Festival of the Arts is held in June featuring visual, performing and culinary arts. There is also a yearly jazz festival. Celebration on the Grand salutes summer, and features free concerts, West Michigan's largest fireworks display and food booths. The annual Fulton Street Farmers Market has been held since 1922, and offers locally grown produce and handmade items.

The Frederik Meijer Gardens and Sculpture Park blends art and nature, maintaining outdoor (on 125 acres) and indoor exhibits. Each spring, visitors marvel at the thousands of butterflies, brought from all over the world and released into the Park's tropical conservatory.

Children enjoy the John Ball Zoo as well as the Grand Rapids Children's Museum, which offers a wide range of entertainment and educational programs for youngsters.

Fall is a very colorful time of year in western Michigan, perhaps compensating for the late spring. During the winter, excessive cloudiness and numerous snow flurries occur with strong westerly winds. Lake Michigan has a tempering effect on cold waves coming in from the west in the winter. Prolonged, severe cold waves are infrequent. The snowfall season extends from mid-November to mid-March and some winters have had continuous snow cover throughout this period.

Rankings

General Rankings

- *US News & World Report* conducted a survey of more than 2,000 people and analyzed the 125 largest metropolitan areas to determine what matters the most when selecting the next place to live. Grand Rapids ranked #12 out of the top 25 as having the best combination of desirable factors. Criteria: cost of living; quality of education; job market, crime rates; and other factors. *realestate.usnews.com, "The 25 Best Places to Live in the U.S. in 2018," April 10, 2018*

- The Grand Rapids metro area was identified as one of America's fastest-growing areas in terms of population and business growth by *MagnifyMoney*. The area ranked #27 out of 35. The 100 most populous metro areas in the U.S. were evaluated on their change from 2011-2016 in the following categories: people and housing; workforce and employment opportunities; growing industry. *www.businessinsider.com, "The 35 Cities in the US with the Biggest Influx of People, the Most Work Opportunities, and the Hottest Business Growth," August 12, 2018*

- The Grand Rapids metro area was identified as one of America's fastest-growing areas in terms of population and economy by *Forbes*. The area ranked #25 out of 25. The 100 most populous metro areas in the U.S. were evaluated on the following criteria: estimated population growth; employment; economic output; wages; home values. *Forbes, "America's Fastest-Growing Cities 2018," February 28, 2018*

- Grand Rapids was selected as one of the best places to live in America by *Outside Magazine*. Criteria included great access to trails and public lands, great for children, delicious food and drink, and welcoming to people of all backgrounds. Three decades of coverage was combined with the expertise of an advisory council to pick the finalists. *Outside Magazine, "The 25 Best Towns of 2017," July 2017*

- The U.S. Conference of Mayors and Waste Management, Inc. sponsor the City Livability Awards Program, which recognize mayors for exemplary leadership in developing and implementing specific programs that improve the quality of life in America's cities. Grand Rapids received an Honorable Mention Citation in the large cities category. *U.S. Conference of Mayors, "2018 City Livability Awards"*

- In their sixth annual survey, Livability.com looked at data for more than 1,000 U.S. cities to determine the rankings for Livability's "Top 100 Best Places to Live" in 2019. Grand Rapids ranked #45. Criteria: median home value capped at $250,000; affordable living; vibrant economy; education, demographics, health care options. transportation & infrastructure; abundant lifestyle amenities. *Livability.com, "Top 100 Best Places to Live 2019" March 2019*

Business/Finance Rankings

- The personal finance site NerdWallet analyzed 183 American metropolitan areas with populations over 250,000 and more than 15,000 businesses to rank where entrepreneurs find the most success. Criteria included area economy, annual income, housing cost, unemployment rate, and the success rate of area businesses. Grand Rapids ranked #150. *www.nerdwallet.com, "Best Places to Start a Business," April 27, 2015*

- The Brookings Institution ranked the nation's largest cities based on income inequality. Grand Rapids was ranked #85 (#1 = greatest inequality). Criteria: the "95/20 ratio," a figure representing the income at which a household earns more than 95 percent of all other households, divided by the income at which a household earns more than only 20 percent of all other households. *Brookings Institution, "Household Income Inequality, Largest Cities of 97 Large U.S. Metro Areas, 2014-2016," February 5, 2018*

- The Brookings Institution ranked the 100 largest metro areas in the U.S. based on income inequality. Grand Rapids was ranked #97 (#1 = greatest inequality). Criteria: the "95/20 ratio," a figure representing the income at which a household earns more than 95 percent of all other households, divided by the income at which a household earns more than only 20 percent of all other households. *Brookings Institution, "Household Income Inequality, 100 Largest U.S. Metro Areas, 2014-2016," February 5, 2018*

- The Grand Rapids metro area was identified as one of the most affordable metropolitan areas in America by *Forbes*. The area ranked #16 out of 20 based on the National Association of Home Builders/Wells Fargo Housing Affordability Index and Sperling's Best Places' cost-of-living index. *Forbes.com, "America's Most Affordable Cities in 2015," March 12, 2015*

- The Grand Rapids metro area appeared on the Milken Institute "2018 Best Performing Cities" list. Rank: #29 out of 200 large metro areas. Criteria: job growth; wage and salary growth; high-tech output growth. *Milken Institute, "Best-Performing Cities 2018," January 24, 2019*

- *Forbes* ranked the 200 most populous metro areas to determine the nation's "Best Places for Business and Careers." The Grand Rapids metro area was ranked #43. Criteria: costs (business and living); job growth (past and projected); income growth; quality of life; educational attainment (college and high school); projected economic growth; cultural and recreational opportunities; net migration patterns; number of highly ranked colleges. *Forbes, "The Best Places for Business and Careers 2018: Seattle Leads the Way," October 24, 2018*

Dating/Romance Rankings

- Grand Rapids was ranked #7 out of 25 cities that stood out for inspiring romance and attracting diners on the website OpenTable.com. Criteria: percentage of people who dined out on Valentine's Day in 2018; percentage of romantic restaurants as rated by OpenTable diner reviews; and percentage of tables seated for two. *OpenTable, "25 Most Romantic Cities in America for 2019," February 7, 2019*

Education Rankings

- Personal finance website *WalletHub* analyzed the 150 largest U.S. metropolitan statistical areas to determine where the most educated Americans are choosing to settle. Criteria: education quality and attainment gap; education levels; percentage of workers with degrees; public school quality rankings; quality and size of each metro area's universities. Grand Rapids was ranked #57 (#1 = most educated city). *www.WalletHub.com, "2018's Most and Least Educated Cities in America," July 24, 2018*

Environmental Rankings

- Niche compiled a list of the nation's snowiest cities, based on the National Oceanic and Atmospheric Administration's 30-year average snowfall data. Among cities with a population of at least 50,000, Grand Rapids ranked #8. *Niche.com, Top 25 Snowiest Cities in America, December 10, 2018*

Food/Drink Rankings

- *Men's Health* ranked 100 major U.S. cities in terms of alcohol intoxication. Grand Rapids ranked #65 (#1 = most sober).Criteria: binge drinking; alcohol-related traffic accidents, arrests, and fatalities. *Men's Health, "America's Drunkest Cities," March 9, 2015*

Health/Fitness Rankings

- The Grand Rapids metro area was identified as one of the worst cities for bed bugs in America by pest control company Orkin. The area ranked #20 out of 50 based on the number of bed bug treatments Orkin performed from December 2017 to November 2018. *Orkin, "Baltimore Remains Front Runner, Atlanta and Philadelphia Break Into Top 10," January 14, 2019*

- Grand Rapids was identified as a "2018 Spring Allergy Capital." The area ranked #36 out of 100. Three groups of factors were used to identify the most challenging cities for people with allergies during the spring season: annual pollen levels; medicine utilization; access to board-certified allergists. *Asthma and Allergy Foundation of America, "Spring Allergy Capitals 2018"*

- Grand Rapids was identified as a "2018 Fall Allergy Capital." The area ranked #33 out of 100. Three groups of factors were used to identify the most challenging cities for people with allergies during the fall season: annual pollen levels; medicine utilization; access to board-certified allergists. *Asthma and Allergy Foundation of America, "Fall Allergy Capitals 2018"*

- Grand Rapids was identified as a "2018 Asthma Capital." The area ranked #66 out of the nation's 100 largest metropolitan areas. Criteria: estimated prevalence; self-reported prevalence; crude death rate for asthma; annual pollen score; annual air quality; public smoking laws; number of board-certified asthma specialists; school inhaler access laws; rescue medication use; controller medication use; ER visits for asthma; uninsured rate; poverty rate. *Asthma and Allergy Foundation of America, "Asthma Capitals 2018: The Most Challenging Places to Live With Asthma"*

- The Grand Rapids metro area ranked #26 out of 189 in The Gallup-Healthways Well-Being Index. Criteria: purpose; social well being; financial health; community and physical health. Results are based on telephone interviews with adults, aged 18 and older, living in metropolitan areas in the 50 U.S. states and the District of Columbia. *Gallup-Healthways, "State of American Well-Being, 2017 Community Well-Being Rankings" March 2018*

Real Estate Rankings

- *WalletHub* compared the most populated U.S. cities, as well as at least two of the most populated cities in each state, for a total of 179, to determine which had the best markets for real estate agents. Grand Rapids ranked #43 where demand was high and pay was the best. Criteria: sales per agent; annual median wage for real-estate agents; monthly average starting salary for real estate agents; real estate job density and competition; unemployment rate; housing-market health index; and other relevant metrics. *www.WalletHub.com, "2018's Best Places to Be a Real Estate Agent," April 25, 2018*

- Despite the national slowdown trend, the Grand Rapids metro area appeared on Realtor.com's list of hot housing markets to watch in 2019. The area ranked #2. Criteria: existing homes inventory and price; new home construction; median household incomes; local economy/population trends. *Realtor.com®, "The 10 Surprising Housing Markets Poised to Rule in 2019," January 2, 2019*

- Grand Rapids was ranked #58 out of 237 metro areas in terms of housing affordability in 2018 by the National Association of Home Builders (#1 = most affordable). Criteria: the share of homes sold in that area affordable to a family earning the local median income, based on standard mortgage underwriting criteria. *National Association of Home Builders®, NAHB-Wells Fargo Housing Opportunity Index, 4th Quarter 2018*

Safety Rankings

- Allstate ranked the 200 largest cities in America in terms of driver safety. Grand Rapids ranked #136. Criteria: internal property damage claims over a two-year period from January 2015 to December 2016. The report helps increase the importance of safety awareness behind the wheel. *Allstate, "Allstate America's Best Drivers Report, 2018" August 28, 2018*

- The National Insurance Crime Bureau ranked 382 metro areas in the U.S. in terms of per capita rates of vehicle theft. The Grand Rapids metro area ranked #332 (#1 = highest rate). Criteria: number of vehicle theft offenses per 100,000 inhabitants in 2017. *National Insurance Crime Bureau, "Hot Spots 2017," July 12, 2018*

Transportation Rankings

- NerdWallet surveyed average annual car insurance premiums in 125 U.S. cities to identify the least expensive U.S. cities in which to insure a car. Locations with no-fault insurance laws was a strong determinant. Grand Rapids came in at #3 for the most expensive rates. *www.nerdwallet.com, "Best Cities for Cheap Car Insurance," February 3, 2014*

Women/Minorities Rankings

- Personal finance website *WalletHub* compared more than 180 U.S. cities—including the 150 most populated U.S. cities, plus at least two of the most populated cities in each state—across two key dimensions, "Hispanic Business-Friendliness" and "Hispanic Purchasing Power", to arrive at the most favorable conditions for Hispanic entrepreneurs. Grand Rapids was ranked #122 out of 182. Criteria includes: share of Hispanic-Owned Businesses; Hispanic entrepreneurship rate to median annual income of Hispanics; Small Business-Friendliness score; cost of living; and number of Hispanics with at least a bachelor's degree. *WalletHub.com, "2018's Best Cities for Hispanic Entrepreneurs," April 26, 2018*

Miscellaneous Rankings

- *MoveHub* ranked the coolest cities, appealing to young people, using its U.S. Hipster İndex and Grand Rapids came out as #9. Criteria: number of thrift stores; density of tattoo parlors, vegan stores and microbreweries; and amount of rent increase. *www.thisisinsider.com, "The 20 Most Hipster Cities in the US-and Why You Should Consider Moving to One," April 10, 2018*

- *WalletHub* compared the 150 most populated U.S. cities to determine their operating efficiency. A "Quality of Services" score was constructed for each city and then divided by the total budget per capita to reveal which were managed the best. Grand Rapids ranked #36. Criteria: financial stability; economy; education; safety; health; infrastructure and pollution. *www.WalletHub.com, "2018's Best- & Worst-Run Cities in America," July 9, 2018*

- Grand Rapids was selected as one of "America's Friendliest Cities." The city ranked #13 in the "Friendliest" category. Respondents to an online survey were asked to rate 38 top urban destinations in the United States as to general friendliness, as well as manners, politeness and warm disposition. *Travel + Leisure, "America's Friendliest Cities," October 20, 2017*

Business Environment

CITY FINANCES

City Government Finances

Component	2016 ($000)	2016 ($ per capita)
Total Revenues	396,535	2,033
Total Expenditures	478,781	2,454
Debt Outstanding	663,817	3,402
Cash and Securities[1]	1,185,033	6,074

Note: (1) Cash and security holdings of a government at the close of its fiscal year, including those of its dependent agencies, utilities, and liquor stores.
Source: U.S. Census Bureau, State & Local Government Finances 2016

City Government Revenue by Source

Source	2016 ($000)	2016 ($ per capita)	2016 (%)
General Revenue			
From Federal Government	32,617	167	8.2
From State Government	37,926	194	9.6
From Local Governments	2,676	14	0.7
Taxes			
Property	54,488	279	13.7
Sales and Gross Receipts	0	0	0.0
Personal Income	88,174	452	22.2
Corporate Income	0	0	0.0
Motor Vehicle License	0	0	0.0
Other Taxes	7,719	40	1.9
Current Charges	111,849	573	28.2
Liquor Store	0	0	0.0
Utility	41,968	215	10.6
Employee Retirement	1,196	6	0.3

Source: U.S. Census Bureau, State & Local Government Finances 2016

City Government Expenditures by Function

Function	2016 ($000)	2016 ($ per capita)	2016 (%)
General Direct Expenditures			
Air Transportation	0	0	0.0
Corrections	0	0	0.0
Education	0	0	0.0
Employment Security Administration	0	0	0.0
Financial Administration	4,021	20	0.8
Fire Protection	28,348	145	5.9
General Public Buildings	0	0	0.0
Governmental Administration, Other	5,319	27	1.1
Health	0	0	0.0
Highways	46,018	235	9.6
Hospitals	0	0	0.0
Housing and Community Development	47,679	244	10.0
Interest on General Debt	22,651	116	4.7
Judicial and Legal	14,359	73	3.0
Libraries	8,488	43	1.8
Parking	10,994	56	2.3
Parks and Recreation	11,165	57	2.3
Police Protection	49,581	254	10.4
Public Welfare	0	0	0.0
Sewerage	38,091	195	8.0
Solid Waste Management	9,866	50	2.1
Veterans' Services	0	0	0.0
Liquor Store	0	0	0.0
Utility	45,560	233	9.5
Employee Retirement	70,327	360	14.7

Source: U.S. Census Bureau, State & Local Government Finances 2016

DEMOGRAPHICS

Population Growth

Area	1990 Census	2000 Census	2010 Census	2017* Estimate	Population Growth (%)	
					1990-2017	2010-2017
City	189,145	197,800	188,040	195,355	3.3	3.9
MSA[1]	645,914	740,482	774,160	1,039,182	60.9	34.2
U.S.	248,709,873	281,421,906	308,745,538	321,004,407	29.1	4.0

Note: (1) Figures cover the Grand Rapids-Wyoming, MI Metropolitan Statistical Area—see Appendix B for areas included; (*) 2013-2017 5-year estimated population
Source: U.S. Census Bureau, 1990 Census, Census 2000, Census 2010, 2013-2017 American Community Survey 5-Year Estimates

Household Size

Area	Persons in Household (%)							Average Household Size
	One	Two	Three	Four	Five	Six	Seven or More	
City	32.5	31.8	14.0	10.9	6.1	2.7	2.0	2.60
MSA[1]	24.6	35.0	15.1	14.3	6.8	2.7	1.5	2.70
U.S.	27.7	33.8	15.7	13.0	6.0	2.3	1.4	2.60

Note: (1) Figures cover the Grand Rapids-Wyoming, MI Metropolitan Statistical Area—see Appendix B for areas included
Source: U.S. Census Bureau, 2013-2017 American Community Survey 5-Year Estimates

Race

Area	White Alone[2] (%)	Black Alone[2] (%)	Asian Alone[2] (%)	AIAN[3] Alone[2] (%)	NHOPI[4] Alone[2] (%)	Other Race Alone[2] (%)	Two or More Races (%)
City	67.6	19.9	2.1	0.4	0.0	5.1	4.8
MSA[1]	84.7	6.5	2.5	0.4	0.0	2.7	3.1
U.S.	73.0	12.7	5.4	0.8	0.2	4.8	3.1

Note: (1) Figures cover the Grand Rapids-Wyoming, MI Metropolitan Statistical Area—see Appendix B for areas included; (2) Alone is defined as not being in combination with one or more other races; (3) American Indian and Alaska Native; (4) Native Hawaiian and Other Pacific Islander
Source: U.S. Census Bureau, 2013-2017 American Community Survey 5-Year Estimates

Hispanic or Latino Origin

Area	Total (%)	Mexican (%)	Puerto Rican (%)	Cuban (%)	Other (%)
City	15.3	9.1	1.3	0.3	4.6
MSA[1]	9.2	6.5	0.8	0.3	1.7
U.S.	17.6	11.1	1.7	0.7	4.1

Note: Persons of Hispanic or Latino origin can be of any race; (1) Figures cover the Grand Rapids-Wyoming, MI Metropolitan Statistical Area—see Appendix B for areas included
Source: U.S. Census Bureau, 2013-2017 American Community Survey 5-Year Estimates

Segregation

Type	Segregation Indices[1]				Percent Change		
	1990	2000	2010	2010 Rank[2]	1990-2000	1990-2010	2000-2010
Black/White	72.7	66.7	64.3	26	-6.0	-8.4	-2.4
Asian/White	34.3	43.7	43.2	37	9.4	8.9	-0.5
Hispanic/White	42.4	52.7	50.4	23	10.3	8.0	-2.3

Note: All figures cover the Metropolitan Statistical Area—see Appendix B for areas included; Figures are based on an analysis of 1990, 2000, and 2010 Census Decennial Census tract data by William H. Frey, Brookings Institution and the University of Michigan Social Science Data Analysis Network. In this analysis all racial groups (whites, blacks, and asians) are non-Hispanic members of those races. Hispanics are shown as a separate category; (1) Segregation Indices are Dissimilarity Indices that measure the degree to which the minority group is distributed differently than whites across census tracts. They range from 0 (complete integration) to 100 (complete segregation) where the value indicates the percentage of the minority group that needs to move to be distributed exactly like whites; (2) Ranges from 1 (most segregated) to 102 (least segregated); n/a not available.
Source: www.CensusScope.org

Ancestry

Area	German	Irish	English	American	Italian	Polish	French[2]	Scottish	Dutch
City	15.4	9.1	6.7	2.6	2.8	6.9	2.7	1.6	14.9
MSA[1]	20.9	10.3	9.1	4.2	3.1	6.6	3.3	1.9	20.1
U.S.	14.1	10.1	7.5	6.6	5.3	2.9	2.5	1.7	1.3

Note: Figures are the percentage of the total population reporting a particular ancestry. The nine most commonly reported ancestries in the U.S. are shown. Figures include multiple ancestries (e.g. if a person reported being Irish and Italian, they were included in both columns); (1) Figures cover the Grand Rapids-Wyoming, MI Metropolitan Statistical Area—see Appendix B for areas included; (2) Excludes Basque
Source: U.S. Census Bureau, 2013-2017 American Community Survey 5-Year Estimates

Foreign-Born Population

Area	Percent of Population Born in								
	Any Foreign Country	Asia	Mexico	Europe	Carribean	Central America[2]	South America	Africa	Canada
City	10.3	2.0	3.2	1.1	0.6	1.8	0.1	1.1	0.4
MSA[1]	6.6	2.0	1.9	1.1	0.4	0.5	0.1	0.4	0.3
U.S.	13.4	4.1	3.6	1.5	1.3	1.0	0.9	0.6	0.3

Note: (1) Figures cover the Grand Rapids-Wyoming, MI Metropolitan Statistical Area—see Appendix B for areas included; (2) Excludes Mexico.
Source: U.S. Census Bureau, 2013-2017 American Community Survey 5-Year Estimates

Marital Status

Area	Never Married	Now Married[2]	Separated	Widowed	Divorced
City	46.4	36.2	1.7	5.2	10.5
MSA[1]	32.1	51.9	1.1	4.9	10.0
U.S.	33.1	48.2	2.0	5.8	10.9

Note: Figures are percentages and cover the population 15 years of age and older; (1) Figures cover the Grand Rapids-Wyoming, MI Metropolitan Statistical Area—see Appendix B for areas included; (2) Excludes separated
Source: U.S. Census Bureau, 2013-2017 American Community Survey 5-Year Estimates

Disability by Age

Area	All Ages	Under 18 Years Old	18 to 64 Years Old	65 Years and Over
City	13.8	5.8	12.5	39.8
MSA[1]	11.8	4.3	10.2	33.5
U.S.	12.6	4.2	10.3	35.5

Note: Figures show percent of the civilian noninstitutionalized population that reported having a disability. Disability status is determined from six types of difficulty: vision, hearing, cognitive, ambulatory, self-care, and independent living. For children under 5 years old, hearing and vision difficulty are used to determine disability status. For children between the ages of 5 and 14, disability status is determined from hearing, vision, cognitive, ambulatory, and self-care difficulties. For people aged 15 years and older, they are considered to have a disability if they have difficulty with any one of the six difficulty types; Note: (1) Figures cover the Grand Rapids-Wyoming, MI Metropolitan Statistical Area—see Appendix B for areas included
Source: U.S. Census Bureau, 2013-2017 American Community Survey 5-Year Estimates

Age

Area	Percent of Population									Median Age
	Under Age 5	Age 5–19	Age 20–34	Age 35–44	Age 45–54	Age 55–64	Age 65–74	Age 75–84	Age 85+	
City	7.4	19.4	29.6	11.3	10.3	10.6	5.7	3.4	2.4	31.1
MSA[1]	6.6	21.0	21.4	12.1	13.1	12.4	7.6	3.8	1.9	35.7
U.S.	6.2	19.5	20.7	12.7	13.4	12.7	8.6	4.4	1.9	37.8

Note: (1) Figures cover the Grand Rapids-Wyoming, MI Metropolitan Statistical Area—see Appendix B for areas included
Source: U.S. Census Bureau, 2013-2017 American Community Survey 5-Year Estimates

Gender

Area	Males	Females	Males per 100 Females
City	96,186	99,169	97.0
MSA[1]	513,783	525,399	97.8
U.S.	158,018,753	162,985,654	97.0

Note: (1) Figures cover the Grand Rapids-Wyoming, MI Metropolitan Statistical Area—see Appendix B for areas included
Source: U.S. Census Bureau, 2013-2017 American Community Survey 5-Year Estimates

Religious Groups by Family

Area	Catholic	Baptist	Non-Den.	Methodist[2]	Lutheran	LDS[3]	Pente-costal	Presby-terian[4]	Muslim[5]	Judaism
MSA[1]	17.2	1.7	8.4	3.1	2.1	0.6	1.1	10.0	1.1	0.1
U.S.	19.1	9.3	4.0	4.0	2.3	2.0	1.9	1.6	0.8	0.7

Note: Figures are the number of adherents as a percentage of the total population; (1) Figures cover the Grand Rapids-Wyoming, MI Metropolitan Statistical Area—see Appendix B for areas included; (2) Methodist/Pietist; (3) Latter Day Saints; (4) Reformed; (5) Figures are estimates
Source: Association of Statisticians of American Religious Bodies, 2010 U.S. Religion Census: Religious Congregations & Membership Study

Religious Groups by Tradition

Area	Catholic	Evangelical Protestant	Mainline Protestant	Other Tradition	Black Protestant	Orthodox
MSA[1]	17.2	20.7	7.6	2.2	1.1	0.2
U.S.	19.1	16.2	7.3	4.3	1.6	0.3

Note: Figures are the number of adherents as a percentage of the total population; (1) Figures cover the Grand Rapids-Wyoming, MI Metropolitan Statistical Area—see Appendix B for areas included
Source: Association of Statisticians of American Religious Bodies, 2010 U.S. Religion Census: Religious Congregations & Membership Study

ECONOMY

Gross Metropolitan Product

Area	2016	2017	2018	2019	Rank[2]
MSA[1]	58.4	61.0	63.9	67.2	53

Note: Figures are in billions of dollars; (1) Figures cover the Grand Rapids-Wyoming, MI Metropolitan Statistical Area—see Appendix B for areas included; (2) Rank is based on 2017 data and ranges from 1 to 381
Source: U.S. Conference of Mayors, U.S. Metro Economies: Economic Growth & Full Employment, June 2018

Economic Growth

Area	2017-2018 (%)	2019-2020 (%)	2021-2022 (%)
MSA[1]	3.5	2.4	1.2

Note: Figures are real gross metropolitan product (GMP) growth rates and represent average annual percent change; (1) Figures cover the Grand Rapids-Wyoming, MI Metropolitan Statistical Area—see Appendix B for areas included
Source: U.S. Conference of Mayors, U.S. Metro Economies: Economic Growth & Full Employment, June 2018

Metropolitan Area Exports

Area	2012	2013	2014	2015	2016	2017	Rank[2]
MSA[1]	3,156.4	5,314.8	5,244.5	5,143.0	5,168.5	5,385.8	54

Note: Figures are in millions of dollars; (1) Figures cover the Grand Rapids-Wyoming, MI Metropolitan Statistical Area—see Appendix B for areas included; (2) Rank is based on 2017 data and ranges from 1 to 387
Source: U.S. Department of Commerce, International Trade Administration, Office of Trade and Economic Analysis, Industry and Analysis, Exports by Metropolitan Area, extracted March 25, 2019

Building Permits

Area	Single-Family			Multi-Family			Total		
	2016	2017	Pct. Chg.	2016	2017	Pct. Chg.	2016	2017	Pct. Chg.
City	69	101	46.4	1,329	777	-41.5	1,398	878	-37.2
MSA[1]	2,649	2,953	11.5	2,068	1,886	-8.8	4,717	4,839	2.6
U.S.	750,800	820,000	9.2	455,800	462,000	1.4	1,206,600	1,282,000	6.2

Note: (1) Figures cover the Grand Rapids-Wyoming, MI Metropolitan Statistical Area—see Appendix B for areas included; Figures represent new, privately-owned housing units authorized (unadjusted data); All permit data are based on estimates with imputation
Source: U.S. Census Bureau, Manufacturing, Mining, and Construction Statistics, Building Permits, 2016, 2017

Bankruptcy Filings

Area	Business Filings			Nonbusiness Filings		
	2017	2018	% Chg.	2017	2018	% Chg.
Kent County	32	28	-12.5	1,072	928	-13.4
U.S.	23,157	22,232	-4.0	765,863	751,186	-1.9

Note: Business filings include Chapter 7, Chapter 11, Chapter 12, and Chapter 13; Nonbusiness filings include Chapter 7, Chapter 11, and Chapter 13
Source: Administrative Office of the U.S. Courts, Business and Nonbusiness Bankruptcy, County Cases Commenced by Chapter of the Bankruptcy Code, During the 12-Month Period Ending December 31, 2017 and Business and Nonbusiness Bankruptcy, County Cases Commenced by Chapter of the Bankruptcy Code, During the 12-Month Period Ending December 31, 2018

Housing Vacancy Rates

Area	Gross Vacancy Rate[2] (%)			Year-Round Vacancy Rate[3] (%)			Rental Vacancy Rate[4] (%)			Homeowner Vacancy Rate[5] (%)		
	2016	2017	2018	2016	2017	2018	2016	2017	2018	2016	2017	2018
MSA[1]	7.1	8.5	8.9	4.4	6.3	6.8	5.1	4.0	6.8	0.5	1.1	0.3
U.S.	12.8	12.7	12.3	9.9	9.9	9.7	6.9	7.2	6.9	1.7	1.6	1.5

Note: (1) Figures cover the Grand Rapids-Wyoming, MI Metropolitan Statistical Area—see Appendix B for areas included; (2) The percentage of the total housing inventory that is vacant; (3) The percentage of the housing inventory (excluding seasonal units) that is year-round vacant; (4) The percentage of rental inventory that is vacant for rent; (5) The percentage of homeowner inventory that is vacant for sale
Source: U.S. Census Bureau, Housing Vacancies and Homeownership Annual Statistics: 2016, 2017, 2018

INCOME

Income

Area	Per Capita ($)	Median Household ($)	Average Household ($)
City	23,225	44,369	58,917
MSA[1]	28,739	58,094	76,101
U.S.	31,177	57,652	81,283

Note: (1) Figures cover the Grand Rapids-Wyoming, MI Metropolitan Statistical Area—see Appendix B for areas included
Source: U.S. Census Bureau, 2013-2017 American Community Survey 5-Year Estimates

Household Income Distribution

Area	Percent of Households Earning							
	Under $15,000	$15,000 -$24,999	$25,000 -$34,999	$35,000 -$49,999	$50,000 -$74,999	$75,000 -$99,999	$100,000 -$149,999	$150,000 and up
City	15.4	12.5	11.6	15.8	19.0	11.6	9.5	4.7
MSA[1]	9.2	9.5	10.0	14.1	20.4	13.7	14.2	9.0
U.S.	11.6	9.8	9.5	13.0	17.7	12.3	14.1	12.1

Note: (1) Figures cover the Grand Rapids-Wyoming, MI Metropolitan Statistical Area—see Appendix B for areas included
Source: U.S. Census Bureau, 2013-2017 American Community Survey 5-Year Estimates

Poverty Rate

Area	All Ages	Under 18 Years Old	18 to 64 Years Old	65 Years and Over
City	22.5	30.6	21.6	9.9
MSA[1]	12.4	15.8	12.3	6.6
U.S.	14.6	20.3	13.7	9.3

Note: Figures are percentage of people whose income during the past 12 months was below the poverty level; (1) Figures cover the Grand Rapids-Wyoming, MI Metropolitan Statistical Area—see Appendix B for areas included
Source: U.S. Census Bureau, 2013-2017 American Community Survey 5-Year Estimates

EMPLOYMENT

Labor Force and Employment

Area	Civilian Labor Force			Workers Employed		
	Dec. 2017	Dec. 2018	% Chg.	Dec. 2017	Dec. 2018	% Chg.
City	103,943	104,567	0.6	99,188	100,721	1.5
MSA[1]	573,055	577,903	0.8	552,982	561,455	1.5
U.S.	159,880,000	162,510,000	1.6	153,602,000	156,481,000	1.9

Note: Data is not seasonally adjusted and covers workers 16 years of age and older; (1) Figures cover the Grand Rapids-Wyoming, MI Metropolitan Statistical Area—see Appendix B for areas included
Source: Bureau of Labor Statistics, Local Area Unemployment Statistics

Unemployment Rate

Area	2018											
	Jan.	Feb.	Mar.	Apr.	May	Jun.	Jul.	Aug.	Sep.	Oct.	Nov.	Dec.
City	5.2	5.1	4.5	4.0	3.8	4.4	4.8	3.6	3.5	3.5	3.3	3.7
MSA[1]	4.0	4.0	3.5	3.0	2.9	3.3	3.6	2.7	2.6	2.6	2.5	2.8
U.S.	4.5	4.4	4.1	3.7	3.6	4.2	4.1	3.9	3.6	3.5	3.5	3.7

Note: Data is not seasonally adjusted and covers workers 16 years of age and older; (1) Figures cover the Grand Rapids-Wyoming, MI Metropolitan Statistical Area—see Appendix B for areas included
Source: Bureau of Labor Statistics, Local Area Unemployment Statistics

Average Wages

Occupation	$/Hr.	Occupation	$/Hr.
Accountants and Auditors	32.80	Maids and Housekeeping Cleaners	12.10
Automotive Mechanics	18.90	Maintenance and Repair Workers	18.90
Bookkeepers	18.20	Marketing Managers	61.40
Carpenters	19.50	Nuclear Medicine Technologists	33.30
Cashiers	11.30	Nurses, Licensed Practical	20.90
Clerks, General Office	17.80	Nurses, Registered	31.70
Clerks, Receptionists/Information	14.40	Nursing Assistants	13.80
Clerks, Shipping/Receiving	15.90	Packers and Packagers, Hand	11.60
Computer Programmers	34.00	Physical Therapists	41.20
Computer Systems Analysts	37.40	Postal Service Mail Carriers	24.60
Computer User Support Specialists	23.20	Real Estate Brokers	32.40
Cooks, Restaurant	12.40	Retail Salespersons	13.00
Dentists	97.50	Sales Reps., Exc. Tech./Scientific	37.80
Electrical Engineers	36.70	Sales Reps., Tech./Scientific	40.40
Electricians	25.00	Secretaries, Exc. Legal/Med./Exec.	17.70
Financial Managers	57.90	Security Guards	13.30
First-Line Supervisors/Managers, Sales	22.10	Surgeons	41.80
Food Preparation Workers	12.20	Teacher Assistants*	13.70
General and Operations Managers	61.60	Teachers, Elementary School*	27.80
Hairdressers/Cosmetologists	14.30	Teachers, Secondary School*	28.40
Internists, General	67.00	Telemarketers	13.00
Janitors and Cleaners	12.60	Truck Drivers, Heavy/Tractor-Trailer	21.10
Landscaping/Groundskeeping Workers	14.80	Truck Drivers, Light/Delivery Svcs.	17.70
Lawyers	46.50	Waiters and Waitresses	13.60

Note: Wage data covers the Grand Rapids-Wyoming, MI Metropolitan Statistical Area—see Appendix B for areas included; (*) Hourly wages for elementary/secondary school teachers and teacher assistants were calculated by the editors from annual wage data based on a 40 hour work week; n/a not available.
Source: Bureau of Labor Statistics, Metro Area Occupational Employment & Wage Estimates, May 2018

Employment by Occupation

Occupation Classification	City (%)	MSA[1] (%)	U.S. (%)
Management, Business, Science, and Arts	34.5	34.7	37.4
Natural Resources, Construction, and Maintenance	7.0	8.0	8.9
Production, Transportation, and Material Moving	16.5	18.2	12.2
Sales and Office	22.0	23.1	23.5
Service	20.0	16.0	18.0

Note: Figures cover employed civilians 16 years of age and older; (1) Figures cover the Grand Rapids-Wyoming, MI Metropolitan Statistical Area—see Appendix B for areas included
Source: U.S. Census Bureau, 2013-2017 American Community Survey 5-Year Estimates

Employment by Industry

Sector	MSA[1]		U.S.
	Number of Employees	Percent of Total	Percent of Total
Construction, Mining, and Logging	25,200	4.4	5.3
Education and Health Services	94,400	16.5	15.9
Financial Activities	26,600	4.7	5.7
Government	50,100	8.8	15.1
Information	6,400	1.1	1.9
Leisure and Hospitality	51,000	8.9	10.7
Manufacturing	119,200	20.9	8.5
Other Services	22,300	3.9	3.9
Professional and Business Services	77,200	13.5	14.1
Retail Trade	50,300	8.8	10.8
Transportation, Warehousing, and Utilities	16,300	2.9	4.2
Wholesale Trade	31,700	5.6	3.9

Note: Figures are non-farm employment as of December 2018. Figures are not seasonally adjusted and include workers 16 years of age and older; (1) Figures cover the Grand Rapids-Wyoming, MI Metropolitan Statistical Area—see Appendix B for areas included
Source: Bureau of Labor Statistics, Current Employment Statistics, Employment, Hours, and Earnings

Occupations with Greatest Projected Employment Growth: 2018 – 2020

Occupation[1]	2018 Employment	2020 Projected Employment	Numeric Employment Change	Percent Employment Change
Combined Food Preparation and Serving Workers, Including Fast Food	121,730	124,870	3,140	2.6
Registered Nurses	99,430	102,150	2,720	2.7
Personal Care Aides	43,960	46,370	2,410	5.5
Laborers and Freight, Stock, and Material Movers, Hand	71,260	73,160	1,900	2.7
Home Health Aides	28,090	29,900	1,810	6.4
Heavy and Tractor-Trailer Truck Drivers	58,310	59,830	1,520	2.6
General and Operations Managers	60,330	61,750	1,420	2.4
Customer Service Representatives	93,100	94,460	1,360	1.5
Mechanical Engineers	43,910	45,230	1,320	3.0
Light Truck or Delivery Services Drivers	31,300	32,510	1,210	3.9

Note: Projections cover Michigan; (1) Sorted by numeric employment change
Source: www.projectionscentral.com, State Occupational Projections, 2018–2020 Short-Term Projections

Fastest Growing Occupations: 2018 – 2020

Occupation[1]	2018 Employment	2020 Projected Employment	Numeric Employment Change	Percent Employment Change
Veterinary Assistants and Laboratory Animal Caretakers	3,200	3,750	550	17.2
Veterinarians	2,870	3,340	470	16.4
Veterinary Technologists and Technicians	3,160	3,670	510	16.1
Dental Laboratory Technicians	1,400	1,610	210	15.0
Credit Counselors	1,080	1,220	140	13.0
Airline Pilots, Copilots, and Flight Engineers	2,930	3,220	290	9.9
Orthotists and Prosthetists	620	680	60	9.7
Reservation and Transportation Ticket Agents and Travel Clerks	4,340	4,710	370	8.5
Nonfarm Animal Caretakers	7,830	8,410	580	7.4
Interpreters and Translators	1,280	1,370	90	7.0

Note: Projections cover Michigan; (1) Sorted by percent employment change and excludes occupations with numeric employment change less than 50
Source: www.projectionscentral.com, State Occupational Projections, 2018–2020 Short-Term Projections

TAXES

State Corporate Income Tax Rates

State	Tax Rate (%)	Income Brackets ($)	Num. of Brackets	Financial Institution Tax Rate (%)[a]	Federal Income Tax Ded.
Michigan	6.0	Flat rate	1	(a)	No

Note: Tax rates as of January 1, 2019; (a) Rates listed are the corporate income tax rate applied to financial institutions or excise taxes based on income. Some states have other taxes based upon the value of deposits or shares.
Source: Federation of Tax Administrators, Range of State Corporate Income Tax Rates, January 1, 2019

State Individual Income Tax Rates

State	Tax Rate (%)	Income Brackets ($)	Personal Exemptions ($)			Standard Ded. ($)	
			Single	Married	Depend.	Single	Married
Michigan (a)	4.25	Flat rate	4,050	8,100	4,050	–	–

Note: Tax rates as of January 1, 2019; Local- and county-level taxes are not included; n/a not applicable; Federal income tax is not deductible on state income tax returns; (a) 19 states have statutory provision for automatically adjusting to the rate of inflation the dollar values of the income tax brackets, standard deductions, and/or personal exemptions. Michigan indexes the personal exemption only. Oregon does not index the income brackets for $125,000 and over.
Source: Federation of Tax Administrators, State Individual Income Tax Rates, January 1, 2019

Various State Sales and Excise Tax Rates

State	State Sales Tax (%)	Gasoline[1] (¢/gal.)	Cigarette[2] ($/pack)	Spirits[3] ($/gal.)	Wine[4] ($/gal.)	Beer[5] ($/gal.)	Recreational Marijuana (%)
Michigan	6	38.41	2.00	11.99 (g)	0.51 (l)	0.2	10.0 (bb)

Note: All tax rates as of January 1, 2019; (1) The American Petroleum Institute has developed a methodology for determining the average tax rate on a gallon of fuel. Rates may include any of the following: excise taxes, environmental fees, storage tank fees, other fees or taxes, general sales tax, and local taxes. In states where gasoline is subject to the general sales tax, or where the fuel tax is based on the average sale price, the average rate determined by API is sensitive to changes in the price of gasoline. States that fully or partially apply general sales taxes to gasoline: CA, CO, GA, IL, IN, MI, NY; (2) The federal excise tax of $1.0066 per pack and local taxes are not included; (3) Rates are those applicable to off-premise sales of 40% alcohol by volume (a.b.v.) distilled spirits in 750ml containers. Local excise taxes are excluded; (4) Rates are those applicable to off-premise sales of 11% a.b.v. non-carbonated wine in 750ml containers; (5) Rates are those applicable to off-premise sales of 4.7% a.b.v. beer in 12 ounce containers; (g) Control states, where the government controls all sales. Products can be subject to ad valorem mark-up as well as excise taxes; (l) Different rates also applicable to alcohol content, place of production, size of container, place purchased (on- or off-premise or on board airlines) or type of wine (carbonated, vermouth, etc.); (bb) 10% excise tax (retail price)
Source: Tax Foundation, 2019 Facts & Figures: How Does Your State Compare?

State Business Tax Climate Index Rankings

State	Overall Rank	Corporate Tax Rank	Individual Income Tax Rank	Sales Tax Rank	Unemployment Insurance Tax Rank	Property Tax Rank
Michigan	13	11	12	11	49	22

Note: The index is a measure of how each state's tax laws affect economic performance. The lower the rank, the more favorable a state's tax system is for business. States without a given tax are given a ranking of 1. The scores/rankings for the District of Columbia do not affect other states. The 2019 index represents the tax climate as of July 1, 2018.
Source: Tax Foundation, State Business Tax Climate Index 2019

COMMERCIAL UTILITIES

Typical Monthly Electric Bills

Area	Commercial Service ($/month)		Industrial Service ($/month)	
	1,500 kWh	40 kW demand 14,000 kWh	1,000 kW demand 200,000 kWh	50,000 kW demand 32,500,000 kWh
City	224	1,924	23,098	2,082,165
Average[1]	203	1,619	25,886	2,540,077

Note: Figures are based on annualized rates; (1) Average based on 187 utilities surveyed
Source: Edison Electric Institute, Typical Bills and Average Rates Report, Summer 2018

TRANSPORTATION

Means of Transportation to Work

Area	Car/Truck/Van		Public Transportation			Bicycle	Walked	Other Means	Worked at Home
	Drove Alone	Car-pooled	Bus	Subway	Railroad				
City	75.0	10.8	4.1	0.1	0.0	1.1	3.8	1.2	3.9
MSA[1]	81.9	9.0	1.5	0.0	0.0	0.5	2.2	0.9	4.1
U.S.	76.4	9.2	2.5	1.9	0.6	0.6	2.7	1.3	4.7

Note: Figures are percentages and cover workers 16 years of age and older; (1) Figures cover the Grand Rapids-Wyoming, MI Metropolitan Statistical Area—see Appendix B for areas included
Source: U.S. Census Bureau, 2013-2017 American Community Survey 5-Year Estimates

Travel Time to Work

Area	Less Than 10 Minutes	10 to 19 Minutes	20 to 29 Minutes	30 to 44 Minutes	45 to 59 Minutes	60 to 89 Minutes	90 Minutes or More
City	16.0	42.0	24.2	11.4	3.0	2.3	1.2
MSA[1]	15.2	34.8	24.9	16.3	4.7	2.5	1.6
U.S.	12.7	28.9	20.9	20.5	8.1	6.2	2.7

Note: Note: Figures are percentages and include workers 16 years old and over; (1) Figures cover the Grand Rapids-Wyoming, MI Metropolitan Statistical Area—see Appendix B for areas included
Source: U.S. Census Bureau, 2013-2017 American Community Survey 5-Year Estimates

Freeway Travel Time Index

Area	1985	1990	1995	2000	2005	2010	2014
Urban Area Rank[1,2]	64	63	59	46	61	57	54
Urban Area Index[1]	1.05	1.08	1.12	1.16	1.16	1.16	1.17
Average Index[3]	1.09	1.11	1.14	1.17	1.20	1.19	1.20

Note: Freeway Travel Time Index—the ratio of travel time in the peak period to the travel time at free-flow conditions. For example, a value of 1.30 indicates a 20-minute free-flow trip takes 26 minutes in the peak (20 minutes x 1.30 = 26 minutes); (1) Covers the Grand Rapids MI urban area; (2) Rank is based on 101 urban areas (#1 = highest travel time index); (3) Average of 101 urban areas
Source: Texas Transportation Institute, 2015 Urban Mobility Scorecard, August 2015

Freeway Commuter Stress Index

Area	1985	1990	1995	2000	2005	2010	2014
Urban Area Rank[1,2]	58	59	55	54	68	58	57
Urban Area Index[1]	1.08	1.11	1.15	1.18	1.18	1.19	1.20
Average Index[3]	1.13	1.16	1.19	1.22	1.25	1.24	1.25

Note: The Freeway Commuter Stress Index is the same as the Freeway Travel Time Index (see table above) except that it includes only the travel in the peak directions during the peak periods; the TTI includes travel in all directions during the peak period. Thus, the CSI is more indicative of the work trip experienced by each commuter on a daily basis; (1) Covers the Grand Rapids MI urban area; (2) Rank is based on 101 urban areas (#1 = highest travel time index); (3) Average of 101 urban areas
Source: Texas Transportation Institute, 2015 Urban Mobility Scorecard, August 2015

Public Transportation

Agency Name / Mode of Transportation	Vehicles Operated in Maximum Service[1]	Annual Unlinked Passenger Trips[2] (in thous.)	Annual Passenger Miles[3] (in thous.)
Interurban Transit Partnership (The Rapid)			
Bus (directly operated)	126	9,760.3	32,209.0
Bus Rapid Transit (directly operated)	8	817.5	2,509.7
Demand Response (purchased transportation)	74	355.3	4,724.5
Vanpool (directly operated)	26	39.9	1,741.0

Note: (1) The number of revenue vehicles operated by the given mode and type of service to meet the annual maximum service requirement. This is the revenue vehicle count during the peak season of the year; on the week and day that maximum service is provided. Vehicles operated in maximum service (VOMS) exclude atypical days and one-time special events; (2) The number of passengers who boarded public transportation vehicles. Passengers are counted each time they board a vehicle no matter how many vehicles they use to travel from their origin to their destination. (3) The sum of the distances ridden by all passengers during the entire fiscal year.
Source: Federal Transit Administration, National Transit Database, 2017

Air Transportation

Airport Name and Code / Type of Service	Passenger Airlines[1]	Passenger Enplanements	Freight Carriers[2]	Freight (lbs)
Gerald R. Ford International (GRR)				
Domestic service (U.S. carriers - 2018)	24	1,631,133	7	47,288,082
International service (U.S. carriers - 2017)	1	2	2	9,870

Note: (1) Includes all U.S.-based major, minor and commuter airlines that carried at least one passenger during the year; (2) Includes all U.S.-based airlines and freight carriers that transported at least one pound of freight during the year.
Source: Bureau of Transportation Statistics, The Intermodal Transportation Database, Air Carriers: T-100 Domestic Market (U.S. Carriers), 2018; Bureau of Transportation Statistics, The Intermodal Transportation Database, Air Carriers: T-100 International Market (U.S. Carriers), 2017

Other Transportation Statistics

Major Highways:	I-96
Amtrak Service:	Yes
Major Waterways/Ports:	Grand River

Source: Amtrak.com; Google Maps

BUSINESSES

Major Business Headquarters

Company Name	Industry	Rankings	
		Fortune[1]	Forbes[2]
Gordon Food Service	Food, Drink & Tobacco	-	22
Meijer	Food Markets	-	19
SpartanNash	Wholesalers: Food and Grocery	351	-

Note: (1) Companies that produce a 10-K are ranked 1 to 500 based on 2017 revenue; (2) All private companies with at least $2 billion in annual revenue through the end of their most current fiscal year are ranked 1 to 229; companies listed are headquartered in the city; dashes indicate no ranking
Source: Fortune, "Fortune 500," June 2018; Forbes, "America's Largest Private Companies," 2018 Rankings

Fast-Growing Businesses

According to *Inc.*, Grand Rapids is home to one of America's 500 fastest-growing private companies: **FormulaFolio Investments** (#385). Criteria: must be an independent, privately-held, for-profit, U.S. corporation, proprietorship or partnership as of December 31, 2017; revenues must be at least $100,000 in 2014 and $2 million in 2017; must have four-year operating/sales history. Holding companies, regulated banks, and utilities were excluded. *Inc.*, "America's 500 Fastest-Growing Private Companies," 2018

Minority- and Women-Owned Businesses

Group	All Firms		Firms with Paid Employees			
	Firms	Sales ($000)	Firms	Sales ($000)	Employees	Payroll ($000)
AIAN[1]	142	104,324	2	(s)	100 - 249	(s)
Asian	509	129,401	147	115,947	1,260	32,363
Black	2,525	74,267	43	(s)	250 - 499	(s)
Hispanic	983	117,780	74	(s)	500 - 999	(s)
NHOPI[2]	n/a	n/a	n/a	n/a	n/a	n/a
Women	6,095	784,577	544	690,172	6,202	130,188
All Firms	16,153	28,419,322	3,518	27,970,918	106,476	4,605,805

Note: Figures cover firms located in the city; minority- and women-owned business are defined as firms in which the corresponding group own 51% or more of the stock or equity of the company; (1) American Indian and Alaska Native; (2) Native Hawaiian and Other Pacific Islander; (s) estimates are suppressed when publication standards are not met; n/a not available
Source: U.S. Census Bureau, 2012 Economic Census, Survey of Business Owners

**HOTELS &
CONVENTION
CENTERS**

Hotels, Motels and Vacation Rentals

Area	5 Star		4 Star		3 Star		2 Star		1 Star		Not Rated	
	Num.	Pct.[3]	Num.	Pct.[3]	Num.	Pct.[3]	Num.	Pct.[3]	Num.	Pct.[3]	Num.	Pct.[3]
City[1]	0	0.0	2	1.0	41	20.6	59	29.6	0	0.0	97	48.7
Total[2]	286	0.4	5,236	7.1	16,715	22.6	10,259	13.9	293	0.4	41,056	55.6

Note: (1) Figures cover Grand Rapids and vicinity; (2) Figures cover all 100 cities in this book; (3) Percentage of hotels which have a given star rating; Star ratings are determined by expedia.com and offer an indication of the general quality of a particular hotel.
Source: www.expedia.com, April 3, 2019

Major Convention Centers

Name	Overall Space (sq. ft.)	Exhibit Space (sq. ft.)	Meeting Space (sq. ft.)	Meeting Rooms
DeVos Place Convention Center	234,000	162,000	n/a	26

Note: Table includes convention centers located in the Grand Rapids-Wyoming, MI metro area; n/a not available
Source: Original research

Living Environment

COST OF LIVING

Cost of Living Index

Composite Index	Groceries	Housing	Utilities	Trans-portation	Health Care	Misc. Goods/Services
97.1	89.7	90.6	98.3	102.2	93.1	104.2

Note: The Cost of Living Index measures regional differences in the cost of consumer goods and services, excluding taxes and non-consumer expenditures, for professional and managerial households in the top income quintile. It is based on more than 50,000 prices covering almost 60 different items for which prices are collected three times a year by chambers of commerce, economic development organizations or university applied economic centers in each participating urban area. The numbers shown should be read as a percentage above or below the national average of 100. For example, a value of 115.4 in the groceries column indicates that grocery prices are 15.4% higher than the national average. Small differences in the index numbers should not be interpreted as significant; Figures cover the Grand Rapids MI urban area.
Source: The Council for Community and Economic Research, ACCRA Cost of Living Index, 2018

Grocery Prices

Area[1]	T-Bone Steak ($/pound)	Frying Chicken ($/pound)	Whole Milk ($/half gal.)	Eggs ($/dozen)	Orange Juice ($/64 oz.)	Coffee ($/11.5 oz.)
City[2]	10.45	1.06	1.77	1.53	3.32	3.36
Avg.	11.35	1.42	1.94	1.81	3.52	4.35
Min.	7.45	0.92	0.80	0.75	2.72	3.06
Max.	15.05	2.76	4.18	4.00	5.36	8.20

Note: (1) Values for the local area are compared with the average, minimum and maximum values for all 291 areas in the Cost of Living Index; (2) Figures cover the Grand Rapids MI urban area; T-Bone Steak (price per pound); Frying Chicken (price per pound, whole fryer); Whole Milk (half gallon carton); Eggs (price per dozen, Grade A, large); Orange Juice (64 oz. Tropicana or Florida Natural); Coffee (11.5 oz. can, vacuum-packed, Maxwell House, Hills Bros, or Folgers).
Source: The Council for Community and Economic Research, ACCRA Cost of Living Index, 2018

Housing and Utility Costs

Area[1]	New Home Price ($)	Apartment Rent ($/month)	All Electric ($/month)	Part Electric ($/month)	Other Energy ($/month)	Telephone ($/month)
City[2]	288,912	1,158	-	98.08	67.91	174.00
Avg.	347,000	1,087	165.93	100.16	67.73	178.70
Min.	200,468	500	93.58	25.64	26.78	163.10
Max.	1,901,222	4,888	388.65	246.86	332.81	197.70

Note: (1) Values for the local area are compared with the average, minimum and maximum values for all 291 areas in the Cost of Living Index; (2) Figures cover the Grand Rapids MI urban area; New Home Price (2,400 sf living area, 8,000 sf lot, in urban area with full utilities); Apartment Rent (950 sf 2 bedroom/1.5 or 2 bath, unfurnished, excluding all utilities except water); All Electric (average monthly cost for an all-electric home); Part Electric (average monthly cost for a part-electric home); Other Energy (average monthly cost for natural gas, fuel oil, coal, wood, and any other forms of energy except electricity); Telephone (price includes the base monthly rate plus taxes and fees for three lines of mobile phone service).
Source: The Council for Community and Economic Research, ACCRA Cost of Living Index, 2018

Health Care, Transportation, and Other Costs

Area[1]	Doctor ($/visit)	Dentist ($/visit)	Optometrist ($/visit)	Gasoline ($/gallon)	Beauty Salon ($/visit)	Men's Shirt ($)
City[2]	96.94	87.78	91.61	2.79	37.61	35.08
Avg.	110.71	95.11	103.74	2.61	37.48	32.03
Min.	33.60	62.55	54.63	1.89	17.00	11.44
Max.	195.97	153.93	225.79	3.59	71.88	58.64

Note: (1) Values for the local area are compared with the average, minimum and maximum values for all 291 areas in the Cost of Living Index; (2) Figures cover the Grand Rapids MI urban area; Doctor (general practitioners routine exam of an established patient); Dentist (adult teeth cleaning and periodic oral examination); Optometrist (full vision eye exam for established adult patient); Gasoline (one gallon regular unleaded, national brand, including all taxes, cash price at self-service pump if available); Beauty Salon (woman's shampoo, trim, and blow-dry); Men's Shirt (cotton/polyester dress shirt, pinpoint weave, long sleeves).
Source: The Council for Community and Economic Research, ACCRA Cost of Living Index, 2018

HOUSING

House Price Index (HPI)

Area	National Ranking[2]	Quarterly Change (%)	One-Year Change (%)	Five-Year Change (%)
MSA[1]	39	1.14	9.07	48.85
U.S.[3]	–	1.12	5.73	32.81

Note: The HPI is a weighted repeat sales index. It measures average price changes in repeat sales or refinancings on the same properties. This information is obtained by reviewing repeat mortgage transactions on single-family properties whose mortgages have been purchased or securitized by Fannie Mae or Freddie Mac in January 1975; (1) Figures cover the Grand Rapids-Wyoming, MI Metropolitan Statistical Area—see Appendix B for areas included; (2) Rankings are based on annual percentage change for all metro areas containing at least 15,000 transactions over the last 10 years and ranges from 1 to 245; (3) figures based on a weighted average of Census Division estimates using a seasonally adjusted, purchase-only index; all figures are for the period ending December 31, 2018
Source: Federal Housing Finance Agency, House Price Index, February 26, 2019

Median Single-Family Home Prices

Area	2016	2017	2018[p]	Percent Change 2017 to 2018
MSA[1]	161.6	177.5	194.6	9.6
U.S. Average	235.5	248.8	261.6	5.1

Note: Figures are median sales prices of existing single-family homes in thousands of dollars; (p) preliminary; (1) Figures cover the Grand Rapids-Wyoming, MI Metropolitan Statistical Area—see Appendix B for areas included
Source: National Association of Realtors, Median Sales Price of Existing Single-Family Homes for Metropolitan Areas, 4th Quarter 2018

Qualifying Income Based on Median Sales Price of Existing Single-Family Homes

Area	With 5% Down ($)	With 10% Down ($)	With 20% Down ($)
MSA[1]	47,191	44,707	39,740
U.S. Average	62,954	59,640	53,013

Note: Figures are preliminary; Qualifying income is based on a mortgage rate of 4.9%. Monthly principal and interest payment is limited to 25% of income; (1) Figures cover the Grand Rapids-Wyoming, MI Metropolitan Statistical Area—see Appendix B for areas included
Source: National Association of Realtors, Qualifying Income Based on Median Sales Price of Existing Single-Family Homes for Metropolitan Areas, 4th Quarter 2018

Median Apartment Condo-Coop Home Prices

Area	2016	2017	2018[p]	Percent Change 2017 to 2018
MSA[1]	n/a	n/a	n/a	n/a
U.S. Average	220.7	234.3	241.0	2.9

Note: Figures are median sales prices of existing apartment condo-coop homes in thousands of dollars; (p) preliminary; n/a not available; (1) Figures cover the Grand Rapids-Wyoming, MI Metropolitan Statistical Area—see Appendix B for areas included
Source: National Association of Realtors, Median Sales Price of Existing Apartment Condo-Coop Homes for Metropolitan Areas, 4th Quarter 2018

Home Value Distribution

Area	Under $50,000	$50,000 -$99,999	$100,000 -$149,999	$150,000 -$199,999	$200,000 -$299,999	$300,000 -$499,999	$500,000 -$999,999	$1,000,000 or more
City	7.7	28.0	32.6	17.6	9.6	3.3	1.1	0.1
MSA[1]	8.4	15.5	23.8	20.6	18.5	9.8	2.7	0.6
U.S.	8.3	13.9	14.7	14.6	18.7	17.3	9.7	2.7

Note: Figures are percentages and cover owner-occupied housing units; (1) Figures cover the Grand Rapids-Wyoming, MI Metropolitan Statistical Area—see Appendix B for areas included
Source: U.S. Census Bureau, 2013-2017 American Community Survey 5-Year Estimates

Homeownership Rate

Area	2010 (%)	2011 (%)	2012 (%)	2013 (%)	2014 (%)	2015 (%)	2016 (%)	2017 (%)	2018 (%)
MSA[1]	76.4	76.4	76.9	73.7	71.6	75.8	76.2	71.7	73.0
U.S.	66.9	66.1	65.4	65.1	64.5	63.7	63.4	63.9	64.4

Note: (1) Figures cover the Grand Rapids-Wyoming, MI Metropolitan Statistical Area—see Appendix B for areas included
Source: U.S. Census Bureau, Housing Vacancies and Homeownership Annual Statistics: 2010-2018

Year Housing Structure Built

Area	2010 or Later	2000 -2009	1990 -1999	1980 -1989	1970 -1979	1960 -1969	1950 -1959	1940 -1949	Before 1940	Median Year
City	1.2	4.2	6.0	7.1	8.8	10.6	15.9	8.9	37.3	1952
MSA[1]	2.4	13.0	16.3	12.5	14.5	9.8	10.8	5.2	15.5	1976
U.S.	3.2	14.5	14.0	13.6	15.5	10.8	10.5	5.1	12.9	1977

Note: Figures are percentages except for Median Year; Note: (1) Figures cover the Grand Rapids-Wyoming, MI Metropolitan Statistical Area—see Appendix B for areas included
Source: U.S. Census Bureau, 2013-2017 American Community Survey 5-Year Estimates

Gross Monthly Rent

Area	Under $500	$500 -$999	$1,000 -$1,499	$1,500 -$1,999	$2,000 -$2,499	$2,500 -$2,999	$3,000 and up	Median ($)
City	11.5	56.8	24.4	5.8	1.2	0.3	0.1	854
MSA[1]	9.0	62.9	21.4	5.0	1.0	0.2	0.5	826
U.S.	10.5	41.1	28.7	11.7	4.5	1.8	1.7	982

Note: Figures are percentages except for Median; Gross rent is the contract rent plus the estimated average monthly cost of utilities (electricity, gas, and water and sewer) and fuels (oil, coal, kerosene, wood, etc.) if these are paid by the renter (or paid for the renter by someone else); (1) Figures cover the Grand Rapids-Wyoming, MI Metropolitan Statistical Area—see Appendix B for areas included
Source: U.S. Census Bureau, 2013-2017 American Community Survey 5-Year Estimates

HEALTH

Health Risk Factors

Category	MSA[1] (%)	U.S. (%)
Adults aged 18–64 who have any kind of health care coverage	90.2	87.3
Adults who reported being in good or better health	86.0	82.4
Adults who have been told they have high blood cholesterol	31.5	33.0
Adults who have been told they have high blood pressure	32.8	32.3
Adults who are current smokers	14.5	17.1
Adults who currently use E-cigarettes	5.0	4.6
Adults who currently use chewing tobacco, snuff, or snus	3.9	4.0
Adults who are heavy drinkers[2]	8.0	6.3
Adults who are binge drinkers[3]	19.9	17.4
Adults who are overweight (BMI 25.0 - 29.9)	32.2	35.3
Adults who are obese (BMI 30.0 - 99.8)	32.3	31.3
Adults who participated in any physical activities in the past month	75.2	74.4
Adults who always or nearly always wears a seat belt	94.5	94.3

Note: (1) Figures cover the Grand Rapids-Wyoming, MI Metropolitan Statistical Area—see Appendix B for areas included; (2) Heavy drinkers are classified as adult men having more than 14 drinks per week and adult women having more than 7 drinks per week; (3) Binge drinkers are classified as males having five or more drinks on one occasion or females having four or more drinks on one occasion
Source: Centers for Disease Control and Prevention, Behaviorial Risk Factor Surveillance System, SMART: Selected Metropolitan Area Risk Trends, 2017

Acute and Chronic Health Conditions

Category	MSA[1] (%)	U.S. (%)
Adults who have ever been told they had a heart attack	2.7	4.2
Adults who have ever been told they have angina or coronary heart disease	2.7	3.9
Adults who have ever been told they had a stroke	3.7	3.0
Adults who have ever been told they have asthma	14.5	14.2
Adults who have ever been told they have arthritis	25.6	24.9
Adults who have ever been told they have diabetes[2]	10.0	10.5
Adults who have ever been told they had skin cancer	6.4	6.2
Adults who have ever been told they had any other types of cancer	5.5	7.1
Adults who have ever been told they have COPD	6.8	6.5
Adults who have ever been told they have kidney disease	3.2	3.0
Adults who have ever been told they have a form of depression	25.0	20.5

Note: (1) Figures cover the Grand Rapids-Wyoming, MI Metropolitan Statistical Area—see Appendix B for areas included; (2) Figures do not include pregnancy-related, borderline, or pre-diabetes
Source: Centers for Disease Control and Prevention, Behaviorial Risk Factor Surveillance System, SMART: Selected Metropolitan Area Risk Trends, 2017

Health Screening and Vaccination Rates

Category	MSA[1] (%)	U.S. (%)
Adults aged 65+ who have had flu shot within the past year	58.8	60.7
Adults aged 65+ who have ever had a pneumonia vaccination	79.1	75.4
Adults who have ever been tested for HIV	37.3	36.1
Adults who have ever had the shingles or zoster vaccine?	32.2	28.9
Adults who have had their blood cholesterol checked within the last five years	92.5	85.9

Note: n/a not available; (1) Figures cover the Grand Rapids-Wyoming, MI Metropolitan Statistical Area—see Appendix B for areas included.
Source: Centers for Disease Control and Prevention, Behavioral Risk Factor Surveillance System, SMART: Selected Metropolitan Area Risk Trends, 2017

Disability Status

Category	MSA[1] (%)	U.S. (%)
Adults who reported being deaf	6.8	6.7
Are you blind or have serious difficulty seeing, even when wearing glasses?	3.4	4.5
Are you limited in any way in any of your usual activities due of arthritis?	13.1	12.9
Do you have difficulty doing errands alone?	7.2	6.8
Do you have difficulty dressing or bathing?	4.3	3.6
Do you have serious difficulty concentrating/remembering/making decisions?	12.1	10.7
Do you have serious difficulty walking or climbing stairs?	14.4	13.6

Note: (1) Figures cover the Grand Rapids-Wyoming, MI Metropolitan Statistical Area—see Appendix B for areas included.
Source: Centers for Disease Control and Prevention, Behavioral Risk Factor Surveillance System, SMART: Selected Metropolitan Area Risk Trends, 2017

Mortality Rates for the Top 10 Causes of Death in the U.S.

ICD-10[a] Sub-Chapter	ICD-10[a] Code	Age-Adjusted Mortality Rate[1] per 100,000 population	
		County[2]	U.S.
Malignant neoplasms	C00-C97	146.9	155.5
Ischaemic heart diseases	I20-I25	104.8	94.8
Other forms of heart disease	I30-I51	41.7	52.9
Chronic lower respiratory diseases	J40-J47	35.3	41.0
Cerebrovascular diseases	I60-I69	32.0	37.5
Other degenerative diseases of the nervous system	G30-G31	44.6	35.0
Other external causes of accidental injury	W00-X59	38.0	33.7
Organic, including symptomatic, mental disorders	F01-F09	38.1	31.0
Hypertensive diseases	I10-I15	25.8	21.9
Diabetes mellitus	E10-E14	11.9	21.2

Note: (a) ICD-10 = International Classification of Diseases 10th Revision; (1) Mortality rates are a three year average covering 2015-2017; (2) Figures cover Kent County.
Source: Centers for Disease Control and Prevention, National Center for Health Statistics. Underlying Cause of Death 1999-2017 on CDC WONDER Online Database

Mortality Rates for Selected Causes of Death

ICD-10[a] Sub-Chapter	ICD-10[a] Code	Age-Adjusted Mortality Rate[1] per 100,000 population	
		County[2]	U.S.
Assault	X85-Y09	2.8	5.9
Diseases of the liver	K70-K76	11.1	14.1
Human immunodeficiency virus (HIV) disease	B20-B24	Suppressed	1.8
Influenza and pneumonia	J09-J18	11.5	14.3
Intentional self-harm	X60-X84	11.3	13.6
Malnutrition	E40-E46	1.6	1.6
Obesity and other hyperalimentation	E65-E68	3.5	2.1
Renal failure	N17-N19	7.7	13.0
Transport accidents	V01-V99	10.8	12.4
Viral hepatitis	B15-B19	1.1	1.6

Note: (a) ICD-10 = International Classification of Diseases 10th Revision; (1) Mortality rates are a three year average covering 2015-2017; (2) Figures cover Kent County; Data are suppressed when the data meet the criteria for confidentiality constraints; Mortality rates are flagged as unreliable when the rate would be calculated with a numerator of 20 or less.
Source: Centers for Disease Control and Prevention, National Center for Health Statistics. Underlying Cause of Death 1999-2017 on CDC WONDER Online Database

Health Insurance Coverage

Area	With Health Insurance	With Private Health Insurance	With Public Health Insurance	Without Health Insurance	Population Under Age 18 Without Health Insurance
City	89.8	61.0	38.9	10.2	3.4
MSA[1]	93.3	74.9	30.7	6.7	3.2
U.S.	89.5	67.2	33.8	10.5	5.7

Note: Figures are percentages that cover the civilian noninstitutionalized population; (1) Figures cover the Grand Rapids-Wyoming, MI Metropolitan Statistical Area—see Appendix B for areas included
Source: U.S. Census Bureau, 2013-2017 American Community Survey 5-Year Estimates

Number of Medical Professionals

Area	MDs[3]	DOs[3,4]	Dentists	Podiatrists	Chiropractors	Optometrists
County[1] (number)	2,097	451	461	31	219	154
County[1] (rate[2])	326.2	70.1	71.1	4.8	33.8	23.7
U.S. (rate[2])	279.3	23.0	68.4	6.0	27.1	16.2

Note: Data as of 2017 unless noted; (1) Data covers Kent County; (2) Rate per 100,000 population; (3) Data as of 2016 and includes all active, non-federal physicians; (4) Doctor of Osteopathic Medicine
Source: U.S. Department of Health and Human Services, Health Resources and Services Administration, Bureau of Health Professions, Area Resource File (ARF) 2017-2018

Best Hospitals

According to *U.S. News,* the Grand Rapids-Wyoming, MI metro area is home to one of the best hospitals in the U.S.: **Spectrum Health-Butterworth and Blodgett Campuses** (6 pediatric specialties). The hospital listed was nationally ranked in at least one of 16 adult or 10 pediatric specialties. Only 170 hospitals nationwide were nationally ranked in one or more adult or pediatric specialty. Twenty hospitals in the U.S. made the Honor Roll. The Best Hospitals Honor Roll takes both the national rankings and the procedure and condition ratings into account. Hospitals received points if they were nationally ranked in one of the 16 adult specialties—the higher they ranked, the more points they got—and how many ratings of "high performing" they earned in the nine procedures and conditions. *U.S. News Online, "America's Best Hospitals 2018-19"*

According to *U.S. News,* the Grand Rapids-Wyoming, MI metro area is home to one of the best children's hospitals in the U.S.: **Spectrum Health Helen DeVos Children's Hospital** (6 pediatric specialties). The hospital listed was highly ranked in at least one of 10 pediatric specialties. Eighty-six children's hospitals in the U.S. were nationally ranked in at least one specialty. Hospitals received points for being ranked in a specialty, and the 10 hospitals with the most points across the 10 specialties make up the Honor Roll. *U.S. News Online, "America's Best Children's Hospitals 2018-19"*

EDUCATION

Public School District Statistics

District Name	Schls	Pupils	Pupil/ Teacher Ratio	Minority Pupils[1] (%)	Free Lunch Eligible[2] (%)	IEP[3] (%)
East Grand Rapids Public Schools	5	2,939	19.3	9.9	3.5	5.6
Forest Hills Public Schools	17	9,908	18.9	19.6	6.2	8.0
Godwin Heights Public Schools	5	2,203	18.2	80.1	78.3	14.0
Grand Rapids Public Schools	49	16,417	15.3	77.4	72.7	19.5
Kelloggsville Public Schools	6	2,248	19.4	66.2	69.3	12.0
Kenowa Hills Public Schools	5	3,146	19.2	27.1	38.7	13.8
Kent ISD	n/a	3,016	16.1	63.4	n/a	0.1
Kentwood Public Schools	17	9,044	19.9	65.2	54.4	13.5
Michigan Virtual Charter Academy	1	2,789	22.1	35.1	58.0	16.1
Northview Public Schools	7	3,392	17.7	23.5	31.7	13.3

Note: Table includes school districts with 2,000 or more students; (1) Percentage of students that are not non-Hispanic white; (2) Percentage of students that are eligible for the free lunch program; (3) Percentage of students that have an Individualized Education Program.
Source: U.S. Department of Education, National Center for Education Statistics, Common Core of Data, Local Education Agency (School District) Universe Survey: School Year 2016-2017; U.S. Department of Education, National Center for Education Statistics, Common Core of Data, Public Elementary/Secondary School Universe Survey: School Year 2016-2017

Best High Schools

According to *U.S. News,* Grand Rapids is home to one of the best high schools in the U.S.: **Grand River Preparatory High School** (#229). More than 20,000 public, magnet and charter schools were ranked based on their performance on state assessments and how well they prepare students for college. Schools with the highest unrounded College Readiness Index values were numerically ranked from 1 to 500 and were classified as gold medal winners. *U.S. News & World Report, "Best High Schools 2018"*

Highest Level of Education

Area	Less than H.S.	H.S. Diploma	Some College, No Deg.	Associate Degree	Bachelor's Degree	Master's Degree	Prof. School Degree	Doctorate Degree
City	14.0	22.3	21.4	7.5	22.5	8.7	1.9	1.5
MSA[1]	9.6	27.2	22.2	9.2	21.0	8.0	1.7	1.1
U.S.	12.7	27.3	20.8	8.3	19.1	8.4	2.0	1.4

Note: Figures cover persons age 25 and over; (1) Figures cover the Grand Rapids-Wyoming, MI Metropolitan Statistical Area—see Appendix B for areas included
Source: U.S. Census Bureau, 2013-2017 American Community Survey 5-Year Estimates

Educational Attainment by Race

Area	High School Graduate or Higher (%)					Bachelor's Degree or Higher (%)				
	Total	White	Black	Asian	Hisp.[2]	Total	White	Black	Asian	Hisp.[2]
City	86.0	90.2	80.3	71.8	49.5	34.7	41.4	14.9	41.3	10.2
MSA[1]	90.4	92.4	82.7	75.8	60.0	31.8	33.3	16.8	36.1	13.4
U.S.	87.3	89.3	84.9	86.5	66.7	30.9	32.2	20.6	52.7	15.2

Note: Figures shown cover persons 25 years old and over; (1) Figures cover the Grand Rapids-Wyoming, MI Metropolitan Statistical Area—see Appendix B for areas included; (2) People of Hispanic origin can be of any race
Source: U.S. Census Bureau, 2013-2017 American Community Survey 5-Year Estimates

School Enrollment by Grade and Control

Area	Preschool (%)		Kindergarten (%)		Grades 1 - 4 (%)		Grades 5 - 8 (%)		Grades 9 - 12 (%)	
	Public	Private	Public	Private	Public	Private	Public	Private	Public	Private
City	61.8	38.2	78.3	21.7	81.0	19.0	85.3	14.7	85.3	14.7
MSA[1]	63.1	36.9	83.3	16.7	84.0	16.0	85.8	14.2	86.5	13.5
U.S.	58.8	41.2	87.7	12.3	89.7	10.3	89.6	10.4	90.3	9.7

Note: Figures shown cover persons 3 years old and over; (1) Figures cover the Grand Rapids-Wyoming, MI Metropolitan Statistical Area—see Appendix B for areas included
Source: U.S. Census Bureau, 2013-2017 American Community Survey 5-Year Estimates

Average Salaries of Public School Classroom Teachers

Area	2016		2017		Change from 2016 to 2017	
	Dollars	Rank[1]	Dollars	Rank[1]	Percent	Rank[2]
Michigan	61,875	12	62,287	12	0.7	39
U.S. Average	58,479	–	59,660	–	2.0	–

Note: (1) Rank ranges from 1 to 51 where 1 indicates highest salary; (2) Rank ranges from 1 to 51 where 1 indicates highest percent change.
Source: National Education Association, Rankings & Estimates: Rankings of the States 2017 and Estimates of School Statistics 2018

Higher Education

Four-Year Colleges			Two-Year Colleges			Medical Schools[1]	Law Schools[2]	Voc/ Tech[3]
Public	Private Non-profit	Private For-profit	Public	Private Non-profit	Private For-profit			
0	7	0	1	0	0	0	0	3

Note: Figures cover institutions located within the city limits and include main campuses only; (1) includes schools accredited by the Liaison Committee on Medical Education and the American Osteopathic Association's Commission on Osteopathic College Accreditation; (2) includes ABA-accredited schools, schools with provisional ABA accreditation, and state accredited schools; (3) includes all schools with programs that are less than 2 years.
Source: National Center for Education Statistics, Integrated Postsecondary Education System (IPEDS), 2017-18; Wikipedia, List of Medical Schools in the United States, accessed April 3, 2019; Wikipedia, List of Law Schools in the United States, accessed April 3, 2019

According to *U.S. News & World Report,* the Grand Rapids-Wyoming, MI metro area is home to one of the best liberal arts colleges in the U.S.: **Hope College** (#103 tie). The indicators used to capture academic quality fall into a number of categories: assessment by administrators at peer institutions; retention of students; faculty resources; student selectivity; financial resources; alumni giving; high school counselor ratings of colleges; and graduation rate. *U.S. News & World Report, "America's Best Colleges 2019"*

PRESIDENTIAL ELECTION

2016 Presidential Election Results

Area	Clinton	Trump	Johnson	Stein	Other
Kent County	44.6	47.7	4.6	1.3	1.9
U.S.	48.0	45.9	3.3	1.1	1.7

Note: Results are percentages and may not add to 100% due to rounding
Source: Dave Leip's Atlas of U.S. Presidential Elections

EMPLOYERS

Major Employers

Company Name	Industry
Alticor	Consumer products, multi-level marketing
Farmers Insurance Group	Insurance
Grand Rapids Public Schools	Public elementary & secondary schools
Herman Miller	Manufacturing & industrial supply
Johnson Controls	Automotive interiors, HVAC equipment
Meijer	Retail, grocery & discount
Spectrum Health	Healthcare
Steelcase	Furniture

Note: Companies shown are located within the Grand Rapids-Wyoming, MI Metropolitan Statistical Area.
Source: Hoovers.com; Wikipedia

PUBLIC SAFETY

Crime Rate

Area	All Crimes	Violent Crimes				Property Crimes		
		Murder	Rape[3]	Robbery	Aggrav. Assault	Burglary	Larceny -Theft	Motor Vehicle Theft
City	2,784.7	6.1	71.3	177.4	456.9	385.6	1,504.0	183.5
Suburbs[1]	1,623.8	2.1	80.0	23.8	129.2	233.1	1,080.0	75.7
Metro[2]	1,840.5	2.8	78.3	52.5	190.3	261.6	1,159.2	95.8
U.S.	2,756.1	5.3	41.7	98.0	248.9	430.4	1,694.4	237.4

Note: Figures are crimes per 100,000 population; (1) All areas within the metro area that are located outside the city limits; (2) Figures cover the Grand Rapids-Wyoming, MI Metropolitan Statistical Area—see Appendix B for areas included; (3) The city and U.S. figures shown were reported using the revised Uniform Crime Reporting (UCR) definition of rape. The suburban and metro area figures shown are an aggregate total of the data submitted using both the revised and legacy UCR definitions.
Source: FBI Uniform Crime Reports, 2017

Hate Crimes

Area	Number of Quarters Reported	Number of Incidents per Bias Motivation					
		Race/Ethnicity/ Ancestry	Religion	Sexual Orientation	Disability	Gender	Gender Identity
City	4	5	1	4	0	0	0
U.S.	4	4,131	1,564	1,130	116	46	119

Source: Federal Bureau of Investigation, Hate Crime Statistics 2017

Identity Theft Consumer Reports

Area	Reports	Reports per 100,000 Population	Rank[2]
MSA[1]	1,317	126	62
U.S.	444,602	135	-

Note: (1) Figures cover the Grand Rapids-Wyoming, MI Metropolitan Statistical Area—see Appendix B for areas included; (2) Rank ranges from 1 to 389 where 1 indicates greatest number of identity theft reports per 100,000 population
Source: Federal Trade Commission, Consumer Sentinel Network Data Book for January–December 2018

Fraud and Other Consumer Reports

Area	Reports	Reports per 100,000 Population	Rank[2]
MSA[1]	4,446	425	288
U.S.	2,552,917	776	-

Note: (1) Figures cover the Grand Rapids-Wyoming, MI Metropolitan Statistical Area—see Appendix B for areas included; (2) Rank ranges from 1 to 389 where 1 indicates greatest number of fraud and other consumer reports per 100,000 population
Source: Federal Trade Commission, Consumer Sentinel Network Data Book for January–December 2018

SPORTS

Professional Sports Teams

Team Name	League	Year Established
No teams are located in the metro area		

Source: Wikipedia, Major Professional Sports Teams of the United States and Canada, April 5, 2019

CLIMATE

Average and Extreme Temperatures

Temperature	Jan	Feb	Mar	Apr	May	Jun	Jul	Aug	Sep	Oct	Nov	Dec	Yr.
Extreme High (°F)	66	67	80	88	92	102	100	100	97	87	81	67	102
Average High (°F)	30	32	42	57	69	79	83	81	73	61	46	34	57
Average Temp. (°F)	23	25	34	47	58	67	72	70	62	51	39	28	48
Average Low (°F)	15	16	25	36	46	56	60	59	51	41	31	21	38
Extreme Low (°F)	-22	-19	-8	3	22	33	41	39	28	18	-10	-18	-22

Note: Figures cover the years 1948-1990
Source: National Climatic Data Center, International Station Meteorological Climate Summary, 9/96

Average Precipitation/Snowfall/Humidity

Precip./Humidity	Jan	Feb	Mar	Apr	May	Jun	Jul	Aug	Sep	Oct	Nov	Dec	Yr.
Avg. Precip. (in.)	1.9	1.6	2.6	3.5	3.0	3.5	3.2	3.2	3.7	2.7	3.1	2.7	34.7
Avg. Snowfall (in.)	21	12	11	3	Tr	0	0	0	Tr	1	8	18	73
Avg. Rel. Hum. 7am (%)	81	80	80	79	79	81	84	88	89	85	83	83	83
Avg. Rel. Hum. 4pm (%)	71	66	61	54	50	52	52	55	58	60	68	74	60

Note: Figures cover the years 1948-1990; Tr = Trace amounts (<0.05 in. of rain; <0.5 in. of snow)
Source: National Climatic Data Center, International Station Meteorological Climate Summary, 9/96

Weather Conditions

Temperature			Daytime Sky			Precipitation		
5°F & below	32°F & below	90°F & above	Clear	Partly cloudy	Cloudy	0.01 inch or more precip.	0.1 inch or more snow/ice	Thunder-storms
15	146	11	67	119	179	142	57	34

Note: Figures are average number of days per year and cover the years 1948-1990
Source: National Climatic Data Center, International Station Meteorological Climate Summary, 9/96

HAZARDOUS WASTE

Superfund Sites

The Grand Rapids-Wyoming, MI metro area is home to nine sites on the EPA's Superfund National Priorities List: **Butterworth #2 Landfill** (final); **Chem Central** (final); **H. Brown Co., Inc.** (final); **Kentwood Landfill** (final); **Organic Chemicals, Inc.** (final); **Southwest Ottawa County Landfill** (final); **Sparta Landfill** (final); **Spartan Chemical Co.** (final); **State Disposal Landfill, Inc.** (final). There are a total of 1,390 Superfund sites with a status of proposed or final on the list in the U.S. *U.S. Environmental Protection Agency, National Priorities List, April 5, 2019*

**AIR & WATER
QUALITY**

Air Quality Trends: Ozone

	1990	1995	2000	2005	2010	2012	2014	2015	2016	2017
MSA[1]	0.102	0.089	0.073	0.085	0.071	0.083	0.069	0.066	0.075	0.065
U.S.	0.088	0.089	0.082	0.080	0.073	0.075	0.067	0.068	0.069	0.068

*Note: (1) Data covers the Grand Rapids-Wyoming, MI Metropolitan Statistical Area—see Appendix B for areas included. The values shown are the composite ozone concentration averages among trend sites based on the highest fourth daily maximum 8-hour concentration in parts per million. These trends are based on sites having an adequate record of monitoring data during the trend period. Data from exceptional events are included.
Source: U.S. Environmental Protection Agency, Air Quality Monitoring Information, "Air Quality Trends by City, 1990-2017"*

Air Quality Index

Area	Percent of Days when Air Quality was...[2]					AQI Statistics[2]	
	Good	Moderate	Unhealthy for Sensitive Groups	Unhealthy	Very Unhealthy	Maximum	Median
MSA[1]	77.8	22.2	0.0	0.0	0.0	100	40

*Note: (1) Data covers the Grand Rapids-Wyoming, MI Metropolitan Statistical Area—see Appendix B for areas included; (2) Based on 365 days with AQI data in 2017. Air Quality Index (AQI) is an index for reporting daily air quality. EPA calculates the AQI for five major air pollutants regulated by the Clean Air Act: ground-level ozone, particle pollution (aka particulate matter), carbon monoxide, sulfur dioxide, and nitrogen dioxide. The AQI runs from 0 to 500. The higher the AQI value, the greater the level of air pollution and the greater the health concern. There are six AQI categories: "Good" AQI is between 0 and 50. Air quality is considered satisfactory; "Moderate" AQI is between 51 and 100. Air quality is acceptable; "Unhealthy for Sensitive Groups" When AQI values are between 101 and 150, members of sensitive groups may experience health effects; "Unhealthy" When AQI values are between 151 and 200 everyone may begin to experience health effects; "Very Unhealthy" AQI values between 201 and 300 trigger a health alert; "Hazardous" AQI values over 300 trigger warnings of emergency conditions (not shown).
Source: U.S. Environmental Protection Agency, Air Quality Index Report, 2017*

Air Quality Index Pollutants

Area	Percent of Days when AQI Pollutant was...[2]					
	Carbon Monoxide	Nitrogen Dioxide	Ozone	Sulfur Dioxide	Particulate Matter 2.5	Particulate Matter 10
MSA[1]	0.0	0.0	65.5	0.3	34.2	0.0

*Note: (1) Data covers the Grand Rapids-Wyoming, MI Metropolitan Statistical Area—see Appendix B for areas included; (2) Based on 365 days with AQI data in 2017. The Air Quality Index (AQI) is an index for reporting daily air quality. EPA calculates the AQI for five major air pollutants regulated by the Clean Air Act: ground-level ozone, particle pollution (also known as particulate matter), carbon monoxide, sulfur dioxide, and nitrogen dioxide. The AQI runs from 0 to 500. The higher the AQI value, the greater the level of air pollution and the greater the health concern.
Source: U.S. Environmental Protection Agency, Air Quality Index Report, 2017*

Maximum Air Pollutant Concentrations: Particulate Matter, Ozone, CO and Lead

	Particulate Matter 10 (ug/m³)	Particulate Matter 2.5 Wtd AM (ug/m³)	Particulate Matter 2.5 24-Hr (ug/m³)	Ozone (ppm)	Carbon Monoxide (ppm)	Lead (ug/m³)
MSA[1] Level	29	9.1	26	0.066	1	0
NAAQS[2]	150	15	35	0.075	9	0.15
Met NAAQS[2]	Yes	Yes	Yes	Yes	Yes	Yes

*Note: (1) Data covers the Grand Rapids-Wyoming, MI Metropolitan Statistical Area—see Appendix B for areas included; Data from exceptional events are included; (2) National Ambient Air Quality Standards; ppm = parts per million; ug/m³ = micrograms per cubic meter; n/a not available.
Concentrations: Particulate Matter 10 (coarse particulate)—highest second maximum 24-hour concentration; Particulate Matter 2.5 Wtd AM (fine particulate)—highest weighted annual mean concentration; Particulate Matter 2.5 24-Hour (fine particulate)—highest 98th percentile 24-hour concentration; Ozone—highest fourth daily maximum 8-hour concentration; Carbon Monoxide—highest second maximum non-overlapping 8-hour concentration; Lead—maximum running 3-month average
Source: U.S. Environmental Protection Agency, Air Quality Monitoring Information, "Air Quality Statistics by City, 2017"*

Maximum Air Pollutant Concentrations: Nitrogen Dioxide and Sulfur Dioxide

	Nitrogen Dioxide AM (ppb)	Nitrogen Dioxide 1-Hr (ppb)	Sulfur Dioxide AM (ppb)	Sulfur Dioxide 1-Hr (ppb)	Sulfur Dioxide 24-Hr (ppb)
MSA[1] Level	n/a	n/a	n/a	21	n/a
NAAQS[2]	53	100	30	75	140
Met NAAQS[2]	n/a	n/a	n/a	Yes	n/a

Note: (1) Data covers the Grand Rapids-Wyoming, MI Metropolitan Statistical Area—see Appendix B for areas included; Data from exceptional events are included; (2) National Ambient Air Quality Standards; ppm = parts per million; ug/m³ = micrograms per cubic meter; n/a not available.
Concentrations: Nitrogen Dioxide AM—highest arithmetic mean concentration; Nitrogen Dioxide 1-Hr—highest 98th percentile 1-hour daily maximum concentration; Sulfur Dioxide AM—highest annual mean concentration; Sulfur Dioxide 1-Hr—highest 99th percentile 1-hour daily maximum concentration; Sulfur Dioxide 24-Hr—highest second maximum 24-hour concentration
Source: U.S. Environmental Protection Agency, Air Quality Monitoring Information, "Air Quality Statistics by City, 2017"

Drinking Water

Water System Name	Pop. Served	Primary Water Source Type	Violations[1] Health Based	Monitoring/ Reporting
Grand Rapids	258,416	Surface	0	0

Note: (1) Based on violation data from January 1, 2018 to December 31, 2018
Source: U.S. Environmental Protection Agency, Office of Ground Water and Drinking Water, Safe Drinking Water Information System (based on data extracted April 5, 2019)

Green Bay, Wisconsin

Background

The city of Green Bay takes its name from an inlet at the mouth of the Fox River, off Lake Michigan. Green Bay is the oldest city in Wisconsin, and the seat of Brown County. The city, laid out on high ground on either side of the river, has always been an important port and, in recent decades, is known to Americans as the home of the nation's oldest professional football team, the Green Bay Packers, who play in Lambeau Field, the longest continuously-occupied stadium in the NFL.

Prior to European settlement, the area had been home to Winnebago and other settled, horticultural tribes. The French explorer Jean Nicolet, who was seeking a route to the Pacific and thence to Asia, was the first recorded European visitor. He landed his canoe in 1634 about 10 miles south of the present city, finding there a community of friendly Winnebago or Oneida, who at first he took to be Chinese.

Later explorers and traders, mostly French, established a trading post at the site, and in 1720, Fort St. Francis was completed at the mouth of the river. In 1745, the first permanent settlement was begun at "Le Baye" in what are the boundaries of the present city. The so-called "Tank House," built by the voyageur Joseph Roy in 1766, is thought to be the oldest house in the state. Green Bay is also home to the oldest Roman Catholic bishopric in the area. Although the French influence was paramount, many of the fur traders who came into the area were associated with the American fur baron John Jacob Astor, who constructed warehouses and other buildings on the site.

Settlers regarded themselves as French citizens until the fort was occupied by the British in 1763. Thereafter, until the War of 1812 and beyond, they were under British control until the Americans garrisoned Fort Howard and brought the city firmly under rule by the new republic. The first newspaper in the state, the *Green Bay Intelligencer,* was established in 1833. In 1854, the city of Green Bay was chartered, and in 1893, the adjoining Fort Howard was incorporated into it. In the late nineteenth century, Green Bay was a major port for the thriving lumber trade.

Forest products, particularly paper, are still a mainstay of the local economy, as are health care, finance, insurance and logistics. The Oneida Tribe of Indians of Wisconsin is headquartered in the region. Tourism is increasingly important, with visitors drawn to the city both for Green Bay Packers football, and for its proximity to some of the most attractive vacation spots in the state.

The city's downtown, like so many others, is undergoing a renaissance. Office space and dwelling units have arrived along the Fox River, as well as a trail along the river's east side. The CityDeck faces the water for four blocks. Similarly, the Broadway corridor has seen a revival. The KI Convention Center was expanded by 35,000 square feet. Recent years also have seen the opening of the 15,000 square foot Children's Museum of Green Bay in the city's downtown.

Other attractions include the National Railroad Museum, which includes the world's largest steam locomotive, and the NEW Zoo, home to more than 200 animals of nearly 90 species.

Green Bay is home to a local campus (1965) of the University of Wisconsin and Bellin College (1909), which specializes in nursing and radiologic sciences.

The weather in Green Bay is a mild version of the general northern plains complex, with four seasons, warm summers, and considerable winter snowfall. High and low temperatures are modified by the city's location on Green Bay, as well as its proximity to Lake Superior and Lake Michigan.

Rankings

Business/Finance Rankings

- The personal finance site NerdWallet analyzed 183 American metropolitan areas with populations over 250,000 and more than 15,000 businesses to rank where entrepreneurs find the most success. Criteria included area economy, annual income, housing cost, unemployment rate, and the success rate of area businesses. Green Bay ranked #8. *www.nerdwallet.com, "Best Places to Start a Business," April 27, 2015*

- Experian's latest annual report on consumer credit ranked cities by the average credit score of its residents. Green Bay was ranked #5 among the ten cities with the highest average credit score, meaning that its residents showed strong credit management. *www.usatoday.com, "Minneapolis Tops List of Cities With Best Average Credit Score; Greenwood Miss., at the Bottom," January 11, 2018*

- Using data from the Council for Community and Economic Research's 2014 cost of living index, NerdWallet ranked the 100 most affordable cities in America. Median income was compared with cost of living to find truly affordable places. Green Bay ranked #93. *NerdWallet.com, "America's Most Affordable Places," May 18, 2015*

- The Green Bay metro area appeared on the Milken Institute "2018 Best Performing Cities" list. Rank: #152 out of 200 large metro areas. Criteria: job growth; wage and salary growth; high-tech output growth. *Milken Institute, "Best-Performing Cities 2018," January 24, 2019*

- *Forbes* ranked the 200 most populous metro areas to determine the nation's "Best Places for Business and Careers." The Green Bay metro area was ranked #122. Criteria: costs (business and living); job growth (past and projected); income growth; quality of life; educational attainment (college and high school); projected economic growth; cultural and recreational opportunities; net migration patterns; number of highly ranked colleges. *Forbes, "The Best Places for Business and Careers 2018: Seattle Leads the Way," October 24, 2018*

Health/Fitness Rankings

- The Green Bay metro area ranked #60 out of 189 in The Gallup-Healthways Well-Being Index. Criteria: purpose; social well being; financial health; community and physical health. Results are based on telephone interviews with adults, aged 18 and older, living in metropolitan areas in the 50 U.S. states and the District of Columbia. *Gallup-Healthways, "State of American Well-Being, 2017 Community Well-Being Rankings" March 2018*

Safety Rankings

- The National Insurance Crime Bureau ranked 382 metro areas in the U.S. in terms of per capita rates of vehicle theft. The Green Bay metro area ranked #341 (#1 = highest rate). Criteria: number of vehicle theft offenses per 100,000 inhabitants in 2017. *National Insurance Crime Bureau, "Hot Spots 2017," July 12, 2018*

Seniors/Retirement Rankings

- From its Best Cities for Successful Aging indexes, the Milken Institute generated rankings for metropolitan areas, weighing data in nine categories—health care, wellness, living arrangements, transportation and convenience, financial characteristics, education, employment, community engagement, and overall livability. The Green Bay metro area was ranked #162 overall in the small metro area category. *Milken Institute, "Best Cities for Successful Aging, 2017" March 14, 2017*

Business Environment

CITY FINANCES

City Government Finances

Component	2016 ($000)	2016 ($ per capita)
Total Revenues	190,323	1,809
Total Expenditures	202,437	1,924
Debt Outstanding	266,935	2,537
Cash and Securities[1]	120,596	1,146

Note: (1) Cash and security holdings of a government at the close of its fiscal year, including those of its dependent agencies, utilities, and liquor stores.
Source: U.S. Census Bureau, State & Local Government Finances 2016

City Government Revenue by Source

Source	2016 ($000)	2016 ($ per capita)	2016 (%)
General Revenue			
From Federal Government	5,136	49	2.7
From State Government	37,472	356	19.7
From Local Governments	7,757	74	4.1
Taxes			
Property	55,196	525	29.0
Sales and Gross Receipts	353	3	0.2
Personal Income	0	0	0.0
Corporate Income	0	0	0.0
Motor Vehicle License	0	0	0.0
Other Taxes	2,975	28	1.6
Current Charges	33,676	320	17.7
Liquor Store	0	0	0.0
Utility	36,167	344	19.0
Employee Retirement	0	0	0.0

Source: U.S. Census Bureau, State & Local Government Finances 2016

City Government Expenditures by Function

Function	2016 ($000)	2016 ($ per capita)	2016 (%)
General Direct Expenditures			
Air Transportation	0	0	0.0
Corrections	0	0	0.0
Education	0	0	0.0
Employment Security Administration	0	0	0.0
Financial Administration	1,616	15	0.8
Fire Protection	22,661	215	11.2
General Public Buildings	503	4	0.2
Governmental Administration, Other	3,981	37	2.0
Health	549	5	0.3
Highways	20,461	194	10.1
Hospitals	0	0	0.0
Housing and Community Development	674	6	0.3
Interest on General Debt	6,822	64	3.4
Judicial and Legal	995	9	0.5
Libraries	0	0	0.0
Parking	2,358	22	1.2
Parks and Recreation	10,730	102	5.3
Police Protection	26,004	247	12.8
Public Welfare	0	0	0.0
Sewerage	18,172	172	9.0
Solid Waste Management	8,700	82	4.3
Veterans' Services	0	0	0.0
Liquor Store	0	0	0.0
Utility	41,487	394	20.5
Employee Retirement	0	0	0.0

Source: U.S. Census Bureau, State & Local Government Finances 2016

DEMOGRAPHICS

Population Growth

Area	1990 Census	2000 Census	2010 Census	2017* Estimate	Population Growth (%)	
					1990-2017	2010-2017
City	96,466	102,313	104,057	104,796	8.6	0.7
MSA[1]	243,698	282,599	306,241	315,847	29.6	3.1
U.S.	248,709,873	281,421,906	308,745,538	321,004,407	29.1	4.0

Note: (1) Figures cover the Green Bay, WI Metropolitan Statistical Area—see Appendix B for areas included;
(*) 2013-2017 5-year estimated population
Source: U.S. Census Bureau, 1990 Census, Census 2000, Census 2010, 2013-2017 American Community Survey 5-Year Estimates

Household Size

Area	Persons in Household (%)							Average Household Size
	One	Two	Three	Four	Five	Six	Seven or More	
City	33.4	33.0	12.4	11.6	6.7	1.5	1.4	2.40
MSA[1]	27.6	37.0	14.1	12.7	6.2	1.5	0.9	2.40
U.S.	27.7	33.8	15.7	13.0	6.0	2.3	1.4	2.60

Note: (1) Figures cover the Green Bay, WI Metropolitan Statistical Area—see Appendix B for areas included
Source: U.S. Census Bureau, 2013-2017 American Community Survey 5-Year Estimates

Race

Area	White Alone[2] (%)	Black Alone[2] (%)	Asian Alone[2] (%)	AIAN[3] Alone[2] (%)	NHOPI[4] Alone[2] (%)	Other Race Alone[2] (%)	Two or More Races (%)
City	77.4	3.8	4.0	3.5	0.0	6.4	4.9
MSA[1]	87.3	1.9	2.6	2.1	0.0	3.2	2.8
U.S.	73.0	12.7	5.4	0.8	0.2	4.8	3.1

Note: (1) Figures cover the Green Bay, WI Metropolitan Statistical Area—see Appendix B for areas included;
(2) Alone is defined as not being in combination with one or more other races; (3) American Indian and Alaska
Native; (4) Native Hawaiian and Other Pacific Islander
Source: U.S. Census Bureau, 2013-2017 American Community Survey 5-Year Estimates

Hispanic or Latino Origin

Area	Total (%)	Mexican (%)	Puerto Rican (%)	Cuban (%)	Other (%)
City	14.4	10.9	1.4	0.2	2.0
MSA[1]	7.2	5.4	0.8	0.1	0.9
U.S.	17.6	11.1	1.7	0.7	4.1

Note: Persons of Hispanic or Latino origin can be of any race; (1) Figures cover the Green Bay, WI
Metropolitan Statistical Area—see Appendix B for areas included
Source: U.S. Census Bureau, 2013-2017 American Community Survey 5-Year Estimates

Segregation

Type	Segregation Indices[1]				Percent Change		
	1990	2000	2010	2010 Rank[2]	1990-2000	1990-2010	2000-2010
Black/White	n/a	n/a	n/a	n/a	n/a	n/a	n/a
Asian/White	n/a	n/a	n/a	n/a	n/a	n/a	n/a
Hispanic/White	n/a	n/a	n/a	n/a	n/a	n/a	n/a

Note: All figures cover the Metropolitan Statistical Area—see Appendix B for areas included; Figures are based
on an analysis of 1990, 2000, and 2010 Census Decennial Census tract data by William H. Frey, Brookings
Institution and the University of Michigan Social Science Data Analysis Network. In this analysis all racial
groups (whites, blacks, and asians) are non-Hispanic members of those races. Hispanics are shown as a
separate category; (1) Segregation Indices are Dissimilarity Indices that measure the degree to which the
minority group is distributed differently than whites across census tracts. They range from 0 (complete
integration) to 100 (complete segregation) where the value indicates the percentage of the minority group that
needs to move to be distributed exactly like whites; (2) Ranges from 1 (most segregated) to 102 (least
segregated); n/a not available.
Source: www.CensusScope.org

Ancestry

Area	German	Irish	English	American	Italian	Polish	French[2]	Scottish	Dutch
City	31.7	8.7	3.4	3.4	2.0	8.1	4.3	0.7	3.5
MSA[1]	37.2	9.4	3.9	3.8	2.3	9.6	4.6	0.8	4.6
U.S.	14.1	10.1	7.5	6.6	5.3	2.9	2.5	1.7	1.3

Note: Figures are the percentage of the total population reporting a particular ancestry. The nine most commonly reported ancestries in the U.S. are shown. Figures include multiple ancestries (e.g. if a person reported being Irish and Italian, they were included in both columns); (1) Figures cover the Green Bay, WI Metropolitan Statistical Area—see Appendix B for areas included; (2) Excludes Basque
Source: U.S. Census Bureau, 2013-2017 American Community Survey 5-Year Estimates

Foreign-Born Population

Area	Percent of Population Born in								
	Any Foreign Country	Asia	Mexico	Europe	Carribean	Central America[2]	South America	Africa	Canada
City	9.1	2.1	4.9	0.6	0.1	0.7	0.2	0.4	0.1
MSA[1]	5.1	1.5	2.3	0.5	0.1	0.3	0.1	0.2	0.1
U.S.	13.4	4.1	3.6	1.5	1.3	1.0	0.9	0.6	0.3

Note: (1) Figures cover the Green Bay, WI Metropolitan Statistical Area—see Appendix B for areas included; (2) Excludes Mexico.
Source: U.S. Census Bureau, 2013-2017 American Community Survey 5-Year Estimates

Marital Status

Area	Never Married	Now Married[2]	Separated	Widowed	Divorced
City	38.7	42.6	1.5	5.0	12.3
MSA[1]	30.5	53.0	1.0	5.1	10.5
U.S.	33.1	48.2	2.0	5.8	10.9

Note: Figures are percentages and cover the population 15 years of age and older; (1) Figures cover the Green Bay, WI Metropolitan Statistical Area—see Appendix B for areas included; (2) Excludes separated
Source: U.S. Census Bureau, 2013-2017 American Community Survey 5-Year Estimates

Disability by Age

Area	All Ages	Under 18 Years Old	18 to 64 Years Old	65 Years and Over
City	13.6	5.5	12.9	34.0
MSA[1]	11.6	4.7	9.8	31.1
U.S.	12.6	4.2	10.3	35.5

Note: Figures show percent of the civilian noninstitutionalized population that reported having a disability. Disability status is determined from six types of difficulty: vision, hearing, cognitive, ambulatory, self-care, and independent living. For children under 5 years old, hearing and vision difficulty are used to determine disability status. For children between the ages of 5 and 14, disability status is determined from hearing, vision, cognitive, ambulatory, and self-care difficulties. For people aged 15 years and older, they are considered to have a disability if they have difficulty with any one of the six difficulty types; Note: (1) Figures cover the Green Bay, WI Metropolitan Statistical Area—see Appendix B for areas included
Source: U.S. Census Bureau, 2013-2017 American Community Survey 5-Year Estimates

Age

Area	Percent of Population									Median Age
	Under Age 5	Age 5–19	Age 20–34	Age 35–44	Age 45–54	Age 55–64	Age 65–74	Age 75–84	Age 85+	
City	7.8	19.8	24.0	11.9	12.5	11.8	6.7	3.6	1.9	34.0
MSA[1]	6.3	19.8	19.4	12.4	14.2	13.4	8.2	4.3	1.9	38.5
U.S.	6.2	19.5	20.7	12.7	13.4	12.7	8.6	4.4	1.9	37.8

Note: (1) Figures cover the Green Bay, WI Metropolitan Statistical Area—see Appendix B for areas included
Source: U.S. Census Bureau, 2013-2017 American Community Survey 5-Year Estimates

Gender

Area	Males	Females	Males per 100 Females
City	51,679	53,117	97.3
MSA[1]	157,496	158,351	99.5
U.S.	158,018,753	162,985,654	97.0

Note: (1) Figures cover the Green Bay, WI Metropolitan Statistical Area—see Appendix B for areas included
Source: U.S. Census Bureau, 2013-2017 American Community Survey 5-Year Estimates

Religious Groups by Family

Area	Catholic	Baptist	Non-Den.	Methodist[2]	Lutheran	LDS[3]	Pente-costal	Presby-terian[4]	Muslim[5]	Judaism
MSA[1]	42.0	0.7	3.4	2.2	12.7	0.4	0.6	1.0	0.1	0.1
U.S.	19.1	9.3	4.0	4.0	2.3	2.0	1.9	1.6	0.8	0.7

Note: Figures are the number of adherents as a percentage of the total population; (1) Figures cover the Green Bay, WI Metropolitan Statistical Area—see Appendix B for areas included; (2) Methodist/Pietist; (3) Latter Day Saints; (4) Reformed; (5) Figures are estimates
Source: Association of Statisticians of American Religious Bodies, 2010 U.S. Religion Census: Religious Congregations & Membership Study

Religious Groups by Tradition

Area	Catholic	Evangelical Protestant	Mainline Protestant	Other Tradition	Black Protestant	Orthodox
MSA[1]	42.0	14.1	8.1	0.6	<0.1	<0.1
U.S.	19.1	16.2	7.3	4.3	1.6	0.3

Note: Figures are the number of adherents as a percentage of the total population; (1) Figures cover the Green Bay, WI Metropolitan Statistical Area—see Appendix B for areas included
Source: Association of Statisticians of American Religious Bodies, 2010 U.S. Religion Census: Religious Congregations & Membership Study

ECONOMY

Gross Metropolitan Product

Area	2016	2017	2018	2019	Rank[2]
MSA[1]	18.7	19.3	20.2	21.2	131

Note: Figures are in billions of dollars; (1) Figures cover the Green Bay, WI Metropolitan Statistical Area—see Appendix B for areas included; (2) Rank is based on 2017 data and ranges from 1 to 381
Source: U.S. Conference of Mayors, U.S. Metro Economies: Economic Growth & Full Employment, June 2018

Economic Growth

Area	2017-2018 (%)	2019-2020 (%)	2021-2022 (%)
MSA[1]	1.8	2.3	1.5

Note: Figures are real gross metropolitan product (GMP) growth rates and represent average annual percent change; (1) Figures cover the Green Bay, WI Metropolitan Statistical Area—see Appendix B for areas included
Source: U.S. Conference of Mayors, U.S. Metro Economies: Economic Growth & Full Employment, June 2018

Metropolitan Area Exports

Area	2012	2013	2014	2015	2016	2017	Rank[2]
MSA[1]	1,031.6	914.8	988.7	968.1	1,044.0	1,054.8	151

Note: Figures are in millions of dollars; (1) Figures cover the Green Bay, WI Metropolitan Statistical Area—see Appendix B for areas included; (2) Rank is based on 2017 data and ranges from 1 to 387
Source: U.S. Department of Commerce, International Trade Administration, Office of Trade and Economic Analysis, Industry and Analysis, Exports by Metropolitan Area, extracted March 25, 2019

Building Permits

Area	Single-Family			Multi-Family			Total		
	2016	2017	Pct. Chg.	2016	2017	Pct. Chg.	2016	2017	Pct. Chg.
City	111	98	-11.7	0	0	0.0	111	98	-11.7
MSA[1]	804	828	3.0	204	348	70.6	1,008	1,176	16.7
U.S.	750,800	820,000	9.2	455,800	462,000	1.4	1,206,600	1,282,000	6.2

Note: (1) Figures cover the Green Bay, WI Metropolitan Statistical Area—see Appendix B for areas included; Figures represent new, privately-owned housing units authorized (unadjusted data); All permit data are based on estimates with imputation
Source: U.S. Census Bureau, Manufacturing, Mining, and Construction Statistics, Building Permits, 2016, 2017

Bankruptcy Filings

Area	Business Filings			Nonbusiness Filings		
	2017	2018	% Chg.	2017	2018	% Chg.
Brown County	21	5	-76.2	617	575	-6.8
U.S.	23,157	22,232	-4.0	765,863	751,186	-1.9

Note: Business filings include Chapter 7, Chapter 11, Chapter 12, and Chapter 13; Nonbusiness filings include Chapter 7, Chapter 11, and Chapter 13
Source: Administrative Office of the U.S. Courts, Business and Nonbusiness Bankruptcy, County Cases Commenced by Chapter of the Bankruptcy Code, During the 12-Month Period Ending December 31, 2017 and Business and Nonbusiness Bankruptcy, County Cases Commenced by Chapter of the Bankruptcy Code, During the 12-Month Period Ending December 31, 2018

Housing Vacancy Rates

Area	Gross Vacancy Rate[2] (%)			Year-Round Vacancy Rate[3] (%)			Rental Vacancy Rate[4] (%)			Homeowner Vacancy Rate[5] (%)		
	2016	2017	2018	2016	2017	2018	2016	2017	2018	2016	2017	2018
MSA[1]	n/a	n/a	n/a	n/a	n/a	n/a	n/a	n/a	n/a	n/a	n/a	n/a
U.S.	12.8	12.7	12.3	9.9	9.9	9.7	6.9	7.2	6.9	1.7	1.6	1.5

Note: (1) Figures cover the Green Bay, WI Metropolitan Statistical Area—see Appendix B for areas included; (2) The percentage of the total housing inventory that is vacant; (3) The percentage of the housing inventory (excluding seasonal units) that is year-round vacant; (4) The percentage of rental inventory that is vacant for rent; (5) The percentage of homeowner inventory that is vacant for sale; n/a not available
Source: U.S. Census Bureau, Housing Vacancies and Homeownership Annual Statistics: 2016, 2017, 2018

INCOME

Income

Area	Per Capita ($)	Median Household ($)	Average Household ($)
City	24,660	45,473	59,780
MSA[1]	29,632	56,831	72,911
U.S.	31,177	57,652	81,283

Note: (1) Figures cover the Green Bay, WI Metropolitan Statistical Area—see Appendix B for areas included
Source: U.S. Census Bureau, 2013-2017 American Community Survey 5-Year Estimates

Household Income Distribution

Area	Percent of Households Earning							
	Under $15,000	$15,000 -$24,999	$25,000 -$34,999	$35,000 -$49,999	$50,000 -$74,999	$75,000 -$99,999	$100,000 -$149,999	$150,000 and up
City	*13.7	12.0	12.6	16.5	18.8	12.4	9.4	4.5
MSA[1]	9.3	9.7	10.3	14.5	19.1	15.1	14.2	7.8
U.S.	11.6	9.8	9.5	13.0	17.7	12.3	14.1	12.1

Note: (1) Figures cover the Green Bay, WI Metropolitan Statistical Area—see Appendix B for areas included
Source: U.S. Census Bureau, 2013-2017 American Community Survey 5-Year Estimates

Poverty Rate

Area	All Ages	Under 18 Years Old	18 to 64 Years Old	65 Years and Over
City	17.2	24.3	15.7	10.5
MSA[1]	10.9	14.9	10.0	8.2
U.S.	14.6	20.3	13.7	9.3

Note: Figures are percentage of people whose income during the past 12 months was below the poverty level; (1) Figures cover the Green Bay, WI Metropolitan Statistical Area—see Appendix B for areas included
Source: U.S. Census Bureau, 2013-2017 American Community Survey 5-Year Estimates

EMPLOYMENT

Labor Force and Employment

Area	Civilian Labor Force			Workers Employed		
	Dec. 2017	Dec. 2018	% Chg.	Dec. 2017	Dec. 2018	% Chg.
City	54,880	54,922	0.1	53,420	53,547	0.2
MSA[1]	173,987	174,287	0.2	169,585	170,033	0.3
U.S.	159,880,000	162,510,000	1.6	153,602,000	156,481,000	1.9

Note: Data is not seasonally adjusted and covers workers 16 years of age and older; (1) Figures cover the Green Bay, WI Metropolitan Statistical Area—see Appendix B for areas included
Source: Bureau of Labor Statistics, Local Area Unemployment Statistics

Unemployment Rate

Area	2018											
	Jan.	Feb.	Mar.	Apr.	May	Jun.	Jul.	Aug.	Sep.	Oct.	Nov.	Dec.
City	3.1	3.3	3.2	2.7	2.6	3.6	3.3	3.3	2.5	2.5	2.5	2.5
MSA[1]	3.0	3.3	3.0	2.6	2.5	3.2	3.0	2.9	2.4	2.4	2.4	2.4
U.S.	4.5	4.4	4.1	3.7	3.6	4.2	4.1	3.9	3.6	3.5	3.5	3.7

Note: Data is not seasonally adjusted and covers workers 16 years of age and older; (1) Figures cover the Green Bay, WI Metropolitan Statistical Area—see Appendix B for areas included
Source: Bureau of Labor Statistics, Local Area Unemployment Statistics

Average Wages

Occupation	$/Hr.	Occupation	$/Hr.
Accountants and Auditors	31.10	Maids and Housekeeping Cleaners	11.50
Automotive Mechanics	20.10	Maintenance and Repair Workers	20.90
Bookkeepers	18.10	Marketing Managers	54.40
Carpenters	24.60	Nuclear Medicine Technologists	n/a
Cashiers	10.10	Nurses, Licensed Practical	20.50
Clerks, General Office	17.00	Nurses, Registered	31.60
Clerks, Receptionists/Information	14.40	Nursing Assistants	14.40
Clerks, Shipping/Receiving	17.30	Packers and Packagers, Hand	12.10
Computer Programmers	33.80	Physical Therapists	41.30
Computer Systems Analysts	41.80	Postal Service Mail Carriers	24.90
Computer User Support Specialists	24.90	Real Estate Brokers	53.30
Cooks, Restaurant	12.10	Retail Salespersons	12.90
Dentists	110.40	Sales Reps., Exc. Tech./Scientific	32.30
Electrical Engineers	39.00	Sales Reps., Tech./Scientific	42.10
Electricians	26.30	Secretaries, Exc. Legal/Med./Exec.	17.90
Financial Managers	57.70	Security Guards	12.90
First-Line Supervisors/Managers, Sales	20.00	Surgeons	n/a
Food Preparation Workers	10.80	Teacher Assistants*	15.60
General and Operations Managers	55.90	Teachers, Elementary School*	25.20
Hairdressers/Cosmetologists	15.20	Teachers, Secondary School*	27.00
Internists, General	n/a	Telemarketers	22.30
Janitors and Cleaners	13.10	Truck Drivers, Heavy/Tractor-Trailer	21.40
Landscaping/Groundskeeping Workers	14.70	Truck Drivers, Light/Delivery Svcs.	15.30
Lawyers	51.80	Waiters and Waitresses	9.80

Note: Wage data covers the Green Bay, WI Metropolitan Statistical Area—see Appendix B for areas included; (*) Hourly wages for elementary/secondary school teachers and teacher assistants were calculated by the editors from annual wage data based on a 40 hour work week; n/a not available.
Source: Bureau of Labor Statistics, Metro Area Occupational Employment & Wage Estimates, May 2018

Employment by Occupation

Occupation Classification	City (%)	MSA[1] (%)	U.S. (%)
Management, Business, Science, and Arts	28.4	33.5	37.4
Natural Resources, Construction, and Maintenance	7.7	9.5	8.9
Production, Transportation, and Material Moving	19.8	17.3	12.2
Sales and Office	24.7	24.0	23.5
Service	19.4	15.7	18.0

Note: Figures cover employed civilians 16 years of age and older; (1) Figures cover the Green Bay, WI Metropolitan Statistical Area—see Appendix B for areas included
Source: U.S. Census Bureau, 2013-2017 American Community Survey 5-Year Estimates

Employment by Industry

Sector	MSA[1]		U.S.
	Number of Employees	Percent of Total	Percent of Total
Construction, Mining, and Logging	7,800	4.3	5.3
Education and Health Services	27,500	15.0	15.9
Financial Activities	12,200	6.6	5.7
Government	22,300	12.2	15.1
Information	1,600	0.9	1.9
Leisure and Hospitality	17,300	9.4	10.7
Manufacturing	31,400	17.1	8.5
Other Services	8,900	4.9	3.9
Professional and Business Services	19,500	10.6	14.1
Retail Trade	17,600	9.6	10.8
Transportation, Warehousing, and Utilities	8,900	4.9	4.2
Wholesale Trade	8,500	4.6	3.9

Note: Figures are non-farm employment as of December 2018. Figures are not seasonally adjusted and include workers 16 years of age and older; (1) Figures cover the Green Bay, WI Metropolitan Statistical Area—see Appendix B for areas included
Source: Bureau of Labor Statistics, Current Employment Statistics, Employment, Hours, and Earnings

Occupations with Greatest Projected Employment Growth: 2018 – 2020

Occupation[1]	2018 Employment	2020 Projected Employment	Numeric Employment Change	Percent Employment Change
Personal Care Aides	67,920	72,730	4,810	7.1
Registered Nurses	58,060	59,770	1,710	2.9
Combined Food Preparation and Serving Workers, Including Fast Food	66,990	68,580	1,590	2.4
Laborers and Freight, Stock, and Material Movers, Hand	58,500	59,990	1,490	2.5
Janitors and Cleaners, Except Maids and Housekeeping Cleaners	48,060	49,400	1,340	2.8
Sales Representatives, Wholesale and Manufacturing, Except Technical and Scientific Products	42,560	43,870	1,310	3.1
Heavy and Tractor-Trailer Truck Drivers	54,640	55,750	1,110	2.0
Carpenters	22,910	23,790	880	3.8
General and Operations Managers	37,480	38,350	870	2.3
Landscaping and Groundskeeping Workers	23,100	23,880	780	3.4

Note: Projections cover Wisconsin; (1) Sorted by numeric employment change
Source: www.projectionscentral.com, State Occupational Projections, 2018–2020 Short-Term Projections

Fastest Growing Occupations: 2018 – 2020

Occupation[1]	2018 Employment	2020 Projected Employment	Numeric Employment Change	Percent Employment Change
Rail-Track Laying and Maintenance Equipment Operators	540	590	50	9.3
Railroad Conductors and Yardmasters	800	870	70	8.8
Locomotive Engineers	1,030	1,120	90	8.7
Helpers—Pipelayers, Plumbers, Pipefitters, and Steamfitters	750	810	60	8.0
Chemical Engineers	660	710	50	7.6
Real Estate Brokers	790	850	60	7.6
Hazardous Materials Removal Workers	660	710	50	7.6
Home Health Aides	7,940	8,510	570	7.2
Plumbers, Pipefitters, and Steamfitters	9,010	9,660	650	7.2
Helpers—Electricians	1,670	1,790	120	7.2

Note: Projections cover Wisconsin; (1) Sorted by percent employment change and excludes occupations with numeric employment change less than 50
Source: www.projectionscentral.com, State Occupational Projections, 2018–2020 Short-Term Projections

TAXES

State Corporate Income Tax Rates

State	Tax Rate (%)	Income Brackets ($)	Num. of Brackets	Financial Institution Tax Rate (%)[a]	Federal Income Tax Ded.
Wisconsin	7.9	Flat rate	1	7.9	No

Note: Tax rates as of January 1, 2019; (a) Rates listed are the corporate income tax rate applied to financial institutions or excise taxes based on income. Some states have other taxes based upon the value of deposits or shares.
Source: Federation of Tax Administrators, Range of State Corporate Income Tax Rates, January 1, 2019

State Individual Income Tax Rates

State	Tax Rate (%)	Income Brackets ($)	Personal Exemptions ($) Single	Married	Depend.	Standard Ded. ($) Single	Married
Wisconsin (a)	4.0 - 7.65	11,760 - 258,950 (w)	700	1,400	700	10,860	20,110 (y)

Note: Tax rates as of January 1, 2019; Local- and county-level taxes are not included; n/a not applicable; Federal income tax is not deductible on state income tax returns; (a) 19 states have statutory provision for automatically adjusting to the rate of inflation the dollar values of the income tax brackets, standard deductions, and/or personal exemptions. Michigan indexes the personal exemption only. Oregon does not index the income brackets for $125,000 and over; (w) The Wisconsin income brackets reported are for single individuals. For married taxpayers filing jointly, the same tax rates apply income brackets ranging from $15,680, to $345,270; (y) Alabama standard deduction is phased out for incomes over $23,000. Rhode Island exemptions & standard deductions phased out for incomes over $203,850; Wisconsin standard deduciton phases out for income over $15,660.
Source: Federation of Tax Administrators, State Individual Income Tax Rates, January 1, 2019

Various State Sales and Excise Tax Rates

State	State Sales Tax (%)	Gasoline[1] (¢/gal.)	Cigarette[2] ($/pack)	Spirits[3] ($/gal.)	Wine[4] ($/gal.)	Beer[5] ($/gal.)	Recreational Marijuana (%)
Wisconsin	5	32.9	2.52	3.25	0.25 (l)	0.06 (q)	Not legal

Note: All tax rates as of January 1, 2019; (1) The American Petroleum Institute has developed a methodology for determining the average tax rate on a gallon of fuel. Rates may include any of the following: excise taxes, environmental fees, storage tank fees, other fees or taxes, general sales tax, and local taxes. In states where gasoline is subject to the general sales tax, or where the fuel tax is based on the average sale price, the average rate determined by API is sensitive to changes in the price of gasoline. States that fully or partially apply general sales taxes to gasoline: CA, CO, GA, IL, IN, MI, NY; (2) The federal excise tax of $1.0066 per pack and local taxes are not included; (3) Rates are those applicable to off-premise sales of 40% alcohol by volume (a.b.v.) distilled spirits in 750ml containers. Local excise taxes are excluded; (4) Rates are those applicable to off-premise sales of 11% a.b.v. non-carbonated wine in 750ml containers; (5) Rates are those applicable to off-premise sales of 4.7% a.b.v. beer in 12 ounce containers; (l) Different rates also applicable to alcohol content, place of production, size of container, place purchased (on- or off-premise or on board airlines) or type of wine (carbonated, vermouth, etc.); (q) Different rates also applicable according to alcohol content, place of production, size of container, or place purchased (on- or off-premise or onboard airlines).
Source: Tax Foundation, 2019 Facts & Figures: How Does Your State Compare?

State Business Tax Climate Index Rankings

State	Overall Rank	Corporate Tax Rank	Individual Income Tax Rank	Sales Tax Rank	Unemployment Insurance Tax Rank	Property Tax Rank
Wisconsin	32	35	39	8	41	21

Note: The index is a measure of how each state's tax laws affect economic performance. The lower the rank, the more favorable a state's tax system is for business. States without a given tax are given a ranking of 1. The scores/rankings for the District of Columbia do not affect other states. The 2019 index represents the tax climate as of July 1, 2018.
Source: Tax Foundation, State Business Tax Climate Index 2019

COMMERCIAL UTILITIES

Typical Monthly Electric Bills

Area	Commercial Service ($/month) 1,500 kWh	40 kW demand 14,000 kWh	Industrial Service ($/month) 1,000 kW demand 200,000 kWh	50,000 kW demand 32,500,000 kWh
City	177	1,364	21,694	2,014,666
Average[1]	203	1,619	25,886	2,540,077

Note: Figures are based on annualized rates; (1) Average based on 187 utilities surveyed
Source: Edison Electric Institute, Typical Bills and Average Rates Report, Summer 2018

TRANSPORTATION

Means of Transportation to Work

| Area | Car/Truck/Van | | Public Transportation | | | Bicycle | Walked | Other Means | Worked at Home |
	Drove Alone	Car-pooled	Bus	Subway	Railroad				
City	79.2	10.3	1.3	0.0	0.0	0.6	3.1	2.2	3.2
MSA[1]	83.3	8.0	0.6	0.0	0.0	0.3	2.3	1.2	4.3
U.S.	76.4	9.2	2.5	1.9	0.6	0.6	2.7	1.3	4.7

Note: Figures are percentages and cover workers 16 years of age and older; (1) Figures cover the Green Bay, WI Metropolitan Statistical Area—see Appendix B for areas included
Source: U.S. Census Bureau, 2013-2017 American Community Survey 5-Year Estimates

Travel Time to Work

Area	Less Than 10 Minutes	10 to 19 Minutes	20 to 29 Minutes	30 to 44 Minutes	45 to 59 Minutes	60 to 89 Minutes	90 Minutes or More
City	18.1	48.4	19.0	7.5	3.8	1.8	1.4
MSA[1]	17.9	39.4	22.0	12.9	4.3	2.1	1.5
U.S.	12.7	28.9	20.9	20.5	8.1	6.2	2.7

Note: Note: Figures are percentages and include workers 16 years old and over; (1) Figures cover the Green Bay, WI Metropolitan Statistical Area—see Appendix B for areas included
Source: U.S. Census Bureau, 2013-2017 American Community Survey 5-Year Estimates

Freeway Travel Time Index

Area	1985	1990	1995	2000	2005	2010	2014
Urban Area Rank[1,2]	n/a	n/a	n/a	n/a	n/a	n/a	n/a
Urban Area Index[1]	n/a	n/a	n/a	n/a	n/a	n/a	n/a
Average Index[3]	1.09	1.11	1.14	1.17	1.20	1.19	1.20

Note: Freeway Travel Time Index—the ratio of travel time in the peak period to the travel time at free-flow conditions. For example, a value of 1.30 indicates a 20-minute free-flow trip takes 26 minutes in the peak (20 minutes x 1.30 = 26 minutes); (1) Data for the Green Bay, WI urban area was not available; (2) Rank is based on 101 urban areas (#1 = highest travel time index); (3) Average of 101 urban areas
Source: Texas Transportation Institute, 2015 Urban Mobility Scorecard, August 2015

Freeway Commuter Stress Index

Area	1985	1990	1995	2000	2005	2010	2014
Urban Area Rank[1,2]	n/a	n/a	n/a	n/a	n/a	n/a	n/a
Urban Area Index[1]	n/a	n/a	n/a	n/a	n/a	n/a	n/a
Average Index[3]	1.13	1.16	1.19	1.22	1.25	1.24	1.25

Note: The Freeway Commuter Stress Index is the same as the Freeway Travel Time Index (see table above) except that it includes only the travel in the peak directions during the peak periods; the TTI includes travel in all directions during the peak period. Thus, the CSI is more indicative of the work trip experienced by each commuter on a daily basis; (1) Data for the Green Bay, WI urban area was not available; (2) Rank is based on 101 urban areas (#1 = highest travel time index); (3) Average of 101 urban areas
Source: Texas Transportation Institute, 2015 Urban Mobility Scorecard, August 2015

Public Transportation

Agency Name / Mode of Transportation	Vehicles Operated in Maximum Service[1]	Annual Unlinked Passenger Trips[2] (in thous.)	Annual Passenger Miles[3] (in thous.)
Green Bay Metro			
Bus (directly operated)	24	1,242.9	3,917.6
Demand Response (purchased transportation)	12	38.5	294.5

Note: (1) The number of revenue vehicles operated by the given mode and type of service to meet the annual maximum service requirement. This is the revenue vehicle count during the peak season of the year; on the week and day that maximum service is provided. Vehicles operated in maximum service (VOMS) exclude atypical days and one-time special events; (2) The number of passengers who boarded public transportation vehicles. Passengers are counted each time they board a vehicle no matter how many vehicles they use to travel from their origin to their destination. (3) The sum of the distances ridden by all passengers during the entire fiscal year.
Source: Federal Transit Administration, National Transit Database, 2017

Air Transportation

Airport Name and Code / Type of Service	Passenger Airlines[1]	Passenger Enplanements	Freight Carriers[2]	Freight (lbs)
Austin-Bergstrom International (GRB)				
Domestic service (U.S. carriers - 2018)	18	313,955	6	100,205
International service (U.S. carriers - 2017)	1	66	1	5,373

Note: (1) Includes all U.S.-based major, minor and commuter airlines that carried at least one passenger during the year; (2) Includes all U.S.-based airlines and freight carriers that transported at least one pound of freight during the year.
Source: Bureau of Transportation Statistics, The Intermodal Transportation Database, Air Carriers: T-100 Domestic Market (U.S. Carriers), 2018; Bureau of Transportation Statistics, The Intermodal Transportation Database, Air Carriers: T-100 International Market (U.S. Carriers), 2017

Other Transportation Statistics

Major Highways:	I-43
Amtrak Service:	Bus connection
Major Waterways/Ports:	Green Bay

Source: Amtrak.com; Google Maps

BUSINESSES

Major Business Headquarters

Company Name	Industry	Rankings Fortune[1]	Rankings Forbes[2]
Schreiber Foods	Food, Drink & Tobacco	-	74
ShopKo Stores	Retailing	-	128

Note: (1) Companies that produce a 10-K are ranked 1 to 500 based on 2017 revenue; (2) All private companies with at least $2 billion in annual revenue through the end of their most current fiscal year are ranked 1 to 229; companies listed are headquartered in the city; dashes indicate no ranking
Source: Fortune, "Fortune 500," June 2018; Forbes, "America's Largest Private Companies," 2018 Rankings

Minority- and Women-Owned Businesses

Group	All Firms Firms	All Firms Sales ($000)	Firms with Paid Employees Firms	Firms with Paid Employees Sales ($000)	Firms with Paid Employees Employees	Firms with Paid Employees Payroll ($000)
AIAN[1]	115	9,412	4	(s)	20 - 99	(s)
Asian	188	15,580	18	12,252	76	6,993
Black	225	8,788	3	4,982	104	2,161
Hispanic	138	13,471	23	(s)	100 - 249	(s)
NHOPI[2]	n/a	n/a	n/a	n/a	n/a	n/a
Women	1,753	244,342	213	206,608	2,681	70,498
All Firms	7,022	15,846,453	1,806	15,592,438	54,522	2,503,556

Note: Figures cover firms located in the city; minority- and women-owned business are defined as firms in which the corresponding group own 51% or more of the stock or equity of the company; (1) American Indian and Alaska Native; (2) Native Hawaiian and Other Pacific Islander; (s) estimates are suppressed when publication standards are not met; n/a not available
Source: U.S. Census Bureau, 2012 Economic Census, Survey of Business Owners

HOTELS & CONVENTION CENTERS

Hotels, Motels and Vacation Rentals

Area	5 Star Num.	5 Star Pct.[3]	4 Star Num.	4 Star Pct.[3]	3 Star Num.	3 Star Pct.[3]	2 Star Num.	2 Star Pct.[3]	1 Star Num.	1 Star Pct.[3]	Not Rated Num.	Not Rated Pct.[3]
City[1]	0	0.0	1	0.5	38	19.9	60	31.4	1	0.5	91	47.6
Total[2]	286	0.4	5,236	7.1	16,715	22.6	10,259	13.9	293	0.4	41,056	55.6

Note: (1) Figures cover Green Bay and vicinity; (2) Figures cover all 100 cities in this book; (3) Percentage of hotels which have a given star rating; Star ratings are determined by expedia.com and offer an indication of the general quality of a particular hotel.
Source: www.expedia.com, April 3, 2019

Major Convention Centers

Name	Overall Space (sq. ft.)	Exhibit Space (sq. ft.)	Meeting Space (sq. ft.)	Meeting Rooms
KI Convention Center	80,000	35,000	n/a	19

Note: Table includes convention centers located in the Green Bay, WI metro area; n/a not available
Source: Original research

Living Environment

COST OF LIVING

Cost of Living Index

Composite Index	Groceries	Housing	Utilities	Trans-portation	Health Care	Misc. Goods/Services
89.6	87.9	81.1	93.4	93.4	102.6	93.9

Note: The Cost of Living Index measures regional differences in the cost of consumer goods and services, excluding taxes and non-consumer expenditures, for professional and managerial households in the top income quintile. It is based on more than 50,000 prices covering almost 60 different items for which prices are collected three times a year by chambers of commerce, economic development organizations or university applied economic centers in each participating urban area. The numbers shown should be read as a percentage above or below the national average of 100. For example, a value of 115.4 in the groceries column indicates that grocery prices are 15.4% higher than the national average. Small differences in the index numbers should not be interpreted as significant; Figures cover the Green Bay WI urban area.
Source: The Council for Community and Economic Research, ACCRA Cost of Living Index, 2018

Grocery Prices

Area[1]	T-Bone Steak ($/pound)	Frying Chicken ($/pound)	Whole Milk ($/half gal.)	Eggs ($/dozen)	Orange Juice ($/64 oz.)	Coffee ($/11.5 oz.)
City[2]	13.06	1.41	1.70	1.08	3.31	4.35
Avg.	11.35	1.42	1.94	1.81	3.52	4.35
Min.	7.45	0.92	0.80	0.75	2.72	3.06
Max.	15.05	2.76	4.18	4.00	5.36	8.20

Note: (1) Values for the local area are compared with the average, minimum and maximum values for all 291 areas in the Cost of Living Index; (2) Figures cover the Green Bay WI urban area; T-Bone Steak (price per pound); Frying Chicken (price per pound, whole fryer); Whole Milk (half gallon carton); Eggs (price per dozen, Grade A, large); Orange Juice (64 oz. Tropicana or Florida Natural); Coffee (11.5 oz. can, vacuum-packed, Maxwell House, Hills Bros, or Folgers).
Source: The Council for Community and Economic Research, ACCRA Cost of Living Index, 2018

Housing and Utility Costs

Area[1]	New Home Price ($)	Apartment Rent ($/month)	All Electric ($/month)	Part Electric ($/month)	Other Energy ($/month)	Telephone ($/month)
City[2]	286,068	805	-	81.59	70.58	172.90
Avg.	347,000	1,087	165.93	100.16	67.73	178.70
Min.	200,468	500	93.58	25.64	26.78	163.10
Max.	1,901,222	4,888	388.65	246.86	332.81	197.70

Note: (1) Values for the local area are compared with the average, minimum and maximum values for all 291 areas in the Cost of Living Index; (2) Figures cover the Green Bay WI urban area; New Home Price (2,400 sf living area, 8,000 sf lot, in urban area with full utilities); Apartment Rent (950 sf 2 bedroom/1.5 or 2 bath, unfurnished, excluding all utilities except water); All Electric (average monthly cost for an all-electric home); Part Electric (average monthly cost for a part-electric home); Other Energy (average monthly cost for natural gas, fuel oil, coal, wood, and any other forms of energy except electricity); Telephone (price includes the base monthly rate plus taxes and fees for three lines of mobile phone service).
Source: The Council for Community and Economic Research, ACCRA Cost of Living Index, 2018

Health Care, Transportation, and Other Costs

Area[1]	Doctor ($/visit)	Dentist ($/visit)	Optometrist ($/visit)	Gasoline ($/gallon)	Beauty Salon ($/visit)	Men's Shirt ($)
City[2]	143.22	89.31	58.89	2.29	22.06	30.86
Avg.	110.71	95.11	103.74	2.61	37.48	32.03
Min.	33.60	62.55	54.63	1.89	17.00	11.44
Max.	195.97	153.93	225.79	3.59	71.88	58.64

Note: (1) Values for the local area are compared with the average, minimum and maximum values for all 291 areas in the Cost of Living Index; (2) Figures cover the Green Bay WI urban area; Doctor (general practitioners routine exam of an established patient); Dentist (adult teeth cleaning and periodic oral examination); Optometrist (full vision eye exam for established adult patient); Gasoline (one gallon regular unleaded, national brand, including all taxes, cash price at self-service pump if available); Beauty Salon (woman's shampoo, trim, and blow-dry); Men's Shirt (cotton/polyester dress shirt, pinpoint weave, long sleeves).
Source: The Council for Community and Economic Research, ACCRA Cost of Living Index, 2018

HOUSING

House Price Index (HPI)

Area	National Ranking[2]	Quarterly Change (%)	One-Year Change (%)	Five-Year Change (%)
MSA[1]	71	0.51	7.79	27.00
U.S.[3]	–	1.12	5.73	32.81

Note: The HPI is a weighted repeat sales index. It measures average price changes in repeat sales or refinancings on the same properties. This information is obtained by reviewing repeat mortgage transactions on single-family properties whose mortgages have been purchased or securitized by Fannie Mae or Freddie Mac in January 1975; (1) Figures cover the Green Bay, WI Metropolitan Statistical Area—see Appendix B for areas included; (2) Rankings are based on annual percentage change for all metro areas containing at least 15,000 transactions over the last 10 years and ranges from 1 to 245; (3) figures based on a weighted average of Census Division estimates using a seasonally adjusted, purchase-only index; all figures are for the period ending December 31, 2018
Source: Federal Housing Finance Agency, House Price Index, February 26, 2019

Median Single-Family Home Prices

Area	2016	2017	2018P	Percent Change 2017 to 2018
MSA[1]	150.6	163.2	177.3	8.6
U.S. Average	235.5	248.8	261.6	5.1

Note: Figures are median sales prices of existing single-family homes in thousands of dollars; (p) preliminary; (1) Figures cover the Green Bay, WI Metropolitan Statistical Area—see Appendix B for areas included
Source: National Association of Realtors, Median Sales Price of Existing Single-Family Homes for Metropolitan Areas, 4th Quarter 2018

Qualifying Income Based on Median Sales Price of Existing Single-Family Homes

Area	With 5% Down ($)	With 10% Down ($)	With 20% Down ($)
MSA[1]	43,256	40,979	36,426
U.S. Average	62,954	59,640	53,013

Note: Figures are preliminary; Qualifying income is based on a mortgage rate of 4.9%. Monthly principal and interest payment is limited to 25% of income; (1) Figures cover the Green Bay, WI Metropolitan Statistical Area—see Appendix B for areas included
Source: National Association of Realtors, Qualifying Income Based on Median Sales Price of Existing Single-Family Homes for Metropolitan Areas, 4th Quarter 2018

Median Apartment Condo-Coop Home Prices

Area	2016	2017	2018P	Percent Change 2017 to 2018
MSA[1]	n/a	n/a	n/a	n/a
U.S. Average	220.7	234.3	241.0	2.9

Note: Figures are median sales prices of existing apartment condo-coop homes in thousands of dollars; (p) preliminary; n/a not available; (1) Figures cover the Green Bay, WI Metropolitan Statistical Area—see Appendix B for areas included
Source: National Association of Realtors, Median Sales Price of Existing Apartment Condo-Coop Homes for Metropolitan Areas, 4th Quarter 2018

Home Value Distribution

Area	Under $50,000	$50,000 -$99,999	$100,000 -$149,999	$150,000 -$199,999	$200,000 -$299,999	$300,000 -$499,999	$500,000 -$999,999	$1,000,000 or more
City	3.5	24.5	37.2	17.9	11.0	4.4	1.1	0.3
MSA[1]	4.4	13.7	25.3	23.3	21.7	9.1	2.2	0.4
U.S.	8.3	13.9	14.7	14.6	18.7	17.3	9.7	2.7

Note: Figures are percentages and cover owner-occupied housing units; (1) Figures cover the Green Bay, WI Metropolitan Statistical Area—see Appendix B for areas included
Source: U.S. Census Bureau, 2013-2017 American Community Survey 5-Year Estimates

Homeownership Rate

Area	2010 (%)	2011 (%)	2012 (%)	2013 (%)	2014 (%)	2015 (%)	2016 (%)	2017 (%)	2018 (%)
MSA[1]	n/a	n/a	n/a	n/a	n/a	n/a	n/a	n/a	n/a
U.S.	66.9	66.1	65.4	65.1	64.5	63.7	63.4	63.9	64.4

Note: (1) Figures cover the Green Bay, WI Metropolitan Statistical Area—see Appendix B for areas included; n/a not available
Source: U.S. Census Bureau, Housing Vacancies and Homeownership Annual Statistics: 2010-2018

Year Housing Structure Built

Area	2010 or Later	2000 -2009	1990 -1999	1980 -1989	1970 -1979	1960 -1969	1950 -1959	1940 -1949	Before 1940	Median Year
City	1.3	7.4	9.7	12.8	17.0	13.7	14.3	6.6	17.3	1969
MSA[1]	3.2	15.8	16.1	12.1	15.9	10.0	9.3	4.5	13.1	1978
U.S.	3.2	14.5	14.0	13.6	15.5	10.8	10.5	5.1	12.9	1977

Note: Figures are percentages except for Median Year; Note: (1) Figures cover the Green Bay, WI Metropolitan Statistical Area—see Appendix B for areas included
Source: U.S. Census Bureau, 2013-2017 American Community Survey 5-Year Estimates

Gross Monthly Rent

Area	Under $500	$500 -$999	$1,000 -$1,499	$1,500 -$1,999	$2,000 -$2,499	$2,500 -$2,999	$3,000 and up	Median ($)
City	16.6	70.5	11.5	0.9	0.2	0.0	0.3	682
MSA[1]	13.2	70.0	14.8	1.3	0.4	0.0	0.3	736
U.S.	10.5	41.1	28.7	11.7	4.5	1.8	1.7	982

Note: Figures are percentages except for Median; Gross rent is the contract rent plus the estimated average monthly cost of utilities (electricity, gas, and water and sewer) and fuels (oil, coal, kerosene, wood, etc.) if these are paid by the renter (or paid for the renter by someone else); (1) Figures cover the Green Bay, WI Metropolitan Statistical Area—see Appendix B for areas included
Source: U.S. Census Bureau, 2013-2017 American Community Survey 5-Year Estimates

HEALTH

Health Risk Factors

Category	MSA[1] (%)	U.S. (%)
Adults aged 18–64 who have any kind of health care coverage	n/a	87.3
Adults who reported being in good or better health	n/a	82.4
Adults who have been told they have high blood cholesterol	n/a	33.0
Adults who have been told they have high blood pressure	n/a	32.3
Adults who are current smokers	n/a	17.1
Adults who currently use E-cigarettes	n/a	4.6
Adults who currently use chewing tobacco, snuff, or snus	n/a	4.0
Adults who are heavy drinkers[2]	n/a	6.3
Adults who are binge drinkers[3]	n/a	17.4
Adults who are overweight (BMI 25.0 - 29.9)	n/a	35.3
Adults who are obese (BMI 30.0 - 99.8)	n/a	31.3
Adults who participated in any physical activities in the past month	n/a	74.4
Adults who always or nearly always wears a seat belt	n/a	94.3

Note: n/a not available; (1) Figures cover the Green Bay, WI Metropolitan Statistical Area—see Appendix B for areas included; (2) Heavy drinkers are classified as adult men having more than 14 drinks per week and adult women having more than 7 drinks per week; (3) Binge drinkers are classified as males having five or more drinks on one occasion or females having four or more drinks on one occasion
Source: Centers for Disease Control and Prevention, Behaviorial Risk Factor Surveillance System, SMART: Selected Metropolitan Area Risk Trends, 2017

Acute and Chronic Health Conditions

Category	MSA[1] (%)	U.S. (%)
Adults who have ever been told they had a heart attack	n/a	4.2
Adults who have ever been told they have angina or coronary heart disease	n/a	3.9
Adults who have ever been told they had a stroke	n/a	3.0
Adults who have ever been told they have asthma	n/a	14.2
Adults who have ever been told they have arthritis	n/a	24.9
Adults who have ever been told they have diabetes[2]	n/a	10.5
Adults who have ever been told they had skin cancer	n/a	6.2
Adults who have ever been told they had any other types of cancer	n/a	7.1
Adults who have ever been told they have COPD	n/a	6.5
Adults who have ever been told they have kidney disease	n/a	3.0
Adults who have ever been told they have a form of depression	n/a	20.5

Note: n/a not available; (1) Figures cover the Green Bay, WI Metropolitan Statistical Area—see Appendix B for areas included; (2) Figures do not include pregnancy-related, borderline, or pre-diabetes
Source: Centers for Disease Control and Prevention, Behaviorial Risk Factor Surveillance System, SMART: Selected Metropolitan Area Risk Trends, 2017

Health Screening and Vaccination Rates

Category	MSA[1] (%)	U.S. (%)
Adults aged 65+ who have had flu shot within the past year	n/a	60.7
Adults aged 65+ who have ever had a pneumonia vaccination	n/a	75.4
Adults who have ever been tested for HIV	n/a	36.1
Adults who have ever had the shingles or zoster vaccine?	n/a	28.9
Adults who have had their blood cholesterol checked within the last five years	n/a	85.9

Note: n/a not available; (1) Figures cover the Green Bay, WI Metropolitan Statistical Area—see Appendix B for areas included.
Source: Centers for Disease Control and Prevention, Behaviorial Risk Factor Surveillance System, SMART: Selected Metropolitan Area Risk Trends, 2017

Disability Status

Category	MSA[1] (%)	U.S. (%)
Adults who reported being deaf	n/a	6.7
Are you blind or have serious difficulty seeing, even when wearing glasses?	n/a	4.5
Are you limited in any way in any of your usual activities due of arthritis?	n/a	12.9
Do you have difficulty doing errands alone?	n/a	6.8
Do you have difficulty dressing or bathing?	n/a	3.6
Do you have serious difficulty concentrating/remembering/making decisions?	n/a	10.7
Do you have serious difficulty walking or climbing stairs?	n/a	13.6

Note: n/a not available; (1) Figures cover the Green Bay, WI Metropolitan Statistical Area—see Appendix B for areas included.
Source: Centers for Disease Control and Prevention, Behaviorial Risk Factor Surveillance System, SMART: Selected Metropolitan Area Risk Trends, 2017

Mortality Rates for the Top 10 Causes of Death in the U.S.

ICD-10[a] Sub-Chapter	ICD-10[a] Code	Age-Adjusted Mortality Rate[1] per 100,000 population	
		County[2]	U.S.
Malignant neoplasms	C00-C97	153.9	155.5
Ischaemic heart diseases	I20-I25	106.5	94.8
Other forms of heart disease	I30-I51	50.0	52.9
Chronic lower respiratory diseases	J40-J47	29.2	41.0
Cerebrovascular diseases	I60-I69	32.5	37.5
Other degenerative diseases of the nervous system	G30-G31	42.5	35.0
Other external causes of accidental injury	W00-X59	33.3	33.7
Organic, including symptomatic, mental disorders	F01-F09	38.7	31.0
Hypertensive diseases	I10-I15	17.6	21.9
Diabetes mellitus	E10-E14	16.7	21.2

Note: (a) ICD-10 = International Classification of Diseases 10th Revision; (1) Mortality rates are a three year average covering 2015-2017; (2) Figures cover Brown County.
Source: Centers for Disease Control and Prevention, National Center for Health Statistics. Underlying Cause of Death 1999-2017 on CDC WONDER Online Database

Mortality Rates for Selected Causes of Death

ICD-10[a] Sub-Chapter	ICD-10[a] Code	Age-Adjusted Mortality Rate[1] per 100,000 population	
		County[2]	U.S.
Assault	X85-Y09	Unreliable	5.9
Diseases of the liver	K70-K76	12.8	14.1
Human immunodeficiency virus (HIV) disease	B20-B24	Suppressed	1.8
Influenza and pneumonia	J09-J18	11.0	14.3
Intentional self-harm	X60-X84	17.9	13.6
Malnutrition	E40-E46	Suppressed	1.6
Obesity and other hyperalimentation	E65-E68	2.3	2.1
Renal failure	N17-N19	11.5	13.0
Transport accidents	V01-V99	8.7	12.4
Viral hepatitis	B15-B19	Suppressed	1.6

Note: (a) ICD-10 = International Classification of Diseases 10th Revision; (1) Mortality rates are a three year average covering 2015-2017; (2) Figures cover Brown County; Data are suppressed when the data meet the criteria for confidentiality constraints; Mortality rates are flagged as unreliable when the rate would be calculated with a numerator of 20 or less.
Source: Centers for Disease Control and Prevention, National Center for Health Statistics. Underlying Cause of Death 1999-2017 on CDC WONDER Online Database

Health Insurance Coverage

Area	With Health Insurance	With Private Health Insurance	With Public Health Insurance	Without Health Insurance	Population Under Age 18 Without Health Insurance
City	91.3	64.4	37.2	8.7	4.0
MSA[1]	93.8	74.3	30.8	6.2	3.6
U.S.	89.5	67.2	33.8	10.5	5.7

Note: Figures are percentages that cover the civilian noninstitutionalized population; (1) Figures cover the Green Bay, WI Metropolitan Statistical Area—see Appendix B for areas included
Source: U.S. Census Bureau, 2013-2017 American Community Survey 5-Year Estimates

Number of Medical Professionals

Area	MDs[3]	DOs[3,4]	Dentists	Podiatrists	Chiropractors	Optometrists
County[1] (number)	626	58	199	9	114	49
County[1] (rate[2])	241.2	22.3	75.9	3.4	43.5	18.7
U.S. (rate[2])	279.3	23.0	68.4	6.0	27.1	16.2

Note: Data as of 2017 unless noted; (1) Data covers Brown County; (2) Rate per 100,000 population; (3) Data as of 2016 and includes all active, non-federal physicians; (4) Doctor of Osteopathic Medicine
Source: U.S. Department of Health and Human Services, Health Resources and Services Administration, Bureau of Health Professions, Area Resource File (ARF) 2017-2018

EDUCATION

Public School District Statistics

District Name	Schls	Pupils	Pupil/ Teacher Ratio	Minority Pupils[1] (%)	Free Lunch Eligible[2] (%)	IEP[3] (%)
Ashwaubenon School District	5	3,339	15.7	22.6	23.5	12.4
Green Bay Area Public SD	42	21,149	14.1	53.6	52.4	15.3
Howard-Suamico School District	9	6,173	16.6	10.9	13.0	11.8

Note: Table includes school districts with 2,000 or more students; (1) Percentage of students that are not non-Hispanic white; (2) Percentage of students that are eligible for the free lunch program; (3) Percentage of students that have an Individualized Education Program.
Source: U.S. Department of Education, National Center for Education Statistics, Common Core of Data, Local Education Agency (School District) Universe Survey: School Year 2016-2017; U.S. Department of Education, National Center for Education Statistics, Common Core of Data, Public Elementary/Secondary School Universe Survey: School Year 2016-2017

Highest Level of Education

Area	Less than H.S.	H.S. Diploma	Some College, No Deg.	Associate Degree	Bachelor's Degree	Master's Degree	Prof. School Degree	Doctorate Degree
City	12.9	31.5	19.4	11.3	18.0	5.1	1.2	0.6
MSA[1]	8.6	32.7	19.5	12.1	19.2	5.9	1.4	0.6
U.S.	12.7	27.3	20.8	8.3	19.1	8.4	2.0	1.4

Note: Figures cover persons age 25 and over; (1) Figures cover the Green Bay, WI Metropolitan Statistical Area—see Appendix B for areas included
Source: U.S. Census Bureau, 2013-2017 American Community Survey 5-Year Estimates

Educational Attainment by Race

Area	High School Graduate or Higher (%)					Bachelor's Degree or Higher (%)				
	Total	White	Black	Asian	Hisp.[2]	Total	White	Black	Asian	Hisp.[2]
City	87.1	90.3	85.9	69.5	47.8	24.9	27.3	9.6	21.6	6.2
MSA[1]	91.4	93.0	86.7	80.5	55.4	27.1	27.9	16.2	41.2	9.0
U.S.	87.3	89.3	84.9	86.5	66.7	30.9	32.2	20.6	52.7	15.2

Note: Figures shown cover persons 25 years old and over; (1) Figures cover the Green Bay, WI Metropolitan Statistical Area—see Appendix B for areas included; (2) People of Hispanic origin can be of any race
Source: U.S. Census Bureau, 2013-2017 American Community Survey 5-Year Estimates

School Enrollment by Grade and Control

Area	Preschool (%)		Kindergarten (%)		Grades 1 - 4 (%)		Grades 5 - 8 (%)		Grades 9 - 12 (%)	
	Public	Private	Public	Private	Public	Private	Public	Private	Public	Private
City	67.7	32.3	86.1	13.9	89.8	10.2	89.4	10.6	91.1	8.9
MSA[1]	68.1	31.9	85.7	14.3	89.0	11.0	90.1	9.9	94.0	6.0
U.S.	58.8	41.2	87.7	12.3	89.7	10.3	89.6	10.4	90.3	9.7

Note: Figures shown cover persons 3 years old and over; (1) Figures cover the Green Bay, WI Metropolitan Statistical Area—see Appendix B for areas included
Source: U.S. Census Bureau, 2013-2017 American Community Survey 5-Year Estimates

Average Salaries of Public School Classroom Teachers

Area	2016		2017		Change from 2016 to 2017	
	Dollars	Rank[1]	Dollars	Rank[1]	Percent	Rank[2]
Wisconsin	54,115	24	54,998	24	1.6	23
U.S. Average	58,479	–	59,660	–	2.0	–

Note: (1) Rank ranges from 1 to 51 where 1 indicates highest salary; (2) Rank ranges from 1 to 51 where 1 indicates highest percent change.
Source: National Education Association, Rankings & Estimates: Rankings of the States 2017 and Estimates of School Statistics 2018

Higher Education

Four-Year Colleges			Two-Year Colleges			Medical Schools[1]	Law Schools[2]	Voc/ Tech[3]
Public	Private Non-profit	Private For-profit	Public	Private Non-profit	Private For-profit			
1	1	1	1	0	0	0	0	1

Note: Figures cover institutions located within the city limits and include main campuses only; (1) includes schools accredited by the Liaison Committee on Medical Education and the American Osteopathic Association's Commission on Osteopathic College Accreditation; (2) includes ABA-accredited schools, schools with provisional ABA accreditation, and state accredited schools; (3) includes all schools with programs that are less than 2 years.
Source: National Center for Education Statistics, Integrated Postsecondary Education System (IPEDS), 2017-18; Wikipedia, List of Medical Schools in the United States, accessed April 3, 2019; Wikipedia, List of Law Schools in the United States, accessed April 3, 2019

According to *U.S. News & World Report,* the Green Bay, WI metro area is home to one of the best liberal arts colleges in the U.S.: **St. Norbert College** (#127 tie). The indicators used to capture academic quality fall into a number of categories: assessment by administrators at peer institutions; retention of students; faculty resources; student selectivity; financial resources; alumni giving; high school counselor ratings of colleges; and graduation rate. *U.S. News & World Report, "America's Best Colleges 2019"*

PRESIDENTIAL ELECTION

2016 Presidential Election Results

Area	Clinton	Trump	Johnson	Stein	Other
Brown County	41.4	52.1	3.9	1.1	1.6
U.S.	48.0	45.9	3.3	1.1	1.7

Note: Results are percentages and may not add to 100% due to rounding
Source: Dave Leip's Atlas of U.S. Presidential Elections

EMPLOYERS

Major Employers

Company Name	Industry
American Foods Group	Food manufacturing
APAC Customer Services	Business management
Associated Bank	Financial services
Aurora Health Care	Healthcare
Bellin Health	Healthcare
Georgia-Pacific	Paper manufacturing
Green Bay Packaging	Paper manufacturing
Green Bay Packers	NFL franchise
H.J. Martin and Son	Interior design
JBS	Food manufacturing
Nicolet National Bank	Financial services
Procter & Gamble Paper Products	Paper manufacturing
Schreiber Foods	Food manufacturing
Schwabe North America	Health products
St. Mary's Hospital Medical Center	Healthcare
St. Vincent Hospital	Healthcare
Wal-Mart Stores	Retail
Wisconsin Public Service	Utilities

Note: Companies shown are located within the Green Bay, WI Metropolitan Statistical Area.
Source: Hoovers.com; Wikipedia

PUBLIC SAFETY

Crime Rate

Area	All Crimes	Violent Crimes				Property Crimes		
		Murder	Rape[3]	Robbery	Aggrav. Assault	Burglary	Larceny-Theft	Motor Vehicle Theft
City	2,511.1	0.0	72.2	61.7	338.9	304.8	1,650.0	83.5
Suburbs[1]	1,131.9	0.0	26.5	4.7	68.4	116.3	885.8	30.2
Metro[2]	1,585.5	0.0	41.5	23.4	157.4	178.3	1,137.1	47.8
U.S.	2,756.1	5.3	41.7	98.0	248.9	430.4	1,694.4	237.4

Note: Figures are crimes per 100,000 population; (1) All areas within the metro area that are located outside the city limits; (2) Figures cover the Green Bay, WI Metropolitan Statistical Area—see Appendix B for areas included; (3) The city and U.S. figures shown were reported using the revised Uniform Crime Reporting (UCR) definition of rape. The suburban and metro area figures shown are an aggregate total of the data submitted using both the revised and legacy UCR definitions.
Source: FBI Uniform Crime Reports, 2017

Hate Crimes

Area	Number of Quarters Reported	Number of Incidents per Bias Motivation					
		Race/Ethnicity/Ancestry	Religion	Sexual Orientation	Disability	Gender	Gender Identity
City	4	0	0	0	0	0	0
U.S.	4	4,131	1,564	1,130	116	46	119

Source: Federal Bureau of Investigation, Hate Crime Statistics 2017

Identity Theft Consumer Reports

Area	Reports	Reports per 100,000 Population	Rank[2]
MSA[1]	201	63	302
U.S.	444,602	135	-

Note: (1) Figures cover the Green Bay, WI Metropolitan Statistical Area—see Appendix B for areas included; (2) Rank ranges from 1 to 389 where 1 indicates greatest number of identity theft reports per 100,000 population
Source: Federal Trade Commission, Consumer Sentinel Network Data Book for January–December 2018

Fraud and Other Consumer Reports

Area	Reports	Reports per 100,000 Population	Rank[2]
MSA[1]	1,345	423	291
U.S.	2,552,917	776	-

Note: (1) Figures cover the Green Bay, WI Metropolitan Statistical Area—see Appendix B for areas included; (2) Rank ranges from 1 to 389 where 1 indicates greatest number of fraud and other consumer reports per 100,000 population
Source: Federal Trade Commission, Consumer Sentinel Network Data Book for January–December 2018

SPORTS

Professional Sports Teams

Team Name	League	Year Established
Green Bay Packers	National Football League (NFL)	1921

Note: Includes teams located in the Green Bay, WI Metropolitan Statistical Area.
Source: Wikipedia, Major Professional Sports Teams of the United States and Canada, April 5, 2019

CLIMATE

Average and Extreme Temperatures

Temperature	Jan	Feb	Mar	Apr	May	Jun	Jul	Aug	Sep	Oct	Nov	Dec	Yr.
Extreme High (°F)	50	55	77	89	91	98	99	99	95	88	72	62	99
Average High (°F)	23	27	38	54	67	76	81	78	70	58	42	28	54
Average Temp. (°F)	15	19	29	44	55	65	70	68	59	48	34	21	44
Average Low (°F)	6	10	21	34	44	53	58	56	48	38	26	13	34
Extreme Low (°F)	-31	-26	-29	7	21	32	40	38	24	15	-9	-27	-31

Note: Figures cover the years 1949-1990
Source: National Climatic Data Center, International Station Meteorological Climate Summary, 9/96

Average Precipitation/Snowfall/Humidity

Precip./Humidity	Jan	Feb	Mar	Apr	May	Jun	Jul	Aug	Sep	Oct	Nov	Dec	Yr.
Avg. Precip. (in.)	1.1	1.1	1.9	2.6	2.9	3.2	3.3	3.3	3.2	2.2	2.0	1.4	28.3
Avg. Snowfall (in.)	11	8	9	2	Tr	0	0	0	Tr	Tr	5	11	46
Avg. Rel. Hum. 6am (%)	77	79	81	79	79	82	86	90	89	85	82	80	83
Avg. Rel. Hum. 3pm (%)	68	65	63	54	52	55	55	58	59	59	67	71	60

Note: Figures cover the years 1949-1990; Tr = Trace amounts (<0.05 in. of rain; <0.5 in. of snow)
Source: National Climatic Data Center, International Station Meteorological Climate Summary, 9/96

Weather Conditions

Temperature			Daytime Sky			Precipitation		
5°F & below	32°F & below	90°F & above	Clear	Partly cloudy	Cloudy	0.01 inch or more precip.	0.1 inch or more snow/ice	Thunder-storms
39	163	7	86	125	154	120	40	33

Note: Figures are average number of days per year and cover the years 1949-1990
Source: National Climatic Data Center, International Station Meteorological Climate Summary, 9/96

HAZARDOUS WASTE

Superfund Sites

The Green Bay, WI metro area is home to three sites on the EPA's Superfund National Priorities List: **Algoma Municipal Landfill** (final); **Better Brite Plating Co. Chrome and Zinc Shops** (final); **Fox River Nrda/Pcb Releases** (proposed). There are a total of 1,390 Superfund sites with a status of proposed or final on the list in the U.S. *U.S. Environmental Protection Agency, National Priorities List, April 5, 2019*

**AIR & WATER
QUALITY**

Air Quality Trends: Ozone

	1990	1995	2000	2005	2010	2012	2014	2015	2016	2017
MSA[1]	n/a	n/a	n/a	n/a	n/a	n/a	n/a	n/a	n/a	n/a
U.S.	0.088	0.089	0.082	0.080	0.073	0.075	0.067	0.068	0.069	0.068

Note: (1) Data covers the Green Bay, WI Metropolitan Statistical Area—see Appendix B for areas included; n/a not available. The values shown are the composite ozone concentration averages among trend sites based on the highest fourth daily maximum 8-hour concentration in parts per million. These trends are based on sites having an adequate record of monitoring data during the trend period. Data from exceptional events are included.
Source: U.S. Environmental Protection Agency, Air Quality Monitoring Information, "Air Quality Trends by City, 1990-2017"

Air Quality Index

Area	Percent of Days when Air Quality was...[2]					AQI Statistics[2]	
	Good	Moderate	Unhealthy for Sensitive Groups	Unhealthy	Very Unhealthy	Maximum	Median
MSA[1]	86.3	13.2	0.5	0.0	0.0	112	37

Note: (1) Data covers the Green Bay, WI Metropolitan Statistical Area—see Appendix B for areas included; (2) Based on 364 days with AQI data in 2017. Air Quality Index (AQI) is an index for reporting daily air quality. EPA calculates the AQI for five major air pollutants regulated by the Clean Air Act: ground-level ozone, particle pollution (aka particulate matter), carbon monoxide, sulfur dioxide, and nitrogen dioxide. The AQI runs from 0 to 500. The higher the AQI value, the greater the level of air pollution and the greater the health concern. There are six AQI categories: "Good" AQI is between 0 and 50. Air quality is considered satisfactory; "Moderate" AQI is between 51 and 100. Air quality is acceptable; "Unhealthy for Sensitive Groups" When AQI values are between 101 and 150, members of sensitive groups may experience health effects; "Unhealthy" When AQI values are between 151 and 200 everyone may begin to experience health effects; "Very Unhealthy" AQI values between 201 and 300 trigger a health alert; "Hazardous" AQI values over 300 trigger warnings of emergency conditions (not shown).
Source: U.S. Environmental Protection Agency, Air Quality Index Report, 2017

Air Quality Index Pollutants

Area	Percent of Days when AQI Pollutant was...[2]					
	Carbon Monoxide	Nitrogen Dioxide	Ozone	Sulfur Dioxide	Particulate Matter 2.5	Particulate Matter 10
MSA[1]	0.0	0.0	60.2	1.4	38.5	0.0

Note: (1) Data covers the Green Bay, WI Metropolitan Statistical Area—see Appendix B for areas included; (2) Based on 364 days with AQI data in 2017. The Air Quality Index (AQI) is an index for reporting daily air quality. EPA calculates the AQI for five major air pollutants regulated by the Clean Air Act: ground-level ozone, particle pollution (also known as particulate matter), carbon monoxide, sulfur dioxide, and nitrogen dioxide. The AQI runs from 0 to 500. The higher the AQI value, the greater the level of air pollution and the greater the health concern.
Source: U.S. Environmental Protection Agency, Air Quality Index Report, 2017

Maximum Air Pollutant Concentrations: Particulate Matter, Ozone, CO and Lead

	Particulate Matter 10 (ug/m^3)	Particulate Matter 2.5 Wtd AM (ug/m^3)	Particulate Matter 2.5 24-Hr (ug/m^3)	Ozone (ppm)	Carbon Monoxide (ppm)	Lead (ug/m^3)
MSA[1] Level	n/a	6.1	16	0.067	n/a	n/a
NAAQS[2]	150	15	35	0.075	9	0.15
Met NAAQS[2]	n/a	Yes	Yes	Yes	n/a	n/a

Note: (1) Data covers the Green Bay, WI Metropolitan Statistical Area—see Appendix B for areas included; Data from exceptional events are included; (2) National Ambient Air Quality Standards; ppm = parts per million; ug/m^3 = micrograms per cubic meter; n/a not available.
Concentrations: Particulate Matter 10 (coarse particulate)—highest second maximum 24-hour concentration; Particulate Matter 2.5 Wtd AM (fine particulate)—highest weighted annual mean concentration; Particulate Matter 2.5 24-Hour (fine particulate)—highest 98th percentile 24-hour concentration; Ozone—highest fourth daily maximum 8-hour concentration; Carbon Monoxide—highest second maximum non-overlapping 8-hour concentration; Lead—maximum running 3-month average
Source: U.S. Environmental Protection Agency, Air Quality Monitoring Information, "Air Quality Statistics by City, 2017"

Maximum Air Pollutant Concentrations: Nitrogen Dioxide and Sulfur Dioxide

	Nitrogen Dioxide AM (ppb)	Nitrogen Dioxide 1-Hr (ppb)	Sulfur Dioxide AM (ppb)	Sulfur Dioxide 1-Hr (ppb)	Sulfur Dioxide 24-Hr (ppb)
MSA[1] Level	n/a	n/a	n/a	11	n/a
NAAQS[2]	53	100	30	75	140
Met NAAQS[2]	n/a	n/a	n/a	Yes	n/a

Note: (1) Data covers the Green Bay, WI Metropolitan Statistical Area—see Appendix B for areas included; Data from exceptional events are included; (2) National Ambient Air Quality Standards; ppm = parts per million; ug/m³ = micrograms per cubic meter; n/a not available.
Concentrations: Nitrogen Dioxide AM—highest arithmetic mean concentration; Nitrogen Dioxide 1-Hr—highest 98th percentile 1-hour daily maximum concentration; Sulfur Dioxide AM—highest annual mean concentration; Sulfur Dioxide 1-Hr—highest 99th percentile 1-hour daily maximum concentration; Sulfur Dioxide 24-Hr—highest second maximum 24-hour concentration
Source: U.S. Environmental Protection Agency, Air Quality Monitoring Information, "Air Quality Statistics by City, 2017"

Drinking Water

Water System Name	Pop. Served	Primary Water Source Type	Violations[1] Health Based	Violations[1] Monitoring/ Reporting
Green Bay Waterworks	104,057	Surface	0	0

Note: (1) Based on violation data from January 1, 2018 to December 31, 2018
Source: U.S. Environmental Protection Agency, Office of Ground Water and Drinking Water, Safe Drinking Water Information System (based on data extracted April 5, 2019)

Indianapolis, Indiana

Background

Indianapolis sits within the boundaries of the Northern manufacturing belt and the midwestern Corn Belt, and its economy reflects both influences. On one side lies the Indianapolis industrial sector, including transportation, airplane and truck parts, paper and rubber products, and computer software. On the other side lies agriculture. Indianapolis is a leading grain market, as well as the largest meat-processing center outside of Chicago.

Despite pollution and other problems of urban decay in the late twentieth century, Indianapolis has made significant strides in this area, completing dozens of major downtown projects, including Dolphin Adventure at the Indianapolis Zoo, Eiteljorg Museum of American Indians and Western Art expansion, Eli Lilly and Company Insulin Finishing Building, the Indianapolis Museum of Art expansion, and Circle Centre, a retail and entertainment complex that draws one million visitors a month.

Known as the "Crossroads of America," Indianapolis is bisected by more interstate highways than any other city in the nation, making it accessible from many locations and within a day's drive of half the country's population. As a result, the city is a popular choice for conventions and offers excellent facilities at the Indiana Convention Center & RCA Dome. The Indianapolis Artsgarden, offering more than 300 free performances and exhibits each year, is linked to the Convention Center by a skywalk, and is a world-class venue for the arts.

The city promotes its living conditions as well as its cultural, recreational, and educational scene. Indianapolis possesses one of the finest children's museums in the United States. The city's 85 parks offer many outdoor activities.

Indianapolis has been called the most underrated food city in the U.S. and the rising (food) star of the Midwest, recognizing Milktooth, Rook, Amelia's, and Bluebeard, all in the Fletcher Place neighborhood. Several Indianapolis chefs and restaurateurs have been semifinalists in the James Beard Foundation Awards in recent years. Microbreweries are quickly becoming a staple in the city. There are now about 50 craft brewers in Indianapolis, with Sun King Brewing being the largest.

Known as the "Racing Capital of the World," Indianapolis hosts the world's three biggest single-day sporting events at the world-famous Indianapolis Motor Speedway: Indy 500; Brickyard 400; and SAP United States Grand Prix. The National Collegiate Athletic Association is also now in Indianapolis, as is the NCAA Hall of Champions. Also, the city's university quarter, housing divisions of Indiana and Purdue Universities, make for a lively learning center.

Indianapolis's Conseco Fieldhouse hosted the Big Ten college basketball tournament from 2008 through 2012. The city hosted the Women's NCAA basketball tournament Final Fours in 2011 and 2016, and the 2012 Super Bowl.

The Indianapolis Art Museum is one of the largest general museums in the United States. Collections include works of Gaugin, Seurat, and Turner. The museum's recent expansion integrates the museum galleries with other properties on its campus, including the Virginia B. Fairbanks Art & Nature Park and the Oldfields-Lilly House.

Indianapolis was initially planned by Alexander Ralston, the American engineer who assisted French architect Pierre L'Enfant in planning Washington, D.C. Thus, like the nation's capital, Indianapolis is laid out on a mile-square grid and is easily navigable. Its centerpiece is Monument Circle, home of the 284-foot Soldiers and Sailors Monument, with a 32-story panoramic view of the Indianapolis skyline.

Indianapolis has a temperate climate, with very warm summers and no dry season. Very cold winter weather sometime occurs with the invasion of continental polar air from northern latitudes. In the summer, tropical air from the Gulf of Mexico brings warm temperatures and moderate humidity.

Rankings

General Rankings

- In its eighth annual survey, *Travel + Leisure* readers nominated their favorite small cities and towns in America—those with 100,000 or fewer residents—voting on numerous attractive features in categories including culture, food and drink, quality of life, style, and people. After 50,000 votes, Indianapolis was ranked #7 among the proposed favorites. *www.travelandleisure.com, "America's Favorite Cities," October 20, 2017*

- Based on more than 425,000 responses, *Condé Nast Traveler* ranked its readers' favorite cities in the U.S. The list was broken into cities over 1 million and cities under 1 million. Indianapolis ranked #15 in the big city category. *Condé Nast Traveler, Readers' Choice Awards 2018, "Best Big Cities in the U.S." October 9, 2018*

- In their sixth annual survey, Livability.com looked at data for more than 1,000 U.S. cities to determine the rankings for Livability's "Top 100 Best Places to Live" in 2019. Indianapolis ranked #75. Criteria: median home value capped at $250,000; affordable living; vibrant economy; education, demographics, health care options. transportation & infrastructure; abundant lifestyle amenities. *Livability.com, "Top 100 Best Places to Live 2019" March 2019*

Business/Finance Rankings

- According to *Business Insider*, the Indianapolis metro area is where startup growth is on the rise. Based on the 2017 Kauffman Index of Growth Entrepreneurship, which measured in-depth national entrepreneurial trends in 40 metro areas, it ranked #10 in highest startup growth. *www.businessinsider.com, "The 21 U.S. Cities with the Highest Startup Growth," October 21, 2017*

- The personal finance site NerdWallet analyzed 183 American metropolitan areas with populations over 250,000 and more than 15,000 businesses to rank where entrepreneurs find the most success. Criteria included area economy, annual income, housing cost, unemployment rate, and the success rate of area businesses. Indianapolis ranked #95. *www.nerdwallet.com, "Best Places to Start a Business," April 27, 2015*

- Based on metro area social media reviews, the employment opinion group Glassdoor surveyed 50 of the largest U.S. metro areas and equally weighed cost of living, hiring opportunity, and job satisfaction to compose a list of "25 Best Cities for Jobs." Median pay and home value, in-demand jobs and number of current job openings was also factored in. The Indianapolis metro area was ranked #3 in overall job satisfaction. *www.glassdoor.com, "Best Cities for Jobs," October 16, 2018*

- In a survey of economic confidence in the nation's 50 largest metropolitan areas conducted January–December 2014, the Indianapolis metro area placed #42, according to Gallup's 2014 Economic Confidence Index. *Gallup, "San Jose and San Francisco Lead in Economic Confidence," March 19, 2015*

- NerdWallet.com identified the 10 most promising cities for job seekers of the nation's 100 largest cities. Indianapolis was ranked #40. Criteria: job availability; annual salary; workforce growth; affordability. *NerdWallet.com, "Best Cities for Job Seekers in 2017," December 19, 2016*

- The Brookings Institution ranked the nation's largest cities based on income inequality. Indianapolis was ranked #72 (#1 = greatest inequality). Criteria: the "95/20 ratio," a figure representing the income at which a household earns more than 95 percent of all other households, divided by the income at which a household earns more than only 20 percent of all other households. *Brookings Institution, "Household Income Inequality, Largest Cities of 97 Large U.S. Metro Areas, 2014-2016," February 5, 2018*

- The Brookings Institution ranked the 100 largest metro areas in the U.S. based on income inequality. Indianapolis was ranked #58 (#1 = greatest inequality). Criteria: the "95/20 ratio," a figure representing the income at which a household earns more than 95 percent of all other households, divided by the income at which a household earns more than only 20 percent of all other households. *Brookings Institution, "Household Income Inequality, 100 Largest U.S. Metro Areas, 2014-2016," February 5, 2018*

- *Forbes* ranked the 100 largest metro areas in the U.S. in terms of the "Best Cities for Young Professionals." The Indianapolis metro area ranked #11 out of 25. (Large metro areas were divided into metro divisions.) Criteria: median rent of a two-bedroom apartment; job growth and unemployment rate; median salary of college graduates with 5 or less years of work experience; networking opportunities; social outlook; percentage of population 25 years of age and older with college degrees. *Forbes.com, "America's 25 Best Cities for Young Professionals in 2017," May 22, 2017*

- The Indianapolis metro area was identified as one of the most affordable metropolitan areas in America by *Forbes*. The area ranked #9 out of 20 based on the National Association of Home Builders/Wells Fargo Housing Affordability Index and Sperling's Best Places' cost-of-living index. *Forbes.com, "America's Most Affordable Cities in 2015," March 12, 2015*

- Indianapolis was identified as one of America's most frugal metro areas by *Coupons.com*. The city ranked #17 out of 25. Criteria: digital coupon usage. *Coupons.com, "America's Most Frugal Cities of 2017," March 22, 2018*

- Indianapolis was identified as one of the happiest cities to work in by CareerBliss.com, an online community for career advancement. The city ranked #7 out of 10. Criteria: an employee's relationship with his or her boss and co-workers; daily tasks; general work environment; compensation; opportunities for advancement; company culture and job reputation; and resources. *Businesswire.com, "CareerBliss Happiest Cities to Work 2019," February 12, 2019*

- The Indianapolis metro area appeared on the Milken Institute "2018 Best Performing Cities" list. Rank: #63 out of 200 large metro areas. Criteria: job growth; wage and salary growth; high-tech output growth. *Milken Institute, "Best-Performing Cities 2018," January 24, 2019*

- *Forbes* ranked the 200 most populous metro areas to determine the nation's "Best Places for Business and Careers." The Indianapolis metro area was ranked #30. Criteria: costs (business and living); job growth (past and projected); income growth; quality of life; educational attainment (college and high school); projected economic growth; cultural and recreational opportunities; net migration patterns; number of highly ranked colleges. *Forbes, "The Best Places for Business and Careers 2018: Seattle Leads the Way," October 24, 2018*

Education Rankings

- Personal finance website *WalletHub* analyzed the 150 largest U.S. metropolitan statistical areas to determine where the most educated Americans are choosing to settle. Criteria: education quality and attainment gap; education levels; percentage of workers with degrees; public school quality rankings; quality and size of each metro area's universities. Indianapolis was ranked #73 (#1 = most educated city). *www.WalletHub.com, "2018's Most and Least Educated Cities in America," July 24, 2018*

- Indianapolis was selected as one of the most well-read cities in America by Amazon.com. The city ranked #18 among the top 20. Cities with populations greater than 500,000 were evaluated based on per capita sales of books, magazines and newspapers (both print and Kindle format). *Amazon.com, "The 20 Most Well-Read Cities in America," May 24, 2016*

- Indianapolis was selected as one of America's most literate cities. The city ranked #29 out of the 82 largest U.S. cities. Criteria: number of booksellers; library resources; Internet resources; educational attainment; periodical publishing resources; newspaper circulation. *Central Connecticut State University, "America's Most Literate Cities, 2016," March 31, 2017*

Environmental Rankings

- The U.S. Environmental Protection Agency (EPA) released a list of U.S. metropolitan areas with the most ENERGY STAR certified buildings in 2017. The Indianapolis metro area was ranked #24 out of 25. *U.S. Environmental Protection Agency, "2018 Energy Star Top Cities," April 11, 2018*

- Indianapolis was highlighted as one of the 25 metro areas most polluted by year-round particle pollution (Annual PM 2.5) in the U.S. during 2014 through 2016. The area ranked #13. *American Lung Association, State of the Air 2018*

- Indianapolis was highlighted as one of the 25 metro areas most polluted by short-term particle pollution (24-hour PM 2.5) in the U.S. during 2014 through 2016. The area ranked #21. *American Lung Association, State of the Air 2018*

Food/Drink Rankings

- The U.S. Chamber of Commerce Foundation conducted an in-depth study on local food truck regulations, surveyed 288 food truck owners, and ranked 20 major American cities based on how friendly they are for operating a food truck. The compiled index assessed the following: procedures for obtaining permits and licenses; complying with restrictions; and financial obligations associated with operating a food truck. Indianapolis ranked #5 overall (1 being the best) for ease in operating a food truck. *www.foodtrucknation.us, "Food Truck Nation," March 20, 2018*

- *Men's Health* ranked 100 major U.S. cities in terms of alcohol intoxication. Indianapolis ranked #61 (#1 = most sober).Criteria: binge drinking; alcohol-related traffic accidents, arrests, and fatalities. *Men's Health, "America's Drunkest Cities," March 9, 2015*

Health/Fitness Rankings

- Analysts who tracked obesity rates in 100 of the nation's most populous areas found that the Indianapolis metro area was one of the ten communities where residents were most likely to be obese, defined as a BMI score of 30 or above. *www.gallup.com, "Colorado Springs Residents Least Likely to Be Obese," May 28, 2015*

- For each of the 100 largest cities in the United States, the American College of Sports Medicine's American Fitness Index evaluated infrastructure, community assets, and policies that encourage healthy and fit lifestyles, including preventive health behaviors, levels of chronic disease conditions, health care access, and community resources and policies that support physical activity. Indianapolis ranked #99 for "community fitness." *www.americanfitnessindex.org, "ACSM American Fitness Index Health and Community Fitness Status of the 100 Largest U.S. Cities," May 2018*

- The Indianapolis metro area was identified as one of the worst cities for bed bugs in America by pest control company Orkin. The area ranked #14 out of 50 based on the number of bed bug treatments Orkin performed from December 2017 to November 2018. *Orkin, "Baltimore Remains Front Runner, Atlanta and Philadelphia Break Into Top 10," January 14, 2019*

- Indianapolis was identified as a "2018 Spring Allergy Capital." The area ranked #68 out of 100. Three groups of factors were used to identify the most challenging cities for people with allergies during the spring season: annual pollen levels; medicine utilization; access to board-certified allergists. *Asthma and Allergy Foundation of America, "Spring Allergy Capitals 2018"*

- Indianapolis was identified as a "2018 Fall Allergy Capital." The area ranked #62 out of 100. Three groups of factors were used to identify the most challenging cities for people with allergies during the fall season: annual pollen levels; medicine utilization; access to board-certified allergists. *Asthma and Allergy Foundation of America, "Fall Allergy Capitals 2018"*

- Indianapolis was identified as a "2018 Asthma Capital." The area ranked #37 out of the nation's 100 largest metropolitan areas. Criteria: estimated prevalence; self-reported prevalence; crude death rate for asthma; annual pollen score; annual air quality; public smoking laws; number of board-certified asthma specialists; school inhaler access laws; rescue medication use; controller medication use; ER visits for asthma; uninsured rate; poverty rate. *Asthma and Allergy Foundation of America, "Asthma Capitals 2018: The Most Challenging Places to Live With Asthma"*

- *Men's Health* ranked 100 major U.S. cities in terms of the best cities for men. Indianapolis ranked #91. Criteria: health; fitness; quality of life. *Men's Health, "The Best & Worst Cities for Men Who Want to Be Fit and Happy," January 1, 2016*

- The Indianapolis metro area ranked #133 out of 189 in The Gallup-Healthways Well-Being Index. Criteria: purpose; social well being; financial health; community and physical health. Results are based on telephone interviews with adults, aged 18 and older, living in metropolitan areas in the 50 U.S. states and the District of Columbia. *Gallup-Healthways, "State of American Well-Being, 2017 Community Well-Being Rankings" March 2018*

Real Estate Rankings

- *WalletHub* compared the most populated U.S. cities, as well as at least two of the most populated cities in each state, for a total of 179, to determine which had the best markets for real estate agents. Indianapolis ranked #127 where demand was high and pay was the best. Criteria: sales per agent; annual median wage for real-estate agents; monthly average starting salary for real estate agents; real estate job density and competition; unemployment rate; housing-market health index; and other relevant metrics. *www.WalletHub.com, "2018's Best Places to Be a Real Estate Agent," April 25, 2018*

- The Indianapolis metro area was identified as one of the top 20 housing markets to invest in for 2019 by *Forbes*. Criteria: strong job and population growth; stable local economy; anticipated home price appreciation; and other factors. *Forbes.com, "The Best Markets for Real Estate Investments In 2019," January 7, 2019*

- The Indianapolis metro area was identified as one of nine best housing markets to invest in. Criteria: single-family rental home investing in the first quarter of 2017 based on first-year returns. The area ranked #7. *The Business Insider, "Here are the 9 Best U.S. Housing Markets for Investment," May 11, 2017*

- The Indianapolis metro area was identified as one of the 10 worst condo markets in the U.S. in 2018. The area ranked #59 out of 61 markets. Criteria: year-over-year change of median sales price of existing apartment condo-coop homes between the 4th quarter of 2017 and the 4th quarter of 2018. *National Association of Realtors®, Median Sales Price of Existing Apartment Condo-Coops Homes for Metropolitan Areas, 4th Quarter 2018*

- Indianapolis was ranked #23 out of 237 metro areas in terms of housing affordability in 2018 by the National Association of Home Builders (#1 = most affordable). Criteria: the share of homes sold in that area affordable to a family earning the local median income, based on standard mortgage underwriting criteria. *National Association of Home Builders®, NAHB-Wells Fargo Housing Opportunity Index, 4th Quarter 2018*

Safety Rankings

- To identify the most dangerous cities in America, 24/7 Wall Street focused on violent crime categories—murder, rape, robbery, and aggravated assault—and property crime as reported in the FBI's 2017 annual Uniform Crime Report. Criteria also included median income from American Community Survey and unemployment figures from Bureau of Labor Statistics. For cities with populations over 100,000, Indianapolis was ranked #13. *247wallst.com, "25 Most Dangerous Cities in America" October 17, 2018*

- Allstate ranked the 200 largest cities in America in terms of driver safety. Indianapolis ranked #80. Criteria: internal property damage claims over a two-year period from January 2015 to December 2016. The report helps increase the importance of safety awareness behind the wheel. *Allstate, "Allstate America's Best Drivers Report, 2018" August 28, 2018*

- Indianapolis was identified as one of "America's Most Dangerous Cities" by *Forbes*. The area ranked #10 out of 10. Criteria: violent crime (murder and non-negligent manslaughter, forcible rape, robbery, and aggravated assault) rates per capita. The editors only considered cities with 200,000 or more residents. *Forbes, "America's Most Dangerous Cities 2015," October 29, 2015*

- Indianapolis was identified as one of the most dangerous cities in America by NeighborhoodScout. The city ranked #27 out of 100. Criteria: number of violent crimes per 1,000 residents. The editors only considered cities with 25,000 or more residents. *NeighborhoodScout.com, "Top 100 Most Dangerous Cities in the U.S. 2019" January 2, 2019*

- The National Insurance Crime Bureau ranked 382 metro areas in the U.S. in terms of per capita rates of vehicle theft. The Indianapolis metro area ranked #53 (#1 = highest rate). Criteria: number of vehicle theft offenses per 100,000 inhabitants in 2017. *National Insurance Crime Bureau, "Hot Spots 2017," July 12, 2018*

Seniors/Retirement Rankings

- From its Best Cities for Successful Aging indexes, the Milken Institute generated rankings for metropolitan areas, weighing data in nine categories—health care, wellness, living arrangements, transportation and convenience, financial characteristics, education, employment, community engagement, and overall livability. The Indianapolis metro area was ranked #44 overall in the large metro area category. *Milken Institute, "Best Cities for Successful Aging, 2017" March 14, 2017*

Sports/Recreation Rankings

- Indianapolis was selected as one of "America's Most Miserable Sports Cities" by *Forbes*. The city was ranked #10. Criteria: postseason losses/misery; years since last title; and number of teams lost to relocation. Contenders were limited to cities with at least 75 cumulative pro seasons of NFL, NBA, NHL, MLS and MLB play. *Forbes, "America's Most Miserable Sports Cities 2016," April 20, 2016*

- Indianapolis was chosen as one of America's best cities for bicycling. The city ranked #30 out of 50. Criteria: cycling infrastructure that is safe and friendly for all ages; energy and bike culture. The editors only considered cities with populations of 100,000 or more. *Bicycling, "The 50 Best Bike Cities in America," October 10, 2018*

Women/Minorities Rankings

- Personal finance website *WalletHub* compared more than 180 U.S. cities—including the 150 most populated U.S. cities, plus at least two of the most populated cities in each state—across two key dimensions, "Hispanic Business-Friendliness" and "Hispanic Purchasing Power", to arrive at the most favorable conditions for Hispanic entrepreneurs. Indianapolis was ranked #112 out of 182. Criteria includes: share of Hispanic-Owned Businesses; Hispanic entrepreneurship rate to median annual income of Hispanics; Small Business-Friendliness score; cost of living; and number of Hispanics with at least a bachelor's degree. *WalletHub.com, "2018's Best Cities for Hispanic Entrepreneurs," April 26, 2018*

Miscellaneous Rankings

- The watchdog site Charity Navigator conducts an annual study of charities in the nation's major markets both to analyze statistical differences in their financial, accountability, and transparency practices and to track year-to-year variations in individual philanthropic communities. Charity Navigator's analysis demonstrated that the financial, accountability and transparency behaviors of America's largest charities can be influenced by the metropolitan market within which the charity operates. The Indianapolis metro area was ranked #29 among the 30 metro markets in the rating category of Overall Score. *www.charitynavigator.org, "2017 Metro Market Study," May 1, 2017*

- *WalletHub* compared the 150 most populated U.S. cities to determine their operating efficiency. A "Quality of Services" score was constructed for each city and then divided by the total budget per capita to reveal which were managed the best. Indianapolis ranked #85. Criteria: financial stability; economy; education; safety; health; infrastructure and pollution. *www.WalletHub.com, "2018's Best- & Worst-Run Cities in America," July 9, 2018*

- Indianapolis was selected as one of "America's Friendliest Cities." The city ranked #6 in the "Friendliest" category. Respondents to an online survey were asked to rate 38 top urban destinations in the United States as to general friendliness, as well as manners, politeness and warm disposition. *Travel + Leisure, "America's Friendliest Cities," October 20, 2017*

Business Environment

CITY FINANCES

City Government Finances

Component	2016 ($000)	2016 ($ per capita)
Total Revenues	3,606,148	4,227
Total Expenditures	4,210,268	4,935
Debt Outstanding	6,625,294	7,765
Cash and Securities[1]	3,109,565	3,645

Note: (1) Cash and security holdings of a government at the close of its fiscal year, including those of its dependent agencies, utilities, and liquor stores.
Source: U.S. Census Bureau, State & Local Government Finances 2016

City Government Revenue by Source

Source	2016 ($000)	2016 ($ per capita)	2016 (%)
General Revenue			
From Federal Government	112,360	132	3.1
From State Government	932,673	1,093	25.9
From Local Governments	12,145	14	0.3
Taxes			
Property	386,399	453	10.7
Sales and Gross Receipts	78,299	92	2.2
Personal Income	217,499	255	6.0
Corporate Income	0	0	0.0
Motor Vehicle License	0	0	0.0
Other Taxes	39,638	46	1.1
Current Charges	1,040,069	1,219	28.8
Liquor Store	0	0	0.0
Utility	641,532	752	17.8
Employee Retirement	5,894	7	0.2

Source: U.S. Census Bureau, State & Local Government Finances 2016

City Government Expenditures by Function

Function	2016 ($000)	2016 ($ per capita)	2016 (%)
General Direct Expenditures			
Air Transportation	119,465	140	2.8
Corrections	215,794	252	5.1
Education	0	0	0.0
Employment Security Administration	0	0	0.0
Financial Administration	36,477	42	0.9
Fire Protection	156,624	183	3.7
General Public Buildings	5,033	5	0.1
Governmental Administration, Other	55,548	65	1.3
Health	95,198	111	2.3
Highways	129,080	151	3.1
Hospitals	1,273,735	1,492	30.3
Housing and Community Development	132,248	155	3.1
Interest on General Debt	174,316	204	4.1
Judicial and Legal	104,343	122	2.5
Libraries	0	0	0.0
Parking	13,533	15	0.3
Parks and Recreation	111,350	130	2.6
Police Protection	200,306	234	4.8
Public Welfare	0	0	0.0
Sewerage	22,060	25	0.5
Solid Waste Management	95,544	112	2.3
Veterans' Services	0	0	0.0
Liquor Store	0	0	0.0
Utility	1,068,713	1,252	25.4
Employee Retirement	12,382	14	0.3

Source: U.S. Census Bureau, State & Local Government Finances 2016

DEMOGRAPHICS

Population Growth

Area	1990 Census	2000 Census	2010 Census	2017* Estimate	Population Growth (%) 1990-2017	2010-2017
City	730,993	781,870	820,445	853,431	16.7	4.0
MSA[1]	1,294,217	1,525,104	1,756,241	1,989,032	53.7	13.3
U.S.	248,709,873	281,421,906	308,745,538	321,004,407	29.1	4.0

Note: (1) Figures cover the Indianapolis-Carmel-Anderson, IN Metropolitan Statistical Area—see Appendix B for areas included; (*) 2013-2017 5-year estimated population
Source: U.S. Census Bureau, 1990 Census, Census 2000, Census 2010, 2013-2017 American Community Survey 5-Year Estimates

Household Size

Area	Persons in Household (%) One	Two	Three	Four	Five	Six	Seven or More	Average Household Size
City	36.0	31.6	13.9	10.6	4.9	2.0	1.1	2.50
MSA[1]	29.4	33.5	15.1	13.1	5.9	2.0	0.9	2.60
U.S.	27.7	33.8	15.7	13.0	6.0	2.3	1.4	2.60

Note: (1) Figures cover the Indianapolis-Carmel-Anderson, IN Metropolitan Statistical Area—see Appendix B for areas included
Source: U.S. Census Bureau, 2013-2017 American Community Survey 5-Year Estimates

Race

Area	White Alone[2] (%)	Black Alone[2] (%)	Asian Alone[2] (%)	AIAN[3] Alone[2] (%)	NHOPI[4] Alone[2] (%)	Other Race Alone[2] (%)	Two or More Races (%)
City	61.8	28.1	3.0	0.3	0.0	3.8	3.0
MSA[1]	77.3	14.9	2.9	0.2	0.0	2.2	2.4
U.S.	73.0	12.7	5.4	0.8	0.2	4.8	3.1

Note: (1) Figures cover the Indianapolis-Carmel-Anderson, IN Metropolitan Statistical Area—see Appendix B for areas included; (2) Alone is defined as not being in combination with one or more other races; (3) American Indian and Alaska Native; (4) Native Hawaiian and Other Pacific Islander
Source: U.S. Census Bureau, 2013-2017 American Community Survey 5-Year Estimates

Hispanic or Latino Origin

Area	Total (%)	Mexican (%)	Puerto Rican (%)	Cuban (%)	Other (%)
City	10.1	7.1	0.6	0.2	2.2
MSA[1]	6.5	4.5	0.4	0.1	1.5
U.S.	17.6	11.1	1.7	0.7	4.1

Note: Persons of Hispanic or Latino origin can be of any race; (1) Figures cover the Indianapolis-Carmel-Anderson, IN Metropolitan Statistical Area—see Appendix B for areas included
Source: U.S. Census Bureau, 2013-2017 American Community Survey 5-Year Estimates

Segregation

Type	Segregation Indices[1] 1990	2000	2010	2010 Rank[2]	Percent Change 1990-2000	1990-2010	2000-2010
Black/White	74.4	72.1	66.4	15	-2.4	-8.0	-5.7
Asian/White	37.8	40.6	41.6	47	2.9	3.9	1.0
Hispanic/White	25.8	43.8	47.3	37	18.0	21.5	3.5

Note: All figures cover the Metropolitan Statistical Area—see Appendix B for areas included; Figures are based on an analysis of 1990, 2000, and 2010 Census Decennial Census tract data by William H. Frey, Brookings Institution and the University of Michigan Social Science Data Analysis Network. In this analysis all racial groups (whites, blacks, and asians) are non-Hispanic members of those races. Hispanics are shown as a separate category; (1) Segregation Indices are Dissimilarity Indices that measure the degree to which the minority group is distributed differently than whites across census tracts. They range from 0 (complete integration) to 100 (complete segregation) where the value indicates the percentage of the minority group that needs to move to be distributed exactly like whites; (2) Ranges from 1 (most segregated) to 102 (least segregated); n/a not available.
Source: www.CensusScope.org

Ancestry

Area	German	Irish	English	American	Italian	Polish	French[2]	Scottish	Dutch
City	15.4	9.4	6.2	6.3	2.3	1.5	1.6	1.6	1.2
MSA[1]	19.4	10.9	8.2	9.5	2.7	2.0	2.0	1.9	1.6
U.S.	14.1	10.1	7.5	6.6	5.3	2.9	2.5	1.7	1.3

Note: Figures are the percentage of the total population reporting a particular ancestry. The nine most commonly reported ancestries in the U.S. are shown. Figures include multiple ancestries (e.g. if a person reported being Irish and Italian, they were included in both columns); (1) Figures cover the Indianapolis-Carmel-Anderson, IN Metropolitan Statistical Area—see Appendix B for areas included; (2) Excludes Basque
Source: U.S. Census Bureau, 2013-2017 American Community Survey 5-Year Estimates

Foreign-Born Population

Area	Any Foreign Country	Asia	Mexico	Europe	Carribean	Central America[2]	South America	Africa	Canada
City	9.3	2.5	3.2	0.5	0.4	1.0	0.2	1.3	0.1
MSA[1]	6.7	2.3	1.8	0.6	0.2	0.5	0.2	0.8	0.1
U.S.	13.4	4.1	3.6	1.5	1.3	1.0	0.9	0.6	0.3

Note: (1) Figures cover the Indianapolis-Carmel-Anderson, IN Metropolitan Statistical Area—see Appendix B for areas included; (2) Excludes Mexico.
Source: U.S. Census Bureau, 2013-2017 American Community Survey 5-Year Estimates

Marital Status

Area	Never Married	Now Married[2]	Separated	Widowed	Divorced
City	41.4	38.3	2.0	5.2	13.1
MSA[1]	32.5	48.3	1.5	5.3	12.4
U.S.	33.1	48.2	2.0	5.8	10.9

Note: Figures are percentages and cover the population 15 years of age and older; (1) Figures cover the Indianapolis-Carmel-Anderson, IN Metropolitan Statistical Area—see Appendix B for areas included; (2) Excludes separated
Source: U.S. Census Bureau, 2013-2017 American Community Survey 5-Year Estimates

Disability by Age

Area	All Ages	Under 18 Years Old	18 to 64 Years Old	65 Years and Over
City	13.7	5.6	12.4	39.3
MSA[1]	12.6	4.8	10.9	36.5
U.S.	12.6	4.2	10.3	35.5

Note: Figures show percent of the civilian noninstitutionalized population that reported having a disability. Disability status is determined from six types of difficulty: vision, hearing, cognitive, ambulatory, self-care, and independent living. For children under 5 years old, hearing and vision difficulty are used to determine disability status. For children between the ages of 5 and 14, disability status is determined from hearing, vision, cognitive, ambulatory, and self-care difficulties. For people aged 15 years and older, they are considered to have a disability if they have difficulty with any one of the six difficulty types; Note: (1) Figures cover the Indianapolis-Carmel-Anderson, IN Metropolitan Statistical Area—see Appendix B for areas included
Source: U.S. Census Bureau, 2013-2017 American Community Survey 5-Year Estimates

Age

Area	Under Age 5	Age 5–19	Age 20–34	Age 35–44	Age 45–54	Age 55–64	Age 65–74	Age 75–84	Age 85+	Median Age
City	7.4	19.7	24.1	12.9	12.6	11.8	6.6	3.4	1.5	34.1
MSA[1]	6.8	20.7	20.7	13.4	13.6	12.2	7.5	3.7	1.6	36.3
U.S.	6.2	19.5	20.7	12.7	13.4	12.7	8.6	4.4	1.9	37.8

Note: (1) Figures cover the Indianapolis-Carmel-Anderson, IN Metropolitan Statistical Area—see Appendix B for areas included
Source: U.S. Census Bureau, 2013-2017 American Community Survey 5-Year Estimates

Gender

Area	Males	Females	Males per 100 Females
City	411,970	441,461	93.3
MSA[1]	971,355	1,017,677	95.4
U.S.	158,018,753	162,985,654	97.0

Note: (1) Figures cover the Indianapolis-Carmel-Anderson, IN Metropolitan Statistical Area—see Appendix B for areas included
Source: U.S. Census Bureau, 2013-2017 American Community Survey 5-Year Estimates

Religious Groups by Family

Area	Catholic	Baptist	Non-Den.	Methodist[2]	Lutheran	LDS[3]	Pentecostal	Presbyterian[4]	Muslim[5]	Judaism
MSA[1]	10.5	10.3	7.2	5.0	1.7	0.7	1.6	1.7	0.2	0.4
U.S.	19.1	9.3	4.0	4.0	2.3	2.0	1.9	1.6	0.8	0.7

Note: Figures are the number of adherents as a percentage of the total population; (1) Figures cover the Indianapolis-Carmel-Anderson, IN Metropolitan Statistical Area—see Appendix B for areas included; (2) Methodist/Pietist; (3) Latter Day Saints; (4) Reformed; (5) Figures are estimates
Source: Association of Statisticians of American Religious Bodies, 2010 U.S. Religion Census: Religious Congregations & Membership Study

Religious Groups by Tradition

Area	Catholic	Evangelical Protestant	Mainline Protestant	Other Tradition	Black Protestant	Orthodox
MSA[1]	10.5	18.3	9.6	1.7	1.9	0.3
U.S.	19.1	16.2	7.3	4.3	1.6	0.3

Note: Figures are the number of adherents as a percentage of the total population; (1) Figures cover the Indianapolis-Carmel-Anderson, IN Metropolitan Statistical Area—see Appendix B for areas included
Source: Association of Statisticians of American Religious Bodies, 2010 U.S. Religion Census: Religious Congregations & Membership Study

ECONOMY

Gross Metropolitan Product

Area	2016	2017	2018	2019	Rank[2]
MSA[1]	136.8	142.9	149.7	158.1	27

Note: Figures are in billions of dollars; (1) Figures cover the Indianapolis-Carmel-Anderson, IN Metropolitan Statistical Area—see Appendix B for areas included; (2) Rank is based on 2017 data and ranges from 1 to 381
Source: U.S. Conference of Mayors, U.S. Metro Economies: Economic Growth & Full Employment, June 2018

Economic Growth

Area	2017-2018 (%)	2019-2020 (%)	2021-2022 (%)
MSA[1]	2.7	2.8	2.1

Note: Figures are real gross metropolitan product (GMP) growth rates and represent average annual percent change; (1) Figures cover the Indianapolis-Carmel-Anderson, IN Metropolitan Statistical Area—see Appendix B for areas included
Source: U.S. Conference of Mayors, U.S. Metro Economies: Economic Growth & Full Employment, June 2018

Metropolitan Area Exports

Area	2012	2013	2014	2015	2016	2017	Rank[2]
MSA[1]	10,436.0	9,747.5	9,539.4	9,809.4	9,655.4	10,544.2	30

Note: Figures are in millions of dollars; (1) Figures cover the Indianapolis-Carmel-Anderson, IN Metropolitan Statistical Area—see Appendix B for areas included; (2) Rank is based on 2017 data and ranges from 1 to 387
Source: U.S. Department of Commerce, International Trade Administration, Office of Trade and Economic Analysis, Industry and Analysis, Exports by Metropolitan Area, extracted March 25, 2019

Building Permits

Area	Single-Family			Multi-Family			Total		
	2016	2017	Pct. Chg.	2016	2017	Pct. Chg.	2016	2017	Pct. Chg.
City	831	914	10.0	1,068	645	-39.6	1,899	1,559	-17.9
MSA[1]	5,828	6,755	15.9	1,945	2,324	19.5	7,773	9,079	16.8
U.S.	750,800	820,000	9.2	455,800	462,000	1.4	1,206,600	1,282,000	6.2

Note: (1) Figures cover the Indianapolis-Carmel-Anderson, IN Metropolitan Statistical Area—see Appendix B for areas included; Figures represent new, privately-owned housing units authorized (unadjusted data); All permit data are based on estimates with imputation
Source: U.S. Census Bureau, Manufacturing, Mining, and Construction Statistics, Building Permits, 2016, 2017

Bankruptcy Filings

Area	Business Filings			Nonbusiness Filings		
	2017	2018	% Chg.	2017	2018	% Chg.
Marion County	68	57	-16.2	4,653	4,546	-2.3
U.S.	23,157	22,232	-4.0	765,863	751,186	-1.9

Note: Business filings include Chapter 7, Chapter 11, Chapter 12, and Chapter 13; Nonbusiness filings include Chapter 7, Chapter 11, and Chapter 13
Source: Administrative Office of the U.S. Courts, Business and Nonbusiness Bankruptcy, County Cases Commenced by Chapter of the Bankruptcy Code, During the 12-Month Period Ending December 31, 2017 and Business and Nonbusiness Bankruptcy, County Cases Commenced by Chapter of the Bankruptcy Code, During the 12-Month Period Ending December 31, 2018

Housing Vacancy Rates

Area	Gross Vacancy Rate[2] (%)			Year-Round Vacancy Rate[3] (%)			Rental Vacancy Rate[4] (%)			Homeowner Vacancy Rate[5] (%)		
	2016	2017	2018	2016	2017	2018	2016	2017	2018	2016	2017	2018
MSA[1]	9.1	10.9	8.7	9.0	10.8	8.6	9.2	11.9	9.9	1.4	1.5	1.5
U.S.	12.8	12.7	12.3	9.9	9.9	9.7	6.9	7.2	6.9	1.7	1.6	1.5

Note: (1) Figures cover the Indianapolis-Carmel-Anderson, IN Metropolitan Statistical Area—see Appendix B for areas included; (2) The percentage of the total housing inventory that is vacant; (3) The percentage of the housing inventory (excluding seasonal units) that is year-round vacant; (4) The percentage of rental inventory that is vacant for rent; (5) The percentage of homeowner inventory that is vacant for sale
Source: U.S. Census Bureau, Housing Vacancies and Homeownership Annual Statistics: 2016, 2017, 2018

INCOME

Income

Area	Per Capita ($)	Median Household ($)	Average Household ($)
City	26,232	44,709	63,698
MSA[1]	30,607	56,528	77,745
U.S.	31,177	57,652	81,283

Note: (1) Figures cover the Indianapolis-Carmel-Anderson, IN Metropolitan Statistical Area—see Appendix B for areas included
Source: U.S. Census Bureau, 2013-2017 American Community Survey 5-Year Estimates

Household Income Distribution

Area	Percent of Households Earning							
	Under $15,000	$15,000 -$24,999	$25,000 -$34,999	$35,000 -$49,999	$50,000 -$74,999	$75,000 -$99,999	$100,000 -$149,999	$150,000 and up
City	15.2	12.2	11.6	15.7	17.8	10.6	10.1	6.7
MSA[1]	10.8	9.8	9.8	14.1	18.4	12.6	14.1	10.5
U.S.	11.6	9.8	9.5	13.0	17.7	12.3	14.1	12.1

Note: (1) Figures cover the Indianapolis-Carmel-Anderson, IN Metropolitan Statistical Area—see Appendix B for areas included
Source: U.S. Census Bureau, 2013-2017 American Community Survey 5-Year Estimates

Poverty Rate

Area	All Ages	Under 18 Years Old	18 to 64 Years Old	65 Years and Over
City	20.1	30.1	18.0	10.0
MSA[1]	13.7	19.6	12.7	7.1
U.S.	14.6	20.3	13.7	9.3

Note: Figures are percentage of people whose income during the past 12 months was below the poverty level; (1) Figures cover the Indianapolis-Carmel-Anderson, IN Metropolitan Statistical Area—see Appendix B for areas included
Source: U.S. Census Bureau, 2013-2017 American Community Survey 5-Year Estimates

EMPLOYMENT

Labor Force and Employment

Area	Civilian Labor Force			Workers Employed		
	Dec. 2017	Dec. 2018	% Chg.	Dec. 2017	Dec. 2018	% Chg.
City	437,038	451,232	3.2	423,438	436,132	3.0
MSA[1]	1,029,258	1,062,644	3.2	999,968	1,029,984	3.0
U.S.	159,880,000	162,510,000	1.6	153,602,000	156,481,000	1.9

Note: Data is not seasonally adjusted and covers workers 16 years of age and older; (1) Figures cover the Indianapolis-Carmel-Anderson, IN Metropolitan Statistical Area—see Appendix B for areas included
Source: Bureau of Labor Statistics, Local Area Unemployment Statistics

Unemployment Rate

Area	2018											
	Jan.	Feb.	Mar.	Apr.	May	Jun.	Jul.	Aug.	Sep.	Oct.	Nov.	Dec.
City	3.4	3.6	3.3	3.0	3.3	3.8	3.6	3.8	3.2	3.6	3.6	3.3
MSA[1]	3.2	3.4	3.0	2.8	3.0	3.4	3.3	3.5	2.9	3.3	3.4	3.1
U.S.	4.5	4.4	4.1	3.7	3.6	4.2	4.1	3.9	3.6	3.5	3.5	3.7

Note: Data is not seasonally adjusted and covers workers 16 years of age and older; (1) Figures cover the Indianapolis-Carmel-Anderson, IN Metropolitan Statistical Area—see Appendix B for areas included
Source: Bureau of Labor Statistics, Local Area Unemployment Statistics

Average Wages

Occupation	$/Hr.	Occupation	$/Hr.
Accountants and Auditors	36.70	Maids and Housekeeping Cleaners	10.80
Automotive Mechanics	21.60	Maintenance and Repair Workers	19.70
Bookkeepers	20.00	Marketing Managers	54.50
Carpenters	24.10	Nuclear Medicine Technologists	35.30
Cashiers	10.40	Nurses, Licensed Practical	22.30
Clerks, General Office	16.80	Nurses, Registered	33.30
Clerks, Receptionists/Information	14.30	Nursing Assistants	13.70
Clerks, Shipping/Receiving	15.10	Packers and Packagers, Hand	12.50
Computer Programmers	40.90	Physical Therapists	40.20
Computer Systems Analysts	39.80	Postal Service Mail Carriers	24.80
Computer User Support Specialists	24.10	Real Estate Brokers	52.40
Cooks, Restaurant	12.20	Retail Salespersons	12.50
Dentists	70.60	Sales Reps., Exc. Tech./Scientific	38.10
Electrical Engineers	42.10	Sales Reps., Tech./Scientific	55.60
Electricians	27.20	Secretaries, Exc. Legal/Med./Exec.	17.00
Financial Managers	65.90	Security Guards	13.90
First-Line Supervisors/Managers, Sales	20.00	Surgeons	127.80
Food Preparation Workers	11.00	Teacher Assistants*	12.20
General and Operations Managers	56.10	Teachers, Elementary School*	27.40
Hairdressers/Cosmetologists	15.00	Teachers, Secondary School*	26.50
Internists, General	115.50	Telemarketers	15.80
Janitors and Cleaners	12.70	Truck Drivers, Heavy/Tractor-Trailer	22.60
Landscaping/Groundskeeping Workers	14.20	Truck Drivers, Light/Delivery Svcs.	17.10
Lawyers	53.60	Waiters and Waitresses	11.30

Note: Wage data covers the Indianapolis-Carmel-Anderson, IN Metropolitan Statistical Area—see Appendix B for areas included; (*) Hourly wages for elementary/secondary school teachers and teacher assistants were calculated by the editors from annual wage data based on a 40 hour work week; n/a not available.
Source: Bureau of Labor Statistics, Metro Area Occupational Employment & Wage Estimates, May 2018

Employment by Occupation

Occupation Classification	City (%)	MSA[1] (%)	U.S. (%)
Management, Business, Science, and Arts	34.8	38.5	37.4
Natural Resources, Construction, and Maintenance	7.3	7.8	8.9
Production, Transportation, and Material Moving	15.1	13.4	12.2
Sales and Office	25.0	24.4	23.5
Service	17.8	15.9	18.0

Note: Figures cover employed civilians 16 years of age and older; (1) Figures cover the Indianapolis-Carmel-Anderson, IN Metropolitan Statistical Area—see Appendix B for areas included
Source: U.S. Census Bureau, 2013-2017 American Community Survey 5-Year Estimates

Employment by Industry

Sector	MSA[1]		U.S.
	Number of Employees	Percent of Total	Percent of Total
Construction	51,900	4.8	4.8
Education and Health Services	163,000	15.1	15.9
Financial Activities	68,100	6.3	5.7
Government	135,900	12.6	15.1
Information	13,200	1.2	1.9
Leisure and Hospitality	103,900	9.6	10.7
Manufacturing	92,500	8.6	8.5
Mining and Logging	700	0.1	0.5
Other Services	46,600	4.3	3.9
Professional and Business Services	174,200	16.1	14.1
Retail Trade	105,000	9.7	10.8
Transportation, Warehousing, and Utilities	73,800	6.8	4.2
Wholesale Trade	50,300	4.7	3.9

Note: Figures are non-farm employment as of December 2018. Figures are not seasonally adjusted and include workers 16 years of age and older; (1) Figures cover the Indianapolis-Carmel-Anderson, IN Metropolitan Statistical Area—see Appendix B for areas included
Source: Bureau of Labor Statistics, Current Employment Statistics, Employment, Hours, and Earnings

Occupations with Greatest Projected Employment Growth: 2018 – 2020

Occupation[1]	2018 Employment	2020 Projected Employment	Numeric Employment Change	Percent Employment Change
Laborers and Freight, Stock, and Material Movers, Hand	76,430	78,940	2,510	3.3
Combined Food Preparation and Serving Workers, Including Fast Food	84,030	86,500	2,470	2.9
Registered Nurses	67,010	69,350	2,340	3.5
Personal Care Aides	29,290	30,960	1,670	5.7
Janitors and Cleaners, Except Maids and Housekeeping Cleaners	48,510	49,760	1,250	2.6
Home Health Aides	13,830	14,930	1,100	8.0
Heavy and Tractor-Trailer Truck Drivers	56,570	57,630	1,060	1.9
Industrial Truck and Tractor Operators	21,430	22,480	1,050	4.9
General and Operations Managers	49,870	50,850	980	2.0
Helpers—Production Workers	17,700	18,520	820	4.6

Note: Projections cover Indiana; (1) Sorted by numeric employment change
Source: www.projectionscentral.com, State Occupational Projections, 2018–2020 Short-Term Projections

Fastest Growing Occupations: 2018 – 2020

Occupation[1]	2018 Employment	2020 Projected Employment	Numeric Employment Change	Percent Employment Change
Flight Attendants	620	680	60	9.7
Home Health Aides	13,830	14,930	1,100	8.0
Airline Pilots, Copilots, and Flight Engineers	670	720	50	7.5
Physician Assistants	1,160	1,240	80	6.9
Software Developers, Applications	8,720	9,300	580	6.7
Nurse Practitioners	4,170	4,440	270	6.5
Computer Numerically Controlled Machine Tool Programmers, Metal and Plastic	960	1,020	60	6.3
Physical Therapist Assistants	2,260	2,390	130	5.8
Personal Care Aides	29,290	30,960	1,670	5.7
Health Specialties Teachers, Postsecondary	3,020	3,190	170	5.6

Note: Projections cover Indiana; (1) Sorted by percent employment change and excludes occupations with numeric employment change less than 50
Source: www.projectionscentral.com, State Occupational Projections, 2018–2020 Short-Term Projections

TAXES

State Corporate Income Tax Rates

State	Tax Rate (%)	Income Brackets ($)	Num. of Brackets	Financial Institution Tax Rate (%)[a]	Federal Income Tax Ded.
Indiana	5.75 (i)	Flat rate	1	6.25	No

Note: Tax rates as of January 1, 2019; (a) Rates listed are the corporate income tax rate applied to financial institutions or excise taxes based on income. Some states have other taxes based upon the value of deposits or shares; (i) The Indiana Corporate tax rate is scheduled to decrease to 5.5% on July 1, 2019. Bank tax rate is scheduled to decrease to 6.0% on 1/1/20.
Source: Federation of Tax Administrators, Range of State Corporate Income Tax Rates, January 1, 2019

State Individual Income Tax Rates

State	Tax Rate (%)	Income Brackets ($)	Personal Exemptions ($)			Standard Ded. ($)	
			Single	Married	Depend.	Single	Married
Indiana	3.23	Flat rate	1,000	2,000	2,500 (j)	–	–

Note: Tax rates as of January 1, 2019; Local- and county-level taxes are not included; n/a not applicable; Federal income tax is not deductible on state income tax returns; (j) In Indiana, includes an additional exemption of $1,500 for each dependent child.
Source: Federation of Tax Administrators, State Individual Income Tax Rates, January 1, 2019

Various State Sales and Excise Tax Rates

State	State Sales Tax (%)	Gasoline[1] (¢/gal.)	Cigarette[2] ($/pack)	Spirits[3] ($/gal.)	Wine[4] ($/gal.)	Beer[5] ($/gal.)	Recreational Marijuana (%)
Indiana	7	42.9	0.995	2.68 (f)	0.47 (l)	0.12	Not legal

Note: All tax rates as of January 1, 2019; (1) The American Petroleum Institute has developed a methodology for determining the average tax rate on a gallon of fuel. Rates may include any of the following: excise taxes, environmental fees, storage tank fees, other fees or taxes, general sales tax, and local taxes. In states where gasoline is subject to the general sales tax, or where the fuel tax is based on the average sale price, the average rate determined by API is sensitive to changes in the price of gasoline. States that fully or partially apply general sales taxes to gasoline: CA, CO, GA, IL, IN, MI, NY; (2) The federal excise tax of $1.0066 per pack and local taxes are not included; (3) Rates are those applicable to off-premise sales of 40% alcohol by volume (a.b.v.) distilled spirits in 750ml containers. Local excise taxes are excluded; (4) Rates are those applicable to off-premise sales of 11% a.b.v. non-carbonated wine in 750ml containers; (5) Rates are those applicable to off-premise sales of 4.7% a.b.v. beer in 12 ounce containers; (f) Different rates also applicable according to alcohol content, place of production, size of container, or place purchased (on- or off-premise or onboard airlines); (l) Different rates also applicable to alcohol content, place of production, size of container, place purchased (on- or off-premise or on board airlines) or type of wine (carbonated, vermouth, etc.).
Source: Tax Foundation, 2019 Facts & Figures: How Does Your State Compare?

State Business Tax Climate Index Rankings

State	Overall Rank	Corporate Tax Rank	Individual Income Tax Rank	Sales Tax Rank	Unemployment Insurance Tax Rank	Property Tax Rank
Indiana	10	18	15	12	11	2

Note: The index is a measure of how each state's tax laws affect economic performance. The lower the rank, the more favorable a state's tax system is for business. States without a given tax are given a ranking of 1. The scores/rankings for the District of Columbia do not affect other states. The 2019 index represents the tax climate as of July 1, 2018.
Source: Tax Foundation, State Business Tax Climate Index 2019

COMMERCIAL REAL ESTATE

Office Market

Market Area	Inventory (sq. ft.)	Vacancy Rate (%)	Under Construction (sq. ft.)	YTD Net Absorption (sq. ft.)	Total Average Asking Rent ($/sq. ft./year)
Indianapolis	61,636,961	9.7	0	-573,543	19.63
National	4,905,867,938	13.1	83,553,714	45,846,470	28.46

Source: Newmark Grubb Knight Frank, National Office Market Report, 4th Quarter 2018

Industrial/Warehouse/R&D Market

Market Area	Inventory (sq. ft.)	Vacancy Rate (%)	Under Construction (sq. ft.)	YTD Net Absorption (sq. ft.)	Total Average Asking Rent ($/sq. ft./year)
Indianapolis	324,226,531	3.8	6,898,359	9,252,941	3.85
National	14,796,839,085	5.0	262,662,294	238,014,726	7.16

Source: Newmark Grubb Knight Frank, National Industrial Market Report, 4th Quarter 2018

COMMERCIAL UTILITIES

Typical Monthly Electric Bills

Area	Commercial Service ($/month)		Industrial Service ($/month)	
	1,500 kWh	40 kW demand 14,000 kWh	1,000 kW demand 200,000 kWh	50,000 kW demand 32,500,000 kWh
City	201	1,515	27,784	2,632,845
Average[1]	203	1,619	25,886	2,540,077

Note: Figures are based on annualized rates; (1) Average based on 187 utilities surveyed
Source: Edison Electric Institute, Typical Bills and Average Rates Report, Summer 2018

TRANSPORTATION

Means of Transportation to Work

Area	Drove Alone	Car-pooled	Bus	Subway	Railroad	Bicycle	Walked	Other Means	Worked at Home
City	82.2	9.3	1.9	0.0	0.0	0.5	1.8	1.1	3.2
MSA[1]	83.9	8.1	0.9	0.0	0.0	0.3	1.5	0.9	4.3
U.S.	76.4	9.2	2.5	1.9	0.6	0.6	2.7	1.3	4.7

Note: Figures are percentages and cover workers 16 years of age and older; (1) Figures cover the Indianapolis-Carmel-Anderson, IN Metropolitan Statistical Area—see Appendix B for areas included
Source: U.S. Census Bureau, 2013-2017 American Community Survey 5-Year Estimates

Travel Time to Work

Area	Less Than 10 Minutes	10 to 19 Minutes	20 to 29 Minutes	30 to 44 Minutes	45 to 59 Minutes	60 to 89 Minutes	90 Minutes or More
City	10.5	30.0	30.4	21.0	4.2	2.5	1.4
MSA[1]	11.9	27.7	24.8	23.4	7.1	3.6	1.5
U.S.	12.7	28.9	20.9	20.5	8.1	6.2	2.7

Note: Note: Figures are percentages and include workers 16 years old and over; (1) Figures cover the Indianapolis-Carmel-Anderson, IN Metropolitan Statistical Area—see Appendix B for areas included
Source: U.S. Census Bureau, 2013-2017 American Community Survey 5-Year Estimates

Freeway Travel Time Index

Area	1985	1990	1995	2000	2005	2010	2014
Urban Area Rank[1,2]	35	41	41	38	51	42	46
Urban Area Index[1]	1.09	1.11	1.14	1.17	1.17	1.18	1.18
Average Index[3]	1.09	1.11	1.14	1.17	1.20	1.19	1.20

Note: Freeway Travel Time Index—the ratio of travel time in the peak period to the travel time at free-flow conditions. For example, a value of 1.30 indicates a 20-minute free-flow trip takes 26 minutes in the peak (20 minutes x 1.30 = 26 minutes); (1) Covers the Indianapolis IN urban area; (2) Rank is based on 101 urban areas (#1 = highest travel time index); (3) Average of 101 urban areas
Source: Texas Transportation Institute, 2015 Urban Mobility Scorecard, August 2015

Freeway Commuter Stress Index

Area	1985	1990	1995	2000	2005	2010	2014
Urban Area Rank[1,2]	48	47	50	54	58	58	61
Urban Area Index[1]	1.10	1.13	1.16	1.18	1.19	1.19	1.19
Average Index[3]	1.13	1.16	1.19	1.22	1.25	1.24	1.25

Note: The Freeway Commuter Stress Index is the same as the Freeway Travel Time Index (see table above) except that it includes only the travel in the peak directions during the peak periods; the TTI includes travel in all directions during the peak period. Thus, the CSI is more indicative of the work trip experienced by each commuter on a daily basis; (1) Covers the Indianapolis IN urban area; (2) Rank is based on 101 urban areas (#1 = highest travel time index); (3) Average of 101 urban areas
Source: Texas Transportation Institute, 2015 Urban Mobility Scorecard, August 2015

Public Transportation

Agency Name / Mode of Transportation	Vehicles Operated in Maximum Service[1]	Annual Unlinked Passenger Trips[2] (in thous.)	Annual Passenger Miles[3] (in thous.)
Indianapolis and Marion County Public Transportation (IndyGo)			
Bus (directly operated)	138	8,754.8	35,935.4
Demand Response (purchased transportation)	71	309.2	3,806.6

Note: (1) The number of revenue vehicles operated by the given mode and type of service to meet the annual maximum service requirement. This is the revenue vehicle count during the peak season of the year; on the week and day that maximum service is provided. Vehicles operated in maximum service (VOMS) exclude atypical days and one-time special events; (2) The number of passengers who boarded public transportation vehicles. Passengers are counted each time they board a vehicle no matter how many vehicles they use to travel from their origin to their destination. (3) The sum of the distances ridden by all passengers during the entire fiscal year.
Source: Federal Transit Administration, National Transit Database, 2017

Air Transportation

Airport Name and Code / Type of Service	Passenger Airlines[1]	Passenger Enplanements	Freight Carriers[2]	Freight (lbs)
Indianapolis International (IND)				
Domestic service (U.S. carriers - 2018)	33	4,580,733	15	990,628,994
International service (U.S. carriers - 2017)	11	10,113	3	50,609,773

Note: (1) Includes all U.S.-based major, minor and commuter airlines that carried at least one passenger during the year; (2) Includes all U.S.-based airlines and freight carriers that transported at least one pound of freight during the year.
Source: Bureau of Transportation Statistics, The Intermodal Transportation Database, Air Carriers: T-100 Domestic Market (U.S. Carriers), 2018; Bureau of Transportation Statistics, The Intermodal Transportation Database, Air Carriers: T-100 International Market (U.S. Carriers), 2017

Other Transportation Statistics

Major Highways:	I-65; I-69; I-70; I-74
Amtrak Service:	Yes
Major Waterways/Ports:	White River

Source: Amtrak.com; Google Maps

BUSINESSES

Major Business Headquarters

Company Name	Industry	Rankings	
		Fortune[1]	Forbes[2]
Anthem	Health Care: Insurance and Managed Care	29	-
Eli Lilly	Pharmaceuticals	129	-
Simon Property Group	Real Estate	493	-

Note: (1) Companies that produce a 10-K are ranked 1 to 500 based on 2017 revenue; (2) All private companies with at least $2 billion in annual revenue through the end of their most current fiscal year are ranked 1 to 229; companies listed are headquartered in the city; dashes indicate no ranking
Source: Fortune, "Fortune 500," June 2018; Forbes, "America's Largest Private Companies," 2018 Rankings

Fast-Growing Businesses

According to *Inc.*, Indianapolis is home to one of America's 500 fastest-growing private companies: **Innovatemap** (#452). Criteria: must be an independent, privately-held, for-profit, U.S. corporation, proprietorship or partnership as of December 31, 2017; revenues must be at least $100,000 in 2014 and $2 million in 2017; must have four-year operating/sales history. Holding companies, regulated banks, and utilities were excluded. *Inc., "America's 500 Fastest-Growing Private Companies," 2018*

Minority Business Opportunity

Indianapolis is home to one company which is on the *Black Enterprise* Industrial/Service list (100 largest companies based on gross sales): **Mays Chemical Co.** (#42). Criteria: operational in previous calendar year; at least 51% black-owned and manufactures/owns the product it sells or provides industrial or consumer services. Brokerages, real estate firms and firms that provide professional services are not eligible. *Black Enterprise, B.E. 100s, 2018*

Indianapolis is home to two companies which are on the *Hispanic Business* 500 list (500 largest U.S. Hispanic-owned companies based on revenue): **Morales Group** (#150); **Garcia**

Construction Group (#205). Companies included must show at least 51 percent ownership by Hispanic U.S. citizens, and must maintain headquarters in one of the 50 states or Washington, D.C. *Hispanic Business, "Hispanic Business 500," June 20, 2013*

Minority- and Women-Owned Businesses

Group	All Firms		Firms with Paid Employees			
	Firms	Sales ($000)	Firms	Sales ($000)	Employees	Payroll ($000)
AIAN[1]	441	49,971	28	39,396	246	10,419
Asian	2,101	1,076,911	651	1,003,996	5,305	132,640
Black	13,322	977,881	521	757,937	7,840	262,939
Hispanic	3,395	617,641	339	512,149	4,224	97,914
NHOPI[2]	48	(s)	12	(s)	20 - 99	(s)
Women	27,668	4,729,023	2,600	4,232,733	28,874	1,054,998
All Firms	69,366	141,782,909	15,252	139,642,415	474,109	23,195,994

Note: Figures cover firms located in the city; minority- and women-owned business are defined as firms in which the corresponding group own 51% or more of the stock or equity of the company; (1) American Indian and Alaska Native; (2) Native Hawaiian and Other Pacific Islander; (s) estimates are suppressed when publication standards are not met
Source: U.S. Census Bureau, 2012 Economic Census, Survey of Business Owners

HOTELS & CONVENTION CENTERS

Hotels, Motels and Vacation Rentals

Area	5 Star		4 Star		3 Star		2 Star		1 Star		Not Rated	
	Num.	Pct.[3]	Num.	Pct.[3]	Num.	Pct.[3]	Num.	Pct.[3]	Num.	Pct.[3]	Num.	Pct.[3]
City[1]	0	0.0	11	2.1	107	20.9	163	31.8	7	1.4	224	43.8
Total[2]	286	0.4	5,236	7.1	16,715	22.6	10,259	13.9	293	0.4	41,056	55.6

Note: (1) Figures cover Indianapolis and vicinity; (2) Figures cover all 100 cities in this book; (3) Percentage of hotels which have a given star rating; Star ratings are determined by expedia.com and offer an indication of the general quality of a particular hotel.
Source: www.expedia.com, April 3, 2019

Major Convention Centers

Name	Overall Space (sq. ft.)	Exhibit Space (sq. ft.)	Meeting Space (sq. ft.)	Meeting Rooms
Indiana Convention Center	n/a	400,000	140,000	48

Note: Table includes convention centers located in the Indianapolis-Carmel-Anderson, IN metro area; n/a not available
Source: Original research

Living Environment

COST OF LIVING

Cost of Living Index

Composite Index	Groceries	Housing	Utilities	Trans-portation	Health Care	Misc. Goods/Services
93.0	94.3	79.5	105.6	94.2	91.5	100.4

Note: The Cost of Living Index measures regional differences in the cost of consumer goods and services, excluding taxes and non-consumer expenditures, for professional and managerial households in the top income quintile. It is based on more than 50,000 prices covering almost 60 different items for which prices are collected three times a year by chambers of commerce, economic development organizations or university applied economic centers in each participating urban area. The numbers shown should be read as a percentage above or below the national average of 100. For example, a value of 115.4 in the groceries column indicates that grocery prices are 15.4% higher than the national average. Small differences in the index numbers should not be interpreted as significant; Figures cover the Indianapolis IN urban area.
Source: The Council for Community and Economic Research, ACCRA Cost of Living Index, 2018

Grocery Prices

Area[1]	T-Bone Steak ($/pound)	Frying Chicken ($/pound)	Whole Milk ($/half gal.)	Eggs ($/dozen)	Orange Juice ($/64 oz.)	Coffee ($/11.5 oz.)
City[2]	11.80	1.38	1.51	1.44	3.40	4.31
Avg.	11.35	1.42	1.94	1.81	3.52	4.35
Min.	7.45	0.92	0.80	0.75	2.72	3.06
Max.	15.05	2.76	4.18	4.00	5.36	8.20

Note: (1) Values for the local area are compared with the average, minimum and maximum values for all 291 areas in the Cost of Living Index; (2) Figures cover the Indianapolis IN urban area; T-Bone Steak (price per pound); Frying Chicken (price per pound, whole fryer); Whole Milk (half gallon carton); Eggs (price per dozen, Grade A, large); Orange Juice (64 oz. Tropicana or Florida Natural); Coffee (11.5 oz. can, vacuum-packed, Maxwell House, Hills Bros, or Folgers).
Source: The Council for Community and Economic Research, ACCRA Cost of Living Index, 2018

Housing and Utility Costs

Area[1]	New Home Price ($)	Apartment Rent ($/month)	All Electric ($/month)	Part Electric ($/month)	Other Energy ($/month)	Telephone ($/month)
City[2]	250,625	1,052	-	105.38	79.02	178.60
Avg.	347,000	1,087	165.93	100.16	67.73	178.70
Min.	200,468	500	93.58	25.64	26.78	163.10
Max.	1,901,222	4,888	388.65	246.86	332.81	197.70

Note: (1) Values for the local area are compared with the average, minimum and maximum values for all 291 areas in the Cost of Living Index; (2) Figures cover the Indianapolis IN urban area; New Home Price (2,400 sf living area, 8,000 sf lot, in urban area with full utilities); Apartment Rent (950 sf 2 bedroom/1.5 or 2 bath, unfurnished, excluding all utilities except water); All Electric (average monthly cost for an all-electric home); Part Electric (average monthly cost for a part-electric home); Other Energy (average monthly cost for natural gas, fuel oil, coal, wood, and any other forms of energy except electricity); Telephone (price includes the base monthly rate plus taxes and fees for three lines of mobile phone service).
Source: The Council for Community and Economic Research, ACCRA Cost of Living Index, 2018

Health Care, Transportation, and Other Costs

Area[1]	Doctor ($/visit)	Dentist ($/visit)	Optometrist ($/visit)	Gasoline ($/gallon)	Beauty Salon ($/visit)	Men's Shirt ($)
City[2]	93.91	92.23	60.20	2.64	39.63	39.87
Avg.	110.71	95.11	103.74	2.61	37.48	32.03
Min.	33.60	62.55	54.63	1.89	17.00	11.44
Max.	195.97	153.93	225.79	3.59	71.88	58.64

Note: (1) Values for the local area are compared with the average, minimum and maximum values for all 291 areas in the Cost of Living Index; (2) Figures cover the Indianapolis IN urban area; Doctor (general practitioners routine exam of an established patient); Dentist (adult teeth cleaning and periodic oral examination); Optometrist (full vision eye exam for established adult patient); Gasoline (one gallon regular unleaded, national brand, including all taxes, cash price at self-service pump if available); Beauty Salon (woman's shampoo, trim, and blow-dry); Men's Shirt (cotton/polyester dress shirt, pinpoint weave, long sleeves).
Source: The Council for Community and Economic Research, ACCRA Cost of Living Index, 2018

HOUSING

House Price Index (HPI)

Area	National Ranking[2]	Quarterly Change (%)	One-Year Change (%)	Five-Year Change (%)
MSA[1]	47	1.62	8.69	32.10
U.S.[3]	–	1.12	5.73	32.81

Note: The HPI is a weighted repeat sales index. It measures average price changes in repeat sales or refinancings on the same properties. This information is obtained by reviewing repeat mortgage transactions on single-family properties whose mortgages have been purchased or securitized by Fannie Mae or Freddie Mac in January 1975; (1) Figures cover the Indianapolis-Carmel-Anderson, IN Metropolitan Statistical Area—see Appendix B for areas included; (2) Rankings are based on annual percentage change for all metro areas containing at least 15,000 transactions over the last 10 years and ranges from 1 to 245; (3) figures based on a weighted average of Census Division estimates using a seasonally adjusted, purchase-only index; all figures are for the period ending December 31, 2018
Source: Federal Housing Finance Agency, House Price Index, February 26, 2019

Median Single-Family Home Prices

Area	2016	2017	2018[p]	Percent Change 2017 to 2018
MSA[1]	159.8	171.5	187.1	9.1
U.S. Average	235.5	248.8	261.6	5.1

Note: Figures are median sales prices of existing single-family homes in thousands of dollars; (p) preliminary; (1) Figures cover the Indianapolis-Carmel-Anderson, IN Metropolitan Statistical Area—see Appendix B for areas included
Source: National Association of Realtors, Median Sales Price of Existing Single-Family Homes for Metropolitan Areas, 4th Quarter 2018

Qualifying Income Based on Median Sales Price of Existing Single-Family Homes

Area	With 5% Down ($)	With 10% Down ($)	With 20% Down ($)
MSA[1]	45,260	42,878	38,114
U.S. Average	62,954	59,640	53,013

Note: Figures are preliminary; Qualifying income is based on a mortgage rate of 4.9%. Monthly principal and interest payment is limited to 25% of income; (1) Figures cover the Indianapolis-Carmel-Anderson, IN Metropolitan Statistical Area—see Appendix B for areas included
Source: National Association of Realtors, Qualifying Income Based on Median Sales Price of Existing Single-Family Homes for Metropolitan Areas, 4th Quarter 2018

Median Apartment Condo-Coop Home Prices

Area	2016	2017	2018[p]	Percent Change 2017 to 2018
MSA[1]	131.0	139.8	147.7	5.7
U.S. Average	220.7	234.3	241.0	2.9

Note: Figures are median sales prices of existing apartment condo-coop homes in thousands of dollars; (p) preliminary; (1) Figures cover the Indianapolis-Carmel-Anderson, IN Metropolitan Statistical Area—see Appendix B for areas included
Source: National Association of Realtors, Median Sales Price of Existing Apartment Condo-Coop Homes for Metropolitan Areas, 4th Quarter 2018

Home Value Distribution

Area	Under $50,000	$50,000 -$99,999	$100,000 -$149,999	$150,000 -$199,999	$200,000 -$299,999	$300,000 -$499,999	$500,000 -$999,999	$1,000,000 or more
City	8.8	26.3	29.0	16.1	10.1	6.7	2.3	0.6
MSA[1]	6.9	18.8	24.9	17.9	16.1	11.0	3.6	0.7
U.S.	8.3	13.9	14.7	14.6	18.7	17.3	9.7	2.7

Note: Figures are percentages and cover owner-occupied housing units; (1) Figures cover the Indianapolis-Carmel-Anderson, IN Metropolitan Statistical Area—see Appendix B for areas included
Source: U.S. Census Bureau, 2013-2017 American Community Survey 5-Year Estimates

Homeownership Rate

Area	2010 (%)	2011 (%)	2012 (%)	2013 (%)	2014 (%)	2015 (%)	2016 (%)	2017 (%)	2018 (%)
MSA[1]	68.8	68.3	67.1	67.5	66.9	64.6	63.9	63.9	64.3
U.S.	66.9	66.1	65.4	65.1	64.5	63.7	63.4	63.9	64.4

Note: (1) Figures cover the Indianapolis-Carmel-Anderson, IN Metropolitan Statistical Area—see Appendix B for areas included
Source: U.S. Census Bureau, Housing Vacancies and Homeownership Annual Statistics: 2010-2018

Year Housing Structure Built

Area	2010 or Later	2000 -2009	1990 -1999	1980 -1989	1970 -1979	1960 -1969	1950 -1959	1940 -1949	Before 1940	Median Year
City	2.2	10.0	13.1	11.9	14.0	13.2	12.8	6.0	16.9	1971
MSA[1]	4.1	16.6	16.8	10.7	12.9	10.9	10.5	4.4	13.1	1979
U.S.	3.2	14.5	14.0	13.6	15.5	10.8	10.5	5.1	12.9	1977

Note: Figures are percentages except for Median Year; Note: (1) Figures cover the Indianapolis-Carmel-Anderson, IN Metropolitan Statistical Area—see Appendix B for areas included
Source: U.S. Census Bureau, 2013-2017 American Community Survey 5-Year Estimates

Gross Monthly Rent

Area	Under $500	$500 -$999	$1,000 -$1,499	$1,500 -$1,999	$2,000 -$2,499	$2,500 -$2,999	$3,000 and up	Median ($)
City	7.4	64.4	23.5	3.5	0.7	0.2	0.3	840
MSA[1]	7.5	60.4	26.0	4.5	1.0	0.3	0.3	859
U.S.	10.5	41.1	28.7	11.7	4.5	1.8	1.7	982

Note: Figures are percentages except for Median; Gross rent is the contract rent plus the estimated average monthly cost of utilities (electricity, gas, and water and sewer) and fuels (oil, coal, kerosene, wood, etc.) if these are paid by the renter (or paid for the renter by someone else); (1) Figures cover the Indianapolis-Carmel-Anderson, IN Metropolitan Statistical Area—see Appendix B for areas included
Source: U.S. Census Bureau, 2013-2017 American Community Survey 5-Year Estimates

HEALTH

Health Risk Factors

Category	MSA[1] (%)	U.S. (%)
Adults aged 18–64 who have any kind of health care coverage	88.5	87.3
Adults who reported being in good or better health	81.9	82.4
Adults who have been told they have high blood cholesterol	33.0	33.0
Adults who have been told they have high blood pressure	34.6	32.3
Adults who are current smokers	19.4	17.1
Adults who currently use E-cigarettes	6.3	4.6
Adults who currently use chewing tobacco, snuff, or snus	3.8	4.0
Adults who are heavy drinkers[2]	6.4	6.3
Adults who are binge drinkers[3]	17.1	17.4
Adults who are overweight (BMI 25.0 - 29.9)	34.3	35.3
Adults who are obese (BMI 30.0 - 99.8)	32.0	31.3
Adults who participated in any physical activities in the past month	71.6	74.4
Adults who always or nearly always wears a seat belt	93.8	94.3

Note: (1) Figures cover the Indianapolis-Carmel-Anderson, IN Metropolitan Statistical Area—see Appendix B for areas included; (2) Heavy drinkers are classified as adult men having more than 14 drinks per week and adult women having more than 7 drinks per week; (3) Binge drinkers are classified as males having five or more drinks on one occasion or females having four or more drinks on one occasion
Source: Centers for Disease Control and Prevention, Behaviorial Risk Factor Surveillance System, SMART: Selected Metropolitan Area Risk Trends, 2017

Acute and Chronic Health Conditions

Category	MSA[1] (%)	U.S. (%)
Adults who have ever been told they had a heart attack	4.3	4.2
Adults who have ever been told they have angina or coronary heart disease	4.2	3.9
Adults who have ever been told they had a stroke	3.4	3.0
Adults who have ever been told they have asthma	14.8	14.2
Adults who have ever been told they have arthritis	25.6	24.9
Adults who have ever been told they have diabetes[2]	11.8	10.5
Adults who have ever been told they had skin cancer	6.6	6.2
Adults who have ever been told they had any other types of cancer	6.9	7.1
Adults who have ever been told they have COPD	7.2	6.5
Adults who have ever been told they have kidney disease	3.4	3.0
Adults who have ever been told they have a form of depression	22.6	20.5

Note: (1) Figures cover the Indianapolis-Carmel-Anderson, IN Metropolitan Statistical Area—see Appendix B for areas included; (2) Figures do not include pregnancy-related, borderline, or pre-diabetes
Source: Centers for Disease Control and Prevention, Behaviorial Risk Factor Surveillance System, SMART: Selected Metropolitan Area Risk Trends, 2017

Health Screening and Vaccination Rates

Category	MSA[1] (%)	U.S. (%)
Adults aged 65+ who have had flu shot within the past year	59.1	60.7
Adults aged 65+ who have ever had a pneumonia vaccination	81.2	75.4
Adults who have ever been tested for HIV	39.3	36.1
Adults who have ever had the shingles or zoster vaccine?	28.3	28.9
Adults who have had their blood cholesterol checked within the last five years	85.3	85.9

Note: n/a not available; (1) Figures cover the Indianapolis-Carmel-Anderson, IN Metropolitan Statistical Area—see Appendix B for areas included.
Source: Centers for Disease Control and Prevention, Behaviorial Risk Factor Surveillance System, SMART: Selected Metropolitan Area Risk Trends, 2017

Disability Status

Category	MSA[1] (%)	U.S. (%)
Adults who reported being deaf	5.1	6.7
Are you blind or have serious difficulty seeing, even when wearing glasses?	4.5	4.5
Are you limited in any way in any of your usual activities due of arthritis?	13.1	12.9
Do you have difficulty doing errands alone?	7.6	6.8
Do you have difficulty dressing or bathing?	3.7	3.6
Do you have serious difficulty concentrating/remembering/making decisions?	10.9	10.7
Do you have serious difficulty walking or climbing stairs?	12.6	13.6

Note: (1) Figures cover the Indianapolis-Carmel-Anderson, IN Metropolitan Statistical Area—see Appendix B for areas included.
Source: Centers for Disease Control and Prevention, Behaviorial Risk Factor Surveillance System, SMART: Selected Metropolitan Area Risk Trends, 2017

Mortality Rates for the Top 10 Causes of Death in the U.S.

ICD-10[a] Sub-Chapter	ICD-10[a] Code	Age-Adjusted Mortality Rate[1] per 100,000 population	
		County[2]	U.S.
Malignant neoplasms	C00-C97	181.8	155.5
Ischaemic heart diseases	I20-I25	97.8	94.8
Other forms of heart disease	I30-I51	59.6	52.9
Chronic lower respiratory diseases	J40-J47	62.1	41.0
Cerebrovascular diseases	I60-I69	41.3	37.5
Other degenerative diseases of the nervous system	G30-G31	32.5	35.0
Other external causes of accidental injury	W00-X59	47.7	33.7
Organic, including symptomatic, mental disorders	F01-F09	43.9	31.0
Hypertensive diseases	I10-I15	25.9	21.9
Diabetes mellitus	E10-E14	27.6	21.2

Note: (a) ICD-10 = International Classification of Diseases 10th Revision; (1) Mortality rates are a three year average covering 2015-2017; (2) Figures cover Marion County.
Source: Centers for Disease Control and Prevention, National Center for Health Statistics. Underlying Cause of Death 1999-2017 on CDC WONDER Online Database

Mortality Rates for Selected Causes of Death

ICD-10[a] Sub-Chapter	ICD-10[a] Code	Age-Adjusted Mortality Rate[1] per 100,000 population	
		County[2]	U.S.
Assault	X85-Y09	17.0	5.9
Diseases of the liver	K70-K76	17.0	14.1
Human immunodeficiency virus (HIV) disease	B20-B24	2.3	1.8
Influenza and pneumonia	J09-J18	11.8	14.3
Intentional self-harm	X60-X84	14.6	13.6
Malnutrition	E40-E46	2.1	1.6
Obesity and other hyperalimentation	E65-E68	2.3	2.1
Renal failure	N17-N19	22.2	13.0
Transport accidents	V01-V99	13.0	12.4
Viral hepatitis	B15-B19	1.7	1.6

Note: (a) ICD-10 = International Classification of Diseases 10th Revision; (1) Mortality rates are a three year average covering 2015-2017; (2) Figures cover Marion County; Data are suppressed when the data meet the criteria for confidentiality constraints; Mortality rates are flagged as unreliable when the rate would be calculated with a numerator of 20 or less.
Source: Centers for Disease Control and Prevention, National Center for Health Statistics. Underlying Cause of Death 1999-2017 on CDC WONDER Online Database

Health Insurance Coverage

Area	With Health Insurance	With Private Health Insurance	With Public Health Insurance	Without Health Insurance	Population Under Age 18 Without Health Insurance
City	87.4	60.5	35.9	12.6	6.1
MSA[1]	90.1	70.4	30.0	9.9	5.6
U.S.	89.5	67.2	33.8	10.5	5.7

Note: Figures are percentages that cover the civilian noninstitutionalized population; (1) Figures cover the Indianapolis-Carmel-Anderson, IN Metropolitan Statistical Area—see Appendix B for areas included
Source: U.S. Census Bureau, 2013-2017 American Community Survey 5-Year Estimates

Number of Medical Professionals

Area	MDs[3]	DOs[3,4]	Dentists	Podiatrists	Chiropractors	Optometrists
County[1] (number)	4,132	205	830	56	142	180
County[1] (rate[2])	437.7	21.7	87.4	5.9	14.9	18.9
U.S. (rate[2])	279.3	23.0	68.4	6.0	27.1	16.2

Note: Data as of 2017 unless noted; (1) Data covers Marion County; (2) Rate per 100,000 population; (3) Data as of 2016 and includes all active, non-federal physicians; (4) Doctor of Osteopathic Medicine
Source: U.S. Department of Health and Human Services, Health Resources and Services Administration, Bureau of Health Professions, Area Resource File (ARF) 2017-2018

Best Hospitals

According to *U.S. News,* the Indianapolis-Carmel-Anderson, IN metro area is home to one of the best hospitals in the U.S.: **Indiana University Health Medical Center** (8 adult specialties and 8 pediatric specialties). The hospital listed was nationally ranked in at least one of 16 adult or 10 pediatric specialties. Only 170 hospitals nationwide were nationally ranked in one or more adult or pediatric specialty. Twenty hospitals in the U.S. made the Honor Roll. The Best Hospitals Honor Roll takes both the national rankings and the procedure and condition ratings into account. Hospitals received points if they were nationally ranked in one of the 16 adult specialties—the higher they ranked, the more points they got—and how many ratings of "high performing" they earned in the nine procedures and conditions. *U.S. News Online, "America's Best Hospitals 2018-19"*

According to *U.S. News,* the Indianapolis-Carmel-Anderson, IN metro area is home to one of the best children's hospitals in the U.S.: **Riley Hospital for Children at IU Health** (8 pediatric specialties). The hospital listed was highly ranked in at least one of 10 pediatric specialties. Eighty-six children's hospitals in the U.S. were nationally ranked in at least one specialty. Hospitals received points for being ranked in a specialty, and the 10 hospitals with the most points across the 10 specialties make up the Honor Roll. *U.S. News Online, "America's Best Children's Hospitals 2018-19"*

EDUCATION

Public School District Statistics

District Name	Schls	Pupils	Pupil/ Teacher Ratio	Minority Pupils[1] (%)	Free Lunch Eligible[2] (%)	IEP[3] (%)
Franklin Township Com Sch Corp	10	9,445	20.2	24.8	27.9	17.7
Hoosier Acad Virtual Charter	1	3,342	42.1	23.1	43.7	13.5
Indiana Connections Academy	1	4,032	39.0	19.0	33.3	17.3
Indiana Virtual School	1	2,947	193.3	34.3	80.3	7.2
Indianapolis Public Schools	67	31,011	14.8	77.9	65.4	19.4
M S D Decatur Township	9	6,477	19.1	28.1	57.8	14.9
M S D Lawrence Township	17	15,379	18.7	73.0	54.2	14.1
M S D Perry Township	17	16,207	20.3	49.7	54.4	14.6
M S D Pike Township	13	11,817	19.2	90.2	61.3	14.5
M S D Warren Township	18	12,865	23.9	72.3	63.0	16.1
M S D Washington Township	13	10,834	17.9	71.4	48.8	16.9
M S D Wayne Township	18	15,472	15.0	65.4	64.4	14.4

Note: Table includes school districts with 2,000 or more students; (1) Percentage of students that are not non-Hispanic white; (2) Percentage of students that are eligible for the free lunch program; (3) Percentage of students that have an Individualized Education Program.
Source: U.S. Department of Education, National Center for Education Statistics, Common Core of Data, Local Education Agency (School District) Universe Survey: School Year 2016-2017; U.S. Department of Education, National Center for Education Statistics, Common Core of Data, Public Elementary/Secondary School Universe Survey: School Year 2016-2017

Best High Schools

According to *U.S. News,* Indianapolis is home to one of the best high schools in the U.S.: **Herron High School** (#252). More than 20,000 public, magnet and charter schools were ranked based on their performance on state assessments and how well they prepare students for college. Schools with the highest unrounded College Readiness Index values were numerically ranked from 1 to 500 and were classified as gold medal winners. *U.S. News & World Report, "Best High Schools 2018"*

Highest Level of Education

Area	Less than H.S.	H.S. Diploma	Some College, No Deg.	Associate Degree	Bachelor's Degree	Master's Degree	Prof. School Degree	Doctorate Degree
City	14.5	28.0	20.7	7.1	19.2	7.3	2.1	1.1
MSA[1]	10.7	28.2	20.2	7.7	21.4	8.4	2.1	1.2
U.S.	12.7	27.3	20.8	8.3	19.1	8.4	2.0	1.4

Note: Figures cover persons age 25 and over; (1) Figures cover the Indianapolis-Carmel-Anderson, IN Metropolitan Statistical Area—see Appendix B for areas included
Source: U.S. Census Bureau, 2013-2017 American Community Survey 5-Year Estimates

Educational Attainment by Race

Area	High School Graduate or Higher (%)					Bachelor's Degree or Higher (%)				
	Total	White	Black	Asian	Hisp.[2]	Total	White	Black	Asian	Hisp.[2]
City	85.5	87.7	84.4	77.7	55.4	29.7	34.8	17.0	47.5	10.8
MSA[1]	89.3	90.8	85.3	83.2	61.0	33.1	35.1	19.7	55.5	14.6
U.S.	87.3	89.3	84.9	86.5	66.7	30.9	32.2	20.6	52.7	15.2

Note: Figures shown cover persons 25 years old and over; (1) Figures cover the Indianapolis-Carmel-Anderson, IN Metropolitan Statistical Area—see Appendix B for areas included; (2) People of Hispanic origin can be of any race
Source: U.S. Census Bureau, 2013-2017 American Community Survey 5-Year Estimates

School Enrollment by Grade and Control

Area	Preschool (%)		Kindergarten (%)		Grades 1 - 4 (%)		Grades 5 - 8 (%)		Grades 9 - 12 (%)	
	Public	Private	Public	Private	Public	Private	Public	Private	Public	Private
City	54.5	45.5	85.2	14.8	88.7	11.3	86.6	13.4	87.7	12.3
MSA[1]	50.4	49.6	86.4	13.6	89.1	10.9	88.4	11.6	89.2	10.8
U.S.	58.8	41.2	87.7	12.3	89.7	10.3	89.6	10.4	90.3	9.7

Note: Figures shown cover persons 3 years old and over; (1) Figures cover the Indianapolis-Carmel-Anderson, IN Metropolitan Statistical Area—see Appendix B for areas included
Source: U.S. Census Bureau, 2013-2017 American Community Survey 5-Year Estimates

Average Salaries of Public School Classroom Teachers

Area	2016		2017		Change from 2016 to 2017	
	Dollars	Rank[1]	Dollars	Rank[1]	Percent	Rank[2]
Indiana	53,645	26	54,308	26	1.2	30
U.S. Average	58,479	–	59,660	–	2.0	–

Note: (1) Rank ranges from 1 to 51 where 1 indicates highest salary; (2) Rank ranges from 1 to 51 where 1 indicates highest percent change.
Source: National Education Association, Rankings & Estimates: Rankings of the States 2017 and Estimates of School Statistics 2018

Higher Education

Four-Year Colleges			Two-Year Colleges			Medical Schools[1]	Law Schools[2]	Voc/ Tech[3]
Public	Private Non-profit	Private For-profit	Public	Private Non-profit	Private For-profit			
1	7	8	1	0	5	2	1	8

Note: Figures cover institutions located within the city limits and include main campuses only; (1) includes schools accredited by the Liaison Committee on Medical Education and the American Osteopathic Association's Commission on Osteopathic College Accreditation; (2) includes ABA-accredited schools, schools with provisional ABA accreditation, and state accredited schools; (3) includes all schools with programs that are less than 2 years.
Source: National Center for Education Statistics, Integrated Postsecondary Education System (IPEDS), 2017-18; Wikipedia, List of Medical Schools in the United States, accessed April 3, 2019; Wikipedia, List of Law Schools in the United States, accessed April 3, 2019

According to *U.S. News & World Report,* the Indianapolis-Carmel-Anderson, IN metro area is home to one of the best national universities in the U.S.: **Indiana University-Purdue**

University—Indianapolis (#194 tie). The indicators used to capture academic quality fall into a number of categories: assessment by administrators at peer institutions; retention of students; faculty resources; student selectivity; financial resources; alumni giving; high school counselor ratings of colleges; and graduation rate. *U.S. News & World Report, "America's Best Colleges 2019"*

According to *U.S. News & World Report,* the Indianapolis-Carmel-Anderson, IN metro area is home to two of the best liberal arts colleges in the U.S.: **DePauw University** (#56 tie); **Franklin College** (#143 tie). The indicators used to capture academic quality fall into a number of categories: assessment by administrators at peer institutions; retention of students; faculty resources; student selectivity; financial resources; alumni giving; high school counselor ratings of colleges; and graduation rate. *U.S. News & World Report, "America's Best Colleges 2019"*

According to *U.S. News & World Report,* the Indianapolis-Carmel-Anderson, IN metro area is home to one of the top 75 medical schools for research in the U.S.: **Indiana University—Indianapolis** (#48 tie). The rankings are based on a weighted average of 11 measures of quality: quality assessment; peer assessment score; assessment score by residency directors; research activity; total research activity; average research activity per faculty member; student selectivity; median MCAT total score; median undergraduate GPA; acceptance rate; and faculty resources. *U.S. News & World Report, "America's Best Graduate Schools, Medical, 2020"*

PRESIDENTIAL ELECTION

2016 Presidential Election Results

Area	Clinton	Trump	Johnson	Stein	Other
Marion County	58.0	35.5	5.0	0.2	1.3
U.S.	48.0	45.9	3.3	1.1	1.7

Note: Results are percentages and may not add to 100% due to rounding
Source: Dave Leip's Atlas of U.S. Presidential Elections

EMPLOYERS

Major Employers

Company Name	Industry
Allison Transmission	Motor vehicle parts & accessories
Ameritech	Local and long distance telephone
Apple American Indiana	Restaurant/family chain
Automotive Components Holdings	Steering mechanisms, motor vehicle
Celadon Trucking Service	Trucking, except local
CNO Financial Group	Insurance services
Communikty Hospitals of Indiana	General medical & surgical hospitals
Conseco Variable Ins Company	Life insurance
Defense Finance and Accounting Services	Accounting, auditing, & bookkeeping
Eli Lilly and Company	Pharmaceutical preparations
Family & Social Svcs Admin	Administration of social and human resources
Federal Express Corporation	Air cargo carrier
GEICO	Auto insurance
Hewlett-Packard Co.	Computer terminals
Indiana Department of Transportation	Regulation administration of transportation
Indiana Police State	General government, state government
Liberty Mutual	Insurance services
Meridian Citizens Mutual Ins Company	Assessment associations: fire, marine & casualty ins
Methodist Hospital	General medical & surgical hospitals
Navient (formerly Sallie Mae)	Financial services
Rolls Royce Corporation	Aircraft engines & engine parts
St. Vincent Hospital and Healthcare Center	General medical & surgical hospitals
The Health Hospital of Marion County	General medical & surgical hospitals
Trustees of indiana University	University
United States Postal Service	U.S. postal service

Note: Companies shown are located within the Indianapolis-Carmel-Anderson, IN Metropolitan Statistical Area.
Source: Hoovers.com; Wikipedia

Best Companies to Work For

Roche Diagnostics, headquartered in Indianapolis, is among the "100 Best Companies for Working Mothers." Criteria: paid time off and leaves; workforce profile; benefits; women's issues and advancement; flexible work; company culture and work life programs. *Working Mother, "100 Best Companies 2018"*

NCAA, headquartered in Indianapolis, is among the "100 Best Places to Work in IT." To qualify, companies had to be U.S.-based organizations or be non-U.S.- based employers that met the following criteria: have a minimum of 300 total employees at a U.S. headquarters and a minimum of 30 IT employees in the U.S., with at least 50% of their IT employees based in the U.S. The best places to work were selected based on compensation, benefits, work/life balance, employee morale, and satisfaction with training and development programs. In addition, *Computerworld* looked at retention efforts, programs for recognizing and rewarding outstanding performances, and benefits such as flextime, elder care and child care, and reimbursement for college tuition and the cost of pursuing technology certifications. *Computerworld, "100 Best Places to Work in IT 2018"*

Anthem; Eli Lilly and Company; Roche Diagnostics, headquartered in Indianapolis, are among the "Top Companies for Executive Women." The 2019 National Association for Female Executives (NAFE) Top Companies for Executive Women application included more than 200 questions on female representation at all levels, but especially the corporate officer and profit-and-loss leadership ranks. The application tracked how many employees have access to programs and policies that promote the advancement of women, and how many employees take advantage of them. The application also examined how companies train managers to help women advance, and how managers are held accountable for the advancement of female employees they oversee. *National Association for Female Executives, "2019 NAFE Top 70 Companies for Executive Women"*

PUBLIC SAFETY

Crime Rate

Area	All Crimes	Violent Crimes				Property Crimes		
		Murder	Rape[3]	Robbery	Aggrav. Assault	Burglary	Larceny -Theft	Motor Vehicle Theft
City	5,745.8	17.9	76.7	400.2	839.1	1,027.2	2,821.5	563.2
Suburbs[1]	1,942.6	1.1	26.9	39.6	145.0	233.5	1,338.8	157.7
Metro[2]	3,576.9	8.3	48.3	194.6	443.3	574.6	1,975.9	331.9
U.S.	2,756.1	5.3	41.7	98.0	248.9	430.4	1,694.4	237.4

Note: Figures are crimes per 100,000 population; (1) All areas within the metro area that are located outside the city limits; (2) Figures cover the Indianapolis-Carmel-Anderson, IN Metropolitan Statistical Area—see Appendix B for areas included; (3) The city and U.S. figures shown were reported using the revised Uniform Crime Reporting (UCR) definition of rape. The suburban and metro area figures shown are an aggregate total of the data submitted using both the revised and legacy UCR definitions.
Source: FBI Uniform Crime Reports, 2017

Hate Crimes

Area	Number of Quarters Reported	Number of Incidents per Bias Motivation					
		Race/Ethnicity/ Ancestry	Religion	Sexual Orientation	Disability	Gender	Gender Identity
City	n/a	n/a	n/a	n/a	n/a	n/a	n/a
U.S.	4	4,131	1,564	1,130	116	46	119

Note: n/a not available.
Source: Federal Bureau of Investigation, Hate Crime Statistics 2017

Identity Theft Consumer Reports

Area	Reports	Reports per 100,000 Population	Rank[2]
MSA[1]	1,961	98	140
U.S.	444,602	135	-

Note: (1) Figures cover the Indianapolis-Carmel-Anderson, IN Metropolitan Statistical Area—see Appendix B for areas included; (2) Rank ranges from 1 to 389 where 1 indicates greatest number of identity theft reports per 100,000 population
Source: Federal Trade Commission, Consumer Sentinel Network Data Book for January–December 2018

Fraud and Other Consumer Reports

Area	Reports	Reports per 100,000 Population	Rank[2]
MSA[1]	11,009	549	106
U.S.	2,552,917	776	-

Note: (1) Figures cover the Indianapolis-Carmel-Anderson, IN Metropolitan Statistical Area—see Appendix B for areas included; (2) Rank ranges from 1 to 389 where 1 indicates greatest number of fraud and other consumer reports per 100,000 population
Source: Federal Trade Commission, Consumer Sentinel Network Data Book for January–December 2018

SPORTS

Professional Sports Teams

Team Name	League	Year Established
Indiana Pacers	National Basketball Association (NBA)	1967
Indianapolis Colts	National Football League (NFL)	1984

Note: Includes teams located in the Indianapolis-Carmel-Anderson, IN Metropolitan Statistical Area.
Source: Wikipedia, Major Professional Sports Teams of the United States and Canada, April 5, 2019

CLIMATE

Average and Extreme Temperatures

Temperature	Jan	Feb	Mar	Apr	May	Jun	Jul	Aug	Sep	Oct	Nov	Dec	Yr.
Extreme High (°F)	71	72	85	89	93	102	104	102	100	90	81	74	104
Average High (°F)	35	39	50	63	73	82	85	84	78	66	51	39	62
Average Temp. (°F)	27	31	41	52	63	72	76	73	67	55	43	31	53
Average Low (°F)	18	22	31	41	52	61	65	63	55	44	33	23	42
Extreme Low (°F)	-22	-21	-7	18	28	39	48	41	34	20	-2	-23	-23

Note: Figures cover the years 1948-1990
Source: National Climatic Data Center, International Station Meteorological Climate Summary, 9/96

Average Precipitation/Snowfall/Humidity

Precip./Humidity	Jan	Feb	Mar	Apr	May	Jun	Jul	Aug	Sep	Oct	Nov	Dec	Yr.
Avg. Precip. (in.)	2.8	2.5	3.6	3.6	4.0	3.9	4.3	3.4	2.9	2.6	3.3	3.3	40.2
Avg. Snowfall (in.)	7	6	4	1	Tr	0	0	0	0	Tr	2	5	25
Avg. Rel. Hum. 7am (%)	81	81	79	77	79	80	84	87	87	85	83	83	82
Avg. Rel. Hum. 4pm (%)	68	64	59	53	53	53	56	56	53	53	63	70	59

Note: Figures cover the years 1948-1990; Tr = Trace amounts (<0.05 in. of rain; <0.5 in. of snow)
Source: National Climatic Data Center, International Station Meteorological Climate Summary, 9/96

Weather Conditions

Temperature			Daytime Sky			Precipitation		
10°F & below	32°F & below	90°F & above	Clear	Partly cloudy	Cloudy	0.01 inch or more precip.	0.1 inch or more snow/ice	Thunder-storms
19	119	19	83	128	154	127	24	43

Note: Figures are average number of days per year and cover the years 1948-1990
Source: National Climatic Data Center, International Station Meteorological Climate Summary, 9/96

HAZARDOUS WASTE

Superfund Sites

The Indianapolis-Carmel-Anderson, IN metro area is home to seven sites on the EPA's Superfund National Priorities List: **Broadway Street Corridor Groundwater Contamination** (final); **Envirochem Corp.** (final); **Keystone Corridor Ground Water Contamination** (final); **Northside Sanitary Landfill, Inc** (final); **Pike and Mulberry Streets PCE Plume** (final); **Reilly Tar & Chemical Corp. (Indianapolis Plant)** (final); **Riverside Ground Water Contamination** (proposed). There are a total of 1,390 Superfund sites with a status of proposed or final on the list in the U.S. *U.S. Environmental Protection Agency, National Priorities List, April 5, 2019*

**AIR & WATER
QUALITY**

Air Quality Trends: Ozone

	1990	1995	2000	2005	2010	2012	2014	2015	2016	2017
MSA[1]	0.086	0.095	0.082	0.080	0.069	0.074	0.063	0.064	0.068	0.066
U.S.	0.088	0.089	0.082	0.080	0.073	0.075	0.067	0.068	0.069	0.068

Note: (1) Data covers the Indianapolis-Carmel-Anderson, IN Metropolitan Statistical Area—see Appendix B for areas included. The values shown are the composite ozone concentration averages among trend sites based on the highest fourth daily maximum 8-hour concentration in parts per million. These trends are based on sites having an adequate record of monitoring data during the trend period. Data from exceptional events are included.
Source: U.S. Environmental Protection Agency, Air Quality Monitoring Information, "Air Quality Trends by City, 1990-2017"

Air Quality Index

Area	Percent of Days when Air Quality was...[2]					AQI Statistics[2]	
	Good	Moderate	Unhealthy for Sensitive Groups	Unhealthy	Very Unhealthy	Maximum	Median
MSA[1]	54.0	43.6	2.5	0.0	0.0	122	48

Note: (1) Data covers the Indianapolis-Carmel-Anderson, IN Metropolitan Statistical Area—see Appendix B for areas included; (2) Based on 365 days with AQI data in 2017. Air Quality Index (AQI) is an index for reporting daily air quality. EPA calculates the AQI for five major air pollutants regulated by the Clean Air Act: ground-level ozone, particle pollution (aka particulate matter), carbon monoxide, sulfur dioxide, and nitrogen dioxide. The AQI runs from 0 to 500. The higher the AQI value, the greater the level of air pollution and the greater the health concern. There are six AQI categories: "Good" AQI is between 0 and 50. Air quality is considered satisfactory; "Moderate" AQI is between 51 and 100. Air quality is acceptable; "Unhealthy for Sensitive Groups" When AQI values are between 101 and 150, members of sensitive groups may experience health effects; "Unhealthy" When AQI values are between 151 and 200 everyone may begin to experience health effects; "Very Unhealthy" AQI values between 201 and 300 trigger a health alert; "Hazardous" AQI values over 300 trigger warnings of emergency conditions (not shown).
Source: U.S. Environmental Protection Agency, Air Quality Index Report, 2017

Air Quality Index Pollutants

Area	Percent of Days when AQI Pollutant was...[2]					
	Carbon Monoxide	Nitrogen Dioxide	Ozone	Sulfur Dioxide	Particulate Matter 2.5	Particulate Matter 10
MSA[1]	0.0	0.8	37.8	2.5	58.9	0.0

Note: (1) Data covers the Indianapolis-Carmel-Anderson, IN Metropolitan Statistical Area—see Appendix B for areas included; (2) Based on 365 days with AQI data in 2017. The Air Quality Index (AQI) is an index for reporting daily air quality. EPA calculates the AQI for five major air pollutants regulated by the Clean Air Act: ground-level ozone, particle pollution (also known as particulate matter), carbon monoxide, sulfur dioxide, and nitrogen dioxide. The AQI runs from 0 to 500. The higher the AQI value, the greater the level of air pollution and the greater the health concern.
Source: U.S. Environmental Protection Agency, Air Quality Index Report, 2017

Maximum Air Pollutant Concentrations: Particulate Matter, Ozone, CO and Lead

	Particulate Matter 10 (ug/m^3)	Particulate Matter 2.5 Wtd AM (ug/m^3)	Particulate Matter 2.5 24-Hr (ug/m^3)	Ozone (ppm)	Carbon Monoxide (ppm)	Lead (ug/m^3)
MSA[1] Level	54	10.1	21	0.069	3	0.02
NAAQS[2]	150	15	35	0.075	9	0.15
Met NAAQS[2]	Yes	Yes	Yes	Yes	Yes	Yes

Note: (1) Data covers the Indianapolis-Carmel-Anderson, IN Metropolitan Statistical Area—see Appendix B for areas included; Data from exceptional events are included; (2) National Ambient Air Quality Standards; ppm = parts per million; ug/m^3 = micrograms per cubic meter; n/a not available.
Concentrations: Particulate Matter 10 (coarse particulate)—highest second maximum 24-hour concentration; Particulate Matter 2.5 Wtd AM (fine particulate)—highest weighted annual mean concentration; Particulate Matter 2.5 24-Hour (fine particulate)—highest 98th percentile 24-hour concentration; Ozone—highest fourth daily maximum 8-hour concentration; Carbon Monoxide—highest second maximum non-overlapping 8-hour concentration; Lead—maximum running 3-month average
Source: U.S. Environmental Protection Agency, Air Quality Monitoring Information, "Air Quality Statistics by City, 2017"

Maximum Air Pollutant Concentrations: Nitrogen Dioxide and Sulfur Dioxide

	Nitrogen Dioxide AM (ppb)	Nitrogen Dioxide 1-Hr (ppb)	Sulfur Dioxide AM (ppb)	Sulfur Dioxide 1-Hr (ppb)	Sulfur Dioxide 24-Hr (ppb)
MSA[1] Level	13	39	n/a	47	n/a
NAAQS[2]	53	100	30	75	140
Met NAAQS[2]	Yes	Yes	n/a	Yes	n/a

Note: (1) Data covers the Indianapolis-Carmel-Anderson, IN Metropolitan Statistical Area—see Appendix B for areas included; Data from exceptional events are included; (2) National Ambient Air Quality Standards; ppm = parts per million; ug/m^3 = micrograms per cubic meter; n/a not available.
Concentrations: Nitrogen Dioxide AM—highest arithmetic mean concentration; Nitrogen Dioxide 1-Hr—highest 98th percentile 1-hour daily maximum concentration; Sulfur Dioxide AM—highest annual mean concentration; Sulfur Dioxide 1-Hr—highest 99th percentile 1-hour daily maximum concentration; Sulfur Dioxide 24-Hr—highest second maximum 24-hour concentration
Source: U.S. Environmental Protection Agency, Air Quality Monitoring Information, "Air Quality Statistics by City, 2017"

Drinking Water

Water System Name	Pop. Served	Primary Water Source Type	Violations[1] Health Based	Monitoring/ Reporting
Citizens Water-Indianapolis	814,338	Surface	0	0

Note: (1) Based on violation data from January 1, 2018 to December 31, 2018
Source: U.S. Environmental Protection Agency, Office of Ground Water and Drinking Water, Safe Drinking Water Information System (based on data extracted April 5, 2019)

Kansas City, Missouri

Background

Kansas City lies on the western boundary of the state. With its sister city of the same name on the other side of the Kansas/Missouri border, both Kansas Cities make up the greater Kansas City metropolitan area.

The territory of the Kansa (or Kaw) tribe received intermittent visits from white settlers during the eighteenth and nineteenth centuries. In 1724, a fort was built in the general vicinity, and in 1804, Meriwether Lewis and William Clark explored the area on behalf of President Jefferson for the Louisiana Purchase. In 1821, the site was a trading post established by *Franois Chouteau*, who established the American Fur Company.

A combination of gold prospectors passing through on their way to California, via steamboat, rail, and coach, and the migration of would-be settlers to California and the Southwest stimulated economic activity in Kansas City during the 1800s. Three major trails—Santa Fe, California, and Oregon—all originated in Jackson County.

It was in this solid Midwestern city that the jazz clubs on 18th Street and Vine gave birth to the careers of Charlie Parker and Count Basie. Today a new generation of artists upholds Kansas City's reputation for great jazz, performing in dozens of clubs featuring live jazz nightly.

Kansas City is also home to more than 100 barbecue restaurants in the metropolitan area and each fall hosts what it claims is the world's biggest barbecue contest.

As one might expect from the heartland of America, Kansas City's major industries are hard wheat and cattle. However, do not be lulled into painting this picture for all of Kansas City. It is a modern urban institution with over 100 parks and playgrounds, suburban areas with an above-average living standard, European statues that line wide stretching boulevards, and a foreign trade zone where foreign countries can store their goods free of import duties. It offers something for everyone, from cultural and sporting events to casinos and gaming, from hot barbecue to even hotter jazz. The Sprint Center arena is a world class home for major league sports, concerts, and events.

Downtown Kansas City is undergoing a period of change, transforming its skyline and incorporating modern skyscrapers among the more traditional nineteenth-century buildings.

The Stowers Institute for Medical Research is a center where genetic studies are underway to find out how cellular and molecular change causes disease.

The Kansas City International Airport and historic Union Station are modern transportation hubs. The station's restored grand hall, with its 95-foot ceilings, shares space with the Science City Museum, theaters, restaurants, and shops.

The city maintains its own symphony, lyric opera and ballet. It boasts about 50 museums and many art galleries. Many of the city's museums have free admission, including the Nelson-Atkins Museum of Art, the Kemper Museum of Contemporary Art and the Kansas City Art Institute's H&R Block Artspace. The Kansas City Zoo offers over 200 acres of exhibits, including the Orangutan Primadome, and has plans to bring penguins to the zoo. Visitors enjoy the Harley-Davidson assembly plant to see how a "Hog" is built, the Children's Peace Pavilion, the Kansas City Renaissance Festival, and Fiesta Hispana, a yearly celebration of Hispanic heritage.

The National Weather Service office at Kansas City is very near the geographical center of the United States. The gently rolling terrain with no topographic impediments allows a free sweep of air from all directions, often with conflict between warm, moist air from the Gulf of Mexico and cold polar air from the north. The summer season is characterized by warm days, mild nights, and moderate humidity. Winters are not severely cold, and sizeable snowfalls are rare.

Rankings

General Rankings

- Kansas City was selected as one of the best places in the world to visit by *National Geographic Traveler*. The list reflects 28 must-see places determined by what's authentic, culturally rich, sustainable, intriguing, and relevant in the world of travel today. Travel experts compiled the best options for the most exciting destinations and best vacation spots for 2019. *National Geographic Traveler, "2019 Best of the World," December 2018/January 2019*

- Kansas City was selected as one of the best places to live in America by *Outside Magazine*. Criteria included great access to trails and public lands, great for children, delicious food and drink, and welcoming to people of all backgrounds. Three decades of coverage was combined with the expertise of an advisory council to pick the finalists. *Outside Magazine, "The 25 Best Towns of 2017," July 2017*

- In their sixth annual survey, Livability.com looked at data for more than 1,000 U.S. cities to determine the rankings for Livability's "Top 100 Best Places to Live" in 2019. Kansas City ranked #49. Criteria: median home value capped at $250,000; affordable living; vibrant economy; education, demographics, health care options. transportation & infrastructure; abundant lifestyle amenities. *Livability.com, "Top 100 Best Places to Live 2019" March 2019*

Business/Finance Rankings

- The personal finance site NerdWallet analyzed 183 American metropolitan areas with populations over 250,000 and more than 15,000 businesses to rank where entrepreneurs find the most success. Criteria included area economy, annual income, housing cost, unemployment rate, and the success rate of area businesses. Kansas City ranked #36. *www.nerdwallet.com, "Best Places to Start a Business," April 27, 2015*

- Kansas City was the #11-ranked city for savers, according to a study by the finance site GOBankingRates, which considered the prospects for people trying to save money. Criteria: average monthly cost of grocery items; median home listing price; median rent; median income; unemployment rate; gas prices; and sales tax in the nation's 60 largest cities. *www.gobankingrates.com, "Best Cities for Saving Money," June 22, 2018*

- Kansas City was ranked #11 among the nation's 60 largest cities for most difficult conditions for savers, according to a study by the finance site GOBankingRates. Criteria: average monthly cost of grocery items; median home listing price; median rent; median income; unemployment rate; gas prices; and sales tax. *www.gobankingrates.com, "Worst Cities for Saving Money," June 22, 2018*

- Recognizing the sizeable percentage of American workers who are self-employed, NerdWallet editors assessed the country's cities according to percentage of freelancers, median rental costs, cell phone plans/taxes, and healthcare affordability and access. By these criteria, Kansas City placed #13 among the best cities for independent workers. *www.nerdwallet.com, "Best Places for Freelance Workers," August 30, 2016*

- Based on metro area social media reviews, the employment opinion group Glassdoor surveyed 50 of the largest U.S. metro areas and equally weighed cost of living, hiring opportunity, and job satisfaction to compose a list of "25 Best Cities for Jobs." Median pay and home value, in-demand jobs and number of current job openings was also factored in. The Kansas City metro area was ranked #11 in overall job satisfaction. *www.glassdoor.com, "Best Cities for Jobs," October 16, 2018*

- In a survey of economic confidence in the nation's 50 largest metropolitan areas conducted January–December 2014, the Kansas City metro area placed #44, according to Gallup's 2014 Economic Confidence Index. *Gallup, "San Jose and San Francisco Lead in Economic Confidence," March 19, 2015*

- NerdWallet.com identified the 10 most promising cities for job seekers of the nation's 100 largest cities. Kansas City was ranked #41. Criteria: job availability; annual salary; workforce growth; affordability. *NerdWallet.com, "Best Cities for Job Seekers in 2017," December 19, 2016*

- The Brookings Institution ranked the nation's largest cities based on income inequality. Kansas City was ranked #77 (#1 = greatest inequality). Criteria: the "95/20 ratio," a figure representing the income at which a household earns more than 95 percent of all other households, divided by the income at which a household earns more than only 20 percent of all other households. *Brookings Institution, "Household Income Inequality, Largest Cities of 97 Large U.S. Metro Areas, 2014-2016," February 5, 2018*

- The Brookings Institution ranked the 100 largest metro areas in the U.S. based on income inequality. Kansas City was ranked #81 (#1 = greatest inequality). Criteria: the "95/20 ratio," a figure representing the income at which a household earns more than 95 percent of all other households, divided by the income at which a household earns more than only 20 percent of all other households. *Brookings Institution, "Household Income Inequality, 100 Largest U.S. Metro Areas, 2014-2016," February 5, 2018*

- Payscale.com ranked the 32 largest metro areas in terms of wage growth. The Kansas City metro area ranked #29. Criteria: private-sector wage growth between the 4th quarter of 2017 and the 4th quarter of 2018. *PayScale, "Wage Trends by Metro Area-4th Quarter," January 8, 2019*

- Kansas City was identified as one of America's most frugal metro areas by *Coupons.com*. The city ranked #18 out of 25. Criteria: digital coupon usage. *Coupons.com, "America's Most Frugal Cities of 2017," March 22, 2018*

- The Kansas City metro area appeared on the Milken Institute "2018 Best Performing Cities" list. Rank: #97 out of 200 large metro areas. Criteria: job growth; wage and salary growth; high-tech output growth. *Milken Institute, "Best-Performing Cities 2018," January 24, 2019*

- *Forbes* ranked the 200 most populous metro areas to determine the nation's "Best Places for Business and Careers." The Kansas City metro area was ranked #49. Criteria: costs (business and living); job growth (past and projected); income growth; quality of life; educational attainment (college and high school); projected economic growth; cultural and recreational opportunities; net migration patterns; number of highly ranked colleges. *Forbes, "The Best Places for Business and Careers 2018: Seattle Leads the Way," October 24, 2018*

Culture/Performing Arts Rankings

- Kansas City was selected as one of the ten best small U.S. cities and towns for moviemakers. Of cities with a population between 100,000 and 400,000 and towns with population less than 100,000, the area ranked #8. Criteria: film community and culture; access to equipment and facilities; film activity in 2018; number of film schools; tax incentives; ease of movement and traffic. *MovieMaker Magazine, "Best Places to Live and Work as a Moviemaker: 2019," January 17, 2019*

- Kansas City was selected as one of "America's Favorite Cities." The city ranked #4 in the "Culture" category. Respondents to an online survey were asked to rate 38 top urban destinations in the U.S. from a visitor's perspective. Criteria: theater scene and community; number of bookstores; live music; and sense of history. *Travelandleisure.com, "These Are America's 20 Most Cultured Cities," October 2016*

- Kansas City was selected as one of "America's Favorite Cities." The city ranked #5 in the "Culture: Galleries " category. Respondents to an online survey were asked to rate 38 top urban destinations in the U.S. from a visitor's perspective. Criteria: number and quality of galleries. *Travelandleisure.com, "America's Favorite Cities," October 11, 2015*

- Kansas City was selected as one of "America's Favorite Cities." The city ranked #4 in the "Culture: Art Scene " category. Respondents to an online survey were asked to rate 38 top urban destinations in the U.S. from a visitor's perspective. Criteria: number and quality of art events. *Travelandleisure.com, "America's Favorite Cities," October 11, 2015*

- Kansas City was selected as one of "America's Favorite Cities." The city ranked #12 in the "Culture: Music Scene " category. Respondents to an online survey were asked to rate 38 top urban destinations in the U.S. from a visitor's perspective. *Travelandleisure.com, "From the Honkytonk Capital to Jazz's Birthplace: America's Best Music Scenes," October 2016*

Dating/Romance Rankings

- *Apartment List* conducted its annual survey of renters to compile a list of cities that have the best opportunities for dating. More than 9,000 respondents, from February 2018 through the end of December 2018, rated their current city or neighborhood for opportunities to date and make friends. Kansas City ranked #62 out of 66 where single residents were very satisfied or somewhat satisfied, making it among the ten worst metros for dating opportunities. Other criteria analyzed included gender and education levels of renters. *Apartment List, "The Best & Worst Cities for Dating 2019," February 8, 2019*

Education Rankings

- Personal finance website *WalletHub* analyzed the 150 largest U.S. metropolitan statistical areas to determine where the most educated Americans are choosing to settle. Criteria: education quality and attainment gap; education levels; percentage of workers with degrees; public school quality rankings; quality and size of each metro area's universities. Kansas City was ranked #32 (#1 = most educated city). *www.WalletHub.com, "2018's Most and Least Educated Cities in America, " July 24, 2018*

- Kansas City was selected as one of America's most literate cities. The city ranked #16 out of the 82 largest U.S. cities. Criteria: number of booksellers; library resources; Internet resources; educational attainment; periodical publishing resources; newspaper circulation. *Central Connecticut State University, "America's Most Literate Cities, 2016," March 31, 2017*

Food/Drink Rankings

- *Men's Health* ranked 100 major U.S. cities in terms of alcohol intoxication. Kansas City ranked #36 (#1 = most sober).Criteria: binge drinking; alcohol-related traffic accidents, arrests, and fatalities. *Men's Health, "America's Drunkest Cities," March 9, 2015*

- Kansas City was selected as one of America's 10 most vegan-friendly cities. The city was ranked #10. *People for the Ethical Treatment of Animals, "Top 10 Vegan-Friendly Cities of 2018," May 16, 2018*

- Kauffman Stadium was selected as one of PETA's "Top 10 Vegan-Friendly Ballparks" for 2018. The park ranked #10. *People for the Ethical Treatment of Animals, "Top 10 Vegan-Friendly Ballparks, " June 4, 2018*

Health/Fitness Rankings

- For each of the 100 largest cities in the United States, the American College of Sports Medicine's American Fitness Index evaluated infrastructure, community assets, and policies that encourage healthy and fit lifestyles, including preventive health behaviors, levels of chronic disease conditions, health care access, and community resources and policies that support physical activity. Kansas City ranked #74 for "community fitness." *www.americanfitnessindex.org, "ACSM American Fitness Index Health and Community Fitness Status of the 100 Largest U.S. Cities," May 2018*

- Kansas City was identified as a "2018 Spring Allergy Capital." The area ranked #72 out of 100. Three groups of factors were used to identify the most challenging cities for people with allergies during the spring season: annual pollen levels; medicine utilization; access to board-certified allergists. *Asthma and Allergy Foundation of America, "Spring Allergy Capitals 2018"*

- Kansas City was identified as a "2018 Fall Allergy Capital." The area ranked #70 out of 100. Three groups of factors were used to identify the most challenging cities for people with allergies during the fall season: annual pollen levels; medicine utilization; access to board-certified allergists. *Asthma and Allergy Foundation of America, "Fall Allergy Capitals 2018"*

- Kansas City was identified as a "2018 Asthma Capital." The area ranked #41 out of the nation's 100 largest metropolitan areas. Criteria: estimated prevalence; self-reported prevalence; crude death rate for asthma; annual pollen score; annual air quality; public smoking laws; number of board-certified asthma specialists; school inhaler access laws; rescue medication use; controller medication use; ER visits for asthma; uninsured rate; poverty rate. *Asthma and Allergy Foundation of America, "Asthma Capitals 2018: The Most Challenging Places to Live With Asthma"*

- *Men's Health* ranked 100 major U.S. cities in terms of the best cities for men. Kansas City ranked #81. Criteria: health; fitness; quality of life. *Men's Health, "The Best & Worst Cities for Men Who Want to Be Fit and Happy," January 1, 2016*

- The Kansas City metro area ranked #87 out of 189 in The Gallup-Healthways Well-Being Index. Criteria: purpose; social well being; financial health; community and physical health. Results are based on telephone interviews with adults, aged 18 and older, living in metropolitan areas in the 50 U.S. states and the District of Columbia. *Gallup-Healthways, "State of American Well-Being, 2017 Community Well-Being Rankings" March 2018*

Real Estate Rankings

- FitSmallBusiness looked at 50 of the largest metropolitan areas in the U.S. to determine which metro was the best to start a real estate business. Data was compiled from such sources as: Zillow, Trulia, U.S. Census Bureau, and the Bureau of Labor Statistics. Criteria: location; inventory; annual wages; median sales price of homes; days on the market; median price cut percentage; and other factors that would influence real estate professional growth. The Kansas City metro area ranked #41. *fitsmallbusiness.com, "The Best Cities to Become a Real Estate Agent in 2018," January 30, 2018*

- *WalletHub* compared the most populated U.S. cities, as well as at least two of the most populated cities in each state, for a total of 179, to determine which had the best markets for real estate agents. Kansas City ranked #104 where demand was high and pay was the best. Criteria: sales per agent; annual median wage for real-estate agents; monthly average starting salary for real estate agents; real estate job density and competition; unemployment rate; housing-market health index; and other relevant metrics. *www.WalletHub.com, "2018's Best Places to Be a Real Estate Agent,"April 25, 2018*

- The Kansas City metro area was identified as one of the top 20 housing markets to invest in for 2019 by *Forbes*. Criteria: strong job and population growth; stable local economy; anticipated home price appreciation; and other factors. *Forbes.com, "The Best Markets for Real Estate Investments In 2019," January 7, 2019*

- Kansas City was ranked #81 out of 237 metro areas in terms of housing affordability in 2018 by the National Association of Home Builders (#1 = most affordable). Criteria: the share of homes sold in that area affordable to a family earning the local median income, based on standard mortgage underwriting criteria. *National Association of Home Builders®, NAHB-Wells Fargo Housing Opportunity Index, 4th Quarter 2018*

Safety Rankings

- To identify the most dangerous cities in America, 24/7 Wall Street focused on violent crime categories—murder, rape, robbery, and aggravated assault—and property crime as reported in the FBI's 2017 annual Uniform Crime Report. Criteria also included median income from American Community Survey and unemployment figures from Bureau of Labor Statistics. For cities with populations over 100,000, Kansas City was ranked #5. *247wallst.com, "25 Most Dangerous Cities in America" October 17, 2018*

- Allstate ranked the 200 largest cities in America in terms of driver safety. Kansas City ranked #32. Criteria: internal property damage claims over a two-year period from January 2015 to December 2016. The report helps increase the importance of safety awareness behind the wheel. *Allstate, "Allstate America's Best Drivers Report, 2018" August 28, 2018*

- Kansas City was identified as one of the most dangerous cities in America by NeighborhoodScout. The city ranked #13 out of 100. Criteria: number of violent crimes per 1,000 residents. The editors only considered cities with 25,000 or more residents. *NeighborhoodScout.com, "Top 100 Most Dangerous Cities in the U.S. 2019" January 2, 2019*

- The National Insurance Crime Bureau ranked 382 metro areas in the U.S. in terms of per capita rates of vehicle theft. The Kansas City metro area ranked #32 (#1 = highest rate). Criteria: number of vehicle theft offenses per 100,000 inhabitants in 2017. *National Insurance Crime Bureau, "Hot Spots 2017," July 12, 2018*

Seniors/Retirement Rankings

- From its Best Cities for Successful Aging indexes, the Milken Institute generated rankings for metropolitan areas, weighing data in nine categories—health care, wellness, living arrangements, transportation and convenience, financial characteristics, education, employment, community engagement, and overall livability. The Kansas City metro area was ranked #26 overall in the large metro area category. *Milken Institute, "Best Cities for Successful Aging, 2017" March 14, 2017*

Women/Minorities Rankings

- Personal finance website *WalletHub* compared more than 180 U.S. cities—including the 150 most populated U.S. cities, plus at least two of the most populated cities in each state—across two key dimensions, "Hispanic Business-Friendliness" and "Hispanic Purchasing Power", to arrive at the most favorable conditions for Hispanic entrepreneurs. Kansas City was ranked #68 out of 182. Criteria includes: share of Hispanic-Owned Businesses; Hispanic entrepreneurship rate to median annual income of Hispanics; Small Business-Friendliness score; cost of living; and number of Hispanics with at least a bachelor's degree. *WalletHub.com, "2018's Best Cities for Hispanic Entrepreneurs," April 26, 2018*

Miscellaneous Rankings

- Kansas City was selected as a 2018 Digital Cities Survey winner. The city ranked #2 in the large city (250,000 to 499,999 population) category. The survey examined and assessed how city governments are utilizing technology to improve transparency, enhance cybersecurity, and solve social challenges. Survey questions focused on ten characteristics: engaged, mobile, open, secure, staffed/supported, efficient, connected, resilient, best practices, and use of innovation. *Center for Digital Government, "2018 Digital Cities Survey," November 2, 2018*

- The watchdog site Charity Navigator conducts an annual study of charities in the nation's major markets both to analyze statistical differences in their financial, accountability, and transparency practices and to track year-to-year variations in individual philanthropic communities. Charity Navigator's analysis demonstrated that the financial, accountability and transparency behaviors of America's largest charities can be influenced by the metropolitan market within which the charity operates. The Kansas City metro area was ranked #9 among the 30 metro markets in the rating category of Overall Score. *www.charitynavigator.org, "2017 Metro Market Study," May 1, 2017*

- *WalletHub* compared the 150 most populated U.S. cities to determine their operating efficiency. A "Quality of Services" score was constructed for each city and then divided by the total budget per capita to reveal which were managed the best. Kansas City ranked #96. Criteria: financial stability; economy; education; safety; health; infrastructure and pollution. *www.WalletHub.com, "2018's Best- & Worst-Run Cities in America," July 9, 2018*

- Kansas City was selected as one of "America's Friendliest Cities." The city ranked #16 in the "Friendliest" category. Respondents to an online survey were asked to rate 38 top urban destinations in the United States as to general friendliness, as well as manners, politeness and warm disposition. *Travel + Leisure, "America's Friendliest Cities," October 20, 2017*

Business Environment

CITY FINANCES

City Government Finances

Component	2016 ($000)	2016 ($ per capita)
Total Revenues	1,654,806	3,481
Total Expenditures	1,964,790	4,133
Debt Outstanding	3,507,155	7,378
Cash and Securities[1]	4,437,062	9,334

Note: (1) Cash and security holdings of a government at the close of its fiscal year, including those of its dependent agencies, utilities, and liquor stores.
Source: U.S. Census Bureau, State & Local Government Finances 2016

City Government Revenue by Source

Source	2016 ($000)	2016 ($ per capita)	2016 (%)
General Revenue			
From Federal Government	43,862	92	2.7
From State Government	26,325	55	1.6
From Local Governments	14,259	30	0.9
Taxes			
Property	118,373	249	7.2
Sales and Gross Receipts	291,153	612	17.6
Personal Income	223,824	471	13.5
Corporate Income	38,144	80	2.3
Motor Vehicle License	4,177	9	0.3
Other Taxes	13,494	28	0.8
Current Charges	414,612	872	25.1
Liquor Store	0	0	0.0
Utility	155,209	326	9.4
Employee Retirement	1,037	2	0.1

Source: U.S. Census Bureau, State & Local Government Finances 2016

City Government Expenditures by Function

Function	2016 ($000)	2016 ($ per capita)	2016 (%)
General Direct Expenditures			
Air Transportation	118,752	249	6.0
Corrections	0	0	0.0
Education	0	0	0.0
Employment Security Administration	0	0	0.0
Financial Administration	17,971	37	0.9
Fire Protection	189,714	399	9.7
General Public Buildings	22,999	48	1.2
Governmental Administration, Other	49,487	104	2.5
Health	53,416	112	2.7
Highways	83,678	176	4.3
Hospitals	0	0	0.0
Housing and Community Development	58,982	124	3.0
Interest on General Debt	80,198	168	4.1
Judicial and Legal	17,952	37	0.9
Libraries	0	0	0.0
Parking	3,805	8	0.2
Parks and Recreation	59,686	125	3.0
Police Protection	219,822	462	11.2
Public Welfare	9,665	20	0.5
Sewerage	161,100	338	8.2
Solid Waste Management	22,399	47	1.1
Veterans' Services	0	0	0.0
Liquor Store	0	0	0.0
Utility	86,054	181	4.4
Employee Retirement	165,544	348	8.4

Source: U.S. Census Bureau, State & Local Government Finances 2016

DEMOGRAPHICS

Population Growth

Area	1990 Census	2000 Census	2010 Census	2017* Estimate	Population Growth (%)	
					1990-2017	2010-2017
City	434,967	441,545	459,787	476,974	9.7	3.7
MSA[1]	1,636,528	1,836,038	2,035,334	2,088,830	27.6	2.6
U.S.	248,709,873	281,421,906	308,745,538	321,004,407	29.1	4.0

Note: (1) Figures cover the Kansas City, MO-KS Metropolitan Statistical Area—see Appendix B for areas included; (*) 2013-2017 5-year estimated population
Source: U.S. Census Bureau, 1990 Census, Census 2000, Census 2010, 2013-2017 American Community Survey 5-Year Estimates

Household Size

Area	Persons in Household (%)							Average Household Size
	One	Two	Three	Four	Five	Six	Seven or More	
City	36.9	31.6	13.6	10.2	4.8	1.7	1.1	2.40
MSA[1]	29.0	33.8	15.1	13.0	5.9	2.0	1.1	2.50
U.S.	27.7	33.8	15.7	13.0	6.0	2.3	1.4	2.60

Note: (1) Figures cover the Kansas City, MO-KS Metropolitan Statistical Area—see Appendix B for areas included
Source: U.S. Census Bureau, 2013-2017 American Community Survey 5-Year Estimates

Race

Area	White Alone[2] (%)	Black Alone[2] (%)	Asian Alone[2] (%)	AIAN[3] Alone[2] (%)	NHOPI[4] Alone[2] (%)	Other Race Alone[2] (%)	Two or More Races (%)
City	60.3	28.7	2.8	0.4	0.1	4.4	3.3
MSA[1]	78.6	12.5	2.7	0.4	0.1	2.6	3.1
U.S.	73.0	12.7	5.4	0.8	0.2	4.8	3.1

Note: (1) Figures cover the Kansas City, MO-KS Metropolitan Statistical Area—see Appendix B for areas included; (2) Alone is defined as not being in combination with one or more other races; (3) American Indian and Alaska Native; (4) Native Hawaiian and Other Pacific Islander
Source: U.S. Census Bureau, 2013-2017 American Community Survey 5-Year Estimates

Hispanic or Latino Origin

Area	Total (%)	Mexican (%)	Puerto Rican (%)	Cuban (%)	Other (%)
City	10.2	7.8	0.3	0.3	1.9
MSA[1]	8.8	6.8	0.3	0.2	1.5
U.S.	17.6	11.1	1.7	0.7	4.1

Note: Persons of Hispanic or Latino origin can be of any race; (1) Figures cover the Kansas City, MO-KS Metropolitan Statistical Area—see Appendix B for areas included
Source: U.S. Census Bureau, 2013-2017 American Community Survey 5-Year Estimates

Segregation

Type	Segregation Indices[1]				Percent Change		
	1990	2000	2010	2010 Rank[2]	1990-2000	1990-2010	2000-2010
Black/White	72.9	70.9	61.2	39	-2.0	-11.7	-9.7
Asian/White	34.4	38.3	38.4	65	3.9	4.0	0.1
Hispanic/White	39.5	45.5	44.4	48	6.0	4.9	-1.2

Note: All figures cover the Metropolitan Statistical Area—see Appendix B for areas included; Figures are based on an analysis of 1990, 2000, and 2010 Census Decennial Census tract data by William H. Frey, Brookings Institution and the University of Michigan Social Science Data Analysis Network. In this analysis all racial groups (whites, blacks, and asians) are non-Hispanic members of those races. Hispanics are shown as a separate category; (1) Segregation Indices are Dissimilarity Indices that measure the degree to which the minority group is distributed differently than whites across census tracts. They range from 0 (complete integration) to 100 (complete segregation) where the value indicates the percentage of the minority group that needs to move to be distributed exactly like whites; (2) Ranges from 1 (most segregated) to 102 (least segregated); n/a not available.
Source: www.CensusScope.org

Ancestry

Area	German	Irish	English	American	Italian	Polish	French[2]	Scottish	Dutch
City	17.2	11.3	7.4	4.6	3.5	1.4	2.3	1.6	1.3
MSA[1]	22.1	12.7	9.8	6.1	3.3	1.6	2.4	1.9	1.5
U.S.	14.1	10.1	7.5	6.6	5.3	2.9	2.5	1.7	1.3

Note: Figures are the percentage of the total population reporting a particular ancestry. The nine most commonly reported ancestries in the U.S. are shown. Figures include multiple ancestries (e.g. if a person reported being Irish and Italian, they were included in both columns); (1) Figures cover the Kansas City, MO-KS Metropolitan Statistical Area—see Appendix B for areas included; (2) Excludes Basque
Source: U.S. Census Bureau, 2013-2017 American Community Survey 5-Year Estimates

Foreign-Born Population

Area	Percent of Population Born in								
	Any Foreign Country	Asia	Mexico	Europe	Carribean	Central America[2]	South America	Africa	Canada
City	7.8	2.3	2.4	0.6	0.4	0.6	0.3	1.1	0.1
MSA[1]	6.6	2.2	2.1	0.6	0.2	0.5	0.2	0.6	0.1
U.S.	13.4	4.1	3.6	1.5	1.3	1.0	0.9	0.6	0.3

Note: (1) Figures cover the Kansas City, MO-KS Metropolitan Statistical Area—see Appendix B for areas included; (2) Excludes Mexico.
Source: U.S. Census Bureau, 2013-2017 American Community Survey 5-Year Estimates

Marital Status

Area	Never Married	Now Married[2]	Separated	Widowed	Divorced
City	39.7	39.6	2.1	5.5	13.1
MSA[1]	30.3	50.5	1.7	5.4	12.1
U.S.	33.1	48.2	2.0	5.8	10.9

Note: Figures are percentages and cover the population 15 years of age and older; (1) Figures cover the Kansas City, MO-KS Metropolitan Statistical Area—see Appendix B for areas included; (2) Excludes separated
Source: U.S. Census Bureau, 2013-2017 American Community Survey 5-Year Estimates

Disability by Age

Area	All Ages	Under 18 Years Old	18 to 64 Years Old	65 Years and Over
City	13.0	3.9	11.8	37.3
MSA[1]	12.2	4.0	10.6	34.7
U.S.	12.6	4.2	10.3	35.5

Note: Figures show percent of the civilian noninstitutionalized population that reported having a disability. Disability status is determined from six types of difficulty: vision, hearing, cognitive, ambulatory, self-care, and independent living. For children under 5 years old, hearing and vision difficulty are used to determine disability status. For children between the ages of 5 and 14, disability status is determined from hearing, vision, cognitive, ambulatory, and self-care difficulties. For people aged 15 years and older, they are considered to have a disability if they have difficulty with any one of the six difficulty types; Note: (1) Figures cover the Kansas City, MO-KS Metropolitan Statistical Area—see Appendix B for areas included
Source: U.S. Census Bureau, 2013-2017 American Community Survey 5-Year Estimates

Age

Area	Percent of Population									Median Age
	Under Age 5	Age 5–19	Age 20–34	Age 35–44	Age 45–54	Age 55–64	Age 65–74	Age 75–84	Age 85+	
City	7.0	18.4	24.4	13.2	12.8	12.0	7.3	3.5	1.7	35.2
MSA[1]	6.7	20.3	20.1	13.2	13.4	12.7	8.0	4.0	1.8	37.1
U.S.	6.2	19.5	20.7	12.7	13.4	12.7	8.6	4.4	1.9	37.8

Note: (1) Figures cover the Kansas City, MO-KS Metropolitan Statistical Area—see Appendix B for areas included
Source: U.S. Census Bureau, 2013-2017 American Community Survey 5-Year Estimates

Gender

Area	Males	Females	Males per 100 Females
City	232,170	244,804	94.8
MSA[1]	1,024,354	1,064,476	96.2
U.S.	158,018,753	162,985,654	97.0

Note: (1) Figures cover the Kansas City, MO-KS Metropolitan Statistical Area—see Appendix B for areas included
Source: U.S. Census Bureau, 2013-2017 American Community Survey 5-Year Estimates

Religious Groups by Family

Area	Catholic	Baptist	Non-Den.	Methodist[2]	Lutheran	LDS[3]	Pente-costal	Presby-terian[4]	Muslim[5]	Judaism
MSA[1]	12.7	13.2	5.2	5.9	2.3	2.5	2.6	1.6	0.3	0.4
U.S.	19.1	9.3	4.0	4.0	2.3	2.0	1.9	1.6	0.8	0.7

Note: Figures are the number of adherents as a percentage of the total population; (1) Figures cover the Kansas City, MO-KS Metropolitan Statistical Area—see Appendix B for areas included; (2) Methodist/Pietist; (3) Latter Day Saints; (4) Reformed; (5) Figures are estimates
Source: Association of Statisticians of American Religious Bodies, 2010 U.S. Religion Census: Religious Congregations & Membership Study

Religious Groups by Tradition

Area	Catholic	Evangelical Protestant	Mainline Protestant	Other Tradition	Black Protestant	Orthodox
MSA[1]	12.7	20.6	10.0	3.7	2.6	0.1
U.S.	19.1	16.2	7.3	4.3	1.6	0.3

Note: Figures are the number of adherents as a percentage of the total population; (1) Figures cover the Kansas City, MO-KS Metropolitan Statistical Area—see Appendix B for areas included
Source: Association of Statisticians of American Religious Bodies, 2010 U.S. Religion Census: Religious Congregations & Membership Study

ECONOMY

Gross Metropolitan Product

Area	2016	2017	2018	2019	Rank[2]
MSA[1]	128.9	133.1	138.9	146.3	32

Note: Figures are in billions of dollars; (1) Figures cover the Kansas City, MO-KS Metropolitan Statistical Area—see Appendix B for areas included; (2) Rank is based on 2017 data and ranges from 1 to 381
Source: U.S. Conference of Mayors, U.S. Metro Economies: Economic Growth & Full Employment, June 2018

Economic Growth

Area	2017-2018 (%)	2019-2020 (%)	2021-2022 (%)
MSA[1]	1.9	2.4	1.9

Note: Figures are real gross metropolitan product (GMP) growth rates and represent average annual percent change; (1) Figures cover the Kansas City, MO-KS Metropolitan Statistical Area—see Appendix B for areas included
Source: U.S. Conference of Mayors, U.S. Metro Economies: Economic Growth & Full Employment, June 2018

Metropolitan Area Exports

Area	2012	2013	2014	2015	2016	2017	Rank[2]
MSA[1]	7,880.8	8,012.1	8,262.9	6,723.2	6,709.8	7,015.0	46

Note: Figures are in millions of dollars; (1) Figures cover the Kansas City, MO-KS Metropolitan Statistical Area—see Appendix B for areas included; (2) Rank is based on 2017 data and ranges from 1 to 387
Source: U.S. Department of Commerce, International Trade Administration, Office of Trade and Economic Analysis, Industry and Analysis, Exports by Metropolitan Area, extracted March 25, 2019

Building Permits

Area	Single-Family			Multi-Family			Total		
	2016	2017	Pct. Chg.	2016	2017	Pct. Chg.	2016	2017	Pct. Chg.
City	825	824	-0.1	2,515	1,542	-38.7	3,340	2,366	-29.2
MSA[1]	5,292	5,951	12.5	5,097	3,900	-23.5	10,389	9,851	-5.2
U.S.	750,800	820,000	9.2	455,800	462,000	1.4	1,206,600	1,282,000	6.2

Note: (1) Figures cover the Kansas City, MO-KS Metropolitan Statistical Area—see Appendix B for areas included; Figures represent new, privately-owned housing units authorized (unadjusted data); All permit data are based on estimates with imputation
Source: U.S. Census Bureau, Manufacturing, Mining, and Construction Statistics, Building Permits, 2016, 2017

Bankruptcy Filings

Area	Business Filings			Nonbusiness Filings		
	2017	2018	% Chg.	2017	2018	% Chg.
Jackson County	31	22	-29.0	2,373	2,192	-7.6
U.S.	23,157	22,232	-4.0	765,863	751,186	-1.9

Note: Business filings include Chapter 7, Chapter 11, Chapter 12, and Chapter 13; Nonbusiness filings include Chapter 7, Chapter 11, and Chapter 13
Source: Administrative Office of the U.S. Courts, Business and Nonbusiness Bankruptcy, County Cases Commenced by Chapter of the Bankruptcy Code, During the 12-Month Period Ending December 31, 2017 and Business and Nonbusiness Bankruptcy, County Cases Commenced by Chapter of the Bankruptcy Code, During the 12-Month Period Ending December 31, 2018

Housing Vacancy Rates

Area	Gross Vacancy Rate[2] (%)			Year-Round Vacancy Rate[3] (%)			Rental Vacancy Rate[4] (%)			Homeowner Vacancy Rate[5] (%)		
	2016	2017	2018	2016	2017	2018	2016	2017	2018	2016	2017	2018
MSA[1]	8.1	8.1	7.8	8.0	7.9	7.7	9.2	9.4	7.9	0.8	0.8	1.2
U.S.	12.8	12.7	12.3	9.9	9.9	9.7	6.9	7.2	6.9	1.7	1.6	1.5

Note: (1) Figures cover the Kansas City, MO-KS Metropolitan Statistical Area—see Appendix B for areas included; (2) The percentage of the total housing inventory that is vacant; (3) The percentage of the housing inventory (excluding seasonal units) that is year-round vacant; (4) The percentage of rental inventory that is vacant for rent; (5) The percentage of homeowner inventory that is vacant for sale
Source: U.S. Census Bureau, Housing Vacancies and Homeownership Annual Statistics: 2016, 2017, 2018

INCOME

Income

Area	Per Capita ($)	Median Household ($)	Average Household ($)
City	29,742	50,136	68,949
MSA[1]	32,962	61,479	82,390
U.S.	31,177	57,652	81,283

Note: (1) Figures cover the Kansas City, MO-KS Metropolitan Statistical Area—see Appendix B for areas included
Source: U.S. Census Bureau, 2013-2017 American Community Survey 5-Year Estimates

Household Income Distribution

Area	Percent of Households Earning							
	Under $15,000	$15,000 -$24,999	$25,000 -$34,999	$35,000 -$49,999	$50,000 -$74,999	$75,000 -$99,999	$100,000 -$149,999	$150,000 and up
City	13.9	11.2	10.6	14.1	18.4	11.7	11.8	8.2
MSA[1]	9.6	8.6	9.3	13.4	18.4	13.6	15.4	11.6
U.S.	11.6	9.8	9.5	13.0	17.7	12.3	14.1	12.1

Note: (1) Figures cover the Kansas City, MO-KS Metropolitan Statistical Area—see Appendix B for areas included
Source: U.S. Census Bureau, 2013-2017 American Community Survey 5-Year Estimates

Poverty Rate

Area	All Ages	Under 18 Years Old	18 to 64 Years Old	65 Years and Over
City	17.3	25.5	15.8	9.9
MSA[1]	11.5	16.2	10.6	7.1
U.S.	14.6	20.3	13.7	9.3

Note: Figures are percentage of people whose income during the past 12 months was below the poverty level; (1) Figures cover the Kansas City, MO-KS Metropolitan Statistical Area—see Appendix B for areas included
Source: U.S. Census Bureau, 2013-2017 American Community Survey 5-Year Estimates

EMPLOYMENT

Labor Force and Employment

Area	Civilian Labor Force			Workers Employed		
	Dec. 2017	Dec. 2018	% Chg.	Dec. 2017	Dec. 2018	% Chg.
City	256,776	259,249	1.0	247,285	250,839	1.4
MSA[1]	1,123,293	1,137,463	1.3	1,086,716	1,102,718	1.5
U.S.	159,880,000	162,510,000	1.6	153,602,000	156,481,000	1.9

Note: Data is not seasonally adjusted and covers workers 16 years of age and older; (1) Figures cover the Kansas City, MO-KS Metropolitan Statistical Area—see Appendix B for areas included
Source: Bureau of Labor Statistics, Local Area Unemployment Statistics

Unemployment Rate

Area	2018											
	Jan.	Feb.	Mar.	Apr.	May	Jun.	Jul.	Aug.	Sep.	Oct.	Nov.	Dec.
City	4.3	3.9	3.9	3.6	3.9	3.8	4.3	3.9	3.0	2.7	2.8	3.2
MSA[1]	4.0	3.8	3.6	3.3	3.6	3.5	3.9	3.5	2.8	2.7	2.7	3.1
U.S.	4.5	4.4	4.1	3.7	3.6	4.2	4.1	3.9	3.6	3.5	3.5	3.7

Note: Data is not seasonally adjusted and covers workers 16 years of age and older; (1) Figures cover the Kansas City, MO-KS Metropolitan Statistical Area—see Appendix B for areas included
Source: Bureau of Labor Statistics, Local Area Unemployment Statistics

Average Wages

Occupation	$/Hr.	Occupation	$/Hr.
Accountants and Auditors	32.80	Maids and Housekeeping Cleaners	10.70
Automotive Mechanics	22.20	Maintenance and Repair Workers	19.40
Bookkeepers	19.50	Marketing Managers	68.70
Carpenters	26.60	Nuclear Medicine Technologists	37.90
Cashiers	11.00	Nurses, Licensed Practical	22.10
Clerks, General Office	15.60	Nurses, Registered	32.40
Clerks, Receptionists/Information	14.10	Nursing Assistants	13.10
Clerks, Shipping/Receiving	16.40	Packers and Packagers, Hand	13.10
Computer Programmers	36.60	Physical Therapists	37.80
Computer Systems Analysts	38.50	Postal Service Mail Carriers	24.50
Computer User Support Specialists	23.70	Real Estate Brokers	25.40
Cooks, Restaurant	12.80	Retail Salespersons	13.50
Dentists	87.20	Sales Reps., Exc. Tech./Scientific	32.90
Electrical Engineers	44.20	Sales Reps., Tech./Scientific	39.20
Electricians	29.20	Secretaries, Exc. Legal/Med./Exec.	18.00
Financial Managers	67.00	Security Guards	18.00
First-Line Supervisors/Managers, Sales	20.60	Surgeons	103.60
Food Preparation Workers	10.80	Teacher Assistants*	13.00
General and Operations Managers	52.90	Teachers, Elementary School*	26.50
Hairdressers/Cosmetologists	13.10	Teachers, Secondary School*	27.60
Internists, General	n/a	Telemarketers	12.50
Janitors and Cleaners	13.60	Truck Drivers, Heavy/Tractor-Trailer	22.80
Landscaping/Groundskeeping Workers	17.30	Truck Drivers, Light/Delivery Svcs.	18.10
Lawyers	59.00	Waiters and Waitresses	10.30

Note: Wage data covers the Kansas City, MO-KS Metropolitan Statistical Area—see Appendix B for areas included; (*) Hourly wages for elementary/secondary school teachers and teacher assistants were calculated by the editors from annual wage data based on a 40 hour work week; n/a not available.
Source: Bureau of Labor Statistics, Metro Area Occupational Employment & Wage Estimates, May 2018

Employment by Occupation

Occupation Classification	City (%)	MSA[1] (%)	U.S. (%)
Management, Business, Science, and Arts	38.6	39.8	37.4
Natural Resources, Construction, and Maintenance	6.5	7.8	8.9
Production, Transportation, and Material Moving	12.1	11.8	12.2
Sales and Office	24.3	24.6	23.5
Service	18.5	16.0	18.0

Note: Figures cover employed civilians 16 years of age and older; (1) Figures cover the Kansas City, MO-KS Metropolitan Statistical Area—see Appendix B for areas included
Source: U.S. Census Bureau, 2013-2017 American Community Survey 5-Year Estimates

Employment by Industry

Sector	MSA[1]		U.S.
	Number of Employees	Percent of Total	Percent of Total
Construction, Mining, and Logging	48,400	4.4	5.3
Education and Health Services	160,000	14.5	15.9
Financial Activities	79,300	7.2	5.7
Government	158,200	14.3	15.1
Information	16,400	1.5	1.9
Leisure and Hospitality	105,600	9.5	10.7
Manufacturing	78,700	7.1	8.5
Other Services	42,700	3.9	3.9
Professional and Business Services	195,000	17.6	14.1
Retail Trade	115,000	10.4	10.8
Transportation, Warehousing, and Utilities	55,900	5.1	4.2
Wholesale Trade	51,700	4.7	3.9

Note: Figures are non-farm employment as of December 2018. Figures are not seasonally adjusted and include workers 16 years of age and older; (1) Figures cover the Kansas City, MO-KS Metropolitan Statistical Area—see Appendix B for areas included
Source: Bureau of Labor Statistics, Current Employment Statistics, Employment, Hours, and Earnings

Occupations with Greatest Projected Employment Growth: 2018 – 2020

Occupation[1]	2018 Employment	2020 Projected Employment	Numeric Employment Change	Percent Employment Change
Personal Care Aides	53,690	56,960	3,270	6.1
Combined Food Preparation and Serving Workers, Including Fast Food	74,280	77,040	2,760	3.7
Registered Nurses	76,570	78,150	1,580	2.1
Laborers and Freight, Stock, and Material Movers, Hand	51,110	52,350	1,240	2.4
General and Operations Managers	46,620	47,750	1,130	2.4
Janitors and Cleaners, Except Maids and Housekeeping Cleaners	47,160	48,290	1,130	2.4
Software Developers, Applications	14,740	15,690	950	6.4
Waiters and Waitresses	52,130	53,070	940	1.8
Customer Service Representatives	61,300	62,210	910	1.5
Construction Laborers	26,060	26,900	840	3.2

Note: Projections cover Missouri; (1) Sorted by numeric employment change
Source: www.projectionscentral.com, State Occupational Projections, 2018–2020 Short-Term Projections

Fastest Growing Occupations: 2018 – 2020

Occupation[1]	2018 Employment	2020 Projected Employment	Numeric Employment Change	Percent Employment Change
Helpers—Pipelayers, Plumbers, Pipefitters, and Steamfitters	700	750	50	7.1
Information Security Analysts	2,910	3,110	200	6.9
Software Developers, Applications	14,740	15,690	950	6.4
Statisticians	970	1,030	60	6.2
Personal Care Aides	53,690	56,960	3,270	6.1
Home Health Aides	12,570	13,310	740	5.9
Dental Laboratory Technicians	870	920	50	5.7
Market Research Analysts and Marketing Specialists	10,590	11,130	540	5.1
Nurse Practitioners	4,210	4,420	210	5.0
Helpers—Carpenters	1,030	1,080	50	4.9

Note: Projections cover Missouri; (1) Sorted by percent employment change and excludes occupations with numeric employment change less than 50
Source: www.projectionscentral.com, State Occupational Projections, 2018–2020 Short-Term Projections

TAXES

State Corporate Income Tax Rates

State	Tax Rate (%)	Income Brackets ($)	Num. of Brackets	Financial Institution Tax Rate (%)[a]	Federal Income Tax Ded.
Missouri	6.25	Flat rate	1	7.0	Yes (j)

Note: Tax rates as of January 1, 2019; (a) Rates listed are the corporate income tax rate applied to financial institutions or excise taxes based on income. Some states have other taxes based upon the value of deposits or shares; (j) 50% of the federal income tax is deductible.
Source: Federation of Tax Administrators, Range of State Corporate Income Tax Rates, January 1, 2019

State Individual Income Tax Rates

State	Tax Rate (%)	Income Brackets ($)	Personal Exemptions ($)			Standard Ded. ($)	
			Single	Married	Depend.	Single	Married
Missouri (a)	1.5 - 5.4	1,053 - 8,424	(d)	(d)	(d)	12,200	24,400 (d)

Note: Tax rates as of January 1, 2019; Local- and county-level taxes are not included; n/a not applicable; The deduction for federal income tax is limited to $5,000 for individuals and $10,000 for joint returns in Missouri and Montana, and to $6,500 for all filers in Oregon; (a) 19 states have statutory provision for automatically adjusting to the rate of inflation the dollar values of the income tax brackets, standard deductions, and/or personal exemptions. Michigan indexes the personal exemption only. Oregon does not index the income brackets for $125,000 and over; (d) These states use the personal exemption/standard deduction amounts provided in the federal Internal Revenue Code. Note, the Tax Cut and Reform Act of 2017 has eliminated personal exemptions from the IRC. CO, ID, NM, ND, SC, and DC have adoptedthe new exemptions and standard deduction amounts. MN conforms to a previous IRC year, while ME adopts the higher standard deduction but retains the exemption amounts.
Source: Federation of Tax Administrators, State Individual Income Tax Rates, January 1, 2019

Various State Sales and Excise Tax Rates

State	State Sales Tax (%)	Gasoline[1] (¢/gal.)	Cigarette[2] ($/pack)	Spirits[3] ($/gal.)	Wine[4] ($/gal.)	Beer[5] ($/gal.)	Recreational Marijuana (%)
Missouri	4.225	17.35	0.17	2	0.42	0.06	Not legal

Note: All tax rates as of January 1, 2019; (1) The American Petroleum Institute has developed a methodology for determining the average tax rate on a gallon of fuel. Rates may include any of the following: excise taxes, environmental fees, storage tank fees, other fees or taxes, general sales tax, and local taxes. In states where gasoline is subject to the general sales tax, or where the fuel tax is based on the average sale price, the average rate determined by API is sensitive to changes in the price of gasoline. States that fully or partially apply general sales taxes to gasoline: CA, CO, GA, IL, IN, MI, NY; (2) The federal excise tax of $1.0066 per pack and local taxes are not included; (3) Rates are those applicable to off-premise sales of 40% alcohol by volume (a.b.v.) distilled spirits in 750ml containers. Local excise taxes are excluded; (4) Rates are those applicable to off-premise sales of 11% a.b.v. non-carbonated wine in 750ml containers; (5) Rates are those applicable to off-premise sales of 4.7% a.b.v. beer in 12 ounce containers.
Source: Tax Foundation, 2019 Facts & Figures: How Does Your State Compare?

State Business Tax Climate Index Rankings

State	Overall Rank	Corporate Tax Rank	Individual Income Tax Rank	Sales Tax Rank	Unemployment Insurance Tax Rank	Property Tax Rank
Missouri	14	4	25	25	8	7

Note: The index is a measure of how each state's tax laws affect economic performance. The lower the rank, the more favorable a state's tax system is for business. States without a given tax are given a ranking of 1. The scores/rankings for the District of Columbia do not affect other states. The 2019 index represents the tax climate as of July 1, 2018.
Source: Tax Foundation, State Business Tax Climate Index 2019

COMMERCIAL REAL ESTATE

Office Market

Market Area	Inventory (sq. ft.)	Vacancy Rate (%)	Under Construction (sq. ft.)	YTD Net Absorption (sq. ft.)	Total Average Asking Rent ($/sq. ft./year)
Kansas City	74,504,092	9.0	280,000	282,190	20.47
National	4,905,867,938	13.1	83,553,714	45,846,470	28.46

Source: Newmark Grubb Knight Frank, National Office Market Report, 4th Quarter 2018

Industrial/Warehouse/R&D Market

Market Area	Inventory (sq. ft.)	Vacancy Rate (%)	Under Construction (sq. ft.)	YTD Net Absorption (sq. ft.)	Total Average Asking Rent ($/sq. ft./year)
Kansas City	278,801,679	5.0	3,387,505	4,371,622	4.82
National	14,796,839,085	5.0	262,662,294	238,014,726	7.16

Source: Newmark Grubb Knight Frank, National Industrial Market Report, 4th Quarter 2018

COMMERCIAL UTILITIES

Typical Monthly Electric Bills

Area	Commercial Service ($/month)		Industrial Service ($/month)	
	1,500 kWh	40 kW demand 14,000 kWh	1,000 kW demand 200,000 kWh	50,000 kW demand 32,500,000 kWh
City	n/a	1,806	32,694	2,592,507
Average[1]	203	1,619	25,886	2,540,077

Note: Figures are based on annualized rates; (1) Average based on 187 utilities surveyed; n/a not available
Source: Edison Electric Institute, Typical Bills and Average Rates Report, Summer 2018

TRANSPORTATION

Means of Transportation to Work

Area	Car/Truck/Van Drove Alone	Car/Truck/Van Car-pooled	Public Transportation Bus	Public Transportation Subway	Public Transportation Railroad	Bicycle	Walked	Other Means	Worked at Home
City	80.4	8.4	2.8	0.0	0.0	0.3	2.1	1.2	4.8
MSA[1]	83.5	8.2	1.0	0.0	0.0	0.2	1.3	0.9	4.9
U.S.	76.4	9.2	2.5	1.9	0.6	0.6	2.7	1.3	4.7

Note: Figures are percentages and cover workers 16 years of age and older; (1) Figures cover the Kansas City, MO-KS Metropolitan Statistical Area—see Appendix B for areas included
Source: U.S. Census Bureau, 2013-2017 American Community Survey 5-Year Estimates

Travel Time to Work

Area	Less Than 10 Minutes	10 to 19 Minutes	20 to 29 Minutes	30 to 44 Minutes	45 to 59 Minutes	60 to 89 Minutes	90 Minutes or More
City	11.5	33.7	28.3	19.2	4.6	1.7	1.0
MSA[1]	12.6	30.9	25.1	21.2	6.6	2.4	1.1
U.S.	12.7	28.9	20.9	20.5	8.1	6.2	2.7

Note: Note: Figures are percentages and include workers 16 years old and over; (1) Figures cover the Kansas City, MO-KS Metropolitan Statistical Area—see Appendix B for areas included
Source: U.S. Census Bureau, 2013-2017 American Community Survey 5-Year Estimates

Freeway Travel Time Index

Area	1985	1990	1995	2000	2005	2010	2014
Urban Area Rank[1,2]	54	46	68	72	77	76	76
Urban Area Index[1]	1.06	1.10	1.11	1.13	1.14	1.14	1.15
Average Index[3]	1.09	1.11	1.14	1.17	1.20	1.19	1.20

Note: Freeway Travel Time Index—the ratio of travel time in the peak period to the travel time at free-flow conditions. For example, a value of 1.30 indicates a 20-minute free-flow trip takes 26 minutes in the peak (20 minutes x 1.30 = 26 minutes); (1) Covers the Kansas City MO-KS urban area; (2) Rank is based on 101 urban areas (#1 = highest travel time index); (3) Average of 101 urban areas
Source: Texas Transportation Institute, 2015 Urban Mobility Scorecard, August 2015

Freeway Commuter Stress Index

Area	1985	1990	1995	2000	2005	2010	2014
Urban Area Rank[1,2]	66	51	71	76	81	82	79
Urban Area Index[1]	1.07	1.12	1.13	1.15	1.16	1.16	1.17
Average Index[3]	1.13	1.16	1.19	1.22	1.25	1.24	1.25

Note: The Freeway Commuter Stress Index is the same as the Freeway Travel Time Index (see table above) except that it includes only the travel in the peak directions during the peak periods; the TTI includes travel in all directions during the peak period. Thus, the CSI is more indicative of the work trip experienced by each commuter on a daily basis; (1) Covers the Kansas City MO-KS urban area; (2) Rank is based on 101 urban areas (#1 = highest travel time index); (3) Average of 101 urban areas
Source: Texas Transportation Institute, 2015 Urban Mobility Scorecard, August 2015

Public Transportation

Agency Name / Mode of Transportation	Vehicles Operated in Maximum Service[1]	Annual Unlinked Passenger Trips[2] (in thous.)	Annual Passenger Miles[3] (in thous.)
Kansas City Area Transportation Authority (KCATA)			
Bus (directly operated)	165	11,888.3	43,395.7
Bus Rapid Transit (directly operated)	12	1,240.9	3,308.9
Demand Response (directly operated)	10	84.3	369.6
Demand Response (purchased transportation)	60	240.8	1,860.2
Demand Response Taxi (purchased transportation)	36	63.2	474.6
Vanpool (directly operated)	17	1.7	74.3
Vanpool (purchased transportation)	25	39.6	1,456.8

Note: (1) The number of revenue vehicles operated by the given mode and type of service to meet the annual maximum service requirement. This is the revenue vehicle count during the peak season of the year; on the week and day that maximum service is provided. Vehicles operated in maximum service (VOMS) exclude atypical days and one-time special events; (2) The number of passengers who boarded public transportation vehicles. Passengers are counted each time they board a vehicle no matter how many vehicles they use to travel from their origin to their destination. (3) The sum of the distances ridden by all passengers during the entire fiscal year.
Source: Federal Transit Administration, National Transit Database, 2017

Air Transportation

Airport Name and Code / Type of Service	Passenger Airlines[1]	Passenger Enplanements	Freight Carriers[2]	Freight (lbs)
Kansas City International (MCI)				
Domestic service (U.S. carriers - 2018)	31	5,747,604	20	109,208,581
International service (U.S. carriers - 2017)	5	14,930	2	280,741

Note: (1) Includes all U.S.-based major, minor and commuter airlines that carried at least one passenger during the year; (2) Includes all U.S.-based airlines and freight carriers that transported at least one pound of freight during the year.
Source: Bureau of Transportation Statistics, The Intermodal Transportation Database, Air Carriers: T-100 Domestic Market (U.S. Carriers), 2018; Bureau of Transportation Statistics, The Intermodal Transportation Database, Air Carriers: T-100 International Market (U.S. Carriers), 2017

Other Transportation Statistics

Major Highways:	I-29; I-35; I-70
Amtrak Service:	Yes
Major Waterways/Ports:	Kansas River; Missouri River

Source: Amtrak.com; Google Maps

BUSINESSES

Major Business Headquarters

Company Name	Industry	Rankings	
		Fortune[1]	Forbes[2]
Bartlett & Co	Food, Drink & Tobacco	-	223
Hallmark Cards	Media	-	105
JE Dunn Construction Group	Construction	-	154

Note: (1) Companies that produce a 10-K are ranked 1 to 500 based on 2017 revenue; (2) All private companies with at least $2 billion in annual revenue through the end of their most current fiscal year are ranked 1 to 229; companies listed are headquartered in the city; dashes indicate no ranking
Source: Fortune, "Fortune 500," June 2018; Forbes, "America's Largest Private Companies," 2018 Rankings

Fast-Growing Businesses

According to *Initiative for a Competitive Inner City (ICIC)*, Kansas City is home to two of America's 100 fastest-growing "inner city" companies: **Vazquez Commercial Contracting** (#6); **DuBois Consultants** (#94). Criteria for inclusion: company must be headquartered in or have 51 percent or more of its physical operations in an economically distressed urban area; must be an independent, for-profit corporation, partnership or proprietorship; must have 10 or more employees and have a five-year sales history that includes sales of at least $200,000 in the base year and at least $1 million in the current year with no decrease in sales over the two most recent years. Companies were ranked overall by revenue growth over the five-year period between 2013 and 2017. *Initiative for a Competitive Inner City (ICIC), "Inner City 100 Companies," 2018*

Minority Business Opportunity

Kansas City is home to one company which is on the *Black Enterprise* Industrial/Service list (100 largest companies based on gross sales): **Alexander Mechanical** (#95). Criteria: operational in previous calendar year; at least 51% black-owned and manufactures/owns the product it sells or provides industrial or consumer services. Brokerages, real estate firms and firms that provide professional services are not eligible. *Black Enterprise, B.E. 100s, 2018*

Kansas City is home to one company which is on the *Hispanic Business* 500 list (500 largest U.S. Hispanic-owned companies based on revenue): **ECCO Select Corp.** (#255). Companies included must show at least 51 percent ownership by Hispanic U.S. citizens, and must maintain headquarters in one of the 50 states or Washington, D.C. *Hispanic Business, "Hispanic Business 500," June 20, 2013*

Minority- and Women-Owned Businesses

Group	All Firms		Firms with Paid Employees			
	Firms	Sales ($000)	Firms	Sales ($000)	Employees	Payroll ($000)
AIAN[1]	383	28,439	40	19,096	212	6,131
Asian	1,655	449,804	394	397,022	2,641	55,413
Black	6,399	285,544	446	184,710	3,071	65,508
Hispanic	1,699	280,269	193	242,365	2,021	62,147
NHOPI[2]	n/a	n/a	n/a	n/a	n/a	n/a
Women	14,564	3,136,838	1,555	2,791,200	12,646	498,565
All Firms	39,486	88,819,944	9,034	87,638,564	287,462	13,831,669

Note: Figures cover firms located in the city; minority- and women-owned business are defined as firms in which the corresponding group own 51% or more of the stock or equity of the company; (1) American Indian and Alaska Native; (2) Native Hawaiian and Other Pacific Islander; n/a not available
Source: U.S. Census Bureau, 2012 Economic Census, Survey of Business Owners

HOTELS & CONVENTION CENTERS

Hotels, Motels and Vacation Rentals

Area	5 Star		4 Star		3 Star		2 Star		1 Star		Not Rated	
	Num.	Pct.[3]	Num.	Pct.[3]	Num.	Pct.[3]	Num.	Pct.[3]	Num.	Pct.[3]	Num.	Pct.[3]
City[1]	0	0.0	18	5.3	53	15.7	105	31.1	2	0.6	160	47.3
Total[2]	286	0.4	5,236	7.1	16,715	22.6	10,259	13.9	293	0.4	41,056	55.6

Note: (1) Figures cover Kansas City and vicinity; (2) Figures cover all 100 cities in this book; (3) Percentage of hotels which have a given star rating; Star ratings are determined by expedia.com and offer an indication of the general quality of a particular hotel.
Source: www.expedia.com, April 3, 2019

Major Convention Centers

Name	Overall Space (sq. ft.)	Exhibit Space (sq. ft.)	Meeting Space (sq. ft.)	Meeting Rooms
Kansas City Convention Center	n/a	388,000	n/a	48
Overland Park Convention Center	140,000	60,000	15,000	n/a

Note: Table includes convention centers located in the Kansas City, MO-KS metro area; n/a not available
Source: Original research

Living Environment

COST OF LIVING

Cost of Living Index

Composite Index	Groceries	Housing	Utilities	Trans-portation	Health Care	Misc. Goods/ Services
95.1	102.7	85.1	99.0	93.7	99.9	99.5

Note: The Cost of Living Index measures regional differences in the cost of consumer goods and services, excluding taxes and non-consumer expenditures, for professional and managerial households in the top income quintile. It is based on more than 50,000 prices covering almost 60 different items for which prices are collected three times a year by chambers of commerce, economic development organizations or university applied economic centers in each participating urban area. The numbers shown should be read as a percentage above or below the national average of 100. For example, a value of 115.4 in the groceries column indicates that grocery prices are 15.4% higher than the national average. Small differences in the index numbers should not be interpreted as significant; Figures cover the Kansas City MO-KS urban area.
Source: The Council for Community and Economic Research, ACCRA Cost of Living Index, 2018

Grocery Prices

Area[1]	T-Bone Steak ($/pound)	Frying Chicken ($/pound)	Whole Milk ($/half gal.)	Eggs ($/dozen)	Orange Juice ($/64 oz.)	Coffee ($/11.5 oz.)
City[2]	11.76	1.44	2.10	1.79	3.35	4.19
Avg.	11.35	1.42	1.94	1.81	3.52	4.35
Min.	7.45	0.92	0.80	0.75	2.72	3.06
Max.	15.05	2.76	4.18	4.00	5.36	8.20

Note: (1) Values for the local area are compared with the average, minimum and maximum values for all 291 areas in the Cost of Living Index; (2) Figures cover the Kansas City MO-KS urban area; T-Bone Steak (price per pound); Frying Chicken (price per pound, whole fryer); Whole Milk (half gallon carton); Eggs (price per dozen, Grade A, large); Orange Juice (64 oz. Tropicana or Florida Natural); Coffee (11.5 oz. can, vacuum-packed, Maxwell House, Hills Bros, or Folgers).
Source: The Council for Community and Economic Research, ACCRA Cost of Living Index, 2018

Housing and Utility Costs

Area[1]	New Home Price ($)	Apartment Rent ($/month)	All Electric ($/month)	Part Electric ($/month)	Other Energy ($/month)	Telephone ($/month)
City[2]	276,197	1,092	-	91.74	68.59	184.50
Avg.	347,000	1,087	165.93	100.16	67.73	178.70
Min.	200,468	500	93.58	25.64	26.78	163.10
Max.	1,901,222	4,888	388.65	246.86	332.81	197.70

Note: (1) Values for the local area are compared with the average, minimum and maximum values for all 291 areas in the Cost of Living Index; (2) Figures cover the Kansas City MO-KS urban area; New Home Price (2,400 sf living area, 8,000 sf lot, in urban area with full utilities); Apartment Rent (950 sf 2 bedroom/1.5 or 2 bath, unfurnished, excluding all utilities except water); All Electric (average monthly cost for an all-electric home); Part Electric (average monthly cost for a part-electric home); Other Energy (average monthly cost for natural gas, fuel oil, coal, wood, and any other forms of energy except electricity); Telephone (price includes the base monthly rate plus taxes and fees for three lines of mobile phone service).
Source: The Council for Community and Economic Research, ACCRA Cost of Living Index, 2018

Health Care, Transportation, and Other Costs

Area[1]	Doctor ($/visit)	Dentist ($/visit)	Optometrist ($/visit)	Gasoline ($/gallon)	Beauty Salon ($/visit)	Men's Shirt ($)
City[2]	94.24	106.60	100.58	2.50	30.23	34.80
Avg.	110.71	95.11	103.74	2.61	37.48	32.03
Min.	33.60	62.55	54.63	1.89	17.00	11.44
Max.	195.97	153.93	225.79	3.59	71.88	58.64

Note: (1) Values for the local area are compared with the average, minimum and maximum values for all 291 areas in the Cost of Living Index; (2) Figures cover the Kansas City MO-KS urban area; Doctor (general practitioners routine exam of an established patient); Dentist (adult teeth cleaning and periodic oral examination); Optometrist (full vision eye exam for established adult patient); Gasoline (one gallon regular unleaded, national brand, including all taxes, cash price at self-service pump if available); Beauty Salon (woman's shampoo, trim, and blow-dry); Men's Shirt (cotton/polyester dress shirt, pinpoint weave, long sleeves).
Source: The Council for Community and Economic Research, ACCRA Cost of Living Index, 2018

HOUSING

House Price Index (HPI)

Area	National Ranking[2]	Quarterly Change (%)	One-Year Change (%)	Five-Year Change (%)
MSA[1]	37	1.59	9.16	37.00
U.S.[3]	–	1.12	5.73	32.81

Note: The HPI is a weighted repeat sales index. It measures average price changes in repeat sales or refinancings on the same properties. This information is obtained by reviewing repeat mortgage transactions on single-family properties whose mortgages have been purchased or securitized by Fannie Mae or Freddie Mac in January 1975; (1) Figures cover the Kansas City, MO-KS Metropolitan Statistical Area—see Appendix B for areas included; (2) Rankings are based on annual percentage change for all metro areas containing at least 15,000 transactions over the last 10 years and ranges from 1 to 245; (3) figures based on a weighted average of Census Division estimates using a seasonally adjusted, purchase-only index; all figures are for the period ending December 31, 2018
Source: Federal Housing Finance Agency, House Price Index, February 26, 2019

Median Single-Family Home Prices

Area	2016	2017	2018[p]	Percent Change 2017 to 2018
MSA[1]	181.3	194.8	206.5	6.0
U.S. Average	235.5	248.8	261.6	5.1

Note: Figures are median sales prices of existing single-family homes in thousands of dollars; (p) preliminary; (1) Figures cover the Kansas City, MO-KS Metropolitan Statistical Area—see Appendix B for areas included
Source: National Association of Realtors, Median Sales Price of Existing Single-Family Homes for Metropolitan Areas, 4th Quarter 2018

Qualifying Income Based on Median Sales Price of Existing Single-Family Homes

Area	With 5% Down ($)	With 10% Down ($)	With 20% Down ($)
MSA[1]	49,854	47,231	41,983
U.S. Average	62,954	59,640	53,013

Note: Figures are preliminary; Qualifying income is based on a mortgage rate of 4.9%. Monthly principal and interest payment is limited to 25% of income; (1) Figures cover the Kansas City, MO-KS Metropolitan Statistical Area—see Appendix B for areas included
Source: National Association of Realtors, Qualifying Income Based on Median Sales Price of Existing Single-Family Homes for Metropolitan Areas, 4th Quarter 2018

Median Apartment Condo-Coop Home Prices

Area	2016	2017	2018[p]	Percent Change 2017 to 2018
MSA[1]	n/a	n/a	n/a	n/a
U.S. Average	220.7	234.3	241.0	2.9

Note: Figures are median sales prices of existing apartment condo-coop homes in thousands of dollars; (p) preliminary; n/a not available; (1) Figures cover the Kansas City, MO-KS Metropolitan Statistical Area—see Appendix B for areas included
Source: National Association of Realtors, Median Sales Price of Existing Apartment Condo-Coop Homes for Metropolitan Areas, 4th Quarter 2018

Home Value Distribution

Area	Under $50,000	$50,000 -$99,999	$100,000 -$149,999	$150,000 -$199,999	$200,000 -$299,999	$300,000 -$499,999	$500,000 -$999,999	$1,000,000 or more
City	12.6	20.9	20.5	17.8	16.7	8.2	2.7	0.6
MSA[1]	7.5	15.4	19.7	19.3	20.6	12.9	3.8	0.8
U.S.	8.3	13.9	14.7	14.6	18.7	17.3	9.7	2.7

Note: Figures are percentages and cover owner-occupied housing units; (1) Figures cover the Kansas City, MO-KS Metropolitan Statistical Area—see Appendix B for areas included
Source: U.S. Census Bureau, 2013-2017 American Community Survey 5-Year Estimates

Homeownership Rate

Area	2010 (%)	2011 (%)	2012 (%)	2013 (%)	2014 (%)	2015 (%)	2016 (%)	2017 (%)	2018 (%)
MSA[1]	68.8	68.5	65.1	65.6	66.1	65.0	62.4	62.4	64.3
U.S.	66.9	66.1	65.4	65.1	64.5	63.7	63.4	63.9	64.4

Note: (1) Figures cover the Kansas City, MO-KS Metropolitan Statistical Area—see Appendix B for areas included
Source: U.S. Census Bureau, Housing Vacancies and Homeownership Annual Statistics: 2010-2018

Year Housing Structure Built

Area	2010 or Later	2000 -2009	1990 -1999	1980 -1989	1970 -1979	1960 -1969	1950 -1959	1940 -1949	Before 1940	Median Year
City	2.8	10.6	9.2	8.5	12.3	13.6	14.7	6.8	21.4	1965
MSA[1]	2.7	14.3	14.5	12.4	16.0	12.1	11.8	4.6	11.6	1976
U.S.	3.2	14.5	14.0	13.6	15.5	10.8	10.5	5.1	12.9	1977

Note: Figures are percentages except for Median Year; Note: (1) Figures cover the Kansas City, MO-KS Metropolitan Statistical Area—see Appendix B for areas included
Source: U.S. Census Bureau, 2013-2017 American Community Survey 5-Year Estimates

Gross Monthly Rent

Area	Under $500	$500 -$999	$1,000 -$1,499	$1,500 -$1,999	$2,000 -$2,499	$2,500 -$2,999	$3,000 and up	Median ($)
City	10.7	55.4	27.3	4.7	1.3	0.2	0.5	862
MSA[1]	9.5	52.6	29.4	6.1	1.5	0.3	0.5	894
U.S.	10.5	41.1	28.7	11.7	4.5	1.8	1.7	982

Note: Figures are percentages except for Median; Gross rent is the contract rent plus the estimated average monthly cost of utilities (electricity, gas, and water and sewer) and fuels (oil, coal, kerosene, wood, etc.) if these are paid by the renter (or paid for the renter by someone else); (1) Figures cover the Kansas City, MO-KS Metropolitan Statistical Area—see Appendix B for areas included
Source: U.S. Census Bureau, 2013-2017 American Community Survey 5-Year Estimates

HEALTH

Health Risk Factors

Category	MSA[1] (%)	U.S. (%)
Adults aged 18–64 who have any kind of health care coverage	85.0	87.3
Adults who reported being in good or better health	85.8	82.4
Adults who have been told they have high blood cholesterol	34.1	33.0
Adults who have been told they have high blood pressure	29.6	32.3
Adults who are current smokers	17.1	17.1
Adults who currently use E-cigarettes	4.5	4.6
Adults who currently use chewing tobacco, snuff, or snus	4.0	4.0
Adults who are heavy drinkers[2]	6.0	6.3
Adults who are binge drinkers[3]	20.7	17.4
Adults who are overweight (BMI 25.0 - 29.9)	36.1	35.3
Adults who are obese (BMI 30.0 - 99.8)	31.2	31.3
Adults who participated in any physical activities in the past month	73.7	74.4
Adults who always or nearly always wears a seat belt	94.9	94.3

Note: (1) Figures cover the Kansas City, MO-KS Metropolitan Statistical Area—see Appendix B for areas included; (2) Heavy drinkers are classified as adult men having more than 14 drinks per week and adult women having more than 7 drinks per week; (3) Binge drinkers are classified as males having five or more drinks on one occasion or females having four or more drinks on one occasion
Source: Centers for Disease Control and Prevention, Behaviorial Risk Factor Surveillance System, SMART: Selected Metropolitan Area Risk Trends, 2017

Acute and Chronic Health Conditions

Category	MSA[1] (%)	U.S. (%)
Adults who have ever been told they had a heart attack	3.9	4.2
Adults who have ever been told they have angina or coronary heart disease	3.8	3.9
Adults who have ever been told they had a stroke	3.4	3.0
Adults who have ever been told they have asthma	13.2	14.2
Adults who have ever been told they have arthritis	23.7	24.9
Adults who have ever been told they have diabetes[2]	9.7	10.5
Adults who have ever been told they had skin cancer	7.0	6.2
Adults who have ever been told they had any other types of cancer	6.4	7.1
Adults who have ever been told they have COPD	6.0	6.5
Adults who have ever been told they have kidney disease	2.5	3.0
Adults who have ever been told they have a form of depression	20.5	20.5

Note: (1) Figures cover the Kansas City, MO-KS Metropolitan Statistical Area—see Appendix B for areas included; (2) Figures do not include pregnancy-related, borderline, or pre-diabetes
Source: Centers for Disease Control and Prevention, Behaviorial Risk Factor Surveillance System, SMART: Selected Metropolitan Area Risk Trends, 2017

Health Screening and Vaccination Rates

Category	MSA[1] (%)	U.S. (%)
Adults aged 65+ who have had flu shot within the past year	60.6	60.7
Adults aged 65+ who have ever had a pneumonia vaccination	78.2	75.4
Adults who have ever been tested for HIV	36.9	36.1
Adults who have ever had the shingles or zoster vaccine?	27.7	28.9
Adults who have had their blood cholesterol checked within the last five years	87.4	85.9

Note: n/a not available; (1) Figures cover the Kansas City, MO-KS Metropolitan Statistical Area—see Appendix B for areas included.
Source: Centers for Disease Control and Prevention, Behaviorial Risk Factor Surveillance System, SMART: Selected Metropolitan Area Risk Trends, 2017

Disability Status

Category	MSA[1] (%)	U.S. (%)
Adults who reported being deaf	5.6	6.7
Are you blind or have serious difficulty seeing, even when wearing glasses?	3.7	4.5
Are you limited in any way in any of your usual activities due of arthritis?	11.2	12.9
Do you have difficulty doing errands alone?	6.5	6.8
Do you have difficulty dressing or bathing?	3.1	3.6
Do you have serious difficulty concentrating/remembering/making decisions?	9.4	10.7
Do you have serious difficulty walking or climbing stairs?	13.0	13.6

Note: (1) Figures cover the Kansas City, MO-KS Metropolitan Statistical Area—see Appendix B for areas included.
Source: Centers for Disease Control and Prevention, Behaviorial Risk Factor Surveillance System, SMART: Selected Metropolitan Area Risk Trends, 2017

Mortality Rates for the Top 10 Causes of Death in the U.S.

ICD-10[a] Sub-Chapter	ICD-10[a] Code	Age-Adjusted Mortality Rate[1] per 100,000 population	
		County[2]	U.S.
Malignant neoplasms	C00-C97	168.3	155.5
Ischaemic heart diseases	I20-I25	78.4	94.8
Other forms of heart disease	I30-I51	75.1	52.9
Chronic lower respiratory diseases	J40-J47	49.6	41.0
Cerebrovascular diseases	I60-I69	39.8	37.5
Other degenerative diseases of the nervous system	G30-G31	26.2	35.0
Other external causes of accidental injury	W00-X59	35.4	33.7
Organic, including symptomatic, mental disorders	F01-F09	46.3	31.0
Hypertensive diseases	I10-I15	24.5	21.9
Diabetes mellitus	E10-E14	19.7	21.2

Note: (a) ICD-10 = International Classification of Diseases 10th Revision; (1) Mortality rates are a three year average covering 2015-2017; (2) Figures cover Jackson County.
Source: Centers for Disease Control and Prevention, National Center for Health Statistics. Underlying Cause of Death 1999-2017 on CDC WONDER Online Database

Mortality Rates for Selected Causes of Death

ICD-10[a] Sub-Chapter	ICD-10[a] Code	Age-Adjusted Mortality Rate[1] per 100,000 population	
		County[2]	U.S.
Assault	X85-Y09	20.9	5.9
Diseases of the liver	K70-K76	14.0	14.1
Human immunodeficiency virus (HIV) disease	B20-B24	1.5	1.8
Influenza and pneumonia	J09-J18	13.5	14.3
Intentional self-harm	X60-X84	19.0	13.6
Malnutrition	E40-E46	3.6	1.6
Obesity and other hyperalimentation	E65-E68	1.6	2.1
Renal failure	N17-N19	24.2	13.0
Transport accidents	V01-V99	14.4	12.4
Viral hepatitis	B15-B19	1.8	1.6

Note: (a) ICD-10 = International Classification of Diseases 10th Revision; (1) Mortality rates are a three year average covering 2015-2017; (2) Figures cover Jackson County; Data are suppressed when the data meet the criteria for confidentiality constraints; Mortality rates are flagged as unreliable when the rate would be calculated with a numerator of 20 or less.
Source: Centers for Disease Control and Prevention, National Center for Health Statistics. Underlying Cause of Death 1999-2017 on CDC WONDER Online Database

Health Insurance Coverage

Area	With Health Insurance	With Private Health Insurance	With Public Health Insurance	Without Health Insurance	Population Under Age 18 Without Health Insurance
City	86.7	66.9	29.2	13.3	6.9
MSA[1]	90.1	74.7	26.6	9.9	5.5
U.S.	89.5	67.2	33.8	10.5	5.7

Note: Figures are percentages that cover the civilian noninstitutionalized population; (1) Figures cover the Kansas City, MO-KS Metropolitan Statistical Area—see Appendix B for areas included
Source: U.S. Census Bureau, 2013-2017 American Community Survey 5-Year Estimates

Number of Medical Professionals

Area	MDs[3]	DOs[3,4]	Dentists	Podiatrists	Chiropractors	Optometrists
County[1] (number)	2,081	415	591	44	305	141
County[1] (rate[2])	300.2	59.9	84.6	6.3	43.6	20.2
U.S. (rate[2])	279.3	23.0	68.4	6.0	27.1	16.2

Note: Data as of 2017 unless noted; (1) Data covers Jackson County; (2) Rate per 100,000 population; (3) Data as of 2016 and includes all active, non-federal physicians; (4) Doctor of Osteopathic Medicine
Source: U.S. Department of Health and Human Services, Health Resources and Services Administration, Bureau of Health Professions, Area Resource File (ARF) 2017-2018

Best Hospitals

According to *U.S. News*, the Kansas City, MO-KS metro area is home to two of the best hospitals in the U.S.: **St. Luke's Hospital** (3 adult specialties); **University of Kansas Hospital** (9 adult specialties). The hospitals listed were nationally ranked in at least one of 16 adult or 10 pediatric specialties. Only 170 hospitals nationwide were nationally ranked in one or more adult or pediatric specialty. Twenty hospitals in the U.S. made the Honor Roll. The Best Hospitals Honor Roll takes both the national rankings and the procedure and condition ratings into account. Hospitals received points if they were nationally ranked in one of the 16 adult specialties—the higher they ranked, the more points they got—and how many ratings of "high performing" they earned in the nine procedures and conditions. *U.S. News Online, "America's Best Hospitals 2018-19"*

According to *U.S. News*, the Kansas City, MO-KS metro area is home to one of the best children's hospitals in the U.S.: **Children's Mercy Kansas City** (10 pediatric specialties). The hospital listed was highly ranked in at least one of 10 pediatric specialties. Eighty-six children's hospitals in the U.S. were nationally ranked in at least one specialty. Hospitals received points for being ranked in a specialty, and the 10 hospitals with the most points across the 10 specialties make up the Honor Roll. *U.S. News Online, "America's Best Children's Hospitals 2018-19"*

EDUCATION

Public School District Statistics

District Name	Schls	Pupils	Pupil/ Teacher Ratio	Minority Pupils[1] (%)	Free Lunch Eligible[2] (%)	IEP[3] (%)
Center 58	8	2,645	12.2	80.6	67.5	14.0
Hickman Mills C-1	15	6,328	13.5	89.4	100.0	13.6
Kansas City 33	35	15,418	14.5	90.1	99.9	13.0
North Kansas City 74	32	20,188	16.1	40.0	37.1	11.5
Park Hill	17	11,659	15.3	30.6	20.5	10.7

Note: Table includes school districts with 2,000 or more students; (1) Percentage of students that are not non-Hispanic white; (2) Percentage of students that are eligible for the free lunch program; (3) Percentage of students that have an Individualized Education Program.
Source: U.S. Department of Education, National Center for Education Statistics, Common Core of Data, Local Education Agency (School District) Universe Survey: School Year 2016-2017; U.S. Department of Education, National Center for Education Statistics, Common Core of Data, Public Elementary/Secondary School Universe Survey: School Year 2016-2017

Highest Level of Education

Area	Less than H.S.	H.S. Diploma	Some College, No Deg.	Associate Degree	Bachelor's Degree	Master's Degree	Prof. School Degree	Doctorate Degree
City	10.9	26.0	22.4	7.3	20.9	9.1	2.3	1.2
MSA[1]	8.5	25.9	22.3	7.6	22.7	9.6	2.3	1.1
U.S.	12.7	27.3	20.8	8.3	19.1	8.4	2.0	1.4

Note: Figures cover persons age 25 and over; (1) Figures cover the Kansas City, MO-KS Metropolitan Statistical Area—see Appendix B for areas included
Source: U.S. Census Bureau, 2013-2017 American Community Survey 5-Year Estimates

Educational Attainment by Race

Area	High School Graduate or Higher (%)					Bachelor's Degree or Higher (%)				
	Total	White	Black	Asian	Hisp.[2]	Total	White	Black	Asian	Hisp.[2]
City	89.1	92.9	85.6	77.1	66.2	33.5	41.7	15.5	45.0	16.2
MSA[1]	91.5	93.2	87.6	84.6	66.3	35.7	38.2	19.3	53.7	16.2
U.S.	87.3	89.3	84.9	86.5	66.7	30.9	32.2	20.6	52.7	15.2

Note: Figures shown cover persons 25 years old and over; (1) Figures cover the Kansas City, MO-KS Metropolitan Statistical Area—see Appendix B for areas included; (2) People of Hispanic origin can be of any race
Source: U.S. Census Bureau, 2013-2017 American Community Survey 5-Year Estimates

School Enrollment by Grade and Control

Area	Preschool (%)		Kindergarten (%)		Grades 1 - 4 (%)		Grades 5 - 8 (%)		Grades 9 - 12 (%)	
	Public	Private	Public	Private	Public	Private	Public	Private	Public	Private
City	56.6	43.4	87.7	12.3	89.1	10.9	87.2	12.8	86.4	13.6
MSA[1]	54.3	45.7	88.5	11.5	89.0	11.0	89.1	10.9	90.0	10.0
U.S.	58.8	41.2	87.7	12.3	89.7	10.3	89.6	10.4	90.3	9.7

Note: Figures shown cover persons 3 years old and over; (1) Figures cover the Kansas City, MO-KS Metropolitan Statistical Area—see Appendix B for areas included
Source: U.S. Census Bureau, 2013-2017 American Community Survey 5-Year Estimates

Average Salaries of Public School Classroom Teachers

Area	2016		2017		Change from 2016 to 2017	
	Dollars	Rank[1]	Dollars	Rank[1]	Percent	Rank[2]
Missouri	47,959	40	48,618	41	1.4	27
U.S. Average	58,479	–	59,660	–	2.0	–

Note: (1) Rank ranges from 1 to 51 where 1 indicates highest salary; (2) Rank ranges from 1 to 51 where 1 indicates highest percent change.
Source: National Education Association, Rankings & Estimates: Rankings of the States 2017 and Estimates of School Statistics 2018

Higher Education

Four-Year Colleges			Two-Year Colleges			Medical Schools[1]	Law Schools[2]	Voc/ Tech[3]
Public	Private Non-profit	Private For-profit	Public	Private Non-profit	Private For-profit			
1	9	4	1	0	6	2	1	3

Note: Figures cover institutions located within the city limits and include main campuses only; (1) includes schools accredited by the Liaison Committee on Medical Education and the American Osteopathic Association's Commission on Osteopathic College Accreditation; (2) includes ABA-accredited schools, schools with provisional ABA accreditation, and state accredited schools; (3) includes all schools with programs that are less than 2 years.
Source: National Center for Education Statistics, Integrated Postsecondary Education System (IPEDS), 2017-18; Wikipedia, List of Medical Schools in the United States, accessed April 3, 2019; Wikipedia, List of Law Schools in the United States, accessed April 3, 2019

According to *U.S. News & World Report,* the Kansas City, MO-KS metro area is home to one of the best liberal arts colleges in the U.S.: **William Jewell College** (#155 tie). The indicators used to capture academic quality fall into a number of categories: assessment by administrators at peer institutions; retention of students; faculty resources; student selectivity; financial resources; alumni giving; high school counselor ratings of colleges; and graduation rate. *U.S. News & World Report, "America's Best Colleges 2019"*

According to *U.S. News & World Report,* the Kansas City, MO-KS metro area is home to one of the top 75 medical schools for research in the U.S.: **University of Kansas Medical Center** (#67 tie). The rankings are based on a weighted average of 11 measures of quality: quality assessment; peer assessment score; assessment score by residency directors; research activity; total research activity; average research activity per faculty member; student selectivity; median MCAT total score; median undergraduate GPA; acceptance rate; and faculty resources. *U.S. News & World Report, "America's Best Graduate Schools, Medical, 2020"*

PRESIDENTIAL ELECTION

2016 Presidential Election Results

Area	Clinton	Trump	Johnson	Stein	Other
Jackson County	55.5	38.1	3.6	1.2	1.7
U.S.	48.0	45.9	3.3	1.1	1.7

Note: Results are percentages and may not add to 100% due to rounding
Source: Dave Leip's Atlas of U.S. Presidential Elections

EMPLOYERS

Major Employers

Company Name	Industry
B&V Baker Guam JV	Engineering services
Black and Veatch Corp	Engineering services
DST Systems	Data processing
Embarq Corporation	Telephone communications
Ford Motor Company	Automobile assembly
Hallmark Cards	Greeting cards
HCA Midwest Division	Hospital management
Honeywell International	Search & navigation equipment
Internal Revenue Service	Taxation department, government
North Kansas City Hospital	General medical & surgical hospitals
Park University	Colleges & universities
Performance Contracting	Drywall
St. Lukes Hospital of Kansas	General medical & surgical hospitals
United Auto Workers	Labor union
University of Kansas	Charitable trust management
University of Kansas	Medical centers
University of Missouri System	General medical & surgical hospitals

Note: Companies shown are located within the Kansas City, MO-KS Metropolitan Statistical Area.
Source: Hoovers.com; Wikipedia

Best Companies to Work For

Burns & McDonnell, headquartered in Kansas City, is among "The 100 Best Companies to Work For." To pick the best companies, *Fortune* partnered with the Great Place to Work Institute. Two-thirds of a company's score is based on the results of the Institute's Trust Index survey, which is sent to a random sample of employees from each company. The questions related to attitudes about management's credibility, job satisfaction, and camaraderie. The other third of the scoring is based on the company's responses to the Institute's Culture Audit, which includes detailed questions about pay and benefit programs, and a series of open-ended questions about hiring practices, internal communication, training, recognition programs, and diversity efforts. Any company that is at least five years old with more than 1,000 U.S. employees is eligible. *Fortune, "The 100 Best Companies to Work For," 2019*

PUBLIC SAFETY

Crime Rate

Area	All Crimes	Violent Crimes				Property Crimes		
		Murder	Rape[3]	Robbery	Aggrav. Assault	Burglary	Larceny -Theft	Motor Vehicle Theft
City	6,268.1	30.9	91.8	383.1	1,218.5	960.5	2,670.4	912.9
Suburbs[1]	n/a	n/a	n/a	n/a	n/a	n/a	n/a	n/a
Metro[2]	n/a	n/a	n/a	n/a	n/a	n/a	n/a	n/a
U.S.	2,756.1	5.3	41.7	98.0	248.9	430.4	1,694.4	237.4

Note: Figures are crimes per 100,000 population; (1) All areas within the metro area that are located outside the city limits; (2) Figures cover the Kansas City, MO-KS Metropolitan Statistical Area—see Appendix B for areas included; n/a not available; (3) The city and U.S. figures shown were reported using the revised Uniform Crime Reporting (UCR) definition of rape. The suburban and metro area figures shown are an aggregate total of the data submitted using both the revised and legacy UCR definitions.
Source: FBI Uniform Crime Reports, 2017

Hate Crimes

Area	Number of Quarters Reported	Number of Incidents per Bias Motivation					
		Race/Ethnicity/ Ancestry	Religion	Sexual Orientation	Disability	Gender	Gender Identity
City	4	34	5	6	0	1	1
U.S.	4	4,131	1,564	1,130	116	46	119

Source: Federal Bureau of Investigation, Hate Crime Statistics 2017

Identity Theft Consumer Reports

Area	Reports	Reports per 100,000 Population	Rank[2]
MSA[1]	1,999	95	154
U.S.	444,602	135	-

Note: (1) Figures cover the Kansas City, MO-KS Metropolitan Statistical Area—see Appendix B for areas included; (2) Rank ranges from 1 to 389 where 1 indicates greatest number of identity theft reports per 100,000 population
Source: Federal Trade Commission, Consumer Sentinel Network Data Book for January–December 2018

Fraud and Other Consumer Reports

Area	Reports	Reports per 100,000 Population	Rank[2]
MSA[1]	12,180	579	74
U.S.	2,552,917	776	-

Note: (1) Figures cover the Kansas City, MO-KS Metropolitan Statistical Area—see Appendix B for areas included; (2) Rank ranges from 1 to 389 where 1 indicates greatest number of fraud and other consumer reports per 100,000 population
Source: Federal Trade Commission, Consumer Sentinel Network Data Book for January–December 2018

SPORTS

Professional Sports Teams

Team Name	League	Year Established
Kansas City Chiefs	National Football League (NFL)	1963
Kansas City Royals	Major League Baseball (MLB)	1969
Sporting Kansas City	Major League Soccer (MLS)	1996

Note: Includes teams located in the Kansas City, MO-KS Metropolitan Statistical Area.
Source: Wikipedia, Major Professional Sports Teams of the United States and Canada, April 5, 2019

CLIMATE

Average and Extreme Temperatures

Temperature	Jan	Feb	Mar	Apr	May	Jun	Jul	Aug	Sep	Oct	Nov	Dec	Yr.
Extreme High (°F)	69	76	86	93	92	105	107	109	102	92	82	70	109
Average High (°F)	35	40	54	65	74	84	90	87	79	66	52	39	64
Average Temp. (°F)	26	31	44	55	64	74	79	77	68	56	43	30	54
Average Low (°F)	17	22	34	44	54	63	69	66	58	45	34	21	44
Extreme Low (°F)	-17	-19	-10	12	30	42	54	43	33	21	1	-23	-23

Note: Figures cover the years 1972-1990
Source: National Climatic Data Center, International Station Meteorological Climate Summary, 9/96

Average Precipitation/Snowfall/Humidity

Precip./Humidity	Jan	Feb	Mar	Apr	May	Jun	Jul	Aug	Sep	Oct	Nov	Dec	Yr.
Avg. Precip. (in.)	1.1	1.2	2.8	3.0	5.5	4.1	3.8	4.1	4.9	3.6	2.1	1.6	38.1
Avg. Snowfall (in.)	6	5	3	1	0	0	0	0	0	Tr	1	5	21
Avg. Rel. Hum. 6am (%)	76	77	78	77	82	84	84	86	86	80	79	78	80
Avg. Rel. Hum. 3pm (%)	58	59	54	50	54	54	51	53	53	51	57	60	54

Note: Figures cover the years 1972-1990; Tr = Trace amounts (<0.05 in. of rain; <0.5 in. of snow)
Source: National Climatic Data Center, International Station Meteorological Climate Summary, 9/96

Weather Conditions

Temperature			Daytime Sky			Precipitation		
10°F & below	32°F & below	90°F & above	Clear	Partly cloudy	Cloudy	0.01 inch or more precip.	0.1 inch or more snow/ice	Thunder-storms
22	110	39	112	134	119	103	17	51

Note: Figures are average number of days per year and cover the years 1972-1990
Source: National Climatic Data Center, International Station Meteorological Climate Summary, 9/96

HAZARDOUS WASTE

Superfund Sites

The Kansas City, MO-KS metro area is home to six sites on the EPA's Superfund National Priorities List: **Armour Road** (final); **Chemical Commodities, Inc.** (final); **Conservation Chemical Co.** (final); **Doepke Disposal (Holliday)** (final); **Lake City Army Ammunition Plant (Northwest Lagoon)** (final); **Lee Chemical** (final). There are a total of 1,390 Superfund sites with a status of proposed or final on the list in the U.S. *U.S. Environmental Protection Agency, National Priorities List, April 5, 2019*

AIR & WATER QUALITY

Air Quality Trends: Ozone

	1990	1995	2000	2005	2010	2012	2014	2015	2016	2017
MSA[1]	0.075	0.098	0.088	0.084	0.072	0.085	0.066	0.063	0.066	0.069
U.S.	0.088	0.089	0.082	0.080	0.073	0.075	0.067	0.068	0.069	0.068

Note: (1) Data covers the Kansas City, MO-KS Metropolitan Statistical Area—see Appendix B for areas included. The values shown are the composite ozone concentration averages among trend sites based on the highest fourth daily maximum 8-hour concentration in parts per million. These trends are based on sites having an adequate record of monitoring data during the trend period. Data from exceptional events are included.
Source: U.S. Environmental Protection Agency, Air Quality Monitoring Information, "Air Quality Trends by City, 1990-2017"

Air Quality Index

Area	Percent of Days when Air Quality was...[2]					AQI Statistics[2]	
	Good	Moderate	Unhealthy for Sensitive Groups	Unhealthy	Very Unhealthy	Maximum	Median
MSA[1]	55.3	42.7	1.9	0.0	0.0	129	48

Note: (1) Data covers the Kansas City, MO-KS Metropolitan Statistical Area—see Appendix B for areas included; (2) Based on 365 days with AQI data in 2017. Air Quality Index (AQI) is an index for reporting daily air quality. EPA calculates the AQI for five major air pollutants regulated by the Clean Air Act: ground-level ozone, particle pollution (aka particulate matter), carbon monoxide, sulfur dioxide, and nitrogen dioxide. The AQI runs from 0 to 500. The higher the AQI value, the greater the level of air pollution and the greater the health concern. There are six AQI categories: "Good" AQI is between 0 and 50. Air quality is considered satisfactory; "Moderate" AQI is between 51 and 100. Air quality is acceptable; "Unhealthy for Sensitive Groups" When AQI values are between 101 and 150, members of sensitive groups may experience health effects; "Unhealthy" When AQI values are between 151 and 200 everyone may begin to experience health effects; "Very Unhealthy" AQI values between 201 and 300 trigger a health alert; "Hazardous" AQI values over 300 trigger warnings of emergency conditions (not shown).
Source: U.S. Environmental Protection Agency, Air Quality Index Report, 2017

Air Quality Index Pollutants

| Area | Percent of Days when AQI Pollutant was...[2] | | | | | |
	Carbon Monoxide	Nitrogen Dioxide	Ozone	Sulfur Dioxide	Particulate Matter 2.5	Particulate Matter 10
MSA[1]	0.0	2.7	46.0	0.5	45.2	5.5

Note: (1) Data covers the Kansas City, MO-KS Metropolitan Statistical Area—see Appendix B for areas included; (2) Based on 365 days with AQI data in 2017. The Air Quality Index (AQI) is an index for reporting daily air quality. EPA calculates the AQI for five major air pollutants regulated by the Clean Air Act: ground-level ozone, particle pollution (also known as particulate matter), carbon monoxide, sulfur dioxide, and nitrogen dioxide. The AQI runs from 0 to 500. The higher the AQI value, the greater the level of air pollution and the greater the health concern.
Source: U.S. Environmental Protection Agency, Air Quality Index Report, 2017

Maximum Air Pollutant Concentrations: Particulate Matter, Ozone, CO and Lead

	Particulate Matter 10 (ug/m³)	Particulate Matter 2.5 Wtd AM (ug/m³)	Particulate Matter 2.5 24-Hr (ug/m³)	Ozone (ppm)	Carbon Monoxide (ppm)	Lead (ug/m³)
MSA[1] Level	117	9.9	23	0.07	1	n/a
NAAQS[2]	150	15	35	0.075	9	0.15
Met NAAQS[2]	Yes	Yes	Yes	Yes	Yes	n/a

Note: (1) Data covers the Kansas City, MO-KS Metropolitan Statistical Area—see Appendix B for areas included; Data from exceptional events are included; (2) National Ambient Air Quality Standards; ppm = parts per million; ug/m³ = micrograms per cubic meter; n/a not available.
Concentrations: Particulate Matter 10 (coarse particulate)—highest second maximum 24-hour concentration; Particulate Matter 2.5 Wtd AM (fine particulate)—highest weighted annual mean concentration; Particulate Matter 2.5 24-Hour (fine particulate)—highest 98th percentile 24-hour concentration; Ozone—highest fourth daily maximum 8-hour concentration; Carbon Monoxide—highest second maximum non-overlapping 8-hour concentration; Lead—maximum running 3-month average
Source: U.S. Environmental Protection Agency, Air Quality Monitoring Information, "Air Quality Statistics by City, 2017"

Maximum Air Pollutant Concentrations: Nitrogen Dioxide and Sulfur Dioxide

	Nitrogen Dioxide AM (ppb)	Nitrogen Dioxide 1-Hr (ppb)	Sulfur Dioxide AM (ppb)	Sulfur Dioxide 1-Hr (ppb)	Sulfur Dioxide 24-Hr (ppb)
MSA[1] Level	12	47	n/a	18	n/a
NAAQS[2]	53	100	30	75	140
Met NAAQS[2]	Yes	Yes	n/a	Yes	n/a

Note: (1) Data covers the Kansas City, MO-KS Metropolitan Statistical Area—see Appendix B for areas included; Data from exceptional events are included; (2) National Ambient Air Quality Standards; ppm = parts per million; ug/m³ = micrograms per cubic meter; n/a not available.
Concentrations: Nitrogen Dioxide AM—highest arithmetic mean concentration; Nitrogen Dioxide 1-Hr—highest 98th percentile 1-hour daily maximum concentration; Sulfur Dioxide AM—highest annual mean concentration; Sulfur Dioxide 1-Hr—highest 99th percentile 1-hour daily maximum concentration; Sulfur Dioxide 24-Hr—highest second maximum 24-hour concentration
Source: U.S. Environmental Protection Agency, Air Quality Monitoring Information, "Air Quality Statistics by City, 2017"

Drinking Water

| Water System Name | Pop. Served | Primary Water Source Type | Violations[1] | |
			Health Based	Monitoring/ Reporting
Kansas City	460,000	Surface	0	0

Note: (1) Based on violation data from January 1, 2018 to December 31, 2018
Source: U.S. Environmental Protection Agency, Office of Ground Water and Drinking Water, Safe Drinking Water Information System (based on data extracted April 5, 2019)

Lincoln, Nebraska

Background

Lincoln, the capital of Nebraska and the seat of Lancaster County is located in the southeastern part of the state. It is a thriving and multifaceted city with a fascinating history and a dynamic and expanding contemporary economy and cultural life. Lincoln today is the second-largest city in Nebraska.

The site first attracted the attention of settlers in 1856 when commercial explorers found saline deposits on the banks of the Salt Creek, and from the bed of what is today known as Capitol Beach Lake. Salt, in fact, constituted the first major commercial activity in the city, with two large salt "boilers," Cox and Peckham, supplying this vital resource to farmers and townspeople in a wide stretch of the Plains region. Captain W.T. Donovan came to the area as a salt company representative, settling there permanently in 1867. He named his claim Lancaster after his home in Pennsylvania, which became the county name.

Omaha had been the capital of Nebraska, but with statehood, a drive began to move the capital south of the Platte River. The new capital, originally to be called simply Capitol City, was sited at Lancaster. State Senator J.H.N. Patrick proposed changing the name to Lincoln, largely because he thought it would discourage Democratic support.

In the 1880s—a dynamic period of Lincoln's early economic growth—William Jennings Bryan came to town as a lawyer and budding politician, and two years later was elected to the U.S. Congress. Another Lincoln luminary from this period was General John J. Pershing, who was an instructor in military science at the recently established University of Nebraska.

Designated as a "refugee-friendly" city by the U.S. Department of State in the 1970s, the city was the twelfth-largest resettlement site per capita in the United States by 2000. Refugee Vietnamese, Karen (Burmese ethnic minority), Sudanese and Yazidi (Iraqi ethnic minority) people, as well as refugees from the Middle East, have been resettled in the city. Lincoln Public Schools took in more than 3,000 students speaking 50 languages during the 2017-2018 school year.

The city's downtown is a modern entertainment, commercial, and office center, and on its west edge is the historic Haymarket District. The state capitol building, designed by Bertram Grosvenor Goodhue in 1919, is an architectural attraction of international repute, and its modernist central white stone column, visible from surrounding prairie hilltops for miles, still uniquely defines the Lincoln skyline. Lincoln is also a city of parks, with 100 parks covering more than 6,000 acres, including a children's zoo and, in cooperation with Lancaster County, a wilderness park. Recent years saw restoration and enhancement to the downtown and improved flood control measures.

The University of Nebraska is city's largest institution of higher learning and its football team attracts crowds of 78,000 to Memorial Stadium. The University of Nebraska is a major hub of cultural activity in the city, and is the site of the State Museum of Natural History. Nebraska Wesleyan University and Union College are also located in Lincoln.

The city offers rich cultural resources that draw on its increasingly cosmopolitan character, as well as on the rural traditions of the state as a whole. The Lied Center for Performing Arts, on the University of Nebraska's downtown campus, features a full range of musical and dramatic performances, and the city also hosts the Nebraska State Fair in early September. In 2010, Lincoln hosted the Special Olympics USA National Games.

Government is the largest employer in Lincoln, with health services the largest non-industrial private sector employer. The city hosts operations of many major employers, and Bryan Medical Center is one of the largest.

The joint County-City Building houses the mayor's office, the city council, Lancaster County commissioner's office, and county, district, and juvenile courts, and the judicial center is connected to the County-City Building by elevated walkways.

The climate in Lincoln is characterized by the robust and dramatic range of the Great Plains area as a whole. Most precipitation falls during April through September, and thunderstorms are predominant in the summer months. Lincoln lies in a valley that affords considerable protection against tornadoes. It still has, however, more than 25 Federal Signal warning sirens in operation throughout the city which are tested every Wednesday morning, except in the winter months.

Rankings

General Rankings

- For its "Best for Vets: Places to Live 2019" rankings, *Military Times* evaluated 599 cities (83 large, 234 medium, 282 small) and compared the locations across three broad categories: veteran and military culture/services; economic indicators; and livability factors such as health, crime, traffic, and school quality. Lincoln ranked #12 out of the top 25, in the large city category (populations of more than 250,000). Data points more specific to veterans and the military weighed more heavily than the rest. *rebootcamp.militarytimes.com, "Military Times Best Places to Live 2019," September 10, 2018*

- In their sixth annual survey, Livability.com looked at data for more than 1,000 U.S. cities to determine the rankings for Livability's "Top 100 Best Places to Live" in 2019. Lincoln ranked #9. Criteria: median home value capped at $250,000; affordable living; vibrant economy; education, demographics, health care options. transportation & infrastructure; abundant lifestyle amenities. *Livability.com, "Top 100 Best Places to Live 2019" March 2019*

Business/Finance Rankings

- The personal finance site NerdWallet analyzed 183 American metropolitan areas with populations over 250,000 and more than 15,000 businesses to rank where entrepreneurs find the most success. Criteria included area economy, annual income, housing cost, unemployment rate, and the success rate of area businesses. Lincoln ranked #25. *www.nerdwallet.com, "Best Places to Start a Business," April 27, 2015*

- Using data from the Council for Community and Economic Research's 2014 cost of living index, NerdWallet ranked the 100 most affordable cities in America. Median income was compared with cost of living to find truly affordable places. Lincoln ranked #27. *NerdWallet.com, "America's Most Affordable Places," May 18, 2015*

- NerdWallet.com identified the 10 most promising cities for job seekers of the nation's 100 largest cities. Lincoln was ranked #8. Criteria: job availability; annual salary; workforce growth; affordability. *NerdWallet.com, "Best Cities for Job Seekers in 2017," December 19, 2016*

- Lincoln was cited as one of America's top metros for new and expanded facility projects in 2018. The area ranked #5 in the mid-sized metro area category (population 200,000 to 1 million). *Site Selection, "Top Metros of 2018," March 2019*

- The Lincoln metro area appeared on the Milken Institute "2018 Best Performing Cities" list. Rank: #126 out of 200 large metro areas. Criteria: job growth; wage and salary growth; high-tech output growth. *Milken Institute, "Best-Performing Cities 2018," January 24, 2019*

- *Forbes* ranked the 200 most populous metro areas to determine the nation's "Best Places for Business and Careers." The Lincoln metro area was ranked #27. Criteria: costs (business and living); job growth (past and projected); income growth; quality of life; educational attainment (college and high school); projected economic growth; cultural and recreational opportunities; net migration patterns; number of highly ranked colleges. *Forbes, "The Best Places for Business and Careers 2018: Seattle Leads the Way," October 24, 2018*

Children/Family Rankings

- Lincoln was selected as one of the most playful cities in the U.S. by KaBOOM! The organization's Playful City USA initiative honors cities and towns across the nation that have made their communities more playable. Criteria: pledging to integrate play as a solution to challenges in their communities; making it easy for children to get active and balanced play; creating more family-friendly and innovative communities as a result. *KaBOOM! National Campaign for Play, "2017 Playful City USA Communities"*

- Lincoln was selected as one of the best cities for newlyweds by *Rent.com*. The city ranked #8 of 15. Criteria: cost of living; availability of rental inventory; annual mean wages; activities and restaurant options; percentage of married couples; percentage of millennials; safety. *Rent.com, "15 Best Cities for Newlyweds," September 11, 2015*

Dating/Romance Rankings

- Lincoln was selected as one of the most romantic cities in the U.S. by video-rental kiosk company Redbox. The city ranked #8 out of 20. Criteria: number of romance-related rentals in 2016. *Redbox, "20 Most Romantic Cities," February 6, 2017*

Education Rankings

- Lincoln was selected as one of America's most literate cities. The city ranked #24 out of the 82 largest U.S. cities. Criteria: number of booksellers; library resources; Internet resources; educational attainment; periodical publishing resources; newspaper circulation. *Central Connecticut State University, "America's Most Literate Cities, 2016," March 31, 2017*

Environmental Rankings

- Lincoln was highlighted as one of the cleanest metro areas for ozone air pollution in the U.S. during 2014 through 2016. The list represents cities with no monitored ozone air pollution in unhealthful ranges. *American Lung Association, State of the Air 2018*

Food/Drink Rankings

- *Men's Health* ranked 100 major U.S. cities in terms of alcohol intoxication. Lincoln ranked #52 (#1 = most sober).Criteria: binge drinking; alcohol-related traffic accidents, arrests, and fatalities. *Men's Health, "America's Drunkest Cities," March 9, 2015*

Health/Fitness Rankings

- For each of the 100 largest cities in the United States, the American College of Sports Medicine's American Fitness Index evaluated infrastructure, community assets, and policies that encourage healthy and fit lifestyles, including preventive health behaviors, levels of chronic disease conditions, health care access, and community resources and policies that support physical activity. Lincoln ranked #17 for "community fitness." *www.americanfitnessindex.org, "ACSM American Fitness Index Health and Community Fitness Status of the 100 Largest U.S. Cities," May 2018*

- *Men's Health* ranked 100 major U.S. cities in terms of the best cities for men. Lincoln ranked #11. Criteria: health; fitness; quality of life. *Men's Health, "The Best & Worst Cities for Men Who Want to Be Fit and Happy," January 1, 2016*

- The Lincoln metro area ranked #58 out of 189 in The Gallup-Healthways Well-Being Index. Criteria: purpose; social well being; financial health; community and physical health. Results are based on telephone interviews with adults, aged 18 and older, living in metropolitan areas in the 50 U.S. states and the District of Columbia. *Gallup-Healthways, "State of American Well-Being, 2017 Community Well-Being Rankings" March 2018*

Real Estate Rankings

- *WalletHub* compared the most populated U.S. cities, as well as at least two of the most populated cities in each state, for a total of 179, to determine which had the best markets for real estate agents. Lincoln ranked #29 where demand was high and pay was the best. Criteria: sales per agent; annual median wage for real-estate agents; monthly average starting salary for real estate agents; real estate job density and competition; unemployment rate; housing-market health index; and other relevant metrics. *www.WalletHub.com, "2018's Best Places to Be a Real Estate Agent,"April 25, 2018*

Safety Rankings

- Allstate ranked the 200 largest cities in America in terms of driver safety. Lincoln ranked #24. Criteria: internal property damage claims over a two-year period from January 2015 to December 2016. The report helps increase the importance of safety awareness behind the wheel. *Allstate, "Allstate America's Best Drivers Report, 2018" August 28, 2018*

- The National Insurance Crime Bureau ranked 382 metro areas in the U.S. in terms of per capita rates of vehicle theft. The Lincoln metro area ranked #281 (#1 = highest rate). Criteria: number of vehicle theft offenses per 100,000 inhabitants in 2017. *National Insurance Crime Bureau, "Hot Spots 2017," July 12, 2018*

Seniors/Retirement Rankings

- From its Best Cities for Successful Aging indexes, the Milken Institute generated rankings for metropolitan areas, weighing data in nine categories—health care, wellness, living arrangements, transportation and convenience, financial characteristics, education, employment, community engagement, and overall livability. The Lincoln metro area was ranked #35 overall in the small metro area category. *Milken Institute, "Best Cities for Successful Aging, 2017" March 14, 2017*

- Lincoln made the 2018 *Forbes* list of "25 Best Places to Retire." Criteria, focused on a high-quality retirement living an affordable price, include: housing/living costs compared to the national average and state taxes; weather and air quality; crime rates; vibrant economy and low unemployment; doctor availability; bikability; walkability; healthy living and volunteering. *Forbes.com, "The Best Places to Retire in 2018," April 23, 2018*

Sports/Recreation Rankings

- Lincoln was chosen as one of America's best cities for bicycling. The city ranked #35 out of 50. Criteria: cycling infrastructure that is safe and friendly for all ages; energy and bike culture. The editors only considered cities with populations of 100,000 or more. *Bicycling, "The 50 Best Bike Cities in America," October 10, 2018*

Women/Minorities Rankings

- Movoto chose the best places for professional women among the largest 100 American cities. Lincoln was among the top ten, at #4, based on commute time, recent job growth, unemployment rank, professional women's groups per capita, and average earnings adjusted for the cost of living. *www.movoto.com, "These Are America's Best Cities for Professional Women," March 5, 2014*

- Personal finance website *WalletHub* compared more than 180 U.S. cities—including the 150 most populated U.S. cities, plus at least two of the most populated cities in each state—across two key dimensions, "Hispanic Business-Friendliness" and "Hispanic Purchasing Power", to arrive at the most favorable conditions for Hispanic entrepreneurs. Lincoln was ranked #78 out of 182. Criteria includes: share of Hispanic-Owned Businesses; Hispanic entrepreneurship rate to median annual income of Hispanics; Small Business-Friendliness score; cost of living; and number of Hispanics with at least a bachelor's degree. *WalletHub.com, "2018's Best Cities for Hispanic Entrepreneurs," April 26, 2018*

Miscellaneous Rankings

- *WalletHub* compared the 150 most populated U.S. cities to determine their operating efficiency. A "Quality of Services" score was constructed for each city and then divided by the total budget per capita to reveal which were managed the best. Lincoln ranked #23. Criteria: financial stability; economy; education; safety; health; infrastructure and pollution. *www.WalletHub.com, "2018's Best- & Worst-Run Cities in America," July 9, 2018*

Business Environment

CITY FINANCES

City Government Finances

Component	2016 ($000)	2016 ($ per capita)
Total Revenues	708,810	2,556
Total Expenditures	667,600	2,407
Debt Outstanding	1,348,770	4,863
Cash and Securities[1]	619,120	2,232

Note: (1) Cash and security holdings of a government at the close of its fiscal year, including those of its dependent agencies, utilities, and liquor stores.
Source: U.S. Census Bureau, State & Local Government Finances 2016

City Government Revenue by Source

Source	2016 ($000)	2016 ($ per capita)	2016 (%)
General Revenue			
From Federal Government	45,997	166	6.5
From State Government	21,611	78	3.0
From Local Governments	8,501	31	1.2
Taxes			
Property	66,657	240	9.4
Sales and Gross Receipts	72,478	261	10.2
Personal Income	0	0	0.0
Corporate Income	0	0	0.0
Motor Vehicle License	5,049	18	0.7
Other Taxes	54,528	197	7.7
Current Charges	64,498	233	9.1
Liquor Store	0	0	0.0
Utility	344,071	1,241	48.5
Employee Retirement	-3,243	-12	-0.5

Source: U.S. Census Bureau, State & Local Government Finances 2016

City Government Expenditures by Function

Function	2016 ($000)	2016 ($ per capita)	2016 (%)
General Direct Expenditures			
Air Transportation	0	0	0.0
Corrections	0	0	0.0
Education	0	0	0.0
Employment Security Administration	0	0	0.0
Financial Administration	5,024	18	0.8
Fire Protection	24,886	89	3.7
General Public Buildings	1,004	3	0.2
Governmental Administration, Other	6,532	23	1.0
Health	23,039	83	3.5
Highways	58,094	209	8.7
Hospitals	0	0	0.0
Housing and Community Development	5,086	18	0.8
Interest on General Debt	5,961	21	0.9
Judicial and Legal	0	0	0.0
Libraries	5,857	21	0.9
Parking	5,974	21	0.9
Parks and Recreation	17,572	63	2.6
Police Protection	38,924	140	5.8
Public Welfare	8,109	29	1.2
Sewerage	23,625	85	3.5
Solid Waste Management	13,985	50	2.1
Veterans' Services	0	0	0.0
Liquor Store	0	0	0.0
Utility	335,036	1,208	50.2
Employee Retirement	11,709	42	1.8

Source: U.S. Census Bureau, State & Local Government Finances 2016

DEMOGRAPHICS

Population Growth

Area	1990 Census	2000 Census	2010 Census	2017* Estimate	Population Growth (%)	
					1990-2017	2010-2017
City	193,629	225,581	258,379	277,315	43.2	7.3
MSA[1]	229,091	266,787	302,157	323,402	41.2	7.0
U.S.	248,709,873	281,421,906	308,745,538	321,004,407	29.1	4.0

Note: (1) Figures cover the Lincoln, NE Metropolitan Statistical Area—see Appendix B for areas included; (*) 2013-2017 5-year estimated population
Source: U.S. Census Bureau, 1990 Census, Census 2000, Census 2010, 2013-2017 American Community Survey 5-Year Estimates

Household Size

Area	Persons in Household (%)							Average Household Size
	One	Two	Three	Four	Five	Six	Seven or More	
City	31.0	35.3	14.4	11.2	5.3	1.8	1.0	2.40
MSA[1]	29.5	36.0	14.3	11.9	5.4	1.9	1.0	2.40
U.S.	27.7	33.8	15.7	13.0	6.0	2.3	1.4	2.60

Note: (1) Figures cover the Lincoln, NE Metropolitan Statistical Area—see Appendix B for areas included
Source: U.S. Census Bureau, 2013-2017 American Community Survey 5-Year Estimates

Race

Area	White Alone[2] (%)	Black Alone[2] (%)	Asian Alone[2] (%)	AIAN[3] Alone[2] (%)	NHOPI[4] Alone[2] (%)	Other Race Alone[2] (%)	Two or More Races (%)
City	85.3	4.4	4.6	0.6	0.1	1.7	3.3
MSA[1]	87.0	3.9	4.0	0.5	0.1	1.5	3.0
U.S.	73.0	12.7	5.4	0.8	0.2	4.8	3.1

Note: (1) Figures cover the Lincoln, NE Metropolitan Statistical Area—see Appendix B for areas included; (2) Alone is defined as not being in combination with one or more other races; (3) American Indian and Alaska Native; (4) Native Hawaiian and Other Pacific Islander
Source: U.S. Census Bureau, 2013-2017 American Community Survey 5-Year Estimates

Hispanic or Latino Origin

Area	Total (%)	Mexican (%)	Puerto Rican (%)	Cuban (%)	Other (%)
City	7.3	5.4	0.2	0.2	1.5
MSA[1]	6.5	4.7	0.2	0.2	1.4
U.S.	17.6	11.1	1.7	0.7	4.1

Note: Persons of Hispanic or Latino origin can be of any race; (1) Figures cover the Lincoln, NE Metropolitan Statistical Area—see Appendix B for areas included
Source: U.S. Census Bureau, 2013-2017 American Community Survey 5-Year Estimates

Segregation

Type	Segregation Indices[1]				Percent Change		
	1990	2000	2010	2010 Rank[2]	1990-2000	1990-2010	2000-2010
Black/White	n/a	n/a	n/a	n/a	n/a	n/a	n/a
Asian/White	n/a	n/a	n/a	n/a	n/a	n/a	n/a
Hispanic/White	n/a	n/a	n/a	n/a	n/a	n/a	n/a

Note: All figures cover the Metropolitan Statistical Area—see Appendix B for areas included; Figures are based on an analysis of 1990, 2000, and 2010 Census Decennial Census tract data by William H. Frey, Brookings Institution and the University of Michigan Social Science Data Analysis Network. In this analysis all racial groups (whites, blacks, and asians) are non-Hispanic members of those races. Hispanics are shown as a separate category; (1) Segregation Indices are Dissimilarity Indices that measure the degree to which the minority group is distributed differently than whites across census tracts. They range from 0 (complete integration) to 100 (complete segregation) where the value indicates the percentage of the minority group that needs to move to be distributed exactly like whites; (2) Ranges from 1 (most segregated) to 102 (least segregated); n/a not available.
Source: www.CensusScope.org

Ancestry

Area	German	Irish	English	American	Italian	Polish	French[2]	Scottish	Dutch
City	36.3	12.1	8.6	4.0	2.2	2.6	2.2	1.7	2.3
MSA[1]	38.2	12.0	8.5	4.1	2.1	2.6	2.2	1.6	2.5
U.S.	14.1	10.1	7.5	6.6	5.3	2.9	2.5	1.7	1.3

Note: Figures are the percentage of the total population reporting a particular ancestry. The nine most commonly reported ancestries in the U.S. are shown. Figures include multiple ancestries (e.g. if a person reported being Irish and Italian, they were included in both columns); (1) Figures cover the Lincoln, NE Metropolitan Statistical Area—see Appendix B for areas included; (2) Excludes Basque
Source: U.S. Census Bureau, 2013-2017 American Community Survey 5-Year Estimates

Foreign-Born Population

Area	Percent of Population Born in								
	Any Foreign Country	Asia	Mexico	Europe	Carribean	Central America[2]	South America	Africa	Canada
City	8.4	4.5	1.4	1.0	0.2	0.3	0.3	0.6	0.2
MSA[1]	7.5	3.9	1.2	0.9	0.2	0.3	0.2	0.6	0.2
U.S.	13.4	4.1	3.6	1.5	1.3	1.0	0.9	0.6	0.3

Note: (1) Figures cover the Lincoln, NE Metropolitan Statistical Area—see Appendix B for areas included; (2) Excludes Mexico.
Source: U.S. Census Bureau, 2013-2017 American Community Survey 5-Year Estimates

Marital Status

Area	Never Married	Now Married[2]	Separated	Widowed	Divorced
City	38.4	45.6	1.1	4.4	10.5
MSA[1]	36.4	48.2	1.1	4.4	10.0
U.S.	33.1	48.2	2.0	5.8	10.9

Note: Figures are percentages and cover the population 15 years of age and older; (1) Figures cover the Lincoln, NE Metropolitan Statistical Area—see Appendix B for areas included; (2) Excludes separated
Source: U.S. Census Bureau, 2013-2017 American Community Survey 5-Year Estimates

Disability by Age

Area	All Ages	Under 18 Years Old	18 to 64 Years Old	65 Years and Over
City	10.8	4.3	8.5	34.4
MSA[1]	10.5	4.1	8.3	33.8
U.S.	12.6	4.2	10.3	35.5

Note: Figures show percent of the civilian noninstitutionalized population that reported having a disability. Disability status is determined from six types of difficulty: vision, hearing, cognitive, ambulatory, self-care, and independent living. For children under 5 years old, hearing and vision difficulty are used to determine disability status. For children between the ages of 5 and 14, disability status is determined from hearing, vision, cognitive, ambulatory, and self-care difficulties. For people aged 15 years and older, they are considered to have a disability if they have difficulty with any one of the six difficulty types; Note: (1) Figures cover the Lincoln, NE Metropolitan Statistical Area—see Appendix B for areas included
Source: U.S. Census Bureau, 2013-2017 American Community Survey 5-Year Estimates

Age

Area	Percent of Population									Median Age
	Under Age 5	Age 5–19	Age 20–34	Age 35–44	Age 45–54	Age 55–64	Age 65–74	Age 75–84	Age 85+	
City	6.7	19.9	26.9	12.2	10.7	11.1	7.2	3.6	1.7	32.4
MSA[1]	6.6	20.3	25.3	12.1	11.3	11.5	7.4	3.7	1.8	33.3
U.S.	6.2	19.5	20.7	12.7	13.4	12.7	8.6	4.4	1.9	37.8

Note: (1) Figures cover the Lincoln, NE Metropolitan Statistical Area—see Appendix B for areas included
Source: U.S. Census Bureau, 2013-2017 American Community Survey 5-Year Estimates

Gender

Area	Males	Females	Males per 100 Females
City	139,057	138,258	100.6
MSA[1]	162,370	161,032	100.8
U.S.	158,018,753	162,985,654	97.0

Note: (1) Figures cover the Lincoln, NE Metropolitan Statistical Area—see Appendix B for areas included
Source: U.S. Census Bureau, 2013-2017 American Community Survey 5-Year Estimates

Religious Groups by Family

Area	Catholic	Baptist	Non-Den.	Methodist[2]	Lutheran	LDS[3]	Pentecostal	Presbyterian[4]	Muslim[5]	Judaism
MSA[1]	14.8	2.4	1.9	7.2	11.3	1.2	1.4	3.9	0.2	0.2
U.S.	19.1	9.3	4.0	4.0	2.3	2.0	1.9	1.6	0.8	0.7

Note: Figures are the number of adherents as a percentage of the total population; (1) Figures cover the Lincoln, NE Metropolitan Statistical Area—see Appendix B for areas included; (2) Methodist/Pietist; (3) Latter Day Saints; (4) Reformed; (5) Figures are estimates
Source: Association of Statisticians of American Religious Bodies, 2010 U.S. Religion Census: Religious Congregations & Membership Study

Religious Groups by Tradition

Area	Catholic	Evangelical Protestant	Mainline Protestant	Other Tradition	Black Protestant	Orthodox
MSA[1]	14.8	14.8	16.2	2.0	0.1	0.1
U.S.	19.1	16.2	7.3	4.3	1.6	0.3

Note: Figures are the number of adherents as a percentage of the total population; (1) Figures cover the Lincoln, NE Metropolitan Statistical Area—see Appendix B for areas included
Source: Association of Statisticians of American Religious Bodies, 2010 U.S. Religion Census: Religious Congregations & Membership Study

ECONOMY

Gross Metropolitan Product

Area	2016	2017	2018	2019	Rank[2]
MSA[1]	19.8	20.3	20.9	22.0	125

Note: Figures are in billions of dollars; (1) Figures cover the Lincoln, NE Metropolitan Statistical Area—see Appendix B for areas included; (2) Rank is based on 2017 data and ranges from 1 to 381
Source: U.S. Conference of Mayors, U.S. Metro Economies: Economic Growth & Full Employment, June 2018

Economic Growth

Area	2017-2018 (%)	2019-2020 (%)	2021-2022 (%)
MSA[1]	0.9	2.1	1.9

Note: Figures are real gross metropolitan product (GMP) growth rates and represent average annual percent change; (1) Figures cover the Lincoln, NE Metropolitan Statistical Area—see Appendix B for areas included
Source: U.S. Conference of Mayors, U.S. Metro Economies: Economic Growth & Full Employment, June 2018

Metropolitan Area Exports

Area	2012	2013	2014	2015	2016	2017	Rank[2]
MSA[1]	904.7	818.4	1,173.9	1,189.3	796.9	860.9	167

Note: Figures are in millions of dollars; (1) Figures cover the Lincoln, NE Metropolitan Statistical Area—see Appendix B for areas included; (2) Rank is based on 2017 data and ranges from 1 to 387
Source: U.S. Department of Commerce, International Trade Administration, Office of Trade and Economic Analysis, Industry and Analysis, Exports by Metropolitan Area, extracted March 25, 2019

Building Permits

Area	Single-Family			Multi-Family			Total		
	2016	2017	Pct. Chg.	2016	2017	Pct. Chg.	2016	2017	Pct. Chg.
City	928	994	7.1	1,238	1,231	-0.6	2,166	2,225	2.7
MSA[1]	1,143	1,271	11.2	1,241	1,237	-0.3	2,384	2,508	5.2
U.S.	750,800	820,000	9.2	455,800	462,000	1.4	1,206,600	1,282,000	6.2

Note: (1) Figures cover the Lincoln, NE Metropolitan Statistical Area—see Appendix B for areas included; Figures represent new, privately-owned housing units authorized (unadjusted data); All permit data are based on estimates with imputation
Source: U.S. Census Bureau, Manufacturing, Mining, and Construction Statistics, Building Permits, 2016, 2017

Bankruptcy Filings

Area	Business Filings			Nonbusiness Filings		
	2017	2018	% Chg.	2017	2018	% Chg.
Lancaster County	17	9	-47.1	692	665	-3.9
U.S.	23,157	22,232	-4.0	765,863	751,186	-1.9

Note: Business filings include Chapter 7, Chapter 11, Chapter 12, and Chapter 13; Nonbusiness filings include Chapter 7, Chapter 11, and Chapter 13
Source: Administrative Office of the U.S. Courts, Business and Nonbusiness Bankruptcy, County Cases Commenced by Chapter of the Bankruptcy Code, During the 12-Month Period Ending December 31, 2017 and Business and Nonbusiness Bankruptcy, County Cases Commenced by Chapter of the Bankruptcy Code, During the 12-Month Period Ending December 31, 2018

Housing Vacancy Rates

Area	Gross Vacancy Rate[2] (%)			Year-Round Vacancy Rate[3] (%)			Rental Vacancy Rate[4] (%)			Homeowner Vacancy Rate[5] (%)		
	2016	2017	2018	2016	2017	2018	2016	2017	2018	2016	2017	2018
MSA[1]	n/a	n/a	n/a	n/a	n/a	n/a	n/a	n/a	n/a	n/a	n/a	n/a
U.S.	12.8	12.7	12.3	9.9	9.9	9.7	6.9	7.2	6.9	1.7	1.6	1.5

Note: (1) Figures cover the Lincoln, NE Metropolitan Statistical Area—see Appendix B for areas included; (2) The percentage of the total housing inventory that is vacant; (3) The percentage of the housing inventory (excluding seasonal units) that is year-round vacant; (4) The percentage of rental inventory that is vacant for rent; (5) The percentage of homeowner inventory that is vacant for sale; n/a not available
Source: U.S. Census Bureau, Housing Vacancies and Homeownership Annual Statistics: 2016, 2017, 2018

INCOME

Income

Area	Per Capita ($)	Median Household ($)	Average Household ($)
City	28,839	53,089	70,721
MSA[1]	29,874	56,132	74,327
U.S.	31,177	57,652	81,283

Note: (1) Figures cover the Lincoln, NE Metropolitan Statistical Area—see Appendix B for areas included
Source: U.S. Census Bureau, 2013-2017 American Community Survey 5-Year Estimates

Household Income Distribution

Area	Percent of Households Earning							
	Under $15,000	$15,000 -$24,999	$25,000 -$34,999	$35,000 -$49,999	$50,000 -$74,999	$75,000 -$99,999	$100,000 -$149,999	$150,000 and up
City	11.1	10.3	11.1	14.4	19.3	12.2	14.1	7.6
MSA[1]	10.3	9.6	10.5	13.9	19.1	12.8	15.1	8.6
U.S.	11.6	9.8	9.5	13.0	17.7	12.3	14.1	12.1

Note: (1) Figures cover the Lincoln, NE Metropolitan Statistical Area—see Appendix B for areas included
Source: U.S. Census Bureau, 2013-2017 American Community Survey 5-Year Estimates

Poverty Rate

Area	All Ages	Under 18 Years Old	18 to 64 Years Old	65 Years and Over
City	15.1	17.0	16.3	5.9
MSA[1]	13.7	15.3	14.8	5.6
U.S.	14.6	20.3	13.7	9.3

Note: Figures are percentage of people whose income during the past 12 months was below the poverty level; (1) Figures cover the Lincoln, NE Metropolitan Statistical Area—see Appendix B for areas included
Source: U.S. Census Bureau, 2013-2017 American Community Survey 5-Year Estimates

EMPLOYMENT

Labor Force and Employment

Area	Civilian Labor Force			Workers Employed		
	Dec. 2017	Dec. 2018	% Chg.	Dec. 2017	Dec. 2018	% Chg.
City	152,563	155,749	2.1	148,759	152,191	2.3
MSA[1]	177,836	181,619	2.1	173,446	177,455	2.3
U.S.	159,880,000	162,510,000	1.6	153,602,000	156,481,000	1.9

Note: Data is not seasonally adjusted and covers workers 16 years of age and older; (1) Figures cover the Lincoln, NE Metropolitan Statistical Area—see Appendix B for areas included
Source: Bureau of Labor Statistics, Local Area Unemployment Statistics

Unemployment Rate

Area	2018											
	Jan.	Feb.	Mar.	Apr.	May	Jun.	Jul.	Aug.	Sep.	Oct.	Nov.	Dec.
City	2.7	2.6	2.6	2.6	2.6	2.9	2.8	2.6	2.4	2.5	2.2	2.3
MSA[1]	2.7	2.6	2.6	2.6	2.6	2.9	2.8	2.6	2.4	2.5	2.2	2.3
U.S.	4.5	4.4	4.1	3.7	3.6	4.2	4.1	3.9	3.6	3.5	3.5	3.7

Note: Data is not seasonally adjusted and covers workers 16 years of age and older; (1) Figures cover the Lincoln, NE Metropolitan Statistical Area—see Appendix B for areas included
Source: Bureau of Labor Statistics, Local Area Unemployment Statistics

Average Wages

Occupation	$/Hr.	Occupation	$/Hr.
Accountants and Auditors	30.10	Maids and Housekeeping Cleaners	11.50
Automotive Mechanics	21.50	Maintenance and Repair Workers	19.00
Bookkeepers	17.70	Marketing Managers	46.50
Carpenters	19.30	Nuclear Medicine Technologists	n/a
Cashiers	10.90	Nurses, Licensed Practical	20.20
Clerks, General Office	13.80	Nurses, Registered	31.00
Clerks, Receptionists/Information	13.30	Nursing Assistants	13.90
Clerks, Shipping/Receiving	17.00	Packers and Packagers, Hand	11.90
Computer Programmers	33.10	Physical Therapists	38.40
Computer Systems Analysts	36.20	Postal Service Mail Carriers	24.70
Computer User Support Specialists	22.20	Real Estate Brokers	26.30
Cooks, Restaurant	13.60	Retail Salespersons	13.00
Dentists	70.30	Sales Reps., Exc. Tech./Scientific	28.90
Electrical Engineers	45.40	Sales Reps., Tech./Scientific	41.90
Electricians	25.20	Secretaries, Exc. Legal/Med./Exec.	17.10
Financial Managers	55.90	Security Guards	16.10
First-Line Supervisors/Managers, Sales	19.80	Surgeons	n/a
Food Preparation Workers	11.70	Teacher Assistants*	13.10
General and Operations Managers	46.50	Teachers, Elementary School*	26.60
Hairdressers/Cosmetologists	11.70	Teachers, Secondary School*	26.70
Internists, General	n/a	Telemarketers	11.70
Janitors and Cleaners	12.80	Truck Drivers, Heavy/Tractor-Trailer	n/a
Landscaping/Groundskeeping Workers	14.10	Truck Drivers, Light/Delivery Svcs.	18.30
Lawyers	48.00	Waiters and Waitresses	11.80

Note: Wage data covers the Lincoln, NE Metropolitan Statistical Area—see Appendix B for areas included; (*) Hourly wages for elementary/secondary school teachers and teacher assistants were calculated by the editors from annual wage data based on a 40 hour work week; n/a not available.
Source: Bureau of Labor Statistics, Metro Area Occupational Employment & Wage Estimates, May 2018

Employment by Occupation

Occupation Classification	City (%)	MSA[1] (%)	U.S. (%)
Management, Business, Science, and Arts	39.6	39.8	37.4
Natural Resources, Construction, and Maintenance	7.3	7.9	8.9
Production, Transportation, and Material Moving	11.5	11.5	12.2
Sales and Office	24.1	23.7	23.5
Service	17.5	17.0	18.0

Note: Figures cover employed civilians 16 years of age and older; (1) Figures cover the Lincoln, NE Metropolitan Statistical Area—see Appendix B for areas included
Source: U.S. Census Bureau, 2013-2017 American Community Survey 5-Year Estimates

Employment by Industry

| Sector | MSA[1] | | U.S. |
	Number of Employees	Percent of Total	Percent of Total
Construction, Mining, and Logging	9,100	4.8	5.3
Education and Health Services	29,700	15.5	15.9
Financial Activities	13,200	6.9	5.7
Government	42,100	22.0	15.1
Information	3,200	1.7	1.9
Leisure and Hospitality	18,900	9.9	10.7
Manufacturing	13,500	7.1	8.5
Other Services	7,200	3.8	3.9
Professional and Business Services	19,700	10.3	14.1
Retail Trade	19,400	10.1	10.8
Transportation, Warehousing, and Utilities	11,200	5.9	4.2
Wholesale Trade	4,100	2.1	3.9

Note: Figures are non-farm employment as of December 2018. Figures are not seasonally adjusted and include workers 16 years of age and older; (1) Figures cover the Lincoln, NE Metropolitan Statistical Area—see Appendix B for areas included
Source: Bureau of Labor Statistics, Current Employment Statistics, Employment, Hours, and Earnings

Occupations with Greatest Projected Employment Growth: 2018 – 2020

Occupation[1]	2018 Employment	2020 Projected Employment	Numeric Employment Change	Percent Employment Change
Combined Food Preparation and Serving Workers, Including Fast Food	23,980	24,800	820	3.4
Registered Nurses	25,360	26,160	800	3.2
Heavy and Tractor-Trailer Truck Drivers	29,280	29,930	650	2.2
Carpenters	12,430	12,880	450	3.6
Janitors and Cleaners, Except Maids and Housekeeping Cleaners	16,140	16,520	380	2.4
Nursing Assistants	14,510	14,870	360	2.5
General and Operations Managers	15,510	15,830	320	2.1
Waiters and Waitresses	16,030	16,350	320	2.0
Accountants and Auditors	10,320	10,600	280	2.7
Software Developers, Applications	5,120	5,400	280	5.5

Note: Projections cover Nebraska; (1) Sorted by numeric employment change
Source: www.projectionscentral.com, State Occupational Projections, 2018–2020 Short-Term Projections

Fastest Growing Occupations: 2018 – 2020

Occupation[1]	2018 Employment	2020 Projected Employment	Numeric Employment Change	Percent Employment Change
Information and Record Clerks, All Other	760	820	60	7.9
Computer Occupations, All Other	1,510	1,610	100	6.6
Home Health Aides	1,990	2,120	130	6.5
Compliance Officers	3,240	3,440	200	6.2
Physician Assistants	1,070	1,130	60	5.6
Management Analysts	3,070	3,240	170	5.5
Software Developers, Applications	5,120	5,400	280	5.5
Medical Assistants	3,280	3,460	180	5.5
Physical Therapists	1,960	2,060	100	5.1
Heating, Air Conditioning, and Refrigeration Mechanics and Installers	2,360	2,480	120	5.1

Note: Projections cover Nebraska; (1) Sorted by percent employment change and excludes occupations with numeric employment change less than 50
Source: www.projectionscentral.com, State Occupational Projections, 2018–2020 Short-Term Projections

TAXES

State Corporate Income Tax Rates

State	Tax Rate (%)	Income Brackets ($)	Num. of Brackets	Financial Institution Tax Rate (%)[a]	Federal Income Tax Ded.
Nebraska	5.58 - 7.81	100,000	2	(a)	No

Note: Tax rates as of January 1, 2019; (a) Rates listed are the corporate income tax rate applied to financial institutions or excise taxes based on income. Some states have other taxes based upon the value of deposits or shares.
Source: Federation of Tax Administrators, Range of State Corporate Income Tax Rates, January 1, 2019

State Individual Income Tax Rates

State	Tax Rate (%)	Income Brackets ($)	Personal Exemptions ($)			Standard Ded. ($)	
			Single	Married	Depend.	Single	Married
Nebraska (a)	2.46 - 6.84	3,230 - 31,160 (b)	137	274 (c)	137 (c)	6,900	13,800

Note: Tax rates as of January 1, 2019; Local- and county-level taxes are not included; n/a not applicable; Federal income tax is not deductible on state income tax returns; (a) 19 states have statutory provision for automatically adjusting to the rate of inflation the dollar values of the income tax brackets, standard deductions, and/or personal exemptions. Michigan indexes the personal exemption only. Oregon does not index the income brackets for $125,000 and over; (b) For joint returns, taxes are twice the tax on half the couple's income; (c) The personal exemption takes the form of a tax credit instead of a deduction
Source: Federation of Tax Administrators, State Individual Income Tax Rates, January 1, 2019

Various State Sales and Excise Tax Rates

State	State Sales Tax (%)	Gasoline[1] (¢/gal.)	Cigarette[2] ($/pack)	Spirits[3] ($/gal.)	Wine[4] ($/gal.)	Beer[5] ($/gal.)	Recreational Marijuana (%)
Nebraska	5.5	30.5	0.64	3.75	0.95 (l)	0.31	Not legal

Note: All tax rates as of January 1, 2019; (1) The American Petroleum Institute has developed a methodology for determining the average tax rate on a gallon of fuel. Rates may include any of the following: excise taxes, environmental fees, storage tank fees, other fees or taxes, general sales tax, and local taxes. In states where gasoline is subject to the general sales tax, or where the fuel tax is based on the average sale price, the average rate determined by API is sensitive to changes in the price of gasoline. States that fully or partially apply general sales taxes to gasoline: CA, CO, GA, IL, IN, MI, NY; (2) The federal excise tax of $1.0066 per pack and local taxes are not included; (3) Rates are those applicable to off-premise sales of 40% alcohol by volume (a.b.v.) distilled spirits in 750ml containers. Local excise taxes are excluded; (4) Rates are those applicable to off-premise sales of 11% a.b.v. non-carbonated wine in 750ml containers; (5) Rates are those applicable to off-premise sales of 4.7% a.b.v. beer in 12 ounce containers; (l) Different rates also applicable to alcohol content, place of production, size of container, place purchased (on- or off-premise or on board airlines) or type of wine (carbonated, vermouth, etc.).
Source: Tax Foundation, 2019 Facts & Figures: How Does Your State Compare?

State Business Tax Climate Index Rankings

State	Overall Rank	Corporate Tax Rank	Individual Income Tax Rank	Sales Tax Rank	Unemployment Insurance Tax Rank	Property Tax Rank
Nebraska	24	28	26	9	9	40

Note: The index is a measure of how each state's tax laws affect economic performance. The lower the rank, the more favorable a state's tax system is for business. States without a given tax are given a ranking of 1. The scores/rankings for the District of Columbia do not affect other states. The 2019 index represents the tax climate as of July 1, 2018.
Source: Tax Foundation, State Business Tax Climate Index 2019

COMMERCIAL UTILITIES

Typical Monthly Electric Bills

Area	General Service, Light ($/month)		General Service, Heavy ($/month)	
	40 kW demand 5,000 kWh	100 kW demand 10,000 kWh	500 kW demand 100,000 kWh	1,500 kW demand 500,000 kWh
City	n/a	n/a	n/a	n/a

Note: Figures are based on rates in effect January 1, 2018
Source: Memphis Light, Gas and Water, 2018 Utility Bill Comparisons for Selected U.S. Cities

TRANSPORTATION

Means of Transportation to Work

Area	Car/Truck/Van		Public Transportation			Bicycle	Walked	Other Means	Worked at Home
	Drove Alone	Car-pooled	Bus	Subway	Railroad				
City	81.5	9.0	1.3	0.0	0.0	1.4	3.1	0.7	3.0
MSA[1]	81.8	8.8	1.1	0.0	0.0	1.2	3.0	0.7	3.4
U.S.	76.4	9.2	2.5	1.9	0.6	0.6	2.7	1.3	4.7

Note: Figures are percentages and cover workers 16 years of age and older; (1) Figures cover the Lincoln, NE Metropolitan Statistical Area—see Appendix B for areas included
Source: U.S. Census Bureau, 2013-2017 American Community Survey 5-Year Estimates

Travel Time to Work

Area	Less Than 10 Minutes	10 to 19 Minutes	20 to 29 Minutes	30 to 44 Minutes	45 to 59 Minutes	60 to 89 Minutes	90 Minutes or More
City	16.5	45.5	22.7	9.7	2.7	2.1	0.8
MSA[1]	16.7	42.5	23.4	11.6	3.0	2.0	0.9
U.S.	12.7	28.9	20.9	20.5	8.1	6.2	2.7

Note: Note: Figures are percentages and include workers 16 years old and over; (1) Figures cover the Lincoln, NE Metropolitan Statistical Area—see Appendix B for areas included
Source: U.S. Census Bureau, 2013-2017 American Community Survey 5-Year Estimates

Freeway Travel Time Index

Area	1985	1990	1995	2000	2005	2010	2014
Urban Area Rank[1,2]	n/a	n/a	n/a	n/a	n/a	n/a	n/a
Urban Area Index[1]	n/a	n/a	n/a	n/a	n/a	n/a	n/a
Average Index[3]	1.09	1.11	1.14	1.17	1.20	1.19	1.20

Note: Freeway Travel Time Index—the ratio of travel time in the peak period to the travel time at free-flow conditions. For example, a value of 1.30 indicates a 20-minute free-flow trip takes 26 minutes in the peak (20 minutes x 1.30 = 26 minutes); (1) Data for the Lincoln, NE urban area was not available; (2) Rank is based on 101 urban areas (#1 = highest travel time index); (3) Average of 101 urban areas
Source: Texas Transportation Institute, 2015 Urban Mobility Scorecard, August 2015

Freeway Commuter Stress Index

Area	1985	1990	1995	2000	2005	2010	2014
Urban Area Rank[1,2]	n/a	n/a	n/a	n/a	n/a	n/a	n/a
Urban Area Index[1]	n/a	n/a	n/a	n/a	n/a	n/a	n/a
Average Index[3]	1.13	1.16	1.19	1.22	1.25	1.24	1.25

Note: The Freeway Commuter Stress Index is the same as the Freeway Travel Time Index (see table above) except that it includes only the travel in the peak directions during the peak periods; the TTI includes travel in all directions during the peak period. Thus, the CSI is more indicative of the work trip experienced by each commuter on a daily basis; (1) Data for the Lincoln, NE urban area was not available; (2) Rank is based on 101 urban areas (#1 = highest travel time index); (3) Average of 101 urban areas
Source: Texas Transportation Institute, 2015 Urban Mobility Scorecard, August 2015

Public Transportation

Agency Name / Mode of Transportation	Vehicles Operated in Maximum Service[1]	Annual Unlinked Passenger Trips[2] (in thous.)	Annual Passenger Miles[3] (in thous.)
StarTran			
Bus (directly operated)	56	2,313.7	6,881.0
Demand Response (directly operated)	9	41.3	195.3
Demand Response Taxi (purchased transportation)	13	23.6	136.6

Note: (1) The number of revenue vehicles operated by the given mode and type of service to meet the annual maximum service requirement. This is the revenue vehicle count during the peak season of the year; on the week and day that maximum service is provided. Vehicles operated in maximum service (VOMS) exclude atypical days and one-time special events; (2) The number of passengers who boarded public transportation vehicles. Passengers are counted each time they board a vehicle no matter how many vehicles they use to travel from their origin to their destination. (3) The sum of the distances ridden by all passengers during the entire fiscal year.
Source: Federal Transit Administration, National Transit Database, 2017

Air Transportation

Airport Name and Code / Type of Service	Passenger Airlines[1]	Passenger Enplanements	Freight Carriers[2]	Freight (lbs)
Lincoln Municipal (LNK)				
Domestic service (U.S. carriers - 2018)	17	149,657	2	15,531
International service (U.S. carriers - 2017)	0	0	0	0

Note: (1) Includes all U.S.-based major, minor and commuter airlines that carried at least one passenger during the year; (2) Includes all U.S.-based airlines and freight carriers that transported at least one pound of freight during the year.
Source: Bureau of Transportation Statistics, The Intermodal Transportation Database, Air Carriers: T-100 Domestic Market (U.S. Carriers), 2018; Bureau of Transportation Statistics, The Intermodal Transportation Database, Air Carriers: T-100 International Market (U.S. Carriers), 2017

Other Transportation Statistics

Major Highways:	I-80
Amtrak Service:	Yes
Major Waterways/Ports:	None

Source: Amtrak.com; Google Maps

BUSINESSES

Major Business Headquarters

Company Name	Industry	Rankings Fortune[1]	Rankings Forbes[2]
No companies listed		-	-

Note: (1) Companies that produce a 10-K are ranked 1 to 500 based on 2017 revenue; (2) All private companies with at least $2 billion in annual revenue through the end of their most current fiscal year are ranked 1 to 229; companies listed are headquartered in the city; dashes indicate no ranking
Source: Fortune, "Fortune 500," June 2018; Forbes, "America's Largest Private Companies," 2018 Rankings

Minority- and Women-Owned Businesses

Group	All Firms Firms	All Firms Sales ($000)	Firms with Paid Employees Firms	Firms with Paid Employees Sales ($000)	Firms with Paid Employees Employees	Firms with Paid Employees Payroll ($000)
AIAN[1]	130	29,599	23	27,877	38	928
Asian	806	105,738	119	87,598	1,339	23,272
Black	455	(s)	38	(s)	250 - 499	(s)
Hispanic	717	136,533	77	116,899	739	16,332
NHOPI[2]	n/a	n/a	n/a	n/a	n/a	n/a
Women	8,174	1,096,265	1,000	930,979	8,882	272,596
All Firms	22,687	27,446,594	5,367	26,843,772	116,653	4,292,071

Note: Figures cover firms located in the city; minority- and women-owned business are defined as firms in which the corresponding group own 51% or more of the stock or equity of the company; (1) American Indian and Alaska Native; (2) Native Hawaiian and Other Pacific Islander; (s) estimates are suppressed when publication standards are not met; n/a not available
Source: U.S. Census Bureau, 2012 Economic Census, Survey of Business Owners

HOTELS & CONVENTION CENTERS

Hotels, Motels and Vacation Rentals

Area	5 Star Num.	5 Star Pct.[3]	4 Star Num.	4 Star Pct.[3]	3 Star Num.	3 Star Pct.[3]	2 Star Num.	2 Star Pct.[3]	1 Star Num.	1 Star Pct.[3]	Not Rated Num.	Not Rated Pct.[3]
City[1]	0	0.0	1	0.7	21	13.8	74	48.7	2	1.3	54	35.5
Total[2]	286	0.4	5,236	7.1	16,715	22.6	10,259	13.9	293	0.4	41,056	55.6

Note: (1) Figures cover Lincoln and vicinity; (2) Figures cover all 100 cities in this book; (3) Percentage of hotels which have a given star rating; Star ratings are determined by expedia.com and offer an indication of the general quality of a particular hotel.
Source: www.expedia.com, April 3, 2019

Major Convention Centers

Name	Overall Space (sq. ft.)	Exhibit Space (sq. ft.)	Meeting Space (sq. ft.)	Meeting Rooms

There are no major convention centers located in the metro area
Source: Original research

Living Environment

COST OF LIVING

Cost of Living Index

Composite Index	Groceries	Housing	Utilities	Trans-portation	Health Care	Misc. Goods/Services
94.5	97.5	81.0	91.0	96.9	103.3	103.8

Note: The Cost of Living Index measures regional differences in the cost of consumer goods and services, excluding taxes and non-consumer expenditures, for professional and managerial households in the top income quintile. It is based on more than 50,000 prices covering almost 60 different items for which prices are collected three times a year by chambers of commerce, economic development organizations or university applied economic centers in each participating urban area. The numbers shown should be read as a percentage above or below the national average of 100. For example, a value of 115.4 in the groceries column indicates that grocery prices are 15.4% higher than the national average. Small differences in the index numbers should not be interpreted as significant; Figures cover the Lincoln NE urban area.
Source: The Council for Community and Economic Research, ACCRA Cost of Living Index, 2018

Grocery Prices

Area[1]	T-Bone Steak ($/pound)	Frying Chicken ($/pound)	Whole Milk ($/half gal.)	Eggs ($/dozen)	Orange Juice ($/64 oz.)	Coffee ($/11.5 oz.)
City[2]	10.96	1.53	2.50	1.93	3.27	3.98
Avg.	11.35	1.42	1.94	1.81	3.52	4.35
Min.	7.45	0.92	0.80	0.75	2.72	3.06
Max.	15.05	2.76	4.18	4.00	5.36	8.20

Note: (1) Values for the local area are compared with the average, minimum and maximum values for all 291 areas in the Cost of Living Index; (2) Figures cover the Lincoln NE urban area; T-Bone Steak (price per pound); Frying Chicken (price per pound, whole fryer); Whole Milk (half gallon carton); Eggs (price per dozen, Grade A, large); Orange Juice (64 oz. Tropicana or Florida Natural); Coffee (11.5 oz. can, vacuum-packed, Maxwell House, Hills Bros, or Folgers).
Source: The Council for Community and Economic Research, ACCRA Cost of Living Index, 2018

Housing and Utility Costs

Area[1]	New Home Price ($)	Apartment Rent ($/month)	All Electric ($/month)	Part Electric ($/month)	Other Energy ($/month)	Telephone ($/month)
City[2]	288,296	827	-	66.38	65.88	190.00
Avg.	347,000	1,087	165.93	100.16	67.73	178.70
Min.	200,468	500	93.58	25.64	26.78	163.10
Max.	1,901,222	4,888	388.65	246.86	332.81	197.70

Note: (1) Values for the local area are compared with the average, minimum and maximum values for all 291 areas in the Cost of Living Index; (2) Figures cover the Lincoln NE urban area; New Home Price (2,400 sf living area, 8,000 sf lot, in urban area with full utilities); Apartment Rent (950 sf 2 bedroom/1.5 or 2 bath, unfurnished, excluding all utilities except water); All Electric (average monthly cost for an all-electric home); Part Electric (average monthly cost for a part-electric home); Other Energy (average monthly cost for natural gas, fuel oil, coal, wood, and any other forms of energy except electricity); Telephone (price includes the base monthly rate plus taxes and fees for three lines of mobile phone service).
Source: The Council for Community and Economic Research, ACCRA Cost of Living Index, 2018

Health Care, Transportation, and Other Costs

Area[1]	Doctor ($/visit)	Dentist ($/visit)	Optometrist ($/visit)	Gasoline ($/gallon)	Beauty Salon ($/visit)	Men's Shirt ($)
City[2]	134.07	86.40	112.02	2.56	39.62	37.92
Avg.	110.71	95.11	103.74	2.61	37.48	32.03
Min.	33.60	62.55	54.63	1.89	17.00	11.44
Max.	195.97	153.93	225.79	3.59	71.88	58.64

Note: (1) Values for the local area are compared with the average, minimum and maximum values for all 291 areas in the Cost of Living Index; (2) Figures cover the Lincoln NE urban area; Doctor (general practitioners routine exam of an established patient); Dentist (adult teeth cleaning and periodic oral examination); Optometrist (full vision eye exam for established adult patient); Gasoline (one gallon regular unleaded, national brand, including all taxes, cash price at self-service pump if available); Beauty Salon (woman's shampoo, trim, and blow-dry); Men's Shirt (cotton/polyester dress shirt, pinpoint weave, long sleeves).
Source: The Council for Community and Economic Research, ACCRA Cost of Living Index, 2018

HOUSING

House Price Index (HPI)

Area	National Ranking[2]	Quarterly Change (%)	One-Year Change (%)	Five-Year Change (%)
MSA[1]	107	-0.15	6.55	30.61
U.S.[3]	–	1.12	5.73	32.81

Note: The HPI is a weighted repeat sales index. It measures average price changes in repeat sales or refinancings on the same properties. This information is obtained by reviewing repeat mortgage transactions on single-family properties whose mortgages have been purchased or securitized by Fannie Mae or Freddie Mac in January 1975; (1) Figures cover the Lincoln, NE Metropolitan Statistical Area—see Appendix B for areas included; (2) Rankings are based on annual percentage change for all metro areas containing at least 15,000 transactions over the last 10 years and ranges from 1 to 245; (3) figures based on a weighted average of Census Division estimates using a seasonally adjusted, purchase-only index; all figures are for the period ending December 31, 2018
Source: Federal Housing Finance Agency, House Price Index, February 26, 2019

Median Single-Family Home Prices

Area	2016	2017	2018p	Percent Change 2017 to 2018
MSA[1]	166.1	175.4	189.8	8.2
U.S. Average	235.5	248.8	261.6	5.1

Note: Figures are median sales prices of existing single-family homes in thousands of dollars; (p) preliminary; (1) Figures cover the Lincoln, NE Metropolitan Statistical Area—see Appendix B for areas included
Source: National Association of Realtors, Median Sales Price of Existing Single-Family Homes for Metropolitan Areas, 4th Quarter 2018

Qualifying Income Based on Median Sales Price of Existing Single-Family Homes

Area	With 5% Down ($)	With 10% Down ($)	With 20% Down ($)
MSA[1]	45,065	42,693	37,949
U.S. Average	62,954	59,640	53,013

Note: Figures are preliminary; Qualifying income is based on a mortgage rate of 4.9%. Monthly principal and interest payment is limited to 25% of income; (1) Figures cover the Lincoln, NE Metropolitan Statistical Area—see Appendix B for areas included
Source: National Association of Realtors, Qualifying Income Based on Median Sales Price of Existing Single-Family Homes for Metropolitan Areas, 4th Quarter 2018

Median Apartment Condo-Coop Home Prices

Area	2016	2017	2018p	Percent Change 2017 to 2018
MSA[1]	n/a	n/a	n/a	n/a
U.S. Average	220.7	234.3	241.0	2.9

Note: Figures are median sales prices of existing apartment condo-coop homes in thousands of dollars; (p) preliminary; n/a not available; (1) Figures cover the Lincoln, NE Metropolitan Statistical Area—see Appendix B for areas included
Source: National Association of Realtors, Median Sales Price of Existing Apartment Condo-Coop Homes for Metropolitan Areas, 4th Quarter 2018

Home Value Distribution

Area	Under $50,000	$50,000 -$99,999	$100,000 -$149,999	$150,000 -$199,999	$200,000 -$299,999	$300,000 -$499,999	$500,000 -$999,999	$1,000,000 or more
City	4.6	11.8	30.0	23.1	20.3	8.3	1.6	0.3
MSA[1]	4.4	11.2	27.7	22.1	21.0	10.7	2.6	0.4
U.S.	8.3	13.9	14.7	14.6	18.7	17.3	9.7	2.7

Note: Figures are percentages and cover owner-occupied housing units; (1) Figures cover the Lincoln, NE Metropolitan Statistical Area—see Appendix B for areas included
Source: U.S. Census Bureau, 2013-2017 American Community Survey 5-Year Estimates

Homeownership Rate

Area	2010 (%)	2011 (%)	2012 (%)	2013 (%)	2014 (%)	2015 (%)	2016 (%)	2017 (%)	2018 (%)
MSA[1]	n/a	n/a	n/a	n/a	n/a	n/a	n/a	n/a	n/a
U.S.	66.9	66.1	65.4	65.1	64.5	63.7	63.4	63.9	64.4

Note: (1) Figures cover the Lincoln, NE Metropolitan Statistical Area—see Appendix B for areas included; n/a not available
Source: U.S. Census Bureau, Housing Vacancies and Homeownership Annual Statistics: 2010-2018

Year Housing Structure Built

Area	2010 or Later	2000 -2009	1990 -1999	1980 -1989	1970 -1979	1960 -1969	1950 -1959	1940 -1949	Before 1940	Median Year
City	4.3	14.9	15.2	11.2	15.2	10.8	11.3	3.4	13.8	1977
MSA[1]	4.5	15.4	15.2	10.7	15.5	10.5	10.5	3.2	14.5	1977
U.S.	3.2	14.5	14.0	13.6	15.5	10.8	10.5	5.1	12.9	1977

Note: Figures are percentages except for Median Year; Note: (1) Figures cover the Lincoln, NE Metropolitan Statistical Area—see Appendix B for areas included
Source: U.S. Census Bureau, 2013-2017 American Community Survey 5-Year Estimates

Gross Monthly Rent

Area	Under $500	$500 -$999	$1,000 -$1,499	$1,500 -$1,999	$2,000 -$2,499	$2,500 -$2,999	$3,000 and up	Median ($)
City	13.8	61.4	20.1	3.0	0.6	0.4	0.8	788
MSA[1]	14.0	61.3	20.0	2.9	0.6	0.4	0.8	784
U.S.	10.5	41.1	28.7	11.7	4.5	1.8	1.7	982

Note: Figures are percentages except for Median; Gross rent is the contract rent plus the estimated average monthly cost of utilities (electricity, gas, and water and sewer) and fuels (oil, coal, kerosene, wood, etc.) if these are paid by the renter (or paid for the renter by someone else); (1) Figures cover the Lincoln, NE Metropolitan Statistical Area—see Appendix B for areas included
Source: U.S. Census Bureau, 2013-2017 American Community Survey 5-Year Estimates

HEALTH

Health Risk Factors

Category	MSA[1] (%)	U.S. (%)
Adults aged 18–64 who have any kind of health care coverage	87.5	87.3
Adults who reported being in good or better health	86.9	82.4
Adults who have been told they have high blood cholesterol	29.3	33.0
Adults who have been told they have high blood pressure	26.5	32.3
Adults who are current smokers	12.2	17.1
Adults who currently use E-cigarettes	3.4	4.6
Adults who currently use chewing tobacco, snuff, or snus	3.3	4.0
Adults who are heavy drinkers[2]	7.5	6.3
Adults who are binge drinkers[3]	24.2	17.4
Adults who are overweight (BMI 25.0 - 29.9)	38.1	35.3
Adults who are obese (BMI 30.0 - 99.8)	28.9	31.3
Adults who participated in any physical activities in the past month	80.1	74.4
Adults who always or nearly always wears a seat belt	92.3	94.3

Note: (1) Figures cover the Lincoln, NE Metropolitan Statistical Area—see Appendix B for areas included; (2) Heavy drinkers are classified as adult men having more than 14 drinks per week and adult women having more than 7 drinks per week; (3) Binge drinkers are classified as males having five or more drinks on one occasion or females having four or more drinks on one occasion
Source: Centers for Disease Control and Prevention, Behaviorial Risk Factor Surveillance System, SMART: Selected Metropolitan Area Risk Trends, 2017

Acute and Chronic Health Conditions

Category	MSA[1] (%)	U.S. (%)
Adults who have ever been told they had a heart attack	3.7	4.2
Adults who have ever been told they have angina or coronary heart disease	3.5	3.9
Adults who have ever been told they had a stroke	2.3	3.0
Adults who have ever been told they have asthma	13.2	14.2
Adults who have ever been told they have arthritis	21.0	24.9
Adults who have ever been told they have diabetes[2]	8.3	10.5
Adults who have ever been told they had skin cancer	5.8	6.2
Adults who have ever been told they had any other types of cancer	6.4	7.1
Adults who have ever been told they have COPD	5.5	6.5
Adults who have ever been told they have kidney disease	2.9	3.0
Adults who have ever been told they have a form of depression	20.7	20.5

Note: (1) Figures cover the Lincoln, NE Metropolitan Statistical Area—see Appendix B for areas included; (2) Figures do not include pregnancy-related, borderline, or pre-diabetes
Source: Centers for Disease Control and Prevention, Behaviorial Risk Factor Surveillance System, SMART: Selected Metropolitan Area Risk Trends, 2017

Health Screening and Vaccination Rates

Category	MSA[1] (%)	U.S. (%)
Adults aged 65+ who have had flu shot within the past year	68.4	60.7
Adults aged 65+ who have ever had a pneumonia vaccination	82.1	75.4
Adults who have ever been tested for HIV	27.1	36.1
Adults who have ever had the shingles or zoster vaccine?	37.7	28.9
Adults who have had their blood cholesterol checked within the last five years	86.2	85.9

Note: n/a not available; (1) Figures cover the Lincoln, NE Metropolitan Statistical Area—see Appendix B for areas included.
Source: Centers for Disease Control and Prevention, Behaviorial Risk Factor Surveillance System, SMART: Selected Metropolitan Area Risk Trends, 2017

Disability Status

Category	MSA[1] (%)	U.S. (%)
Adults who reported being deaf	5.7	6.7
Are you blind or have serious difficulty seeing, even when wearing glasses?	2.5	4.5
Are you limited in any way in any of your usual activities due of arthritis?	9.5	12.9
Do you have difficulty doing errands alone?	3.7	6.8
Do you have difficulty dressing or bathing?	2.4	3.6
Do you have serious difficulty concentrating/remembering/making decisions?	8.0	10.7
Do you have serious difficulty walking or climbing stairs?	8.9	13.6

Note: (1) Figures cover the Lincoln, NE Metropolitan Statistical Area—see Appendix B for areas included.
Source: Centers for Disease Control and Prevention, Behaviorial Risk Factor Surveillance System, SMART: Selected Metropolitan Area Risk Trends, 2017

Mortality Rates for the Top 10 Causes of Death in the U.S.

ICD-10[a] Sub-Chapter	ICD-10[a] Code	Age-Adjusted Mortality Rate[1] per 100,000 population	
		County[2]	U.S.
Malignant neoplasms	C00-C97	145.0	155.5
Ischaemic heart diseases	I20-I25	64.1	94.8
Other forms of heart disease	I30-I51	53.7	52.9
Chronic lower respiratory diseases	J40-J47	55.2	41.0
Cerebrovascular diseases	I60-I69	34.6	37.5
Other degenerative diseases of the nervous system	G30-G31	34.3	35.0
Other external causes of accidental injury	W00-X59	20.3	33.7
Organic, including symptomatic, mental disorders	F01-F09	45.1	31.0
Hypertensive diseases	I10-I15	20.8	21.9
Diabetes mellitus	E10-E14	18.8	21.2

Note: (a) ICD-10 = International Classification of Diseases 10th Revision; (1) Mortality rates are a three year average covering 2015-2017; (2) Figures cover Lancaster County.
Source: Centers for Disease Control and Prevention, National Center for Health Statistics. Underlying Cause of Death 1999-2017 on CDC WONDER Online Database

Mortality Rates for Selected Causes of Death

ICD-10[a] Sub-Chapter	ICD-10[a] Code	Age-Adjusted Mortality Rate[1] per 100,000 population	
		County[2]	U.S.
Assault	X85-Y09	Unreliable	5.9
Diseases of the liver	K70-K76	10.6	14.1
Human immunodeficiency virus (HIV) disease	B20-B24	Suppressed	1.8
Influenza and pneumonia	J09-J18	14.3	14.3
Intentional self-harm	X60-X84	13.8	13.6
Malnutrition	E40-E46	2.5	1.6
Obesity and other hyperalimentation	E65-E68	2.1	2.1
Renal failure	N17-N19	8.8	13.0
Transport accidents	V01-V99	7.5	12.4
Viral hepatitis	B15-B19	Unreliable	1.6

Note: (a) ICD-10 = International Classification of Diseases 10th Revision; (1) Mortality rates are a three year average covering 2015-2017; (2) Figures cover Lancaster County; Data are suppressed when the data meet the criteria for confidentiality constraints; Mortality rates are flagged as unreliable when the rate would be calculated with a numerator of 20 or less.
Source: Centers for Disease Control and Prevention, National Center for Health Statistics. Underlying Cause of Death 1999-2017 on CDC WONDER Online Database

Health Insurance Coverage

Area	With Health Insurance	With Private Health Insurance	With Public Health Insurance	Without Health Insurance	Population Under Age 18 Without Health Insurance
City	91.2	77.1	25.4	8.8	4.6
MSA[1]	91.8	78.5	24.7	8.2	4.2
U.S.	89.5	67.2	33.8	10.5	5.7

Note: Figures are percentages that cover the civilian noninstitutionalized population; (1) Figures cover the Lincoln, NE Metropolitan Statistical Area—see Appendix B for areas included
Source: U.S. Census Bureau, 2013-2017 American Community Survey 5-Year Estimates

Number of Medical Professionals

Area	MDs[3]	DOs[3,4]	Dentists	Podiatrists	Chiropractors	Optometrists
County[1] (number)	664	34	291	17	126	66
County[1] (rate[2])	213.8	10.9	92.6	5.4	40.1	21.0
U.S. (rate[2])	279.3	23.0	68.4	6.0	27.1	16.2

Note: Data as of 2017 unless noted; (1) Data covers Lancaster County; (2) Rate per 100,000 population; (3) Data as of 2016 and includes all active, non-federal physicians; (4) Doctor of Osteopathic Medicine
Source: U.S. Department of Health and Human Services, Health Resources and Services Administration, Bureau of Health Professions, Area Resource File (ARF) 2017-2018

EDUCATION

Public School District Statistics

District Name	Schls	Pupils	Pupil/ Teacher Ratio	Minority Pupils[1] (%)	Free Lunch Eligible[2] (%)	IEP[3] (%)
Lincoln Public Schools	71	40,109	13.4	33.2	39.1	16.3

Note: Table includes school districts with 2,000 or more students; (1) Percentage of students that are not non-Hispanic white; (2) Percentage of students that are eligible for the free lunch program; (3) Percentage of students that have an Individualized Education Program.
Source: U.S. Department of Education, National Center for Education Statistics, Common Core of Data, Local Education Agency (School District) Universe Survey: School Year 2016-2017; U.S. Department of Education, National Center for Education Statistics, Common Core of Data, Public Elementary/Secondary School Universe Survey: School Year 2016-2017

Highest Level of Education

Area	Less than H.S.	H.S. Diploma	Some College, No Deg.	Associate Degree	Bachelor's Degree	Master's Degree	Prof. School Degree	Doctorate Degree
City	7.1	22.2	22.0	11.0	24.2	8.9	2.2	2.5
MSA[1]	6.7	22.6	21.8	11.6	24.0	8.7	2.2	2.4
U.S.	12.7	27.3	20.8	8.3	19.1	8.4	2.0	1.4

Note: Figures cover persons age 25 and over; (1) Figures cover the Lincoln, NE Metropolitan Statistical Area—see Appendix B for areas included
Source: U.S. Census Bureau, 2013-2017 American Community Survey 5-Year Estimates

Educational Attainment by Race

Area	High School Graduate or Higher (%)					Bachelor's Degree or Higher (%)				
	Total	White	Black	Asian	Hisp.[2]	Total	White	Black	Asian	Hisp.[2]
City	92.9	94.7	88.5	80.1	64.9	37.8	39.1	19.0	43.2	16.2
MSA[1]	93.3	94.9	88.5	80.3	64.7	37.3	38.4	19.3	43.2	16.3
U.S.	87.3	89.3	84.9	86.5	66.7	30.9	32.2	20.6	52.7	15.2

Note: Figures shown cover persons 25 years old and over; (1) Figures cover the Lincoln, NE Metropolitan Statistical Area—see Appendix B for areas included; (2) People of Hispanic origin can be of any race
Source: U.S. Census Bureau, 2013-2017 American Community Survey 5-Year Estimates

School Enrollment by Grade and Control

Area	Preschool (%)		Kindergarten (%)		Grades 1 - 4 (%)		Grades 5 - 8 (%)		Grades 9 - 12 (%)	
	Public	Private	Public	Private	Public	Private	Public	Private	Public	Private
City	53.8	46.2	82.7	17.3	84.4	15.6	84.9	15.1	85.7	14.3
MSA[1]	52.6	47.4	82.6	17.4	84.6	15.4	85.3	14.7	86.8	13.2
U.S.	58.8	41.2	87.7	12.3	89.7	10.3	89.6	10.4	90.3	9.7

Note: Figures shown cover persons 3 years old and over; (1) Figures cover the Lincoln, NE Metropolitan Statistical Area—see Appendix B for areas included
Source: U.S. Census Bureau, 2013-2017 American Community Survey 5-Year Estimates

Average Salaries of Public School Classroom Teachers

Area	2016		2017		Change from 2016 to 2017	
	Dollars	Rank[1]	Dollars	Rank[1]	Percent	Rank[2]
Nebraska	51,386	29	52,338	30	1.9	21
U.S. Average	58,479	–	59,660	–	2.0	–

Note: (1) Rank ranges from 1 to 51 where 1 indicates highest salary; (2) Rank ranges from 1 to 51 where 1 indicates highest percent change.
Source: National Education Association, Rankings & Estimates: Rankings of the States 2017 and Estimates of School Statistics 2018

Higher Education

Four-Year Colleges			Two-Year Colleges			Medical Schools[1]	Law Schools[2]	Voc/ Tech[3]
Public	Private Non-profit	Private For-profit	Public	Private Non-profit	Private For-profit			
1	4	1	1	0	5	0	1	0

Note: Figures cover institutions located within the city limits and include main campuses only; (1) includes schools accredited by the Liaison Committee on Medical Education and the American Osteopathic Association's Commission on Osteopathic College Accreditation; (2) includes ABA-accredited schools, schools with provisional ABA accreditation, and state accredited schools; (3) includes all schools with programs that are less than 2 years.
Source: National Center for Education Statistics, Integrated Postsecondary Education System (IPEDS), 2017-18; Wikipedia, List of Medical Schools in the United States, accessed April 3, 2019; Wikipedia, List of Law Schools in the United States, accessed April 3, 2019

According to *U.S. News & World Report,* the Lincoln, NE metro area is home to one of the best national universities in the U.S.: **University of Nebraska—Lincoln** (#129 tie). The indicators used to capture academic quality fall into a number of categories: assessment by administrators at peer institutions; retention of students; faculty resources; student selectivity; financial resources; alumni giving; high school counselor ratings of colleges; and graduation rate. *U.S. News & World Report, "America's Best Colleges 2019"*

According to *U.S. News & World Report,* the Lincoln, NE metro area is home to one of the top 100 law schools in the U.S.: **University of Nebraska—Lincoln** (#77 tie). The rankings are based on a weighted average of 12 measures of quality: peer assessment score; assessment score by lawyers/judges; median LSAT scores; median undergrad GPA; acceptance rate; employment rates for graduates; placement success; bar passage rate; faculty resources; expenditures per student; student/faculty ratio; and library resources. *U.S. News & World Report, "America's Best Graduate Schools, Law, 2020"*

PRESIDENTIAL ELECTION

2016 Presidential Election Results

Area	Clinton	Trump	Johnson	Stein	Other
Lancaster County	45.4	45.2	5.2	1.4	2.7
U.S.	48.0	45.9	3.3	1.1	1.7

Note: Results are percentages and may not add to 100% due to rounding
Source: Dave Leip's Atlas of U.S. Presidential Elections

EMPLOYERS

Major Employers

Company Name	Industry
Bank of the West	Financial services
Cargill Meat Solutions	Food processing
CHI Health Bergan Mercy	Healthcare
CHI Health St Elizabeth	Healthcare
Con Agra Foods Inc	Food manufacturing
Creighton University	Education
First Data	Commerce
Health & Human Svc Dept	Government
JBS USA	Food processing
Methodist Hospital	Healthcare
Mutual of Omaha Insurance Co	Insurance
Nebraska Medical Center	Healthcare
Nebraska Medicine	Healthcare
Offutt AFB	U.S. military
Pay Pal	Payment services
Smithfield Farmland	Agriculture
Tyson Fresh Meats	Food processing
Union Pacific Railroad Co	Railroad
University of NE Medical Ctr	Healthcare
University of Nebraska	Education
West Corp	Communications

Note: Companies shown are located within the Lincoln, NE Metropolitan Statistical Area.
Source: Hoovers.com; Wikipedia

PUBLIC SAFETY

Crime Rate

Area	All Crimes	Violent Crimes				Property Crimes		
		Murder	Rape[3]	Robbery	Aggrav. Assault	Burglary	Larceny-Theft	Motor Vehicle Theft
City	3,463.1	3.6	79.0	67.9	207.4	448.5	2,531.5	125.2
Suburbs[1]	1,218.2	0.0	49.8	2.2	54.1	190.4	852.5	69.2
Metro[2]	3,146.1	3.1	74.8	58.7	185.7	412.1	2,294.5	117.3
U.S.	2,849.1	5.4	40.9	102.9	248.3	468.9	1,745.4	237.3

Note: Figures are crimes per 100,000 population; (1) All areas within the metro area that are located outside the city limits; (2) Figures cover the Lincoln, NE Metropolitan Statistical Area—see Appendix B for areas included; (3) The city and U.S. figures shown were reported using the revised Uniform Crime Reporting (UCR) definition of rape. The suburban and metro area figures shown are an aggregate total of the data submitted using both the revised and legacy UCR definitions.
Source: FBI Uniform Crime Reports, 2016 (data for 2017 was not available)

Hate Crimes

Area	Number of Quarters Reported	Number of Incidents per Bias Motivation					
		Race/Ethnicity/ Ancestry	Religion	Sexual Orientation	Disability	Gender	Gender Identity
City	4	21	5	3	0	0	0
U.S.	4	4,131	1,564	1,130	116	46	119

Source: Federal Bureau of Investigation, Hate Crime Statistics 2017

Identity Theft Consumer Reports

Area	Reports	Reports per 100,000 Population	Rank[2]
MSA[1]	195	60	317
U.S.	444,602	135	

Note: (1) Figures cover the Lincoln, NE Metropolitan Statistical Area—see Appendix B for areas included; (2) Rank ranges from 1 to 389 where 1 indicates greatest number of identity theft reports per 100,000 population
Source: Federal Trade Commission, Consumer Sentinel Network Data Book for January–December 2018

Fraud and Other Consumer Reports

Area	Reports	Reports per 100,000 Population	Rank[2]
MSA[1]	1,348	412	306
U.S.	2,552,917	776	-

Note: (1) Figures cover the Lincoln, NE Metropolitan Statistical Area—see Appendix B for areas included;
(2) Rank ranges from 1 to 389 where 1 indicates greatest number of fraud and other consumer reports per 100,000 population
Source: Federal Trade Commission, Consumer Sentinel Network Data Book for January–December 2018

SPORTS

Professional Sports Teams

Team Name	League	Year Established
No teams are located in the metro area		

Source: Wikipedia, Major Professional Sports Teams of the United States and Canada, April 5, 2019

CLIMATE

Average and Extreme Temperatures

Temperature	Jan	Feb	Mar	Apr	May	Jun	Jul	Aug	Sep	Oct	Nov	Dec	Yr.
Extreme High (°F)	73	77	89	97	99	107	108	107	101	93	82	69	108
Average High (°F)	33	38	50	64	74	85	89	86	78	66	49	36	62
Average Temp. (°F)	22	28	39	52	62	73	78	75	66	53	38	26	51
Average Low (°F)	11	16	27	39	50	60	66	64	53	40	27	16	39
Extreme Low (°F)	-33	-24	-19	3	24	39	45	39	26	11	-5	-27	-33

Note: Figures cover the years 1948-1995
Source: National Climatic Data Center, International Station Meteorological Climate Summary, 9/96

Average Precipitation/Snowfall/Humidity

Precip./Humidity	Jan	Feb	Mar	Apr	May	Jun	Jul	Aug	Sep	Oct	Nov	Dec	Yr.
Avg. Precip. (in.)	0.8	0.8	2.4	2.9	4.1	3.7	3.7	3.4	3.1	1.9	1.4	0.9	29.1
Avg. Snowfall (in.)	6	5	6	1	Tr	0	0	0	Tr	Tr	3	6	27
Avg. Rel. Hum. 6am (%)	78	81	81	80	83	83	83	86	84	80	80	80	82
Avg. Rel. Hum. 3pm (%)	61	60	55	47	51	49	48	51	49	46	54	60	53

Note: Figures cover the years 1948-1995; Tr = Trace amounts (<0.05 in. of rain; <0.5 in. of snow)
Source: National Climatic Data Center, International Station Meteorological Climate Summary, 9/96

Weather Conditions

Temperature			Daytime Sky			Precipitation		
5°F & below	32°F & below	90°F & above	Clear	Partly cloudy	Cloudy	0.01 inch or more precip.	0.1 inch or more snow/ice	Thunder-storms
25	145	40	108	135	122	94	19	46

Note: Figures are average number of days per year and cover the years 1948-1995
Source: National Climatic Data Center, International Station Meteorological Climate Summary, 9/96

HAZARDOUS WASTE

Superfund Sites

The Lincoln, NE metro area has no sites on the EPA's Superfund Final National Priorities List. There are a total of 1,390 Superfund sites with a status of proposed or final on the list in the U.S.
U.S. Environmental Protection Agency, National Priorities List, April 5, 2019

**AIR & WATER
QUALITY**

Air Quality Trends: Ozone

	1990	1995	2000	2005	2010	2012	2014	2015	2016	2017
MSA[1]	0.057	0.060	0.057	0.056	0.050	0.058	0.061	0.061	0.058	0.062
U.S.	0.088	0.089	0.082	0.080	0.073	0.075	0.067	0.068	0.069	0.068

Note: (1) Data covers the Lincoln, NE Metropolitan Statistical Area—see Appendix B for areas included. The values shown are the composite ozone concentration averages among trend sites based on the highest fourth daily maximum 8-hour concentration in parts per million. These trends are based on sites having an adequate record of monitoring data during the trend period. Data from exceptional events are included.
Source: U.S. Environmental Protection Agency, Air Quality Monitoring Information, "Air Quality Trends by City, 1990-2017"

Air Quality Index

Area	Percent of Days when Air Quality was...[2]					AQI Statistics[2]	
	Good	Moderate	Unhealthy for Sensitive Groups	Unhealthy	Very Unhealthy	Maximum	Median
MSA[1]	92.2	7.3	0.6	0.0	0.0	113	33

Note: (1) Data covers the Lincoln, NE Metropolitan Statistical Area—see Appendix B for areas included; (2) Based on 344 days with AQI data in 2017. Air Quality Index (AQI) is an index for reporting daily air quality. EPA calculates the AQI for five major air pollutants regulated by the Clean Air Act: ground-level ozone, particle pollution (aka particulate matter), carbon monoxide, sulfur dioxide, and nitrogen dioxide. The AQI runs from 0 to 500. The higher the AQI value, the greater the level of air pollution and the greater the health concern. There are six AQI categories: "Good" AQI is between 0 and 50. Air quality is considered satisfactory; "Moderate" AQI is between 51 and 100. Air quality is acceptable; "Unhealthy for Sensitive Groups" When AQI values are between 101 and 150, members of sensitive groups may experience health effects; "Unhealthy" When AQI values are between 151 and 200 everyone may begin to experience health effects; "Very Unhealthy" AQI values between 201 and 300 trigger a health alert; "Hazardous" AQI values over 300 trigger warnings of emergency conditions (not shown).
Source: U.S. Environmental Protection Agency, Air Quality Index Report, 2017

Air Quality Index Pollutants

Area	Percent of Days when AQI Pollutant was...[2]					
	Carbon Monoxide	Nitrogen Dioxide	Ozone	Sulfur Dioxide	Particulate Matter 2.5	Particulate Matter 10
MSA[1]	0.0	0.0	57.0	24.4	18.6	0.0

Note: (1) Data covers the Lincoln, NE Metropolitan Statistical Area—see Appendix B for areas included; (2) Based on 344 days with AQI data in 2017. The Air Quality Index (AQI) is an index for reporting daily air quality. EPA calculates the AQI for five major air pollutants regulated by the Clean Air Act: ground-level ozone, particle pollution (also known as particulate matter), carbon monoxide, sulfur dioxide, and nitrogen dioxide. The AQI runs from 0 to 500. The higher the AQI value, the greater the level of air pollution and the greater the health concern.
Source: U.S. Environmental Protection Agency, Air Quality Index Report, 2017

Maximum Air Pollutant Concentrations: Particulate Matter, Ozone, CO and Lead

	Particulate Matter 10 (ug/m³)	Particulate Matter 2.5 Wtd AM (ug/m³)	Particulate Matter 2.5 24-Hr (ug/m³)	Ozone (ppm)	Carbon Monoxide (ppm)	Lead (ug/m³)
MSA[1] Level	n/a	6.7	19	0.062	n/a	n/a
NAAQS[2]	150	15	35	0.075	9	0.15
Met NAAQS[2]	n/a	Yes	Yes	Yes	n/a	n/a

Note: (1) Data covers the Lincoln, NE Metropolitan Statistical Area—see Appendix B for areas included; Data from exceptional events are included; (2) National Ambient Air Quality Standards; ppm = parts per million; ug/m³ = micrograms per cubic meter; n/a not available.
Concentrations: Particulate Matter 10 (coarse particulate)—highest second maximum 24-hour concentration; Particulate Matter 2.5 Wtd AM (fine particulate)—highest weighted annual mean concentration; Particulate Matter 2.5 24-Hour (fine particulate)—highest 98th percentile 24-hour concentration; Ozone—highest fourth daily maximum 8-hour concentration; Carbon Monoxide—highest second maximum non-overlapping 8-hour concentration; Lead—maximum running 3-month average
Source: U.S. Environmental Protection Agency, Air Quality Monitoring Information, "Air Quality Statistics by City, 2017"

Maximum Air Pollutant Concentrations: Nitrogen Dioxide and Sulfur Dioxide

	Nitrogen Dioxide AM (ppb)	Nitrogen Dioxide 1-Hr (ppb)	Sulfur Dioxide AM (ppb)	Sulfur Dioxide 1-Hr (ppb)	Sulfur Dioxide 24-Hr (ppb)
MSA[1] Level	n/a	n/a	n/a	44	n/a
NAAQS[2]	53	100	30	75	140
Met NAAQS[2]	n/a	n/a	n/a	Yes	n/a

Note: (1) Data covers the Lincoln, NE Metropolitan Statistical Area—see Appendix B for areas included; Data from exceptional events are included; (2) National Ambient Air Quality Standards; ppm = parts per million; ug/m³ = micrograms per cubic meter; n/a not available.
Concentrations: Nitrogen Dioxide AM—highest arithmetic mean concentration; Nitrogen Dioxide 1-Hr—highest 98th percentile 1-hour daily maximum concentration; Sulfur Dioxide AM—highest annual mean concentration; Sulfur Dioxide 1-Hr—highest 99th percentile 1-hour daily maximum concentration; Sulfur Dioxide 24-Hr—highest second maximum 24-hour concentration
Source: U.S. Environmental Protection Agency, Air Quality Monitoring Information, "Air Quality Statistics by City, 2017"

Drinking Water

Water System Name	Pop. Served	Primary Water Source Type	Violations[1] Health Based	Violations[1] Monitoring/ Reporting
City of Lincoln	277,348	(2)	0	0

Note: (1) Based on violation data from January 1, 2018 to December 31, 2018; (2) Ground water under direct influence of surface water
Source: U.S. Environmental Protection Agency, Office of Ground Water and Drinking Water, Safe Drinking Water Information System (based on data extracted April 5, 2019)

Little Rock, Arkansas

Background

Little Rock is the capital of Arkansas and the most populous city in the state. It is located along the banks of the Arkansas River and marks the point where the flat Mississippi Delta ends and the foothills of the Quachita Mountains begin. The city is best known for its place in the history of the United States Civil Rights Movement and for its connection to former President William Jefferson Clinton, who served as the Governor of Arkansas before being elected our forty-second President.

The area that is now Little Rock was originally inhabited by Native American tribes including the Quapaw, Choctaw and Cherokee, but the first Europeans in the area were the Spanish, who passed through in the mid-sixteenth century. The city got its name from a rock formation on the southern side of the Arkansas River that was a landmark for river crossings. When French explorer Jean-Baptiste Benard de la Harpe arrived in the area in 1722, he called the area Le pettite roche, or "the little rock," and the nickname stuck. La Harpe built a trading post on the site, but it would be more than 100 years before the city is officially incorporated in 1831. When Arkansas became the 25th American State in 1836, Little Rock was chosen as its capital. Initially the city grew quickly, but many projects, including the railroad between Little Rock and Memphis, were put on hold when the Civil War broke out. Post-war reconstruction, however, brought a wealth of new development so that by the turn of the century, its transformation from a small, sleepy frontier town to a thriving, modern city was complete. After the Great Depression ended in the early 1930s, many residents began to move out to the suburbs and many new roads were built to accommodate the city's changing layout.

In 1957 the city was thrown into the national spotlight with Little Rock Nine—nine African-American students who enrolled in the all-white Central High School, claiming it was their right, based on the U.S. Supreme Court's ruling on *Brown v. Board of Education*. Governor Orval Faubus sent the National Guard to prevent the students from entering the school, but they were eventually admitted under the protection of the U.S. Army sent by President Eisenhower.

Little Rock was again brought to national prominence when then-Governor Bill Clinton started his presidential election campaign in 1992, and gave his election-night acceptance speech from the steps of the Old State House in downtown Little Rock. Clinton has since solidified his link to the city through the William J. Clinton Presidential Center and Park.

Today, the city has a diverse economy built upon manufacturing, education, healthcare and commercial trade. Many major corporations have headquarters in the city. The Little Rock Port is part of a comprehensive industrial business zone on the Arkansas River. In 2016, Little Rock was chosen to join "What Works Cities," a national initiative to help American cities enhance their use of data, improve services, and engage residents.

The Pulaski County Pedestrian and Bicycle Bridge, at 3,463 feet, is the world's longest bridge for pedestrians and bicyclists only. Prominent charitable organization Heifer International has its world headquarters in Little Rock. Dickey-Stephens Park, a 7,000-seat baseball park, is home to minor league team Arkansas Travelers.

Attractions in the city include the MacArthur Museum of Arkansas Military History, the Arkansas Museum of Discovery, and the Old State House Museum. In addition, the William J. Clinton Presidential Center and Park houses the Clinton Presidential Library and the headquarters of the Clinton Foundation. A section of downtown's Main Street, called Creative Corridor, combines the arts, entertainment, business and culture, and is home to the Arkansas Repertory Theatre, Arkansas Symphony Orchestra, and Ballet Arkansas. Other cultural attractions in Little Rock include the Arkansas Arts Center, the Robinson Center Music Hall, and Wildwood Center for the Performing Arts. The city's major institutions of higher learning are the University of Arkansas at Little Rock and the University of Arkansas for Medical Sciences.

Little Rock has a humid subtropical climate, typical of the southern United States. Summers are generally hot, while winters are cooler, but high humidity persists all year round. Rainfall can be heavy at times during the spring and fall but the city rarely receives any snow. In April of 2017, a deadly flood devastated the city. The highest temperature recorded is 114 degrees. A deadly tornado touched down 10 miles west of the city in 2014, when powerful storms killed 16 people in three states.

Rankings

General Rankings

- In their sixth annual survey, Livability.com looked at data for more than 1,000 U.S. cities to determine the rankings for Livability's "Top 100 Best Places to Live" in 2019. Little Rock ranked #90. Criteria: median home value capped at $250,000; affordable living; vibrant economy; education, demographics, health care options. transportation & infrastructure; abundant lifestyle amenities. *Livability.com, "Top 100 Best Places to Live 2019" March 2019*

Business/Finance Rankings

- The personal finance site NerdWallet analyzed 183 American metropolitan areas with populations over 250,000 and more than 15,000 businesses to rank where entrepreneurs find the most success. Criteria included area economy, annual income, housing cost, unemployment rate, and the success rate of area businesses. Little Rock ranked #53. *www.nerdwallet.com, "Best Places to Start a Business," April 27, 2015*

- The Brookings Institution ranked the nation's largest cities based on income inequality. Little Rock was ranked #19 (#1 = greatest inequality). Criteria: the "95/20 ratio," a figure representing the income at which a household earns more than 95 percent of all other households, divided by the income at which a household earns more than only 20 percent of all other households. *Brookings Institution, "Household Income Inequality, Largest Cities of 97 Large U.S. Metro Areas, 2014-2016," February 5, 2018*

- The Brookings Institution ranked the 100 largest metro areas in the U.S. based on income inequality. Little Rock was ranked #48 (#1 = greatest inequality). Criteria: the "95/20 ratio," a figure representing the income at which a household earns more than 95 percent of all other households, divided by the income at which a household earns more than only 20 percent of all other households. *Brookings Institution, "Household Income Inequality, 100 Largest U.S. Metro Areas, 2014-2016," February 5, 2018*

- The Little Rock metro area appeared on the Milken Institute "2018 Best Performing Cities" list. Rank: #155 out of 200 large metro areas. Criteria: job growth; wage and salary growth; high-tech output growth. *Milken Institute, "Best-Performing Cities 2018," January 24, 2019*

- *Forbes* ranked the 200 most populous metro areas to determine the nation's "Best Places for Business and Careers." The Little Rock metro area was ranked #133. Criteria: costs (business and living); job growth (past and projected); income growth; quality of life; educational attainment (college and high school); projected economic growth; cultural and recreational opportunities; net migration patterns; number of highly ranked colleges. *Forbes, "The Best Places for Business and Careers 2018: Seattle Leads the Way," October 24, 2018*

Dating/Romance Rankings

- *Apartment List* conducted its annual survey of renters to compile a list of cities that have the best opportunities for dating. More than 9,000 respondents, from February 2018 through the end of December 2018, rated their current city or neighborhood for opportunities to date and make friends. Little Rock ranked #5 out of 66 where single residents were very satisfied or somewhat satisfied, making it among the ten best metros for dating opportunities. Other criteria analyzed included gender and education levels of renters. *Apartment List, "The Best & Worst Cities for Dating 2019," February 8, 2019*

Education Rankings

- Personal finance website *WalletHub* analyzed the 150 largest U.S. metropolitan statistical areas to determine where the most educated Americans are choosing to settle. Criteria: education quality and attainment gap; education levels; percentage of workers with degrees; public school quality rankings; quality and size of each metro area's universities. Little Rock was ranked #67 (#1 = most educated city). *www.WalletHub.com, "2018's Most and Least Educated Cities in America, " July 24, 2018*

Environmental Rankings

- Little Rock was highlighted as one of the 25 metro areas most polluted by year-round particle pollution (Annual PM 2.5) in the U.S. during 2014 through 2016. The area ranked #24. *American Lung Association, State of the Air 2018*

- Little Rock was highlighted as one of the top 90 cleanest metro areas for short-term particle pollution (24-hour PM 2.5) in the U.S. during 2014 through 2016. Monitors in these cities reported no days with unhealthful PM 2.5 levels. *American Lung Association, State of the Air 2018*

Food/Drink Rankings

- *Men's Health* ranked 100 major U.S. cities in terms of alcohol intoxication. Little Rock ranked #76 (#1 = most sober).Criteria: binge drinking; alcohol-related traffic accidents, arrests, and fatalities. *Men's Health, "America's Drunkest Cities," March 9, 2015*

Health/Fitness Rankings

- Analysts who tracked obesity rates in 100 of the nation's most populous areas found that the Little Rock metro area was one of the ten communities where residents were most likely to be obese, defined as a BMI score of 30 or above. *www.gallup.com, "Colorado Springs Residents Least Likely to Be Obese," May 28, 2015*

- Little Rock was identified as a "2018 Spring Allergy Capital." The area ranked #17 out of 100. Three groups of factors were used to identify the most challenging cities for people with allergies during the spring season: annual pollen levels; medicine utilization; access to board-certified allergists. *Asthma and Allergy Foundation of America, "Spring Allergy Capitals 2018"*

- Little Rock was identified as a "2018 Fall Allergy Capital." The area ranked #21 out of 100. Three groups of factors were used to identify the most challenging cities for people with allergies during the fall season: annual pollen levels; medicine utilization; access to board-certified allergists. *Asthma and Allergy Foundation of America, "Fall Allergy Capitals 2018"*

- Little Rock was identified as a "2018 Asthma Capital." The area ranked #32 out of the nation's 100 largest metropolitan areas. Criteria: estimated prevalence; self-reported prevalence; crude death rate for asthma; annual pollen score; annual air quality; public smoking laws; number of board-certified asthma specialists; school inhaler access laws; rescue medication use; controller medication use; ER visits for asthma; uninsured rate; poverty rate. *Asthma and Allergy Foundation of America, "Asthma Capitals 2018: The Most Challenging Places to Live With Asthma"*

- *Men's Health* ranked 100 major U.S. cities in terms of the best cities for men. Little Rock ranked #89. Criteria: health; fitness; quality of life. *Men's Health, "The Best & Worst Cities for Men Who Want to Be Fit and Happy," January 1, 2016*

- The Little Rock metro area ranked #161 out of 189 in The Gallup-Healthways Well-Being Index. Criteria: purpose; social well being; financial health; community and physical health. Results are based on telephone interviews with adults, aged 18 and older, living in metropolitan areas in the 50 U.S. states and the District of Columbia. *Gallup-Healthways, "State of American Well-Being, 2017 Community Well-Being Rankings" March 2018*

Real Estate Rankings

- *WalletHub* compared the most populated U.S. cities, as well as at least two of the most populated cities in each state, for a total of 179, to determine which had the best markets for real estate agents. Little Rock ranked #165 where demand was high and pay was the best. Criteria: sales per agent; annual median wage for real-estate agents; monthly average starting salary for real estate agents; real estate job density and competition; unemployment rate; housing-market health index; and other relevant metrics. *www.WalletHub.com, "2018's Best Places to Be a Real Estate Agent,"April 25, 2018*

Safety Rankings

- To identify the most dangerous cities in America, 24/7 Wall Street focused on violent crime categories—murder, rape, robbery, and aggravated assault—and property crime as reported in the FBI's 2017 annual Uniform Crime Report. Criteria also included median income from American Community Survey and unemployment figures from Bureau of Labor Statistics. For cities with populations over 100,000, Little Rock was ranked #6. *247wallst.com, "25 Most Dangerous Cities in America" October 17, 2018*

- Allstate ranked the 200 largest cities in America in terms of driver safety. Little Rock ranked #158. Criteria: internal property damage claims over a two-year period from January 2015 to December 2016. The report helps increase the importance of safety awareness behind the wheel. *Allstate, "Allstate America's Best Drivers Report, 2018" August 28, 2018*

- Little Rock was identified as one of the most dangerous cities in America by NeighborhoodScout. The city ranked #15 out of 100. Criteria: number of violent crimes per 1,000 residents. The editors only considered cities with 25,000 or more residents. *NeighborhoodScout.com, "Top 100 Most Dangerous Cities in the U.S. 2019" January 2, 2019*

- The National Insurance Crime Bureau ranked 382 metro areas in the U.S. in terms of per capita rates of vehicle theft. The Little Rock metro area ranked #38 (#1 = highest rate). Criteria: number of vehicle theft offenses per 100,000 inhabitants in 2017. *National Insurance Crime Bureau, "Hot Spots 2017," July 12, 2018*

Seniors/Retirement Rankings

- From its Best Cities for Successful Aging indexes, the Milken Institute generated rankings for metropolitan areas, weighing data in nine categories—health care, wellness, living arrangements, transportation and convenience, financial characteristics, education, employment, community engagement, and overall livability. The Little Rock metro area was ranked #47 overall in the large metro area category. *Milken Institute, "Best Cities for Successful Aging, 2017" March 14, 2017*

Women/Minorities Rankings

- *24/7 Wall St.* compared median earnings over a 12-month period for men and women who worked full-time, year-round, and employment composition by sector to identify the best-paying cities for women. Of the largest 100 U.S. metropolitan areas, Little Rock was ranked #4 in pay disparity. *24/7 Wall St., "The Best (and Worst) Paying Cities for Women," March 27, 2017*

- Personal finance website *WalletHub* compared more than 180 U.S. cities—including the 150 most populated U.S. cities, plus at least two of the most populated cities in each state—across two key dimensions, "Hispanic Business-Friendliness" and "Hispanic Purchasing Power", to arrive at the most favorable conditions for Hispanic entrepreneurs. Little Rock was ranked #108 out of 182. Criteria includes: share of Hispanic-Owned Businesses; Hispanic entrepreneurship rate to median annual income of Hispanics; Small Business-Friendliness score; cost of living; and number of Hispanics with at least a bachelor's degree. *WalletHub.com, "2018's Best Cities for Hispanic Entrepreneurs," April 26, 2018*

Miscellaneous Rankings

- *WalletHub* compared the 150 most populated U.S. cities to determine their operating efficiency. A "Quality of Services" score was constructed for each city and then divided by the total budget per capita to reveal which were managed the best. Little Rock ranked #56. Criteria: financial stability; economy; education; safety; health; infrastructure and pollution. *www.WalletHub.com, "2018's Best- & Worst-Run Cities in America," July 9, 2018*

Business Environment

CITY FINANCES

City Government Finances

Component	2016 ($000)	2016 ($ per capita)
Total Revenues	451,707	2,281
Total Expenditures	493,265	2,491
Debt Outstanding	596,789	3,014
Cash and Securities[1]	544,721	2,751

Note: (1) Cash and security holdings of a government at the close of its fiscal year, including those of its dependent agencies, utilities, and liquor stores.
Source: U.S. Census Bureau, State & Local Government Finances 2016

City Government Revenue by Source

Source	2016 ($000)	2016 ($ per capita)	2016 (%)
General Revenue			
From Federal Government	10,591	53	2.3
From State Government	19,827	100	4.4
From Local Governments	54,204	274	12.0
Taxes			
Property	50,503	255	11.2
Sales and Gross Receipts	121,887	616	27.0
Personal Income	0	0	0.0
Corporate Income	0	0	0.0
Motor Vehicle License	0	0	0.0
Other Taxes	9,011	46	2.0
Current Charges	162,156	819	35.9
Liquor Store	0	0	0.0
Utility	0	0	0.0
Employee Retirement	6,663	34	1.5

Source: U.S. Census Bureau, State & Local Government Finances 2016

City Government Expenditures by Function

Function	2016 ($000)	2016 ($ per capita)	2016 (%)
General Direct Expenditures			
Air Transportation	33,306	168	6.8
Corrections	0	0	0.0
Education	0	0	0.0
Employment Security Administration	0	0	0.0
Financial Administration	8,274	41	1.7
Fire Protection	46,461	234	9.4
General Public Buildings	942	4	0.2
Governmental Administration, Other	5,191	26	1.1
Health	29,496	149	6.0
Highways	32,800	165	6.6
Hospitals	0	0	0.0
Housing and Community Development	8,095	40	1.6
Interest on General Debt	21,283	107	4.3
Judicial and Legal	5,053	25	1.0
Libraries	5,762	29	1.2
Parking	1,244	6	0.3
Parks and Recreation	36,821	186	7.5
Police Protection	72,078	364	14.6
Public Welfare	0	0	0.0
Sewerage	53,101	268	10.8
Solid Waste Management	13,277	67	2.7
Veterans' Services	0	0	0.0
Liquor Store	0	0	0.0
Utility	0	0	0.0
Employee Retirement	22,714	114	4.6

Source: U.S. Census Bureau, State & Local Government Finances 2016

DEMOGRAPHICS

Population Growth

Area	1990 Census	2000 Census	2010 Census	2017* Estimate	Population Growth (%)	
					1990-2017	2010-2017
City	177,519	183,133	193,524	197,780	11.4	2.2
MSA[1]	535,034	610,518	699,757	730,346	36.5	4.4
U.S.	248,709,873	281,421,906	308,745,538	321,004,407	29.1	4.0

Note: (1) Figures cover the Little Rock-North Little Rock-Conway, AR Metropolitan Statistical Area—see Appendix B for areas included; (*) 2013-2017 5-year estimated population
Source: U.S. Census Bureau, 1990 Census, Census 2000, Census 2010, 2013-2017 American Community Survey 5-Year Estimates

Household Size

Area	Persons in Household (%)							Average Household Size
	One	Two	Three	Four	Five	Six	Seven or More	
City	36.8	32.8	13.7	9.9	4.3	1.6	0.9	2.40
MSA[1]	29.8	34.4	16.3	11.6	5.0	1.9	0.9	2.60
U.S.	27.7	33.8	15.7	13.0	6.0	2.3	1.4	2.60

Note: (1) Figures cover the Little Rock-North Little Rock-Conway, AR Metropolitan Statistical Area—see Appendix B for areas included
Source: U.S. Census Bureau, 2013-2017 American Community Survey 5-Year Estimates

Race

Area	White Alone[2] (%)	Black Alone[2] (%)	Asian Alone[2] (%)	AIAN[3] Alone[2] (%)	NHOPI[4] Alone[2] (%)	Other Race Alone[2] (%)	Two or More Races (%)
City	50.8	41.6	3.1	0.2	0.1	1.7	2.6
MSA[1]	71.1	23.0	1.6	0.3	0.1	1.4	2.5
U.S.	73.0	12.7	5.4	0.8	0.2	4.8	3.1

Note: (1) Figures cover the Little Rock-North Little Rock-Conway, AR Metropolitan Statistical Area—see Appendix B for areas included; (2) Alone is defined as not being in combination with one or more other races; (3) American Indian and Alaska Native; (4) Native Hawaiian and Other Pacific Islander
Source: U.S. Census Bureau, 2013-2017 American Community Survey 5-Year Estimates

Hispanic or Latino Origin

Area	Total (%)	Mexican (%)	Puerto Rican (%)	Cuban (%)	Other (%)
City	6.8	4.5	0.4	0.2	1.6
MSA[1]	5.1	3.6	0.3	0.1	1.1
U.S.	17.6	11.1	1.7	0.7	4.1

Note: Persons of Hispanic or Latino origin can be of any race; (1) Figures cover the Little Rock-North Little Rock-Conway, AR Metropolitan Statistical Area—see Appendix B for areas included
Source: U.S. Census Bureau, 2013-2017 American Community Survey 5-Year Estimates

Segregation

Type	Segregation Indices[1]				Percent Change		
	1990	2000	2010	2010 Rank[2]	1990-2000	1990-2010	2000-2010
Black/White	61.1	61.3	58.8	42	0.3	-2.3	-2.5
Asian/White	37.5	38.8	39.7	59	1.3	2.2	0.9
Hispanic/White	23.2	34.7	39.7	68	11.5	16.5	5.0

Note: All figures cover the Metropolitan Statistical Area—see Appendix B for areas included; Figures are based on an analysis of 1990, 2000, and 2010 Census Decennial Census tract data by William H. Frey, Brookings Institution and the University of Michigan Social Science Data Analysis Network. In this analysis all racial groups (whites, blacks, and asians) are non-Hispanic members of those races. Hispanics are shown as a separate category; (1) Segregation Indices are Dissimilarity Indices that measure the degree to which the minority group is distributed differently than whites across census tracts. They range from 0 (complete integration) to 100 (complete segregation) where the value indicates the percentage of the minority group that needs to move to be distributed exactly like whites; (2) Ranges from 1 (most segregated) to 102 (least segregated); n/a not available.
Source: www.CensusScope.org

Ancestry

Area	German	Irish	English	American	Italian	Polish	French[2]	Scottish	Dutch
City	7.8	7.4	7.7	5.9	1.6	1.0	1.9	1.8	0.6
MSA[1]	10.3	9.5	8.9	8.6	1.6	1.0	1.9	2.0	1.0
U.S.	14.1	10.1	7.5	6.6	5.3	2.9	2.5	1.7	1.3

Note: Figures are the percentage of the total population reporting a particular ancestry. The nine most commonly reported ancestries in the U.S. are shown. Figures include multiple ancestries (e.g. if a person reported being Irish and Italian, they were included in both columns); (1) Figures cover the Little Rock-North Little Rock-Conway, AR Metropolitan Statistical Area—see Appendix B for areas included; (2) Excludes Basque
Source: U.S. Census Bureau, 2013-2017 American Community Survey 5-Year Estimates

Foreign-Born Population

Area	Percent of Population Born in								
	Any Foreign Country	Asia	Mexico	Europe	Carribean	Central America[2]	South America	Africa	Canada
City	7.5	2.8	2.0	0.7	0.1	0.9	0.4	0.3	0.2
MSA[1]	4.1	1.4	1.3	0.5	0.1	0.5	0.2	0.2	0.1
U.S.	13.4	4.1	3.6	1.5	1.3	1.0	0.9	0.6	0.3

Note: (1) Figures cover the Little Rock-North Little Rock-Conway, AR Metropolitan Statistical Area—see Appendix B for areas included; (2) Excludes Mexico.
Source: U.S. Census Bureau, 2013-2017 American Community Survey 5-Year Estimates

Marital Status

Area	Never Married	Now Married[2]	Separated	Widowed	Divorced
City	37.3	41.2	2.7	5.8	13.1
MSA[1]	30.5	47.7	2.3	6.0	13.5
U.S.	33.1	48.2	2.0	5.8	10.9

Note: Figures are percentages and cover the population 15 years of age and older; (1) Figures cover the Little Rock-North Little Rock-Conway, AR Metropolitan Statistical Area—see Appendix B for areas included; (2) Excludes separated
Source: U.S. Census Bureau, 2013-2017 American Community Survey 5-Year Estimates

Disability by Age

Area	All Ages	Under 18 Years Old	18 to 64 Years Old	65 Years and Over
City	13.2	6.4	11.2	35.6
MSA[1]	15.2	6.1	13.2	40.0
U.S.	12.6	4.2	10.3	35.5

Note: Figures show percent of the civilian noninstitutionalized population that reported having a disability. Disability status is determined from six types of difficulty: vision, hearing, cognitive, ambulatory, self-care, and independent living. For children under 5 years old, hearing and vision difficulty are used to determine disability status. For children between the ages of 5 and 14, disability status is determined from hearing, vision, cognitive, ambulatory, and self-care difficulties. For people aged 15 years and older, they are considered to have a disability if they have difficulty with any one of the six difficulty types; Note: (1) Figures cover the Little Rock-North Little Rock-Conway, AR Metropolitan Statistical Area—see Appendix B for areas included
Source: U.S. Census Bureau, 2013-2017 American Community Survey 5-Year Estimates

Age

Area	Percent of Population										Median Age
	Under Age 5	Age 5–19	Age 20–34	Age 35–44	Age 45–54	Age 55–64	Age 65–74	Age 75–84	Age 85+	
City	6.5	19.5	22.4	13.3	12.0	13.0	7.8	3.4	2.0	36.0
MSA[1]	6.6	19.9	21.6	13.0	12.7	12.3	8.4	4.0	1.7	36.5
U.S.	6.2	19.5	20.7	12.7	13.4	12.7	8.6	4.4	1.9	37.8

Note: (1) Figures cover the Little Rock-North Little Rock-Conway, AR Metropolitan Statistical Area—see Appendix B for areas included
Source: U.S. Census Bureau, 2013-2017 American Community Survey 5-Year Estimates

Gender

Area	Males	Females	Males per 100 Females
City	95,087	102,693	92.6
MSA[1]	354,144	376,202	94.1
U.S.	158,018,753	162,985,654	97.0

Note: (1) Figures cover the Little Rock-North Little Rock-Conway, AR Metropolitan Statistical Area—see Appendix B for areas included
Source: U.S. Census Bureau, 2013-2017 American Community Survey 5-Year Estimates

Religious Groups by Family

Area	Catholic	Baptist	Non-Den.	Methodist[2]	Lutheran	LDS[3]	Pente-costal	Presby-terian[4]	Muslim[5]	Judaism
MSA[1]	4.5	25.9	6.1	7.3	0.5	0.9	2.9	0.9	0.1	0.1
U.S.	19.1	9.3	4.0	4.0	2.3	2.0	1.9	1.6	0.8	0.7

Note: Figures are the number of adherents as a percentage of the total population; (1) Figures cover the Little Rock-North Little Rock-Conway, AR Metropolitan Statistical Area—see Appendix B for areas included; (2) Methodist/Pietist; (3) Latter Day Saints; (4) Reformed; (5) Figures are estimates
Source: Association of Statisticians of American Religious Bodies, 2010 U.S. Religion Census: Religious Congregations & Membership Study

Religious Groups by Tradition

Area	Catholic	Evangelical Protestant	Mainline Protestant	Other Tradition	Black Protestant	Orthodox
MSA[1]	4.5	33.9	8.2	1.7	3.5	0.1
U.S.	19.1	16.2	7.3	4.3	1.6	0.3

Note: Figures are the number of adherents as a percentage of the total population; (1) Figures cover the Little Rock-North Little Rock-Conway, AR Metropolitan Statistical Area—see Appendix B for areas included
Source: Association of Statisticians of American Religious Bodies, 2010 U.S. Religion Census: Religious Congregations & Membership Study

ECONOMY

Gross Metropolitan Product

Area	2016	2017	2018	2019	Rank[2]
MSA[1]	38.0	39.3	40.6	42.5	74

Note: Figures are in billions of dollars; (1) Figures cover the Little Rock-North Little Rock-Conway, AR Metropolitan Statistical Area—see Appendix B for areas included; (2) Rank is based on 2017 data and ranges from 1 to 381
Source: U.S. Conference of Mayors, U.S. Metro Economies: Economic Growth & Full Employment, June 2018

Economic Growth

Area	2017-2018 (%)	2019-2020 (%)	2021-2022 (%)
MSA[1]	2.7	1.9	1.3

Note: Figures are real gross metropolitan product (GMP) growth rates and represent average annual percent change; (1) Figures cover the Little Rock-North Little Rock-Conway, AR Metropolitan Statistical Area—see Appendix B for areas included
Source: U.S. Conference of Mayors, U.S. Metro Economies: Economic Growth & Full Employment, June 2018

Metropolitan Area Exports

Area	2012	2013	2014	2015	2016	2017	Rank[2]
MSA[1]	2,418.9	2,497.5	2,463.5	1,777.5	1,871.0	2,146.1	93

Note: Figures are in millions of dollars; (1) Figures cover the Little Rock-North Little Rock-Conway, AR Metropolitan Statistical Area—see Appendix B for areas included; (2) Rank is based on 2017 data and ranges from 1 to 387
Source: U.S. Department of Commerce, International Trade Administration, Office of Trade and Economic Analysis, Industry and Analysis, Exports by Metropolitan Area, extracted March 25, 2019

Building Permits

Area	Single-Family			Multi-Family			Total		
	2016	2017	Pct. Chg.	2016	2017	Pct. Chg.	2016	2017	Pct. Chg.
City	330	592	79.4	501	508	1.4	831	1,100	32.4
MSA[1]	1,649	2,087	26.6	678	1,128	66.4	2,327	3,215	38.2
U.S.	750,800	820,000	9.2	455,800	462,000	1.4	1,206,600	1,282,000	6.2

Note: (1) Figures cover the Little Rock-North Little Rock-Conway, AR Metropolitan Statistical Area—see Appendix B for areas included; Figures represent new, privately-owned housing units authorized (unadjusted data); All permit data are based on estimates with imputation
Source: U.S. Census Bureau, Manufacturing, Mining, and Construction Statistics, Building Permits, 2016, 2017

Bankruptcy Filings

Area	Business Filings			Nonbusiness Filings		
	2017	2018	% Chg.	2017	2018	% Chg.
Pulaski County	29	24	-17.2	2,571	2,420	-5.9
U.S.	23,157	22,232	-4.0	765,863	751,186	-1.9

Note: Business filings include Chapter 7, Chapter 11, Chapter 12, and Chapter 13; Nonbusiness filings include Chapter 7, Chapter 11, and Chapter 13
Source: Administrative Office of the U.S. Courts, Business and Nonbusiness Bankruptcy, County Cases Commenced by Chapter of the Bankruptcy Code, During the 12-Month Period Ending December 31, 2017 and Business and Nonbusiness Bankruptcy, County Cases Commenced by Chapter of the Bankruptcy Code, During the 12-Month Period Ending December 31, 2018

Housing Vacancy Rates

Area	Gross Vacancy Rate[2] (%)			Year-Round Vacancy Rate[3] (%)			Rental Vacancy Rate[4] (%)			Homeowner Vacancy Rate[5] (%)		
	2016	2017	2018	2016	2017	2018	2016	2017	2018	2016	2017	2018
MSA[1]	11.8	10.3	10.5	11.8	10.0	10.2	12.2	11.3	10.9	2.4	2.0	1.8
U.S.	12.8	12.7	12.3	9.9	9.9	9.7	6.9	7.2	6.9	1.7	1.6	1.5

Note: (1) Figures cover the Little Rock-North Little Rock-Conway, AR Metropolitan Statistical Area—see Appendix B for areas included; (2) The percentage of the total housing inventory that is vacant; (3) The percentage of the housing inventory (excluding seasonal units) that is year-round vacant; (4) The percentage of rental inventory that is vacant for rent; (5) The percentage of homeowner inventory that is vacant for sale
Source: U.S. Census Bureau, Housing Vacancies and Homeownership Annual Statistics: 2016, 2017, 2018

INCOME

Income

Area	Per Capita ($)	Median Household ($)	Average Household ($)
City	32,719	48,463	77,254
MSA[1]	28,187	51,362	70,449
U.S.	31,177	57,652	81,283

Note: (1) Figures cover the Little Rock-North Little Rock-Conway, AR Metropolitan Statistical Area—see Appendix B for areas included
Source: U.S. Census Bureau, 2013-2017 American Community Survey 5-Year Estimates

Household Income Distribution

Area	Percent of Households Earning							
	Under $15,000	$15,000 -$24,999	$25,000 -$34,999	$35,000 -$49,999	$50,000 -$74,999	$75,000 -$99,999	$100,000 -$149,999	$150,000 and up
City	13.5	12.0	10.8	15.0	16.4	9.9	10.8	11.5
MSA[1]	12.3	10.8	11.1	14.4	18.7	11.8	12.6	8.2
U.S.	11.6	9.8	9.5	13.0	17.7	12.3	14.1	12.1

Note: (1) Figures cover the Little Rock-North Little Rock-Conway, AR Metropolitan Statistical Area—see Appendix B for areas included
Source: U.S. Census Bureau, 2013-2017 American Community Survey 5-Year Estimates

Poverty Rate

Area	All Ages	Under 18 Years Old	18 to 64 Years Old	65 Years and Over
City	17.8	25.3	16.6	9.2
MSA[1]	15.1	20.9	14.4	8.5
U.S.	14.6	20.3	13.7	9.3

Note: Figures are percentage of people whose income during the past 12 months was below the poverty level; (1) Figures cover the Little Rock-North Little Rock-Conway, AR Metropolitan Statistical Area—see Appendix B for areas included
Source: U.S. Census Bureau, 2013-2017 American Community Survey 5-Year Estimates

EMPLOYMENT

Labor Force and Employment

Area	Civilian Labor Force			Workers Employed		
	Dec. 2017	Dec. 2018	% Chg.	Dec. 2017	Dec. 2018	% Chg.
City	97,069	98,167	1.1	94,026	94,836	0.9
MSA[1]	353,050	355,941	0.8	341,315	344,269	0.9
U.S.	159,880,000	162,510,000	1.6	153,602,000	156,481,000	1.9

Note: Data is not seasonally adjusted and covers workers 16 years of age and older; (1) Figures cover the Little Rock-North Little Rock-Conway, AR Metropolitan Statistical Area—see Appendix B for areas included
Source: Bureau of Labor Statistics, Local Area Unemployment Statistics

Unemployment Rate

Area	2018											
	Jan.	Feb.	Mar.	Apr.	May	Jun.	Jul.	Aug.	Sep.	Oct.	Nov.	Dec.
City	3.8	3.8	3.7	3.4	3.3	3.6	3.4	3.2	3.2	3.1	3.1	3.4
MSA[1]	3.8	3.8	3.6	3.2	3.2	3.5	3.3	3.0	3.0	3.0	3.0	3.3
U.S.	4.5	4.4	4.1	3.7	3.6	4.2	4.1	3.9	3.6	3.5	3.5	3.7

Note: Data is not seasonally adjusted and covers workers 16 years of age and older; (1) Figures cover the Little Rock-North Little Rock-Conway, AR Metropolitan Statistical Area—see Appendix B for areas included
Source: Bureau of Labor Statistics, Local Area Unemployment Statistics

Average Wages

Occupation	$/Hr.	Occupation	$/Hr.
Accountants and Auditors	32.30	Maids and Housekeeping Cleaners	10.10
Automotive Mechanics	19.30	Maintenance and Repair Workers	16.10
Bookkeepers	18.30	Marketing Managers	60.80
Carpenters	18.20	Nuclear Medicine Technologists	35.60
Cashiers	10.50	Nurses, Licensed Practical	20.20
Clerks, General Office	15.20	Nurses, Registered	31.30
Clerks, Receptionists/Information	13.80	Nursing Assistants	13.00
Clerks, Shipping/Receiving	15.50	Packers and Packagers, Hand	10.70
Computer Programmers	36.60	Physical Therapists	38.90
Computer Systems Analysts	34.70	Postal Service Mail Carriers	24.90
Computer User Support Specialists	22.50	Real Estate Brokers	32.10
Cooks, Restaurant	11.50	Retail Salespersons	12.50
Dentists	83.50	Sales Reps., Exc. Tech./Scientific	28.20
Electrical Engineers	43.40	Sales Reps., Tech./Scientific	31.30
Electricians	20.70	Secretaries, Exc. Legal/Med./Exec.	16.20
Financial Managers	49.40	Security Guards	14.50
First-Line Supervisors/Managers, Sales	20.40	Surgeons	n/a
Food Preparation Workers	12.10	Teacher Assistants*	10.80
General and Operations Managers	43.70	Teachers, Elementary School*	25.30
Hairdressers/Cosmetologists	11.40	Teachers, Secondary School*	26.10
Internists, General	n/a	Telemarketers	10.90
Janitors and Cleaners	11.40	Truck Drivers, Heavy/Tractor-Trailer	22.40
Landscaping/Groundskeeping Workers	12.70	Truck Drivers, Light/Delivery Svcs.	16.00
Lawyers	46.40	Waiters and Waitresses	10.00

Note: Wage data covers the Little Rock-North Little Rock-Conway, AR Metropolitan Statistical Area—see Appendix B for areas included; (*) Hourly wages for elementary/secondary school teachers and teacher assistants were calculated by the editors from annual wage data based on a 40 hour work week; n/a not available.
Source: Bureau of Labor Statistics, Metro Area Occupational Employment & Wage Estimates, May 2018

Employment by Occupation

Occupation Classification	City (%)	MSA[1] (%)	U.S. (%)
Management, Business, Science, and Arts	43.7	38.4	37.4
Natural Resources, Construction, and Maintenance	5.5	8.6	8.9
Production, Transportation, and Material Moving	9.2	11.0	12.2
Sales and Office	25.0	25.4	23.5
Service	16.6	16.6	18.0

Note: Figures cover employed civilians 16 years of age and older; (1) Figures cover the Little Rock-North Little Rock-Conway, AR Metropolitan Statistical Area—see Appendix B for areas included
Source: U.S. Census Bureau, 2013-2017 American Community Survey 5-Year Estimates

Employment by Industry

Sector	MSA[1] Number of Employees	MSA[1] Percent of Total	U.S. Percent of Total
Construction, Mining, and Logging	16,400	4.5	5.3
Education and Health Services	57,400	15.7	15.9
Financial Activities	21,500	5.9	5.7
Government	71,900	19.7	15.1
Information	4,200	1.2	1.9
Leisure and Hospitality	35,100	9.6	10.7
Manufacturing	21,100	5.8	8.5
Other Services	15,700	4.3	3.9
Professional and Business Services	49,500	13.6	14.1
Retail Trade	40,000	11.0	10.8
Transportation, Warehousing, and Utilities	16,200	4.4	4.2
Wholesale Trade	16,000	4.4	3.9

Note: Figures are non-farm employment as of December 2018. Figures are not seasonally adjusted and include workers 16 years of age and older; (1) Figures cover the Little Rock-North Little Rock-Conway, AR Metropolitan Statistical Area—see Appendix B for areas included
Source: Bureau of Labor Statistics, Current Employment Statistics, Employment, Hours, and Earnings

Occupations with Greatest Projected Employment Growth: 2018 – 2020

Occupation[1]	2018 Employment	2020 Projected Employment	Numeric Employment Change	Percent Employment Change
Combined Food Preparation and Serving Workers, Including Fast Food	34,470	36,030	1,560	4.5
Heavy and Tractor-Trailer Truck Drivers	34,900	36,120	1,220	3.5
Laborers and Freight, Stock, and Material Movers, Hand	24,440	25,580	1,140	4.7
Personal Care Aides	16,820	17,860	1,040	6.2
Farmers, Ranchers, and Other Agricultural Managers	60,960	61,970	1,010	1.7
Registered Nurses	25,610	26,310	700	2.7
Janitors and Cleaners, Except Maids and Housekeeping Cleaners	19,080	19,770	690	3.6
General and Operations Managers	22,770	23,420	650	2.9
Customer Service Representatives	17,270	17,890	620	3.6
Helpers—Production Workers	8,680	9,300	620	7.1

Note: Projections cover Arkansas; (1) Sorted by numeric employment change
Source: www.projectionscentral.com, State Occupational Projections, 2018–2020 Short-Term Projections

Fastest Growing Occupations: 2018 – 2020

Occupation[1]	2018 Employment	2020 Projected Employment	Numeric Employment Change	Percent Employment Change
Insurance Claims and Policy Processing Clerks	1,900	2,090	190	10.0
Sewing Machine Operators	1,750	1,890	140	8.0
Operations Research Analysts	630	680	50	7.9
Agricultural Equipment Operators	1,020	1,100	80	7.8
Mixing and Blending Machine Setters, Operators, and Tenders	1,160	1,250	90	7.8
Farmworkers and Laborers, Crop, Nursery, and Greenhouse	6,830	7,350	520	7.6
Cargo and Freight Agents	930	1,000	70	7.5
Helpers—Production Workers	8,680	9,300	620	7.1
Information Security Analysts	1,900	2,030	130	6.8
Nurse Practitioners	1,900	2,030	130	6.8

Note: Projections cover Arkansas; (1) Sorted by percent employment change and excludes occupations with numeric employment change less than 50
Source: www.projectionscentral.com, State Occupational Projections, 2018–2020 Short-Term Projections

TAXES

State Corporate Income Tax Rates

State	Tax Rate (%)	Income Brackets ($)	Num. of Brackets	Financial Institution Tax Rate (%)[a]	Federal Income Tax Ded.
Arkansas	1.0 - 6.5	3,000 - 100,001	6	1.0 - 6.5	No

Note: Tax rates as of January 1, 2019; (a) Rates listed are the corporate income tax rate applied to financial institutions or excise taxes based on income. Some states have other taxes based upon the value of deposits or shares.
Source: Federation of Tax Administrators, Range of State Corporate Income Tax Rates, January 1, 2019

State Individual Income Tax Rates

State	Tax Rate (%)	Income Brackets ($)	Personal Exemptions ($)			Standard Ded. ($)	
			Single	Married	Depend.	Single	Married
Arkansas (a)	0.9 - 6.9 (f)	4,299 - 35,100	26	52 (c)	26 (c)	2,200	4,400

Note: Tax rates as of January 1, 2019; Local- and county-level taxes are not included; n/a not applicable; Federal income tax is not deductible on state income tax returns; (a) 19 states have statutory provision for automatically adjusting to the rate of inflation the dollar values of the income tax brackets, standard deductions, and/or personal exemptions. Michigan indexes the personal exemption only. Oregon does not index the income brackets for $125,000 and over; (c) The personal exemption takes the form of a tax credit instead of a deduction; (f) Arkansas has separate brackets for taxpayers with income under $75,000 and $21,000. The tax rates for lower income taxpayers are scheduled to decrease beginning in tax year 2019.
Source: Federation of Tax Administrators, State Individual Income Tax Rates, January 1, 2019

Various State Sales and Excise Tax Rates

State	State Sales Tax (%)	Gasoline[1] (¢/gal.)	Cigarette[2] ($/pack)	Spirits[3] ($/gal.)	Wine[4] ($/gal.)	Beer[5] ($/gal.)	Recreational Marijuana (%)
Arkansas	6.5	21.8	1.15	7.73 (i)(j)	1.44 (o)(p)	0.34 (s)(t)	Not legal

Note: All tax rates as of January 1, 2019; (1) The American Petroleum Institute has developed a methodology for determining the average tax rate on a gallon of fuel. Rates may include any of the following: excise taxes, environmental fees, storage tank fees, other fees or taxes, general sales tax, and local taxes. In states where gasoline is subject to the general sales tax, or where the fuel tax is based on the average sale price, the average rate determined by API is sensitive to changes in the price of gasoline. States that fully or partially apply general sales taxes to gasoline: CA, CO, GA, IL, IN, MI, NY; (2) The federal excise tax of $1.0066 per pack and local taxes are not included; (3) Rates are those applicable to off-premise sales of 40% alcohol by volume (a.b.v.) distilled spirits in 750ml containers. Local excise taxes are excluded; (4) Rates are those applicable to off-premise sales of 11% a.b.v. non-carbonated wine in 750ml containers; (5) Rates are those applicable to off-premise sales of 4.7% a.b.v. beer in 12 ounce containers; (i) Includes case fees and/or bottle fees which may vary with size of container; (j) Includes sales taxes specific to alcoholic beverages; (o) Includes case fees and/or bottle fees which may vary with size of container; (p) Includes sales taxes specific to alcoholic beverages; (s) Includes sales taxes specific to alcoholic beverages; (t) Includes case fees and/or bottle fees which may vary with the size of container.
Source: Tax Foundation, 2019 Facts & Figures: How Does Your State Compare?

State Business Tax Climate Index Rankings

State	Overall Rank	Corporate Tax Rank	Individual Income Tax Rank	Sales Tax Rank	Unemployment Insurance Tax Rank	Property Tax Rank
Arkansas	46	40	40	44	34	26

Note: The index is a measure of how each state's tax laws affect economic performance. The lower the rank, the more favorable a state's tax system is for business. States without a given tax are given a ranking of 1. The scores/rankings for the District of Columbia do not affect other states. The 2019 index represents the tax climate as of July 1, 2018.
Source: Tax Foundation, State Business Tax Climate Index 2019

COMMERCIAL UTILITIES

Typical Monthly Electric Bills

Area	Commercial Service ($/month)		Industrial Service ($/month)	
	1,500 kWh	40 kW demand 14,000 kWh	1,000 kW demand 200,000 kWh	50,000 kW demand 32,500,000 kWh
City	101	885	14,462	1,525,200
Average[1]	203	1,619	25,886	2,540,077

Note: Figures are based on annualized rates; (1) Average based on 187 utilities surveyed
Source: Edison Electric Institute, Typical Bills and Average Rates Report, Summer 2018

TRANSPORTATION

Means of Transportation to Work

Area	Car/Truck/Van		Public Transportation			Bicycle	Walked	Other Means	Worked at Home
	Drove Alone	Car-pooled	Bus	Subway	Railroad				
City	82.5	9.9	1.0	0.0	0.0	0.2	1.7	1.1	3.7
MSA[1]	84.1	9.6	0.5	0.0	0.0	0.2	1.3	1.0	3.3
U.S.	76.4	9.2	2.5	1.9	0.6	0.6	2.7	1.3	4.7

Note: Figures are percentages and cover workers 16 years of age and older; (1) Figures cover the Little Rock-North Little Rock-Conway, AR Metropolitan Statistical Area—see Appendix B for areas included
Source: U.S. Census Bureau, 2013-2017 American Community Survey 5-Year Estimates

Travel Time to Work

Area	Less Than 10 Minutes	10 to 19 Minutes	20 to 29 Minutes	30 to 44 Minutes	45 to 59 Minutes	60 to 89 Minutes	90 Minutes or More
City	13.5	43.1	28.6	10.6	1.9	1.1	1.2
MSA[1]	12.7	32.3	24.6	19.4	6.7	3.0	1.2
U.S.	12.7	28.9	20.9	20.5	8.1	6.2	2.7

Note: Note: Figures are percentages and include workers 16 years old and over; (1) Figures cover the Little Rock-North Little Rock-Conway, AR Metropolitan Statistical Area—see Appendix B for areas included
Source: U.S. Census Bureau, 2013-2017 American Community Survey 5-Year Estimates

Freeway Travel Time Index

Area	1985	1990	1995	2000	2005	2010	2014
Urban Area Rank[1,2]	91	94	93	86	86	76	81
Urban Area Index[1]	1.03	1.04	1.06	1.10	1.12	1.14	1.14
Average Index[3]	1.09	1.11	1.14	1.17	1.20	1.19	1.20

Note: Freeway Travel Time Index—the ratio of travel time in the peak period to the travel time at free-flow conditions. For example, a value of 1.30 indicates a 20-minute free-flow trip takes 26 minutes in the peak (20 minutes x 1.30 = 26 minutes); (1) Covers the Little Rock AR urban area; (2) Rank is based on 101 urban areas (#1 = highest travel time index); (3) Average of 101 urban areas
Source: Texas Transportation Institute, 2015 Urban Mobility Scorecard, August 2015

Freeway Commuter Stress Index

Area	1985	1990	1995	2000	2005	2010	2014
Urban Area Rank[1,2]	81	84	88	85	81	74	79
Urban Area Index[1]	1.06	1.08	1.10	1.13	1.16	1.17	1.17
Average Index[3]	1.13	1.16	1.19	1.22	1.25	1.24	1.25

Note: The Freeway Commuter Stress Index is the same as the Freeway Travel Time Index (see table above) except that it includes only the travel in the peak directions during the peak periods; the TTI includes travel in all directions during the peak period. Thus, the CSI is more indicative of the work trip experienced by each commuter on a daily basis; (1) Covers the Little Rock AR urban area; (2) Rank is based on 101 urban areas (#1 = highest travel time index); (3) Average of 101 urban areas
Source: Texas Transportation Institute, 2015 Urban Mobility Scorecard, August 2015

Public Transportation

Agency Name / Mode of Transportation	Vehicles Operated in Maximum Service[1]	Annual Unlinked Passenger Trips[2] (in thous.)	Annual Passenger Miles[3] (in thous.)
Central Arkansas Transit Authority (CATA)			
Bus (directly operated)	49	2,358.4	11,341.5
Demand Response (directly operated)	21	90.5	718.5
Streetcar Rail (directly operated)	3	95.1	244.9

Note: (1) The number of revenue vehicles operated by the given mode and type of service to meet the annual maximum service requirement. This is the revenue vehicle count during the peak season of the year; on the week and day that maximum service is provided. Vehicles operated in maximum service (VOMS) exclude atypical days and one-time special events; (2) The number of passengers who boarded public transportation vehicles. Passengers are counted each time they board a vehicle no matter how many vehicles they use to travel from their origin to their destination. (3) The sum of the distances ridden by all passengers during the entire fiscal year.
Source: Federal Transit Administration, National Transit Database, 2017

Air Transportation

Airport Name and Code / Type of Service	Passenger Airlines[1]	Passenger Enplanements	Freight Carriers[2]	Freight (lbs)
Little Rock National Airport (LIT)				
Domestic service (U.S. carriers - 2018)	20	1,031,053	13	13,581,794
International service (U.S. carriers - 2017)	0	0	4	43,959

Note: (1) Includes all U.S.-based major, minor and commuter airlines that carried at least one passenger during the year; (2) Includes all U.S.-based airlines and freight carriers that transported at least one pound of freight during the year.
Source: Bureau of Transportation Statistics, The Intermodal Transportation Database, Air Carriers: T-100 Domestic Market (U.S. Carriers), 2018; Bureau of Transportation Statistics, The Intermodal Transportation Database, Air Carriers: T-100 International Market (U.S. Carriers), 2017

Other Transportation Statistics

Major Highways:	I-30; I-40
Amtrak Service:	Yes
Major Waterways/Ports:	David D. Terry Lake

Source: Amtrak.com; Google Maps

BUSINESSES

Major Business Headquarters

Company Name	Industry	Rankings	
		Fortune[1]	Forbes[2]
Dillard's	General Merchandisers	439	-
Windstream Holdings	Telecommunications	474	-

Note: (1) Companies that produce a 10-K are ranked 1 to 500 based on 2017 revenue; (2) All private companies with at least $2 billion in annual revenue through the end of their most current fiscal year are ranked 1 to 229; companies listed are headquartered in the city; dashes indicate no ranking
Source: Fortune, "Fortune 500," June 2018; Forbes, "America's Largest Private Companies," 2018 Rankings

Fast-Growing Businesses

According to *Fortune*, Little Rock is home to one of the 100 fastest-growing companies in the world: **Bank OZK** (#85). Companies were ranked by their revenue growth rate; their EPS growth rate; and their three-year annualized total return to investors for the period ending June 30, 2018. Criteria for inclusion: a company, foreign or domestic, must trade on a major U.S. stock exchange; must file quarterly reports with the SEC; must have a minimum market capitalization of $250 million; must have a stock price of at least $5 on June 30, 2018; must have been trading continuously since June 30, 2015; must have revenue and net income for the four quarters ended on or before April 30, 2018, of at least $50 million and $10 million, respectively; and must have posted a compound annual growth in revenue and earnings per share of at least 15% annually over the three years ending on or before April 30, 2018. Real estate investment trusts, limited-liability companies, limited parterships, business development companies, closed-end investment firms, companies about to be acquired, and companies that lost money in the quarter ending April 30, 2018 were excluded. *Fortune, "100 Fastest-Growing Companies," 2018*

According to *Initiative for a Competitive Inner City (ICIC)*, Little Rock is home to one of America's 100 fastest-growing "inner city" companies: **Team SI** (#56). Criteria for inclusion: company must be headquartered in or have 51 percent or more of its physical operations in an economically distressed urban area; must be an independent, for-profit corporation, partnership or proprietorship; must have 10 or more employees and have a five-year sales history that includes sales of at least $200,000 in the base year and at least $1 million in the current year with no decrease in sales over the two most recent years. Companies were ranked overall by revenue growth over the five-year period between 2013 and 2017. *Initiative for a Competitive Inner City (ICIC), "Inner City 100 Companies," 2018*

Minority- and Women-Owned Businesses

Group	All Firms		Firms with Paid Employees			
	Firms	Sales ($000)	Firms	Sales ($000)	Employees	Payroll ($000)
AIAN[1]	146	12,532	25	9,855	103	4,700
Asian	661	641,144	262	623,037	2,252	75,888
Black	4,180	230,893	254	160,948	1,785	37,032
Hispanic	632	142,238	63	121,498	888	18,975
NHOPI[2]	26	(s)	0	(s)	0 - 19	(s)
Women	7,174	972,045	958	852,140	6,026	191,780
All Firms	20,934	42,281,113	6,235	41,457,610	131,640	6,069,077

Note: Figures cover firms located in the city; minority- and women-owned business are defined as firms in which the corresponding group own 51% or more of the stock or equity of the company; (1) American Indian and Alaska Native; (2) Native Hawaiian and Other Pacific Islander; (s) estimates are suppressed when publication standards are not met
Source: U.S. Census Bureau, 2012 Economic Census, Survey of Business Owners

HOTELS & CONVENTION CENTERS

Hotels, Motels and Vacation Rentals

Area	5 Star		4 Star		3 Star		2 Star		1 Star		Not Rated	
	Num.	Pct.[3]	Num.	Pct.[3]	Num.	Pct.[3]	Num.	Pct.[3]	Num.	Pct.[3]	Num.	Pct.[3]
City[1]	0	0.0	3	1.3	44	19.0	96	41.6	1	0.4	87	37.7
Total[2]	286	0.4	5,236	7.1	16,715	22.6	10,259	13.9	293	0.4	41,056	55.6

Note: (1) Figures cover Little Rock and vicinity; (2) Figures cover all 100 cities in this book; (3) Percentage of hotels which have a given star rating; Star ratings are determined by expedia.com and offer an indication of the general quality of a particular hotel.
Source: www.expedia.com, April 3, 2019

Major Convention Centers

Name	Overall Space (sq. ft.)	Exhibit Space (sq. ft.)	Meeting Space (sq. ft.)	Meeting Rooms
Alltell Arena	370,000	n/a	28,000	n/a
Statehouse Convention Center	220,000	n/a	n/a	n/a

Note: Table includes convention centers located in the Little Rock-North Little Rock-Conway, AR metro area; n/a not available
Source: Original research

Living Environment

COST OF LIVING

Cost of Living Index

Composite Index	Groceries	Housing	Utilities	Trans- portation	Health Care	Misc. Goods/ Services
97.4	94.9	88.9	95.5	98.8	87.2	107.0

Note: The Cost of Living Index measures regional differences in the cost of consumer goods and services, excluding taxes and non-consumer expenditures, for professional and managerial households in the top income quintile. It is based on more than 50,000 prices covering almost 60 different items for which prices are collected three times a year by chambers of commerce, economic development organizations or university applied economic centers in each participating urban area. The numbers shown should be read as a percentage above or below the national average of 100. For example, a value of 115.4 in the groceries column indicates that grocery prices are 15.4% higher than the national average. Small differences in the index numbers should not be interpreted as significant; Figures cover the Little Rock-North Little Rock AR urban area.
Source: The Council for Community and Economic Research, ACCRA Cost of Living Index, 2018

Grocery Prices

Area[1]	T-Bone Steak ($/pound)	Frying Chicken ($/pound)	Whole Milk ($/half gal.)	Eggs ($/dozen)	Orange Juice ($/64 oz.)	Coffee ($/11.5 oz.)
City[2]	9.69	1.26	2.16	1.52	3.36	4.04
Avg.	11.35	1.42	1.94	1.81	3.52	4.35
Min.	7.45	0.92	0.80	0.75	2.72	3.06
Max.	15.05	2.76	4.18	4.00	5.36	8.20

*Note: (1) Values for the local area are compared with the average, minimum and maximum values for all 291 areas in the Cost of Living Index; (2) Figures cover the Little Rock-North Little Rock AR urban area; **T-Bone Steak** (price per pound); **Frying Chicken** (price per pound, whole fryer); **Whole Milk** (half gallon carton); **Eggs** (price per dozen, Grade A, large); **Orange Juice** (64 oz. Tropicana or Florida Natural); **Coffee** (11.5 oz. can, vacuum-packed, Maxwell House, Hills Bros, or Folgers).*
Source: The Council for Community and Economic Research, ACCRA Cost of Living Index, 2018

Housing and Utility Costs

Area[1]	New Home Price ($)	Apartment Rent ($/month)	All Electric ($/month)	Part Electric ($/month)	Other Energy ($/month)	Telephone ($/month)
City[2]	339,778	730	-	90.31	59.65	184.40
Avg.	347,000	1,087	165.93	100.16	67.73	178.70
Min.	200,468	500	93.58	25.64	26.78	163.10
Max.	1,901,222	4,888	388.65	246.86	332.81	197.70

*Note: (1) Values for the local area are compared with the average, minimum and maximum values for all 291 areas in the Cost of Living Index; (2) Figures cover the Little Rock-North Little Rock AR urban area; **New Home Price** (2,400 sf living area, 8,000 sf lot, in urban area with full utilities); **Apartment Rent** (950 sf 2 bedroom/1.5 or 2 bath, unfurnished, excluding all utilities except water); **All Electric** (average monthly cost for an all-electric home); **Part Electric** (average monthly cost for a part-electric home); **Other Energy** (average monthly cost for natural gas, fuel oil, coal, wood, and any other forms of energy except electricity); **Telephone** (price includes the base monthly rate plus taxes and fees for three lines of mobile phone service).*
Source: The Council for Community and Economic Research, ACCRA Cost of Living Index, 2018

Health Care, Transportation, and Other Costs

Area[1]	Doctor ($/visit)	Dentist ($/visit)	Optometrist ($/visit)	Gasoline ($/gallon)	Beauty Salon ($/visit)	Men's Shirt ($)
City[2]	114.28	69.92	74.89	2.46	41.43	41.64
Avg.	110.71	95.11	103.74	2.61	37.48	32.03
Min.	33.60	62.55	54.63	1.89	17.00	11.44
Max.	195.97	153.93	225.79	3.59	71.88	58.64

*Note: (1) Values for the local area are compared with the average, minimum and maximum values for all 291 areas in the Cost of Living Index; (2) Figures cover the Little Rock-North Little Rock AR urban area; **Doctor** (general practitioners routine exam of an established patient); **Dentist** (adult teeth cleaning and periodic oral examination); **Optometrist** (full vision eye exam for established adult patient); **Gasoline** (one gallon regular unleaded, national brand, including all taxes, cash price at self-service pump if available); **Beauty Salon** (woman's shampoo, trim, and blow-dry); **Men's Shirt** (cotton/polyester dress shirt, pinpoint weave, long sleeves).*
Source: The Council for Community and Economic Research, ACCRA Cost of Living Index, 2018

HOUSING

House Price Index (HPI)

Area	National Ranking[2]	Quarterly Change (%)	One-Year Change (%)	Five-Year Change (%)
MSA[1]	227	2.46	1.86	12.54
U.S.[3]	–	1.12	5.73	32.81

Note: The HPI is a weighted repeat sales index. It measures average price changes in repeat sales or refinancings on the same properties. This information is obtained by reviewing repeat mortgage transactions on single-family properties whose mortgages have been purchased or securitized by Fannie Mae or Freddie Mac in January 1975; (1) Figures cover the Little Rock-North Little Rock-Conway, AR Metropolitan Statistical Area—see Appendix B for areas included; (2) Rankings are based on annual percentage change for all metro areas containing at least 15,000 transactions over the last 10 years and ranges from 1 to 245; (3) figures based on a weighted average of Census Division estimates using a seasonally adjusted, purchase-only index; all figures are for the period ending December 31, 2018
Source: Federal Housing Finance Agency, House Price Index, February 26, 2019

Median Single-Family Home Prices

Area	2016	2017	2018p	Percent Change 2017 to 2018
MSA[1]	137.8	141.7	146.4	3.3
U.S. Average	235.5	248.8	261.6	5.1

Note: Figures are median sales prices of existing single-family homes in thousands of dollars; (p) preliminary; (1) Figures cover the Little Rock-North Little Rock-Conway, AR Metropolitan Statistical Area—see Appendix B for areas included
Source: National Association of Realtors, Median Sales Price of Existing Single-Family Homes for Metropolitan Areas, 4th Quarter 2018

Qualifying Income Based on Median Sales Price of Existing Single-Family Homes

Area	With 5% Down ($)	With 10% Down ($)	With 20% Down ($)
MSA[1]	35,631	33,756	30,005
U.S. Average	62,954	59,640	53,013

Note: Figures are preliminary; Qualifying income is based on a mortgage rate of 4.9%. Monthly principal and interest payment is limited to 25% of income; (1) Figures cover the Little Rock-North Little Rock-Conway, AR Metropolitan Statistical Area—see Appendix B for areas included
Source: National Association of Realtors, Qualifying Income Based on Median Sales Price of Existing Single-Family Homes for Metropolitan Areas, 4th Quarter 2018

Median Apartment Condo-Coop Home Prices

Area	2016	2017	2018p	Percent Change 2017 to 2018
MSA[1]	n/a	n/a	n/a	n/a
U.S. Average	220.7	234.3	241.0	2.9

Note: Figures are median sales prices of existing apartment condo-coop homes in thousands of dollars; (p) preliminary; n/a not available; (1) Figures cover the Little Rock-North Little Rock-Conway, AR Metropolitan Statistical Area—see Appendix B for areas included
Source: National Association of Realtors, Median Sales Price of Existing Apartment Condo-Coop Homes for Metropolitan Areas, 4th Quarter 2018

Home Value Distribution

Area	Under $50,000	$50,000 -$99,999	$100,000 -$149,999	$150,000 -$199,999	$200,000 -$299,999	$300,000 -$499,999	$500,000 -$999,999	$1,000,000 or more
City	7.4	20.3	18.3	16.8	16.2	14.0	5.4	1.6
MSA[1]	9.2	19.3	23.3	19.0	16.8	8.9	2.7	0.8
U.S.	8.3	13.9	14.7	14.6	18.7	17.3	9.7	2.7

Note: Figures are percentages and cover owner-occupied housing units; (1) Figures cover the Little Rock-North Little Rock-Conway, AR Metropolitan Statistical Area—see Appendix B for areas included
Source: U.S. Census Bureau, 2013-2017 American Community Survey 5-Year Estimates

Homeownership Rate

Area	2010 (%)	2011 (%)	2012 (%)	2013 (%)	2014 (%)	2015 (%)	2016 (%)	2017 (%)	2018 (%)
MSA[1]	n/a	n/a	n/a	n/a	n/a	65.8	64.9	61.0	62.2
U.S.	66.9	66.1	65.4	65.1	64.5	63.7	63.4	63.9	64.4

Note: (1) Figures cover the Little Rock-North Little Rock-Conway, AR Metropolitan Statistical Area—see Appendix B for areas included
Source: U.S. Census Bureau, Housing Vacancies and Homeownership Annual Statistics: 2010-2018

Year Housing Structure Built

Area	2010 or Later	2000 -2009	1990 -1999	1980 -1989	1970 -1979	1960 -1969	1950 -1959	1940 -1949	Before 1940	Median Year
City	3.7	11.1	13.3	17.2	19.8	13.9	9.4	4.7	6.9	1978
MSA[1]	6.3	18.8	18.0	15.1	17.6	10.5	6.9	3.2	3.6	1985
U.S.	3.2	14.5	14.0	13.6	15.5	10.8	10.5	5.1	12.9	1977

Note: Figures are percentages except for Median Year; Note: (1) Figures cover the Little Rock-North Little Rock-Conway, AR Metropolitan Statistical Area—see Appendix B for areas included
Source: U.S. Census Bureau, 2013-2017 American Community Survey 5-Year Estimates

Gross Monthly Rent

Area	Under $500	$500 -$999	$1,000 -$1,499	$1,500 -$1,999	$2,000 -$2,499	$2,500 -$2,999	$3,000 and up	Median ($)
City	9.7	60.1	25.0	3.3	1.1	0.3	0.4	842
MSA[1]	10.7	63.6	21.6	3.1	0.6	0.2	0.3	805
U.S.	10.5	41.1	28.7	11.7	4.5	1.8	1.7	982

Note: Figures are percentages except for Median; Gross rent is the contract rent plus the estimated average monthly cost of utilities (electricity, gas, and water and sewer) and fuels (oil, coal, kerosene, wood, etc.) if these are paid by the renter (or paid for the renter by someone else); (1) Figures cover the Little Rock-North Little Rock-Conway, AR Metropolitan Statistical Area—see Appendix B for areas included
Source: U.S. Census Bureau, 2013-2017 American Community Survey 5-Year Estimates

HEALTH

Health Risk Factors

Category	MSA[1] (%)	U.S. (%)
Adults aged 18–64 who have any kind of health care coverage	85.8	87.3
Adults who reported being in good or better health	76.7	82.4
Adults who have been told they have high blood cholesterol	37.3	33.0
Adults who have been told they have high blood pressure	39.8	32.3
Adults who are current smokers	24.8	17.1
Adults who currently use E-cigarettes	9.1	4.6
Adults who currently use chewing tobacco, snuff, or snus	5.2	4.0
Adults who are heavy drinkers[2]	6.1	6.3
Adults who are binge drinkers[3]	18.2	17.4
Adults who are overweight (BMI 25.0 - 29.9)	31.2	35.3
Adults who are obese (BMI 30.0 - 99.8)	35.4	31.3
Adults who participated in any physical activities in the past month	69.3	74.4
Adults who always or nearly always wears a seat belt	95.2	94.3

Note: (1) Figures cover the Little Rock-North Little Rock-Conway, AR Metropolitan Statistical Area—see Appendix B for areas included; (2) Heavy drinkers are classified as adult men having more than 14 drinks per week and adult women having more than 7 drinks per week; (3) Binge drinkers are classified as males having five or more drinks on one occasion or females having four or more drinks on one occasion
Source: Centers for Disease Control and Prevention, Behaviorial Risk Factor Surveillance System, SMART: Selected Metropolitan Area Risk Trends, 2017

Acute and Chronic Health Conditions

Category	MSA[1] (%)	U.S. (%)
Adults who have ever been told they had a heart attack	4.9	4.2
Adults who have ever been told they have angina or coronary heart disease	5.3	3.9
Adults who have ever been told they had a stroke	3.5	3.0
Adults who have ever been told they have asthma	16.1	14.2
Adults who have ever been told they have arthritis	27.5	24.9
Adults who have ever been told they have diabetes[2]	11.1	10.5
Adults who have ever been told they had skin cancer	7.5	6.2
Adults who have ever been told they had any other types of cancer	8.3	7.1
Adults who have ever been told they have COPD	7.0	6.5
Adults who have ever been told they have kidney disease	4.0	3.0
Adults who have ever been told they have a form of depression	23.3	20.5

Note: (1) Figures cover the Little Rock-North Little Rock-Conway, AR Metropolitan Statistical Area—see Appendix B for areas included; (2) Figures do not include pregnancy-related, borderline, or pre-diabetes
Source: Centers for Disease Control and Prevention, Behaviorial Risk Factor Surveillance System, SMART: Selected Metropolitan Area Risk Trends, 2017

Health Screening and Vaccination Rates

Category	MSA[1] (%)	U.S. (%)
Adults aged 65+ who have had flu shot within the past year	61.5	60.7
Adults aged 65+ who have ever had a pneumonia vaccination	76.1	75.4
Adults who have ever been tested for HIV	40.0	36.1
Adults who have ever had the shingles or zoster vaccine?	32.4	28.9
Adults who have had their blood cholesterol checked within the last five years	83.3	85.9

Note: n/a not available; (1) Figures cover the Little Rock-North Little Rock-Conway, AR Metropolitan Statistical Area—see Appendix B for areas included.
Source: Centers for Disease Control and Prevention, Behaviorial Risk Factor Surveillance System, SMART: Selected Metropolitan Area Risk Trends, 2017

Disability Status

Category	MSA[1] (%)	U.S. (%)
Adults who reported being deaf	7.3	6.7
Are you blind or have serious difficulty seeing, even when wearing glasses?	5.9	4.5
Are you limited in any way in any of your usual activities due of arthritis?	16.7	12.9
Do you have difficulty doing errands alone?	9.5	6.8
Do you have difficulty dressing or bathing?	4.8	3.6
Do you have serious difficulty concentrating/remembering/making decisions?	14.0	10.7
Do you have serious difficulty walking or climbing stairs?	18.7	13.6

Note: (1) Figures cover the Little Rock-North Little Rock-Conway, AR Metropolitan Statistical Area—see Appendix B for areas included.
Source: Centers for Disease Control and Prevention, Behaviorial Risk Factor Surveillance System, SMART: Selected Metropolitan Area Risk Trends, 2017

Mortality Rates for the Top 10 Causes of Death in the U.S.

ICD-10[a] Sub-Chapter	ICD-10[a] Code	Age-Adjusted Mortality Rate[1] per 100,000 population	
		County[2]	U.S.
Malignant neoplasms	C00-C97	166.5	155.5
Ischaemic heart diseases	I20-I25	123.7	94.8
Other forms of heart disease	I30-I51	51.0	52.9
Chronic lower respiratory diseases	J40-J47	41.3	41.0
Cerebrovascular diseases	I60-I69	45.6	37.5
Other degenerative diseases of the nervous system	G30-G31	70.4	35.0
Other external causes of accidental injury	W00-X59	29.6	33.7
Organic, including symptomatic, mental disorders	F01-F09	19.8	31.0
Hypertensive diseases	I10-I15	27.6	21.9
Diabetes mellitus	E10-E14	20.5	21.2

Note: (a) ICD-10 = International Classification of Diseases 10th Revision; (1) Mortality rates are a three year average covering 2015-2017; (2) Figures cover Pulaski County.
Source: Centers for Disease Control and Prevention, National Center for Health Statistics. Underlying Cause of Death 1999-2017 on CDC WONDER Online Database

Mortality Rates for Selected Causes of Death

ICD-10[a] Sub-Chapter	ICD-10[a] Code	Age-Adjusted Mortality Rate[1] per 100,000 population	
		County[2]	U.S.
Assault	X85-Y09	16.8	5.9
Diseases of the liver	K70-K76	15.8	14.1
Human immunodeficiency virus (HIV) disease	B20-B24	3.0	1.8
Influenza and pneumonia	J09-J18	16.1	14.3
Intentional self-harm	X60-X84	16.2	13.6
Malnutrition	E40-E46	3.6	1.6
Obesity and other hyperalimentation	E65-E68	3.4	2.1
Renal failure	N17-N19	19.4	13.0
Transport accidents	V01-V99	14.4	12.4
Viral hepatitis	B15-B19	1.3	1.6

Note: (a) ICD-10 = International Classification of Diseases 10th Revision; (1) Mortality rates are a three year average covering 2015-2017; (2) Figures cover Pulaski County; Data are suppressed when the data meet the criteria for confidentiality constraints; Mortality rates are flagged as unreliable when the rate would be calculated with a numerator of 20 or less.
Source: Centers for Disease Control and Prevention, National Center for Health Statistics. Underlying Cause of Death 1999-2017 on CDC WONDER Online Database

Health Insurance Coverage

Area	With Health Insurance	With Private Health Insurance	With Public Health Insurance	Without Health Insurance	Population Under Age 18 Without Health Insurance
City	89.0	65.1	34.8	11.0	5.7
MSA[1]	90.4	66.7	36.4	9.6	4.9
U.S.	89.5	67.2	33.8	10.5	5.7

Note: Figures are percentages that cover the civilian noninstitutionalized population; (1) Figures cover the Little Rock-North Little Rock-Conway, AR Metropolitan Statistical Area—see Appendix B for areas included
Source: U.S. Census Bureau, 2013-2017 American Community Survey 5-Year Estimates

Number of Medical Professionals

Area	MDs[3]	DOs[3,4]	Dentists	Podiatrists	Chiropractors	Optometrists
County[1] (number)	2,874	65	287	19	83	79
County[1] (rate[2])	730.0	16.5	72.9	4.8	21.1	20.1
U.S. (rate[2])	279.3	23.0	68.4	6.0	27.1	16.2

Note: Data as of 2017 unless noted; (1) Data covers Pulaski County; (2) Rate per 100,000 population; (3) Data as of 2016 and includes all active, non-federal physicians; (4) Doctor of Osteopathic Medicine
Source: U.S. Department of Health and Human Services, Health Resources and Services Administration, Bureau of Health Professions, Area Resource File (ARF) 2017-2018

Best Hospitals

According to *U.S. News,* the Little Rock-North Little Rock-Conway, AR metro area is home to one of the best children's hospitals in the U.S.: **Arkansas Children's Hospital** (4 pediatric specialties). The hospital listed was highly ranked in at least one of 10 pediatric specialties. Eighty-six children's hospitals in the U.S. were nationally ranked in at least one specialty. Hospitals received points for being ranked in a specialty, and the 10 hospitals with the most points across the 10 specialties make up the Honor Roll. *U.S. News Online, "America's Best Children's Hospitals 2018-19"*

EDUCATION

Public School District Statistics

District Name	Schls	Pupils	Pupil/ Teacher Ratio	Minority Pupils[1] (%)	Free Lunch Eligible[2] (%)	IEP[3] (%)
Arkansas Virtual Academy	3	2,092	37.6	20.7	32.1	12.8
Lisa Academy Charter	6	2,041	14.6	75.2	18.9	7.4
Little Rock School District	47	24,383	12.8	82.3	24.7	13.3
Pulaski Co. Special SD	25	12,926	13.9	56.5	19.1	14.2

Note: Table includes school districts with 2,000 or more students; (1) Percentage of students that are not non-Hispanic white; (2) Percentage of students that are eligible for the free lunch program; (3) Percentage of students that have an Individualized Education Program.
Source: U.S. Department of Education, National Center for Education Statistics, Common Core of Data, Local Education Agency (School District) Universe Survey: School Year 2016-2017; U.S. Department of Education, National Center for Education Statistics, Common Core of Data, Public Elementary/Secondary School Universe Survey: School Year 2016-2017

Highest Level of Education

Area	Less than H.S.	H.S. Diploma	Some College, No Deg.	Associate Degree	Bachelor's Degree	Master's Degree	Prof. School Degree	Doctorate Degree
City	8.7	22.5	22.8	5.7	24.0	9.8	3.8	2.7
MSA[1]	9.8	29.4	23.7	7.3	18.8	7.4	2.0	1.5
U.S.	12.7	27.3	20.8	8.3	19.1	8.4	2.0	1.4

Note: Figures cover persons age 25 and over; (1) Figures cover the Little Rock-North Little Rock-Conway, AR Metropolitan Statistical Area—see Appendix B for areas included
Source: U.S. Census Bureau, 2013-2017 American Community Survey 5-Year Estimates

Educational Attainment by Race

Area	High School Graduate or Higher (%)					Bachelor's Degree or Higher (%)				
	Total	White	Black	Asian	Hisp.[2]	Total	White	Black	Asian	Hisp.[2]
City	91.3	94.0	88.2	94.3	60.5	40.3	52.9	20.7	74.8	10.8
MSA[1]	90.2	91.4	87.4	88.5	67.2	29.7	31.9	20.8	58.1	11.9
U.S.	87.3	89.3	84.9	86.5	66.7	30.9	32.2	20.6	52.7	15.2

Note: Figures shown cover persons 25 years old and over; (1) Figures cover the Little Rock-North Little Rock-Conway, AR Metropolitan Statistical Area—see Appendix B for areas included; (2) People of Hispanic origin can be of any race
Source: U.S. Census Bureau, 2013-2017 American Community Survey 5-Year Estimates

School Enrollment by Grade and Control

Area	Preschool (%)		Kindergarten (%)		Grades 1 - 4 (%)		Grades 5 - 8 (%)		Grades 9 - 12 (%)	
	Public	Private	Public	Private	Public	Private	Public	Private	Public	Private
City	49.9	50.1	76.6	23.4	83.4	16.6	78.1	21.9	79.4	20.6
MSA[1]	59.8	40.2	86.1	13.9	89.4	10.6	87.0	13.0	87.2	12.8
U.S.	58.8	41.2	87.7	12.3	89.7	10.3	89.6	10.4	90.3	9.7

Note: Figures shown cover persons 3 years old and over; (1) Figures cover the Little Rock-North Little Rock-Conway, AR Metropolitan Statistical Area—see Appendix B for areas included
Source: U.S. Census Bureau, 2013-2017 American Community Survey 5-Year Estimates

Average Salaries of Public School Classroom Teachers

Area	2016		2017		Change from 2016 to 2017	
	Dollars	Rank[1]	Dollars	Rank[1]	Percent	Rank[2]
Arkansas	48,218	39	48,304	42	0.2	47
U.S. Average	58,479	–	59,660	–	2.0	–

Note: (1) Rank ranges from 1 to 51 where 1 indicates highest salary; (2) Rank ranges from 1 to 51 where 1 indicates highest percent change.
Source: National Education Association, Rankings & Estimates: Rankings of the States 2017 and Estimates of School Statistics 2018

Higher Education

Four-Year Colleges			Two-Year Colleges			Medical Schools[1]	Law Schools[2]	Voc/ Tech[3]
Public	Private Non-profit	Private For-profit	Public	Private Non-profit	Private For-profit			
2	2	2	0	2	0	1	1	5

Note: Figures cover institutions located within the city limits and include main campuses only; (1) includes schools accredited by the Liaison Committee on Medical Education and the American Osteopathic Association's Commission on Osteopathic College Accreditation; (2) includes ABA-accredited schools, schools with provisional ABA accreditation, and state accredited schools; (3) includes all schools with programs that are less than 2 years.
Source: National Center for Education Statistics, Integrated Postsecondary Education System (IPEDS), 2017-18; Wikipedia, List of Medical Schools in the United States, accessed April 3, 2019; Wikipedia, List of Law Schools in the United States, accessed April 3, 2019

According to *U.S. News & World Report,* the Little Rock-North Little Rock-Conway, AR metro area is home to one of the best liberal arts colleges in the U.S.: **Hendrix College** (#76 tie). The indicators used to capture academic quality fall into a number of categories: assessment by administrators at peer institutions; retention of students; faculty resources; student selectivity; financial resources; alumni giving; high school counselor ratings of colleges; and graduation rate. *U.S. News & World Report, "America's Best Colleges 2019"*

PRESIDENTIAL ELECTION

2016 Presidential Election Results

Area	Clinton	Trump	Johnson	Stein	Other
Pulaski County	56.1	38.3	2.7	1.0	1.9
U.S.	48.0	45.9	3.3	1.1	1.7

Note: Results are percentages and may not add to 100% due to rounding
Source: Dave Leip's Atlas of U.S. Presidential Elections

EMPLOYERS

Major Employers

Company Name	Industry
Arkansas Blue Cross and Blue Shield	Hospitals and medical service plans
Arkansas Childrens Hospital	Specialty hospitals, except psychiatric
Baptist Health Systems	General medical & surgical hospitals
Dassault Falcon Jet Corp	Aviation and or aeronautical engineering
Dept of Highway and Trans Arkansas	Regulation, administration of transportation
Dept of Finance & Admin Arkansas	Finance, taxation, and monetary policy
Fidelity Information Systems	Data processing services
Loreal USA	Toilet preparations
Mountaire Farms	Broiler, fryer and roaster chickens
Pulaski County	General practice, attorney
St. Vincent Health System	Medical services organization
United States Dept of Veteran Affairs	General medical & surgical hospitals
University of Arkansas System	Colleges & universities
Valor Telecommunications	Voice telephone communications
Veterans Health Administration	Administration of veterans affairs

Note: Companies shown are located within the Little Rock-North Little Rock-Conway, AR Metropolitan Statistical Area.
Source: Hoovers.com; Wikipedia

PUBLIC SAFETY

Crime Rate

Area	All Crimes	Violent Crimes				Property Crimes		
		Murder	Rape[3]	Robbery	Aggrav. Assault	Burglary	Larceny-Theft	Motor Vehicle Theft
City	8,565.9	27.6	87.8	251.9	1,266.3	1,193.1	5,172.2	566.9
Suburbs[1]	3,533.2	5.9	51.3	64.1	370.1	651.8	2,092.7	297.4
Metro[2]	4,886.7	11.7	61.1	114.6	611.1	797.4	2,920.9	369.9
U.S.	2,756.1	5.3	41.7	98.0	248.9	430.4	1,694.4	237.4

Note: Figures are crimes per 100,000 population; (1) All areas within the metro area that are located outside the city limits; (2) Figures cover the Little Rock-North Little Rock-Conway, AR Metropolitan Statistical Area—see Appendix B for areas included; (3) The city and U.S. figures shown were reported using the revised Uniform Crime Reporting (UCR) definition of rape. The suburban and metro area figures shown are an aggregate total of the data submitted using both the revised and legacy UCR definitions.
Source: FBI Uniform Crime Reports, 2017

Hate Crimes

Area	Number of Quarters Reported	Number of Incidents per Bias Motivation					
		Race/Ethnicity/Ancestry	Religion	Sexual Orientation	Disability	Gender	Gender Identity
City	4	0	0	0	0	0	0
U.S.	4	4,131	1,564	1,130	116	46	119

Source: Federal Bureau of Investigation, Hate Crime Statistics 2017

Identity Theft Consumer Reports

Area	Reports	Reports per 100,000 Population	Rank[2]
MSA[1]	782	106	110
U.S.	444,602	135	-

Note: (1) Figures cover the Little Rock-North Little Rock-Conway, AR Metropolitan Statistical Area—see Appendix B for areas included; (2) Rank ranges from 1 to 389 where 1 indicates greatest number of identity theft reports per 100,000 population
Source: Federal Trade Commission, Consumer Sentinel Network Data Book for January–December 2018

Fraud and Other Consumer Reports

Area	Reports	Reports per 100,000 Population	Rank[2]
MSA[1]	4,263	580	73
U.S.	2,552,917	776	-

Note: (1) Figures cover the Little Rock-North Little Rock-Conway, AR Metropolitan Statistical Area—see Appendix B for areas included; (2) Rank ranges from 1 to 389 where 1 indicates greatest number of fraud and other consumer reports per 100,000 population
Source: Federal Trade Commission, Consumer Sentinel Network Data Book for January–December 2018

SPORTS

Professional Sports Teams

Team Name	League	Year Established
No teams are located in the metro area		

Source: Wikipedia, Major Professional Sports Teams of the United States and Canada, April 5, 2019

CLIMATE

Average and Extreme Temperatures

Temperature	Jan	Feb	Mar	Apr	May	Jun	Jul	Aug	Sep	Oct	Nov	Dec	Yr.
Extreme High (°F)	83	85	91	95	98	105	112	108	103	97	86	80	112
Average High (°F)	50	54	63	73	81	89	92	91	85	75	62	53	73
Average Temp. (°F)	40	45	53	63	71	79	82	81	74	63	52	43	62
Average Low (°F)	30	34	42	51	60	68	72	70	63	51	41	34	51
Extreme Low (°F)	-4	-5	17	28	40	46	54	52	38	29	17	-1	-5

Note: Figures cover the years 1948-1990
Source: National Climatic Data Center, International Station Meteorological Climate Summary, 9/96

Average Precipitation/Snowfall/Humidity

Precip./Humidity	Jan	Feb	Mar	Apr	May	Jun	Jul	Aug	Sep	Oct	Nov	Dec	Yr.
Avg. Precip. (in.)	4.1	4.2	4.9	5.2	5.4	3.6	3.5	3.2	3.8	3.5	4.8	4.5	50.7
Avg. Snowfall (in.)	3	2	1	Tr	0	0	0	0	0	0	Tr	1	5
Avg. Rel. Hum. 6am (%)	80	80	78	81	86	86	87	88	87	86	82	80	84
Avg. Rel. Hum. 3pm (%)	57	54	50	50	53	52	54	52	52	48	52	57	53

Note: Figures cover the years 1948-1990; Tr = Trace amounts (<0.05 in. of rain; <0.5 in. of snow)
Source: National Climatic Data Center, International Station Meteorological Climate Summary, 9/96

Weather Conditions

Temperature			Daytime Sky			Precipitation		
10°F & below	32°F & below	90°F & above	Clear	Partly cloudy	Cloudy	0.01 inch or more precip.	0.1 inch or more snow/ice	Thunder-storms
1	57	73	110	142	113	104	4	57

Note: Figures are average number of days per year and cover the years 1948-1990
Source: National Climatic Data Center, International Station Meteorological Climate Summary, 9/96

HAZARDOUS WASTE

Superfund Sites

The Little Rock-North Little Rock-Conway, AR metro area is home to one site on the EPA's Superfund National Priorities List: **Vertac, Inc.** (final). There are a total of 1,390 Superfund sites with a status of proposed or final on the list in the U.S. *U.S. Environmental Protection Agency, National Priorities List, April 5, 2019*

**AIR & WATER
QUALITY**

Air Quality Trends: Ozone

	1990	1995	2000	2005	2010	2012	2014	2015	2016	2017
MSA[1]	0.080	0.086	0.090	0.083	0.072	0.078	0.066	0.063	0.064	0.060
U.S.	0.088	0.089	0.082	0.080	0.073	0.075	0.067	0.068	0.069	0.068

Note: (1) Data covers the Little Rock-North Little Rock-Conway, AR Metropolitan Statistical Area—see Appendix B for areas included. The values shown are the composite ozone concentration averages among trend sites based on the highest fourth daily maximum 8-hour concentration in parts per million. These trends are based on sites having an adequate record of monitoring data during the trend period. Data from exceptional events are included.
Source: U.S. Environmental Protection Agency, Air Quality Monitoring Information, "Air Quality Trends by City, 1990-2017"

Air Quality Index

Area	Percent of Days when Air Quality was...[2]					AQI Statistics[2]	
	Good	Moderate	Unhealthy for Sensitive Groups	Unhealthy	Very Unhealthy	Maximum	Median
MSA[1]	69.0	30.7	0.3	0.0	0.0	115	44

Note: (1) Data covers the Little Rock-North Little Rock-Conway, AR Metropolitan Statistical Area—see Appendix B for areas included; (2) Based on 365 days with AQI data in 2017. Air Quality Index (AQI) is an index for reporting daily air quality. EPA calculates the AQI for five major air pollutants regulated by the Clean Air Act: ground-level ozone, particle pollution (aka particulate matter), carbon monoxide, sulfur dioxide, and nitrogen dioxide. The AQI runs from 0 to 500. The higher the AQI value, the greater the level of air pollution and the greater the health concern. There are six AQI categories: "Good" AQI is between 0 and 50. Air quality is considered satisfactory; "Moderate" AQI is between 51 and 100. Air quality is acceptable; "Unhealthy for Sensitive Groups" When AQI values are between 101 and 150, members of sensitive groups may experience health effects; "Unhealthy" When AQI values are between 151 and 200 everyone may begin to experience health effects; "Very Unhealthy" AQI values between 201 and 300 trigger a health alert; "Hazardous" AQI values over 300 trigger warnings of emergency conditions (not shown).
Source: U.S. Environmental Protection Agency, Air Quality Index Report, 2017

Air Quality Index Pollutants

Area	Percent of Days when AQI Pollutant was...[2]					
	Carbon Monoxide	Nitrogen Dioxide	Ozone	Sulfur Dioxide	Particulate Matter 2.5	Particulate Matter 10
MSA[1]	0.0	0.5	41.6	0.0	57.8	0.0

Note: (1) Data covers the Little Rock-North Little Rock-Conway, AR Metropolitan Statistical Area—see Appendix B for areas included; (2) Based on 365 days with AQI data in 2017. The Air Quality Index (AQI) is an index for reporting daily air quality. EPA calculates the AQI for five major air pollutants regulated by the Clean Air Act: ground-level ozone, particle pollution (also known as particulate matter), carbon monoxide, sulfur dioxide, and nitrogen dioxide. The AQI runs from 0 to 500. The higher the AQI value, the greater the level of air pollution and the greater the health concern.
Source: U.S. Environmental Protection Agency, Air Quality Index Report, 2017

Maximum Air Pollutant Concentrations: Particulate Matter, Ozone, CO and Lead

	Particulate Matter 10 (ug/m³)	Particulate Matter 2.5 Wtd AM (ug/m³)	Particulate Matter 2.5 24-Hr (ug/m³)	Ozone (ppm)	Carbon Monoxide (ppm)	Lead (ug/m³)
MSA[1] Level	36	9.6	21	0.062	2	n/a
NAAQS[2]	150	15	35	0.075	9	0.15
Met NAAQS[2]	Yes	Yes	Yes	Yes	Yes	n/a

Note: (1) Data covers the Little Rock-North Little Rock-Conway, AR Metropolitan Statistical Area—see Appendix B for areas included; Data from exceptional events are included; (2) National Ambient Air Quality Standards; ppm = parts per million; ug/m³ = micrograms per cubic meter; n/a not available.
Concentrations: Particulate Matter 10 (coarse particulate)—highest second maximum 24-hour concentration; Particulate Matter 2.5 Wtd AM (fine particulate)—highest weighted annual mean concentration; Particulate Matter 2.5 24-Hour (fine particulate)—highest 98th percentile 24-hour concentration; Ozone—highest fourth daily maximum 8-hour concentration; Carbon Monoxide—highest second maximum non-overlapping 8-hour concentration; Lead—maximum running 3-month average
Source: U.S. Environmental Protection Agency, Air Quality Monitoring Information, "Air Quality Statistics by City, 2017"

Maximum Air Pollutant Concentrations: Nitrogen Dioxide and Sulfur Dioxide

	Nitrogen Dioxide AM (ppb)	Nitrogen Dioxide 1-Hr (ppb)	Sulfur Dioxide AM (ppb)	Sulfur Dioxide 1-Hr (ppb)	Sulfur Dioxide 24-Hr (ppb)
MSA[1] Level	8	39	n/a	8	n/a
NAAQS[2]	53	100	30	75	140
Met NAAQS[2]	Yes	Yes	n/a	Yes	n/a

Note: (1) Data covers the Little Rock-North Little Rock-Conway, AR Metropolitan Statistical Area—see Appendix B for areas included; Data from exceptional events are included; (2) National Ambient Air Quality Standards; ppm = parts per million; ug/m³ = micrograms per cubic meter; n/a not available.
Concentrations: Nitrogen Dioxide AM—highest arithmetic mean concentration; Nitrogen Dioxide 1-Hr—highest 98th percentile 1-hour daily maximum concentration; Sulfur Dioxide AM—highest annual mean concentration; Sulfur Dioxide 1-Hr—highest 99th percentile 1-hour daily maximum concentration; Sulfur Dioxide 24-Hr—highest second maximum 24-hour concentration
Source: U.S. Environmental Protection Agency, Air Quality Monitoring Information, "Air Quality Statistics by City, 2017"

Drinking Water

Water System Name	Pop. Served	Primary Water Source Type	Violations[1] Health Based	Violations[1] Monitoring/ Reporting
Central Arkansas Water	330,667	Surface	0	0

Note: (1) Based on violation data from January 1, 2018 to December 31, 2018
Source: U.S. Environmental Protection Agency, Office of Ground Water and Drinking Water, Safe Drinking Water Information System (based on data extracted April 5, 2019)

Madison, Wisconsin

Background

Madison was selected as Wisconsin's territorial capital in 1836 before construction of the city began in 1838. Despite repeated threats to move the capital elsewhere by members of the legislature, it has maintained its status. It was named for President James Madison in 1836, and incorporated into a village in 1856. When Wisconsin attained statehood in 1848, the University of Wisconsin (one of the largest in the country) was established.

Most of the city, including its business center, is situated on an isthmus between Lake Mendota and Lake Minona in the south-central part of the state. Two other lakes, Kengonsa and Waubesa, lie to the south. By ordinance, the city's skyline is dominated by the capitol dome, which weighs 2,500 tons.

Madison serves as the trade center of a rich agricultural and dairy region. Food processing is a major industry. Batteries, dairy equipment, and machine tools are produced there as well.

Wisconsin state government and the University of Wisconsin-Madison remain the two largest Madison employers. However, Madison's economy is evolving from a government-based economy to a consumer services and high-tech base, particularly in the health, biotech, and advertising sectors. Beginning in the early 1990s, the city experienced a steady economic boom fostered by the development of high-tech companies and UW-Madison working with local businesses and entrepreneurs to transfer the results of academic research into real-world applications, especially bio-tech applications.

Many businesses are attracted to Madison's skill base, taking advantage of the area's high level of education. Nearly 50 percent of Madison's population over the age of 25 holds at least a bachelor's degree. *Forbes* magazine reported that Madison has the highest percentage of individuals holding Ph.D.s in the United States.

The city has received numerous awards, beginning as early as 1948 when it was named Best Place to Live in America by *Life* magazine. Although Madison is a progressive, eclectic city, it also offers the atmosphere of a small town with many picturesque communities, four lakes, and over 200 parks. There are a total of 29,000 acres designated for recreational use, including 46 miles of hiking trails, over 150 miles of bicycle trails, 92 miles of shoreline for swimming and boating, and 20 golf courses. Bicycle tourism is an $800 million industry in Wisconsin, which has 20 percent of the nation's bicycling industry manufacturing capacity.

Madison is full of restaurants and boasts a large variety of ethnic food, from Greek and Italian to Japanese, Mexican, and Middle Eastern, as well as many brew pubs.

Cultural life in Madison has long had a center in the downtown, at the Madison Civic Center and its associated sites. Project Overture renovated and redeveloped a variety of cultural venues, including the new Madison Museum of Contemporary Art with innovative design and sculpture-garden rooftop. A new 2,250-seat hall is the home of the Madison Symphony Orchestra, whose old home, the Oscar Meyer Theater, is used by groups such as the CTM Family Theatre and the Wisconsin Chamber group. The goal of these projects is architectural integration and toward that end, the facades of nearby buildings have been refurbished and preserved.

Another major attraction in Madison is the Olbrich Botanical Gardens, with 16 acres of outdoor display gardens, including sunken, perennial, rose, rock, herb, and wildflower gardens. Over 250,000 visitors a year enjoy the gardens, which include a lush, tropical conservatory filled with exotic plants, bright flowers, a rushing waterfall, and free-flying birds.

Madison is home to many institutions of higher learning, including the University of Wisconsin-Madison, Edgewood College, Herzing College, Lakeland College, and Madison Media Institute.

The area has the typical continental climate of interior North America with a large annual temperature range and frequent short-period temperature changes. The city lies in the path of the frequent cyclones and anticyclones, which move eastward over this area during fall, winter, and spring. The most frequent air masses are of polar origin, with occasional influxes of arctic air affecting this area during the winter months. Summers are pleasant, with only occasional periods of extreme heat or high humidity.

Rankings

General Rankings

- *US News & World Report* conducted a survey of more than 2,000 people and analyzed the 125 largest metropolitan areas to determine what matters the most when selecting the next place to live. Madison ranked #16 out of the top 25 as having the best combination of desirable factors. Criteria: cost of living; quality of education; job market, crime rates; and other factors. *realestate.usnews.com, "The 25 Best Places to Live in the U.S. in 2018," April 10, 2018*

- *Insider* listed 33 places in the U.S. that were a must see vacation destination. Whether it is the great beaches, exploring a new city or experiencing the great outdoors, according to the website thisisinsider.com Madison is a place to visit in 2018. *Insider, "33 Trips Everyone Should Take in the U.S. in 2018," November 27, 2017*

- Madison appeared on *Business Insider's* list of the "13 Hottest American Cities for 2016." Criteria: job and population growth; demographics; affordability; livability; residents' health and welfare; technological innovation; sustainability; burgeoning art and food scenes. *www.businessinsider.com, "The Thirteen Hottest American Cities for 2016," December 4, 2015*

- In their sixth annual survey, Livability.com looked at data for more than 1,000 U.S. cities to determine the rankings for Livability's "Top 100 Best Places to Live" in 2019. Madison ranked #3. Criteria: median home value capped at $250,000; affordable living; vibrant economy; education, demographics, health care options. transportation & infrastructure; abundant lifestyle amenities. *Livability.com, "Top 100 Best Places to Live 2019" March 2019*

Business/Finance Rankings

- The personal finance site NerdWallet analyzed 183 American metropolitan areas with populations over 250,000 and more than 15,000 businesses to rank where entrepreneurs find the most success. Criteria included area economy, annual income, housing cost, unemployment rate, and the success rate of area businesses. Madison ranked #40. *www.nerdwallet.com, "Best Places to Start a Business," April 27, 2015*

- Experian's latest annual report on consumer credit ranked cities by the average credit score of its residents. Madison was ranked #10 among the ten cities with the highest average credit score, meaning that its residents showed strong credit management. *www.usatoday.com, "Minneapolis Tops List of Cities With Best Average Credit Score; Greenwood Miss., at the Bottom," January 11, 2018*

- Using data from the Council for Community and Economic Research's 2014 cost of living index, NerdWallet ranked the 100 most affordable cities in America. Median income was compared with cost of living to find truly affordable places. Madison ranked #63. *NerdWallet.com, "America's Most Affordable Places," May 18, 2015*

- NerdWallet.com identified the 10 most promising cities for job seekers of the nation's 100 largest cities. Madison was ranked #29. Criteria: job availability; annual salary; workforce growth; affordability. *NerdWallet.com, "Best Cities for Job Seekers in 2017," December 19, 2016*

- The Brookings Institution ranked the nation's largest cities based on income inequality. Madison was ranked #86 (#1 = greatest inequality). Criteria: the "95/20 ratio," a figure representing the income at which a household earns more than 95 percent of all other households, divided by the income at which a household earns more than only 20 percent of all other households. *Brookings Institution, "Household Income Inequality, Largest Cities of 97 Large U.S. Metro Areas, 2014-2016," February 5, 2018*

- The Brookings Institution ranked the 100 largest metro areas in the U.S. based on income inequality. Madison was ranked #95 (#1 = greatest inequality). Criteria: the "95/20 ratio," a figure representing the income at which a household earns more than 95 percent of all other households, divided by the income at which a household earns more than only 20 percent of all other households. *Brookings Institution, "Household Income Inequality, 100 Largest U.S. Metro Areas, 2014-2016," February 5, 2018*

- Livability.com rated Madison as #10 of ten cities where new college grads' job prospects are brightest. Criteria included: number of 22- to 29-year olds; good job opportunities; affordable housing options; public transportation users; educational attainment; variety of fun things to do. *Livability.com, "2018 Top 10 Best Cities for Recent College Grads," April 26, 2018*

- The Madison metro area appeared on the Milken Institute "2018 Best Performing Cities" list. Rank: #72 out of 200 large metro areas. Criteria: job growth; wage and salary growth; high-tech output growth. *Milken Institute, "Best-Performing Cities 2018," January 24, 2019*

- *Forbes* ranked the 200 most populous metro areas to determine the nation's "Best Places for Business and Careers." The Madison metro area was ranked #48. Criteria: costs (business and living); job growth (past and projected); income growth; quality of life; educational attainment (college and high school); projected economic growth; cultural and recreational opportunities; net migration patterns; number of highly ranked colleges. *Forbes, "The Best Places for Business and Careers 2018: Seattle Leads the Way," October 24, 2018*

Children/Family Rankings

- *Forbes* analyzed data on the 100 largest metropolitan areas in the United States to compile its 2016 ranking of the best cities for raising a family. The Madison metro area was ranked #12. Criteria: median income; childcare costs; percent of population under 18; commuting delays; crime rate; percentage of families owning homes; education quality (mainly test scores). Overall cost of living and housing affordability was also unofficially considered. *Forbes, "America's Best Cities for Raising a Family 2016," August 30, 2016*

Dating/Romance Rankings

- Madison was ranked #15 out of 25 cities that stood out for inspiring romance and attracting diners on the website OpenTable.com. Criteria: percentage of people who dined out on Valentine's Day in 2018; percentage of romantic restaurants as rated by OpenTable diner reviews; and percentage of tables seated for two. *OpenTable, "25 Most Romantic Cities in America for 2019," February 7, 2019*

- Madison was selected as one of America's best cities for singles by the readers of *Travel + Leisure* in their annual "America's Favorite Cities" survey. Criteria included good-looking locals, cool shopping, an active bar scene and hipster-magnet coffee bars. *Travel + Leisure, "Best Cities in America for Singles," July 21, 2017*

Education Rankings

- Personal finance website *WalletHub* analyzed the 150 largest U.S. metropolitan statistical areas to determine where the most educated Americans are choosing to settle. Criteria: education quality and attainment gap; education levels; percentage of workers with degrees; public school quality rankings; quality and size of each metro area's universities. Madison was ranked #6 (#1 = most educated city). *www.WalletHub.com, "2018's Most and Least Educated Cities in America," July 24, 2018*

Food/Drink Rankings

- *Men's Health* ranked 100 major U.S. cities in terms of alcohol intoxication. Madison ranked #15 (#1 = most sober).Criteria: binge drinking; alcohol-related traffic accidents, arrests, and fatalities. *Men's Health, "America's Drunkest Cities," March 9, 2015*

Health/Fitness Rankings

- For each of the 100 largest cities in the United States, the American College of Sports Medicine's American Fitness Index evaluated infrastructure, community assets, and policies that encourage healthy and fit lifestyles, including preventive health behaviors, levels of chronic disease conditions, health care access, and community resources and policies that support physical activity. Madison ranked #4 for "community fitness." *www.americanfitnessindex.org, "ACSM American Fitness Index Health and Community Fitness Status of the 100 Largest U.S. Cities," May 2018*

- Madison was identified as a "2018 Spring Allergy Capital." The area ranked #57 out of 100. Three groups of factors were used to identify the most challenging cities for people with allergies during the spring season: annual pollen levels; medicine utilization; access to board-certified allergists. *Asthma and Allergy Foundation of America, "Spring Allergy Capitals 2018"*

- Madison was identified as a "2018 Fall Allergy Capital." The area ranked #55 out of 100. Three groups of factors were used to identify the most challenging cities for people with allergies during the fall season: annual pollen levels; medicine utilization; access to board-certified allergists. *Asthma and Allergy Foundation of America, "Fall Allergy Capitals 2018"*

- Madison was identified as a "2018 Asthma Capital." The area ranked #59 out of the nation's 100 largest metropolitan areas. Criteria: estimated prevalence; self-reported prevalence; crude death rate for asthma; annual pollen score; annual air quality; public smoking laws; number of board-certified asthma specialists; school inhaler access laws; rescue medication use; controller medication use; ER visits for asthma; uninsured rate; poverty rate. *Asthma and Allergy Foundation of America, "Asthma Capitals 2018: The Most Challenging Places to Live With Asthma"*

- *Men's Health* ranked 100 major U.S. cities in terms of the best cities for men. Madison ranked #3. Criteria: health; fitness; quality of life. *Men's Health, "The Best & Worst Cities for Men Who Want to Be Fit and Happy," January 1, 2016*

- The Madison metro area ranked #61 out of 189 in The Gallup-Healthways Well-Being Index. Criteria: purpose; social well being; financial health; community and physical health. Results are based on telephone interviews with adults, aged 18 and older, living in metropolitan areas in the 50 U.S. states and the District of Columbia. *Gallup-Healthways, "State of American Well-Being, 2017 Community Well-Being Rankings" March 2018*

Real Estate Rankings

- *WalletHub* compared the most populated U.S. cities, as well as at least two of the most populated cities in each state, for a total of 179, to determine which had the best markets for real estate agents. Madison ranked #53 where demand was high and pay was the best. Criteria: sales per agent; annual median wage for real-estate agents; monthly average starting salary for real estate agents; real estate job density and competition; unemployment rate; housing-market health index; and other relevant metrics. *www.WalletHub.com, "2018's Best Places to Be a Real Estate Agent," April 25, 2018*

- Madison was ranked #118 out of 237 metro areas in terms of housing affordability in 2018 by the National Association of Home Builders (#1 = most affordable). Criteria: the share of homes sold in that area affordable to a family earning the local median income, based on standard mortgage underwriting criteria. *National Association of Home Builders®, NAHB-Wells Fargo Housing Opportunity Index, 4th Quarter 2018*

Safety Rankings

- Allstate ranked the 200 largest cities in America in terms of driver safety. Madison ranked #5. Criteria: internal property damage claims over a two-year period from January 2015 to December 2016. The report helps increase the importance of safety awareness behind the wheel. *Allstate, "Allstate America's Best Drivers Report, 2018" August 28, 2018*

- The National Insurance Crime Bureau ranked 382 metro areas in the U.S. in terms of per capita rates of vehicle theft. The Madison metro area ranked #282 (#1 = highest rate). Criteria: number of vehicle theft offenses per 100,000 inhabitants in 2017. *National Insurance Crime Bureau, "Hot Spots 2017," July 12, 2018*

Seniors/Retirement Rankings

- For *U.S. News & World Report's* Best Places rankings, the editors sought out affordable cities where retirees spend the least on housing and can live on $100 a day while still having access to amenities they need, such as health care, utilities, transportation and food. Madison was among the ten cities that best satisfied their criteria. *money.usnews.com, "10 Best Places to Retire on $100 a Day," October 13, 2015*

- From its Best Cities for Successful Aging indexes, the Milken Institute generated rankings for metropolitan areas, weighing data in nine categories—health care, wellness, living arrangements, transportation and convenience, financial characteristics, education, employment, community engagement, and overall livability. The Madison metro area was ranked #2 overall in the large metro area category. *Milken Institute, "Best Cities for Successful Aging, 2017" March 14, 2017*

- Madison made the 2018 *Forbes* list of "25 Best Places to Retire." Criteria, focused on a high-quality retirement living an affordable price, include: housing/living costs compared to the national average and state taxes; weather and air quality; crime rates; vibrant economy and low unemployment; doctor availability; bikability; walkability; healthy living and volunteering. *Forbes.com, "The Best Places to Retire in 2018," April 23, 2018*

Sports/Recreation Rankings

- Madison was chosen as one of America's best cities for bicycling. The city ranked #8 out of 50. Criteria: cycling infrastructure that is safe and friendly for all ages; energy and bike culture. The editors only considered cities with populations of 100,000 or more. *Bicycling, "The 50 Best Bike Cities in America," October 10, 2018*

Women/Minorities Rankings

- Personal finance website *WalletHub* compared more than 180 U.S. cities—including the 150 most populated U.S. cities, plus at least two of the most populated cities in each state—across two key dimensions, "Hispanic Business-Friendliness" and "Hispanic Purchasing Power", to arrive at the most favorable conditions for Hispanic entrepreneurs. Madison was ranked #143 out of 182. Criteria includes: share of Hispanic-Owned Businesses; Hispanic entrepreneurship rate to median annual income of Hispanics; Small Business-Friendliness score; cost of living; and number of Hispanics with at least a bachelor's degree. *WalletHub.com, "2018's Best Cities for Hispanic Entrepreneurs," April 26, 2018*

Miscellaneous Rankings

- *WalletHub* compared the 150 most populated U.S. cities to determine their operating efficiency. A "Quality of Services" score was constructed for each city and then divided by the total budget per capita to reveal which were managed the best. Madison ranked #33. Criteria: financial stability; economy; education; safety; health; infrastructure and pollution. *www.WalletHub.com, "2018's Best- & Worst-Run Cities in America," July 9, 2018*

- Madison appeared on *Travel + Leisure's* list of America's cities with the most attractive people. Criteria: cities were selected by readers in their annual America's Favorite Cities survey. The city ranked #10 out of 10. *Travel + Leisure, "America's Most and Least Attractive People," September 2, 2016*

Business Environment

CITY FINANCES

City Government Finances

Component	2016 ($000)	2016 ($ per capita)
Total Revenues	503,436	2,022
Total Expenditures	553,454	2,223
Debt Outstanding	597,404	2,400
Cash and Securities[1]	522,185	2,098

Note: (1) Cash and security holdings of a government at the close of its fiscal year, including those of its dependent agencies, utilities, and liquor stores.
Source: U.S. Census Bureau, State & Local Government Finances 2016

City Government Revenue by Source

Source	2016 ($000)	2016 ($ per capita)	2016 (%)
General Revenue			
From Federal Government	31,979	128	6.4
From State Government	65,897	265	13.1
From Local Governments	611	2	0.1
Taxes			
Property	213,052	856	42.3
Sales and Gross Receipts	13,820	56	2.7
Personal Income	0	0	0.0
Corporate Income	0	0	0.0
Motor Vehicle License	0	0	0.0
Other Taxes	14,835	60	2.9
Current Charges	92,246	371	18.3
Liquor Store	0	0	0.0
Utility	41,124	165	8.2
Employee Retirement	0	0	0.0

Source: U.S. Census Bureau, State & Local Government Finances 2016

City Government Expenditures by Function

Function	2016 ($000)	2016 ($ per capita)	2016 (%)
General Direct Expenditures			
Air Transportation	0	0	0.0
Corrections	0	0	0.0
Education	0	0	0.0
Employment Security Administration	0	0	0.0
Financial Administration	6,437	25	1.2
Fire Protection	66,120	265	11.9
General Public Buildings	1,864	7	0.3
Governmental Administration, Other	17,135	68	3.1
Health	12,227	49	2.2
Highways	60,320	242	10.9
Hospitals	0	0	0.0
Housing and Community Development	53,481	214	9.7
Interest on General Debt	21,109	84	3.8
Judicial and Legal	3,352	13	0.6
Libraries	15,922	64	2.9
Parking	8,928	35	1.6
Parks and Recreation	45,520	182	8.2
Police Protection	70,360	282	12.7
Public Welfare	0	0	0.0
Sewerage	28,643	115	5.2
Solid Waste Management	16,371	65	3.0
Veterans' Services	0	0	0.0
Liquor Store	0	0	0.0
Utility	82,001	329	14.8
Employee Retirement	0	0	0.0

Source: U.S. Census Bureau, State & Local Government Finances 2016

DEMOGRAPHICS

Population Growth

Area	1990 Census	2000 Census	2010 Census	2017* Estimate	Population Growth (%)	
					1990-2017	2010-2017
City	193,451	208,054	233,209	248,856	28.6	6.7
MSA[1]	432,323	501,774	568,593	640,072	48.1	12.6
U.S.	248,709,873	281,421,906	308,745,538	321,004,407	29.1	4.0

Note: (1) Figures cover the Madison, WI Metropolitan Statistical Area—see Appendix B for areas included; (*) 2013-2017 5-year estimated population
Source: U.S. Census Bureau, 1990 Census, Census 2000, Census 2010, 2013-2017 American Community Survey 5-Year Estimates

Household Size

Area	Persons in Household (%)							Average Household Size
	One	Two	Three	Four	Five	Six	Seven or More	
City	35.1	36.5	13.1	9.8	3.8	1.1	0.5	2.20
MSA[1]	29.5	37.3	14.0	12.2	4.7	1.5	0.7	2.40
U.S.	27.7	33.8	15.7	13.0	6.0	2.3	1.4	2.60

Note: (1) Figures cover the Madison, WI Metropolitan Statistical Area—see Appendix B for areas included
Source: U.S. Census Bureau, 2013-2017 American Community Survey 5-Year Estimates

Race

Area	White Alone[2] (%)	Black Alone[2] (%)	Asian Alone[2] (%)	AIAN[3] Alone[2] (%)	NHOPI[4] Alone[2] (%)	Other Race Alone[2] (%)	Two or More Races (%)
City	78.8	6.5	8.8	0.4	0.0	1.9	3.5
MSA[1]	86.1	4.3	4.7	0.3	0.0	1.7	2.7
U.S.	73.0	12.7	5.4	0.8	0.2	4.8	3.1

Note: (1) Figures cover the Madison, WI Metropolitan Statistical Area—see Appendix B for areas included; (2) Alone is defined as not being in combination with one or more other races; (3) American Indian and Alaska Native; (4) Native Hawaiian and Other Pacific Islander
Source: U.S. Census Bureau, 2013-2017 American Community Survey 5-Year Estimates

Hispanic or Latino Origin

Area	Total (%)	Mexican (%)	Puerto Rican (%)	Cuban (%)	Other (%)
City	7.0	4.6	0.5	0.1	1.7
MSA[1]	5.7	3.8	0.4	0.1	1.3
U.S.	17.6	11.1	1.7	0.7	4.1

Note: Persons of Hispanic or Latino origin can be of any race; (1) Figures cover the Madison, WI Metropolitan Statistical Area—see Appendix B for areas included
Source: U.S. Census Bureau, 2013-2017 American Community Survey 5-Year Estimates

Segregation

Type	Segregation Indices[1]				Percent Change		
	1990	2000	2010	2010 Rank[2]	1990-2000	1990-2010	2000-2010
Black/White	52.1	49.9	49.6	71	-2.2	-2.6	-0.3
Asian/White	54.5	49.5	44.2	29	-5.0	-10.3	-5.3
Hispanic/White	31.1	38.7	40.1	65	7.7	9.1	1.4

Note: All figures cover the Metropolitan Statistical Area—see Appendix B for areas included; Figures are based on an analysis of 1990, 2000, and 2010 Census Decennial Census tract data by William H. Frey, Brookings Institution and the University of Michigan Social Science Data Analysis Network. In this analysis all racial groups (whites, blacks, and asians) are non-Hispanic members of those races. Hispanics are shown as a separate category; (1) Segregation Indices are Dissimilarity Indices that measure the degree to which the minority group is distributed differently than whites across census tracts. They range from 0 (complete integration) to 100 (complete segregation) where the value indicates the percentage of the minority group that needs to move to be distributed exactly like whites; (2) Ranges from 1 (most segregated) to 102 (least segregated); n/a not available.
Source: www.CensusScope.org

Ancestry

Area	German	Irish	English	American	Italian	Polish	French[2]	Scottish	Dutch
City	33.2	13.6	8.3	2.1	4.0	5.8	2.9	1.6	1.9
MSA[1]	38.8	13.6	8.7	2.9	3.6	5.3	2.8	1.6	2.1
U.S.	14.1	10.1	7.5	6.6	5.3	2.9	2.5	1.7	1.3

Note: Figures are the percentage of the total population reporting a particular ancestry. The nine most commonly reported ancestries in the U.S. are shown. Figures include multiple ancestries (e.g. if a person reported being Irish and Italian, they were included in both columns); (1) Figures cover the Madison, WI Metropolitan Statistical Area—see Appendix B for areas included; (2) Excludes Basque
Source: U.S. Census Bureau, 2013-2017 American Community Survey 5-Year Estimates

Foreign-Born Population

Area	Percent of Population Born in								
	Any Foreign Country	Asia	Mexico	Europe	Carribean	Central America[2]	South America	Africa	Canada
City	11.7	6.4	1.8	1.4	0.1	0.3	0.6	0.8	0.2
MSA[1]	7.4	3.5	1.5	1.0	0.1	0.2	0.4	0.5	0.2
U.S.	13.4	4.1	3.6	1.5	1.3	1.0	0.9	0.6	0.3

Note: (1) Figures cover the Madison, WI Metropolitan Statistical Area—see Appendix B for areas included; (2) Excludes Mexico.
Source: U.S. Census Bureau, 2013-2017 American Community Survey 5-Year Estimates

Marital Status

Area	Never Married	Now Married[2]	Separated	Widowed	Divorced
City	49.3	37.8	0.9	3.4	8.5
MSA[1]	36.0	49.2	0.9	4.2	9.6
U.S.	33.1	48.2	2.0	5.8	10.9

Note: Figures are percentages and cover the population 15 years of age and older; (1) Figures cover the Madison, WI Metropolitan Statistical Area—see Appendix B for areas included; (2) Excludes separated
Source: U.S. Census Bureau, 2013-2017 American Community Survey 5-Year Estimates

Disability by Age

Area	All Ages	Under 18 Years Old	18 to 64 Years Old	65 Years and Over
City	8.4	3.4	6.6	28.6
MSA[1]	9.2	3.5	7.4	28.3
U.S.	12.6	4.2	10.3	35.5

Note: Figures show percent of the civilian noninstitutionalized population that reported having a disability. Disability status is determined from six types of difficulty: vision, hearing, cognitive, ambulatory, self-care, and independent living. For children under 5 years old, hearing and vision difficulty are used to determine disability status. For children between the ages of 5 and 14, disability status is determined from hearing, vision, cognitive, ambulatory, and self-care difficulties. For people aged 15 years and older, they are considered to have a disability if they have difficulty with any one of the six difficulty types; Note: (1) Figures cover the Madison, WI Metropolitan Statistical Area—see Appendix B for areas included
Source: U.S. Census Bureau, 2013-2017 American Community Survey 5-Year Estimates

Age

Area	Percent of Population									Median Age
	Under Age 5	Age 5–19	Age 20–34	Age 35–44	Age 45–54	Age 55–64	Age 65–74	Age 75–84	Age 85+	
City	5.2	16.4	35.3	12.0	10.3	9.8	6.4	3.1	1.6	31.0
MSA[1]	5.8	18.5	24.4	12.8	13.0	12.4	7.8	3.6	1.7	35.9
U.S.	6.2	19.5	20.7	12.7	13.4	12.7	8.6	4.4	1.9	37.8

Note: (1) Figures cover the Madison, WI Metropolitan Statistical Area—see Appendix B for areas included
Source: U.S. Census Bureau, 2013-2017 American Community Survey 5-Year Estimates

Gender

Area	Males	Females	Males per 100 Females
City	123,054	125,802	97.8
MSA[1]	318,828	321,244	99.2
U.S.	158,018,753	162,985,654	97.0

Note: (1) Figures cover the Madison, WI Metropolitan Statistical Area—see Appendix B for areas included
Source: U.S. Census Bureau, 2013-2017 American Community Survey 5-Year Estimates

Religious Groups by Family

Area	Catholic	Baptist	Non-Den.	Methodist[2]	Lutheran	LDS[3]	Pentecostal	Presbyterian[4]	Muslim[5]	Judaism
MSA[1]	21.8	1.1	1.6	3.7	12.8	0.5	0.4	2.2	0.5	0.5
U.S.	19.1	9.3	4.0	4.0	2.3	2.0	1.9	1.6	0.8	0.7

Note: Figures are the number of adherents as a percentage of the total population; (1) Figures cover the Madison, WI Metropolitan Statistical Area—see Appendix B for areas included; (2) Methodist/Pietist; (3) Latter Day Saints; (4) Reformed; (5) Figures are estimates
Source: Association of Statisticians of American Religious Bodies, 2010 U.S. Religion Census: Religious Congregations & Membership Study

Religious Groups by Tradition

Area	Catholic	Evangelical Protestant	Mainline Protestant	Other Tradition	Black Protestant	Orthodox
MSA[1]	21.8	7.3	15.4	2.3	0.1	0.1
U.S.	19.1	16.2	7.3	4.3	1.6	0.3

Note: Figures are the number of adherents as a percentage of the total population; (1) Figures cover the Madison, WI Metropolitan Statistical Area—see Appendix B for areas included
Source: Association of Statisticians of American Religious Bodies, 2010 U.S. Religion Census: Religious Congregations & Membership Study

ECONOMY

Gross Metropolitan Product

Area	2016	2017	2018	2019	Rank[2]
MSA[1]	48.1	50.3	52.9	55.9	61

Note: Figures are in billions of dollars; (1) Figures cover the Madison, WI Metropolitan Statistical Area—see Appendix B for areas included; (2) Rank is based on 2017 data and ranges from 1 to 381
Source: U.S. Conference of Mayors, U.S. Metro Economies: Economic Growth & Full Employment, June 2018

Economic Growth

Area	2017-2018 (%)	2019-2020 (%)	2021-2022 (%)
MSA[1]	2.8	2.7	2.1

Note: Figures are real gross metropolitan product (GMP) growth rates and represent average annual percent change; (1) Figures cover the Madison, WI Metropolitan Statistical Area—see Appendix B for areas included
Source: U.S. Conference of Mayors, U.S. Metro Economies: Economic Growth & Full Employment, June 2018

Metropolitan Area Exports

Area	2012	2013	2014	2015	2016	2017	Rank[2]
MSA[1]	2,168.7	2,292.1	2,369.5	2,280.4	2,204.8	2,187.7	92

Note: Figures are in millions of dollars; (1) Figures cover the Madison, WI Metropolitan Statistical Area—see Appendix B for areas included; (2) Rank is based on 2017 data and ranges from 1 to 387
Source: U.S. Department of Commerce, International Trade Administration, Office of Trade and Economic Analysis, Industry and Analysis, Exports by Metropolitan Area, extracted March 25, 2019

Building Permits

Area	Single-Family			Multi-Family			Total		
	2016	2017	Pct. Chg.	2016	2017	Pct. Chg.	2016	2017	Pct. Chg.
City	340	379	11.5	2,041	1,809	-11.4	2,381	2,188	-8.1
MSA[1]	1,613	1,656	2.7	3,340	2,976	-10.9	4,953	4,632	-6.5
U.S.	750,800	820,000	9.2	455,800	462,000	1.4	1,206,600	1,282,000	6.2

Note: (1) Figures cover the Madison, WI Metropolitan Statistical Area—see Appendix B for areas included; Figures represent new, privately-owned housing units authorized (unadjusted data); All permit data are based on estimates with imputation
Source: U.S. Census Bureau, Manufacturing, Mining, and Construction Statistics, Building Permits, 2016, 2017

Bankruptcy Filings

Area	Business Filings			Nonbusiness Filings		
	2017	2018	% Chg.	2017	2018	% Chg.
Dane County	26	22	-15.4	774	772	-0.3
U.S.	23,157	22,232	-4.0	765,863	751,186	-1.9

Note: Business filings include Chapter 7, Chapter 11, Chapter 12, and Chapter 13; Nonbusiness filings include Chapter 7, Chapter 11, and Chapter 13
Source: Administrative Office of the U.S. Courts, Business and Nonbusiness Bankruptcy, County Cases Commenced by Chapter of the Bankruptcy Code, During the 12-Month Period Ending December 31, 2017 and Business and Nonbusiness Bankruptcy, County Cases Commenced by Chapter of the Bankruptcy Code, During the 12-Month Period Ending December 31, 2018

Housing Vacancy Rates

Area	Gross Vacancy Rate[2] (%)			Year-Round Vacancy Rate[3] (%)			Rental Vacancy Rate[4] (%)			Homeowner Vacancy Rate[5] (%)		
	2016	2017	2018	2016	2017	2018	2016	2017	2018	2016	2017	2018
MSA[1]	n/a	n/a	n/a	n/a	n/a	n/a	n/a	n/a	n/a	n/a	n/a	n/a
U.S.	12.8	12.7	12.3	9.9	9.9	9.7	6.9	7.2	6.9	1.7	1.6	1.5

Note: (1) Figures cover the Madison, WI Metropolitan Statistical Area—see Appendix B for areas included; (2) The percentage of the total housing inventory that is vacant; (3) The percentage of the housing inventory (excluding seasonal units) that is year-round vacant; (4) The percentage of rental inventory that is vacant for rent; (5) The percentage of homeowner inventory that is vacant for sale; n/a not available
Source: U.S. Census Bureau, Housing Vacancies and Homeownership Annual Statistics: 2016, 2017, 2018

INCOME

Income

Area	Per Capita ($)	Median Household ($)	Average Household ($)
City	34,740	59,387	79,063
MSA[1]	36,065	66,609	86,307
U.S.	31,177	57,652	81,283

Note: (1) Figures cover the Madison, WI Metropolitan Statistical Area—see Appendix B for areas included
Source: U.S. Census Bureau, 2013-2017 American Community Survey 5-Year Estimates

Household Income Distribution

Area	Percent of Households Earning							
	Under $15,000	$15,000 -$24,999	$25,000 -$34,999	$35,000 -$49,999	$50,000 -$74,999	$75,000 -$99,999	$100,000 -$149,999	$150,000 and up
City	12.2	8.6	8.9	12.9	18.2	13.1	14.8	11.3
MSA[1]	8.8	7.5	8.6	12.4	18.5	14.4	16.8	13.0
U.S.	11.6	9.8	9.5	13.0	17.7	12.3	14.1	12.1

Note: (1) Figures cover the Madison, WI Metropolitan Statistical Area—see Appendix B for areas included
Source: U.S. Census Bureau, 2013-2017 American Community Survey 5-Year Estimates

Poverty Rate

Area	All Ages	Under 18 Years Old	18 to 64 Years Old	65 Years and Over
City	18.3	16.5	20.8	5.7
MSA[1]	11.7	11.8	12.8	5.7
U.S.	14.6	20.3	13.7	9.3

Note: Figures are percentage of people whose income during the past 12 months was below the poverty level; (1) Figures cover the Madison, WI Metropolitan Statistical Area—see Appendix B for areas included
Source: U.S. Census Bureau, 2013-2017 American Community Survey 5-Year Estimates

EMPLOYMENT

Labor Force and Employment

Area	Civilian Labor Force			Workers Employed		
	Dec. 2017	Dec. 2018	% Chg.	Dec. 2017	Dec. 2018	% Chg.
City	157,135	156,294	-0.5	154,210	153,374	-0.5
MSA[1]	390,310	388,149	-0.6	382,618	380,621	-0.5
U.S.	159,880,000	162,510,000	1.6	153,602,000	156,481,000	1.9

Note: Data is not seasonally adjusted and covers workers 16 years of age and older; (1) Figures cover the Madison, WI Metropolitan Statistical Area—see Appendix B for areas included
Source: Bureau of Labor Statistics, Local Area Unemployment Statistics

Unemployment Rate

Area	2018											
	Jan.	Feb.	Mar.	Apr.	May	Jun.	Jul.	Aug.	Sep.	Oct.	Nov.	Dec.
City	2.1	2.1	2.1	1.8	2.1	2.8	2.4	2.3	2.0	2.1	2.0	1.9
MSA[1]	2.3	2.5	2.4	1.9	2.1	2.8	2.4	2.3	2.0	2.1	2.0	1.9
U.S.	4.5	4.4	4.1	3.7	3.6	4.2	4.1	3.9	3.6	3.5	3.5	3.7

Note: Data is not seasonally adjusted and covers workers 16 years of age and older; (1) Figures cover the Madison, WI Metropolitan Statistical Area—see Appendix B for areas included
Source: Bureau of Labor Statistics, Local Area Unemployment Statistics

Average Wages

Occupation	$/Hr.	Occupation	$/Hr.
Accountants and Auditors	33.10	Maids and Housekeeping Cleaners	11.80
Automotive Mechanics	20.60	Maintenance and Repair Workers	20.60
Bookkeepers	19.50	Marketing Managers	60.40
Carpenters	25.80	Nuclear Medicine Technologists	43.90
Cashiers	11.00	Nurses, Licensed Practical	22.90
Clerks, General Office	17.80	Nurses, Registered	38.40
Clerks, Receptionists/Information	15.10	Nursing Assistants	15.80
Clerks, Shipping/Receiving	17.50	Packers and Packagers, Hand	16.80
Computer Programmers	37.10	Physical Therapists	40.00
Computer Systems Analysts	43.80	Postal Service Mail Carriers	24.80
Computer User Support Specialists	27.80	Real Estate Brokers	n/a
Cooks, Restaurant	13.10	Retail Salespersons	12.60
Dentists	112.50	Sales Reps., Exc. Tech./Scientific	32.70
Electrical Engineers	45.60	Sales Reps., Tech./Scientific	33.90
Electricians	28.60	Secretaries, Exc. Legal/Med./Exec.	18.60
Financial Managers	64.00	Security Guards	15.20
First-Line Supervisors/Managers, Sales	22.90	Surgeons	128.40
Food Preparation Workers	12.00	Teacher Assistants*	14.30
General and Operations Managers	61.90	Teachers, Elementary School*	27.80
Hairdressers/Cosmetologists	15.50	Teachers, Secondary School*	27.30
Internists, General	n/a	Telemarketers	13.80
Janitors and Cleaners	14.70	Truck Drivers, Heavy/Tractor-Trailer	23.60
Landscaping/Groundskeeping Workers	16.00	Truck Drivers, Light/Delivery Svcs.	17.20
Lawyers	59.10	Waiters and Waitresses	14.80

Note: Wage data covers the Madison, WI Metropolitan Statistical Area—see Appendix B for areas included; (*) Hourly wages for elementary/secondary school teachers and teacher assistants were calculated by the editors from annual wage data based on a 40 hour work week; n/a not available.
Source: Bureau of Labor Statistics, Metro Area Occupational Employment & Wage Estimates, May 2018

Employment by Occupation

Occupation Classification	City (%)	MSA[1] (%)	U.S. (%)
Management, Business, Science, and Arts	53.1	47.0	37.4
Natural Resources, Construction, and Maintenance	3.3	6.4	8.9
Production, Transportation, and Material Moving	7.2	9.7	12.2
Sales and Office	19.4	21.4	23.5
Service	16.9	15.5	18.0

Note: Figures cover employed civilians 16 years of age and older; (1) Figures cover the Madison, WI Metropolitan Statistical Area—see Appendix B for areas included
Source: U.S. Census Bureau, 2013-2017 American Community Survey 5-Year Estimates

Employment by Industry

Sector	MSA[1]		U.S.
	Number of Employees	Percent of Total	Percent of Total
Construction, Mining, and Logging	18,000	4.4	5.3
Education and Health Services	48,500	11.9	15.9
Financial Activities	23,100	5.7	5.7
Government	87,200	21.4	15.1
Information	17,100	4.2	1.9
Leisure and Hospitality	37,200	9.1	10.7
Manufacturing	35,200	8.6	8.5
Other Services	20,900	5.1	3.9
Professional and Business Services	52,400	12.9	14.1
Retail Trade	42,100	10.3	10.8
Transportation, Warehousing, and Utilities	10,200	2.5	4.2
Wholesale Trade	15,400	3.8	3.9

Note: Figures are non-farm employment as of December 2018. Figures are not seasonally adjusted and include workers 16 years of age and older; (1) Figures cover the Madison, WI Metropolitan Statistical Area—see Appendix B for areas included
Source: Bureau of Labor Statistics, Current Employment Statistics, Employment, Hours, and Earnings

Occupations with Greatest Projected Employment Growth: 2018 – 2020

Occupation[1]	2018 Employment	2020 Projected Employment	Numeric Employment Change	Percent Employment Change
Personal Care Aides	67,920	72,730	4,810	7.1
Registered Nurses	58,060	59,770	1,710	2.9
Combined Food Preparation and Serving Workers, Including Fast Food	66,990	68,580	1,590	2.4
Laborers and Freight, Stock, and Material Movers, Hand	58,500	59,990	1,490	2.5
Janitors and Cleaners, Except Maids and Housekeeping Cleaners	48,060	49,400	1,340	2.8
Sales Representatives, Wholesale and Manufacturing, Except Technical and Scientific Products	42,560	43,870	1,310	3.1
Heavy and Tractor-Trailer Truck Drivers	54,640	55,750	1,110	2.0
Carpenters	22,910	23,790	880	3.8
General and Operations Managers	37,480	38,350	870	2.3
Landscaping and Groundskeeping Workers	23,100	23,880	780	3.4

Note: Projections cover Wisconsin; (1) Sorted by numeric employment change
Source: www.projectionscentral.com, State Occupational Projections, 2018–2020 Short-Term Projections

Fastest Growing Occupations: 2018 – 2020

Occupation[1]	2018 Employment	2020 Projected Employment	Numeric Employment Change	Percent Employment Change
Rail-Track Laying and Maintenance Equipment Operators	540	590	50	9.3
Railroad Conductors and Yardmasters	800	870	70	8.8
Locomotive Engineers	1,030	1,120	90	8.7
Helpers—Pipelayers, Plumbers, Pipefitters, and Steamfitters	750	810	60	8.0
Chemical Engineers	660	710	50	7.6
Real Estate Brokers	790	850	60	7.6
Hazardous Materials Removal Workers	660	710	50	7.6
Home Health Aides	7,940	8,510	570	7.2
Plumbers, Pipefitters, and Steamfitters	9,010	9,660	650	7.2
Helpers—Electricians	1,670	1,790	120	7.2

Note: Projections cover Wisconsin; (1) Sorted by percent employment change and excludes occupations with numeric employment change less than 50
Source: www.projectionscentral.com, State Occupational Projections, 2018–2020 Short-Term Projections

TAXES

State Corporate Income Tax Rates

State	Tax Rate (%)	Income Brackets ($)	Num. of Brackets	Financial Institution Tax Rate (%)[a]	Federal Income Tax Ded.
Wisconsin	7.9	Flat rate	1	7.9	No

Note: Tax rates as of January 1, 2019; (a) Rates listed are the corporate income tax rate applied to financial institutions or excise taxes based on income. Some states have other taxes based upon the value of deposits or shares.
Source: Federation of Tax Administrators, Range of State Corporate Income Tax Rates, January 1, 2019

State Individual Income Tax Rates

State	Tax Rate (%)	Income Brackets ($)	Personal Exemptions ($)			Standard Ded. ($)	
			Single	Married	Depend.	Single	Married
Wisconsin (a)	4.0 - 7.65	11,760 - 258,950 (w)	700	1,400	700	10,860	20,110 (y)

Note: Tax rates as of January 1, 2019; Local- and county-level taxes are not included; n/a not applicable; Federal income tax is not deductible on state income tax returns; (a) 19 states have statutory provision for automatically adjusting to the rate of inflation the dollar values of the income tax brackets, standard deductions, and/or personal exemptions. Michigan indexes the personal exemption only. Oregon does not index the income brackets for $125,000 and over; (w) The Wisconsin income brackets reported are for single individuals. For married taxpayers filing jointly, the same tax rates apply income brackets ranging from $15,680, to $345,270; (y) Alabama standard deduction is phased out for incomes over $23,000. Rhode Island exemptions & standard deductions phased out for incomes over $203,850; Wisconsin standard deduciton phases out for income over $15,660.
Source: Federation of Tax Administrators, State Individual Income Tax Rates, January 1, 2019

Various State Sales and Excise Tax Rates

State	State Sales Tax (%)	Gasoline[1] (¢/gal.)	Cigarette[2] ($/pack)	Spirits[3] ($/gal.)	Wine[4] ($/gal.)	Beer[5] ($/gal.)	Recreational Marijuana (%)
Wisconsin	5	32.9	2.52	3.25	0.25 (l)	0.06 (q)	Not legal

Note: All tax rates as of January 1, 2019; (1) The American Petroleum Institute has developed a methodology for determining the average tax rate on a gallon of fuel. Rates may include any of the following: excise taxes, environmental fees, storage tank fees, other fees or taxes, general sales tax, and local taxes. In states where gasoline is subject to the general sales tax, or where the fuel tax is based on the average sale price, the average rate determined by API is sensitive to changes in the price of gasoline. States that fully or partially apply general sales taxes to gasoline: CA, CO, GA, IL, IN, MI, NY; (2) The federal excise tax of $1.0066 per pack and local taxes are not included; (3) Rates are those applicable to off-premise sales of 40% alcohol by volume (a.b.v.) distilled spirits in 750ml containers. Local excise taxes are excluded; (4) Rates are those applicable to off-premise sales of 11% a.b.v. non-carbonated wine in 750ml containers; (5) Rates are those applicable to off-premise sales of 4.7% a.b.v. beer in 12 ounce containers; (l) Different rates also applicable to alcohol content, place of production, size of container, place purchased (on- or off-premise or on board airlines) or type of wine (carbonated, vermouth, etc.); (q) Different rates also applicable according to alcohol content, place of production, size of container, or place purchased (on- or off-premise or onboard airlines).
Source: Tax Foundation, 2019 Facts & Figures: How Does Your State Compare?

State Business Tax Climate Index Rankings

State	Overall Rank	Corporate Tax Rank	Individual Income Tax Rank	Sales Tax Rank	Unemployment Insurance Tax Rank	Property Tax Rank
Wisconsin	32	35	39	8	41	21

Note: The index is a measure of how each state's tax laws affect economic performance. The lower the rank, the more favorable a state's tax system is for business. States without a given tax are given a ranking of 1. The scores/rankings for the District of Columbia do not affect other states. The 2019 index represents the tax climate as of July 1, 2018.
Source: Tax Foundation, State Business Tax Climate Index 2019

COMMERCIAL UTILITIES

Typical Monthly Electric Bills

Area	Commercial Service ($/month)		Industrial Service ($/month)	
	1,500 kWh	40 kW demand 14,000 kWh	1,000 kW demand 200,000 kWh	50,000 kW demand 32,500,000 kWh
City	215	1,727	29,303	2,820,183
Average[1]	203	1,619	25,886	2,540,077

Note: Figures are based on annualized rates; (1) Average based on 187 utilities surveyed
Source: Edison Electric Institute, Typical Bills and Average Rates Report, Summer 2018

TRANSPORTATION

Means of Transportation to Work

Area	Car/Truck/Van		Public Transportation			Bicycle	Walked	Other Means	Worked at Home
	Drove Alone	Car-pooled	Bus	Subway	Railroad				
City	63.5	7.4	9.4	0.0	0.0	4.8	9.6	1.1	4.2
MSA[1]	74.1	8.2	4.5	0.0	0.0	2.3	5.1	0.9	4.8
U.S.	76.4	9.2	2.5	1.9	0.6	0.6	2.7	1.3	4.7

Note: Figures are percentages and cover workers 16 years of age and older; (1) Figures cover the Madison, WI Metropolitan Statistical Area—see Appendix B for areas included
Source: U.S. Census Bureau, 2013-2017 American Community Survey 5-Year Estimates

Travel Time to Work

Area	Less Than 10 Minutes	10 to 19 Minutes	20 to 29 Minutes	30 to 44 Minutes	45 to 59 Minutes	60 to 89 Minutes	90 Minutes or More
City	15.0	41.0	23.8	14.6	3.0	2.0	0.7
MSA[1]	16.3	32.6	24.0	18.5	5.0	2.5	1.1
U.S.	12.7	28.9	20.9	20.5	8.1	6.2	2.7

Note: Note: Figures are percentages and include workers 16 years old and over; (1) Figures cover the Madison, WI Metropolitan Statistical Area—see Appendix B for areas included
Source: U.S. Census Bureau, 2013-2017 American Community Survey 5-Year Estimates

Freeway Travel Time Index

Area	1985	1990	1995	2000	2005	2010	2014
Urban Area Rank[1,2]	39	63	77	80	72	48	46
Urban Area Index[1]	1.08	1.08	1.09	1.11	1.15	1.17	1.18
Average Index[3]	1.09	1.11	1.14	1.17	1.20	1.19	1.20

Note: Freeway Travel Time Index—the ratio of travel time in the peak period to the travel time at free-flow conditions. For example, a value of 1.30 indicates a 20-minute free-flow trip takes 26 minutes in the peak (20 minutes x 1.30 = 26 minutes); (1) Covers the Madison WI urban area; (2) Rank is based on 101 urban areas (#1 = highest travel time index); (3) Average of 101 urban areas
Source: Texas Transportation Institute, 2015 Urban Mobility Scorecard, August 2015

Freeway Commuter Stress Index

Area	1985	1990	1995	2000	2005	2010	2014
Urban Area Rank[1,2]	42	59	76	81	68	53	52
Urban Area Index[1]	1.11	1.11	1.12	1.14	1.18	1.20	1.21
Average Index[3]	1.13	1.16	1.19	1.22	1.25	1.24	1.25

Note: The Freeway Commuter Stress Index is the same as the Freeway Travel Time Index (see table above) except that it includes only the travel in the peak directions during the peak periods; the TTI includes travel in all directions during the peak period. Thus, the CSI is more indicative of the work trip experienced by each commuter on a daily basis; (1) Covers the Madison WI urban area; (2) Rank is based on 101 urban areas (#1 = highest travel time index); (3) Average of 101 urban areas
Source: Texas Transportation Institute, 2015 Urban Mobility Scorecard, August 2015

Public Transportation

Agency Name / Mode of Transportation	Vehicles Operated in Maximum Service[1]	Annual Unlinked Passenger Trips[2] (in thous.)	Annual Passenger Miles[3] (in thous.)
Metro Transit System (Metro)			
Bus (directly operated)	182	12,817.1	50,606.8
Demand Response (directly operated)	12	52.8	209.3
Demand Response (purchased transportation)	60	238.2	1,499.5

Note: (1) The number of revenue vehicles operated by the given mode and type of service to meet the annual maximum service requirement. This is the revenue vehicle count during the peak season of the year; on the week and day that maximum service is provided. Vehicles operated in maximum service (VOMS) exclude atypical days and one-time special events; (2) The number of passengers who boarded public transportation vehicles. Passengers are counted each time they board a vehicle no matter how many vehicles they use to travel from their origin to their destination. (3) The sum of the distances ridden by all passengers during the entire fiscal year.
Source: Federal Transit Administration, National Transit Database, 2017

Air Transportation

Airport Name and Code / Type of Service	Passenger Airlines[1]	Passenger Enplanements	Freight Carriers[2]	Freight (lbs)
Dane County Regional-Truax Field (MSN)				
Domestic service (U.S. carriers - 2018)	24	1,041,604	7	25,971,318
International service (U.S. carriers - 2017)	0	0	2	47,329

Note: (1) Includes all U.S.-based major, minor and commuter airlines that carried at least one passenger during the year; (2) Includes all U.S.-based airlines and freight carriers that transported at least one pound of freight during the year.
Source: Bureau of Transportation Statistics, The Intermodal Transportation Database, Air Carriers: T-100 Domestic Market (U.S. Carriers), 2018; Bureau of Transportation Statistics, The Intermodal Transportation Database, Air Carriers: T-100 International Market (U.S. Carriers), 2017

Other Transportation Statistics

Major Highways:	I-90; I-94
Amtrak Service:	Bus connection
Major Waterways/Ports:	None

Source: Amtrak.com; Google Maps

BUSINESSES

Major Business Headquarters

Company Name	Industry	Rankings	
		Fortune[1]	Forbes[2]
American Family Insurance Group	Insurance: Property and Casualty (Stock)	311	-

Note: (1) Companies that produce a 10-K are ranked 1 to 500 based on 2017 revenue; (2) All private companies with at least $2 billion in annual revenue through the end of their most current fiscal year are ranked 1 to 229; companies listed are headquartered in the city; dashes indicate no ranking
Source: Fortune, "Fortune 500," June 2018; Forbes, "America's Largest Private Companies," 2018 Rankings

Fast-Growing Businesses

According to *Inc.*, Madison is home to two of America's 500 fastest-growing private companies: **SwanLeap** (#1); **EyeKor** (#484). Criteria: must be an independent, privately-held, for-profit, U.S. corporation, proprietorship or partnership as of December 31, 2017; revenues must be at least $100,000 in 2014 and $2 million in 2017; must have four-year operating/sales history. Holding companies, regulated banks, and utilities were excluded. *Inc., "America's 500 Fastest-Growing Private Companies," 2018*

According to Deloitte, Madison is home to two of North America's 500 fastest-growing high-technology companies: **SwanLeap** (#1); **Exact Sciences Corp** (#8). Companies are ranked by percentage growth in revenue over a four-year period. Criteria for inclusion: company must be headquartered within North America; must own proprietary intellectual property or technology that is sold to customers in products that contributes to a significant portion of the company's operating revenue; must have been in business for a minumum of four years with 2014 operating revenues of at least $50,000 USD/CD and 2017 operating revenues of at least $5 million USD/CD. *Deloitte, 2018 Technology Fast 500*[TM]

Minority Business Opportunity

Madison is home to one company which is on the *Hispanic Business* 500 list (500 largest U.S. Hispanic-owned companies based on revenue): **Cartridge Savers** (#193). Companies included must show at least 51 percent ownership by Hispanic U.S. citizens, and must maintain headquarters in one of the 50 states or Washington, D.C. *Hispanic Business, "Hispanic Business 500," June 20, 2013*

Minority- and Women-Owned Businesses

Group	All Firms		Firms with Paid Employees			
	Firms	Sales ($000)	Firms	Sales ($000)	Employees	Payroll ($000)
AIAN[1]	96	(s)	6	(s)	0 - 19	(s)
Asian	1,073	293,249	185	240,561	1,693	67,928
Black	1,028	38,193	36	25,015	442	8,135
Hispanic	648	492,586	130	(s)	500 - 999	(s)
NHOPI[2]	34	(s)	2	(s)	0 - 19	(s)
Women	7,329	1,379,723	722	1,212,701	8,343	292,151
All Firms	20,714	31,747,001	4,811	31,054,781	133,370	6,237,901

Note: Figures cover firms located in the city; minority- and women-owned business are defined as firms in which the corresponding group own 51% or more of the stock or equity of the company; (1) American Indian and Alaska Native; (2) Native Hawaiian and Other Pacific Islander; (s) estimates are suppressed when publication standards are not met
Source: U.S. Census Bureau, 2012 Economic Census, Survey of Business Owners

**HOTELS &
CONVENTION
CENTERS**

Hotels, Motels and Vacation Rentals

Area	5 Star		4 Star		3 Star		2 Star		1 Star		Not Rated	
	Num.	Pct.[3]	Num.	Pct.[3]	Num.	Pct.[3]	Num.	Pct.[3]	Num.	Pct.[3]	Num.	Pct.[3]
City[1]	0	0.0	6	2.7	47	21.0	64	28.6	0	0.0	107	47.8
Total[2]	286	0.4	5,236	7.1	16,715	22.6	10,259	13.9	293	0.4	41,056	55.6

Note: (1) Figures cover Madison and vicinity; (2) Figures cover all 100 cities in this book; (3) Percentage of hotels which have a given star rating; Star ratings are determined by expedia.com and offer an indication of the general quality of a particular hotel.
Source: www.expedia.com, April 3, 2019

Major Convention Centers

Name	Overall Space (sq. ft.)	Exhibit Space (sq. ft.)	Meeting Space (sq. ft.)	Meeting Rooms
Monona Terrace Convention Center	250,000	37,200	28,000	21

Note: Table includes convention centers located in the Madison, WI metro area
Source: Original research

Living Environment

COST OF LIVING

Cost of Living Index

Composite Index	Groceries	Housing	Utilities	Trans-portation	Health Care	Misc. Goods/ Services
106.1	105.4	109.4	99.4	103.3	118.5	104.4

Note: The Cost of Living Index measures regional differences in the cost of consumer goods and services, excluding taxes and non-consumer expenditures, for professional and managerial households in the top income quintile. It is based on more than 50,000 prices covering almost 60 different items for which prices are collected three times a year by chambers of commerce, economic development organizations or university applied economic centers in each participating urban area. The numbers shown should be read as a percentage above or below the national average of 100. For example, a value of 115.4 in the groceries column indicates that grocery prices are 15.4% higher than the national average. Small differences in the index numbers should not be interpreted as significant; Figures cover the Madison WI urban area.
Source: The Council for Community and Economic Research, ACCRA Cost of Living Index, 2018

Grocery Prices

Area[1]	T-Bone Steak ($/pound)	Frying Chicken ($/pound)	Whole Milk ($/half gal.)	Eggs ($/dozen)	Orange Juice ($/64 oz.)	Coffee ($/11.5 oz.)
City[2]	13.82	1.84	2.32	1.83	3.28	4.65
Avg.	11.35	1.42	1.94	1.81	3.52	4.35
Min.	7.45	0.92	0.80	0.75	2.72	3.06
Max.	15.05	2.76	4.18	4.00	5.36	8.20

Note: (1) Values for the local area are compared with the average, minimum and maximum values for all 291 areas in the Cost of Living Index; (2) Figures cover the Madison WI urban area; T-Bone Steak (price per pound); Frying Chicken (price per pound, whole fryer); Whole Milk (half gallon carton); Eggs (price per dozen, Grade A, large); Orange Juice (64 oz. Tropicana or Florida Natural); Coffee (11.5 oz. can, vacuum-packed, Maxwell House, Hills Bros, or Folgers).
Source: The Council for Community and Economic Research, ACCRA Cost of Living Index, 2018

Housing and Utility Costs

Area[1]	New Home Price ($)	Apartment Rent ($/month)	All Electric ($/month)	Part Electric ($/month)	Other Energy ($/month)	Telephone ($/month)
City[2]	396,381	1,067	-	106.73	63.18	173.00
Avg.	347,000	1,087	165.93	100.16	67.73	178.70
Min.	200,468	500	93.58	25.64	26.78	163.10
Max.	1,901,222	4,888	388.65	246.86	332.81	197.70

Note: (1) Values for the local area are compared with the average, minimum and maximum values for all 291 areas in the Cost of Living Index; (2) Figures cover the Madison WI urban area; New Home Price (2,400 sf living area, 8,000 sf lot, in urban area with full utilities); Apartment Rent (950 sf 2 bedroom/1.5 or 2 bath, unfurnished, excluding all utilities except water); All Electric (average monthly cost for an all-electric home); Part Electric (average monthly cost for a part-electric home); Other Energy (average monthly cost for natural gas, fuel oil, coal, wood, and any other forms of energy except electricity); Telephone (price includes the base monthly rate plus taxes and fees for three lines of mobile phone service).
Source: The Council for Community and Economic Research, ACCRA Cost of Living Index, 2018

Health Care, Transportation, and Other Costs

Area[1]	Doctor ($/visit)	Dentist ($/visit)	Optometrist ($/visit)	Gasoline ($/gallon)	Beauty Salon ($/visit)	Men's Shirt ($)
City[2]	182.00	101.33	59.00	2.51	41.78	31.99
Avg.	110.71	95.11	103.74	2.61	37.48	32.03
Min.	33.60	62.55	54.63	1.89	17.00	11.44
Max.	195.97	153.93	225.79	3.59	71.88	58.64

Note: (1) Values for the local area are compared with the average, minimum and maximum values for all 291 areas in the Cost of Living Index; (2) Figures cover the Madison WI urban area; Doctor (general practitioners routine exam of an established patient); Dentist (adult teeth cleaning and periodic oral examination); Optometrist (full vision eye exam for established adult patient); Gasoline (one gallon regular unleaded, national brand, including all taxes, cash price at self-service pump if available); Beauty Salon (woman's shampoo, trim, and blow-dry); Men's Shirt (cotton/polyester dress shirt, pinpoint weave, long sleeves).
Source: The Council for Community and Economic Research, ACCRA Cost of Living Index, 2018

HOUSING

House Price Index (HPI)

Area	National Ranking[2]	Quarterly Change (%)	One-Year Change (%)	Five-Year Change (%)
MSA[1]	140	-1.20	5.82	26.68
U.S.[3]	–	1.12	5.73	32.81

Note: The HPI is a weighted repeat sales index. It measures average price changes in repeat sales or refinancings on the same properties. This information is obtained by reviewing repeat mortgage transactions on single-family properties whose mortgages have been purchased or securitized by Fannie Mae or Freddie Mac in January 1975; (1) Figures cover the Madison, WI Metropolitan Statistical Area—see Appendix B for areas included; (2) Rankings are based on annual percentage change for all metro areas containing at least 15,000 transactions over the last 10 years and ranges from 1 to 245; (3) figures based on a weighted average of Census Division estimates using a seasonally adjusted, purchase-only index; all figures are for the period ending December 31, 2018
Source: Federal Housing Finance Agency, House Price Index, February 26, 2019

Median Single-Family Home Prices

Area	2016	2017	2018[p]	Percent Change 2017 to 2018
MSA[1]	247.3	267.9	283.7	5.9
U.S. Average	235.5	248.8	261.6	5.1

Note: Figures are median sales prices of existing single-family homes in thousands of dollars; (p) preliminary; (1) Figures cover the Madison, WI Metropolitan Statistical Area—see Appendix B for areas included
Source: National Association of Realtors, Median Sales Price of Existing Single-Family Homes for Metropolitan Areas, 4th Quarter 2018

Qualifying Income Based on Median Sales Price of Existing Single-Family Homes

Area	With 5% Down ($)	With 10% Down ($)	With 20% Down ($)
MSA[1]	68,086	64,502	57,335
U.S. Average	62,954	59,640	53,013

Note: Figures are preliminary; Qualifying income is based on a mortgage rate of 4.9%. Monthly principal and interest payment is limited to 25% of income; (1) Figures cover the Madison, WI Metropolitan Statistical Area—see Appendix B for areas included
Source: National Association of Realtors, Qualifying Income Based on Median Sales Price of Existing Single-Family Homes for Metropolitan Areas, 4th Quarter 2018

Median Apartment Condo-Coop Home Prices

Area	2016	2017	2018[p]	Percent Change 2017 to 2018
MSA[1]	169.2	183.1	195.0	6.5
U.S. Average	220.7	234.3	241.0	2.9

Note: Figures are median sales prices of existing apartment condo-coop homes in thousands of dollars; (p) preliminary; (1) Figures cover the Madison, WI Metropolitan Statistical Area—see Appendix B for areas included
Source: National Association of Realtors, Median Sales Price of Existing Apartment Condo-Coop Homes for Metropolitan Areas, 4th Quarter 2018

Home Value Distribution

Area	Under $50,000	$50,000 -$99,999	$100,000 -$149,999	$150,000 -$199,999	$200,000 -$299,999	$300,000 -$499,999	$500,000 -$999,999	$1,000,000 or more
City	2.3	2.9	11.0	24.0	34.1	20.4	4.7	0.6
MSA[1]	2.9	4.3	11.5	19.9	32.2	22.2	6.0	1.0
U.S.	8.3	13.9	14.7	14.6	18.7	17.3	9.7	2.7

Note: Figures are percentages and cover owner-occupied housing units; (1) Figures cover the Madison, WI Metropolitan Statistical Area—see Appendix B for areas included
Source: U.S. Census Bureau, 2013-2017 American Community Survey 5-Year Estimates

Homeownership Rate

Area	2010 (%)	2011 (%)	2012 (%)	2013 (%)	2014 (%)	2015 (%)	2016 (%)	2017 (%)	2018 (%)
MSA[1]	n/a	n/a	n/a	n/a	n/a	n/a	n/a	n/a	n/a
U.S.	66.9	66.1	65.4	65.1	64.5	63.7	63.4	63.9	64.4

Note: (1) Figures cover the Madison, WI Metropolitan Statistical Area—see Appendix B for areas included; n/a not available
Source: U.S. Census Bureau, Housing Vacancies and Homeownership Annual Statistics: 2010-2018

Year Housing Structure Built

Area	2010 or Later	2000 -2009	1990 -1999	1980 -1989	1970 -1979	1960 -1969	1950 -1959	1940 -1949	Before 1940	Median Year
City	3.8	15.9	13.4	11.4	14.5	11.5	11.1	4.8	13.6	1976
MSA[1]	3.8	17.3	16.0	11.3	15.7	9.5	8.2	3.6	14.6	1979
U.S.	3.2	14.5	14.0	13.6	15.5	10.8	10.5	5.1	12.9	1977

Note: Figures are percentages except for Median Year; Note: (1) Figures cover the Madison, WI Metropolitan Statistical Area—see Appendix B for areas included
Source: U.S. Census Bureau, 2013-2017 American Community Survey 5-Year Estimates

Gross Monthly Rent

Area	Under $500	$500 -$999	$1,000 -$1,499	$1,500 -$1,999	$2,000 -$2,499	$2,500 -$2,999	$3,000 and up	Median ($)
City	4.3	45.0	34.4	11.2	3.2	1.1	0.8	1,008
MSA[1]	5.8	49.6	32.2	8.9	2.3	0.7	0.5	958
U.S.	10.5	41.1	28.7	11.7	4.5	1.8	1.7	982

Note: Figures are percentages except for Median; Gross rent is the contract rent plus the estimated average monthly cost of utilities (electricity, gas, and water and sewer) and fuels (oil, coal, kerosene, wood, etc.) if these are paid by the renter (or paid for the renter by someone else); (1) Figures cover the Madison, WI Metropolitan Statistical Area—see Appendix B for areas included
Source: U.S. Census Bureau, 2013-2017 American Community Survey 5-Year Estimates

HEALTH

Health Risk Factors

Category	MSA[1] (%)	U.S. (%)
Adults aged 18–64 who have any kind of health care coverage	n/a	87.3
Adults who reported being in good or better health	n/a	82.4
Adults who have been told they have high blood cholesterol	n/a	33.0
Adults who have been told they have high blood pressure	n/a	32.3
Adults who are current smokers	n/a	17.1
Adults who currently use E-cigarettes	n/a	4.6
Adults who currently use chewing tobacco, snuff, or snus	n/a	4.0
Adults who are heavy drinkers[2]	n/a	6.3
Adults who are binge drinkers[3]	n/a	17.4
Adults who are overweight (BMI 25.0 - 29.9)	n/a	35.3
Adults who are obese (BMI 30.0 - 99.8)	n/a	31.3
Adults who participated in any physical activities in the past month	n/a	74.4
Adults who always or nearly always wears a seat belt	n/a	94.3

Note: n/a not available; (1) Figures cover the Madison, WI Metropolitan Statistical Area—see Appendix B for areas included; (2) Heavy drinkers are classified as adult men having more than 14 drinks per week and adult women having more than 7 drinks per week; (3) Binge drinkers are classified as males having five or more drinks on one occasion or females having four or more drinks on one occasion
Source: Centers for Disease Control and Prevention, Behaviorial Risk Factor Surveillance System, SMART: Selected Metropolitan Area Risk Trends, 2017

Acute and Chronic Health Conditions

Category	MSA[1] (%)	U.S. (%)
Adults who have ever been told they had a heart attack	n/a	4.2
Adults who have ever been told they have angina or coronary heart disease	n/a	3.9
Adults who have ever been told they had a stroke	n/a	3.0
Adults who have ever been told they have asthma	n/a	14.2
Adults who have ever been told they have arthritis	n/a	24.9
Adults who have ever been told they have diabetes[2]	n/a	10.5
Adults who have ever been told they had skin cancer	n/a	6.2
Adults who have ever been told they had any other types of cancer	n/a	7.1
Adults who have ever been told they have COPD	n/a	6.5
Adults who have ever been told they have kidney disease	n/a	3.0
Adults who have ever been told they have a form of depression	n/a	20.5

Note: n/a not available; (1) Figures cover the Madison, WI Metropolitan Statistical Area—see Appendix B for areas included; (2) Figures do not include pregnancy-related, borderline, or pre-diabetes
Source: Centers for Disease Control and Prevention, Behaviorial Risk Factor Surveillance System, SMART: Selected Metropolitan Area Risk Trends, 2017

Health Screening and Vaccination Rates

Category	MSA[1] (%)	U.S. (%)
Adults aged 65+ who have had flu shot within the past year	n/a	60.7
Adults aged 65+ who have ever had a pneumonia vaccination	n/a	75.4
Adults who have ever been tested for HIV	n/a	36.1
Adults who have ever had the shingles or zoster vaccine?	n/a	28.9
Adults who have had their blood cholesterol checked within the last five years	n/a	85.9

Note: n/a not available; (1) Figures cover the Madison, WI Metropolitan Statistical Area—see Appendix B for areas included.
Source: Centers for Disease Control and Prevention, Behavioral Risk Factor Surveillance System, SMART: Selected Metropolitan Area Risk Trends, 2017

Disability Status

Category	MSA[1] (%)	U.S. (%)
Adults who reported being deaf	n/a	6.7
Are you blind or have serious difficulty seeing, even when wearing glasses?	n/a	4.5
Are you limited in any way in any of your usual activities due of arthritis?	n/a	12.9
Do you have difficulty doing errands alone?	n/a	6.8
Do you have difficulty dressing or bathing?	n/a	3.6
Do you have serious difficulty concentrating/remembering/making decisions?	n/a	10.7
Do you have serious difficulty walking or climbing stairs?	n/a	13.6

Note: n/a not available; (1) Figures cover the Madison, WI Metropolitan Statistical Area—see Appendix B for areas included.
Source: Centers for Disease Control and Prevention, Behavioral Risk Factor Surveillance System, SMART: Selected Metropolitan Area Risk Trends, 2017

Mortality Rates for the Top 10 Causes of Death in the U.S.

ICD-10[a] Sub-Chapter	ICD-10[a] Code	Age-Adjusted Mortality Rate[1] per 100,000 population County[2]	U.S.
Malignant neoplasms	C00-C97	137.7	155.5
Ischaemic heart diseases	I20-I25	65.4	94.8
Other forms of heart disease	I30-I51	42.9	52.9
Chronic lower respiratory diseases	J40-J47	25.4	41.0
Cerebrovascular diseases	I60-I69	29.2	37.5
Other degenerative diseases of the nervous system	G30-G31	40.8	35.0
Other external causes of accidental injury	W00-X59	46.5	33.7
Organic, including symptomatic, mental disorders	F01-F09	34.7	31.0
Hypertensive diseases	I10-I15	13.0	21.9
Diabetes mellitus	E10-E14	14.2	21.2

Note: (a) ICD-10 = International Classification of Diseases 10th Revision; (1) Mortality rates are a three year average covering 2015-2017; (2) Figures cover Dane County.
Source: Centers for Disease Control and Prevention, National Center for Health Statistics. Underlying Cause of Death 1999-2017 on CDC WONDER Online Database

Mortality Rates for Selected Causes of Death

ICD-10[a] Sub-Chapter	ICD-10[a] Code	Age-Adjusted Mortality Rate[1] per 100,000 population County[2]	U.S.
Assault	X85-Y09	2.2	5.9
Diseases of the liver	K70-K76	7.9	14.1
Human immunodeficiency virus (HIV) disease	B20-B24	Suppressed	1.8
Influenza and pneumonia	J09-J18	10.7	14.3
Intentional self-harm	X60-X84	12.8	13.6
Malnutrition	E40-E46	Suppressed	1.6
Obesity and other hyperalimentation	E65-E68	1.8	2.1
Renal failure	N17-N19	6.3	13.0
Transport accidents	V01-V99	8.0	12.4
Viral hepatitis	B15-B19	Suppressed	1.6

Note: (a) ICD-10 = International Classification of Diseases 10th Revision; (1) Mortality rates are a three year average covering 2015-2017; (2) Figures cover Dane County; Data are suppressed when the data meet the criteria for confidentiality constraints; Mortality rates are flagged as unreliable when the rate would be calculated with a numerator of 20 or less.
Source: Centers for Disease Control and Prevention, National Center for Health Statistics. Underlying Cause of Death 1999-2017 on CDC WONDER Online Database

Health Insurance Coverage

Area	With Health Insurance	With Private Health Insurance	With Public Health Insurance	Without Health Insurance	Population Under Age 18 Without Health Insurance
City	94.8	83.2	21.9	5.2	2.8
MSA[1]	95.0	82.8	24.2	5.0	2.7
U.S.	89.5	67.2	33.8	10.5	5.7

Note: Figures are percentages that cover the civilian noninstitutionalized population; (1) Figures cover the Madison, WI Metropolitan Statistical Area—see Appendix B for areas included
Source: U.S. Census Bureau, 2013-2017 American Community Survey 5-Year Estimates

Number of Medical Professionals

Area	MDs[3]	DOs[3,4]	Dentists	Podiatrists	Chiropractors	Optometrists
County[1] (number)	3,114	110	370	26	225	120
County[1] (rate[2])	587.3	20.7	69.0	4.8	41.9	22.4
U.S. (rate[2])	279.3	23.0	68.4	6.0	27.1	16.2

Note: Data as of 2017 unless noted; (1) Data covers Dane County; (2) Rate per 100,000 population; (3) Data as of 2016 and includes all active, non-federal physicians; (4) Doctor of Osteopathic Medicine
Source: U.S. Department of Health and Human Services, Health Resources and Services Administration, Bureau of Health Professions, Area Resource File (ARF) 2017-2018

Best Hospitals

According to *U.S. News,* the Madison, WI metro area is home to one of the best hospitals in the U.S.: **University of Wisconsin Hospitals** (10 adult specialties and 6 pediatric specialties). The hospital listed was nationally ranked in at least one of 16 adult or 10 pediatric specialties. Only 170 hospitals nationwide were nationally ranked in one or more adult or pediatric specialty. Twenty hospitals in the U.S. made the Honor Roll. The Best Hospitals Honor Roll takes both the national rankings and the procedure and condition ratings into account. Hospitals received points if they were nationally ranked in one of the 16 adult specialties—the higher they ranked, the more points they got—and how many ratings of "high performing" they earned in the nine procedures and conditions. *U.S. News Online, "America's Best Hospitals 2018-19"*

According to *U.S. News,* the Madison, WI metro area is home to one of the best children's hospitals in the U.S.: **American Family Children's Hospital** (6 pediatric specialties). The hospital listed was highly ranked in at least one of 10 pediatric specialties. Eighty-six children's hospitals in the U.S. were nationally ranked in at least one specialty. Hospitals received points for being ranked in a specialty, and the 10 hospitals with the most points across the 10 specialties make up the Honor Roll. *U.S. News Online, "America's Best Children's Hospitals 2018-19"*

EDUCATION

Public School District Statistics

District Name	Schls	Pupils	Pupil/ Teacher Ratio	Minority Pupils[1] (%)	Free Lunch Eligible[2] (%)	IEP[3] (%)
Madison Metropolitan SD	53	26,999	12.7	57.1	42.1	13.5

Note: Table includes school districts with 2,000 or more students; (1) Percentage of students that are not non-Hispanic white; (2) Percentage of students that are eligible for the free lunch program; (3) Percentage of students that have an Individualized Education Program.
Source: U.S. Department of Education, National Center for Education Statistics, Common Core of Data, Local Education Agency (School District) Universe Survey: School Year 2016-2017; U.S. Department of Education, National Center for Education Statistics, Common Core of Data, Public Elementary/Secondary School Universe Survey: School Year 2016-2017

Highest Level of Education

Area	Less than H.S.	H.S. Diploma	Some College, No Deg.	Associate Degree	Bachelor's Degree	Master's Degree	Prof. School Degree	Doctorate Degree
City	4.6	14.1	15.8	8.4	32.2	15.5	4.4	5.1
MSA[1]	5.0	21.4	18.5	10.4	27.2	11.5	3.0	3.1
U.S.	12.7	27.3	20.8	8.3	19.1	8.4	2.0	1.4

Note: Figures cover persons age 25 and over; (1) Figures cover the Madison, WI Metropolitan Statistical Area—see Appendix B for areas included
Source: U.S. Census Bureau, 2013-2017 American Community Survey 5-Year Estimates

Educational Attainment by Race

Area	High School Graduate or Higher (%)					Bachelor's Degree or Higher (%)				
	Total	White	Black	Asian	Hisp.[2]	Total	White	Black	Asian	Hisp.[2]
City	95.4	96.8	89.1	89.7	76.3	57.1	59.1	24.0	68.6	33.4
MSA[1]	95.0	96.0	89.3	89.8	73.0	44.8	45.1	23.3	67.2	25.0
U.S.	87.3	89.3	84.9	86.5	66.7	30.9	32.2	20.6	52.7	15.2

Note: Figures shown cover persons 25 years old and over; (1) Figures cover the Madison, WI Metropolitan Statistical Area—see Appendix B for areas included; (2) People of Hispanic origin can be of any race
Source: U.S. Census Bureau, 2013-2017 American Community Survey 5-Year Estimates

School Enrollment by Grade and Control

Area	Preschool (%)		Kindergarten (%)		Grades 1 - 4 (%)		Grades 5 - 8 (%)		Grades 9 - 12 (%)	
	Public	Private	Public	Private	Public	Private	Public	Private	Public	Private
City	51.7	48.3	85.9	14.1	89.0	11.0	84.2	15.8	92.1	7.9
MSA[1]	63.0	37.0	89.5	10.5	90.0	10.0	89.4	10.6	94.7	5.3
U.S.	58.8	41.2	87.7	12.3	89.7	10.3	89.6	10.4	90.3	9.7

Note: Figures shown cover persons 3 years old and over; (1) Figures cover the Madison, WI Metropolitan Statistical Area—see Appendix B for areas included
Source: U.S. Census Bureau, 2013-2017 American Community Survey 5-Year Estimates

Average Salaries of Public School Classroom Teachers

Area	2016		2017		Change from 2016 to 2017	
	Dollars	Rank[1]	Dollars	Rank[1]	Percent	Rank[2]
Wisconsin	54,115	24	54,998	24	1.6	23
U.S. Average	58,479	–	59,660	–	2.0	–

Note: (1) Rank ranges from 1 to 51 where 1 indicates highest salary; (2) Rank ranges from 1 to 51 where 1 indicates highest percent change.
Source: National Education Association, Rankings & Estimates: Rankings of the States 2017 and Estimates of School Statistics 2018

Higher Education

Four-Year Colleges			Two-Year Colleges			Medical Schools[1]	Law Schools[2]	Voc/ Tech[3]
Public	Private Non-profit	Private For-profit	Public	Private Non-profit	Private For-profit			
3	2	1	1	0	2	1	1	3

Note: Figures cover institutions located within the city limits and include main campuses only; (1) includes schools accredited by the Liaison Committee on Medical Education and the American Osteopathic Association's Commission on Osteopathic College Accreditation; (2) includes ABA-accredited schools, schools with provisional ABA accreditation, and state accredited schools; (3) includes all schools with programs that are less than 2 years.
Source: National Center for Education Statistics, Integrated Postsecondary Education System (IPEDS), 2017-18; Wikipedia, List of Medical Schools in the United States, accessed April 3, 2019; Wikipedia, List of Law Schools in the United States, accessed April 3, 2019

According to *U.S. News & World Report,* the Madison, WI metro area is home to two of the best national universities in the U.S.: **University of Wisconsin—Madison** (#49 tie); **Edgewood College** (#165 tie). The indicators used to capture academic quality fall into a number of categories: assessment by administrators at peer institutions; retention of students; faculty resources; student selectivity; financial resources; alumni giving; high school counselor ratings of colleges; and graduation rate. *U.S. News & World Report, "America's Best Colleges 2019"*

According to *U.S. News & World Report,* the Madison, WI metro area is home to one of the top 100 law schools in the U.S.: **University of Wisconsin—Madison** (#34 tie). The rankings are based on a weighted average of 12 measures of quality: peer assessment score; assessment score by lawyers/judges; median LSAT scores; median undergrad GPA; acceptance rate; employment rates for graduates; placement success; bar passage rate; faculty resources; expenditures per student; student/faculty ratio; and library resources. *U.S. News & World Report, "America's Best Graduate Schools, Law, 2020"*

According to *U.S. News & World Report,* the Madison, WI metro area is home to one of the top 75 medical schools for research in the U.S.: **University of Wisconsin—Madison** (#27 tie). The rankings are based on a weighted average of 11 measures of quality: quality assessment; peer assessment score; assessment score by residency directors; research activity; total research activity; average research activity per faculty member; student selectivity; median MCAT total score; median undergraduate GPA; acceptance rate; and faculty resources. *U.S. News & World Report, "America's Best Graduate Schools, Medical, 2020"*

According to *U.S. News & World Report,* the Madison, WI metro area is home to one of the top 75 business schools in the U.S.: **University of Wisconsin—Madison** (#35 tie). The rankings are based on a weighted average of the following nine measures: quality assessment; peer assessment; recruiter assessment; placement success; mean starting salary and bonus; student selectivity; mean GMAT and GRE scores; mean undergraduate GPA; and acceptance rate. *U.S. News & World Report, "America's Best Graduate Schools, Business, 2020"*

PRESIDENTIAL ELECTION

2016 Presidential Election Results

Area	Clinton	Trump	Johnson	Stein	Other
Dane County	70.4	23.0	3.4	1.4	1.8
U.S.	48.0	45.9	3.3	1.1	1.7

Note: Results are percentages and may not add to 100% due to rounding
Source: Dave Leip's Atlas of U.S. Presidential Elections

EMPLOYERS

Major Employers

Company Name	Industry
American Family Mutual Insurance Company	Fire, marine, & casualty insurance
Community Living Alliance	Social services for the handicapped
Covence Laboratories	Druggists preparations
CUNA Mutual Insurance Society	Telephone communication, except radio
Kraft Foods Global	Luncheon meat from purchased meat
University of Wisconsin Hospitals	General medical & surgical hospitals
Veterans Health Administration	General medical & surgical hospitals
WI Dept of Workforce Development	Administration of social & manpower programs
Wisconsin Department of Administration	Administration of general economic programs
Wisconsin Department of Health Services	Administration of public health programs
Wisconsin Department of Natural Resources	Land, mineral, & wildlife conservation
Wisconsin Department of Transportation	State highway patrol
Wisconsin Dept of Natural Resources	Land, mineral, & wildlife conservation
Wisconsin Dept of Transportation	Regulation, administration of transportation
Wisconsin Physicians Srvc Ins Corp	Hospital & medical services plans

Note: Companies shown are located within the Madison, WI Metropolitan Statistical Area.
Source: Hoovers.com; Wikipedia

PUBLIC SAFETY

Crime Rate

Area	All Crimes	Violent Crimes				Property Crimes		
		Murder	Rape[3]	Robbery	Aggrav. Assault	Burglary	Larceny -Theft	Motor Vehicle Theft
City	3,036.5	4.3	37.1	82.9	250.1	362.3	2,130.9	168.8
Suburbs[1]	1,427.7	1.0	24.5	22.2	87.9	195.9	1,023.3	72.9
Metro[2]	2,054.7	2.3	29.4	45.8	151.1	260.8	1,455.0	110.3
U.S.	2,756.1	5.3	41.7	98.0	248.9	430.4	1,694.4	237.4

Note: Figures are crimes per 100,000 population; (1) All areas within the metro area that are located outside the city limits; (2) Figures cover the Madison, WI Metropolitan Statistical Area—see Appendix B for areas included; (3) The city and U.S. figures shown were reported using the revised Uniform Crime Reporting (UCR) definition of rape. The suburban and metro area figures shown are an aggregate total of the data submitted using both the revised and legacy UCR definitions.
Source: FBI Uniform Crime Reports, 2017

Hate Crimes

Area	Number of Quarters Reported	Number of Incidents per Bias Motivation					
		Race/Ethnicity/ Ancestry	Religion	Sexual Orientation	Disability	Gender	Gender Identity
City	4	0	1	1	0	0	0
U.S.	4	4,131	1,564	1,130	116	46	119

Source: Federal Bureau of Investigation, Hate Crime Statistics 2017

Identity Theft Consumer Reports

Area	Reports	Reports per 100,000 Population	Rank[2]
MSA[1]	475	73	253
U.S.	444,602	135	-

Note: (1) Figures cover the Madison, WI Metropolitan Statistical Area—see Appendix B for areas included; (2) Rank ranges from 1 to 389 where 1 indicates greatest number of identity theft reports per 100,000 population
Source: Federal Trade Commission, Consumer Sentinel Network Data Book for January–December 2018

Fraud and Other Consumer Reports

Area	Reports	Reports per 100,000 Population	Rank[2]
MSA[1]	2,968	457	239
U.S.	2,552,917	776	-

Note: (1) Figures cover the Madison, WI Metropolitan Statistical Area—see Appendix B for areas included; (2) Rank ranges from 1 to 389 where 1 indicates greatest number of fraud and other consumer reports per 100,000 population
Source: Federal Trade Commission, Consumer Sentinel Network Data Book for January–December 2018

SPORTS

Professional Sports Teams

Team Name	League	Year Established
No teams are located in the metro area		

Source: Wikipedia, Major Professional Sports Teams of the United States and Canada, April 5, 2019

CLIMATE

Average and Extreme Temperatures

Temperature	Jan	Feb	Mar	Apr	May	Jun	Jul	Aug	Sep	Oct	Nov	Dec	Yr.
Extreme High (°F)	56	61	82	94	93	101	104	102	99	90	76	62	104
Average High (°F)	26	30	42	58	70	79	84	81	72	61	44	30	57
Average Temp. (°F)	17	21	32	46	57	67	72	69	61	50	36	23	46
Average Low (°F)	8	12	22	35	45	54	59	57	49	38	27	14	35
Extreme Low (°F)	-37	-28	-29	0	19	31	36	35	25	13	-8	-25	-37

Note: Figures cover the years 1948-1990
Source: National Climatic Data Center, International Station Meteorological Climate Summary, 9/96

Average Precipitation/Snowfall/Humidity

Precip./Humidity	Jan	Feb	Mar	Apr	May	Jun	Jul	Aug	Sep	Oct	Nov	Dec	Yr.
Avg. Precip. (in.)	1.1	1.1	2.1	2.9	3.2	3.8	3.9	3.9	3.0	2.3	2.0	1.7	31.1
Avg. Snowfall (in.)	10	7	9	2	Tr	0	0	0	Tr	Tr	4	11	42
Avg. Rel. Hum. 6am (%)	78	80	81	80	79	81	85	89	90	85	84	82	83
Avg. Rel. Hum. 3pm (%)	66	63	59	50	50	51	53	55	55	54	64	69	57

Note: Figures cover the years 1948-1990; Tr = Trace amounts (<0.05 in. of rain; <0.5 in. of snow)
Source: National Climatic Data Center, International Station Meteorological Climate Summary, 9/96

Weather Conditions

Temperature			Daytime Sky			Precipitation		
5°F & below	32°F & below	90°F & above	Clear	Partly cloudy	Cloudy	0.01 inch or more precip.	0.1 inch or more snow/ice	Thunder-storms
35	161	14	88	119	158	118	38	40

Note: Figures are average number of days per year and cover the years 1948-1990
Source: National Climatic Data Center, International Station Meteorological Climate Summary, 9/96

HAZARDOUS WASTE

Superfund Sites

The Madison, WI metro area is home to five sites on the EPA's Superfund National Priorities List: **City Disposal Corp. Landfill** (final); **Hagen Farm** (final); **Madison Metropolitan Sewerage District Lagoons** (final); **Refuse Hideaway Landfill** (final); **Stoughton City Landfill** (final). There are a total of 1,390 Superfund sites with a status of proposed or final on the list in the U.S. *U.S. Environmental Protection Agency, National Priorities List, April 5, 2019*

**AIR & WATER
QUALITY**

Air Quality Trends: Ozone

	1990	1995	2000	2005	2010	2012	2014	2015	2016	2017
MSA[1]	0.077	0.084	0.072	0.079	0.062	0.074	0.068	0.064	0.068	0.064
U.S.	0.088	0.089	0.082	0.080	0.073	0.075	0.067	0.068	0.069	0.068

Note: (1) Data covers the Madison, WI Metropolitan Statistical Area—see Appendix B for areas included. The values shown are the composite ozone concentration averages among trend sites based on the highest fourth daily maximum 8-hour concentration in parts per million. These trends are based on sites having an adequate record of monitoring data during the trend period. Data from exceptional events are included.
Source: U.S. Environmental Protection Agency, Air Quality Monitoring Information, "Air Quality Trends by City, 1990-2017"

Air Quality Index

Area	Percent of Days when Air Quality was...[2]					AQI Statistics[2]	
	Good	Moderate	Unhealthy for Sensitive Groups	Unhealthy	Very Unhealthy	Maximum	Median
MSA[1]	80.5	19.5	0.0	0.0	0.0	93	39

Note: (1) Data covers the Madison, WI Metropolitan Statistical Area—see Appendix B for areas included; (2) Based on 365 days with AQI data in 2017. Air Quality Index (AQI) is an index for reporting daily air quality. EPA calculates the AQI for five major air pollutants regulated by the Clean Air Act: ground-level ozone, particle pollution (aka particulate matter), carbon monoxide, sulfur dioxide, and nitrogen dioxide. The AQI runs from 0 to 500. The higher the AQI value, the greater the level of air pollution and the greater the health concern. There are six AQI categories: "Good" AQI is between 0 and 50. Air quality is considered satisfactory; "Moderate" AQI is between 51 and 100. Air quality is acceptable; "Unhealthy for Sensitive Groups" When AQI values are between 101 and 150, members of sensitive groups may experience health effects; "Unhealthy" When AQI values are between 151 and 200 everyone may begin to experience health effects; "Very Unhealthy" AQI values between 201 and 300 trigger a health alert; "Hazardous" AQI values over 300 trigger warnings of emergency conditions (not shown).
Source: U.S. Environmental Protection Agency, Air Quality Index Report, 2017

Air Quality Index Pollutants

Area	Percent of Days when AQI Pollutant was...[2]					
	Carbon Monoxide	Nitrogen Dioxide	Ozone	Sulfur Dioxide	Particulate Matter 2.5	Particulate Matter 10
MSA[1]	0.0	0.0	53.4	1.9	44.7	0.0

Note: (1) Data covers the Madison, WI Metropolitan Statistical Area—see Appendix B for areas included; (2) Based on 365 days with AQI data in 2017. The Air Quality Index (AQI) is an index for reporting daily air quality. EPA calculates the AQI for five major air pollutants regulated by the Clean Air Act: ground-level ozone, particle pollution (also known as particulate matter), carbon monoxide, sulfur dioxide, and nitrogen dioxide. The AQI runs from 0 to 500. The higher the AQI value, the greater the level of air pollution and the greater the health concern.
Source: U.S. Environmental Protection Agency, Air Quality Index Report, 2017

Maximum Air Pollutant Concentrations: Particulate Matter, Ozone, CO and Lead

	Particulate Matter 10 (ug/m^3)	Particulate Matter 2.5 Wtd AM (ug/m^3)	Particulate Matter 2.5 24-Hr (ug/m^3)	Ozone (ppm)	Carbon Monoxide (ppm)	Lead (ug/m^3)
MSA[1] Level	28	7.8	21	0.065	n/a	n/a
NAAQS[2]	150	15	35	0.075	9	0.15
Met NAAQS[2]	Yes	Yes	Yes	Yes	n/a	n/a

Note: (1) Data covers the Madison, WI Metropolitan Statistical Area—see Appendix B for areas included; Data from exceptional events are included; (2) National Ambient Air Quality Standards; ppm = parts per million; ug/m^3 = micrograms per cubic meter; n/a not available.
Concentrations: Particulate Matter 10 (coarse particulate)—highest second maximum 24-hour concentration; Particulate Matter 2.5 Wtd AM (fine particulate)—highest weighted annual mean concentration; Particulate Matter 2.5 24-Hour (fine particulate)—highest 98th percentile 24-hour concentration; Ozone—highest fourth daily maximum 8-hour concentration; Carbon Monoxide—highest second maximum non-overlapping 8-hour concentration; Lead—maximum running 3-month average
Source: U.S. Environmental Protection Agency, Air Quality Monitoring Information, "Air Quality Statistics by City, 2017"

Maximum Air Pollutant Concentrations: Nitrogen Dioxide and Sulfur Dioxide

	Nitrogen Dioxide AM (ppb)	Nitrogen Dioxide 1-Hr (ppb)	Sulfur Dioxide AM (ppb)	Sulfur Dioxide 1-Hr (ppb)	Sulfur Dioxide 24-Hr (ppb)
MSA[1] Level	n/a	n/a	n/a	3	n/a
NAAQS[2]	53	100	30	75	140
Met NAAQS[2]	n/a	n/a	n/a	Yes	n/a

Note: (1) Data covers the Madison, WI Metropolitan Statistical Area—see Appendix B for areas included; Data from exceptional events are included; (2) National Ambient Air Quality Standards; ppm = parts per million; ug/m³ = micrograms per cubic meter; n/a not available.
Concentrations: Nitrogen Dioxide AM—highest arithmetic mean concentration; Nitrogen Dioxide 1-Hr—highest 98th percentile 1-hour daily maximum concentration; Sulfur Dioxide AM—highest annual mean concentration; Sulfur Dioxide 1-Hr—highest 99th percentile 1-hour daily maximum concentration; Sulfur Dioxide 24-Hr—highest second maximum 24-hour concentration
Source: U.S. Environmental Protection Agency, Air Quality Monitoring Information, "Air Quality Statistics by City, 2017"

Drinking Water

Water System Name	Pop. Served	Primary Water Source Type	Violations[1] Health Based	Violations[1] Monitoring/ Reporting
Madison Water Utility	235,000	Ground	0	0

Note: (1) Based on violation data from January 1, 2018 to December 31, 2018
Source: U.S. Environmental Protection Agency, Office of Ground Water and Drinking Water, Safe Drinking Water Information System (based on data extracted April 5, 2019)

Minneapolis, Minnesota

Background

Minneapolis is a vibrant, cosmopolitan city that boasts sunlit skyscrapers and sparkling lakes, as well as theater, museums and abundant recreation. Known for excellence in the fields of performing arts, visual arts, education, finance, advertising, and manufacturing, Minneapolis is also a hub of trade, industry, transportation and finance for the Upper Midwest.

In 1680, a French Franciscan priest, Father Louis Hennepin, was the area's first white man to arrive. In 1819, Fort Snelling was established to protect fur traders from the Sioux and Chippewa tribes. In 1848, two towns, St. Anthony (later named St. Paul), and Minneapolis, grew simultaneously, thus forming the metropolitan area known today as the Twin Cities. A tide of Swedish, German, and Norwegian immigrants came in the late nineteenth century, giving the city a decidedly Scandinavian flavor. Its many lakes gave Minneapolis its name, which comes from the Dakota word "minne," or "of the waters," and the Greek "polis," or city.

Minneapolis's traditional industries were lumber and flour milling. Since the 1950s, technology, including electronics, computers, and other related science industries, has played a vital role in the city's economy, as has printing and advertising.

The city's economy is fueled by an influx of urban dwellers and rapid growth of rental units to house them. The Pillsbury A-Mill Apartment Complex, and the 26 Story Apartment Building are just two of the city's muti-million dollar housing projects.

In addition, the U.S. Bank Stadium was funded by its NFL tenants, the Minnesota Vikings, and the state. During construction of the stadium—built on the site of the old Metrodome—the team played its 2014 and 2015 seasons in the TCF Bank Stadium at the University of Minnesota. Called "Minnesota's biggest-ever public works project," the stadium opened in 2016 with 66,000 seats, and expanded to 70,000 for the 2018 Super Bowl.

Minneapolis has the fourth-highest percentage of gay, lesbian, or bisexual people in the adult population, behind San Francisco, Seattle, and Atlanta. In 2013, the city was among 25 U.S. cities to receive the highest possible score from the Human Rights Campaign, signifying its support for LGBT residents.

Well-known for its cultural and artistic offerings, Minneapolis occupies more theater seats per capita than any U.S. city outside of New York. The Minneapolis Institute of Arts has more than 100,000 pieces of art with renovated African Art galleries. A Michael Graves-designed wing holds contemporary and modern works. Other area attractions include the Science Museum of Minnesota, the Minneapolis Zoo and the Charles A. Lindbergh Historic Site.

More than five miles of downtown Minneapolis are connected by comfortable, climate-controlled glass "skyways" one flight above ground.

Minneapolis is home to award-winning restaurants and chefs. As of 2018, six Minneapolis-based chefs have won James Beard Foundation Awards, causing the city to be named one of the ten best places to visit in the world.

Minneapolis is a major transportation hub. The Minneapolis-St. Paul International Airport is the 16th busiest in North America in terms of number of travelers served, and supports $10.1 billion in business revenue.

The city also hosts a Northstar Corridor commuter line between downtown and Big Lake on existing railroad tracks, and a Green Line linking downtown, the University of Minnesota, and downtown St. Paul. Old rail lines and bridges within the city have been converted for bicycles and pedestrians.

Minneapolis is located at the confluence of the Mississippi and Minnesota rivers. Numerous lakes mark the surrounding region, with 22 within the city park system. The climate is predominantly continental, with extreme swings in seasonal temperatures. Blizzards, freezing rain, tornadoes, wind, and hail storms do occur. Due to the spring snow melt and excessive rain, the Mississippi River sees its share of floods.

Rankings

General Rankings

- *US News & World Report* conducted a survey of more than 2,000 people and analyzed the 125 largest metropolitan areas to determine what matters the most when selecting the next place to live. Minneapolis ranked #9 out of the top 25 as having the best combination of desirable factors. Criteria: cost of living; quality of education; job market, crime rates; and other factors. *realestate.usnews.com, "The 25 Best Places to Live in the U.S. in 2018," April 10, 2018*

- *Insider* listed 33 places in the U.S. that were a must see vacation destination. Whether it is the great beaches, exploring a new city or experiencing the great outdoors, according to the website thisisinsider.com Minneapolis is a place to visit in 2018. *Insider, "33 Trips Everyone Should Take in the U.S. in 2018," November 27, 2017*

- In its eighth annual survey, *Travel + Leisure* readers nominated their favorite small cities and towns in America—those with 100,000 or fewer residents—voting on numerous attractive features in categories including culture, food and drink, quality of life, style, and people. After 50,000 votes, Minneapolis was ranked #12 among the proposed favorites. *www.travelandleisure.com, "America's Favorite Cities," October 20, 2017*

- Minneapolis was selected as one of the best places to live in America by *Outside Magazine*. Criteria included great access to trails and public lands, great for children, delicious food and drink, and welcoming to people of all backgrounds. Three decades of coverage was combined with the expertise of an advisory council to pick the finalists. *Outside Magazine, "The 25 Best Towns of 2017," July 2017*

- Minneapolis was selected as one of the "The 10 Best Places to Live" by *Men's Journal. Men's Journal, "The 10 Best Places to Live," March 8, 2016*

- The human resources consulting firm Mercer ranked 231 major cities worldwide in terms of overall quality of life. Minneapolis ranked #61. Criteria: political, social, economic, and socio-cultural factors; medical and health considerations; schools and education; public services and transportation; recreation; consumer goods; housing; and natural environment. *Mercer, "Mercer 2019 Quality of Living Survey," March 13, 2019*

- Based on more than 425,000 responses, *Condé Nast Traveler* ranked its readers' favorite cities in the U.S. The list was broken into cities over 1 million and cities under 1 million. Minneapolis ranked #14 in the big city category. *Condé Nast Traveler, Readers' Choice Awards 2018, "Best Big Cities in the U.S." October 9, 2018*

- In their sixth annual survey, Livability.com looked at data for more than 1,000 U.S. cities to determine the rankings for Livability's "Top 100 Best Places to Live" in 2019. Minneapolis ranked #13. Criteria: median home value capped at $250,000; affordable living; vibrant economy; education, demographics, health care options. transportation & infrastructure; abundant lifestyle amenities. *Livability.com, "Top 100 Best Places to Live 2019" March 2019*

Business/Finance Rankings

- According to *Business Insider*, the Minneapolis metro area is where startup growth is on the rise. Based on the 2017 Kauffman Index of Growth Entrepreneurship, which measured in-depth national entrepreneurial trends in 40 metro areas, it ranked #9 in highest startup growth. *www.businessinsider.com, "The 21 U.S. Cities with the Highest Startup Growth," October 21, 2017*

- The personal finance site NerdWallet analyzed 183 American metropolitan areas with populations over 250,000 and more than 15,000 businesses to rank where entrepreneurs find the most success. Criteria included area economy, annual income, housing cost, unemployment rate, and the success rate of area businesses. Minneapolis ranked #14. *www.nerdwallet.com, "Best Places to Start a Business," April 27, 2015*

- Experian's latest annual report on consumer credit ranked cities by the average credit score of its residents. Minneapolis was ranked #1 among the ten cities with the highest average credit score, meaning that its residents showed strong credit management. *www.usatoday.com, "Minneapolis Tops List of Cities With Best Average Credit Score; Greenwood Miss., at the Bottom," January 11, 2018*

- Based on metro area social media reviews, the employment opinion group Glassdoor surveyed 50 of the largest U.S. metro areas and equally weighed cost of living, hiring opportunity, and job satisfaction to compose a list of "25 Best Cities for Jobs." Median pay and home value, in-demand jobs and number of current job openings was also factored in. The Minneapolis metro area was ranked #21 in overall job satisfaction. *www.glassdoor.com, "Best Cities for Jobs," October 16, 2018*

- In a survey of economic confidence in the nation's 50 largest metropolitan areas conducted January–December 2014, the Minneapolis metro area placed #4, according to Gallup's 2014 Economic Confidence Index. *Gallup, "San Jose and San Francisco Lead in Economic Confidence," March 19, 2015*

- Using data from the Council for Community and Economic Research's 2014 cost of living index, NerdWallet ranked the 100 most affordable cities in America. Median income was compared with cost of living to find truly affordable places. Minneapolis ranked #88. *NerdWallet.com, "America's Most Affordable Places," May 18, 2015*

- NerdWallet.com identified the 10 most promising cities for job seekers of the nation's 100 largest cities. Minneapolis was ranked #7. Criteria: job availability; annual salary; workforce growth; affordability. *NerdWallet.com, "Best Cities for Job Seekers in 2017," December 19, 2016*

- The Brookings Institution ranked the nation's largest cities based on income inequality. Minneapolis was ranked #31 (#1 = greatest inequality). Criteria: the "95/20 ratio," a figure representing the income at which a household earns more than 95 percent of all other households, divided by the income at which a household earns more than only 20 percent of all other households. *Brookings Institution, "Household Income Inequality, Largest Cities of 97 Large U.S. Metro Areas, 2014-2016," February 5, 2018*

- The Brookings Institution ranked the 100 largest metro areas in the U.S. based on income inequality. Minneapolis was ranked #85 (#1 = greatest inequality). Criteria: the "95/20 ratio," a figure representing the income at which a household earns more than 95 percent of all other households, divided by the income at which a household earns more than only 20 percent of all other households. *Brookings Institution, "Household Income Inequality, 100 Largest U.S. Metro Areas, 2014-2016," February 5, 2018*

- *Forbes* ranked the 100 largest metro areas in the U.S. in terms of the "Best Cities for Young Professionals." The Minneapolis metro area ranked #13 out of 25. (Large metro areas were divided into metro divisions.) Criteria: median rent of a two-bedroom apartment; job growth and unemployment rate; median salary of college graduates with 5 or less years of work experience; networking opportunities; social outlook; percentage of population 25 years of age and older with college degrees. *Forbes.com, "America's 25 Best Cities for Young Professionals in 2017," May 22, 2017*

- Payscale.com ranked the 32 largest metro areas in terms of wage growth. The Minneapolis metro area ranked #10. Criteria: private-sector wage growth between the 4th quarter of 2017 and the 4th quarter of 2018. *PayScale, "Wage Trends by Metro Area-4th Quarter," January 8, 2019*

- The Minneapolis metro area was identified as one of the most debt-ridden places in America by the finance site Credit.com. The metro area was ranked #22. Criteria: residents' average credit card debt as well as median income. *Credit.com, "25 Cities With the Most Credit Card Debt," February 28, 2018*

- The Minneapolis metro area appeared on the Milken Institute "2018 Best Performing Cities" list. Rank: #79 out of 200 large metro areas. Criteria: job growth; wage and salary growth; high-tech output growth. *Milken Institute, "Best-Performing Cities 2018," January 24, 2019*

- *Forbes* ranked the 200 most populous metro areas to determine the nation's "Best Places for Business and Careers." The Minneapolis metro area was ranked #18. Criteria: costs (business and living); job growth (past and projected); income growth; quality of life; educational attainment (college and high school); projected economic growth; cultural and recreational opportunities; net migration patterns; number of highly ranked colleges. *Forbes, "The Best Places for Business and Careers 2018: Seattle Leads the Way," October 24, 2018*

- Mercer Human Resources Consulting ranked 209 cities worldwide in terms of cost-of-living. Minneapolis ranked #102 (the lower the ranking, the higher the cost-of-living). The survey measured the comparative cost of over 200 items (such as housing, food, clothing, household goods, transportation, and entertainment) in each location. *Mercer, "2018 Cost of Living Survey," June 26, 2018*

Children/Family Rankings

- *Forbes* analyzed data on the 100 largest metropolitan areas in the United States to compile its 2016 ranking of the best cities for raising a family. The Minneapolis metro area was ranked #15. Criteria: median income; childcare costs; percent of population under 18; commuting delays; crime rate; percentage of families owning homes; education quality (mainly test scores). Overall cost of living and housing affordability was also unofficially considered. *Forbes, "America's Best Cities for Raising a Family 2016," August 30, 2016*

Culture/Performing Arts Rankings

- Minneapolis was selected as one of "America's Favorite Cities." The city ranked #8 in the "Culture" category. Respondents to an online survey were asked to rate 38 top urban destinations in the U.S. from a visitor's perspective. Criteria: theater scene and community; number of bookstores; live music; and sense of history. *Travelandleisure.com, "These Are America's 20 Most Cultured Cities," October 2016*

- Minneapolis was selected as one of "America's Favorite Cities." The city ranked #3 in the "Culture: Art Scene " category. Respondents to an online survey were asked to rate 38 top urban destinations in the U.S. from a visitor's perspective. Criteria: number and quality of art events. *Travelandleisure.com, "America's Favorite Cities," October 11, 2015*

- Minneapolis was selected as one of "America's Favorite Cities." The city ranked #4 in the "Culture: Concerts " category. Respondents to an online survey were asked to rate 38 top urban destinations in the U.S. from a visitor's perspective. Criteria: number and quality of concerts. *Travelandleisure.com, "America's Favorite Cities," October 11, 2015*

- Minneapolis was selected as one of "America's Favorite Cities." The city ranked #5 in the "Culture: Music Scene " category. Respondents to an online survey were asked to rate 38 top urban destinations in the U.S. from a visitor's perspective. *Travelandleisure.com, "From the Honkytonk Capital to Jazz's Birthplace: America's Best Music Scenes," October 2016*

- Minneapolis was selected as one of "America's Favorite Cities." The city ranked #2 in the "Culture: Theater " category. Respondents to an online survey were asked to rate 38 top urban destinations in the U.S. from a visitor's perspective. Criteria: number and quality of theater offerings. *Travelandleisure.com, "America's Favorite Cities," October 11, 2015*

Dating/Romance Rankings

- *Apartment List* conducted its annual survey of renters to compile a list of cities that have the best opportunities for dating. More than 9,000 respondents, from February 2018 through the end of December 2018, rated their current city or neighborhood for opportunities to date and make friends. Minneapolis ranked #4 out of 66 where single residents were very satisfied or somewhat satisfied, making it among the ten best metros for dating opportunities. Other criteria analyzed included gender and education levels of renters. *Apartment List, "The Best & Worst Cities for Dating 2019," February 8, 2019*

- Minneapolis was selected as one of the best cities for post grads by *Rent.com*. The city ranked #2 of 10. Criteria: millennial population; jobs per capita; unemployment rate; median rent; number of bars and restaurants; access to nightlife and entertainment. *Rent.com, "Top 10 Best Cities for Post Grads," April 3, 2015*

Education Rankings

- Personal finance website *WalletHub* analyzed the 150 largest U.S. metropolitan statistical areas to determine where the most educated Americans are choosing to settle. Criteria: education quality and attainment gap; education levels; percentage of workers with degrees; public school quality rankings; quality and size of each metro area's universities. Minneapolis was ranked #17 (#1 = most educated city). *www.WalletHub.com, "2018's Most and Least Educated Cities in America, " July 24, 2018*

- Minneapolis was selected as one of America's most literate cities. The city ranked #3 out of the 82 largest U.S. cities. Criteria: number of booksellers; library resources; Internet resources; educational attainment; periodical publishing resources; newspaper circulation. *Central Connecticut State University, "America's Most Literate Cities, 2016," March 31, 2017*

Environmental Rankings

- Niche compiled a list of the nation's snowiest cities, based on the National Oceanic and Atmospheric Administration's 30-year average snowfall data. Among cities with a population of at least 50,000, Minneapolis ranked #24. *Niche.com, Top 25 Snowiest Cities in America, December 10, 2018*

- Sperling's BestPlaces assessed the 50 largest metropolitan areas of the United States for the likelihood of dangerously extreme weather events or earthquakes. In general the Southeast and South-Central regions have the highest risk of weather extremes and earthquakes, while the Pacific Northwest enjoys the lowest risk. Of the least risky metropolitan areas, the Minneapolis metro area was ranked #7. *www.bestplaces.net, "Avoid Natural Disasters: BestPlaces Reveals The Top 10 Safest Places to Live," October 25, 2017*

- The U.S. Environmental Protection Agency (EPA) released a list of U.S. metropolitan areas with the most ENERGY STAR certified buildings in 2017. The Minneapolis metro area was ranked #19 out of 25. *U.S. Environmental Protection Agency, "2018 Energy Star Top Cities," April 11, 2018*

- The U.S. Conference of Mayors and Walmart Stores sponsor the Mayors' Climate Protection Awards Program which recognize mayors for outstanding and innovative practices that mayors are taking to increase energy efficiency in their cities, reduce carbon emissions and expand renewable energy. Minneapolis received an Honorable Mention in the large city category. *U.S. Conference of Mayors, "2018 Mayors' Climate Protection Awards Program," June 8, 2018*

Food/Drink Rankings

- The U.S. Chamber of Commerce Foundation conducted an in-depth study on local food truck regulations, surveyed 288 food truck owners, and ranked 20 major American cities based on how friendly they are for operating a food truck. The compiled index assessed the following: procedures for obtaining permits and licenses; complying with restrictions; and financial obligations associated with operating a food truck. Minneapolis ranked #16 overall (1 being the best) for ease in operating a food truck. *www.foodtrucknation.us, "Food Truck Nation," March 20, 2018*

- According to Fodor's Travel, Minneapolis placed among the 14 best U.S. cities for food-truck cuisine. *www.fodors.com, "America's Best Food Truck Cities," August 23, 2016*

- *Men's Health* ranked 100 major U.S. cities in terms of alcohol intoxication. Minneapolis ranked #80 (#1 = most sober).Criteria: binge drinking; alcohol-related traffic accidents, arrests, and fatalities. *Men's Health, "America's Drunkest Cities," March 9, 2015*

- Minneapolis was selected as one of America's 10 most vegan-friendly cities. The city was ranked #4. *People for the Ethical Treatment of Animals, "Top 10 Vegan-Friendly Cities of 2018," May 16, 2018*

- Target Field was selected as one of PETA's "Top 10 Vegan-Friendly Ballparks" for 2018. The park ranked #1. *People for the Ethical Treatment of Animals, "Top 10 Vegan-Friendly Ballparks, " June 4, 2018*

Health/Fitness Rankings

- For each of the 100 largest cities in the United States, the American College of Sports Medicine's American Fitness Index evaluated infrastructure, community assets, and policies that encourage healthy and fit lifestyles, including preventive health behaviors, levels of chronic disease conditions, health care access, and community resources and policies that support physical activity. Minneapolis ranked #2 for "community fitness." *www.americanfitnessindex.org, "ACSM American Fitness Index Health and Community Fitness Status of the 100 Largest U.S. Cities," May 2018*

- Minneapolis was identified as a "2018 Spring Allergy Capital." The area ranked #70 out of 100. Three groups of factors were used to identify the most challenging cities for people with allergies during the spring season: annual pollen levels; medicine utilization; access to board-certified allergists. *Asthma and Allergy Foundation of America, "Spring Allergy Capitals 2018"*

- Minneapolis was identified as a "2018 Fall Allergy Capital." The area ranked #68 out of 100. Three groups of factors were used to identify the most challenging cities for people with allergies during the fall season: annual pollen levels; medicine utilization; access to board-certified allergists. *Asthma and Allergy Foundation of America, "Fall Allergy Capitals 2018"*

- Minneapolis was identified as a "2018 Asthma Capital." The area ranked #95 out of the nation's 100 largest metropolitan areas. Criteria: estimated prevalence; self-reported prevalence; crude death rate for asthma; annual pollen score; annual air quality; public smoking laws; number of board-certified asthma specialists; school inhaler access laws; rescue medication use; controller medication use; ER visits for asthma; uninsured rate; poverty rate. *Asthma and Allergy Foundation of America, "Asthma Capitals 2018: The Most Challenging Places to Live With Asthma"*

- *Men's Health* ranked 100 major U.S. cities in terms of the best cities for men. Minneapolis ranked #14. Criteria: health; fitness; quality of life. *Men's Health, "The Best & Worst Cities for Men Who Want to Be Fit and Happy," January 1, 2016*

- The Minneapolis metro area ranked #41 out of 189 in The Gallup-Healthways Well-Being Index. Criteria: purpose; social well being; financial health; community and physical health. Results are based on telephone interviews with adults, aged 18 and older, living in metropolitan areas in the 50 U.S. states and the District of Columbia. *Gallup-Healthways, "State of American Well-Being, 2017 Community Well-Being Rankings" March 2018*

Pet Rankings

- Minneapolis was selected as one of the best cities for dogs in America by *Dog Fancy*. Criteria: dog-friendly open spaces and dog parks; events celebrating dogs and their owners; vet-to-dog ratios; abundant pet supply and other services; municipal laws that support and protect all pets. *Dog Fancy, "DogTown USA 2014," July 16, 2014*

Real Estate Rankings

- FitSmallBusiness looked at 50 of the largest metropolitan areas in the U.S. to determine which metro was the best to start a real estate business. Data was compiled from such sources as: Zillow, Trulia, U.S. Census Bureau, and the Bureau of Labor Statistics. Criteria: location; inventory; annual wages; median sales price of homes; days on the market; median price cut percentage; and other factors that would influence real estate professional growth. The Minneapolis metro area ranked #22. *fitsmallbusiness.com, "The Best Cities to Become a Real Estate Agent in 2018," January 30, 2018*

- *WalletHub* compared the most populated U.S. cities, as well as at least two of the most populated cities in each state, for a total of 179, to determine which had the best markets for real estate agents. Minneapolis ranked #75 where demand was high and pay was the best. Criteria: sales per agent; annual median wage for real-estate agents; monthly average starting salary for real estate agents; real estate job density and competition; unemployment rate; housing-market health index; and other relevant metrics. *www.WalletHub.com, "2018's Best Places to Be a Real Estate Agent," April 25, 2018*

- The Minneapolis metro area was identified as one of the top 20 housing markets to invest in for 2019 by *Forbes*. Criteria: strong job and population growth; stable local economy; anticipated home price appreciation; and other factors. *Forbes.com, "The Best Markets for Real Estate Investments In 2019," January 7, 2019*

- Minneapolis was ranked #87 out of 237 metro areas in terms of housing affordability in 2018 by the National Association of Home Builders (#1 = most affordable). Criteria: the share of homes sold in that area affordable to a family earning the local median income, based on standard mortgage underwriting criteria. *National Association of Home Builders®, NAHB-Wells Fargo Housing Opportunity Index, 4th Quarter 2018*

Safety Rankings

- To identify the most dangerous cities in America, 24/7 Wall Street focused on violent crime categories—murder, rape, robbery, and aggravated assault—and property crime as reported in the FBI's 2017 annual Uniform Crime Report. Criteria also included median income from American Community Survey and unemployment figures from Bureau of Labor Statistics. For cities with populations over 100,000, Minneapolis was ranked #20. *247wallst.com, "25 Most Dangerous Cities in America" October 17, 2018*

- Allstate ranked the 200 largest cities in America in terms of driver safety. Minneapolis ranked #127. Criteria: internal property damage claims over a two-year period from January 2015 to December 2016. The report helps increase the importance of safety awareness behind the wheel. *Allstate, "Allstate America's Best Drivers Report, 2018" August 28, 2018*

- Minneapolis was identified as one of the most dangerous cities in America by NeighborhoodScout. The city ranked #56 out of 100. Criteria: number of violent crimes per 1,000 residents. The editors only considered cities with 25,000 or more residents. *NeighborhoodScout.com, "Top 100 Most Dangerous Cities in the U.S. 2019" January 2, 2019*

- The National Insurance Crime Bureau ranked 382 metro areas in the U.S. in terms of per capita rates of vehicle theft. The Minneapolis metro area ranked #139 (#1 = highest rate). Criteria: number of vehicle theft offenses per 100,000 inhabitants in 2017. *National Insurance Crime Bureau, "Hot Spots 2017," July 12, 2018*

Seniors/Retirement Rankings

- For *U.S. News & World Report's* Best Places rankings, the editors sought out affordable cities where retirees spend the least on housing and can live on $100 a day while still having access to amenities they need, such as health care, utilities, transportation and food. Minneapolis was among the ten cities that best satisfied their criteria. *money.usnews.com, "10 Best Places to Retire on $100 a Day," October 13, 2015*

- From its Best Cities for Successful Aging indexes, the Milken Institute generated rankings for metropolitan areas, weighing data in nine categories—health care, wellness, living arrangements, transportation and convenience, financial characteristics, education, employment, community engagement, and overall livability. The Minneapolis metro area was ranked #14 overall in the large metro area category. *Milken Institute, "Best Cities for Successful Aging, 2017" March 14, 2017*

Sports/Recreation Rankings

- Minneapolis was selected as one of "America's Most Miserable Sports Cities" by *Forbes*. The city was ranked #4. Criteria: postseason losses/misery; years since last title; and number of teams lost to relocation. Contenders were limited to cities with at least 75 cumulative pro seasons of NFL, NBA, NHL, MLS and MLB play. *Forbes, "America's Most Miserable Sports Cities 2016," April 20, 2016*

- Minneapolis was chosen as one of America's best cities for bicycling. The city ranked #4 out of 50. Criteria: cycling infrastructure that is safe and friendly for all ages; energy and bike culture. The editors only considered cities with populations of 100,000 or more. *Bicycling, "The 50 Best Bike Cities in America," October 10, 2018*

Transportation Rankings

- Business Insider presented an AllTransit Performance Score ranking of public transportation in major U.S. cities and towns, with populations over 250,000, in which Minneapolis earned the #12-ranked "Transit Score," awarded for frequency of service, access to jobs, quality and number of stops, and affordability. *www.businessinsider.com, "The 17 Major U.S. Cities with the Best Public Transportation," April 17, 2018*

- NerdWallet surveyed average annual car insurance premiums in 125 U.S. cities to identify the least expensive U.S. cities in which to insure a car. Locations with no-fault insurance laws was a strong determinant. Minneapolis came in at #18 for the most expensive rates. *www.nerdwallet.com, "Best Cities for Cheap Car Insurance," February 3, 2014*

Women/Minorities Rankings

- Minneapolis was selected as one of "America's Favorite Cities." The city ranked #1 in the "Type of Trip: Gay-friendly Vacation" category. Respondents to an online survey were asked to rate 38 top urban destinations in the United States from visitor's perspective. Criteria: gay-friendly. *Travel + Leisure, "America's Favorite Cities 2015"*

- NerdWallet examined data for 529 U.S. cities and ranked them based on the environment for working women. Minneapolis ranked #2. Criteria: women's earnings; labor force participation rate; cost of living; unemployment rate. *www.nerdwallet.com, "Best Cities for Women in the Workforce 2016," April 4, 2016*

- Minneapolis was selected as one of the gayest cities in America by *The Advocate*. The city ranked #22 out of 25. Criteria, among many: Trans Pride parades/festivals; gay rugby teams; lesbian bars; LGBT centers; theater screenings of "Moonlight"; LGBT-inclusive nondiscrimination ordinances; and gay bowling teams. *The Advocate, "Queerest Cities in America 2017" January 12, 2017*

- Personal finance website *WalletHub* compared more than 180 U.S. cities—including the 150 most populated U.S. cities, plus at least two of the most populated cities in each state—across two key dimensions, "Hispanic Business-Friendliness" and "Hispanic Purchasing Power", to arrive at the most favorable conditions for Hispanic entrepreneurs. Minneapolis was ranked #154 out of 182. Criteria includes: share of Hispanic-Owned Businesses; Hispanic entrepreneurship rate to median annual income of Hispanics; Small Business-Friendliness score; cost of living; and number of Hispanics with at least a bachelor's degree. *WalletHub.com, "2018's Best Cities for Hispanic Entrepreneurs," April 26, 2018*

Miscellaneous Rankings

- The watchdog site Charity Navigator conducts an annual study of charities in the nation's major markets both to analyze statistical differences in their financial, accountability, and transparency practices and to track year-to-year variations in individual philanthropic communities. Charity Navigator's analysis demonstrated that the financial, accountability and transparency behaviors of America's largest charities can be influenced by the metropolitan market within which the charity operates. The Minneapolis metro area was ranked #8 among the 30 metro markets in the rating category of Overall Score. *www.charitynavigator.org, "2017 Metro Market Study," May 1, 2017*

- *WalletHub* compared the 150 most populated U.S. cities to determine their operating efficiency. A "Quality of Services" score was constructed for each city and then divided by the total budget per capita to reveal which were managed the best. Minneapolis ranked #90. Criteria: financial stability; economy; education; safety; health; infrastructure and pollution. *www.WalletHub.com, "2018's Best- & Worst-Run Cities in America," July 9, 2018*

- Minneapolis was selected as one of "America's Friendliest Cities." The city ranked #18 in the "Friendliest" category. Respondents to an online survey were asked to rate 38 top urban destinations in the United States as to general friendliness, as well as manners, politeness and warm disposition. *Travel + Leisure, "America's Friendliest Cities," October 20, 2017*

- The National Alliance to End Homelessness listed the 25 most populous metro areas with the highest rate of homelessness. The Minneapolis metro area had a high rate of homelessness. Criteria: number of homeless people per 10,000 population in 2016. *National Alliance to End Homelessness, "Homelessness in the 25 Most Populous U.S. Metro Areas," September 1, 2017*

Business Environment

CITY FINANCES

City Government Finances

Component	2016 ($000)	2016 ($ per capita)
Total Revenues	1,175,257	2,860
Total Expenditures	1,154,508	2,809
Debt Outstanding	2,968,320	7,223
Cash and Securities[1]	3,029,974	7,373

Note: (1) Cash and security holdings of a government at the close of its fiscal year, including those of its dependent agencies, utilities, and liquor stores.
Source: U.S. Census Bureau, State & Local Government Finances 2016

City Government Revenue by Source

Source	2016 ($000)	2016 ($ per capita)	2016 (%)
General Revenue			
From Federal Government	26,218	64	2.2
From State Government	91,280	222	7.8
From Local Governments	94,010	229	8.0
Taxes			
Property	302,153	735	25.7
Sales and Gross Receipts	92,094	224	7.8
Personal Income	0	0	0.0
Corporate Income	0	0	0.0
Motor Vehicle License	0	0	0.0
Other Taxes	46,114	112	3.9
Current Charges	308,897	752	26.3
Liquor Store	0	0	0.0
Utility	72,658	177	6.2
Employee Retirement	0	0	0.0

Source: U.S. Census Bureau, State & Local Government Finances 2016

City Government Expenditures by Function

Function	2016 ($000)	2016 ($ per capita)	2016 (%)
General Direct Expenditures			
Air Transportation	0	0	0.0
Corrections	0	0	0.0
Education	0	0	0.0
Employment Security Administration	0	0	0.0
Financial Administration	27,305	66	2.4
Fire Protection	61,315	149	5.3
General Public Buildings	0	0	0.0
Governmental Administration, Other	0	0	0.0
Health	23,462	57	2.0
Highways	130,445	317	11.3
Hospitals	0	0	0.0
Housing and Community Development	199,641	485	17.3
Interest on General Debt	117,969	287	10.2
Judicial and Legal	0	0	0.0
Libraries	4,571	11	0.4
Parking	40,601	98	3.5
Parks and Recreation	146,341	356	12.7
Police Protection	168,310	409	14.6
Public Welfare	0	0	0.0
Sewerage	85,516	208	7.4
Solid Waste Management	34,166	83	3.0
Veterans' Services	0	0	0.0
Liquor Store	0	0	0.0
Utility	57,806	140	5.0
Employee Retirement	0	0	0.0

Source: U.S. Census Bureau, State & Local Government Finances 2016

DEMOGRAPHICS

Population Growth

Area	1990 Census	2000 Census	2010 Census	2017* Estimate	Population Growth (%)	
					1990-2017	2010-2017
City	368,383	382,618	382,578	411,452	11.7	7.5
MSA[1]	2,538,834	2,968,806	3,279,833	3,526,149	38.9	7.5
U.S.	248,709,873	281,421,906	308,745,538	321,004,407	29.1	4.0

Note: (1) Figures cover the Minneapolis-St. Paul-Bloomington, MN-WI Metropolitan Statistical Area—see Appendix B for areas included; (*) 2013-2017 5-year estimated population
Source: U.S. Census Bureau, 1990 Census, Census 2000, Census 2010, 2013-2017 American Community Survey 5-Year Estimates

Household Size

Area	Persons in Household (%)							Average Household Size
	One	Two	Three	Four	Five	Six	Seven or More	
City	40.4	31.0	11.9	9.3	3.8	1.9	1.6	2.30
MSA[1]	27.8	34.0	14.9	13.8	5.9	2.1	1.3	2.60
U.S.	27.7	33.8	15.7	13.0	6.0	2.3	1.4	2.60

Note: (1) Figures cover the Minneapolis-St. Paul-Bloomington, MN-WI Metropolitan Statistical Area—see Appendix B for areas included
Source: U.S. Census Bureau, 2013-2017 American Community Survey 5-Year Estimates

Race

Area	White Alone[2] (%)	Black Alone[2] (%)	Asian Alone[2] (%)	AIAN[3] Alone[2] (%)	NHOPI[4] Alone[2] (%)	Other Race Alone[2] (%)	Two or More Races (%)
City	63.9	18.9	6.0	1.2	0.0	4.9	4.9
MSA[1]	79.6	8.0	6.4	0.6	0.0	2.1	3.3
U.S.	73.0	12.7	5.4	0.8	0.2	4.8	3.1

Note: (1) Figures cover the Minneapolis-St. Paul-Bloomington, MN-WI Metropolitan Statistical Area—see Appendix B for areas included; (2) Alone is defined as not being in combination with one or more other races; (3) American Indian and Alaska Native; (4) Native Hawaiian and Other Pacific Islander
Source: U.S. Census Bureau, 2013-2017 American Community Survey 5-Year Estimates

Hispanic or Latino Origin

Area	Total (%)	Mexican (%)	Puerto Rican (%)	Cuban (%)	Other (%)
City	9.8	6.1	0.5	0.2	3.1
MSA[1]	5.7	3.8	0.3	0.1	1.5
U.S.	17.6	11.1	1.7	0.7	4.1

Note: Persons of Hispanic or Latino origin can be of any race; (1) Figures cover the Minneapolis-St. Paul-Bloomington, MN-WI Metropolitan Statistical Area—see Appendix B for areas included
Source: U.S. Census Bureau, 2013-2017 American Community Survey 5-Year Estimates

Segregation

Type	Segregation Indices[1]				Percent Change		
	1990	2000	2010	2010 Rank[2]	1990-2000	1990-2010	2000-2010
Black/White	62.3	60.1	52.9	60	-2.3	-9.4	-7.2
Asian/White	41.6	44.8	42.8	39	3.2	1.2	-2.0
Hispanic/White	35.5	46.5	42.5	54	11.0	7.0	-4.0

Note: All figures cover the Metropolitan Statistical Area—see Appendix B for areas included; Figures are based on an analysis of 1990, 2000, and 2010 Census Decennial Census tract data by William H. Frey, Brookings Institution and the University of Michigan Social Science Data Analysis Network. In this analysis all racial groups (whites, blacks, and asians) are non-Hispanic members of those races. Hispanics are shown as a separate category; (1) Segregation Indices are Dissimilarity Indices that measure the degree to which the minority group is distributed differently than whites across census tracts. They range from 0 (complete integration) to 100 (complete segregation) where the value indicates the percentage of the minority group that needs to move to be distributed exactly like whites; (2) Ranges from 1 (most segregated) to 102 (least segregated); n/a not available.
Source: www.CensusScope.org

Ancestry

Area	German	Irish	English	American	Italian	Polish	French[2]	Scottish	Dutch
City	22.1	10.3	5.7	1.9	2.6	3.8	2.8	1.4	1.4
MSA[1]	30.7	11.2	5.7	3.1	2.7	4.5	3.5	1.3	1.5
U.S.	14.1	10.1	7.5	6.6	5.3	2.9	2.5	1.7	1.3

Note: Figures are the percentage of the total population reporting a particular ancestry. The nine most commonly reported ancestries in the U.S. are shown. Figures include multiple ancestries (e.g. if a person reported being Irish and Italian, they were included in both columns); (1) Figures cover the Minneapolis-St. Paul-Bloomington, MN-WI Metropolitan Statistical Area—see Appendix B for areas included; (2) Excludes Basque
Source: U.S. Census Bureau, 2013-2017 American Community Survey 5-Year Estimates

Foreign-Born Population

Area	Any Foreign Country	Asia	Mexico	Europe	Carribean	Central America[2]	South America	Africa	Canada
City	15.9	4.0	2.9	1.1	0.3	0.4	1.3	5.4	0.3
MSA[1]	10.4	4.1	1.4	1.1	0.2	0.4	0.5	2.5	0.2
U.S.	13.4	4.1	3.6	1.5	1.3	1.0	0.9	0.6	0.3

Note: (1) Figures cover the Minneapolis-St. Paul-Bloomington, MN-WI Metropolitan Statistical Area—see Appendix B for areas included; (2) Excludes Mexico.
Source: U.S. Census Bureau, 2013-2017 American Community Survey 5-Year Estimates

Marital Status

Area	Never Married	Now Married[2]	Separated	Widowed	Divorced
City	51.0	34.3	1.7	3.1	10.0
MSA[1]	33.0	51.5	1.2	4.4	10.0
U.S.	33.1	48.2	2.0	5.8	10.9

Note: Figures are percentages and cover the population 15 years of age and older; (1) Figures cover the Minneapolis-St. Paul-Bloomington, MN-WI Metropolitan Statistical Area—see Appendix B for areas included; (2) Excludes separated
Source: U.S. Census Bureau, 2013-2017 American Community Survey 5-Year Estimates

Disability by Age

Area	All Ages	Under 18 Years Old	18 to 64 Years Old	65 Years and Over
City	11.2	4.5	10.2	34.0
MSA[1]	9.8	3.6	8.0	30.7
U.S.	12.6	4.2	10.3	35.5

Note: Figures show percent of the civilian noninstitutionalized population that reported having a disability. Disability status is determined from six types of difficulty: vision, hearing, cognitive, ambulatory, self-care, and independent living. For children under 5 years old, hearing and vision difficulty are used to determine disability status. For children between the ages of 5 and 14, disability status is determined from hearing, vision, cognitive, ambulatory, and self-care difficulties. For people aged 15 years and older, they are considered to have a disability if they have difficulty with any one of the six difficulty types; Note: (1) Figures cover the Minneapolis-St. Paul-Bloomington, MN-WI Metropolitan Statistical Area—see Appendix B for areas included
Source: U.S. Census Bureau, 2013-2017 American Community Survey 5-Year Estimates

Age

Area	Under Age 5	Age 5–19	Age 20–34	Age 35–44	Age 45–54	Age 55–64	Age 65–74	Age 75–84	Age 85+	Median Age
City	6.7	16.8	32.1	13.7	11.5	10.1	5.8	2.3	1.1	32.1
MSA[1]	6.6	19.9	21.0	13.1	14.0	12.7	7.4	3.6	1.7	36.8
U.S.	6.2	19.5	20.7	12.7	13.4	12.7	8.6	4.4	1.9	37.8

Note: (1) Figures cover the Minneapolis-St. Paul-Bloomington, MN-WI Metropolitan Statistical Area—see Appendix B for areas included
Source: U.S. Census Bureau, 2013-2017 American Community Survey 5-Year Estimates

Gender

Area	Males	Females	Males per 100 Females
City	208,322	203,130	102.6
MSA[1]	1,745,774	1,780,375	98.1
U.S.	158,018,753	162,985,654	97.0

Note: (1) Figures cover the Minneapolis-St. Paul-Bloomington, MN-WI Metropolitan Statistical Area—see Appendix B for areas included
Source: U.S. Census Bureau, 2013-2017 American Community Survey 5-Year Estimates

Religious Groups by Family

Area	Catholic	Baptist	Non-Den.	Methodist[2]	Lutheran	LDS[3]	Pente-costal	Presby-terian[4]	Muslim[5]	Judaism
MSA[1]	21.7	2.5	3.0	2.8	14.5	0.6	1.8	1.9	0.4	0.7
U.S.	19.1	9.3	4.0	4.0	2.3	2.0	1.9	1.6	0.8	0.7

Note: Figures are the number of adherents as a percentage of the total population; (1) Figures cover the Minneapolis-St. Paul-Bloomington, MN-WI Metropolitan Statistical Area—see Appendix B for areas included; (2) Methodist/Pietist; (3) Latter Day Saints; (4) Reformed; (5) Figures are estimates
Source: Association of Statisticians of American Religious Bodies, 2010 U.S. Religion Census: Religious Congregations & Membership Study

Religious Groups by Tradition

Area	Catholic	Evangelical Protestant	Mainline Protestant	Other Tradition	Black Protestant	Orthodox
MSA[1]	21.7	12.9	14.5	2.3	0.5	0.2
U.S.	19.1	16.2	7.3	4.3	1.6	0.3

Note: Figures are the number of adherents as a percentage of the total population; (1) Figures cover the Minneapolis-St. Paul-Bloomington, MN-WI Metropolitan Statistical Area—see Appendix B for areas included
Source: Association of Statisticians of American Religious Bodies, 2010 U.S. Religion Census: Religious Congregations & Membership Study

ECONOMY

Gross Metropolitan Product

Area	2016	2017	2018	2019	Rank[2]
MSA[1]	249.4	259.5	268.3	282.1	15

Note: Figures are in billions of dollars; (1) Figures cover the Minneapolis-St. Paul-Bloomington, MN-WI Metropolitan Statistical Area—see Appendix B for areas included; (2) Rank is based on 2017 data and ranges from 1 to 381
Source: U.S. Conference of Mayors, U.S. Metro Economies: Economic Growth & Full Employment, June 2018

Economic Growth

Area	2017-2018 (%)	2019-2020 (%)	2021-2022 (%)
MSA[1]	2.8	2.5	1.8

Note: Figures are real gross metropolitan product (GMP) growth rates and represent average annual percent change; (1) Figures cover the Minneapolis-St. Paul-Bloomington, MN-WI Metropolitan Statistical Area—see Appendix B for areas included
Source: U.S. Conference of Mayors, U.S. Metro Economies: Economic Growth & Full Employment, June 2018

Metropolitan Area Exports

Area	2012	2013	2014	2015	2016	2017	Rank[2]
MSA[1]	25,155.7	23,747.5	21,198.2	19,608.6	18,329.2	19,070.9	18

Note: Figures are in millions of dollars; (1) Figures cover the Minneapolis-St. Paul-Bloomington, MN-WI Metropolitan Statistical Area—see Appendix B for areas included; (2) Rank is based on 2017 data and ranges from 1 to 387
Source: U.S. Department of Commerce, International Trade Administration, Office of Trade and Economic Analysis, Industry and Analysis, Exports by Metropolitan Area, extracted March 25, 2019

Building Permits

Area	Single-Family			Multi-Family			Total		
	2016	2017	Pct. Chg.	2016	2017	Pct. Chg.	2016	2017	Pct. Chg.
City	169	137	-18.9	2,739	2,117	-22.7	2,908	2,254	-22.5
MSA[1]	7,889	8,782	11.3	6,271	6,318	0.7	14,160	15,100	6.6
U.S.	750,800	820,000	9.2	455,800	462,000	1.4	1,206,600	1,282,000	6.2

Note: (1) Figures cover the Minneapolis-St. Paul-Bloomington, MN-WI Metropolitan Statistical Area—see Appendix B for areas included; Figures represent new, privately-owned housing units authorized (unadjusted data); All permit data are based on estimates with imputation
Source: U.S. Census Bureau, Manufacturing, Mining, and Construction Statistics, Building Permits, 2016, 2017

Bankruptcy Filings

Area	Business Filings			Nonbusiness Filings		
	2017	2018	% Chg.	2017	2018	% Chg.
Hennepin County	83	61	-26.5	2,112	2,124	0.6
U.S.	23,157	22,232	-4.0	765,863	751,186	-1.9

Note: Business filings include Chapter 7, Chapter 11, Chapter 12, and Chapter 13; Nonbusiness filings include Chapter 7, Chapter 11, and Chapter 13
Source: Administrative Office of the U.S. Courts, Business and Nonbusiness Bankruptcy, County Cases Commenced by Chapter of the Bankruptcy Code, During the 12-Month Period Ending December 31, 2017 and Business and Nonbusiness Bankruptcy, County Cases Commenced by Chapter of the Bankruptcy Code, During the 12-Month Period Ending December 31, 2018

Housing Vacancy Rates

Area	Gross Vacancy Rate[2] (%)			Year-Round Vacancy Rate[3] (%)			Rental Vacancy Rate[4] (%)			Homeowner Vacancy Rate[5] (%)		
	2016	2017	2018	2016	2017	2018	2016	2017	2018	2016	2017	2018
MSA[1]	5.3	4.5	3.9	4.7	4.1	3.3	3.8	4.2	4.1	0.8	0.9	0.4
U.S.	12.8	12.7	12.3	9.9	9.9	9.7	6.9	7.2	6.9	1.7	1.6	1.5

Note: (1) Figures cover the Minneapolis-St. Paul-Bloomington, MN-WI Metropolitan Statistical Area—see Appendix B for areas included; (2) The percentage of the total housing inventory that is vacant; (3) The percentage of the housing inventory (excluding seasonal units) that is year-round vacant; (4) The percentage of rental inventory that is vacant for rent; (5) The percentage of homeowner inventory that is vacant for sale
Source: U.S. Census Bureau, Housing Vacancies and Homeownership Annual Statistics: 2016, 2017, 2018

INCOME

Income

Area	Per Capita ($)	Median Household ($)	Average Household ($)
City	35,259	55,720	81,550
MSA[1]	37,866	73,735	96,530
U.S.	31,177	57,652	81,283

Note: (1) Figures cover the Minneapolis-St. Paul-Bloomington, MN-WI Metropolitan Statistical Area—see Appendix B for areas included
Source: U.S. Census Bureau, 2013-2017 American Community Survey 5-Year Estimates

Household Income Distribution

Area	Percent of Households Earning							
	Under $15,000	$15,000 -$24,999	$25,000 -$34,999	$35,000 -$49,999	$50,000 -$74,999	$75,000 -$99,999	$100,000 -$149,999	$150,000 and up
City	14.9	9.8	8.8	12.1	16.3	11.6	13.9	12.7
MSA[1]	7.5	7.1	7.4	11.3	17.6	14.1	18.6	16.5
U.S.	11.6	9.8	9.5	13.0	17.7	12.3	14.1	12.1

Note: (1) Figures cover the Minneapolis-St. Paul-Bloomington, MN-WI Metropolitan Statistical Area—see Appendix B for areas included
Source: U.S. Census Bureau, 2013-2017 American Community Survey 5-Year Estimates

Poverty Rate

Area	All Ages	Under 18 Years Old	18 to 64 Years Old	65 Years and Over
City	20.7	28.1	19.7	12.6
MSA[1]	9.4	12.3	8.8	6.5
U.S.	14.6	20.3	13.7	9.3

Note: Figures are percentage of people whose income during the past 12 months was below the poverty level; (1) Figures cover the Minneapolis-St. Paul-Bloomington, MN-WI Metropolitan Statistical Area—see Appendix B for areas included
Source: U.S. Census Bureau, 2013-2017 American Community Survey 5-Year Estimates

EMPLOYMENT

Labor Force and Employment

Area	Civilian Labor Force			Workers Employed		
	Dec. 2017	Dec. 2018	% Chg.	Dec. 2017	Dec. 2018	% Chg.
City	237,197	240,306	1.3	230,805	234,326	1.5
MSA[1]	1,983,313	2,008,040	1.2	1,924,623	1,952,456	1.4
U.S.	159,880,000	162,510,000	1.6	153,602,000	156,481,000	1.9

Note: Data is not seasonally adjusted and covers workers 16 years of age and older; (1) Figures cover the Minneapolis-St. Paul-Bloomington, MN-WI Metropolitan Statistical Area—see Appendix B for areas included
Source: Bureau of Labor Statistics, Local Area Unemployment Statistics

Unemployment Rate

Area	2018											
	Jan.	Feb.	Mar.	Apr.	May	Jun.	Jul.	Aug.	Sep.	Oct.	Nov.	Dec.
City	3.0	2.9	2.9	2.5	2.3	2.9	2.7	2.5	2.2	2.1	1.9	2.5
MSA[1]	3.4	3.4	3.3	2.7	2.3	2.8	2.6	2.5	2.2	2.1	2.0	2.8
U.S.	4.5	4.4	4.1	3.7	3.6	4.2	4.1	3.9	3.6	3.5	3.5	3.7

Note: Data is not seasonally adjusted and covers workers 16 years of age and older; (1) Figures cover the Minneapolis-St. Paul-Bloomington, MN-WI Metropolitan Statistical Area—see Appendix B for areas included
Source: Bureau of Labor Statistics, Local Area Unemployment Statistics

Average Wages

Occupation	$/Hr.	Occupation	$/Hr.
Accountants and Auditors	36.00	Maids and Housekeeping Cleaners	14.20
Automotive Mechanics	21.50	Maintenance and Repair Workers	22.50
Bookkeepers	22.40	Marketing Managers	68.50
Carpenters	26.40	Nuclear Medicine Technologists	41.10
Cashiers	12.10	Nurses, Licensed Practical	23.50
Clerks, General Office	18.70	Nurses, Registered	40.20
Clerks, Receptionists/Information	15.50	Nursing Assistants	17.00
Clerks, Shipping/Receiving	18.30	Packers and Packagers, Hand	13.70
Computer Programmers	42.70	Physical Therapists	40.30
Computer Systems Analysts	45.60	Postal Service Mail Carriers	25.20
Computer User Support Specialists	27.30	Real Estate Brokers	30.20
Cooks, Restaurant	14.60	Retail Salespersons	14.10
Dentists	111.50	Sales Reps., Exc. Tech./Scientific	36.30
Electrical Engineers	48.20	Sales Reps., Tech./Scientific	42.00
Electricians	37.20	Secretaries, Exc. Legal/Med./Exec.	20.50
Financial Managers	67.80	Security Guards	16.70
First-Line Supervisors/Managers, Sales	22.10	Surgeons	n/a
Food Preparation Workers	13.30	Teacher Assistants*	15.80
General and Operations Managers	58.80	Teachers, Elementary School*	33.30
Hairdressers/Cosmetologists	15.00	Teachers, Secondary School*	32.70
Internists, General	120.70	Telemarketers	16.30
Janitors and Cleaners	15.60	Truck Drivers, Heavy/Tractor-Trailer	25.10
Landscaping/Groundskeeping Workers	18.10	Truck Drivers, Light/Delivery Svcs.	20.80
Lawyers	59.60	Waiters and Waitresses	12.60

Note: Wage data covers the Minneapolis-St. Paul-Bloomington, MN-WI Metropolitan Statistical Area—see Appendix B for areas included; (*) Hourly wages for elementary/secondary school teachers and teacher assistants were calculated by the editors from annual wage data based on a 40 hour work week; n/a not available.
Source: Bureau of Labor Statistics, Metro Area Occupational Employment & Wage Estimates, May 2018

Employment by Occupation

Occupation Classification	City (%)	MSA[1] (%)	U.S. (%)
Management, Business, Science, and Arts	48.9	43.3	37.4
Natural Resources, Construction, and Maintenance	3.9	6.6	8.9
Production, Transportation, and Material Moving	8.9	11.4	12.2
Sales and Office	19.8	23.2	23.5
Service	18.5	15.6	18.0

Note: Figures cover employed civilians 16 years of age and older; (1) Figures cover the Minneapolis-St. Paul-Bloomington, MN-WI Metropolitan Statistical Area—see Appendix B for areas included
Source: U.S. Census Bureau, 2013-2017 American Community Survey 5-Year Estimates

Employment by Industry

Sector	MSA[1] Number of Employees	Percent of Total	U.S. Percent of Total
Construction, Mining, and Logging	77,800	3.9	5.3
Education and Health Services	336,400	16.7	15.9
Financial Activities	149,300	7.4	5.7
Government	250,200	12.4	15.1
Information	37,400	1.9	1.9
Leisure and Hospitality	184,100	9.2	10.7
Manufacturing	199,500	9.9	8.5
Other Services	78,300	3.9	3.9
Professional and Business Services	325,800	16.2	14.1
Retail Trade	198,600	9.9	10.8
Transportation, Warehousing, and Utilities	78,100	3.9	4.2
Wholesale Trade	95,400	4.7	3.9

Note: Figures are non-farm employment as of December 2018. Figures are not seasonally adjusted and include workers 16 years of age and older; (1) Figures cover the Minneapolis-St. Paul-Bloomington, MN-WI Metropolitan Statistical Area—see Appendix B for areas included
Source: Bureau of Labor Statistics, Current Employment Statistics, Employment, Hours, and Earnings

Occupations with Greatest Projected Employment Growth: 2018 – 2020

Occupation[1]	2018 Employment	2020 Projected Employment	Numeric Employment Change	Percent Employment Change
Personal Care Aides	71,130	74,150	3,020	4.2
Registered Nurses	63,910	66,090	2,180	3.4
Janitors and Cleaners, Except Maids and Housekeeping Cleaners	47,680	48,880	1,200	2.5
Heavy and Tractor-Trailer Truck Drivers	35,950	36,930	980	2.7
Combined Food Preparation and Serving Workers, Including Fast Food	65,710	66,600	890	1.4
General and Operations Managers	44,110	44,980	870	2.0
Home Health Aides	25,920	26,660	740	2.9
Light Truck or Delivery Services Drivers	16,260	16,990	730	4.5
Elementary School Teachers, Except Special Education	30,690	31,400	710	2.3
Teacher Assistants	34,480	35,190	710	2.1

Note: Projections cover Minnesota; (1) Sorted by numeric employment change
Source: www.projectionscentral.com, State Occupational Projections, 2018–2020 Short-Term Projections

Fastest Growing Occupations: 2018 – 2020

Occupation[1]	2018 Employment	2020 Projected Employment	Numeric Employment Change	Percent Employment Change
Wind Turbine Service Technicians	260	310	50	19.2
Couriers and Messengers	1,140	1,230	90	7.9
Physician Assistants	2,060	2,200	140	6.8
Plumbers, Pipefitters, and Steamfitters	9,300	9,910	610	6.6
Statisticians	970	1,030	60	6.2
Roofers	2,380	2,520	140	5.9
Operations Research Analysts	2,820	2,980	160	5.7
Nurse Practitioners	3,670	3,880	210	5.7
Structural Iron and Steel Workers	1,610	1,700	90	5.6
Cement Masons and Concrete Finishers	5,410	5,700	290	5.4

Note: Projections cover Minnesota; (1) Sorted by percent employment change and excludes occupations with numeric employment change less than 50
Source: www.projectionscentral.com, State Occupational Projections, 2018–2020 Short-Term Projections

TAXES

State Corporate Income Tax Rates

State	Tax Rate (%)	Income Brackets ($)	Num. of Brackets	Financial Institution Tax Rate (%)[a]	Federal Income Tax Ded.
Minnesota	9.8 (n)	Flat rate	1	9.8 (n)	No

Note: Tax rates as of January 1, 2019; (a) Rates listed are the corporate income tax rate applied to financial institutions or excise taxes based on income. Some states have other taxes based upon the value of deposits or shares; (n) In addition, Minnesota levies a 5.8% tentative minimum tax on Alternative Minimum Taxable Income.
Source: Federation of Tax Administrators, Range of State Corporate Income Tax Rates, January 1, 2019

State Individual Income Tax Rates

State	Tax Rate (%)	Income Brackets ($)	Personal Exemptions ($)			Standard Ded. ($)	
			Single	Married	Depend.	Single	Married
Minnesota (a)	5.35 - 9.85	26,520 - 163,890 (n)	4,150	8,300 (d)	4,150 (d)	6,500	3,000 (d)

Note: Tax rates as of January 1, 2019; Local- and county-level taxes are not included; n/a not applicable; Federal income tax is not deductible on state income tax returns; (a) 19 states have statutory provision for automatically adjusting to the rate of inflation the dollar values of the income tax brackets, standard deductions, and/or personal exemptions. Michigan indexes the personal exemption only. Oregon does not index the income brackets for $125,000 and over; (d) These states use the personal exemption/standard deduction amounts provided in the federal Internal Revenue Code. Note, the Tax Cut and Reform Act of 2017 has eliminated personal exemptions from the IRC. CO, ID, NM, ND, SC, and DC have adoptedthe new exemptions and standard deduction amounts. MN conforms to a previous IRC year, while ME adopts the higher standard deduction but retains the exemption amounts; (n) The income brackets reported for Minnesota are for single individuals. For married couples filing jointly, the same tax rates apply to income brackets ranging from $38,770 to $273,150.
Source: Federation of Tax Administrators, State Individual Income Tax Rates, January 1, 2019

Various State Sales and Excise Tax Rates

State	State Sales Tax (%)	Gasoline[1] (¢/gal.)	Cigarette[2] ($/pack)	Spirits[3] ($/gal.)	Wine[4] ($/gal.)	Beer[5] ($/gal.)	Recreational Marijuana (%)
Minnesota	6.875	28.6	3.04	8.96 (i)(j)	1.20 (o)(p)	0.49 (q)(s)	Not legal

Note: All tax rates as of January 1, 2019; (1) The American Petroleum Institute has developed a methodology for determining the average tax rate on a gallon of fuel. Rates may include any of the following: excise taxes, environmental fees, storage tank fees, other fees or taxes, general sales tax, and local taxes. In states where gasoline is subject to the general sales tax, or where the fuel tax is based on the average sale price, the average rate determined by API is sensitive to changes in the price of gasoline. States that fully or partially apply general sales taxes to gasoline: CA, CO, GA, IL, IN, MI, NY; (2) The federal excise tax of $1.0066 per pack and local taxes are not included; (3) Rates are those applicable to off-premise sales of 40% alcohol by volume (a.b.v.) distilled spirits in 750ml containers. Local excise taxes are excluded; (4) Rates are those applicable to off-premise sales of 11% a.b.v. non-carbonated wine in 750ml containers; (5) Rates are those applicable to off-premise sales of 4.7% a.b.v. beer in 12 ounce containers; (i) Includes case fees and/or bottle fees which may vary with size of container; (j) Includes sales taxes specific to alcoholic beverages; (o) Includes case fees and/or bottle fees which may vary with size of container; (p) Includes sales taxes specific to alcoholic beverages; (q) Different rates also applicable according to alcohol content, place of production, size of container, or place purchased (on- or off-premise or onboard airlines); (s) Includes sales taxes specific to alcoholic beverages.
Source: Tax Foundation, 2019 Facts & Figures: How Does Your State Compare?

State Business Tax Climate Index Rankings

State	Overall Rank	Corporate Tax Rank	Individual Income Tax Rank	Sales Tax Rank	Unemployment Insurance Tax Rank	Property Tax Rank
Minnesota	43	42	46	27	25	31

Note: The index is a measure of how each state's tax laws affect economic performance. The lower the rank, the more favorable a state's tax system is for business. States without a given tax are given a ranking of 1. The scores/rankings for the District of Columbia do not affect other states. The 2019 index represents the tax climate as of July 1, 2018.
Source: Tax Foundation, State Business Tax Climate Index 2019

COMMERCIAL REAL ESTATE

Office Market

Market Area	Inventory (sq. ft.)	Vacancy Rate (%)	Under Construction (sq. ft.)	YTD Net Absorption (sq. ft.)	Total Average Asking Rent ($/sq. ft./year)
Minneapolis	118,903,531	11.2	1,203,275	2,302,096	19.80
National	4,905,867,938	13.1	83,553,714	45,846,470	28.46

Source: Newmark Grubb Knight Frank, National Office Market Report, 4th Quarter 2018

Industrial/Warehouse/R&D Market

Market Area	Inventory (sq. ft.)	Vacancy Rate (%)	Under Construction (sq. ft.)	YTD Net Absorption (sq. ft.)	Total Average Asking Rent ($/sq. ft./year)
Minneapolis	383,883,087	3.5	2,031,632	3,165,257	6.90
National	14,796,839,085	5.0	262,662,294	238,014,726	7.16

Source: Newmark Grubb Knight Frank, National Industrial Market Report, 4th Quarter 2018

COMMERCIAL UTILITIES

Typical Monthly Electric Bills

Area	Commercial Service ($/month)		Industrial Service ($/month)	
	1,500 kWh	40 kW demand 14,000 kWh	1,000 kW demand 200,000 kWh	50,000 kW demand 32,500,000 kWh
City	191	1,484	25,497	2,536,929
Average[1]	203	1,619	25,886	2,540,077

Note: Figures are based on annualized rates; (1) Average based on 187 utilities surveyed
Source: Edison Electric Institute, Typical Bills and Average Rates Report, Summer 2018

TRANSPORTATION

Means of Transportation to Work

Area	Car/Truck/Van Drove Alone	Car/Truck/Van Car-pooled	Public Transportation Bus	Public Transportation Subway	Public Transportation Railroad	Bicycle	Walked	Other Means	Worked at Home
City	61.0	7.9	11.9	1.0	0.2	4.1	7.0	1.5	5.4
MSA[1]	77.7	8.2	4.3	0.2	0.2	0.9	2.2	1.0	5.3
U.S.	76.4	9.2	2.5	1.9	0.6	0.6	2.7	1.3	4.7

Note: Figures are percentages and cover workers 16 years of age and older; (1) Figures cover the Minneapolis-St. Paul-Bloomington, MN-WI Metropolitan Statistical Area—see Appendix B for areas included
Source: U.S. Census Bureau, 2013-2017 American Community Survey 5-Year Estimates

Travel Time to Work

Area	Less Than 10 Minutes	10 to 19 Minutes	20 to 29 Minutes	30 to 44 Minutes	45 to 59 Minutes	60 to 89 Minutes	90 Minutes or More
City	8.4	33.0	30.2	20.1	4.2	3.0	1.2
MSA[1]	10.5	27.6	24.9	23.3	8.1	4.3	1.3
U.S.	12.7	28.9	20.9	20.5	8.1	6.2	2.7

Note: Note: Figures are percentages and include workers 16 years old and over; (1) Figures cover the Minneapolis-St. Paul-Bloomington, MN-WI Metropolitan Statistical Area—see Appendix B for areas included
Source: U.S. Census Bureau, 2013-2017 American Community Survey 5-Year Estimates

Freeway Travel Time Index

Area	1985	1990	1995	2000	2005	2010	2014
Urban Area Rank[1,2]	26	25	18	11	17	21	21
Urban Area Index[1]	1.10	1.14	1.21	1.27	1.28	1.25	1.26
Average Index[3]	1.09	1.11	1.14	1.17	1.20	1.19	1.20

Note: Freeway Travel Time Index—the ratio of travel time in the peak period to the travel time at free-flow conditions. For example, a value of 1.30 indicates a 20-minute free-flow trip takes 26 minutes in the peak (20 minutes x 1.30 = 26 minutes); (1) Covers the Minneapolis-St. Paul MN-WI urban area; (2) Rank is based on 101 urban areas (#1 = highest travel time index); (3) Average of 101 urban areas
Source: Texas Transportation Institute, 2015 Urban Mobility Scorecard, August 2015

Freeway Commuter Stress Index

Area	1985	1990	1995	2000	2005	2010	2014
Urban Area Rank[1,2]	33	33	23	17	18	25	27
Urban Area Index[1]	1.14	1.18	1.26	1.31	1.33	1.30	1.31
Average Index[3]	1.13	1.16	1.19	1.22	1.25	1.24	1.25

Note: The Freeway Commuter Stress Index is the same as the Freeway Travel Time Index (see table above) except that it includes only the travel in the peak directions during the peak periods; the TTI includes travel in all directions during the peak period. Thus, the CSI is more indicative of the work trip experienced by each commuter on a daily basis; (1) Covers the Minneapolis-St. Paul MN-WI urban area; (2) Rank is based on 101 urban areas (#1 = highest travel time index); (3) Average of 101 urban areas
Source: Texas Transportation Institute, 2015 Urban Mobility Scorecard, August 2015

Public Transportation

Agency Name / Mode of Transportation	Vehicles Operated in Maximum Service[1]	Annual Unlinked Passenger Trips[2] (in thous.)	Annual Passenger Miles[3] (in thous.)
Metro Transit			
Bus (directly operated)	754	57,322.6	237,929.5
Commuter Rail (purchased transportation)	20	793.8	19,441.5
Light Rail (directly operated)	76	23,811.0	102,035.2

Note: (1) The number of revenue vehicles operated by the given mode and type of service to meet the annual maximum service requirement. This is the revenue vehicle count during the peak season of the year; on the week and day that maximum service is provided. Vehicles operated in maximum service (VOMS) exclude atypical days and one-time special events; (2) The number of passengers who boarded public transportation vehicles. Passengers are counted each time they board a vehicle no matter how many vehicles they use to travel from their origin to their destination. (3) The sum of the distances ridden by all passengers during the entire fiscal year.
Source: Federal Transit Administration, National Transit Database, 2017

Air Transportation

Airport Name and Code / Type of Service	Passenger Airlines[1]	Passenger Enplanements	Freight Carriers[2]	Freight (lbs)
Minneapolis-St. Paul International (MSP)				
Domestic service (U.S. carriers - 2018)	36	16,879,197	23	186,918,896
International service (U.S. carriers - 2017)	12	1,276,805	3	23,637,410

Note: (1) Includes all U.S.-based major, minor and commuter airlines that carried at least one passenger during the year; (2) Includes all U.S.-based airlines and freight carriers that transported at least one pound of freight during the year.
Source: Bureau of Transportation Statistics, The Intermodal Transportation Database, Air Carriers: T-100 Domestic Market (U.S. Carriers), 2018; Bureau of Transportation Statistics, The Intermodal Transportation Database, Air Carriers: T-100 International Market (U.S. Carriers), 2017

Other Transportation Statistics

Major Highways:	I-35; I-94
Amtrak Service:	Yes (station is located in St. Paul)
Major Waterways/Ports:	Port of Minneapolis

Source: Amtrak.com; Google Maps

BUSINESSES

Major Business Headquarters

Company Name	Industry	Rankings Fortune[1]	Forbes[2]
Ameriprise Financial	Diversified Financials	252	-
Cargill	Food, Drink & Tobacco	-	1
General Mills	Food Consumer Products	182	-
Mortenson	Construction	-	106
Target	General Merchandisers	39	-
Thrivent Financial for Lutherans	Insurance: Life, Health (Mutual)	343	-
U.S. Bancorp	Commercial Banks	122	-
Xcel Energy	Utilities: Gas and Electric	266	-

Note: (1) Companies that produce a 10-K are ranked 1 to 500 based on 2017 revenue; (2) All private companies with at least $2 billion in annual revenue through the end of their most current fiscal year are ranked 1 to 229; companies listed are headquartered in the city; dashes indicate no ranking
Source: Fortune, "Fortune 500," June 2018; Forbes, "America's Largest Private Companies," 2018 Rankings

Fast-Growing Businesses

According to *Inc.*, Minneapolis is home to two of America's 500 fastest-growing private companies: **Love Your Melon** (#106); **ChromebookParts.com** (#416). Criteria: must be an independent, privately-held, for-profit, U.S. corporation, proprietorship or partnership as of December 31, 2017; revenues must be at least $100,000 in 2014 and $2 million in 2017; must have four-year operating/sales history. Holding companies, regulated banks, and utilities were excluded. *Inc., "America's 500 Fastest-Growing Private Companies," 2018*

Minority Business Opportunity

Minneapolis is home to one company which is on the *Black Enterprise* Industrial/Service list (100 largest companies based on gross sales): **THOR Cos.** (#11). Criteria: operational in previous calendar year; at least 51% black-owned and manufactures/owns the product it sells or provides industrial or consumer services. Brokerages, real estate firms and firms that provide professional services are not eligible. *Black Enterprise, B.E. 100s, 2018*

Minority- and Women-Owned Businesses

Group	All Firms Firms	Sales ($000)	Firms with Paid Employees Firms	Sales ($000)	Employees	Payroll ($000)
AIAN[1]	629	56,171	31	(s)	500 - 999	(s)
Asian	1,633	483,166	420	448,249	3,658	93,512
Black	6,009	641,492	294	(s)	5,000 - 9,999	(s)
Hispanic	1,333	163,280	145	120,458	1,620	33,314
NHOPI[2]	59	(s)	0	(s)	0 - 19	(s)
Women	16,547	1,901,149	1,602	1,479,305	19,696	549,893
All Firms	44,702	95,129,881	9,209	93,644,436	299,777	18,398,078

Note: Figures cover firms located in the city; minority- and women-owned business are defined as firms in which the corresponding group own 51% or more of the stock or equity of the company; (1) American Indian and Alaska Native; (2) Native Hawaiian and Other Pacific Islander; (s) estimates are suppressed when publication standards are not met
Source: U.S. Census Bureau, 2012 Economic Census, Survey of Business Owners

HOTELS & CONVENTION CENTERS

Hotels, Motels and Vacation Rentals

Area	5 Star Num.	Pct.[3]	4 Star Num.	Pct.[3]	3 Star Num.	Pct.[3]	2 Star Num.	Pct.[3]	1 Star Num.	Pct.[3]	Not Rated Num.	Pct.[3]
City[1]	0	0.0	29	8.7	70	21.0	29	8.7	1	0.3	204	61.3
Total[2]	286	0.4	5,236	7.1	16,715	22.6	10,259	13.9	293	0.4	41,056	55.6

Note: (1) Figures cover Minneapolis and vicinity; (2) Figures cover all 100 cities in this book; (3) Percentage of hotels which have a given star rating; Star ratings are determined by expedia.com and offer an indication of the general quality of a particular hotel.
Source: www.expedia.com, April 3, 2019

The Minneapolis-St. Paul-Bloomington, MN-WI metro area is home to one of the best city hotels in the continental U.S. according to *Travel & Leisure*: **Hewing Hotel**. Magazine readers were surveyed and asked to rate hotels on the following criteria: rooms/facilities; location; service; food; and value. The list includes the top 15 city hotels in the continental U.S. *Travel & Leisure, "The World's Best Awards 2018"*

Major Convention Centers

Name	Overall Space (sq. ft.)	Exhibit Space (sq. ft.)	Meeting Space (sq. ft.)	Meeting Rooms
Minneapolis Convention Center	n/a	475,000	95,458	87
Saint Paul River Centre	n/a	100,000	n/a	15

Note: Table includes convention centers located in the Minneapolis-St. Paul-Bloomington, MN-WI metro area; n/a not available
Source: Original research

Living Environment

COST OF LIVING

Cost of Living Index

Composite Index	Groceries	Housing	Utilities	Trans-portation	Health Care	Misc. Goods/ Services
106.4	105.3	104.0	97.6	107.9	105.8	110.9

Note: The Cost of Living Index measures regional differences in the cost of consumer goods and services, excluding taxes and non-consumer expenditures, for professional and managerial households in the top income quintile. It is based on more than 50,000 prices covering almost 60 different items for which prices are collected three times a year by chambers of commerce, economic development organizations or university applied economic centers in each participating urban area. The numbers shown should be read as a percentage above or below the national average of 100. For example, a value of 115.4 in the groceries column indicates that grocery prices are 15.4% higher than the national average. Small differences in the index numbers should not be interpreted as significant; Figures cover the Minneapolis MN urban area.
Source: The Council for Community and Economic Research, ACCRA Cost of Living Index, 2018

Grocery Prices

Area[1]	T-Bone Steak ($/pound)	Frying Chicken ($/pound)	Whole Milk ($/half gal.)	Eggs ($/dozen)	Orange Juice ($/64 oz.)	Coffee ($/11.5 oz.)
City[2]	13.75	2.10	2.51	1.82	3.68	4.70
Avg.	11.35	1.42	1.94	1.81	3.52	4.35
Min.	7.45	0.92	0.80	0.75	2.72	3.06
Max.	15.05	2.76	4.18	4.00	5.36	8.20

Note: (1) Values for the local area are compared with the average, minimum and maximum values for all 291 areas in the Cost of Living Index; (2) Figures cover the Minneapolis MN urban area; T-Bone Steak (price per pound); Frying Chicken (price per pound, whole fryer); Whole Milk (half gallon carton); Eggs (price per dozen, Grade A, large); Orange Juice (64 oz. Tropicana or Florida Natural); Coffee (11.5 oz. can, vacuum-packed, Maxwell House, Hills Bros, or Folgers).
Source: The Council for Community and Economic Research, ACCRA Cost of Living Index, 2018

Housing and Utility Costs

Area[1]	New Home Price ($)	Apartment Rent ($/month)	All Electric ($/month)	Part Electric ($/month)	Other Energy ($/month)	Telephone ($/month)
City[2]	362,307	1,158	-	95.34	66.40	176.70
Avg.	347,000	1,087	165.93	100.16	67.73	178.70
Min.	200,468	500	93.58	25.64	26.78	163.10
Max.	1,901,222	4,888	388.65	246.86	332.81	197.70

Note: (1) Values for the local area are compared with the average, minimum and maximum values for all 291 areas in the Cost of Living Index; (2) Figures cover the Minneapolis MN urban area; New Home Price (2,400 sf living area, 8,000 sf lot, in urban area with full utilities); Apartment Rent (950 sf 2 bedroom/1.5 or 2 bath, unfurnished, excluding all utilities except water); All Electric (average monthly cost for an all-electric home); Part Electric (average monthly cost for a part-electric home); Other Energy (average monthly cost for natural gas, fuel oil, coal, wood, and any other forms of energy except electricity); Telephone (price includes the base monthly rate plus taxes and fees for three lines of mobile phone service).
Source: The Council for Community and Economic Research, ACCRA Cost of Living Index, 2018

Health Care, Transportation, and Other Costs

Area[1]	Doctor ($/visit)	Dentist ($/visit)	Optometrist ($/visit)	Gasoline ($/gallon)	Beauty Salon ($/visit)	Men's Shirt ($)
City[2]	144.82	85.76	88.91	2.57	34.88	34.24
Avg.	110.71	95.11	103.74	2.61	37.48	32.03
Min.	33.60	62.55	54.63	1.89	17.00	11.44
Max.	195.97	153.93	225.79	3.59	71.88	58.64

Note: (1) Values for the local area are compared with the average, minimum and maximum values for all 291 areas in the Cost of Living Index; (2) Figures cover the Minneapolis MN urban area; Doctor (general practitioners routine exam of an established patient); Dentist (adult teeth cleaning and periodic oral examination); Optometrist (full vision eye exam for established adult patient); Gasoline (one gallon regular unleaded, national brand, including all taxes, cash price at self-service pump if available); Beauty Salon (woman's shampoo, trim, and blow-dry); Men's Shirt (cotton/polyester dress shirt, pinpoint weave, long sleeves).
Source: The Council for Community and Economic Research, ACCRA Cost of Living Index, 2018

HOUSING

House Price Index (HPI)

Area	National Ranking[2]	Quarterly Change (%)	One-Year Change (%)	Five-Year Change (%)
MSA[1]	122	-0.88	6.31	31.91
U.S.[3]	–	1.12	5.73	32.81

Note: The HPI is a weighted repeat sales index. It measures average price changes in repeat sales or refinancings on the same properties. This information is obtained by reviewing repeat mortgage transactions on single-family properties whose mortgages have been purchased or securitized by Fannie Mae or Freddie Mac in January 1975; (1) Figures cover the Minneapolis-St. Paul-Bloomington, MN-WI Metropolitan Statistical Area—see Appendix B for areas included; (2) Rankings are based on annual percentage change for all metro areas containing at least 15,000 transactions over the last 10 years and ranges from 1 to 245; (3) figures based on a weighted average of Census Division estimates using a seasonally adjusted, purchase-only index; all figures are for the period ending December 31, 2018
Source: Federal Housing Finance Agency, House Price Index, February 26, 2019

Median Single-Family Home Prices

Area	2016	2017	2018[p]	Percent Change 2017 to 2018
MSA[1]	237.0	252.1	273.4	8.4
U.S. Average	235.5	248.8	261.6	5.1

Note: Figures are median sales prices of existing single-family homes in thousands of dollars; (p) preliminary; (1) Figures cover the Minneapolis-St. Paul-Bloomington, MN-WI Metropolitan Statistical Area—see Appendix B for areas included
Source: National Association of Realtors, Median Sales Price of Existing Single-Family Homes for Metropolitan Areas, 4th Quarter 2018

Qualifying Income Based on Median Sales Price of Existing Single-Family Homes

Area	With 5% Down ($)	With 10% Down ($)	With 20% Down ($)
MSA[1]	66,277	62,789	55,812
U.S. Average	62,954	59,640	53,013

Note: Figures are preliminary; Qualifying income is based on a mortgage rate of 4.9%. Monthly principal and interest payment is limited to 25% of income; (1) Figures cover the Minneapolis-St. Paul-Bloomington, MN-WI Metropolitan Statistical Area—see Appendix B for areas included
Source: National Association of Realtors, Qualifying Income Based on Median Sales Price of Existing Single-Family Homes for Metropolitan Areas, 4th Quarter 2018

Median Apartment Condo-Coop Home Prices

Area	2016	2017	2018[p]	Percent Change 2017 to 2018
MSA[1]	n/a	n/a	n/a	n/a
U.S. Average	220.7	234.3	241.0	2.9

Note: Figures are median sales prices of existing apartment condo-coop homes in thousands of dollars; (p) preliminary; n/a not available; (1) Figures cover the Minneapolis-St. Paul-Bloomington, MN-WI Metropolitan Statistical Area—see Appendix B for areas included
Source: National Association of Realtors, Median Sales Price of Existing Apartment Condo-Coop Homes for Metropolitan Areas, 4th Quarter 2018

Home Value Distribution

Area	Under $50,000	$50,000 -$99,999	$100,000 -$149,999	$150,000 -$199,999	$200,000 -$299,999	$300,000 -$499,999	$500,000 -$999,999	$1,000,000 or more
City	2.2	6.0	14.1	19.7	28.9	19.3	8.2	1.6
MSA[1]	3.6	4.1	11.6	20.0	30.4	21.9	7.1	1.2
U.S.	8.3	13.9	14.7	14.6	18.7	17.3	9.7	2.7

Note: Figures are percentages and cover owner-occupied housing units; (1) Figures cover the Minneapolis-St. Paul-Bloomington, MN-WI Metropolitan Statistical Area—see Appendix B for areas included
Source: U.S. Census Bureau, 2013-2017 American Community Survey 5-Year Estimates

Homeownership Rate

Area	2010 (%)	2011 (%)	2012 (%)	2013 (%)	2014 (%)	2015 (%)	2016 (%)	2017 (%)	2018 (%)
MSA[1]	71.2	69.1	70.8	71.7	69.7	67.9	69.1	70.1	67.8
U.S.	66.9	66.1	65.4	65.1	64.5	63.7	63.4	63.9	64.4

Note: (1) Figures cover the Minneapolis-St. Paul-Bloomington, MN-WI Metropolitan Statistical Area—see Appendix B for areas included
Source: U.S. Census Bureau, Housing Vacancies and Homeownership Annual Statistics: 2010-2018

Year Housing Structure Built

Area	2010 or Later	2000 -2009	1990 -1999	1980 -1989	1970 -1979	1960 -1969	1950 -1959	1940 -1949	Before 1940	Median Year
City	3.3	7.4	3.3	6.2	9.2	7.5	10.0	7.3	45.8	1946
MSA[1]	3.0	14.9	14.5	14.7	15.0	9.9	9.9	3.8	14.4	1978
U.S.	3.2	14.5	14.0	13.6	15.5	10.8	10.5	5.1	12.9	1977

Note: Figures are percentages except for Median Year; Note: (1) Figures cover the Minneapolis-St. Paul-Bloomington, MN-WI Metropolitan Statistical Area—see Appendix B for areas included
Source: U.S. Census Bureau, 2013-2017 American Community Survey 5-Year Estimates

Gross Monthly Rent

Area	Under $500	$500 -$999	$1,000 -$1,499	$1,500 -$1,999	$2,000 -$2,499	$2,500 -$2,999	$3,000 and up	Median ($)
City	14.1	42.0	28.1	10.8	3.5	0.9	0.5	941
MSA[1]	9.8	40.1	32.7	12.7	3.1	0.9	0.7	1,001
U.S.	10.5	41.1	28.7	11.7	4.5	1.8	1.7	982

Note: Figures are percentages except for Median; Gross rent is the contract rent plus the estimated average monthly cost of utilities (electricity, gas, and water and sewer) and fuels (oil, coal, kerosene, wood, etc.) if these are paid by the renter (or paid for the renter by someone else); (1) Figures cover the Minneapolis-St. Paul-Bloomington, MN-WI Metropolitan Statistical Area—see Appendix B for areas included
Source: U.S. Census Bureau, 2013-2017 American Community Survey 5-Year Estimates

HEALTH

Health Risk Factors

Category	MSA[1] (%)	U.S. (%)
Adults aged 18–64 who have any kind of health care coverage	91.0	87.3
Adults who reported being in good or better health	88.5	82.4
Adults who have been told they have high blood cholesterol	28.1	33.0
Adults who have been told they have high blood pressure	24.8	32.3
Adults who are current smokers	13.2	17.1
Adults who currently use E-cigarettes	3.4	4.6
Adults who currently use chewing tobacco, snuff, or snus	3.9	4.0
Adults who are heavy drinkers[2]	6.6	6.3
Adults who are binge drinkers[3]	20.5	17.4
Adults who are overweight (BMI 25.0 - 29.9)	35.6	35.3
Adults who are obese (BMI 30.0 - 99.8)	26.0	31.3
Adults who participated in any physical activities in the past month	78.1	74.4
Adults who always or nearly always wears a seat belt	97.3	94.3

Note: (1) Figures cover the Minneapolis-St. Paul-Bloomington, MN-WI Metropolitan Statistical Area—see Appendix B for areas included; (2) Heavy drinkers are classified as adult men having more than 14 drinks per week and adult women having more than 7 drinks per week; (3) Binge drinkers are classified as males having five or more drinks on one occasion or females having four or more drinks on one occasion
Source: Centers for Disease Control and Prevention, Behavioral Risk Factor Surveillance System, SMART: Selected Metropolitan Area Risk Trends, 2017

Acute and Chronic Health Conditions

Category	MSA[1] (%)	U.S. (%)
Adults who have ever been told they had a heart attack	3.0	4.2
Adults who have ever been told they have angina or coronary heart disease	3.0	3.9
Adults who have ever been told they had a stroke	2.0	3.0
Adults who have ever been told they have asthma	10.8	14.2
Adults who have ever been told they have arthritis	17.4	24.9
Adults who have ever been told they have diabetes[2]	6.7	10.5
Adults who have ever been told they had skin cancer	5.7	6.2
Adults who have ever been told they had any other types of cancer	6.3	7.1
Adults who have ever been told they have COPD	3.9	6.5
Adults who have ever been told they have kidney disease	2.5	3.0
Adults who have ever been told they have a form of depression	19.2	20.5

Note: (1) Figures cover the Minneapolis-St. Paul-Bloomington, MN-WI Metropolitan Statistical Area—see Appendix B for areas included; (2) Figures do not include pregnancy-related, borderline, or pre-diabetes
Source: Centers for Disease Control and Prevention, Behavioral Risk Factor Surveillance System, SMART: Selected Metropolitan Area Risk Trends, 2017

Health Screening and Vaccination Rates

Category	MSA[1] (%)	U.S. (%)
Adults aged 65+ who have had flu shot within the past year	65.7	60.7
Adults aged 65+ who have ever had a pneumonia vaccination	78.7	75.4
Adults who have ever been tested for HIV	35.8	36.1
Adults who have ever had the shingles or zoster vaccine?	33.6	28.9
Adults who have had their blood cholesterol checked within the last five years	87.9	85.9

Note: n/a not available; (1) Figures cover the Minneapolis-St. Paul-Bloomington, MN-WI Metropolitan Statistical Area—see Appendix B for areas included.
Source: Centers for Disease Control and Prevention, Behaviorial Risk Factor Surveillance System, SMART: Selected Metropolitan Area Risk Trends, 2017

Disability Status

Category	MSA[1] (%)	U.S. (%)
Adults who reported being deaf	5.6	6.7
Are you blind or have serious difficulty seeing, even when wearing glasses?	2.6	4.5
Are you limited in any way in any of your usual activities due of arthritis?	8.1	12.9
Do you have difficulty doing errands alone?	4.8	6.8
Do you have difficulty dressing or bathing?	2.5	3.6
Do you have serious difficulty concentrating/remembering/making decisions?	9.2	10.7
Do you have serious difficulty walking or climbing stairs?	9.1	13.6

Note: (1) Figures cover the Minneapolis-St. Paul-Bloomington, MN-WI Metropolitan Statistical Area—see Appendix B for areas included.
Source: Centers for Disease Control and Prevention, Behaviorial Risk Factor Surveillance System, SMART: Selected Metropolitan Area Risk Trends, 2017

Mortality Rates for the Top 10 Causes of Death in the U.S.

ICD-10[a] Sub-Chapter	ICD-10[a] Code	Age-Adjusted Mortality Rate[1] per 100,000 population	
		County[2]	U.S.
Malignant neoplasms	C00-C97	144.4	155.5
Ischaemic heart diseases	I20-I25	48.1	94.8
Other forms of heart disease	I30-I51	40.6	52.9
Chronic lower respiratory diseases	J40-J47	32.8	41.0
Cerebrovascular diseases	I60-I69	31.9	37.5
Other degenerative diseases of the nervous system	G30-G31	32.7	35.0
Other external causes of accidental injury	W00-X59	40.2	33.7
Organic, including symptomatic, mental disorders	F01-F09	52.7	31.0
Hypertensive diseases	I10-I15	14.9	21.9
Diabetes mellitus	E10-E14	18.4	21.2

Note: (a) ICD-10 = International Classification of Diseases 10th Revision; (1) Mortality rates are a three year average covering 2015-2017; (2) Figures cover Hennepin County.
Source: Centers for Disease Control and Prevention, National Center for Health Statistics. Underlying Cause of Death 1999-2017 on CDC WONDER Online Database

Mortality Rates for Selected Causes of Death

ICD-10[a] Sub-Chapter	ICD-10[a] Code	Age-Adjusted Mortality Rate[1] per 100,000 population	
		County[2]	U.S.
Assault	X85-Y09	4.2	5.9
Diseases of the liver	K70-K76	12.9	14.1
Human immunodeficiency virus (HIV) disease	B20-B24	1.4	1.8
Influenza and pneumonia	J09-J18	9.6	14.3
Intentional self-harm	X60-X84	11.1	13.6
Malnutrition	E40-E46	1.2	1.6
Obesity and other hyperalimentation	E65-E68	1.8	2.1
Renal failure	N17-N19	8.6	13.0
Transport accidents	V01-V99	4.8	12.4
Viral hepatitis	B15-B19	1.0	1.6

Note: (a) ICD-10 = International Classification of Diseases 10th Revision; (1) Mortality rates are a three year average covering 2015-2017; (2) Figures cover Hennepin County; Data are suppressed when the data meet the criteria for confidentiality constraints; Mortality rates are flagged as unreliable when the rate would be calculated with a numerator of 20 or less.
Source: Centers for Disease Control and Prevention, National Center for Health Statistics. Underlying Cause of Death 1999-2017 on CDC WONDER Online Database

Health Insurance Coverage

Area	With Health Insurance	With Private Health Insurance	With Public Health Insurance	Without Health Insurance	Population Under Age 18 Without Health Insurance
City	91.5	66.6	32.8	8.5	4.9
MSA[1]	94.7	78.0	28.1	5.3	3.5
U.S.	89.5	67.2	33.8	10.5	5.7

Note: Figures are percentages that cover the civilian noninstitutionalized population; (1) Figures cover the Minneapolis-St. Paul-Bloomington, MN-WI Metropolitan Statistical Area—see Appendix B for areas included
Source: U.S. Census Bureau, 2013-2017 American Community Survey 5-Year Estimates

Number of Medical Professionals

Area	MDs[3]	DOs[3,4]	Dentists	Podiatrists	Chiropractors	Optometrists
County[1] (number)	6,199	239	1,184	57	871	240
County[1] (rate[2])	501.1	19.3	94.6	4.6	69.6	19.2
U.S. (rate[2])	279.3	23.0	68.4	6.0	27.1	16.2

Note: Data as of 2017 unless noted; (1) Data covers Hennepin County; (2) Rate per 100,000 population; (3) Data as of 2016 and includes all active, non-federal physicians; (4) Doctor of Osteopathic Medicine
Source: U.S. Department of Health and Human Services, Health Resources and Services Administration, Bureau of Health Professions, Area Resource File (ARF) 2017-2018

Best Hospitals

According to *U.S. News,* the Minneapolis-St. Paul-Bloomington, MN-WI metro area is home to three of the best hospitals in the U.S.: **Abbott Northwestern Hospital** (8 adult specialties); **United Hospital** (1 adult specialty); **University of Minnesota Medical Center** (2 adult specialties and 5 pediatric specialties). The hospitals listed were nationally ranked in at least one of 16 adult or 10 pediatric specialties. Only 170 hospitals nationwide were nationally ranked in one or more adult or pediatric specialty. Twenty hospitals in the U.S. made the Honor Roll. The Best Hospitals Honor Roll takes both the national rankings and the procedure and condition ratings into account. Hospitals received points if they were nationally ranked in one of the 16 adult specialties—the higher they ranked, the more points they got—and how many ratings of "high performing" they earned in the nine procedures and conditions. *U.S. News Online, "America's Best Hospitals 2018-19"*

According to *U.S. News,* the Minneapolis-St. Paul-Bloomington, MN-WI metro area is home to two of the best children's hospitals in the U.S.: **Children's Hospitals and Clinics of Minnesota** (2 pediatric specialties); **University of Minnesota Masonic Children's Hospital** (5 pediatric specialties). The hospitals listed were highly ranked in at least one of 10 pediatric specialties. Eighty-six children's hospitals in the U.S. were nationally ranked in at least one specialty. Hospitals received points for being ranked in a specialty, and the 10 hospitals with the most points across the 10 specialties make up the Honor Roll. *U.S. News Online, "America's Best Children's Hospitals 2018-19"*

EDUCATION

Public School District Statistics

District Name	Schls	Pupils	Pupil/ Teacher Ratio	Minority Pupils[1] (%)	Free Lunch Eligible[2] (%)	IEP[3] (%)
Minneapolis Public School Dist.	104	36,675	13.4	66.1	56.4	18.5
Minnesota Transitions Charter Sch	7	3,041	20.3	40.2	45.1	14.8

Note: Table includes school districts with 2,000 or more students; (1) Percentage of students that are not non-Hispanic white; (2) Percentage of students that are eligible for the free lunch program; (3) Percentage of students that have an Individualized Education Program.
Source: U.S. Department of Education, National Center for Education Statistics, Common Core of Data, Local Education Agency (School District) Universe Survey: School Year 2016-2017; U.S. Department of Education, National Center for Education Statistics, Common Core of Data, Public Elementary/Secondary School Universe Survey: School Year 2016-2017

Highest Level of Education

Area	Less than H.S.	H.S. Diploma	Some College, No Deg.	Associate Degree	Bachelor's Degree	Master's Degree	Prof. School Degree	Doctorate Degree
City	10.7	16.4	17.5	7.1	29.3	12.7	3.9	2.5
MSA[1]	6.6	21.9	20.6	10.3	26.5	9.8	2.5	1.6
U.S.	12.7	27.3	20.8	8.3	19.1	8.4	2.0	1.4

Note: Figures cover persons age 25 and over; (1) Figures cover the Minneapolis-St. Paul-Bloomington, MN-WI Metropolitan Statistical Area—see Appendix B for areas included
Source: U.S. Census Bureau, 2013-2017 American Community Survey 5-Year Estimates

Educational Attainment by Race

Area	High School Graduate or Higher (%)					Bachelor's Degree or Higher (%)				
	Total	White	Black	Asian	Hisp.[2]	Total	White	Black	Asian	Hisp.[2]
City	89.3	95.6	74.9	80.4	56.1	48.3	58.7	14.4	50.0	16.6
MSA[1]	93.4	95.9	82.2	80.2	66.5	40.5	42.6	20.9	43.7	18.5
U.S.	87.3	89.3	84.9	86.5	66.7	30.9	32.2	20.6	52.7	15.2

Note: Figures shown cover persons 25 years old and over; (1) Figures cover the Minneapolis-St. Paul-Bloomington, MN-WI Metropolitan Statistical Area—see Appendix B for areas included; (2) People of Hispanic origin can be of any race
Source: U.S. Census Bureau, 2013-2017 American Community Survey 5-Year Estimates

School Enrollment by Grade and Control

Area	Preschool (%)		Kindergarten (%)		Grades 1 - 4 (%)		Grades 5 - 8 (%)		Grades 9 - 12 (%)	
	Public	Private	Public	Private	Public	Private	Public	Private	Public	Private
City	57.8	42.2	85.7	14.3	87.3	12.7	86.7	13.3	87.6	12.4
MSA[1]	59.6	40.4	87.5	12.5	89.0	11.0	89.6	10.4	91.0	9.0
U.S.	58.8	41.2	87.7	12.3	89.7	10.3	89.6	10.4	90.3	9.7

Note: Figures shown cover persons 3 years old and over; (1) Figures cover the Minneapolis-St. Paul-Bloomington, MN-WI Metropolitan Statistical Area—see Appendix B for areas included
Source: U.S. Census Bureau, 2013-2017 American Community Survey 5-Year Estimates

Average Salaries of Public School Classroom Teachers

Area	2016		2017		Change from 2016 to 2017	
	Dollars	Rank[1]	Dollars	Rank[1]	Percent	Rank[2]
Minnesota	56,913	17	57,346	20	0.8	36
U.S. Average	58,479	–	59,660	–	2.0	–

Note: (1) Rank ranges from 1 to 51 where 1 indicates highest salary; (2) Rank ranges from 1 to 51 where 1 indicates highest percent change.
Source: National Education Association, Rankings & Estimates: Rankings of the States 2017 and Estimates of School Statistics 2018

Higher Education

Four-Year Colleges			Two-Year Colleges			Medical Schools[1]	Law Schools[2]	Voc/ Tech[3]
Public	Private Non-profit	Private For-profit	Public	Private Non-profit	Private For-profit			
1	6	5	1	0	0	1	2	3

Note: Figures cover institutions located within the city limits and include main campuses only; (1) includes schools accredited by the Liaison Committee on Medical Education and the American Osteopathic Association's Commission on Osteopathic College Accreditation; (2) includes ABA-accredited schools, schools with provisional ABA accreditation, and state accredited schools; (3) includes all schools with programs that are less than 2 years.
Source: National Center for Education Statistics, Integrated Postsecondary Education System (IPEDS), 2017-18; Wikipedia, List of Medical Schools in the United States, accessed April 3, 2019; Wikipedia, List of Law Schools in the United States, accessed April 3, 2019

According to *U.S. News & World Report,* the Minneapolis-St. Paul-Bloomington, MN-WI metro area is home to two of the best national universities in the U.S.: **University of Minnesota—Twin Cities** (#76 tie); **University of St. Thomas** (#124 tie). The indicators used to capture academic quality fall into a number of categories: assessment by administrators at peer institutions; retention of students; faculty resources; student selectivity; financial resources; alumni giving; high school counselor ratings of colleges; and graduation rate. *U.S. News & World Report, "America's Best Colleges 2019"*

According to *U.S. News & World Report,* the Minneapolis-St. Paul-Bloomington, MN-WI metro area is home to three of the best liberal arts colleges in the U.S.: **Carleton College** (#5 tie); **Macalester College** (#27 tie); **St. Olaf College** (#61 tie). The indicators used to capture academic quality fall into a number of categories: assessment by administrators at peer institutions; retention of students; faculty resources; student selectivity; financial resources; alumni giving; high school counselor ratings of colleges; and graduation rate. *U.S. News & World Report, "America's Best Colleges 2019"*

According to *U.S. News & World Report,* the Minneapolis-St. Paul-Bloomington, MN-WI metro area is home to one of the top 100 law schools in the U.S.: **University of Minnesota** (#20). The rankings are based on a weighted average of 12 measures of quality: peer assessment score; assessment score by lawyers/judges; median LSAT scores; median undergrad GPA; acceptance rate; employment rates for graduates; placement success; bar passage rate; faculty resources; expenditures per student; student/faculty ratio; and library resources. *U.S. News & World Report, "America's Best Graduate Schools, Law, 2020"*

According to *U.S. News & World Report,* the Minneapolis-St. Paul-Bloomington, MN-WI metro area is home to one of the top 75 medical schools for research in the U.S.: **University of Minnesota** (#43 tie). The rankings are based on a weighted average of 11 measures of quality: quality assessment; peer assessment score; assessment score by residency directors; research activity; total research activity; average research activity per faculty member; student selectivity; median MCAT total score; median undergraduate GPA; acceptance rate; and faculty resources. *U.S. News & World Report, "America's Best Graduate Schools, Medical, 2020"*

According to *U.S. News & World Report,* the Minneapolis-St. Paul-Bloomington, MN-WI metro area is home to one of the top 75 business schools in the U.S.: **University of Minnesota—Twin Cities (Carlson)** (#35 tie). The rankings are based on a weighted average of the following nine measures: quality assessment; peer assessment; recruiter assessment; placement success; mean starting salary and bonus; student selectivity; mean GMAT and GRE scores; mean undergraduate GPA; and acceptance rate. *U.S. News & World Report, "America's Best Graduate Schools, Business, 2020"*

PRESIDENTIAL ELECTION

2016 Presidential Election Results

Area	Clinton	Trump	Johnson	Stein	Other
Hennepin County	63.1	28.2	3.6	1.5	3.6
U.S.	48.0	45.9	3.3	1.1	1.7

Note: Results are percentages and may not add to 100% due to rounding
Source: Dave Leip's Atlas of U.S. Presidential Elections

EMPLOYERS

Major Employers

Company Name	Industry
3M Company	Adhesives, sealants
Ameriprise Financial	Investment advice
Anderson Corporation	Millwork
Aware Integrated	Hospital & medical services plans
Bethesda Healtheast Hospital	General medical & surgical hospitals
Carlson Holdings	Hotels & motels
City of Minneapolis	General government, local government
County of Hennepin	General government, county government
Hennepin County	County government
Honeywell International	Aircraft engines & engine parts
Lawson Software	Application computer software
Medtronic	Electromedical equipment
Minnesota Department of Human Services	Family services agency
Minnesota Department of Transportation	Regulation, administration of transportation
North Memorial Hospital	General medical & surgical hospitals
Regents of the University of Minnesota	Specialty outpatient clinics, nec
Rosemount Apple Valley and Eagan	Personal service agents, brokers, & bureaus
St. Paul Fire and marine Insurance Company	Fire, marine, & casualty insurance
Thomson Legal Regulatory	Books, publishing & printing
United Parcel Service	Package delivery services
Wells Fargo	Mortgage bankers
West Publishing Corporation	Data base information retrieval

Note: Companies shown are located within the Minneapolis-St. Paul-Bloomington, MN-WI Metropolitan Statistical Area.
Source: Hoovers.com; Wikipedia

Best Companies to Work For

Ceridian; General Mills, headquartered in Minneapolis, are among the "100 Best Companies for Working Mothers." Criteria: paid time off and leaves; workforce profile; benefits; women's issues and advancement; flexible work; company culture and work life programs. *Working Mother, "100 Best Companies 2018"*

General Mills; U.S. Bank, headquartered in Minneapolis, are among the "Best Companies for Multicultural Women." *Working Mother* selected 24 companies based on a detailed application completed by public and private firms based in the United States, excluding government agencies, companies in the human resources field and non-autonomous divisions. Companies supplied data about the hiring, pay, and promotion of multicultural employees. Applications focused on representation of multicultural women, recruitment, retention and advancement programs, and company culture. *Working Mother, "2018 Best Companies for Multicultural Women"*

General Mills, headquartered in Minneapolis, is among the "Top Companies for Executive Women." The 2019 National Association for Female Executives (NAFE) Top Companies for Executive Women application included more than 200 questions on female representation at all levels, but especially the corporate officer and profit-and-loss leadership ranks. The application tracked how many employees have access to programs and policies that promote the advancement of women, and how many employees take advantage of them. The application also examined how companies train managers to help women advance, and how managers are held accountable for the advancement of female employees they oversee. *National Association for Female Executives, "2019 NAFE Top 70 Companies for Executive Women"*

PUBLIC SAFETY

Crime Rate

Area	All Crimes	Violent Crimes				Property Crimes		
		Murder	Rape[3]	Robbery	Aggrav. Assault	Burglary	Larceny-Theft	Motor Vehicle Theft
City	5,742.6	10.0	122.7	434.2	534.4	897.9	3,173.5	570.0
Suburbs[1]	2,286.0	1.7	32.8	46.7	94.0	281.4	1,661.8	167.7
Metro[2]	2,688.6	2.6	43.3	91.8	145.3	353.2	1,837.8	214.5
U.S.	2,756.1	5.3	41.7	98.0	248.9	430.4	1,694.4	237.4

Note: Figures are crimes per 100,000 population; (1) All areas within the metro area that are located outside the city limits; (2) Figures cover the Minneapolis-St. Paul-Bloomington, MN-WI Metropolitan Statistical Area—see Appendix B for areas included; (3) The city and U.S. figures shown were reported using the revised Uniform Crime Reporting (UCR) definition of rape. The suburban and metro area figures shown are an aggregate total of the data submitted using both the revised and legacy UCR definitions.
Source: FBI Uniform Crime Reports, 2017

Hate Crimes

Area	Number of Quarters Reported	Number of Incidents per Bias Motivation					
		Race/Ethnicity/Ancestry	Religion	Sexual Orientation	Disability	Gender	Gender Identity
City	4	16	7	8	0	0	0
U.S.	4	4,131	1,564	1,130	116	46	119

Source: Federal Bureau of Investigation, Hate Crime Statistics 2017

Identity Theft Consumer Reports

Area	Reports	Reports per 100,000 Population	Rank[2]
MSA[1]	3,006	85	207
U.S.	444,602	135	-

Note: (1) Figures cover the Minneapolis-St. Paul-Bloomington, MN-WI Metropolitan Statistical Area—see Appendix B for areas included; (2) Rank ranges from 1 to 389 where 1 indicates greatest number of identity theft reports per 100,000 population
Source: Federal Trade Commission, Consumer Sentinel Network Data Book for January–December 2018

Fraud and Other Consumer Reports

Area	Reports	Reports per 100,000 Population	Rank[2]
MSA[1]	17,825	502	175
U.S.	2,552,917	776	-

Note: (1) Figures cover the Minneapolis-St. Paul-Bloomington, MN-WI Metropolitan Statistical Area—see Appendix B for areas included; (2) Rank ranges from 1 to 389 where 1 indicates greatest number of fraud and other consumer reports per 100,000 population
Source: Federal Trade Commission, Consumer Sentinel Network Data Book for January–December 2018

SPORTS

Professional Sports Teams

Team Name	League	Year Established
Minnesota Timberwolves	National Basketball Association (NBA)	1989
Minnesota Twins	Major League Baseball (MLB)	1961
Minnesota United FC	Major League Soccer (MLS)	2017
Minnesota Vikings	National Football League (NFL)	1961
Minnesota Wild	National Hockey League (NHL)	2000

Note: Includes teams located in the Minneapolis-St. Paul-Bloomington, MN-WI Metropolitan Statistical Area.
Source: Wikipedia, Major Professional Sports Teams of the United States and Canada, April 5, 2019

CLIMATE

Average and Extreme Temperatures

Temperature	Jan	Feb	Mar	Apr	May	Jun	Jul	Aug	Sep	Oct	Nov	Dec	Yr.
Extreme High (°F)	57	60	83	95	96	102	105	101	98	89	74	63	105
Average High (°F)	21	27	38	56	69	79	84	81	71	59	41	26	54
Average Temp. (°F)	12	18	30	46	59	69	74	71	61	50	33	19	45
Average Low (°F)	3	9	21	36	48	58	63	61	50	39	25	11	35
Extreme Low (°F)	-34	-28	-32	2	18	37	43	39	26	15	-17	-29	-34

Note: Figures cover the years 1948-1990
Source: National Climatic Data Center, International Station Meteorological Climate Summary, 9/96

Average Precipitation/Snowfall/Humidity

Precip./Humidity	Jan	Feb	Mar	Apr	May	Jun	Jul	Aug	Sep	Oct	Nov	Dec	Yr.
Avg. Precip. (in.)	0.8	0.8	1.9	2.2	3.1	4.0	3.8	3.6	2.5	1.9	1.4	1.0	27.1
Avg. Snowfall (in.)	11	9	12	3	Tr	0	0	0	Tr	Tr	7	10	52
Avg. Rel. Hum. 6am (%)	75	76	77	75	75	79	81	84	85	81	80	79	79
Avg. Rel. Hum. 3pm (%)	64	62	58	48	47	50	50	52	53	52	62	68	55

Note: Figures cover the years 1948-1990; Tr = Trace amounts (<0.05 in. of rain; <0.5 in. of snow)
Source: National Climatic Data Center, International Station Meteorological Climate Summary, 9/96

Weather Conditions

Temperature			Daytime Sky			Precipitation		
5°F & below	32°F & below	90°F & above	Clear	Partly cloudy	Cloudy	0.01 inch or more precip.	0.1 inch or more snow/ice	Thunder-storms
45	156	16	93	125	147	113	41	37

Note: Figures are average number of days per year and cover the years 1948-1990
Source: National Climatic Data Center, International Station Meteorological Climate Summary, 9/96

HAZARDOUS WASTE

Superfund Sites

The Minneapolis-St. Paul-Bloomington, MN-WI metro area is home to 16 sites on the EPA's Superfund National Priorities List: **Baytown Township Ground Water Plume** (final); **Fmc Corp. (Fridley Plant)** (final); **Freeway Sanitary Landfill** (final); **Fridley Commons Park Well Field** (final); **General Mills/Henkel Corp.** (final); **Joslyn Manufacturing & Supply Co.** (final); **Koppers Coke** (final); **Kurt Manufacturing Co.** (final); **Macgillis & Gibbs Co./Bell Lumber & Pole Co.** (final); **Naval Industrial Reserve Ordnance Plant** (final); **New Brighton/Arden Hills/Tcaap (USARMY)** (final); **Oakdale Dump** (final); **Reilly Tar & Chemical Corp. (Saint Louis Park Plant)** (final); **South Andover Site** (final); **South Minneapolis Residential Soil Contamination** (final); **Spring Park Municipal Well Field** (final). There are a total of 1,390

Superfund sites with a status of proposed or final on the list in the U.S. *U.S. Environmental Protection Agency, National Priorities List, April 5, 2019*

AIR & WATER QUALITY

Air Quality Trends: Ozone

	1990	1995	2000	2005	2010	2012	2014	2015	2016	2017
MSA[1]	0.068	0.084	0.065	0.074	0.066	0.073	0.063	0.061	0.061	0.062
U.S.	0.088	0.089	0.082	0.080	0.073	0.075	0.067	0.068	0.069	0.068

Note: (1) Data covers the Minneapolis-St. Paul-Bloomington, MN-WI Metropolitan Statistical Area—see Appendix B for areas included. The values shown are the composite ozone concentration averages among trend sites based on the highest fourth daily maximum 8-hour concentration in parts per million. These trends are based on sites having an adequate record of monitoring data during the trend period. Data from exceptional events are included.
Source: U.S. Environmental Protection Agency, Air Quality Monitoring Information, "Air Quality Trends by City, 1990-2017"

Air Quality Index

Area	Percent of Days when Air Quality was...[2]					AQI Statistics[2]	
	Good	Moderate	Unhealthy for Sensitive Groups	Unhealthy	Very Unhealthy	Maximum	Median
MSA[1]	47.7	52.1	0.3	0.0	0.0	115	51

Note: (1) Data covers the Minneapolis-St. Paul-Bloomington, MN-WI Metropolitan Statistical Area—see Appendix B for areas included; (2) Based on 365 days with AQI data in 2017. Air Quality Index (AQI) is an index for reporting daily air quality. EPA calculates the AQI for five major air pollutants regulated by the Clean Air Act: ground-level ozone, particle pollution (aka particulate matter), carbon monoxide, sulfur dioxide, and nitrogen dioxide. The AQI runs from 0 to 500. The higher the AQI value, the greater the level of air pollution and the greater the health concern. There are six AQI categories: "Good" AQI is between 0 and 50. Air quality is considered satisfactory; "Moderate" AQI is between 51 and 100. Air quality is acceptable; "Unhealthy for Sensitive Groups" When AQI values are between 101 and 150, members of sensitive groups may experience health effects; "Unhealthy" When AQI values are between 151 and 200 everyone may begin to experience health effects; "Very Unhealthy" AQI values between 201 and 300 trigger a health alert; "Hazardous" AQI values over 300 trigger warnings of emergency conditions (not shown).
Source: U.S. Environmental Protection Agency, Air Quality Index Report, 2017

Air Quality Index Pollutants

Area	Percent of Days when AQI Pollutant was...[2]					
	Carbon Monoxide	Nitrogen Dioxide	Ozone	Sulfur Dioxide	Particulate Matter 2.5	Particulate Matter 10
MSA[1]	0.0	1.6	26.8	0.0	36.2	35.3

Note: (1) Data covers the Minneapolis-St. Paul-Bloomington, MN-WI Metropolitan Statistical Area—see Appendix B for areas included; (2) Based on 365 days with AQI data in 2017. The Air Quality Index (AQI) is an index for reporting daily air quality. EPA calculates the AQI for five major air pollutants regulated by the Clean Air Act: ground-level ozone, particle pollution (also known as particulate matter), carbon monoxide, sulfur dioxide, and nitrogen dioxide. The AQI runs from 0 to 500. The higher the AQI value, the greater the level of air pollution and the greater the health concern.
Source: U.S. Environmental Protection Agency, Air Quality Index Report, 2017

Maximum Air Pollutant Concentrations: Particulate Matter, Ozone, CO and Lead

	Particulate Matter 10 (ug/m^3)	Particulate Matter 2.5 Wtd AM (ug/m^3)	Particulate Matter 2.5 24-Hr (ug/m^3)	Ozone (ppm)	Carbon Monoxide (ppm)	Lead (ug/m^3)
MSA[1] Level	150	8.7	20	0.063	4	0.11
NAAQS[2]	150	15	35	0.075	9	0.15
Met NAAQS[2]	Yes	Yes	Yes	Yes	Yes	Yes

Note: (1) Data covers the Minneapolis-St. Paul-Bloomington, MN-WI Metropolitan Statistical Area—see Appendix B for areas included; Data from exceptional events are included; (2) National Ambient Air Quality Standards; ppm = parts per million; ug/m^3 = micrograms per cubic meter; n/a not available.
Concentrations: Particulate Matter 10 (coarse particulate)—highest second maximum 24-hour concentration; Particulate Matter 2.5 Wtd AM (fine particulate)—highest weighted annual mean concentration; Particulate Matter 2.5 24-Hour (fine particulate)—highest 98th percentile 24-hour concentration; Ozone—highest fourth daily maximum 8-hour concentration; Carbon Monoxide—highest second maximum non-overlapping 8-hour concentration; Lead—maximum running 3-month average
Source: U.S. Environmental Protection Agency, Air Quality Monitoring Information, "Air Quality Statistics by City, 2017"

Maximum Air Pollutant Concentrations: Nitrogen Dioxide and Sulfur Dioxide

	Nitrogen Dioxide AM (ppb)	Nitrogen Dioxide 1-Hr (ppb)	Sulfur Dioxide AM (ppb)	Sulfur Dioxide 1-Hr (ppb)	Sulfur Dioxide 24-Hr (ppb)
MSA[1] Level	13	44	n/a	18	n/a
NAAQS[2]	53	100	30	75	140
Met NAAQS[2]	Yes	Yes	n/a	Yes	n/a

Note: (1) Data covers the Minneapolis-St. Paul-Bloomington, MN-WI Metropolitan Statistical Area—see Appendix B for areas included; Data from exceptional events are included; (2) National Ambient Air Quality Standards; ppm = parts per million; ug/m³ = micrograms per cubic meter; n/a not available.
Concentrations: Nitrogen Dioxide AM—highest arithmetic mean concentration; Nitrogen Dioxide 1-Hr—highest 98th percentile 1-hour daily maximum concentration; Sulfur Dioxide AM—highest annual mean concentration; Sulfur Dioxide 1-Hr—highest 99th percentile 1-hour daily maximum concentration; Sulfur Dioxide 24-Hr—highest second maximum 24-hour concentration
Source: U.S. Environmental Protection Agency, Air Quality Monitoring Information, "Air Quality Statistics by City, 2017"

Drinking Water

Water System Name	Pop. Served	Primary Water Source Type	Violations[1] Health Based	Violations[1] Monitoring/ Reporting
Minneapolis	423,990	Surface	0	0

Note: (1) Based on violation data from January 1, 2018 to December 31, 2018
Source: U.S. Environmental Protection Agency, Office of Ground Water and Drinking Water, Safe Drinking Water Information System (based on data extracted April 5, 2019)

Oklahoma City, Oklahoma

Background

The 1992 film *Far and Away,* directed by Ron Howard, shows Tom Cruise charging away on his horse to claim land in the Oklahoma Territory. That dramatic scene depicted a true event from the great Oklahoma land run of 1889. A pistol was fired from the Oklahoma Station house of the Santa Fe Railroad and 10,000 homesteaders raced away to stake land claims in central Oklahoma territory. Overnight, Oklahoma City, "OKC" as the locals like to call their town, had been founded.

The town grew quickly along the tracks of the Santa Fe Railroad. Soon it became a distribution center for the territory's crops and livestock. Today, the city still functions as a major transportation center for the state's farm produce and livestock industry. By 1910 the city had become the state capital, which also furthered growth. But in 1928, growth went through the ceiling when oil was discovered within the city limits, forever changing the economic face of Oklahoma City from one of livestock and feed to one of livestock, feed, and oil.

After World War II, Oklahoma City, like many other cities, entered industry, most notably aircraft and related industries. The Tinker Air Force Base and the Federal Aviation Administration's Mike Monroney Aeronautical Center—home to the largest concentration of Dept. of Transportation personnel outside of Washington, D.C.—have made Oklahoma City a leading aviation center and, combined, employ more than 30,000 federal and civil contract workers. Major economic sectors for the Greater Oklahoma City region—the geographic center of the continent—also include energy, bioscience, and logistics.

The area caters to a Western lifestyle. The town is the home of the National Cowboy and Western Heritage Museum, with its famous 18-foot tall sculpture, "End of the Trail," by James Earle Fraser. The Oklahoma History Center, affiliated with the Smithsonian Institute, occupies a 215,000 square foot building on an 18-acre campus. The Red Earth Museum features 1,400 items of Native American art and a research center. To the north of Oklahoma City's Capitol building is the Tribal Flag Plaza, displaying the 39 native tribal flags of Oklahoma. Each September the State Fair is held in Oklahoma City, and each January the International Finals Rodeo is held at the State Fair Park. If swinging a bat is more your style than riding a bronco, there's the National Softball Hall of Fame and Museum.

Oklahoma City hired famous architect I.M. Pei to redesign its downtown area. Taking inspiration from the Tivoli Gardens of Copenhagen, the downtown boasts of the Myriad Gardens, a 12-acre recreational park with gardens, an amphitheater, and the seven-story Crystal Bridge Tropical Conservatory.

The city is also home to the Oklahoma City Thunder, a team that's become a leading NBA contender in recent years, often making the playoffs.

A national tragedy that played out in Oklahoma City remains present in the memory of the city and the country. On April 19, 1995, Oklahoma City suffered a deadly terrorist incident when a truck bomb destroyed part of the Alfred P. Murray Federal Building in the downtown area, leaving 168 people dead and more than 500 injured. In the face of such tragedy, the world marveled at how Oklahoma City and the state of Oklahoma carried itself with dignity and generosity. The Oklahoma City National Memorial commemorates those people whose lives were ended or forever changed on that day.

Oklahoma City's weather is changeable. There are pronounced daily and seasonal temperature changes and considerable variation in seasonal and annual precipitation. Summers are long and usually hot, while winters are comparatively mild and short. The city is located in Tornado Alley, which is frequently visited in the springtime by violent thunderstorms producing damaging winds, large hail, and tornadoes.

Rankings

General Rankings

- For its "Best for Vets: Places to Live 2019" rankings, *Military Times* evaluated 599 cities (83 large, 234 medium, 282 small) and compared the locations across three broad categories: veteran and military culture/services; economic indicators; and livability factors such as health, crime, traffic, and school quality. Oklahoma City ranked #6 out of the top 25, in the large city category (populations of more than 250,000). Data points more specific to veterans and the military weighed more heavily than the rest. *rebootcamp.militarytimes.com, "Military Times Best Places to Live 2019," September 10, 2018*

- The Oklahoma City metro area was identified as one of America's fastest-growing areas in terms of population and business growth by *MagnifyMoney*. The area ranked #31 out of 35. The 100 most populous metro areas in the U.S. were evaluated on their change from 2011-2016 in the following categories: people and housing; workforce and employment opportunities; growing industry. *www.businessinsider.com, "The 35 Cities in the US with the Biggest Influx of People, the Most Work Opportunities, and the Hottest Business Growth," August 12, 2018*

- In their sixth annual survey, Livability.com looked at data for more than 1,000 U.S. cities to determine the rankings for Livability's "Top 100 Best Places to Live" in 2019. Oklahoma City ranked #89. Criteria: median home value capped at $250,000; affordable living; vibrant economy; education, demographics, health care options. transportation & infrastructure; abundant lifestyle amenities. *Livability.com, "Top 100 Best Places to Live 2019" March 2019*

Business/Finance Rankings

- The personal finance site NerdWallet analyzed 183 American metropolitan areas with populations over 250,000 and more than 15,000 businesses to rank where entrepreneurs find the most success. Criteria included area economy, annual income, housing cost, unemployment rate, and the success rate of area businesses. Oklahoma City ranked #33. *www.nerdwallet.com, "Best Places to Start a Business," April 27, 2015*

- Oklahoma City was the #3-ranked city for savers, according to a study by the finance site GOBankingRates, which considered the prospects for people trying to save money. Criteria: average monthly cost of grocery items; median home listing price; median rent; median income; unemployment rate; gas prices; and sales tax in the nation's 60 largest cities. *www.gobankingrates.com, "Best Cities for Saving Money," June 22, 2018*

- Oklahoma City was ranked #3 among the nation's 60 largest cities for most difficult conditions for savers, according to a study by the finance site GOBankingRates. Criteria: average monthly cost of grocery items; median home listing price; median rent; median income; unemployment rate; gas prices; and sales tax. *www.gobankingrates.com, "Worst Cities for Saving Money," June 22, 2018*

- Recognizing the sizeable percentage of American workers who are self-employed, NerdWallet editors assessed the country's cities according to percentage of freelancers, median rental costs, cell phone plans/taxes, and healthcare affordability and access. By these criteria, Oklahoma City placed #14 among the best cities for independent workers. *www.nerdwallet.com, "Best Places for Freelance Workers," August 30, 2016*

- USAA and Hiring Our Heroes worked with Sperlings's BestPlaces and the Institute for Veterans and Military Families at Syracuse University to rank major metropolitan areas where military-skills-related employment is strongest. Criteria for veterans *pursuing entrepreneurship* included veteran-owned businesses per capita; percentage of small businesses; colleges; certification/license transfers; airports nearby; and accessible health resources. Metro areas with a higher than national average crime or unemployment rate were excluded. At #9, the Oklahoma City metro area made the top ten. *www.usaa.com, "2015 Best Places for Veterans"*

- USAA and Hiring Our Heroes worked with Sperlings's BestPlaces and the Institute for Veterans and Military Families at Syracuse University to rank major metropolitan areas where military-skills-related employment is strongest. Criteria for *mid-career* veterans included veteran wage growth; recent job growth; stability; and accessible health resources. Metro areas with a higher than national average crime or unemployment rate were excluded. At #1, the Oklahoma City metro area made the top ten. *www.usaa.com, "2015 Best Places for Veterans"*

- Based on metro area social media reviews, the employment opinion group Glassdoor surveyed 50 of the largest U.S. metro areas and equally weighed cost of living, hiring opportunity, and job satisfaction to compose a list of "25 Best Cities for Jobs." Median pay and home value, in-demand jobs and number of current job openings was also factored in. The Oklahoma City metro area was ranked #20 in overall job satisfaction. *www.glassdoor.com, "Best Cities for Jobs," October 16, 2018*

- In a survey of economic confidence in the nation's 50 largest metropolitan areas conducted January–December 2014, the Oklahoma City metro area placed #48, according to Gallup's 2014 Economic Confidence Index. *Gallup, "San Jose and San Francisco Lead in Economic Confidence," March 19, 2015*

- Using data from the Council for Community and Economic Research's 2014 cost of living index, NerdWallet ranked the 100 most affordable cities in America. Median income was compared with cost of living to find truly affordable places. Oklahoma City ranked #42. *NerdWallet.com, "America's Most Affordable Places," May 18, 2015*

- NerdWallet.com identified the 10 most promising cities for job seekers of the nation's 100 largest cities. Oklahoma City was ranked #56. Criteria: job availability; annual salary; workforce growth; affordability. *NerdWallet.com, "Best Cities for Job Seekers in 2017," December 19, 2016*

- The Brookings Institution ranked the nation's largest cities based on income inequality. Oklahoma City was ranked #70 (#1 = greatest inequality). Criteria: the "95/20 ratio," a figure representing the income at which a household earns more than 95 percent of all other households, divided by the income at which a household earns more than only 20 percent of all other households. *Brookings Institution, "Household Income Inequality, Largest Cities of 97 Large U.S. Metro Areas, 2014-2016," February 5, 2018*

- The Brookings Institution ranked the 100 largest metro areas in the U.S. based on income inequality. Oklahoma City was ranked #47 (#1 = greatest inequality). Criteria: the "95/20 ratio," a figure representing the income at which a household earns more than 95 percent of all other households, divided by the income at which a household earns more than only 20 percent of all other households. *Brookings Institution, "Household Income Inequality, 100 Largest U.S. Metro Areas, 2014-2016," February 5, 2018*

- The Oklahoma City metro area was identified as one of the most affordable metropolitan areas in America by *Forbes*. The area ranked #4 out of 20 based on the National Association of Home Builders/Wells Fargo Housing Affordability Index and Sperling's Best Places' cost-of-living index. *Forbes.com, "America's Most Affordable Cities in 2015," March 12, 2015*

- For its annual survey of the "10 Cheapest U.S. Cities to Live In," Kiplinger applied Cost of Living Index statistics developed by the Council for Community and Economic Research to U.S. Census Bureau population and median household income data for cities with populations above 50,000. In the resulting ranking, Oklahoma City ranked #9. *Kiplinger.com, "10 Cheapest U.S. Cities to Live In," March 19, 2018*

- The Oklahoma City metro area appeared on the Milken Institute "2018 Best Performing Cities" list. Rank: #147 out of 200 large metro areas. Criteria: job growth; wage and salary growth; high-tech output growth. *Milken Institute, "Best-Performing Cities 2018," January 24, 2019*

- *Forbes* ranked the 200 most populous metro areas to determine the nation's "Best Places for Business and Careers." The Oklahoma City metro area was ranked #50. Criteria: costs (business and living); job growth (past and projected); income growth; quality of life; educational attainment (college and high school); projected economic growth; cultural and recreational opportunities; net migration patterns; number of highly ranked colleges. *Forbes, "The Best Places for Business and Careers 2018: Seattle Leads the Way," October 24, 2018*

Culture/Performing Arts Rankings

- Oklahoma City was selected as one of the twenty best large U.S. cities for moviemakers. Of cities with a population over 400,000, the city was ranked #13. Criteria: film community and culture; access to equipment and facilities; film activity in 2018; number of film schools; tax incentives. ease of movement and traffic. *MovieMaker Magazine, "Best Places to Live and Work as a Moviemaker: 2019," January 16, 2019*

Dating/Romance Rankings

- Oklahoma City was ranked #18 out of 25 cities that stood out for inspiring romance and attracting diners on the website OpenTable.com. Criteria: percentage of people who dined out on Valentine's Day in 2018; percentage of romantic restaurants as rated by OpenTable diner reviews; and percentage of tables seated for two. *OpenTable, "25 Most Romantic Cities in America for 2019," February 7, 2019*

Education Rankings

- Personal finance website *WalletHub* analyzed the 150 largest U.S. metropolitan statistical areas to determine where the most educated Americans are choosing to settle. Criteria: education quality and attainment gap; education levels; percentage of workers with degrees; public school quality rankings; quality and size of each metro area's universities. Oklahoma City was ranked #68 (#1 = most educated city). *www.WalletHub.com, "2018's Most and Least Educated Cities in America," July 24, 2018*

- Oklahoma City was selected as one of America's most literate cities. The city ranked #41 out of the 82 largest U.S. cities. Criteria: number of booksellers; library resources; Internet resources; educational attainment; periodical publishing resources; newspaper circulation. *Central Connecticut State University, "America's Most Literate Cities, 2016," March 31, 2017*

Environmental Rankings

- Sperling's BestPlaces assessed the 50 largest metropolitan areas of the United States for the likelihood of dangerously extreme weather events or earthquakes. In general the Southeast and South-Central regions have the highest risk of weather extremes and earthquakes, while the Pacific Northwest enjoys the lowest risk. Of the most risky metropolitan areas, the Oklahoma City metro area was ranked #3. *www.bestplaces.net, "Avoid Natural Disasters: BestPlaces Reveals The Top 10 Safest Places to Live," October 25, 2017*

- Oklahoma City was highlighted as one of the top 90 cleanest metro areas for short-term particle pollution (24-hour PM 2.5) in the U.S. during 2014 through 2016. Monitors in these cities reported no days with unhealthful PM 2.5 levels. *American Lung Association, State of the Air 2018*

Food/Drink Rankings

- *Men's Health* ranked 100 major U.S. cities in terms of alcohol intoxication. Oklahoma City ranked #31 (#1 = most sober).Criteria: binge drinking; alcohol-related traffic accidents, arrests, and fatalities. *Men's Health, "America's Drunkest Cities," March 9, 2015*

Health/Fitness Rankings

- For each of the 100 largest cities in the United States, the American College of Sports Medicine's American Fitness Index evaluated infrastructure, community assets, and policies that encourage healthy and fit lifestyles, including preventive health behaviors, levels of chronic disease conditions, health care access, and community resources and policies that support physical activity. Oklahoma City ranked #100 for "community fitness." *www.americanfitnessindex.org, "ACSM American Fitness Index Health and Community Fitness Status of the 100 Largest U.S. Cities," May 2018*

- Oklahoma City was identified as a "2018 Spring Allergy Capital." The area ranked #9 out of 100. Three groups of factors were used to identify the most challenging cities for people with allergies during the spring season: annual pollen levels; medicine utilization; access to board-certified allergists. *Asthma and Allergy Foundation of America, "Spring Allergy Capitals 2018"*

- Oklahoma City was identified as a "2018 Fall Allergy Capital." The area ranked #9 out of 100. Three groups of factors were used to identify the most challenging cities for people with allergies during the fall season: annual pollen levels; medicine utilization; access to board-certified allergists. *Asthma and Allergy Foundation of America, "Fall Allergy Capitals 2018"*

- Oklahoma City was identified as a "2018 Asthma Capital." The area ranked #34 out of the nation's 100 largest metropolitan areas. Criteria: estimated prevalence; self-reported prevalence; crude death rate for asthma; annual pollen score; annual air quality; public smoking laws; number of board-certified asthma specialists; school inhaler access laws; rescue medication use; controller medication use; ER visits for asthma; uninsured rate; poverty rate. *Asthma and Allergy Foundation of America, "Asthma Capitals 2018: The Most Challenging Places to Live With Asthma"*

- *Men's Health* ranked 100 major U.S. cities in terms of the best cities for men. Oklahoma City ranked #86. Criteria: health; fitness; quality of life. *Men's Health, "The Best & Worst Cities for Men Who Want to Be Fit and Happy," January 1, 2016*

- The Oklahoma City metro area ranked #173 out of 189 in The Gallup-Healthways Well-Being Index. Criteria: purpose; social well being; financial health; community and physical health. Results are based on telephone interviews with adults, aged 18 and older, living in metropolitan areas in the 50 U.S. states and the District of Columbia. *Gallup-Healthways, "State of American Well-Being, 2017 Community Well-Being Rankings" March 2018*

Real Estate Rankings

- FitSmallBusiness looked at 50 of the largest metropolitan areas in the U.S. to determine which metro was the best to start a real estate business. Data was compiled from such sources as: Zillow, Trulia, U.S. Census Bureau, and the Bureau of Labor Statistics. Criteria: location; inventory; annual wages; median sales price of homes; days on the market; median price cut percentage; and other factors that would influence real estate professional growth. The Oklahoma City metro area ranked #35. *fitsmallbusiness.com, "The Best Cities to Become a Real Estate Agent in 2018," January 30, 2018*

- *WalletHub* compared the most populated U.S. cities, as well as at least two of the most populated cities in each state, for a total of 179, to determine which had the best markets for real estate agents. Oklahoma City ranked #162 where demand was high and pay was the best. Criteria: sales per agent; annual median wage for real-estate agents; monthly average starting salary for real estate agents; real estate job density and competition; unemployment rate; housing-market health index; and other relevant metrics. *www.WalletHub.com, "2018's Best Places to Be a Real Estate Agent,"April 25, 2018*

- The Oklahoma City metro area was identified as one of nine best housing markets to invest in. Criteria: single-family rental home investing in the first quarter of 2017 based on first-year returns. The area ranked #6. *The Business Insider, "Here are the 9 Best U.S. Housing Markets for Investment," May 11, 2017*

- Oklahoma City was ranked #48 out of 237 metro areas in terms of housing affordability in 2018 by the National Association of Home Builders (#1 = most affordable). Criteria: the share of homes sold in that area affordable to a family earning the local median income, based on standard mortgage underwriting criteria. *National Association of Home Builders®, NAHB-Wells Fargo Housing Opportunity Index, 4th Quarter 2018*

Safety Rankings

- Allstate ranked the 200 largest cities in America in terms of driver safety. Oklahoma City ranked #52. Criteria: internal property damage claims over a two-year period from January 2015 to December 2016. The report helps increase the importance of safety awareness behind the wheel. *Allstate, "Allstate America's Best Drivers Report, 2018" August 28, 2018*

- The National Insurance Crime Bureau ranked 382 metro areas in the U.S. in terms of per capita rates of vehicle theft. The Oklahoma City metro area ranked #69 (#1 = highest rate). Criteria: number of vehicle theft offenses per 100,000 inhabitants in 2017. *National Insurance Crime Bureau, "Hot Spots 2017," July 12, 2018*

Seniors/Retirement Rankings

- From its Best Cities for Successful Aging indexes, the Milken Institute generated rankings for metropolitan areas, weighing data in nine categories—health care, wellness, living arrangements, transportation and convenience, financial characteristics, education, employment, community engagement, and overall livability. The Oklahoma City metro area was ranked #28 overall in the large metro area category. *Milken Institute, "Best Cities for Successful Aging, 2017" March 14, 2017*

Miscellaneous Rankings

- *WalletHub* compared the 150 most populated U.S. cities to determine their operating efficiency. A "Quality of Services" score was constructed for each city and then divided by the total budget per capita to reveal which were managed the best. Oklahoma City ranked #10. Criteria: financial stability; economy; education; safety; health; infrastructure and pollution. *www.WalletHub.com, "2018's Best- & Worst-Run Cities in America," July 9, 2018*

Business Environment

CITY FINANCES

City Government Finances

Component	2016 ($000)	2016 ($ per capita)
Total Revenues	1,482,279	2,348
Total Expenditures	1,533,813	2,429
Debt Outstanding	1,655,123	2,622
Cash and Securities[1]	2,371,354	3,756

Note: (1) Cash and security holdings of a government at the close of its fiscal year, including those of its dependent agencies, utilities, and liquor stores.
Source: U.S. Census Bureau, State & Local Government Finances 2016

City Government Revenue by Source

Source	2016 ($000)	2016 ($ per capita)	2016 (%)
General Revenue			
From Federal Government	41,784	66	2.8
From State Government	58,421	93	3.9
From Local Governments	149,318	237	10.1
Taxes			
Property	104,043	165	7.0
Sales and Gross Receipts	510,525	809	34.4
Personal Income	0	0	0.0
Corporate Income	0	0	0.0
Motor Vehicle License	0	0	0.0
Other Taxes	23,616	37	1.6
Current Charges	262,360	416	17.7
Liquor Store	0	0	0.0
Utility	144,258	228	9.7
Employee Retirement	10,429	17	0.7

Source: U.S. Census Bureau, State & Local Government Finances 2016

City Government Expenditures by Function

Function	2016 ($000)	2016 ($ per capita)	2016 (%)
General Direct Expenditures			
Air Transportation	94,185	149	6.1
Corrections	8,684	13	0.6
Education	0	0	0.0
Employment Security Administration	0	0	0.0
Financial Administration	23,694	37	1.5
Fire Protection	142,085	225	9.3
General Public Buildings	0	0	0.0
Governmental Administration, Other	13,147	20	0.9
Health	5,192	8	0.3
Highways	77,839	123	5.1
Hospitals	0	0	0.0
Housing and Community Development	50,839	80	3.3
Interest on General Debt	35,720	56	2.3
Judicial and Legal	21,416	33	1.4
Libraries	0	0	0.0
Parking	6,326	10	0.4
Parks and Recreation	199,444	315	13.0
Police Protection	171,202	271	11.2
Public Welfare	0	0	0.0
Sewerage	27,465	43	1.8
Solid Waste Management	52,097	82	3.4
Veterans' Services	0	0	0.0
Liquor Store	0	0	0.0
Utility	410,092	649	26.7
Employee Retirement	54,026	85	3.5

Source: U.S. Census Bureau, State & Local Government Finances 2016

DEMOGRAPHICS

Population Growth

Area	1990 Census	2000 Census	2010 Census	2017* Estimate	Population Growth (%) 1990-2017	2010-2017
City	445,065	506,132	579,999	629,191	41.4	8.5
MSA[1]	971,042	1,095,421	1,252,987	1,353,504	39.4	8.0
U.S.	248,709,873	281,421,906	308,745,538	321,004,407	29.1	4.0

Note: (1) Figures cover the Oklahoma City, OK Metropolitan Statistical Area—see Appendix B for areas included; (*) 2013-2017 5-year estimated population
Source: U.S. Census Bureau, 1990 Census, Census 2000, Census 2010, 2013-2017 American Community Survey 5-Year Estimates

Household Size

Area	Persons in Household (%) One	Two	Three	Four	Five	Six	Seven or More	Average Household Size
City	31.0	32.1	15.0	12.2	6.0	2.6	1.3	2.60
MSA[1]	28.3	34.1	15.6	12.6	5.9	2.3	1.2	2.60
U.S.	27.7	33.8	15.7	13.0	6.0	2.3	1.4	2.60

Note: (1) Figures cover the Oklahoma City, OK Metropolitan Statistical Area—see Appendix B for areas included
Source: U.S. Census Bureau, 2013-2017 American Community Survey 5-Year Estimates

Race

Area	White Alone[2] (%)	Black Alone[2] (%)	Asian Alone[2] (%)	AIAN[3] Alone[2] (%)	NHOPI[4] Alone[2] (%)	Other Race Alone[2] (%)	Two or More Races (%)
City	67.7	14.5	4.5	2.8	0.1	3.9	6.5
MSA[1]	73.9	10.2	3.1	3.4	0.1	2.6	6.6
U.S.	73.0	12.7	5.4	0.8	0.2	4.8	3.1

Note: (1) Figures cover the Oklahoma City, OK Metropolitan Statistical Area—see Appendix B for areas included; (2) Alone is defined as not being in combination with one or more other races; (3) American Indian and Alaska Native; (4) Native Hawaiian and Other Pacific Islander
Source: U.S. Census Bureau, 2013-2017 American Community Survey 5-Year Estimates

Hispanic or Latino Origin

Area	Total (%)	Mexican (%)	Puerto Rican (%)	Cuban (%)	Other (%)
City	19.1	16.0	0.3	0.1	2.7
MSA[1]	12.8	10.5	0.3	0.1	1.9
U.S.	17.6	11.1	1.7	0.7	4.1

Note: Persons of Hispanic or Latino origin can be of any race; (1) Figures cover the Oklahoma City, OK Metropolitan Statistical Area—see Appendix B for areas included
Source: U.S. Census Bureau, 2013-2017 American Community Survey 5-Year Estimates

Segregation

Type	Segregation Indices[1] 1990	2000	2010	2010 Rank[2]	Percent Change 1990-2000	1990-2010	2000-2010
Black/White	60.2	55.3	51.4	67	-4.8	-8.8	-4.0
Asian/White	39.8	40.8	39.2	60	1.0	-0.6	-1.7
Hispanic/White	33.4	44.2	47.0	38	10.7	13.6	2.9

Note: All figures cover the Metropolitan Statistical Area—see Appendix B for areas included; Figures are based on an analysis of 1990, 2000, and 2010 Census tract data by William H. Frey, Brookings Institution and the University of Michigan Social Science Data Analysis Network. In this analysis all racial groups (whites, blacks, and asians) are non-Hispanic members of those races. Hispanics are shown as a separate category; (1) Segregation Indices are Dissimilarity Indices that measure the degree to which the minority group is distributed differently than whites across census tracts. They range from 0 (complete integration) to 100 (complete segregation) where the value indicates the percentage of the minority group that needs to move to be distributed exactly like whites; (2) Ranges from 1 (most segregated) to 102 (least segregated); n/a not available.
Source: www.CensusScope.org

Ancestry

Area	German	Irish	English	American	Italian	Polish	French[2]	Scottish	Dutch
City	11.7	9.1	6.6	5.9	1.9	0.9	1.9	1.6	1.2
MSA[1]	13.4	10.1	7.6	7.6	2.0	1.0	2.0	1.8	1.4
U.S.	14.1	10.1	7.5	6.6	5.3	2.9	2.5	1.7	1.3

Note: Figures are the percentage of the total population reporting a particular ancestry. The nine most commonly reported ancestries in the U.S. are shown. Figures include multiple ancestries (e.g. if a person reported being Irish and Italian, they were included in both columns); (1) Figures cover the Oklahoma City, OK Metropolitan Statistical Area—see Appendix B for areas included; (2) Excludes Basque
Source: U.S. Census Bureau, 2013-2017 American Community Survey 5-Year Estimates

Foreign-Born Population

Area	Any Foreign Country	Percent of Population Born in							
		Asia	Mexico	Europe	Carribean	Central America[2]	South America	Africa	Canada
City	12.1	3.4	6.1	0.4	0.1	1.1	0.3	0.5	0.1
MSA[1]	8.0	2.5	3.6	0.4	0.1	0.7	0.2	0.4	0.1
U.S.	13.4	4.1	3.6	1.5	1.3	1.0	0.9	0.6	0.3

Note: (1) Figures cover the Oklahoma City, OK Metropolitan Statistical Area—see Appendix B for areas included; (2) Excludes Mexico.
Source: U.S. Census Bureau, 2013-2017 American Community Survey 5-Year Estimates

Marital Status

Area	Never Married	Now Married[2]	Separated	Widowed	Divorced
City	32.8	46.2	2.3	5.6	13.0
MSA[1]	30.8	48.8	2.1	5.6	12.7
U.S.	33.1	48.2	2.0	5.8	10.9

Note: Figures are percentages and cover the population 15 years of age and older; (1) Figures cover the Oklahoma City, OK Metropolitan Statistical Area—see Appendix B for areas included; (2) Excludes separated
Source: U.S. Census Bureau, 2013-2017 American Community Survey 5-Year Estimates

Disability by Age

Area	All Ages	Under 18 Years Old	18 to 64 Years Old	65 Years and Over
City	13.5	4.7	12.3	39.4
MSA[1]	13.7	4.5	12.2	39.6
U.S.	12.6	4.2	10.3	35.5

Note: Figures show percent of the civilian noninstitutionalized population that reported having a disability. Disability status is determined from six types of difficulty: vision, hearing, cognitive, ambulatory, self-care, and independent living. For children under 5 years old, hearing and vision difficulty are used to determine disability status. For children between the ages of 5 and 14, disability status is determined from hearing, vision, cognitive, ambulatory, and self-care difficulties. For people aged 15 years and older, they are considered to have a disability if they have difficulty with any one of the six difficulty types; Note: (1) Figures cover the Oklahoma City, OK Metropolitan Statistical Area—see Appendix B for areas included
Source: U.S. Census Bureau, 2013-2017 American Community Survey 5-Year Estimates

Age

Area	Percent of Population									Median Age
	Under Age 5	Age 5–19	Age 20–34	Age 35–44	Age 45–54	Age 55–64	Age 65–74	Age 75–84	Age 85+	
City	7.8	20.2	23.4	13.2	12.0	11.5	7.0	3.4	1.5	34.1
MSA[1]	7.1	20.5	22.6	12.8	12.2	11.9	7.6	3.8	1.5	34.9
U.S.	6.2	19.5	20.7	12.7	13.4	12.7	8.6	4.4	1.9	37.8

Note: (1) Figures cover the Oklahoma City, OK Metropolitan Statistical Area—see Appendix B for areas included
Source: U.S. Census Bureau, 2013-2017 American Community Survey 5-Year Estimates

Gender

Area	Males	Females	Males per 100 Females
City	309,360	319,831	96.7
MSA[1]	667,697	685,807	97.4
U.S.	158,018,753	162,985,654	97.0

Note: (1) Figures cover the Oklahoma City, OK Metropolitan Statistical Area—see Appendix B for areas included
Source: U.S. Census Bureau, 2013-2017 American Community Survey 5-Year Estimates

Religious Groups by Family

Area	Catholic	Baptist	Non-Den.	Methodist[2]	Lutheran	LDS[3]	Pentecostal	Presbyterian[4]	Muslim[5]	Judaism
MSA[1]	6.4	25.4	7.1	10.6	0.7	1.3	3.2	1.0	0.2	0.1
U.S.	19.1	9.3	4.0	4.0	2.3	2.0	1.9	1.6	0.8	0.7

Note: Figures are the number of adherents as a percentage of the total population; (1) Figures cover the Oklahoma City, OK Metropolitan Statistical Area—see Appendix B for areas included; (2) Methodist/Pietist; (3) Latter Day Saints; (4) Reformed; (5) Figures are estimates
Source: Association of Statisticians of American Religious Bodies, 2010 U.S. Religion Census: Religious Congregations & Membership Study

Religious Groups by Tradition

Area	Catholic	Evangelical Protestant	Mainline Protestant	Other Tradition	Black Protestant	Orthodox
MSA[1]	6.4	39.1	9.9	2.8	1.9	0.2
U.S.	19.1	16.2	7.3	4.3	1.6	0.3

Note: Figures are the number of adherents as a percentage of the total population; (1) Figures cover the Oklahoma City, OK Metropolitan Statistical Area—see Appendix B for areas included
Source: Association of Statisticians of American Religious Bodies, 2010 U.S. Religion Census: Religious Congregations & Membership Study

ECONOMY

Gross Metropolitan Product

Area	2016	2017	2018	2019	Rank[2]
MSA[1]	69.7	73.0	77.1	81.1	49

Note: Figures are in billions of dollars; (1) Figures cover the Oklahoma City, OK Metropolitan Statistical Area—see Appendix B for areas included; (2) Rank is based on 2017 data and ranges from 1 to 381
Source: U.S. Conference of Mayors, U.S. Metro Economies: Economic Growth & Full Employment, June 2018

Economic Growth

Area	2017-2018 (%)	2019-2020 (%)	2021-2022 (%)
MSA[1]	2.9	2.9	2.1

Note: Figures are real gross metropolitan product (GMP) growth rates and represent average annual percent change; (1) Figures cover the Oklahoma City, OK Metropolitan Statistical Area—see Appendix B for areas included
Source: U.S. Conference of Mayors, U.S. Metro Economies: Economic Growth & Full Employment, June 2018

Metropolitan Area Exports

Area	2012	2013	2014	2015	2016	2017	Rank[2]
MSA[1]	1,574.6	1,581.7	1,622.0	1,353.1	1,260.0	1,278.8	129

Note: Figures are in millions of dollars; (1) Figures cover the Oklahoma City, OK Metropolitan Statistical Area—see Appendix B for areas included; (2) Rank is based on 2017 data and ranges from 1 to 387
Source: U.S. Department of Commerce, International Trade Administration, Office of Trade and Economic Analysis, Industry and Analysis, Exports by Metropolitan Area, extracted March 25, 2019

Building Permits

Area	Single-Family			Multi-Family			Total		
	2016	2017	Pct. Chg.	2016	2017	Pct. Chg.	2016	2017	Pct. Chg.
City	2,899	2,707	-6.6	291	48	-83.5	3,190	2,755	-13.6
MSA[1]	5,039	5,132	1.8	1,701	287	-83.1	6,740	5,419	-19.6
U.S.	750,800	820,000	9.2	455,800	462,000	1.4	1,206,600	1,282,000	6.2

Note: (1) Figures cover the Oklahoma City, OK Metropolitan Statistical Area—see Appendix B for areas included; Figures represent new, privately-owned housing units authorized (unadjusted data); All permit data are based on estimates with imputation
Source: U.S. Census Bureau, Manufacturing, Mining, and Construction Statistics, Building Permits, 2016, 2017

Bankruptcy Filings

Area	Business Filings			Nonbusiness Filings		
	2017	2018	% Chg.	2017	2018	% Chg.
Oklahoma County	59	63	6.8	2,098	2,255	7.5
U.S.	23,157	22,232	-4.0	765,863	751,186	-1.9

Note: Business filings include Chapter 7, Chapter 11, Chapter 12, and Chapter 13; Nonbusiness filings include Chapter 7, Chapter 11, and Chapter 13
Source: Administrative Office of the U.S. Courts, Business and Nonbusiness Bankruptcy, County Cases Commenced by Chapter of the Bankruptcy Code, During the 12-Month Period Ending December 31, 2017 and Business and Nonbusiness Bankruptcy, County Cases Commenced by Chapter of the Bankruptcy Code, During the 12-Month Period Ending December 31, 2018

Housing Vacancy Rates

Area	Gross Vacancy Rate[2] (%)			Year-Round Vacancy Rate[3] (%)			Rental Vacancy Rate[4] (%)			Homeowner Vacancy Rate[5] (%)		
	2016	2017	2018	2016	2017	2018	2016	2017	2018	2016	2017	2018
MSA[1]	11.9	11.1	11.5	11.6	10.8	11.2	10.9	9.9	11.8	1.6	1.9	2.7
U.S.	12.8	12.7	12.3	9.9	9.9	9.7	6.9	7.2	6.9	1.7	1.6	1.5

Note: (1) Figures cover the Oklahoma City, OK Metropolitan Statistical Area—see Appendix B for areas included; (2) The percentage of the total housing inventory that is vacant; (3) The percentage of the housing inventory (excluding seasonal units) that is year-round vacant; (4) The percentage of rental inventory that is vacant for rent; (5) The percentage of homeowner inventory that is vacant for sale
Source: U.S. Census Bureau, Housing Vacancies and Homeownership Annual Statistics: 2016, 2017, 2018

INCOME

Income

Area	Per Capita ($)	Median Household ($)	Average Household ($)
City	28,365	51,581	72,393
MSA[1]	28,963	54,946	74,813
U.S.	31,177	57,652	81,283

Note: (1) Figures cover the Oklahoma City, OK Metropolitan Statistical Area—see Appendix B for areas included
Source: U.S. Census Bureau, 2013-2017 American Community Survey 5-Year Estimates

Household Income Distribution

Area	Percent of Households Earning							
	Under $15,000	$15,000 -$24,999	$25,000 -$34,999	$35,000 -$49,999	$50,000 -$74,999	$75,000 -$99,999	$100,000 -$149,999	$150,000 and up
City	12.1	10.1	11.3	15.0	17.9	11.9	12.4	9.2
MSA[1]	11.1	9.7	10.5	14.2	19.1	12.7	13.1	9.5
U.S.	11.6	9.8	9.5	13.0	17.7	12.3	14.1	12.1

Note: (1) Figures cover the Oklahoma City, OK Metropolitan Statistical Area—see Appendix B for areas included
Source: U.S. Census Bureau, 2013-2017 American Community Survey 5-Year Estimates

Poverty Rate

Area	All Ages	Under 18 Years Old	18 to 64 Years Old	65 Years and Over
City	17.1	25.8	15.1	8.2
MSA[1]	14.6	20.6	13.7	7.2
U.S.	14.6	20.3	13.7	9.3

Note: Figures are percentage of people whose income during the past 12 months was below the poverty level; (1) Figures cover the Oklahoma City, OK Metropolitan Statistical Area—see Appendix B for areas included
Source: U.S. Census Bureau, 2013-2017 American Community Survey 5-Year Estimates

EMPLOYMENT

Labor Force and Employment

Area	Civilian Labor Force			Workers Employed		
	Dec. 2017	Dec. 2018	% Chg.	Dec. 2017	Dec. 2018	% Chg.
City	315,790	315,289	-0.2	304,263	306,285	0.7
MSA[1]	674,115	672,568	-0.2	650,461	653,952	0.5
U.S.	159,880,000	162,510,000	1.6	153,602,000	156,481,000	1.9

Note: Data is not seasonally adjusted and covers workers 16 years of age and older; (1) Figures cover the Oklahoma City, OK Metropolitan Statistical Area—see Appendix B for areas included
Source: Bureau of Labor Statistics, Local Area Unemployment Statistics

Unemployment Rate

Area	2018											
	Jan.	Feb.	Mar.	Apr.	May	Jun.	Jul.	Aug.	Sep.	Oct.	Nov.	Dec.
City	4.0	3.8	3.6	3.5	3.7	3.7	3.4	3.3	2.9	2.9	2.7	2.9
MSA[1]	3.8	3.7	3.6	3.5	3.6	3.7	3.3	3.2	2.8	2.8	2.6	2.8
U.S.	4.5	4.4	4.1	3.7	3.6	4.2	4.1	3.9	3.6	3.5	3.5	3.7

Note: Data is not seasonally adjusted and covers workers 16 years of age and older; (1) Figures cover the Oklahoma City, OK Metropolitan Statistical Area—see Appendix B for areas included
Source: Bureau of Labor Statistics, Local Area Unemployment Statistics

Average Wages

Occupation	$/Hr.	Occupation	$/Hr.
Accountants and Auditors	36.30	Maids and Housekeeping Cleaners	10.10
Automotive Mechanics	21.40	Maintenance and Repair Workers	16.80
Bookkeepers	19.10	Marketing Managers	57.20
Carpenters	20.50	Nuclear Medicine Technologists	35.70
Cashiers	10.40	Nurses, Licensed Practical	20.60
Clerks, General Office	14.00	Nurses, Registered	31.30
Clerks, Receptionists/Information	13.80	Nursing Assistants	12.80
Clerks, Shipping/Receiving	15.70	Packers and Packagers, Hand	11.00
Computer Programmers	39.70	Physical Therapists	41.50
Computer Systems Analysts	35.90	Postal Service Mail Carriers	24.60
Computer User Support Specialists	23.00	Real Estate Brokers	n/a
Cooks, Restaurant	12.10	Retail Salespersons	14.00
Dentists	73.70	Sales Reps., Exc. Tech./Scientific	29.20
Electrical Engineers	46.50	Sales Reps., Tech./Scientific	40.90
Electricians	26.30	Secretaries, Exc. Legal/Med./Exec.	15.80
Financial Managers	54.10	Security Guards	15.80
First-Line Supervisors/Managers, Sales	21.20	Surgeons	129.10
Food Preparation Workers	9.80	Teacher Assistants*	9.80
General and Operations Managers	54.40	Teachers, Elementary School*	20.50
Hairdressers/Cosmetologists	12.40	Teachers, Secondary School*	21.20
Internists, General	85.90	Telemarketers	14.30
Janitors and Cleaners	11.70	Truck Drivers, Heavy/Tractor-Trailer	21.00
Landscaping/Groundskeeping Workers	13.50	Truck Drivers, Light/Delivery Svcs.	16.20
Lawyers	55.00	Waiters and Waitresses	10.00

Note: Wage data covers the Oklahoma City, OK Metropolitan Statistical Area—see Appendix B for areas included; (*) Hourly wages for elementary/secondary school teachers and teacher assistants were calculated by the editors from annual wage data based on a 40 hour work week; n/a not available.
Source: Bureau of Labor Statistics, Metro Area Occupational Employment & Wage Estimates, May 2018

Employment by Occupation

Occupation Classification	City (%)	MSA[1] (%)	U.S. (%)
Management, Business, Science, and Arts	36.0	36.9	37.4
Natural Resources, Construction, and Maintenance	10.9	10.7	8.9
Production, Transportation, and Material Moving	11.0	10.7	12.2
Sales and Office	24.8	24.8	23.5
Service	17.2	16.9	18.0

Note: Figures cover employed civilians 16 years of age and older; (1) Figures cover the Oklahoma City, OK Metropolitan Statistical Area—see Appendix B for areas included
Source: U.S. Census Bureau, 2013-2017 American Community Survey 5-Year Estimates

Employment by Industry

Sector	MSA[1]		U.S.
	Number of Employees	Percent of Total	Percent of Total
Construction	31,500	4.8	4.8
Education and Health Services	93,900	14.2	15.9
Financial Activities	33,800	5.1	5.7
Government	132,100	20.0	15.1
Information	7,300	1.1	1.9
Leisure and Hospitality	74,700	11.3	10.7
Manufacturing	33,900	5.1	8.5
Mining and Logging	22,600	3.4	0.5
Other Services	29,300	4.4	3.9
Professional and Business Services	84,800	12.8	14.1
Retail Trade	68,000	10.3	10.8
Transportation, Warehousing, and Utilities	23,200	3.5	4.2
Wholesale Trade	25,200	3.8	3.9

Note: Figures are non-farm employment as of December 2018. Figures are not seasonally adjusted and include workers 16 years of age and older; (1) Figures cover the Oklahoma City, OK Metropolitan Statistical Area—see Appendix B for areas included
Source: Bureau of Labor Statistics, Current Employment Statistics, Employment, Hours, and Earnings

Occupations with Greatest Projected Employment Growth: 2018 – 2020

Occupation[1]	2018 Employment	2020 Projected Employment	Numeric Employment Change	Percent Employment Change
Combined Food Preparation and Serving Workers, Including Fast Food	35,080	36,780	1,700	4.8
Laborers and Freight, Stock, and Material Movers, Hand	28,610	29,800	1,190	4.2
Retail Salespersons	48,310	49,410	1,100	2.3
Waiters and Waitresses	28,480	29,370	890	3.1
General and Operations Managers	29,600	30,440	840	2.8
Personal Care Aides	13,570	14,370	800	5.9
Heavy and Tractor-Trailer Truck Drivers	26,700	27,430	730	2.7
Janitors and Cleaners, Except Maids and Housekeeping Cleaners	23,090	23,670	580	2.5
Cooks, Restaurant	13,990	14,550	560	4.0
Customer Service Representatives	30,220	30,740	520	1.7

Note: Projections cover Oklahoma; (1) Sorted by numeric employment change
Source: www.projectionscentral.com, State Occupational Projections, 2018–2020 Short-Term Projections

Fastest Growing Occupations: 2018 – 2020

Occupation[1]	2018 Employment	2020 Projected Employment	Numeric Employment Change	Percent Employment Change
Veterinary Assistants and Laboratory Animal Caretakers	1,620	1,730	110	6.8
Software Developers, Applications	4,770	5,050	280	5.9
Personal Care Aides	13,570	14,370	800	5.9
Home Health Aides	8,450	8,940	490	5.8
Helpers—Pipelayers, Plumbers, Pipefitters, and Steamfitters	1,410	1,490	80	5.7
Veterinary Technologists and Technicians	910	960	50	5.5
Nonfarm Animal Caretakers	2,800	2,950	150	5.4
Veterinarians	1,160	1,220	60	5.2
Industrial Truck and Tractor Operators	7,760	8,150	390	5.0
Machine Feeders and Offbearers	1,000	1,050	50	5.0

Note: Projections cover Oklahoma; (1) Sorted by percent employment change and excludes occupations with numeric employment change less than 50
Source: www.projectionscentral.com, State Occupational Projections, 2018–2020 Short-Term Projections

TAXES

State Corporate Income Tax Rates

State	Tax Rate (%)	Income Brackets ($)	Num. of Brackets	Financial Institution Tax Rate (%)[a]	Federal Income Tax Ded.
Oklahoma	6.0	Flat rate	1	6.0	No

Note: Tax rates as of January 1, 2019; (a) Rates listed are the corporate income tax rate applied to financial institutions or excise taxes based on income. Some states have other taxes based upon the value of deposits or shares.
Source: Federation of Tax Administrators, Range of State Corporate Income Tax Rates, January 1, 2019

State Individual Income Tax Rates

State	Tax Rate (%)	Income Brackets ($)	Personal Exemptions ($)			Standard Ded. ($)	
			Single	Married	Depend.	Single	Married
Oklahoma	0.5 - 5.0	1,000 - 7,200 (t)	1,000	2,000	1,000	6,350	12,700

Note: Tax rates as of January 1, 2019; Local- and county-level taxes are not included; n/a not applicable; Federal income tax is not deductible on state income tax returns; (t) The income brackets reported for Oklahoma are for single persons. For married persons filing jointly, the same tax rates apply to income brackets ranging from $2,000, to $12,200.
Source: Federation of Tax Administrators, State Individual Income Tax Rates, January 1, 2019

Various State Sales and Excise Tax Rates

State	State Sales Tax (%)	Gasoline[1] (¢/gal.)	Cigarette[2] ($/pack)	Spirits[3] ($/gal.)	Wine[4] ($/gal.)	Beer[5] ($/gal.)	Recreational Marijuana (%)
Oklahoma	4.5	20	2.03	5.56	0.72 (l)	0.40 (q)	Not legal

Note: All tax rates as of January 1, 2019; (1) The American Petroleum Institute has developed a methodology for determining the average tax rate on a gallon of fuel. Rates may include any of the following: excise taxes, environmental fees, storage tank fees, other fees or taxes, general sales tax, and local taxes. In states where gasoline is subject to the general sales tax, or where the fuel tax is based on the average sale price, the average rate determined by API is sensitive to changes in the price of gasoline. States that fully or partially apply general sales taxes to gasoline: CA, CO, GA, IL, IN, MI, NY; (2) The federal excise tax of $1.0066 per pack and local taxes are not included; (3) Rates are those applicable to off-premise sales of 40% alcohol by volume (a.b.v.) distilled spirits in 750ml containers. Local excise taxes are excluded; (4) Rates are those applicable to off-premise sales of 11% a.b.v. non-carbonated wine in 750ml containers; (5) Rates are those applicable to off-premise sales of 4.7% a.b.v. beer in 12 ounce containers; (l) Different rates also applicable to alcohol content, place of production, size of container, place purchased (on- or off-premise or on board airlines) or type of wine (carbonated, vermouth, etc.); (q) Different rates also applicable according to alcohol content, place of production, size of container, or place purchased (on- or off-premise or onboard airlines).
Source: Tax Foundation, 2019 Facts & Figures: How Does Your State Compare?

State Business Tax Climate Index Rankings

State	Overall Rank	Corporate Tax Rank	Individual Income Tax Rank	Sales Tax Rank	Unemployment Insurance Tax Rank	Property Tax Rank
Oklahoma	26	9	33	39	1	19

Note: The index is a measure of how each state's tax laws affect economic performance. The lower the rank, the more favorable a state's tax system is for business. States without a given tax are given a ranking of 1. The scores/rankings for the District of Columbia do not affect other states. The 2019 index represents the tax climate as of July 1, 2018.
Source: Tax Foundation, State Business Tax Climate Index 2019

COMMERCIAL REAL ESTATE

Office Market

Market Area	Inventory (sq. ft.)	Vacancy Rate (%)	Under Construction (sq. ft.)	YTD Net Absorption (sq. ft.)	Total Average Asking Rent ($/sq. ft./year)
Oklahoma City	15,012,402	23.1	0	7,671	19.69
National	4,905,867,938	13.1	83,553,714	45,846,470	28.46

Source: Newmark Grubb Knight Frank, National Office Market Report, 4th Quarter 2018

COMMERCIAL
UTILITIES

Typical Monthly Electric Bills

Area	Commercial Service ($/month)		Industrial Service ($/month)	
	1,500 kWh	40 kW demand 14,000 kWh	1,000 kW demand 200,000 kWh	50,000 kW demand 32,500,000 kWh
City	167	1,046	14,388	1,266,656
Average[1]	203	1,619	25,886	2,540,077

Note: Figures are based on annualized rates; (1) Average based on 187 utilities surveyed
Source: Edison Electric Institute, Typical Bills and Average Rates Report, Summer 2018

TRANSPORTATION

Means of Transportation to Work

Area	Car/Truck/Van		Public Transportation			Bicycle	Walked	Other Means	Worked at Home
	Drove Alone	Car-pooled	Bus	Subway	Railroad				
City	82.3	11.2	0.5	0.0	0.0	0.2	1.4	0.8	3.5
MSA[1]	83.3	9.9	0.4	0.0	0.0	0.3	1.5	0.9	3.7
U.S.	76.4	9.2	2.5	1.9	0.6	0.6	2.7	1.3	4.7

Note: Figures are percentages and cover workers 16 years of age and older; (1) Figures cover the Oklahoma City, OK Metropolitan Statistical Area—see Appendix B for areas included
Source: U.S. Census Bureau, 2013-2017 American Community Survey 5-Year Estimates

Travel Time to Work

Area	Less Than 10 Minutes	10 to 19 Minutes	20 to 29 Minutes	30 to 44 Minutes	45 to 59 Minutes	60 to 89 Minutes	90 Minutes or More
City	11.5	36.1	29.3	17.1	2.8	1.5	1.6
MSA[1]	13.0	32.5	25.6	19.9	5.2	2.3	1.6
U.S.	12.7	28.9	20.9	20.5	8.1	6.2	2.7

Note: Note: Figures are percentages and include workers 16 years old and over; (1) Figures cover the Oklahoma City, OK Metropolitan Statistical Area—see Appendix B for areas included
Source: U.S. Census Bureau, 2013-2017 American Community Survey 5-Year Estimates

Freeway Travel Time Index

Area	1985	1990	1995	2000	2005	2010	2014
Urban Area Rank[1,2]	54	63	68	46	42	42	42
Urban Area Index[1]	1.06	1.08	1.11	1.16	1.18	1.18	1.19
Average Index[3]	1.09	1.11	1.14	1.17	1.20	1.19	1.20

Note: Freeway Travel Time Index—the ratio of travel time in the peak period to the travel time at free-flow conditions. For example, a value of 1.30 indicates a 20-minute free-flow trip takes 26 minutes in the peak (20 minutes x 1.30 = 26 minutes); (1) Covers the Oklahoma City OK urban area; (2) Rank is based on 101 urban areas (#1 = highest travel time index); (3) Average of 101 urban areas
Source: Texas Transportation Institute, 2015 Urban Mobility Scorecard, August 2015

Freeway Commuter Stress Index

Area	1985	1990	1995	2000	2005	2010	2014
Urban Area Rank[1,2]	66	75	71	54	53	58	52
Urban Area Index[1]	1.07	1.09	1.13	1.18	1.20	1.19	1.21
Average Index[3]	1.13	1.16	1.19	1.22	1.25	1.24	1.25

Note: The Freeway Commuter Stress Index is the same as the Freeway Travel Time Index (see table above) except that it includes only the travel in the peak directions during the peak periods; the TTI includes travel in all directions during the peak period. Thus, the CSI is more indicative of the work trip experienced by each commuter on a daily basis; (1) Covers the Oklahoma City OK urban area; (2) Rank is based on 101 urban areas (#1 = highest travel time index); (3) Average of 101 urban areas
Source: Texas Transportation Institute, 2015 Urban Mobility Scorecard, August 2015

Public Transportation

Agency Name / Mode of Transportation	Vehicles Operated in Maximum Service[1]	Annual Unlinked Passenger Trips[2] (in thous.)	Annual Passenger Miles[3] (in thous.)
Central Oklahoma Transportation & Parking Authority (COTPA)			
Bus (directly operated)	49	3,128.3	16,125.8
Bus (purchased transportation)	4	0.8	5.3
Demand Response (directly operated)	17	54.4	499.1
Demand Response Taxi (purchased transportation)	6	7.1	37.7
Ferryboat (purchased transportation)	2	13.4	30.3
Vanpool (purchased transportation)	2	1.7	47.2

Note: (1) The number of revenue vehicles operated by the given mode and type of service to meet the annual maximum service requirement. This is the revenue vehicle count during the peak season of the year; on the week and day that maximum service is provided. Vehicles operated in maximum service (VOMS) exclude atypical days and one-time special events; (2) The number of passengers who boarded public transportation vehicles. Passengers are counted each time they board a vehicle no matter how many vehicles they use to travel from their origin to their destination. (3) The sum of the distances ridden by all passengers during the entire fiscal year.
Source: Federal Transit Administration, National Transit Database, 2017

Air Transportation

Airport Name and Code / Type of Service	Passenger Airlines[1]	Passenger Enplanements	Freight Carriers[2]	Freight (lbs)
Will Rogers World Airport (OKC)				
Domestic service (U.S. carriers - 2018)	29	2,083,910	12	29,888,344
International service (U.S. carriers - 2017)	2	303	1	60,995

Note: (1) Includes all U.S.-based major, minor and commuter airlines that carried at least one passenger during the year; (2) Includes all U.S.-based airlines and freight carriers that transported at least one pound of freight during the year.
Source: Bureau of Transportation Statistics, The Intermodal Transportation Database, Air Carriers: T-100 Domestic Market (U.S. Carriers), 2018; Bureau of Transportation Statistics, The Intermodal Transportation Database, Air Carriers: T-100 International Market (U.S. Carriers), 2017

Other Transportation Statistics

Major Highways: I-35; I-40; I-44;
Amtrak Service: Yes
Major Waterways/Ports: None
Source: Amtrak.com; Google Maps

BUSINESSES

Major Business Headquarters

Company Name	Industry	Rankings	
		Fortune[1]	Forbes[2]
Chesapeake Energy	Mining, Crude-Oil Production	314	-
Devon Energy	Mining, Crude-Oil Production	213	-
Hobby Lobby Stores	Retailing	-	91
Love's Travel Stops & Country Stores	Convenience Stores & Gas Stations	-	16

Note: (1) Companies that produce a 10-K are ranked 1 to 500 based on 2017 revenue; (2) All private companies with at least $2 billion in annual revenue through the end of their most current fiscal year are ranked 1 to 229; companies listed are headquartered in the city; dashes indicate no ranking
Source: Fortune, "Fortune 500," June 2018; Forbes, "America's Largest Private Companies," 2018 Rankings

Fast-Growing Businesses

According to *Fortune*, Oklahoma City is home to one of the 100 fastest-growing companies in the world: **Paycom Software** (#5). Companies were ranked by their revenue growth rate; their EPS growth rate; and their three-year annualized total return to investors for the period ending June 30, 2018. Criteria for inclusion: a company, foreign or domestic, must trade on a major U.S. stock exchange; must file quarterly reports with the SEC; must have a minimum market capitalization of $250 million; must have a stock price of at least $5 on June 30, 2018; must have been trading continuously since June 30, 2015; must have revenue and net income for the four quarters ended on or before April 30, 2018, of at least $50 million and $10 million, respectively; and must have posted a compound annual growth in revenue and earnings per share of at least 15% annually over the three years ending on or before April 30, 2018. Real estate investment trusts, limited-liability companies, limited parterships, business development companies, closed-end investment firms, companies about to be acquired, and companies that lost money in the quarter ending April 30, 2018 were excluded. *Fortune, "100 Fastest-Growing Companies," 2018*

According to Deloitte, Oklahoma City is home to one of North America's 500 fastest-growing high-technology companies: **Paycom** (#414). Companies are ranked by percentage growth in revenue over a four-year period. Criteria for inclusion: company must be headquartered within North America; must own proprietary intellectual property or technology that is sold to customers in products that contributes to a significant portion of the company's operating revenue; must have been in business for a minumum of four years with 2014 operating revenues of at least $50,000 USD/CD and 2017 operating revenues of at least $5 million USD/CD. *Deloitte, 2018 Technology Fast 500*™

Minority Business Opportunity

Oklahoma City is home to one company which is on the *Hispanic Business* 500 list (500 largest U.S. Hispanic-owned companies based on revenue): **Lopez Foods** (#17). Companies included must show at least 51 percent ownership by Hispanic U.S. citizens, and must maintain headquarters in one of the 50 states or Washington, D.C. *Hispanic Business, "Hispanic Business 500," June 20, 2013*

Minority- and Women-Owned Businesses

Group	All Firms		Firms with Paid Employees			
	Firms	Sales ($000)	Firms	Sales ($000)	Employees	Payroll ($000)
AIAN[1]	2,870	716,870	413	596,089	4,227	193,808
Asian	3,475	714,106	630	589,326	5,443	102,323
Black	5,208	305,422	289	215,201	3,043	89,435
Hispanic	4,920	1,092,474	430	885,775	3,845	111,618
NHOPI[2]	35	3,784	6	(s)	20 - 99	(s)
Women	20,163	5,106,277	2,624	4,596,994	24,353	933,230
All Firms	58,815	132,726,309	14,488	130,383,497	301,903	13,914,882

Note: Figures cover firms located in the city; minority- and women-owned business are defined as firms in which the corresponding group own 51% or more of the stock or equity of the company; (1) American Indian and Alaska Native; (2) Native Hawaiian and Other Pacific Islander; (s) estimates are suppressed when publication standards are not met
Source: U.S. Census Bureau, 2012 Economic Census, Survey of Business Owners

HOTELS & CONVENTION CENTERS

Hotels, Motels and Vacation Rentals

Area	5 Star		4 Star		3 Star		2 Star		1 Star		Not Rated	
	Num.	Pct.[3]	Num.	Pct.[3]	Num.	Pct.[3]	Num.	Pct.[3]	Num.	Pct.[3]	Num.	Pct.[3]
City[1]	0	0.0	7	1.8	62	16.4	183	48.3	6	1.6	121	31.9
Total[2]	286	0.4	5,236	7.1	16,715	22.6	10,259	13.9	293	0.4	41,056	55.6

Note: (1) Figures cover Oklahoma City and vicinity; (2) Figures cover all 100 cities in this book; (3) Percentage of hotels which have a given star rating; Star ratings are determined by expedia.com and offer an indication of the general quality of a particular hotel.
Source: www.expedia.com, April 3, 2019

Major Convention Centers

Name	Overall Space (sq. ft.)	Exhibit Space (sq. ft.)	Meeting Space (sq. ft.)	Meeting Rooms
Cox Convention Center	n/a	100,000	30,000	26

Note: Table includes convention centers located in the Oklahoma City, OK metro area; n/a not available
Source: Original research

Living Environment

COST OF LIVING

Cost of Living Index

Composite Index	Groceries	Housing	Utilities	Trans-portation	Health Care	Misc. Goods/ Services
84.7	92.1	72.1	94.5	85.6	92.9	88.8

Note: The Cost of Living Index measures regional differences in the cost of consumer goods and services, excluding taxes and non-consumer expenditures, for professional and managerial households in the top income quintile. It is based on more than 50,000 prices covering almost 60 different items for which prices are collected three times a year by chambers of commerce, economic development organizations or university applied economic centers in each participating urban area. The numbers shown should be read as a percentage above or below the national average of 100. For example, a value of 115.4 in the groceries column indicates that grocery prices are 15.4% higher than the national average. Small differences in the index numbers should not be interpreted as significant; Figures cover the Oklahoma City OK urban area.
Source: The Council for Community and Economic Research, ACCRA Cost of Living Index, 2018

Grocery Prices

Area[1]	T-Bone Steak ($/pound)	Frying Chicken ($/pound)	Whole Milk ($/half gal.)	Eggs ($/dozen)	Orange Juice ($/64 oz.)	Coffee ($/11.5 oz.)
City[2]	10.29	1.27	1.90	1.50	3.28	3.96
Avg.	11.35	1.42	1.94	1.81	3.52	4.35
Min.	7.45	0.92	0.80	0.75	2.72	3.06
Max.	15.05	2.76	4.18	4.00	5.36	8.20

Note: (1) Values for the local area are compared with the average, minimum and maximum values for all 291 areas in the Cost of Living Index; (2) Figures cover the Oklahoma City OK urban area; T-Bone Steak (price per pound); Frying Chicken (price per pound, whole fryer); Whole Milk (half gallon carton); Eggs (price per dozen, Grade A, large); Orange Juice (64 oz. Tropicana or Florida Natural); Coffee (11.5 oz. can, vacuum-packed, Maxwell House, Hills Bros, or Folgers).
Source: The Council for Community and Economic Research, ACCRA Cost of Living Index, 2018

Housing and Utility Costs

Area[1]	New Home Price ($)	Apartment Rent ($/month)	All Electric ($/month)	Part Electric ($/month)	Other Energy ($/month)	Telephone ($/month)
City[2]	244,210	828	-	87.20	63.38	179.30
Avg.	347,000	1,087	165.93	100.16	67.73	178.70
Min.	200,468	500	93.58	25.64	26.78	163.10
Max.	1,901,222	4,888	388.65	246.86	332.81	197.70

Note: (1) Values for the local area are compared with the average, minimum and maximum values for all 291 areas in the Cost of Living Index; (2) Figures cover the Oklahoma City OK urban area; New Home Price (2,400 sf living area, 8,000 sf lot, in urban area with full utilities); Apartment Rent (950 sf 2 bedroom/1.5 or 2 bath, unfurnished, excluding all utilities except water); All Electric (average monthly cost for an all-electric home); Part Electric (average monthly cost for a part-electric home); Other Energy (average monthly cost for natural gas, fuel oil, coal, wood, and any other forms of energy except electricity); Telephone (price includes the base monthly rate plus taxes and fees for three lines of mobile phone service).
Source: The Council for Community and Economic Research, ACCRA Cost of Living Index, 2018

Health Care, Transportation, and Other Costs

Area[1]	Doctor ($/visit)	Dentist ($/visit)	Optometrist ($/visit)	Gasoline ($/gallon)	Beauty Salon ($/visit)	Men's Shirt ($)
City[2]	89.82	91.21	97.00	2.24	35.63	20.12
Avg.	110.71	95.11	103.74	2.61	37.48	32.03
Min.	33.60	62.55	54.63	1.89	17.00	11.44
Max.	195.97	153.93	225.79	3.59	71.88	58.64

Note: (1) Values for the local area are compared with the average, minimum and maximum values for all 291 areas in the Cost of Living Index; (2) Figures cover the Oklahoma City OK urban area; Doctor (general practitioners routine exam of an established patient); Dentist (adult teeth cleaning and periodic oral examination); Optometrist (full vision eye exam for established adult patient); Gasoline (one gallon regular unleaded, national brand, including all taxes, cash price at self-service pump if available); Beauty Salon (woman's shampoo, trim, and blow-dry); Men's Shirt (cotton/polyester dress shirt, pinpoint weave, long sleeves).
Source: The Council for Community and Economic Research, ACCRA Cost of Living Index, 2018

HOUSING

House Price Index (HPI)

Area	National Ranking[2]	Quarterly Change (%)	One-Year Change (%)	Five-Year Change (%)
MSA[1]	191	0.26	3.87	21.60
U.S.[3]	–	1.12	5.73	32.81

Note: The HPI is a weighted repeat sales index. It measures average price changes in repeat sales or refinancings on the same properties. This information is obtained by reviewing repeat mortgage transactions on single-family properties whose mortgages have been purchased or securitized by Fannie Mae or Freddie Mac in January 1975; (1) Figures cover the Oklahoma City, OK Metropolitan Statistical Area—see Appendix B for areas included; (2) Rankings are based on annual percentage change for all metro areas containing at least 15,000 transactions over the last 10 years and ranges from 1 to 245; (3) figures based on a weighted average of Census Division estimates using a seasonally adjusted, purchase-only index; all figures are for the period ending December 31, 2018
Source: Federal Housing Finance Agency, House Price Index, February 26, 2019

Median Single-Family Home Prices

Area	2016	2017	2018p	Percent Change 2017 to 2018
MSA[1]	150.8	154.3	159.5	3.4
U.S. Average	235.5	248.8	261.6	5.1

Note: Figures are median sales prices of existing single-family homes in thousands of dollars; (p) preliminary; (1) Figures cover the Oklahoma City, OK Metropolitan Statistical Area—see Appendix B for areas included
Source: National Association of Realtors, Median Sales Price of Existing Single-Family Homes for Metropolitan Areas, 4th Quarter 2018

Qualifying Income Based on Median Sales Price of Existing Single-Family Homes

Area	With 5% Down ($)	With 10% Down ($)	With 20% Down ($)
MSA[1]	39,346	37,275	33,133
U.S. Average	62,954	59,640	53,013

Note: Figures are preliminary; Qualifying income is based on a mortgage rate of 4.9%. Monthly principal and interest payment is limited to 25% of income; (1) Figures cover the Oklahoma City, OK Metropolitan Statistical Area—see Appendix B for areas included
Source: National Association of Realtors, Qualifying Income Based on Median Sales Price of Existing Single-Family Homes for Metropolitan Areas, 4th Quarter 2018

Median Apartment Condo-Coop Home Prices

Area	2016	2017	2018p	Percent Change 2017 to 2018
MSA[1]	n/a	n/a	n/a	n/a
U.S. Average	220.7	234.3	241.0	2.9

Note: Figures are median sales prices of existing apartment condo-coop homes in thousands of dollars; (p) preliminary; n/a not available; (1) Figures cover the Oklahoma City, OK Metropolitan Statistical Area—see Appendix B for areas included
Source: National Association of Realtors, Median Sales Price of Existing Apartment Condo-Coop Homes for Metropolitan Areas, 4th Quarter 2018

Home Value Distribution

Area	Under $50,000	$50,000 -$99,999	$100,000 -$149,999	$150,000 -$199,999	$200,000 -$299,999	$300,000 -$499,999	$500,000 -$999,999	$1,000,000 or more
City	8.7	19.9	22.1	20.0	17.1	8.6	2.9	0.7
MSA[1]	8.7	20.0	22.8	19.3	16.7	8.9	2.9	0.8
U.S.	8.3	13.9	14.7	14.6	18.7	17.3	9.7	2.7

Note: Figures are percentages and cover owner-occupied housing units; (1) Figures cover the Oklahoma City, OK Metropolitan Statistical Area—see Appendix B for areas included
Source: U.S. Census Bureau, 2013-2017 American Community Survey 5-Year Estimates

Homeownership Rate

Area	2010 (%)	2011 (%)	2012 (%)	2013 (%)	2014 (%)	2015 (%)	2016 (%)	2017 (%)	2018 (%)
MSA[1]	70.0	69.6	67.3	67.6	65.7	61.4	63.1	64.7	64.6
U.S.	66.9	66.1	65.4	65.1	64.5	63.7	63.4	63.9	64.4

Note: (1) Figures cover the Oklahoma City, OK Metropolitan Statistical Area—see Appendix B for areas included
Source: U.S. Census Bureau, Housing Vacancies and Homeownership Annual Statistics: 2010-2018

Year Housing Structure Built

Area	2010 or Later	2000 -2009	1990 -1999	1980 -1989	1970 -1979	1960 -1969	1950 -1959	1940 -1949	Before 1940	Median Year
City	6.2	13.9	10.0	15.3	15.9	13.0	10.8	6.2	8.8	1977
MSA[1]	6.2	15.6	11.5	15.1	17.4	12.4	9.9	5.3	6.5	1979
U.S.	3.2	14.5	14.0	13.6	15.5	10.8	10.5	5.1	12.9	1977

Note: Figures are percentages except for Median Year; Note: (1) Figures cover the Oklahoma City, OK Metropolitan Statistical Area—see Appendix B for areas included
Source: U.S. Census Bureau, 2013-2017 American Community Survey 5-Year Estimates

Gross Monthly Rent

Area	Under $500	$500 -$999	$1,000 -$1,499	$1,500 -$1,999	$2,000 -$2,499	$2,500 -$2,999	$3,000 and up	Median ($)
City	9.7	61.7	21.8	5.2	1.1	0.3	0.3	819
MSA[1]	9.4	61.1	22.6	5.3	1.0	0.3	0.3	827
U.S.	10.5	41.1	28.7	11.7	4.5	1.8	1.7	982

Note: Figures are percentages except for Median; Gross rent is the contract rent plus the estimated average monthly cost of utilities (electricity, gas, and water and sewer) and fuels (oil, coal, kerosene, wood, etc.) if these are paid by the renter (or paid for the renter by someone else); (1) Figures cover the Oklahoma City, OK Metropolitan Statistical Area—see Appendix B for areas included
Source: U.S. Census Bureau, 2013-2017 American Community Survey 5-Year Estimates

HEALTH

Health Risk Factors

Category	MSA[1] (%)	U.S. (%)
Adults aged 18–64 who have any kind of health care coverage	80.7	87.3
Adults who reported being in good or better health	80.8	82.4
Adults who have been told they have high blood cholesterol	35.9	33.0
Adults who have been told they have high blood pressure	34.7	32.3
Adults who are current smokers	17.1	17.1
Adults who currently use E-cigarettes	6.6	4.6
Adults who currently use chewing tobacco, snuff, or snus	5.8	4.0
Adults who are heavy drinkers[2]	4.4	6.3
Adults who are binge drinkers[3]	14.7	17.4
Adults who are overweight (BMI 25.0 - 29.9)	33.5	35.3
Adults who are obese (BMI 30.0 - 99.8)	34.6	31.3
Adults who participated in any physical activities in the past month	71.9	74.4
Adults who always or nearly always wears a seat belt	94.9	94.3

Note: (1) Figures cover the Oklahoma City, OK Metropolitan Statistical Area—see Appendix B for areas included; (2) Heavy drinkers are classified as adult men having more than 14 drinks per week and adult women having more than 7 drinks per week; (3) Binge drinkers are classified as males having five or more drinks on one occasion or females having four or more drinks on one occasion
Source: Centers for Disease Control and Prevention, Behaviorial Risk Factor Surveillance System, SMART: Selected Metropolitan Area Risk Trends, 2017

Acute and Chronic Health Conditions

Category	MSA[1] (%)	U.S. (%)
Adults who have ever been told they had a heart attack	4.9	4.2
Adults who have ever been told they have angina or coronary heart disease	5.1	3.9
Adults who have ever been told they had a stroke	3.4	3.0
Adults who have ever been told they have asthma	14.2	14.2
Adults who have ever been told they have arthritis	26.9	24.9
Adults who have ever been told they have diabetes[2]	12.1	10.5
Adults who have ever been told they had skin cancer	5.9	6.2
Adults who have ever been told they had any other types of cancer	7.0	7.1
Adults who have ever been told they have COPD	7.2	6.5
Adults who have ever been told they have kidney disease	4.1	3.0
Adults who have ever been told they have a form of depression	23.1	20.5

Note: (1) Figures cover the Oklahoma City, OK Metropolitan Statistical Area—see Appendix B for areas included; (2) Figures do not include pregnancy-related, borderline, or pre-diabetes
Source: Centers for Disease Control and Prevention, Behaviorial Risk Factor Surveillance System, SMART: Selected Metropolitan Area Risk Trends, 2017

Health Screening and Vaccination Rates

Category	MSA[1] (%)	U.S. (%)
Adults aged 65+ who have had flu shot within the past year	70.4	60.7
Adults aged 65+ who have ever had a pneumonia vaccination	82.0	75.4
Adults who have ever been tested for HIV	32.8	36.1
Adults who have ever had the shingles or zoster vaccine?	30.7	28.9
Adults who have had their blood cholesterol checked within the last five years	83.2	85.9

Note: n/a not available; (1) Figures cover the Oklahoma City, OK Metropolitan Statistical Area—see Appendix B for areas included.
Source: Centers for Disease Control and Prevention, Behavioral Risk Factor Surveillance System, SMART: Selected Metropolitan Area Risk Trends, 2017

Disability Status

Category	MSA[1] (%)	U.S. (%)
Adults who reported being deaf	7.9	6.7
Are you blind or have serious difficulty seeing, even when wearing glasses?	6.3	4.5
Are you limited in any way in any of your usual activities due of arthritis?	15.0	12.9
Do you have difficulty doing errands alone?	9.9	6.8
Do you have difficulty dressing or bathing?	5.9	3.6
Do you have serious difficulty concentrating/remembering/making decisions?	14.7	10.7
Do you have serious difficulty walking or climbing stairs?	17.4	13.6

Note: (1) Figures cover the Oklahoma City, OK Metropolitan Statistical Area—see Appendix B for areas included.
Source: Centers for Disease Control and Prevention, Behavioral Risk Factor Surveillance System, SMART: Selected Metropolitan Area Risk Trends, 2017

Mortality Rates for the Top 10 Causes of Death in the U.S.

ICD-10[a] Sub-Chapter	ICD-10[a] Code	Age-Adjusted Mortality Rate[1] per 100,000 population	
		County[2]	U.S.
Malignant neoplasms	C00-C97	178.4	155.5
Ischaemic heart diseases	I20-I25	119.3	94.8
Other forms of heart disease	I30-I51	51.3	52.9
Chronic lower respiratory diseases	J40-J47	61.2	41.0
Cerebrovascular diseases	I60-I69	46.2	37.5
Other degenerative diseases of the nervous system	G30-G31	49.3	35.0
Other external causes of accidental injury	W00-X59	48.5	33.7
Organic, including symptomatic, mental disorders	F01-F09	32.0	31.0
Hypertensive diseases	I10-I15	48.8	21.9
Diabetes mellitus	E10-E14	34.4	21.2

Note: (a) ICD-10 = International Classification of Diseases 10th Revision; (1) Mortality rates are a three year average covering 2015-2017; (2) Figures cover Oklahoma County.
Source: Centers for Disease Control and Prevention, National Center for Health Statistics. Underlying Cause of Death 1999-2017 on CDC WONDER Online Database

Mortality Rates for Selected Causes of Death

ICD-10[a] Sub-Chapter	ICD-10[a] Code	Age-Adjusted Mortality Rate[1] per 100,000 population	
		County[2]	U.S.
Assault	X85-Y09	12.1	5.9
Diseases of the liver	K70-K76	20.3	14.1
Human immunodeficiency virus (HIV) disease	B20-B24	2.3	1.8
Influenza and pneumonia	J09-J18	11.1	14.3
Intentional self-harm	X60-X84	17.7	13.6
Malnutrition	E40-E46	2.5	1.6
Obesity and other hyperalimentation	E65-E68	1.7	2.1
Renal failure	N17-N19	12.1	13.0
Transport accidents	V01-V99	14.2	12.4
Viral hepatitis	B15-B19	3.3	1.6

Note: (a) ICD-10 = International Classification of Diseases 10th Revision; (1) Mortality rates are a three year average covering 2015-2017; (2) Figures cover Oklahoma County; Data are suppressed when the data meet the criteria for confidentiality constraints; Mortality rates are flagged as unreliable when the rate would be calculated with a numerator of 20 or less.
Source: Centers for Disease Control and Prevention, National Center for Health Statistics. Underlying Cause of Death 1999-2017 on CDC WONDER Online Database

Health Insurance Coverage

Area	With Health Insurance	With Private Health Insurance	With Public Health Insurance	Without Health Insurance	Population Under Age 18 Without Health Insurance
City	84.1	62.7	31.7	15.9	7.5
MSA[1]	86.6	67.6	30.3	13.4	6.8
U.S.	89.5	67.2	33.8	10.5	5.7

Note: Figures are percentages that cover the civilian noninstitutionalized population; (1) Figures cover the Oklahoma City, OK Metropolitan Statistical Area—see Appendix B for areas included
Source: U.S. Census Bureau, 2013-2017 American Community Survey 5-Year Estimates

Number of Medical Professionals

Area	MDs[3]	DOs[3,4]	Dentists	Podiatrists	Chiropractors	Optometrists
County[1] (number)	3,166	351	800	38	205	143
County[1] (rate[2])	403.7	44.8	101.5	4.8	26.0	18.1
U.S. (rate[2])	279.3	23.0	68.4	6.0	27.1	16.2

Note: Data as of 2017 unless noted; (1) Data covers Oklahoma County; (2) Rate per 100,000 population; (3) Data as of 2016 and includes all active, non-federal physicians; (4) Doctor of Osteopathic Medicine
Source: U.S. Department of Health and Human Services, Health Resources and Services Administration, Bureau of Health Professions, Area Resource File (ARF) 2017-2018

EDUCATION

Public School District Statistics

District Name	Schls	Pupils	Pupil/ Teacher Ratio	Minority Pupils[1] (%)	Free Lunch Eligible[2] (%)	IEP[3] (%)
Epic Charter Schools	3	9,077	45.5	34.6	54.6	11.9
Oklahoma City	78	39,806	16.8	85.9	81.2	13.8
Santa Fe South (Charter)	5	2,414	19.2	96.1	76.0	9.5
Western Heights	8	3,580	14.5	75.1	82.1	12.7

Note: Table includes school districts with 2,000 or more students; (1) Percentage of students that are not non-Hispanic white; (2) Percentage of students that are eligible for the free lunch program; (3) Percentage of students that have an Individualized Education Program.
Source: U.S. Department of Education, National Center for Education Statistics, Common Core of Data, Local Education Agency (School District) Universe Survey: School Year 2016-2017; U.S. Department of Education, National Center for Education Statistics, Common Core of Data, Public Elementary/Secondary School Universe Survey: School Year 2016-2017

Best High Schools

According to *U.S. News,* Oklahoma City is home to three of the best high schools in the U.S.: **Harding Charter Preparatory High School** (#150); **Dove Science Academy OKC** (#251); **Classen Hs Of Advanced Studies** (#495). More than 20,000 public, magnet and charter schools were ranked based on their performance on state assessments and how well they prepare students for college. Schools with the highest unrounded College Readiness Index values were numerically ranked from 1 to 500 and were classified as gold medal winners. *U.S. News & World Report, "Best High Schools 2018"*

Highest Level of Education

Area	Less than H.S.	H.S. Diploma	Some College, No Deg.	Associate Degree	Bachelor's Degree	Master's Degree	Prof. School Degree	Doctorate Degree
City	14.4	25.3	23.4	7.2	19.5	7.0	2.1	1.0
MSA[1]	11.6	27.2	24.3	7.4	19.4	7.2	1.8	1.2
U.S.	12.7	27.3	20.8	8.3	19.1	8.4	2.0	1.4

Note: Figures cover persons age 25 and over; (1) Figures cover the Oklahoma City, OK Metropolitan Statistical Area—see Appendix B for areas included
Source: U.S. Census Bureau, 2013-2017 American Community Survey 5-Year Estimates

Educational Attainment by Race

Area	High School Graduate or Higher (%)					Bachelor's Degree or Higher (%)				
	Total	White	Black	Asian	Hisp.[2]	Total	White	Black	Asian	Hisp.[2]
City	85.6	86.8	88.6	80.2	52.5	29.6	32.1	19.7	40.4	9.3
MSA[1]	88.4	89.4	89.8	82.9	58.9	29.6	31.0	20.7	44.3	12.0
U.S.	87.3	89.3	84.9	86.5	66.7	30.9	32.2	20.6	52.7	15.2

Note: Figures shown cover persons 25 years old and over; (1) Figures cover the Oklahoma City, OK Metropolitan Statistical Area—see Appendix B for areas included; (2) People of Hispanic origin can be of any race
Source: U.S. Census Bureau, 2013-2017 American Community Survey 5-Year Estimates

School Enrollment by Grade and Control

Area	Preschool (%)		Kindergarten (%)		Grades 1 - 4 (%)		Grades 5 - 8 (%)		Grades 9 - 12 (%)	
	Public	Private	Public	Private	Public	Private	Public	Private	Public	Private
City	70.8	29.2	91.6	8.4	91.4	8.6	89.6	10.4	90.6	9.4
MSA[1]	71.7	28.3	89.4	10.6	91.1	8.9	90.4	9.6	91.6	8.4
U.S.	58.8	41.2	87.7	12.3	89.7	10.3	89.6	10.4	90.3	9.7

Note: Figures shown cover persons 3 years old and over; (1) Figures cover the Oklahoma City, OK Metropolitan Statistical Area—see Appendix B for areas included
Source: U.S. Census Bureau, 2013-2017 American Community Survey 5-Year Estimates

Average Salaries of Public School Classroom Teachers

Area	2016		2017		Change from 2016 to 2017	
	Dollars	Rank[1]	Dollars	Rank[1]	Percent	Rank[2]
Oklahoma	45,276	49	45,292	50	0.0	49
U.S. Average	58,479	–	59,660	–	2.0	–

Note: (1) Rank ranges from 1 to 51 where 1 indicates highest salary; (2) Rank ranges from 1 to 51 where 1 indicates highest percent change.
Source: National Education Association, Rankings & Estimates: Rankings of the States 2017 and Estimates of School Statistics 2018

Higher Education

Four-Year Colleges			Two-Year Colleges			Medical Schools[1]	Law Schools[2]	Voc/ Tech[3]
Public	Private Non-profit	Private For-profit	Public	Private Non-profit	Private For-profit			
2	2	2	2	0	2	1	1	6

Note: Figures cover institutions located within the city limits and include main campuses only; (1) includes schools accredited by the Liaison Committee on Medical Education and the American Osteopathic Association's Commission on Osteopathic College Accreditation; (2) includes ABA-accredited schools, schools with provisional ABA accreditation, and state accredited schools; (3) includes all schools with programs that are less than 2 years.
Source: National Center for Education Statistics, Integrated Postsecondary Education System (IPEDS), 2017-18; Wikipedia, List of Medical Schools in the United States, accessed April 3, 2019; Wikipedia, List of Law Schools in the United States, accessed April 3, 2019

According to U.S. News & World Report, the Oklahoma City, OK metro area is home to one of the top 100 law schools in the U.S.: **University of Oklahoma** (#71 tie). The rankings are based on a weighted average of 12 measures of quality: peer assessment score; assessment score by lawyers/judges; median LSAT scores; median undergrad GPA; acceptance rate; employment rates for graduates; placement success; bar passage rate; faculty resources; expenditures per student; student/faculty ratio; and library resources. U.S. News & World Report, "America's Best Graduate Schools, Law, 2020"

According to U.S. News & World Report, the Oklahoma City, OK metro area is home to one of the top 75 business schools in the U.S.: **University of Oklahoma (Price)** (#58 tie). The rankings are based on a weighted average of the following nine measures: quality assessment; peer assessment; recruiter assessment; placement success; mean starting salary and bonus; student selectivity; mean GMAT and GRE scores; mean undergraduate GPA; and acceptance rate. U.S. News & World Report, "America's Best Graduate Schools, Business, 2020"

**PRESIDENTIAL
ELECTION**

2016 Presidential Election Results

Area	Clinton	Trump	Johnson	Stein	Other
Oklahoma County	41.2	51.7	7.1	0.0	0.0
U.S.	48.0	45.9	3.3	1.1	1.7

Note: Results are percentages and may not add to 100% due to rounding
Source: Dave Leip's Atlas of U.S. Presidential Elections

EMPLOYERS

Major Employers

Company Name	Industry
AT&T	Telecommunications
Chesapeake Energy Corp	Oil & gas
City of Oklahoma City	Government
Devon Energy Corp	Oil & gas
FAA Mike Monroney Aeronautical Center	Aerospace
Hobby Lobby Stores	Wholesale & retail
INTEGRIS Health	Health care
Mercy Health Center	Health care
Norman Regional Hospital	Health care
OGE Energy Corp	Utility
Oklahoma City Community College	Education
OU Medical Center	Health care
Sonic Corp	Wholesale & retail
SSM Health Care of Oklahoma	Health care
State of Oklahoma	State government
The Boeing Company	Aerospace
Tinker Air Force Base	U.S. military
University of Central Oklahoma	Higher education
University of Oklahoma - Norman	Higher education
University of Oklahoma Health Sci Ctr	Higher education

Note: Companies shown are located within the Oklahoma City, OK Metropolitan Statistical Area.
Source: Hoovers.com; Wikipedia

Best Companies to Work For

American Fidelity Assurance, headquartered in Oklahoma City, is among "The 100 Best Companies to Work For." To pick the best companies, *Fortune* partnered with the Great Place to Work Institute. Two-thirds of a company's score is based on the results of the Institute's Trust Index survey, which is sent to a random sample of employees from each company. The questions related to attitudes about management's credibility, job satisfaction, and camaraderie. The other third of the scoring is based on the company's responses to the Institute's Culture Audit, which includes detailed questions about pay and benefit programs, and a series of open-ended questions about hiring practices, internal communication, training, recognition programs, and diversity efforts. Any company that is at least five years old with more than 1,000 U.S. employees is eligible. *Fortune, "The 100 Best Companies to Work For," 2019*

American Fidelity Assurance, headquartered in Oklahoma City, is among the "100 Best Places to Work in IT." To qualify, companies had to be U.S.-based organizations or be non-U.S.- based employers that met the following criteria: have a minimum of 300 total employees at a U.S. headquarters and a minimum of 30 IT employees in the U.S., with at least 50% of their IT employees based in the U.S. The best places to work were selected based on compensation, benefits, work/life balance, employee morale, and satisfaction with training and development programs. In addition, *Computerworld* looked at retention efforts, programs for recognizing and rewarding outstanding performances, and benefits such as flextime, elder care and child care, and reimbursement for college tuition and the cost of pursuing technology certifications. *Computerworld, "100 Best Places to Work in IT 2018"*

PUBLIC SAFETY

Crime Rate

Area	All Crimes	Violent Crimes				Property Crimes		
		Murder	Rape[3]	Robbery	Aggrav. Assault	Burglary	Larceny -Theft	Motor Vehicle Theft
City	4,539.8	12.5	73.1	172.8	529.0	941.8	2,378.8	431.9
Suburbs[1]	2,391.4	3.3	45.0	43.2	152.9	481.4	1,477.0	188.6
Metro[2]	3,396.3	7.6	58.2	103.8	328.8	696.7	1,898.8	302.4
U.S.	2,756.1	5.3	41.7	98.0	248.9	430.4	1,694.4	237.4

Note: Figures are crimes per 100,000 population; (1) All areas within the metro area that are located outside the city limits; (2) Figures cover the Oklahoma City, OK Metropolitan Statistical Area—see Appendix B for areas included; (3) The city and U.S. figures shown were reported using the revised Uniform Crime Reporting (UCR) definition of rape. The suburban and metro area figures shown are an aggregate total of the data submitted using both the revised and legacy UCR definitions.
Source: FBI Uniform Crime Reports, 2017

Hate Crimes

Area	Number of Quarters Reported	Number of Incidents per Bias Motivation					
		Race/Ethnicity/ Ancestry	Religion	Sexual Orientation	Disability	Gender	Gender Identity
City	4	0	0	0	0	0	0
U.S.	4	4,131	1,564	1,130	116	46	119

Source: Federal Bureau of Investigation, Hate Crime Statistics 2017

Identity Theft Consumer Reports

Area	Reports	Reports per 100,000 Population	Rank[2]
MSA[1]	1,271	93	162
U.S.	444,602	135	-

Note: (1) Figures cover the Oklahoma City, OK Metropolitan Statistical Area—see Appendix B for areas included; (2) Rank ranges from 1 to 389 where 1 indicates greatest number of identity theft reports per 100,000 population
Source: Federal Trade Commission, Consumer Sentinel Network Data Book for January–December 2018

Fraud and Other Consumer Reports

Area	Reports	Reports per 100,000 Population	Rank[2]
MSA[1]	6,049	441	263
U.S.	2,552,917	776	-

Note: (1) Figures cover the Oklahoma City, OK Metropolitan Statistical Area—see Appendix B for areas included; (2) Rank ranges from 1 to 389 where 1 indicates greatest number of fraud and other consumer reports per 100,000 population
Source: Federal Trade Commission, Consumer Sentinel Network Data Book for January–December 2018

SPORTS

Professional Sports Teams

Team Name	League	Year Established
Oklahoma City Thunder	National Basketball Association (NBA)	2008

Note: Includes teams located in the Oklahoma City, OK Metropolitan Statistical Area.
Source: Wikipedia, Major Professional Sports Teams of the United States and Canada, April 5, 2019

CLIMATE

Average and Extreme Temperatures

Temperature	Jan	Feb	Mar	Apr	May	Jun	Jul	Aug	Sep	Oct	Nov	Dec	Yr.
Extreme High (°F)	80	84	93	100	104	105	109	110	104	96	87	86	110
Average High (°F)	47	52	61	72	79	87	93	92	84	74	60	50	71
Average Temp. (°F)	36	41	50	60	69	77	82	81	73	62	49	40	60
Average Low (°F)	26	30	38	49	58	66	71	70	62	51	38	29	49
Extreme Low (°F)	-4	-3	1	20	32	47	53	51	36	22	11	-8	-8

Note: Figures cover the years 1948-1990
Source: National Climatic Data Center, International Station Meteorological Climate Summary, 9/96

Average Precipitation/Snowfall/Humidity

Precip./Humidity	Jan	Feb	Mar	Apr	May	Jun	Jul	Aug	Sep	Oct	Nov	Dec	Yr.
Avg. Precip. (in.)	1.2	1.5	2.5	2.8	5.6	4.4	2.8	2.5	3.5	3.1	1.6	1.3	32.8
Avg. Snowfall (in.)	3	3	2	Tr	0	0	0	0	0	Tr	1	2	10
Avg. Rel. Hum. 6am (%)	78	78	76	77	84	84	81	81	82	79	78	77	80
Avg. Rel. Hum. 3pm (%)	53	52	47	46	52	51	46	44	47	46	48	52	49

Note: Figures cover the years 1948-1990; Tr = Trace amounts (<0.05 in. of rain; <0.5 in. of snow)
Source: National Climatic Data Center, International Station Meteorological Climate Summary, 9/96

Weather Conditions

Temperature			Daytime Sky			Precipitation		
10°F & below	32°F & below	90°F & above	Clear	Partly cloudy	Cloudy	0.01 inch or more precip.	0.1 inch or more snow/ice	Thunder-storms
5	79	70	124	131	110	80	8	50

Note: Figures are average number of days per year and cover the years 1948-1990
Source: National Climatic Data Center, International Station Meteorological Climate Summary, 9/96

HAZARDOUS WASTE

Superfund Sites

The Oklahoma City, OK metro area is home to three sites on the EPA's Superfund National Priorities List: **Eagle Industries** (final); **Hardage/Criner** (final); **Tinker Air Force Base (Soldier Creek/Building 3001)** (final). There are a total of 1,390 Superfund sites with a status of proposed or final on the list in the U.S. *U.S. Environmental Protection Agency, National Priorities List, April 5, 2019*

AIR & WATER QUALITY

Air Quality Trends: Ozone

	1990	1995	2000	2005	2010	2012	2014	2015	2016	2017
MSA[1]	0.078	0.086	0.082	0.077	0.071	0.080	0.068	0.067	0.066	0.069
U.S.	0.088	0.089	0.082	0.080	0.073	0.075	0.067	0.068	0.069	0.068

Note: (1) Data covers the Oklahoma City, OK Metropolitan Statistical Area—see Appendix B for areas included. The values shown are the composite ozone concentration averages among trend sites based on the highest fourth daily maximum 8-hour concentration in parts per million. These trends are based on sites having an adequate record of monitoring data during the trend period. Data from exceptional events are included.
Source: U.S. Environmental Protection Agency, Air Quality Monitoring Information, "Air Quality Trends by City, 1990-2017"

Air Quality Index

Area	Percent of Days when Air Quality was...[2]					AQI Statistics[2]	
	Good	Moderate	Unhealthy for Sensitive Groups	Unhealthy	Very Unhealthy	Maximum	Median
MSA[1]	62.2	35.9	1.9	0.0	0.0	119	47

Note: (1) Data covers the Oklahoma City, OK Metropolitan Statistical Area—see Appendix B for areas included; (2) Based on 365 days with AQI data in 2017. Air Quality Index (AQI) is an index for reporting daily air quality. EPA calculates the AQI for five major air pollutants regulated by the Clean Air Act: ground-level ozone, particle pollution (aka particulate matter), carbon monoxide, sulfur dioxide, and nitrogen dioxide. The AQI runs from 0 to 500. The higher the AQI value, the greater the level of air pollution and the greater the health concern. There are six AQI categories: "Good" AQI is between 0 and 50. Air quality is considered satisfactory; "Moderate" AQI is between 51 and 100. Air quality is acceptable; "Unhealthy for Sensitive Groups" When AQI values are between 101 and 150, members of sensitive groups may experience health effects; "Unhealthy" When AQI values are between 151 and 200 everyone may begin to experience health effects; "Very Unhealthy" AQI values between 201 and 300 trigger a health alert; "Hazardous" AQI values over 300 trigger warnings of emergency conditions (not shown).
Source: U.S. Environmental Protection Agency, Air Quality Index Report, 2017

Air Quality Index Pollutants

Area	Percent of Days when AQI Pollutant was...[2]					
	Carbon Monoxide	Nitrogen Dioxide	Ozone	Sulfur Dioxide	Particulate Matter 2.5	Particulate Matter 10
MSA[1]	0.0	4.7	60.5	0.0	34.8	0.0

Note: (1) Data covers the Oklahoma City, OK Metropolitan Statistical Area—see Appendix B for areas included; (2) Based on 365 days with AQI data in 2017. The Air Quality Index (AQI) is an index for reporting daily air quality. EPA calculates the AQI for five major air pollutants regulated by the Clean Air Act: ground-level ozone, particle pollution (also known as particulate matter), carbon monoxide, sulfur dioxide, and nitrogen dioxide. The AQI runs from 0 to 500. The higher the AQI value, the greater the level of air pollution and the greater the health concern.
Source: U.S. Environmental Protection Agency, Air Quality Index Report, 2017

Maximum Air Pollutant Concentrations: Particulate Matter, Ozone, CO and Lead

	Particulate Matter 10 (ug/m^3)	Particulate Matter 2.5 Wtd AM (ug/m^3)	Particulate Matter 2.5 24-Hr (ug/m^3)	Ozone (ppm)	Carbon Monoxide (ppm)	Lead (ug/m^3)
MSA[1] Level	52	7.8	16	0.071	1	n/a
NAAQS[2]	150	15	35	0.075	9	0.15
Met NAAQS[2]	Yes	Yes	Yes	Yes	Yes	n/a

Note: (1) Data covers the Oklahoma City, OK Metropolitan Statistical Area—see Appendix B for areas included; Data from exceptional events are included; (2) National Ambient Air Quality Standards; ppm = parts per million; ug/m^3 = micrograms per cubic meter; n/a not available.
Concentrations: Particulate Matter 10 (coarse particulate)—highest second maximum 24-hour concentration; Particulate Matter 2.5 Wtd AM (fine particulate)—highest weighted annual mean concentration; Particulate Matter 2.5 24-Hour (fine particulate)—highest 98th percentile 24-hour concentration; Ozone—highest fourth daily maximum 8-hour concentration; Carbon Monoxide—highest second maximum non-overlapping 8-hour concentration; Lead—maximum running 3-month average
Source: U.S. Environmental Protection Agency, Air Quality Monitoring Information, "Air Quality Statistics by City, 2017"

Maximum Air Pollutant Concentrations: Nitrogen Dioxide and Sulfur Dioxide

	Nitrogen Dioxide AM (ppb)	Nitrogen Dioxide 1-Hr (ppb)	Sulfur Dioxide AM (ppb)	Sulfur Dioxide 1-Hr (ppb)	Sulfur Dioxide 24-Hr (ppb)
MSA[1] Level	16	43	n/a	2	n/a
NAAQS[2]	53	100	30	75	140
Met NAAQS[2]	Yes	Yes	n/a	Yes	n/a

Note: (1) Data covers the Oklahoma City, OK Metropolitan Statistical Area—see Appendix B for areas included; Data from exceptional events are included; (2) National Ambient Air Quality Standards; ppm = parts per million; ug/m^3 = micrograms per cubic meter; n/a not available.
Concentrations: Nitrogen Dioxide AM—highest arithmetic mean concentration; Nitrogen Dioxide 1-Hr—highest 98th percentile 1-hour daily maximum concentration; Sulfur Dioxide AM—highest annual mean concentration; Sulfur Dioxide 1-Hr—highest 99th percentile 1-hour daily maximum concentration; Sulfur Dioxide 24-Hr—highest second maximum 24-hour concentration
Source: U.S. Environmental Protection Agency, Air Quality Monitoring Information, "Air Quality Statistics by City, 2017"

Drinking Water

Water System Name	Pop. Served	Primary Water Source Type	Violations[1]	
			Health Based	Monitoring/ Reporting
Oklahoma City	630,000	Surface	0	0

Note: (1) Based on violation data from January 1, 2018 to December 31, 2018
Source: U.S. Environmental Protection Agency, Office of Ground Water and Drinking Water, Safe Drinking Water Information System (based on data extracted April 5, 2019)

Omaha, Nebraska

Background

Omaha's central location in the heartland of the United States has been important to its strong economy. Located on the western banks of the Missouri River, the city has been a significant agricultural and transportation center since its establishment in 1854. In its earliest history, Omaha was a trading center and "Gateway to the West." From these roots, Omaha has seen steady growth.

There are nearly 20,000 businesses located in the metropolitan area, including Fortune 500 companies such as ConAgra Foods, Mutual of Omaha, Union Pacific Railroad, Kiewit Corporation, and Berkshire Hathaway, the last of which is headed by Omaha's most prominent businessman, Warren Buffet, famously recognized as one of the richest men in the world.

Additional Fortune 500 companies have manufacturing plants or service centers in the metropolitan area. The headquarters of insurance companies, direct response/telemarketing centers and other national and international firms call Omaha home. The city is also a regional service and trade center. Services and trade combined comprise 57 percent of metro area employment.

Omaha is large enough to offer a variety of cosmopolitan attractions, yet small enough to provide a relaxed lifestyle. Recreational activities abound, and Omaha residents enjoy a low cost of living, outstanding health care and a low crime rate.

The Omaha metropolitan area is served by several public and private school systems, and offers 11 colleges and universities, including Gallup University, offering courses that support leaders, managers, and sales professionals.

The community also has access to excellent cultural programs worthy of a much larger city, including the professional Omaha Symphony, Omaha Theater Ballet, and Opera Omaha. Performances by these groups and other touring companies are held in the magnificent Orpheum Theater, a restored 1920s vaudeville house. The Bemis Center for Contemporary Arts, the largest urban artist colony in the world, plays host to artists from all over the world.

Omaha is home to world-famous Father Flanagan's Boys and Girls Town, and the award-winning Henry Doorly Zoo, which includes the world's largest indoor rainforest and a collection of rare white tigers. Other attractions include the Strategic Air & Space Museum and the birthplaces of Malcom X and former President Gerald R. Ford.

Omaha celebrated its 150th birthday in 2004, and continues to devote much effort to new projects. The acreage fronting the Missouri River, is home to several new developments including a 2,700-foot bridge with a 506-foot span across the river connecting nearly 150 miles of trails in Nebraska and Iowa. The Midwestern headquarters for the National Park Service is in Omaha, the first building in Nebraska to be rated tops under the Leadership in Energy and Environmental Design system, or LEED. The nearby Riverfront Place is a six-acre urban neighborhood that includes residential units, commercial space, a public plaza, riverfront access, and connections to miles of walking trails.

Omaha's weather shows the usual contrasts of a continental climate, with cold, dry winters and warm summers. The city is situated between two climatic zones, the humid east and the dry west, and fluctuation between these zones produce for weather periods characteristic of either zone or combinations of both. Most precipitation falls between April and September in the form of sharp thunderstorms or evening lightning shows.

Rankings

General Rankings

- For its "Best for Vets: Places to Live 2019" rankings, *Military Times* evaluated 599 cities (83 large, 234 medium, 282 small) and compared the locations across three broad categories: veteran and military culture/services; economic indicators; and livability factors such as health, crime, traffic, and school quality. Omaha ranked #9 out of the top 25, in the large city category (populations of more than 250,000). Data points more specific to veterans and the military weighed more heavily than the rest. *rebootcamp.militarytimes.com, "Military Times Best Places to Live 2019," September 10, 2018*

- The Omaha metro area was identified as one of America's fastest-growing areas in terms of population and business growth by *MagnifyMoney*. The area ranked #33 out of 35. The 100 most populous metro areas in the U.S. were evaluated on their change from 2011-2016 in the following categories: people and housing; workforce and employment opportunities; growing industry. *www.businessinsider.com, "The 35 Cities in the US with the Biggest Influx of People, the Most Work Opportunities, and the Hottest Business Growth," August 12, 2018*

- In their sixth annual survey, Livability.com looked at data for more than 1,000 U.S. cities to determine the rankings for Livability's "Top 100 Best Places to Live" in 2019. Omaha ranked #20. Criteria: median home value capped at $250,000; affordable living; vibrant economy; education, demographics, health care options. transportation & infrastructure; abundant lifestyle amenities. *Livability.com, "Top 100 Best Places to Live 2019" March 2019*

Business/Finance Rankings

- The personal finance site NerdWallet analyzed 183 American metropolitan areas with populations over 250,000 and more than 15,000 businesses to rank where entrepreneurs find the most success. Criteria included area economy, annual income, housing cost, unemployment rate, and the success rate of area businesses. Omaha ranked #16. *www.nerdwallet.com, "Best Places to Start a Business," April 27, 2015*

- Omaha was the #9-ranked city for savers, according to a study by the finance site GOBankingRates, which considered the prospects for people trying to save money. Criteria: average monthly cost of grocery items; median home listing price; median rent; median income; unemployment rate; gas prices; and sales tax in the nation's 60 largest cities. *www.gobankingrates.com, "Best Cities for Saving Money," June 22, 2018*

- Omaha was ranked #9 among the nation's 60 largest cities for most difficult conditions for savers, according to a study by the finance site GOBankingRates. Criteria: average monthly cost of grocery items; median home listing price; median rent; median income; unemployment rate; gas prices; and sales tax. *www.gobankingrates.com, "Worst Cities for Saving Money," June 22, 2018*

- Recognizing the sizeable percentage of American workers who are self-employed, NerdWallet editors assessed the country's cities according to percentage of freelancers, median rental costs, cell phone plans/taxes, and healthcare affordability and access. By these criteria, Omaha placed #11 among the best cities for independent workers. *www.nerdwallet.com, "Best Places for Freelance Workers," August 30, 2016*

- Using data from the Council for Community and Economic Research's 2014 cost of living index, NerdWallet ranked the 100 most affordable cities in America. Median income was compared with cost of living to find truly affordable places. Omaha ranked #26. *NerdWallet.com, "America's Most Affordable Places," May 18, 2015*

- NerdWallet.com identified the 10 most promising cities for job seekers of the nation's 100 largest cities. Omaha was ranked #24. Criteria: job availability; annual salary; workforce growth; affordability. *NerdWallet.com, "Best Cities for Job Seekers in 2017," December 19, 2016*

- The Brookings Institution ranked the nation's largest cities based on income inequality. Omaha was ranked #67 (#1 = greatest inequality). Criteria: the "95/20 ratio," a figure representing the income at which a household earns more than 95 percent of all other households, divided by the income at which a household earns more than only 20 percent of all other households. *Brookings Institution, "Household Income Inequality, Largest Cities of 97 Large U.S. Metro Areas, 2014-2016," February 5, 2018*

- The Brookings Institution ranked the 100 largest metro areas in the U.S. based on income inequality. Omaha was ranked #90 (#1 = greatest inequality). Criteria: the "95/20 ratio," a figure representing the income at which a household earns more than 95 percent of all other households, divided by the income at which a household earns more than only 20 percent of all other households. *Brookings Institution, "Household Income Inequality, 100 Largest U.S. Metro Areas, 2014-2016," February 5, 2018*

- *Forbes* ranked the 100 largest metro areas in the U.S. in terms of the "Best Cities for Young Professionals." The Omaha metro area ranked #19 out of 25. (Large metro areas were divided into metro divisions.) Criteria: median rent of a two-bedroom apartment; job growth and unemployment rate; median salary of college graduates with 5 or less years of work experience; networking opportunities; social outlook; percentage of population 25 years of age and older with college degrees. *Forbes.com, "America's 25 Best Cities for Young Professionals in 2017," May 22, 2017*

- Omaha was cited as one of America's top metros for new and expanded facility projects in 2018. The area ranked #1 in the mid-sized metro area category (population 200,000 to 1 million). *Site Selection, "Top Metros of 2018," March 2019*

- The Omaha metro area appeared on the Milken Institute "2018 Best Performing Cities" list. Rank: #134 out of 200 large metro areas. Criteria: job growth; wage and salary growth; high-tech output growth. *Milken Institute, "Best-Performing Cities 2018," January 24, 2019*

- *Forbes* ranked the 200 most populous metro areas to determine the nation's "Best Places for Business and Careers." The Omaha metro area was ranked #44. Criteria: costs (business and living); job growth (past and projected); income growth; quality of life; educational attainment (college and high school); projected economic growth; cultural and recreational opportunities; net migration patterns; number of highly ranked colleges. *Forbes, "The Best Places for Business and Careers 2018: Seattle Leads the Way," October 24, 2018*

Dating/Romance Rankings

- Omaha was ranked #19 out of 25 cities that stood out for inspiring romance and attracting diners on the website OpenTable.com. Criteria: percentage of people who dined out on Valentine's Day in 2018; percentage of romantic restaurants as rated by OpenTable diner reviews; and percentage of tables seated for two. *OpenTable, "25 Most Romantic Cities in America for 2019," February 7, 2019*

Education Rankings

- Personal finance website *WalletHub* analyzed the 150 largest U.S. metropolitan statistical areas to determine where the most educated Americans are choosing to settle. Criteria: education quality and attainment gap; education levels; percentage of workers with degrees; public school quality rankings; quality and size of each metro area's universities. Omaha was ranked #34 (#1 = most educated city). *www.WalletHub.com, "2018's Most and Least Educated Cities in America," July 24, 2018*

- Omaha was selected as one of America's most literate cities. The city ranked #33 out of the 82 largest U.S. cities. Criteria: number of booksellers; library resources; Internet resources; educational attainment; periodical publishing resources; newspaper circulation. *Central Connecticut State University, "America's Most Literate Cities, 2016," March 31, 2017*

Food/Drink Rankings

- In compiling its list of "Top 10 Best Foodie Cities, 2015," the lifestyle website Livability analyzed data for cities with high concentrations of restaurants and bars. Looking at access to healthy food and farmers' markets, adult obesity rates, and other factors like Yelp reviews and James Beard Award winners, Livability chose Omaha as the #2 American foodie town. *livability.com, "Top 10 Best Foodie Cities, 2015," July 6, 2015*

- *Men's Health* ranked 100 major U.S. cities in terms of alcohol intoxication. Omaha ranked #39 (#1 = most sober).Criteria: binge drinking; alcohol-related traffic accidents, arrests, and fatalities. *Men's Health, "America's Drunkest Cities," March 9, 2015*

- Omaha was selected as one of America's 10 most vegan-friendly cities. The city was ranked #8. *People for the Ethical Treatment of Animals, "Top 10 Vegan-Friendly Cities of 2018," May 16, 2018*

Health/Fitness Rankings

- For each of the 100 largest cities in the United States, the American College of Sports Medicine's American Fitness Index evaluated infrastructure, community assets, and policies that encourage healthy and fit lifestyles, including preventive health behaviors, levels of chronic disease conditions, health care access, and community resources and policies that support physical activity. Omaha ranked #33 for "community fitness." *www.americanfitnessindex.org, "ACSM American Fitness Index Health and Community Fitness Status of the 100 Largest U.S. Cities," May 2018*

- The Omaha metro area was identified as one of the worst cities for bed bugs in America by pest control company Orkin. The area ranked #37 out of 50 based on the number of bed bug treatments Orkin performed from December 2017 to November 2018. *Orkin, "Baltimore Remains Front Runner, Atlanta and Philadelphia Break Into Top 10," January 14, 2019*

- Omaha was identified as a "2018 Spring Allergy Capital." The area ranked #58 out of 100. Three groups of factors were used to identify the most challenging cities for people with allergies during the spring season: annual pollen levels; medicine utilization; access to board-certified allergists. *Asthma and Allergy Foundation of America, "Spring Allergy Capitals 2018"*

- Omaha was identified as a "2018 Fall Allergy Capital." The area ranked #45 out of 100. Three groups of factors were used to identify the most challenging cities for people with allergies during the fall season: annual pollen levels; medicine utilization; access to board-certified allergists. *Asthma and Allergy Foundation of America, "Fall Allergy Capitals 2018"*

- Omaha was identified as a "2018 Asthma Capital." The area ranked #12 out of the nation's 100 largest metropolitan areas. Criteria: estimated prevalence; self-reported prevalence; crude death rate for asthma; annual pollen score; annual air quality; public smoking laws; number of board-certified asthma specialists; school inhaler access laws; rescue medication use; controller medication use; ER visits for asthma; uninsured rate; poverty rate. *Asthma and Allergy Foundation of America, "Asthma Capitals 2018: The Most Challenging Places to Live With Asthma"*

- *Men's Health* ranked 100 major U.S. cities in terms of the best cities for men. Omaha ranked #33. Criteria: health; fitness; quality of life. *Men's Health, "The Best & Worst Cities for Men Who Want to Be Fit and Happy," January 1, 2016*

- The Omaha metro area ranked #82 out of 189 in The Gallup-Healthways Well-Being Index. Criteria: purpose; social well being; financial health; community and physical health. Results are based on telephone interviews with adults, aged 18 and older, living in metropolitan areas in the 50 U.S. states and the District of Columbia. *Gallup-Healthways, "State of American Well-Being, 2017 Community Well-Being Rankings" March 2018*

Real Estate Rankings

- *WalletHub* compared the most populated U.S. cities, as well as at least two of the most populated cities in each state, for a total of 179, to determine which had the best markets for real estate agents. Omaha ranked #64 where demand was high and pay was the best. Criteria: sales per agent; annual median wage for real-estate agents; monthly average starting salary for real estate agents; real estate job density and competition; unemployment rate; housing-market health index; and other relevant metrics. *www.WalletHub.com, "2018's Best Places to Be a Real Estate Agent," April 25, 2018*

- The Omaha metro area was identified as one of the 20 best housing markets in the U.S. in 2018. The area ranked #14 out of 178 markets. Criteria: year-over-year change of median sales price of existing single-family homes between the 4th quarter of 2017 and the 4th quarter of 2018. *National Association of Realtors®, Median Sales Price of Existing Single-Family Homes for Metropolitan Areas, 4th Quarter 2018*

Safety Rankings

- Allstate ranked the 200 largest cities in America in terms of driver safety. Omaha ranked #41. Criteria: internal property damage claims over a two-year period from January 2015 to December 2016. The report helps increase the importance of safety awareness behind the wheel. *Allstate, "Allstate America's Best Drivers Report, 2018" August 28, 2018*

- The National Insurance Crime Bureau ranked 382 metro areas in the U.S. in terms of per capita rates of vehicle theft. The Omaha metro area ranked #39 (#1 = highest rate). Criteria: number of vehicle theft offenses per 100,000 inhabitants in 2017. *National Insurance Crime Bureau, "Hot Spots 2017," July 12, 2018*

Seniors/Retirement Rankings

- From its Best Cities for Successful Aging indexes, the Milken Institute generated rankings for metropolitan areas, weighing data in nine categories—health care, wellness, living arrangements, transportation and convenience, financial characteristics, education, employment, community engagement, and overall livability. The Omaha metro area was ranked #7 overall in the large metro area category. *Milken Institute, "Best Cities for Successful Aging, 2017" March 14, 2017*

Sports/Recreation Rankings

- Omaha was chosen as one of America's best cities for bicycling. The city ranked #45 out of 50. Criteria: cycling infrastructure that is safe and friendly for all ages; energy and bike culture. The editors only considered cities with populations of 100,000 or more. *Bicycling, "The 50 Best Bike Cities in America," October 10, 2018*

Women/Minorities Rankings

- Movoto chose the best places for professional women among the largest 100 American cities. Omaha was among the top ten, at #2, based on commute time, recent job growth, unemployment rank, professional women's groups per capita, and average earnings adjusted for the cost of living. *www.movoto.com, "These Are America's Best Cities for Professional Women," March 5, 2014*

- Personal finance website *WalletHub* compared more than 180 U.S. cities—including the 150 most populated U.S. cities, plus at least two of the most populated cities in each state—across two key dimensions, "Hispanic Business-Friendliness" and "Hispanic Purchasing Power", to arrive at the most favorable conditions for Hispanic entrepreneurs. Omaha was ranked #103 out of 182. Criteria includes: share of Hispanic-Owned Businesses; Hispanic entrepreneurship rate to median annual income of Hispanics; Small Business-Friendliness score; cost of living; and number of Hispanics with at least a bachelor's degree. *WalletHub.com, "2018's Best Cities for Hispanic Entrepreneurs," April 26, 2018*

Miscellaneous Rankings

- *WalletHub* compared the 150 most populated U.S. cities to determine their operating efficiency. A "Quality of Services" score was constructed for each city and then divided by the total budget per capita to reveal which were managed the best. Omaha ranked #80. Criteria: financial stability; economy; education; safety; health; infrastructure and pollution. *www.WalletHub.com, "2018's Best- & Worst-Run Cities in America," July 9, 2018*

Business Environment

CITY FINANCES

City Government Finances

Component	2016 ($000)	2016 ($ per capita)
Total Revenues	704,162	1,586
Total Expenditures	670,809	1,511
Debt Outstanding	1,401,066	3,156
Cash and Securities[1]	939,885	2,117

Note: (1) Cash and security holdings of a government at the close of its fiscal year, including those of its dependent agencies, utilities, and liquor stores.
Source: U.S. Census Bureau, State & Local Government Finances 2016

City Government Revenue by Source

Source	2016 ($000)	2016 ($ per capita)	2016 (%)
General Revenue			
From Federal Government	13,260	30	1.9
From State Government	44,604	100	6.3
From Local Governments	17,974	40	2.6
Taxes			
Property	150,161	338	21.3
Sales and Gross Receipts	151,786	342	21.6
Personal Income	0	0	0.0
Corporate Income	0	0	0.0
Motor Vehicle License	30,695	69	4.4
Other Taxes	72,321	163	10.3
Current Charges	179,699	405	25.5
Liquor Store	0	0	0.0
Utility	0	0	0.0
Employee Retirement	38,966	88	5.5

Source: U.S. Census Bureau, State & Local Government Finances 2016

City Government Expenditures by Function

Function	2016 ($000)	2016 ($ per capita)	2016 (%)
General Direct Expenditures			
Air Transportation	0	0	0.0
Corrections	0	0	0.0
Education	0	0	0.0
Employment Security Administration	0	0	0.0
Financial Administration	9,358	21	1.4
Fire Protection	74,885	168	11.2
General Public Buildings	6,398	14	1.0
Governmental Administration, Other	14,739	33	2.2
Health	0	0	0.0
Highways	77,637	174	11.6
Hospitals	0	0	0.0
Housing and Community Development	665	1	0.1
Interest on General Debt	41,880	94	6.2
Judicial and Legal	4,093	9	0.6
Libraries	15,144	34	2.3
Parking	2,505	5	0.4
Parks and Recreation	30,542	68	4.6
Police Protection	101,646	229	15.2
Public Welfare	0	0	0.0
Sewerage	114,182	257	17.0
Solid Waste Management	20,992	47	3.1
Veterans' Services	0	0	0.0
Liquor Store	0	0	0.0
Utility	0	0	0.0
Employee Retirement	108,578	244	16.2

Source: U.S. Census Bureau, State & Local Government Finances 2016

DEMOGRAPHICS

Population Growth

Area	1990 Census	2000 Census	2010 Census	2017* Estimate	Population Growth (%)	
					1990-2017	2010-2017
City	371,972	390,007	408,958	463,081	24.5	13.2
MSA[1]	685,797	767,041	865,350	914,190	33.3	5.6
U.S.	248,709,873	281,421,906	308,745,538	321,004,407	29.1	4.0

Note: (1) Figures cover the Omaha-Council Bluffs, NE-IA Metropolitan Statistical Area—see Appendix B for areas included; (*) 2013-2017 5-year estimated population
Source: U.S. Census Bureau, 1990 Census, Census 2000, Census 2010, 2013-2017 American Community Survey 5-Year Estimates

Household Size

Area	Persons in Household (%)							Average Household Size
	One	Two	Three	Four	Five	Six	Seven or More	
City	32.8	31.7	14.1	11.4	5.9	2.6	1.6	2.50
MSA[1]	28.5	33.5	14.7	13.0	6.3	2.6	1.4	2.50
U.S.	27.7	33.8	15.7	13.0	6.0	2.3	1.4	2.60

Note: (1) Figures cover the Omaha-Council Bluffs, NE-IA Metropolitan Statistical Area—see Appendix B for areas included
Source: U.S. Census Bureau, 2013-2017 American Community Survey 5-Year Estimates

Race

Area	White Alone[2] (%)	Black Alone[2] (%)	Asian Alone[2] (%)	AIAN[3] Alone[2] (%)	NHOPI[4] Alone[2] (%)	Other Race Alone[2] (%)	Two or More Races (%)
City	78.2	12.3	3.5	0.5	0.1	2.3	3.1
MSA[1]	84.7	7.6	2.6	0.4	0.1	1.8	2.8
U.S.	73.0	12.7	5.4	0.8	0.2	4.8	3.1

Note: (1) Figures cover the Omaha-Council Bluffs, NE-IA Metropolitan Statistical Area—see Appendix B for areas included; (2) Alone is defined as not being in combination with one or more other races; (3) American Indian and Alaska Native; (4) Native Hawaiian and Other Pacific Islander
Source: U.S. Census Bureau, 2013-2017 American Community Survey 5-Year Estimates

Hispanic or Latino Origin

Area	Total (%)	Mexican (%)	Puerto Rican (%)	Cuban (%)	Other (%)
City	13.7	10.6	0.3	0.2	2.5
MSA[1]	10.1	7.8	0.3	0.1	1.8
U.S.	17.6	11.1	1.7	0.7	4.1

Note: Persons of Hispanic or Latino origin can be of any race; (1) Figures cover the Omaha-Council Bluffs, NE-IA Metropolitan Statistical Area—see Appendix B for areas included
Source: U.S. Census Bureau, 2013-2017 American Community Survey 5-Year Estimates

Segregation

Type	Segregation Indices[1]				Percent Change		
	1990	2000	2010	2010 Rank[2]	1990-2000	1990-2010	2000-2010
Black/White	71.4	67.3	61.3	38	-4.1	-10.1	-6.0
Asian/White	34.2	36.0	36.3	74	1.8	2.1	0.3
Hispanic/White	38.5	48.9	48.8	30	10.4	10.3	-0.1

Note: All figures cover the Metropolitan Statistical Area—see Appendix B for areas included; Figures are based on an analysis of 1990, 2000, and 2010 Census Decennial Census tract data by William H. Frey, Brookings Institution and the University of Michigan Social Science Data Analysis Network. In this analysis all racial groups (whites, blacks, and asians) are non-Hispanic members of those races. Hispanics are shown as a separate category; (1) Segregation Indices are Dissimilarity Indices that measure the degree to which the minority group is distributed differently than whites across census tracts. They range from 0 (complete integration) to 100 (complete segregation) where the value indicates the percentage of the minority group that needs to move to be distributed exactly like whites; (2) Ranges from 1 (most segregated) to 102 (least segregated); n/a not available.
Source: www.CensusScope.org

Ancestry

Area	German	Irish	English	American	Italian	Polish	French[2]	Scottish	Dutch
City	26.1	13.8	6.5	3.2	4.3	3.8	2.2	1.3	1.5
MSA[1]	30.4	14.5	7.8	3.8	4.1	3.8	2.4	1.3	1.8
U.S.	14.1	10.1	7.5	6.6	5.3	2.9	2.5	1.7	1.3

Note: Figures are the percentage of the total population reporting a particular ancestry. The nine most commonly reported ancestries in the U.S. are shown. Figures include multiple ancestries (e.g. if a person reported being Irish and Italian, they were included in both columns); (1) Figures cover the Omaha-Council Bluffs, NE-IA Metropolitan Statistical Area—see Appendix B for areas included; (2) Excludes Basque
Source: U.S. Census Bureau, 2013-2017 American Community Survey 5-Year Estimates

Foreign-Born Population

Area	Percent of Population Born in								
	Any Foreign Country	Asia	Mexico	Europe	Carribean	Central America[2]	South America	Africa	Canada
City	10.3	3.0	4.0	0.7	0.2	1.0	0.2	1.1	0.1
MSA[1]	7.2	2.2	2.7	0.6	0.1	0.6	0.2	0.7	0.1
U.S.	13.4	4.1	3.6	1.5	1.3	1.0	0.9	0.6	0.3

Note: (1) Figures cover the Omaha-Council Bluffs, NE-IA Metropolitan Statistical Area—see Appendix B for areas included; (2) Excludes Mexico.
Source: U.S. Census Bureau, 2013-2017 American Community Survey 5-Year Estimates

Marital Status

Area	Never Married	Now Married[2]	Separated	Widowed	Divorced
City	36.0	45.8	1.7	5.0	11.4
MSA[1]	31.0	51.7	1.4	5.0	10.9
U.S.	33.1	48.2	2.0	5.8	10.9

Note: Figures are percentages and cover the population 15 years of age and older; (1) Figures cover the Omaha-Council Bluffs, NE-IA Metropolitan Statistical Area—see Appendix B for areas included; (2) Excludes separated
Source: U.S. Census Bureau, 2013-2017 American Community Survey 5-Year Estimates

Disability by Age

Area	All Ages	Under 18 Years Old	18 to 64 Years Old	65 Years and Over
City	11.1	3.6	9.7	34.2
MSA[1]	10.9	3.5	9.6	33.3
U.S.	12.6	4.2	10.3	35.5

Note: Figures show percent of the civilian noninstitutionalized population that reported having a disability. Disability status is determined from six types of difficulty: vision, hearing, cognitive, ambulatory, self-care, and independent living. For children under 5 years old, hearing and vision difficulty are used to determine disability status. For children between the ages of 5 and 14, disability status is determined from hearing, vision, cognitive, ambulatory, and self-care difficulties. For people aged 15 years and older, they are considered to have a disability if they have difficulty with any one of the six difficulty types; Note: (1) Figures cover the Omaha-Council Bluffs, NE-IA Metropolitan Statistical Area—see Appendix B for areas included
Source: U.S. Census Bureau, 2013-2017 American Community Survey 5-Year Estimates

Age

Area	Percent of Population									Median Age
	Under Age 5	Age 5–19	Age 20–34	Age 35–44	Age 45–54	Age 55–64	Age 65–74	Age 75–84	Age 85+	
City	7.3	20.6	23.2	12.5	12.4	11.9	7.1	3.5	1.7	34.3
MSA[1]	7.3	21.0	21.1	13.0	12.9	12.0	7.4	3.6	1.6	35.4
U.S.	6.2	19.5	20.7	12.7	13.4	12.7	8.6	4.4	1.9	37.8

Note: (1) Figures cover the Omaha-Council Bluffs, NE-IA Metropolitan Statistical Area—see Appendix B for areas included
Source: U.S. Census Bureau, 2013-2017 American Community Survey 5-Year Estimates

Gender

Area	Males	Females	Males per 100 Females
City	228,597	234,484	97.5
MSA[1]	452,361	461,829	97.9
U.S.	158,018,753	162,985,654	97.0

Note: (1) Figures cover the Omaha-Council Bluffs, NE-IA Metropolitan Statistical Area—see Appendix B for areas included
Source: U.S. Census Bureau, 2013-2017 American Community Survey 5-Year Estimates

Religious Groups by Family

Area	Catholic	Baptist	Non-Den.	Methodist[2]	Lutheran	LDS[3]	Pente-costal	Presby-terian[4]	Muslim[5]	Judaism
MSA[1]	21.6	4.6	1.8	3.9	7.9	1.8	1.3	2.3	0.5	0.4
U.S.	19.1	9.3	4.0	4.0	2.3	2.0	1.9	1.6	0.8	0.7

Note: Figures are the number of adherents as a percentage of the total population; (1) Figures cover the Omaha-Council Bluffs, NE-IA Metropolitan Statistical Area—see Appendix B for areas included; (2) Methodist/Pietist; (3) Latter Day Saints; (4) Reformed; (5) Figures are estimates
Source: Association of Statisticians of American Religious Bodies, 2010 U.S. Religion Census: Religious Congregations & Membership Study

Religious Groups by Tradition

Area	Catholic	Evangelical Protestant	Mainline Protestant	Other Tradition	Black Protestant	Orthodox
MSA[1]	21.6	12.1	10.8	3.3	1.5	0.1
U.S.	19.1	16.2	7.3	4.3	1.6	0.3

Note: Figures are the number of adherents as a percentage of the total population; (1) Figures cover the Omaha-Council Bluffs, NE-IA Metropolitan Statistical Area—see Appendix B for areas included
Source: Association of Statisticians of American Religious Bodies, 2010 U.S. Religion Census: Religious Congregations & Membership Study

ECONOMY

Gross Metropolitan Product

Area	2016	2017	2018	2019	Rank[2]
MSA[1]	63.2	64.8	67.1	70.2	51

Note: Figures are in billions of dollars; (1) Figures cover the Omaha-Council Bluffs, NE-IA Metropolitan Statistical Area—see Appendix B for areas included; (2) Rank is based on 2017 data and ranges from 1 to 381
Source: U.S. Conference of Mayors, U.S. Metro Economies: Economic Growth & Full Employment, June 2018

Economic Growth

Area	2017-2018 (%)	2019-2020 (%)	2021-2022 (%)
MSA[1]	1.1	1.9	1.9

Note: Figures are real gross metropolitan product (GMP) growth rates and represent average annual percent change; (1) Figures cover the Omaha-Council Bluffs, NE-IA Metropolitan Statistical Area—see Appendix B for areas included
Source: U.S. Conference of Mayors, U.S. Metro Economies: Economic Growth & Full Employment, June 2018

Metropolitan Area Exports

Area	2012	2013	2014	2015	2016	2017	Rank[2]
MSA[1]	3,529.3	4,255.9	4,528.5	3,753.4	3,509.7	3,756.2	65

Note: Figures are in millions of dollars; (1) Figures cover the Omaha-Council Bluffs, NE-IA Metropolitan Statistical Area—see Appendix B for areas included; (2) Rank is based on 2017 data and ranges from 1 to 387
Source: U.S. Department of Commerce, International Trade Administration, Office of Trade and Economic Analysis, Industry and Analysis, Exports by Metropolitan Area, extracted March 25, 2019

Building Permits

Area	Single-Family			Multi-Family			Total		
	2016	2017	Pct. Chg.	2016	2017	Pct. Chg.	2016	2017	Pct. Chg.
City	1,427	1,533	7.4	1,137	1,697	49.3	2,564	3,230	26.0
MSA[1]	2,906	3,158	8.7	1,334	1,797	34.7	4,240	4,955	16.9
U.S.	750,800	820,000	9.2	455,800	462,000	1.4	1,206,600	1,282,000	6.2

Note: (1) Figures cover the Omaha-Council Bluffs, NE-IA Metropolitan Statistical Area—see Appendix B for areas included; Figures represent new, privately-owned housing units authorized (unadjusted data); All permit data are based on estimates with imputation
Source: U.S. Census Bureau, Manufacturing, Mining, and Construction Statistics, Building Permits, 2016, 2017

Bankruptcy Filings

Area	Business Filings			Nonbusiness Filings		
	2017	2018	% Chg.	2017	2018	% Chg.
Douglas County	38	23	-39.5	1,225	1,189	-2.9
U.S.	23,157	22,232	-4.0	765,863	751,186	-1.9

Note: Business filings include Chapter 7, Chapter 11, Chapter 12, and Chapter 13; Nonbusiness filings include Chapter 7, Chapter 11, and Chapter 13
Source: Administrative Office of the U.S. Courts, Business and Nonbusiness Bankruptcy, County Cases Commenced by Chapter of the Bankruptcy Code, During the 12-Month Period Ending December 31, 2017 and Business and Nonbusiness Bankruptcy, County Cases Commenced by Chapter of the Bankruptcy Code, During the 12-Month Period Ending December 31, 2018

Housing Vacancy Rates

Area	Gross Vacancy Rate[2] (%)			Year-Round Vacancy Rate[3] (%)			Rental Vacancy Rate[4] (%)			Homeowner Vacancy Rate[5] (%)		
	2016	2017	2018	2016	2017	2018	2016	2017	2018	2016	2017	2018
MSA[1]	6.9	5.9	7.1	6.2	5.4	6.1	6.7	4.7	7.1	0.7	0.9	0.7
U.S.	12.8	12.7	12.3	9.9	9.9	9.7	6.9	7.2	6.9	1.7	1.6	1.5

Note: (1) Figures cover the Omaha-Council Bluffs, NE-IA Metropolitan Statistical Area—see Appendix B for areas included; (2) The percentage of the total housing inventory that is vacant; (3) The percentage of the housing inventory (excluding seasonal units) that is year-round vacant; (4) The percentage of rental inventory that is vacant for rent; (5) The percentage of homeowner inventory that is vacant for sale
Source: U.S. Census Bureau, Housing Vacancies and Homeownership Annual Statistics: 2016, 2017, 2018

INCOME

Income

Area	Per Capita ($)	Median Household ($)	Average Household ($)
City	30,222	53,789	74,931
MSA[1]	31,895	62,345	81,192
U.S.	31,177	57,652	81,283

Note: (1) Figures cover the Omaha-Council Bluffs, NE-IA Metropolitan Statistical Area—see Appendix B for areas included
Source: U.S. Census Bureau, 2013-2017 American Community Survey 5-Year Estimates

Household Income Distribution

Area	Percent of Households Earning							
	Under $15,000	$15,000 -$24,999	$25,000 -$34,999	$35,000 -$49,999	$50,000 -$74,999	$75,000 -$99,999	$100,000 -$149,999	$150,000 and up
City	11.9	10.0	9.7	14.8	18.5	12.1	13.1	9.9
MSA[1]	9.4	8.4	8.8	13.6	19.0	13.7	15.9	11.4
U.S.	11.6	9.8	9.5	13.0	17.7	12.3	14.1	12.1

Note: (1) Figures cover the Omaha-Council Bluffs, NE-IA Metropolitan Statistical Area—see Appendix B for areas included
Source: U.S. Census Bureau, 2013-2017 American Community Survey 5-Year Estimates

Poverty Rate

Area	All Ages	Under 18 Years Old	18 to 64 Years Old	65 Years and Over
City	15.1	21.4	13.8	8.6
MSA[1]	11.2	14.9	10.4	7.2
U.S.	14.6	20.3	13.7	9.3

Note: Figures are percentage of people whose income during the past 12 months was below the poverty level; (1) Figures cover the Omaha-Council Bluffs, NE-IA Metropolitan Statistical Area—see Appendix B for areas included
Source: U.S. Census Bureau, 2013-2017 American Community Survey 5-Year Estimates

EMPLOYMENT

Labor Force and Employment

Area	Civilian Labor Force			Workers Employed		
	Dec. 2017	Dec. 2018	% Chg.	Dec. 2017	Dec. 2018	% Chg.
City	229,225	236,434	3.1	222,137	229,428	3.3
MSA[1]	478,265	492,493	3.0	464,636	479,337	3.2
U.S.	159,880,000	162,510,000	1.6	153,602,000	156,481,000	1.9

Note: Data is not seasonally adjusted and covers workers 16 years of age and older; (1) Figures cover the Omaha-Council Bluffs, NE-IA Metropolitan Statistical Area—see Appendix B for areas included
Source: Bureau of Labor Statistics, Local Area Unemployment Statistics

Unemployment Rate

Area	2018											
	Jan.	Feb.	Mar.	Apr.	May	Jun.	Jul.	Aug.	Sep.	Oct.	Nov.	Dec.
City	3.4	3.3	3.3	3.2	3.1	3.4	3.5	3.1	2.9	3.0	2.8	3.0
MSA[1]	3.2	3.1	3.0	2.9	2.8	3.1	3.1	2.8	2.6	2.6	2.5	2.7
U.S.	4.5	4.4	4.1	3.7	3.6	4.2	4.1	3.9	3.6	3.5	3.5	3.7

Note: Data is not seasonally adjusted and covers workers 16 years of age and older; (1) Figures cover the Omaha-Council Bluffs, NE-IA Metropolitan Statistical Area—see Appendix B for areas included
Source: Bureau of Labor Statistics, Local Area Unemployment Statistics

Average Wages

Occupation	$/Hr.	Occupation	$/Hr.
Accountants and Auditors	33.70	Maids and Housekeeping Cleaners	11.60
Automotive Mechanics	21.80	Maintenance and Repair Workers	20.30
Bookkeepers	19.20	Marketing Managers	50.90
Carpenters	19.90	Nuclear Medicine Technologists	33.80
Cashiers	11.40	Nurses, Licensed Practical	21.50
Clerks, General Office	16.40	Nurses, Registered	31.60
Clerks, Receptionists/Information	14.10	Nursing Assistants	14.00
Clerks, Shipping/Receiving	16.30	Packers and Packagers, Hand	12.40
Computer Programmers	38.50	Physical Therapists	37.80
Computer Systems Analysts	37.80	Postal Service Mail Carriers	25.00
Computer User Support Specialists	24.90	Real Estate Brokers	31.10
Cooks, Restaurant	13.30	Retail Salespersons	13.20
Dentists	72.00	Sales Reps., Exc. Tech./Scientific	28.80
Electrical Engineers	42.20	Sales Reps., Tech./Scientific	33.20
Electricians	25.50	Secretaries, Exc. Legal/Med./Exec.	17.20
Financial Managers	56.00	Security Guards	17.00
First-Line Supervisors/Managers, Sales	20.20	Surgeons	137.50
Food Preparation Workers	11.80	Teacher Assistants*	12.70
General and Operations Managers	49.00	Teachers, Elementary School*	28.10
Hairdressers/Cosmetologists	14.70	Teachers, Secondary School*	27.80
Internists, General	126.00	Telemarketers	12.80
Janitors and Cleaners	13.20	Truck Drivers, Heavy/Tractor-Trailer	21.30
Landscaping/Groundskeeping Workers	15.30	Truck Drivers, Light/Delivery Svcs.	17.10
Lawyers	55.40	Waiters and Waitresses	12.70

Note: Wage data covers the Omaha-Council Bluffs, NE-IA Metropolitan Statistical Area—see Appendix B for areas included; (*) Hourly wages for elementary/secondary school teachers and teacher assistants were calculated by the editors from annual wage data based on a 40 hour work week; n/a not available.
Source: Bureau of Labor Statistics, Metro Area Occupational Employment & Wage Estimates, May 2018

Employment by Occupation

Occupation Classification	City (%)	MSA[1] (%)	U.S. (%)
Management, Business, Science, and Arts	38.6	39.4	37.4
Natural Resources, Construction, and Maintenance	7.8	8.5	8.9
Production, Transportation, and Material Moving	11.0	11.1	12.2
Sales and Office	25.5	25.0	23.5
Service	17.1	16.0	18.0

Note: Figures cover employed civilians 16 years of age and older; (1) Figures cover the Omaha-Council Bluffs, NE-IA Metropolitan Statistical Area—see Appendix B for areas included
Source: U.S. Census Bureau, 2013-2017 American Community Survey 5-Year Estimates

Employment by Industry

Sector	MSA[1]		U.S.
	Number of Employees	Percent of Total	Percent of Total
Construction, Mining, and Logging	29,000	5.7	5.3
Education and Health Services	81,300	16.0	15.9
Financial Activities	45,400	8.9	5.7
Government	67,500	13.3	15.1
Information	11,000	2.2	1.9
Leisure and Hospitality	49,300	9.7	10.7
Manufacturing	33,900	6.7	8.5
Other Services	18,000	3.5	3.9
Professional and Business Services	73,800	14.5	14.1
Retail Trade	55,700	11.0	10.8
Transportation, Warehousing, and Utilities	26,700	5.3	4.2
Wholesale Trade	16,800	3.3	3.9

Note: Figures are non-farm employment as of December 2018. Figures are not seasonally adjusted and include workers 16 years of age and older; (1) Figures cover the Omaha-Council Bluffs, NE-IA Metropolitan Statistical Area—see Appendix B for areas included
Source: Bureau of Labor Statistics, Current Employment Statistics, Employment, Hours, and Earnings

Occupations with Greatest Projected Employment Growth: 2018 – 2020

Occupation[1]	2018 Employment	2020 Projected Employment	Numeric Employment Change	Percent Employment Change
Combined Food Preparation and Serving Workers, Including Fast Food	23,980	24,800	820	3.4
Registered Nurses	25,360	26,160	800	3.2
Heavy and Tractor-Trailer Truck Drivers	29,280	29,930	650	2.2
Carpenters	12,430	12,880	450	3.6
Janitors and Cleaners, Except Maids and Housekeeping Cleaners	16,140	16,520	380	2.4
Nursing Assistants	14,510	14,870	360	2.5
General and Operations Managers	15,510	15,830	320	2.1
Waiters and Waitresses	16,030	16,350	320	2.0
Accountants and Auditors	10,320	10,600	280	2.7
Software Developers, Applications	5,120	5,400	280	5.5

Note: Projections cover Nebraska; (1) Sorted by numeric employment change
Source: www.projectionscentral.com, State Occupational Projections, 2018–2020 Short-Term Projections

Fastest Growing Occupations: 2018 – 2020

Occupation[1]	2018 Employment	2020 Projected Employment	Numeric Employment Change	Percent Employment Change
Information and Record Clerks, All Other	760	820	60	7.9
Computer Occupations, All Other	1,510	1,610	100	6.6
Home Health Aides	1,990	2,120	130	6.5
Compliance Officers	3,240	3,440	200	6.2
Physician Assistants	1,070	1,130	60	5.6
Management Analysts	3,070	3,240	170	5.5
Software Developers, Applications	5,120	5,400	280	5.5
Medical Assistants	3,280	3,460	180	5.5
Physical Therapists	1,960	2,060	100	5.1
Heating, Air Conditioning, and Refrigeration Mechanics and Installers	2,360	2,480	120	5.1

Note: Projections cover Nebraska; (1) Sorted by percent employment change and excludes occupations with numeric employment change less than 50
Source: www.projectionscentral.com, State Occupational Projections, 2018–2020 Short-Term Projections

TAXES

State Corporate Income Tax Rates

State	Tax Rate (%)	Income Brackets ($)	Num. of Brackets	Financial Institution Tax Rate (%)[a]	Federal Income Tax Ded.
Nebraska	5.58 - 7.81	100,000	2	(a)	No

Note: Tax rates as of January 1, 2019; (a) Rates listed are the corporate income tax rate applied to financial institutions or excise taxes based on income. Some states have other taxes based upon the value of deposits or shares.
Source: Federation of Tax Administrators, Range of State Corporate Income Tax Rates, January 1, 2019

State Individual Income Tax Rates

State	Tax Rate (%)	Income Brackets ($)	Personal Exemptions ($)			Standard Ded. ($)	
			Single	Married	Depend.	Single	Married
Nebraska (a)	2.46 - 6.84	3,230 - 31,160 (b)	137	274 (c)	137 (c)	6,900	13,800

Note: Tax rates as of January 1, 2019; Local- and county-level taxes are not included; n/a not applicable; Federal income tax is not deductible on state income tax returns; (a) 19 states have statutory provision for automatically adjusting to the rate of inflation the dollar values of the income tax brackets, standard deductions, and/or personal exemptions. Michigan indexes the personal exemption only. Oregon does not index the income brackets for $125,000 and over; (b) For joint returns, taxes are twice the tax on half the couple's income; (c) The personal exemption takes the form of a tax credit instead of a deduction
Source: Federation of Tax Administrators, State Individual Income Tax Rates, January 1, 2019

Various State Sales and Excise Tax Rates

State	State Sales Tax (%)	Gasoline[1] (¢/gal.)	Cigarette[2] ($/pack)	Spirits[3] ($/gal.)	Wine[4] ($/gal.)	Beer[5] ($/gal.)	Recreational Marijuana (%)
Nebraska	5.5	30.5	0.64	3.75	0.95 (l)	0.31	Not legal

Note: All tax rates as of January 1, 2019; (1) The American Petroleum Institute has developed a methodology for determining the average tax rate on a gallon of fuel. Rates may include any of the following: excise taxes, environmental fees, storage tank fees, other fees or taxes, general sales tax, and local taxes. In states where gasoline is subject to the general sales tax, or where the fuel tax is based on the average sale price, the average rate determined by API is sensitive to changes in the price of gasoline. States that fully or partially apply general sales taxes to gasoline: CA, CO, GA, IL, IN, MI, NY; (2) The federal excise tax of $1.0066 per pack and local taxes are not included; (3) Rates are those applicable to off-premise sales of 40% alcohol by volume (a.b.v.) distilled spirits in 750ml containers. Local excise taxes are excluded; (4) Rates are those applicable to off-premise sales of 11% a.b.v. non-carbonated wine in 750ml containers; (5) Rates are those applicable to off-premise sales of 4.7% a.b.v. beer in 12 ounce containers; (l) Different rates also applicable to alcohol content, place of production, size of container, place purchased (on- or off-premise or on board airlines) or type of wine (carbonated, vermouth, etc.).
Source: Tax Foundation, 2019 Facts & Figures: How Does Your State Compare?

State Business Tax Climate Index Rankings

State	Overall Rank	Corporate Tax Rank	Individual Income Tax Rank	Sales Tax Rank	Unemployment Insurance Tax Rank	Property Tax Rank
Nebraska	24	28	26	9	9	40

Note: The index is a measure of how each state's tax laws affect economic performance. The lower the rank, the more favorable a state's tax system is for business. States without a given tax are given a ranking of 1. The scores/rankings for the District of Columbia do not affect other states. The 2019 index represents the tax climate as of July 1, 2018.
Source: Tax Foundation, State Business Tax Climate Index 2019

COMMERCIAL UTILITIES

Typical Monthly Electric Bills

Area	General Service, Light ($/month)		General Service, Heavy ($/month)	
	40 kW demand 5,000 kWh	100 kW demand 10,000 kWh	500 kW demand 100,000 kWh	1,500 kW demand 500,000 kWh
City	398	1,186	8,996	38,345

Note: Figures are based on rates in effect January 1, 2018
Source: Memphis Light, Gas and Water, 2018 Utility Bill Comparisons for Selected U.S. Cities

TRANSPORTATION

Means of Transportation to Work

| Area | Car/Truck/Van | | Public Transportation | | | Bicycle | Walked | Other Means | Worked at Home |
	Drove Alone	Car-pooled	Bus	Subway	Railroad				
City	82.1	9.1	1.4	0.0	0.0	0.3	2.4	1.2	3.6
MSA[1]	84.0	8.4	0.9	0.0	0.0	0.2	1.8	1.0	3.7
U.S.	76.4	9.2	2.5	1.9	0.6	0.6	2.7	1.3	4.7

Note: Figures are percentages and cover workers 16 years of age and older; (1) Figures cover the Omaha-Council Bluffs, NE-IA Metropolitan Statistical Area—see Appendix B for areas included
Source: U.S. Census Bureau, 2013-2017 American Community Survey 5-Year Estimates

Travel Time to Work

Area	Less Than 10 Minutes	10 to 19 Minutes	20 to 29 Minutes	30 to 44 Minutes	45 to 59 Minutes	60 to 89 Minutes	90 Minutes or More
City	14.5	41.3	27.7	12.3	2.1	1.3	0.8
MSA[1]	14.3	36.7	27.0	15.9	3.5	1.6	1.0
U.S.	12.7	28.9	20.9	20.5	8.1	6.2	2.7

Note: Note: Figures are percentages and include workers 16 years old and over; (1) Figures cover the Omaha-Council Bluffs, NE-IA Metropolitan Statistical Area—see Appendix B for areas included
Source: U.S. Census Bureau, 2013-2017 American Community Survey 5-Year Estimates

Freeway Travel Time Index

Area	1985	1990	1995	2000	2005	2010	2014
Urban Area Rank[1,2]	64	63	73	72	72	57	65
Urban Area Index[1]	1.05	1.08	1.10	1.13	1.15	1.16	1.16
Average Index[3]	1.09	1.11	1.14	1.17	1.20	1.19	1.20

Note: Freeway Travel Time Index—the ratio of travel time in the peak period to the travel time at free-flow conditions. For example, a value of 1.30 indicates a 20-minute free-flow trip takes 26 minutes in the peak (20 minutes x 1.30 = 26 minutes); (1) Covers the Omaha NE-IA urban area; (2) Rank is based on 101 urban areas (#1 = highest travel time index); (3) Average of 101 urban areas
Source: Texas Transportation Institute, 2015 Urban Mobility Scorecard, August 2015

Freeway Commuter Stress Index

Area	1985	1990	1995	2000	2005	2010	2014
Urban Area Rank[1,2]	53	51	61	54	58	53	57
Urban Area Index[1]	1.09	1.12	1.14	1.18	1.19	1.20	1.20
Average Index[3]	1.13	1.16	1.19	1.22	1.25	1.24	1.25

Note: The Freeway Commuter Stress Index is the same as the Freeway Travel Time Index (see table above) except that it includes only the travel in the peak directions during the peak periods; the TTI includes travel in all directions during the peak period. Thus, the CSI is more indicative of the work trip experienced by each commuter on a daily basis; (1) Covers the Omaha NE-IA urban area; (2) Rank is based on 101 urban areas (#1 = highest travel time index); (3) Average of 101 urban areas
Source: Texas Transportation Institute, 2015 Urban Mobility Scorecard, August 2015

Public Transportation

Agency Name / Mode of Transportation	Vehicles Operated in Maximum Service[1]	Annual Unlinked Passenger Trips[2] (in thous.)	Annual Passenger Miles[3] (in thous.)
Transit Authority of Omaha (MAT)			
Bus (directly operated)	90	3,592.5	13,456.0
Demand Response (directly operated)	21	114.1	729.0

Note: (1) The number of revenue vehicles operated by the given mode and type of service to meet the annual maximum service requirement. This is the revenue vehicle count during the peak season of the year; on the week and day that maximum service is provided. Vehicles operated in maximum service (VOMS) exclude atypical days and one-time special events; (2) The number of passengers who boarded public transportation vehicles. Passengers are counted each time they board a vehicle no matter how many vehicles they use to travel from their origin to their destination. (3) The sum of the distances ridden by all passengers during the entire fiscal year.
Source: Federal Transit Administration, National Transit Database, 2017

Air Transportation

Airport Name and Code / Type of Service	Passenger Airlines[1]	Passenger Enplanements	Freight Carriers[2]	Freight (lbs)
Eppley Airfield (OMA)				
Domestic service (U.S. carriers - 2018)	29	2,446,896	11	63,015,294
International service (U.S. carriers - 2017)	3	53	1	64,116

Note: (1) Includes all U.S.-based major, minor and commuter airlines that carried at least one passenger during the year; (2) Includes all U.S.-based airlines and freight carriers that transported at least one pound of freight during the year.
Source: Bureau of Transportation Statistics, The Intermodal Transportation Database, Air Carriers: T-100 Domestic Market (U.S. Carriers), 2018; Bureau of Transportation Statistics, The Intermodal Transportation Database, Air Carriers: T-100 International Market (U.S. Carriers), 2017

Other Transportation Statistics

Major Highways:	I-80
Amtrak Service:	Yes
Major Waterways/Ports:	Port of Omaha (serves the Missouri River basin)

Source: Amtrak.com; Google Maps

BUSINESSES

Major Business Headquarters

Company Name	Industry	Rankings	
		Fortune[1]	Forbes[2]
Berkshire Hathaway	Insurance: Property and Casualty (Stock)	3	-
Kiewit Corporation	Construction	-	41
Mutual of Omaha Insurance	Insurance: Life, Health (stock)	337	-
Peter Kiewit Sons'	Engineering, Construction	339	-
Scoular	Food, Drink & Tobacco	-	94
Tenaska	Multicompany	-	26
Union Pacific	Railroads	141	-

Note: (1) Companies that produce a 10-K are ranked 1 to 500 based on 2017 revenue; (2) All private companies with at least $2 billion in annual revenue through the end of their most current fiscal year are ranked 1 to 229; companies listed are headquartered in the city; dashes indicate no ranking
Source: Fortune, "Fortune 500," June 2018; Forbes, "America's Largest Private Companies," 2018 Rankings

Fast-Growing Businesses

According to *Inc.*, Omaha is home to one of America's 500 fastest-growing private companies: **Flywheel** (#344). Criteria: must be an independent, privately-held, for-profit, U.S. corporation, proprietorship or partnership as of December 31, 2017; revenues must be at least $100,000 in 2014 and $2 million in 2017; must have four-year operating/sales history. Holding companies, regulated banks, and utilities were excluded. *Inc., "America's 500 Fastest-Growing Private Companies," 2018*

Minority Business Opportunity

Omaha is home to one company which is on the *Black Enterprise* Industrial/Service list (100 largest companies based on gross sales): **All American Meats** (#50). Criteria: operational in previous calendar year; at least 51% black-owned and manufactures/owns the product it sells or provides industrial or consumer services. Brokerages, real estate firms and firms that provide professional services are not eligible. *Black Enterprise, B.E. 100s, 2018*

Omaha is home to one company which is on the *Hispanic Business* 500 list (500 largest U.S. Hispanic-owned companies based on revenue): **Midwest Maintenance Co.** (#317). Companies included must show at least 51 percent ownership by Hispanic U.S. citizens, and must maintain headquarters in one of the 50 states or Washington, D.C. *Hispanic Business, "Hispanic Business 500," June 20, 2013*

Minority- and Women-Owned Businesses

Group	All Firms		Firms with Paid Employees			
	Firms	Sales ($000)	Firms	Sales ($000)	Employees	Payroll ($000)
AIAN[1]	254	9,161	15	3,675	32	371
Asian	1,150	224,709	230	194,717	1,913	44,163
Black	3,349	137,711	168	77,071	918	18,750
Hispanic	2,021	447,845	170	356,891	1,709	49,522
NHOPI[2]	n/a	n/a	n/a	n/a	n/a	n/a
Women	12,869	2,379,340	1,494	2,107,314	13,828	479,154
All Firms	37,664	91,113,564	10,126	89,879,746	320,226	14,447,769

Note: Figures cover firms located in the city; minority- and women-owned business are defined as firms in which the corresponding group own 51% or more of the stock or equity of the company; (1) American Indian and Alaska Native; (2) Native Hawaiian and Other Pacific Islander; n/a not available
Source: U.S. Census Bureau, 2012 Economic Census, Survey of Business Owners

HOTELS & CONVENTION CENTERS

Hotels, Motels and Vacation Rentals

Area	5 Star		4 Star		3 Star		2 Star		1 Star		Not Rated	
	Num.	Pct.[3]	Num.	Pct.[3]	Num.	Pct.[3]	Num.	Pct.[3]	Num.	Pct.[3]	Num.	Pct.[3]
City[1]	0	0.0	4	2.2	33	18.4	69	38.5	0	0.0	73	40.8
Total[2]	286	0.4	5,236	7.1	16,715	22.6	10,259	13.9	293	0.4	41,056	55.6

Note: (1) Figures cover Omaha and vicinity; (2) Figures cover all 100 cities in this book; (3) Percentage of hotels which have a given star rating; Star ratings are determined by expedia.com and offer an indication of the general quality of a particular hotel.
Source: www.expedia.com, April 3, 2019

Major Convention Centers

Name	Overall Space (sq. ft.)	Exhibit Space (sq. ft.)	Meeting Space (sq. ft.)	Meeting Rooms
Quest Center Omaha	n/a	194,000	63,000	n/a

Note: Table includes convention centers located in the Omaha-Council Bluffs, NE-IA metro area; n/a not available
Source: Original research

Living Environment

COST OF LIVING

Cost of Living Index

Composite Index	Groceries	Housing	Utilities	Trans-portation	Health Care	Misc. Goods/ Services
95.1	97.1	89.0	99.7	103.2	98.4	95.7

Note: The Cost of Living Index measures regional differences in the cost of consumer goods and services, excluding taxes and non-consumer expenditures, for professional and managerial households in the top income quintile. It is based on more than 50,000 prices covering almost 60 different items for which prices are collected three times a year by chambers of commerce, economic development organizations or university applied economic centers in each participating urban area. The numbers shown should be read as a percentage above or below the national average of 100. For example, a value of 115.4 in the groceries column indicates that grocery prices are 15.4% higher than the national average. Small differences in the index numbers should not be interpreted as significant; Figures cover the Omaha NE urban area.
Source: The Council for Community and Economic Research, ACCRA Cost of Living Index, 2018

Grocery Prices

Area[1]	T-Bone Steak ($/pound)	Frying Chicken ($/pound)	Whole Milk ($/half gal.)	Eggs ($/dozen)	Orange Juice ($/64 oz.)	Coffee ($/11.5 oz.)
City[2]	11.65	1.61	1.67	1.64	3.32	4.03
Avg.	11.35	1.42	1.94	1.81	3.52	4.35
Min.	7.45	0.92	0.80	0.75	2.72	3.06
Max.	15.05	2.76	4.18	4.00	5.36	8.20

Note: (1) Values for the local area are compared with the average, minimum and maximum values for all 291 areas in the Cost of Living Index; (2) Figures cover the Omaha NE urban area; T-Bone Steak (price per pound); Frying Chicken (price per pound, whole fryer); Whole Milk (half gallon carton); Eggs (price per dozen, Grade A, large); Orange Juice (64 oz. Tropicana or Florida Natural); Coffee (11.5 oz. can, vacuum-packed, Maxwell House, Hills Bros, or Folgers).
Source: The Council for Community and Economic Research, ACCRA Cost of Living Index, 2018

Housing and Utility Costs

Area[1]	New Home Price ($)	Apartment Rent ($/month)	All Electric ($/month)	Part Electric ($/month)	Other Energy ($/month)	Telephone ($/month)
City[2]	294,858	1,086	-	89.69	69.18	189.30
Avg.	347,000	1,087	165.93	100.16	67.73	178.70
Min.	200,468	500	93.58	25.64	26.78	163.10
Max.	1,901,222	4,888	388.65	246.86	332.81	197.70

Note: (1) Values for the local area are compared with the average, minimum and maximum values for all 291 areas in the Cost of Living Index; (2) Figures cover the Omaha NE urban area; New Home Price (2,400 sf living area, 8,000 sf lot, in urban area with full utilities); Apartment Rent (950 sf 2 bedroom/1.5 or 2 bath, unfurnished, excluding all utilities except water); All Electric (average monthly cost for an all-electric home); Part Electric (average monthly cost for a part-electric home); Other Energy (average monthly cost for natural gas, fuel oil, coal, wood, and any other forms of energy except electricity); Telephone (price includes the base monthly rate plus taxes and fees for three lines of mobile phone service).
Source: The Council for Community and Economic Research, ACCRA Cost of Living Index, 2018

Health Care, Transportation, and Other Costs

Area[1]	Doctor ($/visit)	Dentist ($/visit)	Optometrist ($/visit)	Gasoline ($/gallon)	Beauty Salon ($/visit)	Men's Shirt ($)
City[2]	138.94	74.45	99.55	2.51	37.03	27.33
Avg.	110.71	95.11	103.74	2.61	37.48	32.03
Min.	33.60	62.55	54.63	1.89	17.00	11.44
Max.	195.97	153.93	225.79	3.59	71.88	58.64

Note: (1) Values for the local area are compared with the average, minimum and maximum values for all 291 areas in the Cost of Living Index; (2) Figures cover the Omaha NE urban area; Doctor (general practitioners routine exam of an established patient); Dentist (adult teeth cleaning and periodic oral examination); Optometrist (full vision eye exam for established adult patient); Gasoline (one gallon regular unleaded, national brand, including all taxes, cash price at self-service pump if available); Beauty Salon (woman's shampoo, trim, and blow-dry); Men's Shirt (cotton/polyester dress shirt, pinpoint weave, long sleeves).
Source: The Council for Community and Economic Research, ACCRA Cost of Living Index, 2018

HOUSING

House Price Index (HPI)

Area	National Ranking[2]	Quarterly Change (%)	One-Year Change (%)	Five-Year Change (%)
MSA[1]	120	-0.24	6.33	27.96
U.S.[3]	—	1.12	5.73	32.81

Note: The HPI is a weighted repeat sales index. It measures average price changes in repeat sales or refinancings on the same properties. This information is obtained by reviewing repeat mortgage transactions on single-family properties whose mortgages have been purchased or securitized by Fannie Mae or Freddie Mac in January 1975; (1) Figures cover the Omaha-Council Bluffs, NE-IA Metropolitan Statistical Area—see Appendix B for areas included; (2) Rankings are based on annual percentage change for all metro areas containing at least 15,000 transactions over the last 10 years and ranges from 1 to 245; (3) figures based on a weighted average of Census Division estimates using a seasonally adjusted, purchase-only index; all figures are for the period ending December 31, 2018
Source: Federal Housing Finance Agency, House Price Index, February 26, 2019

Median Single-Family Home Prices

Area	2016	2017	2018[p]	Percent Change 2017 to 2018
MSA[1]	168.8	175.9	191.7	9.0
U.S. Average	235.5	248.8	261.6	5.1

Note: Figures are median sales prices of existing single-family homes in thousands of dollars; (p) preliminary; (1) Figures cover the Omaha-Council Bluffs, NE-IA Metropolitan Statistical Area—see Appendix B for areas included
Source: National Association of Realtors, Median Sales Price of Existing Single-Family Homes for Metropolitan Areas, 4th Quarter 2018

Qualifying Income Based on Median Sales Price of Existing Single-Family Homes

Area	With 5% Down ($)	With 10% Down ($)	With 20% Down ($)
MSA[1]	46,897	44,429	39,493
U.S. Average	62,954	59,640	53,013

Note: Figures are preliminary; Qualifying income is based on a mortgage rate of 4.9%. Monthly principal and interest payment is limited to 25% of income; (1) Figures cover the Omaha-Council Bluffs, NE-IA Metropolitan Statistical Area—see Appendix B for areas included
Source: National Association of Realtors, Qualifying Income Based on Median Sales Price of Existing Single-Family Homes for Metropolitan Areas, 4th Quarter 2018

Median Apartment Condo-Coop Home Prices

Area	2016	2017	2018[p]	Percent Change 2017 to 2018
MSA[1]	n/a	n/a	n/a	n/a
U.S. Average	220.7	234.3	241.0	2.9

Note: Figures are median sales prices of existing apartment condo-coop homes in thousands of dollars; (p) preliminary; n/a not available; (1) Figures cover the Omaha-Council Bluffs, NE-IA Metropolitan Statistical Area—see Appendix B for areas included
Source: National Association of Realtors, Median Sales Price of Existing Apartment Condo-Coop Homes for Metropolitan Areas, 4th Quarter 2018

Home Value Distribution

Area	Under $50,000	$50,000 -$99,999	$100,000 -$149,999	$150,000 -$199,999	$200,000 -$299,999	$300,000 -$499,999	$500,000 -$999,999	$1,000,000 or more
City	5.4	17.0	29.8	19.8	16.6	8.2	2.7	0.6
MSA[1]	4.9	14.0	27.3	20.0	19.6	10.8	2.8	0.6
U.S.	8.3	13.9	14.7	14.6	18.7	17.3	9.7	2.7

Note: Figures are percentages and cover owner-occupied housing units; (1) Figures cover the Omaha-Council Bluffs, NE-IA Metropolitan Statistical Area—see Appendix B for areas included
Source: U.S. Census Bureau, 2013-2017 American Community Survey 5-Year Estimates

Homeownership Rate

Area	2010 (%)	2011 (%)	2012 (%)	2013 (%)	2014 (%)	2015 (%)	2016 (%)	2017 (%)	2018 (%)
MSA[1]	73.2	71.6	72.4	70.6	68.7	69.6	69.2	65.5	67.8
U.S.	66.9	66.1	65.4	65.1	64.5	63.7	63.4	63.9	64.4

Note: (1) Figures cover the Omaha-Council Bluffs, NE-IA Metropolitan Statistical Area—see Appendix B for areas included
Source: U.S. Census Bureau, Housing Vacancies and Homeownership Annual Statistics: 2010-2018

Year Housing Structure Built

Area	2010 or Later	2000 -2009	1990 -1999	1980 -1989	1970 -1979	1960 -1969	1950 -1959	1940 -1949	Before 1940	Median Year
City	2.2	6.7	12.4	11.0	15.9	14.6	11.7	4.7	20.8	1969
MSA[1]	4.4	15.0	12.9	10.1	14.8	11.9	9.1	3.8	17.9	1975
U.S.	3.2	14.5	14.0	13.6	15.5	10.8	10.5	5.1	12.9	1977

Note: Figures are percentages except for Median Year; Note: (1) Figures cover the Omaha-Council Bluffs, NE-IA Metropolitan Statistical Area—see Appendix B for areas included
Source: U.S. Census Bureau, 2013-2017 American Community Survey 5-Year Estimates

Gross Monthly Rent

Area	Under $500	$500 -$999	$1,000 -$1,499	$1,500 -$1,999	$2,000 -$2,499	$2,500 -$2,999	$3,000 and up	Median ($)
City	9.3	57.0	26.9	4.7	1.3	0.4	0.3	861
MSA[1]	9.5	56.3	26.6	5.3	1.4	0.3	0.6	865
U.S.	10.5	41.1	28.7	11.7	4.5	1.8	1.7	982

Note: Figures are percentages except for Median; Gross rent is the contract rent plus the estimated average monthly cost of utilities (electricity, gas, and water and sewer) and fuels (oil, coal, kerosene, wood, etc.) if these are paid by the renter (or paid for the renter by someone else); (1) Figures cover the Omaha-Council Bluffs, NE-IA Metropolitan Statistical Area—see Appendix B for areas included
Source: U.S. Census Bureau, 2013-2017 American Community Survey 5-Year Estimates

HEALTH

Health Risk Factors

Category	MSA[1] (%)	U.S. (%)
Adults aged 18–64 who have any kind of health care coverage	86.6	87.3
Adults who reported being in good or better health	85.7	82.4
Adults who have been told they have high blood cholesterol	33.2	33.0
Adults who have been told they have high blood pressure	31.8	32.3
Adults who are current smokers	16.6	17.1
Adults who currently use E-cigarettes	4.9	4.6
Adults who currently use chewing tobacco, snuff, or snus	4.1	4.0
Adults who are heavy drinkers[2]	7.5	6.3
Adults who are binge drinkers[3]	20.6	17.4
Adults who are overweight (BMI 25.0 - 29.9)	35.2	35.3
Adults who are obese (BMI 30.0 - 99.8)	33.3	31.3
Adults who participated in any physical activities in the past month	76.9	74.4
Adults who always or nearly always wears a seat belt	91.6	94.3

Note: (1) Figures cover the Omaha-Council Bluffs, NE-IA Metropolitan Statistical Area—see Appendix B for areas included; (2) Heavy drinkers are classified as adult men having more than 14 drinks per week and adult women having more than 7 drinks per week; (3) Binge drinkers are classified as males having five or more drinks on one occasion or females having four or more drinks on one occasion
Source: Centers for Disease Control and Prevention, Behaviorial Risk Factor Surveillance System, SMART: Selected Metropolitan Area Risk Trends, 2017

Acute and Chronic Health Conditions

Category	MSA[1] (%)	U.S. (%)
Adults who have ever been told they had a heart attack	3.7	4.2
Adults who have ever been told they have angina or coronary heart disease	3.5	3.9
Adults who have ever been told they had a stroke	2.8	3.0
Adults who have ever been told they have asthma	12.0	14.2
Adults who have ever been told they have arthritis	23.1	24.9
Adults who have ever been told they have diabetes[2]	10.3	10.5
Adults who have ever been told they had skin cancer	5.5	6.2
Adults who have ever been told they had any other types of cancer	5.7	7.1
Adults who have ever been told they have COPD	5.9	6.5
Adults who have ever been told they have kidney disease	2.5	3.0
Adults who have ever been told they have a form of depression	20.6	20.5

Note: (1) Figures cover the Omaha-Council Bluffs, NE-IA Metropolitan Statistical Area—see Appendix B for areas included; (2) Figures do not include pregnancy-related, borderline, or pre-diabetes
Source: Centers for Disease Control and Prevention, Behaviorial Risk Factor Surveillance System, SMART: Selected Metropolitan Area Risk Trends, 2017

Health Screening and Vaccination Rates

Category	MSA[1] (%)	U.S. (%)
Adults aged 65+ who have had flu shot within the past year	67.3	60.7
Adults aged 65+ who have ever had a pneumonia vaccination	81.9	75.4
Adults who have ever been tested for HIV	31.2	36.1
Adults who have ever had the shingles or zoster vaccine?	35.0	28.9
Adults who have had their blood cholesterol checked within the last five years	86.0	85.9

Note: n/a not available; (1) Figures cover the Omaha-Council Bluffs, NE-IA Metropolitan Statistical Area—see Appendix B for areas included.
Source: Centers for Disease Control and Prevention, Behaviorial Risk Factor Surveillance System, SMART: Selected Metropolitan Area Risk Trends, 2017

Disability Status

Category	MSA[1] (%)	U.S. (%)
Adults who reported being deaf	5.9	6.7
Are you blind or have serious difficulty seeing, even when wearing glasses?	3.5	4.5
Are you limited in any way in any of your usual activities due of arthritis?	11.2	12.9
Do you have difficulty doing errands alone?	6.1	6.8
Do you have difficulty dressing or bathing?	3.4	3.6
Do you have serious difficulty concentrating/remembering/making decisions?	10.0	10.7
Do you have serious difficulty walking or climbing stairs?	11.4	13.6

Note: (1) Figures cover the Omaha-Council Bluffs, NE-IA Metropolitan Statistical Area—see Appendix B for areas included.
Source: Centers for Disease Control and Prevention, Behaviorial Risk Factor Surveillance System, SMART: Selected Metropolitan Area Risk Trends, 2017

Mortality Rates for the Top 10 Causes of Death in the U.S.

ICD-10[a] Sub-Chapter	ICD-10[a] Code	Age-Adjusted Mortality Rate[1] per 100,000 population	
		County[2]	U.S.
Malignant neoplasms	C00-C97	165.3	155.5
Ischaemic heart diseases	I20-I25	69.6	94.8
Other forms of heart disease	I30-I51	52.8	52.9
Chronic lower respiratory diseases	J40-J47	52.1	41.0
Cerebrovascular diseases	I60-I69	35.3	37.5
Other degenerative diseases of the nervous system	G30-G31	38.0	35.0
Other external causes of accidental injury	W00-X59	26.6	33.7
Organic, including symptomatic, mental disorders	F01-F09	39.7	31.0
Hypertensive diseases	I10-I15	20.4	21.9
Diabetes mellitus	E10-E14	26.4	21.2

Note: (a) ICD-10 = International Classification of Diseases 10th Revision; (1) Mortality rates are a three year average covering 2015-2017; (2) Figures cover Douglas County.
Source: Centers for Disease Control and Prevention, National Center for Health Statistics. Underlying Cause of Death 1999-2017 on CDC WONDER Online Database

Mortality Rates for Selected Causes of Death

ICD-10[a] Sub-Chapter	ICD-10[a] Code	Age-Adjusted Mortality Rate[1] per 100,000 population	
		County[2]	U.S.
Assault	X85-Y09	6.6	5.9
Diseases of the liver	K70-K76	13.7	14.1
Human immunodeficiency virus (HIV) disease	B20-B24	Unreliable	1.8
Influenza and pneumonia	J09-J18	16.2	14.3
Intentional self-harm	X60-X84	11.7	13.6
Malnutrition	E40-E46	3.6	1.6
Obesity and other hyperalimentation	E65-E68	2.3	2.1
Renal failure	N17-N19	11.1	13.0
Transport accidents	V01-V99	9.9	12.4
Viral hepatitis	B15-B19	1.7	1.6

Note: (a) ICD-10 = International Classification of Diseases 10th Revision; (1) Mortality rates are a three year average covering 2015-2017; (2) Figures cover Douglas County; Data are suppressed when the data meet the criteria for confidentiality constraints; Mortality rates are flagged as unreliable when the rate would be calculated with a numerator of 20 or less.
Source: Centers for Disease Control and Prevention, National Center for Health Statistics. Underlying Cause of Death 1999-2017 on CDC WONDER Online Database

Health Insurance Coverage

Area	With Health Insurance	With Private Health Insurance	With Public Health Insurance	Without Health Insurance	Population Under Age 18 Without Health Insurance
City	88.9	70.5	27.9	11.1	5.6
MSA[1]	91.5	75.9	26.3	8.5	4.2
U.S.	89.5	67.2	33.8	10.5	5.7

Note: Figures are percentages that cover the civilian noninstitutionalized population; (1) Figures cover the Omaha-Council Bluffs, NE-IA Metropolitan Statistical Area—see Appendix B for areas included
Source: U.S. Census Bureau, 2013-2017 American Community Survey 5-Year Estimates

Number of Medical Professionals

Area	MDs[3]	DOs[3,4]	Dentists	Podiatrists	Chiropractors	Optometrists
County[1] (number)	2,953	170	522	31	221	109
County[1] (rate[2])	531.2	30.6	92.9	5.5	39.4	19.4
U.S. (rate[2])	279.3	23.0	68.4	6.0	27.1	16.2

Note: Data as of 2017 unless noted; (1) Data covers Douglas County; (2) Rate per 100,000 population; (3) Data as of 2016 and includes all active, non-federal physicians; (4) Doctor of Osteopathic Medicine
Source: U.S. Department of Health and Human Services, Health Resources and Services Administration, Bureau of Health Professions, Area Resource File (ARF) 2017-2018

Best Hospitals

According to *U.S. News,* the Omaha-Council Bluffs, NE-IA metro area is home to one of the best hospitals in the U.S.: **Nebraska Medicine-Nebraska Medical Center** (1 adult specialty). The hospital listed was nationally ranked in at least one of 16 adult or 10 pediatric specialties. Only 170 hospitals nationwide were nationally ranked in one or more adult or pediatric specialty. Twenty hospitals in the U.S. made the Honor Roll. The Best Hospitals Honor Roll takes both the national rankings and the procedure and condition ratings into account. Hospitals received points if they were nationally ranked in one of the 16 adult specialties—the higher they ranked, the more points they got—and how many ratings of "high performing" they earned in the nine procedures and conditions. *U.S. News Online, "America's Best Hospitals 2018-19"*

According to *U.S. News,* the Omaha-Council Bluffs, NE-IA metro area is home to one of the best children's hospitals in the U.S.: **Children's Hospital and Medical Center** (5 pediatric specialties). The hospital listed was highly ranked in at least one of 10 pediatric specialties. Eighty-six children's hospitals in the U.S. were nationally ranked in at least one specialty. Hospitals received points for being ranked in a specialty, and the 10 hospitals with the most points across the 10 specialties make up the Honor Roll. *U.S. News Online, "America's Best Children's Hospitals 2018-19"*

EDUCATION

Public School District Statistics

District Name	Schls	Pupils	Pupil/ Teacher Ratio	Minority Pupils[1] (%)	Free Lunch Eligible[2] (%)	IEP[3] (%)
Millard Public Schools	36	23,980	16.2	21.5	15.8	11.8
Omaha Public Schools	106	52,344	14.5	72.1	59.3	19.2
Westside Community Schools	14	5,999	13.9	27.0	27.9	11.5

Note: Table includes school districts with 2,000 or more students; (1) Percentage of students that are not non-Hispanic white; (2) Percentage of students that are eligible for the free lunch program; (3) Percentage of students that have an Individualized Education Program.
Source: U.S. Department of Education, National Center for Education Statistics, Common Core of Data, Local Education Agency (School District) Universe Survey: School Year 2016-2017; U.S. Department of Education, National Center for Education Statistics, Common Core of Data, Public Elementary/Secondary School Universe Survey: School Year 2016-2017

Best High Schools

According to *U.S. News,* Omaha is home to one of the best high schools in the U.S.: **Elkhorn South High School** (#386). More than 20,000 public, magnet and charter schools were ranked based on their performance on state assessments and how well they prepare students for college. Schools with the highest unrounded College Readiness Index values were numerically ranked from 1 to 500 and were classified as gold medal winners. *U.S. News & World Report, "Best High Schools 2018"*

Highest Level of Education

Area	Less than H.S.	H.S. Diploma	Some College, No Deg.	Associate Degree	Bachelor's Degree	Master's Degree	Prof. School Degree	Doctorate Degree
City	11.6	22.5	22.9	7.4	23.0	8.4	2.8	1.5
MSA[1]	8.8	24.0	23.5	8.6	23.1	8.6	2.2	1.2
U.S.	12.7	27.3	20.8	8.3	19.1	8.4	2.0	1.4

Note: Figures cover persons age 25 and over; (1) Figures cover the Omaha-Council Bluffs, NE-IA Metropolitan Statistical Area—see Appendix B for areas included
Source: U.S. Census Bureau, 2013-2017 American Community Survey 5-Year Estimates

Educational Attainment by Race

Area	High School Graduate or Higher (%)					Bachelor's Degree or Higher (%)				
	Total	White	Black	Asian	Hisp.[2]	Total	White	Black	Asian	Hisp.[2]
City	88.4	90.3	85.6	69.9	48.7	35.6	38.3	18.6	48.0	10.2
MSA[1]	91.2	92.6	87.3	75.9	56.3	35.1	36.3	21.8	49.9	13.6
U.S.	87.3	89.3	84.9	86.5	66.7	30.9	32.2	20.6	52.7	15.2

Note: Figures shown cover persons 25 years old and over; (1) Figures cover the Omaha-Council Bluffs, NE-IA Metropolitan Statistical Area—see Appendix B for areas included; (2) People of Hispanic origin can be of any race
Source: U.S. Census Bureau, 2013-2017 American Community Survey 5-Year Estimates

School Enrollment by Grade and Control

Area	Preschool (%)		Kindergarten (%)		Grades 1 - 4 (%)		Grades 5 - 8 (%)		Grades 9 - 12 (%)	
	Public	Private	Public	Private	Public	Private	Public	Private	Public	Private
City	57.9	42.1	83.0	17.0	85.9	14.1	87.0	13.0	84.8	15.2
MSA[1]	58.4	41.6	85.7	14.3	87.6	12.4	88.3	11.7	87.7	12.3
U.S.	58.8	41.2	87.7	12.3	89.7	10.3	89.6	10.4	90.3	9.7

Note: Figures shown cover persons 3 years old and over; (1) Figures cover the Omaha-Council Bluffs, NE-IA Metropolitan Statistical Area—see Appendix B for areas included
Source: U.S. Census Bureau, 2013-2017 American Community Survey 5-Year Estimates

Average Salaries of Public School Classroom Teachers

Area	2016		2017		Change from 2016 to 2017	
	Dollars	Rank[1]	Dollars	Rank[1]	Percent	Rank[2]
Nebraska	51,386	29	52,338	30	1.9	21
U.S. Average	58,479	–	59,660	–	2.0	–

Note: (1) Rank ranges from 1 to 51 where 1 indicates highest salary; (2) Rank ranges from 1 to 51 where 1 indicates highest percent change.
Source: National Education Association, Rankings & Estimates: Rankings of the States 2017 and Estimates of School Statistics 2018

Higher Education

Four-Year Colleges			Two-Year Colleges			Medical Schools[1]	Law Schools[2]	Voc/ Tech[3]
Public	Private Non-profit	Private For-profit	Public	Private Non-profit	Private For-profit			
2	5	2	1	2	3	2	1	0

Note: Figures cover institutions located within the city limits and include main campuses only; (1) includes schools accredited by the Liaison Committee on Medical Education and the American Osteopathic Association's Commission on Osteopathic College Accreditation; (2) includes ABA-accredited schools, schools with provisional ABA accreditation, and state accredited schools; (3) includes all schools with programs that are less than 2 years.
Source: National Center for Education Statistics, Integrated Postsecondary Education System (IPEDS), 2017-18; Wikipedia, List of Medical Schools in the United States, accessed April 3, 2019; Wikipedia, List of Law Schools in the United States, accessed April 3, 2019

According to *U.S. News & World Report,* the Omaha-Council Bluffs, NE-IA metro area is home to one of the top 75 medical schools for research in the U.S.: **University of Nebraska Medical Center** (#65 tie). The rankings are based on a weighted average of 11 measures of quality: quality assessment; peer assessment score; assessment score by residency directors; research activity; total research activity; average research activity per faculty member; student selectivity; median MCAT total score; median undergraduate GPA; acceptance rate; and faculty resources. *U.S. News & World Report, "America's Best Graduate Schools, Medical, 2020"*

**PRESIDENTIAL
ELECTION**

2016 Presidential Election Results

Area	Clinton	Trump	Johnson	Stein	Other
Douglas County	47.3	45.0	4.3	1.2	2.2
U.S.	48.0	45.9	3.3	1.1	1.7

Note: Results are percentages and may not add to 100% due to rounding
Source: Dave Leip's Atlas of U.S. Presidential Elections

EMPLOYERS

Major Employers

Company Name	Industry
Alegent Health	General medical & surgical hospitals
Alegent Health-Immanuel Medical Center	Hospital, ama approved residency
City of Omaha	City & town managers' office
Creighton St. Joseph Reg Healthcare Sys	General medical & surgical hospitals
Creighton University	Colleges & universities
Drivers Management	Truck driver services
First Data Resources	Data processing service
Harveys Iowa Management Company	Casino hotels
Kiewit Offshore Services	Fabricated structural metal
Metropolitan Community College	Community college
Mutual of Omaha Insurance Company	Life insurance
Nebraska Furniture Mart	Furniture stores
Omaha Public Power District	Electric services
The Archbishop Bergan Mercy Hospital	General medical & surgical hospitals
The Nebraska Medical Center	General medical & surgical hospitals
The Pacesetter Corporation	General remodeling, single-family houses
Tyson Foods	Meats & meat products
Valmont Industries	Irrigation equipment, self-propelled

Note: Companies shown are located within the Omaha-Council Bluffs, NE-IA Metropolitan Statistical Area.
Source: Hoovers.com; Wikipedia

PUBLIC SAFETY

Crime Rate

Area	All Crimes	Violent Crimes				Property Crimes		
		Murder	Rape[3]	Robbery	Aggrav. Assault	Burglary	Larceny-Theft	Motor Vehicle Theft
City	4,527.5	6.9	91.2	139.1	410.1	464.6	2,636.7	778.8
Suburbs[1]	1,870.1	0.8	30.8	24.2	84.7	259.2	1,272.1	198.3
Metro[2]	3,149.4	3.7	59.9	79.5	241.4	358.1	1,929.0	477.8
U.S.	2,756.1	5.3	41.7	98.0	248.9	430.4	1,694.4	237.4

Note: Figures are crimes per 100,000 population; (1) All areas within the metro area that are located outside the city limits; (2) Figures cover the Omaha-Council Bluffs, NE-IA Metropolitan Statistical Area—see Appendix B for areas included; (3) The city and U.S. figures shown were reported using the revised Uniform Crime Reporting (UCR) definition of rape. The suburban and metro area figures shown are an aggregate total of the data submitted using both the revised and legacy UCR definitions.
Source: FBI Uniform Crime Reports, 2017

Hate Crimes

Area	Number of Quarters Reported	Number of Incidents per Bias Motivation					
		Race/Ethnicity/Ancestry	Religion	Sexual Orientation	Disability	Gender	Gender Identity
City	4	2	1	0	0	0	0
U.S.	4	4,131	1,564	1,130	116	46	119

Source: Federal Bureau of Investigation, Hate Crime Statistics 2017

Identity Theft Consumer Reports

Area	Reports	Reports per 100,000 Population	Rank[2]
MSA[1]	797	86	192
U.S.	444,602	135	-

Note: (1) Figures cover the Omaha-Council Bluffs, NE-IA Metropolitan Statistical Area—see Appendix B for areas included; (2) Rank ranges from 1 to 389 where 1 indicates greatest number of identity theft reports per 100,000 population
Source: Federal Trade Commission, Consumer Sentinel Network Data Book for January–December 2018

Fraud and Other Consumer Reports

Area	Reports	Reports per 100,000 Population	Rank[2]
MSA[1]	4,573	495	191
U.S.	2,552,917	776	-

Note: (1) Figures cover the Omaha-Council Bluffs, NE-IA Metropolitan Statistical Area—see Appendix B for areas included; (2) Rank ranges from 1 to 389 where 1 indicates greatest number of fraud and other consumer reports per 100,000 population
Source: Federal Trade Commission, Consumer Sentinel Network Data Book for January–December 2018

SPORTS

Professional Sports Teams

Team Name	League	Year Established
No teams are located in the metro area		

Source: Wikipedia, Major Professional Sports Teams of the United States and Canada, April 5, 2019

CLIMATE

Average and Extreme Temperatures

Temperature	Jan	Feb	Mar	Apr	May	Jun	Jul	Aug	Sep	Oct	Nov	Dec	Yr.
Extreme High (°F)	67	77	89	97	98	105	110	107	103	95	80	69	110
Average High (°F)	31	37	48	64	74	84	88	85	77	66	49	36	62
Average Temp. (°F)	22	27	38	52	63	73	77	75	66	54	39	27	51
Average Low (°F)	11	17	27	40	52	61	66	64	54	42	29	17	40
Extreme Low (°F)	-23	-21	-16	5	27	38	44	43	25	13	-9	-23	-23

Note: Figures cover the years 1948-1992
Source: National Climatic Data Center, International Station Meteorological Climate Summary, 9/96

Average Precipitation/Snowfall/Humidity

Precip./Humidity	Jan	Feb	Mar	Apr	May	Jun	Jul	Aug	Sep	Oct	Nov	Dec	Yr.
Avg. Precip. (in.)	0.8	0.9	2.0	2.8	4.3	4.0	3.7	3.8	3.4	2.1	1.5	0.9	30.1
Avg. Snowfall (in.)	7	6	7	1	Tr	0	0	0	Tr	Tr	3	6	29
Avg. Rel. Hum. 6am (%)	78	80	79	77	80	82	84	86	85	81	79	80	81
Avg. Rel. Hum. 3pm (%)	61	59	54	46	49	50	51	53	51	47	55	61	53

Note: Figures cover the years 1948-1992; Tr = Trace amounts (<0.05 in. of rain; <0.5 in. of snow)
Source: National Climatic Data Center, International Station Meteorological Climate Summary, 9/96

Weather Conditions

Temperature			Daytime Sky			Precipitation		
5°F & below	32°F & below	90°F & above	Clear	Partly cloudy	Cloudy	0.01 inch or more precip.	0.1 inch or more snow/ice	Thunder-storms
23	139	35	100	142	123	97	20	46

Note: Figures are average number of days per year and cover the years 1948-1992
Source: National Climatic Data Center, International Station Meteorological Climate Summary, 9/96

HAZARDOUS WASTE

Superfund Sites

The Omaha-Council Bluffs, NE-IA metro area is home to three sites on the EPA's Superfund National Priorities List: **Nebraska Ordnance Plant (Former)** (final); **Old Hwy 275 and N 288th Street** (final); **Omaha Lead** (final). There are a total of 1,390 Superfund sites with a status of proposed or final on the list in the U.S. *U.S. Environmental Protection Agency, National Priorities List, April 5, 2019*

**AIR & WATER
QUALITY**

Air Quality Trends: Ozone

	1990	1995	2000	2005	2010	2012	2014	2015	2016	2017
MSA[1]	0.054	0.075	0.063	0.069	0.058	0.066	0.059	0.055	0.063	0.061
U.S.	0.088	0.089	0.082	0.080	0.073	0.075	0.067	0.068	0.069	0.068

Note: (1) Data covers the Omaha-Council Bluffs, NE-IA Metropolitan Statistical Area—see Appendix B for areas included. The values shown are the composite ozone concentration averages among trend sites based on the highest fourth daily maximum 8-hour concentration in parts per million. These trends are based on sites having an adequate record of monitoring data during the trend period. Data from exceptional events are included.
Source: U.S. Environmental Protection Agency, Air Quality Monitoring Information, "Air Quality Trends by City, 1990-2017"

Air Quality Index

Area	Percent of Days when Air Quality was...[2]					AQI Statistics[2]	
	Good	Moderate	Unhealthy for Sensitive Groups	Unhealthy	Very Unhealthy	Maximum	Median
MSA[1]	54.2	45.2	0.5	0.0	0.0	114	48

Note: (1) Data covers the Omaha-Council Bluffs, NE-IA Metropolitan Statistical Area—see Appendix B for areas included; (2) Based on 365 days with AQI data in 2017. Air Quality Index (AQI) is an index for reporting daily air quality. EPA calculates the AQI for five major air pollutants regulated by the Clean Air Act: ground-level ozone, particle pollution (aka particulate matter), carbon monoxide, sulfur dioxide, and nitrogen dioxide. The AQI runs from 0 to 500. The higher the AQI value, the greater the level of air pollution and the greater the health concern. There are six AQI categories: "Good" AQI is between 0 and 50. Air quality is considered satisfactory; "Moderate" AQI is between 51 and 100. Air quality is acceptable; "Unhealthy for Sensitive Groups" When AQI values are between 101 and 150, members of sensitive groups may experience health effects; "Unhealthy" When AQI values are between 151 and 200 everyone may begin to experience health effects; "Very Unhealthy" AQI values between 201 and 300 trigger a health alert; "Hazardous" AQI values over 300 trigger warnings of emergency conditions (not shown).
Source: U.S. Environmental Protection Agency, Air Quality Index Report, 2017

Air Quality Index Pollutants

Area	Percent of Days when AQI Pollutant was...[2]					
	Carbon Monoxide	Nitrogen Dioxide	Ozone	Sulfur Dioxide	Particulate Matter 2.5	Particulate Matter 10
MSA[1]	0.0	0.0	33.7	6.0	48.5	11.8

Note: (1) Data covers the Omaha-Council Bluffs, NE-IA Metropolitan Statistical Area—see Appendix B for areas included; (2) Based on 365 days with AQI data in 2017. The Air Quality Index (AQI) is an index for reporting daily air quality. EPA calculates the AQI for five major air pollutants regulated by the Clean Air Act: ground-level ozone, particle pollution (also known as particulate matter), carbon monoxide, sulfur dioxide, and nitrogen dioxide. The AQI runs from 0 to 500. The higher the AQI value, the greater the level of air pollution and the greater the health concern.
Source: U.S. Environmental Protection Agency, Air Quality Index Report, 2017

Maximum Air Pollutant Concentrations: Particulate Matter, Ozone, CO and Lead

	Particulate Matter 10 (ug/m³)	Particulate Matter 2.5 Wtd AM (ug/m³)	Particulate Matter 2.5 24-Hr (ug/m³)	Ozone (ppm)	Carbon Monoxide (ppm)	Lead (ug/m³)
MSA[1] Level	113	9.7	21	0.064	2	0.05
NAAQS[2]	150	15	35	0.075	9	0.15
Met NAAQS[2]	Yes	Yes	Yes	Yes	Yes	Yes

Note: (1) Data covers the Omaha-Council Bluffs, NE-IA Metropolitan Statistical Area—see Appendix B for areas included; Data from exceptional events are included; (2) National Ambient Air Quality Standards; ppm = parts per million; ug/m³ = micrograms per cubic meter; n/a not available.
Concentrations: Particulate Matter 10 (coarse particulate)—highest second maximum 24-hour concentration; Particulate Matter 2.5 Wtd AM (fine particulate)—highest weighted annual mean concentration; Particulate Matter 2.5 24-Hour (fine particulate)—highest 98th percentile 24-hour concentration; Ozone—highest fourth daily maximum 8-hour concentration; Carbon Monoxide—highest second maximum non-overlapping 8-hour concentration; Lead—maximum running 3-month average
Source: U.S. Environmental Protection Agency, Air Quality Monitoring Information, "Air Quality Statistics by City, 2017"

Maximum Air Pollutant Concentrations: Nitrogen Dioxide and Sulfur Dioxide

	Nitrogen Dioxide AM (ppb)	Nitrogen Dioxide 1-Hr (ppb)	Sulfur Dioxide AM (ppb)	Sulfur Dioxide 1-Hr (ppb)	Sulfur Dioxide 24-Hr (ppb)
MSA[1] Level	n/a	n/a	n/a	55	n/a
NAAQS[2]	53	100	30	75	140
Met NAAQS[2]	n/a	n/a	n/a	Yes	n/a

Note: (1) Data covers the Omaha-Council Bluffs, NE-IA Metropolitan Statistical Area—see Appendix B for areas included; Data from exceptional events are included; (2) National Ambient Air Quality Standards; ppm = parts per million; ug/m³ = micrograms per cubic meter; n/a not available.
Concentrations: Nitrogen Dioxide AM—highest arithmetic mean concentration; Nitrogen Dioxide 1-Hr—highest 98th percentile 1-hour daily maximum concentration; Sulfur Dioxide AM—highest annual mean concentration; Sulfur Dioxide 1-Hr—highest 99th percentile 1-hour daily maximum concentration; Sulfur Dioxide 24-Hr—highest second maximum 24-hour concentration
Source: U.S. Environmental Protection Agency, Air Quality Monitoring Information, "Air Quality Statistics by City, 2017"

Drinking Water

Water System Name	Pop. Served	Primary Water Source Type	Violations[1] Health Based	Violations[1] Monitoring/ Reporting
Metropolitan Utilities District	600,000	Surface	0	0

Note: (1) Based on violation data from January 1, 2018 to December 31, 2018
Source: U.S. Environmental Protection Agency, Office of Ground Water and Drinking Water, Safe Drinking Water Information System (based on data extracted April 5, 2019)

Peoria, Illinois

Background

Like most Midwestern cities at the turn of the 19th century, Peoria started out as a military fort. Originally built in 1680 by French explorers, Fort Clark burned to the ground only to be rebuilt in 1813, following the War of 1812. By 1825, Fort Clark was renamed Peoria—the name of a local tribe of Native Americans. By 1845, Peoria was incorporated as a city.

Industry came to Peoria in 1830 when John Hamlin constructed a flour mill. Other industries soon followed including foundries, carriage factories, and furniture makers. In 1837, Andrew Eitle and Almiron S. Cole founded a distillery that made Peoria a world leader in liquor production, with the greatest liquor tax revenues of any other district in the country. In fact, at the turn of the century, the federal government received 42 percent of its revenue from liquor taxes—a major factor in the prohibition debate. And nobody produced more liquor than Peoria. According to The Peoria Historical Society, between the years of 1837 and 1919, Peoria had 24 breweries and 73 distilleries. The city took a huge financial hit during prohibition, although it became a bootleg capital with the dubious distinction of being home to mobsters such as the Shelton Brothers. This economic growth due to tax revenues would draw other industries to the area, the largest being farm equipment manufacturing, which included everything from wire fencing to wheels. Today, Keystone Steel & Wire is still the nation's leader in wire manufacturing after more than 120 years. Other top manufacturers in Peoria include Caterpillar Tractor Company and Komatsu-Dresser.

The health care industry employs over 25 percent of Peoria's work force, and reflects some of Peoria's greatest contributions to national health. During World War II, the "Peoria Plan for Human Rehabilitation" called for the creation of the Institute of Physical Medicine and Rehabilitation, one of the first such institutions designed to rehabilitate polio victims, and to help injured veterans integrate back into civilian life and work. In 1943, a moldy cantaloupe found in Peoria would produce the world's first Penicillium chrysogenum, used in producing industrial penicillin at the USDA's National Center for Agricultural Utilization Research, located in Peoria.

In the 1850s, German immigrants brought the concept of the public hall to Peoria, providing theater, music and the concomitant lectures and debates. At the time it was considered great success if an act could "play in Peoria." Perhaps Peoria's reputation for theater and debate is what brought Abraham Lincoln to the city in October of 1864, a first step in his journey to the White House and the Emancipation Proclamation in his three-hour response to the Kansas-Nebraska Act.

Peoria citizenry was largely divided during the Civil War. However, a local merchant, Moses Pettengill, opened his home to the Underground Railroad, and Peoria's Camp Lyon was a Union training ground for over 7500 Union soldiers.

Other notable events include Charles Lindbergh's connection with his first airmail route. Locals debate that, had Peoria provided backing for his transatlantic flight, Lindbergh's plane might have been called the "Spirit of Peoria." Music icon, Richard Whiting was from Peoria, and wrote an extraordinary number of hits, including "Til We Meet Again," "On the Good Ship Lollipop," "Hooray for Hollywood," and "Ain't We Got Fun." He was only 46 when he died.

The Glen Oak Park is a 100-acre park featuring a zoo, conservatory and gardens. Peoria has numerous performing arts venues that include the Peoria Symphony (the 10th oldest in the nation), Peoria Ballet Company, and Opera Illinois. The Lakeview Museum of Arts and Sciences displays folk art and African art, and also features a planetarium and children's science museum. A new museum square, The Block, houses the Peoria Riverfront Museum, a planetarium, and the Caterpillar World Visitors Center.

The best time to visit Peoria is between May and October when the weather is usually mild and dry.

Rankings

Business/Finance Rankings

- The personal finance site NerdWallet analyzed 183 American metropolitan areas with populations over 250,000 and more than 15,000 businesses to rank where entrepreneurs find the most success. Criteria included area economy, annual income, housing cost, unemployment rate, and the success rate of area businesses. Peoria ranked #10. *www.nerdwallet.com, "Best Places to Start a Business," April 27, 2015*

- The Peoria metro area appeared on the Milken Institute "2018 Best Performing Cities" list. Rank: #199 out of 200 large metro areas. Criteria: job growth; wage and salary growth; high-tech output growth. *Milken Institute, "Best-Performing Cities 2018," January 24, 2019*

- *Forbes* ranked the 200 most populous metro areas to determine the nation's "Best Places for Business and Careers." The Peoria metro area was ranked #168. Criteria: costs (business and living); job growth (past and projected); income growth; quality of life; educational attainment (college and high school); projected economic growth; cultural and recreational opportunities; net migration patterns; number of highly ranked colleges. *Forbes, "The Best Places for Business and Careers 2018: Seattle Leads the Way," October 24, 2018*

Education Rankings

- Personal finance website *WalletHub* analyzed the 150 largest U.S. metropolitan statistical areas to determine where the most educated Americans are choosing to settle. Criteria: education quality and attainment gap; education levels; percentage of workers with degrees; public school quality rankings; quality and size of each metro area's universities. Peoria was ranked #88 (#1 = most educated city). *www.WalletHub.com, "2018's Most and Least Educated Cities in America," July 24, 2018*

Health/Fitness Rankings

- The Peoria metro area ranked #139 out of 189 in The Gallup-Healthways Well-Being Index. Criteria: purpose; social well being; financial health; community and physical health. Results are based on telephone interviews with adults, aged 18 and older, living in metropolitan areas in the 50 U.S. states and the District of Columbia. *Gallup-Healthways, "State of American Well-Being, 2017 Community Well-Being Rankings" March 2018*

Real Estate Rankings

- The Peoria metro area was identified as one of the 20 worst housing markets in the U.S. in 2018. The area ranked #175 out of 178 markets. Criteria: year-over-year change of median sales price of existing single-family homes between the 4th quarter of 2017 and the 4th quarter of 2018. *National Association of Realtors®, Median Sales Price of Existing Single-Family Homes for Metropolitan Areas, 4th Quarter 2018*

- The Peoria metro area was identified as one of the 20 most affordable housing markets in the U.S. in 2018. The area ranked #6 out of 180 markets. Criteria: qualification for a mortgage loan on a typical home. *National Association of Realtors®, Qualifying Income Based on Sales Price of Existing Single-Family Homes for Metropolitan Areas, 2018*

- Peoria was ranked #27 out of 237 metro areas in terms of housing affordability in 2018 by the National Association of Home Builders (#1 = most affordable). Criteria: the share of homes sold in that area affordable to a family earning the local median income, based on standard mortgage underwriting criteria. *National Association of Home Builders®, NAHB-Wells Fargo Housing Opportunity Index, 4th Quarter 2018*

- The nation's largest metro areas were analyzed in terms of the percentage of households entering some stage of foreclosure in 2018. The Peoria metro area ranked #5 out of 10 (#1 = highest foreclosure rate). *ATTOM Data Solutions, "2018 Year-End U.S. Foreclosure Market Report™," January 17, 2019*

Safety Rankings

- The National Insurance Crime Bureau ranked 382 metro areas in the U.S. in terms of per capita rates of vehicle theft. The Peoria metro area ranked #262 (#1 = highest rate). Criteria: number of vehicle theft offenses per 100,000 inhabitants in 2017. *National Insurance Crime Bureau, "Hot Spots 2017," July 12, 2018*

Seniors/Retirement Rankings

- From its Best Cities for Successful Aging indexes, the Milken Institute generated rankings for metropolitan areas, weighing data in nine categories—health care, wellness, living arrangements, transportation and convenience, financial characteristics, education, employment, community engagement, and overall livability. The Peoria metro area was ranked #134 overall in the small metro area category. *Milken Institute, "Best Cities for Successful Aging, 2017" March 14, 2017*

Business Environment

CITY FINANCES

City Government Finances

Component	2016 ($000)	2016 ($ per capita)
Total Revenues	173,545	1,508
Total Expenditures	209,565	1,821
Debt Outstanding	194,445	1,690
Cash and Securities[1]	315,080	2,738

Note: (1) Cash and security holdings of a government at the close of its fiscal year, including those of its dependent agencies, utilities, and liquor stores.
Source: U.S. Census Bureau, State & Local Government Finances 2016

City Government Revenue by Source

Source	2016 ($000)	2016 ($ per capita)	2016 (%)
General Revenue			
From Federal Government	2,443	21	1.4
From State Government	60,940	530	35.1
From Local Governments	0	0	0.0
Taxes			
Property	31,564	274	18.2
Sales and Gross Receipts	42,362	368	24.4
Personal Income	0	0	0.0
Corporate Income	0	0	0.0
Motor Vehicle License	0	0	0.0
Other Taxes	2,685	23	1.5
Current Charges	19,129	166	11.0
Liquor Store	0	0	0.0
Utility	0	0	0.0
Employee Retirement	2,963	26	1.7

Source: U.S. Census Bureau, State & Local Government Finances 2016

City Government Expenditures by Function

Function	2016 ($000)	2016 ($ per capita)	2016 (%)
General Direct Expenditures			
Air Transportation	0	0	0.0
Corrections	0	0	0.0
Education	0	0	0.0
Employment Security Administration	0	0	0.0
Financial Administration	2,996	26	1.4
Fire Protection	31,236	271	14.9
General Public Buildings	1,554	13	0.7
Governmental Administration, Other	2,513	21	1.2
Health	0	0	0.0
Highways	35,078	304	16.7
Hospitals	0	0	0.0
Housing and Community Development	2,067	18	1.0
Interest on General Debt	7,936	69	3.8
Judicial and Legal	0	0	0.0
Libraries	7,913	68	3.8
Parking	1,554	13	0.7
Parks and Recreation	0	0	0.0
Police Protection	38,407	333	18.3
Public Welfare	0	0	0.0
Sewerage	3,605	31	1.7
Solid Waste Management	7,189	62	3.4
Veterans' Services	0	0	0.0
Liquor Store	0	0	0.0
Utility	0	0	0.0
Employee Retirement	25,872	224	12.3

Source: U.S. Census Bureau, State & Local Government Finances 2016

DEMOGRAPHICS

Population Growth

Area	1990 Census	2000 Census	2010 Census	2017* Estimate	Population Growth (%)	
					1990-2017	2010-2017
City	114,341	112,936	115,007	115,424	0.9	0.4
MSA[1]	358,552	366,899	379,186	377,258	5.2	-0.5
U.S.	248,709,873	281,421,906	308,745,538	321,004,407	29.1	4.0

Note: (1) Figures cover the Peoria, IL Metropolitan Statistical Area—see Appendix B for areas included; (*) 2013-2017 5-year estimated population
Source: U.S. Census Bureau, 1990 Census, Census 2000, Census 2010, 2013-2017 American Community Survey 5-Year Estimates

Household Size

Area	Persons in Household (%)							Average Household Size
	One	Two	Three	Four	Five	Six	Seven or More	
City	37.1	31.0	14.1	10.3	4.2	2.1	1.2	2.40
MSA[1]	30.3	35.7	14.2	11.7	4.9	2.1	1.1	2.40
U.S.	27.7	33.8	15.7	13.0	6.0	2.3	1.4	2.60

Note: (1) Figures cover the Peoria, IL Metropolitan Statistical Area—see Appendix B for areas included
Source: U.S. Census Bureau, 2013-2017 American Community Survey 5-Year Estimates

Race

Area	White Alone[2] (%)	Black Alone[2] (%)	Asian Alone[2] (%)	AIAN[3] Alone[2] (%)	NHOPI[4] Alone[2] (%)	Other Race Alone[2] (%)	Two or More Races (%)
City	60.3	26.7	5.6	0.3	0.0	2.5	4.7
MSA[1]	84.8	9.2	2.4	0.2	0.0	1.0	2.5
U.S.	73.0	12.7	5.4	0.8	0.2	4.8	3.1

Note: (1) Figures cover the Peoria, IL Metropolitan Statistical Area—see Appendix B for areas included; (2) Alone is defined as not being in combination with one or more other races; (3) American Indian and Alaska Native; (4) Native Hawaiian and Other Pacific Islander
Source: U.S. Census Bureau, 2013-2017 American Community Survey 5-Year Estimates

Hispanic or Latino Origin

Area	Total (%)	Mexican (%)	Puerto Rican (%)	Cuban (%)	Other (%)
City	6.0	4.7	0.3	0.1	0.9
MSA[1]	3.4	2.6	0.2	0.1	0.5
U.S.	17.6	11.1	1.7	0.7	4.1

Note: Persons of Hispanic or Latino origin can be of any race; (1) Figures cover the Peoria, IL Metropolitan Statistical Area—see Appendix B for areas included
Source: U.S. Census Bureau, 2013-2017 American Community Survey 5-Year Estimates

Segregation

Type	Segregation Indices[1]				Percent Change		
	1990	2000	2010	2010 Rank[2]	1990-2000	1990-2010	2000-2010
Black/White	n/a	n/a	n/a	n/a	n/a	n/a	n/a
Asian/White	n/a	n/a	n/a	n/a	n/a	n/a	n/a
Hispanic/White	n/a	n/a	n/a	n/a	n/a	n/a	n/a

Note: All figures cover the Metropolitan Statistical Area—see Appendix B for areas included; Figures are based on an analysis of 1990, 2000, and 2010 Census Decennial Census tract data by William H. Frey, Brookings Institution and the University of Michigan Social Science Data Analysis Network. In this analysis all racial groups (whites, blacks, and asians) are non-Hispanic members of those races. Hispanics are shown as a separate category; (1) Segregation Indices are Dissimilarity Indices that measure the degree to which the minority group is distributed differently than whites across census tracts. They range from 0 (complete integration) to 100 (complete segregation) where the value indicates the percentage of the minority group that needs to move to be distributed exactly like whites; (2) Ranges from 1 (most segregated) to 102 (least segregated); n/a not available.
Source: www.CensusScope.org

Ancestry

Area	German	Irish	English	American	Italian	Polish	French[2]	Scottish	Dutch
City	19.7	11.3	7.0	5.6	3.4	2.0	1.7	1.6	1.1
MSA[1]	29.3	13.0	9.1	7.0	4.2	2.1	2.3	2.0	1.6
U.S.	14.1	10.1	7.5	6.6	5.3	2.9	2.5	1.7	1.3

Note: Figures are the percentage of the total population reporting a particular ancestry. The nine most commonly reported ancestries in the U.S. are shown. Figures include multiple ancestries (e.g. if a person reported being Irish and Italian, they were included in both columns); (1) Figures cover the Peoria, IL Metropolitan Statistical Area—see Appendix B for areas included; (2) Excludes Basque
Source: U.S. Census Bureau, 2013-2017 American Community Survey 5-Year Estimates

Foreign-Born Population

Area	Percent of Population Born in								
	Any Foreign Country	Asia	Mexico	Europe	Carribean	Central America[2]	South America	Africa	Canada
City	8.3	4.6	1.7	0.8	0.1	0.1	0.4	0.3	0.1
MSA[1]	3.8	1.9	0.7	0.6	0.1	0.1	0.2	0.1	0.1
U.S.	13.4	4.1	3.6	1.5	1.3	1.0	0.9	0.6	0.3

Note: (1) Figures cover the Peoria, IL Metropolitan Statistical Area—see Appendix B for areas included; (2) Excludes Mexico.
Source: U.S. Census Bureau, 2013-2017 American Community Survey 5-Year Estimates

Marital Status

Area	Never Married	Now Married[2]	Separated	Widowed	Divorced
City	40.2	40.3	1.3	6.2	12.0
MSA[1]	29.6	51.3	1.1	6.7	11.3
U.S.	33.1	48.2	2.0	5.8	10.9

Note: Figures are percentages and cover the population 15 years of age and older; (1) Figures cover the Peoria, IL Metropolitan Statistical Area—see Appendix B for areas included; (2) Excludes separated
Source: U.S. Census Bureau, 2013-2017 American Community Survey 5-Year Estimates

Disability by Age

Area	All Ages	Under 18 Years Old	18 to 64 Years Old	65 Years and Over
City	12.4	3.3	11.1	34.3
MSA[1]	11.5	3.3	9.1	32.7
U.S.	12.6	4.2	10.3	35.5

Note: Figures show percent of the civilian noninstitutionalized population that reported having a disability. Disability status is determined from six types of difficulty: vision, hearing, cognitive, ambulatory, self-care, and independent living. For children under 5 years old, hearing and vision difficulty are used to determine disability status. For children between the ages of 5 and 14, disability status is determined from hearing, vision, cognitive, ambulatory, and self-care difficulties. For people aged 15 years and older, they are considered to have a disability if they have difficulty with any one of the six difficulty types; Note: (1) Figures cover the Peoria, IL Metropolitan Statistical Area—see Appendix B for areas included
Source: U.S. Census Bureau, 2013-2017 American Community Survey 5-Year Estimates

Age

Area	Percent of Population									Median Age
	Under Age 5	Age 5–19	Age 20–34	Age 35–44	Age 45–54	Age 55–64	Age 65–74	Age 75–84	Age 85+	
City	7.6	20.4	22.9	11.8	11.4	11.6	7.9	4.1	2.3	34.3
MSA[1]	6.5	19.5	19.0	12.3	12.9	13.4	9.1	5.0	2.5	39.0
U.S.	6.2	19.5	20.7	12.7	13.4	12.7	8.6	4.4	1.9	37.8

Note: (1) Figures cover the Peoria, IL Metropolitan Statistical Area—see Appendix B for areas included
Source: U.S. Census Bureau, 2013-2017 American Community Survey 5-Year Estimates

Gender

Area	Males	Females	Males per 100 Females
City	54,890	60,534	90.7
MSA[1]	184,718	192,540	95.9
U.S.	158,018,753	162,985,654	97.0

Note: (1) Figures cover the Peoria, IL Metropolitan Statistical Area—see Appendix B for areas included
Source: U.S. Census Bureau, 2013-2017 American Community Survey 5-Year Estimates

Religious Groups by Family

Area	Catholic	Baptist	Non-Den.	Methodist[2]	Lutheran	LDS[3]	Pente-costal	Presby-terian[4]	Muslim[5]	Judaism
MSA[1]	11.5	5.5	5.3	5.0	6.1	0.5	1.5	2.8	5.2	0.1
U.S.	19.1	9.3	4.0	4.0	2.3	2.0	1.9	1.6	0.8	0.7

Note: Figures are the number of adherents as a percentage of the total population; (1) Figures cover the Peoria, IL Metropolitan Statistical Area—see Appendix B for areas included; (2) Methodist/Pietist; (3) Latter Day Saints; (4) Reformed; (5) Figures are estimates
Source: Association of Statisticians of American Religious Bodies, 2010 U.S. Religion Census: Religious Congregations & Membership Study

Religious Groups by Tradition

Area	Catholic	Evangelical Protestant	Mainline Protestant	Other Tradition	Black Protestant	Orthodox
MSA[1]	11.5	18.9	11.1	6.2	0.9	0.1
U.S.	19.1	16.2	7.3	4.3	1.6	0.3

Note: Figures are the number of adherents as a percentage of the total population; (1) Figures cover the Peoria, IL Metropolitan Statistical Area—see Appendix B for areas included
Source: Association of Statisticians of American Religious Bodies, 2010 U.S. Religion Census: Religious Congregations & Membership Study

ECONOMY

Gross Metropolitan Product

Area	2016	2017	2018	2019	Rank[2]
MSA[1]	20.1	20.5	21.3	22.3	124

Note: Figures are in billions of dollars; (1) Figures cover the Peoria, IL Metropolitan Statistical Area—see Appendix B for areas included; (2) Rank is based on 2017 data and ranges from 1 to 381
Source: U.S. Conference of Mayors, U.S. Metro Economies: Economic Growth & Full Employment, June 2018

Economic Growth

Area	2017-2018 (%)	2019-2020 (%)	2021-2022 (%)
MSA[1]	0.8	1.8	1.0

Note: Figures are real gross metropolitan product (GMP) growth rates and represent average annual percent change; (1) Figures cover the Peoria, IL Metropolitan Statistical Area—see Appendix B for areas included
Source: U.S. Conference of Mayors, U.S. Metro Economies: Economic Growth & Full Employment, June 2018

Metropolitan Area Exports

Area	2012	2013	2014	2015	2016	2017	Rank[2]
MSA[1]	17,838.0	12,184.5	11,234.8	9,826.9	7,260.1	9,403.6	33

Note: Figures are in millions of dollars; (1) Figures cover the Peoria, IL Metropolitan Statistical Area—see Appendix B for areas included; (2) Rank is based on 2017 data and ranges from 1 to 387
Source: U.S. Department of Commerce, International Trade Administration, Office of Trade and Economic Analysis, Industry and Analysis, Exports by Metropolitan Area, extracted March 25, 2019

Building Permits

Area	Single-Family			Multi-Family			Total		
	2016	2017	Pct. Chg.	2016	2017	Pct. Chg.	2016	2017	Pct. Chg.
City	39	32	-17.9	0	0	0.0	39	32	-17.9
MSA[1]	326	247	-24.2	24	10	-58.3	350	257	-26.6
U.S.	750,800	820,000	9.2	455,800	462,000	1.4	1,206,600	1,282,000	6.2

Note: (1) Figures cover the Peoria, IL Metropolitan Statistical Area—see Appendix B for areas included; Figures represent new, privately-owned housing units authorized (unadjusted data); All permit data are based on estimates with imputation
Source: U.S. Census Bureau, Manufacturing, Mining, and Construction Statistics, Building Permits, 2016, 2017

Bankruptcy Filings

Area	Business Filings			Nonbusiness Filings		
	2017	2018	% Chg.	2017	2018	% Chg.
Peoria County	11	14	27.3	533	555	4.1
U.S.	23,157	22,232	-4.0	765,863	751,186	-1.9

Note: Business filings include Chapter 7, Chapter 11, Chapter 12, and Chapter 13; Nonbusiness filings include Chapter 7, Chapter 11, and Chapter 13
Source: Administrative Office of the U.S. Courts, Business and Nonbusiness Bankruptcy, County Cases Commenced by Chapter of the Bankruptcy Code, During the 12-Month Period Ending December 31, 2017 and Business and Nonbusiness Bankruptcy, County Cases Commenced by Chapter of the Bankruptcy Code, During the 12-Month Period Ending December 31, 2018

Housing Vacancy Rates

Area	Gross Vacancy Rate[2] (%)			Year-Round Vacancy Rate[3] (%)			Rental Vacancy Rate[4] (%)			Homeowner Vacancy Rate[5] (%)		
	2016	2017	2018	2016	2017	2018	2016	2017	2018	2016	2017	2018
MSA[1]	n/a	n/a	n/a	n/a	n/a	n/a	n/a	n/a	n/a	n/a	n/a	n/a
U.S.	12.8	12.7	12.3	9.9	9.9	9.7	6.9	7.2	6.9	1.7	1.6	1.5

Note: (1) Figures cover the Peoria, IL Metropolitan Statistical Area—see Appendix B for areas included; (2) The percentage of the total housing inventory that is vacant; (3) The percentage of the housing inventory (excluding seasonal units) that is year-round vacant; (4) The percentage of rental inventory that is vacant for rent; (5) The percentage of homeowner inventory that is vacant for sale; n/a not available
Source: U.S. Census Bureau, Housing Vacancies and Homeownership Annual Statistics: 2016, 2017, 2018

INCOME

Income

Area	Per Capita ($)	Median Household ($)	Average Household ($)
City	28,507	47,697	68,524
MSA[1]	30,990	57,301	75,829
U.S.	31,177	57,652	81,283

Note: (1) Figures cover the Peoria, IL Metropolitan Statistical Area—see Appendix B for areas included
Source: U.S. Census Bureau, 2013-2017 American Community Survey 5-Year Estimates

Household Income Distribution

Area	Percent of Households Earning							
	Under $15,000	$15,000 -$24,999	$25,000 -$34,999	$35,000 -$49,999	$50,000 -$74,999	$75,000 -$99,999	$100,000 -$149,999	$150,000 and up
City	16.6	12.2	10.6	12.4	16.7	11.4	11.5	8.6
MSA[1]	9.9	9.4	10.0	14.0	19.2	13.8	14.3	9.3
U.S.	11.6	9.8	9.5	13.0	17.7	12.3	14.1	12.1

Note: (1) Figures cover the Peoria, IL Metropolitan Statistical Area—see Appendix B for areas included
Source: U.S. Census Bureau, 2013-2017 American Community Survey 5-Year Estimates

Poverty Rate

Area	All Ages	Under 18 Years Old	18 to 64 Years Old	65 Years and Over
City	20.9	28.0	20.4	10.2
MSA[1]	12.0	16.6	11.8	6.1
U.S.	14.6	20.3	13.7	9.3

Note: Figures are percentage of people whose income during the past 12 months was below the poverty level; (1) Figures cover the Peoria, IL Metropolitan Statistical Area—see Appendix B for areas included
Source: U.S. Census Bureau, 2013-2017 American Community Survey 5-Year Estimates

EMPLOYMENT

Labor Force and Employment

Area	Civilian Labor Force			Workers Employed		
	Dec. 2017	Dec. 2018	% Chg.	Dec. 2017	Dec. 2018	% Chg.
City	51,182	51,811	1.2	48,530	48,559	0.1
MSA[1]	174,815	176,606	1.0	166,398	166,484	0.1
U.S.	159,880,000	162,510,000	1.6	153,602,000	156,481,000	1.9

Note: Data is not seasonally adjusted and covers workers 16 years of age and older; (1) Figures cover the Peoria, IL Metropolitan Statistical Area—see Appendix B for areas included
Source: Bureau of Labor Statistics, Local Area Unemployment Statistics

Unemployment Rate

Area	2018											
	Jan.	Feb.	Mar.	Apr.	May	Jun.	Jul.	Aug.	Sep.	Oct.	Nov.	Dec.
City	5.5	5.0	5.3	4.6	4.9	5.7	5.6	5.6	5.0	5.6	5.6	6.3
MSA[1]	5.4	5.0	5.0	4.1	4.2	5.0	4.9	4.9	4.4	4.8	4.8	5.7
U.S.	4.5	4.4	4.1	3.7	3.6	4.2	4.1	3.9	3.6	3.5	3.5	3.7

Note: Data is not seasonally adjusted and covers workers 16 years of age and older; (1) Figures cover the Peoria, IL Metropolitan Statistical Area—see Appendix B for areas included
Source: Bureau of Labor Statistics, Local Area Unemployment Statistics

Average Wages

Occupation	$/Hr.	Occupation	$/Hr.
Accountants and Auditors	37.30	Maids and Housekeeping Cleaners	11.80
Automotive Mechanics	21.40	Maintenance and Repair Workers	20.00
Bookkeepers	18.30	Marketing Managers	66.10
Carpenters	27.20	Nuclear Medicine Technologists	n/a
Cashiers	10.70	Nurses, Licensed Practical	21.10
Clerks, General Office	16.60	Nurses, Registered	32.10
Clerks, Receptionists/Information	12.60	Nursing Assistants	12.80
Clerks, Shipping/Receiving	16.20	Packers and Packagers, Hand	12.50
Computer Programmers	36.00	Physical Therapists	40.60
Computer Systems Analysts	42.90	Postal Service Mail Carriers	25.00
Computer User Support Specialists	23.60	Real Estate Brokers	n/a
Cooks, Restaurant	12.40	Retail Salespersons	14.80
Dentists	80.40	Sales Reps., Exc. Tech./Scientific	28.40
Electrical Engineers	n/a	Sales Reps., Tech./Scientific	42.60
Electricians	30.20	Secretaries, Exc. Legal/Med./Exec.	16.60
Financial Managers	61.90	Security Guards	16.20
First-Line Supervisors/Managers, Sales	19.40	Surgeons	n/a
Food Preparation Workers	11.00	Teacher Assistants*	11.90
General and Operations Managers	54.70	Teachers, Elementary School*	23.00
Hairdressers/Cosmetologists	14.50	Teachers, Secondary School*	27.30
Internists, General	n/a	Telemarketers	16.70
Janitors and Cleaners	14.00	Truck Drivers, Heavy/Tractor-Trailer	19.90
Landscaping/Groundskeeping Workers	12.20	Truck Drivers, Light/Delivery Svcs.	18.10
Lawyers	59.90	Waiters and Waitresses	10.00

Note: Wage data covers the Peoria, IL Metropolitan Statistical Area—see Appendix B for areas included; (*) Hourly wages for elementary/secondary school teachers and teacher assistants were calculated by the editors from annual wage data based on a 40 hour work week; n/a not available.
Source: Bureau of Labor Statistics, Metro Area Occupational Employment & Wage Estimates, May 2018

Employment by Occupation

Occupation Classification	City (%)	MSA[1] (%)	U.S. (%)
Management, Business, Science, and Arts	41.8	36.8	37.4
Natural Resources, Construction, and Maintenance	4.7	8.2	8.9
Production, Transportation, and Material Moving	10.0	13.0	12.2
Sales and Office	24.1	24.3	23.5
Service	19.4	17.7	18.0

Note: Figures cover employed civilians 16 years of age and older; (1) Figures cover the Peoria, IL Metropolitan Statistical Area—see Appendix B for areas included
Source: U.S. Census Bureau, 2013-2017 American Community Survey 5-Year Estimates

Employment by Industry

Sector	MSA[1]		U.S.
	Number of Employees	Percent of Total	Percent of Total
Construction, Mining, and Logging	7,200	4.1	5.3
Education and Health Services	31,900	18.1	15.9
Financial Activities	7,200	4.1	5.7
Government	21,400	12.1	15.1
Information	2,000	1.1	1.9
Leisure and Hospitality	17,900	10.1	10.7
Manufacturing	23,700	13.4	8.5
Other Services	7,700	4.4	3.9
Professional and Business Services	24,900	14.1	14.1
Retail Trade	18,100	10.3	10.8
Transportation, Warehousing, and Utilities	7,100	4.0	4.2
Wholesale Trade	7,300	4.1	3.9

Note: Figures are non-farm employment as of December 2018. Figures are not seasonally adjusted and include workers 16 years of age and older; (1) Figures cover the Peoria, IL Metropolitan Statistical Area—see Appendix B for areas included
Source: Bureau of Labor Statistics, Current Employment Statistics, Employment, Hours, and Earnings

Occupations with Greatest Projected Employment Growth: 2018 – 2020

Occupation[1]	2018 Employment	2020 Projected Employment	Numeric Employment Change	Percent Employment Change
Combined Food Preparation and Serving Workers, Including Fast Food	139,870	145,560	5,690	4.1
Laborers and Freight, Stock, and Material Movers, Hand	153,200	158,690	5,490	3.6
Registered Nurses	126,530	130,420	3,890	3.1
General and Operations Managers	122,420	125,420	3,000	2.5
Waiters and Waitresses	91,610	93,810	2,200	2.4
Heavy and Tractor-Trailer Truck Drivers	71,040	73,220	2,180	3.1
Personal Care Aides	50,390	52,470	2,080	4.1
Light Truck or Delivery Services Drivers	50,560	52,420	1,860	3.7
Software Developers, Applications	27,370	29,190	1,820	6.6
Management Analysts	41,280	42,960	1,680	4.1

Note: Projections cover Illinois; (1) Sorted by numeric employment change
Source: www.projectionscentral.com, State Occupational Projections, 2018–2020 Short-Term Projections

Fastest Growing Occupations: 2018 – 2020

Occupation[1]	2018 Employment	2020 Projected Employment	Numeric Employment Change	Percent Employment Change
Statisticians	1,340	1,440	100	7.5
Nurse Practitioners	7,960	8,530	570	7.2
Computer Numerically Controlled Machine Tool Programmers, Metal and Plastic	1,320	1,410	90	6.8
Software Developers, Applications	27,370	29,190	1,820	6.6
Operations Research Analysts	6,770	7,200	430	6.4
Computer and Information Research Scientists	970	1,030	60	6.2
Physician Assistants	3,700	3,930	230	6.2
Locker Room, Coatroom, and Dressing Room Attendants	850	900	50	5.9
Occupational Therapy Aides	1,780	1,880	100	5.6
Market Research Analysts and Marketing Specialists	23,210	24,420	1,210	5.2

Note: Projections cover Illinois; (1) Sorted by percent employment change and excludes occupations with numeric employment change less than 50
Source: www.projectionscentral.com, State Occupational Projections, 2018–2020 Short-Term Projections

TAXES

State Corporate Income Tax Rates

State	Tax Rate (%)	Income Brackets ($)	Num. of Brackets	Financial Institution Tax Rate (%)[a]	Federal Income Tax Ded.
Illinois	9.5 (h)	Flat rate	1	9.5 (h)	No

Note: Tax rates as of January 1, 2019; (a) Rates listed are the corporate income tax rate applied to financial institutions or excise taxes based on income. Some states have other taxes based upon the value of deposits or shares; (h) The Illinois rate of 9.5% is the sum of a corporate income tax rate of 7.0% plus a replacement tax of 2.5%.
Source: Federation of Tax Administrators, Range of State Corporate Income Tax Rates, January 1, 2019

State Individual Income Tax Rates

State	Tax Rate (%)	Income Brackets ($)	Personal Exemptions ($)			Standard Ded. ($)	
			Single	Married	Depend.	Single	Married
Illinois (a)	4.95	Flat rate	2,225	4,450	2,225	–	–

Note: Tax rates as of January 1, 2019; Local- and county-level taxes are not included; n/a not applicable; Federal income tax is not deductible on state income tax returns; (a) 19 states have statutory provision for automatically adjusting to the rate of inflation the dollar values of the income tax brackets, standard deductions, and/or personal exemptions. Michigan indexes the personal exemption only. Oregon does not index the income brackets for $125,000 and over.
Source: Federation of Tax Administrators, State Individual Income Tax Rates, January 1, 2019

Various State Sales and Excise Tax Rates

State	State Sales Tax (%)	Gasoline[1] (¢/gal.)	Cigarette[2] ($/pack)	Spirits[3] ($/gal.)	Wine[4] ($/gal.)	Beer[5] ($/gal.)	Recreational Marijuana (%)
Illinois	6.25	31.98	1.98	8.55 (f)	1.39 (l)	0.23	Not legal

Note: All tax rates as of January 1, 2019; (1) The American Petroleum Institute has developed a methodology for determining the average tax rate on a gallon of fuel. Rates may include any of the following: excise taxes, environmental fees, storage tank fees, other fees or taxes, general sales tax, and local taxes. In states where gasoline is subject to the general sales tax, or where the fuel tax is based on the average sale price, the average rate determined by API is sensitive to changes in the price of gasoline. States that fully or partially apply general sales taxes to gasoline: CA, CO, GA, IL, IN, MI, NY; (2) The federal excise tax of $1.0066 per pack and local taxes are not included; (3) Rates are those applicable to off-premise sales of 40% alcohol by volume (a.b.v.) distilled spirits in 750ml containers. Local excise taxes are excluded; (4) Rates are those applicable to off-premise sales of 11% a.b.v. non-carbonated wine in 750ml containers; (5) Rates are those applicable to off-premise sales of 4.7% a.b.v. beer in 12 ounce containers; (f) Different rates also applicable according to alcohol content, place of production, size of container, or place purchased (on- or off-premise or onboard airlines); (l) Different rates also applicable to alcohol content, place of production, size of container, place purchased (on- or off-premise or on board airlines) or type of wine (carbonated, vermouth, etc.).
Source: Tax Foundation, 2019 Facts & Figures: How Does Your State Compare?

State Business Tax Climate Index Rankings

State	Overall Rank	Corporate Tax Rank	Individual Income Tax Rank	Sales Tax Rank	Unemployment Insurance Tax Rank	Property Tax Rank
Illinois	36	39	13	36	42	45

Note: The index is a measure of how each state's tax laws affect economic performance. The lower the rank, the more favorable a state's tax system is for business. States without a given tax are given a ranking of 1. The scores/rankings for the District of Columbia do not affect other states. The 2019 index represents the tax climate as of July 1, 2018.
Source: Tax Foundation, State Business Tax Climate Index 2019

COMMERCIAL UTILITIES

Typical Monthly Electric Bills

Area	Commercial Service ($/month)		Industrial Service ($/month)	
	1,500 kWh	40 kW demand 14,000 kWh	1,000 kW demand 200,000 kWh	50,000 kW demand 32,500,000 kWh
City	156	1,371	n/a	n/a
Average[1]	203	1,619	25,886	2,540,077

Note: Figures are based on annualized rates; (1) Average based on 187 utilities surveyed; n/a not available
Source: Edison Electric Institute, Typical Bills and Average Rates Report, Summer 2018

TRANSPORTATION

Means of Transportation to Work

Area	Car/Truck/Van		Public Transportation			Bicycle	Walked	Other Means	Worked at Home
	Drove Alone	Car-pooled	Bus	Subway	Railroad				
City	79.7	8.9	3.8	0.0	0.0	0.5	3.2	1.1	2.8
MSA[1]	84.7	7.6	1.4	0.0	0.0	0.3	2.1	0.9	3.0
U.S.	76.4	9.2	2.5	1.9	0.6	0.6	2.7	1.3	4.7

Note: Figures are percentages and cover workers 16 years of age and older; (1) Figures cover the Peoria, IL Metropolitan Statistical Area—see Appendix B for areas included
Source: U.S. Census Bureau, 2013-2017 American Community Survey 5-Year Estimates

Travel Time to Work

Area	Less Than 10 Minutes	10 to 19 Minutes	20 to 29 Minutes	30 to 44 Minutes	45 to 59 Minutes	60 to 89 Minutes	90 Minutes or More
City	17.6	48.3	20.8	8.1	2.2	2.1	1.0
MSA[1]	17.1	35.8	24.8	15.4	3.6	1.8	1.5
U.S.	12.7	28.9	20.9	20.5	8.1	6.2	2.7

Note: Note: Figures are percentages and include workers 16 years old and over; (1) Figures cover the Peoria, IL Metropolitan Statistical Area—see Appendix B for areas included
Source: U.S. Census Bureau, 2013-2017 American Community Survey 5-Year Estimates

Freeway Travel Time Index

Area	1985	1990	1995	2000	2005	2010	2014
Urban Area Rank[1,2]	n/a	n/a	n/a	n/a	n/a	n/a	n/a
Urban Area Index[1]	n/a	n/a	n/a	n/a	n/a	n/a	n/a
Average Index[3]	1.09	1.11	1.14	1.17	1.20	1.19	1.20

Note: Freeway Travel Time Index—the ratio of travel time in the peak period to the travel time at free-flow conditions. For example, a value of 1.30 indicates a 20-minute free-flow trip takes 26 minutes in the peak (20 minutes x 1.30 = 26 minutes); (1) Data for the Peoria, IL urban area was not available; (2) Rank is based on 101 urban areas (#1 = highest travel time index); (3) Average of 101 urban areas
Source: Texas Transportation Institute, 2015 Urban Mobility Scorecard, August 2015

Freeway Commuter Stress Index

Area	1985	1990	1995	2000	2005	2010	2014
Urban Area Rank[1,2]	n/a	n/a	n/a	n/a	n/a	n/a	n/a
Urban Area Index[1]	n/a	n/a	n/a	n/a	n/a	n/a	n/a
Average Index[3]	1.13	1.16	1.19	1.22	1.25	1.24	1.25

Note: The Freeway Commuter Stress Index is the same as the Freeway Travel Time Index (see table above) except that it includes only the travel in the peak directions during the peak periods; the TTI includes travel in all directions during the peak period. Thus, the CSI is more indicative of the work trip experienced by each commuter on a daily basis; (1) Data for the Peoria, IL urban area was not available; (2) Rank is based on 101 urban areas (#1 = highest travel time index); (3) Average of 101 urban areas
Source: Texas Transportation Institute, 2015 Urban Mobility Scorecard, August 2015

Public Transportation

Agency Name / Mode of Transportation	Vehicles Operated in Maximum Service[1]	Annual Unlinked Passenger Trips[2] (in thous.)	Annual Passenger Miles[3] (in thous.)
Greater Peoria Mass Transit District			
Bus (directly operated)	45	2,711.7	16,541.5
Demand Response (purchased transportation)	37	138.6	889.8

Note: (1) The number of revenue vehicles operated by the given mode and type of service to meet the annual maximum service requirement. This is the revenue vehicle count during the peak season of the year; on the week and day that maximum service is provided. Vehicles operated in maximum service (VOMS) exclude atypical days and one-time special events; (2) The number of passengers who boarded public transportation vehicles. Passengers are counted each time they board a vehicle no matter how many vehicles they use to travel from their origin to their destination. (3) The sum of the distances ridden by all passengers during the entire fiscal year.
Source: Federal Transit Administration, National Transit Database, 2017

Air Transportation

Airport Name and Code / Type of Service	Passenger Airlines[1]	Passenger Enplanements	Freight Carriers[2]	Freight (lbs)
General Wayne A. Downing Peoria International Airport (PIA)				
Domestic service (U.S. carriers - 2018)	11	328,504	4	16,639,117
International service (U.S. carriers - 2017)	0	0	0	0

Note: (1) Includes all U.S.-based major, minor and commuter airlines that carried at least one passenger during the year; (2) Includes all U.S.-based airlines and freight carriers that transported at least one pound of freight during the year.
Source: Bureau of Transportation Statistics, The Intermodal Transportation Database, Air Carriers: T-100 Domestic Market (U.S. Carriers), 2018; Bureau of Transportation Statistics, The Intermodal Transportation Database, Air Carriers: T-100 International Market (U.S. Carriers), 2017

Other Transportation Statistics

Major Highways:	I-74; I-474
Amtrak Service:	Yes
Major Waterways/Ports:	Illinois River

Source: Amtrak.com; Google Maps

BUSINESSES

Major Business Headquarters

Company Name	Industry	Rankings	
		Fortune[1]	Forbes[2]
Caterpillar	Construction and Farm Machinery	65	-

Note: (1) Companies that produce a 10-K are ranked 1 to 500 based on 2017 revenue; (2) All private companies with at least $2 billion in annual revenue through the end of their most current fiscal year are ranked 1 to 229; companies listed are headquartered in the city; dashes indicate no ranking
Source: Fortune, "Fortune 500," June 2018; Forbes, "America's Largest Private Companies," 2018 Rankings

Minority- and Women-Owned Businesses

Group	All Firms		Firms with Paid Employees			
	Firms	Sales ($000)	Firms	Sales ($000)	Employees	Payroll ($000)
AIAN[1]	75	(s)	22	(s)	100 - 249	(s)
Asian	292	165,321	134	161,366	1,421	37,138
Black	1,295	44,510	37	21,608	228	5,459
Hispanic	186	(s)	44	(s)	250 - 499	(s)
NHOPI[2]	n/a	n/a	n/a	n/a	n/a	n/a
Women	2,741	527,889	393	461,825	3,548	105,789
All Firms	8,053	17,242,461	2,812	17,046,888	93,399	5,965,582

Note: Figures cover firms located in the city; minority- and women-owned business are defined as firms in which the corresponding group own 51% or more of the stock or equity of the company; (1) American Indian and Alaska Native; (2) Native Hawaiian and Other Pacific Islander; (s) estimates are suppressed when publication standards are not met; n/a not available
Source: U.S. Census Bureau, 2012 Economic Census, Survey of Business Owners

HOTELS & CONVENTION CENTERS

Hotels, Motels and Vacation Rentals

Area	5 Star		4 Star		3 Star		2 Star		1 Star		Not Rated	
	Num.	Pct.[3]	Num.	Pct.[3]	Num.	Pct.[3]	Num.	Pct.[3]	Num.	Pct.[3]	Num.	Pct.[3]
City[1]	0	0.0	1	1.5	16	23.9	38	56.7	1	1.5	11	16.4
Total[2]	286	0.4	5,236	7.1	16,715	22.6	10,259	13.9	293	0.4	41,056	55.6

Note: (1) Figures cover Peoria and vicinity; (2) Figures cover all 100 cities in this book; (3) Percentage of hotels which have a given star rating; Star ratings are determined by expedia.com and offer an indication of the general quality of a particular hotel.
Source: www.expedia.com, April 3, 2019

Major Convention Centers

Name	Overall Space (sq. ft.)	Exhibit Space (sq. ft.)	Meeting Space (sq. ft.)	Meeting Rooms
Peoria Civic Center	900,000	110,000	n/a	16

Note: Table includes convention centers located in the Peoria, IL metro area; n/a not available
Source: Original research

Living Environment

COST OF LIVING

Cost of Living Index

Composite Index	Groceries	Housing	Utilities	Trans-portation	Health Care	Misc. Goods/Services
95.2	94.9	82.8	92.7	100.0	98.0	104.8

Note: The Cost of Living Index measures regional differences in the cost of consumer goods and services, excluding taxes and non-consumer expenditures, for professional and managerial households in the top income quintile. It is based on more than 50,000 prices covering almost 60 different items for which prices are collected three times a year by chambers of commerce, economic development organizations or university applied economic centers in each participating urban area. The numbers shown should be read as a percentage above or below the national average of 100. For example, a value of 115.4 in the groceries column indicates that grocery prices are 15.4% higher than the national average. Small differences in the index numbers should not be interpreted as significant; Figures cover the Peoria IL urban area.
Source: The Council for Community and Economic Research, ACCRA Cost of Living Index, 2018

Grocery Prices

Area[1]	T-Bone Steak ($/pound)	Frying Chicken ($/pound)	Whole Milk ($/half gal.)	Eggs ($/dozen)	Orange Juice ($/64 oz.)	Coffee ($/11.5 oz.)
City[2]	12.16	1.78	0.80	1.53	3.86	4.17
Avg.	11.35	1.42	1.94	1.81	3.52	4.35
Min.	7.45	0.92	0.80	0.75	2.72	3.06
Max.	15.05	2.76	4.18	4.00	5.36	8.20

*Note: (1) Values for the local area are compared with the average, minimum and maximum values for all 291 areas in the Cost of Living Index; (2) Figures cover the Peoria IL urban area; **T-Bone Steak** (price per pound); **Frying Chicken** (price per pound, whole fryer); **Whole Milk** (half gallon carton); **Eggs** (price per dozen, Grade A, large); **Orange Juice** (64 oz. Tropicana or Florida Natural); **Coffee** (11.5 oz. can, vacuum-packed, Maxwell House, Hills Bros, or Folgers).*
Source: The Council for Community and Economic Research, ACCRA Cost of Living Index, 2018

Housing and Utility Costs

Area[1]	New Home Price ($)	Apartment Rent ($/month)	All Electric ($/month)	Part Electric ($/month)	Other Energy ($/month)	Telephone ($/month)
City[2]	308,294	769	-	75.05	65.31	185.70
Avg.	347,000	1,087	165.93	100.16	67.73	178.70
Min.	200,468	500	93.58	25.64	26.78	163.10
Max.	1,901,222	4,888	388.65	246.86	332.81	197.70

*Note: (1) Values for the local area are compared with the average, minimum and maximum values for all 291 areas in the Cost of Living Index; (2) Figures cover the Peoria IL urban area; **New Home Price** (2,400 sf living area, 8,000 sf lot, in urban area with full utilities); **Apartment Rent** (950 sf 2 bedroom/1.5 or 2 bath, unfurnished, excluding all utilities except water); **All Electric** (average monthly cost for an all-electric home); **Part Electric** (average monthly cost for a part-electric home); **Other Energy** (average monthly cost for natural gas, fuel oil, coal, wood, and any other forms of energy except electricity); **Telephone** (price includes the base monthly rate plus taxes and fees for three lines of mobile phone service).*
Source: The Council for Community and Economic Research, ACCRA Cost of Living Index, 2018

Health Care, Transportation, and Other Costs

Area[1]	Doctor ($/visit)	Dentist ($/visit)	Optometrist ($/visit)	Gasoline ($/gallon)	Beauty Salon ($/visit)	Men's Shirt ($)
City[2]	103.07	93.47	119.16	2.67	28.80	34.58
Avg.	110.71	95.11	103.74	2.61	37.48	32.03
Min.	33.60	62.55	54.63	1.89	17.00	11.44
Max.	195.97	153.93	225.79	3.59	71.88	58.64

*Note: (1) Values for the local area are compared with the average, minimum and maximum values for all 291 areas in the Cost of Living Index; (2) Figures cover the Peoria IL urban area; **Doctor** (general practitioners routine exam of an established patient); **Dentist** (adult teeth cleaning and periodic oral examination); **Optometrist** (full vision eye exam for established adult patient); **Gasoline** (one gallon regular unleaded, national brand, including all taxes, cash price at self-service pump if available); **Beauty Salon** (woman's shampoo, trim, and blow-dry); **Men's Shirt** (cotton/polyester dress shirt, pinpoint weave, long sleeves).*
Source: The Council for Community and Economic Research, ACCRA Cost of Living Index, 2018

HOUSING

House Price Index (HPI)

Area	National Ranking[2]	Quarterly Change (%)	One-Year Change (%)	Five-Year Change (%)
MSA[1]	221	1.82	2.14	3.12
U.S.[3]	—	1.12	5.73	32.81

Note: The HPI is a weighted repeat sales index. It measures average price changes in repeat sales or refinancings on the same properties. This information is obtained by reviewing repeat mortgage transactions on single-family properties whose mortgages have been purchased or securitized by Fannie Mae or Freddie Mac in January 1975; (1) Figures cover the Peoria, IL Metropolitan Statistical Area—see Appendix B for areas included; (2) Rankings are based on annual percentage change for all metro areas containing at least 15,000 transactions over the last 10 years and ranges from 1 to 245; (3) figures based on a weighted average of Census Division estimates using a seasonally adjusted, purchase-only index; all figures are for the period ending December 31, 2018
Source: Federal Housing Finance Agency, House Price Index, February 26, 2019

Median Single-Family Home Prices

Area	2016	2017	2018[p]	Percent Change 2017 to 2018
MSA[1]	118.0	122.6	124.3	1.4
U.S. Average	235.5	248.8	261.6	5.1

Note: Figures are median sales prices of existing single-family homes in thousands of dollars; (p) preliminary; (1) Figures cover the Peoria, IL Metropolitan Statistical Area—see Appendix B for areas included
Source: National Association of Realtors, Median Sales Price of Existing Single-Family Homes for Metropolitan Areas, 4th Quarter 2018

Qualifying Income Based on Median Sales Price of Existing Single-Family Homes

Area	With 5% Down ($)	With 10% Down ($)	With 20% Down ($)
MSA[1]	28,300	26,810	23,831
U.S. Average	62,954	59,640	53,013

Note: Figures are preliminary; Qualifying income is based on a mortgage rate of 4.9%. Monthly principal and interest payment is limited to 25% of income; (1) Figures cover the Peoria, IL Metropolitan Statistical Area—see Appendix B for areas included
Source: National Association of Realtors, Qualifying Income Based on Median Sales Price of Existing Single-Family Homes for Metropolitan Areas, 4th Quarter 2018

Median Apartment Condo-Coop Home Prices

Area	2016	2017	2018[p]	Percent Change 2017 to 2018
MSA[1]	n/a	n/a	n/a	n/a
U.S. Average	220.7	234.3	241.0	2.9

Note: Figures are median sales prices of existing apartment condo-coop homes in thousands of dollars; (p) preliminary; n/a not available; (1) Figures cover the Peoria, IL Metropolitan Statistical Area—see Appendix B for areas included
Source: National Association of Realtors, Median Sales Price of Existing Apartment Condo-Coop Homes for Metropolitan Areas, 4th Quarter 2018

Home Value Distribution

Area	Under $50,000	$50,000 -$99,999	$100,000 -$149,999	$150,000 -$199,999	$200,000 -$299,999	$300,000 -$499,999	$500,000 -$999,999	$1,000,000 or more
City	13.1	26.5	21.1	15.8	14.5	6.4	2.3	0.3
MSA[1]	8.1	25.5	24.0	18.0	15.4	7.0	1.7	0.4
U.S.	8.3	13.9	14.7	14.6	18.7	17.3	9.7	2.7

Note: Figures are percentages and cover owner-occupied housing units; (1) Figures cover the Peoria, IL Metropolitan Statistical Area—see Appendix B for areas included
Source: U.S. Census Bureau, 2013-2017 American Community Survey 5-Year Estimates

Homeownership Rate

Area	2010 (%)	2011 (%)	2012 (%)	2013 (%)	2014 (%)	2015 (%)	2016 (%)	2017 (%)	2018 (%)
MSA[1]	n/a	n/a	n/a	n/a	n/a	n/a	n/a	n/a	n/a
U.S.	66.9	66.1	65.4	65.1	64.5	63.7	63.4	63.9	64.4

Note: (1) Figures cover the Peoria, IL Metropolitan Statistical Area—see Appendix B for areas included; n/a not available
Source: U.S. Census Bureau, Housing Vacancies and Homeownership Annual Statistics: 2010-2018

Year Housing Structure Built

Area	2010 or Later	2000 -2009	1990 -1999	1980 -1989	1970 -1979	1960 -1969	1950 -1959	1940 -1949	Before 1940	Median Year
City	2.1	8.7	7.3	6.9	14.6	13.7	15.8	8.3	22.6	1962
MSA[1]	2.2	9.0	8.7	6.2	17.3	13.3	15.3	8.2	19.9	1965
U.S.	3.2	14.5	14.0	13.6	15.5	10.8	10.5	5.1	12.9	1977

Note: Figures are percentages except for Median Year; Note: (1) Figures cover the Peoria, IL Metropolitan Statistical Area—see Appendix B for areas included
Source: U.S. Census Bureau, 2013-2017 American Community Survey 5-Year Estimates

Gross Monthly Rent

Area	Under $500	$500 -$999	$1,000 -$1,499	$1,500 -$1,999	$2,000 -$2,499	$2,500 -$2,999	$3,000 and up	Median ($)
City	17.7	60.6	15.4	4.1	1.3	0.5	0.4	756
MSA[1]	16.7	63.2	14.8	2.9	1.2	0.5	0.7	739
U.S.	10.5	41.1	28.7	11.7	4.5	1.8	1.7	982

Note: Figures are percentages except for Median; Gross rent is the contract rent plus the estimated average monthly cost of utilities (electricity, gas, and water and sewer) and fuels (oil, coal, kerosene, wood, etc.) if these are paid by the renter (or paid for the renter by someone else); (1) Figures cover the Peoria, IL Metropolitan Statistical Area—see Appendix B for areas included
Source: U.S. Census Bureau, 2013-2017 American Community Survey 5-Year Estimates

HEALTH

Health Risk Factors

Category	MSA[1] (%)	U.S. (%)
Adults aged 18–64 who have any kind of health care coverage	n/a	87.3
Adults who reported being in good or better health	n/a	82.4
Adults who have been told they have high blood cholesterol	n/a	33.0
Adults who have been told they have high blood pressure	n/a	32.3
Adults who are current smokers	n/a	17.1
Adults who currently use E-cigarettes	n/a	4.6
Adults who currently use chewing tobacco, snuff, or snus	n/a	4.0
Adults who are heavy drinkers[2]	n/a	6.3
Adults who are binge drinkers[3]	n/a	17.4
Adults who are overweight (BMI 25.0 - 29.9)	n/a	35.3
Adults who are obese (BMI 30.0 - 99.8)	n/a	31.3
Adults who participated in any physical activities in the past month	n/a	74.4
Adults who always or nearly always wears a seat belt	n/a	94.3

Note: n/a not available; (1) Figures cover the Peoria, IL Metropolitan Statistical Area—see Appendix B for areas included; (2) Heavy drinkers are classified as adult men having more than 14 drinks per week and adult women having more than 7 drinks per week; (3) Binge drinkers are classified as males having five or more drinks on one occasion or females having four or more drinks on one occasion
Source: Centers for Disease Control and Prevention, Behaviorial Risk Factor Surveillance System, SMART: Selected Metropolitan Area Risk Trends, 2017

Acute and Chronic Health Conditions

Category	MSA[1] (%)	U.S. (%)
Adults who have ever been told they had a heart attack	n/a	4.2
Adults who have ever been told they have angina or coronary heart disease	n/a	3.9
Adults who have ever been told they had a stroke	n/a	3.0
Adults who have ever been told they have asthma	n/a	14.2
Adults who have ever been told they have arthritis	n/a	24.9
Adults who have ever been told they have diabetes[2]	n/a	10.5
Adults who have ever been told they had skin cancer	n/a	6.2
Adults who have ever been told they had any other types of cancer	n/a	7.1
Adults who have ever been told they have COPD	n/a	6.5
Adults who have ever been told they have kidney disease	n/a	3.0
Adults who have ever been told they have a form of depression	n/a	20.5

Note: n/a not available; (1) Figures cover the Peoria, IL Metropolitan Statistical Area—see Appendix B for areas included; (2) Figures do not include pregnancy-related, borderline, or pre-diabetes
Source: Centers for Disease Control and Prevention, Behaviorial Risk Factor Surveillance System, SMART: Selected Metropolitan Area Risk Trends, 2017

Health Screening and Vaccination Rates

Category	MSA[1] (%)	U.S. (%)
Adults aged 65+ who have had flu shot within the past year	n/a	60.7
Adults aged 65+ who have ever had a pneumonia vaccination	n/a	75.4
Adults who have ever been tested for HIV	n/a	36.1
Adults who have ever had the shingles or zoster vaccine?	n/a	28.9
Adults who have had their blood cholesterol checked within the last five years	n/a	85.9

Note: n/a not available; (1) Figures cover the Peoria, IL Metropolitan Statistical Area—see Appendix B for areas included.
Source: Centers for Disease Control and Prevention, Behaviorial Risk Factor Surveillance System, SMART: Selected Metropolitan Area Risk Trends, 2017

Disability Status

Category	MSA[1] (%)	U.S. (%)
Adults who reported being deaf	n/a	6.7
Are you blind or have serious difficulty seeing, even when wearing glasses?	n/a	4.5
Are you limited in any way in any of your usual activities due of arthritis?	n/a	12.9
Do you have difficulty doing errands alone?	n/a	6.8
Do you have difficulty dressing or bathing?	n/a	3.6
Do you have serious difficulty concentrating/remembering/making decisions?	n/a	10.7
Do you have serious difficulty walking or climbing stairs?	n/a	13.6

Note: n/a not available; (1) Figures cover the Peoria, IL Metropolitan Statistical Area—see Appendix B for areas included.
Source: Centers for Disease Control and Prevention, Behaviorial Risk Factor Surveillance System, SMART: Selected Metropolitan Area Risk Trends, 2017

Mortality Rates for the Top 10 Causes of Death in the U.S.

ICD-10[a] Sub-Chapter	ICD-10[a] Code	Age-Adjusted Mortality Rate[1] per 100,000 population	
		County[2]	U.S.
Malignant neoplasms	C00-C97	174.2	155.5
Ischaemic heart diseases	I20-I25	93.4	94.8
Other forms of heart disease	I30-I51	55.6	52.9
Chronic lower respiratory diseases	J40-J47	49.5	41.0
Cerebrovascular diseases	I60-I69	44.6	37.5
Other degenerative diseases of the nervous system	G30-G31	24.2	35.0
Other external causes of accidental injury	W00-X59	38.7	33.7
Organic, including symptomatic, mental disorders	F01-F09	49.4	31.0
Hypertensive diseases	I10-I15	17.3	21.9
Diabetes mellitus	E10-E14	19.4	21.2

Note: (a) ICD-10 = International Classification of Diseases 10th Revision; (1) Mortality rates are a three year average covering 2015-2017; (2) Figures cover Peoria County.
Source: Centers for Disease Control and Prevention, National Center for Health Statistics. Underlying Cause of Death 1999-2017 on CDC WONDER Online Database

Mortality Rates for Selected Causes of Death

ICD-10[a] Sub-Chapter	ICD-10[a] Code	Age-Adjusted Mortality Rate[1] per 100,000 population	
		County[2]	U.S.
Assault	X85-Y09	7.9	5.9
Diseases of the liver	K70-K76	11.4	14.1
Human immunodeficiency virus (HIV) disease	B20-B24	Suppressed	1.8
Influenza and pneumonia	J09-J18	24.7	14.3
Intentional self-harm	X60-X84	14.8	13.6
Malnutrition	E40-E46	Suppressed	1.6
Obesity and other hyperalimentation	E65-E68	Suppressed	2.1
Renal failure	N17-N19	13.5	13.0
Transport accidents	V01-V99	9.3	12.4
Viral hepatitis	B15-B19	Suppressed	1.6

Note: (a) ICD-10 = International Classification of Diseases 10th Revision; (1) Mortality rates are a three year average covering 2015-2017; (2) Figures cover Peoria County; Data are suppressed when the data meet the criteria for confidentiality constraints; Mortality rates are flagged as unreliable when the rate would be calculated with a numerator of 20 or less.
Source: Centers for Disease Control and Prevention, National Center for Health Statistics. Underlying Cause of Death 1999-2017 on CDC WONDER Online Database

Health Insurance Coverage

Area	With Health Insurance	With Private Health Insurance	With Public Health Insurance	Without Health Insurance	Population Under Age 18 Without Health Insurance
City	92.8	63.4	41.1	7.2	2.1
MSA[1]	94.5	73.9	35.3	5.5	2.7
U.S.	89.5	67.2	33.8	10.5	5.7

Note: Figures are percentages that cover the civilian noninstitutionalized population; (1) Figures cover the Peoria, IL Metropolitan Statistical Area—see Appendix B for areas included
Source: U.S. Census Bureau, 2013-2017 American Community Survey 5-Year Estimates

Number of Medical Professionals

Area	MDs[3]	DOs[3,4]	Dentists	Podiatrists	Chiropractors	Optometrists
County[1] (number)	1,009	88	150	15	90	36
County[1] (rate[2])	544.5	47.5	82.0	8.2	49.2	19.7
U.S. (rate[2])	279.3	23.0	68.4	6.0	27.1	16.2

Note: Data as of 2017 unless noted; (1) Data covers Peoria County; (2) Rate per 100,000 population; (3) Data as of 2016 and includes all active, non-federal physicians; (4) Doctor of Osteopathic Medicine
Source: U.S. Department of Health and Human Services, Health Resources and Services Administration, Bureau of Health Professions, Area Resource File (ARF) 2017-2018

Best Hospitals

According to *U.S. News,* the Peoria, IL metro area is home to one of the best hospitals in the U.S.: **OSF HealthCare St. Francis Medical Center** (1 pediatric specialty). The hospital listed was nationally ranked in at least one of 16 adult or 10 pediatric specialties. Only 170 hospitals nationwide were nationally ranked in one or more adult or pediatric specialty. Twenty hospitals in the U.S. made the Honor Roll. The Best Hospitals Honor Roll takes both the national rankings and the procedure and condition ratings into account. Hospitals received points if they were nationally ranked in one of the 16 adult specialties—the higher they ranked, the more points they got—and how many ratings of "high performing" they earned in the nine procedures and conditions. *U.S. News Online, "America's Best Hospitals 2018-19"*

According to *U.S. News,* the Peoria, IL metro area is home to one of the best children's hospitals in the U.S.: **OSF HealthCare Children's Hospital of Illinois** (1 pediatric specialty). The hospital listed was highly ranked in at least one of 10 pediatric specialties. Eighty-six children's hospitals in the U.S. were nationally ranked in at least one specialty. Hospitals received points for being ranked in a specialty, and the 10 hospitals with the most points across the 10 specialties make up the Honor Roll. *U.S. News Online, "America's Best Children's Hospitals 2018-19"*

EDUCATION

Public School District Statistics

District Name	Schls	Pupils	Pupil/ Teacher Ratio	Minority Pupils[1] (%)	Free Lunch Eligible[2] (%)	IEP[3] (%)
Dunlap Cusd 323	8	4,597	17.9	34.7	8.7	12.3
Peoria SD 150	29	13,329	13.6	78.5	72.1	18.4

Note: Table includes school districts with 2,000 or more students; (1) Percentage of students that are not non-Hispanic white; (2) Percentage of students that are eligible for the free lunch program; (3) Percentage of students that have an Individualized Education Program.
Source: U.S. Department of Education, National Center for Education Statistics, Common Core of Data, Local Education Agency (School District) Universe Survey: School Year 2016-2017; U.S. Department of Education, National Center for Education Statistics, Common Core of Data, Public Elementary/Secondary School Universe Survey: School Year 2016-2017

Highest Level of Education

Area	Less than H.S.	H.S. Diploma	Some College, No Deg.	Associate Degree	Bachelor's Degree	Master's Degree	Prof. School Degree	Doctorate Degree
City	11.8	23.9	20.6	9.2	20.9	9.8	2.7	1.1
MSA[1]	8.4	30.2	23.0	10.3	18.7	7.2	1.4	0.8
U.S.	12.7	27.3	20.8	8.3	19.1	8.4	2.0	1.4

Note: Figures cover persons age 25 and over; (1) Figures cover the Peoria, IL Metropolitan Statistical Area—see Appendix B for areas included
Source: U.S. Census Bureau, 2013-2017 American Community Survey 5-Year Estimates

Educational Attainment by Race

Area	High School Graduate or Higher (%)					Bachelor's Degree or Higher (%)				
	Total	White	Black	Asian	Hisp.[2]	Total	White	Black	Asian	Hisp.[2]
City	88.2	92.0	78.9	95.4	62.2	34.4	38.9	12.8	74.9	21.7
MSA[1]	91.6	92.9	79.6	94.2	71.7	28.2	28.4	12.9	71.7	20.7
U.S.	87.3	89.3	84.9	86.5	66.7	30.9	32.2	20.6	52.7	15.2

Note: Figures shown cover persons 25 years old and over; (1) Figures cover the Peoria, IL Metropolitan Statistical Area—see Appendix B for areas included; (2) People of Hispanic origin can be of any race
Source: U.S. Census Bureau, 2013-2017 American Community Survey 5-Year Estimates

School Enrollment by Grade and Control

Area	Preschool (%)		Kindergarten (%)		Grades 1 - 4 (%)		Grades 5 - 8 (%)		Grades 9 - 12 (%)	
	Public	Private	Public	Private	Public	Private	Public	Private	Public	Private
City	70.0	30.0	71.8	28.2	83.2	16.8	80.0	20.0	84.1	15.9
MSA[1]	61.3	38.7	82.3	17.7	87.9	12.1	86.6	13.4	88.9	11.1
U.S.	58.8	41.2	87.7	12.3	89.7	10.3	89.6	10.4	90.3	9.7

Note: Figures shown cover persons 3 years old and over; (1) Figures cover the Peoria, IL Metropolitan Statistical Area—see Appendix B for areas included
Source: U.S. Census Bureau, 2013-2017 American Community Survey 5-Year Estimates

Average Salaries of Public School Classroom Teachers

Area	2016		2017		Change from 2016 to 2017	
	Dollars	Rank[1]	Dollars	Rank[1]	Percent	Rank[2]
Illinois	63,475	11	64,933	11	2.3	19
U.S. Average	58,479	–	59,660	–	2.0	–

Note: (1) Rank ranges from 1 to 51 where 1 indicates highest salary; (2) Rank ranges from 1 to 51 where 1 indicates highest percent change.
Source: National Education Association, Rankings & Estimates: Rankings of the States 2017 and Estimates of School Statistics 2018

Higher Education

Four-Year Colleges			Two-Year Colleges			Medical Schools[1]	Law Schools[2]	Voc/ Tech[3]
Public	Private Non-profit	Private For-profit	Public	Private Non-profit	Private For-profit			
0	3	1	0	0	0	0	0	1

Note: Figures cover institutions located within the city limits and include main campuses only; (1) includes schools accredited by the Liaison Committee on Medical Education and the American Osteopathic Association's Commission on Osteopathic College Accreditation; (2) includes ABA-accredited schools, schools with provisional ABA accreditation, and state accredited schools; (3) includes all schools with programs that are less than 2 years.
Source: National Center for Education Statistics, Integrated Postsecondary Education System (IPEDS), 2017-18; Wikipedia, List of Medical Schools in the United States, accessed April 3, 2019; Wikipedia, List of Law Schools in the United States, accessed April 3, 2019

PRESIDENTIAL ELECTION

2016 Presidential Election Results

Area	Clinton	Trump	Johnson	Stein	Other
Peoria County	48.1	45.0	4.7	1.4	0.8
U.S.	48.0	45.9	3.3	1.1	1.7

Note: Results are percentages and may not add to 100% due to rounding
Source: Dave Leip's Atlas of U.S. Presidential Elections

EMPLOYERS

Major Employers

Company Name	Industry
Advanced Technology Services	Technical job training
Ameren Illinois	Utility
Bradley University	Education
CEFCU	Banking and financial services
City of Peoria	Government
G&D Integrated	Transportation, distribution
Health Professionals Ltd.	Healthcare
HGS USA (Formerly Affina)	Customer support
Hostess Brands	Food manufacturing
Illinois Central College	Education
Keystone Steel and Wire Co	Steel & wire production
Kmart Corp.	Retail
Komatsu Mining Systems	Coal business
Kroger Company	Supermarkets
Matcor Metal Fabrication	Manufacturer
Methodist Medical Center	Healthcare
OSF Saint Francis Medical Center	Healthcare
Par-A-Dice Hotel/Casino	Gambling
Pekin Hospital	Education
Pekin Insurance & Farmers Auto Insurance	Insurance
Peoria County	Government
Peoria Journal Star	Newspapers, publishing & printing
Peoria School District	Education
Proctor Hospital	Healthcare
Wal-Mart Stores	Retail

Note: Companies shown are located within the Peoria, IL Metropolitan Statistical Area.
Source: Hoovers.com; Wikipedia

PUBLIC SAFETY

Crime Rate

Area	All Crimes	Violent Crimes				Property Crimes		
		Murder	Rape[3]	Robbery	Aggrav. Assault	Burglary	Larceny -Theft	Motor Vehicle Theft
City	4,973.0	10.5	56.9	246.2	445.9	980.2	2,940.7	292.6
Suburbs[1]	1,755.3	0.8	52.7	19.9	163.8	350.2	1,090.4	77.5
Metro[2]	2,732.2	3.7	54.0	88.6	249.5	541.5	1,652.1	142.8
U.S.	2,756.1	5.3	41.7	98.0	248.9	430.4	1,694.4	237.4

Note: Figures are crimes per 100,000 population; (1) All areas within the metro area that are located outside the city limits; (2) Figures cover the Peoria, IL Metropolitan Statistical Area—see Appendix B for areas included; (3) The city and U.S. figures shown were reported using the revised Uniform Crime Reporting (UCR) definition of rape. The suburban and metro area figures shown are an aggregate total of the data submitted using both the revised and legacy UCR definitions.
Source: FBI Uniform Crime Reports, 2017

Hate Crimes

Area	Number of Quarters Reported	Number of Incidents per Bias Motivation					
		Race/Ethnicity/ Ancestry	Religion	Sexual Orientation	Disability	Gender	Gender Identity
City	4	0	0	1	0	0	0
U.S.	4	4,131	1,564	1,130	116	46	119

Source: Federal Bureau of Investigation, Hate Crime Statistics 2017

Identity Theft Consumer Reports

Area	Reports	Reports per 100,000 Population	Rank[2]
MSA[1]	273	73	256
U.S.	444,602	135	-

*Note: (1) Figures cover the Peoria, IL Metropolitan Statistical Area—see Appendix B for areas included;
(2) Rank ranges from 1 to 389 where 1 indicates greatest number of identity theft reports per 100,000
population*
Source: Federal Trade Commission, Consumer Sentinel Network Data Book for January–December 2018

Fraud and Other Consumer Reports

Area	Reports	Reports per 100,000 Population	Rank[2]
MSA[1]	1,507	401	318
U.S.	2,552,917	776	-

*Note: (1) Figures cover the Peoria, IL Metropolitan Statistical Area—see Appendix B for areas included;
(2) Rank ranges from 1 to 389 where 1 indicates greatest number of fraud and other consumer reports per
100,000 population*
Source: Federal Trade Commission, Consumer Sentinel Network Data Book for January–December 2018

SPORTS

Professional Sports Teams

Team Name	League	Year Established
No teams are located in the metro area		

Source: Wikipedia, Major Professional Sports Teams of the United States and Canada, April 5, 2019

CLIMATE

Average and Extreme Temperatures

Temperature	Jan	Feb	Mar	Apr	May	Jun	Jul	Aug	Sep	Oct	Nov	Dec	Yr.
Extreme High (°F)	71	74	87	92	104	105	113	106	102	92	81	71	113
Average High (°F)	32	36	48	62	73	82	86	84	77	65	49	36	61
Average Temp. (°F)	24	28	39	51	62	72	76	74	66	55	41	29	51
Average Low (°F)	16	19	29	41	51	60	65	63	55	43	32	21	41
Extreme Low (°F)	-25	-26	-11	14	25	39	46	41	24	13	-2	-24	-26

Note: Figures cover the years 1948-1995
Source: National Climatic Data Center, International Station Meteorological Climate Summary, 9/96

Average Precipitation/Snowfall/Humidity

Precip./Humidity	Jan	Feb	Mar	Apr	May	Jun	Jul	Aug	Sep	Oct	Nov	Dec	Yr.
Avg. Precip. (in.)	1.8	1.6	2.8	3.8	4.0	3.9	3.8	3.1	3.6	2.6	2.5	2.0	35.4
Avg. Snowfall (in.)	6	5	4	1	Tr	0	0	0	Tr	Tr	2	5	23
Avg. Rel. Hum. 6am (%)	80	81	81	78	80	82	86	89	87	84	83	83	83
Avg. Rel. Hum. 3pm (%)	67	64	58	52	52	52	55	56	52	52	61	69	57

Note: Figures cover the years 1948-1995; Tr = Trace amounts (<0.05 in. of rain; <0.5 in. of snow)
Source: National Climatic Data Center, International Station Meteorological Climate Summary, 9/96

Weather Conditions

Temperature			Daytime Sky			Precipitation		
5°F & below	32°F & below	90°F & above	Clear	Partly cloudy	Cloudy	0.01 inch or more precip.	0.1 inch or more snow/ice	Thunder-storms
16	127	27	89	127	149	115	22	49

Note: Figures are average number of days per year and cover the years 1948-1995
Source: National Climatic Data Center, International Station Meteorological Climate Summary, 9/96

HAZARDOUS WASTE

Superfund Sites

The Peoria, IL metro area has no sites on the EPA's Superfund Final National Priorities List. There
are a total of 1,390 Superfund sites with a status of proposed or final on the list in the U.S. *U.S.
Environmental Protection Agency, National Priorities List, April 5, 2019*

**AIR & WATER
QUALITY**

Air Quality Trends: Ozone

	1990	1995	2000	2005	2010	2012	2014	2015	2016	2017
MSA[1]	0.071	0.082	0.072	0.075	0.064	0.072	0.064	0.062	0.067	0.066
U.S.	0.088	0.089	0.082	0.080	0.073	0.075	0.067	0.068	0.069	0.068

Note: (1) Data covers the Peoria, IL Metropolitan Statistical Area—see Appendix B for areas included. The values shown are the composite ozone concentration averages among trend sites based on the highest fourth daily maximum 8-hour concentration in parts per million. These trends are based on sites having an adequate record of monitoring data during the trend period. Data from exceptional events are included.
Source: U.S. Environmental Protection Agency, Air Quality Monitoring Information, "Air Quality Trends by City, 1990-2017"

Air Quality Index

Area	Percent of Days when Air Quality was...[2]					AQI Statistics[2]	
	Good	Moderate	Unhealthy for Sensitive Groups	Unhealthy	Very Unhealthy	Maximum	Median
MSA[1]	70.7	28.5	0.8	0.0	0.0	115	44

Note: (1) Data covers the Peoria, IL Metropolitan Statistical Area—see Appendix B for areas included; (2) Based on 365 days with AQI data in 2017. Air Quality Index (AQI) is an index for reporting daily air quality. EPA calculates the AQI for five major air pollutants regulated by the Clean Air Act: ground-level ozone, particle pollution (aka particulate matter), carbon monoxide, sulfur dioxide, and nitrogen dioxide. The AQI runs from 0 to 500. The higher the AQI value, the greater the level of air pollution and the greater the health concern. There are six AQI categories: "Good" AQI is between 0 and 50. Air quality is considered satisfactory; "Moderate" AQI is between 51 and 100. Air quality is acceptable; "Unhealthy for Sensitive Groups" When AQI values are between 101 and 150, members of sensitive groups may experience health effects; "Unhealthy" When AQI values are between 151 and 200 everyone may begin to experience health effects; "Very Unhealthy" AQI values between 201 and 300 trigger a health alert; "Hazardous" AQI values over 300 trigger warnings of emergency conditions (not shown).
Source: U.S. Environmental Protection Agency, Air Quality Index Report, 2017

Air Quality Index Pollutants

Area	Percent of Days when AQI Pollutant was...[2]					
	Carbon Monoxide	Nitrogen Dioxide	Ozone	Sulfur Dioxide	Particulate Matter 2.5	Particulate Matter 10
MSA[1]	0.0	0.0	57.0	1.1	41.9	0.0

Note: (1) Data covers the Peoria, IL Metropolitan Statistical Area—see Appendix B for areas included; (2) Based on 365 days with AQI data in 2017. The Air Quality Index (AQI) is an index for reporting daily air quality. EPA calculates the AQI for five major air pollutants regulated by the Clean Air Act: ground-level ozone, particle pollution (also known as particulate matter), carbon monoxide, sulfur dioxide, and nitrogen dioxide. The AQI runs from 0 to 500. The higher the AQI value, the greater the level of air pollution and the greater the health concern.
Source: U.S. Environmental Protection Agency, Air Quality Index Report, 2017

Maximum Air Pollutant Concentrations: Particulate Matter, Ozone, CO and Lead

	Particulate Matter 10 (ug/m^3)	Particulate Matter 2.5 Wtd AM (ug/m^3)	Particulate Matter 2.5 24-Hr (ug/m^3)	Ozone (ppm)	Carbon Monoxide (ppm)	Lead (ug/m^3)
MSA[1] Level	n/a	8.3	22	0.066	n/a	n/a
NAAQS[2]	150	15	35	0.075	9	0.15
Met NAAQS[2]	n/a	Yes	Yes	Yes	n/a	n/a

Note: (1) Data covers the Peoria, IL Metropolitan Statistical Area—see Appendix B for areas included; Data from exceptional events are included; (2) National Ambient Air Quality Standards; ppm = parts per million; ug/m^3 = micrograms per cubic meter; n/a not available.
Concentrations: Particulate Matter 10 (coarse particulate)—highest second maximum 24-hour concentration; Particulate Matter 2.5 Wtd AM (fine particulate)—highest weighted annual mean concentration; Particulate Matter 2.5 24-Hour (fine particulate)—highest 98th percentile 24-hour concentration; Ozone—highest fourth daily maximum 8-hour concentration; Carbon Monoxide—highest second maximum non-overlapping 8-hour concentration; Lead—maximum running 3-month average
Source: U.S. Environmental Protection Agency, Air Quality Monitoring Information, "Air Quality Statistics by City, 2017"

Maximum Air Pollutant Concentrations: Nitrogen Dioxide and Sulfur Dioxide

	Nitrogen Dioxide AM (ppb)	Nitrogen Dioxide 1-Hr (ppb)	Sulfur Dioxide AM (ppb)	Sulfur Dioxide 1-Hr (ppb)	Sulfur Dioxide 24-Hr (ppb)
MSA[1] Level	n/a	n/a	n/a	23	n/a
NAAQS[2]	53	100	30	75	140
Met NAAQS[2]	n/a	n/a	n/a	Yes	n/a

Note: (1) Data covers the Peoria, IL Metropolitan Statistical Area—see Appendix B for areas included; Data from exceptional events are included; (2) National Ambient Air Quality Standards; ppm = parts per million; ug/m³ = micrograms per cubic meter; n/a not available.
Concentrations: Nitrogen Dioxide AM—highest arithmetic mean concentration; Nitrogen Dioxide 1-Hr—highest 98th percentile 1-hour daily maximum concentration; Sulfur Dioxide AM—highest annual mean concentration; Sulfur Dioxide 1-Hr—highest 99th percentile 1-hour daily maximum concentration; Sulfur Dioxide 24-Hr—highest second maximum 24-hour concentration
Source: U.S. Environmental Protection Agency, Air Quality Monitoring Information, "Air Quality Statistics by City, 2017"

Drinking Water

Water System Name	Pop. Served	Primary Water Source Type	Violations[1] Health Based	Violations[1] Monitoring/ Reporting
Illinois American-Peoria	121,478	Surface	0	0

Note: (1) Based on violation data from January 1, 2018 to December 31, 2018
Source: U.S. Environmental Protection Agency, Office of Ground Water and Drinking Water, Safe Drinking Water Information System (based on data extracted April 5, 2019)

Rochester, Minnesota

Background

Rochester, Minnesota is often characterized as a medical Mecca, as the city's history is full of major breakthroughs in modern medicine. Before Dr. William Mayo arrived in 1864, as an examining physician for Civil War draftees, Rochester was basically a transportation hub for the wheat markets of southeastern Minnesota. However, Rochester's destiny was set when a pioneer of medicine, a determined sister of the Order of St. Francis, and a devastating tornado converged on the evening of August 21, 1883.

Dr. William Worrall (W.W.) Mayo had been schooled in Manchester England, migrated to the U.S. and worked as many things before finishing his medical training in Indiana. In 1864, he and his young family settled in Rochester and, following the Civil War, set up a medical practice.

A deadly tornado hit Rochester on August 21, 1883, killing dozens and injuring hundreds. The Mayos (father and two sons, Will and Charlie) and other Rochester physicians called upon the Sisters of St. Francis who worked tirelessly with the Drs. Mayo, and further, established St. Mary's Hospital in 1889, in spite of the Mayos' insistence that Rochester was too small for such a hospital. In 1914, St. Mary's Hospital would become the Mayo Clinic which today is a medical model of integrated medicine consisting of teamwork, pooled knowledge, and resources among physicians, used throughout the world. Dr. Mayo personally trained his students, assuming that the best way to learn medicine is by studying large numbers of cases, and by hands-on experience, known today as residency training, a standard in medical education.

The Mayo Clinic is still a world pioneer, making Rochester a "medical destination," and employing over 30,000 in Rochester alone. Additional Mayo facilities have been established in Arizona and Florida. The Mayo Clinic is the largest not-for-profit medical practice in the world. In 1973, Mayo opened its medical school, the most selective in the country.

IBM is also important to Rochester's economy, employing over 4,400 employees. IBM's nickname "Big Blue" was based on the Rochester facility, which is constructed of blue panels designed to reflect the Minnesota sky. The building is the largest IBM facility under one roof in the world. In 1990, the National Building Museum acknowledged the facility for its historic significance and innovation.

For those interested in history, the Mayo Clinic offers history and art tours, and The History Center of Olmsted County offers an impressive variety of programs, including research facilities and rare collections. Venues include tours of the historic 38-room, Mayowood Mansion and gardens—once the home of the Mayo family. Much of the architecture was the handiwork of W. W. Mayo himself.

The oldest cultural arts institution in the community, Rochester Symphony Orchestra & Chorale was founded in 1919 as a professional performing arts organization. Its earliest ensemble—the Lawler-Dodge Orchestra—was founded in 1912 as a volunteer orchestra, driven by Daisy Plummer, wife of world-famous Mayo Clinic physician, Dr. Henry Plummer, and directed by Harold Cooke. The Orchestra performed in the former Chateau Theatre where they played background music for silent movies.

The Rochester Downtown Alliance created the Summer Market and Music Festival, and STYLE, the Runway Experience. StyleICE is a unique celebration in which local downtown bars produce an all-ice experience. Everything from glasses to couches is created out of ice, and features special lighting effects and live music.

Minnesota has one of the most extensive state park systems in the nation. Likewise, Rochester's city park system is large, with more than 100 sites covering five square miles. The city also maintains 85 miles of paved trails in addition to state trails such as the Douglas State Trail. The nearest state park is Whitewater State Park.

Rochester features a humid continental climate, four distinct seasons. Summers are very warm and winters are very cold. Rochester sees an annual average of 30 inches of rainfall and 48 inches of snowfall. Significant snow accumulation is common during the winter months. Spring and fall are transitional, with a warming trend during the spring and a cooling trend during the fall. It is not uncommon to see snowfall during early spring and late fall.

Rankings

General Rankings

- In their sixth annual survey, Livability.com looked at data for more than 1,000 U.S. cities to determine the rankings for Livability's "Top 100 Best Places to Live" in 2019. Rochester ranked #5. Criteria: median home value capped at $250,000; affordable living; vibrant economy; education, demographics, health care options. transportation & infrastructure; abundant lifestyle amenities. *Livability.com, "Top 100 Best Places to Live 2019" March 2019*

Business/Finance Rankings

- Experian's latest annual report on consumer credit ranked cities by the average credit score of its residents. Rochester was ranked #2 among the ten cities with the highest average credit score, meaning that its residents showed strong credit management. *www.usatoday.com, "Minneapolis Tops List of Cities With Best Average Credit Score; Greenwood Miss., at the Bottom," January 11, 2018*

- The Rochester metro area appeared on the Milken Institute "2018 Best Performing Cities" list. Rank: #81 out of 201 small metro areas. Criteria: job growth; wage and salary growth; high-tech output growth. *Milken Institute, "Best-Performing Cities 2018," January 24, 2019*

- *Forbes* ranked 200 smaller metro areas (population under 265,400) to determine the nation's "Best Small Places for Business and Careers." The Rochester metro area was ranked #43. Criteria: costs (business and living); job growth (past and projected); income growth; quality of life; educational attainment (college and high school); projected economic growth; cultural and recreational opportunities; net migration patterns; number of highly ranked colleges. *Forbes, "The Best Small Cities for Business and Careers 2018," October, 24 2018*

Environmental Rankings

- Rochester was highlighted as one of the cleanest metro areas for ozone air pollution in the U.S. during 2014 through 2016. The list represents cities with no monitored ozone air pollution in unhealthful ranges. *American Lung Association, State of the Air 2018*

Safety Rankings

- The National Insurance Crime Bureau ranked 382 metro areas in the U.S. in terms of per capita rates of vehicle theft. The Rochester metro area ranked #314 (#1 = highest rate). Criteria: number of vehicle theft offenses per 100,000 inhabitants in 2017. *National Insurance Crime Bureau, "Hot Spots 2017," July 12, 2018*

Seniors/Retirement Rankings

- From its Best Cities for Successful Aging indexes, the Milken Institute generated rankings for metropolitan areas, weighing data in nine categories—health care, wellness, living arrangements, transportation and convenience, financial characteristics, education, employment, community engagement, and overall livability. The Rochester metro area was ranked #24 overall in the small metro area category. *Milken Institute, "Best Cities for Successful Aging, 2017" March 14, 2017*

Sports/Recreation Rankings

- Rochester was chosen as a bicycle friendly community by the League of American Bicyclists. A "Bicycle Friendly Community" welcomes cyclists by providing safe and supportive accommodation for cycling and encouraging people to bike for transportation and recreation. There are five award levels: Diamond; Platinum; Gold; Silver; and Bronze. The community achieved an award level of Bronze. *League of American Bicyclists, "Fall 2018 Awards-Bicycle Friendly Community Master List," December 6, 2018*

Women/Minorities Rankings

- NerdWallet examined data for 529 U.S. cities and ranked them based on the environment for working women. Rochester ranked #1. Criteria: women's earnings; labor force participation rate; cost of living; unemployment rate. *www.nerdwallet.com, "Best Cities for Women in the Workforce 2016," April 4, 2016*

Business Environment

CITY FINANCES

City Government Finances

Component	2016 ($000)	2016 ($ per capita)
Total Revenues	483,186	4,306
Total Expenditures	372,092	3,316
Debt Outstanding	2,531,900	22,561
Cash and Securities[1]	2,429,477	21,648

Note: (1) Cash and security holdings of a government at the close of its fiscal year, including those of its dependent agencies, utilities, and liquor stores.
Source: U.S. Census Bureau, State & Local Government Finances 2016

City Government Revenue by Source

Source	2016 ($000)	2016 ($ per capita)	2016 (%)
General Revenue			
From Federal Government	1,065	9	0.2
From State Government	52,256	466	10.8
From Local Governments	878	8	0.2
Taxes			
Property	54,588	486	11.3
Sales and Gross Receipts	21,351	190	4.4
Personal Income	0	0	0.0
Corporate Income	0	0	0.0
Motor Vehicle License	0	0	0.0
Other Taxes	3,783	34	0.8
Current Charges	51,462	459	10.7
Liquor Store	0	0	0.0
Utility	156,185	1,392	32.3
Employee Retirement	0	0	0.0

Source: U.S. Census Bureau, State & Local Government Finances 2016

City Government Expenditures by Function

Function	2016 ($000)	2016 ($ per capita)	2016 (%)
General Direct Expenditures			
Air Transportation	3,840	34	1.0
Corrections	0	0	0.0
Education	0	0	0.0
Employment Security Administration	0	0	0.0
Financial Administration	1,518	13	0.4
Fire Protection	15,539	138	4.2
General Public Buildings	583	5	0.2
Governmental Administration, Other	3,621	32	1.0
Health	376	3	0.1
Highways	10,193	90	2.7
Hospitals	0	0	0.0
Housing and Community Development	584	5	0.2
Interest on General Debt	71,144	633	19.1
Judicial and Legal	1,578	14	0.4
Libraries	7,393	65	2.0
Parking	4,106	36	1.1
Parks and Recreation	16,554	147	4.4
Police Protection	24,608	219	6.6
Public Welfare	0	0	0.0
Sewerage	12,579	112	3.4
Solid Waste Management	0	0	0.0
Veterans' Services	0	0	0.0
Liquor Store	0	0	0.0
Utility	187,775	1,673	50.5
Employee Retirement	0	0	0.0

Source: U.S. Census Bureau, State & Local Government Finances 2016

DEMOGRAPHICS

Population Growth

Area	1990 Census	2000 Census	2010 Census	2017* Estimate	Population Growth (%)	
					1990-2017	2010-2017
City	74,151	85,806	106,769	112,683	52.0	5.5
MSA[1]	141,945	163,618	186,011	214,485	51.1	15.3
U.S.	248,709,873	281,421,906	308,745,538	321,004,407	29.1	4.0

Note: (1) Figures cover the Rochester, MN Metropolitan Statistical Area—see Appendix B for areas included; (*) 2013-2017 5-year estimated population
Source: U.S. Census Bureau, 1990 Census, Census 2000, Census 2010, 2013-2017 American Community Survey 5-Year Estimates

Household Size

Area	Persons in Household (%)							Average Household Size
	One	Two	Three	Four	Five	Six	Seven or More	
City	29.2	33.8	14.8	14.0	5.0	1.8	1.4	2.40
MSA[1]	26.0	36.8	14.4	14.0	5.4	2.2	1.2	2.50
U.S.	27.7	33.8	15.7	13.0	6.0	2.3	1.4	2.60

Note: (1) Figures cover the Rochester, MN Metropolitan Statistical Area—see Appendix B for areas included
Source: U.S. Census Bureau, 2013-2017 American Community Survey 5-Year Estimates

Race

Area	White Alone[2] (%)	Black Alone[2] (%)	Asian Alone[2] (%)	AIAN[3] Alone[2] (%)	NHOPI[4] Alone[2] (%)	Other Race Alone[2] (%)	Two or More Races (%)
City	80.7	7.4	7.3	0.4	0.0	1.2	3.0
MSA[1]	88.3	4.1	4.3	0.3	0.0	0.8	2.2
U.S.	73.0	12.7	5.4	0.8	0.2	4.8	3.1

Note: (1) Figures cover the Rochester, MN Metropolitan Statistical Area—see Appendix B for areas included; (2) Alone is defined as not being in combination with one or more other races; (3) American Indian and Alaska Native; (4) Native Hawaiian and Other Pacific Islander
Source: U.S. Census Bureau, 2013-2017 American Community Survey 5-Year Estimates

Hispanic or Latino Origin

Area	Total (%)	Mexican (%)	Puerto Rican (%)	Cuban (%)	Other (%)
City	5.8	4.0	0.5	0.1	1.2
MSA[1]	4.3	3.1	0.3	0.1	0.8
U.S.	17.6	11.1	1.7	0.7	4.1

Note: Persons of Hispanic or Latino origin can be of any race; (1) Figures cover the Rochester, MN Metropolitan Statistical Area—see Appendix B for areas included
Source: U.S. Census Bureau, 2013-2017 American Community Survey 5-Year Estimates

Segregation

Type	Segregation Indices[1]				Percent Change		
	1990	2000	2010	2010 Rank[2]	1990-2000	1990-2010	2000-2010
Black/White	n/a	n/a	n/a	n/a	n/a	n/a	n/a
Asian/White	n/a	n/a	n/a	n/a	n/a	n/a	n/a
Hispanic/White	n/a	n/a	n/a	n/a	n/a	n/a	n/a

Note: All figures cover the Metropolitan Statistical Area—see Appendix B for areas included; Figures are based on an analysis of 1990, 2000, and 2010 Census Decennial Census tract data by William H. Frey, Brookings Institution and the University of Michigan Social Science Data Analysis Network. In this analysis all racial groups (whites, blacks, and asians) are non-Hispanic members of those races. Hispanics are shown as a separate category; (1) Segregation Indices are Dissimilarity Indices that measure the degree to which the minority group is distributed differently than whites across census tracts. They range from 0 (complete integration) to 100 (complete segregation) where the value indicates the percentage of the minority group that needs to move to be distributed exactly like whites; (2) Ranges from 1 (most segregated) to 102 (least segregated); n/a not available.
Source: www.CensusScope.org

Ancestry

Area	German	Irish	English	American	Italian	Polish	French[2]	Scottish	Dutch
City	30.9	11.3	6.3	3.2	2.2	3.8	2.0	1.3	1.5
MSA[1]	36.7	11.8	6.3	3.6	1.7	3.4	2.3	1.2	2.0
U.S.	14.1	10.1	7.5	6.6	5.3	2.9	2.5	1.7	1.3

Note: Figures are the percentage of the total population reporting a particular ancestry. The nine most commonly reported ancestries in the U.S. are shown. Figures include multiple ancestries (e.g. if a person reported being Irish and Italian, they were included in both columns); (1) Figures cover the Rochester, MN Metropolitan Statistical Area—see Appendix B for areas included; (2) Excludes Basque
Source: U.S. Census Bureau, 2013-2017 American Community Survey 5-Year Estimates

Foreign-Born Population

Area	Percent of Population Born in								
	Any Foreign Country	Asia	Mexico	Europe	Carribean	Central America[2]	South America	Africa	Canada
City	13.6	5.7	1.8	1.7	0.2	0.2	0.2	3.4	0.3
MSA[1]	8.1	3.3	1.2	1.1	0.1	0.2	0.2	1.8	0.2
U.S.	13.4	4.1	3.6	1.5	1.3	1.0	0.9	0.6	0.3

Note: (1) Figures cover the Rochester, MN Metropolitan Statistical Area—see Appendix B for areas included; (2) Excludes Mexico.
Source: U.S. Census Bureau, 2013-2017 American Community Survey 5-Year Estimates

Marital Status

Area	Never Married	Now Married[2]	Separated	Widowed	Divorced
City	31.6	52.8	1.0	4.7	9.9
MSA[1]	27.3	57.6	0.8	4.9	9.3
U.S.	33.1	48.2	2.0	5.8	10.9

Note: Figures are percentages and cover the population 15 years of age and older; (1) Figures cover the Rochester, MN Metropolitan Statistical Area—see Appendix B for areas included; (2) Excludes separated
Source: U.S. Census Bureau, 2013-2017 American Community Survey 5-Year Estimates

Disability by Age

Area	All Ages	Under 18 Years Old	18 to 64 Years Old	65 Years and Over
City	10.7	4.3	8.8	30.5
MSA[1]	10.3	3.9	7.9	30.5
U.S.	12.6	4.2	10.3	35.5

Note: Figures show percent of the civilian noninstitutionalized population that reported having a disability. Disability status is determined from six types of difficulty: vision, hearing, cognitive, ambulatory, self-care, and independent living. For children under 5 years old, hearing and vision difficulty are used to determine disability status. For children between the ages of 5 and 14, disability status is determined from hearing, vision, cognitive, ambulatory, and self-care difficulties. For people aged 15 years and older, they are considered to have a disability if they have difficulty with any one of the six difficulty types; Note: (1) Figures cover the Rochester, MN Metropolitan Statistical Area—see Appendix B for areas included
Source: U.S. Census Bureau, 2013-2017 American Community Survey 5-Year Estimates

Age

Area	Under Age 5	Age 5–19	Age 20–34	Age 35–44	Age 45–54	Age 55–64	Age 65–74	Age 75–84	Age 85+	Median Age
City	7.3	18.9	22.9	12.8	12.4	11.4	7.4	4.5	2.2	35.5
MSA[1]	6.8	19.8	19.2	12.4	13.3	13.3	8.2	4.8	2.2	38.4
U.S.	6.2	19.5	20.7	12.7	13.4	12.7	8.6	4.4	1.9	37.8

Note: (1) Figures cover the Rochester, MN Metropolitan Statistical Area—see Appendix B for areas included
Source: U.S. Census Bureau, 2013-2017 American Community Survey 5-Year Estimates

Gender

Area	Males	Females	Males per 100 Females
City	54,584	58,099	93.9
MSA[1]	105,686	108,799	97.1
U.S.	158,018,753	162,985,654	97.0

Note: (1) Figures cover the Rochester, MN Metropolitan Statistical Area—see Appendix B for areas included
Source: U.S. Census Bureau, 2013-2017 American Community Survey 5-Year Estimates

Religious Groups by Family

Area	Catholic	Baptist	Non-Den.	Methodist[2]	Lutheran	LDS[3]	Pentecostal	Presbyterian[4]	Muslim[5]	Judaism
MSA[1]	23.4	1.7	4.7	4.9	21.1	1.1	1.3	2.9	0.3	0.2
U.S.	19.1	9.3	4.0	4.0	2.3	2.0	1.9	1.6	0.8	0.7

Note: Figures are the number of adherents as a percentage of the total population; (1) Figures cover the Rochester, MN Metropolitan Statistical Area—see Appendix B for areas included; (2) Methodist/Pietist; (3) Latter Day Saints; (4) Reformed; (5) Figures are estimates
Source: Association of Statisticians of American Religious Bodies, 2010 U.S. Religion Census: Religious Congregations & Membership Study

Religious Groups by Tradition

Area	Catholic	Evangelical Protestant	Mainline Protestant	Other Tradition	Black Protestant	Orthodox
MSA[1]	23.4	19.0	21.1	2.1	<0.1	0.1
U.S.	19.1	16.2	7.3	4.3	1.6	0.3

Note: Figures are the number of adherents as a percentage of the total population; (1) Figures cover the Rochester, MN Metropolitan Statistical Area—see Appendix B for areas included
Source: Association of Statisticians of American Religious Bodies, 2010 U.S. Religion Census: Religious Congregations & Membership Study

ECONOMY

Gross Metropolitan Product

Area	2016	2017	2018	2019	Rank[2]
MSA[1]	12.1	12.5	12.9	13.5	181

Note: Figures are in billions of dollars; (1) Figures cover the Rochester, MN Metropolitan Statistical Area—see Appendix B for areas included; (2) Rank is based on 2017 data and ranges from 1 to 381
Source: U.S. Conference of Mayors, U.S. Metro Economies: Economic Growth & Full Employment, June 2018

Economic Growth

Area	2017-2018 (%)	2019-2020 (%)	2021-2022 (%)
MSA[1]	1.6	1.7	1.2

Note: Figures are real gross metropolitan product (GMP) growth rates and represent average annual percent change; (1) Figures cover the Rochester, MN Metropolitan Statistical Area—see Appendix B for areas included
Source: U.S. Conference of Mayors, U.S. Metro Economies: Economic Growth & Full Employment, June 2018

Metropolitan Area Exports

Area	2012	2013	2014	2015	2016	2017	Rank[2]
MSA[1]	1,023.7	1,061.0	720.5	530.2	398.0	495.3	209

Note: Figures are in millions of dollars; (1) Figures cover the Rochester, MN Metropolitan Statistical Area—see Appendix B for areas included; (2) Rank is based on 2017 data and ranges from 1 to 387
Source: U.S. Department of Commerce, International Trade Administration, Office of Trade and Economic Analysis, Industry and Analysis, Exports by Metropolitan Area, extracted March 25, 2019

Building Permits

Area	Single-Family			Multi-Family			Total		
	2016	2017	Pct. Chg.	2016	2017	Pct. Chg.	2016	2017	Pct. Chg.
City	403	437	8.4	993	617	-37.9	1,396	1,054	-24.5
MSA[1]	744	818	9.9	993	631	-36.5	1,737	1,449	-16.6
U.S.	750,800	820,000	9.2	455,800	462,000	1.4	1,206,600	1,282,000	6.2

Note: (1) Figures cover the Rochester, MN Metropolitan Statistical Area—see Appendix B for areas included; Figures represent new, privately-owned housing units authorized (unadjusted data); All permit data are based on estimates with imputation
Source: U.S. Census Bureau, Manufacturing, Mining, and Construction Statistics, Building Permits, 2016, 2017

Bankruptcy Filings

Area	Business Filings			Nonbusiness Filings		
	2017	2018	% Chg.	2017	2018	% Chg.
Olmsted County	4	5	25.0	146	169	15.8
U.S.	23,157	22,232	-4.0	765,863	751,186	-1.9

Note: Business filings include Chapter 7, Chapter 11, Chapter 12, and Chapter 13; Nonbusiness filings include Chapter 7, Chapter 11, and Chapter 13
Source: Administrative Office of the U.S. Courts, Business and Nonbusiness Bankruptcy, County Cases Commenced by Chapter of the Bankruptcy Code, During the 12-Month Period Ending December 31, 2017 and Business and Nonbusiness Bankruptcy, County Cases Commenced by Chapter of the Bankruptcy Code, During the 12-Month Period Ending December 31, 2018

Housing Vacancy Rates

Area	Gross Vacancy Rate[2] (%)			Year-Round Vacancy Rate[3] (%)			Rental Vacancy Rate[4] (%)			Homeowner Vacancy Rate[5] (%)		
	2016	2017	2018	2016	2017	2018	2016	2017	2018	2016	2017	2018
MSA[1]	n/a	n/a	n/a	n/a	n/a	n/a	n/a	n/a	n/a	n/a	n/a	n/a
U.S.	12.8	12.7	12.3	9.9	9.9	9.7	6.9	7.2	6.9	1.7	1.6	1.5

Note: (1) Figures cover the Rochester, MN Metropolitan Statistical Area—see Appendix B for areas included; (2) The percentage of the total housing inventory that is vacant; (3) The percentage of the housing inventory (excluding seasonal units) that is year-round vacant; (4) The percentage of rental inventory that is vacant for rent; (5) The percentage of homeowner inventory that is vacant for sale; n/a not available
Source: U.S. Census Bureau, Housing Vacancies and Homeownership Annual Statistics: 2016, 2017, 2018

INCOME

Income

Area	Per Capita ($)	Median Household ($)	Average Household ($)
City	36,659	68,574	90,446
MSA[1]	35,842	69,003	89,677
U.S.	31,177	57,652	81,283

Note: (1) Figures cover the Rochester, MN Metropolitan Statistical Area—see Appendix B for areas included
Source: U.S. Census Bureau, 2013-2017 American Community Survey 5-Year Estimates

Household Income Distribution

Area	Percent of Households Earning							
	Under $15,000	$15,000 -$24,999	$25,000 -$34,999	$35,000 -$49,999	$50,000 -$74,999	$75,000 -$99,999	$100,000 -$149,999	$150,000 and up
City	8.4	7.3	8.8	11.6	18.0	14.6	16.9	14.4
MSA[1]	7.6	7.2	8.6	11.7	19.0	14.5	18.0	13.4
U.S.	11.6	9.8	9.5	13.0	17.7	12.3	14.1	12.1

Note: (1) Figures cover the Rochester, MN Metropolitan Statistical Area—see Appendix B for areas included
Source: U.S. Census Bureau, 2013-2017 American Community Survey 5-Year Estimates

Poverty Rate

Area	All Ages	Under 18 Years Old	18 to 64 Years Old	65 Years and Over
City	10.4	13.0	10.6	4.6
MSA[1]	8.6	11.0	8.4	5.6
U.S.	14.6	20.3	13.7	9.3

Note: Figures are percentage of people whose income during the past 12 months was below the poverty level; (1) Figures cover the Rochester, MN Metropolitan Statistical Area—see Appendix B for areas included
Source: U.S. Census Bureau, 2013-2017 American Community Survey 5-Year Estimates

EMPLOYMENT

Labor Force and Employment

Area	Civilian Labor Force			Workers Employed		
	Dec. 2017	Dec. 2018	% Chg.	Dec. 2017	Dec. 2018	% Chg.
City	63,515	63,316	-0.3	61,863	61,747	-0.2
MSA[1]	121,410	120,953	-0.4	117,927	117,605	-0.3
U.S.	159,880,000	162,510,000	1.6	153,602,000	156,481,000	1.9

Note: Data is not seasonally adjusted and covers workers 16 years of age and older; (1) Figures cover the Rochester, MN Metropolitan Statistical Area—see Appendix B for areas included
Source: Bureau of Labor Statistics, Local Area Unemployment Statistics

Unemployment Rate

Area	2018											
	Jan.	Feb.	Mar.	Apr.	May	Jun.	Jul.	Aug.	Sep.	Oct.	Nov.	Dec.
City	3.0	3.0	2.8	2.4	2.0	2.4	2.1	2.0	1.9	1.8	1.8	2.5
MSA[1]	3.6	3.6	3.4	2.8	2.1	2.6	2.3	2.2	1.9	1.9	1.9	2.8
U.S.	4.5	4.4	4.1	3.7	3.6	4.2	4.1	3.9	3.6	3.5	3.5	3.7

Note: Data is not seasonally adjusted and covers workers 16 years of age and older; (1) Figures cover the Rochester, MN Metropolitan Statistical Area—see Appendix B for areas included
Source: Bureau of Labor Statistics, Local Area Unemployment Statistics

Average Wages

Occupation	$/Hr.	Occupation	$/Hr.
Accountants and Auditors	29.80	Maids and Housekeeping Cleaners	11.90
Automotive Mechanics	19.40	Maintenance and Repair Workers	20.20
Bookkeepers	19.20	Marketing Managers	67.70
Carpenters	25.20	Nuclear Medicine Technologists	n/a
Cashiers	11.90	Nurses, Licensed Practical	22.80
Clerks, General Office	17.20	Nurses, Registered	36.40
Clerks, Receptionists/Information	12.20	Nursing Assistants	n/a
Clerks, Shipping/Receiving	18.00	Packers and Packagers, Hand	13.20
Computer Programmers	46.30	Physical Therapists	40.00
Computer Systems Analysts	40.70	Postal Service Mail Carriers	24.80
Computer User Support Specialists	26.10	Real Estate Brokers	n/a
Cooks, Restaurant	13.40	Retail Salespersons	13.20
Dentists	109.70	Sales Reps., Exc. Tech./Scientific	31.80
Electrical Engineers	43.40	Sales Reps., Tech./Scientific	41.40
Electricians	30.80	Secretaries, Exc. Legal/Med./Exec.	16.50
Financial Managers	53.10	Security Guards	14.60
First-Line Supervisors/Managers, Sales	19.70	Surgeons	n/a
Food Preparation Workers	12.10	Teacher Assistants*	15.00
General and Operations Managers	42.10	Teachers, Elementary School*	26.20
Hairdressers/Cosmetologists	13.90	Teachers, Secondary School*	31.40
Internists, General	n/a	Telemarketers	n/a
Janitors and Cleaners	15.10	Truck Drivers, Heavy/Tractor-Trailer	23.10
Landscaping/Groundskeeping Workers	15.70	Truck Drivers, Light/Delivery Svcs.	16.60
Lawyers	39.50	Waiters and Waitresses	10.60

Note: Wage data covers the Rochester, MN Metropolitan Statistical Area—see Appendix B for areas included; (*) Hourly wages for elementary/secondary school teachers and teacher assistants were calculated by the editors from annual wage data based on a 40 hour work week; n/a not available.
Source: Bureau of Labor Statistics, Metro Area Occupational Employment & Wage Estimates, May 2018

Employment by Occupation

Occupation Classification	City (%)	MSA[1] (%)	U.S. (%)
Management, Business, Science, and Arts	50.8	45.3	37.4
Natural Resources, Construction, and Maintenance	5.4	8.3	8.9
Production, Transportation, and Material Moving	8.7	10.9	12.2
Sales and Office	18.7	19.7	23.5
Service	16.5	15.8	18.0

Note: Figures cover employed civilians 16 years of age and older; (1) Figures cover the Rochester, MN Metropolitan Statistical Area—see Appendix B for areas included
Source: U.S. Census Bureau, 2013-2017 American Community Survey 5-Year Estimates

Employment by Industry

Sector	MSA[1]		U.S.
	Number of Employees	Percent of Total	Percent of Total
Construction, Mining, and Logging	4,700	3.8	5.3
Education and Health Services	51,000	41.5	15.9
Financial Activities	2,700	2.2	5.7
Government	13,300	10.8	15.1
Information	1,600	1.3	1.9
Leisure and Hospitality	11,000	9.0	10.7
Manufacturing	10,800	8.8	8.5
Other Services	3,800	3.1	3.9
Professional and Business Services	6,000	4.9	14.1
Retail Trade	12,500	10.2	10.8
Transportation, Warehousing, and Utilities	2,700	2.2	4.2
Wholesale Trade	2,800	2.3	3.9

Note: Figures are non-farm employment as of December 2018. Figures are not seasonally adjusted and include workers 16 years of age and older; (1) Figures cover the Rochester, MN Metropolitan Statistical Area—see Appendix B for areas included
Source: Bureau of Labor Statistics, Current Employment Statistics, Employment, Hours, and Earnings

Occupations with Greatest Projected Employment Growth: 2018 – 2020

Occupation[1]	2018 Employment	2020 Projected Employment	Numeric Employment Change	Percent Employment Change
Personal Care Aides	71,130	74,150	3,020	4.2
Registered Nurses	63,910	66,090	2,180	3.4
Janitors and Cleaners, Except Maids and Housekeeping Cleaners	47,680	48,880	1,200	2.5
Heavy and Tractor-Trailer Truck Drivers	35,950	36,930	980	2.7
Combined Food Preparation and Serving Workers, Including Fast Food	65,710	66,600	890	1.4
General and Operations Managers	44,110	44,980	870	2.0
Home Health Aides	25,920	26,660	740	2.9
Light Truck or Delivery Services Drivers	16,260	16,990	730	4.5
Elementary School Teachers, Except Special Education	30,690	31,400	710	2.3
Teacher Assistants	34,480	35,190	710	2.1

Note: Projections cover Minnesota; (1) Sorted by numeric employment change
Source: www.projectionscentral.com, State Occupational Projections, 2018–2020 Short-Term Projections

Fastest Growing Occupations: 2018 – 2020

Occupation[1]	2018 Employment	2020 Projected Employment	Numeric Employment Change	Percent Employment Change
Wind Turbine Service Technicians	260	310	50	19.2
Couriers and Messengers	1,140	1,230	90	7.9
Physician Assistants	2,060	2,200	140	6.8
Plumbers, Pipefitters, and Steamfitters	9,300	9,910	610	6.6
Statisticians	970	1,030	60	6.2
Roofers	2,380	2,520	140	5.9
Operations Research Analysts	2,820	2,980	160	5.7
Nurse Practitioners	3,670	3,880	210	5.7
Structural Iron and Steel Workers	1,610	1,700	90	5.6
Cement Masons and Concrete Finishers	5,410	5,700	290	5.4

Note: Projections cover Minnesota; (1) Sorted by percent employment change and excludes occupations with numeric employment change less than 50
Source: www.projectionscentral.com, State Occupational Projections, 2018–2020 Short-Term Projections

TAXES

State Corporate Income Tax Rates

State	Tax Rate (%)	Income Brackets ($)	Num. of Brackets	Financial Institution Tax Rate (%)[a]	Federal Income Tax Ded.
Minnesota	9.8 (n)	Flat rate	1	9.8 (n)	No

Note: Tax rates as of January 1, 2019; (a) Rates listed are the corporate income tax rate applied to financial institutions or excise taxes based on income. Some states have other taxes based upon the value of deposits or shares; (n) In addition, Minnesota levies a 5.8% tentative minimum tax on Alternative Minimum Taxable Income.
Source: Federation of Tax Administrators, Range of State Corporate Income Tax Rates, January 1, 2019

State Individual Income Tax Rates

State	Tax Rate (%)	Income Brackets ($)	Personal Exemptions ($)			Standard Ded. ($)	
			Single	Married	Depend.	Single	Married
Minnesota (a)	5.35 - 9.85	26,520 - 163,890 (n)	4,150	8,300 (d)	4,150 (d)	6,500	3,000 (d)

Note: Tax rates as of January 1, 2019; Local- and county-level taxes are not included; n/a not applicable; Federal income tax is not deductible on state income tax returns; (a) 19 states have statutory provision for automatically adjusting to the rate of inflation the dollar values of the income tax brackets, standard deductions, and/or personal exemptions. Michigan indexes the personal exemption only. Oregon does not index the income brackets for $125,000 and over; (d) These states use the personal exemption/standard deduction amounts provided in the federal Internal Revenue Code. Note, the Tax Cut and Reform Act of 2017 has eliminated personal exemptions from the IRC. CO, ID, NM, ND, SC, and DC have adopted the new exemptions and standard deduction amounts. MN conforms to a previous IRC year, while ME adopts the higher standard deduction but retains the exemption amounts; (n) The income brackets reported for Minnesota are for single individuals. For married couples filing jointly, the same tax rates apply to income brackets ranging from $38,770 to $273,150.
Source: Federation of Tax Administrators, State Individual Income Tax Rates, January 1, 2019

Various State Sales and Excise Tax Rates

State	State Sales Tax (%)	Gasoline[1] (¢/gal.)	Cigarette[2] ($/pack)	Spirits[3] ($/gal.)	Wine[4] ($/gal.)	Beer[5] ($/gal.)	Recreational Marijuana (%)
Minnesota	6.875	28.6	3.04	8.96 (i)(j)	1.20 (o)(p)	0.49 (q)(s)	Not legal

Note: All tax rates as of January 1, 2019; (1) The American Petroleum Institute has developed a methodology for determining the average tax rate on a gallon of fuel. Rates may include any of the following: excise taxes, environmental fees, storage tank fees, other fees or taxes, general sales tax, and local taxes. In states where gasoline is subject to the general sales tax, or where the fuel tax is based on the average sale price, the average rate determined by API is sensitive to changes in the price of gasoline. States that fully or partially apply general sales taxes to gasoline: CA, CO, GA, IL, IN, MI, NY; (2) The federal excise tax of $1.0066 per pack and local taxes are not included; (3) Rates are those applicable to off-premise sales of 40% alcohol by volume (a.b.v.) distilled spirits in 750ml containers. Local excise taxes are excluded; (4) Rates are those applicable to off-premise sales of 11% a.b.v. non-carbonated wine in 750ml containers; (5) Rates are those applicable to off-premise sales of 4.7% a.b.v. beer in 12 ounce containers; (i) Includes case fees and/or bottle fees which may vary with size of container; (j) Includes sales taxes specific to alcoholic beverages; (o) Includes case fees and/or bottle fees which may vary with size of container; (p) Includes sales taxes specific to alcoholic beverages; (q) Different rates also applicable according to alcohol content, place of production, size of container, or place purchased (on- or off-premise or onboard airlines); (s) Includes sales taxes specific to alcoholic beverages.
Source: Tax Foundation, 2019 Facts & Figures: How Does Your State Compare?

State Business Tax Climate Index Rankings

State	Overall Rank	Corporate Tax Rank	Individual Income Tax Rank	Sales Tax Rank	Unemployment Insurance Tax Rank	Property Tax Rank
Minnesota	43	42	46	27	25	31

Note: The index is a measure of how each state's tax laws affect economic performance. The lower the rank, the more favorable a state's tax system is for business. States without a given tax are given a ranking of 1. The scores/rankings for the District of Columbia do not affect other states. The 2019 index represents the tax climate as of July 1, 2018.
Source: Tax Foundation, State Business Tax Climate Index 2019

COMMERCIAL UTILITIES

Typical Monthly Electric Bills

Area	Commercial Service ($/month)		Industrial Service ($/month)	
	1,500 kWh	40 kW demand 14,000 kWh	1,000 kW demand 200,000 kWh	50,000 kW demand 32,500,000 kWh
City	n/a	n/a	n/a	n/a
Average[1]	203	1,619	25,886	2,540,077

Note: Figures are based on annualized rates; (1) Average based on 187 utilities surveyed; n/a not available
Source: Edison Electric Institute, Typical Bills and Average Rates Report, Summer 2018

TRANSPORTATION

Means of Transportation to Work

Area	Car/Truck/Van		Public Transportation			Bicycle	Walked	Other Means	Worked at Home
	Drove Alone	Car-pooled	Bus	Subway	Railroad				
City	71.7	11.7	6.7	0.0	0.0	1.1	4.3	0.8	3.7
MSA[1]	74.6	11.0	4.4	0.0	0.0	0.7	3.6	0.8	4.9
U.S.	76.4	9.2	2.5	1.9	0.6	0.6	2.7	1.3	4.7

Note: Figures are percentages and cover workers 16 years of age and older; (1) Figures cover the Rochester, MN Metropolitan Statistical Area—see Appendix B for areas included
Source: U.S. Census Bureau, 2013-2017 American Community Survey 5-Year Estimates

Travel Time to Work

Area	Less Than 10 Minutes	10 to 19 Minutes	20 to 29 Minutes	30 to 44 Minutes	45 to 59 Minutes	60 to 89 Minutes	90 Minutes or More
City	19.7	56.6	12.5	6.2	2.2	1.7	1.2
MSA[1]	19.0	42.2	18.5	12.4	3.8	2.4	1.6
U.S.	12.7	28.9	20.9	20.5	8.1	6.2	2.7

Note: Note: Figures are percentages and include workers 16 years old and over; (1) Figures cover the Rochester, MN Metropolitan Statistical Area—see Appendix B for areas included
Source: U.S. Census Bureau, 2013-2017 American Community Survey 5-Year Estimates

Freeway Travel Time Index

Area	1985	1990	1995	2000	2005	2010	2014
Urban Area Rank[1,2]	n/a	n/a	n/a	n/a	n/a	n/a	n/a
Urban Area Index[1]	n/a	n/a	n/a	n/a	n/a	n/a	n/a
Average Index[3]	1.09	1.11	1.14	1.17	1.20	1.19	1.20

Note: Freeway Travel Time Index—the ratio of travel time in the peak period to the travel time at free-flow conditions. For example, a value of 1.30 indicates a 20-minute free-flow trip takes 26 minutes in the peak (20 minutes x 1.30 = 26 minutes); (1) Data for the Rochester, MN urban area was not available; (2) Rank is based on 101 urban areas (#1 = highest travel time index); (3) Average of 101 urban areas
Source: Texas Transportation Institute, 2015 Urban Mobility Scorecard, August 2015

Freeway Commuter Stress Index

Area	1985	1990	1995	2000	2005	2010	2014
Urban Area Rank[1,2]	n/a	n/a	n/a	n/a	n/a	n/a	n/a
Urban Area Index[1]	n/a	n/a	n/a	n/a	n/a	n/a	n/a
Average Index[3]	1.13	1.16	1.19	1.22	1.25	1.24	1.25

Note: The Freeway Commuter Stress Index is the same as the Freeway Travel Time Index (see table above) except that it includes only the travel in the peak directions during the peak periods; the TTI includes travel in all directions during the peak period. Thus, the CSI is more indicative of the work trip experienced by each commuter on a daily basis; (1) Data for the Rochester, MN urban area was not available; (2) Rank is based on 101 urban areas (#1 = highest travel time index); (3) Average of 101 urban areas
Source: Texas Transportation Institute, 2015 Urban Mobility Scorecard, August 2015

Public Transportation

Agency Name / Mode of Transportation	Vehicles Operated in Maximum Service[1]	Annual Unlinked Passenger Trips[2] (in thous.)	Annual Passenger Miles[3] (in thous.)
City of Rochester Public Transportation			
Bus (purchased transportation)	38	1,838.0	6,624.2
Demand Response (purchased transportation)	5	32.0	224.5
Demand Response Taxi (purchased transportation)	1	16.2	66.4

Note: (1) The number of revenue vehicles operated by the given mode and type of service to meet the annual maximum service requirement. This is the revenue vehicle count during the peak season of the year; on the week and day that maximum service is provided. Vehicles operated in maximum service (VOMS) exclude atypical days and one-time special events; (2) The number of passengers who boarded public transportation vehicles. Passengers are counted each time they board a vehicle no matter how many vehicles they use to travel from their origin to their destination. (3) The sum of the distances ridden by all passengers during the entire fiscal year.
Source: Federal Transit Administration, National Transit Database, 2017

Air Transportation

Airport Name and Code / Type of Service	Passenger Airlines[1]	Passenger Enplanements	Freight Carriers[2]	Freight (lbs)
Rochester International Airport (RST)				
Domestic service (U.S. carriers - 2018)	11	182,243	2	11,041,409
International service (U.S. carriers - 2017)	0	0	0	0

Note: (1) Includes all U.S.-based major, minor and commuter airlines that carried at least one passenger during the year; (2) Includes all U.S.-based airlines and freight carriers that transported at least one pound of freight during the year.
Source: Bureau of Transportation Statistics, The Intermodal Transportation Database, Air Carriers: T-100 Domestic Market (U.S. Carriers), 2018; Bureau of Transportation Statistics, The Intermodal Transportation Database, Air Carriers: T-100 International Market (U.S. Carriers), 2017

Other Transportation Statistics

Major Highways:	I-90
Amtrak Service:	No
Major Waterways/Ports:	None

Source: Amtrak.com; Google Maps

BUSINESSES

Major Business Headquarters

Company Name	Industry	Rankings	
		Fortune[1]	Forbes[2]
No companies listed	-	-	-

Note: (1) Companies that produce a 10-K are ranked 1 to 500 based on 2017 revenue; (2) All private companies with at least $2 billion in annual revenue through the end of their most current fiscal year are ranked 1 to 229; companies listed are headquartered in the city; dashes indicate no ranking
Source: Fortune, "Fortune 500," June 2018; Forbes, "America's Largest Private Companies," 2018 Rankings

Fast-Growing Businesses

According to *Inc.*, Rochester is home to two of America's 500 fastest-growing private companies: **The Media Manager** (#103); **Trbhi** (#485). Criteria: must be an independent, privately-held, for-profit, U.S. corporation, proprietorship or partnership as of December 31, 2017; revenues must be at least $100,000 in 2014 and $2 million in 2017; must have four-year operating/sales history. Holding companies, regulated banks, and utilities were excluded. *Inc., "America's 500 Fastest-Growing Private Companies," 2018*

Minority- and Women-Owned Businesses

Group	All Firms		Firms with Paid Employees			
	Firms	Sales ($000)	Firms	Sales ($000)	Employees	Payroll ($000)
AIAN[1]	39	(s)	0	(s)	0 - 19	(s)
Asian	478	45,980	72	36,275	451	7,310
Black	431	(s)	35	(s)	1,000 - 2,499	(s)
Hispanic	219	(s)	9	(s)	20 - 99	(s)
NHOPI[2]	n/a	n/a	n/a	n/a	n/a	n/a
Women	2,801	488,834	291	422,196	2,461	59,817
All Firms	8,900	12,577,132	2,349	12,256,680	73,568	3,032,558

Note: Figures cover firms located in the city; minority- and women-owned business are defined as firms in which the corresponding group own 51% or more of the stock or equity of the company; (1) American Indian and Alaska Native; (2) Native Hawaiian and Other Pacific Islander; (s) estimates are suppressed when publication standards are not met; n/a not available
Source: U.S. Census Bureau, 2012 Economic Census, Survey of Business Owners

HOTELS & CONVENTION CENTERS

Hotels, Motels and Vacation Rentals

Area	5 Star		4 Star		3 Star		2 Star		1 Star		Not Rated	
	Num.	Pct.[3]	Num.	Pct.[3]	Num.	Pct.[3]	Num.	Pct.[3]	Num.	Pct.[3]	Num.	Pct.[3]
City[1]	0	0.0	3	1.5	33	16.9	55	28.2	2	1.0	102	52.3
Total[2]	286	0.4	5,236	7.1	16,715	22.6	10,259	13.9	293	0.4	41,056	55.6

Note: (1) Figures cover Rochester and vicinity; (2) Figures cover all 100 cities in this book; (3) Percentage of hotels which have a given star rating; Star ratings are determined by expedia.com and offer an indication of the general quality of a particular hotel.
Source: www.expedia.com, April 3, 2019

Major Convention Centers

Name	Overall Space (sq. ft.)	Exhibit Space (sq. ft.)	Meeting Space (sq. ft.)	Meeting Rooms
Mayo Civic Center	n/a	25,200	n/a	4

Note: Table includes convention centers located in the Rochester, MN metro area; n/a not available
Source: Original research

Living Environment

COST OF LIVING

Cost of Living Index

Composite Index	Groceries	Housing	Utilities	Trans-portation	Health Care	Misc. Goods/Services
n/a	n/a	n/a	n/a	n/a	n/a	n/a

Note: The Cost of Living Index measures regional differences in the cost of consumer goods and services, excluding taxes and non-consumer expenditures, for professional and managerial households in the top income quintile. It is based on more than 50,000 prices covering almost 60 different items for which prices are collected three times a year by chambers of commerce, economic development organizations or university applied economic centers in each participating urban area. The numbers shown should be read as a percentage above or below the national average of 100. For example, a value of 115.4 in the groceries column indicates that grocery prices are 15.4% higher than the national average. Small differences in the index numbers should not be interpreted as significant; n/a not available.
Source: The Council for Community and Economic Research, ACCRA Cost of Living Index, 2018

Grocery Prices

Area[1]	T-Bone Steak ($/pound)	Frying Chicken ($/pound)	Whole Milk ($/half gal.)	Eggs ($/dozen)	Orange Juice ($/64 oz.)	Coffee ($/11.5 oz.)
City[2]	n/a	n/a	n/a	n/a	n/a	n/a
Avg.	11.35	1.42	1.94	1.81	3.52	4.35
Min.	7.45	0.92	0.80	0.75	2.72	3.06
Max.	15.05	2.76	4.18	4.00	5.36	8.20

Note: (1) Values for the local area are compared with the average, minimum and maximum values for all 291 areas in the Cost of Living Index; (2) Figures cover the Rochester MN urban area; n/a not available; T-Bone Steak (price per pound); Frying Chicken (price per pound, whole fryer); Whole Milk (half gallon carton); Eggs (price per dozen, Grade A, large); Orange Juice (64 oz. Tropicana or Florida Natural); Coffee (11.5 oz. can, vacuum-packed, Maxwell House, Hills Bros, or Folgers).
Source: The Council for Community and Economic Research, ACCRA Cost of Living Index, 2018

Housing and Utility Costs

Area[1]	New Home Price ($)	Apartment Rent ($/month)	All Electric ($/month)	Part Electric ($/month)	Other Energy ($/month)	Telephone ($/month)
City[2]	n/a	n/a	n/a	n/a	n/a	n/a
Avg.	347,000	1,087	165.93	100.16	67.73	178.70
Min.	200,468	500	93.58	25.64	26.78	163.10
Max.	1,901,222	4,888	388.65	246.86	332.81	197.70

Note: (1) Values for the local area are compared with the average, minimum and maximum values for all 291 areas in the Cost of Living Index; (2) Figures cover the Rochester MN urban area; n/a not available; New Home Price (2,400 sf living area, 8,000 sf lot, in urban area with full utilities); Apartment Rent (950 sf 2 bedroom/1.5 or 2 bath, unfurnished, excluding all utilities except water); All Electric (average monthly cost for an all-electric home); Part Electric (average monthly cost for a part-electric home); Other Energy (average monthly cost for natural gas, fuel oil, coal, wood, and any other forms of energy except electricity); Telephone (price includes the base monthly rate plus taxes and fees for three lines of mobile phone service).
Source: The Council for Community and Economic Research, ACCRA Cost of Living Index, 2018

Health Care, Transportation, and Other Costs

Area[1]	Doctor ($/visit)	Dentist ($/visit)	Optometrist ($/visit)	Gasoline ($/gallon)	Beauty Salon ($/visit)	Men's Shirt ($)
City[2]	n/a	n/a	n/a	n/a	n/a	n/a
Avg.	110.71	95.11	103.74	2.61	37.48	32.03
Min.	33.60	62.55	54.63	1.89	17.00	11.44
Max.	195.97	153.93	225.79	3.59	71.88	58.64

Note: (1) Values for the local area are compared with the average, minimum and maximum values for all 291 areas in the Cost of Living Index; (2) Figures cover the Rochester MN urban area; n/a not available; Doctor (general practitioners routine exam of an established patient); Dentist (adult teeth cleaning and periodic oral examination); Optometrist (full vision eye exam for established adult patient); Gasoline (one gallon regular unleaded, national brand, including all taxes, cash price at self-service pump if available); Beauty Salon (woman's shampoo, trim, and blow-dry); Men's Shirt (cotton/polyester dress shirt, pinpoint weave, long sleeves).
Source: The Council for Community and Economic Research, ACCRA Cost of Living Index, 2018

HOUSING

House Price Index (HPI)

Area	National Ranking[2]	Quarterly Change (%)	One-Year Change (%)	Five-Year Change (%)
MSA[1]	91	1.02	7.08	33.87
U.S.[3]	—	1.12	5.73	32.81

Note: The HPI is a weighted repeat sales index. It measures average price changes in repeat sales or refinancings on the same properties. This information is obtained by reviewing repeat mortgage transactions on single-family properties whose mortgages have been purchased or securitized by Fannie Mae or Freddie Mac in January 1975; (1) Figures cover the Rochester, MN Metropolitan Statistical Area—see Appendix B for areas included; (2) Rankings are based on annual percentage change for all metro areas containing at least 15,000 transactions over the last 10 years and ranges from 1 to 245; (3) figures based on a weighted average of Census Division estimates using a seasonally adjusted, purchase-only index; all figures are for the period ending December 31, 2018
Source: Federal Housing Finance Agency, House Price Index, February 26, 2019

Median Single-Family Home Prices

Area	2016	2017	2018[p]	Percent Change 2017 to 2018
MSA[1]	n/a	n/a	n/a	n/a
U.S. Average	235.5	248.8	261.6	5.1

Note: Figures are median sales prices of existing single-family homes in thousands of dollars; (p) preliminary; n/a not available; (1) Figures cover the Rochester, MN Metropolitan Statistical Area—see Appendix B for areas included
Source: National Association of Realtors, Median Sales Price of Existing Single-Family Homes for Metropolitan Areas, 4th Quarter 2018

Qualifying Income Based on Median Sales Price of Existing Single-Family Homes

Area	With 5% Down ($)	With 10% Down ($)	With 20% Down ($)
MSA[1]	n/a	n/a	n/a
U.S. Average	62,954	59,640	53,013

Note: Figures are preliminary; Qualifying income is based on a mortgage rate of 4.9%. Monthly principal and interest payment is limited to 25% of income; n/a not available; (1) Figures cover the Rochester, MN Metropolitan Statistical Area—see Appendix B for areas included
Source: National Association of Realtors, Qualifying Income Based on Median Sales Price of Existing Single-Family Homes for Metropolitan Areas, 4th Quarter 2018

Median Apartment Condo-Coop Home Prices

Area	2016	2017	2018[p]	Percent Change 2017 to 2018
MSA[1]	n/a	n/a	n/a	n/a
U.S. Average	220.7	234.3	241.0	2.9

Note: Figures are median sales prices of existing apartment condo-coop homes in thousands of dollars; (p) preliminary; n/a not available; (1) Figures cover the Rochester, MN Metropolitan Statistical Area—see Appendix B for areas included
Source: National Association of Realtors, Median Sales Price of Existing Apartment Condo-Coop Homes for Metropolitan Areas, 4th Quarter 2018

Home Value Distribution

Area	Under $50,000	$50,000 -$99,999	$100,000 -$149,999	$150,000 -$199,999	$200,000 -$299,999	$300,000 -$499,999	$500,000 -$999,999	$1,000,000 or more
City	4.6	7.3	22.1	26.5	23.0	13.7	2.4	0.5
MSA[1]	5.9	8.8	20.0	22.9	21.7	15.7	4.1	1.0
U.S.	8.3	13.9	14.7	14.6	18.7	17.3	9.7	2.7

Note: Figures are percentages and cover owner-occupied housing units; (1) Figures cover the Rochester, MN Metropolitan Statistical Area—see Appendix B for areas included
Source: U.S. Census Bureau, 2013-2017 American Community Survey 5-Year Estimates

Homeownership Rate

Area	2010 (%)	2011 (%)	2012 (%)	2013 (%)	2014 (%)	2015 (%)	2016 (%)	2017 (%)	2018 (%)
MSA[1]	n/a	n/a	n/a	n/a	n/a	n/a	n/a	n/a	n/a
U.S.	66.9	66.1	65.4	65.1	64.5	63.7	63.4	63.9	64.4

Note: (1) Figures cover the Rochester, MN Metropolitan Statistical Area—see Appendix B for areas included; n/a not available
Source: U.S. Census Bureau, Housing Vacancies and Homeownership Annual Statistics: 2010-2018

Year Housing Structure Built

Area	2010 or Later	2000 -2009	1990 -1999	1980 -1989	1970 -1979	1960 -1969	1950 -1959	1940 -1949	Before 1940	Median Year
City	4.8	19.5	14.7	14.3	13.8	11.6	9.7	3.6	8.1	1982
MSA[1]	4.0	18.6	14.9	12.2	13.8	9.8	8.1	3.7	15.0	1980
U.S.	3.2	14.5	14.0	13.6	15.5	10.8	10.5	5.1	12.9	1977

Note: Figures are percentages except for Median Year; Note: (1) Figures cover the Rochester, MN Metropolitan Statistical Area—see Appendix B for areas included
Source: U.S. Census Bureau, 2013-2017 American Community Survey 5-Year Estimates

Gross Monthly Rent

Area	Under $500	$500 -$999	$1,000 -$1,499	$1,500 -$1,999	$2,000 -$2,499	$2,500 -$2,999	$3,000 and up	Median ($)
City	10.8	47.7	28.2	9.6	2.0	0.4	1.3	891
MSA[1]	14.0	50.5	24.6	7.7	1.8	0.3	1.0	835
U.S.	10.5	41.1	28.7	11.7	4.5	1.8	1.7	982

Note: Figures are percentages except for Median; Gross rent is the contract rent plus the estimated average monthly cost of utilities (electricity, gas, and water and sewer) and fuels (oil, coal, kerosene, wood, etc.) if these are paid by the renter (or paid for the renter by someone else); (1) Figures cover the Rochester, MN Metropolitan Statistical Area—see Appendix B for areas included
Source: U.S. Census Bureau, 2013-2017 American Community Survey 5-Year Estimates

HEALTH

Health Risk Factors

Category	MSA[1] (%)	U.S. (%)
Adults aged 18–64 who have any kind of health care coverage	90.6	87.3
Adults who reported being in good or better health	90.8	82.4
Adults who have been told they have high blood cholesterol	30.6	33.0
Adults who have been told they have high blood pressure	26.2	32.3
Adults who are current smokers	12.4	17.1
Adults who currently use E-cigarettes	n/a	4.6
Adults who currently use chewing tobacco, snuff, or snus	3.3	4.0
Adults who are heavy drinkers[2]	5.9	6.3
Adults who are binge drinkers[3]	15.7	17.4
Adults who are overweight (BMI 25.0 - 29.9)	37.2	35.3
Adults who are obese (BMI 30.0 - 99.8)	30.5	31.3
Adults who participated in any physical activities in the past month	74.9	74.4
Adults who always or nearly always wears a seat belt	97.5	94.3

Note: n/a not available; (1) Figures cover the Rochester, MN Metropolitan Statistical Area—see Appendix B for areas included; (2) Heavy drinkers are classified as adult men having more than 14 drinks per week and adult women having more than 7 drinks per week; (3) Binge drinkers are classified as males having five or more drinks on one occasion or females having four or more drinks on one occasion
Source: Centers for Disease Control and Prevention, Behavioral Risk Factor Surveillance System, SMART: Selected Metropolitan Area Risk Trends, 2017

Acute and Chronic Health Conditions

Category	MSA[1] (%)	U.S. (%)
Adults who have ever been told they had a heart attack	3.3	4.2
Adults who have ever been told they have angina or coronary heart disease	3.8	3.9
Adults who have ever been told they had a stroke	2.2	3.0
Adults who have ever been told they have asthma	12.8	14.2
Adults who have ever been told they have arthritis	21.7	24.9
Adults who have ever been told they have diabetes[2]	9.2	10.5
Adults who have ever been told they had skin cancer	7.0	6.2
Adults who have ever been told they had any other types of cancer	5.8	7.1
Adults who have ever been told they have COPD	5.4	6.5
Adults who have ever been told they have kidney disease	2.6	3.0
Adults who have ever been told they have a form of depression	19.2	20.5

Note: (1) Figures cover the Rochester, MN Metropolitan Statistical Area—see Appendix B for areas included; (2) Figures do not include pregnancy-related, borderline, or pre-diabetes
Source: Centers for Disease Control and Prevention, Behavioral Risk Factor Surveillance System, SMART: Selected Metropolitan Area Risk Trends, 2017

Health Screening and Vaccination Rates

Category	MSA[1] (%)	U.S. (%)
Adults aged 65+ who have had flu shot within the past year	73.6	60.7
Adults aged 65+ who have ever had a pneumonia vaccination	85.4	75.4
Adults who have ever been tested for HIV	23.8	36.1
Adults who have ever had the shingles or zoster vaccine?	40.5	28.9
Adults who have had their blood cholesterol checked within the last five years	86.1	85.9

Note: n/a not available; (1) Figures cover the Rochester, MN Metropolitan Statistical Area—see Appendix B for areas included.
Source: Centers for Disease Control and Prevention, Behaviorial Risk Factor Surveillance System, SMART: Selected Metropolitan Area Risk Trends, 2017

Disability Status

Category	MSA[1] (%)	U.S. (%)
Adults who reported being deaf	7.9	6.7
Are you blind or have serious difficulty seeing, even when wearing glasses?	3.2	4.5
Are you limited in any way in any of your usual activities due of arthritis?	10.6	12.9
Do you have difficulty doing errands alone?	3.6	6.8
Do you have difficulty dressing or bathing?	2.3	3.6
Do you have serious difficulty concentrating/remembering/making decisions?	8.5	10.7
Do you have serious difficulty walking or climbing stairs?	10.0	13.6

Note: (1) Figures cover the Rochester, MN Metropolitan Statistical Area—see Appendix B for areas included.
Source: Centers for Disease Control and Prevention, Behaviorial Risk Factor Surveillance System, SMART: Selected Metropolitan Area Risk Trends, 2017

Mortality Rates for the Top 10 Causes of Death in the U.S.

ICD-10[a] Sub-Chapter	ICD-10[a] Code	Age-Adjusted Mortality Rate[1] per 100,000 population	
		County[2]	U.S.
Malignant neoplasms	C00-C97	125.5	155.5
Ischaemic heart diseases	I20-I25	78.2	94.8
Other forms of heart disease	I30-I51	31.7	52.9
Chronic lower respiratory diseases	J40-J47	30.5	41.0
Cerebrovascular diseases	I60-I69	28.3	37.5
Other degenerative diseases of the nervous system	G30-G31	45.3	35.0
Other external causes of accidental injury	W00-X59	27.3	33.7
Organic, including symptomatic, mental disorders	F01-F09	41.8	31.0
Hypertensive diseases	I10-I15	16.0	21.9
Diabetes mellitus	E10-E14	8.7	21.2

Note: (a) ICD-10 = International Classification of Diseases 10th Revision; (1) Mortality rates are a three year average covering 2015-2017; (2) Figures cover Olmsted County.
Source: Centers for Disease Control and Prevention, National Center for Health Statistics. Underlying Cause of Death 1999-2017 on CDC WONDER Online Database

Mortality Rates for Selected Causes of Death

ICD-10[a] Sub-Chapter	ICD-10[a] Code	Age-Adjusted Mortality Rate[1] per 100,000 population	
		County[2]	U.S.
Assault	X85-Y09	Suppressed	5.9
Diseases of the liver	K70-K76	8.1	14.1
Human immunodeficiency virus (HIV) disease	B20-B24	Suppressed	1.8
Influenza and pneumonia	J09-J18	4.9	14.3
Intentional self-harm	X60-X84	9.7	13.6
Malnutrition	E40-E46	Suppressed	1.6
Obesity and other hyperalimentation	E65-E68	Suppressed	2.1
Renal failure	N17-N19	Unreliable	13.0
Transport accidents	V01-V99	8.5	12.4
Viral hepatitis	B15-B19	Unreliable	1.6

Note: (a) ICD-10 = International Classification of Diseases 10th Revision; (1) Mortality rates are a three year average covering 2015-2017; (2) Figures cover Olmsted County; Data are suppressed when the data meet the criteria for confidentiality constraints; Mortality rates are flagged as unreliable when the rate would be calculated with a numerator of 20 or less.
Source: Centers for Disease Control and Prevention, National Center for Health Statistics. Underlying Cause of Death 1999-2017 on CDC WONDER Online Database

Health Insurance Coverage

Area	With Health Insurance	With Private Health Insurance	With Public Health Insurance	Without Health Insurance	Population Under Age 18 Without Health Insurance
City	95.0	78.9	29.5	5.0	2.8
MSA[1]	94.9	79.8	29.3	5.1	3.5
U.S.	89.5	67.2	33.8	10.5	5.7

Note: Figures are percentages that cover the civilian noninstitutionalized population; (1) Figures cover the Rochester, MN Metropolitan Statistical Area—see Appendix B for areas included
Source: U.S. Census Bureau, 2013-2017 American Community Survey 5-Year Estimates

Number of Medical Professionals

Area	MDs[3]	DOs[3,4]	Dentists	Podiatrists	Chiropractors	Optometrists
County[1] (number)	3,696	87	174	10	68	34
County[1] (rate[2])	2,412.8	56.8	112.3	6.5	43.9	21.9
U.S. (rate[2])	279.3	23.0	68.4	6.0	27.1	16.2

Note: Data as of 2017 unless noted; (1) Data covers Olmsted County; (2) Rate per 100,000 population; (3) Data as of 2016 and includes all active, non-federal physicians; (4) Doctor of Osteopathic Medicine
Source: U.S. Department of Health and Human Services, Health Resources and Services Administration, Bureau of Health Professions, Area Resource File (ARF) 2017-2018

Best Hospitals

According to *U.S. News,* the Rochester, MN metro area is home to one of the best hospitals in the U.S.: **Mayo Clinic** (Honor Roll/15 adult specialties and 7 pediatric specialties). The hospital listed was nationally ranked in at least one of 16 adult or 10 pediatric specialties. Only 170 hospitals nationwide were nationally ranked in one or more adult or pediatric specialty. Twenty hospitals in the U.S. made the Honor Roll. The Best Hospitals Honor Roll takes both the national rankings and the procedure and condition ratings into account. Hospitals received points if they were nationally ranked in one of the 16 adult specialties—the higher they ranked, the more points they got—and how many ratings of "high performing" they earned in the nine procedures and conditions. *U.S. News Online, "America's Best Hospitals 2018-19"*

According to *U.S. News,* the Rochester, MN metro area is home to one of the best children's hospitals in the U.S.: **Mayo Clinic Children's Center** (7 pediatric specialties). The hospital listed was highly ranked in at least one of 10 pediatric specialties. Eighty-six children's hospitals in the U.S. were nationally ranked in at least one specialty. Hospitals received points for being ranked in a specialty, and the 10 hospitals with the most points across the 10 specialties make up the Honor Roll. *U.S. News Online, "America's Best Children's Hospitals 2018-19"*

EDUCATION

Public School District Statistics

District Name	Schls	Pupils	Pupil/ Teacher Ratio	Minority Pupils[1] (%)	Free Lunch Eligible[2] (%)	IEP[3] (%)
Rochester Public School District	40	17,449	15.0	38.2	30.5	16.3

Note: Table includes school districts with 2,000 or more students; (1) Percentage of students that are not non-Hispanic white; (2) Percentage of students that are eligible for the free lunch program; (3) Percentage of students that have an Individualized Education Program.
Source: U.S. Department of Education, National Center for Education Statistics, Common Core of Data, Local Education Agency (School District) Universe Survey: School Year 2016-2017; U.S. Department of Education, National Center for Education Statistics, Common Core of Data, Public Elementary/Secondary School Universe Survey: School Year 2016-2017

Highest Level of Education

Area	Less than H.S.	H.S. Diploma	Some College, No Deg.	Associate Degree	Bachelor's Degree	Master's Degree	Prof. School Degree	Doctorate Degree
City	6.0	19.4	19.1	10.8	24.7	11.1	5.1	3.9
MSA[1]	6.0	24.7	20.7	11.7	21.9	8.9	3.6	2.5
U.S.	12.7	27.3	20.8	8.3	19.1	8.4	2.0	1.4

Note: Figures cover persons age 25 and over; (1) Figures cover the Rochester, MN Metropolitan Statistical Area—see Appendix B for areas included
Source: U.S. Census Bureau, 2013-2017 American Community Survey 5-Year Estimates

Educational Attainment by Race

Area	High School Graduate or Higher (%)					Bachelor's Degree or Higher (%)				
	Total	White	Black	Asian	Hisp.[2]	Total	White	Black	Asian	Hisp.[2]
City	94.0	96.0	82.2	83.3	72.8	44.7	45.4	22.5	57.8	23.8
MSA[1]	94.0	95.1	82.7	83.5	72.4	36.9	36.6	22.6	56.6	20.9
U.S.	87.3	89.3	84.9	86.5	66.7	30.9	32.2	20.6	52.7	15.2

Note: Figures shown cover persons 25 years old and over; (1) Figures cover the Rochester, MN Metropolitan Statistical Area—see Appendix B for areas included; (2) People of Hispanic origin can be of any race
Source: U.S. Census Bureau, 2013-2017 American Community Survey 5-Year Estimates

School Enrollment by Grade and Control

Area	Preschool (%)		Kindergarten (%)		Grades 1 - 4 (%)		Grades 5 - 8 (%)		Grades 9 - 12 (%)	
	Public	Private	Public	Private	Public	Private	Public	Private	Public	Private
City	51.3	48.7	78.8	21.2	85.0	15.0	83.9	16.1	93.6	6.4
MSA[1]	60.8	39.2	83.3	16.7	87.0	13.0	87.3	12.7	93.3	6.7
U.S.	58.8	41.2	87.7	12.3	89.7	10.3	89.6	10.4	90.3	9.7

Note: Figures shown cover persons 3 years old and over; (1) Figures cover the Rochester, MN Metropolitan Statistical Area—see Appendix B for areas included
Source: U.S. Census Bureau, 2013-2017 American Community Survey 5-Year Estimates

Average Salaries of Public School Classroom Teachers

Area	2016		2017		Change from 2016 to 2017	
	Dollars	Rank[1]	Dollars	Rank[1]	Percent	Rank[2]
Minnesota	56,913	17	57,346	20	0.8	36
U.S. Average	58,479	–	59,660	–	2.0	–

Note: (1) Rank ranges from 1 to 51 where 1 indicates highest salary; (2) Rank ranges from 1 to 51 where 1 indicates highest percent change.
Source: National Education Association, Rankings & Estimates: Rankings of the States 2017 and Estimates of School Statistics 2018

Higher Education

Four-Year Colleges			Two-Year Colleges			Medical Schools[1]	Law Schools[2]	Voc/ Tech[3]
Public	Private Non-profit	Private For-profit	Public	Private Non-profit	Private For-profit			
1	3	1	1	0	0	1	0	2

Note: Figures cover institutions located within the city limits and include main campuses only; (1) includes schools accredited by the Liaison Committee on Medical Education and the American Osteopathic Association's Commission on Osteopathic College Accreditation; (2) includes ABA-accredited schools, schools with provisional ABA accreditation, and state accredited schools; (3) includes all schools with programs that are less than 2 years.
Source: National Center for Education Statistics, Integrated Postsecondary Education System (IPEDS), 2017-18; Wikipedia, List of Medical Schools in the United States, accessed April 3, 2019; Wikipedia, List of Law Schools in the United States, accessed April 3, 2019

According to *U.S. News & World Report,* the Rochester, MN metro area is home to one of the top 75 medical schools for research in the U.S.: **Mayo Clinic School of Medicine (Alix)** (#9 tie). The rankings are based on a weighted average of 11 measures of quality: quality assessment; peer assessment score; assessment score by residency directors; research activity; total research activity; average research activity per faculty member; student selectivity; median MCAT total score; median undergraduate GPA; acceptance rate; and faculty resources. *U.S. News & World Report, "America's Best Graduate Schools, Medical, 2020"*

PRESIDENTIAL ELECTION

2016 Presidential Election Results

Area	Clinton	Trump	Johnson	Stein	Other
Olmsted County	45.3	44.5	4.4	1.4	4.4
U.S.	48.0	45.9	3.3	1.1	1.7

Note: Results are percentages and may not add to 100% due to rounding
Source: Dave Leip's Atlas of U.S. Presidential Elections

EMPLOYERS

Major Employers

Company Name	Industry
Benchmark Electronics	Contract mfg/design/engineering
Cardinal of Minnesota	Res. services/dev. disabilities
Charter Communications	Cable & other pay television services
City of Rochester	Municipal government
Crenlo	Fabricated metal
Federal Medical Center	Corrections/medical
Halcon	Furniture manufacturer
Hiawatha Homes	Res. services/dev. disabilities
IBM	Electronics
Interstate Hotels & Resorts	Hotel/restaurant services
Kemps	Food processing
Mayo Clinic	Healthcare
McNeilus Steel	Steel fabrication
McNeilus Truck	Mobile concrete mixers, garbage trucks
Olmstead County	Government
Olmstead Medical Center	Healthcare
Pace Dairy	Food processing
RCTC	Post-secondary education
Reichel Foods	Refrigerated lunch & snacks
Rochester Meat Company	Meat processor
Rochester Medical Corp	Medical device manufacturer
Rochester Public Schools	Education
Samaritan Bethany	Health care of the aging
Seneca Food	Food processing
Think Bank	Banking and financial services

Note: Companies shown are located within the Rochester, MN Metropolitan Statistical Area.
Source: Hoovers.com; Wikipedia

PUBLIC SAFETY

Crime Rate

Area	All Crimes	Violent Crimes				Property Crimes		
		Murder	Rape[3]	Robbery	Aggrav. Assault	Burglary	Larceny -Theft	Motor Vehicle Theft
City	2,054.2	0.9	52.9	39.9	100.7	249.9	1,524.8	85.0
Suburbs[1]	782.8	0.0	24.3	4.9	62.2	131.1	506.0	54.4
Metro[2]	1,454.3	0.5	39.4	23.4	82.5	193.9	1,044.1	70.6
U.S.	2,756.1	5.3	41.7	98.0	248.9	430.4	1,694.4	237.4

Note: Figures are crimes per 100,000 population; (1) All areas within the metro area that are located outside the city limits; (2) Figures cover the Rochester, MN Metropolitan Statistical Area—see Appendix B for areas included; (3) The city and U.S. figures shown were reported using the revised Uniform Crime Reporting (UCR) definition of rape. The suburban and metro area figures shown are an aggregate total of the data submitted using both the revised and legacy UCR definitions.
Source: FBI Uniform Crime Reports, 2017

Hate Crimes

Area	Number of Quarters Reported	Number of Incidents per Bias Motivation					
		Race/Ethnicity/ Ancestry	Religion	Sexual Orientation	Disability	Gender	Gender Identity
City	4	10	3	0	0	0	0
U.S.	4	4,131	1,564	1,130	116	46	119

Source: Federal Bureau of Investigation, Hate Crime Statistics 2017

Identity Theft Consumer Reports

Area	Reports	Reports per 100,000 Population	Rank[2]
MSA[1]	164	76	242
U.S.	444,602	135	-

Note: (1) Figures cover the Rochester, MN Metropolitan Statistical Area—see Appendix B for areas included; (2) Rank ranges from 1 to 389 where 1 indicates greatest number of identity theft reports per 100,000 population
Source: Federal Trade Commission, Consumer Sentinel Network Data Book for January–December 2018

Fraud and Other Consumer Reports

Area	Reports	Reports per 100,000 Population	Rank[2]
MSA[1]	873	404	315
U.S.	2,552,917	776	-

Note: (1) Figures cover the Rochester, MN Metropolitan Statistical Area—see Appendix B for areas included; (2) Rank ranges from 1 to 389 where 1 indicates greatest number of fraud and other consumer reports per 100,000 population
Source: Federal Trade Commission, Consumer Sentinel Network Data Book for January–December 2018

SPORTS

Professional Sports Teams

Team Name	League	Year Established

No teams are located in the metro area
Source: Wikipedia, Major Professional Sports Teams of the United States and Canada, April 5, 2019

CLIMATE

Average and Extreme Temperatures

Temperature	Jan	Feb	Mar	Apr	May	Jun	Jul	Aug	Sep	Oct	Nov	Dec	Yr.
Extreme High (°F)	55	63	79	91	92	101	102	100	97	90	74	62	102
Average High (°F)	21	26	38	55	68	78	82	79	70	59	40	26	54
Average Temp. (°F)	12	18	29	45	57	67	71	69	60	48	32	19	44
Average Low (°F)	3	8	20	34	46	56	60	58	48	38	24	10	34
Extreme Low (°F)	-40	-29	-31	5	21	35	42	35	23	11	-20	-33	-40

Note: Figures cover the years 1948-1995
Source: National Climatic Data Center, International Station Meteorological Climate Summary, 9/96

Average Precipitation/Snowfall/Humidity

Precip./Humidity	Jan	Feb	Mar	Apr	May	Jun	Jul	Aug	Sep	Oct	Nov	Dec	Yr.
Avg. Precip. (in.)	0.8	0.8	1.8	2.8	3.4	4.0	4.2	3.9	3.1	2.0	1.7	1.0	29.4
Avg. Snowfall (in.)	9	8	10	4	Tr	0	0	0	Tr	1	6	10	47
Avg. Rel. Hum. 6am (%)	80	81	82	80	80	82	86	88	87	82	83	83	83
Avg. Rel. Hum. 3pm (%)	72	68	65	54	52	53	56	57	56	54	66	74	61

Note: Figures cover the years 1948-1995; Tr = Trace amounts (<0.05 in. of rain; <0.5 in. of snow)
Source: National Climatic Data Center, International Station Meteorological Climate Summary, 9/96

Weather Conditions

Temperature			Daytime Sky			Precipitation		
5°F & below	32°F & below	90°F & above	Clear	Partly cloudy	Cloudy	0.01 inch or more precip.	0.1 inch or more snow/ice	Thunder-storms
46	165	9	87	126	152	114	40	41

Note: Figures are average number of days per year and cover the years 1948-1995
Source: National Climatic Data Center, International Station Meteorological Climate Summary, 9/96

HAZARDOUS WASTE

Superfund Sites

The Rochester, MN metro area has no sites on the EPA's Superfund Final National Priorities List. There are a total of 1,390 Superfund sites with a status of proposed or final on the list in the U.S.
U.S. Environmental Protection Agency, National Priorities List, April 5, 2019

**AIR & WATER
QUALITY**

Air Quality Trends: Ozone

	1990	1995	2000	2005	2010	2012	2014	2015	2016	2017
MSA[1]	n/a	n/a	n/a	n/a	n/a	n/a	n/a	n/a	n/a	n/a
U.S.	0.088	0.089	0.082	0.080	0.073	0.075	0.067	0.068	0.069	0.068

Note: (1) Data covers the Rochester, MN Metropolitan Statistical Area—see Appendix B for areas included; n/a not available. The values shown are the composite ozone concentration averages among trend sites based on the highest fourth daily maximum 8-hour concentration in parts per million. These trends are based on sites having an adequate record of monitoring data during the trend period. Data from exceptional events are included.
Source: U.S. Environmental Protection Agency, Air Quality Monitoring Information, "Air Quality Trends by City, 1990-2017"

Air Quality Index

Area	Percent of Days when Air Quality was...[2]					AQI Statistics[2]	
	Good	Moderate	Unhealthy for Sensitive Groups	Unhealthy	Very Unhealthy	Maximum	Median
MSA[1]	85.5	14.5	0.0	0.0	0.0	87	37

Note: (1) Data covers the Rochester, MN Metropolitan Statistical Area—see Appendix B for areas included; (2) Based on 365 days with AQI data in 2017. Air Quality Index (AQI) is an index for reporting daily air quality. EPA calculates the AQI for five major air pollutants regulated by the Clean Air Act: ground-level ozone, particle pollution (aka particulate matter), carbon monoxide, sulfur dioxide, and nitrogen dioxide. The AQI runs from 0 to 500. The higher the AQI value, the greater the level of air pollution and the greater the health concern. There are six AQI categories: "Good" AQI is between 0 and 50. Air quality is considered satisfactory; "Moderate" AQI is between 51 and 100. Air quality is acceptable; "Unhealthy for Sensitive Groups" When AQI values are between 101 and 150, members of sensitive groups may experience health effects; "Unhealthy" When AQI values are between 151 and 200 everyone may begin to experience health effects; "Very Unhealthy" AQI values between 201 and 300 trigger a health alert; "Hazardous" AQI values over 300 trigger warnings of emergency conditions (not shown).
Source: U.S. Environmental Protection Agency, Air Quality Index Report, 2017

Air Quality Index Pollutants

Area	Percent of Days when AQI Pollutant was...[2]					
	Carbon Monoxide	Nitrogen Dioxide	Ozone	Sulfur Dioxide	Particulate Matter 2.5	Particulate Matter 10
MSA[1]	0.0	0.0	56.4	0.0	43.6	0.0

Note: (1) Data covers the Rochester, MN Metropolitan Statistical Area—see Appendix B for areas included; (2) Based on 365 days with AQI data in 2017. The Air Quality Index (AQI) is an index for reporting daily air quality. EPA calculates the AQI for five major air pollutants regulated by the Clean Air Act: ground-level ozone, particle pollution (also known as particulate matter), carbon monoxide, sulfur dioxide, and nitrogen dioxide. The AQI runs from 0 to 500. The higher the AQI value, the greater the level of air pollution and the greater the health concern.
Source: U.S. Environmental Protection Agency, Air Quality Index Report, 2017

Maximum Air Pollutant Concentrations: Particulate Matter, Ozone, CO and Lead

	Particulate Matter 10 (ug/m³)	Particulate Matter 2.5 Wtd AM (ug/m³)	Particulate Matter 2.5 24-Hr (ug/m³)	Ozone (ppm)	Carbon Monoxide (ppm)	Lead (ug/m³)
MSA[1] Level	n/a	6.9	18	0.062	n/a	n/a
NAAQS[2]	150	15	35	0.075	9	0.15
Met NAAQS[2]	n/a	Yes	Yes	Yes	n/a	n/a

Note: (1) Data covers the Rochester, MN Metropolitan Statistical Area—see Appendix B for areas included; Data from exceptional events are included; (2) National Ambient Air Quality Standards; ppm = parts per million; ug/m³ = micrograms per cubic meter; n/a not available.
Concentrations: Particulate Matter 10 (coarse particulate)—highest second maximum 24-hour concentration; Particulate Matter 2.5 Wtd AM (fine particulate)—highest weighted annual mean concentration; Particulate Matter 2.5 24-Hour (fine particulate)—highest 98th percentile 24-hour concentration; Ozone—highest fourth daily maximum 8-hour concentration; Carbon Monoxide—highest second maximum non-overlapping 8-hour concentration; Lead—maximum running 3-month average
Source: U.S. Environmental Protection Agency, Air Quality Monitoring Information, "Air Quality Statistics by City, 2017"

Maximum Air Pollutant Concentrations: Nitrogen Dioxide and Sulfur Dioxide

	Nitrogen Dioxide AM (ppb)	Nitrogen Dioxide 1-Hr (ppb)	Sulfur Dioxide AM (ppb)	Sulfur Dioxide 1-Hr (ppb)	Sulfur Dioxide 24-Hr (ppb)
MSA[1] Level	n/a	n/a	n/a	n/a	n/a
NAAQS[2]	53	100	30	75	140
Met NAAQS[2]	n/a	n/a	n/a	n/a	n/a

Note: (1) Data covers the Rochester, MN Metropolitan Statistical Area—see Appendix B for areas included; Data from exceptional events are included; (2) National Ambient Air Quality Standards; ppm = parts per million; ug/m³ = micrograms per cubic meter; n/a not available.
Concentrations: Nitrogen Dioxide AM—highest arithmetic mean concentration; Nitrogen Dioxide 1-Hr—highest 98th percentile 1-hour daily maximum concentration; Sulfur Dioxide AM—highest annual mean concentration; Sulfur Dioxide 1-Hr—highest 99th percentile 1-hour daily maximum concentration; Sulfur Dioxide 24-Hr—highest second maximum 24-hour concentration
Source: U.S. Environmental Protection Agency, Air Quality Monitoring Information, "Air Quality Statistics by City, 2017"

Drinking Water

Water System Name	Pop. Served	Primary Water Source Type	Violations[1] Health Based	Violations[1] Monitoring/ Reporting
Rochester	114,011	Ground	0	0

Note: (1) Based on violation data from January 1, 2018 to December 31, 2018
Source: U.S. Environmental Protection Agency, Office of Ground Water and Drinking Water, Safe Drinking Water Information System (based on data extracted April 5, 2019)

Sioux Falls, South Dakota

Background

Sioux Falls, in southeastern South Dakota, is named for the falls on the Big Sioux River where it is located. It is the seat of Minnehaha County and overlaps Lincoln County, as well. Sioux Falls is a Great Plains city, rich in history and scenic attractions, a dynamic economic center, and a splendid family town, offering an extensive range of outdoor activities.

The city was founded prior to the Civil War by settlers who were attracted by the nearby stone quarries and the possibility of harnessing the river for water power. Many Scottish, English, and Norwegian immigrants came to the area and used their skills as stonecutters. The community was incorporated as a village in 1877 and as a city in 1883.

At the city's popular Falls Park, the remains of a water-driven mill testify to the importance of the river. The city has preserved much of its early architectural charm, with five separate historical districts preserving buildings of considerable interest. Of particular interest are the R.F. Pettigrew home, residence of the state's first U.S. senator, and the Minnehaha County Courthouse.

Sioux Falls's restoration efforts have culminated in the "Phillips to the Falls" program, which extends Phillips Avenue north to Falls Park and expands the park to the south, truly joining the park to the rest of downtown.

Sioux Falls offers one of the Midwest's most dynamic business environments, partly due to the lack of a state corporate income tax, and is home to industry leaders in agri-business, distribution and trade, financial services, high-tech manufacturing, health care, retail and tourism. City infrastructure work continues on 23,000 acres, an area larger than half the present size of the city, in eastern Sioux Falls, to prepare the area for growth. Two of this city's largest companies are Wells Fargo and Citigroup.

The city is at the heart of a large agricultural and stock-raising area, producing corn and soybeans, and serving as a great regional center for stockyards and meat-packing plants. Industries in Sioux Falls also produce computer components, electronics, and artificial flowers. Some of the nation's leading credit card operations are based in the city, and it is a regional center for retail, tourism, marketing, and medical care. Employment opportunities are varied and abundant, and the city's unemployment rate is generally half that of the state as a whole. Air travel is available through the Sioux Falls Regional Airport, which connects conveniently to major air hubs.

Sioux Falls is an important center of higher education, home to the University of South Dakota, Dakota State University, South Dakota State University, Northern State University, Augustana College, National American University, Colorado Technical University at Sioux Falls, and Southeast Technical Institute. Also, the Federal Earth Resource Observation System operates a major data collection and analysis site nearby.

The city and its environs are home to a variety of recreation, such as the Catfish Bay Water Ski & Stage Show, Empire Golf Sport Dome, Great Bear Recreation Park, Huset's Speedway, and Wild Water West, the state's largest water and amusement park. The Downtown River Greenway Project includes significant greenway reconstruction on the east bank of the Big Sioux River.

The modern Washington Pavilion of Arts and Science in the Sioux Falls historic downtown district features a performing arts space, a domed Omni theater, a science museum, and display areas for the city's active Fine Arts Center. The Sioux Falls Jazz and Blues Festival celebrated its 25 year in 2016.

The climate is continental with frequent daily or weekly weather changes as the area is visited by differing, usually cold, air masses, which move in very rapidly. During the late fall and winter, cold fronts accompanied by strong, gusty winds can cause temperatures to drop significantly during a 24-hour period. Rainfall is heavier during the spring and summer, and thunderstorms are frequent. Summer daytime temperatures can be high, but the nights are usually comfortable.

Rankings

General Rankings

- In their sixth annual survey, Livability.com looked at data for more than 1,000 U.S. cities to determine the rankings for Livability's "Top 100 Best Places to Live" in 2019. Sioux Falls ranked #7. Criteria: median home value capped at $250,000; affordable living; vibrant economy; education, demographics, health care options. transportation & infrastructure; abundant lifestyle amenities. *Livability.com, "Top 100 Best Places to Live 2019" March 2019*

Business/Finance Rankings

- Experian's latest annual report on consumer credit ranked cities by the average credit score of its residents. Sioux Falls was ranked #7 among the ten cities with the highest average credit score, meaning that its residents showed strong credit management. *www.usatoday.com, "Minneapolis Tops List of Cities With Best Average Credit Score; Greenwood Miss., at the Bottom," January 11, 2018*

- Using data from the Council for Community and Economic Research's 2014 cost of living index, NerdWallet ranked the 100 most affordable cities in America. Median income was compared with cost of living to find truly affordable places. Sioux Falls ranked #36. *NerdWallet.com, "America's Most Affordable Places," May 18, 2015*

- The Sioux Falls metro area appeared on the Milken Institute "2018 Best Performing Cities" list. Rank: #21 out of 201 small metro areas. Criteria: job growth; wage and salary growth; high-tech output growth. *Milken Institute, "Best-Performing Cities 2018," January 24, 2019*

- *Forbes* ranked 200 smaller metro areas (population under 265,400) to determine the nation's "Best Small Places for Business and Careers." The Sioux Falls metro area was ranked #1. Criteria: costs (business and living); job growth (past and projected); income growth; quality of life; educational attainment (college and high school); projected economic growth; cultural and recreational opportunities; net migration patterns; number of highly ranked colleges. *Forbes, "The Best Small Cities for Business and Careers 2018," October, 24 2018*

Dating/Romance Rankings

- Sioux Falls was selected as one of the most romantic cities in the U.S. by video-rental kiosk company Redbox. The city ranked #7 out of 20. Criteria: number of romance-related rentals in 2016. *Redbox, "20 Most Romantic Cities," February 6, 2017*

Food/Drink Rankings

- *Men's Health* ranked 100 major U.S. cities in terms of alcohol intoxication. Sioux Falls ranked #69 (#1 = most sober).Criteria: binge drinking; alcohol-related traffic accidents, arrests, and fatalities. *Men's Health, "America's Drunkest Cities," March 9, 2015*

Health/Fitness Rankings

- *Men's Health* ranked 100 major U.S. cities in terms of the best cities for men. Sioux Falls ranked #50. Criteria: health; fitness; quality of life. *Men's Health, "The Best & Worst Cities for Men Who Want to Be Fit and Happy," January 1, 2016*

Real Estate Rankings

- *WalletHub* compared the most populated U.S. cities, as well as at least two of the most populated cities in each state, for a total of 179, to determine which had the best markets for real estate agents. Sioux Falls ranked #36 where demand was high and pay was the best. Criteria: sales per agent; annual median wage for real-estate agents; monthly average starting salary for real estate agents; real estate job density and competition; unemployment rate; housing-market health index; and other relevant metrics. *www.WalletHub.com, "2018's Best Places to Be a Real Estate Agent,"April 25, 2018*

Safety Rankings

- Allstate ranked the 200 largest cities in America in terms of driver safety. Sioux Falls ranked #79. Criteria: internal property damage claims over a two-year period from January 2015 to December 2016. The report helps increase the importance of safety awareness behind the wheel. *Allstate, "Allstate America's Best Drivers Report, 2018" August 28, 2018*

- The National Insurance Crime Bureau ranked 382 metro areas in the U.S. in terms of per capita rates of vehicle theft. The Sioux Falls metro area ranked #205 (#1 = highest rate). Criteria: number of vehicle theft offenses per 100,000 inhabitants in 2017. *National Insurance Crime Bureau, "Hot Spots 2017," July 12, 2018*

Seniors/Retirement Rankings

- From its Best Cities for Successful Aging indexes, the Milken Institute generated rankings for metropolitan areas, weighing data in nine categories—health care, wellness, living arrangements, transportation and convenience, financial characteristics, education, employment, community engagement, and overall livability. The Sioux Falls metro area was ranked #5 overall in the small metro area category. *Milken Institute, "Best Cities for Successful Aging, 2017" March 14, 2017*

Women/Minorities Rankings

- *Women's Health*, together with the site Yelp, identified the 15 "Wellthiest" spots in the U.S. Sioux Falls appeared among the top for happiest, healthiest, outdoorsiest and Zen-iest. *Women's Health, "The 15 Wellthiest Cities in the U.S." July 5, 2017*

- Personal finance website *WalletHub* compared more than 180 U.S. cities—including the 150 most populated U.S. cities, plus at least two of the most populated cities in each state—across two key dimensions, "Hispanic Business-Friendliness" and "Hispanic Purchasing Power", to arrive at the most favorable conditions for Hispanic entrepreneurs. Sioux Falls was ranked #14 out of 182. Criteria includes: share of Hispanic-Owned Businesses; Hispanic entrepreneurship rate to median annual income of Hispanics; Small Business-Friendliness score; cost of living; and number of Hispanics with at least a bachelor's degree. *WalletHub.com, "2018's Best Cities for Hispanic Entrepreneurs," April 26, 2018*

Miscellaneous Rankings

- *WalletHub* compared the 150 most populated U.S. cities to determine their operating efficiency. A "Quality of Services" score was constructed for each city and then divided by the total budget per capita to reveal which were managed the best. Sioux Falls ranked #6. Criteria: financial stability; economy; education; safety; health; infrastructure and pollution. *www.WalletHub.com, "2018's Best- & Worst-Run Cities in America," July 9, 2018*

Business Environment

CITY FINANCES

City Government Finances

Component	2016 ($000)	2016 ($ per capita)
Total Revenues	349,492	2,037
Total Expenditures	342,196	1,995
Debt Outstanding	365,366	2,130
Cash and Securities[1]	731,023	4,261

Note: (1) Cash and security holdings of a government at the close of its fiscal year, including those of its dependent agencies, utilities, and liquor stores.
Source: U.S. Census Bureau, State & Local Government Finances 2016

City Government Revenue by Source

Source	2016 ($000)	2016 ($ per capita)	2016 (%)
General Revenue			
From Federal Government	40,423	236	11.6
From State Government	7,286	42	2.1
From Local Governments	349	2	0.1
Taxes			
Property	55,408	323	15.9
Sales and Gross Receipts	134,978	787	38.6
Personal Income	0	0	0.0
Corporate Income	0	0	0.0
Motor Vehicle License	0	0	0.0
Other Taxes	6,011	35	1.7
Current Charges	51,642	301	14.8
Liquor Store	0	0	0.0
Utility	41,844	244	12.0
Employee Retirement	4,312	25	1.2

Source: U.S. Census Bureau, State & Local Government Finances 2016

City Government Expenditures by Function

Function	2016 ($000)	2016 ($ per capita)	2016 (%)
General Direct Expenditures			
Air Transportation	0	0	0.0
Corrections	0	0	0.0
Education	0	0	0.0
Employment Security Administration	0	0	0.0
Financial Administration	2,600	15	0.8
Fire Protection	27,929	162	8.2
General Public Buildings	4,367	25	1.3
Governmental Administration, Other	11,798	68	3.4
Health	10,772	62	3.1
Highways	60,007	349	17.5
Hospitals	0	0	0.0
Housing and Community Development	2,771	16	0.8
Interest on General Debt	8,453	49	2.5
Judicial and Legal	1,612	9	0.5
Libraries	7,383	43	2.2
Parking	2,336	13	0.7
Parks and Recreation	33,474	195	9.8
Police Protection	32,776	191	9.6
Public Welfare	0	0	0.0
Sewerage	16,044	93	4.7
Solid Waste Management	7,379	43	2.2
Veterans' Services	0	0	0.0
Liquor Store	0	0	0.0
Utility	47,361	276	13.8
Employee Retirement	46,160	269	13.5

Source: U.S. Census Bureau, State & Local Government Finances 2016

DEMOGRAPHICS

Population Growth

Area	1990 Census	2000 Census	2010 Census	2017* Estimate	Population Growth (%)	
					1990-2017	2010-2017
City	102,262	123,975	153,888	170,401	66.6	10.7
MSA[1]	153,500	187,093	228,261	250,564	63.2	9.8
U.S.	248,709,873	281,421,906	308,745,538	321,004,407	29.1	4.0

Note: (1) Figures cover the Sioux Falls, SD Metropolitan Statistical Area—see Appendix B for areas included; (*) 2013-2017 5-year estimated population
Source: U.S. Census Bureau, 1990 Census, Census 2000, Census 2010, 2013-2017 American Community Survey 5-Year Estimates

Household Size

Area	Persons in Household (%)							Average Household Size
	One	Two	Three	Four	Five	Six	Seven or More	
City	32.3	34.0	13.5	11.2	5.4	2.2	1.3	2.40
MSA[1]	28.7	35.0	14.0	12.6	6.2	2.4	1.2	2.50
U.S.	27.7	33.8	15.7	13.0	6.0	2.3	1.4	2.60

Note: (1) Figures cover the Sioux Falls, SD Metropolitan Statistical Area—see Appendix B for areas included
Source: U.S. Census Bureau, 2013-2017 American Community Survey 5-Year Estimates

Race

Area	White Alone[2] (%)	Black Alone[2] (%)	Asian Alone[2] (%)	AIAN[3] Alone[2] (%)	NHOPI[4] Alone[2] (%)	Other Race Alone[2] (%)	Two or More Races (%)
City	85.0	5.4	2.3	2.4	0.0	1.8	3.1
MSA[1]	88.7	3.8	1.6	1.9	0.0	1.3	2.6
U.S.	73.0	12.7	5.4	0.8	0.2	4.8	3.1

Note: (1) Figures cover the Sioux Falls, SD Metropolitan Statistical Area—see Appendix B for areas included; (2) Alone is defined as not being in combination with one or more other races; (3) American Indian and Alaska Native; (4) Native Hawaiian and Other Pacific Islander
Source: U.S. Census Bureau, 2013-2017 American Community Survey 5-Year Estimates

Hispanic or Latino Origin

Area	Total (%)	Mexican (%)	Puerto Rican (%)	Cuban (%)	Other (%)
City	5.0	2.9	0.3	0.0	1.8
MSA[1]	4.0	2.3	0.2	0.0	1.4
U.S.	17.6	11.1	1.7	0.7	4.1

Note: Persons of Hispanic or Latino origin can be of any race; (1) Figures cover the Sioux Falls, SD Metropolitan Statistical Area—see Appendix B for areas included
Source: U.S. Census Bureau, 2013-2017 American Community Survey 5-Year Estimates

Segregation

Type	Segregation Indices[1]				Percent Change		
	1990	2000	2010	2010 Rank[2]	1990-2000	1990-2010	2000-2010
Black/White	n/a	n/a	n/a	n/a	n/a	n/a	n/a
Asian/White	n/a	n/a	n/a	n/a	n/a	n/a	n/a
Hispanic/White	n/a	n/a	n/a	n/a	n/a	n/a	n/a

Note: All figures cover the Metropolitan Statistical Area—see Appendix B for areas included; Figures are based on an analysis of 1990, 2000, and 2010 Census Decennial Census tract data by William H. Frey, Brookings Institution and the University of Michigan Social Science Data Analysis Network. In this analysis all racial groups (whites, blacks, and asians) are non-Hispanic members of those races. Hispanics are shown as a separate category; (1) Segregation Indices are Dissimilarity Indices that measure the degree to which the minority group is distributed differently than whites across census tracts. They range from 0 (complete integration) to 100 (complete segregation) where the value indicates the percentage of the minority group that needs to move to be distributed exactly like whites; (2) Ranges from 1 (most segregated) to 102 (least segregated); n/a not available.
Source: www.CensusScope.org

Ancestry

Area	German	Irish	English	American	Italian	Polish	French[2]	Scottish	Dutch
City	36.5	10.6	5.1	3.9	1.5	1.8	2.2	1.1	5.9
MSA[1]	39.1	10.4	5.2	4.3	1.3	1.6	2.1	1.0	6.8
U.S.	14.1	10.1	7.5	6.6	5.3	2.9	2.5	1.7	1.3

Note: Figures are the percentage of the total population reporting a particular ancestry. The nine most commonly reported ancestries in the U.S. are shown. Figures include multiple ancestries (e.g. if a person reported being Irish and Italian, they were included in both columns); (1) Figures cover the Sioux Falls, SD Metropolitan Statistical Area—see Appendix B for areas included; (2) Excludes Basque
Source: U.S. Census Bureau, 2013-2017 American Community Survey 5-Year Estimates

Foreign-Born Population

Area	Any Foreign Country	Asia	Mexico	Europe	Carribean	Central America[2]	South America	Africa	Canada
City	7.3	2.1	0.4	0.8	0.1	0.9	0.1	2.7	0.1
MSA[1]	5.4	1.5	0.4	0.7	0.1	0.7	0.1	1.9	0.1
U.S.	13.4	4.1	3.6	1.5	1.3	1.0	0.9	0.6	0.3

Note: (1) Figures cover the Sioux Falls, SD Metropolitan Statistical Area—see Appendix B for areas included; (2) Excludes Mexico.
Source: U.S. Census Bureau, 2013-2017 American Community Survey 5-Year Estimates

Marital Status

Area	Never Married	Now Married[2]	Separated	Widowed	Divorced
City	34.0	48.6	1.4	5.1	10.8
MSA[1]	30.4	53.2	1.3	5.1	10.1
U.S.	33.1	48.2	2.0	5.8	10.9

Note: Figures are percentages and cover the population 15 years of age and older; (1) Figures cover the Sioux Falls, SD Metropolitan Statistical Area—see Appendix B for areas included; (2) Excludes separated
Source: U.S. Census Bureau, 2013-2017 American Community Survey 5-Year Estimates

Disability by Age

Area	All Ages	Under 18 Years Old	18 to 64 Years Old	65 Years and Over
City	10.2	3.1	9.2	30.9
MSA[1]	9.9	3.2	8.8	30.5
U.S.	12.6	4.2	10.3	35.5

Note: Figures show percent of the civilian noninstitutionalized population that reported having a disability. Disability status is determined from six types of difficulty: vision, hearing, cognitive, ambulatory, self-care, and independent living. For children under 5 years old, hearing and vision difficulty are used to determine disability status. For children between the ages of 5 and 14, disability status is determined from hearing, vision, cognitive, ambulatory, and self-care difficulties. For people aged 15 years and older, they are considered to have a disability if they have difficulty with any one of the six difficulty types; Note: (1) Figures cover the Sioux Falls, SD Metropolitan Statistical Area—see Appendix B for areas included
Source: U.S. Census Bureau, 2013-2017 American Community Survey 5-Year Estimates

Age

Area	Under Age 5	Age 5–19	Age 20–34	Age 35–44	Age 45–54	Age 55–64	Age 65–74	Age 75–84	Age 85+	Median Age
City	7.7	19.7	23.8	13.2	11.9	11.9	6.9	3.3	1.8	34.3
MSA[1]	7.7	20.5	21.8	13.2	12.5	11.9	7.1	3.4	1.9	35.0
U.S.	6.2	19.5	20.7	12.7	13.4	12.7	8.6	4.4	1.9	37.8

Note: (1) Figures cover the Sioux Falls, SD Metropolitan Statistical Area—see Appendix B for areas included
Source: U.S. Census Bureau, 2013-2017 American Community Survey 5-Year Estimates

Gender

Area	Males	Females	Males per 100 Females
City	84,964	85,437	99.4
MSA[1]	125,534	125,030	100.4
U.S.	158,018,753	162,985,654	97.0

Note: (1) Figures cover the Sioux Falls, SD Metropolitan Statistical Area—see Appendix B for areas included
Source: U.S. Census Bureau, 2013-2017 American Community Survey 5-Year Estimates

Religious Groups by Family

Area	Catholic	Baptist	Non-Den.	Methodist[2]	Lutheran	LDS[3]	Pente-costal	Presby-terian[4]	Muslim[5]	Judaism
MSA[1]	14.9	3.0	1.5	3.9	21.4	0.7	1.1	6.2	0.3	0.1
U.S.	19.1	9.3	4.0	4.0	2.3	2.0	1.9	1.6	0.8	0.7

Note: Figures are the number of adherents as a percentage of the total population; (1) Figures cover the Sioux Falls, SD Metropolitan Statistical Area—see Appendix B for areas included; (2) Methodist/Pietist; (3) Latter Day Saints; (4) Reformed; (5) Figures are estimates
Source: Association of Statisticians of American Religious Bodies, 2010 U.S. Religion Census: Religious Congregations & Membership Study

Religious Groups by Tradition

Area	Catholic	Evangelical Protestant	Mainline Protestant	Other Tradition	Black Protestant	Orthodox
MSA[1]	14.9	12.9	28.1	1.2	0.1	0.1
U.S.	19.1	16.2	7.3	4.3	1.6	0.3

Note: Figures are the number of adherents as a percentage of the total population; (1) Figures cover the Sioux Falls, SD Metropolitan Statistical Area—see Appendix B for areas included
Source: Association of Statisticians of American Religious Bodies, 2010 U.S. Religion Census: Religious Congregations & Membership Study

ECONOMY

Gross Metropolitan Product

Area	2016	2017	2018	2019	Rank[2]
MSA[1]	18.9	19.6	20.5	21.6	128

Note: Figures are in billions of dollars; (1) Figures cover the Sioux Falls, SD Metropolitan Statistical Area—see Appendix B for areas included; (2) Rank is based on 2017 data and ranges from 1 to 381
Source: U.S. Conference of Mayors, U.S. Metro Economies: Economic Growth & Full Employment, June 2018

Economic Growth

Area	2017-2018 (%)	2019-2020 (%)	2021-2022 (%)
MSA[1]	1.5	2.9	2.2

Note: Figures are real gross metropolitan product (GMP) growth rates and represent average annual percent change; (1) Figures cover the Sioux Falls, SD Metropolitan Statistical Area—see Appendix B for areas included
Source: U.S. Conference of Mayors, U.S. Metro Economies: Economic Growth & Full Employment, June 2018

Metropolitan Area Exports

Area	2012	2013	2014	2015	2016	2017	Rank[2]
MSA[1]	439.5	433.0	455.3	375.0	334.3	386.8	230

Note: Figures are in millions of dollars; (1) Figures cover the Sioux Falls, SD Metropolitan Statistical Area—see Appendix B for areas included; (2) Rank is based on 2017 data and ranges from 1 to 387
Source: U.S. Department of Commerce, International Trade Administration, Office of Trade and Economic Analysis, Industry and Analysis, Exports by Metropolitan Area, extracted March 25, 2019

Building Permits

Area	Single-Family			Multi-Family			Total		
	2016	2017	Pct. Chg.	2016	2017	Pct. Chg.	2016	2017	Pct. Chg.
City	1,059	1,192	12.6	1,451	1,202	-17.2	2,510	2,394	-4.6
MSA[1]	1,431	1,533	7.1	1,653	1,381	-16.5	3,084	2,914	-5.5
U.S.	750,800	820,000	9.2	455,800	462,000	1.4	1,206,600	1,282,000	6.2

Note: (1) Figures cover the Sioux Falls, SD Metropolitan Statistical Area—see Appendix B for areas included; Figures represent new, privately-owned housing units authorized (unadjusted data); All permit data are based on estimates with imputation
Source: U.S. Census Bureau, Manufacturing, Mining, and Construction Statistics, Building Permits, 2016, 2017

Bankruptcy Filings

Area	Business Filings			Nonbusiness Filings		
	2017	2018	% Chg.	2017	2018	% Chg.
Minnehaha County	8	10	25.0	327	343	4.9
U.S.	23,157	22,232	-4.0	765,863	751,186	-1.9

Note: Business filings include Chapter 7, Chapter 11, Chapter 12, and Chapter 13; Nonbusiness filings include Chapter 7, Chapter 11, and Chapter 13
Source: Administrative Office of the U.S. Courts, Business and Nonbusiness Bankruptcy, County Cases Commenced by Chapter of the Bankruptcy Code, During the 12-Month Period Ending December 31, 2017 and Business and Nonbusiness Bankruptcy, County Cases Commenced by Chapter of the Bankruptcy Code, During the 12-Month Period Ending December 31, 2018

Housing Vacancy Rates

Area	Gross Vacancy Rate[2] (%)			Year-Round Vacancy Rate[3] (%)			Rental Vacancy Rate[4] (%)			Homeowner Vacancy Rate[5] (%)		
	2016	2017	2018	2016	2017	2018	2016	2017	2018	2016	2017	2018
MSA[1]	n/a	n/a	n/a	n/a	n/a	n/a	n/a	n/a	n/a	n/a	n/a	n/a
U.S.	12.8	12.7	12.3	9.9	9.9	9.7	6.9	7.2	6.9	1.7	1.6	1.5

Note: (1) Figures cover the Sioux Falls, SD Metropolitan Statistical Area—see Appendix B for areas included; (2) The percentage of the total housing inventory that is vacant; (3) The percentage of the housing inventory (excluding seasonal units) that is year-round vacant; (4) The percentage of rental inventory that is vacant for rent; (5) The percentage of homeowner inventory that is vacant for sale; n/a not available
Source: U.S. Census Bureau, Housing Vacancies and Homeownership Annual Statistics: 2016, 2017, 2018

INCOME

Income

Area	Per Capita ($)	Median Household ($)	Average Household ($)
City	31,161	56,714	75,241
MSA[1]	31,578	62,047	78,853
U.S.	31,177	57,652	81,283

Note: (1) Figures cover the Sioux Falls, SD Metropolitan Statistical Area—see Appendix B for areas included
Source: U.S. Census Bureau, 2013-2017 American Community Survey 5-Year Estimates

Household Income Distribution

Area	Percent of Households Earning							
	Under $15,000	$15,000 -$24,999	$25,000 -$34,999	$35,000 -$49,999	$50,000 -$74,999	$75,000 -$99,999	$100,000 -$149,999	$150,000 and up
City	10.1	8.9	10.9	14.5	19.0	14.4	13.2	9.1
MSA[1]	8.6	8.0	10.1	13.8	19.2	15.9	14.9	9.5
U.S.	11.6	9.8	9.5	13.0	17.7	12.3	14.1	12.1

Note: (1) Figures cover the Sioux Falls, SD Metropolitan Statistical Area—see Appendix B for areas included
Source: U.S. Census Bureau, 2013-2017 American Community Survey 5-Year Estimates

Poverty Rate

Area	All Ages	Under 18 Years Old	18 to 64 Years Old	65 Years and Over
City	11.1	14.1	10.5	8.3
MSA[1]	9.2	11.4	8.7	7.2
U.S.	14.6	20.3	13.7	9.3

Note: Figures are percentage of people whose income during the past 12 months was below the poverty level; (1) Figures cover the Sioux Falls, SD Metropolitan Statistical Area—see Appendix B for areas included
Source: U.S. Census Bureau, 2013-2017 American Community Survey 5-Year Estimates

EMPLOYMENT

Labor Force and Employment

Area	Civilian Labor Force			Workers Employed		
	Dec. 2017	Dec. 2018	% Chg.	Dec. 2017	Dec. 2018	% Chg.
City	102,100	103,935	1.8	99,008	101,225	2.2
MSA[1]	149,739	152,386	1.8	145,340	148,590	2.2
U.S.	159,880,000	162,510,000	1.6	153,602,000	156,481,000	1.9

Note: Data is not seasonally adjusted and covers workers 16 years of age and older; (1) Figures cover the Sioux Falls, SD Metropolitan Statistical Area—see Appendix B for areas included
Source: Bureau of Labor Statistics, Local Area Unemployment Statistics

Unemployment Rate

Area	2018											
	Jan.	Feb.	Mar.	Apr.	May	Jun.	Jul.	Aug.	Sep.	Oct.	Nov.	Dec.
City	3.5	3.5	3.2	3.0	2.5	2.5	2.1	2.4	2.2	2.2	2.4	2.6
MSA[1]	3.4	3.4	3.1	2.9	2.4	2.4	2.1	2.3	2.2	2.2	2.3	2.5
U.S.	4.5	4.4	4.1	3.7	3.6	4.2	4.1	3.9	3.6	3.5	3.5	3.7

Note: Data is not seasonally adjusted and covers workers 16 years of age and older; (1) Figures cover the Sioux Falls, SD Metropolitan Statistical Area—see Appendix B for areas included
Source: Bureau of Labor Statistics, Local Area Unemployment Statistics

Average Wages

Occupation	$/Hr.	Occupation	$/Hr.
Accountants and Auditors	32.40	Maids and Housekeeping Cleaners	11.10
Automotive Mechanics	20.50	Maintenance and Repair Workers	17.90
Bookkeepers	16.70	Marketing Managers	64.50
Carpenters	17.80	Nuclear Medicine Technologists	30.50
Cashiers	11.10	Nurses, Licensed Practical	18.70
Clerks, General Office	12.40	Nurses, Registered	28.30
Clerks, Receptionists/Information	13.60	Nursing Assistants	13.10
Clerks, Shipping/Receiving	15.80	Packers and Packagers, Hand	11.80
Computer Programmers	28.00	Physical Therapists	34.20
Computer Systems Analysts	35.60	Postal Service Mail Carriers	25.10
Computer User Support Specialists	19.30	Real Estate Brokers	n/a
Cooks, Restaurant	12.40	Retail Salespersons	14.90
Dentists	99.80	Sales Reps., Exc. Tech./Scientific	33.10
Electrical Engineers	37.30	Sales Reps., Tech./Scientific	43.70
Electricians	22.00	Secretaries, Exc. Legal/Med./Exec.	14.30
Financial Managers	69.80	Security Guards	13.90
First-Line Supervisors/Managers, Sales	23.50	Surgeons	n/a
Food Preparation Workers	11.50	Teacher Assistants*	11.80
General and Operations Managers	67.10	Teachers, Elementary School*	21.90
Hairdressers/Cosmetologists	14.10	Teachers, Secondary School*	22.10
Internists, General	140.10	Telemarketers	n/a
Janitors and Cleaners	12.40	Truck Drivers, Heavy/Tractor-Trailer	20.70
Landscaping/Groundskeeping Workers	14.10	Truck Drivers, Light/Delivery Svcs.	16.90
Lawyers	67.20	Waiters and Waitresses	10.60

Note: Wage data covers the Sioux Falls, SD Metropolitan Statistical Area—see Appendix B for areas included; (*) Hourly wages for elementary/secondary school teachers and teacher assistants were calculated by the editors from annual wage data based on a 40 hour work week; n/a not available.
Source: Bureau of Labor Statistics, Metro Area Occupational Employment & Wage Estimates, May 2018

Employment by Occupation

Occupation Classification	City (%)	MSA[1] (%)	U.S. (%)
Management, Business, Science, and Arts	36.3	36.7	37.4
Natural Resources, Construction, and Maintenance	8.0	9.4	8.9
Production, Transportation, and Material Moving	13.3	12.7	12.2
Sales and Office	26.9	26.0	23.5
Service	15.5	15.3	18.0

Note: Figures cover employed civilians 16 years of age and older; (1) Figures cover the Sioux Falls, SD Metropolitan Statistical Area—see Appendix B for areas included
Source: U.S. Census Bureau, 2013-2017 American Community Survey 5-Year Estimates

Employment by Industry

Sector	MSA[1]		U.S.
	Number of Employees	Percent of Total	Percent of Total
Construction, Mining, and Logging	8,500	5.3	5.3
Education and Health Services	33,400	20.8	15.9
Financial Activities	15,800	9.8	5.7
Government	14,700	9.1	15.1
Information	2,600	1.6	1.9
Leisure and Hospitality	15,300	9.5	10.7
Manufacturing	14,400	9.0	8.5
Other Services	6,000	3.7	3.9
Professional and Business Services	16,200	10.1	14.1
Retail Trade	19,600	12.2	10.8
Transportation, Warehousing, and Utilities	5,900	3.7	4.2
Wholesale Trade	8,400	5.2	3.9

Note: Figures are non-farm employment as of December 2018. Figures are not seasonally adjusted and include workers 16 years of age and older; (1) Figures cover the Sioux Falls, SD Metropolitan Statistical Area—see Appendix B for areas included
Source: Bureau of Labor Statistics, Current Employment Statistics, Employment, Hours, and Earnings

Occupations with Greatest Projected Employment Growth: 2018 – 2020

Occupation[1]	2018 Employment	2020 Projected Employment	Numeric Employment Change	Percent Employment Change
Registered Nurses	12,800	13,310	510	4.0
Combined Food Preparation and Serving Workers, Including Fast Food	9,750	10,110	360	3.7
Janitors and Cleaners, Except Maids and Housekeeping Cleaners	10,200	10,520	320	3.1
Laborers and Freight, Stock, and Material Movers, Hand	7,250	7,470	220	3.0
Personal Care Aides	3,020	3,230	210	7.0
Sales Representatives, Wholesale and Manufacturing, Except Technical and Scientific Products	5,530	5,740	210	3.8
Heavy and Tractor-Trailer Truck Drivers	8,540	8,750	210	2.5
Welders, Cutters, Solderers, and Brazers	3,430	3,610	180	5.2
Accountants and Auditors	5,190	5,350	160	3.1
Childcare Workers	6,250	6,400	150	2.4

Note: Projections cover South Dakota; (1) Sorted by numeric employment change
Source: www.projectionscentral.com, State Occupational Projections, 2018–2020 Short-Term Projections

Fastest Growing Occupations: 2018 – 2020

Occupation[1]	2018 Employment	2020 Projected Employment	Numeric Employment Change	Percent Employment Change
Software Developers, Applications	1,280	1,400	120	9.4
Home Health Aides	1,160	1,250	90	7.8
Emergency Medical Technicians and Paramedics	1,100	1,180	80	7.3
Personal Care Aides	3,020	3,230	210	7.0
Slaughterers and Meat Packers	910	960	50	5.5
Welders, Cutters, Solderers, and Brazers	3,430	3,610	180	5.2
Residential Advisors	2,520	2,640	120	4.8
Medical Assistants	1,070	1,120	50	4.7
Sales Representatives, Wholesale and Manufacturing, Technical and Scientific Products	1,500	1,570	70	4.7
Management Analysts	3,060	3,190	130	4.2

Note: Projections cover South Dakota; (1) Sorted by percent employment change and excludes occupations with numeric employment change less than 50
Source: www.projectionscentral.com, State Occupational Projections, 2018–2020 Short-Term Projections

TAXES

State Corporate Income Tax Rates

State	Tax Rate (%)	Income Brackets ($)	Num. of Brackets	Financial Institution Tax Rate (%)[a]	Federal Income Tax Ded.
South Dakota	None	–	–	6.0-0.25 (b)	No

Note: Tax rates as of January 1, 2019; (a) Rates listed are the corporate income tax rate applied to financial institutions or excise taxes based on income. Some states have other taxes based upon the value of deposits or shares; (b) Minimum tax is $800 in California, $250 in District of Columbia, $50 in Arizona and North Dakota (banks), $400 in Rhode Island, $200 per location in South Dakota (banks), $100 in Utah, $300 in Vermont.
Source: Federation of Tax Administrators, Range of State Corporate Income Tax Rates, January 1, 2019

State Individual Income Tax Rates

State	Tax Rate (%)	Income Brackets ($)	Personal Exemptions ($)			Standard Ded. ($)	
			Single	Married	Depend.	Single	Married
South Dakota					– No state income tax –		

Note: Tax rates as of January 1, 2019; Local- and county-level taxes are not included; n/a not applicable;

Source: Federation of Tax Administrators, State Individual Income Tax Rates, January 1, 2019

Various State Sales and Excise Tax Rates

State	State Sales Tax (%)	Gasoline[1] (¢/gal.)	Cigarette[2] ($/pack)	Spirits[3] ($/gal.)	Wine[4] ($/gal.)	Beer[5] ($/gal.)	Recreational Marijuana (%)
South Dakota	4.5 (c)	30	1.53	4.67 (f)(j)	1.31 (l)(p)	0.27	Not legal

Note: All tax rates as of January 1, 2019; (1) The American Petroleum Institute has developed a methodology for determining the average tax rate on a gallon of fuel. Rates may include any of the following: excise taxes, environmental fees, storage tank fees, other fees or taxes, general sales tax, and local taxes. In states where gasoline is subject to the general sales tax, or where the fuel tax is based on the average sale price, the average rate determined by API is sensitive to changes in the price of gasoline. States that fully or partially apply general sales taxes to gasoline: CA, CO, GA, IL, IN, MI, NY; (2) The federal excise tax of $1.0066 per pack and local taxes are not included; (3) Rates are those applicable to off-premise sales of 40% alcohol by volume (a.b.v.) distilled spirits in 750ml containers. Local excise taxes are excluded; (4) Rates are those applicable to off-premise sales of 11% a.b.v. non-carbonated wine in 750ml containers; (5) Rates are those applicable to off-premise sales of 4.7% a.b.v. beer in 12 ounce containers; (c) The sales taxes in Hawaii, New Mexico, North Dakota, and South Dakota have broad bases that include many business-to-business services; (f) Different rates also applicable according to alcohol content, place of production, size of container, or place purchased (on- or off-premise or onboard airlines); (j) Includes sales taxes specific to alcoholic beverages; (l) Different rates also applicable to alcohol content, place of production, size of container, place purchased (on- or off-premise or on board airlines) or type of wine (carbonated, vermouth, etc.); (p) Includes sales taxes specific to alcoholic beverages.
Source: Tax Foundation, 2019 Facts & Figures: How Does Your State Compare?

State Business Tax Climate Index Rankings

State	Overall Rank	Corporate Tax Rank	Individual Income Tax Rank	Sales Tax Rank	Unemployment Insurance Tax Rank	Property Tax Rank
South Dakota	3	1	1	33	39	28

Note: The index is a measure of how each state's tax laws affect economic performance. The lower the rank, the more favorable a state's tax system is for business. States without a given tax are given a ranking of 1. The scores/rankings for the District of Columbia do not affect other states. The 2019 index represents the tax climate as of July 1, 2018.
Source: Tax Foundation, State Business Tax Climate Index 2019

COMMERCIAL UTILITIES

Typical Monthly Electric Bills

Area	Commercial Service ($/month)		Industrial Service ($/month)	
	1,500 kWh	40 kW demand 14,000 kWh	1,000 kW demand 200,000 kWh	50,000 kW demand 32,500,000 kWh
City	209	1,591	24,670	1,945,760
Average[1]	203	1,619	25,886	2,540,077

Note: Figures are based on annualized rates; (1) Average based on 187 utilities surveyed
Source: Edison Electric Institute, Typical Bills and Average Rates Report, Summer 2018

TRANSPORTATION

Means of Transportation to Work

Area	Car/Truck/Van		Public Transportation			Bicycle	Walked	Other Means	Worked at Home
	Drove Alone	Car-pooled	Bus	Subway	Railroad				
City	83.9	8.8	1.0	0.0	0.0	0.5	2.0	0.9	3.0
MSA[1]	84.3	8.1	0.7	0.0	0.0	0.3	2.0	0.8	3.8
U.S.	76.4	9.2	2.5	1.9	0.6	0.6	2.7	1.3	4.7

Note: Figures are percentages and cover workers 16 years of age and older; (1) Figures cover the Sioux Falls, SD Metropolitan Statistical Area—see Appendix B for areas included
Source: U.S. Census Bureau, 2013-2017 American Community Survey 5-Year Estimates

Travel Time to Work

Area	Less Than 10 Minutes	10 to 19 Minutes	20 to 29 Minutes	30 to 44 Minutes	45 to 59 Minutes	60 to 89 Minutes	90 Minutes or More
City	17.0	52.1	21.6	5.2	1.6	1.6	1.0
MSA[1]	17.0	43.7	24.5	9.8	2.3	1.6	1.2
U.S.	12.7	28.9	20.9	20.5	8.1	6.2	2.7

Note: Note: Figures are percentages and include workers 16 years old and over; (1) Figures cover the Sioux Falls, SD Metropolitan Statistical Area—see Appendix B for areas included
Source: U.S. Census Bureau, 2013-2017 American Community Survey 5-Year Estimates

Freeway Travel Time Index

Area	1985	1990	1995	2000	2005	2010	2014
Urban Area Rank[1,2]	n/a	n/a	n/a	n/a	n/a	n/a	n/a
Urban Area Index[1]	n/a	n/a	n/a	n/a	n/a	n/a	n/a
Average Index[3]	1.09	1.11	1.14	1.17	1.20	1.19	1.20

Note: Freeway Travel Time Index—the ratio of travel time in the peak period to the travel time at free-flow conditions. For example, a value of 1.30 indicates a 20-minute free-flow trip takes 26 minutes in the peak (20 minutes x 1.30 = 26 minutes); (1) Data for the Sioux Falls, SD urban area was not available; (2) Rank is based on 101 urban areas (#1 = highest travel time index); (3) Average of 101 urban areas
Source: Texas Transportation Institute, 2015 Urban Mobility Scorecard, August 2015

Freeway Commuter Stress Index

Area	1985	1990	1995	2000	2005	2010	2014
Urban Area Rank[1,2]	n/a	n/a	n/a	n/a	n/a	n/a	n/a
Urban Area Index[1]	n/a	n/a	n/a	n/a	n/a	n/a	n/a
Average Index[3]	1.13	1.16	1.19	1.22	1.25	1.24	1.25

Note: The Freeway Commuter Stress Index is the same as the Freeway Travel Time Index (see table above) except that it includes only the travel in the peak directions during the peak periods; the TTI includes travel in all directions during the peak period. Thus, the CSI is more indicative of the work trip experienced by each commuter on a daily basis; (1) Data for the Sioux Falls, SD urban area was not available; (2) Rank is based on 101 urban areas (#1 = highest travel time index); (3) Average of 101 urban areas
Source: Texas Transportation Institute, 2015 Urban Mobility Scorecard, August 2015

Public Transportation

Agency Name / Mode of Transportation	Vehicles Operated in Maximum Service[1]	Annual Unlinked Passenger Trips[2] (in thous.)	Annual Passenger Miles[3] (in thous.)
Sioux Falls Transit			
Bus (directly operated)	22	795.0	3,325.5
Demand Response (directly operated)	20	99.8	725.2

Note: (1) The number of revenue vehicles operated by the given mode and type of service to meet the annual maximum service requirement. This is the revenue vehicle count during the peak season of the year; on the week and day that maximum service is provided. Vehicles operated in maximum service (VOMS) exclude atypical days and one-time special events; (2) The number of passengers who boarded public transportation vehicles. Passengers are counted each time they board a vehicle no matter how many vehicles they use to travel from their origin to their destination. (3) The sum of the distances ridden by all passengers during the entire fiscal year.
Source: Federal Transit Administration, National Transit Database, 2017

Air Transportation

Airport Name and Code / Type of Service	Passenger Airlines[1]	Passenger Enplanements	Freight Carriers[2]	Freight (lbs)
Joe Foss Field (FSD)				
Domestic service (U.S. carriers - 2018)	19	529,215	8	36,002,489
International service (U.S. carriers - 2017)	3	60	1	12,711,482

Note: (1) Includes all U.S.-based major, minor and commuter airlines that carried at least one passenger during the year; (2) Includes all U.S.-based airlines and freight carriers that transported at least one pound of freight during the year.
Source: Bureau of Transportation Statistics, The Intermodal Transportation Database, Air Carriers: T-100 Domestic Market (U.S. Carriers), 2018; Bureau of Transportation Statistics, The Intermodal Transportation Database, Air Carriers: T-100 International Market (U.S. Carriers), 2017

Other Transportation Statistics

Major Highways: I-29; I-90
Amtrak Service: No
Major Waterways/Ports: None
Source: Amtrak.com; Google Maps

BUSINESSES

Major Business Headquarters

Company Name	Industry	Rankings	
		Fortune[1]	Forbes[2]
No companies listed	-	-	-

Note: (1) Companies that produce a 10-K are ranked 1 to 500 based on 2017 revenue; (2) All private companies with at least $2 billion in annual revenue through the end of their most current fiscal year are ranked 1 to 229; companies listed are headquartered in the city; dashes indicate no ranking
Source: Fortune, "Fortune 500," June 2018; Forbes, "America's Largest Private Companies," 2018 Rankings

Fast-Growing Businesses

According to *Fortune*, Sioux Falls is home to one of the 100 fastest-growing companies in the world: **Meta Financial Group** (#24). Companies were ranked by their revenue growth rate; their EPS growth rate; and their three-year annualized total return to investors for the period ending June 30, 2018. Criteria for inclusion: a company, foreign or domestic, must trade on a major U.S. stock exchange; must file quarterly reports with the SEC; must have a minimum market capitalization of $250 million; must have a stock price of at least $5 on June 30, 2018; must have been trading continuously since June 30, 2015; must have revenue and net income for the four quarters ended on or before April 30, 2018, of at least $50 million and $10 million, respectively; and must have posted a compound annual growth in revenue and earnings per share of at least 15% annually over the three years ending on or before April 30, 2018. Real estate investment trusts, limited-liability companies, limited parterships, business development companies, closed-end investment firms, companies about to be acquired, and companies that lost money in the quarter ending April 30, 2018 were excluded. *Fortune, "100 Fastest-Growing Companies," 2018*

Minority- and Women-Owned Businesses

Group	All Firms		Firms with Paid Employees			
	Firms	Sales ($000)	Firms	Sales ($000)	Employees	Payroll ($000)
AIAN[1]	79	19,348	11	16,165	39	1,411
Asian	289	42,962	59	34,299	185	6,123
Black	274	12,216	7	4,501	99	1,298
Hispanic	241	(s)	11	(s)	500 - 999	(s)
NHOPI[2]	n/a	n/a	n/a	n/a	n/a	n/a
Women	4,164	736,156	459	644,347	4,910	135,921
All Firms	15,083	26,509,536	4,125	25,969,295	106,961	4,173,394

Note: Figures cover firms located in the city; minority- and women-owned business are defined as firms in which the corresponding group own 51% or more of the stock or equity of the company; (1) American Indian and Alaska Native; (2) Native Hawaiian and Other Pacific Islander; (s) estimates are suppressed when publication standards are not met; n/a not available
Source: U.S. Census Bureau, 2012 Economic Census, Survey of Business Owners

HOTELS & CONVENTION CENTERS

Hotels, Motels and Vacation Rentals

Area	5 Star		4 Star		3 Star		2 Star		1 Star		Not Rated	
	Num.	Pct.[3]	Num.	Pct.[3]	Num.	Pct.[3]	Num.	Pct.[3]	Num.	Pct.[3]	Num.	Pct.[3]
City[1]	0	0.0	1	1.4	13	18.6	43	61.4	0	0.0	13	18.6
Total[2]	286	0.4	5,236	7.1	16,715	22.6	10,259	13.9	293	0.4	41,056	55.6

Note: (1) Figures cover Sioux Falls and vicinity; (2) Figures cover all 100 cities in this book; (3) Percentage of hotels which have a given star rating; Star ratings are determined by expedia.com and offer an indication of the general quality of a particular hotel.
Source: www.expedia.com, April 3, 2019

Major Convention Centers

Name	Overall Space (sq. ft.)	Exhibit Space (sq. ft.)	Meeting Space (sq. ft.)	Meeting Rooms
Sioux Falls Convention Center	100,000	50,000	n/a	12

Note: Table includes convention centers located in the Sioux Falls, SD metro area; n/a not available
Source: Original research

Living Environment

COST OF LIVING

Cost of Living Index

Composite Index	Groceries	Housing	Utilities	Trans-portation	Health Care	Misc. Goods/ Services
97.0	98.0	85.5	92.8	95.4	112.2	105.9

Note: The Cost of Living Index measures regional differences in the cost of consumer goods and services, excluding taxes and non-consumer expenditures, for professional and managerial households in the top income quintile. It is based on more than 50,000 prices covering almost 60 different items for which prices are collected three times a year by chambers of commerce, economic development organizations or university applied economic centers in each participating urban area. The numbers shown should be read as a percentage above or below the national average of 100. For example, a value of 115.4 in the groceries column indicates that grocery prices are 15.4% higher than the national average. Small differences in the index numbers should not be interpreted as significant; Figures cover the Sioux Falls SD urban area.
Source: The Council for Community and Economic Research, ACCRA Cost of Living Index, 2018

Grocery Prices

Area[1]	T-Bone Steak ($/pound)	Frying Chicken ($/pound)	Whole Milk ($/half gal.)	Eggs ($/dozen)	Orange Juice ($/64 oz.)	Coffee ($/11.5 oz.)
City[2]	10.07	1.83	2.04	1.53	3.15	4.53
Avg.	11.35	1.42	1.94	1.81	3.52	4.35
Min.	7.45	0.92	0.80	0.75	2.72	3.06
Max.	15.05	2.76	4.18	4.00	5.36	8.20

*Note: (1) Values for the local area are compared with the average, minimum and maximum values for all 291 areas in the Cost of Living Index; (2) Figures cover the Sioux Falls SD urban area; **T-Bone Steak** (price per pound); **Frying Chicken** (price per pound, whole fryer); **Whole Milk** (half gallon carton); **Eggs** (price per dozen, Grade A, large); **Orange Juice** (64 oz. Tropicana or Florida Natural); **Coffee** (11.5 oz. can, vacuum-packed, Maxwell House, Hills Bros, or Folgers).*
Source: The Council for Community and Economic Research, ACCRA Cost of Living Index, 2018

Housing and Utility Costs

Area[1]	New Home Price ($)	Apartment Rent ($/month)	All Electric ($/month)	Part Electric ($/month)	Other Energy ($/month)	Telephone ($/month)
City[2]	308,639	850	-	96.79	46.96	181.80
Avg.	347,000	1,087	165.93	100.16	67.73	178.70
Min.	200,468	500	93.58	25.64	26.78	163.10
Max.	1,901,222	4,888	388.65	246.86	332.81	197.70

*Note: (1) Values for the local area are compared with the average, minimum and maximum values for all 291 areas in the Cost of Living Index; (2) Figures cover the Sioux Falls SD urban area; **New Home Price** (2,400 sf living area, 8,000 sf lot, in urban area with full utilities); **Apartment Rent** (950 sf 2 bedroom/1.5 or 2 bath, unfurnished, excluding all utilities except water); **All Electric** (average monthly cost for an all-electric home); **Part Electric** (average monthly cost for a part-electric home); **Other Energy** (average monthly cost for natural gas, fuel oil, coal, wood, and any other forms of energy except electricity); **Telephone** (price includes the base monthly rate plus taxes and fees for three lines of mobile phone service).*
Source: The Council for Community and Economic Research, ACCRA Cost of Living Index, 2018

Health Care, Transportation, and Other Costs

Area[1]	Doctor ($/visit)	Dentist ($/visit)	Optometrist ($/visit)	Gasoline ($/gallon)	Beauty Salon ($/visit)	Men's Shirt ($)
City[2]	147.74	96.51	132.58	2.61	28.07	37.09
Avg.	110.71	95.11	103.74	2.61	37.48	32.03
Min.	33.60	62.55	54.63	1.89	17.00	11.44
Max.	195.97	153.93	225.79	3.59	71.88	58.64

*Note: (1) Values for the local area are compared with the average, minimum and maximum values for all 291 areas in the Cost of Living Index; (2) Figures cover the Sioux Falls SD urban area; **Doctor** (general practitioners routine exam of an established patient); **Dentist** (adult teeth cleaning and periodic oral examination); **Optometrist** (full vision eye exam for established adult patient); **Gasoline** (one gallon regular unleaded, national brand, including all taxes, cash price at self-service pump if available); **Beauty Salon** (woman's shampoo, trim, and blow-dry); **Men's Shirt** (cotton/polyester dress shirt, pinpoint weave, long sleeves).*
Source: The Council for Community and Economic Research, ACCRA Cost of Living Index, 2018

HOUSING

House Price Index (HPI)

Area	National Ranking[2]	Quarterly Change (%)	One-Year Change (%)	Five-Year Change (%)
MSA[1]	144	-0.10	5.68	29.97
U.S.[3]	–	1.12	5.73	32.81

Note: The HPI is a weighted repeat sales index. It measures average price changes in repeat sales or refinancings on the same properties. This information is obtained by reviewing repeat mortgage transactions on single-family properties whose mortgages have been purchased or securitized by Fannie Mae or Freddie Mac in January 1975; (1) Figures cover the Sioux Falls, SD Metropolitan Statistical Area—see Appendix B for areas included; (2) Rankings are based on annual percentage change for all metro areas containing at least 15,000 transactions over the last 10 years and ranges from 1 to 245; (3) figures based on a weighted average of Census Division estimates using a seasonally adjusted, purchase-only index; all figures are for the period ending December 31, 2018
Source: Federal Housing Finance Agency, House Price Index, February 26, 2019

Median Single-Family Home Prices

Area	2016	2017	2018[p]	Percent Change 2017 to 2018
MSA[1]	185.8	194.4	209.3	7.7
U.S. Average	235.5	248.8	261.6	5.1

Note: Figures are median sales prices of existing single-family homes in thousands of dollars; (p) preliminary; (1) Figures cover the Sioux Falls, SD Metropolitan Statistical Area—see Appendix B for areas included
Source: National Association of Realtors, Median Sales Price of Existing Single-Family Homes for Metropolitan Areas, 4th Quarter 2018

Qualifying Income Based on Median Sales Price of Existing Single-Family Homes

Area	With 5% Down ($)	With 10% Down ($)	With 20% Down ($)
MSA[1]	49,463	46,860	41,653
U.S. Average	62,954	59,640	53,013

Note: Figures are preliminary; Qualifying income is based on a mortgage rate of 4.9%. Monthly principal and interest payment is limited to 25% of income; (1) Figures cover the Sioux Falls, SD Metropolitan Statistical Area—see Appendix B for areas included
Source: National Association of Realtors, Qualifying Income Based on Median Sales Price of Existing Single-Family Homes for Metropolitan Areas, 4th Quarter 2018

Median Apartment Condo-Coop Home Prices

Area	2016	2017	2018[p]	Percent Change 2017 to 2018
MSA[1]	n/a	n/a	n/a	n/a
U.S. Average	220.7	234.3	241.0	2.9

Note: Figures are median sales prices of existing apartment condo-coop homes in thousands of dollars; (p) preliminary; n/a not available; (1) Figures cover the Sioux Falls, SD Metropolitan Statistical Area—see Appendix B for areas included
Source: National Association of Realtors, Median Sales Price of Existing Apartment Condo-Coop Homes for Metropolitan Areas, 4th Quarter 2018

Home Value Distribution

Area	Under $50,000	$50,000 -$99,999	$100,000 -$149,999	$150,000 -$199,999	$200,000 -$299,999	$300,000 -$499,999	$500,000 -$999,999	$1,000,000 or more
City	6.7	8.9	22.3	25.9	21.3	11.2	2.8	0.8
MSA[1]	6.6	10.0	20.8	24.1	22.0	12.5	3.2	0.8
U.S.	8.3	13.9	14.7	14.6	18.7	17.3	9.7	2.7

Note: Figures are percentages and cover owner-occupied housing units; (1) Figures cover the Sioux Falls, SD Metropolitan Statistical Area—see Appendix B for areas included
Source: U.S. Census Bureau, 2013-2017 American Community Survey 5-Year Estimates

Homeownership Rate

Area	2010 (%)	2011 (%)	2012 (%)	2013 (%)	2014 (%)	2015 (%)	2016 (%)	2017 (%)	2018 (%)
MSA[1]	n/a	n/a	n/a	n/a	n/a	n/a	n/a	n/a	n/a
U.S.	66.9	66.1	65.4	65.1	64.5	63.7	63.4	63.9	64.4

Note: (1) Figures cover the Sioux Falls, SD Metropolitan Statistical Area—see Appendix B for areas included; n/a not available
Source: U.S. Census Bureau, Housing Vacancies and Homeownership Annual Statistics: 2010-2018

Year Housing Structure Built

Area	2010 or Later	2000 -2009	1990 -1999	1980 -1989	1970 -1979	1960 -1969	1950 -1959	1940 -1949	Before 1940	Median Year
City	8.8	19.3	15.9	11.3	14.6	7.7	8.9	4.8	8.7	1985
MSA[1]	7.7	20.1	15.6	10.1	14.6	7.2	8.0	4.4	12.2	1983
U.S.	3.2	14.5	14.0	13.6	15.5	10.8	10.5	5.1	12.9	1977

Note: Figures are percentages except for Median Year; Note: (1) Figures cover the Sioux Falls, SD Metropolitan Statistical Area—see Appendix B for areas included
Source: U.S. Census Bureau, 2013-2017 American Community Survey 5-Year Estimates

Gross Monthly Rent

Area	Under $500	$500 -$999	$1,000 -$1,499	$1,500 -$1,999	$2,000 -$2,499	$2,500 -$2,999	$3,000 and up	Median ($)
City	11.3	68.2	16.5	2.5	0.4	0.7	0.5	771
MSA[1]	12.1	67.2	16.6	2.5	0.4	0.7	0.5	771
U.S.	10.5	41.1	28.7	11.7	4.5	1.8	1.7	982

Note: Figures are percentages except for Median; Gross rent is the contract rent plus the estimated average monthly cost of utilities (electricity, gas, and water and sewer) and fuels (oil, coal, kerosene, wood, etc.) if these are paid by the renter (or paid for the renter by someone else); (1) Figures cover the Sioux Falls, SD Metropolitan Statistical Area—see Appendix B for areas included
Source: U.S. Census Bureau, 2013-2017 American Community Survey 5-Year Estimates

HEALTH

Health Risk Factors

Category	MSA[1] (%)	U.S. (%)
Adults aged 18–64 who have any kind of health care coverage	83.5	87.3
Adults who reported being in good or better health	88.4	82.4
Adults who have been told they have high blood cholesterol	28.8	33.0
Adults who have been told they have high blood pressure	27.8	32.3
Adults who are current smokers	20.3	17.1
Adults who currently use E-cigarettes	n/a	4.6
Adults who currently use chewing tobacco, snuff, or snus	4.0	4.0
Adults who are heavy drinkers[2]	7.8	6.3
Adults who are binge drinkers[3]	19.4	17.4
Adults who are overweight (BMI 25.0 - 29.9)	35.5	35.3
Adults who are obese (BMI 30.0 - 99.8)	29.1	31.3
Adults who participated in any physical activities in the past month	75.1	74.4
Adults who always or nearly always wears a seat belt	88.1	94.3

Note: n/a not available; (1) Figures cover the Sioux Falls, SD Metropolitan Statistical Area—see Appendix B for areas included; (2) Heavy drinkers are classified as adult men having more than 14 drinks per week and adult women having more than 7 drinks per week; (3) Binge drinkers are classified as males having five or more drinks on one occasion or females having four or more drinks on one occasion
Source: Centers for Disease Control and Prevention, Behaviorial Risk Factor Surveillance System, SMART: Selected Metropolitan Area Risk Trends, 2017

Acute and Chronic Health Conditions

Category	MSA[1] (%)	U.S. (%)
Adults who have ever been told they had a heart attack	5.0	4.2
Adults who have ever been told they have angina or coronary heart disease	4.7	3.9
Adults who have ever been told they had a stroke	2.0	3.0
Adults who have ever been told they have asthma	9.5	14.2
Adults who have ever been told they have arthritis	19.7	24.9
Adults who have ever been told they have diabetes[2]	8.8	10.5
Adults who have ever been told they had skin cancer	3.2	6.2
Adults who have ever been told they had any other types of cancer	6.4	7.1
Adults who have ever been told they have COPD	4.4	6.5
Adults who have ever been told they have kidney disease	1.6	3.0
Adults who have ever been told they have a form of depression	18.0	20.5

Note: (1) Figures cover the Sioux Falls, SD Metropolitan Statistical Area—see Appendix B for areas included; (2) Figures do not include pregnancy-related, borderline, or pre-diabetes
Source: Centers for Disease Control and Prevention, Behaviorial Risk Factor Surveillance System, SMART: Selected Metropolitan Area Risk Trends, 2017

Health Screening and Vaccination Rates

Category	MSA[1] (%)	U.S. (%)
Adults aged 65+ who have had flu shot within the past year	69.1	60.7
Adults aged 65+ who have ever had a pneumonia vaccination	77.7	75.4
Adults who have ever been tested for HIV	29.3	36.1
Adults who have ever had the shingles or zoster vaccine?	41.7	28.9
Adults who have had their blood cholesterol checked within the last five years	79.3	85.9

Note: n/a not available; (1) Figures cover the Sioux Falls, SD Metropolitan Statistical Area—see Appendix B for areas included.
Source: Centers for Disease Control and Prevention, Behaviorial Risk Factor Surveillance System, SMART: Selected Metropolitan Area Risk Trends, 2017

Disability Status

Category	MSA[1] (%)	U.S. (%)
Adults who reported being deaf	6.9	6.7
Are you blind or have serious difficulty seeing, even when wearing glasses?	n/a	4.5
Are you limited in any way in any of your usual activities due of arthritis?	8.8	12.9
Do you have difficulty doing errands alone?	6.0	6.8
Do you have difficulty dressing or bathing?	3.1	3.6
Do you have serious difficulty concentrating/remembering/making decisions?	8.5	10.7
Do you have serious difficulty walking or climbing stairs?	8.4	13.6

Note: n/a not available; (1) Figures cover the Sioux Falls, SD Metropolitan Statistical Area—see Appendix B for areas included.
Source: Centers for Disease Control and Prevention, Behaviorial Risk Factor Surveillance System, SMART: Selected Metropolitan Area Risk Trends, 2017

Mortality Rates for the Top 10 Causes of Death in the U.S.

ICD-10[a] Sub-Chapter	ICD-10[a] Code	Age-Adjusted Mortality Rate[1] per 100,000 population	
		County[2]	U.S.
Malignant neoplasms	C00-C97	165.1	155.5
Ischaemic heart diseases	I20-I25	89.9	94.8
Other forms of heart disease	I30-I51	29.5	52.9
Chronic lower respiratory diseases	J40-J47	45.7	41.0
Cerebrovascular diseases	I60-I69	38.1	37.5
Other degenerative diseases of the nervous system	G30-G31	51.8	35.0
Other external causes of accidental injury	W00-X59	34.2	33.7
Organic, including symptomatic, mental disorders	F01-F09	19.0	31.0
Hypertensive diseases	I10-I15	35.2	21.9
Diabetes mellitus	E10-E14	16.7	21.2

Note: (a) ICD-10 = International Classification of Diseases 10th Revision; (1) Mortality rates are a three year average covering 2015-2017; (2) Figures cover Minnehaha County.
Source: Centers for Disease Control and Prevention, National Center for Health Statistics. Underlying Cause of Death 1999-2017 on CDC WONDER Online Database

Mortality Rates for Selected Causes of Death

ICD-10[a] Sub-Chapter	ICD-10[a] Code	Age-Adjusted Mortality Rate[1] per 100,000 population	
		County[2]	U.S.
Assault	X85-Y09	3.9	5.9
Diseases of the liver	K70-K76	14.2	14.1
Human immunodeficiency virus (HIV) disease	B20-B24	Suppressed	1.8
Influenza and pneumonia	J09-J18	13.5	14.3
Intentional self-harm	X60-X84	20.5	13.6
Malnutrition	E40-E46	Unreliable	1.6
Obesity and other hyperalimentation	E65-E68	Suppressed	2.1
Renal failure	N17-N19	5.8	13.0
Transport accidents	V01-V99	8.5	12.4
Viral hepatitis	B15-B19	Suppressed	1.6

Note: (a) ICD-10 = International Classification of Diseases 10th Revision; (1) Mortality rates are a three year average covering 2015-2017; (2) Figures cover Minnehaha County; Data are suppressed when the data meet the criteria for confidentiality constraints; Mortality rates are flagged as unreliable when the rate would be calculated with a numerator of 20 or less.
Source: Centers for Disease Control and Prevention, National Center for Health Statistics. Underlying Cause of Death 1999-2017 on CDC WONDER Online Database

Health Insurance Coverage

Area	With Health Insurance	With Private Health Insurance	With Public Health Insurance	Without Health Insurance	Population Under Age 18 Without Health Insurance
City	92.1	77.1	26.1	7.9	4.1
MSA[1]	92.9	79.5	24.6	7.1	4.0
U.S.	89.5	67.2	33.8	10.5	5.7

Note: Figures are percentages that cover the civilian noninstitutionalized population; (1) Figures cover the Sioux Falls, SD Metropolitan Statistical Area—see Appendix B for areas included
Source: U.S. Census Bureau, 2013-2017 American Community Survey 5-Year Estimates

Number of Medical Professionals

Area	MDs[3]	DOs[3,4]	Dentists	Podiatrists	Chiropractors	Optometrists
County[1] (number)	658	49	100	11	105	37
County[1] (rate[2])	353.7	26.3	53.0	5.8	55.7	19.6
U.S. (rate[2])	279.3	23.0	68.4	6.0	27.1	16.2

Note: Data as of 2017 unless noted; (1) Data covers Minnehaha County; (2) Rate per 100,000 population; (3) Data as of 2016 and includes all active, non-federal physicians; (4) Doctor of Osteopathic Medicine
Source: U.S. Department of Health and Human Services, Health Resources and Services Administration, Bureau of Health Professions, Area Resource File (ARF) 2017-2018

Best Hospitals

According to *U.S. News,* the Sioux Falls, SD metro area is home to two of the best hospitals in the U.S.: **Avera McKennan Hospital and University Health Center** (1 adult specialty); **Sanford USD Medical Center** (1 adult specialty). The hospitals listed were nationally ranked in at least one of 16 adult or 10 pediatric specialties. Only 170 hospitals nationwide were nationally ranked in one or more adult or pediatric specialty. Twenty hospitals in the U.S. made the Honor Roll. The Best Hospitals Honor Roll takes both the national rankings and the procedure and condition ratings into account. Hospitals received points if they were nationally ranked in one of the 16 adult specialties—the higher they ranked, the more points they got—and how many ratings of "high performing" they earned in the nine procedures and conditions. *U.S. News Online, "America's Best Hospitals 2018-19"*

EDUCATION

Public School District Statistics

District Name	Schls	Pupils	Pupil/ Teacher Ratio	Minority Pupils[1] (%)	Free Lunch Eligible[2] (%)	IEP[3] (%)
Sioux Falls School District 49-5	44	24,662	15.5	35.6	35.6	15.4

Note: Table includes school districts with 2,000 or more students; (1) Percentage of students that are not non-Hispanic white; (2) Percentage of students that are eligible for the free lunch program; (3) Percentage of students that have an Individualized Education Program.
Source: U.S. Department of Education, National Center for Education Statistics, Common Core of Data, Local Education Agency (School District) Universe Survey: School Year 2016-2017; U.S. Department of Education, National Center for Education Statistics, Common Core of Data, Public Elementary/Secondary School Universe Survey: School Year 2016-2017

Highest Level of Education

Area	Less than H.S.	H.S. Diploma	Some College, No Deg.	Associate Degree	Bachelor's Degree	Master's Degree	Prof. School Degree	Doctorate Degree
City	8.3	25.6	21.6	10.8	23.0	7.4	2.3	1.1
MSA[1]	7.5	26.6	21.4	12.1	22.7	6.7	2.0	1.0
U.S.	12.7	27.3	20.8	8.3	19.1	8.4	2.0	1.4

Note: Figures cover persons age 25 and over; (1) Figures cover the Sioux Falls, SD Metropolitan Statistical Area—see Appendix B for areas included
Source: U.S. Census Bureau, 2013-2017 American Community Survey 5-Year Estimates

Educational Attainment by Race

Area	High School Graduate or Higher (%)					Bachelor's Degree or Higher (%)				
	Total	White	Black	Asian	Hisp.[2]	Total	White	Black	Asian	Hisp.[2]
City	91.7	93.9	74.2	70.8	62.6	33.8	35.9	14.5	34.8	11.4
MSA[1]	92.5	94.1	74.9	72.2	64.7	32.5	33.8	15.1	35.9	13.5
U.S.	87.3	89.3	84.9	86.5	66.7	30.9	32.2	20.6	52.7	15.2

Note: Figures shown cover persons 25 years old and over; (1) Figures cover the Sioux Falls, SD Metropolitan Statistical Area—see Appendix B for areas included; (2) People of Hispanic origin can be of any race
Source: U.S. Census Bureau, 2013-2017 American Community Survey 5-Year Estimates

School Enrollment by Grade and Control

Area	Preschool (%)		Kindergarten (%)		Grades 1 - 4 (%)		Grades 5 - 8 (%)		Grades 9 - 12 (%)	
	Public	Private	Public	Private	Public	Private	Public	Private	Public	Private
City	52.2	47.8	84.5	15.5	88.7	11.3	89.6	10.4	85.4	14.6
MSA[1]	54.9	45.1	86.0	14.0	89.1	10.9	90.7	9.3	87.9	12.1
U.S.	58.8	41.2	87.7	12.3	89.7	10.3	89.6	10.4	90.3	9.7

Note: Figures shown cover persons 3 years old and over; (1) Figures cover the Sioux Falls, SD Metropolitan Statistical Area—see Appendix B for areas included
Source: U.S. Census Bureau, 2013-2017 American Community Survey 5-Year Estimates

Average Salaries of Public School Classroom Teachers

Area	2016		2017		Change from 2016 to 2017	
	Dollars	Rank[1]	Dollars	Rank[1]	Percent	Rank[2]
South Dakota	42,025	51	46,979	48	11.8	1
U.S. Average	58,479	–	59,660	–	2.0	–

Note: (1) Rank ranges from 1 to 51 where 1 indicates highest salary; (2) Rank ranges from 1 to 51 where 1 indicates highest percent change.
Source: National Education Association, Rankings & Estimates: Rankings of the States 2017 and Estimates of School Statistics 2018

Higher Education

Four-Year Colleges			Two-Year Colleges			Medical Schools[1]	Law Schools[2]	Voc/Tech[3]
Public	Private Non-profit	Private For-profit	Public	Private Non-profit	Private For-profit			
0	3	1	1	2	1	1	0	0

Note: Figures cover institutions located within the city limits and include main campuses only; (1) includes schools accredited by the Liaison Committee on Medical Education and the American Osteopathic Association's Commission on Osteopathic College Accreditation; (2) includes ABA-accredited schools, schools with provisional ABA accreditation, and state accredited schools; (3) includes all schools with programs that are less than 2 years.
Source: National Center for Education Statistics, Integrated Postsecondary Education System (IPEDS), 2017-18; Wikipedia, List of Medical Schools in the United States, accessed April 3, 2019; Wikipedia, List of Law Schools in the United States, accessed April 3, 2019

PRESIDENTIAL ELECTION

2016 Presidential Election Results

Area	Clinton	Trump	Johnson	Stein	Other
Minnehaha County	39.1	53.7	6.1	0.0	1.1
U.S.	48.0	45.9	3.3	1.1	1.7

Note: Results are percentages and may not add to 100% due to rounding
Source: Dave Leip's Atlas of U.S. Presidential Elections

EMPLOYERS

Major Employers

Company Name	Industry
Avera Health	Health care
Billion Automotive	Auto dealership
Capital One	Financial/credit card processing
CIGNA	Mail order pharmacy
Citi	Credit card processing
City of Sioux Falls	Government
Department of Veterans Affairs	Government medical facilities
Esurance	Insurance service center
Evangelical Lutheran Good Samaritan Society	Health care
First PREMIER Bank/PREMIER Bankcard	Financial/credit card processing
Hy-Vee Food Stores	Retail grocery
John Morrell & Co.	Meat processing
Lewis Drug	Retail pharmacy
LifeScape	Health care
Midcontinent Communications	Telecommunications/cable services
Minnehaha County	Government
Raven Industries	Manufacturing
Sammons Financial Group/Midland National	Insurance
Sanford Health	Health care
Sioux Falls School District 49-5	Education
StarMark Cabinetry	Manufacturing
United States Postal Service	U.S. postal service
USGS EROS Data Center/SGT	Satellite info processing
Wal-Mart and Sam's Club	Retail & wholesale
Wells Fargo	Financial/credit card/student loans

Note: Companies shown are located within the Sioux Falls, SD Metropolitan Statistical Area.
Source: Hoovers.com; Wikipedia

PUBLIC SAFETY

Crime Rate

Area	All Crimes	Violent Crimes				Property Crimes		
		Murder	Rape[3]	Robbery	Aggrav. Assault	Burglary	Larceny -Theft	Motor Vehicle Theft
City	3,307.7	2.2	68.0	56.2	323.8	368.2	2,225.6	263.6
Suburbs[1]	1,146.9	2.5	32.0	2.5	110.8	224.0	710.1	65.2
Metro[2]	2,630.1	2.3	56.7	39.4	257.0	323.0	1,750.3	201.4
U.S.	2,756.1	5.3	41.7	98.0	248.9	430.4	1,694.4	237.4

Note: Figures are crimes per 100,000 population; (1) All areas within the metro area that are located outside the city limits; (2) Figures cover the Sioux Falls, SD Metropolitan Statistical Area—see Appendix B for areas included; (3) The city and U.S. figures shown were reported using the revised Uniform Crime Reporting (UCR) definition of rape. The suburban and metro area figures shown are an aggregate total of the data submitted using both the revised and legacy UCR definitions.
Source: FBI Uniform Crime Reports, 2017

Hate Crimes

Area	Number of Quarters Reported	Number of Incidents per Bias Motivation					
		Race/Ethnicity/ Ancestry	Religion	Sexual Orientation	Disability	Gender	Gender Identity
City	4	1	2	2	0	0	0
U.S.	4	4,131	1,564	1,130	116	46	119

Source: Federal Bureau of Investigation, Hate Crime Statistics 2017

Identity Theft Consumer Reports

Area	Reports	Reports per 100,000 Population	Rank[2]
MSA[1]	159	62	306
U.S.	444,602	135	-

Note: (1) Figures cover the Sioux Falls, SD Metropolitan Statistical Area—see Appendix B for areas included; (2) Rank ranges from 1 to 389 where 1 indicates greatest number of identity theft reports per 100,000 population
Source: Federal Trade Commission, Consumer Sentinel Network Data Book for January–December 2018

Fraud and Other Consumer Reports

Area	Reports	Reports per 100,000 Population	Rank[2]
MSA[1]	1,007	394	322
U.S.	2,552,917	776	-

Note: (1) Figures cover the Sioux Falls, SD Metropolitan Statistical Area—see Appendix B for areas included; (2) Rank ranges from 1 to 389 where 1 indicates greatest number of fraud and other consumer reports per 100,000 population
Source: Federal Trade Commission, Consumer Sentinel Network Data Book for January–December 2018

SPORTS

Professional Sports Teams

Team Name	League	Year Established

No teams are located in the metro area
Source: Wikipedia, Major Professional Sports Teams of the United States and Canada, April 5, 2019

CLIMATE

Average and Extreme Temperatures

Temperature	Jan	Feb	Mar	Apr	May	Jun	Jul	Aug	Sep	Oct	Nov	Dec	Yr.
Extreme High (°F)	66	70	88	94	104	110	110	109	104	94	76	62	110
Average High (°F)	25	30	41	59	71	80	86	84	74	62	43	29	57
Average Temp. (°F)	15	20	32	47	59	69	75	72	62	50	33	20	46
Average Low (°F)	5	10	22	35	47	57	62	60	49	38	23	10	35
Extreme Low (°F)	-36	-31	-23	4	17	33	38	34	22	9	-17	-28	-36

Note: Figures cover the years 1932-1990
Source: National Climatic Data Center, International Station Meteorological Climate Summary, 9/96

Average Precipitation/Snowfall/Humidity

Precip./Humidity	Jan	Feb	Mar	Apr	May	Jun	Jul	Aug	Sep	Oct	Nov	Dec	Yr.
Avg. Precip. (in.)	0.6	0.8	1.6	2.4	3.3	3.9	2.8	3.2	2.8	1.5	1.0	0.7	24.6
Avg. Snowfall (in.)	7	8	9	2	Tr	0	0	0	Tr	Tr	5	7	38
Avg. Rel. Hum. 6am (%)	n/a	n/a	n/a	n/a	n/a	n/a	n/a	n/a	n/a	n/a	n/a	n/a	n/a
Avg. Rel. Hum. 3pm (%)	n/a	n/a	n/a	n/a	n/a	n/a	n/a	n/a	n/a	n/a	n/a	n/a	n/a

Note: Figures cover the years 1932-1990; Tr = Trace amounts (<0.05 in. of rain; <0.5 in. of snow)
Source: National Climatic Data Center, International Station Meteorological Climate Summary, 9/96

Weather Conditions

Temperature			Daytime Sky			Precipitation		
5°F & below	32°F & below	90°F & above	Clear	Partly cloudy	Cloudy	0.01 inch or more precip.	0.1 inch or more snow/ice	Thunder-storms
n/a	n/a	n/a	95	136	134	n/a	n/a	n/a

Note: Figures are average number of days per year and cover the years 1932-1990
Source: National Climatic Data Center, International Station Meteorological Climate Summary, 9/96

HAZARDOUS WASTE

Superfund Sites

The Sioux Falls, SD metro area has no sites on the EPA's Superfund Final National Priorities List. There are a total of 1,390 Superfund sites with a status of proposed or final on the list in the U.S.
U.S. Environmental Protection Agency, National Priorities List, April 5, 2019

**AIR & WATER
QUALITY**

Air Quality Trends: Ozone

	1990	1995	2000	2005	2010	2012	2014	2015	2016	2017
MSA[1]	n/a	n/a	n/a	n/a	n/a	n/a	n/a	n/a	n/a	n/a
U.S.	0.088	0.089	0.082	0.080	0.073	0.075	0.067	0.068	0.069	0.068

*Note: (1) Data covers the Sioux Falls, SD Metropolitan Statistical Area—see Appendix B for areas included;
n/a not available. The values shown are the composite ozone concentration averages among trend sites based
on the highest fourth daily maximum 8-hour concentration in parts per million. These trends are based on sites
having an adequate record of monitoring data during the trend period. Data from exceptional events are
included.
Source: U.S. Environmental Protection Agency, Air Quality Monitoring Information, "Air Quality Trends by
City, 1990-2017"*

Air Quality Index

Area	Percent of Days when Air Quality was...[2]					AQI Statistics[2]	
	Good	Moderate	Unhealthy for Sensitive Groups	Unhealthy	Very Unhealthy	Maximum	Median
MSA[1]	87.1	12.9	0.0	0.0	0.0	97	35

*Note: (1) Data covers the Sioux Falls, SD Metropolitan Statistical Area—see Appendix B for areas included;
(2) Based on 365 days with AQI data in 2017. Air Quality Index (AQI) is an index for reporting daily air
quality. EPA calculates the AQI for five major air pollutants regulated by the Clean Air Act: ground-level
ozone, particle pollution (aka particulate matter), carbon monoxide, sulfur dioxide, and nitrogen dioxide. The
AQI runs from 0 to 500. The higher the AQI value, the greater the level of air pollution and the greater the
health concern. There are six AQI categories: "Good" AQI is between 0 and 50. Air quality is considered
satisfactory; "Moderate" AQI is between 51 and 100. Air quality is acceptable; "Unhealthy for Sensitive
Groups" When AQI values are between 101 and 150, members of sensitive groups may experience health
effects; "Unhealthy" When AQI values are between 151 and 200 everyone may begin to experience health
effects; "Very Unhealthy" AQI values between 201 and 300 trigger a health alert; "Hazardous" AQI values
over 300 trigger warnings of emergency conditions (not shown).
Source: U.S. Environmental Protection Agency, Air Quality Index Report, 2017*

Air Quality Index Pollutants

Area	Percent of Days when AQI Pollutant was...[2]					
	Carbon Monoxide	Nitrogen Dioxide	Ozone	Sulfur Dioxide	Particulate Matter 2.5	Particulate Matter 10
MSA[1]	0.0	1.1	72.3	0.0	24.4	2.2

*Note: (1) Data covers the Sioux Falls, SD Metropolitan Statistical Area—see Appendix B for areas included;
(2) Based on 365 days with AQI data in 2017. The Air Quality Index (AQI) is an index for reporting daily air
quality. EPA calculates the AQI for five major air pollutants regulated by the Clean Air Act: ground-level
ozone, particle pollution (also known as particulate matter), carbon monoxide, sulfur dioxide, and nitrogen
dioxide. The AQI runs from 0 to 500. The higher the AQI value, the greater the level of air pollution and the
greater the health concern.
Source: U.S. Environmental Protection Agency, Air Quality Index Report, 2017*

Maximum Air Pollutant Concentrations: Particulate Matter, Ozone, CO and Lead

	Particulate Matter 10 (ug/m^3)	Particulate Matter 2.5 Wtd AM (ug/m^3)	Particulate Matter 2.5 24-Hr (ug/m^3)	Ozone (ppm)	Carbon Monoxide (ppm)	Lead (ug/m^3)
MSA[1] Level	54	5.6	14	0.066	1	n/a
NAAQS[2]	150	15	35	0.075	9	0.15
Met NAAQS[2]	Yes	Yes	Yes	Yes	Yes	n/a

*Note: (1) Data covers the Sioux Falls, SD Metropolitan Statistical Area—see Appendix B for areas included;
Data from exceptional events are included; (2) National Ambient Air Quality Standards; ppm = parts per
million; ug/m^3 = micrograms per cubic meter; n/a not available.
Concentrations: Particulate Matter 10 (coarse particulate)—highest second maximum 24-hour concentration;
Particulate Matter 2.5 Wtd AM (fine particulate)—highest weighted annual mean concentration; Particulate
Matter 2.5 24-Hour (fine particulate)—highest 98th percentile 24-hour concentration; Ozone—highest fourth
daily maximum 8-hour concentration; Carbon Monoxide—highest second maximum non-overlapping 8-hour
concentration; Lead—maximum running 3-month average
Source: U.S. Environmental Protection Agency, Air Quality Monitoring Information, "Air Quality Statistics by
City, 2017"*

Maximum Air Pollutant Concentrations: Nitrogen Dioxide and Sulfur Dioxide

	Nitrogen Dioxide AM (ppb)	Nitrogen Dioxide 1-Hr (ppb)	Sulfur Dioxide AM (ppb)	Sulfur Dioxide 1-Hr (ppb)	Sulfur Dioxide 24-Hr (ppb)
MSA[1] Level	4	30	n/a	5	n/a
NAAQS[2]	53	100	30	75	140
Met NAAQS[2]	Yes	Yes	n/a	Yes	n/a

Note: (1) Data covers the Sioux Falls, SD Metropolitan Statistical Area—see Appendix B for areas included; Data from exceptional events are included; (2) National Ambient Air Quality Standards; ppm = parts per million; ug/m³ = micrograms per cubic meter; n/a not available.
Concentrations: Nitrogen Dioxide AM—highest arithmetic mean concentration; Nitrogen Dioxide 1-Hr—highest 98th percentile 1-hour daily maximum concentration; Sulfur Dioxide AM—highest annual mean concentration; Sulfur Dioxide 1-Hr—highest 99th percentile 1-hour daily maximum concentration; Sulfur Dioxide 24-Hr—highest second maximum 24-hour concentration
Source: U.S. Environmental Protection Agency, Air Quality Monitoring Information, "Air Quality Statistics by City, 2017"

Drinking Water

Water System Name	Pop. Served	Primary Water Source Type	Violations[1] Health Based	Violations[1] Monitoring/ Reporting
Sioux Falls	173,300	Surface	0	0

Note: (1) Based on violation data from January 1, 2018 to December 31, 2018
Source: U.S. Environmental Protection Agency, Office of Ground Water and Drinking Water, Safe Drinking Water Information System (based on data extracted April 5, 2019)

Springfield, Illinois

Background

Springfield, Illinois is located the Midwest region of the United States. In the early 1800s, hunter and sugar maker Robert Pullman traveled with a small team to unexplored areas north of his home and discovered Sugar Creek, with an abundance of sugar maple trees and rich soil. Pullman built a cabin in the area in October 1817 and became its first European settler. He returned to his home in southern Illinois the following spring with the maple sugar and furs he had harvested. After Illinois entered the Union in 1818, Elisha Kelly from North Carolina discovered the Sugar Creek area and relocated his family and some friends there. They named the area Calhoun in honor of Senator John C. Calhoun of South Carolina. Another influential settler was businessman Elijah Iles who, in 1821, relocated his family there from Missouri. Iles opened the first general store. Calhoun was renamed Springfield in 1832 after that city in Massachusetts which was a thriving town that Iles aspired to.

Abraham Lincoln is synonymous with Springfield, Illinois. Although known as Springfield's most prominent citizen, Lincoln was actually born in Hodgenville, Kentucky in 1809. He moved to the Springfield area in 1831, and into the city itself in 1837 where he practiced law and politics. Lincoln's famous farewell speech, and one of his earliest published speeches, his Lyceum address, was delivered in Springfield in January of 1838. In 1839, Springfield became the capital of Illinois due to Lincoln's efforts. In 1852, Springfield connected with the railroad system which led to its economic expansion. After Lincoln became President of the United States in 1861, and with the advent of the Civil War, Springfield became a solider training area and Confederate prisoner camp. By 1900 Springfield emerged as a major player in the coal and farming industries, and a hub for the Illinois railroad.

Another celebrity resident of Springfield is architect Frank Lloyd Wright, who built the Dana Thomas House for the silver mine heiress Susan Lawrence Dana in 1902. Actually a "remodel" of Dana's Victorian mansion, this 12,000 square foot, 35-room house is the best preserved example of Lloyd's "Prairie" houses. The Dana Thomas House has the largest known collection of Wright's site-specific furniture and glass art throughout its 16 levels. It has been thoroughly renovated and is currently a museum. Other famous Springfield residents include Olympian swimmers Michael Phelps and Ryan Held, and many professional athletes and authors, including Vachel Lindsay, Edgar Lee Masters, John Hay, Virginia Eiffert and Robert Fitzgerald.

Springfield is an American history buff's dream for all things Lincoln. The city houses Lincoln's home and law office, which are open to the public and listed as National Historic sites. The Abraham Lincoln Presidential Library and Museum, built in 2005, houses the original Gettysburg Address and the largest collection of Lincoln biographical works. The nearby Capital Building is not only where Lincoln served in the House of Representatives, but also where mourners passed his body as it laid in state in 1865. Just a short walk away is Oak Ridge Cemetery where Lincoln and his immediate family are buried at Lincoln's Tomb. A more recent presidential fact—former President Obama announced both his candidacy for the presidency and his choice for running mate Joe Biden at the State Capitol building in Springfield.

Two popular annual events hosted by the city are the Old Capitol Art Fair and the Route 66 Film Festival. Springfield is home to the Hoogland Center for the Arts, Springfield Theatre Center, Springfield Ballet Company, Illinois Symphony Orchestra and the Springfield Municipal Opera. And, the Illinois state legislature adopted a resolution proclaiming Springfield the "Chili Capital of the Civilized World."

Springfield has a humid, continental climate and was hit by two tornadoes in 2006.

Rankings

Business/Finance Rankings

- Using data from the Council for Community and Economic Research's 2014 cost of living index, NerdWallet ranked the 100 most affordable cities in America. Median income was compared with cost of living to find truly affordable places. Springfield ranked #24. *NerdWallet.com, "America's Most Affordable Places," May 18, 2015*

- The Springfield metro area appeared on the Milken Institute "2018 Best Performing Cities" list. Rank: #184 out of 201 small metro areas. Criteria: job growth; wage and salary growth; high-tech output growth. *Milken Institute, "Best-Performing Cities 2018," January 24, 2019*

- *Forbes* ranked 200 smaller metro areas (population under 265,400) to determine the nation's "Best Small Places for Business and Careers." The Springfield metro area was ranked #60. Criteria: costs (business and living); job growth (past and projected); income growth; quality of life; educational attainment (college and high school); projected economic growth; cultural and recreational opportunities; net migration patterns; number of highly ranked colleges. *Forbes, "The Best Small Cities for Business and Careers 2018," October, 24 2018*

Real Estate Rankings

- The Springfield metro area was identified as one of the 20 most affordable housing markets in the U.S. in 2018. The area ranked #16 out of 180 markets. Criteria: qualification for a mortgage loan on a typical home. *National Association of Realtors®, Qualifying Income Based on Sales Price of Existing Single-Family Homes for Metropolitan Areas, 2018*

- Springfield was ranked #10 out of 237 metro areas in terms of housing affordability in 2018 by the National Association of Home Builders (#1 = most affordable). Criteria: the share of homes sold in that area affordable to a family earning the local median income, based on standard mortgage underwriting criteria. *National Association of Home Builders®, NAHB-Wells Fargo Housing Opportunity Index, 4th Quarter 2018*

Safety Rankings

- Springfield was identified as one of the most dangerous cities in America by NeighborhoodScout. The city ranked #61 out of 100. Criteria: number of violent crimes per 1,000 residents. The editors only considered cities with 25,000 or more residents. *NeighborhoodScout.com, "Top 100 Most Dangerous Cities in the U.S. 2019" January 2, 2019*

- The National Insurance Crime Bureau ranked 382 metro areas in the U.S. in terms of per capita rates of vehicle theft. The Springfield metro area ranked #146 (#1 = highest rate). Criteria: number of vehicle theft offenses per 100,000 inhabitants in 2017. *National Insurance Crime Bureau, "Hot Spots 2017," July 12, 2018*

Seniors/Retirement Rankings

- From its Best Cities for Successful Aging indexes, the Milken Institute generated rankings for metropolitan areas, weighing data in nine categories—health care, wellness, living arrangements, transportation and convenience, financial characteristics, education, employment, community engagement, and overall livability. The Springfield metro area was ranked #92 overall in the small metro area category. *Milken Institute, "Best Cities for Successful Aging, 2017" March 14, 2017*

Business Environment

CITY FINANCES

City Government Finances

Component	2016 ($000)	2016 ($ per capita)
Total Revenues	427,191	3,665
Total Expenditures	483,224	4,146
Debt Outstanding	748,804	6,424
Cash and Securities[1]	558,970	4,795

Note: (1) Cash and security holdings of a government at the close of its fiscal year, including those of its dependent agencies, utilities, and liquor stores.
Source: U.S. Census Bureau, State & Local Government Finances 2016

City Government Revenue by Source

Source	2016 ($000)	2016 ($ per capita)	2016 (%)
General Revenue			
From Federal Government	1,519	13	0.4
From State Government	63,639	546	14.9
From Local Governments	517	4	0.1
Taxes			
Property	27,858	239	6.5
Sales and Gross Receipts	55,632	477	13.0
Personal Income	0	0	0.0
Corporate Income	0	0	0.0
Motor Vehicle License	0	0	0.0
Other Taxes	1,490	13	0.3
Current Charges	16,928	145	4.0
Liquor Store	0	0	0.0
Utility	266,141	2,283	62.3
Employee Retirement	-8,500	-73	-2.0

Source: U.S. Census Bureau, State & Local Government Finances 2016

City Government Expenditures by Function

Function	2016 ($000)	2016 ($ per capita)	2016 (%)
General Direct Expenditures			
Air Transportation	0	0	0.0
Corrections	0	0	0.0
Education	0	0	0.0
Employment Security Administration	0	0	0.0
Financial Administration	1,938	16	0.4
Fire Protection	37,006	317	7.7
General Public Buildings	2,677	23	0.6
Governmental Administration, Other	6,798	58	1.4
Health	0	0	0.0
Highways	52,955	454	11.0
Hospitals	0	0	0.0
Housing and Community Development	13,056	112	2.7
Interest on General Debt	4,090	35	0.8
Judicial and Legal	1,591	13	0.3
Libraries	4,420	37	0.9
Parking	925	7	0.2
Parks and Recreation	58	< 1	< 0.1
Police Protection	43,853	376	9.1
Public Welfare	0	0	0.0
Sewerage	10,792	92	2.2
Solid Waste Management	0	0	0.0
Veterans' Services	0	0	0.0
Liquor Store	0	0	0.0
Utility	245,698	2,107	50.8
Employee Retirement	25,738	220	5.3

Source: U.S. Census Bureau, State & Local Government Finances 2016

DEMOGRAPHICS

Population Growth

Area	1990 Census	2000 Census	2010 Census	2017* Estimate	Population Growth (%)	
					1990-2017	2010-2017
City	108,997	111,454	116,250	116,313	6.7	0.1
MSA[1]	189,550	201,437	210,170	210,550	11.1	0.2
U.S.	248,709,873	281,421,906	308,745,538	321,004,407	29.1	4.0

Note: (1) Figures cover the Springfield, IL Metropolitan Statistical Area—see Appendix B for areas included; (*) 2013-2017 5-year estimated population
Source: U.S. Census Bureau, 1990 Census, Census 2000, Census 2010, 2013-2017 American Community Survey 5-Year Estimates

Household Size

Area	Persons in Household (%)							Average Household Size
	One	Two	Three	Four	Five	Six	Seven or More	
City	36.7	33.6	14.8	9.5	3.2	1.3	1.0	2.20
MSA[1]	31.6	35.9	14.9	11.1	4.2	1.6	0.8	2.30
U.S.	27.7	33.8	15.7	13.0	6.0	2.3	1.4	2.60

Note: (1) Figures cover the Springfield, IL Metropolitan Statistical Area—see Appendix B for areas included
Source: U.S. Census Bureau, 2013-2017 American Community Survey 5-Year Estimates

Race

Area	White Alone[2] (%)	Black Alone[2] (%)	Asian Alone[2] (%)	AIAN[3] Alone[2] (%)	NHOPI[4] Alone[2] (%)	Other Race Alone[2] (%)	Two or More Races (%)
City	73.2	19.9	2.8	0.1	0.0	0.8	3.2
MSA[1]	83.1	12.0	1.8	0.1	0.1	0.6	2.3
U.S.	73.0	12.7	5.4	0.8	0.2	4.8	3.1

Note: (1) Figures cover the Springfield, IL Metropolitan Statistical Area—see Appendix B for areas included; (2) Alone is defined as not being in combination with one or more other races; (3) American Indian and Alaska Native; (4) Native Hawaiian and Other Pacific Islander
Source: U.S. Census Bureau, 2013-2017 American Community Survey 5-Year Estimates

Hispanic or Latino Origin

Area	Total (%)	Mexican (%)	Puerto Rican (%)	Cuban (%)	Other (%)
City	2.6	1.5	0.5	0.1	0.5
MSA[1]	2.2	1.3	0.4	0.1	0.4
U.S.	17.6	11.1	1.7	0.7	4.1

Note: Persons of Hispanic or Latino origin can be of any race; (1) Figures cover the Springfield, IL Metropolitan Statistical Area—see Appendix B for areas included
Source: U.S. Census Bureau, 2013-2017 American Community Survey 5-Year Estimates

Segregation

Type	Segregation Indices[1]				Percent Change		
	1990	2000	2010	2010 Rank[2]	1990-2000	1990-2010	2000-2010
Black/White	n/a	n/a	n/a	n/a	n/a	n/a	n/a
Asian/White	n/a	n/a	n/a	n/a	n/a	n/a	n/a
Hispanic/White	n/a	n/a	n/a	n/a	n/a	n/a	n/a

Note: All figures cover the Metropolitan Statistical Area—see Appendix B for areas included; Figures are based on an analysis of 1990, 2000, and 2010 Census Decennial Census tract data by William H. Frey, Brookings Institution and the University of Michigan Social Science Data Analysis Network. In this analysis all racial groups (whites, blacks, and asians) are non-Hispanic members of those races. Hispanics are shown as a separate category; (1) Segregation Indices are Dissimilarity Indices that measure the degree to which the minority group is distributed differently than whites across census tracts. They range from 0 (complete integration) to 100 (complete segregation) where the value indicates the percentage of the minority group that needs to move to be distributed exactly like whites; (2) Ranges from 1 (most segregated) to 102 (least segregated); n/a not available.
Source: www.CensusScope.org

Ancestry

Area	German	Irish	English	American	Italian	Polish	French[2]	Scottish	Dutch
City	22.2	14.0	9.5	5.3	5.0	2.0	2.2	1.6	1.3
MSA[1]	25.9	14.8	10.7	6.4	5.3	2.0	2.5	1.8	1.4
U.S.	14.1	10.1	7.5	6.6	5.3	2.9	2.5	1.7	1.3

Note: Figures are the percentage of the total population reporting a particular ancestry. The nine most commonly reported ancestries in the U.S. are shown. Figures include multiple ancestries (e.g. if a person reported being Irish and Italian, they were included in both columns); (1) Figures cover the Springfield, IL Metropolitan Statistical Area—see Appendix B for areas included; (2) Excludes Basque
Source: U.S. Census Bureau, 2013-2017 American Community Survey 5-Year Estimates

Foreign-Born Population

Area	Percent of Population Born in								
	Any Foreign Country	Asia	Mexico	Europe	Carribean	Central America[2]	South America	Africa	Canada
City	4.1	2.3	0.4	0.5	0.2	0.1	0.1	0.5	0.1
MSA[1]	2.9	1.6	0.3	0.4	0.1	0.1	0.1	0.3	0.1
U.S.	13.4	4.1	3.6	1.5	1.3	1.0	0.9	0.6	0.3

Note: (1) Figures cover the Springfield, IL Metropolitan Statistical Area—see Appendix B for areas included; (2) Excludes Mexico.
Source: U.S. Census Bureau, 2013-2017 American Community Survey 5-Year Estimates

Marital Status

Area	Never Married	Now Married[2]	Separated	Widowed	Divorced
City	36.0	41.8	1.5	6.4	14.3
MSA[1]	30.8	48.6	1.2	6.1	13.3
U.S.	33.1	48.2	2.0	5.8	10.9

Note: Figures are percentages and cover the population 15 years of age and older; (1) Figures cover the Springfield, IL Metropolitan Statistical Area—see Appendix B for areas included; (2) Excludes separated
Source: U.S. Census Bureau, 2013-2017 American Community Survey 5-Year Estimates

Disability by Age

Area	All Ages	Under 18 Years Old	18 to 64 Years Old	65 Years and Over
City	15.1	5.8	13.1	36.3
MSA[1]	13.9	5.8	11.6	35.0
U.S.	12.6	4.2	10.3	35.5

Note: Figures show percent of the civilian noninstitutionalized population that reported having a disability. Disability status is determined from six types of difficulty: vision, hearing, cognitive, ambulatory, self-care, and independent living. For children under 5 years old, hearing and vision difficulty are used to determine disability status. For children between the ages of 5 and 14, disability status is determined from hearing, vision, cognitive, ambulatory, and self-care difficulties. For people aged 15 years and older, they are considered to have a disability if they have difficulty with any one of the six difficulty types; Note: (1) Figures cover the Springfield, IL Metropolitan Statistical Area—see Appendix B for areas included
Source: U.S. Census Bureau, 2013-2017 American Community Survey 5-Year Estimates

Age

Area	Percent of Population									Median Age
	Under Age 5	Age 5–19	Age 20–34	Age 35–44	Age 45–54	Age 55–64	Age 65–74	Age 75–84	Age 85+	
City	6.1	18.5	20.7	11.6	12.9	13.9	9.0	4.7	2.4	38.9
MSA[1]	5.8	19.3	18.6	12.2	13.7	14.1	9.3	4.8	2.2	40.2
U.S.	6.2	19.5	20.7	12.7	13.4	12.7	8.6	4.4	1.9	37.8

Note: (1) Figures cover the Springfield, IL Metropolitan Statistical Area—see Appendix B for areas included
Source: U.S. Census Bureau, 2013-2017 American Community Survey 5-Year Estimates

Gender

Area	Males	Females	Males per 100 Females
City	55,284	61,029	90.6
MSA[1]	101,183	109,367	92.5
U.S.	158,018,753	162,985,654	97.0

Note: (1) Figures cover the Springfield, IL Metropolitan Statistical Area—see Appendix B for areas included
Source: U.S. Census Bureau, 2013-2017 American Community Survey 5-Year Estimates

Religious Groups by Family

Area	Catholic	Baptist	Non-Den.	Methodist[2]	Lutheran	LDS[3]	Pente-costal	Presby-terian[4]	Muslim[5]	Judaism
MSA[1]	15.6	11.7	2.7	6.8	5.6	0.8	5.0	2.0	1.6	0.2
U.S.	19.1	9.3	4.0	4.0	2.3	2.0	1.9	1.6	0.8	0.7

Note: Figures are the number of adherents as a percentage of the total population; (1) Figures cover the Springfield, IL Metropolitan Statistical Area—see Appendix B for areas included; (2) Methodist/Pietist; (3) Latter Day Saints; (4) Reformed; (5) Figures are estimates
Source: Association of Statisticians of American Religious Bodies, 2010 U.S. Religion Census: Religious Congregations & Membership Study

Religious Groups by Tradition

Area	Catholic	Evangelical Protestant	Mainline Protestant	Other Tradition	Black Protestant	Orthodox
MSA[1]	15.6	21.5	11.7	3.2	2.1	0.1
U.S.	19.1	16.2	7.3	4.3	1.6	0.3

Note: Figures are the number of adherents as a percentage of the total population; (1) Figures cover the Springfield, IL Metropolitan Statistical Area—see Appendix B for areas included
Source: Association of Statisticians of American Religious Bodies, 2010 U.S. Religion Census: Religious Congregations & Membership Study

ECONOMY

Gross Metropolitan Product

Area	2016	2017	2018	2019	Rank[2]
MSA[1]	10.0	10.1	10.3	10.7	205

Note: Figures are in billions of dollars; (1) Figures cover the Springfield, IL Metropolitan Statistical Area—see Appendix B for areas included; (2) Rank is based on 2017 data and ranges from 1 to 381
Source: U.S. Conference of Mayors, U.S. Metro Economies: Economic Growth & Full Employment, June 2018

Economic Growth

Area	2017-2018 (%)	2019-2020 (%)	2021-2022 (%)
MSA[1]	-0.2	1.1	0.6

Note: Figures are real gross metropolitan product (GMP) growth rates and represent average annual percent change; (1) Figures cover the Springfield, IL Metropolitan Statistical Area—see Appendix B for areas included
Source: U.S. Conference of Mayors, U.S. Metro Economies: Economic Growth & Full Employment, June 2018

Metropolitan Area Exports

Area	2012	2013	2014	2015	2016	2017	Rank[2]
MSA[1]	99.5	97.5	94.4	111.7	88.3	107.5	335

Note: Figures are in millions of dollars; (1) Figures cover the Springfield, IL Metropolitan Statistical Area—see Appendix B for areas included; (2) Rank is based on 2017 data and ranges from 1 to 387
Source: U.S. Department of Commerce, International Trade Administration, Office of Trade and Economic Analysis, Industry and Analysis, Exports by Metropolitan Area, extracted March 25, 2019

Building Permits

Area	Single-Family			Multi-Family			Total		
	2016	2017	Pct. Chg.	2016	2017	Pct. Chg.	2016	2017	Pct. Chg.
City	74	57	-23.0	94	94	0.0	168	151	-10.1
MSA[1]	274	210	-23.4	152	112	-26.3	426	322	-24.4
U.S.	750,800	820,000	9.2	455,800	462,000	1.4	1,206,600	1,282,000	6.2

Note: (1) Figures cover the Springfield, IL Metropolitan Statistical Area—see Appendix B for areas included; Figures represent new, privately-owned housing units authorized (unadjusted data); All permit data are based on estimates with imputation
Source: U.S. Census Bureau, Manufacturing, Mining, and Construction Statistics, Building Permits, 2016, 2017

Bankruptcy Filings

Area	Business Filings			Nonbusiness Filings		
	2017	2018	% Chg.	2017	2018	% Chg.
Sangamon County	9	8	-11.1	553	472	-14.6
U.S.	23,157	22,232	-4.0	765,863	751,186	-1.9

Note: Business filings include Chapter 7, Chapter 11, Chapter 12, and Chapter 13; Nonbusiness filings include Chapter 7, Chapter 11, and Chapter 13
Source: Administrative Office of the U.S. Courts, Business and Nonbusiness Bankruptcy, County Cases Commenced by Chapter of the Bankruptcy Code, During the 12-Month Period Ending December 31, 2017 and Business and Nonbusiness Bankruptcy, County Cases Commenced by Chapter of the Bankruptcy Code, During the 12-Month Period Ending December 31, 2018

Housing Vacancy Rates

Area	Gross Vacancy Rate[2] (%)			Year-Round Vacancy Rate[3] (%)			Rental Vacancy Rate[4] (%)			Homeowner Vacancy Rate[5] (%)		
	2016	2017	2018	2016	2017	2018	2016	2017	2018	2016	2017	2018
MSA[1]	n/a	n/a	n/a	n/a	n/a	n/a	n/a	n/a	n/a	n/a	n/a	n/a
U.S.	12.8	12.7	12.3	9.9	9.9	9.7	6.9	7.2	6.9	1.7	1.6	1.5

Note: (1) Figures cover the Springfield, IL Metropolitan Statistical Area—see Appendix B for areas included; (2) The percentage of the total housing inventory that is vacant; (3) The percentage of the housing inventory (excluding seasonal units) that is year-round vacant; (4) The percentage of rental inventory that is vacant for rent; (5) The percentage of homeowner inventory that is vacant for sale; n/a not available
Source: U.S. Census Bureau, Housing Vacancies and Homeownership Annual Statistics: 2016, 2017, 2018

INCOME

Income

Area	Per Capita ($)	Median Household ($)	Average Household ($)
City	32,162	51,789	73,023
MSA[1]	33,251	58,956	78,020
U.S.	31,177	57,652	81,283

Note: (1) Figures cover the Springfield, IL Metropolitan Statistical Area—see Appendix B for areas included
Source: U.S. Census Bureau, 2013-2017 American Community Survey 5-Year Estimates

Household Income Distribution

Area	Percent of Households Earning							
	Under $15,000	$15,000 -$24,999	$25,000 -$34,999	$35,000 -$49,999	$50,000 -$74,999	$75,000 -$99,999	$100,000 -$149,999	$150,000 and up
City	14.6	12.0	9.3	12.6	17.3	12.2	12.0	9.9
MSA[1]	11.3	10.3	8.6	12.6	18.2	13.6	14.5	10.8
U.S.	11.6	9.8	9.5	13.0	17.7	12.3	14.1	12.1

Note: (1) Figures cover the Springfield, IL Metropolitan Statistical Area—see Appendix B for areas included
Source: U.S. Census Bureau, 2013-2017 American Community Survey 5-Year Estimates

Poverty Rate

Area	All Ages	Under 18 Years Old	18 to 64 Years Old	65 Years and Over
City	20.3	31.9	19.2	7.9
MSA[1]	15.4	24.3	14.4	6.6
U.S.	14.6	20.3	13.7	9.3

Note: Figures are percentage of people whose income during the past 12 months was below the poverty level; (1) Figures cover the Springfield, IL Metropolitan Statistical Area—see Appendix B for areas included
Source: U.S. Census Bureau, 2013-2017 American Community Survey 5-Year Estimates

EMPLOYMENT

Labor Force and Employment

Area	Civilian Labor Force			Workers Employed		
	Dec. 2017	Dec. 2018	% Chg.	Dec. 2017	Dec. 2018	% Chg.
City	57,636	57,912	0.5	55,303	54,991	-0.6
MSA[1]	108,369	108,970	0.6	104,156	103,567	-0.6
U.S.	159,880,000	162,510,000	1.6	153,602,000	156,481,000	1.9

Note: Data is not seasonally adjusted and covers workers 16 years of age and older; (1) Figures cover the Springfield, IL Metropolitan Statistical Area—see Appendix B for areas included
Source: Bureau of Labor Statistics, Local Area Unemployment Statistics

Unemployment Rate

| Area | 2018 | | | | | | | | | | | |
	Jan.	Feb.	Mar.	Apr.	May	Jun.	Jul.	Aug.	Sep.	Oct.	Nov.	Dec.
City	4.4	4.0	4.1	3.4	3.5	4.7	4.5	4.7	4.0	4.4	4.4	5.0
MSA[1]	4.4	4.0	4.1	3.2	3.4	4.2	4.0	4.2	3.7	4.1	4.2	5.0
U.S.	4.5	4.4	4.1	3.7	3.6	4.2	4.1	3.9	3.6	3.5	3.5	3.7

Note: Data is not seasonally adjusted and covers workers 16 years of age and older; (1) Figures cover the Springfield, IL Metropolitan Statistical Area—see Appendix B for areas included
Source: Bureau of Labor Statistics, Local Area Unemployment Statistics

Average Wages

Occupation	$/Hr.	Occupation	$/Hr.
Accountants and Auditors	36.50	Maids and Housekeeping Cleaners	11.20
Automotive Mechanics	18.80	Maintenance and Repair Workers	18.90
Bookkeepers	19.40	Marketing Managers	56.10
Carpenters	24.40	Nuclear Medicine Technologists	n/a
Cashiers	10.60	Nurses, Licensed Practical	21.20
Clerks, General Office	18.20	Nurses, Registered	32.80
Clerks, Receptionists/Information	12.10	Nursing Assistants	14.10
Clerks, Shipping/Receiving	15.40	Packers and Packagers, Hand	n/a
Computer Programmers	40.50	Physical Therapists	42.00
Computer Systems Analysts	43.40	Postal Service Mail Carriers	24.90
Computer User Support Specialists	22.30	Real Estate Brokers	n/a
Cooks, Restaurant	12.30	Retail Salespersons	13.40
Dentists	70.00	Sales Reps., Exc. Tech./Scientific	27.20
Electrical Engineers	44.80	Sales Reps., Tech./Scientific	28.80
Electricians	32.20	Secretaries, Exc. Legal/Med./Exec.	17.40
Financial Managers	61.20	Security Guards	23.30
First-Line Supervisors/Managers, Sales	19.60	Surgeons	n/a
Food Preparation Workers	11.20	Teacher Assistants*	11.80
General and Operations Managers	45.40	Teachers, Elementary School*	25.70
Hairdressers/Cosmetologists	19.00	Teachers, Secondary School*	26.90
Internists, General	n/a	Telemarketers	n/a
Janitors and Cleaners	15.20	Truck Drivers, Heavy/Tractor-Trailer	22.30
Landscaping/Groundskeeping Workers	14.60	Truck Drivers, Light/Delivery Svcs.	15.40
Lawyers	56.60	Waiters and Waitresses	10.50

Note: Wage data covers the Springfield, IL Metropolitan Statistical Area—see Appendix B for areas included; (*) Hourly wages for elementary/secondary school teachers and teacher assistants were calculated by the editors from annual wage data based on a 40 hour work week; n/a not available.
Source: Bureau of Labor Statistics, Metro Area Occupational Employment & Wage Estimates, May 2018

Employment by Occupation

Occupation Classification	City (%)	MSA[1] (%)	U.S. (%)
Management, Business, Science, and Arts	42.5	41.1	37.4
Natural Resources, Construction, and Maintenance	5.0	6.9	8.9
Production, Transportation, and Material Moving	8.5	8.9	12.2
Sales and Office	24.5	25.1	23.5
Service	19.6	18.1	18.0

Note: Figures cover employed civilians 16 years of age and older; (1) Figures cover the Springfield, IL Metropolitan Statistical Area—see Appendix B for areas included
Source: U.S. Census Bureau, 2013-2017 American Community Survey 5-Year Estimates

Employment by Industry

Sector	MSA[1]		U.S.
	Number of Employees	Percent of Total	Percent of Total
Construction, Mining, and Logging	3,200	2.8	5.3
Education and Health Services	21,500	18.7	15.9
Financial Activities	6,400	5.6	5.7
Government	30,000	26.1	15.1
Information	2,700	2.3	1.9
Leisure and Hospitality	10,700	9.3	10.7
Manufacturing	3,500	3.0	8.5
Other Services	6,800	5.9	3.9
Professional and Business Services	12,300	10.7	14.1
Retail Trade	12,600	10.9	10.8
Transportation, Warehousing, and Utilities	2,100	1.8	4.2
Wholesale Trade	3,300	2.9	3.9

Note: Figures are non-farm employment as of December 2018. Figures are not seasonally adjusted and include workers 16 years of age and older; (1) Figures cover the Springfield, IL Metropolitan Statistical Area—see Appendix B for areas included
Source: Bureau of Labor Statistics, Current Employment Statistics, Employment, Hours, and Earnings

Occupations with Greatest Projected Employment Growth: 2018 – 2020

Occupation[1]	2018 Employment	2020 Projected Employment	Numeric Employment Change	Percent Employment Change
Combined Food Preparation and Serving Workers, Including Fast Food	139,870	145,560	5,690	4.1
Laborers and Freight, Stock, and Material Movers, Hand	153,200	158,690	5,490	3.6
Registered Nurses	126,530	130,420	3,890	3.1
General and Operations Managers	122,420	125,420	3,000	2.5
Waiters and Waitresses	91,610	93,810	2,200	2.4
Heavy and Tractor-Trailer Truck Drivers	71,040	73,220	2,180	3.1
Personal Care Aides	50,390	52,470	2,080	4.1
Light Truck or Delivery Services Drivers	50,560	52,420	1,860	3.7
Software Developers, Applications	27,370	29,190	1,820	6.6
Management Analysts	41,280	42,960	1,680	4.1

Note: Projections cover Illinois; (1) Sorted by numeric employment change
Source: www.projectionscentral.com, State Occupational Projections, 2018–2020 Short-Term Projections

Fastest Growing Occupations: 2018 – 2020

Occupation[1]	2018 Employment	2020 Projected Employment	Numeric Employment Change	Percent Employment Change
Statisticians	1,340	1,440	100	7.5
Nurse Practitioners	7,960	8,530	570	7.2
Computer Numerically Controlled Machine Tool Programmers, Metal and Plastic	1,320	1,410	90	6.8
Software Developers, Applications	27,370	29,190	1,820	6.6
Operations Research Analysts	6,770	7,200	430	6.4
Computer and Information Research Scientists	970	1,030	60	6.2
Physician Assistants	3,700	3,930	230	6.2
Locker Room, Coatroom, and Dressing Room Attendants	850	900	50	5.9
Occupational Therapy Aides	1,780	1,880	100	5.6
Market Research Analysts and Marketing Specialists	23,210	24,420	1,210	5.2

Note: Projections cover Illinois; (1) Sorted by percent employment change and excludes occupations with numeric employment change less than 50
Source: www.projectionscentral.com, State Occupational Projections, 2018–2020 Short-Term Projections

TAXES

State Corporate Income Tax Rates

State	Tax Rate (%)	Income Brackets ($)	Num. of Brackets	Financial Institution Tax Rate (%)[a]	Federal Income Tax Ded.
Illinois	9.5 (h)	Flat rate	1	9.5 (h)	No

Note: Tax rates as of January 1, 2019; (a) Rates listed are the corporate income tax rate applied to financial institutions or excise taxes based on income. Some states have other taxes based upon the value of deposits or shares; (h) The Illinois rate of 9.5% is the sum of a corporate income tax rate of 7.0% plus a replacement tax of 2.5%.
Source: Federation of Tax Administrators, Range of State Corporate Income Tax Rates, January 1, 2019

State Individual Income Tax Rates

State	Tax Rate (%)	Income Brackets ($)	Personal Exemptions ($) Single	Married	Depend.	Standard Ded. ($) Single	Married
Illinois (a)	4.95	Flat rate	2,225	4,450	2,225	–	–

Note: Tax rates as of January 1, 2019; Local- and county-level taxes are not included; n/a not applicable; Federal income tax is not deductible on state income tax returns; (a) 19 states have statutory provision for automatically adjusting to the rate of inflation the dollar values of the income tax brackets, standard deductions, and/or personal exemptions. Michigan indexes the personal exemption only. Oregon does not index the income brackets for $125,000 and over.
Source: Federation of Tax Administrators, State Individual Income Tax Rates, January 1, 2019

Various State Sales and Excise Tax Rates

State	State Sales Tax (%)	Gasoline[1] (¢/gal.)	Cigarette[2] ($/pack)	Spirits[3] ($/gal.)	Wine[4] ($/gal.)	Beer[5] ($/gal.)	Recreational Marijuana (%)
Illinois	6.25	31.98	1.98	8.55 (f)	1.39 (l)	0.23	Not legal

Note: All tax rates as of January 1, 2019; (1) The American Petroleum Institute has developed a methodology for determining the average tax rate on a gallon of fuel. Rates may include any of the following: excise taxes, environmental fees, storage tank fees, other fees or taxes, general sales tax, and local taxes. In states where gasoline is subject to the general sales tax, or where the fuel tax is based on the average sale price, the average rate determined by API is sensitive to changes in the price of gasoline. States that fully or partially apply general sales taxes to gasoline: CA, CO, GA, IL, IN, MI, NY; (2) The federal excise tax of $1.0066 per pack and local taxes are not included; (3) Rates are those applicable to off-premise sales of 40% alcohol by volume (a.b.v.) distilled spirits in 750ml containers. Local excise taxes are excluded; (4) Rates are those applicable to off-premise sales of 11% a.b.v. non-carbonated wine in 750ml containers; (5) Rates are those applicable to off-premise sales of 4.7% a.b.v. beer in 12 ounce containers; (f) Different rates also applicable according to alcohol content, place of production, size of container, or place purchased (on- or off-premise or onboard airlines); (l) Different rates also applicable to alcohol content, place of production, size of container, place purchased (on- or off-premise or on board airlines) or type of wine (carbonated, vermouth, etc.).
Source: Tax Foundation, 2019 Facts & Figures: How Does Your State Compare?

State Business Tax Climate Index Rankings

State	Overall Rank	Corporate Tax Rank	Individual Income Tax Rank	Sales Tax Rank	Unemployment Insurance Tax Rank	Property Tax Rank
Illinois	36	39	13	36	42	45

Note: The index is a measure of how each state's tax laws affect economic performance. The lower the rank, the more favorable a state's tax system is for business. States without a given tax are given a ranking of 1. The scores/rankings for the District of Columbia do not affect other states. The 2019 index represents the tax climate as of July 1, 2018.
Source: Tax Foundation, State Business Tax Climate Index 2019

COMMERCIAL UTILITIES

Typical Monthly Electric Bills

Area	General Service, Light ($/month) 40 kW demand 5,000 kWh	100 kW demand 10,000 kWh	General Service, Heavy ($/month) 500 kW demand 100,000 kWh	1,500 kW demand 500,000 kWh
City	n/a	n/a	n/a	n/a

Note: Figures are based on rates in effect January 1, 2018
Source: Memphis Light, Gas and Water, 2018 Utility Bill Comparisons for Selected U.S. Cities

TRANSPORTATION

Means of Transportation to Work

Area	Car/Truck/Van		Public Transportation			Bicycle	Walked	Other Means	Worked at Home
	Drove Alone	Car-pooled	Bus	Subway	Railroad				
City	81.9	7.9	2.2	0.1	0.0	0.5	2.5	1.2	3.6
MSA[1]	83.3	7.8	1.4	0.1	0.0	0.4	2.0	1.1	3.9
U.S.	76.4	9.2	2.5	1.9	0.6	0.6	2.7	1.3	4.7

Note: Figures are percentages and cover workers 16 years of age and older; (1) Figures cover the Springfield, IL Metropolitan Statistical Area—see Appendix B for areas included
Source: U.S. Census Bureau, 2013-2017 American Community Survey 5-Year Estimates

Travel Time to Work

Area	Less Than 10 Minutes	10 to 19 Minutes	20 to 29 Minutes	30 to 44 Minutes	45 to 59 Minutes	60 to 89 Minutes	90 Minutes or More
City	19.1	50.0	19.1	5.7	2.2	2.4	1.4
MSA[1]	16.5	41.0	23.7	11.6	3.2	2.6	1.5
U.S.	12.7	28.9	20.9	20.5	8.1	6.2	2.7

Note: Note: Figures are percentages and include workers 16 years old and over; (1) Figures cover the Springfield, IL Metropolitan Statistical Area—see Appendix B for areas included
Source: U.S. Census Bureau, 2013-2017 American Community Survey 5-Year Estimates

Freeway Travel Time Index

Area	1985	1990	1995	2000	2005	2010	2014
Urban Area Rank[1,2]	n/a	n/a	n/a	n/a	n/a	n/a	n/a
Urban Area Index[1]	n/a	n/a	n/a	n/a	n/a	n/a	n/a
Average Index[3]	1.09	1.11	1.14	1.17	1.20	1.19	1.20

Note: Freeway Travel Time Index—the ratio of travel time in the peak period to the travel time at free-flow conditions. For example, a value of 1.30 indicates a 20-minute free-flow trip takes 26 minutes in the peak (20 minutes x 1.30 = 26 minutes); (1) Data for the Springfield, IL urban area was not available; (2) Rank is based on 101 urban areas (#1 = highest travel time index); (3) Average of 101 urban areas
Source: Texas Transportation Institute, 2015 Urban Mobility Scorecard, August 2015

Freeway Commuter Stress Index

Area	1985	1990	1995	2000	2005	2010	2014
Urban Area Rank[1,2]	n/a	n/a	n/a	n/a	n/a	n/a	n/a
Urban Area Index[1]	n/a	n/a	n/a	n/a	n/a	n/a	n/a
Average Index[3]	1.13	1.16	1.19	1.22	1.25	1.24	1.25

Note: The Freeway Commuter Stress Index is the same as the Freeway Travel Time Index (see table above) except that it includes only the travel in the peak directions during the peak periods; the TTI includes travel in all directions during the peak period. Thus, the CSI is more indicative of the work trip experienced by each commuter on a daily basis; (1) Data for the Springfield, IL urban area was not available; (2) Rank is based on 101 urban areas (#1 = highest travel time index); (3) Average of 101 urban areas
Source: Texas Transportation Institute, 2015 Urban Mobility Scorecard, August 2015

Public Transportation

Agency Name / Mode of Transportation	Vehicles Operated in Maximum Service[1]	Annual Unlinked Passenger Trips[2] (in thous.)	Annual Passenger Miles[3] (in thous.)
Springfield Mass Transit District (SMTD)			
Bus (directly operated)	46	1,647.9	6,056.7
Demand Response (directly operated)	12	78.0	474.4

Note: (1) The number of revenue vehicles operated by the given mode and type of service to meet the annual maximum service requirement. This is the revenue vehicle count during the peak season of the year; on the week and day that maximum service is provided. Vehicles operated in maximum service (VOMS) exclude atypical days and one-time special events; (2) The number of passengers who boarded public transportation vehicles. Passengers are counted each time they board a vehicle no matter how many vehicles they use to travel from their origin to their destination. (3) The sum of the distances ridden by all passengers during the entire fiscal year.
Source: Federal Transit Administration, National Transit Database, 2017

Air Transportation

Airport Name and Code / Type of Service	Passenger Airlines[1]	Passenger Enplanements	Freight Carriers[2]	Freight (lbs)
Capital Airport (SPI)				
Domestic service (U.S. carriers - 2018)	7	76,645	1	119
International service (U.S. carriers - 2017)	0	0	0	0

Note: (1) Includes all U.S.-based major, minor and commuter airlines that carried at least one passenger during the year; (2) Includes all U.S.-based airlines and freight carriers that transported at least one pound of freight during the year.
Source: Bureau of Transportation Statistics, The Intermodal Transportation Database, Air Carriers: T-100 Domestic Market (U.S. Carriers), 2018; Bureau of Transportation Statistics, The Intermodal Transportation Database, Air Carriers: T-100 International Market (U.S. Carriers), 2017

Other Transportation Statistics

Major Highways:	I-55; I-72
Amtrak Service:	Yes
Major Waterways/Ports:	None

Source: Amtrak.com; Google Maps

BUSINESSES

Major Business Headquarters

Company Name	Industry	Rankings Fortune[1]	Forbes[2]
No companies listed		-	-

Note: (1) Companies that produce a 10-K are ranked 1 to 500 based on 2017 revenue; (2) All private companies with at least $2 billion in annual revenue through the end of their most current fiscal year are ranked 1 to 229; companies listed are headquartered in the city; dashes indicate no ranking
Source: Fortune, "Fortune 500," June 2018; Forbes, "America's Largest Private Companies," 2018 Rankings

Minority- and Women-Owned Businesses

Group	All Firms Firms	Sales ($000)	Firms with Paid Employees Firms	Sales ($000)	Employees	Payroll ($000)
AIAN[1]	25	177	0	0	0	0
Asian	291	81,769	68	75,121	658	18,643
Black	1,329	21,480	37	7,705	225	2,490
Hispanic	181	(s)	36	(s)	500 - 999	(s)
NHOPI[2]	n/a	n/a	n/a	n/a	n/a	n/a
Women	3,787	601,391	437	556,184	4,192	155,176
All Firms	9,006	14,243,891	2,655	14,048,329	66,577	2,516,800

Note: Figures cover firms located in the city; minority- and women-owned business are defined as firms in which the corresponding group own 51% or more of the stock or equity of the company; (1) American Indian and Alaska Native; (2) Native Hawaiian and Other Pacific Islander; (s) estimates are suppressed when publication standards are not met; n/a not available
Source: U.S. Census Bureau, 2012 Economic Census, Survey of Business Owners

HOTELS & CONVENTION CENTERS

Hotels, Motels and Vacation Rentals

Area	5 Star Num.	Pct.[3]	4 Star Num.	Pct.[3]	3 Star Num.	Pct.[3]	2 Star Num.	Pct.[3]	1 Star Num.	Pct.[3]	Not Rated Num.	Pct.[3]
City[1]	0	0.0	2	2.5	16	20.0	51	63.8	1	1.3	10	12.5
Total[2]	286	0.4	5,236	7.1	16,715	22.6	10,259	13.9	293	0.4	41,056	55.6

Note: (1) Figures cover Springfield and vicinity; (2) Figures cover all 100 cities in this book; (3) Percentage of hotels which have a given star rating; Star ratings are determined by expedia.com and offer an indication of the general quality of a particular hotel.
Source: www.expedia.com, April 3, 2019

Major Convention Centers

Name	Overall Space (sq. ft.)	Exhibit Space (sq. ft.)	Meeting Space (sq. ft.)	Meeting Rooms
Prairie Capital Convention Center	n/a	44,000	21,000	n/a

Note: Table includes convention centers located in the Springfield, IL metro area; n/a not available
Source: Original research

Living Environment

COST OF LIVING

Cost of Living Index

Composite Index	Groceries	Housing	Utilities	Trans-portation	Health Care	Misc. Goods/ Services
n/a	n/a	n/a	n/a	n/a	n/a	n/a

Note: The Cost of Living Index measures regional differences in the cost of consumer goods and services, excluding taxes and non-consumer expenditures, for professional and managerial households in the top income quintile. It is based on more than 50,000 prices covering almost 60 different items for which prices are collected three times a year by chambers of commerce, economic development organizations or university applied economic centers in each participating urban area. The numbers shown should be read as a percentage above or below the national average of 100. For example, a value of 115.4 in the groceries column indicates that grocery prices are 15.4% higher than the national average. Small differences in the index numbers should not be interpreted as significant; n/a not available.
Source: The Council for Community and Economic Research, ACCRA Cost of Living Index, 2018

Grocery Prices

Area[1]	T-Bone Steak ($/pound)	Frying Chicken ($/pound)	Whole Milk ($/half gal.)	Eggs ($/dozen)	Orange Juice ($/64 oz.)	Coffee ($/11.5 oz.)
City[2]	n/a	n/a	n/a	n/a	n/a	n/a
Avg.	11.35	1.42	1.94	1.81	3.52	4.35
Min.	7.45	0.92	0.80	0.75	2.72	3.06
Max.	15.05	2.76	4.18	4.00	5.36	8.20

Note: (1) Values for the local area are compared with the average, minimum and maximum values for all 291 areas in the Cost of Living Index; (2) Figures cover the Springfield IL urban area; n/a not available; **T-Bone Steak** (price per pound); **Frying Chicken** (price per pound, whole fryer); **Whole Milk** (half gallon carton); **Eggs** (price per dozen, Grade A, large); **Orange Juice** (64 oz. Tropicana or Florida Natural); **Coffee** (11.5 oz. can, vacuum-packed, Maxwell House, Hills Bros, or Folgers).
Source: The Council for Community and Economic Research, ACCRA Cost of Living Index, 2018

Housing and Utility Costs

Area[1]	New Home Price ($)	Apartment Rent ($/month)	All Electric ($/month)	Part Electric ($/month)	Other Energy ($/month)	Telephone ($/month)
City[2]	n/a	n/a	n/a	n/a	n/a	n/a
Avg.	347,000	1,087	165.93	100.16	67.73	178.70
Min.	200,468	500	93.58	25.64	26.78	163.10
Max.	1,901,222	4,888	388.65	246.86	332.81	197.70

Note: (1) Values for the local area are compared with the average, minimum and maximum values for all 291 areas in the Cost of Living Index; (2) Figures cover the Springfield IL urban area; n/a not available; **New Home Price** (2,400 sf living area, 8,000 sf lot, in urban area with full utilities); **Apartment Rent** (950 sf 2 bedroom/1.5 or 2 bath, unfurnished, excluding all utilities except water); **All Electric** (average monthly cost for an all-electric home); **Part Electric** (average monthly cost for a part-electric home); **Other Energy** (average monthly cost for natural gas, fuel oil, coal, wood, and any other forms of energy except electricity); **Telephone** (price includes the base monthly rate plus taxes and fees for three lines of mobile phone service).
Source: The Council for Community and Economic Research, ACCRA Cost of Living Index, 2018

Health Care, Transportation, and Other Costs

Area[1]	Doctor ($/visit)	Dentist ($/visit)	Optometrist ($/visit)	Gasoline ($/gallon)	Beauty Salon ($/visit)	Men's Shirt ($)
City[2]	n/a	n/a	n/a	n/a	n/a	n/a
Avg.	110.71	95.11	103.74	2.61	37.48	32.03
Min.	33.60	62.55	54.63	1.89	17.00	11.44
Max.	195.97	153.93	225.79	3.59	71.88	58.64

Note: (1) Values for the local area are compared with the average, minimum and maximum values for all 291 areas in the Cost of Living Index; (2) Figures cover the Springfield IL urban area; n/a not available; **Doctor** (general practitioners routine exam of an established patient); **Dentist** (adult teeth cleaning and periodic oral examination); **Optometrist** (full vision eye exam for established adult patient); **Gasoline** (one gallon regular unleaded, national brand, including all taxes, cash price at self-service pump if available); **Beauty Salon** (woman's shampoo, trim, and blow-dry); **Men's Shirt** (cotton/polyester dress shirt, pinpoint weave, long sleeves).
Source: The Council for Community and Economic Research, ACCRA Cost of Living Index, 2018

HOUSING

House Price Index (HPI)

Area	National Ranking[2]	Quarterly Change (%)	One-Year Change (%)	Five-Year Change (%)
MSA[1]	213	0.80	2.77	9.93
U.S.[3]	–	1.12	5.73	32.81

Note: The HPI is a weighted repeat sales index. It measures average price changes in repeat sales or refinancings on the same properties. This information is obtained by reviewing repeat mortgage transactions on single-family properties whose mortgages have been purchased or securitized by Fannie Mae or Freddie Mac in January 1975; (1) Figures cover the Springfield, IL Metropolitan Statistical Area—see Appendix B for areas included; (2) Rankings are based on annual percentage change for all metro areas containing at least 15,000 transactions over the last 10 years and ranges from 1 to 245; (3) figures based on a weighted average of Census Division estimates using a seasonally adjusted, purchase-only index; all figures are for the period ending December 31, 2018
Source: Federal Housing Finance Agency, House Price Index, February 26, 2019

Median Single-Family Home Prices

Area	2016	2017	2018[p]	Percent Change 2017 to 2018
MSA[1]	135.0	132.4	133.5	0.8
U.S. Average	235.5	248.8	261.6	5.1

Note: Figures are median sales prices of existing single-family homes in thousands of dollars; (p) preliminary; (1) Figures cover the Springfield, IL Metropolitan Statistical Area—see Appendix B for areas included
Source: National Association of Realtors, Median Sales Price of Existing Single-Family Homes for Metropolitan Areas, 4th Quarter 2018

Qualifying Income Based on Median Sales Price of Existing Single-Family Homes

Area	With 5% Down ($)	With 10% Down ($)	With 20% Down ($)
MSA[1]	32,576	30,862	27,433
U.S. Average	62,954	59,640	53,013

Note: Figures are preliminary; Qualifying income is based on a mortgage rate of 4.9%. Monthly principal and interest payment is limited to 25% of income; (1) Figures cover the Springfield, IL Metropolitan Statistical Area—see Appendix B for areas included
Source: National Association of Realtors, Qualifying Income Based on Median Sales Price of Existing Single-Family Homes for Metropolitan Areas, 4th Quarter 2018

Median Apartment Condo-Coop Home Prices

Area	2016	2017	2018[p]	Percent Change 2017 to 2018
MSA[1]	n/a	n/a	n/a	n/a
U.S. Average	220.7	234.3	241.0	2.9

Note: Figures are median sales prices of existing apartment condo-coop homes in thousands of dollars; (p) preliminary; n/a not available; (1) Figures cover the Springfield, IL Metropolitan Statistical Area—see Appendix B for areas included
Source: National Association of Realtors, Median Sales Price of Existing Apartment Condo-Coop Homes for Metropolitan Areas, 4th Quarter 2018

Home Value Distribution

Area	Under $50,000	$50,000 -$99,999	$100,000 -$149,999	$150,000 -$199,999	$200,000 -$299,999	$300,000 -$499,999	$500,000 -$999,999	$1,000,000 or more
City	11.8	26.0	24.1	15.1	14.4	6.2	2.1	0.2
MSA[1]	9.7	23.8	22.8	17.5	17.2	6.9	1.9	0.3
U.S.	8.3	13.9	14.7	14.6	18.7	17.3	9.7	2.7

Note: Figures are percentages and cover owner-occupied housing units; (1) Figures cover the Springfield, IL Metropolitan Statistical Area—see Appendix B for areas included
Source: U.S. Census Bureau, 2013-2017 American Community Survey 5-Year Estimates

Homeownership Rate

Area	2010 (%)	2011 (%)	2012 (%)	2013 (%)	2014 (%)	2015 (%)	2016 (%)	2017 (%)	2018 (%)
MSA[1]	n/a	n/a	n/a	n/a	n/a	n/a	n/a	n/a	n/a
U.S.	66.9	66.1	65.4	65.1	64.5	63.7	63.4	63.9	64.4

Note: (1) Figures cover the Springfield, IL Metropolitan Statistical Area—see Appendix B for areas included; n/a not available
Source: U.S. Census Bureau, Housing Vacancies and Homeownership Annual Statistics: 2010-2018

Year Housing Structure Built

Area	2010 or Later	2000 -2009	1990 -1999	1980 -1989	1970 -1979	1960 -1969	1950 -1959	1940 -1949	Before 1940	Median Year
City	1.5	9.2	12.8	9.9	15.0	13.4	11.9	7.0	19.2	1969
MSA[1]	2.2	10.3	13.4	9.4	15.8	12.5	12.2	6.9	17.3	1971
U.S.	3.2	14.5	14.0	13.6	15.5	10.8	10.5	5.1	12.9	1977

Note: Figures are percentages except for Median Year; Note: (1) Figures cover the Springfield, IL Metropolitan Statistical Area—see Appendix B for areas included
Source: U.S. Census Bureau, 2013-2017 American Community Survey 5-Year Estimates

Gross Monthly Rent

Area	Under $500	$500 -$999	$1,000 -$1,499	$1,500 -$1,999	$2,000 -$2,499	$2,500 -$2,999	$3,000 and up	Median ($)
City	14.8	64.8	16.7	2.4	0.7	0.5	0.1	765
MSA[1]	13.3	65.0	17.7	2.7	0.5	0.6	0.1	777
U.S.	10.5	41.1	28.7	11.7	4.5	1.8	1.7	982

Note: Figures are percentages except for Median; Gross rent is the contract rent plus the estimated average monthly cost of utilities (electricity, gas, and water and sewer) and fuels (oil, coal, kerosene, wood, etc.) if these are paid by the renter (or paid for the renter by someone else); (1) Figures cover the Springfield, IL Metropolitan Statistical Area—see Appendix B for areas included
Source: U.S. Census Bureau, 2013-2017 American Community Survey 5-Year Estimates

HEALTH

Health Risk Factors

Category	MSA[1] (%)	U.S. (%)
Adults aged 18–64 who have any kind of health care coverage	n/a	87.3
Adults who reported being in good or better health	n/a	82.4
Adults who have been told they have high blood cholesterol	n/a	33.0
Adults who have been told they have high blood pressure	n/a	32.3
Adults who are current smokers	n/a	17.1
Adults who currently use E-cigarettes	n/a	4.6
Adults who currently use chewing tobacco, snuff, or snus	n/a	4.0
Adults who are heavy drinkers[2]	n/a	6.3
Adults who are binge drinkers[3]	n/a	17.4
Adults who are overweight (BMI 25.0 - 29.9)	n/a	35.3
Adults who are obese (BMI 30.0 - 99.8)	n/a	31.3
Adults who participated in any physical activities in the past month	n/a	74.4
Adults who always or nearly always wears a seat belt	n/a	94.3

Note: n/a not available; (1) Figures cover the Springfield, IL Metropolitan Statistical Area—see Appendix B for areas included; (2) Heavy drinkers are classified as adult men having more than 14 drinks per week and adult women having more than 7 drinks per week; (3) Binge drinkers are classified as males having five or more drinks on one occasion or females having four or more drinks on one occasion
Source: Centers for Disease Control and Prevention, Behavioral Risk Factor Surveillance System, SMART: Selected Metropolitan Area Risk Trends, 2017

Acute and Chronic Health Conditions

Category	MSA[1] (%)	U.S. (%)
Adults who have ever been told they had a heart attack	n/a	4.2
Adults who have ever been told they have angina or coronary heart disease	n/a	3.9
Adults who have ever been told they had a stroke	n/a	3.0
Adults who have ever been told they have asthma	n/a	14.2
Adults who have ever been told they have arthritis	n/a	24.9
Adults who have ever been told they have diabetes[2]	n/a	10.5
Adults who have ever been told they had skin cancer	n/a	6.2
Adults who have ever been told they had any other types of cancer	n/a	7.1
Adults who have ever been told they have COPD	n/a	6.5
Adults who have ever been told they have kidney disease	n/a	3.0
Adults who have ever been told they have a form of depression	n/a	20.5

Note: n/a not available; (1) Figures cover the Springfield, IL Metropolitan Statistical Area—see Appendix B for areas included; (2) Figures do not include pregnancy-related, borderline, or pre-diabetes
Source: Centers for Disease Control and Prevention, Behavioral Risk Factor Surveillance System, SMART: Selected Metropolitan Area Risk Trends, 2017

Health Screening and Vaccination Rates

Category	MSA[1] (%)	U.S. (%)
Adults aged 65+ who have had flu shot within the past year	n/a	60.7
Adults aged 65+ who have ever had a pneumonia vaccination	n/a	75.4
Adults who have ever been tested for HIV	n/a	36.1
Adults who have ever had the shingles or zoster vaccine?	n/a	28.9
Adults who have had their blood cholesterol checked within the last five years	n/a	85.9

Note: n/a not available; (1) Figures cover the Springfield, IL Metropolitan Statistical Area—see Appendix B for areas included.
Source: Centers for Disease Control and Prevention, Behaviorial Risk Factor Surveillance System, SMART: Selected Metropolitan Area Risk Trends, 2017

Disability Status

Category	MSA[1] (%)	U.S. (%)
Adults who reported being deaf	n/a	6.7
Are you blind or have serious difficulty seeing, even when wearing glasses?	n/a	4.5
Are you limited in any way in any of your usual activities due of arthritis?	n/a	12.9
Do you have difficulty doing errands alone?	n/a	6.8
Do you have difficulty dressing or bathing?	n/a	3.6
Do you have serious difficulty concentrating/remembering/making decisions?	n/a	10.7
Do you have serious difficulty walking or climbing stairs?	n/a	13.6

Note: n/a not available; (1) Figures cover the Springfield, IL Metropolitan Statistical Area—see Appendix B for areas included.
Source: Centers for Disease Control and Prevention, Behaviorial Risk Factor Surveillance System, SMART: Selected Metropolitan Area Risk Trends, 2017

Mortality Rates for the Top 10 Causes of Death in the U.S.

ICD-10[a] Sub-Chapter	ICD-10[a] Code	Age-Adjusted Mortality Rate[1] per 100,000 population	
		County[2]	U.S.
Malignant neoplasms	C00-C97	173.0	155.5
Ischaemic heart diseases	I20-I25	86.9	94.8
Other forms of heart disease	I30-I51	61.6	52.9
Chronic lower respiratory diseases	J40-J47	35.3	41.0
Cerebrovascular diseases	I60-I69	40.5	37.5
Other degenerative diseases of the nervous system	G30-G31	22.0	35.0
Other external causes of accidental injury	W00-X59	40.2	33.7
Organic, including symptomatic, mental disorders	F01-F09	41.1	31.0
Hypertensive diseases	I10-I15	22.2	21.9
Diabetes mellitus	E10-E14	20.5	21.2

Note: (a) ICD-10 = International Classification of Diseases 10th Revision; (1) Mortality rates are a three year average covering 2015-2017; (2) Figures cover Sangamon County.
Source: Centers for Disease Control and Prevention, National Center for Health Statistics. Underlying Cause of Death 1999-2017 on CDC WONDER Online Database

Mortality Rates for Selected Causes of Death

ICD-10[a] Sub-Chapter	ICD-10[a] Code	Age-Adjusted Mortality Rate[1] per 100,000 population	
		County[2]	U.S.
Assault	X85-Y09	6.1	5.9
Diseases of the liver	K70-K76	14.9	14.1
Human immunodeficiency virus (HIV) disease	B20-B24	Suppressed	1.8
Influenza and pneumonia	J09-J18	16.3	14.3
Intentional self-harm	X60-X84	16.8	13.6
Malnutrition	E40-E46	Unreliable	1.6
Obesity and other hyperalimentation	E65-E68	Unreliable	2.1
Renal failure	N17-N19	13.5	13.0
Transport accidents	V01-V99	10.0	12.4
Viral hepatitis	B15-B19	Suppressed	1.6

Note: (a) ICD-10 = International Classification of Diseases 10th Revision; (1) Mortality rates are a three year average covering 2015-2017; (2) Figures cover Sangamon County; Data are suppressed when the data meet the criteria for confidentiality constraints; Mortality rates are flagged as unreliable when the rate would be calculated with a numerator of 20 or less.
Source: Centers for Disease Control and Prevention, National Center for Health Statistics. Underlying Cause of Death 1999-2017 on CDC WONDER Online Database

Health Insurance Coverage

Area	With Health Insurance	With Private Health Insurance	With Public Health Insurance	Without Health Insurance	Population Under Age 18 Without Health Insurance
City	94.2	68.1	40.8	5.8	1.8
MSA[1]	95.1	73.6	36.5	4.9	1.6
U.S.	89.5	67.2	33.8	10.5	5.7

Note: Figures are percentages that cover the civilian noninstitutionalized population; (1) Figures cover the Springfield, IL Metropolitan Statistical Area—see Appendix B for areas included
Source: U.S. Census Bureau, 2013-2017 American Community Survey 5-Year Estimates

Number of Medical Professionals

Area	MDs[3]	DOs[3,4]	Dentists	Podiatrists	Chiropractors	Optometrists
County[1] (number)	1,231	45	167	11	77	43
County[1] (rate[2])	623.0	22.8	85.0	5.6	39.2	21.9
U.S. (rate[2])	279.3	23.0	68.4	6.0	27.1	16.2

Note: Data as of 2017 unless noted; (1) Data covers Sangamon County; (2) Rate per 100,000 population; (3) Data as of 2016 and includes all active, non-federal physicians; (4) Doctor of Osteopathic Medicine
Source: U.S. Department of Health and Human Services, Health Resources and Services Administration, Bureau of Health Professions, Area Resource File (ARF) 2017-2018

EDUCATION

Public School District Statistics

District Name	Schls	Pupils	Pupil/ Teacher Ratio	Minority Pupils[1] (%)	Free Lunch Eligible[2] (%)	IEP[3] (%)
Springfield SD 186	34	14,903	14.6	55.8	62.9	22.1

Note: Table includes school districts with 2,000 or more students; (1) Percentage of students that are not non-Hispanic white; (2) Percentage of students that are eligible for the free lunch program; (3) Percentage of students that have an Individualized Education Program.
Source: U.S. Department of Education, National Center for Education Statistics, Common Core of Data, Local Education Agency (School District) Universe Survey: School Year 2016-2017; U.S. Department of Education, National Center for Education Statistics, Common Core of Data, Public Elementary/Secondary School Universe Survey: School Year 2016-2017

Highest Level of Education

Area	Less than H.S.	H.S. Diploma	Some College, No Deg.	Associate Degree	Bachelor's Degree	Master's Degree	Prof. School Degree	Doctorate Degree
City	8.6	26.2	22.0	7.3	21.6	9.7	3.2	1.3
MSA[1]	7.6	28.1	22.7	8.0	21.2	8.7	2.6	1.1
U.S.	12.7	27.3	20.8	8.3	19.1	8.4	2.0	1.4

Note: Figures cover persons age 25 and over; (1) Figures cover the Springfield, IL Metropolitan Statistical Area—see Appendix B for areas included
Source: U.S. Census Bureau, 2013-2017 American Community Survey 5-Year Estimates

Educational Attainment by Race

Area	High School Graduate or Higher (%)					Bachelor's Degree or Higher (%)				
	Total	White	Black	Asian	Hisp.[2]	Total	White	Black	Asian	Hisp.[2]
City	91.4	92.8	84.3	91.1	85.9	35.8	38.2	19.9	67.7	30.5
MSA[1]	92.4	93.4	84.2	91.6	86.5	33.6	34.6	19.9	65.4	31.0
U.S.	87.3	89.3	84.9	86.5	66.7	30.9	32.2	20.6	52.7	15.2

Note: Figures shown cover persons 25 years old and over; (1) Figures cover the Springfield, IL Metropolitan Statistical Area—see Appendix B for areas included; (2) People of Hispanic origin can be of any race
Source: U.S. Census Bureau, 2013-2017 American Community Survey 5-Year Estimates

School Enrollment by Grade and Control

Area	Preschool (%)		Kindergarten (%)		Grades 1 - 4 (%)		Grades 5 - 8 (%)		Grades 9 - 12 (%)	
	Public	Private	Public	Private	Public	Private	Public	Private	Public	Private
City	65.3	34.7	81.2	18.8	82.6	17.4	84.6	15.4	85.9	14.1
MSA[1]	65.3	34.7	85.4	14.6	87.4	12.6	87.4	12.6	90.3	9.7
U.S.	58.8	41.2	87.7	12.3	89.7	10.3	89.6	10.4	90.3	9.7

Note: Figures shown cover persons 3 years old and over; (1) Figures cover the Springfield, IL Metropolitan Statistical Area—see Appendix B for areas included
Source: U.S. Census Bureau, 2013-2017 American Community Survey 5-Year Estimates

Average Salaries of Public School Classroom Teachers

Area	2016		2017		Change from 2016 to 2017	
	Dollars	Rank[1]	Dollars	Rank[1]	Percent	Rank[2]
Illinois	63,475	11	64,933	11	2.3	19
U.S. Average	58,479	–	59,660	–	2.0	–

Note: (1) Rank ranges from 1 to 51 where 1 indicates highest salary; (2) Rank ranges from 1 to 51 where 1 indicates highest percent change.
Source: National Education Association, Rankings & Estimates: Rankings of the States 2017 and Estimates of School Statistics 2018

Higher Education

Four-Year Colleges			Two-Year Colleges			Medical Schools[1]	Law Schools[2]	Voc/ Tech[3]
Public	Private Non-profit	Private For-profit	Public	Private Non-profit	Private For-profit			
1	1	0	1	0	0	1	0	4

Note: Figures cover institutions located within the city limits and include main campuses only; (1) includes schools accredited by the Liaison Committee on Medical Education and the American Osteopathic Association's Commission on Osteopathic College Accreditation; (2) includes ABA-accredited schools, schools with provisional ABA accreditation, and state accredited schools; (3) includes all schools with programs that are less than 2 years.
Source: National Center for Education Statistics, Integrated Postsecondary Education System (IPEDS), 2017-18; Wikipedia, List of Medical Schools in the United States, accessed April 3, 2019; Wikipedia, List of Law Schools in the United States, accessed April 3, 2019

PRESIDENTIAL ELECTION

2016 Presidential Election Results

Area	Clinton	Trump	Johnson	Stein	Other
Sangamon County	41.6	50.8	4.6	1.5	1.6
U.S.	48.0	45.9	3.3	1.1	1.7

Note: Results are percentages and may not add to 100% due to rounding
Source: Dave Leip's Atlas of U.S. Presidential Elections

EMPLOYERS

Major Employers

Company Name	Industry
BlueCross BlueShield of Illinois	Insurance
Horace Mann Insurance Company	Insurance
Illinois National Guard	U.S. military
Memorial Health System	Healthcare
Southern Illinois University School of Med	Education
Springfield Clinic	Healthcare
Springfield School District #186	Education
St. John's Medical	Healthcare
State of Illinois	State government
U.S. Postal Service	Government/postal service
University of Illinois at Springfield	Education

Note: Companies shown are located within the Springfield, IL Metropolitan Statistical Area.
Source: Hoovers.com; Wikipedia

PUBLIC SAFETY

Crime Rate

Area	All Crimes	Violent Crimes				Property Crimes		
		Murder	Rape[3]	Robbery	Aggrav. Assault	Burglary	Larceny -Theft	Motor Vehicle Theft
City	5,810.4	9.5	80.5	217.2	747.6	1,047.0	3,437.8	270.8
Suburbs[1]	1,582.4	2.1	47.6	21.2	205.3	333.4	860.6	112.2
Metro[2]	3,908.7	6.2	65.7	129.0	503.7	726.0	2,278.6	199.5
U.S.	2,756.1	5.3	41.7	98.0	248.9	430.4	1,694.4	237.4

Note: Figures are crimes per 100,000 population; (1) All areas within the metro area that are located outside the city limits; (2) Figures cover the Springfield, IL Metropolitan Statistical Area—see Appendix B for areas included; (3) The city and U.S. figures shown were reported using the revised Uniform Crime Reporting (UCR) definition of rape. The suburban and metro area figures shown are an aggregate total of the data submitted using both the revised and legacy UCR definitions.
Source: FBI Uniform Crime Reports, 2017

Hate Crimes

Area	Number of Quarters Reported	Number of Incidents per Bias Motivation					
		Race/Ethnicity/ Ancestry	Religion	Sexual Orientation	Disability	Gender	Gender Identity
City	4	2	0	1	0	0	0
U.S.	4	4,131	1,564	1,130	116	46	119

Source: Federal Bureau of Investigation, Hate Crime Statistics 2017

Identity Theft Consumer Reports

Area	Reports	Reports per 100,000 Population	Rank[2]
MSA[1]	175	83	215
U.S.	444,602	135	-

Note: (1) Figures cover the Springfield, IL Metropolitan Statistical Area—see Appendix B for areas included; (2) Rank ranges from 1 to 389 where 1 indicates greatest number of identity theft reports per 100,000 population
Source: Federal Trade Commission, Consumer Sentinel Network Data Book for January–December 2018

Fraud and Other Consumer Reports

Area	Reports	Reports per 100,000 Population	Rank[2]
MSA[1]	925	440	264
U.S.	2,552,917	776	-

Note: (1) Figures cover the Springfield, IL Metropolitan Statistical Area—see Appendix B for areas included; (2) Rank ranges from 1 to 389 where 1 indicates greatest number of fraud and other consumer reports per 100,000 population
Source: Federal Trade Commission, Consumer Sentinel Network Data Book for January–December 2018

SPORTS

Professional Sports Teams

Team Name	League	Year Established
No teams are located in the metro area		

Source: Wikipedia, Major Professional Sports Teams of the United States and Canada, April 5, 2019

CLIMATE

Average and Extreme Temperatures

Temperature	Jan	Feb	Mar	Apr	May	Jun	Jul	Aug	Sep	Oct	Nov	Dec	Yr.
Extreme High (°F)	73	78	91	90	101	104	112	108	101	93	83	74	112
Average High (°F)	35	38	50	63	74	84	88	85	79	67	51	38	63
Average Temp. (°F)	27	30	41	53	64	73	78	75	68	57	43	31	54
Average Low (°F)	19	22	32	43	53	63	67	65	57	46	34	24	44
Extreme Low (°F)	-21	-24	-12	17	28	40	48	43	32	13	-3	-21	-24

Note: Figures cover the years 1948-1995
Source: National Climatic Data Center, International Station Meteorological Climate Summary, 9/96

Average Precipitation/Snowfall/Humidity

Precip./Humidity	Jan	Feb	Mar	Apr	May	Jun	Jul	Aug	Sep	Oct	Nov	Dec	Yr.
Avg. Precip. (in.)	1.8	1.7	3.1	3.6	3.8	3.9	3.3	3.1	3.3	2.6	2.4	2.1	34.9
Avg. Snowfall (in.)	6	6	4	1	Tr	0	0	0	0	Tr	1	5	21
Avg. Rel. Hum. 6am (%)	80	81	81	79	81	82	85	89	87	83	82	82	83
Avg. Rel. Hum. 3pm (%)	67	65	59	52	51	51	54	56	50	50	60	69	57

Note: Figures cover the years 1948-1995; Tr = Trace amounts (<0.05 in. of rain; <0.5 in. of snow)
Source: National Climatic Data Center, International Station Meteorological Climate Summary, 9/96

Weather Conditions

Temperature			Daytime Sky			Precipitation		
10°F & below	32°F & below	90°F & above	Clear	Partly cloudy	Cloudy	0.01 inch or more precip.	0.1 inch or more snow/ice	Thunder-storms
19	111	34	96	126	143	111	18	49

Note: Figures are average number of days per year and cover the years 1948-1995
Source: National Climatic Data Center, International Station Meteorological Climate Summary, 9/96

HAZARDOUS WASTE

Superfund Sites

The Springfield, IL metro area has no sites on the EPA's Superfund Final National Priorities List. There are a total of 1,390 Superfund sites with a status of proposed or final on the list in the U.S.
U.S. Environmental Protection Agency, National Priorities List, April 5, 2019

AIR & WATER QUALITY

Air Quality Trends: Ozone

	1990	1995	2000	2005	2010	2012	2014	2015	2016	2017
MSA[1]	n/a	n/a	n/a	n/a	n/a	n/a	n/a	n/a	n/a	n/a
U.S.	0.088	0.089	0.082	0.080	0.073	0.075	0.067	0.068	0.069	0.068

Note: (1) Data covers the Springfield, IL Metropolitan Statistical Area—see Appendix B for areas included; n/a not available. The values shown are the composite ozone concentration averages among trend sites based on the highest fourth daily maximum 8-hour concentration in parts per million. These trends are based on sites having an adequate record of monitoring data during the trend period. Data from exceptional events are included.
Source: U.S. Environmental Protection Agency, Air Quality Monitoring Information, "Air Quality Trends by City, 1990-2017"

Air Quality Index

Area	Percent of Days when Air Quality was...[2]					AQI Statistics[2]	
	Good	Moderate	Unhealthy for Sensitive Groups	Unhealthy	Very Unhealthy	Maximum	Median
MSA[1]	81.9	17.6	0.5	0.0	0.0	115	40

Note: (1) Data covers the Springfield, IL Metropolitan Statistical Area—see Appendix B for areas included; (2) Based on 364 days with AQI data in 2017. Air Quality Index (AQI) is an index for reporting daily air quality. EPA calculates the AQI for five major air pollutants regulated by the Clean Air Act: ground-level ozone, particle pollution (aka particulate matter), carbon monoxide, sulfur dioxide, and nitrogen dioxide. The AQI runs from 0 to 500. The higher the AQI value, the greater the level of air pollution and the greater the health concern. There are six AQI categories: "Good" AQI is between 0 and 50. Air quality is considered satisfactory; "Moderate" AQI is between 51 and 100. Air quality is acceptable; "Unhealthy for Sensitive Groups" When AQI values are between 101 and 150, members of sensitive groups may experience health effects; "Unhealthy" When AQI values are between 151 and 200 everyone may begin to experience health effects; "Very Unhealthy" AQI values between 201 and 300 trigger a health alert; "Hazardous" AQI values over 300 trigger warnings of emergency conditions (not shown).
Source: U.S. Environmental Protection Agency, Air Quality Index Report, 2017

Air Quality Index Pollutants

Area	Percent of Days when AQI Pollutant was...[2]					
	Carbon Monoxide	Nitrogen Dioxide	Ozone	Sulfur Dioxide	Particulate Matter 2.5	Particulate Matter 10
MSA[1]	0.0	0.0	76.6	0.0	23.4	0.0

Note: (1) Data covers the Springfield, IL Metropolitan Statistical Area—see Appendix B for areas included; (2) Based on 364 days with AQI data in 2017. The Air Quality Index (AQI) is an index for reporting daily air quality. EPA calculates the AQI for five major air pollutants regulated by the Clean Air Act: ground-level ozone, particle pollution (also known as particulate matter), carbon monoxide, sulfur dioxide, and nitrogen dioxide. The AQI runs from 0 to 500. The higher the AQI value, the greater the level of air pollution and the greater the health concern.
Source: U.S. Environmental Protection Agency, Air Quality Index Report, 2017

Maximum Air Pollutant Concentrations: Particulate Matter, Ozone, CO and Lead

	Particulate Matter 10 (ug/m^3)	Particulate Matter 2.5 Wtd AM (ug/m^3)	Particulate Matter 2.5 24-Hr (ug/m^3)	Ozone (ppm)	Carbon Monoxide (ppm)	Lead (ug/m^3)
MSA[1] Level	n/a	8.6	21	0.069	n/a	n/a
NAAQS[2]	150	15	35	0.075	9	0.15
Met NAAQS[2]	n/a	Yes	Yes	Yes	n/a	n/a

Note: (1) Data covers the Springfield, IL Metropolitan Statistical Area—see Appendix B for areas included; Data from exceptional events are included; (2) National Ambient Air Quality Standards; ppm = parts per million; ug/m³ = micrograms per cubic meter; n/a not available.
Concentrations: Particulate Matter 10 (coarse particulate)—highest second maximum 24-hour concentration; Particulate Matter 2.5 Wtd AM (fine particulate)—highest weighted annual mean concentration; Particulate Matter 2.5 24-Hour (fine particulate)—highest 98th percentile 24-hour concentration; Ozone—highest fourth daily maximum 8-hour concentration; Carbon Monoxide—highest second maximum non-overlapping 8-hour concentration; Lead—maximum running 3-month average
Source: U.S. Environmental Protection Agency, Air Quality Monitoring Information, "Air Quality Statistics by City, 2017"

Maximum Air Pollutant Concentrations: Nitrogen Dioxide and Sulfur Dioxide

	Nitrogen Dioxide AM (ppb)	Nitrogen Dioxide 1-Hr (ppb)	Sulfur Dioxide AM (ppb)	Sulfur Dioxide 1-Hr (ppb)	Sulfur Dioxide 24-Hr (ppb)
MSA[1] Level	n/a	n/a	n/a	n/a	n/a
NAAQS[2]	53	100	30	75	140
Met NAAQS[2]	n/a	n/a	n/a	n/a	n/a

Note: (1) Data covers the Springfield, IL Metropolitan Statistical Area—see Appendix B for areas included; Data from exceptional events are included; (2) National Ambient Air Quality Standards; ppm = parts per million; ug/m³ = micrograms per cubic meter; n/a not available.
Concentrations: Nitrogen Dioxide AM—highest arithmetic mean concentration; Nitrogen Dioxide 1-Hr—highest 98th percentile 1-hour daily maximum concentration; Sulfur Dioxide AM—highest annual mean concentration; Sulfur Dioxide 1-Hr—highest 99th percentile 1-hour daily maximum concentration; Sulfur Dioxide 24-Hr—highest second maximum 24-hour concentration
Source: U.S. Environmental Protection Agency, Air Quality Monitoring Information, "Air Quality Statistics by City, 2017"

Drinking Water

Water System Name	Pop. Served	Primary Water Source Type	Violations[1]	
			Health Based	Monitoring/ Reporting
Springfield	119,395	Surface	0	0

Note: (1) Based on violation data from January 1, 2018 to December 31, 2018
Source: U.S. Environmental Protection Agency, Office of Ground Water and Drinking Water, Safe Drinking Water Information System (based on data extracted April 5, 2019)

Topeka, Kansas

Background

Water might not be the first thing that comes to mind when one thinks of Topeka, the capital of Kansas, but "Kansa" is the language of the Native American tribe known as the "people of water." Topeka sits atop rich, river-bottom soil deposited along the Kansas River. Rich soil makes great farm land and "Topeka" means "a good place to dig." First used by the Native American Kaw as a natural ford over the Kansas River, the city would become a key element in the westward expansion super highway known today as the Oregon Trail—an opportunity seized by three French-Canadian brothers and their three Kaw brides, who made a life for themselves ferrying westbound pioneers across the Kansas River. In fact, transportation remains a defining industry for Topeka.

Just as Topeka originated as a natural ford for Native American wanderers, it became a natural draw for railroads, and the industry that followed. The Atchison, Topeka and Santa Fe Railroad was only one in a series of rail enterprises in Topeka. Today, Burlington Northern Railroad still maintains one of the largest rail shops in the world in Topeka Kansas.

Topeka has been the site of race relations conflict since its inception. Anti-slavery (Topeka) and pro-slavery (Lecompton) factions across the Kansas territory clashed in the 1800s, foreshadowing the civil war soon followed. Nearly one hundred years later, a black elementary-school girl from Topeka, Linda Brown, put Topeka at the center of—the Supreme Court case *Brown v. Board of Education*. This landmark case forever changed the tenor of race relations in America, instituting school desegregation across the country.

The city was home to other civil rights milestones, including the Women's Suffrage Movement in Kansas, Topeka native Charles Curtis being the only Vice President of Native American descent, and Topeka native Georgia Neese Clark Gray being the first woman to be appointed U.S. Treasurer.

GoTopeka and the Topeka Chamber of Commerce have been instrumental in attracting a variety of industries. Topeka is home to the Goodyear Tire and Rubber, Collective Brands (a.k.a. Payless ShoeSource), PTs Coffee Roasting Co., Frito-Lay, and a division of Mars Chocolate North America.

Redevelopment continues along areas of the Kansas River. Downtown Topeka has seen recent improvements to its streetscape, facades, and development of apartments and condominium lofts. Historic North Topeka saw the renovation of the Great Overland Station, regarded as the greatest representation of classic railroad architecture in the state, and which is located across the river from the State Capitol, which itself is undergoing a $283 million, eight-year renovation.

Topeka is home to Washburn University, a public institution with over 6,900 students and more than 200 academic programs. Washburn participates in an academic common market, meaning students in neighboring states (Colorado, Texas, Oklahoma, Missouri and Nebraska) are offered the same tuition discounts as Kansas residents. Washburn is often ranked as a top midwestern college.

Topeka climate is between continental and subtropical. It has hot, somewhat humid summers and cool to cold, fairly dry winters. Daily average temperature ranges from 29.7 °F in January to 79.0 °F in July. The city receives nearly 36.5 inches of precipitation during an average year, with the largest share in May and June. Thunderstorms can be severe, producing frequent lightning, large hail, and sometimes tornadoes. Kansas sits in the heart of tornado alley, and in 1966 a tornado ripped through downtown Topeka, narrowly missing the Capital building. Topeka has also seen its share of floods, including a fatal event in 1905, and another devastating flood in 1951. Topeka has since built a series of flood control damns to help reign in the powerful Kansas River.

Rankings

Business/Finance Rankings

- According to data by the Bureau of Economic Analysis (BEA) and the Bureau of Labor Statistics (BLS), the Topeka metro area has the fastest-shrinking GDP (gross domestic product) and negative employment trends, at #6. *247wallst.com, "Cities With the Fastest Growing (and Shrinking) Economies," September 26, 2016*

- The Topeka metro area appeared on the Milken Institute "2018 Best Performing Cities" list. Rank: #162 out of 201 small metro areas. Criteria: job growth; wage and salary growth; high-tech output growth. *Milken Institute, "Best-Performing Cities 2018," January 24, 2019*

- *Forbes* ranked 200 smaller metro areas (population under 265,400) to determine the nation's "Best Small Places for Business and Careers." The Topeka metro area was ranked #150. Criteria: costs (business and living); job growth (past and projected); income growth; quality of life; educational attainment (college and high school); projected economic growth; cultural and recreational opportunities; net migration patterns; number of highly ranked colleges. *Forbes, "The Best Small Cities for Business and Careers 2018," October, 24 2018*

Real Estate Rankings

- The Topeka metro area was identified as one of the 20 most affordable housing markets in the U.S. in 2018. The area ranked #12 out of 180 markets. Criteria: qualification for a mortgage loan on a typical home. *National Association of Realtors®, Qualifying Income Based on Sales Price of Existing Single-Family Homes for Metropolitan Areas, 2018*

Safety Rankings

- The National Insurance Crime Bureau ranked 382 metro areas in the U.S. in terms of per capita rates of vehicle theft. The Topeka metro area ranked #34 (#1 = highest rate). Criteria: number of vehicle theft offenses per 100,000 inhabitants in 2017. *National Insurance Crime Bureau, "Hot Spots 2017," July 12, 2018*

Seniors/Retirement Rankings

- From its Best Cities for Successful Aging indexes, the Milken Institute generated rankings for metropolitan areas, weighing data in nine categories—health care, wellness, living arrangements, transportation and convenience, financial characteristics, education, employment, community engagement, and overall livability. The Topeka metro area was ranked #134 overall in the small metro area category. *Milken Institute, "Best Cities for Successful Aging, 2017" March 14, 2017*

Miscellaneous Rankings

- *WalletHub* compared the 150 most populated U.S. cities to determine their operating efficiency. A "Quality of Services" score was constructed for each city and then divided by the total budget per capita to reveal which were managed the best. Topeka ranked #44. Criteria: financial stability; economy; education; safety; health; infrastructure and pollution. *www.WalletHub.com, "2018's Best- & Worst-Run Cities in America," July 9, 2018*

Business Environment

CITY FINANCES

City Government Finances

Component	2016 ($000)	2016 ($ per capita)
Total Revenues	218,194	1,714
Total Expenditures	214,921	1,689
Debt Outstanding	326,919	2,569
Cash and Securities[1]	170,710	1,341

Note: (1) Cash and security holdings of a government at the close of its fiscal year, including those of its dependent agencies, utilities, and liquor stores.
Source: U.S. Census Bureau, State & Local Government Finances 2016

City Government Revenue by Source

Source	2016 ($000)	2016 ($ per capita)	2016 (%)
General Revenue			
From Federal Government	7,478	59	3.4
From State Government	16,022	126	7.3
From Local Governments	35	0	0.0
Taxes			
Property	46,506	365	21.3
Sales and Gross Receipts	72,467	569	33.2
Personal Income	0	0	0.0
Corporate Income	0	0	0.0
Motor Vehicle License	0	0	0.0
Other Taxes	1,721	14	0.8
Current Charges	36,190	284	16.6
Liquor Store	0	0	0.0
Utility	29,479	232	13.5
Employee Retirement	0	0	0.0

Source: U.S. Census Bureau, State & Local Government Finances 2016

City Government Expenditures by Function

Function	2016 ($000)	2016 ($ per capita)	2016 (%)
General Direct Expenditures			
Air Transportation	0	0	0.0
Corrections	823	6	0.4
Education	0	0	0.0
Employment Security Administration	0	0	0.0
Financial Administration	2,331	18	1.1
Fire Protection	27,871	219	13.0
General Public Buildings	1,431	11	0.7
Governmental Administration, Other	2,632	20	1.2
Health	0	0	0.0
Highways	27,789	218	12.9
Hospitals	0	0	0.0
Housing and Community Development	5,136	40	2.4
Interest on General Debt	3,217	25	1.5
Judicial and Legal	1,688	13	0.8
Libraries	0	0	0.0
Parking	3,523	27	1.6
Parks and Recreation	2,908	22	1.4
Police Protection	39,376	309	18.3
Public Welfare	619	4	0.3
Sewerage	31,717	249	14.8
Solid Waste Management	0	0	0.0
Veterans' Services	0	0	0.0
Liquor Store	0	0	0.0
Utility	42,720	335	19.9
Employee Retirement	0	0	0.0

Source: U.S. Census Bureau, State & Local Government Finances 2016

DEMOGRAPHICS

Population Growth

Area	1990 Census	2000 Census	2010 Census	2017* Estimate	Population Growth (%)	
					1990-2017	2010-2017
City	121,197	122,377	127,473	127,139	4.9	-0.3
MSA[1]	210,257	224,551	233,870	233,382	11.0	-0.2
U.S.	248,709,873	281,421,906	308,745,538	321,004,407	29.1	4.0

Note: (1) Figures cover the Topeka, KS Metropolitan Statistical Area—see Appendix B for areas included; (*) 2013-2017 5-year estimated population
Source: U.S. Census Bureau, 1990 Census, Census 2000, Census 2010, 2013-2017 American Community Survey 5-Year Estimates

Household Size

Area	Persons in Household (%)							Average Household Size
	One	Two	Three	Four	Five	Six	Seven or More	
City	37.3	32.2	13.0	10.4	4.7	1.8	0.7	2.30
MSA[1]	30.5	36.0	13.5	11.7	5.2	2.1	1.0	2.40
U.S.	27.7	33.8	15.7	13.0	6.0	2.3	1.4	2.60

Note: (1) Figures cover the Topeka, KS Metropolitan Statistical Area—see Appendix B for areas included
Source: U.S. Census Bureau, 2013-2017 American Community Survey 5-Year Estimates

Race

Area	White Alone[2] (%)	Black Alone[2] (%)	Asian Alone[2] (%)	AIAN[3] Alone[2] (%)	NHOPI[4] Alone[2] (%)	Other Race Alone[2] (%)	Two or More Races (%)
City	78.9	10.4	1.5	0.8	0.1	2.9	5.4
MSA[1]	85.5	6.2	1.0	1.1	0.1	1.8	4.4
U.S.	73.0	12.7	5.4	0.8	0.2	4.8	3.1

Note: (1) Figures cover the Topeka, KS Metropolitan Statistical Area—see Appendix B for areas included; (2) Alone is defined as not being in combination with one or more other races; (3) American Indian and Alaska Native; (4) Native Hawaiian and Other Pacific Islander
Source: U.S. Census Bureau, 2013-2017 American Community Survey 5-Year Estimates

Hispanic or Latino Origin

Area	Total (%)	Mexican (%)	Puerto Rican (%)	Cuban (%)	Other (%)
City	14.3	12.3	0.7	0.1	1.2
MSA[1]	9.9	8.5	0.5	0.1	0.8
U.S.	17.6	11.1	1.7	0.7	4.1

Note: Persons of Hispanic or Latino origin can be of any race; (1) Figures cover the Topeka, KS Metropolitan Statistical Area—see Appendix B for areas included
Source: U.S. Census Bureau, 2013-2017 American Community Survey 5-Year Estimates

Segregation

Type	Segregation Indices[1]				Percent Change		
	1990	2000	2010	2010 Rank[2]	1990-2000	1990-2010	2000-2010
Black/White	n/a	n/a	n/a	n/a	n/a	n/a	n/a
Asian/White	n/a	n/a	n/a	n/a	n/a	n/a	n/a
Hispanic/White	n/a	n/a	n/a	n/a	n/a	n/a	n/a

Note: All figures cover the Metropolitan Statistical Area—see Appendix B for areas included; Figures are based on an analysis of 1990, 2000, and 2010 Census Decennial Census tract data by William H. Frey, Brookings Institution and the University of Michigan Social Science Data Analysis Network. In this analysis all racial groups (whites, blacks, and asians) are non-Hispanic members of those races. Hispanics are shown as a separate category; (1) Segregation Indices are Dissimilarity Indices that measure the degree to which the minority group is distributed differently than whites across census tracts. They range from 0 (complete integration) to 100 (complete segregation) where the value indicates the percentage of the minority group that needs to move to be distributed exactly like whites; (2) Ranges from 1 (most segregated) to 102 (least segregated); n/a not available.
Source: www.CensusScope.org

Ancestry

Area	German	Irish	English	American	Italian	Polish	French[2]	Scottish	Dutch
City	22.7	10.6	12.9	5.0	2.3	1.2	2.2	1.8	1.3
MSA[1]	27.4	12.0	12.2	6.0	1.8	1.3	2.8	2.0	1.6
U.S.	14.1	10.1	7.5	6.6	5.3	2.9	2.5	1.7	1.3

Note: Figures are the percentage of the total population reporting a particular ancestry. The nine most commonly reported ancestries in the U.S. are shown. Figures include multiple ancestries (e.g. if a person reported being Irish and Italian, they were included in both columns); (1) Figures cover the Topeka, KS Metropolitan Statistical Area—see Appendix B for areas included; (2) Excludes Basque
Source: U.S. Census Bureau, 2013-2017 American Community Survey 5-Year Estimates

Foreign-Born Population

Area	Percent of Population Born in								
	Any Foreign Country	Asia	Mexico	Europe	Carribean	Central America[2]	South America	Africa	Canada
City	5.3	1.3	2.7	0.4	0.1	0.3	0.2	0.1	0.0
MSA[1]	3.4	0.9	1.6	0.3	0.1	0.2	0.1	0.1	0.1
U.S.	13.4	4.1	3.6	1.5	1.3	1.0	0.9	0.6	0.3

Note: (1) Figures cover the Topeka, KS Metropolitan Statistical Area—see Appendix B for areas included; (2) Excludes Mexico.
Source: U.S. Census Bureau, 2013-2017 American Community Survey 5-Year Estimates

Marital Status

Area	Never Married	Now Married[2]	Separated	Widowed	Divorced
City	31.8	44.7	1.5	7.2	14.8
MSA[1]	26.6	52.9	1.2	6.7	12.5
U.S.	33.1	48.2	2.0	5.8	10.9

Note: Figures are percentages and cover the population 15 years of age and older; (1) Figures cover the Topeka, KS Metropolitan Statistical Area—see Appendix B for areas included; (2) Excludes separated
Source: U.S. Census Bureau, 2013-2017 American Community Survey 5-Year Estimates

Disability by Age

Area	All Ages	Under 18 Years Old	18 to 64 Years Old	65 Years and Over
City	15.8	4.1	14.3	39.0
MSA[1]	14.5	4.4	12.7	35.9
U.S.	12.6	4.2	10.3	35.5

Note: Figures show percent of the civilian noninstitutionalized population that reported having a disability. Disability status is determined from six types of difficulty: vision, hearing, cognitive, ambulatory, self-care, and independent living. For children under 5 years old, hearing and vision difficulty are used to determine disability status. For children between the ages of 5 and 14, disability status is determined from hearing, vision, cognitive, ambulatory, and self-care difficulties. For people aged 15 years and older, they are considered to have a disability if they have difficulty with any one of the six difficulty types; Note: (1) Figures cover the Topeka, KS Metropolitan Statistical Area—see Appendix B for areas included
Source: U.S. Census Bureau, 2013-2017 American Community Survey 5-Year Estimates

Age

Area	Percent of Population									Median Age
	Under Age 5	Age 5–19	Age 20–34	Age 35–44	Age 45–54	Age 55–64	Age 65–74	Age 75–84	Age 85+	
City	7.2	18.8	21.2	11.6	12.3	12.9	8.7	4.9	2.7	37.2
MSA[1]	6.4	20.1	17.9	11.5	13.1	14.2	9.5	5.0	2.4	39.9
U.S.	6.2	19.5	20.7	12.7	13.4	12.7	8.6	4.4	1.9	37.8

Note: (1) Figures cover the Topeka, KS Metropolitan Statistical Area—see Appendix B for areas included
Source: U.S. Census Bureau, 2013-2017 American Community Survey 5-Year Estimates

Gender

Area	Males	Females	Males per 100 Females
City	60,948	66,191	92.1
MSA[1]	114,091	119,291	95.6
U.S.	158,018,753	162,985,654	97.0

Note: (1) Figures cover the Topeka, KS Metropolitan Statistical Area—see Appendix B for areas included
Source: U.S. Census Bureau, 2013-2017 American Community Survey 5-Year Estimates

Religious Groups by Family

Area	Catholic	Baptist	Non-Den.	Methodist[2]	Lutheran	LDS[3]	Pente-costal	Presby-terian[4]	Muslim[5]	Judaism
MSA[1]	12.8	9.1	4.1	7.3	3.6	1.5	2.0	1.7	0.1	0.1
U.S.	19.1	9.3	4.0	4.0	2.3	2.0	1.9	1.6	0.8	0.7

Note: Figures are the number of adherents as a percentage of the total population; (1) Figures cover the Topeka, KS Metropolitan Statistical Area—see Appendix B for areas included; (2) Methodist/Pietist; (3) Latter Day Saints; (4) Reformed; (5) Figures are estimates
Source: Association of Statisticians of American Religious Bodies, 2010 U.S. Religion Census: Religious Congregations & Membership Study

Religious Groups by Tradition

Area	Catholic	Evangelical Protestant	Mainline Protestant	Other Tradition	Black Protestant	Orthodox
MSA[1]	12.8	15.5	12.9	1.8	2.8	<0.1
U.S.	19.1	16.2	7.3	4.3	1.6	0.3

Note: Figures are the number of adherents as a percentage of the total population; (1) Figures cover the Topeka, KS Metropolitan Statistical Area—see Appendix B for areas included
Source: Association of Statisticians of American Religious Bodies, 2010 U.S. Religion Census: Religious Congregations & Membership Study

ECONOMY

Gross Metropolitan Product

Area	2016	2017	2018	2019	Rank[2]
MSA[1]	10.6	10.8	11.1	11.5	196

Note: Figures are in billions of dollars; (1) Figures cover the Topeka, KS Metropolitan Statistical Area—see Appendix B for areas included; (2) Rank is based on 2017 data and ranges from 1 to 381
Source: U.S. Conference of Mayors, U.S. Metro Economies: Economic Growth & Full Employment, June 2018

Economic Growth

Area	2017-2018 (%)	2019-2020 (%)	2021-2022 (%)
MSA[1]	0.4	0.8	0.1

Note: Figures are real gross metropolitan product (GMP) growth rates and represent average annual percent change; (1) Figures cover the Topeka, KS Metropolitan Statistical Area—see Appendix B for areas included
Source: U.S. Conference of Mayors, U.S. Metro Economies: Economic Growth & Full Employment, June 2018

Metropolitan Area Exports

Area	2012	2013	2014	2015	2016	2017	Rank[2]
MSA[1]	265.0	303.3	365.0	363.5	305.2	300.7	252

Note: Figures are in millions of dollars; (1) Figures cover the Topeka, KS Metropolitan Statistical Area—see Appendix B for areas included; (2) Rank is based on 2017 data and ranges from 1 to 387
Source: U.S. Department of Commerce, International Trade Administration, Office of Trade and Economic Analysis, Industry and Analysis, Exports by Metropolitan Area, extracted March 25, 2019

Building Permits

Area	Single-Family			Multi-Family			Total		
	2016	2017	Pct. Chg.	2016	2017	Pct. Chg.	2016	2017	Pct. Chg.
City	100	85	-15.0	12	0	-100.0	112	85	-24.1
MSA[1]	368	327	-11.1	20	8	-60.0	388	335	-13.7
U.S.	750,800	820,000	9.2	455,800	462,000	1.4	1,206,600	1,282,000	6.2

Note: (1) Figures cover the Topeka, KS Metropolitan Statistical Area—see Appendix B for areas included; Figures represent new, privately-owned housing units authorized (unadjusted data); All permit data are based on estimates with imputation
Source: U.S. Census Bureau, Manufacturing, Mining, and Construction Statistics, Building Permits, 2016, 2017

Bankruptcy Filings

Area	Business Filings			Nonbusiness Filings		
	2017	2018	% Chg.	2017	2018	% Chg.
Shawnee County	39	6	-84.6	871	923	6.0
U.S.	23,157	22,232	-4.0	765,863	751,186	-1.9

Note: Business filings include Chapter 7, Chapter 11, Chapter 12, and Chapter 13; Nonbusiness filings include Chapter 7, Chapter 11, and Chapter 13
Source: Administrative Office of the U.S. Courts, Business and Nonbusiness Bankruptcy, County Cases Commenced by Chapter of the Bankruptcy Code, During the 12-Month Period Ending December 31, 2017 and Business and Nonbusiness Bankruptcy, County Cases Commenced by Chapter of the Bankruptcy Code, During the 12-Month Period Ending December 31, 2018

Housing Vacancy Rates

Area	Gross Vacancy Rate[2] (%)			Year-Round Vacancy Rate[3] (%)			Rental Vacancy Rate[4] (%)			Homeowner Vacancy Rate[5] (%)		
	2016	2017	2018	2016	2017	2018	2016	2017	2018	2016	2017	2018
MSA[1]	n/a	n/a	n/a	n/a	n/a	n/a	n/a	n/a	n/a	n/a	n/a	n/a
U.S.	12.8	12.7	12.3	9.9	9.9	9.7	6.9	7.2	6.9	1.7	1.6	1.5

Note: (1) Figures cover the Topeka, KS Metropolitan Statistical Area—see Appendix B for areas included; (2) The percentage of the total housing inventory that is vacant; (3) The percentage of the housing inventory (excluding seasonal units) that is year-round vacant; (4) The percentage of rental inventory that is vacant for rent; (5) The percentage of homeowner inventory that is vacant for sale; n/a not available
Source: U.S. Census Bureau, Housing Vacancies and Homeownership Annual Statistics: 2016, 2017, 2018

INCOME

Income

Area	Per Capita ($)	Median Household ($)	Average Household ($)
City	26,048	46,087	60,359
MSA[1]	28,190	55,194	68,649
U.S.	31,177	57,652	81,283

Note: (1) Figures cover the Topeka, KS Metropolitan Statistical Area—see Appendix B for areas included
Source: U.S. Census Bureau, 2013-2017 American Community Survey 5-Year Estimates

Household Income Distribution

Area	Percent of Households Earning							
	Under $15,000	$15,000 -$24,999	$25,000 -$34,999	$35,000 -$49,999	$50,000 -$74,999	$75,000 -$99,999	$100,000 -$149,999	$150,000 and up
City	13.2	12.7	12.3	14.9	19.8	11.9	10.8	4.3
MSA[1]	10.2	10.5	10.6	14.0	20.3	14.1	14.4	5.9
U.S.	11.6	9.8	9.5	13.0	17.7	12.3	14.1	12.1

Note: (1) Figures cover the Topeka, KS Metropolitan Statistical Area—see Appendix B for areas included
Source: U.S. Census Bureau, 2013-2017 American Community Survey 5-Year Estimates

Poverty Rate

Area	All Ages	Under 18 Years Old	18 to 64 Years Old	65 Years and Over
City	16.7	21.7	16.9	8.3
MSA[1]	12.4	15.8	12.5	6.7
U.S.	14.6	20.3	13.7	9.3

Note: Figures are percentage of people whose income during the past 12 months was below the poverty level; (1) Figures cover the Topeka, KS Metropolitan Statistical Area—see Appendix B for areas included
Source: U.S. Census Bureau, 2013-2017 American Community Survey 5-Year Estimates

EMPLOYMENT

Labor Force and Employment

Area	Civilian Labor Force			Workers Employed		
	Dec. 2017	Dec. 2018	% Chg.	Dec. 2017	Dec. 2018	% Chg.
City	62,249	62,486	0.4	60,176	60,220	0.1
MSA[1]	118,135	118,696	0.5	114,515	114,734	0.2
U.S.	159,880,000	162,510,000	1.6	153,602,000	156,481,000	1.9

Note: Data is not seasonally adjusted and covers workers 16 years of age and older; (1) Figures cover the Topeka, KS Metropolitan Statistical Area—see Appendix B for areas included
Source: Bureau of Labor Statistics, Local Area Unemployment Statistics

Unemployment Rate

Area	2018											
	Jan.	Feb.	Mar.	Apr.	May	Jun.	Jul.	Aug.	Sep.	Oct.	Nov.	Dec.
City	3.8	4.1	3.7	3.5	3.6	4.0	4.3	3.9	3.3	3.4	3.4	3.6
MSA[1]	3.7	3.8	3.5	3.2	3.3	3.7	4.0	3.5	3.0	3.2	3.1	3.3
U.S.	4.5	4.4	4.1	3.7	3.6	4.2	4.1	3.9	3.6	3.5	3.5	3.7

Note: Data is not seasonally adjusted and covers workers 16 years of age and older; (1) Figures cover the Topeka, KS Metropolitan Statistical Area—see Appendix B for areas included
Source: Bureau of Labor Statistics, Local Area Unemployment Statistics

Average Wages

Occupation	$/Hr.	Occupation	$/Hr.
Accountants and Auditors	28.60	Maids and Housekeeping Cleaners	10.10
Automotive Mechanics	17.40	Maintenance and Repair Workers	18.30
Bookkeepers	17.30	Marketing Managers	61.40
Carpenters	19.80	Nuclear Medicine Technologists	n/a
Cashiers	10.40	Nurses, Licensed Practical	21.00
Clerks, General Office	14.70	Nurses, Registered	31.40
Clerks, Receptionists/Information	13.70	Nursing Assistants	12.80
Clerks, Shipping/Receiving	19.40	Packers and Packagers, Hand	13.80
Computer Programmers	33.80	Physical Therapists	44.30
Computer Systems Analysts	33.80	Postal Service Mail Carriers	24.00
Computer User Support Specialists	22.20	Real Estate Brokers	n/a
Cooks, Restaurant	11.20	Retail Salespersons	12.30
Dentists	113.80	Sales Reps., Exc. Tech./Scientific	30.60
Electrical Engineers	42.70	Sales Reps., Tech./Scientific	36.10
Electricians	24.80	Secretaries, Exc. Legal/Med./Exec.	16.00
Financial Managers	58.60	Security Guards	13.20
First-Line Supervisors/Managers, Sales	20.20	Surgeons	n/a
Food Preparation Workers	10.30	Teacher Assistants*	12.40
General and Operations Managers	40.00	Teachers, Elementary School*	23.00
Hairdressers/Cosmetologists	n/a	Teachers, Secondary School*	23.90
Internists, General	n/a	Telemarketers	n/a
Janitors and Cleaners	12.00	Truck Drivers, Heavy/Tractor-Trailer	20.70
Landscaping/Groundskeeping Workers	15.60	Truck Drivers, Light/Delivery Svcs.	18.30
Lawyers	46.00	Waiters and Waitresses	10.10

Note: Wage data covers the Topeka, KS Metropolitan Statistical Area—see Appendix B for areas included; (*) Hourly wages for elementary/secondary school teachers and teacher assistants were calculated by the editors from annual wage data based on a 40 hour work week; n/a not available.
Source: Bureau of Labor Statistics, Metro Area Occupational Employment & Wage Estimates, May 2018

Employment by Occupation

Occupation Classification	City (%)	MSA[1] (%)	U.S. (%)
Management, Business, Science, and Arts	35.7	36.9	37.4
Natural Resources, Construction, and Maintenance	8.0	9.9	8.9
Production, Transportation, and Material Moving	13.4	13.3	12.2
Sales and Office	23.8	23.2	23.5
Service	19.0	16.7	18.0

Note: Figures cover employed civilians 16 years of age and older; (1) Figures cover the Topeka, KS Metropolitan Statistical Area—see Appendix B for areas included
Source: U.S. Census Bureau, 2013-2017 American Community Survey 5-Year Estimates

Employment by Industry

Sector	MSA[1]		U.S.
	Number of Employees	Percent of Total	Percent of Total
Construction, Mining, and Logging	5,400	4.8	5.3
Education and Health Services	18,800	16.6	15.9
Financial Activities	7,900	7.0	5.7
Government	26,900	23.7	15.1
Information	1,400	1.2	1.9
Leisure and Hospitality	8,700	7.7	10.7
Manufacturing	7,900	7.0	8.5
Other Services	4,900	4.3	3.9
Professional and Business Services	13,800	12.2	14.1
Retail Trade	10,800	9.5	10.8
Transportation, Warehousing, and Utilities	3,900	3.4	4.2
Wholesale Trade	2,900	2.6	3.9

Note: Figures are non-farm employment as of December 2018. Figures are not seasonally adjusted and include workers 16 years of age and older; (1) Figures cover the Topeka, KS Metropolitan Statistical Area—see Appendix B for areas included
Source: Bureau of Labor Statistics, Current Employment Statistics, Employment, Hours, and Earnings

Occupations with Greatest Projected Employment Growth: 2018 – 2020

Occupation[1]	2018 Employment	2020 Projected Employment	Numeric Employment Change	Percent Employment Change
Personal Care Aides	18,800	19,770	970	5.2
Combined Food Preparation and Serving Workers, Including Fast Food	25,590	26,510	920	3.6
Registered Nurses	29,930	30,800	870	2.9
Laborers and Freight, Stock, and Material Movers, Hand	20,880	21,530	650	3.1
Janitors and Cleaners, Except Maids and Housekeeping Cleaners	21,410	21,900	490	2.3
Nursing Assistants	24,130	24,600	470	1.9
Waiters and Waitresses	22,450	22,910	460	2.0
General and Operations Managers	20,180	20,590	410	2.0
Customer Service Representatives	30,080	30,480	400	1.3
Heavy and Tractor-Trailer Truck Drivers	21,670	22,070	400	1.8

Note: Projections cover Kansas; (1) Sorted by numeric employment change
Source: www.projectionscentral.com, State Occupational Projections, 2018–2020 Short-Term Projections

Fastest Growing Occupations: 2018 – 2020

Occupation[1]	2018 Employment	2020 Projected Employment	Numeric Employment Change	Percent Employment Change
Cargo and Freight Agents	690	740	50	7.2
Home Health Aides	4,210	4,490	280	6.7
Physician Assistants	1,110	1,180	70	6.3
Nurse Practitioners	1,910	2,020	110	5.8
Industrial Engineers	2,230	2,350	120	5.4
Respiratory Therapists	1,290	1,360	70	5.4
Operations Research Analysts	1,130	1,190	60	5.3
Aircraft Mechanics and Service Technicians	1,690	1,780	90	5.3
Personal Care Aides	18,800	19,770	970	5.2
Aerospace Engineers	2,280	2,390	110	4.8

Note: Projections cover Kansas; (1) Sorted by percent employment change and excludes occupations with numeric employment change less than 50
Source: www.projectionscentral.com, State Occupational Projections, 2018–2020 Short-Term Projections

TAXES

State Corporate Income Tax Rates

State	Tax Rate (%)	Income Brackets ($)	Num. of Brackets	Financial Institution Tax Rate (%)[a]	Federal Income Tax Ded.
Kansas	4.0 (k)	Flat rate	1	2.25 (k)	No

Note: Tax rates as of January 1, 2019; (a) Rates listed are the corporate income tax rate applied to financial institutions or excise taxes based on income. Some states have other taxes based upon the value of deposits or shares; (k) In addition to the flat 4% corporate income tax, Kansas levies a 3.0% surtax on taxable income over $50,000. Banks pay a privilege tax of 2.25% of net income, plus a surtax of 2.125% (2.25% for savings and loans, trust companies, and federally chartered savings banks) on net income in excess of $25,000; (l) The state franchise tax on financial institutions is either (1) the sum of 1% of the Maine net income of the financial institution for the taxable year, plus 8¢ per $1,000 of the institut
Source: Federation of Tax Administrators, Range of State Corporate Income Tax Rates, January 1, 2019

State Individual Income Tax Rates

State	Tax Rate (%)	Income Brackets ($)	Personal Exemptions ($)			Standard Ded. ($)	
			Single	Married	Depend.	Single	Married
Kansas	3.1 - 5.7	15,000 - 30,000 (b)	2,250	4,500	2,250	3,000	7,500

Note: Tax rates as of January 1, 2019; Local- and county-level taxes are not included; n/a not applicable; Federal income tax is not deductible on state income tax returns; (b) For joint returns, taxes are twice the tax on half the couple's income.
Source: Federation of Tax Administrators, State Individual Income Tax Rates, January 1, 2019

Various State Sales and Excise Tax Rates

State	State Sales Tax (%)	Gasoline[1] (¢/gal.)	Cigarette[2] ($/pack)	Spirits[3] ($/gal.)	Wine[4] ($/gal.)	Beer[5] ($/gal.)	Recreational Marijuana (%)
Kansas	6.5	24.03	1.29	2.5	0.30 (l)	0.18 (q)	Not legal

Note: All tax rates as of January 1, 2019; (1) The American Petroleum Institute has developed a methodology for determining the average tax rate on a gallon of fuel. Rates may include any of the following: excise taxes, environmental fees, storage tank fees, other fees or taxes, general sales tax, and local taxes. In states where gasoline is subject to the general sales tax, or where the fuel tax is based on the average sale price, the average rate determined by API is sensitive to changes in the price of gasoline. States that fully or partially apply general sales taxes to gasoline: CA, CO, GA, IL, IN, MI, NY; (2) The federal excise tax of $1.0066 per pack and local taxes are not included; (3) Rates are those applicable to off-premise sales of 40% alcohol by volume (a.b.v.) distilled spirits in 750ml containers. Local excise taxes are excluded; (4) Rates are those applicable to off-premise sales of 11% a.b.v. non-carbonated wine in 750ml containers; (5) Rates are those applicable to off-premise sales of 4.7% a.b.v. beer in 12 ounce containers; (l) Different rates also applicable to alcohol content, place of production, size of container, place purchased (on- or off-premise or on board airlines) or type of wine (carbonated, vermouth, etc.); (q) Different rates also applicable according to alcohol content, place of production, size of container, or place purchased (on- or off-premise or onboard airlines).
Source: Tax Foundation, 2019 Facts & Figures: How Does Your State Compare?

State Business Tax Climate Index Rankings

State	Overall Rank	Corporate Tax Rank	Individual Income Tax Rank	Sales Tax Rank	Unemployment Insurance Tax Rank	Property Tax Rank
Kansas	28	34	21	31	15	20

Note: The index is a measure of how each state's tax laws affect economic performance. The lower the rank, the more favorable a state's tax system is for business. States without a given tax are given a ranking of 1. The scores/rankings for the District of Columbia do not affect other states. The 2019 index represents the tax climate as of July 1, 2018.
Source: Tax Foundation, State Business Tax Climate Index 2019

COMMERCIAL UTILITIES

Typical Monthly Electric Bills

Area	Commercial Service ($/month)		Industrial Service ($/month)	
	1,500 kWh	40 kW demand 14,000 kWh	1,000 kW demand 200,000 kWh	50,000 kW demand 32,500,000 kWh
City	175	1,454	26,628	2,161,984
Average[1]	203	1,619	25,886	2,540,077

Note: Figures are based on annualized rates; (1) Average based on 187 utilities surveyed
Source: Edison Electric Institute, Typical Bills and Average Rates Report, Summer 2018

TRANSPORTATION

Means of Transportation to Work

| Area | Car/Truck/Van | | Public Transportation | | | Bicycle | Walked | Other Means | Worked at Home |
	Drove Alone	Car-pooled	Bus	Subway	Railroad				
City	81.4	10.8	1.2	0.0	0.0	0.3	2.4	1.5	2.4
MSA[1]	83.0	9.8	0.7	0.0	0.0	0.2	1.8	1.1	3.3
U.S.	76.4	9.2	2.5	1.9	0.6	0.6	2.7	1.3	4.7

Note: Figures are percentages and cover workers 16 years of age and older; (1) Figures cover the Topeka, KS Metropolitan Statistical Area—see Appendix B for areas included
Source: U.S. Census Bureau, 2013-2017 American Community Survey 5-Year Estimates

Travel Time to Work

Area	Less Than 10 Minutes	10 to 19 Minutes	20 to 29 Minutes	30 to 44 Minutes	45 to 59 Minutes	60 to 89 Minutes	90 Minutes or More
City	18.4	54.4	14.5	7.5	1.6	2.5	1.0
MSA[1]	16.5	42.5	19.2	13.5	3.8	3.0	1.5
U.S.	12.7	28.9	20.9	20.5	8.1	6.2	2.7

Note: Note: Figures are percentages and include workers 16 years old and over; (1) Figures cover the Topeka, KS Metropolitan Statistical Area—see Appendix B for areas included
Source: U.S. Census Bureau, 2013-2017 American Community Survey 5-Year Estimates

Freeway Travel Time Index

Area	1985	1990	1995	2000	2005	2010	2014
Urban Area Rank[1,2]	n/a	n/a	n/a	n/a	n/a	n/a	n/a
Urban Area Index[1]	n/a	n/a	n/a	n/a	n/a	n/a	n/a
Average Index[3]	1.09	1.11	1.14	1.17	1.20	1.19	1.20

Note: Freeway Travel Time Index—the ratio of travel time in the peak period to the travel time at free-flow conditions. For example, a value of 1.30 indicates a 20-minute free-flow trip takes 26 minutes in the peak (20 minutes x 1.30 = 26 minutes); (1) Data for the Topeka, KS urban area was not available; (2) Rank is based on 101 urban areas (#1 = highest travel time index); (3) Average of 101 urban areas
Source: Texas Transportation Institute, 2015 Urban Mobility Scorecard, August 2015

Freeway Commuter Stress Index

Area	1985	1990	1995	2000	2005	2010	2014
Urban Area Rank[1,2]	n/a	n/a	n/a	n/a	n/a	n/a	n/a
Urban Area Index[1]	n/a	n/a	n/a	n/a	n/a	n/a	n/a
Average Index[3]	1.13	1.16	1.19	1.22	1.25	1.24	1.25

Note: The Freeway Commuter Stress Index is the same as the Freeway Travel Time Index (see table above) except that it includes only the travel in the peak directions during the peak periods; the TTI includes travel in all directions during the peak period. Thus, the CSI is more indicative of the work trip experienced by each commuter on a daily basis; (1) Data for the Topeka, KS urban area was not available; (2) Rank is based on 101 urban areas (#1 = highest travel time index); (3) Average of 101 urban areas
Source: Texas Transportation Institute, 2015 Urban Mobility Scorecard, August 2015

Public Transportation

Agency Name / Mode of Transportation	Vehicles Operated in Maximum Service[1]	Annual Unlinked Passenger Trips[2] (in thous.)	Annual Passenger Miles[3] (in thous.)
Topeka Metropolitan Transit Authority			
Bus (directly operated)	24	1,197.3	4,994.2
Demand Response (directly operated)	7	25.4	102.0
Demand Response Taxi (purchased transportation)	7	26.2	142.3

Note: (1) The number of revenue vehicles operated by the given mode and type of service to meet the annual maximum service requirement. This is the revenue vehicle count during the peak season of the year; on the week and day that maximum service is provided. Vehicles operated in maximum service (VOMS) exclude atypical days and one-time special events; (2) The number of passengers who boarded public transportation vehicles. Passengers are counted each time they board a vehicle no matter how many vehicles they use to travel from their origin to their destination. (3) The sum of the distances ridden by all passengers during the entire fiscal year.
Source: Federal Transit Administration, National Transit Database, 2017

Air Transportation

Airport Name and Code / Type of Service	Passenger Airlines[1]	Passenger Enplanements	Freight Carriers[2]	Freight (lbs)
Topeka Regional Airport (FOE)				
Domestic service (U.S. carriers - 2018)	11	2,297	1	4,614
International service (U.S. carriers - 2017)	1	590	0	0

Note: (1) Includes all U.S.-based major, minor and commuter airlines that carried at least one passenger during the year; (2) Includes all U.S.-based airlines and freight carriers that transported at least one pound of freight during the year.
Source: Bureau of Transportation Statistics, The Intermodal Transportation Database, Air Carriers: T-100 Domestic Market (U.S. Carriers), 2018; Bureau of Transportation Statistics, The Intermodal Transportation Database, Air Carriers: T-100 International Market (U.S. Carriers), 2017

Other Transportation Statistics

Major Highways:	I-70; I-335; I-470
Amtrak Service:	Yes
Major Waterways/Ports:	Kansas River

Source: Amtrak.com; Google Maps

BUSINESSES

Major Business Headquarters

Company Name	Industry	Rankings Fortune[1]	Rankings Forbes[2]
Payless Holdings	Retailing	-	156

Note: (1) Companies that produce a 10-K are ranked 1 to 500 based on 2017 revenue; (2) All private companies with at least $2 billion in annual revenue through the end of their most current fiscal year are ranked 1 to 229; companies listed are headquartered in the city; dashes indicate no ranking
Source: Fortune, "Fortune 500," June 2018; Forbes, "America's Largest Private Companies," 2018 Rankings

Minority- and Women-Owned Businesses

Group	All Firms Firms	All Firms Sales ($000)	Firms with Paid Employees Firms	Firms with Paid Employees Sales ($000)	Firms with Paid Employees Employees	Firms with Paid Employees Payroll ($000)
AIAN[1]	107	3,424	11	2,022	30	504
Asian	217	172,137	109	168,622	1,438	66,306
Black	481	19,770	11	11,199	118	2,858
Hispanic	451	23,305	58	15,060	299	5,398
NHOPI[2]	n/a	n/a	n/a	n/a	n/a	n/a
Women	2,981	442,677	373	386,506	2,843	84,644
All Firms	8,993	16,942,793	2,869	16,712,755	63,760	2,636,157

Note: Figures cover firms located in the city; minority- and women-owned business are defined as firms in which the corresponding group own 51% or more of the stock or equity of the company; (1) American Indian and Alaska Native; (2) Native Hawaiian and Other Pacific Islander; n/a not available
Source: U.S. Census Bureau, 2012 Economic Census, Survey of Business Owners

HOTELS & CONVENTION CENTERS

Hotels, Motels and Vacation Rentals

Area	5 Star Num.	5 Star Pct.[3]	4 Star Num.	4 Star Pct.[3]	3 Star Num.	3 Star Pct.[3]	2 Star Num.	2 Star Pct.[3]	1 Star Num.	1 Star Pct.[3]	Not Rated Num.	Not Rated Pct.[3]
City[1]	0	0.0	1	0.8	26	21.0	55	44.4	3	2.4	39	31.5
Total[2]	286	0.4	5,236	7.1	16,715	22.6	10,259	13.9	293	0.4	41,056	55.6

Note: (1) Figures cover Topeka and vicinity; (2) Figures cover all 100 cities in this book; (3) Percentage of hotels which have a given star rating; Star ratings are determined by expedia.com and offer an indication of the general quality of a particular hotel.
Source: www.expedia.com, April 3, 2019

Major Convention Centers

Name	Overall Space (sq. ft.)	Exhibit Space (sq. ft.)	Meeting Space (sq. ft.)	Meeting Rooms
Kansas Expocentre Exhibition Hall	n/a	44,500	n/a	n/a

Note: Table includes convention centers located in the Topeka, KS metro area; n/a not available
Source: Original research

Living Environment

COST OF LIVING

Cost of Living Index

Composite Index	Groceries	Housing	Utilities	Trans-portation	Health Care	Misc. Goods/ Services
90.9	97.1	79.4	100.4	95.4	93.4	94.3

Note: The Cost of Living Index measures regional differences in the cost of consumer goods and services, excluding taxes and non-consumer expenditures, for professional and managerial households in the top income quintile. It is based on more than 50,000 prices covering almost 60 different items for which prices are collected three times a year by chambers of commerce, economic development organizations or university applied economic centers in each participating urban area. The numbers shown should be read as a percentage above or below the national average of 100. For example, a value of 115.4 in the groceries column indicates that grocery prices are 15.4% higher than the national average. Small differences in the index numbers should not be interpreted as significant; Figures cover the Topeka KS urban area.
Source: The Council for Community and Economic Research, ACCRA Cost of Living Index, 2018

Grocery Prices

Area[1]	T-Bone Steak ($/pound)	Frying Chicken ($/pound)	Whole Milk ($/half gal.)	Eggs ($/dozen)	Orange Juice ($/64 oz.)	Coffee ($/11.5 oz.)
City[2]	10.28	1.74	1.56	1.22	3.51	4.61
Avg.	11.35	1.42	1.94	1.81	3.52	4.35
Min.	7.45	0.92	0.80	0.75	2.72	3.06
Max.	15.05	2.76	4.18	4.00	5.36	8.20

*Note: (1) Values for the local area are compared with the average, minimum and maximum values for all 291 areas in the Cost of Living Index; (2) Figures cover the Topeka KS urban area; **T-Bone Steak** (price per pound); **Frying Chicken** (price per pound, whole fryer); **Whole Milk** (half gallon carton); **Eggs** (price per dozen, Grade A, large); **Orange Juice** (64 oz. Tropicana or Florida Natural); **Coffee** (11.5 oz. can, vacuum-packed, Maxwell House, Hills Bros, or Folgers).*
Source: The Council for Community and Economic Research, ACCRA Cost of Living Index, 2018

Housing and Utility Costs

Area[1]	New Home Price ($)	Apartment Rent ($/month)	All Electric ($/month)	Part Electric ($/month)	Other Energy ($/month)	Telephone ($/month)
City[2]	287,385	794	-	96.10	67.76	185.30
Avg.	347,000	1,087	165.93	100.16	67.73	178.70
Min.	200,468	500	93.58	25.64	26.78	163.10
Max.	1,901,222	4,888	388.65	246.86	332.81	197.70

*Note: (1) Values for the local area are compared with the average, minimum and maximum values for all 291 areas in the Cost of Living Index; (2) Figures cover the Topeka KS urban area; **New Home Price** (2,400 sf living area, 8,000 sf lot, in urban area with full utilities); **Apartment Rent** (950 sf 2 bedroom/1.5 or 2 bath, unfurnished, excluding all utilities except water); **All Electric** (average monthly cost for an all-electric home); **Part Electric** (average monthly cost for a part-electric home); **Other Energy** (average monthly cost for natural gas, fuel oil, coal, wood, and any other forms of energy except electricity); **Telephone** (price includes the base monthly rate plus taxes and fees for three lines of mobile phone service).*
Source: The Council for Community and Economic Research, ACCRA Cost of Living Index, 2018

Health Care, Transportation, and Other Costs

Area[1]	Doctor ($/visit)	Dentist ($/visit)	Optometrist ($/visit)	Gasoline ($/gallon)	Beauty Salon ($/visit)	Men's Shirt ($)
City[2]	88.42	88.44	121.81	2.41	32.67	33.63
Avg.	110.71	95.11	103.74	2.61	37.48	32.03
Min.	33.60	62.55	54.63	1.89	17.00	11.44
Max.	195.97	153.93	225.79	3.59	71.88	58.64

*Note: (1) Values for the local area are compared with the average, minimum and maximum values for all 291 areas in the Cost of Living Index; (2) Figures cover the Topeka KS urban area; **Doctor** (general practitioners routine exam of an established patient); **Dentist** (adult teeth cleaning and periodic oral examination); **Optometrist** (full vision eye exam for established adult patient); **Gasoline** (one gallon regular unleaded, national brand, including all taxes, cash price at self-service pump if available); **Beauty Salon** (woman's shampoo, trim, and blow-dry); **Men's Shirt** (cotton/polyester dress shirt, pinpoint weave, long sleeves).*
Source: The Council for Community and Economic Research, ACCRA Cost of Living Index, 2018

HOUSING

House Price Index (HPI)

Area	National Ranking[2]	Quarterly Change (%)	One-Year Change (%)	Five-Year Change (%)
MSA[1]	113	2.47	6.42	16.66
U.S.[3]	–	1.12	5.73	32.81

Note: The HPI is a weighted repeat sales index. It measures average price changes in repeat sales or refinancings on the same properties. This information is obtained by reviewing repeat mortgage transactions on single-family properties whose mortgages have been purchased or securitized by Fannie Mae or Freddie Mac in January 1975; (1) Figures cover the Topeka, KS Metropolitan Statistical Area—see Appendix B for areas included; (2) Rankings are based on annual percentage change for all metro areas containing at least 15,000 transactions over the last 10 years and ranges from 1 to 245; (3) figures based on a weighted average of Census Division estimates using a seasonally adjusted, purchase-only index; all figures are for the period ending December 31, 2018
Source: Federal Housing Finance Agency, House Price Index, February 26, 2019

Median Single-Family Home Prices

Area	2016	2017	2018[p]	Percent Change 2017 to 2018
MSA[1]	124.0	128.6	132.1	2.7
U.S. Average	235.5	248.8	261.6	5.1

Note: Figures are median sales prices of existing single-family homes in thousands of dollars; (p) preliminary; (1) Figures cover the Topeka, KS Metropolitan Statistical Area—see Appendix B for areas included
Source: National Association of Realtors, Median Sales Price of Existing Single-Family Homes for Metropolitan Areas, 4th Quarter 2018

Qualifying Income Based on Median Sales Price of Existing Single-Family Homes

Area	With 5% Down ($)	With 10% Down ($)	With 20% Down ($)
MSA[1]	30,695	29,079	25,848
U.S. Average	62,954	59,640	53,013

Note: Figures are preliminary; Qualifying income is based on a mortgage rate of 4.9%. Monthly principal and interest payment is limited to 25% of income; (1) Figures cover the Topeka, KS Metropolitan Statistical Area—see Appendix B for areas included
Source: National Association of Realtors, Qualifying Income Based on Median Sales Price of Existing Single-Family Homes for Metropolitan Areas, 4th Quarter 2018

Median Apartment Condo-Coop Home Prices

Area	2016	2017	2018[p]	Percent Change 2017 to 2018
MSA[1]	n/a	n/a	n/a	n/a
U.S. Average	220.7	234.3	241.0	2.9

Note: Figures are median sales prices of existing apartment condo-coop homes in thousands of dollars; (p) preliminary; n/a not available; (1) Figures cover the Topeka, KS Metropolitan Statistical Area—see Appendix B for areas included
Source: National Association of Realtors, Median Sales Price of Existing Apartment Condo-Coop Homes for Metropolitan Areas, 4th Quarter 2018

Home Value Distribution

Area	Under $50,000	$50,000 -$99,999	$100,000 -$149,999	$150,000 -$199,999	$200,000 -$299,999	$300,000 -$499,999	$500,000 -$999,999	$1,000,000 or more
City	14.6	35.2	23.5	14.2	8.8	2.6	0.8	0.3
MSA[1]	11.1	26.0	23.5	18.1	14.1	5.8	1.3	0.2
U.S.	8.3	13.9	14.7	14.6	18.7	17.3	9.7	2.7

Note: Figures are percentages and cover owner-occupied housing units; (1) Figures cover the Topeka, KS Metropolitan Statistical Area—see Appendix B for areas included
Source: U.S. Census Bureau, 2013-2017 American Community Survey 5-Year Estimates

Homeownership Rate

Area	2010 (%)	2011 (%)	2012 (%)	2013 (%)	2014 (%)	2015 (%)	2016 (%)	2017 (%)	2018 (%)
MSA[1]	n/a	n/a	n/a	n/a	n/a	n/a	n/a	n/a	n/a
U.S.	66.9	66.1	65.4	65.1	64.5	63.7	63.4	63.9	64.4

Note: (1) Figures cover the Topeka, KS Metropolitan Statistical Area—see Appendix B for areas included; n/a not available
Source: U.S. Census Bureau, Housing Vacancies and Homeownership Annual Statistics: 2010-2018

Year Housing Structure Built

Area	2010 or Later	2000 -2009	1990 -1999	1980 -1989	1970 -1979	1960 -1969	1950 -1959	1940 -1949	Before 1940	Median Year
City	0.9	7.3	9.8	9.9	14.5	16.1	16.4	6.7	18.5	1965
MSA[1]	1.3	9.7	12.7	10.6	16.5	13.7	12.2	5.2	18.0	1971
U.S.	3.2	14.5	14.0	13.6	15.5	10.8	10.5	5.1	12.9	1977

Note: Figures are percentages except for Median Year; Note: (1) Figures cover the Topeka, KS Metropolitan Statistical Area—see Appendix B for areas included
Source: U.S. Census Bureau, 2013-2017 American Community Survey 5-Year Estimates

Gross Monthly Rent

Area	Under $500	$500 -$999	$1,000 -$1,499	$1,500 -$1,999	$2,000 -$2,499	$2,500 -$2,999	$3,000 and up	Median ($)
City	16.9	61.9	15.8	3.1	1.8	0.2	0.3	751
MSA[1]	18.0	59.9	16.2	3.3	1.8	0.2	0.7	751
U.S.	10.5	41.1	28.7	11.7	4.5	1.8	1.7	982

Note: Figures are percentages except for Median; Gross rent is the contract rent plus the estimated average monthly cost of utilities (electricity, gas, and water and sewer) and fuels (oil, coal, kerosene, wood, etc.) if these are paid by the renter (or paid for the renter by someone else); (1) Figures cover the Topeka, KS Metropolitan Statistical Area—see Appendix B for areas included
Source: U.S. Census Bureau, 2013-2017 American Community Survey 5-Year Estimates

HEALTH

Health Risk Factors

Category	MSA[1] (%)	U.S. (%)
Adults aged 18–64 who have any kind of health care coverage	87.5	87.3
Adults who reported being in good or better health	81.7	82.4
Adults who have been told they have high blood cholesterol	38.8	33.0
Adults who have been told they have high blood pressure	37.8	32.3
Adults who are current smokers	20.8	17.1
Adults who currently use E-cigarettes	5.8	4.6
Adults who currently use chewing tobacco, snuff, or snus	5.0	4.0
Adults who are heavy drinkers[2]	5.8	6.3
Adults who are binge drinkers[3]	16.3	17.4
Adults who are overweight (BMI 25.0 - 29.9)	32.5	35.3
Adults who are obese (BMI 30.0 - 99.8)	37.1	31.3
Adults who participated in any physical activities in the past month	72.6	74.4
Adults who always or nearly always wears a seat belt	94.0	94.3

Note: (1) Figures cover the Topeka, KS Metropolitan Statistical Area—see Appendix B for areas included; (2) Heavy drinkers are classified as adult men having more than 14 drinks per week and adult women having more than 7 drinks per week; (3) Binge drinkers are classified as males having five or more drinks on one occasion or females having four or more drinks on one occasion
Source: Centers for Disease Control and Prevention, Behaviorial Risk Factor Surveillance System, SMART: Selected Metropolitan Area Risk Trends, 2017

Acute and Chronic Health Conditions

Category	MSA[1] (%)	U.S. (%)
Adults who have ever been told they had a heart attack	4.3	4.2
Adults who have ever been told they have angina or coronary heart disease	4.6	3.9
Adults who have ever been told they had a stroke	2.9	3.0
Adults who have ever been told they have asthma	15.9	14.2
Adults who have ever been told they have arthritis	26.5	24.9
Adults who have ever been told they have diabetes[2]	12.4	10.5
Adults who have ever been told they had skin cancer	7.9	6.2
Adults who have ever been told they had any other types of cancer	7.6	7.1
Adults who have ever been told they have COPD	7.9	6.5
Adults who have ever been told they have kidney disease	4.2	3.0
Adults who have ever been told they have a form of depression	23.7	20.5

Note: (1) Figures cover the Topeka, KS Metropolitan Statistical Area—see Appendix B for areas included; (2) Figures do not include pregnancy-related, borderline, or pre-diabetes
Source: Centers for Disease Control and Prevention, Behaviorial Risk Factor Surveillance System, SMART: Selected Metropolitan Area Risk Trends, 2017

Health Screening and Vaccination Rates

Category	MSA[1] (%)	U.S. (%)
Adults aged 65+ who have had flu shot within the past year	61.8	60.7
Adults aged 65+ who have ever had a pneumonia vaccination	81.8	75.4
Adults who have ever been tested for HIV	28.1	36.1
Adults who have ever had the shingles or zoster vaccine?	33.0	28.9
Adults who have had their blood cholesterol checked within the last five years	86.2	85.9

Note: n/a not available; (1) Figures cover the Topeka, KS Metropolitan Statistical Area—see Appendix B for areas included.
Source: Centers for Disease Control and Prevention, Behaviorial Risk Factor Surveillance System, SMART: Selected Metropolitan Area Risk Trends, 2017

Disability Status

Category	MSA[1] (%)	U.S. (%)
Adults who reported being deaf	8.3	6.7
Are you blind or have serious difficulty seeing, even when wearing glasses?	4.4	4.5
Are you limited in any way in any of your usual activities due of arthritis?	12.8	12.9
Do you have difficulty doing errands alone?	6.4	6.8
Do you have difficulty dressing or bathing?	3.7	3.6
Do you have serious difficulty concentrating/remembering/making decisions?	12.7	10.7
Do you have serious difficulty walking or climbing stairs?	15.4	13.6

Note: (1) Figures cover the Topeka, KS Metropolitan Statistical Area—see Appendix B for areas included.
Source: Centers for Disease Control and Prevention, Behaviorial Risk Factor Surveillance System, SMART: Selected Metropolitan Area Risk Trends, 2017

Mortality Rates for the Top 10 Causes of Death in the U.S.

ICD-10[a] Sub-Chapter	ICD-10[a] Code	Age-Adjusted Mortality Rate[1] per 100,000 population County[2]	U.S.
Malignant neoplasms	C00-C97	172.0	155.5
Ischaemic heart diseases	I20-I25	79.7	94.8
Other forms of heart disease	I30-I51	46.9	52.9
Chronic lower respiratory diseases	J40-J47	56.6	41.0
Cerebrovascular diseases	I60-I69	38.0	37.5
Other degenerative diseases of the nervous system	G30-G31	34.3	35.0
Other external causes of accidental injury	W00-X59	35.1	33.7
Organic, including symptomatic, mental disorders	F01-F09	46.6	31.0
Hypertensive diseases	I10-I15	28.3	21.9
Diabetes mellitus	E10-E14	22.5	21.2

Note: (a) ICD-10 = International Classification of Diseases 10th Revision; (1) Mortality rates are a three year average covering 2015-2017; (2) Figures cover Shawnee County.
Source: Centers for Disease Control and Prevention, National Center for Health Statistics. Underlying Cause of Death 1999-2017 on CDC WONDER Online Database

Mortality Rates for Selected Causes of Death

ICD-10[a] Sub-Chapter	ICD-10[a] Code	Age-Adjusted Mortality Rate[1] per 100,000 population County[2]	U.S.
Assault	X85-Y09	12.3	5.9
Diseases of the liver	K70-K76	15.5	14.1
Human immunodeficiency virus (HIV) disease	B20-B24	Suppressed	1.8
Influenza and pneumonia	J09-J18	15.7	14.3
Intentional self-harm	X60-X84	23.4	13.6
Malnutrition	E40-E46	Unreliable	1.6
Obesity and other hyperalimentation	E65-E68	Unreliable	2.1
Renal failure	N17-N19	12.8	13.0
Transport accidents	V01-V99	13.6	12.4
Viral hepatitis	B15-B19	Suppressed	1.6

Note: (a) ICD-10 = International Classification of Diseases 10th Revision; (1) Mortality rates are a three year average covering 2015-2017; (2) Figures cover Shawnee County; Data are suppressed when the data meet the criteria for confidentiality constraints; Mortality rates are flagged as unreliable when the rate would be calculated with a numerator of 20 or less.
Source: Centers for Disease Control and Prevention, National Center for Health Statistics. Underlying Cause of Death 1999-2017 on CDC WONDER Online Database

Health Insurance Coverage

Area	With Health Insurance	With Private Health Insurance	With Public Health Insurance	Without Health Insurance	Population Under Age 18 Without Health Insurance
City	89.2	69.9	35.1	10.8	6.1
MSA[1]	91.4	75.2	32.2	8.6	4.9
U.S.	89.5	67.2	33.8	10.5	5.7

Note: Figures are percentages that cover the civilian noninstitutionalized population; (1) Figures cover the Topeka, KS Metropolitan Statistical Area—see Appendix B for areas included
Source: U.S. Census Bureau, 2013-2017 American Community Survey 5-Year Estimates

Number of Medical Professionals

Area	MDs[3]	DOs[3,4]	Dentists	Podiatrists	Chiropractors	Optometrists
County[1] (number)	357	45	110	10	45	44
County[1] (rate[2])	200.4	25.3	61.7	5.6	25.3	24.7
U.S. (rate[2])	279.3	23.0	68.4	6.0	27.1	16.2

Note: Data as of 2017 unless noted; (1) Data covers Shawnee County; (2) Rate per 100,000 population; (3) Data as of 2016 and includes all active, non-federal physicians; (4) Doctor of Osteopathic Medicine
Source: U.S. Department of Health and Human Services, Health Resources and Services Administration, Bureau of Health Professions, Area Resource File (ARF) 2017-2018

EDUCATION

Public School District Statistics

District Name	Schls	Pupils	Pupil/ Teacher Ratio	Minority Pupils[1] (%)	Free Lunch Eligible[2] (%)	IEP[3] (%)
Auburn Washburn	9	6,333	14.3	27.4	24.7	12.9
Seaman USD 345	7	3,849	13.7	17.4	28.0	16.0
Topeka Public Schools	28	13,791	11.8	62.2	66.8	20.3

Note: Table includes school districts with 2,000 or more students; (1) Percentage of students that are not non-Hispanic white; (2) Percentage of students that are eligible for the free lunch program; (3) Percentage of students that have an Individualized Education Program.
Source: U.S. Department of Education, National Center for Education Statistics, Common Core of Data, Local Education Agency (School District) Universe Survey: School Year 2016-2017; U.S. Department of Education, National Center for Education Statistics, Common Core of Data, Public Elementary/Secondary School Universe Survey: School Year 2016-2017

Highest Level of Education

Area	Less than H.S.	H.S. Diploma	Some College, No Deg.	Associate Degree	Bachelor's Degree	Master's Degree	Prof. School Degree	Doctorate Degree
City	10.3	31.4	24.2	5.9	17.4	7.5	2.0	1.3
MSA[1]	8.1	32.7	24.1	7.0	18.0	7.4	1.6	1.1
U.S.	12.7	27.3	20.8	8.3	19.1	8.4	2.0	1.4

Note: Figures cover persons age 25 and over; (1) Figures cover the Topeka, KS Metropolitan Statistical Area—see Appendix B for areas included
Source: U.S. Census Bureau, 2013-2017 American Community Survey 5-Year Estimates

Educational Attainment by Race

Area	High School Graduate or Higher (%)					Bachelor's Degree or Higher (%)				
	Total	White	Black	Asian	Hisp.[2]	Total	White	Black	Asian	Hisp.[2]
City	89.7	91.1	83.9	89.1	71.6	28.2	30.2	12.4	64.9	11.2
MSA[1]	91.9	92.9	84.0	86.6	75.0	28.1	29.3	13.0	59.4	13.4
U.S.	87.3	89.3	84.9	86.5	66.7	30.9	32.2	20.6	52.7	15.2

Note: Figures shown cover persons 25 years old and over; (1) Figures cover the Topeka, KS Metropolitan Statistical Area—see Appendix B for areas included; (2) People of Hispanic origin can be of any race
Source: U.S. Census Bureau, 2013-2017 American Community Survey 5-Year Estimates

School Enrollment by Grade and Control

Area	Preschool (%)		Kindergarten (%)		Grades 1 - 4 (%)		Grades 5 - 8 (%)		Grades 9 - 12 (%)	
	Public	Private	Public	Private	Public	Private	Public	Private	Public	Private
City	67.9	32.1	93.1	6.9	89.2	10.8	88.8	11.2	92.7	7.3
MSA[1]	71.3	28.7	92.1	7.9	90.1	9.9	88.6	11.4	92.2	7.8
U.S.	58.8	41.2	87.7	12.3	89.7	10.3	89.6	10.4	90.3	9.7

Note: Figures shown cover persons 3 years old and over; (1) Figures cover the Topeka, KS Metropolitan Statistical Area—see Appendix B for areas included
Source: U.S. Census Bureau, 2013-2017 American Community Survey 5-Year Estimates

Average Salaries of Public School Classroom Teachers

Area	2016		2017		Change from 2016 to 2017	
	Dollars	Rank[1]	Dollars	Rank[1]	Percent	Rank[2]
Kansas	47,755	42	49,422	40	3.5	4
U.S. Average	58,479	–	59,660	–	2.0	–

Note: (1) Rank ranges from 1 to 51 where 1 indicates highest salary; (2) Rank ranges from 1 to 51 where 1 indicates highest percent change.
Source: National Education Association, Rankings & Estimates: Rankings of the States 2017 and Estimates of School Statistics 2018

Higher Education

Four-Year Colleges			Two-Year Colleges			Medical Schools[1]	Law Schools[2]	Voc/ Tech[3]
Public	Private Non-profit	Private For-profit	Public	Private Non-profit	Private For-profit			
1	0	1	0	0	1	0	1	1

Note: Figures cover institutions located within the city limits and include main campuses only; (1) includes schools accredited by the Liaison Committee on Medical Education and the American Osteopathic Association's Commission on Osteopathic College Accreditation; (2) includes ABA-accredited schools, schools with provisional ABA accreditation, and state accredited schools; (3) includes all schools with programs that are less than 2 years.
Source: National Center for Education Statistics, Integrated Postsecondary Education System (IPEDS), 2017-18; Wikipedia, List of Medical Schools in the United States, accessed April 3, 2019; Wikipedia, List of Law Schools in the United States, accessed April 3, 2019

PRESIDENTIAL ELECTION

2016 Presidential Election Results

Area	Clinton	Trump	Johnson	Stein	Other
Shawnee County	44.2	46.8	4.4	2.3	2.3
U.S.	48.0	45.9	3.3	1.1	1.7

Note: Results are percentages and may not add to 100% due to rounding
Source: Dave Leip's Atlas of U.S. Presidential Elections

EMPLOYERS

Major Employers

Company Name	Industry
Auburn Washburn USD 437	Education
BlueCross BlueShield of Kansas	Healthcare
BNSF Railway Company	Transportation
City of Topeka	Government
Dillon Stores	Retail
Frito-Lay	Manufacturing & distribution
Goodyear Tire and Rubber Company	Manufacturing & distribution
Hill's Pet Nutrition	Retail
Joint Force Hdqrtrs/KS Army Natl Guard	U.S. military
Midwest Health Management	Healthcare
Payless ShoeSource	Retail
Reser's Fine Foods	Manufacturing & distribution
Seaman USD 345	Education
Security Benefit	Insurance & financial
Shawnee County Government	Government
Shawnee Heights USD 450	Education
St. Francis Health Care	Healthcare
State of Kansas	State government
Stormont-Vail HealthCare	Healthcare
Target Distribution Center	Manufacturing & distribution
Topeka USD 501	Education
United States Government	Federal government
Wal-Mart and Sam's Club	Retail
Washburn University	Education
Westar Energy	Utility

Note: Companies shown are located within the Topeka, KS Metropolitan Statistical Area.
Source: Hoovers.com; Wikipedia

PUBLIC SAFETY

Crime Rate

Area	All Crimes	Violent Crimes				Property Crimes		
		Murder	Rape[3]	Robbery	Aggrav. Assault	Burglary	Larceny -Theft	Motor Vehicle Theft
City	5,742.2	21.3	44.2	212.4	335.6	790.5	3,731.5	606.5
Suburbs[1]	1,805.3	4.7	27.4	14.1	128.3	331.1	1,144.1	155.6
Metro[2]	3,948.1	13.8	36.5	122.1	241.1	581.0	2,552.4	401.0
U.S.	2,756.1	5.3	41.7	98.0	248.9	430.4	1,694.4	237.4

Note: Figures are crimes per 100,000 population; (1) All areas within the metro area that are located outside the city limits; (2) Figures cover the Topeka, KS Metropolitan Statistical Area—see Appendix B for areas included; (3) The city and U.S. figures shown were reported using the revised Uniform Crime Reporting (UCR) definition of rape. The suburban and metro area figures shown are an aggregate total of the data submitted using both the revised and legacy UCR definitions.
Source: FBI Uniform Crime Reports, 2017

Hate Crimes

Area	Number of Quarters Reported	Number of Incidents per Bias Motivation					
		Race/Ethnicity/ Ancestry	Religion	Sexual Orientation	Disability	Gender	Gender Identity
City	4	1	0	0	0	0	0
U.S.	4	4,131	1,564	1,130	116	46	119

Source: Federal Bureau of Investigation, Hate Crime Statistics 2017

Identity Theft Consumer Reports

Area	Reports	Reports per 100,000 Population	Rank[2]
MSA[1]	207	89	177
U.S.	444,602	135	-

Note: (1) Figures cover the Topeka, KS Metropolitan Statistical Area—see Appendix B for areas included;
(2) Rank ranges from 1 to 389 where 1 indicates greatest number of identity theft reports per 100,000 population
Source: Federal Trade Commission, Consumer Sentinel Network Data Book for January–December 2018

Fraud and Other Consumer Reports

Area	Reports	Reports per 100,000 Population	Rank[2]
MSA[1]	1,380	592	64
U.S.	2,552,917	776	-

Note: (1) Figures cover the Topeka, KS Metropolitan Statistical Area—see Appendix B for areas included;
(2) Rank ranges from 1 to 389 where 1 indicates greatest number of fraud and other consumer reports per 100,000 population
Source: Federal Trade Commission, Consumer Sentinel Network Data Book for January–December 2018

SPORTS

Professional Sports Teams

Team Name	League	Year Established

No teams are located in the metro area
Source: Wikipedia, Major Professional Sports Teams of the United States and Canada, April 5, 2019

CLIMATE

Average and Extreme Temperatures

Temperature	Jan	Feb	Mar	Apr	May	Jun	Jul	Aug	Sep	Oct	Nov	Dec	Yr.
Extreme High (°F)	73	80	89	95	97	107	110	110	104	96	85	73	110
Average High (°F)	37	43	54	67	76	85	89	88	81	70	54	41	66
Average Temp. (°F)	27	33	43	55	65	74	79	77	69	57	43	32	55
Average Low (°F)	17	22	31	43	53	63	67	65	56	44	32	21	43
Extreme Low (°F)	-20	-23	-7	10	26	42	43	41	29	19	2	-26	-26

Note: Figures cover the years 1948-1990
Source: National Climatic Data Center, International Station Meteorological Climate Summary, 9/96

Average Precipitation/Snowfall/Humidity

Precip./Humidity	Jan	Feb	Mar	Apr	May	Jun	Jul	Aug	Sep	Oct	Nov	Dec	Yr.
Avg. Precip. (in.)	1.0	1.1	2.4	3.0	4.3	5.3	4.1	3.9	3.4	2.9	1.7	1.3	34.4
Avg. Snowfall (in.)	6	5	4	1	0	0	0	0	0	Tr	1	5	21
Avg. Rel. Hum. 6am (%)	77	79	79	79	84	86	86	87	87	83	80	80	82
Avg. Rel. Hum. 3pm (%)	58	57	51	48	52	54	53	52	50	47	51	58	53

Note: Figures cover the years 1948-1990; Tr = Trace amounts (<0.05 in. of rain; <0.5 in. of snow)
Source: National Climatic Data Center, International Station Meteorological Climate Summary, 9/96

Weather Conditions

Temperature			Daytime Sky			Precipitation		
10°F & below	32°F & below	90°F & above	Clear	Partly cloudy	Cloudy	0.01 inch or more precip.	0.1 inch or more snow/ice	Thunder-storms
20	123	45	111	127	127	96	15	54

Note: Figures are average number of days per year and cover the years 1948-1990
Source: National Climatic Data Center, International Station Meteorological Climate Summary, 9/96

HAZARDOUS WASTE

Superfund Sites

The Topeka, KS metro area has no sites on the EPA's Superfund Final National Priorities List. There are a total of 1,390 Superfund sites with a status of proposed or final on the list in the U.S. *U.S. Environmental Protection Agency, National Priorities List, April 5, 2019*

AIR & WATER QUALITY

Air Quality Trends: Ozone

	1990	1995	2000	2005	2010	2012	2014	2015	2016	2017
MSA[1]	n/a	n/a	n/a	n/a	n/a	n/a	n/a	n/a	n/a	n/a
U.S.	0.088	0.089	0.082	0.080	0.073	0.075	0.067	0.068	0.069	0.068

Note: (1) Data covers the Topeka, KS Metropolitan Statistical Area—see Appendix B for areas included; n/a not available. The values shown are the composite ozone concentration averages among trend sites based on the highest fourth daily maximum 8-hour concentration in parts per million. These trends are based on sites having an adequate record of monitoring data during the trend period. Data from exceptional events are included.
Source: U.S. Environmental Protection Agency, Air Quality Monitoring Information, "Air Quality Trends by City, 1990-2017"

Air Quality Index

Area	Percent of Days when Air Quality was...[2]					AQI Statistics[2]	
	Good	Moderate	Unhealthy for Sensitive Groups	Unhealthy	Very Unhealthy	Maximum	Median
MSA[1]	82.8	17.2	0.0	0.0	0.0	93	39

Note: (1) Data covers the Topeka, KS Metropolitan Statistical Area—see Appendix B for areas included; (2) Based on 361 days with AQI data in 2017. Air Quality Index (AQI) is an index for reporting daily air quality. EPA calculates the AQI for five major air pollutants regulated by the Clean Air Act: ground-level ozone, particle pollution (aka particulate matter), carbon monoxide, sulfur dioxide, and nitrogen dioxide. The AQI runs from 0 to 500. The higher the AQI value, the greater the level of air pollution and the greater the health concern. There are six AQI categories: "Good" AQI is between 0 and 50. Air quality is considered satisfactory; "Moderate" AQI is between 51 and 100. Air quality is acceptable; "Unhealthy for Sensitive Groups" When AQI values are between 101 and 150, members of sensitive groups may experience health effects; "Unhealthy" When AQI values are between 151 and 200 everyone may begin to experience health effects; "Very Unhealthy" AQI values between 201 and 300 trigger a health alert; "Hazardous" AQI values over 300 trigger warnings of emergency conditions (not shown).
Source: U.S. Environmental Protection Agency, Air Quality Index Report, 2017

Air Quality Index Pollutants

Area	Percent of Days when AQI Pollutant was...[2]					
	Carbon Monoxide	Nitrogen Dioxide	Ozone	Sulfur Dioxide	Particulate Matter 2.5	Particulate Matter 10
MSA[1]	0.0	0.0	64.5	0.0	34.9	0.6

Note: (1) Data covers the Topeka, KS Metropolitan Statistical Area—see Appendix B for areas included; (2) Based on 361 days with AQI data in 2017. The Air Quality Index (AQI) is an index for reporting daily air quality. EPA calculates the AQI for five major air pollutants regulated by the Clean Air Act: ground-level ozone, particle pollution (also known as particulate matter), carbon monoxide, sulfur dioxide, and nitrogen dioxide. The AQI runs from 0 to 500. The higher the AQI value, the greater the level of air pollution and the greater the health concern.
Source: U.S. Environmental Protection Agency, Air Quality Index Report, 2017

Maximum Air Pollutant Concentrations: Particulate Matter, Ozone, CO and Lead

	Particulate Matter 10 (ug/m³)	Particulate Matter 2.5 Wtd AM (ug/m³)	Particulate Matter 2.5 24-Hr (ug/m³)	Ozone (ppm)	Carbon Monoxide (ppm)	Lead (ug/m³)
MSA[1] Level	49	8.8	21	0.062	n/a	n/a
NAAQS[2]	150	15	35	0.075	9	0.15
Met NAAQS[2]	Yes	Yes	Yes	Yes	n/a	n/a

Note: (1) Data covers the Topeka, KS Metropolitan Statistical Area—see Appendix B for areas included; Data from exceptional events are included; (2) National Ambient Air Quality Standards; ppm = parts per million; ug/m³ = micrograms per cubic meter; n/a not available.
Concentrations: Particulate Matter 10 (coarse particulate)—highest second maximum 24-hour concentration; Particulate Matter 2.5 Wtd AM (fine particulate)—highest weighted annual mean concentration; Particulate Matter 2.5 24-Hour (fine particulate)—highest 98th percentile 24-hour concentration; Ozone—highest fourth daily maximum 8-hour concentration; Carbon Monoxide—highest second maximum non-overlapping 8-hour concentration; Lead—maximum running 3-month average
Source: U.S. Environmental Protection Agency, Air Quality Monitoring Information, "Air Quality Statistics by City, 2017"

Maximum Air Pollutant Concentrations: Nitrogen Dioxide and Sulfur Dioxide

	Nitrogen Dioxide AM (ppb)	Nitrogen Dioxide 1-Hr (ppb)	Sulfur Dioxide AM (ppb)	Sulfur Dioxide 1-Hr (ppb)	Sulfur Dioxide 24-Hr (ppb)
MSA[1] Level	n/a	n/a	n/a	n/a	n/a
NAAQS[2]	53	100	30	75	140
Met NAAQS[2]	n/a	n/a	n/a	n/a	n/a

Note: (1) Data covers the Topeka, KS Metropolitan Statistical Area—see Appendix B for areas included; Data from exceptional events are included; (2) National Ambient Air Quality Standards; ppm = parts per million; ug/m³ = micrograms per cubic meter; n/a not available.
Concentrations: Nitrogen Dioxide AM—highest arithmetic mean concentration; Nitrogen Dioxide 1-Hr—highest 98th percentile 1-hour daily maximum concentration; Sulfur Dioxide AM—highest annual mean concentration; Sulfur Dioxide 1-Hr—highest 99th percentile 1-hour daily maximum concentration; Sulfur Dioxide 24-Hr—highest second maximum 24-hour concentration
Source: U.S. Environmental Protection Agency, Air Quality Monitoring Information, "Air Quality Statistics by City, 2017"

Drinking Water

Water System Name	Pop. Served	Primary Water Source Type	Violations[1] Health Based	Violations[1] Monitoring/ Reporting
City of Topeka	126,587	Surface	1	0

Note: (1) Based on violation data from January 1, 2018 to December 31, 2018
Source: U.S. Environmental Protection Agency, Office of Ground Water and Drinking Water, Safe Drinking Water Information System (based on data extracted April 5, 2019)

Appendixes

Appendix A: Comparative Statistics

Table of Contents

Population Growth: City

Area	1990 Census	2000 Census	2010 Census	2017* Estimate	Population Growth (%)	
					1990-2017	2010-2017
Albany, NY	100,756	95,658	97,856	98,498	-2.2	0.7
Albuquerque, NM	388,375	448,607	545,852	556,718	43.3	2.0
Allentown, PA	105,066	106,632	118,032	120,128	14.3	1.8
Anchorage, AK	226,338	260,283	291,826	298,225	31.8	2.2
Ann Arbor, MI	111,018	114,024	113,934	119,303	7.5	4.7
Athens, GA	86,561	100,266	115,452	122,292	41.3	5.9
Atlanta, GA	394,092	416,474	420,003	465,230	18.1	10.8
Austin, TX	499,053	656,562	790,390	916,906	83.7	16.0
Baton Rouge, LA	223,299	227,818	229,493	227,549	1.9	-0.8
Billings, MT	81,812	89,847	104,170	109,082	33.3	4.7
Boise City, ID	144,317	185,787	205,671	220,859	53.0	7.4
Boston, MA	574,283	589,141	617,594	669,158	16.5	8.3
Boulder, CO	87,737	94,673	97,385	106,271	21.1	9.1
Cape Coral, FL	75,507	102,286	154,305	173,679	130.0	12.6
Cedar Rapids, IA	110,829	120,758	126,326	130,330	17.6	3.2
Charleston, SC	96,102	96,650	120,083	131,204	36.5	9.3
Charlotte, NC	428,283	540,828	731,424	826,060	92.9	12.9
Chicago, IL	2,783,726	2,896,016	2,695,598	2,722,586	-2.2	1.0
Clarksville, TN	78,569	103,455	132,929	147,771	88.1	11.2
College Station, TX	53,318	67,890	93,857	107,445	101.5	14.5
Colorado Springs, CO	283,798	360,890	416,427	450,000	58.6	8.1
Columbia, MO	71,069	84,531	108,500	118,620	66.9	9.3
Columbia, SC	115,475	116,278	129,272	132,236	14.5	2.3
Columbus, OH	648,656	711,470	787,033	852,144	31.4	8.3
Dallas, TX	1,006,971	1,188,580	1,197,816	1,300,122	29.1	8.5
Denver, CO	467,153	554,636	600,158	678,467	45.2	13.0
Des Moines, IA	193,569	198,682	203,433	214,778	11.0	5.6
Durham, NC	151,737	187,035	228,330	257,232	69.5	12.7
Edison, NJ	88,680	97,687	99,967	102,304	15.4	2.3
El Paso, TX	515,541	563,662	649,121	678,266	31.6	4.5
Eugene, OR	118,073	137,893	156,185	163,135	38.2	4.4
Evansville, IN	126,272	121,582	117,429	119,806	-5.1	2.0
Fargo, ND	74,372	90,599	105,549	118,099	58.8	11.9
Fayetteville, NC	118,247	121,015	200,564	210,324	77.9	4.9
Fort Collins, CO	89,555	118,652	143,986	159,150	77.7	10.5
Fort Wayne, IN	205,671	205,727	253,691	262,450	27.6	3.5
Fort Worth, TX	448,311	534,694	741,206	835,129	86.3	12.7
Gainesville, FL	90,519	95,447	124,354	129,394	42.9	4.1
Grand Rapids, MI	189,145	197,800	188,040	195,355	3.3	3.9
Greeley, CO	60,887	76,930	92,889	100,760	65.5	8.5
Green Bay, WI	96,466	102,313	104,057	104,796	8.6	0.7
Greensboro, NC	193,389	223,891	269,666	284,816	47.3	5.6
Honolulu, HI	376,465	371,657	337,256	350,788	-6.8	4.0
Houston, TX	1,697,610	1,953,631	2,099,451	2,267,336	33.6	8.0
Huntsville, AL	161,842	158,216	180,105	190,501	17.7	5.8
Indianapolis, IN	730,993	781,870	820,445	853,431	16.7	4.0
Jacksonville, FL	635,221	735,617	821,784	867,313	36.5	5.5
Kansas City, MO	434,967	441,545	459,787	476,974	9.7	3.7
Lafayette, LA	104,735	110,257	120,623	126,476	20.8	4.9
Las Cruces, NM	63,267	74,267	97,618	101,014	59.7	3.5
Las Vegas, NV	261,374	478,434	583,756	621,662	137.8	6.5
Lexington, KY	225,366	260,512	295,803	315,109	39.8	6.5
Lincoln, NE	193,629	225,581	258,379	277,315	43.2	7.3
Little Rock, AR	177,519	183,133	193,524	197,780	11.4	2.2
Los Angeles, CA	3,487,671	3,694,820	3,792,621	3,949,776	13.2	4.1

Table continued on next page.

Area	1990 Census	2000 Census	2010 Census	2017* Estimate	Population Growth (%)	
					1990-2017	2010-2017
Louisville, KY	269,160	256,231	597,337	615,478	128.7	3.0
Madison, WI	193,451	208,054	233,209	248,856	28.6	6.7
Manchester, NH	99,567	107,006	109,565	110,601	11.1	0.9
McAllen, TX	86,145	106,414	129,877	139,838	62.3	7.7
Miami, FL	358,843	362,470	399,457	443,007	23.5	10.9
Midland, TX	89,358	94,996	111,147	131,286	46.9	18.1
Minneapolis, MN	368,383	382,618	382,578	411,452	11.7	7.5
Nashville, TN	488,364	545,524	601,222	654,187	34.0	8.8
New Orleans, LA	496,938	484,674	343,829	388,182	-21.9	12.9
New York, NY	7,322,552	8,008,278	8,175,133	8,560,072	16.9	4.7
Oklahoma City, OK	445,065	506,132	579,999	629,191	41.4	8.5
Omaha, NE	371,972	390,007	408,958	463,081	24.5	13.2
Orlando, FL	161,172	185,951	238,300	269,414	67.2	13.1
Peoria, IL	114,341	112,936	115,007	115,424	0.9	0.4
Philadelphia, PA	1,585,577	1,517,550	1,526,006	1,569,657	-1.0	2.9
Phoenix, AZ	989,873	1,321,045	1,445,632	1,574,421	59.1	8.9
Pittsburgh, PA	369,785	334,563	305,704	305,012	-17.5	-0.2
Portland, OR	485,833	529,121	583,776	630,331	29.7	8.0
Providence, RI	160,734	173,618	178,042	179,509	11.7	0.8
Provo, UT	87,148	105,166	112,488	116,199	33.3	3.3
Raleigh, NC	226,841	276,093	403,892	449,477	98.1	11.3
Reno, NV	139,950	180,480	225,221	239,732	71.3	6.4
Richmond, VA	202,783	197,790	204,214	220,892	8.9	8.2
Roanoke, VA	96,415	94,911	97,032	99,572	3.3	2.6
Rochester, MN	74,151	85,806	106,769	112,683	52.0	5.5
Salem, OR	112,046	136,924	154,637	163,654	46.1	5.8
Salt Lake City, UT	159,796	181,743	186,440	194,188	21.5	4.2
San Antonio, TX	997,258	1,144,646	1,327,407	1,461,623	46.6	10.1
San Diego, CA	1,111,048	1,223,400	1,307,402	1,390,966	25.2	6.4
San Francisco, CA	723,959	776,733	805,235	864,263	19.4	7.3
San Jose, CA	784,324	894,943	945,942	1,023,031	30.4	8.1
Santa Rosa, CA	123,297	147,595	167,815	174,244	41.3	3.8
Savannah, GA	138,038	131,510	136,286	145,094	5.1	6.5
Seattle, WA	516,262	563,374	608,660	688,245	33.3	13.1
Sioux Falls, SD	102,262	123,975	153,888	170,401	66.6	10.7
Springfield, IL	108,997	111,454	116,250	116,313	6.7	0.1
Tallahassee, FL	128,014	150,624	181,376	188,463	47.2	3.9
Tampa, FL	279,960	303,447	335,709	368,087	31.5	9.6
Topeka, KS	121,197	122,377	127,473	127,139	4.9	-0.3
Tyler, TX	77,653	83,650	96,900	102,561	32.1	5.8
Virginia Beach, VA	393,069	425,257	437,994	450,057	14.5	2.8
Visalia, CA	78,398	91,565	124,442	130,047	65.9	4.5
Washington, DC	606,900	572,059	601,723	672,391	10.8	11.7
Wilmington, NC	64,609	75,838	106,476	115,261	78.4	8.3
Winston-Salem, NC	168,139	185,776	229,617	240,193	42.9	4.6
U.S.	248,709,873	281,421,906	308,745,538	321,004,407	29.1	4.0

Note: (*) 2013-2017 5-year estimated population
Source: U.S. Census Bureau, 1990 Census, Census 2000, Census 2010, 2013-2017 American Community Survey 5-Year Estimates

Population Growth: Metro Area

Area	1990 Census	2000 Census	2010 Census	2017* Estimate	Population Growth (%)	
					1990-2017	2010-2017
Albany, NY	809,443	825,875	870,716	881,862	8.9	1.3
Albuquerque, NM	599,416	729,649	887,077	905,049	51.0	2.0
Allentown, PA	686,666	740,395	821,173	832,790	21.3	1.4
Anchorage, AK	266,021	319,605	380,821	399,360	50.1	4.9
Ann Arbor, MI	282,937	322,895	344,791	361,509	27.8	4.8
Athens, GA	136,025	166,079	192,541	202,780	49.1	5.3
Atlanta, GA	3,069,411	4,247,981	5,268,860	5,700,990	85.7	8.2
Austin, TX	846,217	1,249,763	1,716,289	2,000,590	136.4	16.6
Baton Rouge, LA	623,853	705,973	802,484	828,741	32.8	3.3
Billings, MT	121,499	138,904	158,050	167,545	37.9	6.0
Boise City, ID	319,596	464,840	616,561	677,346	111.9	9.9
Boston, MA	4,133,895	4,391,344	4,552,402	4,771,936	15.4	4.8
Boulder, CO	208,898	269,758	294,567	316,782	51.6	7.5
Cape Coral, FL	335,113	440,888	618,754	700,165	108.9	13.2
Cedar Rapids, IA	210,640	237,230	257,940	266,122	26.3	3.2
Charleston, SC	506,875	549,033	664,607	744,195	46.8	12.0
Charlotte, NC	1,024,331	1,330,448	1,758,038	2,427,024	136.9	38.1
Chicago, IL	8,182,076	9,098,316	9,461,105	9,549,229	16.7	0.9
Clarksville, TN	189,277	232,000	273,949	278,844	47.3	1.8
College Station, TX	150,998	184,885	228,660	248,554	64.6	8.7
Colorado Springs, CO	409,482	537,484	645,613	698,595	70.6	8.2
Columbia, MO	122,010	145,666	172,786	174,589	43.1	1.0
Columbia, SC	548,325	647,158	767,598	808,377	47.4	5.3
Columbus, OH	1,405,176	1,612,694	1,836,536	2,023,695	44.0	10.2
Dallas, TX	3,989,294	5,161,544	6,371,773	7,104,415	78.1	11.5
Denver, CO	1,666,935	2,179,296	2,543,482	2,798,684	67.9	10.0
Des Moines, IA	416,346	481,394	569,633	623,113	49.7	9.4
Durham, NC	344,646	426,493	504,357	550,281	59.7	9.1
Edison, NJ	16,845,992	18,323,002	18,897,109	20,192,042	19.9	6.9
El Paso, TX	591,610	679,622	800,647	838,527	41.7	4.7
Eugene, OR	282,912	322,959	351,715	363,471	28.5	3.3
Evansville, IN	324,858	342,815	358,676	315,263	-3.0	-12.1
Fargo, ND	153,296	174,367	208,777	232,660	51.8	11.4
Fayetteville, NC	297,422	336,609	366,383	385,337	29.6	5.2
Fort Collins, CO	186,136	251,494	299,630	330,976	77.8	10.5
Fort Wayne, IN	354,435	390,156	416,257	429,060	21.1	3.1
Fort Worth, TX	3,989,294	5,161,544	6,371,773	7,104,415	78.1	11.5
Gainesville, FL	191,263	232,392	264,275	277,056	44.9	4.8
Grand Rapids, MI	645,914	740,482	774,160	1,039,182	60.9	34.2
Greeley, CO	131,816	180,926	252,825	285,729	116.8	13.0
Green Bay, WI	243,698	282,599	306,241	315,847	29.6	3.1
Greensboro, NC	540,257	643,430	723,801	751,590	39.1	3.8
Honolulu, HI	836,231	876,156	953,207	990,060	18.4	3.9
Houston, TX	3,767,335	4,715,407	5,946,800	6,636,208	76.2	11.6
Huntsville, AL	293,047	342,376	417,593	444,908	51.8	6.5
Indianapolis, IN	1,294,217	1,525,104	1,756,241	1,989,032	53.7	13.3
Jacksonville, FL	925,213	1,122,750	1,345,596	1,447,884	56.5	7.6
Kansas City, MO	1,636,528	1,836,038	2,035,334	2,088,830	27.6	2.6
Lafayette, LA	208,740	239,086	273,738	487,633	133.6	78.1
Las Cruces, NM	135,510	174,682	209,233	213,849	57.8	2.2
Las Vegas, NV	741,459	1,375,765	1,951,269	2,112,436	184.9	8.3
Lexington, KY	348,428	408,326	472,099	500,689	43.7	6.1
Lincoln, NE	229,091	266,787	302,157	323,402	41.2	7.0
Little Rock, AR	535,034	610,518	699,757	730,346	36.5	4.4
Los Angeles, CA	11,273,720	12,365,627	12,828,837	13,261,538	17.6	3.4

Table continued on next page.

Area	1990 Census	2000 Census	2010 Census	2017* Estimate	Population Growth (%)	
					1990-2017	2010-2017
Louisville, KY	1,055,973	1,161,975	1,283,566	1,278,203	21.0	-0.4
Madison, WI	432,323	501,774	568,593	640,072	48.1	12.6
Manchester, NH	336,073	380,841	400,721	406,371	20.9	1.4
McAllen, TX	383,545	569,463	774,769	839,539	118.9	8.4
Miami, FL	4,056,100	5,007,564	5,564,635	6,019,790	48.4	8.2
Midland, TX	106,611	116,009	136,872	165,430	55.2	20.9
Minneapolis, MN	2,538,834	2,968,806	3,279,833	3,526,149	38.9	.7.5
Nashville, TN	1,048,218	1,311,789	1,589,934	1,830,410	74.6	15.1
New Orleans, LA	1,264,391	1,316,510	1,167,764	1,260,660	-0.3	8.0
New York, NY	16,845,992	18,323,002	18,897,109	20,192,042	19.9	6.9
Oklahoma City, OK	971,042	1,095,421	1,252,987	1,353,504	39.4	8.0
Omaha, NE	685,797	767,041	865,350	914,190	33.3	5.6
Orlando, FL	1,224,852	1,644,561	2,134,411	2,390,859	95.2	12.0
Peoria, IL	358,552	366,899	379,186	377,258	5.2	-0.5
Philadelphia, PA	5,435,470	5,687,147	5,965,343	6,065,644	11.6	1.7
Phoenix, AZ	2,238,480	3,251,876	4,192,887	4,561,038	103.8	8.8
Pittsburgh, PA	2,468,289	2,431,087	2,356,285	2,348,143	-4.9	-0.3
Portland, OR	1,523,741	1,927,881	2,226,009	2,382,037	56.3	7.0
Providence, RI	1,509,789	1,582,997	1,600,852	1,613,154	6.8	0.8
Provo, UT	269,407	376,774	526,810	587,190	118.0	11.5
Raleigh, NC	541,081	797,071	1,130,490	1,273,985	135.5	12.7
Reno, NV	257,193	342,885	425,417	449,442	74.7	5.6
Richmond, VA	949,244	1,096,957	1,258,251	1,270,158	33.8	0.9
Roanoke, VA	268,465	288,309	308,707	313,069	16.6	1.4
Rochester, MN	141,945	163,618	186,011	214,485	51.1	15.3
Salem, OR	278,024	347,214	390,738	410,119	47.5	5.0
Salt Lake City, UT	768,075	968,858	1,124,197	1,170,057	52.3	4.1
San Antonio, TX	1,407,745	1,711,703	2,142,508	2,377,507	68.9	11.0
San Diego, CA	2,498,016	2,813,833	3,095,313	3,283,665	31.5	6.1
San Francisco, CA	3,686,592	4,123,740	4,335,391	4,641,820	25.9	7.1
San Jose, CA	1,534,280	1,735,819	1,836,911	1,969,897	28.4	7.2
Santa Rosa, CA	388,222	458,614	483,878	500,943	29.0	3.5
Savannah, GA	258,060	293,000	347,611	377,476	46.3	8.6
Seattle, WA	2,559,164	3,043,878	3,439,809	3,735,216	46.0	8.6
Sioux Falls, SD	153,500	187,093	228,261	250,564	63.2	9.8
Springfield, IL	189,550	201,437	210,170	210,550	11.1	0.2
Tallahassee, FL	259,096	320,304	367,413	377,674	45.8	2.8
Tampa, FL	2,067,959	2,395,997	2,783,243	2,978,209	44.0	7.0
Topeka, KS	210,257	224,551	233,870	233,382	11.0	-0.2
Tyler, TX	151,309	174,706	209,714	222,277	46.9	6.0
Virginia Beach, VA	1,449,389	1,576,370	1,671,683	1,717,708	18.5	2.8
Visalia, CA	311,823	368,021	442,179	458,809	47.1	3.8
Washington, DC	4,122,914	4,796,183	5,582,170	6,090,196	47.7	9.1
Wilmington, NC	200,124	274,532	362,315	277,496	38.7	-23.4
Winston-Salem, NC	361,091	421,961	477,717	658,195	82.3	37.8
U.S.	248,709,873	281,421,906	308,745,538	321,004,407	29.1	4.0

Note: (*) 2013-2017 5-year estimated population; Figures cover the Metropolitan Statistical Area (MSA)—see Appendix B for areas included
Source: U.S. Census Bureau, 1990 Census, Census 2000, Census 2010, 2013-2017 American Community Survey 5-Year Estimates

Household Size: City

City	Persons in Household (%)							Average Household Size
	One	Two	Three	Four	Five	Six	Seven or More	
Albany, NY	45.0	30.6	12.1	7.1	3.2	1.2	0.6	2.14
Albuquerque, NM	33.7	33.0	14.5	11.1	4.9	1.7	0.9	2.49
Allentown, PA	27.9	28.7	15.7	13.4	8.0	3.4	2.6	2.74
Anchorage, AK	24.5	33.5	18.0	13.5	6.0	2.1	2.0	2.74
Ann Arbor, MI	35.7	35.8	12.2	10.7	3.1	1.4	0.8	2.27
Athens, GA	34.9	34.7	14.2	10.3	3.4	1.4	0.7	2.44
Atlanta, GA	47.4	29.7	10.5	7.4	3.1	1.1	0.6	2.24
Austin, TX	34.2	32.9	14.3	11.2	4.5	1.6	1.0	2.48
Baton Rouge, LA	36.4	32.9	15.0	8.6	4.1	1.7	1.0	2.54
Billings, MT	32.1	34.7	14.4	11.1	4.5	1.8	1.1	2.32
Boise City, ID	33.3	34.3	15.0	10.3	4.3	1.4	1.1	2.45
Boston, MA	36.6	31.7	15.2	10.0	3.8	1.6	0.8	2.36
Boulder, CO	33.2	37.4	14.2	11.1	3.0	0.5	0.2	2.25
Cape Coral, FL	23.2	42.7	15.0	11.3	5.5	1.5	0.4	2.77
Cedar Rapids, IA	33.5	34.2	14.1	11.4	3.6	2.0	0.9	2.34
Charleston, SC	35.2	37.1	14.4	9.2	2.7	0.7	0.3	2.33
Charlotte, NC	31.8	31.8	15.8	12.3	5.3	1.7	1.0	2.57
Chicago, IL	36.6	29.1	13.9	10.4	5.5	2.4	1.8	2.54
Clarksville, TN	23.4	32.8	19.5	14.4	6.1	2.0	1.4	2.70
College Station, TX	29.0	34.1	16.1	14.8	3.5	1.6	0.5	2.48
Colorado Springs, CO	28.5	34.7	14.7	12.8	5.9	2.0	1.0	2.52
Columbia, MO	33.0	33.4	14.4	12.6	4.9	1.1	0.3	2.33
Columbia, SC	40.3	32.7	12.9	8.6	4.1	0.6	0.5	2.24
Columbus, OH	35.3	31.7	14.8	10.3	4.7	1.8	1.1	2.40
Dallas, TX	34.4	29.0	14.3	11.3	6.3	2.6	1.8	2.58
Denver, CO	38.7	32.0	12.3	9.4	4.3	1.7	1.3	2.31
Des Moines, IA	33.0	30.6	15.2	11.2	5.7	2.4	1.5	2.50
Durham, NC	34.6	32.8	15.1	10.8	4.0	1.6	0.7	2.35
Edison, NJ	19.7	28.3	21.7	20.6	6.3	2.0	1.0	2.87
El Paso, TX	24.3	28.1	18.4	16.0	8.2	3.3	1.5	3.01
Eugene, OR	32.9	35.1	14.9	10.8	4.1	1.1	0.7	2.33
Evansville, IN	37.9	33.0	13.2	9.2	4.0	1.2	1.2	2.24
Fargo, ND	36.6	33.3	15.1	8.8	4.3	1.1	0.4	2.14
Fayetteville, NC	33.9	33.3	14.9	11.0	4.2	1.6	0.8	2.45
Fort Collins, CO	24.9	37.6	18.6	12.8	4.1	1.1	0.5	2.46
Fort Wayne, IN	32.4	31.8	15.1	11.2	5.8	2.2	1.1	2.46
Fort Worth, TX	26.4	28.8	15.9	14.9	8.1	3.3	2.2	2.88
Gainesville, FL	42.1	33.0	13.6	7.5	2.4	0.9	0.2	2.32
Grand Rapids, MI	32.4	31.7	14.0	10.8	6.1	2.7	2.0	2.56
Greeley, CO	25.6	32.3	15.9	13.2	8.0	2.9	1.8	2.70
Green Bay, WI	33.4	33.0	12.3	11.5	6.6	1.4	1.4	2.38
Greensboro, NC	34.2	33.4	15.2	10.2	4.7	1.2	0.7	2.37
Honolulu, HI	33.0	30.5	15.2	11.0	4.8	2.5	2.8	2.62
Houston, TX	32.2	28.9	15.2	12.1	6.7	2.7	1.9	2.66
Huntsville, AL	36.4	33.4	14.0	9.9	4.1	1.3	0.6	2.25
Indianapolis, IN	36.0	31.5	13.8	10.5	4.9	1.9	1.0	2.51
Jacksonville, FL	30.2	34.0	16.3	11.6	5.0	1.7	0.9	2.59
Kansas City, MO	36.9	31.6	13.6	10.1	4.8	1.6	1.1	2.35
Lafayette, LA	33.9	35.1	14.6	9.9	4.3	1.2	0.7	2.46
Las Cruces, NM	29.3	33.0	18.1	11.3	5.3	1.9	0.8	2.49
Las Vegas, NV	29.3	31.7	15.5	11.9	6.6	3.0	1.7	2.77
Lexington, KY	31.4	35.7	15.2	10.8	4.7	1.4	0.6	2.37
Lincoln, NE	31.0	35.2	14.3	11.2	5.2	1.8	0.9	2.39
Little Rock, AR	36.7	32.7	13.7	9.9	4.3	1.5	0.9	2.42

Table continued on next page.

City	Persons in Household (%)							Average Household Size
	One	Two	Three	Four	Five	Six	Seven or More	
Los Angeles, CA	30.1	28.5	15.2	13.2	6.9	3.1	2.6	2.83
Louisville, KY	33.5	32.9	15.1	10.8	4.8	1.6	0.9	2.44
Madison, WI	35.1	36.5	13.1	9.7	3.7	1.1	0.5	2.20
Manchester, NH	31.0	35.2	16.1	10.5	4.5	1.3	1.0	2.35
McAllen, TX	19.6	28.4	19.1	16.1	9.8	4.2	2.5	3.15
Miami, FL	38.0	29.7	15.3	9.6	4.3	1.6	1.1	2.63
Midland, TX	24.8	32.4	16.0	15.0	7.0	2.8	1.7	2.84
Minneapolis, MN	40.4	31.0	11.9	9.3	3.7	1.8	1.6	2.29
Nashville, TN	34.2	33.1	15.2	10.1	4.2	1.7	1.1	2.40
New Orleans, LA	43.4	29.8	13.3	8.2	3.2	1.1	0.8	2.42
New York, NY	32.3	28.1	16.2	12.4	6.0	2.5	2.1	2.67
Oklahoma City, OK	30.9	32.0	14.9	12.1	5.9	2.5	1.2	2.59
Omaha, NE	32.7	31.6	14.1	11.3	5.8	2.6	1.5	2.48
Orlando, FL	34.2	33.2	16.1	10.4	3.5	1.6	0.6	2.44
Peoria, IL	37.1	31.0	14.0	10.2	4.2	2.0	1.1	2.40
Philadelphia, PA	39.3	28.3	14.3	10.1	4.5	1.9	1.2	2.57
Phoenix, AZ	28.3	30.0	15.0	12.8	7.1	3.9	2.7	2.86
Pittsburgh, PA	42.0	32.6	12.8	7.8	2.9	1.0	0.6	2.08
Portland, OR	33.9	33.8	14.7	10.7	4.2	1.4	1.0	2.35
Providence, RI	32.5	27.7	16.9	12.7	6.7	1.7	1.5	2.66
Provo, UT	14.1	33.5	18.1	15.2	8.2	6.4	4.3	3.20
Raleigh, NC	33.3	31.8	15.4	12.3	4.6	1.6	0.7	2.43
Reno, NV	34.4	31.7	14.7	10.8	4.7	1.9	1.4	2.43
Richmond, VA	42.8	31.1	13.1	7.4	3.4	1.2	0.7	2.35
Roanoke, VA	37.4	33.3	14.6	8.3	3.9	1.4	0.7	2.30
Rochester, MN	29.2	33.7	14.7	14.0	5.0	1.7	1.3	2.44
Salem, OR	29.1	32.0	14.6	13.4	5.8	3.0	1.8	2.64
Salt Lake City, UT	34.8	32.2	14.5	10.0	4.4	2.1	1.7	2.45
San Antonio, TX	28.6	29.4	16.6	13.2	7.1	2.8	1.9	2.91
San Diego, CA	27.7	32.8	16.3	13.0	5.8	2.5	1.6	2.72
San Francisco, CA	36.6	33.6	13.8	9.3	3.5	1.4	1.4	2.35
San Jose, CA	19.6	28.2	18.2	18.1	8.4	3.6	3.5	3.15
Santa Rosa, CA	29.4	32.0	14.7	13.6	5.7	2.3	2.2	2.65
Savannah, GA	33.7	33.3	15.6	9.2	4.8	1.9	1.2	2.50
Seattle, WA	39.1	34.9	12.2	9.1	3.0	0.7	0.7	2.11
Sioux Falls, SD	32.3	34.0	13.5	11.2	5.4	2.2	1.2	2.39
Springfield, IL	36.6	33.5	14.8	9.4	3.1	1.2	1.0	2.22
Tallahassee, FL	33.4	33.8	17.8	9.8	3.6	0.9	0.2	2.33
Tampa, FL	36.3	31.6	14.8	10.7	4.2	1.4	0.7	2.42
Topeka, KS	37.2	32.1	12.9	10.4	4.6	1.7	0.7	2.31
Tyler, TX	32.7	33.2	13.3	11.9	5.4	1.9	1.4	2.67
Virginia Beach, VA	24.3	33.4	18.2	14.8	6.1	1.9	0.9	2.62
Visalia, CA	21.6	28.5	15.4	17.9	9.4	4.3	2.5	3.04
Washington, DC	43.5	30.5	12.3	8.1	3.3	1.2	0.8	2.28
Wilmington, NC	38.2	34.5	14.0	8.8	3.0	0.7	0.5	2.18
Winston-Salem, NC	34.8	30.9	14.8	10.9	5.5	1.9	0.9	2.45
U.S.	27.6	33.8	15.7	13.0	6.0	2.3	1.4	2.63

U.S. Census Bureau, 2013-2017 American Community Survey 5-Year Estimates

Household Size: Metro Area

Metro Area	Persons in Household (%)							Average Household Size
	One	Two	Three	Four	Five	Six	Seven or More	
Albany, NY	32.0	35.1	15.2	11.3	4.2	1.4	0.5	2.43
Albuquerque, NM	30.8	34.2	14.7	11.3	5.4	2.1	1.2	2.58
Allentown, PA	25.9	35.2	16.0	13.5	6.1	2.0	1.0	2.54
Anchorage, AK	24.3	33.7	17.3	13.6	6.3	2.4	2.2	2.85
Ann Arbor, MI	30.1	35.7	13.8	12.4	4.8	1.7	1.1	2.46
Athens, GA	29.6	35.3	15.4	12.1	4.9	1.7	0.7	2.55
Atlanta, GA	26.5	31.3	17.1	14.4	6.5	2.5	1.4	2.77
Austin, TX	27.8	33.3	15.6	13.7	5.9	2.1	1.3	2.70
Baton Rouge, LA	28.1	33.9	17.0	12.0	5.8	1.9	1.0	2.67
Billings, MT	29.4	36.7	14.2	11.2	4.9	2.0	1.3	2.38
Boise City, ID	28.0	33.9	14.3	12.5	6.8	2.4	1.8	2.69
Boston, MA	27.7	32.7	16.7	14.5	5.6	1.7	0.8	2.55
Boulder, CO	27.9	36.7	15.4	13.0	4.7	1.4	0.5	2.44
Cape Coral, FL	28.0	44.3	11.9	8.7	4.2	1.6	0.8	2.61
Cedar Rapids, IA	28.7	36.8	14.1	12.6	4.7	2.0	0.9	2.41
Charleston, SC	28.8	35.3	16.9	11.8	4.6	1.5	0.8	2.59
Charlotte, NC	26.6	33.8	16.9	13.8	5.7	1.9	0.9	2.64
Chicago, IL	28.5	30.7	15.7	13.9	6.8	2.5	1.5	2.70
Clarksville, TN	23.8	33.2	18.4	14.2	6.4	2.4	1.2	2.68
College Station, TX	27.4	34.0	16.2	13.6	5.2	2.2	1.1	2.58
Colorado Springs, CO	24.7	35.2	16.0	13.8	6.5	2.3	1.1	2.62
Columbia, MO	29.9	34.7	14.8	13.3	5.2	1.1	0.7	2.40
Columbia, SC	29.4	34.3	16.1	12.2	5.3	1.5	0.8	2.53
Columbus, OH	28.4	33.7	15.9	13.1	5.7	1.9	1.0	2.54
Dallas, TX	24.8	30.8	16.8	15.2	7.5	2.9	1.7	2.81
Denver, CO	28.2	33.9	15.0	13.3	5.7	2.2	1.3	2.57
Des Moines, IA	27.5	34.2	15.0	13.5	6.4	2.1	0.9	2.53
Durham, NC	30.8	35.7	15.1	11.4	4.5	1.4	0.7	2.42
Edison, NJ	27.8	29.2	17.0	14.6	6.6	2.5	1.9	2.76
El Paso, TX	22.5	27.5	18.4	16.6	9.1	3.6	1.9	3.12
Eugene, OR	29.5	37.9	14.7	11.0	4.1	1.6	0.9	2.39
Evansville, IN	30.0	36.4	14.3	11.5	4.9	1.5	1.0	2.40
Fargo, ND	31.0	34.8	14.9	11.9	5.0	1.4	0.6	2.32
Fayetteville, NC	30.5	32.4	16.6	12.0	5.4	1.8	1.0	2.60
Fort Collins, CO	24.2	39.7	16.6	12.2	4.7	1.6	0.6	2.46
Fort Wayne, IN	28.8	33.9	14.8	12.5	6.1	2.3	1.3	2.53
Fort Worth, TX	24.8	30.8	16.8	15.2	7.5	2.9	1.7	2.81
Gainesville, FL	34.4	35.1	14.5	10.0	3.3	1.8	0.5	2.50
Grand Rapids, MI	24.5	34.9	15.1	14.3	6.8	2.6	1.4	2.65
Greeley, CO	20.5	33.7	16.8	16.1	8.0	2.8	1.8	2.80
Green Bay, WI	27.6	37.0	14.0	12.7	6.1	1.4	0.9	2.42
Greensboro, NC	29.6	35.0	16.0	11.2	5.3	1.7	1.0	2.49
Honolulu, HI	23.4	29.9	17.3	13.9	7.2	3.6	4.5	3.06
Houston, TX	24.2	29.6	17.1	15.5	8.2	3.2	2.0	2.89
Huntsville, AL	29.7	34.3	15.9	12.6	5.0	1.5	0.7	2.48
Indianapolis, IN	29.4	33.4	15.1	13.1	5.8	2.0	0.9	2.57
Jacksonville, FL	27.2	35.6	16.3	12.5	5.3	1.9	0.8	2.62
Kansas City, MO	29.0	33.7	15.1	12.9	5.9	2.0	1.1	2.52
Lafayette, LA	27.1	33.6	17.4	12.8	5.9	2.0	0.9	2.67
Las Cruces, NM	24.5	33.1	17.9	12.9	6.4	2.9	1.9	2.72
Las Vegas, NV	28.2	32.5	15.4	12.5	6.6	2.8	1.7	2.79
Lexington, KY	28.0	35.9	16.3	12.2	5.0	1.6	0.7	2.44
Lincoln, NE	29.4	36.0	14.2	11.8	5.4	1.9	1.0	2.42
Little Rock, AR	29.8	34.3	16.3	11.6	4.9	1.8	0.9	2.57

Table continued on next page.

Metro Area	Persons in Household (%)							Average Household Size
	One	Two	Three	Four	Five	Six	Seven or More	
Los Angeles, CA	24.5	28.4	16.9	15.4	8.1	3.6	2.9	3.02
Louisville, KY	30.1	34.3	15.6	12.0	5.2	1.6	0.8	2.51
Madison, WI	29.5	37.3	14.0	12.1	4.7	1.5	0.7	2.35
Manchester, NH	24.6	36.3	17.3	13.5	5.3	1.6	1.0	2.52
McAllen, TX	15.3	25.0	17.8	17.7	13.1	5.8	5.0	3.57
Miami, FL	28.3	32.1	16.8	13.5	5.7	2.1	1.2	2.86
Midland, TX	24.3	32.1	15.6	15.5	7.3	2.7	2.2	2.88
Minneapolis, MN	27.8	34.0	14.9	13.7	5.9	2.1	1.3	2.55
Nashville, TN	26.6	34.4	16.7	13.4	5.6	2.0	1.1	2.60
New Orleans, LA	32.3	32.4	15.9	11.9	4.7	1.6	1.0	2.58
New York, NY	27.8	29.2	17.0	14.6	6.6	2.5	1.9	2.76
Oklahoma City, OK	28.2	34.1	15.5	12.5	5.9	2.3	1.2	2.61
Omaha, NE	28.4	33.4	14.6	12.9	6.3	2.6	1.3	2.54
Orlando, FL	25.4	34.4	17.1	13.7	5.7	2.2	1.1	2.81
Peoria, IL	30.3	35.6	14.2	11.6	4.9	2.1	1.0	2.44
Philadelphia, PA	29.4	31.8	16.2	13.5	5.7	2.0	1.0	2.62
Phoenix, AZ	26.7	34.3	14.3	12.6	6.6	3.0	2.0	2.76
Pittsburgh, PA	32.6	35.5	14.7	11.0	4.0	1.3	0.5	2.28
Portland, OR	26.9	34.7	15.7	13.4	5.6	2.1	1.4	2.57
Providence, RI	29.6	32.9	16.8	13.2	5.0	1.5	0.7	2.48
Provo, UT	11.9	27.8	15.8	15.8	12.4	9.3	6.6	3.60
Raleigh, NC	25.1	33.0	17.5	15.3	5.9	2.0	0.9	2.65
Reno, NV	29.4	34.6	15.2	11.7	5.1	2.3	1.4	2.53
Richmond, VA	28.6	34.4	16.5	12.4	5.2	1.7	0.8	2.57
Roanoke, VA	30.6	37.3	14.8	10.5	4.2	1.4	0.8	2.35
Rochester, MN	25.9	36.8	14.3	13.9	5.4	2.2	1.1	2.48
Salem, OR	25.2	34.4	15.0	13.2	6.7	3.0	2.0	2.74
Salt Lake City, UT	22.3	30.1	15.9	14.3	8.9	4.9	3.2	3.02
San Antonio, TX	25.5	31.0	16.9	14.1	7.3	2.9	1.9	2.94
San Diego, CA	23.9	32.5	17.1	14.6	6.8	2.8	1.9	2.87
San Francisco, CA	26.7	31.6	16.8	14.5	6.1	2.3	1.7	2.71
San Jose, CA	20.6	29.9	18.5	17.9	7.3	2.9	2.5	2.99
Santa Rosa, CA	28.1	34.1	15.4	13.0	5.6	2.0	1.5	2.59
Savannah, GA	27.3	34.3	17.0	12.7	5.5	1.9	1.0	2.62
Seattle, WA	27.7	34.2	15.9	13.4	5.3	2.0	1.2	2.53
Sioux Falls, SD	28.6	35.0	13.9	12.5	6.2	2.3	1.2	2.48
Springfield, IL	31.5	35.8	14.8	11.0	4.2	1.6	0.7	2.32
Tallahassee, FL	29.4	34.9	17.7	11.4	4.4	1.2	0.7	2.42
Tampa, FL	31.1	36.6	14.5	10.8	4.4	1.5	0.8	2.48
Topeka, KS	30.4	36.0	13.4	11.7	5.2	2.0	1.0	2.43
Tyler, TX	26.7	36.1	14.7	12.4	5.6	2.5	1.7	2.79
Virginia Beach, VA	26.8	34.0	17.6	13.1	5.4	1.8	0.9	2.59
Visalia, CA	17.6	25.7	16.5	17.9	11.6	5.9	4.5	3.35
Washington, DC	26.9	30.5	16.7	14.7	6.5	2.6	1.6	2.76
Wilmington, NC	32.5	36.2	14.5	10.8	3.7	1.4	0.5	2.39
Winston-Salem, NC	29.0	35.6	15.3	12.0	5.1	1.8	0.8	2.47
U.S.	27.6	33.8	15.7	13.0	6.0	2.3	1.4	2.63

Note: Figures cover the Metropolitan Statistical Area (MSA)—see Appendix B for areas included
Source: U.S. Census Bureau, 2013-2017 American Community Survey 5-Year Estimates

Race: City

City	White Alone[1] (%)	Black Alone[1] (%)	Asian Alone[1] (%)	AIAN[2] Alone[1] (%)	NHOPI[3] Alone[1] (%)	Other Race Alone[1] (%)	Two or More Races (%)
Albany, NY	55.1	28.7	7.4	0.3	0.0	2.8	5.6
Albuquerque, NM	73.6	3.3	2.7	4.4	0.1	11.6	4.3
Allentown, PA	59.2	14.1	2.1	0.5	0.1	19.5	4.6
Anchorage, AK	63.7	5.5	9.3	7.3	2.4	2.2	9.7
Ann Arbor, MI	72.0	7.0	15.9	0.4	0.0	0.5	4.2
Athens, GA	63.2	27.5	4.3	0.1	0.0	2.6	2.2
Atlanta, GA	40.1	52.3	4.0	0.3	0.0	1.0	2.3
Austin, TX	75.0	7.6	7.0	0.5	0.1	6.7	3.1
Baton Rouge, LA	38.6	54.8	3.6	0.3	0.0	1.3	1.3
Billings, MT	90.1	0.9	0.6	4.4	0.1	0.8	3.0
Boise City, ID	88.8	1.9	3.3	0.7	0.1	1.6	3.5
Boston, MA	52.8	25.3	9.5	0.4	0.0	7.2	4.9
Boulder, CO	87.9	1.1	5.3	0.3	0.1	1.7	3.5
Cape Coral, FL	90.1	4.4	1.6	0.3	0.0	2.2	1.5
Cedar Rapids, IA	85.8	6.4	3.0	0.2	0.1	1.2	3.2
Charleston, SC	74.4	21.9	1.6	0.1	0.0	0.3	1.6
Charlotte, NC	50.0	35.0	6.2	0.3	0.1	5.5	2.9
Chicago, IL	49.1	30.5	6.2	0.3	0.0	11.2	2.6
Clarksville, TN	66.6	23.4	2.3	0.7	0.5	1.6	4.9
College Station, TX	77.5	8.1	9.8	0.3	0.0	1.7	2.5
Colorado Springs, CO	78.2	6.4	2.9	0.7	0.3	5.9	5.6
Columbia, MO	77.4	10.4	6.0	0.3	0.1	1.0	4.8
Columbia, SC	52.3	40.9	2.6	0.1	0.2	1.2	2.6
Columbus, OH	60.5	28.3	5.2	0.2	0.0	1.7	4.1
Dallas, TX	61.8	24.3	3.4	0.3	0.0	7.7	2.6
Denver, CO	76.9	9.5	3.6	1.0	0.1	5.5	3.4
Des Moines, IA	76.1	11.0	6.0	0.5	0.1	2.5	3.9
Durham, NC	48.0	39.7	5.2	0.3	0.0	3.9	3.0
Edison, NJ	36.4	7.1	49.0	0.3	0.0	4.0	3.3
El Paso, TX	82.0	3.8	1.3	0.6	0.1	9.8	2.4
Eugene, OR	84.0	1.9	4.3	1.0	0.3	3.0	5.4
Evansville, IN	81.7	12.6	0.7	0.3	0.2	1.2	3.3
Fargo, ND	86.2	5.5	3.6	1.1	0.0	0.6	2.9
Fayetteville, NC	45.9	41.5	2.9	0.9	0.3	2.6	5.8
Fort Collins, CO	89.0	1.6	3.1	0.8	0.1	1.9	3.6
Fort Wayne, IN	74.2	15.0	4.3	0.2	0.1	2.1	4.2
Fort Worth, TX	64.4	18.8	3.9	0.4	0.1	9.1	3.4
Gainesville, FL	66.0	22.0	6.9	0.3	0.1	0.9	3.8
Grand Rapids, MI	67.6	19.9	2.1	0.4	0.0	5.1	4.8
Greeley, CO	84.7	2.2	1.3	1.0	0.0	7.9	2.9
Green Bay, WI	77.4	3.8	4.0	3.5	0.0	6.4	4.9
Greensboro, NC	48.0	41.8	4.4	0.4	0.1	2.7	2.5
Honolulu, HI	17.7	1.7	54.1	0.1	8.1	0.9	17.4
Houston, TX	58.5	22.9	6.7	0.3	0.1	9.5	2.0
Huntsville, AL	62.3	30.8	2.6	0.3	0.1	1.3	2.5
Indianapolis, IN	61.8	28.1	3.0	0.3	0.0	3.8	3.0
Jacksonville, FL	59.2	31.0	4.8	0.2	0.1	1.5	3.3
Kansas City, MO	60.3	28.7	2.8	0.4	0.1	4.4	3.3
Lafayette, LA	63.5	31.7	2.1	0.2	0.0	0.6	1.9
Las Cruces, NM	87.1	2.6	1.7	1.5	0.0	4.2	2.9
Las Vegas, NV	62.7	12.2	6.7	0.7	0.7	12.3	4.8
Lexington, KY	75.6	14.5	3.6	0.3	0.1	2.7	3.2
Lincoln, NE	85.3	4.4	4.6	0.6	0.1	1.7	3.3
Little Rock, AR	50.8	41.6	3.1	0.2	0.1	1.7	2.6

Table continued on next page.

City	White Alone[1] (%)	Black Alone[1] (%)	Asian Alone[1] (%)	AIAN[2] Alone[1] (%)	NHOPI[3] Alone[1] (%)	Other Race Alone[1] (%)	Two or More Races (%)
Los Angeles, CA	52.2	8.9	11.7	0.7	0.2	22.9	3.5
Louisville, KY	70.5	23.2	2.5	0.1	0.1	0.7	2.9
Madison, WI	78.8	6.5	8.8	0.4	0.0	1.9	3.5
Manchester, NH	86.5	4.9	4.8	0.2	0.0	1.2	2.4
McAllen, TX	80.1	1.0	2.6	0.3	0.1	14.7	1.2
Miami, FL	75.4	18.4	0.9	0.3	0.0	3.3	1.7
Midland, TX	80.9	7.4	2.1	0.4	0.1	6.9	2.3
Minneapolis, MN	63.9	18.9	6.0	1.2	0.0	4.9	4.9
Nashville, TN	63.1	27.8	3.6	0.3	0.1	2.7	2.5
New Orleans, LA	34.1	59.8	3.0	0.2	0.0	1.2	1.8
New York, NY	42.8	24.3	14.0	0.4	0.1	15.1	3.3
Oklahoma City, OK	67.7	14.5	4.5	2.8	0.1	3.9	6.5
Omaha, NE	78.2	12.3	3.5	0.5	0.1	2.3	3.1
Orlando, FL	60.7	26.1	4.3	0.2	0.0	5.7	2.9
Peoria, IL	60.3	26.7	5.6	0.3	0.0	2.5	4.7
Philadelphia, PA	41.6	42.6	7.1	0.4	0.1	5.6	2.8
Phoenix, AZ	71.9	6.9	3.6	2.0	0.2	11.7	3.7
Pittsburgh, PA	66.6	23.6	5.6	0.2	0.0	0.5	3.4
Portland, OR	77.4	5.7	7.8	0.8	0.6	2.3	5.5
Providence, RI	52.9	15.6	6.2	1.3	0.2	19.5	4.2
Provo, UT	88.7	0.6	2.5	0.6	1.3	2.6	3.6
Raleigh, NC	59.0	28.9	4.6	0.3	0.1	4.6	2.6
Reno, NV	77.5	2.6	6.4	1.2	0.8	6.8	4.7
Richmond, VA	44.7	48.2	2.1	0.4	0.0	1.1	3.5
Roanoke, VA	63.0	28.3	3.0	0.2	0.2	1.9	3.4
Rochester, MN	80.7	7.4	7.3	0.4	0.0	1.2	3.0
Salem, OR	81.0	1.5	2.8	1.1	1.5	5.1	7.0
Salt Lake City, UT	73.7	2.0	5.4	1.3	1.7	12.8	3.1
San Antonio, TX	80.1	7.0	2.7	0.7	0.1	6.7	2.7
San Diego, CA	64.7	6.4	16.8	0.4	0.4	6.2	5.1
San Francisco, CA	47.2	5.3	34.2	0.4	0.4	7.5	5.1
San Jose, CA	40.7	3.0	34.8	0.6	0.4	15.5	5.1
Santa Rosa, CA	68.8	2.5	5.4	1.9	0.6	14.1	6.5
Savannah, GA	39.1	54.7	2.2	0.2	0.1	1.0	2.6
Seattle, WA	68.6	7.1	14.5	0.6	0.4	2.2	6.6
Sioux Falls, SD	85.0	5.4	2.3	2.4	0.0	1.8	3.1
Springfield, IL	73.2	19.9	2.8	0.1	0.0	0.8	3.2
Tallahassee, FL	56.9	35.2	4.2	0.2	0.0	1.0	2.5
Tampa, FL	65.2	24.2	4.2	0.3	0.1	2.6	3.4
Topeka, KS	78.9	10.4	1.5	0.8	0.1	2.9	5.4
Tyler, TX	67.8	24.8	2.4	0.3	0.2	2.6	1.9
Virginia Beach, VA	67.2	19.0	6.6	0.2	0.1	1.7	5.1
Visalia, CA	78.3	2.0	5.7	1.2	0.1	8.1	4.6
Washington, DC	40.7	47.7	3.8	0.3	0.0	4.6	2.9
Wilmington, NC	76.7	18.4	1.4	0.4	0.1	1.2	1.8
Winston-Salem, NC	56.2	34.7	2.2	0.3	0.1	4.1	2.3
U.S.	73.0	12.7	5.4	0.8	0.2	4.8	3.1

Note: (1) Alone is defined as not being in combination with one or more other races; (2) American Indian and Alaska Native; (3) Native Hawaiian and Other Pacific Islander
Source: U.S. Census Bureau, 2013-2017 American Community Survey 5-Year Estimates

Race: Metro Area

Metro Area	White Alone[1] (%)	Black Alone[1] (%)	Asian Alone[1] (%)	AIAN[2] Alone[1] (%)	NHOPI[3] Alone[1] (%)	Other Race Alone[1] (%)	Two or More Races (%)
Albany, NY	83.3	7.8	4.3	0.2	0.0	1.4	3.0
Albuquerque, NM	74.3	2.6	2.1	5.8	0.1	11.0	4.1
Allentown, PA	84.1	5.6	2.8	0.2	0.0	4.4	2.8
Anchorage, AK	68.6	4.4	7.3	6.7	1.8	1.8	9.4
Ann Arbor, MI	73.9	11.9	8.7	0.3	0.0	0.7	4.4
Athens, GA	72.0	20.1	3.6	0.1	0.0	2.1	2.0
Atlanta, GA	54.6	33.7	5.6	0.3	0.0	3.2	2.5
Austin, TX	77.7	7.3	5.5	0.4	0.1	5.8	3.3
Baton Rouge, LA	59.6	35.4	2.1	0.2	0.0	1.0	1.7
Billings, MT	91.3	0.7	0.6	4.0	0.1	0.6	2.7
Boise City, ID	89.8	1.0	2.0	0.8	0.2	3.3	3.0
Boston, MA	77.0	8.1	7.5	0.2	0.0	4.0	3.2
Boulder, CO	88.6	0.9	4.5	0.5	0.1	2.4	2.9
Cape Coral, FL	84.7	8.7	1.6	0.2	0.1	3.0	1.8
Cedar Rapids, IA	90.2	4.3	1.9	0.2	0.1	0.8	2.5
Charleston, SC	67.6	26.3	1.7	0.3	0.0	1.4	2.5
Charlotte, NC	67.9	22.3	3.4	0.3	0.0	3.5	2.4
Chicago, IL	66.0	16.7	6.3	0.2	0.0	8.1	2.5
Clarksville, TN	72.4	19.4	1.9	0.6	0.4	1.2	4.1
College Station, TX	75.2	11.2	5.2	0.4	0.0	5.0	2.9
Colorado Springs, CO	80.1	6.0	2.7	0.7	0.4	4.6	5.6
Columbia, MO	81.4	8.5	4.2	0.3	0.1	1.0	4.4
Columbia, SC	60.2	33.3	2.0	0.2	0.1	1.7	2.6
Columbus, OH	76.6	15.1	3.8	0.2	0.0	1.1	3.2
Dallas, TX	69.4	15.4	6.3	0.4	0.1	5.4	2.9
Denver, CO	81.7	5.6	4.1	0.8	0.1	4.3	3.5
Des Moines, IA	87.0	5.1	3.9	0.2	0.1	1.2	2.5
Durham, NC	61.9	26.8	4.8	0.3	0.0	3.3	2.8
Edison, NJ	58.3	17.1	10.9	0.3	0.0	10.5	2.9
El Paso, TX	81.1	3.4	1.1	0.7	0.1	11.2	2.3
Eugene, OR	87.7	1.1	2.6	1.1	0.2	2.3	5.0
Evansville, IN	88.6	6.8	1.3	0.2	0.1	0.8	2.3
Fargo, ND	89.3	3.9	2.5	1.1	0.0	0.6	2.6
Fayetteville, NC	50.3	36.1	2.3	2.3	0.2	2.9	5.8
Fort Collins, CO	91.2	0.9	2.1	0.6	0.1	1.9	3.2
Fort Wayne, IN	81.9	9.9	3.1	0.2	0.0	1.6	3.2
Fort Worth, TX	69.4	15.4	6.3	0.4	0.1	5.4	2.9
Gainesville, FL	70.9	19.3	5.5	0.3	0.1	0.8	3.1
Grand Rapids, MI	84.7	6.5	2.5	0.4	0.0	2.7	3.1
Greeley, CO	88.8	1.1	1.4	0.7	0.1	5.2	2.7
Green Bay, WI	87.3	1.9	2.6	2.1	0.0	3.2	2.8
Greensboro, NC	64.0	26.7	3.6	0.4	0.1	3.1	2.2
Honolulu, HI	21.1	2.3	42.9	0.1	9.4	1.0	23.2
Houston, TX	65.7	17.2	7.5	0.4	0.1	6.8	2.3
Huntsville, AL	71.2	21.9	2.3	0.7	0.1	1.1	2.8
Indianapolis, IN	77.3	14.9	2.9	0.2	0.0	2.2	2.4
Jacksonville, FL	70.0	21.5	3.8	0.2	0.1	1.3	3.1
Kansas City, MO	78.6	12.5	2.7	0.4	0.1	2.6	3.1
Lafayette, LA	70.7	24.6	1.7	0.2	0.0	0.9	2.0
Las Cruces, NM	88.3	1.8	1.0	1.1	0.0	5.9	1.9
Las Vegas, NV	61.6	11.2	9.6	0.6	0.7	11.2	5.0
Lexington, KY	81.2	10.9	2.6	0.3	0.0	2.2	2.8
Lincoln, NE	87.0	3.9	4.0	0.5	0.1	1.5	3.0
Little Rock, AR	71.1	23.0	1.6	0.3	0.1	1.4	2.5

Table continued on next page.

Metro Area	White Alone[1] (%)	Black Alone[1] (%)	Asian Alone[1] (%)	AIAN[2] Alone[1] (%)	NHOPI[3] Alone[1] (%)	Other Race Alone[1] (%)	Two or More Races (%)
Los Angeles, CA	54.2	6.7	15.7	0.6	0.3	18.7	3.8
Louisville, KY	80.3	14.2	1.9	0.2	0.0	0.8	2.6
Madison, WI	86.1	4.3	4.7	0.3	0.0	1.7	2.7
Manchester, NH	90.3	2.5	3.8	0.1	0.0	0.9	2.3
McAllen, TX	88.9	0.6	1.0	0.2	0.0	8.1	1.2
Miami, FL	70.9	21.4	2.5	0.2	0.0	2.9	2.2
Midland, TX	82.8	6.0	1.9	0.5	0.1	6.6	2.1
Minneapolis, MN	79.6	8.0	6.4	0.6	0.0	2.1	3.3
Nashville, TN	78.1	15.2	2.6	0.3	0.1	1.6	2.2
New Orleans, LA	57.8	35.0	2.9	0.3	0.0	2.0	1.9
New York, NY	58.3	17.1	10.9	0.3	0.0	10.5	2.9
Oklahoma City, OK	73.9	10.2	3.1	3.4	0.1	2.6	6.6
Omaha, NE	84.7	7.6	2.6	0.4	0.1	1.8	2.8
Orlando, FL	70.5	16.4	4.2	0.3	0.1	5.2	3.3
Peoria, IL	84.8	9.2	2.4	0.2	0.0	1.0	2.5
Philadelphia, PA	67.3	21.0	5.8	0.2	0.0	3.1	2.6
Phoenix, AZ	78.2	5.3	3.7	2.2	0.2	6.9	3.5
Pittsburgh, PA	86.9	8.1	2.2	0.1	0.0	0.3	2.3
Portland, OR	81.6	2.8	6.3	0.8	0.5	3.2	4.8
Providence, RI	82.5	5.6	3.0	0.4	0.1	5.6	2.9
Provo, UT	92.0	0.6	1.5	0.5	0.8	1.9	2.7
Raleigh, NC	68.2	19.9	5.3	0.4	0.0	3.4	2.7
Reno, NV	79.7	2.3	5.3	1.6	0.6	6.2	4.3
Richmond, VA	61.6	29.8	3.7	0.3	0.0	1.6	3.0
Roanoke, VA	81.3	13.1	2.1	0.2	0.1	1.0	2.2
Rochester, MN	88.3	4.1	4.3	0.3	0.0	0.8	2.2
Salem, OR	83.5	1.1	2.0	1.0	0.7	5.5	6.1
Salt Lake City, UT	80.7	1.7	3.7	0.8	1.5	8.7	3.0
San Antonio, TX	80.7	6.7	2.4	0.6	0.1	6.5	3.1
San Diego, CA	70.8	5.0	11.7	0.6	0.4	6.3	5.1
San Francisco, CA	50.9	7.5	25.3	0.5	0.7	9.2	5.9
San Jose, CA	46.6	2.5	34.2	0.5	0.4	11.0	4.9
Santa Rosa, CA	75.3	1.6	3.9	1.1	0.3	12.4	5.3
Savannah, GA	59.6	33.5	2.2	0.3	0.1	1.6	2.6
Seattle, WA	70.2	5.6	12.8	0.9	0.9	3.2	6.5
Sioux Falls, SD	88.7	3.8	1.6	1.9	0.0	1.3	2.6
Springfield, IL	83.1	12.0	1.8	0.1	0.1	0.6	2.3
Tallahassee, FL	61.2	33.0	2.6	0.2	0.0	0.9	2.1
Tampa, FL	78.4	12.0	3.3	0.3	0.1	2.9	2.9
Topeka, KS	85.5	6.2	1.0	1.1	0.1	1.8	4.4
Tyler, TX	76.9	17.6	1.6	0.4	0.1	1.9	1.6
Virginia Beach, VA	59.6	30.6	3.8	0.3	0.1	1.6	4.1
Visalia, CA	78.9	1.6	3.5	1.3	0.1	11.5	3.1
Washington, DC	54.6	25.4	9.9	0.3	0.1	5.8	3.9
Wilmington, NC	80.0	14.5	1.1	0.3	0.1	1.8	2.2
Winston-Salem, NC	76.0	17.7	1.7	0.3	0.1	2.4	1.8
U.S.	73.0	12.7	5.4	0.8	0.2	4.8	3.1

Note: (1) Figures cover the Metropolitan Statistical Area (MSA)—see Appendix B for areas included; (1) Alone is defined as not being in combination with one or more other races; (2) American Indian and Alaska Native; (3) Native Hawaiian & Other Pacific Islander
Source: U.S. Census Bureau, 2013-2017 American Community Survey 5-Year Estimates

Hispanic Origin: City

City	Hispanic or Latino (%)	Mexican (%)	Puerto Rican (%)	Cuban (%)	Other Hispanic or Latino (%)
Albany, NY	9.8	0.8	5.4	0.3	3.2
Albuquerque, NM	48.5	28.8	0.7	0.4	18.7
Allentown, PA	50.6	1.8	28.7	0.6	19.6
Anchorage, AK	8.9	5.0	1.1	0.1	2.6
Ann Arbor, MI	4.4	1.9	0.3	0.2	1.9
Athens, GA	10.7	6.9	0.9	0.3	2.7
Atlanta, GA	4.6	2.3	0.7	0.3	1.3
Austin, TX	34.5	28.3	0.8	0.6	4.8
Baton Rouge, LA	3.4	1.2	0.2	0.2	1.8
Billings, MT	6.3	4.5	0.4	0.2	1.2
Boise City, ID	8.7	7.2	0.2	0.1	1.2
Boston, MA	19.4	1.0	5.2	0.4	12.7
Boulder, CO	9.3	5.8	0.4	0.3	2.8
Cape Coral, FL	20.2	2.0	5.1	6.3	6.8
Cedar Rapids, IA	3.8	2.9	0.1	0.0	0.8
Charleston, SC	2.9	1.3	0.4	0.2	0.9
Charlotte, NC	14.0	5.6	1.0	0.5	6.8
Chicago, IL	29.0	21.7	3.8	0.3	3.2
Clarksville, TN	11.3	5.1	3.6	0.3	2.3
College Station, TX	14.8	11.0	0.4	0.4	3.1
Colorado Springs, CO	17.6	11.1	1.3	0.4	4.8
Columbia, MO	3.2	2.0	0.1	0.1	1.0
Columbia, SC	5.8	2.5	1.3	0.3	1.6
Columbus, OH	6.0	3.4	0.8	0.1	1.6
Dallas, TX	41.7	36.0	0.5	0.3	4.9
Denver, CO	30.5	24.7	0.6	0.2	5.0
Des Moines, IA	13.1	10.2	0.3	0.2	2.4
Durham, NC	14.0	6.8	0.9	0.2	6.0
Edison, NJ	9.6	1.3	2.5	0.8	5.0
El Paso, TX	80.8	76.4	1.1	0.1	3.1
Eugene, OR	9.5	7.4	0.4	0.1	1.6
Evansville, IN	3.0	2.5	0.2	0.0	0.2
Fargo, ND	2.8	1.8	0.3	0.0	0.7
Fayetteville, NC	12.0	4.2	3.8	0.4	3.6
Fort Collins, CO	11.8	8.2	0.4	0.1	3.0
Fort Wayne, IN	8.7	6.2	0.6	0.1	1.8
Fort Worth, TX	34.8	30.8	1.0	0.2	2.8
Gainesville, FL	10.7	1.3	3.1	2.4	4.0
Grand Rapids, MI	15.3	9.1	1.3	0.3	4.6
Greeley, CO	39.4	30.8	0.5	0.3	7.9
Green Bay, WI	14.4	10.9	1.4	0.2	2.0
Greensboro, NC	7.3	4.6	0.7	0.2	1.8
Honolulu, HI	7.0	1.9	1.8	0.2	3.0
Houston, TX	44.5	32.3	0.5	0.7	10.8
Huntsville, AL	5.5	3.5	0.6	0.1	1.2
Indianapolis, IN	10.1	7.1	0.6	0.2	2.2
Jacksonville, FL	9.1	1.9	2.9	1.1	3.2
Kansas City, MO	10.2	7.8	0.3	0.3	1.9
Lafayette, LA	4.1	1.9	0.4	0.2	1.6
Las Cruces, NM	58.6	53.1	0.7	0.1	4.8
Las Vegas, NV	32.7	24.7	1.0	1.3	5.6
Lexington, KY	7.0	4.7	0.8	0.2	1.3
Lincoln, NE	7.3	5.4	0.2	0.2	1.5
Little Rock, AR	6.8	4.5	0.4	0.2	1.6
Los Angeles, CA	48.7	32.7	0.5	0.4	15.2

Table continued on next page.

City	Hispanic or Latino (%)	Mexican (%)	Puerto Rican (%)	Cuban (%)	Other Hispanic or Latino (%)
Louisville, KY	5.2	2.2	0.4	1.5	1.0
Madison, WI	7.0	4.6	0.5	0.1	1.7
Manchester, NH	9.4	1.8	3.7	0.1	3.8
McAllen, TX	85.2	80.7	0.6	0.3	3.6
Miami, FL	72.2	1.9	3.4	35.6	31.3
Midland, TX	42.8	39.9	0.5	0.3	2.2
Minneapolis, MN	9.8	6.1	0.5	0.2	3.1
Nashville, TN	10.4	6.1	0.6	0.4	3.2
New Orleans, LA	5.5	1.2	0.3	0.4	3.7
New York, NY	29.1	4.0	8.4	0.5	16.2
Oklahoma City, OK	19.1	16.0	0.3	0.1	2.7
Omaha, NE	13.7	10.6	0.3	0.2	2.5
Orlando, FL	29.7	1.7	14.9	2.7	10.3
Peoria, IL	6.0	4.7	0.3	0.1	0.9
Philadelphia, PA	14.1	1.3	8.7	0.3	3.9
Phoenix, AZ	42.5	38.6	0.6	0.3	2.9
Pittsburgh, PA	2.9	0.9	0.8	0.2	1.1
Portland, OR	9.7	7.1	0.4	0.3	1.9
Providence, RI	42.0	1.8	8.2	0.3	31.7
Provo, UT	16.3	11.2	0.3	0.2	4.6
Raleigh, NC	11.0	5.5	0.9	0.3	4.3
Reno, NV	25.2	19.5	0.5	0.2	5.0
Richmond, VA	6.5	1.8	0.7	0.2	3.8
Roanoke, VA	6.0	2.3	0.9	0.6	2.3
Rochester, MN	5.8	4.0	0.5	0.1	1.2
Salem, OR	22.4	20.0	0.5	0.1	1.8
Salt Lake City, UT	21.3	17.0	0.3	0.2	3.8
San Antonio, TX	64.0	57.6	1.1	0.2	5.0
San Diego, CA	30.0	26.4	0.7	0.2	2.7
San Francisco, CA	15.3	7.8	0.6	0.3	6.6
San Jose, CA	32.3	28.1	0.5	0.2	3.5
Santa Rosa, CA	31.8	28.2	0.6	0.1	3.0
Savannah, GA	4.8	1.8	1.2	0.3	1.5
Seattle, WA	6.5	3.8	0.4	0.3	2.0
Sioux Falls, SD	5.0	2.9	0.3	0.0	1.8
Springfield, IL	2.6	1.5	0.5	0.1	0.5
Tallahassee, FL	6.8	1.2	1.5	1.4	2.7
Tampa, FL	25.1	3.3	7.7	7.4	6.8
Topeka, KS	14.3	12.3	0.7	0.1	1.2
Tyler, TX	22.3	19.9	0.4	0.1	1.9
Virginia Beach, VA	7.8	2.3	2.4	0.3	2.8
Visalia, CA	50.3	47.7	0.3	0.1	2.1
Washington, DC	10.7	2.0	0.7	0.4	7.5
Wilmington, NC	6.3	3.2	0.5	0.2	2.5
Winston-Salem, NC	14.9	9.4	1.5	0.2	3.7
U.S.	17.6	11.1	1.7	0.7	4.1

Note: Persons of Hispanic or Latino origin can be of any race
Source: U.S. Census Bureau, 2013-2017 American Community Survey 5-Year Estimates

Hispanic Origin: Metro Area

Metro Area	Hispanic or Latino (%)	Mexican (%)	Puerto Rican (%)	Cuban (%)	Other Hispanic or Latino (%)
Albany, NY	4.9	0.7	2.3	0.2	1.6
Albuquerque, NM	48.5	28.6	0.6	0.3	19.0
Allentown, PA	15.8	1.2	8.7	0.3	5.5
Anchorage, AK	7.8	4.4	1.0	0.1	2.3
Ann Arbor, MI	4.5	2.4	0.3	0.2	1.7
Athens, GA	8.3	5.2	0.7	0.2	2.2
Atlanta, GA	10.5	5.8	1.0	0.4	3.4
Austin, TX	32.2	26.9	0.8	0.5	4.0
Baton Rouge, LA	3.8	1.7	0.3	0.1	1.6
Billings, MT	5.2	3.9	0.3	0.1	0.9
Boise City, ID	13.3	11.5	0.3	0.1	1.4
Boston, MA	10.6	0.7	2.8	0.2	6.8
Boulder, CO	13.8	10.3	0.4	0.3	2.8
Cape Coral, FL	20.2	5.8	4.3	3.9	6.2
Cedar Rapids, IA	2.8	2.1	0.1	0.0	0.6
Charleston, SC	5.4	2.8	0.8	0.1	1.6
Charlotte, NC	9.8	4.8	0.9	0.4	3.8
Chicago, IL	21.8	17.2	2.1	0.2	2.2
Clarksville, TN	8.7	4.3	2.4	0.3	1.7
College Station, TX	24.4	21.0	0.2	0.2	3.0
Colorado Springs, CO	16.1	9.9	1.5	0.3	4.4
Columbia, MO	3.3	2.2	0.1	0.2	0.8
Columbia, SC	5.4	2.8	1.0	0.2	1.4
Columbus, OH	3.9	2.1	0.6	0.1	1.2
Dallas, TX	28.4	23.8	0.7	0.2	3.7
Denver, CO	22.9	17.6	0.5	0.2	4.6
Des Moines, IA	7.2	5.4	0.2	0.1	1.4
Durham, NC	11.4	6.2	0.7	0.2	4.3
Edison, NJ	24.1	3.1	6.3	0.7	14.0
El Paso, TX	82.2	78.0	1.1	0.1	3.0
Eugene, OR	8.4	6.5	0.3	0.1	1.5
Evansville, IN	2.2	1.6	0.2	0.1	0.4
Fargo, ND	3.0	2.1	0.2	0.0	0.6
Fayetteville, NC	11.4	4.5	3.8	0.3	2.9
Fort Collins, CO	11.2	8.5	0.3	0.1	2.4
Fort Wayne, IN	6.5	4.6	0.5	0.1	1.3
Fort Worth, TX	28.4	23.8	0.7	0.2	3.7
Gainesville, FL	9.0	1.5	2.5	1.8	3.2
Grand Rapids, MI	9.2	6.5	0.8	0.3	1.7
Greeley, CO	29.0	23.5	0.4	0.2	4.9
Green Bay, WI	7.2	5.4	0.8	0.1	0.9
Greensboro, NC	8.1	5.7	0.6	0.2	1.6
Honolulu, HI	9.6	2.8	3.0	0.2	3.6
Houston, TX	36.7	27.8	0.6	0.5	7.7
Huntsville, AL	5.0	3.1	0.7	0.2	1.0
Indianapolis, IN	6.5	4.5	0.4	0.1	1.5
Jacksonville, FL	8.2	1.8	2.7	1.0	2.7
Kansas City, MO	8.8	6.8	0.3	0.2	1.5
Lafayette, LA	3.9	2.2	0.3	0.1	1.2
Las Cruces, NM	67.7	63.2	0.5	0.2	3.8
Las Vegas, NV	30.7	23.0	1.1	1.3	5.3
Lexington, KY	6.0	4.1	0.6	0.1	1.2
Lincoln, NE	6.5	4.7	0.2	0.2	1.4
Little Rock, AR	5.1	3.6	0.3	0.1	1.1
Los Angeles, CA	45.0	35.1	0.4	0.4	9.1

Table continued on next page.

Metro Area	Hispanic or Latino (%)	Mexican (%)	Puerto Rican (%)	Cuban (%)	Other Hispanic or Latino (%)
Louisville, KY	4.5	2.3	0.4	0.8	0.9
Madison, WI	5.7	3.8	0.4	0.1	1.3
Manchester, NH	6.3	1.4	2.1	0.2	2.6
McAllen, TX	91.8	88.7	0.3	0.1	2.7
Miami, FL	44.2	2.5	3.9	18.9	18.9
Midland, TX	43.3	40.6	0.5	0.3	1.9
Minneapolis, MN	5.7	3.8	0.3	0.1	1.5
Nashville, TN	7.0	4.4	0.5	0.2	1.9
New Orleans, LA	8.7	1.9	0.5	0.6	5.7
New York, NY	24.1	3.1	6.3	0.7	14.0
Oklahoma City, OK	12.8	10.5	0.3	0.1	1.9
Omaha, NE	10.1	7.8	0.3	0.1	1.8
Orlando, FL	29.0	2.9	14.8	2.2	9.1
Peoria, IL	3.4	2.6	0.2	0.1	0.5
Philadelphia, PA	9.0	1.8	4.5	0.2	2.5
Phoenix, AZ	30.5	27.1	0.7	0.2	2.5
Pittsburgh, PA	1.6	0.5	0.5	0.1	0.6
Portland, OR	11.6	9.3	0.3	0.2	1.8
Providence, RI	12.1	0.8	3.9	0.2	7.2
Provo, UT	11.2	7.7	0.2	0.1	3.3
Raleigh, NC	10.4	5.7	1.1	0.3	3.2
Reno, NV	23.7	18.6	0.5	0.2	4.5
Richmond, VA	5.8	1.6	1.0	0.2	3.1
Roanoke, VA	3.7	1.7	0.5	0.3	1.2
Rochester, MN	4.3	3.1	0.3	0.1	0.8
Salem, OR	23.6	21.3	0.5	0.1	1.7
Salt Lake City, UT	17.6	13.1	0.4	0.1	4.0
San Antonio, TX	55.1	49.1	1.2	0.2	4.5
San Diego, CA	33.4	29.8	0.7	0.2	2.7
San Francisco, CA	21.9	14.4	0.7	0.2	6.6
San Jose, CA	27.0	23.0	0.5	0.1	3.4
Santa Rosa, CA	26.4	22.6	0.5	0.1	3.2
Savannah, GA	5.9	2.7	1.4	0.2	1.6
Seattle, WA	9.7	6.9	0.5	0.2	2.1
Sioux Falls, SD	4.0	2.3	0.2	0.0	1.4
Springfield, IL	2.2	1.3	0.4	0.1	0.4
Tallahassee, FL	6.3	1.8	1.3	1.1	2.2
Tampa, FL	18.4	3.7	6.1	3.7	5.0
Topeka, KS	9.9	8.5	0.5	0.1	0.8
Tyler, TX	19.0	17.2	0.4	0.1	1.4
Virginia Beach, VA	6.4	2.0	2.0	0.3	2.1
Visalia, CA	63.6	61.4	0.2	0.1	1.8
Washington, DC	15.3	2.2	1.0	0.3	11.7
Wilmington, NC	5.7	3.2	0.5	0.2	1.8
Winston-Salem, NC	10.0	6.5	0.9	0.2	2.4
U.S.	17.6	11.1	1.7	0.7	4.1

Note: Persons of Hispanic or Latino origin can be of any race; Figures cover the Metropolitan Statistical Area (MSA)—see Appendix B for areas included
Source: U.S. Census Bureau, 2013-2017 American Community Survey 5-Year Estimates

Age: City

City	Under Age 5	Age 5–19	Age 20–34	Age 35–44	Age 45–54	Age 55–64	Age 65–74	Age 75–84	Age 85+	Median Age
Albany, NY	5.5	18.1	32.4	10.5	10.6	10.3	6.7	3.4	2.4	30.9
Albuquerque, NM	6.3	19.2	22.9	12.9	12.4	12.2	8.1	4.3	1.7	36.2
Allentown, PA	7.6	22.8	24.4	12.3	11.4	9.8	6.1	3.7	2.0	31.8
Anchorage, AK	7.4	19.7	25.7	12.8	12.9	12.0	6.2	2.3	0.9	33.1
Ann Arbor, MI	4.1	18.9	38.7	9.5	8.7	8.9	6.5	3.2	1.6	27.5
Athens, GA	5.5	20.9	35.2	11.0	8.8	8.8	5.8	2.7	1.3	27.2
Atlanta, GA	5.8	16.8	30.1	14.2	12.2	9.6	6.8	3.2	1.3	33.5
Austin, TX	6.7	17.3	30.3	15.7	12.0	9.6	5.2	2.2	1.0	32.7
Baton Rouge, LA	6.6	19.1	29.7	10.2	10.4	11.0	7.4	3.8	1.7	31.1
Billings, MT	6.5	18.4	22.2	12.3	11.7	12.6	8.6	4.9	2.6	37.0
Boise City, ID	5.8	19.4	23.4	13.7	12.5	12.2	7.8	3.4	1.9	36.0
Boston, MA	5.2	15.7	34.6	12.5	11.1	9.9	6.2	3.2	1.5	32.0
Boulder, CO	3.4	18.8	37.0	11.4	9.9	9.2	6.0	2.7	1.8	28.6
Cape Coral, FL	4.5	17.5	15.1	11.5	14.7	14.9	12.8	6.1	3.0	45.9
Cedar Rapids, IA	6.9	19.0	22.9	12.7	12.2	12.1	7.6	4.4	2.3	36.0
Charleston, SC	5.9	15.4	29.8	12.2	10.7	12.2	8.6	3.4	1.9	34.4
Charlotte, NC	6.9	19.8	24.9	15.2	13.1	10.3	5.9	2.7	1.1	33.9
Chicago, IL	6.6	17.6	27.4	14.0	12.1	10.7	6.7	3.5	1.4	34.1
Clarksville, TN	9.2	20.5	31.0	12.7	10.3	8.2	5.0	2.4	0.6	29.4
College Station, TX	5.3	22.7	44.7	8.7	6.9	5.8	3.7	1.6	0.7	22.7
Colorado Springs, CO	6.7	19.7	24.2	12.6	12.5	11.6	7.5	3.7	1.5	34.6
Columbia, MO	5.9	18.7	36.0	10.8	9.6	9.2	5.5	3.0	1.3	27.6
Columbia, SC	5.1	23.0	32.3	10.5	10.0	9.4	5.8	2.8	1.2	28.3
Columbus, OH	7.4	18.4	29.2	13.1	11.9	10.4	5.8	2.6	1.3	32.2
Dallas, TX	7.8	20.0	26.3	13.9	12.0	10.3	5.8	2.8	1.2	32.5
Denver, CO	6.4	16.0	28.7	15.7	11.6	10.3	6.6	3.1	1.6	34.4
Des Moines, IA	7.3	20.1	24.1	13.0	12.2	11.6	6.7	3.3	1.6	33.9
Durham, NC	7.0	18.5	26.9	14.3	12.0	10.6	6.5	2.8	1.5	33.6
Edison, NJ	6.2	17.5	19.3	15.6	14.1	13.3	7.8	4.1	2.0	39.3
El Paso, TX	7.6	22.5	22.7	12.5	12.0	10.5	6.7	3.9	1.6	32.8
Eugene, OR	4.7	18.0	28.4	11.8	10.6	11.5	8.8	3.7	2.5	34.1
Evansville, IN	6.4	17.6	23.2	11.8	12.6	12.9	8.2	4.5	2.8	37.2
Fargo, ND	6.9	17.8	32.7	11.2	10.1	10.2	5.7	3.4	2.0	30.3
Fayetteville, NC	7.5	19.2	30.7	11.0	10.3	9.9	6.3	3.6	1.3	30.0
Fort Collins, CO	5.4	19.5	33.7	11.9	9.9	9.5	5.8	2.9	1.4	29.2
Fort Wayne, IN	7.2	21.1	22.0	12.3	12.2	11.9	7.9	3.6	1.9	34.9
Fort Worth, TX	8.1	23.0	23.5	14.0	12.4	9.8	5.6	2.6	1.1	32.2
Gainesville, FL	3.8	18.8	42.0	8.7	8.1	9.0	5.6	2.7	1.5	26.0
Grand Rapids, MI	7.4	19.4	29.6	11.3	10.3	10.6	5.7	3.4	2.4	31.1
Greeley, CO	6.9	23.9	24.5	11.9	10.9	10.1	6.5	3.5	1.7	30.7
Green Bay, WI	7.8	19.8	24.0	11.9	12.5	11.8	6.7	3.6	1.9	34.0
Greensboro, NC	6.2	19.6	24.3	12.7	12.7	11.3	7.7	3.8	1.8	35.0
Honolulu, HI	5.2	14.1	22.4	12.8	13.3	12.9	9.7	5.6	4.0	41.4
Houston, TX	7.8	19.8	26.0	14.0	12.0	10.3	6.0	2.9	1.2	32.9
Huntsville, AL	6.6	17.7	23.4	11.5	13.0	12.7	8.3	5.0	1.9	36.9
Indianapolis, IN	7.4	19.7	24.1	12.9	12.6	11.8	6.6	3.4	1.5	34.1
Jacksonville, FL	6.9	18.5	23.4	12.7	13.3	12.3	7.7	3.4	1.6	35.8
Kansas City, MO	7.0	18.4	24.4	13.2	12.8	12.0	7.3	3.5	1.7	35.2
Lafayette, LA	5.6	19.0	25.9	11.0	12.5	12.9	7.4	4.1	1.6	34.7
Las Cruces, NM	6.8	20.7	26.2	10.7	10.2	10.5	8.2	4.8	1.8	32.6
Las Vegas, NV	6.4	19.9	20.5	13.7	13.6	11.7	8.6	4.2	1.3	37.4
Lexington, KY	6.2	18.4	26.4	13.2	12.2	11.4	7.2	3.4	1.6	34.3
Lincoln, NE	6.7	19.9	26.9	12.2	10.7	11.1	7.2	3.6	1.7	32.4
Little Rock, AR	6.5	19.5	22.4	13.3	12.0	13.0	7.8	3.4	2.0	36.0

Table continued on next page.

| City | Percent of Population | | | | | | | | | Median Age |
	Under Age 5	Age 5–19	Age 20–34	Age 35–44	Age 45–54	Age 55–64	Age 65–74	Age 75–84	Age 85+	
Los Angeles, CA	6.2	17.9	25.6	14.5	13.3	10.9	6.5	3.5	1.7	35.2
Louisville, KY	6.6	18.7	21.6	12.4	13.3	13.2	8.0	4.1	1.9	37.2
Madison, WI	5.2	16.4	35.3	12.0	10.3	9.8	6.4	3.1	1.6	31.0
Manchester, NH	5.6	16.2	25.8	12.6	14.0	12.4	7.2	3.7	2.3	36.5
McAllen, TX	7.9	23.8	21.2	13.4	11.4	9.8	6.7	4.2	1.5	32.9
Miami, FL	6.2	13.4	22.8	15.1	14.3	11.5	8.6	5.3	2.7	40.0
Midland, TX	8.5	21.3	24.6	12.6	11.5	10.8	5.6	3.3	1.7	32.1
Minneapolis, MN	6.7	16.8	32.1	13.7	11.5	10.1	5.8	2.3	1.1	32.1
Nashville, TN	6.9	17.1	27.3	13.8	12.2	11.4	6.6	3.3	1.3	34.1
New Orleans, LA	6.0	16.8	25.7	12.8	12.6	13.1	7.8	3.5	1.6	35.9
New York, NY	6.5	16.7	24.9	13.8	13.0	11.5	7.6	4.1	1.9	36.2
Oklahoma City, OK	7.8	20.2	23.4	13.2	12.0	11.5	7.0	3.4	1.5	34.1
Omaha, NE	7.3	20.6	23.2	12.5	12.4	11.9	7.1	3.5	1.7	34.3
Orlando, FL	7.1	16.2	29.6	14.9	12.2	9.6	6.3	2.8	1.4	33.3
Peoria, IL	7.6	20.4	22.9	11.8	11.4	11.6	7.9	4.1	2.3	34.3
Philadelphia, PA	6.9	18.1	26.3	12.2	12.0	11.5	7.2	3.9	1.8	34.1
Phoenix, AZ	7.5	21.8	23.1	13.9	13.0	10.5	6.1	2.7	1.2	33.3
Pittsburgh, PA	4.9	15.6	33.0	10.4	10.1	11.8	7.5	4.3	2.5	32.9
Portland, OR	5.6	14.8	26.0	16.9	13.0	11.7	7.4	3.0	1.6	36.8
Providence, RI	6.3	21.9	29.5	12.4	11.0	9.2	5.2	2.8	1.6	29.8
Provo, UT	8.0	20.9	46.2	8.2	5.5	5.3	3.0	2.0	0.9	23.7
Raleigh, NC	6.2	19.4	27.6	14.9	12.7	9.5	5.8	2.7	1.2	33.1
Reno, NV	6.4	18.4	24.5	12.4	12.7	11.8	8.5	3.8	1.5	35.5
Richmond, VA	6.1	16.0	30.4	11.5	11.9	12.3	7.0	3.3	1.8	33.5
Roanoke, VA	6.9	17.0	21.7	12.8	13.0	13.2	8.7	4.0	2.7	38.4
Rochester, MN	7.3	18.9	22.9	12.8	12.4	11.4	7.4	4.5	2.2	35.5
Salem, OR	6.7	20.6	22.5	13.4	12.3	11.2	7.6	3.7	2.1	35.2
Salt Lake City, UT	6.8	16.8	32.0	13.5	10.3	9.8	6.2	3.0	1.3	31.9
San Antonio, TX	7.1	21.3	24.1	13.2	12.2	10.6	6.7	3.4	1.5	33.2
San Diego, CA	6.3	17.0	27.9	13.6	12.5	10.8	6.8	3.5	1.7	34.3
San Francisco, CA	4.5	10.4	28.9	15.9	13.5	11.9	7.9	4.5	2.4	38.3
San Jose, CA	6.4	18.8	22.5	14.8	14.0	11.5	6.8	3.6	1.5	36.4
Santa Rosa, CA	6.0	18.6	21.2	13.0	12.6	12.8	8.9	4.2	2.5	38.1
Savannah, GA	6.5	19.3	28.3	11.3	10.8	10.8	7.2	3.7	1.9	32.3
Seattle, WA	4.9	13.0	30.8	15.8	12.4	11.1	7.1	3.1	1.9	35.7
Sioux Falls, SD	7.7	19.7	23.8	13.2	11.9	11.9	6.9	3.3	1.8	34.3
Springfield, IL	6.1	18.5	20.7	11.6	12.9	13.9	9.0	4.7	2.4	38.9
Tallahassee, FL	5.0	19.1	39.0	10.0	8.5	8.9	5.7	2.7	1.2	26.6
Tampa, FL	6.2	18.9	23.9	13.4	13.8	11.4	7.2	3.5	1.5	35.6
Topeka, KS	7.2	18.8	21.2	11.6	12.3	12.9	8.7	4.9	2.7	37.2
Tyler, TX	7.4	20.4	24.6	10.7	10.9	10.9	7.6	5.3	2.3	33.4
Virginia Beach, VA	6.5	18.5	24.2	12.9	13.4	11.8	7.5	3.6	1.6	35.6
Visalia, CA	9.0	24.1	21.0	12.9	11.4	10.1	6.9	3.0	1.6	31.9
Washington, DC	6.5	14.3	31.5	14.2	11.4	10.3	6.8	3.4	1.7	33.9
Wilmington, NC	4.6	17.2	26.9	11.9	11.7	12.2	9.0	4.3	2.3	36.0
Winston-Salem, NC	6.7	20.9	22.1	12.5	12.4	11.8	7.7	4.3	1.8	35.3
U.S.	6.2	19.5	20.7	12.7	13.4	12.7	8.6	4.4	1.9	37.8

Source: U.S. Census Bureau, 2013-2017 American Community Survey 5-Year Estimates

Age: Metro Area

Metro Area	Percent of Population									Median Age
	Under Age 5	Age 5–19	Age 20–34	Age 35–44	Age 45–54	Age 55–64	Age 65–74	Age 75–84	Age 85+	
Albany, NY	5.3	18.3	20.6	11.9	14.2	13.7	9.2	4.5	2.4	40.0
Albuquerque, NM	5.9	19.6	20.9	12.5	12.9	13.1	9.0	4.4	1.6	37.7
Allentown, PA	5.3	18.9	18.4	12.0	14.5	13.9	9.3	5.0	2.7	41.3
Anchorage, AK	7.4	20.4	24.4	12.9	13.0	12.3	6.4	2.4	0.8	33.5
Ann Arbor, MI	5.1	19.8	27.3	11.5	12.3	11.6	7.6	3.4	1.5	33.4
Athens, GA	5.5	21.0	27.5	12.1	11.1	10.6	7.4	3.3	1.4	31.8
Atlanta, GA	6.5	21.4	20.6	14.4	14.5	11.4	7.1	3.0	1.1	36.1
Austin, TX	6.6	20.1	24.6	15.4	12.9	10.5	6.2	2.6	1.0	34.2
Baton Rouge, LA	6.6	20.3	23.3	12.5	12.6	12.0	7.8	3.6	1.3	34.9
Billings, MT	6.3	19.0	19.5	12.2	12.8	13.9	9.3	4.7	2.2	39.0
Boise City, ID	6.6	22.2	20.0	13.4	12.7	11.7	8.2	3.6	1.5	35.8
Boston, MA	5.4	18.0	22.0	12.6	14.4	13.0	8.3	4.3	2.1	38.7
Boulder, CO	4.8	19.6	24.0	12.8	13.4	12.7	7.7	3.4	1.5	36.2
Cape Coral, FL	4.8	15.5	15.9	10.5	12.3	14.0	15.2	8.6	3.2	47.8
Cedar Rapids, IA	6.2	19.9	19.8	12.6	13.5	12.8	8.4	4.6	2.3	38.1
Charleston, SC	6.2	18.6	22.7	12.9	13.2	12.6	8.7	3.6	1.5	36.6
Charlotte, NC	6.4	20.5	20.0	14.3	14.4	11.8	7.8	3.6	1.3	37.3
Chicago, IL	6.2	19.9	21.2	13.4	13.7	12.5	7.7	3.9	1.8	37.0
Clarksville, TN	8.7	20.8	27.8	12.5	10.9	9.3	6.0	3.1	1.0	30.5
College Station, TX	6.2	20.9	33.8	10.5	9.7	8.9	5.8	2.8	1.3	27.2
Colorado Springs, CO	6.8	20.6	23.4	12.5	12.8	12.0	7.4	3.4	1.2	34.4
Columbia, MO	6.0	19.5	30.6	11.4	11.0	10.7	6.5	3.3	1.2	30.6
Columbia, SC	5.9	20.4	21.9	12.5	13.1	12.5	8.4	3.8	1.4	36.3
Columbus, OH	6.7	19.9	22.2	13.5	13.4	12.0	7.4	3.5	1.5	35.8
Dallas, TX	7.1	22.1	21.3	14.3	13.7	11.0	6.5	3.0	1.1	34.6
Denver, CO	6.3	19.4	22.2	14.6	13.6	12.1	7.3	3.2	1.4	36.3
Des Moines, IA	7.2	20.7	21.1	13.6	13.2	11.6	7.2	3.6	1.7	35.7
Durham, NC	5.9	18.8	23.0	13.3	13.0	12.4	8.3	3.7	1.7	36.7
Edison, NJ	6.1	18.0	21.4	13.2	14.1	12.5	8.1	4.4	2.2	38.2
El Paso, TX	7.9	23.3	23.0	12.6	11.7	10.2	6.3	3.6	1.4	31.9
Eugene, OR	5.0	17.3	22.4	11.6	11.9	14.0	10.6	4.8	2.4	39.4
Evansville, IN	6.1	19.2	19.7	11.9	13.2	14.0	9.0	4.7	2.2	39.3
Fargo, ND	7.1	19.5	27.7	12.2	11.2	10.8	6.1	3.4	1.8	32.3
Fayetteville, NC	7.9	20.5	27.4	12.0	11.4	10.2	6.4	3.2	1.1	31.2
Fort Collins, CO	5.4	18.7	25.1	12.1	11.7	12.8	8.6	3.9	1.6	35.7
Fort Wayne, IN	7.0	21.3	19.8	12.3	12.9	12.7	8.1	3.9	2.0	36.4
Fort Worth, TX	7.1	22.1	21.3	14.3	13.7	11.0	6.5	3.0	1.1	34.6
Gainesville, FL	5.4	18.4	30.6	10.5	10.5	11.4	7.9	3.6	1.8	31.7
Grand Rapids, MI	6.6	21.0	21.4	12.1	13.1	12.4	7.6	3.8	1.9	35.7
Greeley, CO	7.3	22.4	21.3	13.4	12.6	11.6	7.0	3.1	1.2	34.2
Green Bay, WI	6.3	19.8	19.4	12.4	14.2	13.4	8.2	4.3	1.9	38.5
Greensboro, NC	5.8	19.7	19.8	12.6	14.1	12.8	8.9	4.5	1.8	38.8
Honolulu, HI	6.5	17.2	23.0	12.6	12.5	11.9	8.8	4.8	2.8	37.6
Houston, TX	7.5	22.0	21.9	14.2	13.1	11.1	6.4	2.8	1.0	34.0
Huntsville, AL	5.8	19.3	20.4	12.5	15.0	12.9	8.2	4.4	1.5	38.4
Indianapolis, IN	6.8	20.7	20.7	13.4	13.6	12.2	7.5	3.7	1.6	36.3
Jacksonville, FL	6.2	18.8	20.9	12.7	13.8	13.1	8.9	4.0	1.7	38.1
Kansas City, MO	6.7	20.3	20.1	13.2	13.4	12.7	8.0	4.0	1.8	37.1
Lafayette, LA	7.0	20.3	21.9	12.4	12.9	12.5	7.5	3.8	1.5	35.4
Las Cruces, NM	6.9	22.2	23.7	10.7	11.0	11.0	8.3	4.6	1.5	32.9
Las Vegas, NV	6.4	19.5	21.4	14.0	13.5	11.6	8.6	3.9	1.3	36.9
Lexington, KY	6.3	19.2	23.4	13.2	13.0	12.0	7.8	3.6	1.6	35.8
Lincoln, NE	6.6	20.3	25.3	12.1	11.3	11.5	7.4	3.7	1.8	33.3
Little Rock, AR	6.6	19.9	21.6	13.0	12.7	12.3	8.4	4.0	1.7	36.5

Table continued on next page.

Metro Area	Percent of Population									Median Age
	Under Age 5	Age 5–19	Age 20–34	Age 35–44	Age 45–54	Age 55–64	Age 65–74	Age 75–84	Age 85+	
Los Angeles, CA	6.2	19.0	22.8	13.7	13.9	11.6	7.2	3.8	1.8	36.4
Louisville, KY	6.2	19.0	19.7	12.9	13.9	13.5	8.7	4.2	1.9	38.8
Madison, WI	5.8	18.5	24.4	12.8	13.0	12.4	7.8	3.6	1.7	35.9
Manchester, NH	5.4	18.4	19.3	12.5	15.8	14.2	8.4	4.1	1.9	40.5
McAllen, TX	9.6	27.2	21.0	13.0	10.6	8.1	5.8	3.4	1.2	28.9
Miami, FL	5.6	17.1	19.6	13.3	14.6	12.4	9.0	5.5	2.7	40.7
Midland, TX	8.6	22.0	24.3	12.4	11.3	11.0	5.6	3.2	1.5	31.8
Minneapolis, MN	6.6	19.9	21.0	13.1	14.0	12.7	7.4	3.6	1.7	36.8
Nashville, TN	6.5	19.6	22.0	13.7	13.7	12.1	7.6	3.5	1.3	36.3
New Orleans, LA	6.2	18.4	21.6	12.6	13.4	13.5	8.5	4.0	1.7	37.7
New York, NY	6.1	18.0	21.4	13.2	14.1	12.5	8.1	4.4	2.2	38.2
Oklahoma City, OK	7.1	20.5	22.6	12.8	12.2	11.9	7.6	3.8	1.5	34.9
Omaha, NE	7.3	21.0	21.1	13.0	12.9	12.0	7.4	3.6	1.6	35.4
Orlando, FL	5.9	19.0	22.3	13.6	13.6	11.6	8.2	4.1	1.7	36.9
Peoria, IL	6.5	19.5	19.0	12.3	12.9	13.4	9.1	5.0	2.5	39.0
Philadelphia, PA	5.9	18.9	20.8	12.3	14.0	13.2	8.3	4.4	2.2	38.6
Phoenix, AZ	6.6	20.6	21.0	13.2	12.7	11.3	8.5	4.3	1.7	36.2
Pittsburgh, PA	5.1	16.7	19.2	11.4	13.8	15.1	10.0	5.7	3.0	43.0
Portland, OR	6.0	18.5	21.2	14.6	13.5	12.7	8.3	3.6	1.7	37.8
Providence, RI	5.2	18.3	20.4	12.0	14.5	13.7	8.9	4.6	2.6	40.2
Provo, UT	10.0	28.5	26.9	12.3	8.3	6.6	4.3	2.3	0.7	24.6
Raleigh, NC	6.4	21.1	20.5	15.1	14.6	11.3	6.9	3.0	1.1	36.3
Reno, NV	6.0	18.5	21.3	12.2	13.4	13.4	9.7	4.0	1.5	38.2
Richmond, VA	5.9	18.9	20.6	12.8	14.2	13.2	8.6	3.9	1.8	38.5
Roanoke, VA	5.5	17.6	18.0	11.8	14.0	14.4	10.8	5.5	2.4	42.6
Rochester, MN	6.8	19.8	19.2	12.4	13.3	13.3	8.2	4.8	2.2	38.4
Salem, OR	6.6	21.2	20.4	12.3	12.1	12.3	8.8	4.3	2.0	36.3
Salt Lake City, UT	8.0	22.8	23.6	14.3	11.3	10.1	5.9	2.8	1.1	32.3
San Antonio, TX	7.0	21.6	22.1	13.2	12.7	11.1	7.3	3.6	1.4	34.4
San Diego, CA	6.5	18.5	24.4	13.2	12.9	11.6	7.3	3.8	1.8	35.4
San Francisco, CA	5.6	16.7	21.9	14.5	14.2	12.6	8.2	4.1	2.1	38.8
San Jose, CA	6.3	18.9	21.9	14.7	14.2	11.5	7.0	3.8	1.7	36.9
Santa Rosa, CA	5.2	17.6	19.3	12.3	13.5	14.6	10.5	4.6	2.3	41.4
Savannah, GA	6.7	19.8	23.5	12.8	12.4	11.7	8.0	3.6	1.6	35.0
Seattle, WA	6.2	17.9	22.7	14.2	13.9	12.5	7.5	3.4	1.6	37.1
Sioux Falls, SD	7.7	20.5	21.8	13.2	12.5	11.9	7.1	3.4	1.9	35.0
Springfield, IL	5.8	19.3	18.6	12.2	13.7	14.1	9.3	4.8	2.2	40.2
Tallahassee, FL	5.2	18.7	28.2	11.4	11.7	11.8	8.0	3.5	1.4	33.3
Tampa, FL	5.5	17.2	18.8	12.3	13.9	13.4	10.6	5.8	2.6	42.0
Topeka, KS	6.4	20.1	17.9	11.5	13.1	14.2	9.5	5.0	2.4	39.9
Tyler, TX	6.9	20.9	20.7	11.8	12.1	12.1	8.7	5.1	1.8	36.6
Virginia Beach, VA	6.4	18.8	23.7	12.1	13.2	12.3	7.9	3.9	1.7	35.7
Visalia, CA	8.6	25.8	21.6	12.4	11.3	9.6	6.2	3.1	1.4	30.6
Washington, DC	6.6	19.1	21.7	14.4	14.5	11.9	7.2	3.3	1.4	36.7
Wilmington, NC	5.3	17.6	21.6	12.8	13.1	13.1	10.0	4.8	1.8	39.6
Winston-Salem, NC	5.8	19.7	18.0	12.4	14.4	13.4	9.4	5.1	1.7	40.4
U.S.	6.2	19.5	20.7	12.7	13.4	12.7	8.6	4.4	1.9	37.8

Note: Figures cover the Metropolitan Statistical Area (MSA)—see Appendix B for areas included
Source: U.S. Census Bureau, 2013-2017 American Community Survey 5-Year Estimates

Segregation

Metro Area	Black/White		Asian/White		Hispanic/White	
	Index[1]	Rank[2]	Index[1]	Rank[2]	Index[1]	Rank[2]
Albany, NY	61.3	37	43.1	38	38.9	70
Albuquerque, NM	30.9	99	28.5	93	36.4	79
Allentown, PA	47.2	78	38.0	67	55.4	11
Anchorage, AK	n/a	n/a	n/a	n/a	n/a	n/a
Ann Arbor, MI	n/a	n/a	n/a	n/a	n/a	n/a
Athens, GA	n/a	n/a	n/a	n/a	n/a	n/a
Atlanta, GA	59.0	41	48.5	10	49.5	27
Austin, TX	50.1	70	41.2	49	43.2	51
Baton Rouge, LA	57.5	45	50.8	5	32.7	88
Billings, MT	n/a	n/a	n/a	n/a	n/a	n/a
Boise City, ID	30.2	101	27.6	95	36.2	80
Boston, MA	64.0	27	45.4	23	59.6	5
Boulder, CO	n/a	n/a	n/a	n/a	n/a	n/a
Cape Coral, FL	61.6	35	25.3	96	40.2	63
Cedar Rapids, IA	n/a	n/a	n/a	n/a	n/a	n/a
Charleston, SC	41.5	88	33.4	84	39.8	66
Charlotte, NC	53.8	56	43.6	34	47.6	35
Chicago, IL	76.4	3	44.9	26	56.3	10
Clarksville, TN	n/a	n/a	n/a	n/a	n/a	n/a
College Station, TX	n/a	n/a	n/a	n/a	n/a	n/a
Colorado Springs, CO	39.3	92	24.1	98	30.3	95
Columbia, MO	n/a	n/a	n/a	n/a	n/a	n/a
Columbia, SC	48.8	74	41.9	46	34.9	82
Columbus, OH	62.2	33	43.3	35	41.5	59
Dallas, TX	56.6	48	46.6	19	50.3	24
Denver, CO	62.6	31	33.4	83	48.8	31
Des Moines, IA	51.6	66	35.5	76	46.7	40
Durham, NC	48.1	75	44.0	30	48.0	33
Edison, NJ	78.0	2	51.9	3	62.0	3
El Paso, TX	30.7	100	22.2	100	43.3	50
Eugene, OR	n/a	n/a	n/a	n/a	n/a	n/a
Evansville, IN	n/a	n/a	n/a	n/a	n/a	n/a
Fargo, ND	n/a	n/a	n/a	n/a	n/a	n/a
Fayetteville, NC	n/a	n/a	n/a	n/a	n/a	n/a
Fort Collins, CO	n/a	n/a	n/a	n/a	n/a	n/a
Fort Wayne, IN	n/a	n/a	n/a	n/a	n/a	n/a
Fort Worth, TX	56.6	48	46.6	19	50.3	24
Gainesville, FL	n/a	n/a	n/a	n/a	n/a	n/a
Grand Rapids, MI	64.3	26	43.2	37	50.4	23
Greeley, CO	n/a	n/a	n/a	n/a	n/a	n/a
Green Bay, WI	n/a	n/a	n/a	n/a	n/a	n/a
Greensboro, NC	54.7	53	47.7	14	41.1	61
Honolulu, HI	36.9	95	42.1	44	31.9	91
Houston, TX	61.4	36	50.4	7	52.5	18
Huntsville, AL	n/a	n/a	n/a	n/a	n/a	n/a
Indianapolis, IN	66.4	15	41.6	47	47.3	37
Jacksonville, FL	53.1	59	37.5	71	27.6	98
Kansas City, MO	61.2	39	38.4	65	44.4	48
Lafayette, LA	n/a	n/a	n/a	n/a	n/a	n/a
Las Cruces, NM	n/a	n/a	n/a	n/a	n/a	n/a
Las Vegas, NV	37.6	94	28.8	92	42.0	58
Lexington, KY	n/a	n/a	n/a	n/a	n/a	n/a
Lincoln, NE	n/a	n/a	n/a	n/a	n/a	n/a
Little Rock, AR	58.8	42	39.7	59	39.7	68
Los Angeles, CA	67.8	10	48.4	12	62.2	2

Table continued on next page.

Metro Area	Black/White Index[1]	Black/White Rank[2]	Asian/White Index[1]	Asian/White Rank[2]	Hispanic/White Index[1]	Hispanic/White Rank[2]
Louisville, KY	58.1	43	42.2	43	38.7	73
Madison, WI	49.6	71	44.2	29	40.1	65
Manchester, NH	n/a	n/a	n/a	n/a	n/a	n/a
McAllen, TX	40.7	90	46.7	17	39.2	69
Miami, FL	64.8	23	34.2	80	57.4	8
Midland, TX	n/a	n/a	n/a	n/a	n/a	n/a
Minneapolis, MN	52.9	60	42.8	39	42.5	54
Nashville, TN	56.2	49	41.0	51	47.9	34
New Orleans, LA	63.9	28	48.6	9	38.3	74
New York, NY	78.0	2	51.9	3	62.0	3
Oklahoma City, OK	51.4	67	39.2	60	47.0	38
Omaha, NE	61.3	38	36.3	74	48.8	30
Orlando, FL	50.7	69	33.9	81	40.2	64
Peoria, IL	n/a	n/a	n/a	n/a	n/a	n/a
Philadelphia, PA	68.4	9	42.3	42	55.1	12
Phoenix, AZ	43.6	86	32.7	85	49.3	28
Pittsburgh, PA	65.8	17	52.4	2	28.6	97
Portland, OR	46.0	81	35.8	75	34.3	83
Providence, RI	53.5	57	40.1	55	60.1	4
Provo, UT	21.9	102	28.2	94	30.9	93
Raleigh, NC	42.1	87	46.7	16	37.1	76
Reno, NV	n/a	n/a	n/a	n/a	n/a	n/a
Richmond, VA	52.4	63	43.9	32	44.9	46
Roanoke, VA	n/a	n/a	n/a	n/a	n/a	n/a
Rochester, MN	n/a	n/a	n/a	n/a	n/a	n/a
Salem, OR	n/a	n/a	n/a	n/a	n/a	n/a
Salt Lake City, UT	39.3	93	31.0	88	42.9	53
San Antonio, TX	49.0	73	38.3	66	46.1	43
San Diego, CA	51.2	68	48.2	13	49.6	25
San Francisco, CA	62.0	34	46.6	18	49.6	26
San Jose, CA	40.9	89	45.0	25	47.6	36
Santa Rosa, CA	n/a	n/a	n/a	n/a	n/a	n/a
Savannah, GA	n/a	n/a	n/a	n/a	n/a	n/a
Seattle, WA	49.1	72	37.6	69	32.8	87
Sioux Falls, SD	n/a	n/a	n/a	n/a	n/a	n/a
Springfield, IL	n/a	n/a	n/a	n/a	n/a	n/a
Tallahassee, FL	n/a	n/a	n/a	n/a	n/a	n/a
Tampa, FL	56.2	50	35.3	78	40.7	62
Topeka, KS	n/a	n/a	n/a	n/a	n/a	n/a
Tyler, TX	n/a	n/a	n/a	n/a	n/a	n/a
Virginia Beach, VA	47.8	76	34.3	79	32.2	90
Visalia, CA	n/a	n/a	n/a	n/a	n/a	n/a
Washington, DC	62.3	32	38.9	64	48.3	32
Wilmington, NC	n/a	n/a	n/a	n/a	n/a	n/a
Winston-Salem, NC	n/a	n/a	n/a	n/a	n/a	n/a

Note: Figures are based on an analysis of 1990, 2000, and 2010 Census Decennial Census tract data by William H. Frey, Brookings Institution and the University of Michigan Social Science Data Analysis Network. In this analysis all racial groups (whites, blacks, and asians) are non-Hispanic members of those races. Hispanics are shown as a separate category; All figures cover the Metropolitan Statistical Area (see Appendix B for areas included); (1) Segregation Indices are Dissimilarity Indices that measure the degree to which the minority group is distributed differently than whites across census tracts. They range from 0 (complete integration) to 100 (complete [segregation) where the value indicates the percentage of the minority group that needs to move to be distributed exactly like whites; (2) Ranges from 1 (most segregated) to 102 (least segregated); n/a not available.
Source: www.CensusScope.org

Religious Groups by Family

Area[1]	Catholic	Baptist	Non-Den.	Methodist[2]	Lutheran	LDS[3]	Pentecostal	Presbyterian[4]	Muslim[5]	Judaism
Albany, NY	26.8	1.2	2.2	2.9	1.5	0.3	0.5	2.1	1.2	1.0
Albuquerque, NM	27.1	3.7	4.2	1.4	0.9	2.3	1.4	1.0	0.2	0.2
Allentown, PA	23.1	0.4	1.9	3.9	7.9	0.3	0.4	6.2	0.6	0.6
Anchorage, AK	6.9	5.0	6.4	1.3	1.9	5.1	1.8	0.6	0.2	0.1
Ann Arbor, MI	12.3	2.2	1.5	3.0	2.8	0.8	1.9	2.9	1.2	0.9
Athens, GA	4.4	16.2	2.2	8.3	0.3	0.8	2.8	2.0	0.3	0.2
Atlanta, GA	7.4	17.4	6.8	7.8	0.5	0.7	2.6	1.8	0.7	0.5
Austin, TX	16.0	10.3	4.5	3.6	1.9	1.1	0.8	1.0	1.2	0.2
Baton Rouge, LA	22.5	18.2	9.6	4.6	0.2	0.7	1.1	0.6	0.2	0.1
Billings, MT	12.0	2.4	3.7	2.1	6.1	4.9	4.0	1.8	<0.1	<0.1
Boise City, ID	8.0	2.9	4.1	2.1	1.1	15.8	2.3	0.6	0.1	0.1
Boston, MA	44.3	1.1	1.0	0.9	0.3	0.4	0.6	1.6	0.4	1.4
Boulder, CO	20.1	2.3	4.7	1.7	3.0	2.9	0.4	2.0	0.1	0.7
Cape Coral, FL	16.2	4.9	3.0	2.5	1.1	0.5	4.3	1.4	0.9	0.2
Cedar Rapids, IA	18.8	2.3	3.0	7.3	11.3	0.8	1.8	3.2	0.5	0.1
Charleston, SC	6.1	12.4	7.0	10.0	1.1	0.9	2.0	2.3	0.1	0.3
Charlotte, NC	5.9	17.2	6.7	8.6	1.3	0.7	3.2	4.5	0.2	0.3
Chicago, IL	34.2	3.2	4.4	1.9	3.0	0.3	1.2	1.9	3.2	0.8
Clarksville, TN	4.0	30.9	2.2	6.1	0.5	1.5	1.8	1.0	0.1	<0.1
College Station, TX	11.7	15.6	3.9	4.7	1.5	1.2	0.6	0.9	1.1	<0.1
Colorado Springs, CO	8.3	4.3	7.4	2.4	1.9	3.0	1.0	2.0	<0.1	0.1
Columbia, MO	6.6	14.6	5.4	4.3	1.7	1.3	1.0	2.3	0.3	0.2
Columbia, SC	3.1	18.0	5.2	9.3	3.4	1.0	2.6	3.3	0.1	0.2
Columbus, OH	11.7	5.3	3.5	4.7	2.4	0.7	1.9	2.0	0.8	0.5
Dallas, TX	13.3	18.7	7.7	5.2	0.7	1.1	2.1	0.9	2.4	0.3
Denver, CO	16.0	2.9	4.6	1.7	2.1	2.4	1.2	1.5	0.5	0.6
Des Moines, IA	13.6	4.7	3.3	6.9	8.2	0.9	2.3	2.9	0.3	0.3
Durham, NC	5.0	13.8	5.6	8.1	0.4	0.7	1.3	2.5	0.4	0.5
Edison, NJ	36.9	1.8	1.7	1.3	0.7	0.3	0.8	1.0	2.3	4.7
El Paso, TX	43.2	3.7	4.9	0.8	0.3	1.5	1.4	0.2	<0.1	0.2
Eugene, OR	6.1	3.1	1.9	0.8	1.3	3.7	3.2	0.6	<0.1	0.3
Evansville, IN	14.7	16.7	5.6	5.6	1.4	0.5	1.9	3.0	<0.1	<0.1
Fargo, ND	17.4	0.4	0.4	3.3	32.5	0.6	1.5	1.8	0.1	<0.1
Fayetteville, NC	2.6	14.1	10.4	6.2	0.1	1.4	4.8	2.1	0.1	<0.1
Fort Collins, CO	11.8	2.2	6.3	4.3	3.4	2.9	4.7	1.9	0.1	<0.1
Fort Wayne, IN	14.2	6.0	6.8	5.1	8.5	0.4	1.4	1.6	0.2	0.1
Fort Worth, TX	13.3	18.7	7.7	5.2	0.7	1.1	2.1	0.9	2.4	0.3
Gainesville, FL	7.5	12.2	4.3	6.3	0.5	1.0	3.4	1.0	1.0	0.4
Grand Rapids, MI	17.1	1.7	8.3	3.0	2.1	0.5	1.1	9.9	1.0	0.1
Greeley, CO	13.5	1.8	1.5	2.6	2.0	1.9	1.8	1.4	0.1	<0.1
Green Bay, WI	42.0	0.7	3.4	2.2	12.7	0.3	0.6	1.0	0.1	<0.1
Greensboro, NC	2.6	12.8	7.4	9.8	0.6	0.8	2.4	3.1	0.6	0.4
Honolulu, HI	18.2	1.9	2.2	0.8	0.3	5.1	4.1	1.4	<0.1	<0.1
Houston, TX	17.0	16.0	7.2	4.8	1.0	1.1	1.5	0.8	2.6	0.3
Huntsville, AL	3.9	27.6	3.1	7.5	0.7	1.1	1.2	1.7	0.2	0.1
Indianapolis, IN	10.5	10.2	7.1	4.9	1.6	0.7	1.6	1.6	0.2	0.3
Jacksonville, FL	9.8	18.5	7.7	4.5	0.6	1.1	1.9	1.6	0.6	0.4
Kansas City, MO	12.6	13.1	5.2	5.8	2.2	2.4	2.6	1.6	0.3	0.4
Lafayette, LA	47.0	14.7	3.9	2.5	0.2	0.4	2.9	0.1	0.1	<0.1
Las Cruces, NM	31.7	5.7	1.2	2.0	0.5	2.1	2.7	0.6	0.2	0.2
Las Vegas, NV	18.1	2.9	3.0	0.4	0.7	6.3	1.5	0.2	<0.1	0.3
Lexington, KY	6.7	24.9	2.3	5.9	0.4	1.0	2.1	1.3	0.1	0.3
Lincoln, NE	14.7	2.4	1.9	7.1	11.2	1.1	1.4	3.9	0.2	0.1
Little Rock, AR	4.5	25.9	6.0	7.3	0.5	0.9	2.8	0.8	0.1	0.1
Los Angeles, CA	33.8	2.7	3.6	1.0	0.6	1.7	1.7	0.9	0.7	0.9

Table continued on next page.

Area[1]	Catholic	Baptist	Non-Den.	Methodist[2]	Lutheran	LDS[3]	Pentecostal	Presbyterian[4]	Muslim[5]	Judaism
Louisville, KY	13.6	25.0	1.7	3.7	0.6	0.8	0.9	1.1	0.5	0.4
Madison, WI	21.8	1.1	1.5	3.6	12.7	0.5	0.3	2.1	0.4	0.4
Manchester, NH	31.1	1.3	2.3	1.1	0.5	0.6	0.4	2.0	0.3	0.5
McAllen, TX	34.7	4.4	2.8	1.2	0.4	1.3	1.2	0.1	0.9	<0.1
Miami, FL	18.5	5.3	4.1	1.2	0.4	0.5	1.7	0.6	0.9	1.5
Midland, TX	22.4	25.2	8.8	4.2	0.6	1.2	1.6	1.8	3.7	<0.1
Minneapolis, MN	21.7	2.4	2.9	2.7	14.4	0.6	1.7	1.8	0.4	0.7
Nashville, TN	4.1	25.2	5.8	6.1	0.3	0.7	2.1	2.1	0.3	0.1
New Orleans, LA	31.5	8.4	3.7	2.6	0.8	0.5	2.1	0.5	0.4	0.5
New York, NY	36.9	1.8	1.7	1.3	0.7	0.3	0.8	1.0	2.3	4.7
Oklahoma City, OK	6.3	25.3	7.0	10.6	0.7	1.2	3.1	0.9	0.2	0.1
Omaha, NE	21.6	4.5	1.8	3.9	7.8	1.7	1.2	2.2	0.5	0.4
Orlando, FL	13.2	6.9	5.6	2.9	0.9	0.9	3.2	1.3	1.3	0.2
Peoria, IL	11.4	5.5	5.2	4.9	6.1	0.5	1.5	2.8	5.2	0.1
Philadelphia, PA	33.4	3.9	2.8	2.9	1.8	0.3	0.8	2.1	1.2	1.3
Phoenix, AZ	13.3	3.4	5.1	1.0	1.6	6.1	2.9	0.6	0.1	0.3
Pittsburgh, PA	32.8	2.3	2.8	5.6	3.3	0.3	1.1	4.6	0.3	0.7
Portland, OR	10.5	2.3	4.5	1.0	1.6	3.7	2.0	0.9	0.1	0.3
Providence, RI	47.0	1.4	1.2	0.8	0.5	0.3	0.5	1.0	0.1	0.7
Provo, UT	1.3	<0.1	<0.1	0.1	<0.1	88.5	0.1	<0.1	<0.1	<0.1
Raleigh, NC	9.1	12.1	5.9	6.7	0.9	0.8	2.2	2.2	0.9	0.3
Reno, NV	14.3	1.5	3.1	0.9	0.7	4.6	1.9	0.4	<0.1	0.1
Richmond, VA	5.9	19.9	5.4	6.1	0.6	0.9	1.8	2.1	2.7	0.3
Roanoke, VA	3.7	22.4	4.5	7.2	1.4	1.1	2.7	2.5	2.2	0.2
Rochester, MN	23.3	1.6	4.6	4.8	21.0	1.1	1.2	2.9	0.2	0.2
Salem, OR	16.6	2.1	2.9	1.1	1.6	3.8	3.4	0.7	<0.1	<0.1
Salt Lake City, UT	8.9	0.8	0.5	0.5	0.5	58.9	0.6	0.3	0.4	0.1
San Antonio, TX	28.4	8.5	6.0	3.0	1.6	1.4	1.3	0.7	0.9	0.2
San Diego, CA	25.9	2.0	4.8	1.1	0.9	2.3	1.0	0.9	0.7	0.5
San Francisco, CA	20.7	2.5	2.4	1.9	0.5	1.5	1.2	1.1	1.2	0.8
San Jose, CA	26.0	1.3	4.2	1.0	0.5	1.4	1.1	0.7	1.0	0.6
Santa Rosa, CA	22.2	1.3	1.5	0.9	0.9	1.9	0.6	0.9	0.4	0.4
Savannah, GA	7.0	19.6	6.9	8.9	1.6	0.9	2.3	1.0	0.1	0.8
Seattle, WA	12.3	2.1	5.0	1.2	2.0	3.3	2.8	1.4	0.4	0.4
Sioux Falls, SD	14.9	3.0	1.5	3.8	21.4	0.7	1.0	6.2	0.3	<0.1
Springfield, IL	15.5	11.7	2.7	6.8	5.6	0.7	4.9	2.0	1.5	0.2
Tallahassee, FL	4.8	16.0	6.7	9.1	0.4	1.0	2.1	1.5	0.8	0.3
Tampa, FL	10.8	7.0	3.7	3.4	0.9	0.6	2.1	0.9	1.2	0.4
Topeka, KS	12.7	9.0	4.1	7.3	3.6	1.4	2.0	1.6	<0.1	0.1
Tyler, TX	12.1	33.5	8.9	6.3	0.5	1.1	5.0	0.6	0.3	0.1
Virginia Beach, VA	6.4	11.5	6.1	5.2	0.7	0.9	1.9	2.0	2.0	0.3
Visalia, CA	23.2	2.6	2.5	0.8	0.5	1.7	3.6	0.9	0.3	<0.1
Washington, DC	14.5	7.3	4.8	4.5	1.2	1.1	1.0	1.3	2.3	1.1
Wilmington, NC	6.1	14.4	4.6	8.4	0.9	1.0	1.1	2.5	0.2	0.1
Winston-Salem, NC	3.5	17.4	9.3	12.4	0.7	0.6	2.5	2.2	0.3	0.1
U.S.	19.1	9.3	4.0	4.0	2.3	2.0	1.9	1.6	0.8	0.7

Note: Figures are the number of adherents as a percentage of the total population; (1) Figures cover the Metropolitan Statistical Area—see Appendix B for areas included; (2) Methodist/Pietist; (3) Latter Day Saints; (4) Reformed; (5) Figures are estimates
Source: Association of Statisticians of American Religious Bodies, 2010 U.S. Religion Census: Religious Congregations & Membership Study

Religious Groups by Tradition

Area	Catholic	Evangelical Protestant	Mainline Protestant	Other Tradition	Black Protestant	Orthodox
Albany, NY	26.8	4.5	7.3	3.1	0.5	0.3
Albuquerque, NM	27.1	11.2	3.2	3.9	0.2	0.1
Allentown, PA	23.1	5.3	17.7	3.0	0.1	0.6
Anchorage, AK	6.9	15.6	3.5	6.8	0.3	0.6
Ann Arbor, MI	12.3	7.3	7.5	3.7	1.5	0.2
Athens, GA	4.4	21.1	9.7	1.7	2.4	0.1
Atlanta, GA	7.4	26.0	9.8	2.9	3.1	0.2
Austin, TX	16.0	16.1	6.3	3.9	1.3	0.1
Baton Rouge, LA	22.5	24.8	5.6	1.5	5.1	<0.1
Billings, MT	12.0	13.6	8.1	5.1	<0.1	<0.1
Boise City, ID	8.0	12.9	4.3	16.7	<0.1	<0.1
Boston, MA	44.3	3.2	4.5	3.4	0.1	1.0
Boulder, CO	20.1	9.7	6.4	4.8	<0.1	0.2
Cape Coral, FL	16.2	14.3	4.6	2.0	0.3	0.1
Cedar Rapids, IA	18.8	13.7	17.5	1.9	0.1	0.2
Charleston, SC	6.1	19.6	11.1	1.8	7.3	0.1
Charlotte, NC	5.9	27.5	13.3	1.6	2.7	0.4
Chicago, IL	34.2	9.7	5.1	5.0	2.0	0.9
Clarksville, TN	4.0	35.3	7.2	1.6	2.4	<0.1
College Station, TX	11.7	20.6	6.6	2.5	0.9	<0.1
Colorado Springs, CO	8.3	15.2	5.3	3.7	0.4	0.1
Columbia, MO	6.6	19.9	10.4	2.3	0.4	0.1
Columbia, SC	3.1	25.5	13.4	2.1	5.4	0.1
Columbus, OH	11.7	11.8	9.5	3.1	1.1	0.2
Dallas, TX	13.3	28.3	6.9	4.7	1.7	0.1
Denver, CO	16.0	11.0	4.5	4.6	0.3	0.3
Des Moines, IA	13.6	12.3	16.8	1.8	0.9	0.1
Durham, NC	5.0	19.3	11.7	2.9	3.1	<0.1
Edison, NJ	36.9	3.9	4.1	8.3	1.2	0.9
El Paso, TX	43.2	10.8	1.2	2.0	0.2	<0.1
Eugene, OR	6.1	9.6	3.4	5.4	<0.1	<0.1
Evansville, IN	14.7	24.0	9.9	0.8	1.8	<0.1
Fargo, ND	17.4	10.7	30.8	0.8	<0.1	<0.1
Fayetteville, NC	2.6	26.7	7.8	1.7	4.3	0.1
Fort Collins, CO	11.8	18.8	5.9	3.9	<0.1	0.1
Fort Wayne, IN	14.2	24.6	9.1	0.9	2.4	0.2
Fort Worth, TX	13.3	28.3	6.9	4.7	1.7	0.1
Gainesville, FL	7.5	20.4	6.9	4.1	2.1	<0.1
Grand Rapids, MI	17.1	20.7	7.5	2.1	1.0	0.2
Greeley, CO	13.5	9.2	3.8	2.1	<0.1	<0.1
Green Bay, WI	42.0	14.1	8.1	0.6	<0.1	<0.1
Greensboro, NC	2.6	23.2	14.0	2.1	2.6	<0.1
Honolulu, HI	18.2	9.6	2.9	8.4	<0.1	<0.1
Houston, TX	17.0	24.9	6.6	4.9	1.3	0.2
Huntsville, AL	3.9	33.3	9.6	1.8	1.8	<0.1
Indianapolis, IN	10.5	18.2	9.6	1.6	1.8	0.2
Jacksonville, FL	9.8	27.1	5.6	2.9	4.2	0.2
Kansas City, MO	12.6	20.5	9.9	3.6	2.6	0.1
Lafayette, LA	47.0	12.7	3.2	0.7	9.2	<0.1
Las Cruces, NM	31.7	10.5	3.1	3.2	0.1	<0.1
Las Vegas, NV	18.1	7.7	1.3	7.6	0.4	0.4
Lexington, KY	6.7	28.3	10.2	1.7	2.0	0.1
Lincoln, NE	14.7	14.8	16.2	2.0	0.1	<0.1
Little Rock, AR	4.5	33.9	8.1	1.7	3.4	<0.1
Los Angeles, CA	33.8	9.0	2.3	4.6	0.8	0.6

Table continued on next page.

Area	Catholic	Evangelical Protestant	Mainline Protestant	Other Tradition	Black Protestant	Orthodox
Louisville, KY	13.6	24.5	7.1	2.0	2.9	<0.1
Madison, WI	21.8	7.2	15.3	2.2	0.1	<0.1
Manchester, NH	31.1	5.1	4.4	1.8	<0.1	0.7
McAllen, TX	34.7	9.7	1.8	2.3	<0.1	<0.1
Miami, FL	18.5	11.4	2.4	3.5	1.7	0.2
Midland, TX	22.4	35.4	7.2	5.3	1.0	<0.1
Minneapolis, MN	21.7	12.8	14.5	2.2	0.4	0.2
Nashville, TN	4.1	32.9	8.0	1.7	3.3	0.4
New Orleans, LA	31.5	12.7	4.0	2.1	2.9	0.1
New York, NY	36.9	3.9	4.1	8.3	1.2	0.9
Oklahoma City, OK	6.3	39.0	9.8	2.7	1.9	0.1
Omaha, NE	21.6	12.1	10.7	3.2	1.4	0.1
Orlando, FL	13.2	17.8	4.7	3.2	1.2	0.3
Peoria, IL	11.4	18.9	11.1	6.1	0.9	0.1
Philadelphia, PA	33.4	6.3	8.9	3.7	1.7	0.4
Phoenix, AZ	13.3	13.2	2.6	7.8	0.1	0.3
Pittsburgh, PA	32.8	7.3	13.8	2.0	0.8	0.6
Portland, OR	10.5	11.6	3.6	5.2	0.1	0.3
Providence, RI	47.0	2.8	4.7	1.6	<0.1	0.5
Provo, UT	1.3	0.4	<0.1	88.8	<0.1	<0.1
Raleigh, NC	9.1	19.9	10.1	3.2	1.7	0.2
Reno, NV	14.3	7.6	1.9	5.1	0.2	0.1
Richmond, VA	5.9	23.6	13.3	4.5	2.4	0.1
Roanoke, VA	3.7	31.7	13.1	3.9	1.2	0.1
Rochester, MN	23.3	18.9	21.0	2.0	<0.1	0.1
Salem, OR	16.6	14.1	3.8	4.1	<0.1	<0.1
Salt Lake City, UT	8.9	2.6	1.2	60.0	0.1	0.4
San Antonio, TX	28.4	16.9	5.0	3.1	0.4	<0.1
San Diego, CA	25.9	9.7	2.4	5.2	0.3	0.2
San Francisco, CA	20.7	6.1	3.8	5.2	1.0	0.6
San Jose, CA	26.0	8.2	2.4	6.8	0.1	0.4
Santa Rosa, CA	22.2	5.3	2.3	4.8	<0.1	0.2
Savannah, GA	7.0	25.0	9.4	2.6	8.5	0.1
Seattle, WA	12.3	11.9	4.6	5.9	0.3	0.4
Sioux Falls, SD	14.9	12.9	28.0	1.2	0.1	0.1
Springfield, IL	15.5	21.4	11.6	3.1	2.1	0.1
Tallahassee, FL	4.8	21.9	6.3	2.9	9.1	0.1
Tampa, FL	10.8	13.6	5.1	3.1	1.1	0.8
Topeka, KS	12.7	15.5	12.8	1.7	2.7	<0.1
Tyler, TX	12.1	45.5	7.4	1.7	4.1	<0.1
Virginia Beach, VA	6.4	18.0	9.4	3.9	2.2	0.3
Visalia, CA	23.2	12.0	1.9	3.1	0.1	0.1
Washington, DC	14.5	12.4	8.7	5.9	2.3	0.6
Wilmington, NC	6.1	20.3	10.7	1.6	3.1	0.1
Winston-Salem, NC	3.5	29.1	15.6	1.2	2.2	0.2
U.S.	19.1	16.2	7.3	4.3	1.6	0.3

Note: Figures are the number of adherents as a percentage of the total population; (1) Figures cover the Metropolitan Statistical Area—see Appendix B for areas included
Source: Association of Statisticians of American Religious Bodies, 2010 U.S. Religion Census: Religious Congregations & Membership Study

Ancestry: City

City	German	Irish	English	American	Italian	Polish	French[1]	Scottish	Dutch
Albany, NY	10.2	14.8	5.2	2.0	12.3	3.9	2.6	0.9	1.3
Albuquerque, NM	9.7	7.1	6.0	3.8	3.0	1.2	1.8	1.7	0.8
Allentown, PA	11.9	6.4	2.0	2.5	4.5	1.9	0.9	0.5	1.2
Anchorage, AK	15.1	9.6	8.0	4.5	2.8	2.1	2.7	2.5	1.6
Ann Arbor, MI	17.6	9.4	9.8	4.9	5.0	6.6	3.2	2.6	2.2
Athens, GA	8.8	8.5	9.0	5.5	3.2	1.6	1.7	2.9	0.9
Atlanta, GA	5.8	5.3	7.0	6.0	2.3	1.3	1.6	1.7	0.5
Austin, TX	11.2	7.3	7.6	3.3	2.9	1.7	2.3	2.0	0.8
Baton Rouge, LA	5.5	5.1	5.2	6.2	3.1	0.6	7.3	1.2	0.3
Billings, MT	25.3	10.8	9.7	12.0	3.0	1.9	2.9	2.7	1.5
Boise City, ID	17.8	11.7	18.3	4.7	3.7	1.6	2.7	4.0	1.8
Boston, MA	4.5	13.9	4.5	3.4	7.9	2.4	1.9	1.3	0.5
Boulder, CO	20.0	13.8	11.3	2.9	6.1	3.5	3.0	3.6	1.4
Cape Coral, FL	15.1	11.6	7.8	14.7	9.8	3.7	2.9	1.9	1.3
Cedar Rapids, IA	33.8	14.7	8.5	4.8	1.7	1.5	2.4	1.5	2.2
Charleston, SC	10.9	11.0	10.8	19.9	3.9	1.8	2.3	3.1	0.6
Charlotte, NC	9.3	7.2	6.7	4.5	3.5	1.7	1.4	1.9	0.6
Chicago, IL	7.4	7.5	2.4	2.0	3.9	5.9	1.0	0.6	0.5
Clarksville, TN	11.8	9.3	5.5	9.2	3.0	2.0	1.9	1.5	1.0
College Station, TX	17.8	9.4	8.9	3.6	3.5	2.7	3.5	2.8	0.8
Colorado Springs, CO	20.4	11.9	10.0	4.7	4.9	2.4	3.0	2.6	1.8
Columbia, MO	25.1	12.6	9.7	5.4	3.5	2.3	2.7	2.1	1.3
Columbia, SC	9.4	7.8	8.8	6.1	2.8	1.4	2.0	2.4	0.7
Columbus, OH	18.4	10.6	6.3	4.3	5.1	2.1	1.8	1.7	0.9
Dallas, TX	5.6	4.1	4.8	3.2	1.4	0.8	1.3	1.2	0.5
Denver, CO	14.3	9.7	7.9	3.0	4.4	2.6	2.4	2.0	1.4
Des Moines, IA	20.3	11.5	6.9	4.5	3.9	1.1	2.1	1.5	2.8
Durham, NC	7.2	5.9	7.1	4.6	2.7	1.8	1.4	1.8	0.6
Edison, NJ	4.9	6.9	1.5	1.9	8.6	4.8	0.7	0.6	0.4
El Paso, TX	3.6	2.3	1.6	2.9	1.2	0.4	0.7	0.4	0.3
Eugene, OR	17.5	12.9	11.1	3.9	4.5	2.2	3.4	3.4	2.0
Evansville, IN	25.7	11.6	11.3	7.1	1.5	1.2	1.7	1.5	1.1
Fargo, ND	38.7	8.8	4.1	2.1	1.2	2.9	3.8	1.4	1.1
Fayetteville, NC	9.2	7.5	6.6	4.8	3.2	1.4	1.7	1.8	0.6
Fort Collins, CO	24.4	13.5	11.3	3.8	6.1	3.2	3.5	2.8	1.9
Fort Wayne, IN	26.1	9.5	6.5	6.4	2.7	1.9	3.2	1.8	1.4
Fort Worth, TX	8.4	6.8	6.0	5.2	1.9	1.0	1.8	1.5	0.7
Gainesville, FL	11.3	10.4	8.2	4.0	6.2	2.8	2.7	2.4	1.3
Grand Rapids, MI	15.4	9.1	6.7	2.6	2.8	6.9	2.7	1.6	14.9
Greeley, CO	19.7	8.6	6.8	3.8	2.7	1.5	1.9	1.8	1.2
Green Bay, WI	31.7	8.7	3.4	3.4	2.0	8.1	4.3	0.7	3.5
Greensboro, NC	7.5	5.4	7.0	5.0	2.1	1.1	1.2	1.9	0.7
Honolulu, HI	4.0	3.4	2.8	1.2	1.9	0.7	1.1	0.7	0.4
Houston, TX	5.0	3.7	3.9	4.0	1.5	0.9	1.6	0.9	0.4
Huntsville, AL	9.4	8.7	9.5	10.1	2.7	0.9	1.8	2.2	1.0
Indianapolis, IN	15.4	9.4	6.2	6.3	2.3	1.5	1.6	1.6	1.2
Jacksonville, FL	8.9	8.5	6.7	5.7	4.0	1.6	1.7	1.7	0.9
Kansas City, MO	17.2	11.3	7.4	4.6	3.5	1.4	2.3	1.6	1.3
Lafayette, LA	7.5	5.6	6.4	7.1	3.6	0.5	19.8	0.9	0.6
Las Cruces, NM	7.6	5.3	4.9	2.6	2.1	1.1	1.3	1.3	0.6
Las Vegas, NV	9.6	8.2	5.6	3.6	5.8	2.2	1.8	1.4	0.8
Lexington, KY	14.5	12.2	11.2	11.0	2.8	1.5	1.8	2.9	1.3
Lincoln, NE	36.3	12.1	8.6	4.0	2.2	2.6	2.2	1.7	2.3
Little Rock, AR	7.8	7.4	7.7	5.9	1.6	1.0	1.9	1.8	0.6
Los Angeles, CA	4.1	3.6	3.0	3.1	2.7	1.5	1.1	0.7	0.4
Louisville, KY	15.5	11.6	8.2	11.4	2.5	0.9	1.8	1.6	0.9

Table continued on next page.

City	German	Irish	English	American	Italian	Polish	French[1]	Scottish	Dutch
Madison, WI	33.2	13.6	8.3	2.1	4.0	5.8	2.9	1.6	1.9
Manchester, NH	6.5	19.2	8.6	3.5	9.1	3.9	15.5	2.7	0.6
McAllen, TX	3.2	1.7	1.6	3.9	0.8	0.2	0.8	0.7	0.3
Miami, FL	1.7	1.3	0.9	3.8	2.1	0.6	0.9	0.3	0.2
Midland, TX	8.9	7.2	6.3	4.8	1.3	0.5	1.5	1.9	0.7
Minneapolis, MN	22.1	10.3	5.7	1.9	2.6	3.8	2.8	1.4	1.4
Nashville, TN	8.4	8.0	7.5	8.2	2.4	1.2	1.7	2.0	0.9
New Orleans, LA	6.5	5.8	4.2	2.4	4.0	0.9	5.8	1.1	0.4
New York, NY	3.0	4.4	1.6	4.7	6.4	2.4	0.8	0.4	0.2
Oklahoma City, OK	11.7	9.1	6.6	5.9	1.9	0.9	1.9	1.6	1.2
Omaha, NE	26.1	13.8	6.5	3.2	4.3	3.8	2.2	1.3	1.5
Orlando, FL	6.7	5.9	4.9	5.5	4.4	1.7	1.8	1.3	0.7
Peoria, IL	19.7	11.3	7.0	5.6	3.4	2.0	1.7	1.6	1.1
Philadelphia, PA	6.7	10.7	2.5	2.5	7.4	3.3	0.7	0.6	0.3
Phoenix, AZ	10.8	7.5	5.6	3.2	3.9	2.1	1.9	1.4	1.0
Pittsburgh, PA	19.5	16.1	5.3	4.3	12.4	7.3	1.4	1.4	0.6
Portland, OR	17.1	11.6	10.6	4.5	4.6	2.5	3.2	3.2	2.1
Providence, RI	3.3	8.0	3.9	3.2	8.5	1.9	3.1	0.9	0.3
Provo, UT	10.9	4.5	24.1	3.1	2.2	0.5	1.8	4.5	1.8
Raleigh, NC	9.1	7.7	9.0	12.8	4.0	1.9	1.7	2.6	0.7
Reno, NV	13.3	11.2	8.7	5.0	5.8	1.9	2.7	2.2	1.4
Richmond, VA	7.0	6.3	7.6	3.9	3.2	1.2	1.4	2.1	0.6
Roanoke, VA	9.2	9.2	8.0	10.7	1.9	1.4	1.3	2.1	1.1
Rochester, MN	30.9	11.3	6.3	3.2	2.2	3.8	2.0	1.3	1.5
Salem, OR	18.2	9.9	9.4	4.6	3.2	1.5	3.0	2.8	1.7
Salt Lake City, UT	10.5	6.8	15.7	3.7	3.2	1.4	2.1	3.5	2.0
San Antonio, TX	7.5	4.5	3.7	2.9	1.8	1.1	1.3	0.9	0.5
San Diego, CA	9.0	7.2	5.7	2.6	4.1	1.8	1.9	1.5	0.9
San Francisco, CA	7.5	8.0	5.3	2.8	4.8	1.8	2.3	1.5	0.8
San Jose, CA	5.5	4.3	3.8	1.6	3.6	1.0	1.2	0.8	0.6
Santa Rosa, CA	11.7	10.2	9.0	2.9	7.5	1.4	3.1	2.2	1.1
Savannah, GA	6.5	7.4	4.9	3.7	2.8	1.3	1.4	1.4	0.6
Seattle, WA	15.7	11.3	10.5	2.6	4.3	2.7	3.1	3.3	1.6
Sioux Falls, SD	36.5	10.6	5.1	3.9	1.5	1.8	2.2	1.1	5.9
Springfield, IL	22.2	14.0	9.5	5.3	5.0	2.0	2.2	1.6	1.3
Tallahassee, FL	9.3	8.6	7.7	4.1	3.9	2.0	2.0	2.2	0.8
Tampa, FL	8.8	8.5	6.0	5.8	5.9	2.0	2.3	1.6	0.7
Topeka, KS	22.7	10.6	12.9	5.0	2.3	1.2	2.2	1.8	1.3
Tyler, TX	7.5	6.9	7.2	11.9	1.5	0.8	1.4	1.8	0.7
Virginia Beach, VA	12.5	11.1	9.3	10.8	5.7	2.6	2.4	2.5	1.0
Visalia, CA	7.0	5.8	4.3	2.7	2.2	0.7	1.2	1.2	1.6
Washington, DC	7.0	6.7	5.0	2.3	3.9	2.2	1.5	1.3	0.6
Wilmington, NC	10.0	9.4	11.1	14.7	4.6	1.8	2.0	2.9	0.9
Winston-Salem, NC	9.4	6.9	8.4	5.7	2.7	1.1	1.5	2.0	0.9
U.S.	14.1	10.1	7.5	6.6	5.3	2.9	2.5	1.7	1.3

Note: Figures are the percentage of the total population reporting a particular ancestry. The nine most commonly reported ancestries in the U.S. are shown. Figures include multiple ancestries (e.g. if a person reported being Irish and Italian, they were included in both columns); (1) Excludes Basque
Source: U.S. Census Bureau, 2013-2017 American Community Survey 5-Year Estimates

Ancestry: Metro Area

Metro Area	German	Irish	English	American	Italian	Polish	French[1]	Scottish	Dutch
Albany, NY	15.7	21.7	9.5	4.5	17.0	6.6	6.2	1.9	3.3
Albuquerque, NM	9.5	7.0	6.3	4.1	2.9	1.4	1.7	1.7	0.8
Allentown, PA	25.5	13.7	6.0	4.8	12.9	5.5	1.6	1.1	2.5
Anchorage, AK	16.2	10.0	8.2	4.8	3.0	2.1	2.9	2.6	1.6
Ann Arbor, MI	20.1	10.5	10.3	7.2	4.7	6.8	3.2	2.6	2.2
Athens, GA	8.6	9.3	10.0	9.4	2.9	1.4	1.7	2.9	1.0
Atlanta, GA	6.9	7.1	7.3	9.5	2.5	1.3	1.4	1.8	0.7
Austin, TX	13.0	7.7	8.1	4.1	2.8	1.6	2.5	2.1	0.9
Baton Rouge, LA	7.3	7.4	5.6	7.7	4.9	0.6	13.2	1.2	0.4
Billings, MT	26.7	10.7	9.7	12.4	2.8	1.9	2.9	2.9	1.6
Boise City, ID	16.9	9.4	18.0	5.6	3.1	1.3	2.3	3.1	1.9
Boston, MA	6.1	21.7	9.7	3.9	13.7	3.5	5.0	2.4	0.6
Boulder, CO	20.8	12.7	12.5	4.1	5.8	3.5	3.1	3.7	1.9
Cape Coral, FL	14.3	11.0	8.5	14.1	7.5	3.3	2.8	1.9	1.4
Cedar Rapids, IA	37.0	15.3	8.1	5.5	1.7	1.3	2.4	1.6	2.1
Charleston, SC	10.6	10.6	8.6	12.9	3.5	1.8	2.3	2.5	0.8
Charlotte, NC	11.9	8.9	8.0	9.1	3.9	1.7	1.7	2.2	1.0
Chicago, IL	14.9	11.0	4.2	2.8	6.8	9.0	1.5	1.0	1.2
Clarksville, TN	11.2	9.7	6.8	11.3	2.8	1.6	1.7	1.6	1.0
College Station, TX	14.9	8.7	7.5	4.2	2.8	2.1	2.7	2.2	0.7
Colorado Springs, CO	20.7	11.9	9.9	5.1	5.0	2.6	3.0	2.8	1.8
Columbia, MO	25.2	12.5	10.4	6.5	3.5	1.9	2.6	2.1	1.4
Columbia, SC	10.8	8.0	8.0	9.1	2.4	1.2	1.7	2.0	0.8
Columbus, OH	23.6	13.2	8.8	6.5	5.5	2.3	2.0	2.2	1.4
Dallas, TX	9.5	7.3	7.1	6.5	2.1	1.1	1.8	1.7	0.9
Denver, CO	18.5	11.0	9.6	4.4	5.0	2.6	2.6	2.4	1.6
Des Moines, IA	27.7	13.2	8.7	4.7	3.4	1.4	2.0	1.8	3.4
Durham, NC	9.5	7.7	9.5	6.1	3.2	1.9	1.8	2.5	0.9
Edison, NJ	6.7	9.7	2.9	4.8	12.8	3.9	1.0	0.7	0.6
El Paso, TX	3.4	2.2	1.5	2.7	1.1	0.4	0.6	0.4	0.3
Eugene, OR	18.7	13.0	11.4	4.8	4.2	1.9	3.2	3.4	2.1
Evansville, IN	28.2	11.6	11.4	10.4	1.9	1.1	1.9	1.8	1.2
Fargo, ND	39.4	8.0	4.1	2.0	1.2	2.8	3.4	1.3	1.2
Fayetteville, NC	8.8	7.3	6.8	6.3	3.0	1.3	1.6	1.9	0.6
Fort Collins, CO	26.3	13.6	12.4	4.5	5.3	2.8	3.6	3.1	2.1
Fort Wayne, IN	28.8	9.4	7.1	7.8	2.8	2.0	3.5	1.8	1.5
Fort Worth, TX	9.5	7.3	7.1	6.5	2.1	1.1	1.8	1.7	0.9
Gainesville, FL	11.8	10.8	9.0	5.2	5.2	2.6	2.6	2.3	1.2
Grand Rapids, MI	20.9	10.3	9.1	4.2	3.1	6.6	3.3	1.9	20.1
Greeley, CO	22.8	10.0	8.5	4.8	3.5	2.1	2.2	1.8	1.7
Green Bay, WI	37.2	9.4	3.9	3.8	2.3	9.6	4.6	0.8	4.6
Greensboro, NC	8.6	6.6	8.4	8.7	2.2	1.1	1.2	2.1	0.8
Honolulu, HI	5.3	4.0	3.3	1.3	2.1	0.9	1.1	0.9	0.5
Houston, TX	8.3	5.7	5.4	4.5	2.1	1.2	2.2	1.2	0.6
Huntsville, AL	9.8	9.7	10.0	11.6	2.2	1.0	1.9	2.2	0.9
Indianapolis, IN	19.4	10.9	8.2	9.5	2.7	2.0	2.0	1.9	1.6
Jacksonville, FL	10.7	10.0	8.4	7.9	4.8	2.0	2.3	2.1	1.0
Kansas City, MO	22.1	12.7	9.8	6.1	3.3	1.6	2.4	1.9	1.5
Lafayette, LA	6.9	4.5	4.2	10.7	2.7	0.5	20.5	0.7	0.3
Las Cruces, NM	6.0	4.4	3.9	2.5	1.5	0.7	1.0	1.0	0.5
Las Vegas, NV	9.6	7.6	5.6	3.5	5.4	2.1	1.9	1.3	0.8
Lexington, KY	13.8	12.4	11.4	15.3	2.6	1.4	1.8	2.8	1.3
Lincoln, NE	38.2	12.0	8.5	4.1	2.1	2.6	2.2	1.6	2.5
Little Rock, AR	10.3	9.5	8.9	8.6	1.6	1.0	1.9	2.0	1.0
Los Angeles, CA	5.6	4.4	4.0	3.4	2.9	1.3	1.3	0.9	0.6
Louisville, KY	17.9	12.4	9.2	13.1	2.4	1.1	2.1	1.9	1.0

Table continued on next page.

Metro Area	German	Irish	English	American	Italian	Polish	French[1]	Scottish	Dutch
Madison, WI	38.8	13.6	8.7	2.9	3.6	5.3	2.8	1.6	2.1
Manchester, NH	8.4	20.6	12.8	3.8	10.4	4.7	13.7	3.4	0.8
McAllen, TX	1.9	1.0	0.9	2.4	0.5	0.2	0.5	0.3	0.2
Miami, FL	4.7	4.5	2.9	6.0	5.1	2.0	1.3	0.7	0.4
Midland, TX	9.0	7.1	6.1	4.8	1.2	0.6	1.5	1.8	0.6
Minneapolis, MN	30.7	11.2	5.7	3.1	2.7	4.5	3.5	1.3	1.5
Nashville, TN	10.3	10.1	9.5	12.5	2.7	1.4	1.9	2.3	1.0
New Orleans, LA	10.1	7.6	4.6	5.0	8.2	0.7	12.8	1.1	0.4
New York, NY	6.7	9.7	2.9	4.8	12.8	3.9	1.0	0.7	0.6
Oklahoma City, OK	13.4	10.1	7.6	7.6	2.0	1.0	2.0	1.8	1.4
Omaha, NE	30.4	14.5	7.8	3.8	4.1	3.8	2.4	1.3	1.8
Orlando, FL	9.0	7.9	6.4	7.3	5.2	2.0	2.0	1.4	0.9
Peoria, IL	29.3	13.0	9.1	7.0	4.2	2.1	2.3	2.0	1.6
Philadelphia, PA	15.4	18.7	7.0	3.8	13.5	5.2	1.4	1.3	0.8
Phoenix, AZ	13.5	8.6	7.9	4.2	4.5	2.5	2.2	1.7	1.2
Pittsburgh, PA	27.1	18.0	8.0	4.0	16.1	8.6	1.8	1.9	1.2
Portland, OR	18.8	11.0	10.8	4.8	4.0	1.9	3.1	3.1	2.0
Providence, RI	4.8	18.0	10.4	3.4	14.4	3.9	10.0	1.7	0.4
Provo, UT	11.0	5.0	28.2	4.9	2.4	0.7	2.0	5.3	1.8
Raleigh, NC	11.0	9.7	10.2	10.9	4.9	2.1	1.9	2.6	1.0
Reno, NV	14.5	11.5	9.3	5.0	6.3	2.0	2.8	2.5	1.4
Richmond, VA	9.7	8.2	11.0	7.0	3.6	1.5	1.7	2.2	0.8
Roanoke, VA	12.9	10.5	11.0	14.1	2.6	1.3	1.7	2.2	1.1
Rochester, MN	36.7	11.8	6.3	3.6	1.7	3.4	2.3	1.2	2.0
Salem, OR	18.3	9.3	9.9	4.7	2.8	1.4	2.9	2.7	1.8
Salt Lake City, UT	10.7	5.7	21.0	4.3	3.1	0.9	2.0	4.0	2.2
San Antonio, TX	10.8	5.8	5.2	3.4	2.1	1.5	1.8	1.2	0.6
San Diego, CA	10.2	8.1	7.0	2.8	4.3	1.8	2.1	1.6	1.0
San Francisco, CA	8.1	7.6	5.9	2.5	5.0	1.5	2.0	1.5	0.9
San Jose, CA	6.5	5.0	4.7	1.8	3.9	1.2	1.5	1.1	0.7
Santa Rosa, CA	13.4	12.0	10.2	3.0	9.0	1.8	3.3	2.5	1.4
Savannah, GA	9.6	10.6	7.2	6.7	3.4	1.4	1.9	2.0	0.7
Seattle, WA	15.9	10.2	9.8	3.4	3.7	2.0	3.0	2.7	1.7
Sioux Falls, SD	39.1	10.4	5.2	4.3	1.3	1.6	2.1	1.0	6.8
Springfield, IL	25.9	14.8	10.7	6.4	5.3	2.0	2.5	1.8	1.4
Tallahassee, FL	9.5	9.0	8.2	5.6	3.3	1.6	2.0	2.4	1.0
Tampa, FL	12.6	11.0	7.9	9.7	7.5	3.1	2.7	1.8	1.1
Topeka, KS	27.4	12.0	12.2	6.0	1.8	1.3	2.8	2.0	1.6
Tyler, TX	8.8	8.3	8.2	15.0	1.7	0.7	2.3	2.0	0.9
Virginia Beach, VA	10.5	9.1	9.1	9.5	4.2	1.9	2.0	1.9	0.9
Visalia, CA	4.5	3.7	3.0	2.0	1.5	0.3	0.8	0.8	1.0
Washington, DC	10.0	8.7	7.0	4.4	4.4	2.3	1.6	1.7	0.8
Wilmington, NC	11.3	10.7	10.5	13.4	5.1	2.1	2.3	2.9	1.0
Winston-Salem, NC	12.5	8.0	9.5	10.7	2.6	1.0	1.5	2.3	1.2
U.S.	14.1	10.1	7.5	6.6	5.3	2.9	2.5	1.7	1.3

Note: Figures are the percentage of the total population reporting a particular ancestry. The nine most commonly reported ancestries in the U.S. are shown. Figures include multiple ancestries (e.g. if a person reported being Irish and Italian, they were included in both columns); Figures cover the Metropolitan Statistical Area—see Appendix B for areas included; (1) Excludes Basque
Source: U.S. Census Bureau, 2013-2017 American Community Survey 5-Year Estimates

Foreign-Born Population: City

City	Any Foreign Country	Asia	Mexico	Europe	Carribean	Central America[1]	South America	Africa	Canada
						Percent of Population Born in			
Albany, NY	12.7	6.1	0.2	2.0	2.0	0.2	1.0	1.0	0.2
Albuquerque, NM	9.9	2.3	5.6	0.8	0.3	0.2	0.3	0.3	0.2
Allentown, PA	17.4	3.1	0.8	0.6	8.4	1.3	2.3	0.6	0.1
Anchorage, AK	10.5	6.0	0.8	1.2	0.6	0.1	0.5	0.5	0.4
Ann Arbor, MI	18.6	11.9	0.4	3.3	0.2	0.2	0.8	0.8	0.8
Athens, GA	10.4	3.3	3.3	1.0	0.3	1.0	0.7	0.5	0.2
Atlanta, GA	6.9	2.7	0.9	1.1	0.6	0.2	0.4	0.6	0.2
Austin, TX	18.4	5.4	8.1	1.2	0.5	1.6	0.6	0.6	0.3
Baton Rouge, LA	5.5	3.0	0.6	0.4	0.2	0.7	0.3	0.3	0.1
Billings, MT	2.4	0.7	0.4	0.5	0.1	0.2	0.0	0.2	0.3
Boise City, ID	7.0	2.9	1.3	1.5	0.0	0.1	0.2	0.7	0.2
Boston, MA	28.3	7.4	0.3	3.6	8.3	2.9	2.4	3.1	0.4
Boulder, CO	11.2	4.4	1.4	2.9	0.0	0.2	1.0	0.2	0.6
Cape Coral, FL	14.7	1.3	0.7	2.5	5.6	1.3	2.6	0.1	0.6
Cedar Rapids, IA	5.0	2.5	0.9	0.4	0.2	0.1	0.1	0.7	0.1
Charleston, SC	4.1	1.4	0.4	1.2	0.2	0.2	0.1	0.3	0.2
Charlotte, NC	16.4	5.1	2.9	1.2	1.0	2.6	1.5	1.9	0.2
Chicago, IL	20.7	4.9	8.9	3.5	0.4	0.9	1.0	0.9	0.2
Clarksville, TN	5.5	1.6	1.3	1.0	0.4	0.3	0.5	0.3	0.1
College Station, TX	12.8	7.4	1.8	1.0	0.1	0.6	1.0	0.7	0.3
Colorado Springs, CO	7.5	2.1	2.1	1.6	0.3	0.3	0.3	0.4	0.3
Columbia, MO	7.8	4.8	0.3	1.0	0.1	0.1	0.4	0.7	0.3
Columbia, SC	5.6	2.3	0.9	0.9	0.2	0.3	0.5	0.4	0.1
Columbus, OH	11.8	4.6	1.4	0.8	0.4	0.4	0.3	3.7	0.1
Dallas, TX	24.4	2.9	15.8	0.7	0.4	2.4	0.5	1.6	0.2
Denver, CO	15.8	3.0	8.2	1.4	0.2	0.7	0.6	1.4	0.3
Des Moines, IA	12.3	4.1	3.5	1.0	0.1	1.1	0.1	2.2	0.1
Durham, NC	14.7	4.3	3.5	1.1	0.5	2.9	0.6	1.3	0.4
Edison, NJ	46.9	38.0	0.8	2.9	1.6	0.2	2.0	1.3	0.2
El Paso, TX	24.5	1.1	21.8	0.6	0.2	0.3	0.3	0.2	0.0
Eugene, OR	8.2	3.4	2.1	1.1	0.1	0.4	0.3	0.3	0.5
Evansville, IN	2.7	0.7	0.9	0.5	0.1	0.1	0.0	0.2	0.1
Fargo, ND	8.2	3.5	0.2	1.1	0.1	0.1	0.3	2.8	0.2
Fayetteville, NC	6.6	2.5	0.6	0.9	0.8	0.8	0.4	0.4	0.1
Fort Collins, CO	6.4	2.6	1.2	1.2	0.1	0.2	0.5	0.3	0.2
Fort Wayne, IN	7.8	3.5	1.9	0.9	0.1	0.7	0.3	0.2	0.1
Fort Worth, TX	16.9	3.1	10.3	0.7	0.3	0.8	0.4	1.0	0.2
Gainesville, FL	11.1	4.8	0.4	1.4	1.4	0.3	2.0	0.6	0.2
Grand Rapids, MI	10.3	2.0	3.2	1.1	0.6	1.8	0.1	1.1	0.4
Greeley, CO	11.2	1.1	7.6	0.4	0.2	0.8	0.3	0.7	0.1
Green Bay, WI	9.1	2.1	4.9	0.6	0.1	0.7	0.2	0.4	0.1
Greensboro, NC	10.5	3.7	2.1	1.0	0.4	0.5	0.6	2.0	0.2
Honolulu, HI	27.1	23.0	0.2	0.8	0.1	0.1	0.2	0.1	0.2
Houston, TX	29.2	5.9	12.2	1.2	0.9	5.9	1.1	1.7	0.2
Huntsville, AL	6.6	2.3	1.6	0.8	0.5	0.6	0.2	0.5	0.1
Indianapolis, IN	9.3	2.5	3.2	0.5	0.4	1.0	0.2	1.3	0.1
Jacksonville, FL	10.6	4.1	0.6	1.7	1.7	0.6	1.1	0.5	0.2
Kansas City, MO	7.8	2.3	2.4	0.6	0.4	0.6	0.3	1.1	0.1
Lafayette, LA	4.9	1.8	0.9	0.7	0.3	0.5	0.1	0.3	0.2
Las Cruces, NM	11.4	2.1	7.8	0.5	0.1	0.3	0.1	0.5	0.1
Las Vegas, NV	21.2	5.2	9.7	1.5	1.1	2.1	0.8	0.4	0.3
Lexington, KY	9.1	3.5	2.4	0.9	0.2	0.5	0.3	1.0	0.2
Lincoln, NE	8.4	4.5	1.4	1.0	0.2	0.3	0.3	0.6	0.2
Little Rock, AR	7.5	2.8	2.0	0.7	0.1	0.9	0.4	0.3	0.2

Table continued on next page.

City	Percent of Population Born in								
	Any Foreign Country	Asia	Mexico	Europe	Carribean	Central America[1]	South America	Africa	Canada
Los Angeles, CA	37.6	11.2	13.2	2.4	0.3	8.3	1.1	0.6	0.4
Louisville, KY	7.1	2.2	0.8	0.9	1.4	0.2	0.3	1.2	0.1
Madison, WI	11.7	6.4	1.8	1.4	0.1	0.3	0.6	0.8	0.2
Manchester, NH	13.2	4.9	0.8	2.3	1.1	0.8	0.8	1.5	1.0
McAllen, TX	27.4	2.0	23.7	0.3	0.2	0.4	0.6	0.0	0.1
Miami, FL	58.0	0.9	0.9	1.9	33.0	12.1	8.8	0.2	0.1
Midland, TX	12.4	1.7	8.2	0.3	0.7	0.2	0.4	0.4	0.4
Minneapolis, MN	15.9	4.0	2.9	1.1	0.3	0.4	1.3	5.4	0.3
Nashville, TN	12.8	3.9	3.0	0.7	0.4	1.7	0.4	2.4	0.2
New Orleans, LA	5.9	2.0	0.3	0.8	0.3	1.6	0.4	0.3	0.1
New York, NY	37.2	10.8	2.1	5.5	10.3	1.4	4.9	1.7	0.3
Oklahoma City, OK	12.1	3.4	6.1	0.4	0.1	1.1	0.3	0.5	0.1
Omaha, NE	10.3	3.0	4.0	0.7	0.2	1.0	0.2	1.1	0.1
Orlando, FL	19.8	3.1	0.5	1.5	6.3	1.2	6.4	0.6	0.3
Peoria, IL	8.3	4.6	1.7	0.8	0.1	0.1	0.4	0.3	0.1
Philadelphia, PA	13.4	5.3	0.5	2.2	2.4	0.6	0.8	1.4	0.1
Phoenix, AZ	19.6	3.3	12.4	1.3	0.3	0.8	0.4	0.7	0.4
Pittsburgh, PA	8.6	4.9	0.2	1.8	0.2	0.1	0.4	0.7	0.2
Portland, OR	14.0	5.7	2.4	2.9	0.2	0.4	0.4	1.1	0.5
Providence, RI	29.2	4.5	0.8	2.2	11.8	5.3	1.7	2.7	0.2
Provo, UT	10.5	1.7	4.4	0.5	0.1	0.6	2.1	0.3	0.4
Raleigh, NC	13.4	3.9	3.1	1.4	0.7	1.4	0.6	1.8	0.4
Reno, NV	16.5	5.0	7.0	1.1	0.1	1.9	0.6	0.3	0.3
Richmond, VA	6.4	1.4	0.8	0.6	0.3	2.0	0.4	0.7	0.1
Roanoke, VA	7.6	2.8	0.7	0.6	1.1	1.2	0.1	0.7	0.2
Rochester, MN	13.6	5.7	1.8	1.7	0.2	0.2	0.2	3.4	0.3
Salem, OR	11.5	1.8	7.2	1.1	0.1	0.2	0.2	0.2	0.3
Salt Lake City, UT	16.4	4.3	6.4	2.0	0.2	0.6	1.2	0.8	0.4
San Antonio, TX	14.2	2.4	9.3	0.6	0.2	0.7	0.4	0.3	0.1
San Diego, CA	26.4	12.0	9.3	2.3	0.2	0.5	0.7	0.8	0.5
San Francisco, CA	34.8	22.5	2.6	4.5	0.2	2.6	1.0	0.5	0.6
San Jose, CA	39.4	24.7	9.6	2.1	0.1	1.0	0.6	0.7	0.4
Santa Rosa, CA	19.4	4.2	10.9	1.6	0.1	0.8	0.2	0.9	0.3
Savannah, GA	5.6	2.1	0.8	1.0	0.4	0.3	0.5	0.3	0.2
Seattle, WA	18.0	10.0	1.2	2.6	0.1	0.4	0.5	2.1	0.9
Sioux Falls, SD	7.3	2.1	0.4	0.8	0.1	0.9	0.1	2.7	0.1
Springfield, IL	4.1	2.3	0.4	0.5	0.2	0.1	0.1	0.5	0.1
Tallahassee, FL	7.9	3.3	0.2	1.0	1.2	0.4	0.7	0.8	0.2
Tampa, FL	16.2	3.5	1.3	1.3	6.3	1.1	1.8	0.6	0.4
Topeka, KS	5.3	1.3	2.7	0.4	0.1	0.3	0.2	0.1	0.0
Tyler, TX	10.9	1.7	7.0	0.4	0.2	0.6	0.1	0.5	0.2
Virginia Beach, VA	9.1	4.9	0.5	1.5	0.6	0.5	0.5	0.5	0.2
Visalia, CA	13.9	3.5	8.4	0.7	0.1	0.6	0.2	0.2	0.2
Washington, DC	14.0	2.8	0.6	2.6	1.2	2.7	1.5	2.2	0.3
Wilmington, NC	5.8	1.2	1.4	1.3	0.2	0.9	0.4	0.2	0.2
Winston-Salem, NC	9.8	1.9	4.2	0.9	0.4	1.5	0.5	0.4	0.1
U.S.	13.4	4.1	3.6	1.5	1.3	1.0	0.9	0.6	0.3

Note: (1) Excludes Mexico
Source: U.S. Census Bureau, 2013-2017 American Community Survey 5-Year Estimates

Foreign-Born Population: Metro Area

Metro Area	Any Foreign Country	Percent of Population Born in							
		Asia	Mexico	Europe	Carribean	Central America[1]	South America	Africa	Canada
Albany, NY	7.7	3.3	0.2	1.7	0.6	0.1	1.0	0.5	0.2
Albuquerque, NM	9.3	1.7	5.7	0.7	0.2	0.2	0.3	0.2	0.2
Allentown, PA	8.7	2.6	0.4	1.6	1.9	0.6	1.1	0.4	0.1
Anchorage, AK	8.7	4.8	0.6	1.3	0.5	0.1	0.4	0.4	0.4
Ann Arbor, MI	12.0	7.0	0.4	2.1	0.2	0.4	0.5	0.7	0.6
Athens, GA	8.1	2.7	2.4	0.9	0.2	0.9	0.5	0.4	0.2
Atlanta, GA	13.6	4.3	2.8	1.2	1.4	1.1	1.0	1.5	0.2
Austin, TX	14.9	4.2	6.8	1.0	0.4	1.1	0.5	0.6	0.2
Baton Rouge, LA	3.9	1.6	0.7	0.3	0.2	0.6	0.2	0.2	0.1
Billings, MT	2.1	0.6	0.4	0.5	0.0	0.1	0.0	0.1	0.2
Boise City, ID	6.4	1.6	2.8	1.1	0.0	0.2	0.2	0.3	0.2
Boston, MA	18.2	5.8	0.2	3.3	3.2	1.5	1.9	1.6	0.5
Boulder, CO	10.8	3.5	3.0	2.3	0.1	0.3	0.7	0.2	0.5
Cape Coral, FL	16.1	1.2	2.5	2.2	5.2	1.9	1.9	0.2	1.0
Cedar Rapids, IA	3.5	1.6	0.6	0.4	0.1	0.0	0.1	0.5	0.2
Charleston, SC	5.0	1.3	1.1	1.0	0.3	0.4	0.5	0.2	0.2
Charlotte, NC	9.8	2.7	2.2	1.0	0.6	1.3	0.9	0.8	0.2
Chicago, IL	17.7	5.0	6.7	3.8	0.3	0.5	0.6	0.6	0.2
Clarksville, TN	4.2	1.4	0.9	0.7	0.3	0.3	0.3	0.3	0.1
College Station, TX	12.4	4.0	5.7	0.7	0.1	0.6	0.5	0.5	0.2
Colorado Springs, CO	6.7	1.9	1.7	1.6	0.3	0.3	0.3	0.3	0.3
Columbia, MO	6.0	3.4	0.4	0.9	0.1	0.1	0.3	0.5	0.3
Columbia, SC	5.1	1.6	1.2	0.8	0.2	0.5	0.2	0.4	0.1
Columbus, OH	7.5	3.2	0.8	0.8	0.2	0.2	0.2	1.9	0.1
Dallas, TX	18.1	4.9	8.7	0.8	0.3	1.4	0.5	1.3	0.2
Denver, CO	12.3	3.2	5.3	1.5	0.1	0.5	0.4	0.9	0.3
Des Moines, IA	7.8	2.9	1.7	1.3	0.1	0.6	0.2	1.1	0.1
Durham, NC	12.2	3.7	3.1	1.3	0.4	1.9	0.5	0.8	0.4
Edison, NJ	28.9	8.4	1.6	4.4	6.7	1.9	4.2	1.3	0.2
El Paso, TX	25.5	1.0	23.1	0.5	0.2	0.3	0.2	0.2	0.0
Eugene, OR	5.9	2.0	1.7	0.9	0.0	0.4	0.2	0.2	0.3
Evansville, IN	2.6	1.2	0.5	0.5	0.1	0.2	0.1	0.1	0.1
Fargo, ND	5.9	2.6	0.2	0.7	0.1	0.1	0.2	1.8	0.3
Fayetteville, NC	6.0	1.9	1.0	0.9	0.7	0.7	0.4	0.3	0.1
Fort Collins, CO	5.4	1.7	1.3	1.2	0.1	0.1	0.5	0.2	0.2
Fort Wayne, IN	5.7	2.6	1.3	0.7	0.1	0.5	0.2	0.2	0.1
Fort Worth, TX	18.1	4.9	8.7	0.8	0.3	1.4	0.5	1.3	0.2
Gainesville, FL	9.5	4.0	0.4	1.3	1.4	0.3	1.4	0.4	0.3
Grand Rapids, MI	6.6	2.0	1.9	1.1	0.4	0.5	0.1	0.4	0.3
Greeley, CO	8.8	1.0	5.9	0.4	0.2	0.5	0.2	0.3	0.1
Green Bay, WI	5.1	1.5	2.3	0.5	0.1	0.3	0.1	0.2	0.1
Greensboro, NC	8.7	2.9	2.6	0.7	0.3	0.6	0.4	1.0	0.2
Honolulu, HI	19.4	16.0	0.2	0.7	0.1	0.1	0.2	0.1	0.2
Houston, TX	23.2	5.8	9.4	1.1	0.7	3.5	1.2	1.2	0.3
Huntsville, AL	5.2	1.9	1.2	0.7	0.3	0.4	0.1	0.3	0.1
Indianapolis, IN	6.7	2.3	1.8	0.6	0.2	0.5	0.2	0.8	0.1
Jacksonville, FL	8.8	3.2	0.5	1.6	1.4	0.5	0.9	0.4	0.2
Kansas City, MO	6.6	2.2	2.1	0.6	0.2	0.5	0.2	0.6	0.1
Lafayette, LA	3.3	1.1	0.9	0.3	0.1	0.5	0.1	0.2	0.1
Las Cruces, NM	17.2	1.3	14.7	0.5	0.0	0.2	0.1	0.3	0.1
Las Vegas, NV	22.3	7.2	8.6	1.6	1.1	1.9	0.7	0.7	0.4
Lexington, KY	7.1	2.5	2.1	0.8	0.2	0.4	0.2	0.7	0.2
Lincoln, NE	7.5	3.9	1.2	0.9	0.2	0.3	0.2	0.6	0.2
Little Rock, AR	4.1	1.4	1.3	0.5	0.1	0.5	0.2	0.2	0.1

Table continued on next page.

Metro Area	Percent of Population Born in								
	Any Foreign Country	Asia	Mexico	Europe	Carribean	Central America[1]	South America	Africa	Canada
Los Angeles, CA	33.4	12.7	12.7	1.7	0.3	4.2	0.9	0.6	0.3
Louisville, KY	5.2	1.6	0.9	0.7	0.8	0.2	0.2	0.7	0.1
Madison, WI	7.4	3.5	1.5	1.0	0.1	0.2	0.4	0.5	0.2
Manchester, NH	9.3	3.3	0.5	1.7	0.8	0.4	0.8	0.7	0.9
McAllen, TX	27.3	0.8	25.5	0.1	0.1	0.4	0.3	0.0	0.1
Miami, FL	40.0	2.1	1.1	2.3	21.0	4.2	8.3	0.4	0.6
Midland, TX	12.2	1.5	8.6	0.4	0.6	0.2	0.3	0.3	0.3
Minneapolis, MN	10.4	4.1	1.4	1.1	0.2	0.4	0.5	2.5	0.2
Nashville, TN	7.8	2.5	2.0	0.7	0.2	0.8	0.3	1.1	0.2
New Orleans, LA	7.6	2.1	0.6	0.6	0.7	2.7	0.5	0.3	0.1
New York, NY	28.9	8.4	1.6	4.4	6.7	1.9	4.2	1.3	0.2
Oklahoma City, OK	8.0	2.5	3.6	0.4	0.1	0.7	0.2	0.4	0.1
Omaha, NE	7.2	2.2	2.7	0.6	0.1	0.6	0.2	0.7	0.1
Orlando, FL	17.3	3.0	1.2	1.5	5.3	1.1	4.4	0.6	0.3
Peoria, IL	3.8	1.9	0.7	0.6	0.1	0.1	0.2	0.1	0.1
Philadelphia, PA	10.5	4.4	0.9	1.9	1.2	0.4	0.6	1.0	0.1
Phoenix, AZ	14.3	3.2	7.5	1.3	0.2	0.5	0.3	0.5	0.7
Pittsburgh, PA	3.8	1.9	0.1	1.0	0.1	0.1	0.2	0.3	0.1
Portland, OR	12.6	4.7	3.4	2.4	0.2	0.4	0.3	0.5	0.4
Providence, RI	13.3	2.3	0.2	4.4	2.2	1.4	1.1	1.5	0.2
Provo, UT	7.1	1.1	2.9	0.5	0.1	0.5	1.3	0.2	0.3
Raleigh, NC	12.1	4.2	3.0	1.2	0.5	1.0	0.6	1.1	0.4
Reno, NV	14.3	3.9	6.5	1.0	0.1	1.6	0.5	0.3	0.3
Richmond, VA	7.4	3.0	0.6	1.0	0.4	1.2	0.4	0.6	0.1
Roanoke, VA	4.9	1.9	0.6	0.7	0.5	0.4	0.2	0.4	0.2
Rochester, MN	8.1	3.3	1.2	1.1	0.1	0.2	0.2	1.8	0.2
Salem, OR	11.9	1.5	8.0	1.1	0.0	0.3	0.2	0.2	0.3
Salt Lake City, UT	12.0	2.9	4.7	1.3	0.1	0.6	1.1	0.5	0.3
San Antonio, TX	11.7	2.0	7.4	0.7	0.2	0.6	0.4	0.3	0.1
San Diego, CA	23.6	9.0	10.4	1.9	0.2	0.5	0.6	0.5	0.4
San Francisco, CA	30.5	17.1	5.2	2.9	0.2	2.5	0.9	0.7	0.4
San Jose, CA	38.1	24.5	7.6	3.0	0.1	0.9	0.7	0.6	0.5
Santa Rosa, CA	16.6	3.0	9.4	1.9	0.1	0.8	0.4	0.4	0.4
Savannah, GA	5.7	1.9	1.1	0.9	0.4	0.4	0.4	0.3	0.2
Seattle, WA	17.8	9.3	2.4	2.7	0.1	0.5	0.4	1.3	0.7
Sioux Falls, SD	5.4	1.5	0.4	0.7	0.1	0.7	0.1	1.9	0.1
Springfield, IL	2.9	1.6	0.3	0.4	0.1	0.1	0.1	0.3	0.1
Tallahassee, FL	6.0	2.1	0.4	0.8	0.9	0.5	0.5	0.5	0.2
Tampa, FL	13.2	2.7	1.4	2.2	3.4	0.7	1.8	0.4	0.7
Topeka, KS	3.4	0.9	1.6	0.3	0.1	0.2	0.1	0.1	0.1
Tyler, TX	8.3	1.1	5.8	0.3	0.1	0.4	0.1	0.3	0.1
Virginia Beach, VA	6.4	2.9	0.4	1.1	0.5	0.6	0.4	0.5	0.1
Visalia, CA	22.4	2.2	18.4	0.7	0.1	0.6	0.1	0.1	0.1
Washington, DC	22.6	8.2	0.8	1.9	1.1	4.8	2.3	3.3	0.2
Wilmington, NC	4.8	0.9	1.3	1.1	0.2	0.7	0.3	0.2	0.2
Winston-Salem, NC	6.7	1.3	2.9	0.6	0.2	0.9	0.3	0.2	0.1
U.S.	13.4	4.1	3.6	1.5	1.3	1.0	0.9	0.6	0.3

Note: Figures cover the Metropolitan Statistical Area—see Appendix B for areas included; (1) Excludes Mexico
Source: U.S. Census Bureau, 2013-2017 American Community Survey 5-Year Estimates

Marital Status: City

City	Never Married	Now Married[1]	Separated	Widowed	Divorced
Albany, NY	59.4	24.6	1.9	5.5	8.5
Albuquerque, NM	37.0	41.8	1.7	5.6	13.9
Allentown, PA	46.3	33.6	3.9	5.4	10.8
Anchorage, AK	34.4	48.9	1.6	3.4	11.7
Ann Arbor, MI	55.3	34.0	0.7	2.7	7.3
Athens, GA	55.5	30.9	1.6	3.8	8.1
Atlanta, GA	54.3	27.1	2.0	5.7	10.9
Austin, TX	43.5	40.3	1.9	3.1	11.1
Baton Rouge, LA	48.7	30.6	2.5	6.8	11.3
Billings, MT	29.3	48.9	1.2	6.5	14.1
Boise City, ID	34.2	46.6	1.1	4.4	13.7
Boston, MA	55.9	29.7	2.8	4.1	7.5
Boulder, CO	55.2	32.8	0.7	2.7	8.6
Cape Coral, FL	24.6	51.5	2.2	7.8	13.9
Cedar Rapids, IA	34.2	47.0	1.3	6.0	11.5
Charleston, SC	41.6	40.5	1.8	5.0	11.2
Charlotte, NC	40.5	42.5	2.7	4.1	10.2
Chicago, IL	49.0	35.1	2.3	5.2	8.4
Clarksville, TN	28.8	52.1	2.7	4.1	12.3
College Station, TX	61.1	30.8	0.9	2.1	5.1
Colorado Springs, CO	30.3	50.2	1.7	4.7	13.1
Columbia, MO	49.1	37.6	1.1	3.3	8.9
Columbia, SC	56.0	27.9	3.0	4.3	8.8
Columbus, OH	44.7	36.5	2.1	4.4	12.2
Dallas, TX	41.1	40.0	3.4	4.6	10.9
Denver, CO	42.2	39.2	2.0	4.2	12.4
Des Moines, IA	37.0	41.2	2.0	5.5	14.2
Durham, NC	42.6	39.9	2.6	4.5	10.5
Edison, NJ	25.5	60.7	1.5	6.2	6.1
El Paso, TX	33.9	45.7	3.4	5.9	11.1
Eugene, OR	42.3	39.7	1.4	4.5	12.0
Evansville, IN	34.3	39.4	1.6	7.0	17.7
Fargo, ND	43.9	41.4	1.1	4.5	9.1
Fayetteville, NC	37.2	42.4	3.8	5.1	11.6
Fort Collins, CO	45.6	41.5	0.9	3.2	8.8
Fort Wayne, IN	34.8	44.7	1.4	5.9	13.2
Fort Worth, TX	34.9	45.9	2.5	4.6	12.1
Gainesville, FL	61.0	24.9	1.7	3.7	8.7
Grand Rapids, MI	46.4	36.2	1.7	5.2	10.5
Greeley, CO	35.8	46.2	1.5	5.0	11.5
Green Bay, WI	38.7	42.6	1.5	5.0	12.3
Greensboro, NC	42.0	39.0	2.4	5.6	11.0
Honolulu, HI	35.7	45.9	1.3	7.0	10.1
Houston, TX	40.5	41.6	3.2	4.7	10.0
Huntsville, AL	34.8	43.9	2.2	6.0	13.1
Indianapolis, IN	41.4	38.3	2.0	5.2	13.1
Jacksonville, FL	34.6	43.1	2.6	5.9	13.8
Kansas City, MO	39.7	39.6	2.1	5.5	13.1
Lafayette, LA	43.3	37.9	2.2	5.6	11.0
Las Cruces, NM	38.6	41.8	1.6	5.4	12.5
Las Vegas, NV	34.8	43.0	2.6	5.4	14.1
Lexington, KY	38.8	42.8	1.8	4.5	12.2
Lincoln, NE	38.4	45.6	1.1	4.4	10.5
Little Rock, AR	37.3	41.2	2.7	5.8	13.1
Los Angeles, CA	45.8	38.6	2.7	4.6	8.3
Louisville, KY	35.9	41.8	2.1	6.3	13.8

Table continued on next page.

City	Never Married	Now Married[1]	Separated	Widowed	Divorced
Madison, WI	49.3	37.8	0.9	3.4	8.5
Manchester, NH	38.1	40.3	2.0	5.4	14.2
McAllen, TX	31.7	50.6	3.5	5.0	9.2
Miami, FL	40.9	34.7	4.0	6.6	13.9
Midland, TX	29.4	52.1	1.9	5.0	11.7
Minneapolis, MN	51.0	34.3	1.7	3.1	10.0
Nashville, TN	40.4	40.3	2.2	4.8	12.3
New Orleans, LA	48.8	29.8	3.0	6.0	12.5
New York, NY	43.9	39.5	3.1	5.6	7.8
Oklahoma City, OK	32.8	46.2	2.3	5.6	13.0
Omaha, NE	36.0	45.8	1.7	5.0	11.4
Orlando, FL	43.2	35.3	3.4	4.5	13.7
Peoria, IL	40.2	40.3	1.3	6.2	12.0
Philadelphia, PA	51.7	29.6	3.4	6.3	9.1
Phoenix, AZ	39.1	41.9	2.2	4.3	12.6
Pittsburgh, PA	51.8	31.2	2.0	6.0	9.0
Portland, OR	40.3	41.3	1.8	4.1	12.5
Providence, RI	52.9	31.4	2.8	4.4	8.5
Provo, UT	45.7	46.4	0.9	2.1	4.8
Raleigh, NC	42.7	40.3	2.6	3.8	10.6
Reno, NV	35.6	41.8	2.3	5.2	15.1
Richmond, VA	52.0	26.6	3.3	6.0	12.1
Roanoke, VA	36.7	37.9	3.0	7.7	14.7
Rochester, MN	31.6	52.8	1.0	4.7	9.9
Salem, OR	33.9	44.9	2.1	5.3	13.9
Salt Lake City, UT	41.4	42.1	1.7	4.1	10.7
San Antonio, TX	37.6	41.9	3.1	5.2	12.1
San Diego, CA	40.1	43.8	1.8	4.2	10.0
San Francisco, CA	45.8	39.8	1.4	4.7	8.3
San Jose, CA	35.2	50.7	1.7	4.3	8.1
Santa Rosa, CA	34.3	44.1	1.8	6.0	13.9
Savannah, GA	46.7	31.2	2.7	6.4	13.1
Seattle, WA	44.1	40.8	1.2	3.7	10.1
Sioux Falls, SD	34.0	48.6	1.4	5.1	10.8
Springfield, IL	36.0	41.8	1.5	6.4	14.3
Tallahassee, FL	55.9	29.9	1.2	3.5	9.5
Tampa, FL	41.4	37.3	2.9	5.2	13.2
Topeka, KS	31.8	44.7	1.5	7.2	14.8
Tyler, TX	35.2	42.8	2.1	7.0	13.0
Virginia Beach, VA	31.0	50.1	2.7	5.0	11.2
Visalia, CA	34.6	48.1	2.0	4.7	10.7
Washington, DC	55.8	28.5	2.2	4.4	9.1
Wilmington, NC	42.4	38.6	2.6	5.3	11.1
Winston-Salem, NC	39.8	40.6	3.0	5.9	10.8
U.S.	33.1	48.2	2.0	5.8	10.9

Note: Figures are percentages and cover the population 15 years of age and older; (1) Excludes separated
Source: U.S. Census Bureau, 2013-2017 American Community Survey 5-Year Estimates

Marital Status: Metro Area

Metro Area	Never Married	Now Married[1]	Separated	Widowed	Divorced
Albany, NY	36.2	46.0	1.9	6.0	9.9
Albuquerque, NM	34.6	44.6	1.6	5.7	13.4
Allentown, PA	31.3	50.0	2.3	6.5	9.9
Anchorage, AK	33.6	49.2	1.7	3.6	11.9
Ann Arbor, MI	42.7	43.7	0.9	3.8	8.9
Athens, GA	43.3	40.9	1.7	5.0	9.1
Atlanta, GA	35.0	47.4	2.1	4.6	11.0
Austin, TX	36.2	47.4	1.8	3.7	10.9
Baton Rouge, LA	36.5	43.5	2.2	6.2	11.7
Billings, MT	26.9	52.6	1.3	6.1	13.2
Boise City, ID	29.3	52.7	1.2	4.7	12.2
Boston, MA	36.9	47.5	1.7	5.2	8.8
Boulder, CO	37.6	47.0	0.9	3.6	10.9
Cape Coral, FL	26.1	50.8	1.9	8.2	13.0
Cedar Rapids, IA	28.9	53.2	1.2	5.8	10.9
Charleston, SC	33.9	46.5	2.7	5.6	11.3
Charlotte, NC	32.0	49.6	2.6	5.3	10.5
Chicago, IL	36.9	47.0	1.7	5.5	8.9
Clarksville, TN	27.9	52.7	2.4	5.0	12.0
College Station, TX	46.5	39.4	2.1	4.1	8.0
Colorado Springs, CO	28.7	53.7	1.6	4.1	11.9
Columbia, MO	41.8	43.5	1.3	3.8	9.7
Columbia, SC	36.2	44.2	3.1	5.8	10.7
Columbus, OH	34.3	47.5	1.8	4.9	11.6
Dallas, TX	32.0	50.5	2.3	4.5	10.8
Denver, CO	32.5	49.9	1.5	4.1	11.9
Des Moines, IA	29.5	52.4	1.3	5.0	11.7
Durham, NC	37.4	45.3	2.3	4.9	10.0
Edison, NJ	38.1	45.8	2.4	5.8	7.9
El Paso, TX	34.5	46.1	3.4	5.5	10.5
Eugene, OR	33.8	45.6	1.6	5.5	13.4
Evansville, IN	27.9	50.7	1.2	6.3	13.9
Fargo, ND	37.5	48.6	0.9	4.3	8.7
Fayetteville, NC	34.1	45.9	3.5	5.2	11.2
Fort Collins, CO	34.2	50.6	1.0	3.9	10.2
Fort Wayne, IN	30.4	50.6	1.2	5.8	12.0
Fort Worth, TX	32.0	50.5	2.3	4.5	10.8
Gainesville, FL	45.5	37.6	1.6	4.8	10.4
Grand Rapids, MI	32.1	51.9	1.1	4.9	10.0
Greeley, CO	27.8	55.7	1.3	4.3	11.0
Green Bay, WI	30.5	53.0	1.0	5.1	10.5
Greensboro, NC	33.2	46.6	2.8	6.3	11.1
Honolulu, HI	33.6	50.3	1.2	6.3	8.6
Houston, TX	33.3	50.1	2.5	4.5	9.6
Huntsville, AL	30.1	50.3	1.9	5.8	11.9
Indianapolis, IN	32.5	48.3	1.5	5.3	12.4
Jacksonville, FL	30.9	48.0	2.2	5.9	13.0
Kansas City, MO	30.3	50.5	1.7	5.4	12.1
Lafayette, LA	34.8	45.4	2.3	5.9	11.5
Las Cruces, NM	35.9	46.9	2.2	5.0	10.0
Las Vegas, NV	34.4	44.3	2.5	5.2	13.7
Lexington, KY	34.0	47.0	1.9	4.8	12.3
Lincoln, NE	36.4	48.2	1.1	4.4	10.0
Little Rock, AR	30.5	47.7	2.3	6.0	13.5
Los Angeles, CA	39.9	44.4	2.3	4.9	8.5
Louisville, KY	31.3	47.4	1.8	6.3	13.3

Table continued on next page.

Metro Area	Never Married	Now Married[1]	Separated	Widowed	Divorced
Madison, WI	36.0	49.2	0.9	4.2	9.6
Manchester, NH	29.9	51.6	1.3	5.2	11.9
McAllen, TX	33.6	49.7	3.9	5.1	7.8
Miami, FL	34.6	42.9	3.0	6.6	12.9
Midland, TX	28.8	52.8	2.0	4.8	11.7
Minneapolis, MN	33.0	51.5	1.2	4.4	10.0
Nashville, TN	31.4	50.1	1.8	5.0	11.6
New Orleans, LA	37.5	41.6	2.4	6.4	12.2
New York, NY	38.1	45.8	2.4	5.8	7.9
Oklahoma City, OK	30.8	48.8	2.1	5.6	12.7
Omaha, NE	31.0	51.7	1.4	5.0	10.9
Orlando, FL	34.8	46.0	2.3	5.3	11.7
Peoria, IL	29.6	51.3	1.1	6.7	11.3
Philadelphia, PA	37.4	45.1	2.2	6.2	9.0
Phoenix, AZ	33.8	47.3	1.7	5.1	12.2
Pittsburgh, PA	31.6	49.3	1.7	7.5	9.8
Portland, OR	31.5	49.9	1.7	4.6	12.2
Providence, RI	35.3	45.7	1.7	6.3	11.0
Provo, UT	31.8	58.8	1.0	2.6	5.8
Raleigh, NC	31.6	51.8	2.5	4.3	9.8
Reno, NV	31.1	47.8	1.9	5.2	14.1
Richmond, VA	34.4	46.2	2.5	5.9	11.1
Roanoke, VA	28.0	49.9	2.3	7.5	12.3
Rochester, MN	27.3	57.6	0.8	4.9	9.3
Salem, OR	30.8	49.5	2.0	5.3	12.4
Salt Lake City, UT	31.3	52.4	1.8	4.0	10.5
San Antonio, TX	33.9	46.7	2.7	5.2	11.5
San Diego, CA	35.7	47.4	1.8	4.8	10.3
San Francisco, CA	36.1	48.3	1.6	4.9	9.1
San Jose, CA	33.3	53.0	1.5	4.2	7.9
Santa Rosa, CA	32.3	47.6	1.7	5.3	13.2
Savannah, GA	34.7	45.1	2.1	5.8	12.2
Seattle, WA	32.3	50.6	1.5	4.4	11.2
Sioux Falls, SD	30.4	53.2	1.3	5.1	10.1
Springfield, IL	30.8	48.6	1.2	6.1	13.3
Tallahassee, FL	43.4	39.8	1.6	4.5	10.8
Tampa, FL	30.8	46.3	2.2	7.1	13.6
Topeka, KS	26.6	52.9	1.2	6.7	12.5
Tyler, TX	28.9	50.5	2.2	6.7	11.7
Virginia Beach, VA	33.7	46.9	2.9	5.5	11.1
Visalia, CA	36.9	47.1	2.3	5.0	8.7
Washington, DC	36.1	48.7	2.1	4.3	8.9
Wilmington, NC	33.5	46.7	2.6	5.9	11.4
Winston-Salem, NC	29.5	50.0	2.7	6.6	11.2
U.S.	33.1	48.2	2.0	5.8	10.9

Note: Figures are percentages and cover the population 15 years of age and older; Figures cover the Metropolitan Statistical Area—see Appendix B for areas included; (1) Excludes separated
Source: U.S. Census Bureau, 2013-2017 American Community Survey 5-Year Estimates

Disability by Age: City

City	All Ages	Under 18 Years Old	18 to 64 Years Old	65 Years and Over
Albany, NY	12.1	3.7	10.3	34.6
Albuquerque, NM	13.3	3.5	11.7	37.1
Allentown, PA	18.3	10.3	17.9	39.5
Anchorage, AK	10.9	3.7	9.8	37.7
Ann Arbor, MI	6.9	1.7	4.8	26.9
Athens, GA	10.5	3.6	9.1	33.7
Atlanta, GA	12.1	4.2	9.9	38.9
Austin, TX	8.7	3.8	7.3	32.9
Baton Rouge, LA	16.1	8.2	13.2	43.9
Billings, MT	13.0	5.6	10.5	33.7
Boise City, ID	11.2	4.0	9.5	32.3
Boston, MA	12.3	5.1	9.6	41.7
Boulder, CO	6.8	2.2	4.7	28.5
Cape Coral, FL	12.8	2.8	9.8	30.2
Cedar Rapids, IA	10.4	3.9	8.4	30.0
Charleston, SC	9.6	3.0	7.6	28.4
Charlotte, NC	8.7	2.9	7.5	32.3
Chicago, IL	10.6	3.0	8.4	37.8
Clarksville, TN	14.7	4.7	15.5	43.8
College Station, TX	6.0	3.2	4.6	31.5
Colorado Springs, CO	12.8	4.3	11.6	34.5
Columbia, MO	9.6	3.2	7.8	36.3
Columbia, SC	11.7	3.5	10.0	36.6
Columbus, OH	11.9	4.9	10.8	36.9
Dallas, TX	9.6	3.1	8.2	36.0
Denver, CO	9.6	2.9	7.6	34.5
Des Moines, IA	13.7	5.1	13.0	36.2
Durham, NC	9.9	3.4	8.3	34.3
Edison, NJ	8.1	3.1	5.2	30.1
El Paso, TX	13.7	4.4	11.5	45.0
Eugene, OR	13.5	4.8	11.0	35.7
Evansville, IN	17.9	6.1	16.5	41.2
Fargo, ND	10.4	3.0	8.6	36.2
Fayetteville, NC	16.7	6.7	15.4	44.1
Fort Collins, CO	8.0	2.8	6.0	32.6
Fort Wayne, IN	13.3	5.7	12.3	33.4
Fort Worth, TX	10.5	3.6	9.7	37.5
Gainesville, FL	10.0	2.9	8.0	36.1
Grand Rapids, MI	13.8	5.8	12.5	39.8
Greeley, CO	11.3	3.0	9.8	38.2
Green Bay, WI	13.6	5.5	12.9	34.0
Greensboro, NC	10.0	3.6	7.7	32.1
Honolulu, HI	11.3	2.5	7.3	32.5
Houston, TX	9.6	3.3	7.8	36.8
Huntsville, AL	13.2	4.4	10.9	35.4
Indianapolis, IN	13.7	5.6	12.4	39.3
Jacksonville, FL	13.6	4.9	11.8	38.7
Kansas City, MO	13.0	3.9	11.8	37.3
Lafayette, LA	12.0	3.1	10.6	34.6
Las Cruces, NM	13.6	4.1	10.9	39.8
Las Vegas, NV	13.1	3.9	11.3	36.5
Lexington, KY	11.9	4.1	10.1	35.4
Lincoln, NE	10.8	4.3	8.5	34.4
Little Rock, AR	13.2	6.4	11.2	35.6
Los Angeles, CA	10.0	3.0	7.4	38.3

Table continued on next page.

City	All Ages	Under 18 Years Old	18 to 64 Years Old	65 Years and Over
Louisville, KY	14.8	5.0	13.3	37.7
Madison, WI	8.4	3.4	6.6	28.6
Manchester, NH	14.7	6.2	12.3	40.5
McAllen, TX	13.2	4.9	10.8	46.1
Miami, FL	12.0	3.7	8.3	36.1
Midland, TX	9.3	2.7	7.6	37.0
Minneapolis, MN	11.2	4.5	10.2	34.0
Nashville, TN	11.8	3.8	10.3	37.0
New Orleans, LA	13.8	4.4	12.1	38.1
New York, NY	10.8	3.5	7.9	36.4
Oklahoma City, OK	13.5	4.7	12.3	39.4
Omaha, NE	11.1	3.6	9.7	34.2
Orlando, FL	10.3	5.3	8.1	35.5
Peoria, IL	12.4	3.3	11.1	34.3
Philadelphia, PA	15.9	6.0	14.1	42.2
Phoenix, AZ	10.3	3.8	9.2	35.5
Pittsburgh, PA	13.8	5.9	10.8	37.6
Portland, OR	12.7	4.4	10.8	37.3
Providence, RI	12.7	6.0	11.4	38.8
Provo, UT	8.3	3.7	7.4	35.8
Raleigh, NC	8.6	4.4	6.7	32.4
Reno, NV	12.2	4.7	10.5	32.5
Richmond, VA	15.5	7.9	13.9	37.1
Roanoke, VA	16.3	6.5	14.0	40.7
Rochester, MN	10.7	4.3	8.8	30.5
Salem, OR	14.7	5.4	13.4	38.4
Salt Lake City, UT	10.6	3.2	8.9	36.5
San Antonio, TX	14.3	5.4	12.7	43.3
San Diego, CA	9.0	3.1	6.5	33.4
San Francisco, CA	10.6	2.3	6.8	36.7
San Jose, CA	8.4	2.5	5.8	34.7
Santa Rosa, CA	12.2	3.5	10.1	33.5
Savannah, GA	14.4	5.5	11.7	42.7
Seattle, WA	9.4	2.6	7.0	33.0
Sioux Falls, SD	10.2	3.1	9.2	30.9
Springfield, IL	15.1	5.8	13.1	36.3
Tallahassee, FL	10.2	4.9	8.6	32.9
Tampa, FL	12.1	4.1	9.9	38.2
Topeka, KS	15.8	4.1	14.3	39.0
Tyler, TX	12.4	4.8	9.4	37.9
Virginia Beach, VA	10.7	3.7	8.7	32.4
Visalia, CA	13.7	5.6	12.2	43.0
Washington, DC	11.7	4.3	9.7	35.2
Wilmington, NC	13.0	3.6	10.3	35.6
Winston-Salem, NC	10.5	3.1	8.6	32.4
U.S.	12.6	4.2	10.3	35.5

Note: Figures show percent of the civilian noninstitutionalized population that reported having a disability. Disability status is determined from from six types of difficulty: vision, hearing, cognitive, ambulatory, self-care, and independent living. For children under 5 years old, hearing and vision difficulty are used to determine disability status. For children between the ages of 5 and 14, disability status is determined from hearing, vision, cognitive, ambulatory, and self-care difficulties. For people aged 15 years and older, they are considered to have a disability if they have difficulty with any one of the six difficulty types.
Source: U.S. Census Bureau, 2013-2017 American Community Survey 5-Year Estimates

Disability by Age: Metro Area

Metro Area	All Ages	Under 18 Years Old	18 to 64 Years Old	65 Years and Over
Albany, NY	12.3	4.4	10.0	31.7
Albuquerque, NM	14.0	3.6	12.4	37.1
Allentown, PA	13.4	5.8	10.8	32.9
Anchorage, AK	11.2	3.6	10.2	37.8
Ann Arbor, MI	8.8	2.9	6.8	29.0
Athens, GA	11.9	4.4	10.1	34.8
Atlanta, GA	10.1	3.4	8.7	33.9
Austin, TX	9.2	3.7	7.7	32.6
Baton Rouge, LA	14.1	5.7	12.1	39.8
Billings, MT	13.1	5.6	10.7	33.3
Boise City, ID	11.6	4.2	10.2	32.9
Boston, MA	10.6	4.0	8.0	32.0
Boulder, CO	8.3	2.9	6.5	26.8
Cape Coral, FL	13.8	3.9	9.9	28.6
Cedar Rapids, IA	10.3	4.0	8.1	29.3
Charleston, SC	12.0	4.1	9.9	34.7
Charlotte, NC	11.0	3.6	9.4	33.9
Chicago, IL	9.9	3.0	7.7	33.6
Clarksville, TN	15.2	4.9	15.3	42.4
College Station, TX	9.4	3.9	7.1	38.2
Colorado Springs, CO	12.3	4.0	11.4	33.8
Columbia, MO	11.3	4.1	9.6	35.7
Columbia, SC	13.4	3.8	11.8	36.7
Columbus, OH	11.9	4.6	10.3	34.6
Dallas, TX	9.6	3.4	8.1	34.9
Denver, CO	9.3	3.0	7.6	31.7
Des Moines, IA	10.5	3.9	9.2	31.3
Durham, NC	11.1	3.7	9.2	32.3
Edison, NJ	10.2	3.3	7.4	33.0
El Paso, TX	13.9	5.0	12.0	46.3
Eugene, OR	16.8	5.4	14.4	37.7
Evansville, IN	15.2	5.5	13.4	36.6
Fargo, ND	9.9	3.2	8.1	34.7
Fayetteville, NC	16.5	6.6	15.6	45.2
Fort Collins, CO	9.8	3.3	7.6	29.5
Fort Wayne, IN	12.7	4.7	11.5	33.4
Fort Worth, TX	9.6	3.4	8.1	34.9
Gainesville, FL	11.2	3.5	8.6	35.6
Grand Rapids, MI	11.8	4.3	10.2	33.5
Greeley, CO	10.2	2.9	8.8	35.4
Green Bay, WI	11.6	4.7	9.8	31.1
Greensboro, NC	12.4	3.9	10.4	33.6
Honolulu, HI	11.0	2.8	7.6	33.9
Houston, TX	9.5	3.4	8.0	35.7
Huntsville, AL	13.4	4.8	11.0	38.1
Indianapolis, IN	12.6	4.8	10.9	36.5
Jacksonville, FL	13.3	4.7	11.3	35.9
Kansas City, MO	12.2	4.0	10.6	34.7
Lafayette, LA	14.1	4.5	12.8	40.3
Las Cruces, NM	12.6	3.5	10.1	39.5
Las Vegas, NV	12.4	3.8	10.5	35.7
Lexington, KY	12.8	4.2	11.1	36.4
Lincoln, NE	10.5	4.1	8.3	33.8
Little Rock, AR	15.2	6.1	13.2	40.0
Los Angeles, CA	9.6	2.9	7.0	35.2

Table continued on next page.

Metro Area	All Ages	Under 18 Years Old	18 to 64 Years Old	65 Years and Over
Louisville, KY	14.4	4.7	12.7	37.0
Madison, WI	9.2	3.5	7.4	28.3
Manchester, NH	11.5	4.7	9.2	32.4
McAllen, TX	13.0	5.2	10.7	50.3
Miami, FL	11.0	3.4	7.4	33.3
Midland, TX	9.3	2.6	7.6	38.4
Minneapolis, MN	9.8	3.6	8.0	30.7
Nashville, TN	12.1	3.8	10.6	36.2
New Orleans, LA	13.7	4.7	11.7	37.2
New York, NY	10.2	3.3	7.4	33.0
Oklahoma City, OK	13.7	4.5	12.2	39.6
Omaha, NE	10.9	3.5	9.6	33.3
Orlando, FL	11.8	4.7	9.5	34.1
Peoria, IL	11.5	3.3	9.1	32.7
Philadelphia, PA	12.4	4.6	10.1	33.8
Phoenix, AZ	11.3	3.6	9.2	33.3
Pittsburgh, PA	14.2	5.2	11.1	34.1
Portland, OR	12.2	4.0	10.3	35.3
Providence, RI	13.5	5.0	11.1	34.7
Provo, UT	7.6	3.2	7.1	33.1
Raleigh, NC	9.6	3.8	7.9	33.1
Reno, NV	12.2	4.4	10.3	32.0
Richmond, VA	12.2	4.9	10.2	32.8
Roanoke, VA	14.4	5.1	11.7	34.0
Rochester, MN	10.3	3.9	7.9	30.5
Salem, OR	14.7	5.3	12.9	37.7
Salt Lake City, UT	9.4	3.4	8.2	34.2
San Antonio, TX	13.8	5.0	12.1	40.6
San Diego, CA	9.8	3.0	7.2	34.3
San Francisco, CA	10.0	2.9	7.2	32.7
San Jose, CA	7.9	2.3	5.3	32.5
Santa Rosa, CA	12.0	3.4	9.8	30.2
Savannah, GA	13.2	4.9	11.1	38.5
Seattle, WA	11.0	3.5	9.1	34.6
Sioux Falls, SD	9.9	3.2	8.8	30.5
Springfield, IL	13.9	5.8	11.6	35.0
Tallahassee, FL	12.7	5.9	10.4	35.0
Tampa, FL	14.0	4.4	10.9	34.4
Topeka, KS	14.5	4.4	12.7	35.9
Tyler, TX	13.6	5.3	11.4	35.7
Virginia Beach, VA	12.4	4.4	10.5	34.4
Visalia, CA	12.3	4.1	11.0	44.4
Washington, DC	8.5	3.0	6.7	29.6
Wilmington, NC	13.4	4.2	11.2	33.8
Winston-Salem, NC	12.9	4.2	10.6	34.7
U.S.	12.6	4.2	10.3	35.5

Note: Figures show percent of the civilian noninstitutionalized population that reported having a disability. Disability status is determined from from six types of difficulty: vision, hearing, cognitive, ambulatory, self-care, and independent living. For children under 5 years old, hearing and vision difficulty are used to determine disability status. For children between the ages of 5 and 14, disability status is determined from hearing, vision, cognitive, ambulatory, and self-care difficulties. For people aged 15 years and older, they are considered to have a disability if they have difficulty with any one of the six difficulty types; Figures cover the Metropolitan Statistical Area—see Appendix B for areas included
Source: U.S. Census Bureau, 2013-2017 American Community Survey 5-Year Estimates

Male/Female Ratio: City

City	Males	Females	Males per 100 Females
Albany, NY	46,249	52,249	88.5
Albuquerque, NM	271,465	285,253	95.2
Allentown, PA	58,145	61,983	93.8
Anchorage, AK	152,311	145,914	104.4
Ann Arbor, MI	59,344	59,959	99.0
Athens, GA	58,197	64,095	90.8
Atlanta, GA	228,038	237,192	96.1
Austin, TX	463,869	453,037	102.4
Baton Rouge, LA	108,014	119,535	90.4
Billings, MT	52,955	56,127	94.3
Boise City, ID	109,423	111,436	98.2
Boston, MA	321,703	347,455	92.6
Boulder, CO	55,395	50,876	108.9
Cape Coral, FL	84,138	89,541	94.0
Cedar Rapids, IA	63,400	66,930	94.7
Charleston, SC	62,890	68,314	92.1
Charlotte, NC	395,854	430,206	92.0
Chicago, IL	1,321,621	1,400,965	94.3
Clarksville, TN	73,898	73,873	100.0
College Station, TX	54,425	53,020	102.6
Colorado Springs, CO	224,484	225,516	99.5
Columbia, MO	56,935	61,685	92.3
Columbia, SC	67,861	64,375	105.4
Columbus, OH	415,208	436,936	95.0
Dallas, TX	644,344	655,778	98.3
Denver, CO	339,400	339,067	100.1
Des Moines, IA	105,981	108,797	97.4
Durham, NC	120,795	136,437	88.5
Edison, NJ	49,950	52,354	95.4
El Paso, TX	330,360	347,906	95.0
Eugene, OR	80,505	82,630	97.4
Evansville, IN	57,153	62,653	91.2
Fargo, ND	59,777	58,322	102.5
Fayetteville, NC	106,042	104,282	101.7
Fort Collins, CO	79,742	79,408	100.4
Fort Wayne, IN	126,804	135,646	93.5
Fort Worth, TX	408,803	426,326	95.9
Gainesville, FL	62,173	67,221	92.5
Grand Rapids, MI	96,186	99,169	97.0
Greeley, CO	49,599	51,161	96.9
Green Bay, WI	51,679	53,117	97.3
Greensboro, NC	132,805	152,011	87.4
Honolulu, HI	173,063	177,725	97.4
Houston, TX	1,135,634	1,131,702	100.3
Huntsville, AL	92,044	98,457	93.5
Indianapolis, IN	411,970	441,461	93.3
Jacksonville, FL	419,756	447,557	93.8
Kansas City, MO	232,170	244,804	94.8
Lafayette, LA	61,985	64,491	96.1
Las Cruces, NM	49,468	51,546	96.0
Las Vegas, NV	310,539	311,123	99.8
Lexington, KY	154,530	160,579	96.2
Lincoln, NE	139,057	138,258	100.6
Little Rock, AR	95,087	102,693	92.6
Los Angeles, CA	1,953,844	1,995,932	97.9

Table continued on next page.

City	Males	Females	Males per 100 Females
Louisville, KY	297,551	317,927	93.6
Madison, WI	123,054	125,802	97.8
Manchester, NH	56,555	54,046	104.6
McAllen, TX	69,425	70,413	98.6
Miami, FL	219,009	223,998	97.8
Midland, TX	66,129	65,157	101.5
Minneapolis, MN	208,322	203,130	102.6
Nashville, TN	315,266	338,921	93.0
New Orleans, LA	185,063	203,119	91.1
New York, NY	4,079,907	4,480,165	91.1
Oklahoma City, OK	309,360	319,831	96.7
Omaha, NE	228,597	234,484	97.5
Orlando, FL	130,347	139,067	93.7
Peoria, IL	54,890	60,534	90.7
Philadelphia, PA	742,412	827,245	89.7
Phoenix, AZ	784,828	789,593	99.4
Pittsburgh, PA	149,303	155,709	95.9
Portland, OR	312,021	318,310	98.0
Providence, RI	86,442	93,067	92.9
Provo, UT	58,177	58,022	100.3
Raleigh, NC	217,048	232,429	93.4
Reno, NV	121,150	118,582	102.2
Richmond, VA	104,853	116,039	90.4
Roanoke, VA	47,736	51,836	92.1
Rochester, MN	54,584	58,099	93.9
Salem, OR	81,919	81,735	100.2
Salt Lake City, UT	100,038	94,150	106.3
San Antonio, TX	719,677	741,946	97.0
San Diego, CA	700,029	690,937	101.3
San Francisco, CA	440,633	423,630	104.0
San Jose, CA	516,124	506,907	101.8
Santa Rosa, CA	84,326	89,918	93.8
Savannah, GA	68,627	76,467	89.7
Seattle, WA	345,628	342,617	100.9
Sioux Falls, SD	84,964	85,437	99.4
Springfield, IL	55,284	61,029	90.6
Tallahassee, FL	89,060	99,403	89.6
Tampa, FL	177,778	190,309	93.4
Topeka, KS	60,948	66,191	92.1
Tyler, TX	48,565	53,996	89.9
Virginia Beach, VA	221,350	228,707	96.8
Visalia, CA	62,580	67,467	92.8
Washington, DC	319,046	353,345	90.3
Wilmington, NC	54,045	61,216	88.3
Winston-Salem, NC	112,867	127,326	88.6
U.S.	158,018,753	162,985,654	97.0

Source: U.S. Census Bureau, 2013-2017 American Community Survey 5-Year Estimates

Male/Female Ratio: Metro Area

Metro Area	Males	Females	Males per 100 Females
Albany, NY	431,315	450,547	95.7
Albuquerque, NM	444,821	460,228	96.7
Allentown, PA	407,842	424,948	96.0
Anchorage, AK	205,078	194,282	105.6
Ann Arbor, MI	178,949	182,560	98.0
Athens, GA	98,156	104,624	93.8
Atlanta, GA	2,759,925	2,941,065	93.8
Austin, TX	1,001,806	998,784	100.3
Baton Rouge, LA	406,015	422,726	96.0
Billings, MT	82,512	85,033	97.0
Boise City, ID	338,305	339,041	99.8
Boston, MA	2,317,311	2,454,625	94.4
Boulder, CO	159,112	157,670	100.9
Cape Coral, FL	342,731	357,434	95.9
Cedar Rapids, IA	131,848	134,274	98.2
Charleston, SC	363,546	380,649	95.5
Charlotte, NC	1,177,333	1,249,691	94.2
Chicago, IL	4,671,861	4,877,368	95.8
Clarksville, TN	141,675	137,169	103.3
College Station, TX	125,550	123,004	102.1
Colorado Springs, CO	352,044	346,551	101.6
Columbia, MO	84,812	89,777	94.5
Columbia, SC	392,671	415,706	94.5
Columbus, OH	995,328	1,028,367	96.8
Dallas, TX	3,493,829	3,610,586	96.8
Denver, CO	1,396,026	1,402,658	99.5
Des Moines, IA	306,668	316,445	96.9
Durham, NC	263,517	286,764	91.9
Edison, NJ	9,762,858	10,429,184	93.6
El Paso, TX	411,040	427,487	96.2
Eugene, OR	179,116	184,355	97.2
Evansville, IN	153,544	161,719	94.9
Fargo, ND	116,897	115,763	101.0
Fayetteville, NC	191,780	193,557	99.1
Fort Collins, CO	164,920	166,056	99.3
Fort Wayne, IN	209,819	219,241	95.7
Fort Worth, TX	3,493,829	3,610,586	96.8
Gainesville, FL	134,695	142,361	94.6
Grand Rapids, MI	513,783	525,399	97.8
Greeley, CO	143,783	141,946	101.3
Green Bay, WI	157,496	158,351	99.5
Greensboro, NC	359,693	391,897	91.8
Honolulu, HI	498,993	491,067	101.6
Houston, TX	3,297,364	3,338,844	98.8
Huntsville, AL	218,457	226,451	96.5
Indianapolis, IN	971,355	1,017,677	95.4
Jacksonville, FL	705,474	742,410	95.0
Kansas City, MO	1,024,354	1,064,476	96.2
Lafayette, LA	238,051	249,582	95.4
Las Cruces, NM	105,094	108,755	96.6
Las Vegas, NV	1,056,002	1,056,434	100.0
Lexington, KY	245,089	255,600	95.9
Lincoln, NE	162,370	161,032	100.8
Little Rock, AR	354,144	376,202	94.1
Los Angeles, CA	6,537,886	6,723,652	97.2

Table continued on next page.

Metro Area	Males	Females	Males per 100 Females
Louisville, KY	623,967	654,236	95.4
Madison, WI	318,828	321,244	99.2
Manchester, NH	201,775	204,596	98.6
McAllen, TX	410,383	429,156	95.6
Miami, FL	2,923,416	3,096,374	94.4
Midland, TX	83,194	82,236	101.2
Minneapolis, MN	1,745,774	1,780,375	98.1
Nashville, TN	893,066	937,344	95.3
New Orleans, LA	609,832	650,828	93.7
New York, NY	9,762,858	10,429,184	93.6
Oklahoma City, OK	667,697	685,807	97.4
Omaha, NE	452,361	461,829	97.9
Orlando, FL	1,169,047	1,221,812	95.7
Peoria, IL	184,718	192,540	95.9
Philadelphia, PA	2,932,332	3,133,312	93.6
Phoenix, AZ	2,267,129	2,293,909	98.8
Pittsburgh, PA	1,141,403	1,206,740	94.6
Portland, OR	1,178,136	1,203,901	97.9
Providence, RI	782,300	830,854	94.2
Provo, UT	296,365	290,825	101.9
Raleigh, NC	620,902	653,083	95.1
Reno, NV	226,106	223,336	101.2
Richmond, VA	615,033	655,125	93.9
Roanoke, VA	151,071	161,998	93.3
Rochester, MN	105,686	108,799	97.1
Salem, OR	203,322	206,797	98.3
Salt Lake City, UT	587,531	582,526	100.9
San Antonio, TX	1,173,885	1,203,622	97.5
San Diego, CA	1,651,147	1,632,518	101.1
San Francisco, CA	2,292,525	2,349,295	97.6
San Jose, CA	992,525	977,372	101.6
Santa Rosa, CA	245,381	255,562	96.0
Savannah, GA	183,354	194,122	94.5
Seattle, WA	1,865,943	1,869,273	99.8
Sioux Falls, SD	125,534	125,030	100.4
Springfield, IL	101,183	109,367	92.5
Tallahassee, FL	182,931	194,743	93.9
Tampa, FL	1,442,886	1,535,323	94.0
Topeka, KS	114,091	119,291	95.6
Tyler, TX	107,355	114,922	93.4
Virginia Beach, VA	845,945	871,763	97.0
Visalia, CA	229,488	229,321	100.1
Washington, DC	2,975,354	3,114,842	95.5
Wilmington, NC	133,775	143,721	93.1
Winston-Salem, NC	316,610	341,585	92.7
U.S.	158,018,753	162,985,654	97.0

Note: Figures cover the Metropolitan Statistical Area (MSA)—see Appendix B for areas included
Source: U.S. Census Bureau, 2013-2017 American Community Survey 5-Year Estimates

Gross Metropolitan Product

MSA[1]	2016	2017	2018	2019	Rank[2]
Albany, NY	52.8	54.5	56.3	58.8	57
Albuquerque, NM	43.2	44.8	46.8	48.7	63
Allentown, PA	42.6	44.1	46.1	48.3	64
Anchorage, AK	27.2	28.7	31.2	32.0	93
Ann Arbor, MI	22.0	22.8	23.7	25.0	114
Athens, GA	8.8	9.3	9.7	10.1	218
Atlanta, GA	368.8	384.3	402.8	425.7	10
Austin, TX	133.7	142.9	153.3	162.8	26
Baton Rouge, LA	52.0	53.7	56.3	59.2	59
Billings, MT	10.1	10.4	10.8	11.3	201
Boise City, ID	32.3	34.2	36.0	38.1	79
Boston, MA	422.7	441.4	461.9	486.3	9
Boulder, CO	24.0	25.3	26.7	28.1	106
Cape Coral, FL	27.4	28.7	30.2	32.3	94
Cedar Rapids, IA	18.3	18.6	19.1	19.9	134
Charleston, SC	39.0	40.7	42.6	45.2	73
Charlotte, NC	163.9	172.3	181.0	192.4	20
Chicago, IL	655.7	675.8	703.9	737.3	3
Clarksville, TN	10.7	10.9	11.5	12.1	194
College Station, TX	9.4	10.1	10.9	11.6	206
Colorado Springs, CO	31.4	33.0	34.8	36.9	82
Columbia, MO	8.9	9.2	9.4	9.9	220
Columbia, SC	40.3	41.6	43.2	45.6	71
Columbus, OH	130.5	137.2	143.9	151.8	29
Dallas, TX	506.8	541.1	579.3	613.4	4
Denver, CO	198.0	209.4	221.5	233.9	18
Des Moines, IA	52.3	54.4	55.9	58.9	58
Durham, NC	43.9	45.9	48.3	51.7	62
Edison, NJ	1,667.3	1,718.2	1,788.3	1,876.6	1
El Paso, TX	28.4	29.8	31.3	32.7	89
Eugene, OR	15.4	16.0	16.7	17.5	156
Evansville, IN	17.1	17.8	18.6	19.5	143
Fargo, ND	15.8	16.5	17.2	18.1	154
Fayetteville, NC	17.3	17.6	18.3	19.2	144
Fort Collins, CO	15.9	17.2	18.3	19.5	146
Fort Wayne, IN	21.1	21.9	22.7	23.8	115
Fort Worth, TX	506.8	541.1	579.3	613.4	4
Gainesville, FL	12.5	13.1	13.8	14.5	177
Grand Rapids, MI	58.4	61.0	63.9	67.2	53
Greeley, CO	11.2	12.3	13.7	14.9	185
Green Bay, WI	18.7	19.3	20.2	21.2	131
Greensboro, NC	40.0	40.9	42.4	44.3	72
Honolulu, HI	65.5	67.8	70.4	72.7	50
Houston, TX	474.1	500.8	544.6	580.0	7
Huntsville, AL	24.8	25.9	27.2	28.7	104
Indianapolis, IN	136.8	142.9	149.7	158.1	27
Jacksonville, FL	71.7	75.0	79.0	83.7	47
Kansas City, MO	128.9	133.1	138.9	146.3	32
Lafayette, LA	20.9	21.6	23.0	24.3	117
Las Cruces, NM	6.9	7.1	7.4	7.8	251
Las Vegas, NV	111.6	117.3	124.9	133.2	36
Lexington, KY	28.8	29.9	31.2	32.7	88
Lincoln, NE	19.8	20.3	20.9	22.0	125
Little Rock, AR	38.0	39.3	40.6	42.5	74
Los Angeles, CA	1,008.2	1,048.6	1,094.1	1,152.4	2
Louisville, KY	74.6	77.5	80.2	84.0	46

Table continued on next page.

MSA[1]	2016	2017	2018	2019	Rank[2]
Madison, WI	48.1	50.3	52.9	55.9	61
Manchester, NH	26.8	27.8	29.1	30.5	98
McAllen, TX	19.4	20.5	21.7	22.7	123
Miami, FL	329.7	340.9	356.6	376.6	12
Midland, TX	24.0	26.9	32.7	35.4	100
Minneapolis, MN	249.4	259.5	268.3	282.1	15
Nashville, TN	125.5	132.2	139.5	148.2	33
New Orleans, LA	78.0	80.5	84.4	88.1	45
New York, NY	1,667.3	1,718.2	1,788.3	1,876.6	1
Oklahoma City, OK	69.7	73.0	77.1	81.1	49
Omaha, NE	63.2	64.8	67.1	70.2	51
Orlando, FL	127.3	133.6	141.0	149.7	31
Peoria, IL	20.1	20.5	21.3	22.3	124
Philadelphia, PA	430.6	447.6	467.8	490.3	8
Phoenix, AZ	231.1	243.7	260.0	277.6	16
Pittsburgh, PA	138.0	143.8	150.5	157.4	25
Portland, OR	164.9	171.8	181.4	192.5	21
Providence, RI	80.2	82.8	86.6	90.6	44
Provo, UT	23.4	25.0	26.4	28.2	108
Raleigh, NC	79.9	84.0	88.7	94.8	42
Reno, NV	26.0	27.8	29.8	31.7	99
Richmond, VA	80.2	82.9	86.8	91.3	43
Roanoke, VA	15.2	15.4	16.0	16.7	158
Rochester, MN	12.1	12.5	12.9	13.5	181
Salem, OR	16.1	16.7	17.6	18.5	149
Salt Lake City, UT	85.4	89.5	94.3	100.3	40
San Antonio, TX	115.4	122.3	129.7	136.4	35
San Diego, CA	216.7	227.6	239.8	254.4	17
San Francisco, CA	473.6	501.9	529.8	563.3	6
San Jose, CA	254.1	267.7	282.2	298.6	13
Santa Rosa, CA	27.5	29.1	30.4	32.0	91
Savannah, GA	17.9	18.6	19.1	20.0	135
Seattle, WA	335.5	357.5	376.1	396.4	11
Sioux Falls, SD	18.9	19.6	20.5	21.6	128
Springfield, IL	10.0	10.1	10.3	10.7	205
Tallahassee, FL	15.8	16.5	17.3	18.3	153
Tampa, FL	143.2	148.6	156.2	165.6	24
Topeka, KS	10.6	10.8	11.1	11.5	196
Tyler, TX	13.4	14.1	15.4	16.0	169
Virginia Beach, VA	92.2	95.1	99.3	104.4	39
Visalia, CA	15.8	16.7	17.6	18.6	152
Washington, DC	508.6	528.9	555.4	585.9	5
Wilmington, NC	14.2	14.7	15.3	16.2	163
Winston-Salem, NC	28.8	29.4	30.6	32.1	90

Note: Figures are in billions of dollars; (1) Metropolitan Statistical Area—see Appendix B for areas included; (2) Rank is based on 2017 data and ranges from 1 to 381.
Source: The U.S. Conference of Mayors, U.S. Metro Economies: Economic Growth & Full Employment, June 2018

Economic Growth

MSA[1]	2017-2018 (%)	2019-2020 (%)	2021-2022 (%)
Albany, NY	1.8	1.8	0.9
Albuquerque, NM	2.5	1.9	1.6
Allentown, PA	1.9	1.9	1.3
Anchorage, AK	1.5	1.5	1.6
Ann Arbor, MI	2.8	2.4	1.5
Athens, GA	2.6	1.7	1.1
Atlanta, GA	2.8	2.8	2.0
Austin, TX	4.9	3.4	2.9
Baton Rouge, LA	1.9	2.8	2.6
Billings, MT	1.8	1.9	1.3
Boise City, ID	3.7	3.1	2.2
Boston, MA	2.6	2.5	1.7
Boulder, CO	3.2	2.7	1.7
Cape Coral, FL	3.5	4.0	2.9
Cedar Rapids, IA	0.7	1.8	1.5
Charleston, SC	3.0	3.2	2.3
Charlotte, NC	3.5	3.3	2.3
Chicago, IL	1.6	1.9	1.0
Clarksville, TN	1.7	2.4	1.4
College Station, TX	4.9	2.8	2.1
Colorado Springs, CO	3.3	3.1	2.1
Columbia, MO	1.4	2.4	2.2
Columbia, SC	2.1	2.8	2.0
Columbus, OH	3.1	2.6	1.7
Dallas, TX	4.6	3.1	2.3
Denver, CO	3.0	2.8	2.1
Des Moines, IA	2.3	2.5	2.3
Durham, NC	3.1	4.0	2.8
Edison, NJ	2.0	2.1	1.3
El Paso, TX	3.5	2.0	1.5
Eugene, OR	2.3	2.0	1.3
Evansville, IN	2.4	1.9	1.0
Fargo, ND	0.4	1.6	1.5
Fayetteville, NC	0.7	2.3	1.5
Fort Collins, CO	4.8	4.0	2.7
Fort Wayne, IN	2.0	1.9	1.1
Fort Worth, TX	4.6	3.1	2.3
Gainesville, FL	3.1	2.5	1.8
Grand Rapids, MI	3.5	2.4	1.2
Greeley, CO	6.3	5.3	3.2
Green Bay, WI	1.8	2.3	1.5
Greensboro, NC	1.1	1.9	1.1
Honolulu, HI	1.2	1.2	1.2
Houston, TX	3.6	4.1	2.8
Huntsville, AL	3.6	2.7	2.9
Indianapolis, IN	2.7	2.8	2.1
Jacksonville, FL	3.6	3.0	2.3
Kansas City, MO	1.9	2.4	1.9
Lafayette, LA	0.8	3.4	2.6
Las Cruces, NM	0.5	2.3	2.4
Las Vegas, NV	3.1	3.6	2.6
Lexington, KY	2.2	2.0	1.1
Lincoln, NE	0.9	2.1	1.9
Little Rock, AR	2.7	1.9	1.3
Los Angeles, CA	2.1	2.5	1.5
Louisville, KY	2.4	1.9	1.1

Table continued on next page.

MSA[1]	2017-2018 (%)	2019-2020 (%)	2021-2022 (%)
Madison, WI	2.8	2.7	2.1
Manchester, NH	2.1	2.4	1.6
McAllen, TX	3.8	2.4	2.3
Miami, FL	2.7	2.8	1.9
Midland, TX	7.6	6.9	4.7
Minneapolis, MN	2.8	2.5	1.8
Nashville, TN	3.5	3.2	2.2
New Orleans, LA	1.5	2.2	1.9
New York, NY	2.0	2.1	1.3
Oklahoma City, OK	2.9	2.9	2.1
Omaha, NE	1.1	1.9	1.9
Orlando, FL	3.9	3.3	2.5
Peoria, IL	0.8	1.8	1.0
Philadelphia, PA	2.3	2.0	1.4
Phoenix, AZ	3.4	3.8	2.5
Pittsburgh, PA	1.9	1.7	1.1
Portland, OR	2.9	3.0	1.9
Providence, RI	1.8	1.9	1.1
Provo, UT	4.6	4.4	3.3
Raleigh, NC	3.7	4.0	3.0
Reno, NV	4.1	3.5	1.9
Richmond, VA	2.0	2.3	1.5
Roanoke, VA	0.5	1.5	0.8
Rochester, MN	1.6	1.7	1.2
Salem, OR	2.4	2.6	1.8
Salt Lake City, UT	3.3	3.5	2.5
San Antonio, TX	3.4	2.5	2.2
San Diego, CA	3.0	3.2	2.1
San Francisco, CA	3.8	3.4	2.2
San Jose, CA	3.5	3.1	2.3
Santa Rosa, CA	2.9	2.2	1.2
Savannah, GA	1.3	1.7	0.8
Seattle, WA	4.0	2.8	2.0
Sioux Falls, SD	1.5	2.9	2.2
Springfield, IL	-0.2	1.1	0.6
Tallahassee, FL	2.9	2.6	1.9
Tampa, FL	3.2	3.1	2.2
Topeka, KS	0.4	0.8	0.1
Tyler, TX	1.7	2.4	1.9
Virginia Beach, VA	1.6	2.1	1.6
Visalia, CA	2.0	3.0	2.3
Washington, DC	2.3	2.4	2.0
Wilmington, NC	2.1	3.0	2.0
Winston-Salem, NC	1.3	2.2	1.1

Note: Figures are real gross metropolitan product (GMP) growth rates and represent annual average percent change;
(1) Metropolitan Statistical Area—see Appendix B for areas included
Source: The U.S. Conference of Mayors, U.S. Metro Economies: Economic Growth & Full Employment, June 2018

Metropolitan Area Exports

Area	2012	2013	2014	2015	2016	2017	Rank[2]
Albany, NY	3,420.1	3,946.1	4,547.0	4,470.3	4,135.0	3,883.2	64
Albuquerque, NM	1,790.6	1,389.6	1,564.0	1,761.2	999.7	624.2	189
Allentown, PA	2,939.0	2,949.9	3,152.5	3,439.9	3,657.2	3,639.4	67
Anchorage, AK	416.4	518.0	571.8	421.9	1,215.4	1,675.9	114
Ann Arbor, MI	1,053.4	1,156.2	1,213.6	1,053.0	1,207.9	1,447.4	120
Athens, GA	229.7	286.0	320.8	327.4	332.1	297.7	253
Atlanta, GA	18,169.1	18,827.9	19,870.3	19,163.9	20,480.1	21,748.0	14
Austin, TX	8,976.6	8,870.8	9,400.0	10,094.5	10,682.7	12,451.5	27
Baton Rouge, LA	5,820.2	6,261.5	7,528.3	6,505.4	6,580.5	8,830.3	40
Billings, MT	141.4	139.8	133.2	66.8	50.7	78.8	349
Boise City, ID	4,088.2	3,657.9	3,143.4	2,668.0	3,021.7	2,483.3	86
Boston, MA	21,234.8	22,212.8	23,378.5	21,329.5	21,168.0	23,116.2	13
Boulder, CO	1,128.0	1,046.0	1,016.1	1,039.1	956.3	1,012.0	157
Cape Coral, FL	509.8	442.6	496.6	487.3	540.3	592.3	193
Cedar Rapids, IA	889.1	930.2	879.0	873.5	945.0	1,071.6	149
Charleston, SC	2,429.8	3,464.3	5,866.7	6,457.5	9,508.1	8,845.2	39
Charlotte, NC	6,322.6	10,684.1	12,885.3	13,985.8	11,944.1	13,122.5	24
Chicago, IL	40,568.0	44,910.6	47,340.1	44,820.9	43,932.7	46,140.2	5
Clarksville, TN	326.3	315.9	323.7	296.5	376.1	360.2	235
College Station, TX	103.6	108.7	129.7	122.5	113.2	145.4	319
Colorado Springs, CO	1,044.6	1,065.4	856.6	832.4	786.9	819.7	171
Columbia, MO	296.6	423.9	237.7	214.0	213.7	224.0	294
Columbia, SC	1,543.6	1,681.3	2,007.9	2,011.8	2,007.7	2,123.9	95
Columbus, OH	5,488.6	5,731.4	6,245.6	6,201.6	5,675.4	5,962.2	50
Dallas, TX	27,820.9	27,596.0	28,669.4	27,372.9	27,187.8	30,269.1	9
Denver, CO	3,355.8	3,618.4	4,958.6	3,909.5	3,649.3	3,954.7	63
Des Moines, IA	1,183.2	1,279.4	1,361.8	1,047.8	1,052.2	1,141.2	142
Durham, NC	2,723.2	2,971.7	2,934.0	2,807.2	2,937.4	3,128.4	76
Edison, NJ	102,298.0	106,922.8	105,266.6	95,645.4	89,649.5	93,693.7	2
El Paso, TX	12,796.9	14,359.7	20,079.3	24,560.9	26,452.8	25,814.1	12
Eugene, OR	482.2	476.0	495.7	400.2	371.8	391.3	229
Evansville, IN	4,025.3	3,865.6	3,756.5	4,483.7	3,022.4	4,001.9	62
Fargo, ND	785.9	817.9	782.8	543.2	474.5	519.5	205
Fayetteville, NC	322.3	344.0	375.8	256.3	179.8	231.6	290
Fort Collins, CO	861.7	986.1	1,037.4	990.7	993.8	1,034.1	153
Fort Wayne, IN	1,353.5	1,441.8	1,581.1	1,529.0	1,322.2	1,422.8	121
Fort Worth, TX	27,820.9	27,596.0	28,669.4	27,372.9	27,187.8	30,269.1	9
Gainesville, FL	348.6	295.0	304.3	291.6	277.3	292.1	255
Grand Rapids, MI	3,156.4	5,314.8	5,244.5	5,143.0	5,168.5	5,385.8	54
Greeley, CO	1,381.4	1,287.5	1,343.6	1,240.1	1,539.6	1,492.8	118
Green Bay, WI	1,031.6	914.8	988.7	968.1	1,044.0	1,054.8	151
Greensboro, NC	4,281.9	4,278.3	3,505.5	3,286.1	3,730.4	3,537.9	68
Honolulu, HI	306.3	323.2	765.5	446.4	330.3	393.6	228
Houston, TX	110,297.8	114,962.6	118,966.0	97,054.3	84,105.5	95,760.3	1
Huntsville, AL	1,491.5	1,518.7	1,440.4	1,344.7	1,827.3	1,889.2	105
Indianapolis, IN	10,436.0	9,747.5	9,539.4	9,809.4	9,655.4	10,544.2	30
Jacksonville, FL	2,595.0	2,467.8	2,473.7	2,564.4	2,159.0	2,141.7	94
Kansas City, MO	7,880.8	8,012.1	8,262.9	6,723.2	6,709.8	7,015.0	46
Lafayette, LA	726.0	1,261.8	1,532.7	1,165.2	1,335.2	954.8	162
Las Cruces, NM	746.1	433.0	1,346.3	1,593.7	1,568.6	1,390.2	122
Las Vegas, NV	1,811.5	2,008.2	2,509.7	2,916.2	2,312.3	2,710.6	80
Lexington, KY	2,462.1	2,294.0	2,191.4	2,065.7	2,069.6	2,119.8	96
Lincoln, NE	904.7	818.4	1,173.9	1,189.3	796.9	860.9	167
Little Rock, AR	2,418.9	2,497.5	2,463.5	1,777.5	1,871.0	2,146.1	93
Los Angeles, CA	75,007.5	76,305.7	75,471.2	61,758.7	61,245.7	63,752.9	3
Louisville, KY	7,706.7	8,898.0	8,877.3	8,037.9	7,793.3	8,925.9	38

Table continued on next page.

Area	2012	2013	2014	2015	2016	2017	Rank[2]
Madison, WI	2,168.7	2,292.1	2,369.5	2,280.4	2,204.8	2,187.7	92
Manchester, NH	1,634.9	1,445.8	1,575.4	1,556.6	1,465.2	1,714.7	111
McAllen, TX	5,198.5	5,265.5	5,316.0	5,327.1	5,214.3	5,659.0	52
Miami, FL	47,858.7	41,771.5	37,969.5	33,258.5	32,734.5	34,780.5	7
Midland, TX	104.4	164.1	122.7	110.1	69.6	69.4	353
Minneapolis, MN	25,155.7	23,747.5	21,198.2	19,608.6	18,329.2	19,070.9	18
Nashville, TN	6,402.1	8,702.8	9,620.9	9,353.0	9,460.1	10,164.3	31
New Orleans, LA	24,359.5	30,030.9	34,881.5	27,023.3	29,518.8	31,648.5	8
New York, NY	102,298.0	106,922.8	105,266.6	95,645.4	89,649.5	93,693.7	2
Oklahoma City, OK	1,574.6	1,581.7	1,622.0	1,353.1	1,260.0	1,278.8	129
Omaha, NE	3,529.3	4,255.9	4,528.5	3,753.4	3,509.7	3,756.2	65
Orlando, FL	3,850.6	3,227.7	3,134.8	3,082.7	3,363.9	3,196.7	75
Peoria, IL	17,838.0	12,184.5	11,234.8	9,826.9	7,260.1	9,403.6	33
Philadelphia, PA	22,991.6	24,929.2	26,321.3	24,236.1	21,359.9	21,689.7	15
Phoenix, AZ	10,834.3	11,473.5	12,764.4	13,821.5	12,838.2	13,223.1	23
Pittsburgh, PA	14,134.7	10,444.4	10,015.8	9,137.1	7,971.0	9,322.7	34
Portland, OR	20,337.7	17,606.8	18,667.2	18,847.8	20,256.8	20,788.8	17
Providence, RI	5,830.8	6,609.0	6,595.1	5,048.8	6,595.7	7,125.4	45
Provo, UT	2,058.1	2,789.2	2,533.4	2,216.4	1,894.8	2,065.3	100
Raleigh, NC	2,308.1	2,280.6	2,713.1	2,553.4	2,620.4	2,865.8	78
Reno, NV	2,019.0	2,117.4	2,138.9	1,943.3	2,382.1	2,517.3	85
Richmond, VA	4,328.1	4,337.2	3,307.0	3,325.9	3,525.7	3,663.7	66
Roanoke, VA	716.6	746.5	690.9	637.6	613.3	616.2	190
Rochester, MN	1,023.7	1,061.0	720.5	530.2	398.0	495.3	209
Salem, OR	437.3	414.4	374.8	385.4	358.2	339.0	238
Salt Lake City, UT	15,990.0	11,867.2	8,361.5	10,380.5	8,653.7	7,916.9	43
San Antonio, TX	14,010.2	19,287.6	25,781.8	15,919.2	5,621.2	9,184.1	35
San Diego, CA	17,183.3	17,885.5	18,585.7	17,439.7	18,086.6	18,637.1	19
San Francisco, CA	23,031.7	25,305.3	26,863.7	25,061.1	24,506.3	29,103.8	10
San Jose, CA	26,687.7	23,413.1	21,128.8	19,827.2	21,716.8	21,464.7	16
Santa Rosa, CA	1,059.1	1,044.8	1,103.7	1,119.8	1,194.3	1,168.2	138
Savannah, GA	4,116.5	5,436.4	5,093.4	5,447.5	4,263.4	4,472.0	59
Seattle, WA	50,301.7	56,686.4	61,938.4	67,226.4	61,881.0	59,007.0	4
Sioux Falls, SD	439.5	433.0	455.3	375.0	334.3	386.8	230
Springfield, IL	99.5	97.5	94.4	111.7	88.3	107.5	335
Tallahassee, FL	130.8	122.5	174.0	191.2	223.1	241.1	284
Tampa, FL	7,190.0	6,673.0	5,817.3	5,660.4	5,702.9	6,256.0	49
Topeka, KS	265.0	303.3	365.0	363.5	305.2	300.7	252
Tyler, TX	221.1	219.6	301.1	207.3	176.7	234.5	287
Virginia Beach, VA	2,735.0	2,539.2	3,573.2	3,556.4	3,291.1	3,307.2	70
Visalia, CA	1,113.4	1,178.7	1,323.7	1,086.8	1,097.1	1,371.6	124
Washington, DC	14,609.7	16,225.0	13,053.6	13,900.4	13,582.4	12,736.1	26
Wilmington, NC	923.5	766.7	571.9	617.3	598.7	759.8	177
Winston-Salem, NC	1,148.1	1,660.1	1,441.9	1,267.4	1,234.6	1,131.7	144

Note: Figures are in millions of dollars; (1) Metropolitan Statistical Area—see Appendix B for areas included; (2) Rank is based on 2017 data and ranges from 1 to 387
Source: U.S. Department of Commerce, International Trade Administration, Office of Trade and Economic Analysis, Industry and Analysis, Exports by Metropolitan Area, extracted March 25, 2019

Building Permits: City

City	Single-Family			Multi-Family			Total		
	2016	2017	Pct. Chg.	2016	2017	Pct. Chg.	2016	2017	Pct. Chg.
Albany, NY	10	9	-10.0	93	109	17.2	103	118	14.6
Albuquerque, NM	913	1,088	19.2	379	184	-51.5	1,292	1,272	-1.5
Allentown, PA	16	15	-6.3	0	0	0.0	16	15	-6.3
Anchorage, AK	719	800	11.3	211	219	3.8	930	1,019	9.6
Ann Arbor, MI	25	105	320.0	0	7	–	25	112	348.0
Athens, GA	115	189	64.3	4	176	4,300.0	119	365	206.7
Atlanta, GA	855	922	7.8	7,176	4,179	-41.8	8,031	5,101	-36.5
Austin, TX	3,705	4,440	19.8	5,198	7,139	37.3	8,903	11,579	30.1
Baton Rouge, LA	284	253	-10.9	0	0	0.0	284	253	-10.9
Billings, MT	525	432	-17.7	12	60	400.0	537	492	-8.4
Boise City, ID	682	810	18.8	717	350	-51.2	1,399	1,160	-17.1
Boston, MA	56	52	-7.1	3,292	5,033	52.9	3,348	5,085	51.9
Boulder, CO	85	74	-12.9	16	128	700.0	101	202	100.0
Cape Coral, FL	1,443	1,842	27.7	144	708	391.7	1,587	2,550	60.7
Cedar Rapids, IA	268	219	-18.3	127	313	146.5	395	532	34.7
Charleston, SC	692	766	10.7	350	303	-13.4	1,042	1,069	2.6
Charlotte, NC	n/a	n/a	n/a	n/a	n/a	n/a	n/a	n/a	n/a
Chicago, IL	613	525	-14.4	8,491	8,414	-0.9	9,104	8,939	-1.8
Clarksville, TN	788	806	2.3	256	227	-11.3	1,044	1,033	-1.1
College Station, TX	735	594	-19.2	1,165	1,319	13.2	1,900	1,913	0.7
Colorado Springs, CO	n/a	n/a	n/a	n/a	n/a	n/a	n/a	n/a	n/a
Columbia, MO	568	403	-29.0	405	861	112.6	973	1,264	29.9
Columbia, SC	251	341	35.9	0	8	–	251	349	39.0
Columbus, OH	649	650	0.2	3,071	3,579	16.5	3,720	4,229	13.7
Dallas, TX	1,640	2,100	28.0	8,697	5,151	-40.8	10,337	7,251	-29.9
Denver, CO	1,887	2,370	25.6	5,955	8,155	36.9	7,842	10,525	34.2
Des Moines, IA	236	173	-26.7	1,209	1,124	-7.0	1,445	1,297	-10.2
Durham, NC	1,647	1,783	8.3	1,332	1,179	-11.5	2,979	2,962	-0.6
Edison, NJ	70	58	-17.1	0	0	0.0	70	58	-17.1
El Paso, TX	2,014	2,020	0.3	829	897	8.2	2,843	2,917	2.6
Eugene, OR	324	364	12.3	423	15	-96.5	747	379	-49.3
Evansville, IN	96	72	-25.0	80	6	-92.5	176	78	-55.7
Fargo, ND	474	444	-6.3	859	781	-9.1	1,333	1,225	-8.1
Fayetteville, NC	296	257	-13.2	0	56	–	296	313	5.7
Fort Collins, CO	488	657	34.6	1,386	720	-48.1	1,874	1,377	-26.5
Fort Wayne, IN	n/a	n/a	n/a	n/a	n/a	n/a	n/a	n/a	n/a
Fort Worth, TX	3,459	5,042	45.8	3,949	3,814	-3.4	7,408	8,856	19.5
Gainesville, FL	76	118	55.3	247	1,200	385.8	323	1,318	308.0
Grand Rapids, MI	69	101	46.4	1,329	777	-41.5	1,398	878	-37.2
Greeley, CO	263	120	-54.4	312	229	-26.6	575	349	-39.3
Green Bay, WI	111	98	-11.7	0	0	0.0	111	98	-11.7
Greensboro, NC	549	728	32.6	960	881	-8.2	1,509	1,609	6.6
Honolulu, HI	n/a	n/a	n/a	n/a	n/a	n/a	n/a	n/a	n/a
Houston, TX	4,169	5,326	27.8	5,329	4,346	-18.4	9,498	9,672	1.8
Huntsville, AL	1,091	1,144	4.9	672	380	-43.5	1,763	1,524	-13.6
Indianapolis, IN	831	914	10.0	1,068	645	-39.6	1,899	1,559	-17.9
Jacksonville, FL	2,678	3,005	12.2	2,839	2,874	1.2	5,517	5,879	6.6
Kansas City, MO	825	824	-0.1	2,515	1,542	-38.7	3,340	2,366	-29.2
Lafayette, LA	n/a	n/a	n/a	n/a	n/a	n/a	n/a	n/a	n/a
Las Cruces, NM	418	478	14.4	13	315	2,323.1	431	793	84.0
Las Vegas, NV	1,454	1,605	10.4	826	276	-66.6	2,280	1,881	-17.5
Lexington, KY	670	743	10.9	695	605	-12.9	1,365	1,348	-1.2
Lincoln, NE	928	994	7.1	1,238	1,231	-0.6	2,166	2,225	2.7
Little Rock, AR	330	592	79.4	501	508	1.4	831	1,100	32.4

Table continued on next page.

City	Single-Family			Multi-Family			Total		
	2016	2017	Pct. Chg.	2016	2017	Pct. Chg.	2016	2017	Pct. Chg.
Los Angeles, CA	1,796	2,360	31.4	12,094	12,486	3.2	13,890	14,846	6.9
Louisville, KY	1,072	1,236	15.3	1,736	2,056	18.4	2,808	3,292	17.2
Madison, WI	340	379	11.5	2,041	1,809	-11.4	2,381	2,188	-8.1
Manchester, NH	141	149	5.7	157	95	-39.5	298	244	-18.1
McAllen, TX	450	438	-2.7	173	200	15.6	623	638	2.4
Miami, FL	87	90	3.4	3,823	4,671	22.2	3,910	4,761	21.8
Midland, TX	632	761	20.4	40	0	-100.0	672	761	13.2
Minneapolis, MN	169	137	-18.9	2,739	2,117	-22.7	2,908	2,254	-22.5
Nashville, TN	3,712	3,827	3.1	5,751	2,423	-57.9	9,463	6,250	-34.0
New Orleans, LA	280	447	59.6	328	213	-35.1	608	660	8.6
New York, NY	561	483	-13.9	15,719	21,618	37.5	16,280	22,101	35.8
Oklahoma City, OK	2,899	2,707	-6.6	291	48	-83.5	3,190	2,755	-13.6
Omaha, NE	1,427	1,533	7.4	1,137	1,697	49.3	2,564	3,230	26.0
Orlando, FL	730	828	13.4	930	818	-12.0	1,660	1,646	-0.8
Peoria, IL	39	32	-17.9	0	0	0.0	39	32	-17.9
Philadelphia, PA	904	783	-13.4	2,271	2,606	14.8	3,175	3,389	6.7
Phoenix, AZ	2,479	2,932	18.3	4,493	3,900	-13.2	6,972	6,832	-2.0
Pittsburgh, PA	63	66	4.8	373	410	9.9	436	476	9.2
Portland, OR	831	703	-15.4	4,098	6,086	48.5	4,929	6,789	37.7
Providence, RI	11	2	-81.8	51	2	-96.1	62	4	-93.5
Provo, UT	186	223	19.9	73	17	-76.7	259	240	-7.3
Raleigh, NC	1,412	1,365	-3.3	2,036	1,851	-9.1	3,448	3,216	-6.7
Reno, NV	1,059	1,124	6.1	1,315	1,210	-8.0	2,374	2,334	-1.7
Richmond, VA	280	326	16.4	230	991	330.9	510	1,317	158.2
Roanoke, VA	15	18	20.0	138	156	13.0	153	174	13.7
Rochester, MN	403	437	8.4	993	617	-37.9	1,396	1,054	-24.5
Salem, OR	302	319	5.6	490	655	33.7	792	974	23.0
Salt Lake City, UT	90	88	-2.2	3,175	542	-82.9	3,265	630	-80.7
San Antonio, TX	2,152	2,489	15.7	4,211	3,711	-11.9	6,363	6,200	-2.6
San Diego, CA	823	1,138	38.3	5,789	4,554	-21.3	6,612	5,692	-13.9
San Francisco, CA	123	43	-65.0	3,964	3,991	0.7	4,087	4,034	-1.3
San Jose, CA	222	177	-20.3	2,506	2,264	-9.7	2,728	2,441	-10.5
Santa Rosa, CA	104	232	123.1	134	112	-16.4	238	344	44.5
Savannah, GA	300	384	28.0	0	0	0.0	300	384	28.0
Seattle, WA	797	593	-25.6	9,202	9,294	1.0	9,999	9,887	-1.1
Sioux Falls, SD	1,059	1,192	12.6	1,451	1,202	-17.2	2,510	2,394	-4.6
Springfield, IL	74	57	-23.0	94	94	0.0	168	151	-10.1
Tallahassee, FL	330	379	14.8	539	1,156	114.5	869	1,535	76.6
Tampa, FL	934	1,010	8.1	3,328	2,165	-34.9	4,262	3,175	-25.5
Topeka, KS	100	85	-15.0	12	0	-100.0	112	85	-24.1
Tyler, TX	305	313	2.6	93	48	-48.4	398	361	-9.3
Virginia Beach, VA	768	646	-15.9	815	877	7.6	1,583	1,523	-3.8
Visalia, CA	613	517	-15.7	92	32	-65.2	705	549	-22.1
Washington, DC	336	352	4.8	4,354	5,685	30.6	4,690	6,037	28.7
Wilmington, NC	n/a	n/a	n/a	n/a	n/a	n/a	n/a	n/a	n/a
Winston-Salem, NC	453	1,183	161.1	443	777	75.4	896	1,960	118.8
U.S.	750,800	820,000	9.2	455,800	462,000	1.4	1,206,600	1,282,000	6.2

Note: Figures represent new, privately-owned housing units authorized (unadjusted data); All permit data are based on estimates with imputation
Source: U.S. Census Bureau, Manufacturing, Mining, and Construction Statistics, Building Permits, 2016, 2017

Building Permits: Metro Area

Metro Area	Single-Family			Multi-Family			Total		
	2016	2017	Pct. Chg.	2016	2017	Pct. Chg.	2016	2017	Pct. Chg.
Albany, NY	1,380	1,212	-12.2	1,473	1,134	-23.0	2,853	2,346	-17.8
Albuquerque, NM	1,931	1,996	3.4	534	260	-51.3	2,465	2,256	-8.5
Allentown, PA	1,059	938	-11.4	204	180	-11.8	1,263	1,118	-11.5
Anchorage, AK	751	851	13.3	295	297	0.7	1,046	1,148	9.8
Ann Arbor, MI	438	583	33.1	0	74	–	438	657	50.0
Athens, GA	523	581	11.1	61	190	211.5	584	771	32.0
Atlanta, GA	23,100	24,973	8.1	13,257	8,859	-33.2	36,357	33,832	-6.9
Austin, TX	13,327	16,119	20.9	8,534	10,581	24.0	21,861	26,700	22.1
Baton Rouge, LA	3,402	3,586	5.4	24	53	120.8	3,426	3,639	6.2
Billings, MT	1,054	992	-5.9	152	233	53.3	1,206	1,225	1.6
Boise City, ID	5,383	6,275	16.6	1,375	1,634	18.8	6,758	7,909	17.0
Boston, MA	5,243	4,949	-5.6	8,004	9,808	22.5	13,247	14,757	11.4
Boulder, CO	716	808	12.8	1,133	859	-24.2	1,849	1,667	-9.8
Cape Coral, FL	4,092	4,841	18.3	1,325	2,113	59.5	5,417	6,954	28.4
Cedar Rapids, IA	555	537	-3.2	232	455	96.1	787	992	26.0
Charleston, SC	4,787	4,726	-1.3	2,187	2,541	16.2	6,974	7,267	4.2
Charlotte, NC	14,041	15,247	8.6	6,533	7,622	16.7	20,574	22,869	11.2
Chicago, IL	8,032	8,416	4.8	11,909	13,716	15.2	19,941	22,132	11.0
Clarksville, TN	1,316	1,558	18.4	363	255	-29.8	1,679	1,813	8.0
College Station, TX	1,218	1,155	-5.2	1,642	1,928	17.4	2,860	3,083	7.8
Colorado Springs, CO	3,610	3,852	6.7	1,556	1,113	-28.5	5,166	4,965	-3.9
Columbia, MO	863	769	-10.9	441	865	96.1	1,304	1,634	25.3
Columbia, SC	3,916	4,072	4.0	711	557	-21.7	4,627	4,629	0.0
Columbus, OH	4,157	4,295	3.3	4,480	4,597	2.6	8,637	8,892	3.0
Dallas, TX	29,703	34,604	16.5	26,097	27,920	7.0	55,800	62,524	12.1
Denver, CO	10,247	10,978	7.1	11,700	11,757	0.5	21,947	22,735	3.6
Des Moines, IA	3,760	3,697	-1.7	2,937	2,670	-9.1	6,697	6,367	-4.9
Durham, NC	2,951	3,268	10.7	1,431	1,656	15.7	4,382	4,924	12.4
Edison, NJ	10,397	11,289	8.6	32,834	39,289	19.7	43,231	50,578	17.0
El Paso, TX	2,219	2,373	6.9	835	904	8.3	3,054	3,277	7.3
Eugene, OR	736	821	11.5	438	21	-95.2	1,174	842	-28.3
Evansville, IN	633	618	-2.4	314	303	-3.5	947	921	-2.7
Fargo, ND	1,192	1,065	-10.7	1,287	826	-35.8	2,479	1,891	-23.7
Fayetteville, NC	833	874	4.9	120	61	-49.2	953	935	-1.9
Fort Collins, CO	1,622	2,027	25.0	1,910	908	-52.5	3,532	2,935	-16.9
Fort Wayne, IN	1,076	1,222	13.6	460	500	8.7	1,536	1,722	12.1
Fort Worth, TX	29,703	34,604	16.5	26,097	27,920	7.0	55,800	62,524	12.1
Gainesville, FL	609	684	12.3	501	1,585	216.4	1,110	2,269	104.4
Grand Rapids, MI	2,649	2,953	11.5	2,068	1,886	-8.8	4,717	4,839	2.6
Greeley, CO	2,463	2,777	12.7	546	869	59.2	3,009	3,646	21.2
Green Bay, WI	804	828	3.0	204	348	70.6	1,008	1,176	16.7
Greensboro, NC	1,635	2,012	23.1	1,100	1,043	-5.2	2,735	3,055	11.7
Honolulu, HI	846	1,028	21.5	812	940	15.8	1,658	1,968	18.7
Houston, TX	35,367	36,348	2.8	9,365	6,047	-35.4	44,732	42,395	-5.2
Huntsville, AL	2,320	2,577	11.1	672	382	-43.2	2,992	2,959	-1.1
Indianapolis, IN	5,828	6,755	15.9	1,945	2,324	19.5	7,773	9,079	16.8
Jacksonville, FL	8,597	9,833	14.4	3,171	3,126	-1.4	11,768	12,959	10.1
Kansas City, MO	5,292	5,951	12.5	5,097	3,900	-23.5	10,389	9,851	-5.2
Lafayette, LA	1,518	1,746	15.0	180	25	-86.1	1,698	1,771	4.3
Las Cruces, NM	757	803	6.1	13	323	2,384.6	770	1,126	46.2
Las Vegas, NV	8,805	9,812	11.4	4,772	4,261	-10.7	13,577	14,073	3.7
Lexington, KY	1,480	1,602	8.2	1,252	724	-42.2	2,732	2,326	-14.9
Lincoln, NE	1,143	1,271	11.2	1,241	1,237	-0.3	2,384	2,508	5.2
Little Rock, AR	1,649	2,087	26.6	678	1,128	66.4	2,327	3,215	38.2

Table continued on next page.

Metro Area	Single-Family			Multi-Family			Total		
	2016	2017	Pct. Chg.	2016	2017	Pct. Chg.	2016	2017	Pct. Chg.
Los Angeles, CA	9,379	10,587	12.9	22,735	20,497	-9.8	32,114	31,084	-3.2
Louisville, KY	3,127	3,446	10.2	2,022	2,339	15.7	5,149	5,785	12.4
Madison, WI	1,613	1,656	2.7	3,340	2,976	-10.9	4,953	4,632	-6.5
Manchester, NH	701	717	2.3	396	316	-20.2	1,097	1,033	-5.8
McAllen, TX	2,921	2,698	-7.6	1,647	1,599	-2.9	4,568	4,297	-5.9
Miami, FL	6,705	6,655	-0.7	12,037	13,068	8.6	18,742	19,723	5.2
Midland, TX	636	766	20.4	40	0	-100.0	676	766	13.3
Minneapolis, MN	7,889	8,782	11.3	6,271	6,318	0.7	14,160	15,100	6.6
Nashville, TN	12,830	13,650	6.4	7,352	6,981	-5.0	20,182	20,631	2.2
New Orleans, LA	2,494	2,720	9.1	492	246	-50.0	2,986	2,966	-0.7
New York, NY	10,397	11,289	8.6	32,834	39,289	19.7	43,231	50,578	17.0
Oklahoma City, OK	5,039	5,132	1.8	1,701	287	-83.1	6,740	5,419	-19.6
Omaha, NE	2,906	3,158	8.7	1,334	1,797	34.7	4,240	4,955	16.9
Orlando, FL	14,227	14,431	1.4	9,027	4,634	-48.7	23,254	19,065	-18.0
Peoria, IL	326	247	-24.2	24	10	-58.3	350	257	-26.6
Philadelphia, PA	7,016	7,233	3.1	5,229	6,311	20.7	12,245	13,544	10.6
Phoenix, AZ	18,433	20,471	11.1	10,150	8,841	-12.9	28,583	29,312	2.6
Pittsburgh, PA	3,015	2,988	-0.9	1,388	1,340	-3.5	4,403	4,328	-1.7
Portland, OR	7,397	6,211	-16.0	7,332	9,772	33.3	14,729	15,983	8.5
Providence, RI	1,662	1,722	3.6	902	288	-68.1	2,564	2,010	-21.6
Provo, UT	4,429	5,090	14.9	888	2,155	142.7	5,317	7,245	36.3
Raleigh, NC	9,442	10,752	13.9	4,072	3,428	-15.8	13,514	14,180	4.9
Reno, NV	1,868	2,091	11.9	1,732	2,473	42.8	3,600	4,564	26.8
Richmond, VA	4,003	4,614	15.3	916	2,531	176.3	4,919	7,145	45.3
Roanoke, VA	380	424	11.6	162	168	3.7	542	592	9.2
Rochester, MN	744	818	9.9	993	631	-36.5	1,737	1,449	-16.6
Salem, OR	814	790	-2.9	664	765	15.2	1,478	1,555	5.2
Salt Lake City, UT	4,351	4,918	13.0	4,380	2,449	-44.1	8,731	7,367	-15.6
San Antonio, TX	6,464	7,535	16.6	5,777	4,981	-13.8	12,241	12,516	2.2
San Diego, CA	2,351	4,056	72.5	8,440	6,385	-24.3	10,791	10,441	-3.2
San Francisco, CA	4,967	4,777	-3.8	9,820	12,175	24.0	14,787	16,952	14.6
San Jose, CA	2,099	2,592	23.5	4,068	5,947	46.2	6,167	8,539	38.5
Santa Rosa, CA	621	840	35.3	298	338	13.4	919	1,178	28.2
Savannah, GA	1,769	1,898	7.3	202	220	8.9	1,971	2,118	7.5
Seattle, WA	9,425	9,997	6.1	16,064	17,337	7.9	25,489	27,334	7.2
Sioux Falls, SD	1,431	1,533	7.1	1,653	1,381	-16.5	3,084	2,914	-5.5
Springfield, IL	274	210	-23.4	152	112	-26.3	426	322	-24.4
Tallahassee, FL	810	1,897	134.2	803	1,156	44.0	1,613	3,053	89.3
Tampa, FL	10,685	12,732	19.2	7,067	5,536	-21.7	17,752	18,268	2.9
Topeka, KS	368	327	-11.1	20	8	-60.0	388	335	-13.7
Tyler, TX	454	472	4.0	127	206	62.2	581	678	16.7
Virginia Beach, VA	4,095	4,404	7.5	2,118	1,778	-16.1	6,213	6,182	-0.5
Visalia, CA	1,190	1,162	-2.4	126	152	20.6	1,316	1,314	-0.2
Washington, DC	13,384	14,225	6.3	12,303	13,040	6.0	25,687	27,265	6.1
Wilmington, NC	1,774	2,193	23.6	1,173	569	-51.5	2,947	2,762	-6.3
Winston-Salem, NC	2,243	2,784	24.1	484	981	102.7	2,727	3,765	38.1
U.S.	750,800	820,000	9.2	455,800	462,000	1.4	1,206,600	1,282,000	6.2

Note: Figures cover the Metropolitan Statistical Area—see Appendix B for areas included; Figures represent new, privately-owned housing units authorized (unadjusted data); All permit data are based on estimates with imputation
Source: U.S. Census Bureau, Manufacturing, Mining, and Construction Statistics, Building Permits, 2016, 2017

Housing Vacancy Rates

Metro Area[1]	Gross Vacancy Rate[2] (%)			Year-Round Vacancy Rate[3] (%)			Rental Vacancy Rate[4] (%)			Homeowner Vacancy Rate[5] (%)		
	2016	2017	2018	2016	2017	2018	2016	2017	2018	2016	2017	2018
Albany, NY	11.8	10.5	11.6	8.7	8.3	10.4	3.8	8.5	10.8	2.1	2.1	1.7
Albuquerque, NM	9.2	8.9	8.3	8.9	8.6	7.9	8.1	9.0	7.8	1.9	2.1	1.8
Allentown, PA	7.4	9.5	9.3	5.2	8.5	7.1	4.2	5.3	5.7	1.1	1.7	0.9
Anchorage, AK	n/a	n/a	n/a	n/a	n/a	n/a	n/a	n/a	n/a	n/a	n/a	n/a
Ann Arbor, MI	n/a	n/a	n/a	n/a	n/a	n/a	n/a	n/a	n/a	n/a	n/a	n/a
Athens, GA	n/a	n/a	n/a	n/a	n/a	n/a	n/a	n/a	n/a	n/a	n/a	n/a
Atlanta, GA	9.7	8.9	7.8	9.4	8.4	7.4	6.2	7.0	6.6	1.6	1.0	1.1
Austin, TX	8.2	10.4	9.7	7.6	9.3	8.7	5.5	6.1	7.0	1.0	2.0	1.2
Baton Rouge, LA	12.3	13.6	13.0	12.0	13.0	11.8	7.4	8.7	7.6	1.5	1.0	1.4
Billings, MT	n/a	n/a	n/a	n/a	n/a	n/a	n/a	n/a	n/a	n/a	n/a	n/a
Boise City, ID	n/a	n/a	n/a	n/a	n/a	n/a	n/a	n/a	n/a	n/a	n/a	n/a
Boston, MA	7.8	7.6	7.5	6.5	6.5	6.5	3.7	4.8	3.8	0.9	0.6	1.0
Boulder, CO	n/a	n/a	n/a	n/a	n/a	n/a	n/a	n/a	n/a	n/a	n/a	n/a
Cape Coral, FL	38.5	39.1	41.5	17.8	20.2	16.6	5.8	4.3	5.8	3.0	2.9	3.0
Cedar Rapids, IA	n/a	n/a	n/a	n/a	n/a	n/a	n/a	n/a	n/a	n/a	n/a	n/a
Charleston, SC	14.8	16.5	16.0	13.6	16.1	14.5	12.2	17.9	17.0	2.4	1.6	3.4
Charlotte, NC	7.7	6.9	8.5	7.5	6.8	8.1	7.4	5.4	5.6	1.1	0.8	1.7
Chicago, IL	8.6	8.4	7.5	8.5	8.3	7.4	6.4	7.0	7.0	2.3	1.8	1.6
Clarksville, TN	n/a	n/a	n/a	n/a	n/a	n/a	n/a	n/a	n/a	n/a	n/a	n/a
College Station, TX	n/a	n/a	n/a	n/a	n/a	n/a	n/a	n/a	n/a	n/a	n/a	n/a
Colorado Springs, CO	n/a	n/a	n/a	n/a	n/a	n/a	n/a	n/a	n/a	n/a	n/a	n/a
Columbia, MO	n/a	n/a	n/a	n/a	n/a	n/a	n/a	n/a	n/a	n/a	n/a	n/a
Columbia, SC	10.2	11.0	8.9	10.1	10.7	8.8	5.2	6.3	9.4	0.9	2.4	1.9
Columbus, OH	8.0	6.6	7.4	7.8	6.0	7.4	6.1	6.3	8.6	1.0	1.1	1.5
Dallas, TX	7.9	7.8	7.8	7.7	7.6	7.6	6.8	7.1	7.4	1.4	0.8	1.4
Denver, CO	6.4	7.8	8.0	5.2	6.9	7.4	4.5	5.9	3.8	1.1	0.7	0.9
Des Moines, IA	n/a	n/a	n/a	n/a	n/a	n/a	n/a	n/a	n/a	n/a	n/a	n/a
Durham, NC	n/a	n/a	n/a	n/a	n/a	n/a	n/a	n/a	n/a	n/a	n/a	n/a
Edison, NJ	10.3	10.7	10.3	9.1	9.6	9.1	4.7	4.6	4.5	2.2	1.9	1.6
El Paso, TX	n/a	n/a	n/a	n/a	n/a	n/a	n/a	n/a	n/a	n/a	n/a	n/a
Eugene, OR	n/a	n/a	n/a	n/a	n/a	n/a	n/a	n/a	n/a	n/a	n/a	n/a
Evansville, IN	n/a	n/a	n/a	n/a	n/a	n/a	n/a	n/a	n/a	n/a	n/a	n/a
Fargo, ND	n/a	n/a	n/a	n/a	n/a	n/a	n/a	n/a	n/a	n/a	n/a	n/a
Fayetteville, NC	n/a	n/a	n/a	n/a	n/a	n/a	n/a	n/a	n/a	n/a	n/a	n/a
Fort Collins, CO	n/a	n/a	n/a	n/a	n/a	n/a	n/a	n/a	n/a	n/a	n/a	n/a
Fort Wayne, IN	n/a	n/a	n/a	n/a	n/a	n/a	n/a	n/a	n/a	n/a	n/a	n/a
Fort Worth, TX	7.9	7.8	7.8	7.7	7.6	7.6	6.8	7.1	7.4	1.4	0.8	1.4
Gainesville, FL	n/a	n/a	n/a	n/a	n/a	n/a	n/a	n/a	n/a	n/a	n/a	n/a
Grand Rapids, MI	7.1	8.5	8.9	4.4	6.3	6.8	5.1	4.0	6.8	0.5	1.1	0.3
Greeley, CO	n/a	n/a	n/a	n/a	n/a	n/a	n/a	n/a	n/a	n/a	n/a	n/a
Green Bay, WI	n/a	n/a	n/a	n/a	n/a	n/a	n/a	n/a	n/a	n/a	n/a	n/a
Greensboro, NC	10.9	10.2	11.6	10.9	9.6	11.5	12.5	10.2	11.4	1.7	1.2	1.0
Honolulu, HI	13.7	13.9	14.0	12.5	12.4	12.9	9.4	8.0	6.5	1.1	0.9	1.4
Houston, TX	8.6	9.3	8.8	8.0	8.9	8.2	9.3	9.9	8.8	1.8	1.5	2.0
Huntsville, AL	n/a	n/a	n/a	n/a	n/a	n/a	n/a	n/a	n/a	n/a	n/a	n/a
Indianapolis, IN	9.1	10.9	8.7	9.0	10.8	8.6	9.2	11.9	9.9	1.4	1.5	1.5
Jacksonville, FL	14.5	12.5	10.1	14.0	12.0	9.3	8.3	8.5	5.6	1.6	1.5	1.3
Kansas City, MO	8.1	8.1	7.8	8.0	7.9	7.7	9.2	9.4	7.9	0.8	0.8	1.2
Lafayette, LA	n/a	n/a	n/a	n/a	n/a	n/a	n/a	n/a	n/a	n/a	n/a	n/a
Las Cruces, NM	n/a	n/a	n/a	n/a	n/a	n/a	n/a	n/a	n/a	n/a	n/a	n/a
Las Vegas, NV	11.8	12.6	11.4	10.7	11.0	10.4	6.6	7.0	6.8	2.0	2.4	0.9
Lexington, KY	n/a	n/a	n/a	n/a	n/a	n/a	n/a	n/a	n/a	n/a	n/a	n/a
Lincoln, NE	n/a	n/a	n/a	n/a	n/a	n/a	n/a	n/a	n/a	n/a	n/a	n/a
Little Rock, AR	11.8	10.3	10.5	11.8	10.0	10.2	12.2	11.3	10.9	2.4	2.0	1.8

Table continued on next page.

Metro Area[1]	Gross Vacancy Rate[2] (%)			Year-Round Vacancy Rate[3] (%)			Rental Vacancy Rate[4] (%)			Homeowner Vacancy Rate[5] (%)		
	2016	2017	2018	2016	2017	2018	2016	2017	2018	2016	2017	2018
Los Angeles, CA	5.0	6.3	6.6	4.7	5.9	6.2	2.9	4.1	4.0	0.8	0.9	1.2
Louisville, KY	7.6	7.3	7.6	7.2	7.2	7.4	5.0	7.8	7.7	1.5	0.6	1.4
Madison, WI	n/a	n/a	n/a	n/a	n/a	n/a	n/a	n/a	n/a	n/a	n/a	n/a
Manchester, NH	n/a	n/a	n/a	n/a	n/a	n/a	n/a	n/a	n/a	n/a	n/a	n/a
McAllen, TX	n/a	n/a	n/a	n/a	n/a	n/a	n/a	n/a	n/a	n/a	n/a	n/a
Miami, FL	17.9	17.8	14.9	9.5	9.2	7.9	7.2	7.0	7.4	1.4	1.9	1.9
Midland, TX	n/a	n/a	n/a	n/a	n/a	n/a	n/a	n/a	n/a	n/a	n/a	n/a
Minneapolis, MN	5.3	4.5	3.9	4.7	4.1	3.3	3.8	4.2	4.1	0.8	0.9	0.4
Nashville, TN	6.6	6.2	5.9	6.4	6.1	5.8	4.8	7.6	7.5	1.5	0.6	0.8
New Orleans, LA	13.6	12.8	11.9	12.7	12.2	11.8	11.1	10.8	9.7	2.6	2.5	1.7
New York, NY	10.3	10.7	10.3	9.1	9.6	9.1	4.7	4.6	4.5	2.2	1.9	1.6
Oklahoma City, OK	11.9	11.1	11.5	11.6	10.8	11.2	10.9	9.9	11.8	1.6	1.9	2.7
Omaha, NE	6.9	5.9	7.1	6.2	5.4	6.1	6.7	4.7	7.1	0.7	0.9	0.7
Orlando, FL	13.2	14.3	19.4	10.3	10.5	16.2	6.6	6.9	5.8	2.1	1.5	2.6
Peoria, IL	n/a	n/a	n/a	n/a	n/a	n/a	n/a	n/a	n/a	n/a	n/a	n/a
Philadelphia, PA	9.3	8.6	9.0	8.6	8.3	8.9	6.8	7.3	6.4	1.4	1.6	1.2
Phoenix, AZ	13.9	13.7	12.6	8.8	8.1	7.8	5.8	6.0	6.2	1.6	1.5	1.4
Pittsburgh, PA	17.7	13.6	10.2	17.4	13.4	9.9	7.4	9.7	6.3	1.8	2.2	2.2
Portland, OR	6.7	6.4	6.8	6.2	6.1	6.0	5.0	4.8	3.8	1.0	1.1	1.4
Providence, RI	11.1	11.3	10.3	7.5	8.1	8.5	3.8	4.2	5.0	1.3	1.2	1.1
Provo, UT	n/a	n/a	n/a	n/a	n/a	n/a	n/a	n/a	n/a	n/a	n/a	n/a
Raleigh, NC	6.8	8.0	6.7	6.7	7.8	6.6	4.3	5.8	6.4	1.9	1.7	0.9
Reno, NV	n/a	n/a	n/a	n/a	n/a	n/a	n/a	n/a	n/a	n/a	n/a	n/a
Richmond, VA	6.9	9.1	8.0	6.8	9.1	8.0	5.8	7.2	5.4	1.7	1.2	2.1
Roanoke, VA	n/a	n/a	n/a	n/a	n/a	n/a	n/a	n/a	n/a	n/a	n/a	n/a
Rochester, MN	n/a	n/a	n/a	n/a	n/a	n/a	n/a	n/a	n/a	n/a	n/a	n/a
Salem, OR	n/a	n/a	n/a	n/a	n/a	n/a	n/a	n/a	n/a	n/a	n/a	n/a
Salt Lake City, UT	5.4	5.0	5.0	5.0	4.8	4.7	6.4	6.2	6.1	0.5	0.6	0.5
San Antonio, TX	9.9	9.9	6.7	8.6	8.8	5.8	10.3	11.5	7.4	1.9	1.8	0.6
San Diego, CA	7.5	6.4	7.6	6.9	6.0	7.4	2.9	3.9	4.5	1.2	0.6	0.7
San Francisco, CA	6.0	6.0	7.5	5.9	5.9	7.4	3.6	4.2	5.4	0.7	0.7	0.9
San Jose, CA	6.1	6.0	5.8	5.8	5.9	5.8	4.5	3.2	4.6	0.8	0.7	0.5
Santa Rosa, CA	n/a	n/a	n/a	n/a	n/a	n/a	n/a	n/a	n/a	n/a	n/a	n/a
Savannah, GA	n/a	n/a	n/a	n/a	n/a	n/a	n/a	n/a	n/a	n/a	n/a	n/a
Seattle, WA	5.6	6.0	5.9	5.3	5.4	5.4	3.3	3.4	4.8	0.9	0.5	0.8
Sioux Falls, SD	n/a	n/a	n/a	n/a	n/a	n/a	n/a	n/a	n/a	n/a	n/a	n/a
Springfield, IL	n/a	n/a	n/a	n/a	n/a	n/a	n/a	n/a	n/a	n/a	n/a	n/a
Tallahassee, FL	n/a	n/a	n/a	n/a	n/a	n/a	n/a	n/a	n/a	n/a	n/a	n/a
Tampa, FL	16.1	16.2	16.1	12.8	12.5	11.9	8.7	9.6	9.9	2.5	2.4	2.1
Topeka, KS	n/a	n/a	n/a	n/a	n/a	n/a	n/a	n/a	n/a	n/a	n/a	n/a
Tyler, TX	n/a	n/a	n/a	n/a	n/a	n/a	n/a	n/a	n/a	n/a	n/a	n/a
Virginia Beach, VA	12.0	9.4	8.9	9.6	8.9	7.6	8.2	8.2	7.1	2.1	2.5	1.2
Visalia, CA	n/a	n/a	n/a	n/a	n/a	n/a	n/a	n/a	n/a	n/a	n/a	n/a
Washington, DC	8.2	7.4	7.0	7.9	7.1	6.7	6.0	6.2	6.2	1.7	1.2	1.1
Wilmington, NC	n/a	n/a	n/a	n/a	n/a	n/a	n/a	n/a	n/a	n/a	n/a	n/a
Winston-Salem, NC	n/a	n/a	n/a	n/a	n/a	n/a	n/a	n/a	n/a	n/a	n/a	n/a
U.S.	12.8	12.7	12.3	9.9	9.9	9.7	6.9	7.2	6.9	1.7	1.6	1.5

Note: (1) Metropolitan Statistical Area—see Appendix B for areas included; (2) The percentage of the total housing inventory that is vacant; (3) The percentage of the housing inventory (excluding seasonal units) that is year-round vacant; (4) The percentage of rental inventory that is vacant for rent; (5) The percentage of homeowner inventory that is vacant for sale; n/a not available
Source: U.S. Census Bureau, Housing Vacancies and Homeownership Annual Statistics: 2016, 2017, 2018

Bankruptcy Filings

City	Area Covered	Business Filings			Nonbusiness Filings		
		2017	2018	% Chg.	2017	2018	% Chg.
Albany, NY	Albany County	14	12	-14.3	505	513	1.6
Albuquerque, NM	Bernalillo County	53	38	-28.3	1,166	1,118	-4.1
Allentown, PA	Lehigh County	25	27	8.0	603	585	-3.0
Anchorage, AK	Anchorage Borough	18	18	0.0	176	212	20.5
Ann Arbor, MI	Washtenaw County	15	18	20.0	650	645	-0.8
Athens, GA	Clarke County	4	5	25.0	390	368	-5.6
Atlanta, GA	Fulton County	145	108	-25.5	4,655	4,600	-1.2
Austin, TX	Travis County	113	122	8.0	705	714	1.3
Baton Rouge, LA	East Baton Rouge Parish	22	21	-4.5	728	616	-15.4
Billings, MT	Yellowstone County	9	2	-77.8	222	215	-3.2
Boise City, ID	Ada County	27	35	29.6	861	946	9.9
Boston, MA	Suffolk County	56	48	-14.3	615	594	-3.4
Boulder, CO	Boulder County	27	23	-14.8	407	392	-3.7
Cape Coral, FL	Lee County	55	80	45.5	1,071	1,130	5.5
Cedar Rapids, IA	Linn County	7	9	28.6	283	289	2.1
Charleston, SC	Charleston County	16	11	-31.3	378	386	2.1
Charlotte, NC	Mecklenburg County	49	81	65.3	1,312	1,262	-3.8
Chicago, IL	Cook County	424	435	2.6	31,634	29,321	-7.3
Clarksville, TN	Montgomery County	13	7	-46.2	855	858	0.4
College Station, TX	Brazos County	5	6	20.0	71	68	-4.2
Colorado Springs, CO	El Paso County	36	49	36.1	1,737	1,672	-3.7
Columbia, MO	Boone County	3	6	100.0	394	427	8.4
Columbia, SC	Richland County	11	12	9.1	675	712	5.5
Columbus, OH	Franklin County	58	70	20.7	4,463	4,479	0.4
Dallas, TX	Dallas County	332	306	-7.8	3,955	3,997	1.1
Denver, CO	Denver County	102	78	-23.5	1,598	1,420	-11.1
Des Moines, IA	Polk County	34	20	-41.2	807	820	1.6
Durham, NC	Durham County	16	14	-12.5	459	439	-4.4
Edison, NJ	Middlesex County	62	55	-11.3	1,895	1,945	2.6
El Paso, TX	El Paso County	66	49	-25.8	2,058	2,108	2.4
Eugene, OR	Lane County	23	20	-13.0	858	905	5.5
Evansville, IN	Vanderburgh County	7	10	42.9	651	648	-0.5
Fargo, ND	Cass County	7	14	100.0	188	177	-5.9
Fayetteville, NC	Cumberland County	9	14	55.6	786	781	-0.6
Fort Collins, CO	Larimer County	17	32	88.2	630	605	-4.0
Fort Wayne, IN	Allen County	30	16	-46.7	1,507	1,386	-8.0
Fort Worth, TX	Tarrant County	231	204	-11.7	4,050	3,983	-1.7
Gainesville, FL	Alachua County	15	13	-13.3	236	238	0.8
Grand Rapids, MI	Kent County	38	32	-15.8	1,249	1,072	-14.2
Greeley, CO	Weld County	13	22	69.2	764	726	-5.0
Green Bay, WI	Brown County	13	21	61.5	539	617	14.5
Greensboro, NC	Guilford County	15	27	80.0	714	766	7.3
Honolulu, HI	Honolulu County	33	32	-3.0	934	934	0.0
Houston, TX	Harris County	489	447	-8.6	4,530	4,681	3.3
Huntsville, AL	Madison County	33	21	-36.4	1,397	1,432	2.5
Indianapolis, IN	Marion County	76	68	-10.5	4,510	4,653	3.2
Jacksonville, FL	Duval County	83	94	13.3	2,329	2,169	-6.9
Kansas City, MO	Jackson County	45	31	-31.1	2,457	2,373	-3.4
Lafayette, LA	Lafayette Parish	30	61	103.3	520	561	7.9
Las Cruces, NM	Dona Ana County	8	19	137.5	329	377	14.6
Las Vegas, NV	Clark County	225	216	-4.0	7,115	7,041	-1.0
Lexington, KY	Fayette County	23	16	-30.4	815	824	1.1
Lincoln, NE	Lancaster County	17	17	0.0	655	692	5.6
Little Rock, AR	Pulaski County	30	29	-3.3	2,563	2,571	0.3
Los Angeles, CA	Los Angeles County	1,072	1,168	9.0	20,697	19,176	-7.3

Table continued on next page.

City	Area Covered	Business Filings			Nonbusiness Filings		
		2017	2018	% Chg.	2017	2018	% Chg.
Louisville, KY	Jefferson County	48	44	-8.3	2,890	2,886	-0.1
Madison, WI	Dane County	28	26	-7.1	748	774	3.5
Manchester, NH	Hillsborough County	47	30	-36.2	545	591	8.4
McAllen, TX	Hidalgo County	46	40	-13.0	504	455	-9.7
Miami, FL	Miami-Dade County	246	231	-6.1	8,616	7,726	-10.3
Midland, TX	Midland County	22	12	-45.5	69	79	14.5
Minneapolis, MN	Hennepin County	84	83	-1.2	2,025	2,112	4.3
Nashville, TN	Davidson County	73	59	-19.2	2,558	2,274	-11.1
New Orleans, LA	Orleans Parish	46	59	28.3	631	561	-11.1
New York, NY	Bronx County	43	49	14.0	1,991	2,108	5.9
New York, NY	Kings County	165	165	0.0	2,264	2,526	11.6
New York, NY	New York County	310	430	38.7	1,047	1,099	5.0
New York, NY	Queens County	124	198	59.7	2,807	3,326	18.5
New York, NY	Richmond County	18	31	72.2	591	716	21.2
Oklahoma City, OK	Oklahoma County	110	59	-46.4	2,113	2,098	-0.7
Omaha, NE	Douglas County	34	38	11.8	1,307	1,225	-6.3
Orlando, FL	Orange County	134	137	2.2	3,256	2,801	-14.0
Peoria, IL	Peoria County	12	11	-8.3	542	533	-1.7
Philadelphia, PA	Philadelphia County	58	76	31.0	2,658	2,555	-3.9
Phoenix, AZ	Maricopa County	413	385	-6.8	10,064	10,423	3.6
Pittsburgh, PA	Allegheny County	131	120	-8.4	2,299	2,583	12.4
Portland, OR	Multnomah County	70	38	-45.7	1,545	1,468	-5.0
Providence, RI	Providence County	30	38	26.7	1,443	1,425	-1.2
Provo, UT	Utah County	41	36	-12.2	1,588	1,598	0.6
Raleigh, NC	Wake County	76	79	3.9	1,539	1,458	-5.3
Reno, NV	Washoe County	32	43	34.4	1,037	920	-11.3
Richmond, VA	Richmond city	10	10	0.0	920	914	-0.7
Roanoke, VA	Roanoke city	5	6	20.0	299	308	3.0
Rochester, MN	Olmsted County	3	4	33.3	171	146	-14.6
Salem, OR	Marion County	9	11	22.2	957	1,103	15.3
Salt Lake City, UT	Salt Lake County	70	94	34.3	5,045	4,775	-5.4
San Antonio, TX	Bexar County	173	109	-37.0	2,240	2,239	0.0
San Diego, CA	San Diego County	290	296	2.1	7,553	7,405	-2.0
San Francisco, CA	San Francisco County	83	78	-6.0	621	550	-11.4
San Jose, CA	Santa Clara County	92	99	7.6	2,067	1,843	-10.8
Santa Rosa, CA	Sonoma County	40	28	-30.0	538	528	-1.9
Savannah, GA	Chatham County	19	12	-36.8	1,320	1,252	-5.2
Seattle, WA	King County	129	142	10.1	3,161	2,633	-16.7
Sioux Falls, SD	Minnehaha County	5	8	60.0	328	327	-0.3
Springfield, IL	Sangamon County	10	9	-10.0	539	553	2.6
Tallahassee, FL	Leon County	30	23	-23.3	326	355	8.9
Tampa, FL	Hillsborough County	152	136	-10.5	3,021	2,950	-2.4
Topeka, KS	Shawnee County	9	39	333.3	873	871	-0.2
Tyler, TX	Smith County	15	19	26.7	274	309	12.8
Virginia Beach, VA	Virginia Beach city	27	15	-44.4	1,559	1,650	5.8
Visalia, CA	Tulare County	20	26	30.0	738	792	7.3
Washington, DC	District of Columbia	38	30	-21.1	625	685	9.6
Wilmington, NC	New Hanover County	19	21	10.5	305	260	-14.8
Winston-Salem, NC	Forsyth County	19	11	-42.1	530	555	4.7
U.S.	U.S.	24,114	23,157	-4.0	770,846	765,863	-0.6

Note: Business filings include Chapter 7, Chapter 11,
Chapter 12, and Chapter 13; Nonbusiness filings include Chapter 7, Chapter 11, and Chapter 13
Source: Administrative Office of the U.S. Courts, Business and Nonbusiness Bankruptcy, County Cases Commenced by Chapter of the
Bankruptcy Code, During the 12- Month Period Ending December 31, 2017 and Business and Nonbusiness Bankruptcy, County Cases
Commenced by Chapter of the Bankruptcy Code, During the 12- Month Period Ending December 31, 2018

Income: City

City	Per Capita ($)	Median Household ($)	Average Household ($)
Albany, NY	27,632	43,790	63,120
Albuquerque, NM	28,229	49,878	67,881
Allentown, PA	19,024	38,522	51,893
Anchorage, AK	38,977	82,271	105,010
Ann Arbor, MI	39,253	61,247	89,295
Athens, GA	21,111	34,258	53,394
Atlanta, GA	40,595	51,701	92,186
Austin, TX	37,888	63,717	91,811
Baton Rouge, LA	25,876	40,948	63,669
Billings, MT	31,854	55,585	74,949
Boise City, ID	32,147	54,547	76,984
Boston, MA	39,686	62,021	95,114
Boulder, CO	40,895	64,183	98,899
Cape Coral, FL	26,446	53,653	68,090
Cedar Rapids, IA	31,585	56,828	73,859
Charleston, SC	38,126	61,367	88,467
Charlotte, NC	34,687	58,202	87,225
Chicago, IL	32,560	52,497	81,061
Clarksville, TN	23,377	51,164	61,610
College Station, TX	24,640	39,430	66,254
Colorado Springs, CO	31,333	58,158	77,814
Columbia, MO	28,253	47,236	69,694
Columbia, SC	27,730	43,650	69,516
Columbus, OH	26,778	49,478	63,554
Dallas, TX	31,260	47,285	78,925
Denver, CO	38,991	60,098	88,779
Des Moines, IA	26,494	49,999	64,820
Durham, NC	32,305	54,284	77,357
Edison, NJ	41,441	95,622	117,009
El Paso, TX	21,120	44,431	60,383
Eugene, OR	28,602	47,489	67,468
Evansville, IN	22,375	36,956	50,350
Fargo, ND	31,866	50,561	71,030
Fayetteville, NC	23,853	43,439	57,059
Fort Collins, CO	31,686	60,110	80,591
Fort Wayne, IN	25,066	45,853	60,942
Fort Worth, TX	27,191	57,309	76,309
Gainesville, FL	21,111	34,004	51,019
Grand Rapids, MI	23,225	44,369	58,917
Greeley, CO	24,678	52,887	68,355
Green Bay, WI	24,660	45,473	59,780
Greensboro, NC	27,849	44,978	66,683
Honolulu, HI	34,613	65,707	89,543
Houston, TX	30,547	49,399	79,344
Huntsville, AL	33,070	51,926	75,789
Indianapolis, IN	26,232	44,709	63,698
Jacksonville, FL	27,486	50,555	68,733
Kansas City, MO	29,742	50,136	68,949
Lafayette, LA	30,988	48,533	74,381
Las Cruces, NM	23,131	40,924	57,527
Las Vegas, NV	27,650	53,159	72,694
Lexington, KY	31,653	53,013	76,300
Lincoln, NE	28,839	53,089	70,721
Little Rock, AR	32,719	48,463	77,254
Los Angeles, CA	31,563	54,501	86,758
Louisville, KY	28,975	49,439	69,805

Table continued on next page.

City	Per Capita ($)	Median Household ($)	Average Household ($)
Madison, WI	34,740	59,387	79,063
Manchester, NH	29,681	56,467	70,077
McAllen, TX	21,683	45,057	66,023
Miami, FL	25,067	33,999	60,341
Midland, TX	39,499	75,646	109,351
Minneapolis, MN	35,259	55,720	81,550
Nashville, TN	31,109	52,858	74,021
New Orleans, LA	29,275	38,721	67,224
New York, NY	35,761	57,782	93,196
Oklahoma City, OK	28,365	51,581	72,393
Omaha, NE	30,222	53,789	74,931
Orlando, FL	28,117	45,436	65,450
Peoria, IL	28,507	47,697	68,524
Philadelphia, PA	24,811	40,649	60,517
Phoenix, AZ	26,528	52,080	73,092
Pittsburgh, PA	30,397	44,092	66,639
Portland, OR	36,492	61,532	85,335
Providence, RI	24,052	40,366	64,839
Provo, UT	19,385	44,312	64,998
Raleigh, NC	35,094	61,505	86,374
Reno, NV	29,821	52,106	71,604
Richmond, VA	30,113	42,356	68,295
Roanoke, VA	24,697	41,483	55,976
Rochester, MN	36,659	68,574	90,446
Salem, OR	24,755	51,666	66,507
Salt Lake City, UT	32,954	54,009	79,834
San Antonio, TX	24,325	49,711	66,799
San Diego, CA	37,112	71,535	98,632
San Francisco, CA	59,508	96,265	137,761
San Jose, CA	40,275	96,662	124,356
Santa Rosa, CA	33,360	67,144	86,806
Savannah, GA	22,497	39,386	56,370
Seattle, WA	51,872	79,565	111,232
Sioux Falls, SD	31,161	56,714	75,241
Springfield, IL	32,162	51,789	73,023
Tallahassee, FL	25,471	42,418	61,645
Tampa, FL	32,869	48,245	78,953
Topeka, KS	26,048	46,087	60,359
Tyler, TX	26,620	46,463	69,882
Virginia Beach, VA	34,607	70,500	89,528
Visalia, CA	24,359	54,934	73,305
Washington, DC	50,832	77,649	116,090
Wilmington, NC	30,601	43,867	67,718
Winston-Salem, NC	26,668	42,219	66,187
U.S.	31,177	57,652	81,283

Source: U.S. Census Bureau, 2013-2017 American Community Survey 5-Year Estimates

Income: Metro Area

Metro Area	Per Capita ($)	Median Household ($)	Average Household ($)
Albany, NY	34,770	65,743	85,015
Albuquerque, NM	27,388	50,781	68,397
Allentown, PA	31,939	62,479	81,785
Anchorage, AK	36,807	80,724	101,305
Ann Arbor, MI	37,455	65,618	92,429
Athens, GA	24,581	42,418	63,569
Atlanta, GA	31,784	61,733	85,937
Austin, TX	35,949	69,717	94,724
Baton Rouge, LA	28,962	55,329	75,819
Billings, MT	32,226	57,812	77,471
Boise City, ID	27,506	54,120	72,902
Boston, MA	43,348	81,838	111,548
Boulder, CO	42,119	75,669	104,898
Cape Coral, FL	30,233	52,052	74,000
Cedar Rapids, IA	32,504	62,399	79,045
Charleston, SC	31,542	57,666	79,452
Charlotte, NC	31,525	57,871	81,709
Chicago, IL	34,624	65,757	91,944
Clarksville, TN	24,006	50,369	63,127
College Station, TX	25,328	45,078	66,928
Colorado Springs, CO	31,345	62,751	81,510
Columbia, MO	28,495	52,005	70,887
Columbia, SC	27,694	52,728	69,810
Columbus, OH	31,649	60,170	80,496
Dallas, TX	32,463	63,870	89,486
Denver, CO	38,018	71,884	96,371
Des Moines, IA	34,537	65,971	86,866
Durham, NC	34,342	57,600	84,882
Edison, NJ	39,182	72,205	106,398
El Paso, TX	19,917	43,170	58,772
Eugene, OR	27,032	47,710	64,571
Evansville, IN	28,086	49,873	67,860
Fargo, ND	32,574	59,074	78,102
Fayetteville, NC	23,085	44,883	58,255
Fort Collins, CO	34,087	64,980	85,429
Fort Wayne, IN	26,951	51,642	67,688
Fort Worth, TX	32,463	63,870	89,486
Gainesville, FL	26,103	45,323	65,637
Grand Rapids, MI	28,739	58,094	76,101
Greeley, CO	29,226	66,489	81,655
Green Bay, WI	29,632	56,831	72,911
Greensboro, NC	26,659	47,145	66,019
Honolulu, HI	33,776	80,078	101,194
Houston, TX	32,308	62,922	91,350
Huntsville, AL	32,676	59,583	80,893
Indianapolis, IN	30,607	56,528	77,745
Jacksonville, FL	30,451	56,449	77,552
Kansas City, MO	32,962	61,479	82,390
Lafayette, LA	26,768	49,514	69,156
Las Cruces, NM	21,050	39,114	57,160
Las Vegas, NV	27,719	54,882	73,247
Lexington, KY	30,560	54,436	75,656
Lincoln, NE	29,874	56,132	74,327
Little Rock, AR	28,187	51,362	70,449
Los Angeles, CA	32,417	65,331	95,055
Louisville, KY	30,124	54,624	74,474

Table continued on next page.

Metro Area	Per Capita ($)	Median Household ($)	Average Household ($)
Madison, WI	36,065	66,609	86,307
Manchester, NH	37,622	75,777	94,966
McAllen, TX	15,883	37,097	54,348
Miami, FL	29,499	51,758	78,886
Midland, TX	38,210	75,570	107,458
Minneapolis, MN	37,866	73,735	96,530
Nashville, TN	31,873	59,365	81,795
New Orleans, LA	29,298	50,154	72,656
New York, NY	39,182	72,205	106,398
Oklahoma City, OK	28,963	54,946	74,813
Omaha, NE	31,895	62,345	81,192
Orlando, FL	26,966	52,261	72,452
Peoria, IL	30,990	57,301	75,829
Philadelphia, PA	35,652	66,285	92,455
Phoenix, AZ	29,542	57,935	79,498
Pittsburgh, PA	33,182	56,073	76,614
Portland, OR	34,476	66,657	87,759
Providence, RI	33,001	61,536	82,080
Provo, UT	23,157	66,742	83,695
Raleigh, NC	34,821	68,870	91,708
Reno, NV	31,919	58,654	79,370
Richmond, VA	33,544	63,599	85,350
Roanoke, VA	29,393	52,609	69,257
Rochester, MN	35,842	69,003	89,677
Salem, OR	25,012	54,304	68,403
Salt Lake City, UT	29,805	67,838	87,705
San Antonio, TX	27,154	56,495	76,281
San Diego, CA	34,350	70,588	96,153
San Francisco, CA	48,538	92,714	129,577
San Jose, CA	48,133	105,809	141,951
Santa Rosa, CA	37,767	71,769	96,675
Savannah, GA	28,566	55,021	74,008
Seattle, WA	40,699	77,269	102,558
Sioux Falls, SD	31,578	62,047	78,853
Springfield, IL	33,251	58,956	78,020
Tallahassee, FL	26,709	48,618	67,419
Tampa, FL	29,632	50,567	71,311
Topeka, KS	28,190	55,194	68,649
Tyler, TX	26,270	50,742	70,687
Virginia Beach, VA	31,082	61,889	79,683
Visalia, CA	18,962	44,871	62,325
Washington, DC	46,267	97,148	125,230
Wilmington, NC	30,522	51,137	72,671
Winston-Salem, NC	26,896	47,099	66,378
U.S.	31,177	57,652	81,283

Note: Figures cover the Metropolitan Statistical Area (MSA)—see Appendix B for areas included
Source: U.S. Census Bureau, 2013-2017 American Community Survey 5-Year Estimates

Household Income Distribution: City

City	Percent of Households Earning							
	Under $15,000	$15,000 -$24,999	$25,000 -$34,999	$35,000 -$49,999	$50,000 -$74,999	$75,000 -$99,999	$100,000 -$149,999	$150,000 and up
Albany, NY	19.5	12.5	10.1	12.4	17.3	9.6	10.6	8.0
Albuquerque, NM	14.0	11.6	10.6	13.9	17.4	11.9	12.5	8.1
Allentown, PA	19.2	13.9	12.9	14.4	19.4	10.1	7.1	3.0
Anchorage, AK	5.4	5.4	6.0	10.6	17.7	14.5	20.7	19.7
Ann Arbor, MI	14.0	8.0	8.2	11.2	15.6	11.4	14.9	16.6
Athens, GA	24.6	14.6	11.5	13.4	13.2	8.1	9.0	5.6
Atlanta, GA	17.0	10.6	9.1	11.8	15.1	9.6	11.5	15.3
Austin, TX	9.9	7.7	8.6	12.9	18.3	12.2	15.1	15.3
Baton Rouge, LA	20.3	13.1	11.5	13.7	15.0	8.3	9.9	8.3
Billings, MT	10.1	11.3	10.0	13.4	21.4	12.4	12.3	9.1
Boise City, ID	11.8	10.9	9.6	13.3	18.0	12.8	13.2	10.4
Boston, MA	17.9	8.6	7.0	9.2	14.3	9.9	15.1	17.9
Boulder, CO	14.2	8.4	8.3	10.4	14.0	11.3	14.2	19.3
Cape Coral, FL	9.9	9.4	10.8	14.7	22.7	13.4	12.1	6.9
Cedar Rapids, IA	9.8	9.2	10.4	14.3	19.6	13.7	14.8	8.1
Charleston, SC	12.7	8.5	7.9	12.5	16.5	12.1	15.6	14.2
Charlotte, NC	10.0	9.4	10.1	13.8	18.1	11.8	13.4	13.4
Chicago, IL	15.8	10.9	9.2	11.9	15.8	10.9	12.7	12.9
Clarksville, TN	11.7	9.2	11.2	16.4	23.3	13.8	10.1	4.4
College Station, TX	23.6	12.7	9.6	11.7	12.5	9.5	11.8	8.6
Colorado Springs, CO	9.9	9.1	9.8	13.6	19.1	12.8	15.0	10.7
Columbia, MO	18.3	10.6	9.5	13.2	15.5	10.9	12.4	9.7
Columbia, SC	19.0	10.9	11.3	13.2	16.6	10.1	9.4	9.6
Columbus, OH	14.1	10.5	11.0	14.7	19.4	12.2	12.2	5.8
Dallas, TX	13.8	12.0	11.5	14.9	17.2	9.6	9.7	11.4
Denver, CO	11.8	8.5	8.9	12.8	17.1	12.2	14.0	14.7
Des Moines, IA	13.6	10.9	10.3	15.1	20.8	12.7	10.5	5.9
Durham, NC	12.1	9.7	10.1	13.8	17.5	12.3	13.3	11.2
Edison, NJ	5.7	4.8	5.9	8.2	14.0	14.0	20.6	26.8
El Paso, TX	15.6	12.5	11.8	15.4	18.2	10.4	10.2	5.9
Eugene, OR	17.7	11.7	9.9	13.1	17.5	10.5	11.3	8.4
Evansville, IN	17.5	15.0	14.9	15.8	18.0	8.9	6.5	3.4
Fargo, ND	11.9	11.1	11.6	14.8	18.2	12.7	11.8	8.0
Fayetteville, NC	14.6	12.2	13.6	16.5	19.2	10.5	8.8	4.6
Fort Collins, CO	11.2	9.2	8.9	13.9	15.7	13.3	15.8	11.9
Fort Wayne, IN	13.4	12.1	12.5	15.8	19.7	11.9	9.3	5.3
Fort Worth, TX	11.7	9.2	9.7	12.7	19.0	13.2	14.5	9.9
Gainesville, FL	25.7	14.1	11.2	12.2	15.8	9.0	7.6	4.5
Grand Rapids, MI	15.4	12.5	11.6	15.8	19.0	11.6	9.5	4.7
Greeley, CO	12.8	10.4	9.1	14.8	20.5	13.1	12.5	6.9
Green Bay, WI	13.7	12.0	12.6	16.5	18.8	12.4	9.4	4.5
Greensboro, NC	14.7	12.0	11.9	15.8	17.6	10.7	9.6	7.6
Honolulu, HI	10.7	7.7	7.2	12.2	18.7	13.2	15.4	14.8
Houston, TX	13.5	12.2	11.0	13.7	16.7	9.7	10.9	12.2
Huntsville, AL	14.9	11.2	9.9	12.3	16.1	10.2	14.0	11.3
Indianapolis, IN	15.2	12.2	11.6	15.7	17.8	10.6	10.1	6.7
Jacksonville, FL	12.9	10.0	11.3	15.2	18.9	12.5	11.6	7.6
Kansas City, MO	13.9	11.2	10.6	14.1	18.4	11.7	11.8	8.2
Lafayette, LA	15.9	12.0	10.7	12.6	16.2	9.6	11.3	11.7
Las Cruces, NM	19.3	13.1	11.9	14.4	16.1	9.8	9.6	5.7
Las Vegas, NV	11.8	10.2	10.9	14.4	18.5	12.6	12.8	8.8
Lexington, KY	13.8	10.6	10.1	12.9	17.5	11.8	12.8	10.4
Lincoln, NE	11.1	10.3	11.1	14.4	19.3	12.2	14.1	7.6
Little Rock, AR	13.5	12.0	10.8	15.0	16.4	9.9	10.8	11.5

Table continued on next page.

City	Percent of Households Earning							
	Under $15,000	$15,000 -$24,999	$25,000 -$34,999	$35,000 -$49,999	$50,000 -$74,999	$75,000 -$99,999	$100,000 -$149,999	$150,000 and up
Los Angeles, CA	13.9	10.8	9.7	12.2	15.8	10.7	12.8	14.2
Louisville, KY	14.1	11.4	10.5	14.5	17.8	11.7	11.5	8.5
Madison, WI	12.2	8.6	8.9	12.9	18.2	13.1	14.8	11.3
Manchester, NH	11.0	9.8	10.5	12.7	20.5	13.6	14.6	7.3
McAllen, TX	18.1	13.9	9.9	11.6	17.0	10.4	10.6	8.5
Miami, FL	23.4	15.4	12.2	13.0	13.5	7.6	7.5	7.5
Midland, TX	6.3	6.9	8.0	11.0	17.5	13.0	17.8	19.4
Minneapolis, MN	14.9	9.8	8.8	12.1	16.3	11.6	13.9	12.7
Nashville, TN	11.5	10.0	10.3	15.1	19.4	12.4	12.1	9.2
New Orleans, LA	22.9	13.0	10.7	12.3	13.7	8.8	9.2	9.5
New York, NY	15.7	9.8	8.4	10.9	15.0	10.9	13.5	15.8
Oklahoma City, OK	12.1	10.1	11.3	15.0	17.9	11.9	12.4	9.2
Omaha, NE	11.9	10.0	9.7	14.8	18.5	12.1	13.1	9.9
Orlando, FL	14.0	12.1	12.8	15.7	18.3	9.6	9.4	7.9
Peoria, IL	16.6	12.2	10.6	12.4	16.7	11.4	11.5	8.6
Philadelphia, PA	21.9	12.1	10.6	13.4	15.5	9.5	9.8	7.2
Phoenix, AZ	12.5	10.4	10.4	14.6	18.6	11.4	12.3	9.7
Pittsburgh, PA	19.0	12.4	10.7	12.5	16.5	10.1	10.3	8.7
Portland, OR	12.5	8.5	8.7	12.0	16.9	12.7	15.1	13.7
Providence, RI	22.6	12.2	10.1	11.9	16.1	9.7	8.8	8.5
Provo, UT	13.7	13.5	13.7	14.0	18.2	9.6	11.0	6.4
Raleigh, NC	8.5	8.2	9.3	14.5	19.1	12.9	14.5	12.9
Reno, NV	11.9	11.5	10.5	14.1	18.5	11.9	13.0	8.6
Richmond, VA	19.6	11.8	10.8	14.1	16.0	9.0	9.8	8.8
Roanoke, VA	17.8	13.5	11.8	15.1	18.6	11.0	7.3	4.9
Rochester, MN	8.4	7.3	8.8	11.6	18.0	14.6	16.9	14.4
Salem, OR	11.1	10.9	11.6	14.8	19.6	13.4	12.1	6.5
Salt Lake City, UT	13.4	9.9	10.3	13.2	17.8	12.0	12.1	11.3
San Antonio, TX	13.6	11.1	11.0	14.6	19.0	11.3	11.8	7.6
San Diego, CA	9.2	7.5	7.6	11.1	16.8	12.6	16.9	18.4
San Francisco, CA	11.2	6.6	5.4	7.1	11.1	9.7	16.7	32.0
San Jose, CA	7.1	5.6	5.4	8.6	13.4	11.4	18.6	30.0
Santa Rosa, CA	8.2	7.5	7.7	12.1	20.0	14.4	16.2	14.0
Savannah, GA	19.7	13.4	12.0	15.2	15.8	9.6	8.9	5.4
Seattle, WA	9.9	6.3	6.5	9.7	15.1	11.9	17.3	23.3
Sioux Falls, SD	10.1	8.9	10.9	14.5	19.0	14.4	13.2	9.1
Springfield, IL	14.6	12.0	9.3	12.6	17.3	12.2	12.0	9.9
Tallahassee, FL	18.5	11.8	11.4	15.3	15.8	9.6	10.2	7.4
Tampa, FL	16.3	11.5	10.4	13.0	15.6	9.8	11.1	12.2
Topeka, KS	13.2	12.7	12.3	14.9	19.8	11.9	10.8	4.3
Tyler, TX	13.9	12.7	11.1	15.0	18.5	10.1	9.7	9.0
Virginia Beach, VA	6.1	6.3	7.7	13.0	20.2	15.5	18.3	13.0
Visalia, CA	11.7	10.8	9.0	14.2	18.3	12.5	14.3	9.2
Washington, DC	14.1	7.0	6.4	8.2	13.1	10.7	16.0	24.6
Wilmington, NC	18.1	12.5	11.1	13.1	16.6	8.9	10.7	9.0
Winston-Salem, NC	16.9	12.9	12.4	14.4	16.6	10.0	9.1	7.6
U.S.	11.6	9.8	9.5	13.0	17.7	12.3	14.1	12.1

Source: U.S. Census Bureau, 2013-2017 American Community Survey 5-Year Estimates

Household Income Distribution: Metro Area

Metro Area	Percent of Households Earning							
	Under $15,000	$15,000 -$24,999	$25,000 -$34,999	$35,000 -$49,999	$50,000 -$74,999	$75,000 -$99,999	$100,000 -$149,999	$150,000 and up
Albany, NY	9.4	8.4	8.4	12.1	17.8	13.6	17.2	13.1
Albuquerque, NM	13.7	11.6	10.2	13.9	17.9	12.0	12.4	8.4
Allentown, PA	9.0	9.2	8.9	12.8	18.9	13.6	15.7	11.8
Anchorage, AK	6.1	5.8	6.1	10.7	17.5	14.6	20.6	18.6
Ann Arbor, MI	10.7	8.0	7.9	12.1	16.7	11.5	16.4	16.7
Athens, GA	18.9	13.0	10.8	13.8	15.1	9.5	11.2	7.7
Atlanta, GA	9.8	8.6	9.1	13.1	18.3	12.8	14.9	13.4
Austin, TX	8.3	7.2	7.9	12.2	18.1	13.4	16.9	16.0
Baton Rouge, LA	13.6	10.3	9.2	12.7	16.8	11.7	14.9	10.7
Billings, MT	9.4	10.5	9.7	13.5	20.7	13.1	13.5	9.5
Boise City, ID	11.3	9.7	10.0	14.7	19.9	12.8	13.0	8.6
Boston, MA	9.6	6.9	6.4	9.0	14.6	12.1	18.2	23.1
Boulder, CO	9.4	6.9	7.4	10.5	15.4	12.5	16.6	21.2
Cape Coral, FL	11.1	10.3	11.4	14.7	20.0	12.0	11.6	8.9
Cedar Rapids, IA	8.4	8.6	9.6	13.5	18.8	15.0	16.2	9.9
Charleston, SC	11.5	9.1	9.5	13.0	18.8	12.9	14.3	10.9
Charlotte, NC	10.4	9.5	9.8	13.7	18.2	12.6	13.9	11.9
Chicago, IL	10.4	8.6	8.2	11.6	16.8	12.8	16.0	15.7
Clarksville, TN	12.5	9.8	10.9	16.4	21.4	12.9	10.7	5.5
College Station, TX	17.9	11.5	10.4	13.5	15.9	11.1	11.4	8.2
Colorado Springs, CO	8.7	8.1	9.1	13.1	19.6	13.5	16.1	11.8
Columbia, MO	15.0	9.8	9.7	13.3	17.7	12.1	13.1	9.2
Columbia, SC	12.8	9.9	10.8	13.8	19.1	13.0	12.6	7.8
Columbus, OH	10.5	9.0	9.3	13.0	18.5	13.0	15.3	11.3
Dallas, TX	8.9	8.3	9.0	12.7	18.2	12.6	15.6	14.6
Denver, CO	7.8	6.8	7.8	11.9	17.8	13.7	17.5	16.7
Des Moines, IA	8.3	7.8	8.4	12.5	19.4	14.6	16.2	12.8
Durham, NC	11.2	9.8	9.2	13.2	17.3	12.0	13.5	13.8
Edison, NJ	11.3	8.2	7.5	10.0	14.7	11.5	16.1	20.8
El Paso, TX	15.9	12.8	12.1	15.9	17.9	10.2	9.8	5.3
Eugene, OR	14.6	11.7	11.1	14.6	18.6	11.8	10.9	6.6
Evansville, IN	12.7	11.3	11.7	14.3	18.1	12.2	12.3	7.2
Fargo, ND	9.9	9.5	9.8	13.3	18.7	14.5	14.3	9.9
Fayetteville, NC	14.4	12.1	12.7	16.1	18.8	11.5	9.6	4.8
Fort Collins, CO	8.6	8.9	8.7	13.0	17.0	14.4	16.4	13.0
Fort Wayne, IN	10.7	10.5	11.3	15.4	20.6	13.2	11.8	6.4
Fort Worth, TX	8.9	8.3	9.0	12.7	18.2	12.6	15.6	14.6
Gainesville, FL	18.4	11.9	10.5	12.8	17.1	10.5	10.4	8.6
Grand Rapids, MI	9.2	9.5	10.0	14.1	20.4	13.7	14.2	9.0
Greeley, CO	8.5	7.7	8.2	12.5	19.3	16.2	17.1	10.6
Green Bay, WI	9.3	9.7	10.3	14.5	19.1	15.1	14.2	7.8
Greensboro, NC	13.5	11.7	11.9	15.3	18.2	11.4	10.6	7.3
Honolulu, HI	7.5	5.6	6.2	10.3	17.1	14.4	19.8	19.1
Houston, TX	9.7	9.1	9.1	12.2	17.2	11.8	15.1	15.7
Huntsville, AL	11.7	9.6	9.4	12.0	16.8	12.1	15.8	12.6
Indianapolis, IN	10.8	9.8	9.8	14.1	18.4	12.6	14.1	10.5
Jacksonville, FL	11.0	9.0	10.4	14.1	18.8	12.9	13.5	10.4
Kansas City, MO	9.6	8.6	9.3	13.4	18.4	13.6	15.4	11.6
Lafayette, LA	14.7	12.0	10.5	13.2	16.7	11.1	13.1	8.7
Las Cruces, NM	18.5	15.5	11.9	14.6	15.6	8.9	9.3	5.9
Las Vegas, NV	10.6	9.6	10.8	14.6	19.7	12.9	13.1	8.6
Lexington, KY	12.9	10.3	10.1	13.1	18.0	12.4	13.3	9.8
Lincoln, NE	10.3	9.6	10.5	13.9	19.1	12.8	15.1	8.6
Little Rock, AR	12.3	10.8	11.1	14.4	18.7	11.8	12.6	8.2

Table continued on next page.

Metro Area	Percent of Households Earning							
	Under $15,000	$15,000 -$24,999	$25,000 -$34,999	$35,000 -$49,999	$50,000 -$74,999	$75,000 -$99,999	$100,000 -$149,999	$150,000 and up
Los Angeles, CA	10.6	8.9	8.4	11.5	16.2	12.0	15.3	17.0
Louisville, KY	11.5	10.1	9.8	14.5	18.7	12.8	13.3	9.3
Madison, WI	8.8	7.5	8.6	12.4	18.5	14.4	16.8	13.0
Manchester, NH	7.0	7.0	7.7	11.0	16.9	14.1	19.4	17.0
McAllen, TX	20.9	14.9	12.0	13.2	16.0	9.4	8.8	4.9
Miami, FL	13.2	11.1	10.3	13.7	17.1	11.1	12.2	11.2
Midland, TX	6.2	7.0	8.2	11.1	17.4	13.0	18.1	19.0
Minneapolis, MN	7.5	7.1	7.4	11.3	17.6	14.1	18.6	16.5
Nashville, TN	9.5	9.1	9.4	14.0	19.3	13.3	14.2	11.3
New Orleans, LA	15.5	11.2	10.3	12.8	16.5	11.1	12.4	10.1
New York, NY	11.3	8.2	7.5	10.0	14.7	11.5	16.1	20.8
Oklahoma City, OK	11.1	9.7	10.5	14.2	19.1	12.7	13.1	9.5
Omaha, NE	9.4	8.4	8.8	13.6	19.0	13.7	15.9	11.4
Orlando, FL	11.2	10.4	11.0	15.1	19.2	11.8	12.0	9.2
Peoria, IL	9.9	9.4	10.0	14.0	19.2	13.8	14.3	9.3
Philadelphia, PA	11.3	8.4	8.1	11.3	16.1	12.2	16.2	16.5
Phoenix, AZ	10.6	9.2	9.6	13.8	18.7	12.7	14.2	11.2
Pittsburgh, PA	11.8	10.6	9.8	12.8	18.0	12.7	14.1	10.3
Portland, OR	8.9	8.0	8.3	12.2	18.1	13.9	16.8	13.7
Providence, RI	12.4	9.5	8.5	11.6	16.2	13.0	16.0	12.8
Provo, UT	7.3	7.0	8.2	12.8	20.8	15.4	17.4	11.0
Raleigh, NC	7.8	7.3	8.3	12.7	17.8	13.6	17.0	15.6
Reno, NV	10.0	9.9	9.2	13.8	18.9	13.0	14.6	10.5
Richmond, VA	9.9	7.9	8.5	13.0	17.9	13.6	16.1	13.0
Roanoke, VA	12.5	10.1	10.7	14.2	19.8	13.0	12.3	7.5
Rochester, MN	7.6	7.2	8.6	11.7	19.0	14.5	18.0	13.4
Salem, OR	10.5	10.2	10.5	14.7	20.2	13.8	13.4	6.7
Salt Lake City, UT	7.3	7.0	8.2	12.5	20.2	15.0	17.0	12.6
San Antonio, TX	11.3	9.6	9.8	13.4	18.9	12.5	14.2	10.3
San Diego, CA	8.9	7.6	8.0	11.4	16.8	12.9	17.0	17.5
San Francisco, CA	8.1	6.2	5.8	8.4	13.2	11.4	17.9	29.0
San Jose, CA	6.3	5.0	5.1	7.6	12.3	10.8	18.4	34.6
Santa Rosa, CA	8.1	7.3	7.5	11.1	18.0	14.1	16.7	17.2
Savannah, GA	12.4	9.9	9.6	13.7	18.0	12.9	13.8	9.7
Seattle, WA	8.0	6.2	6.9	10.7	16.8	13.5	18.4	19.3
Sioux Falls, SD	8.6	8.0	10.1	13.8	19.2	15.9	14.9	9.5
Springfield, IL	11.3	10.3	8.6	12.6	18.2	13.6	14.5	10.8
Tallahassee, FL	14.7	10.5	11.0	14.8	17.5	11.6	11.7	8.2
Tampa, FL	12.3	11.5	10.9	14.8	18.1	11.7	11.8	9.0
Topeka, KS	10.2	10.5	10.6	14.0	20.3	14.1	14.4	5.9
Tyler, TX	11.6	11.7	11.1	15.0	17.9	11.6	12.5	8.6
Virginia Beach, VA	9.4	8.5	8.7	13.2	19.5	13.8	16.1	10.8
Visalia, CA	14.4	13.9	11.3	15.3	17.2	10.3	10.9	6.7
Washington, DC	6.2	4.6	5.2	8.1	14.5	12.7	20.2	28.4
Wilmington, NC	14.0	10.8	10.5	13.4	17.7	11.5	12.5	9.6
Winston-Salem, NC	13.7	12.0	11.5	15.2	18.0	12.0	10.5	6.9
U.S.	11.6	9.8	9.5	13.0	17.7	12.3	14.1	12.1

Note: Figures cover the Metropolitan Statistical Area (MSA)—see Appendix B for areas included
Source: Source: U.S. Census Bureau, 2013-2017 American Community Survey 5-Year Estimates

Poverty Rate: City

City	All Ages	Under 18 Years Old	18 to 64 Years Old	65 Years and Over
Albany, NY	24.5	30.5	25.4	11.2
Albuquerque, NM	18.2	25.5	17.3	9.9
Allentown, PA	27.3	39.9	24.1	14.1
Anchorage, AK	8.1	11.5	7.2	5.0
Ann Arbor, MI	22.1	10.8	26.9	7.2
Athens, GA	34.4	39.8	36.4	10.8
Atlanta, GA	22.4	35.7	19.8	15.0
Austin, TX	15.4	21.4	14.3	9.7
Baton Rouge, LA	26.0	34.6	25.9	12.6
Billings, MT	10.8	11.8	11.4	7.1
Boise City, ID	14.0	15.2	14.4	9.8
Boston, MA	20.5	29.7	18.3	20.5
Boulder, CO	21.6	8.2	26.3	6.9
Cape Coral, FL	12.7	17.0	12.8	8.7
Cedar Rapids, IA	11.4	13.6	11.8	6.2
Charleston, SC	14.6	16.5	15.7	6.9
Charlotte, NC	14.9	21.0	13.5	8.9
Chicago, IL	20.6	30.7	18.1	16.2
Clarksville, TN	15.3	19.6	14.3	8.3
College Station, TX	31.8	17.5	37.5	7.0
Colorado Springs, CO	12.8	16.9	12.4	7.2
Columbia, MO	22.9	15.9	27.4	4.9
Columbia, SC	22.3	28.3	22.1	13.7
Columbus, OH	20.8	31.1	18.7	11.2
Dallas, TX	21.8	34.2	18.1	14.1
Denver, CO	15.1	22.8	13.5	10.7
Des Moines, IA	18.1	27.5	15.8	11.0
Durham, NC	17.4	26.0	15.9	8.3
Edison, NJ	5.3	4.5	5.2	7.5
El Paso, TX	20.3	28.5	17.0	18.4
Eugene, OR	21.7	17.7	25.6	9.4
Evansville, IN	23.3	37.3	21.5	10.8
Fargo, ND	13.9	13.4	15.1	7.1
Fayetteville, NC	19.3	29.3	16.9	10.8
Fort Collins, CO	17.0	10.2	20.4	6.8
Fort Wayne, IN	17.8	27.1	16.2	7.3
Fort Worth, TX	16.9	23.4	14.7	11.1
Gainesville, FL	33.6	27.2	37.9	10.0
Grand Rapids, MI	22.5	30.6	21.6	9.9
Greeley, CO	17.5	20.2	17.7	10.2
Green Bay, WI	17.2	24.3	15.7	10.5
Greensboro, NC	19.2	27.2	18.3	10.0
Honolulu, HI	11.6	14.2	11.2	10.8
Houston, TX	21.2	33.3	17.6	13.8
Huntsville, AL	18.3	28.7	17.2	8.1
Indianapolis, IN	20.1	30.1	18.0	10.0
Jacksonville, FL	16.4	24.8	14.5	10.8
Kansas City, MO	17.3	25.5	15.8	9.9
Lafayette, LA	19.1	26.1	18.3	11.5
Las Cruces, NM	24.4	32.4	25.4	7.9
Las Vegas, NV	16.2	23.7	14.7	9.7
Lexington, KY	18.6	22.9	19.1	8.0
Lincoln, NE	15.1	17.0	16.3	5.9
Little Rock, AR	17.8	25.3	16.6	9.2
Los Angeles, CA	20.4	29.5	18.2	15.9

Table continued on next page.

City	All Ages	Under 18 Years Old	18 to 64 Years Old	65 Years and Over
Louisville, KY	16.7	24.4	15.5	9.5
Madison, WI	18.3	16.5	20.8	5.7
Manchester, NH	14.9	21.4	14.3	8.6
McAllen, TX	25.2	36.6	20.6	20.8
Miami, FL	25.8	36.0	21.9	30.3
Midland, TX	8.7	11.4	7.4	9.6
Minneapolis, MN	20.7	28.1	19.7	12.6
Nashville, TN	17.2	28.2	15.0	8.7
New Orleans, LA	25.4	38.3	23.0	16.9
New York, NY	19.6	27.8	17.2	18.4
Oklahoma City, OK	17.1	25.8	15.1	8.2
Omaha, NE	15.1	21.4	13.8	8.6
Orlando, FL	19.1	28.0	17.0	14.9
Peoria, IL	20.9	28.0	20.4	10.2
Philadelphia, PA	25.8	36.0	23.9	17.6
Phoenix, AZ	20.9	30.5	18.4	11.2
Pittsburgh, PA	22.0	30.5	22.1	12.3
Portland, OR	16.2	19.3	16.2	11.9
Providence, RI	26.9	36.0	24.7	19.3
Provo, UT	25.4	17.0	29.9	8.0
Raleigh, NC	14.0	19.7	13.2	6.6
Reno, NV	16.2	19.8	16.6	8.5
Richmond, VA	25.2	40.5	23.3	13.1
Roanoke, VA	21.6	33.3	19.7	12.2
Rochester, MN	10.4	13.0	10.6	4.6
Salem, OR	16.2	21.2	15.9	8.1
Salt Lake City, UT	17.8	22.4	17.5	11.0
San Antonio, TX	18.6	27.2	16.2	12.6
San Diego, CA	14.5	18.6	14.1	9.6
San Francisco, CA	11.7	11.4	11.3	13.6
San Jose, CA	10.0	11.6	9.5	9.8
Santa Rosa, CA	11.8	16.9	11.3	6.5
Savannah, GA	24.0	34.8	22.9	11.7
Seattle, WA	12.5	13.4	12.4	11.5
Sioux Falls, SD	11.1	14.1	10.5	8.3
Springfield, IL	20.3	31.9	19.2	7.9
Tallahassee, FL	27.1	23.4	30.6	7.9
Tampa, FL	20.0	28.7	17.8	16.6
Topeka, KS	16.7	21.7	16.9	8.3
Tyler, TX	20.2	27.4	19.6	10.9
Virginia Beach, VA	8.0	11.4	7.4	5.4
Visalia, CA	20.3	27.2	18.8	9.4
Washington, DC	17.4	25.5	15.8	14.3
Wilmington, NC	23.2	29.9	24.4	10.9
Winston-Salem, NC	23.3	35.0	21.4	10.9
U.S.	14.6	20.3	13.7	9.3

Note: Figures are percentage of people whose income during the past 12 months was below the poverty level;
Source: U.S. Census Bureau, 2013-2017 American Community Survey 5-Year Estimates

Poverty Rate: Metro Area

Metro Area	All Ages	Under 18 Years Old	18 to 64 Years Old	65 Years and Over
Albany, NY	11.0	14.9	10.8	6.4
Albuquerque, NM	17.9	24.9	17.1	10.5
Allentown, PA	11.1	17.3	10.2	6.4
Anchorage, AK	8.5	11.5	7.9	5.2
Ann Arbor, MI	14.5	12.7	16.7	6.1
Athens, GA	25.4	29.4	27.1	9.2
Atlanta, GA	13.9	20.1	12.4	8.9
Austin, TX	12.3	15.6	11.8	7.4
Baton Rouge, LA	16.9	22.6	16.0	10.5
Billings, MT	10.2	11.9	10.2	7.7
Boise City, ID	13.8	16.6	13.4	10.2
Boston, MA	10.0	12.5	9.5	8.9
Boulder, CO	13.1	11.6	14.8	6.4
Cape Coral, FL	14.9	24.9	15.0	7.8
Cedar Rapids, IA	9.4	11.3	9.4	6.0
Charleston, SC	13.9	20.1	12.9	8.6
Charlotte, NC	13.4	18.7	12.4	8.5
Chicago, IL	13.1	18.6	11.8	9.3
Clarksville, TN	15.6	20.4	14.5	9.5
College Station, TX	24.4	23.1	27.1	9.5
Colorado Springs, CO	11.0	14.0	10.6	6.6
Columbia, MO	18.7	15.2	21.8	6.9
Columbia, SC	15.6	21.3	15.0	8.5
Columbus, OH	14.0	19.8	13.0	7.8
Dallas, TX	13.3	19.2	11.7	8.4
Denver, CO	10.2	13.7	9.5	7.0
Des Moines, IA	10.3	13.6	9.5	7.3
Durham, NC	15.5	20.6	15.6	7.4
Edison, NJ	13.8	19.3	12.4	11.8
El Paso, TX	21.8	30.3	18.1	19.7
Eugene, OR	18.8	20.3	21.2	8.7
Evansville, IN	15.4	22.4	14.5	9.0
Fargo, ND	11.5	11.4	12.5	6.3
Fayetteville, NC	18.7	26.9	16.6	10.8
Fort Collins, CO	12.4	10.9	14.4	5.6
Fort Wayne, IN	14.1	21.1	12.9	6.2
Fort Worth, TX	13.3	19.2	11.7	8.4
Gainesville, FL	23.1	22.8	26.2	8.7
Grand Rapids, MI	12.4	15.8	12.3	6.6
Greeley, CO	11.2	13.4	10.9	8.0
Green Bay, WI	10.9	14.9	10.0	8.2
Greensboro, NC	16.9	24.7	16.0	9.3
Honolulu, HI	9.1	11.3	8.7	7.7
Houston, TX	14.8	21.5	12.7	10.0
Huntsville, AL	13.9	20.0	12.9	8.5
Indianapolis, IN	13.7	19.6	12.7	7.1
Jacksonville, FL	13.9	19.9	13.0	8.7
Kansas City, MO	11.5	16.2	10.6	7.1
Lafayette, LA	18.1	24.7	16.3	14.0
Las Cruces, NM	27.9	41.0	26.0	12.3
Las Vegas, NV	14.6	21.2	13.4	8.7
Lexington, KY	17.2	22.7	17.3	7.6
Lincoln, NE	13.7	15.3	14.8	5.6
Little Rock, AR	15.1	20.9	14.4	8.5
Los Angeles, CA	15.8	22.2	14.3	12.3

Table continued on next page.

Metro Area	All Ages	Under 18 Years Old	18 to 64 Years Old	65 Years and Over
Louisville, KY	13.2	18.8	12.4	8.0
Madison, WI	11.7	11.8	12.8	5.7
Manchester, NH	8.6	10.9	8.4	5.7
McAllen, TX	31.8	43.8	26.3	23.0
Miami, FL	16.1	22.2	14.4	14.9
Midland, TX	8.6	11.4	7.3	9.2
Minneapolis, MN	9.4	12.3	8.8	6.5
Nashville, TN	12.8	18.2	11.8	7.7
New Orleans, LA	18.0	26.6	16.2	12.3
New York, NY	13.8	19.3	12.4	11.8
Oklahoma City, OK	14.6	20.6	13.7	7.2
Omaha, NE	11.2	14.9	10.4	7.2
Orlando, FL	15.4	22.1	14.2	10.1
Peoria, IL	12.0	16.6	11.8	6.1
Philadelphia, PA	13.1	17.8	12.4	8.9
Phoenix, AZ	15.7	22.4	14.7	8.4
Pittsburgh, PA	11.8	16.3	11.6	8.0
Portland, OR	12.3	15.5	12.1	8.0
Providence, RI	13.0	18.3	12.1	9.6
Provo, UT	11.8	10.6	13.4	5.7
Raleigh, NC	11.1	15.1	10.2	6.8
Reno, NV	13.3	16.9	13.3	7.7
Richmond, VA	12.4	17.9	11.7	6.8
Roanoke, VA	13.6	20.2	12.9	8.5
Rochester, MN	8.6	11.0	8.4	5.6
Salem, OR	15.8	22.2	15.3	7.5
Salt Lake City, UT	10.3	12.7	9.7	7.0
San Antonio, TX	15.2	21.8	13.5	10.4
San Diego, CA	13.3	17.1	12.9	9.0
San Francisco, CA	10.1	11.7	10.0	8.6
San Jose, CA	8.7	9.9	8.3	8.5
Santa Rosa, CA	10.7	13.1	11.0	6.7
Savannah, GA	15.8	22.6	14.9	8.0
Seattle, WA	10.4	13.0	9.9	8.1
Sioux Falls, SD	9.2	11.4	8.7	7.2
Springfield, IL	15.4	24.3	14.4	6.6
Tallahassee, FL	20.2	21.6	22.2	7.8
Tampa, FL	14.6	20.3	14.1	9.9
Topeka, KS	12.4	15.8	12.5	6.7
Tyler, TX	16.3	22.1	15.7	9.2
Virginia Beach, VA	12.2	18.2	11.1	6.9
Visalia, CA	27.1	36.2	24.5	14.3
Washington, DC	8.3	10.7	7.6	7.2
Wilmington, NC	17.5	22.0	18.3	9.1
Winston-Salem, NC	17.3	26.2	16.0	9.1
U.S.	14.6	20.3	13.7	9.3

Note: Figures are percentage of people whose income during the past 12 months was below the poverty level; Figures cover the Metropolitan Statistical Area—see Appendix B for areas included
Source: U.S. Census Bureau, 2013-2017 American Community Survey 5-Year Estimates

Employment by Industry

Metro Area[1]	(A)	(B)	(C)	(D)	(E)	(F)	(G)	(H)	(I)	(J)	(K)	(L)	(M)	(N)
Albany, NY	4.0	n/a	20.6	5.4	21.4	1.7	8.8	5.5	n/a	4.0	11.9	10.4	3.0	2.7
Albuquerque, NM	5.9	n/a	16.8	4.7	20.6	1.7	11.0	4.0	n/a	3.0	15.4	10.7	2.7	2.9
Allentown, PA	3.6	n/a	20.8	3.7	10.8	1.4	9.9	10.1	n/a	3.8	12.5	10.6	8.5	3.8
Anchorage, AK	7.0	5.3	18.3	4.5	19.9	2.3	11.1	1.1	1.6	3.6	10.5	12.0	6.5	2.8
Ann Arbor, MI	1.9	n/a	12.2	3.0	38.0	2.3	7.7	6.7	n/a	2.8	13.3	7.2	1.7	2.7
Athens, GA	n/a	n/a	n/a	n/a	29.7	n/a	11.3	n/a	n/a	n/a	9.3	11.0	n/a	n/a
Atlanta, GA	4.6	4.5	12.7	6.1	11.9	3.4	10.6	6.1	<0.1	3.4	19.0	10.6	5.7	5.4
Austin, TX	5.8	n/a	11.7	5.8	16.8	3.1	11.8	5.6	n/a	4.1	17.3	10.3	2.1	4.8
Baton Rouge, LA	13.3	13.0	12.7	4.5	18.5	1.2	9.6	7.2	0.2	4.0	11.4	10.2	3.7	3.3
Billings, MT	n/a	n/a	18.1	n/a	11.5	n/a	13.5	n/a	n/a	n/a	11.0	n/a	n/a	n/a
Boise City, ID	7.1	n/a	14.6	5.5	14.5	1.3	9.9	8.7	n/a	3.5	15.0	11.5	3.4	4.5
Boston, MA[4]	3.7	n/a	22.5	8.1	10.6	3.2	9.6	4.2	n/a	3.6	20.4	8.1	2.4	3.1
Boulder, CO	2.9	n/a	13.2	3.5	20.0	4.1	10.9	9.6	n/a	3.2	18.8	9.1	0.9	3.2
Cape Coral, FL	11.4	n/a	11.0	4.8	15.5	1.0	15.5	2.2	n/a	4.1	13.8	15.5	1.9	2.6
Cedar Rapids, IA	5.3	n/a	14.6	7.4	11.7	2.5	8.1	13.6	n/a	3.5	10.5	10.4	7.9	4.1
Charleston, SC	6.0	n/a	11.4	4.3	17.9	1.7	12.9	7.4	n/a	3.8	15.4	12.0	4.2	2.6
Charlotte, NC	5.2	n/a	10.3	7.9	12.6	2.4	11.4	8.9	n/a	3.4	17.0	10.7	5.1	4.7
Chicago, IL[2]	3.3	3.2	15.9	7.0	11.0	1.7	9.9	7.5	<0.1	4.2	18.7	9.4	5.8	5.0
Clarksville, TN	3.5	n/a	12.8	3.4	20.4	1.1	12.2	14.0	n/a	3.2	9.8	13.6	2.7	n/a
College Station, TX	6.4	n/a	10.2	3.3	35.6	1.0	14.0	4.6	n/a	2.8	7.7	10.2	1.5	2.2
Colorado Springs, CO	6.1	n/a	13.8	6.2	18.2	1.9	12.5	3.9	n/a	5.9	15.7	11.7	1.8	1.9
Columbia, MO	n/a	n/a	n/a	n/a	30.3	n/a	n/a	n/a	n/a	n/a	n/a	10.9	n/a	n/a
Columbia, SC	4.4	n/a	11.7	7.5	21.4	1.3	9.8	7.4	n/a	4.0	13.1	10.9	4.4	3.7
Columbus, OH	3.7	n/a	15.4	7.7	15.9	1.5	9.5	6.7	n/a	3.7	16.5	9.2	5.9	3.7
Dallas, TX[2]	5.5	n/a	11.9	9.0	11.4	2.6	10.1	6.8	n/a	3.2	18.9	9.9	4.7	5.6
Denver, CO	7.1	n/a	12.6	7.2	13.2	3.2	10.8	4.6	n/a	3.9	18.2	9.4	4.3	4.8
Des Moines, IA	5.5	n/a	14.4	15.0	12.1	1.8	9.2	5.6	n/a	3.4	13.6	11.0	3.1	4.8
Durham, NC	2.7	n/a	22.0	4.7	21.6	1.3	8.6	8.8	n/a	3.4	14.5	7.8	1.5	2.6
Edison, NJ[2]	3.7	n/a	21.2	8.6	13.0	3.4	9.4	2.8	n/a	4.2	16.1	9.4	3.8	3.8
El Paso, TX	5.1	n/a	14.5	3.9	22.8	1.4	11.2	5.1	n/a	2.8	11.1	12.7	5.2	3.8
Eugene, OR	5.0	4.4	17.1	5.0	18.4	1.4	10.6	9.0	0.5	3.2	11.1	12.5	2.2	4.0
Evansville, IN	6.0	n/a	17.6	3.3	10.7	0.9	9.7	14.5	n/a	5.1	12.3	10.7	4.9	3.8
Fargo, ND	5.6	n/a	17.5	7.7	14.3	2.1	9.5	7.2	n/a	3.5	10.9	10.9	4.2	6.2
Fayetteville, NC	4.3	n/a	11.4	2.8	31.0	0.9	12.3	6.2	n/a	3.3	9.1	13.0	3.4	1.7
Fort Collins, CO	6.7	n/a	10.6	4.0	24.0	1.7	12.3	8.5	n/a	3.7	12.1	11.3	1.9	2.8
Fort Wayne, IN	4.8	n/a	19.0	5.3	9.6	1.1	9.0	16.4	n/a	5.0	9.9	10.8	3.9	4.7
Fort Worth, TX[2]	7.0	n/a	12.8	5.8	13.0	1.0	11.3	9.4	n/a	3.5	10.6	11.6	8.6	5.0
Gainesville, FL	4.0	n/a	18.0	4.5	30.0	1.0	10.7	3.1	n/a	2.9	10.0	10.7	2.4	2.2
Grand Rapids, MI	4.4	n/a	16.5	4.6	8.7	1.1	8.9	20.8	n/a	3.9	13.5	8.8	2.8	5.5
Greeley, CO	17.6	n/a	9.4	4.0	16.7	0.6	8.1	12.7	n/a	3.2	9.6	9.5	4.2	3.9
Green Bay, WI	4.2	n/a	14.9	6.6	12.1	0.8	9.4	17.1	n/a	4.8	10.6	9.5	4.8	4.6
Greensboro, NC	4.3	n/a	14.3	5.1	12.4	1.2	9.7	15.1	n/a	3.4	12.9	10.7	5.3	5.2
Honolulu, HI	5.5	n/a	13.5	4.5	21.0	1.7	15.4	2.3	n/a	4.4	13.4	9.9	5.0	2.9
Houston, TX	9.6	7.1	12.7	5.2	13.4	1.0	10.3	7.5	2.5	3.5	15.9	10.0	5.0	5.5
Huntsville, AL	3.8	n/a	9.0	2.8	21.3	1.0	9.1	10.6	n/a	3.3	23.9	10.7	1.3	2.5
Indianapolis, IN	4.8	4.8	15.1	6.3	12.5	1.2	9.6	8.5	<0.1	4.3	16.1	9.7	6.8	4.6
Jacksonville, FL	6.3	6.2	15.1	9.2	11.0	1.3	12.0	4.4	<0.1	3.7	15.1	12.4	5.4	3.6
Kansas City, MO	4.3	n/a	14.4	7.1	14.2	1.4	9.5	7.1	n/a	3.8	17.6	10.3	5.0	4.6
Lafayette, LA	11.0	4.7	15.8	5.3	13.4	1.1	10.7	7.6	6.2	3.4	10.5	13.4	2.9	4.3
Las Cruces, NM	4.9	n/a	21.5	3.4	27.3	0.9	11.2	3.3	n/a	2.0	10.7	9.9	2.9	1.6
Las Vegas, NV	6.5	6.4	10.2	5.2	10.3	1.0	28.3	2.4	<0.1	3.2	14.2	11.0	4.8	2.3
Lexington, KY	4.5	n/a	13.1	3.5	18.6	1.0	11.0	10.9	n/a	3.4	14.5	11.0	4.1	3.8
Lincoln, NE	4.7	n/a	15.5	6.9	22.0	1.6	9.8	7.0	n/a	3.7	10.3	10.1	5.8	2.1
Little Rock, AR	4.4	n/a	15.7	5.8	19.7	1.1	9.6	5.7	n/a	4.3	13.5	10.9	4.4	4.3
Los Angeles, CA[2]	3.2	3.2	18.3	4.8	13.0	4.8	11.7	7.4	<0.1	3.5	13.7	9.6	4.6	4.9
Louisville, KY	4.5	n/a	14.4	6.8	11.1	1.3	9.6	12.4	n/a	3.8	12.9	10.0	8.5	4.2

Table continued on next page.

Metro Area[1]	(A)	(B)	(C)	(D)	(E)	(F)	(G)	(H)	(I)	(J)	(K)	(L)	(M)	(N)
Madison, WI	4.4	n/a	11.9	5.6	21.4	4.2	9.1	8.6	n/a	5.1	12.8	10.3	2.5	3.7
Manchester, NH[3]	4.5	n/a	22.2	7.0	10.3	3.0	8.7	6.9	n/a	4.2	15.1	11.2	2.4	3.9
McAllen, TX	3.0	n/a	28.0	3.3	23.0	1.0	9.4	2.6	n/a	2.1	6.5	14.0	3.2	3.3
Miami, FL[2]	4.3	4.3	15.6	6.7	11.7	1.6	11.9	3.4	<0.1	4.2	14.8	12.6	6.6	6.0
Midland, TX	34.9	n/a	6.6	4.0	8.7	0.8	9.1	3.8	n/a	3.2	8.8	8.8	4.5	6.2
Minneapolis, MN	3.8	n/a	16.7	7.4	12.4	1.8	9.1	9.9	n/a	3.8	16.2	9.8	3.8	4.7
Nashville, TN	4.5	n/a	14.9	6.6	11.9	2.2	11.2	8.0	n/a	4.1	16.5	10.2	5.3	4.0
New Orleans, LA	6.0	5.3	17.4	4.9	12.3	1.2	16.0	5.1	0.7	4.2	13.0	10.6	5.1	3.7
New York, NY[2]	3.7	n/a	21.2	8.6	13.0	3.4	9.4	2.8	n/a	4.2	16.1	9.4	3.8	3.8
Oklahoma City, OK	8.1	4.7	14.2	5.1	20.0	1.1	11.3	5.1	3.4	4.4	12.8	10.3	3.5	3.8
Omaha, NE	5.7	n/a	15.9	8.9	13.2	2.1	9.7	6.6	n/a	3.5	14.5	10.9	5.2	3.3
Orlando, FL	6.3	6.3	11.9	5.8	9.8	1.9	20.1	3.5	<0.1	3.3	18.3	11.7	3.4	3.5
Peoria, IL	4.0	n/a	18.0	4.0	12.1	1.1	10.1	13.4	n/a	4.3	14.1	10.2	4.0	4.1
Philadelphia, PA[2]	2.5	n/a	31.1	6.1	13.3	1.5	10.0	3.4	n/a	4.0	13.6	7.7	4.0	2.4
Phoenix, AZ	6.2	6.0	15.4	8.9	11.2	1.8	10.7	6.0	0.1	3.2	16.8	11.2	4.2	3.8
Pittsburgh, PA	5.9	5.0	21.6	6.3	9.7	1.6	9.9	7.2	0.9	4.2	15.1	10.2	4.1	3.6
Portland, OR	6.1	6.0	15.2	5.9	12.6	2.1	10.3	10.6	0.1	3.5	14.9	10.1	3.6	4.7
Providence, RI[3]	4.1	4.1	21.7	6.2	12.2	1.2	10.6	8.4	<0.1	4.6	12.7	11.3	3.2	3.2
Provo, UT	8.8	n/a	20.9	3.3	12.5	5.0	8.0	7.6	n/a	2.0	14.4	12.9	1.4	2.7
Raleigh, NC	6.3	n/a	12.4	5.2	15.6	3.4	10.8	5.6	n/a	3.8	18.5	11.6	2.3	4.0
Reno, NV	7.3	7.2	10.8	4.3	12.2	1.1	15.0	10.0	0.1	2.5	14.2	10.2	8.0	3.9
Richmond, VA	5.7	n/a	14.5	7.5	16.7	1.0	9.0	4.7	n/a	4.7	17.0	10.0	4.4	4.1
Roanoke, VA	5.0	n/a	17.2	4.9	14.2	0.8	8.8	9.4	n/a	4.8	13.9	10.5	5.3	4.7
Rochester, MN	3.8	n/a	41.5	2.2	10.8	1.3	8.9	8.7	n/a	3.0	4.8	10.1	2.2	2.2
Salem, OR	6.9	6.6	17.0	4.2	24.8	0.7	9.1	7.5	0.3	3.2	8.8	11.6	3.2	2.4
Salt Lake City, UT	5.7	n/a	11.3	8.1	15.0	2.8	8.8	7.8	n/a	2.9	16.9	10.6	5.3	4.4
San Antonio, TX	5.9	4.9	15.5	8.6	16.2	1.9	12.7	4.7	0.9	3.5	13.4	10.9	2.9	3.4
San Diego, CA	5.5	5.5	14.2	5.0	16.7	1.5	13.3	7.6	<0.1	3.7	16.5	10.2	2.3	2.9
San Francisco, CA[2]	3.6	3.6	12.2	7.0	11.2	7.5	12.3	3.2	<0.1	3.6	25.1	7.2	4.2	2.3
San Jose, CA	4.2	4.2	15.3	3.3	8.7	8.3	9.1	15.2	<0.1	2.5	20.9	7.8	1.5	2.7
Santa Rosa, CA	7.2	7.1	17.0	4.1	15.0	1.2	11.6	11.2	0.1	3.3	10.9	12.1	2.1	3.6
Savannah, GA	4.7	n/a	14.3	3.5	13.5	1.0	14.1	10.1	n/a	3.8	11.0	12.3	7.6	3.5
Seattle, WA[2]	6.0	5.9	12.9	4.9	12.3	6.7	9.9	9.4	<0.1	3.4	15.1	11.2	3.5	4.1
Sioux Falls, SD	5.2	n/a	20.7	9.8	9.1	1.6	9.5	8.9	n/a	3.7	10.0	12.1	3.6	5.2
Springfield, IL	2.7	n/a	18.6	5.5	26.0	2.3	9.3	3.0	n/a	5.9	10.6	10.9	1.8	2.8
Tallahassee, FL	4.5	n/a	12.9	4.2	33.0	1.6	11.2	1.7	n/a	5.2	11.5	10.5	1.3	2.0
Tampa, FL	5.6	5.6	15.4	8.8	11.4	1.8	11.6	4.9	<0.1	3.4	18.1	12.2	2.4	3.8
Topeka, KS	4.7	n/a	16.5	6.9	23.7	1.2	7.6	6.9	n/a	4.3	12.1	9.5	3.4	2.5
Tyler, TX	6.2	n/a	22.6	3.9	13.9	1.3	10.7	5.0	n/a	3.7	10.1	12.6	4.7	4.7
Virginia Beach, VA	4.8	n/a	14.3	4.8	20.4	1.3	11.2	7.3	n/a	4.5	14.3	11.1	3.2	2.3
Visalia, CA	4.7	n/a	12.7	3.1	25.7	0.7	9.1	10.0	n/a	2.6	8.4	13.4	5.7	3.4
Washington, DC[2]	4.6	n/a	12.9	4.3	21.7	2.2	10.2	1.3	n/a	6.7	23.2	8.1	2.4	1.8
Wilmington, NC	6.7	n/a	11.6	4.7	18.7	2.5	15.2	4.6	n/a	3.8	12.2	13.7	2.4	3.4
Winston-Salem, NC	4.0	n/a	20.5	4.9	11.9	0.6	10.4	12.1	n/a	3.1	13.7	11.5	3.6	3.1
U.S.	5.3	4.8	15.9	5.7	15.1	1.9	10.7	8.5	0.5	3.9	14.1	10.8	4.2	3.9

Note: All figures are percentages covering non-farm employment as of December 2018 and are not seasonally adjusted;
(1) Figures cover the Metropolitan Statistical Area (MSA) except where noted. See Appendix B for areas included; (2) Metropolitan Division; (3) New England City and Town Area; (4) New England City and Town Area Division; (A) Construction, Mining, and Logging (some areas report Construction separate from Mining and Logging); (B) Construction; (C) Education and Health Services; (D) Financial Activities; (E) Government; (F) Information; (G) Leisure and Hospitality; (H) Manufacturing; (I) Mining and Logging; (J) Other Services; (K) Professional and Business Services; (L) Retail Trade; (M) Transportation and Utilities; (N) Wholesale Trade; n/a not available
Source: Bureau of Labor Statistics, Current Employment Statistics, Employment, Hours, and Earnings, December 2018

Labor Force, Employment and Job Growth: City

City	Civilian Labor Force			Workers Employed		
	Dec. 2017	Dec. 2018	% Chg.	Dec. 2017	Dec. 2018	% Chg.
Albany, NY	46,643	47,704	2.2	44,459	45,976	3.4
Albuquerque, NM	278,343	287,128	3.1	264,846	274,874	3.7
Allentown, PA	54,030	54,927	1.6	50,624	51,750	2.2
Anchorage, AK	156,235	153,126	-1.9	147,186	145,328	-1.2
Ann Arbor, MI	65,171	65,503	0.5	63,515	64,041	0.8
Athens, GA	60,911	62,570	2.7	58,343	60,290	3.3
Atlanta, GA	252,504	255,674	1.2	240,597	245,200	1.9
Austin, TX	578,582	599,854	3.6	564,005	584,814	3.6
Baton Rouge, LA	114,467	114,228	-0.2	110,218	109,416	-0.7
Billings, MT	56,572	56,666	0.1	54,593	54,787	0.3
Boise City, ID	127,840	131,138	2.5	124,833	128,133	2.6
Boston, MA	372,444	393,079	5.5	362,346	383,962	5.9
Boulder, CO	64,429	66,564	3.3	62,976	64,432	2.3
Cape Coral, FL	87,362	89,615	2.5	84,383	86,784	2.8
Cedar Rapids, IA	70,152	70,700	0.7	67,761	68,658	1.3
Charleston, SC	72,422	73,601	1.6	70,111	71,740	2.3
Charlotte, NC	483,182	490,050	1.4	463,433	473,059	2.0
Chicago, IL	1,361,078	1,335,474	-1.8	1,288,701	1,283,431	-0.4
Clarksville, TN	59,588	61,309	2.8	57,442	59,226	3.1
College Station, TX	59,536	60,885	2.2	58,011	59,187	2.0
Colorado Springs, CO	233,297	247,687	6.1	225,458	236,593	4.9
Columbia, MO	66,863	67,317	0.6	65,375	65,918	0.8
Columbia, SC	59,440	59,882	0.7	56,706	57,719	1.7
Columbus, OH	465,421	467,223	0.3	448,071	448,562	0.1
Dallas, TX	685,232	710,627	3.7	662,456	686,384	3.6
Denver, CO	401,313	411,708	2.5	389,719	396,286	1.6
Des Moines, IA	111,536	115,184	3.2	107,681	111,687	3.7
Durham, NC	142,841	145,434	1.8	137,308	140,582	2.3
Edison, NJ	54,808	54,865	0.1	53,232	53,523	0.5
El Paso, TX	297,041	303,631	2.2	285,407	291,848	2.2
Eugene, OR	85,893	84,904	-1.1	82,759	81,544	-1.4
Evansville, IN	58,960	59,887	1.5	57,218	57,922	1.2
Fargo, ND	69,596	68,580	-1.4	68,045	67,103	-1.3
Fayetteville, NC	76,094	76,808	0.9	71,557	72,716	1.6
Fort Collins, CO	98,374	102,737	4.4	96,051	99,566	3.6
Fort Wayne, IN	124,295	128,942	3.7	120,667	124,877	3.4
Fort Worth, TX	416,976	430,412	3.2	403,226	415,732	3.1
Gainesville, FL	67,232	68,434	1.7	64,845	66,131	1.9
Grand Rapids, MI	103,943	104,567	0.6	99,188	100,721	1.5
Greeley, CO	53,136	54,936	3.3	51,634	52,884	2.4
Green Bay, WI	54,880	54,922	0.0	53,420	53,547	0.2
Greensboro, NC	143,681	144,756	0.7	137,008	138,976	1.4
Honolulu, HI	471,688	468,609	-0.6	463,613	458,462	-1.1
Houston, TX	1,155,275	1,193,791	3.3	1,107,177	1,148,266	3.7
Huntsville, AL	94,181	98,508	4.5	91,263	95,413	4.5
Indianapolis, IN	437,038	451,232	3.2	423,438	436,132	3.0
Jacksonville, FL	457,717	464,256	1.4	441,382	449,181	1.7
Kansas City, MO	256,776	259,249	0.9	247,285	250,839	1.4
Lafayette, LA	59,801	59,450	-0.5	57,509	57,050	-0.8
Las Cruces, NM	45,773	46,276	1.1	43,256	44,063	1.8
Las Vegas, NV	306,426	317,238	3.5	290,781	302,680	4.0
Lexington, KY	174,457	176,120	0.9	169,534	171,118	0.9
Lincoln, NE	152,563	155,749	2.0	148,759	152,191	2.3
Little Rock, AR	97,069	98,167	1.1	94,026	94,836	0.8
Los Angeles, CA	2,070,235	2,093,984	1.1	1,984,993	1,997,076	0.6

Table continued on next page.

City	Civilian Labor Force			Workers Employed		
	Dec. 2017	Dec. 2018	% Chg.	Dec. 2017	Dec. 2018	% Chg.
Louisville, KY	394,322	395,478	0.2	380,983	381,300	0.0
Madison, WI	157,135	156,294	-0.5	154,210	153,374	-0.5
Manchester, NH	61,554	63,695	3.4	60,096	62,362	3.7
McAllen, TX	65,733	67,123	2.1	62,813	64,102	2.0
Miami, FL	231,034	231,547	0.2	220,564	223,501	1.3
Midland, TX	76,140	81,038	6.4	74,430	79,340	6.6
Minneapolis, MN	237,197	240,306	1.3	230,805	234,326	1.5
Nashville, TN	389,865	398,504	2.2	381,000	389,436	2.2
New Orleans, LA	179,260	180,224	0.5	172,059	172,588	0.3
New York, NY	4,097,111	4,120,012	0.5	3,930,027	3,956,181	0.6
Oklahoma City, OK	315,790	315,289	-0.1	304,263	306,285	0.6
Omaha, NE	229,225	236,434	3.1	222,137	229,428	3.2
Orlando, FL	166,522	172,311	3.4	161,476	167,611	3.8
Peoria, IL	51,182	51,811	1.2	48,530	48,559	0.0
Philadelphia, PA	699,144	716,864	2.5	659,824	681,673	3.3
Phoenix, AZ	821,300	857,747	4.4	788,157	819,226	3.9
Pittsburgh, PA	155,985	157,113	0.7	149,377	151,228	1.2
Portland, OR	378,785	379,135	0.0	366,371	365,951	-0.1
Providence, RI	86,558	87,407	0.9	82,383	83,483	1.3
Provo, UT	68,212	68,301	0.1	66,711	66,683	0.0
Raleigh, NC	253,520	259,281	2.2	243,568	250,554	2.8
Reno, NV	131,602	138,852	5.5	126,818	134,139	5.7
Richmond, VA	115,459	117,002	1.3	110,771	113,308	2.2
Roanoke, VA	48,370	49,186	1.6	46,536	47,881	2.8
Rochester, MN	63,515	63,316	-0.3	61,863	61,747	-0.1
Salem, OR	81,089	80,206	-1.0	77,833	76,682	-1.4
Salt Lake City, UT	114,107	113,951	-0.1	111,105	110,875	-0.2
San Antonio, TX	719,253	729,331	1.4	697,791	706,404	1.2
San Diego, CA	713,826	730,204	2.2	690,518	707,716	2.4
San Francisco, CA	571,462	585,540	2.4	557,616	572,810	2.7
San Jose, CA	555,312	574,518	3.4	539,945	560,113	3.7
Santa Rosa, CA	89,803	91,470	1.8	87,147	89,089	2.2
Savannah, GA	67,349	66,715	-0.9	64,307	64,028	-0.4
Seattle, WA	448,837	456,935	1.8	434,295	443,165	2.0
Sioux Falls, SD	102,100	103,935	1.8	99,008	101,225	2.2
Springfield, IL	57,636	57,912	0.4	55,303	54,991	-0.5
Tallahassee, FL	100,181	102,424	2.2	96,633	98,960	2.4
Tampa, FL	197,563	200,096	1.2	190,512	193,524	1.5
Topeka, KS	62,249	62,486	0.3	60,176	60,220	0.0
Tyler, TX	51,203	52,965	3.4	49,397	51,146	3.5
Virginia Beach, VA	228,851	232,737	1.7	221,361	226,637	2.3
Visalia, CA	60,030	61,666	2.7	57,134	58,689	2.7
Washington, DC	401,070	401,943	0.2	379,474	382,184	0.7
Wilmington, NC	61,254	61,633	0.6	58,646	59,149	0.8
Winston-Salem, NC	116,513	118,049	1.3	111,333	113,512	1.9
U.S.	159,880,000	162,510,000	1.6	153,602,000	156,481,000	1.9

Note: Data is not seasonally adjusted and covers workers 16 years of age and older
Source: Bureau of Labor Statistics, Local Area Unemployment Statistics

Labor Force, Employment and Job Growth: Metro Area

Metro Area[1]	Civilian Labor Force			Workers Employed		
	Dec. 2017	Dec. 2018	% Chg.	Dec. 2017	Dec. 2018	% Chg.
Albany, NY	445,967	457,216	2.5	427,121	442,048	3.4
Albuquerque, NM	430,911	444,200	3.0	408,815	424,436	3.8
Allentown, PA	429,942	437,716	1.8	411,484	420,069	2.0
Anchorage, AK	203,924	199,540	-2.1	190,759	188,393	-1.2
Ann Arbor, MI	194,270	195,123	0.4	188,260	189,818	0.8
Athens, GA	100,971	103,672	2.6	96,987	100,137	3.2
Atlanta, GA	3,056,722	3,097,603	1.3	2,931,140	2,986,890	1.9
Austin, TX	1,164,240	1,207,936	3.7	1,133,101	1,174,961	3.6
Baton Rouge, LA	418,468	416,996	-0.3	403,814	400,928	-0.7
Billings, MT	86,898	87,078	0.2	83,788	84,119	0.4
Boise City, ID	351,551	360,557	2.5	342,090	351,071	2.6
Boston, MA[4]	1,597,698	1,686,499	5.5	1,556,045	1,648,872	5.9
Boulder, CO	189,048	194,860	3.0	184,248	188,507	2.3
Cape Coral, FL	334,489	343,149	2.5	323,111	332,304	2.8
Cedar Rapids, IA	141,463	142,627	0.8	136,902	138,776	1.3
Charleston, SC	373,329	379,429	1.6	360,371	368,841	2.3
Charlotte, NC	1,325,794	1,343,634	1.3	1,271,766	1,297,622	2.0
Chicago, IL[2]	3,739,557	3,718,529	-0.5	3,578,093	3,586,035	0.2
Clarksville, TN	110,843	114,018	2.8	106,720	109,983	3.0
College Station, TX	131,772	134,501	2.0	128,210	130,738	1.9
Colorado Springs, CO	341,600	362,668	6.1	329,935	346,215	4.9
Columbia, MO	97,854	98,566	0.7	95,671	96,465	0.8
Columbia, SC	398,003	400,750	0.6	381,547	388,371	1.7
Columbus, OH	1,080,007	1,083,998	0.3	1,039,735	1,040,444	0.0
Dallas, TX[2]	2,585,893	2,682,088	3.7	2,504,449	2,594,961	3.6
Denver, CO	1,607,274	1,648,629	2.5	1,561,361	1,587,640	1.6
Des Moines, IA	344,073	355,975	3.4	335,149	347,559	3.7
Durham, NC	293,411	298,927	1.8	282,262	289,010	2.3
Edison, NJ[2]	7,115,615	7,151,776	0.5	6,832,994	6,887,158	0.7
El Paso, TX	355,795	363,598	2.1	341,342	349,017	2.2
Eugene, OR	184,824	182,636	-1.1	177,308	174,706	-1.4
Evansville, IN	160,568	162,866	1.4	156,131	157,860	1.1
Fargo, ND	137,092	135,806	-0.9	133,678	132,655	-0.7
Fayetteville, NC	147,423	148,870	0.9	139,257	141,505	1.6
Fort Collins, CO	196,349	205,101	4.4	191,451	198,457	3.6
Fort Wayne, IN	209,676	217,559	3.7	203,947	211,085	3.5
Fort Worth, TX[2]	1,241,227	1,280,488	3.1	1,201,876	1,238,690	3.0
Gainesville, FL	142,110	144,576	1.7	137,447	140,175	1.9
Grand Rapids, MI	573,055	577,903	0.8	552,982	561,455	1.5
Greeley, CO	160,310	165,552	3.2	156,034	159,811	2.4
Green Bay, WI	173,987	174,287	0.1	169,585	170,033	0.2
Greensboro, NC	366,857	369,553	0.7	350,147	355,120	1.4
Honolulu, HI	471,688	468,609	-0.6	463,613	458,462	-1.1
Houston, TX	3,343,410	3,453,216	3.2	3,199,215	3,317,794	3.7
Huntsville, AL	216,297	226,125	4.5	209,920	219,378	4.5
Indianapolis, IN	1,029,258	1,062,644	3.2	999,968	1,029,984	3.0
Jacksonville, FL	764,461	775,809	1.4	738,808	751,739	1.7
Kansas City, MO	1,123,293	1,137,463	1.2	1,086,716	1,102,718	1.4
Lafayette, LA	210,893	209,429	-0.6	201,965	200,424	-0.7
Las Cruces, NM	94,214	95,377	1.2	88,285	89,932	1.8
Las Vegas, NV	1,082,372	1,121,105	3.5	1,028,603	1,070,694	4.0
Lexington, KY	270,791	273,538	1.0	262,893	265,503	0.9
Lincoln, NE	177,836	181,619	2.1	173,446	177,455	2.3
Little Rock, AR	353,050	355,941	0.8	341,315	344,269	0.8
Los Angeles, CA[2]	5,101,061	5,165,908	1.2	4,880,342	4,930,006	1.0

Table continued on next page.

Metro Area[1]	Civilian Labor Force			Workers Employed		
	Dec. 2017	Dec. 2018	% Chg.	Dec. 2017	Dec. 2018	% Chg.
Louisville, KY	659,783	663,187	0.5	638,249	640,174	0.3
Madison, WI	390,310	388,149	-0.5	382,618	380,621	-0.5
Manchester, NH[3]	115,281	119,355	3.5	112,778	117,030	3.7
McAllen, TX	343,867	351,108	2.1	321,005	327,595	2.0
Miami, FL[2]	1,387,642	1,403,293	1.1	1,327,905	1,353,811	1.9
Midland, TX	94,704	100,757	6.3	92,563	98,626	6.5
Minneapolis, MN	1,983,313	2,008,040	1.2	1,924,623	1,952,456	1.4
Nashville, TN	1,015,902	1,037,452	2.1	991,652	1,013,224	2.1
New Orleans, LA	596,570	599,617	0.5	574,236	576,006	0.3
New York, NY[2]	7,115,615	7,151,776	0.5	6,832,994	6,887,158	0.7
Oklahoma City, OK	674,115	672,568	-0.2	650,461	653,952	0.5
Omaha, NE	478,265	492,493	2.9	464,636	479,337	3.1
Orlando, FL	1,312,511	1,358,231	3.4	1,269,679	1,317,910	3.8
Peoria, IL	174,815	176,606	1.0	166,398	166,484	0.0
Philadelphia, PA[2]	992,557	1,014,933	2.2	941,721	969,053	2.9
Phoenix, AZ	2,333,423	2,437,324	4.4	2,239,985	2,328,539	3.9
Pittsburgh, PA	1,200,452	1,209,534	0.7	1,146,911	1,161,821	1.3
Portland, OR	1,324,396	1,329,963	0.4	1,276,346	1,279,680	0.2
Providence, RI[3]	685,055	696,587	1.6	657,109	670,946	2.1
Provo, UT	304,146	304,414	0.0	296,661	296,534	0.0
Raleigh, NC	696,216	712,202	2.3	669,860	688,965	2.8
Reno, NV	245,311	258,836	5.5	236,289	249,934	5.7
Richmond, VA	669,505	679,381	1.4	645,440	660,541	2.3
Roanoke, VA	155,015	158,189	2.0	149,756	154,286	3.0
Rochester, MN	121,410	120,953	-0.3	117,927	117,605	-0.2
Salem, OR	202,072	199,854	-1.1	194,142	191,272	-1.4
Salt Lake City, UT	661,109	660,018	-0.1	643,138	641,797	-0.2
San Antonio, TX	1,171,978	1,188,172	1.3	1,136,835	1,150,484	1.2
San Diego, CA	1,583,042	1,620,080	2.3	1,530,168	1,568,277	2.4
San Francisco, CA[2]	1,026,081	1,051,734	2.5	1,002,221	1,029,473	2.7
San Jose, CA	1,078,824	1,115,934	3.4	1,049,364	1,088,429	3.7
Santa Rosa, CA	262,817	268,011	1.9	255,330	261,020	2.2
Savannah, GA	184,906	183,341	-0.8	177,538	176,766	-0.4
Seattle, WA[2]	1,659,565	1,693,796	2.0	1,600,578	1,636,187	2.2
Sioux Falls, SD	149,739	152,386	1.7	145,340	148,590	2.2
Springfield, IL	108,369	108,970	0.5	104,156	103,567	-0.5
Tallahassee, FL	190,403	194,727	2.2	183,898	188,401	2.4
Tampa, FL	1,510,641	1,531,562	1.3	1,458,656	1,482,283	1.6
Topeka, KS	118,135	118,696	0.4	114,515	114,734	0.1
Tyler, TX	106,787	110,590	3.5	103,079	106,728	3.5
Virginia Beach, VA	834,501	847,145	1.5	802,950	821,768	2.3
Visalia, CA	202,360	206,453	2.0	181,688	186,633	2.7
Washington, DC[2]	2,688,714	2,709,342	0.7	2,597,010	2,630,947	1.3
Wilmington, NC	144,433	144,997	0.3	138,263	139,416	0.8
Winston-Salem, NC	323,295	327,665	1.3	309,920	315,939	1.9
U.S.	159,880,000	162,510,000	1.6	153,602,000	156,481,000	1.9

Note: Data is not seasonally adjusted and covers workers 16 years of age and older; (1) Figures cover the Metropolitan Statistical Area (MSA) except where noted. See Appendix B for areas included; (2) Metropolitan Division; (3) New England City and Town Area; (4) New England City and Town Area Division
Source: Bureau of Labor Statistics, Local Area Unemployment Statistics

Unemployment Rate: City

City	2018											
	Jan.	Feb.	Mar.	Apr.	May	Jun.	Jul.	Aug.	Sep.	Oct.	Nov.	Dec.
Albany, NY	5.4	5.2	4.8	4.6	4.2	5.0	4.9	4.8	4.1	3.8	3.5	3.6
Albuquerque, NM	5.0	4.8	4.4	3.9	3.6	4.6	4.5	4.4	4.3	4.1	4.1	4.3
Allentown, PA	7.4	7.7	7.4	6.7	6.2	6.8	7.2	7.2	6.5	6.4	5.9	5.8
Anchorage, AK	6.4	6.7	6.4	6.2	5.8	5.7	5.0	4.7	4.9	4.9	5.1	5.1
Ann Arbor, MI	3.0	3.0	2.5	2.3	2.5	2.9	3.3	2.5	2.3	2.4	2.2	2.2
Athens, GA	4.3	4.5	4.0	3.6	3.4	4.5	4.1	3.7	3.2	3.6	3.2	3.6
Atlanta, GA	5.0	4.9	4.5	4.0	3.9	4.5	4.3	4.1	3.5	3.8	3.6	4.1
Austin, TX	2.8	2.8	2.9	2.6	2.6	2.9	2.8	2.8	2.7	2.5	2.5	2.5
Baton Rouge, LA	4.2	3.8	4.1	4.1	4.6	6.0	5.9	5.6	4.9	4.6	4.3	4.2
Billings, MT	4.2	4.2	3.9	3.0	2.5	3.4	3.3	3.0	3.0	3.0	3.2	3.3
Boise City, ID	3.1	2.7	2.6	2.3	2.2	2.3	2.4	2.0	2.0	2.0	2.2	2.3
Boston, MA	3.3	3.2	3.1	2.8	3.1	3.9	3.8	3.4	3.0	2.7	2.4	2.3
Boulder, CO	2.5	2.6	2.4	2.1	1.9	2.6	2.6	3.2	2.7	2.7	2.8	3.2
Cape Coral, FL	3.9	3.5	3.5	3.1	3.1	3.7	3.8	3.6	2.9	3.0	3.0	3.2
Cedar Rapids, IA	3.9	3.8	3.3	2.9	2.7	3.1	3.0	2.9	2.6	2.4	2.5	2.9
Charleston, SC	3.9	3.5	3.1	2.1	2.2	2.9	2.8	2.9	2.6	2.6	2.4	2.5
Charlotte, NC	4.5	4.4	4.1	3.6	3.6	4.0	3.9	3.8	2.9	3.3	3.3	3.5
Chicago, IL	5.9	5.6	4.5	3.9	3.6	4.7	4.5	4.3	4.0	4.4	4.0	3.9
Clarksville, TN	4.3	4.0	3.9	3.3	3.5	4.9	5.0	4.6	4.4	4.3	3.8	3.4
College Station, TX	2.9	2.9	2.8	2.5	2.6	3.5	3.3	3.3	2.9	2.7	2.6	2.8
Colorado Springs, CO	3.8	3.8	3.4	3.0	2.7	3.4	3.6	3.9	3.6	3.5	3.9	4.5
Columbia, MO	2.8	2.5	2.5	2.3	2.4	2.5	2.9	2.6	1.9	1.5	1.8	2.1
Columbia, SC	5.4	4.7	4.5	3.1	3.2	4.3	4.2	4.3	3.7	3.6	3.4	3.6
Columbus, OH	3.8	3.7	3.4	3.4	3.5	4.5	4.1	3.9	3.7	3.8	3.6	4.0
Dallas, TX	3.8	3.9	3.8	3.5	3.5	3.9	3.8	3.7	3.6	3.4	3.3	3.4
Denver, CO	3.3	3.2	2.8	2.5	2.4	2.9	3.0	3.3	3.0	3.0	3.3	3.7
Des Moines, IA	4.4	4.3	3.7	2.9	2.6	2.8	2.7	2.6	2.4	2.3	2.4	3.0
Durham, NC	4.1	3.9	3.8	3.4	3.4	3.9	3.7	3.5	2.8	3.1	3.1	3.3
Edison, NJ	3.1	3.2	3.1	2.9	2.8	3.4	3.5	3.2	3.0	2.6	2.1	2.4
El Paso, TX	4.4	4.4	4.4	4.0	4.0	4.5	4.3	4.2	4.1	3.8	3.8	3.9
Eugene, OR	3.9	4.2	4.2	3.8	3.5	4.1	4.3	4.3	3.9	4.1	3.9	4.0
Evansville, IN	3.3	3.6	3.1	2.9	3.2	3.6	3.5	3.8	3.2	3.6	3.5	3.3
Fargo, ND	2.9	2.8	2.8	2.5	2.0	2.5	2.1	2.2	2.1	1.8	2.0	2.2
Fayetteville, NC	6.4	6.3	6.0	5.2	5.1	5.9	6.0	5.8	4.5	4.9	5.0	5.3
Fort Collins, CO	2.7	2.7	2.4	2.1	1.9	2.4	2.4	2.9	2.5	2.6	2.8	3.1
Fort Wayne, IN	3.4	3.6	3.1	2.8	3.2	3.5	3.4	3.6	2.8	3.4	3.4	3.2
Fort Worth, TX	3.8	3.8	3.9	3.5	3.5	4.0	3.9	3.8	3.5	3.3	3.3	3.4
Gainesville, FL	4.3	3.8	3.8	3.4	3.3	4.2	4.1	3.7	2.9	3.0	3.0	3.4
Grand Rapids, MI	5.2	5.1	4.5	4.0	3.8	4.4	4.8	3.6	3.5	3.5	3.3	3.7
Greeley, CO	3.4	3.4	3.0	2.6	2.3	2.9	3.0	3.4	3.0	3.0	3.2	3.7
Green Bay, WI	3.1	3.3	3.2	2.7	2.6	3.6	3.3	3.3	2.5	2.5	2.5	2.5
Greensboro, NC	5.1	5.0	4.7	4.1	4.1	4.7	4.6	4.3	3.3	3.6	3.7	4.0
Honolulu, HI	2.0	1.9	1.9	1.9	1.9	2.6	2.0	2.1	2.4	2.3	2.5	2.2
Houston, TX	4.6	4.6	4.5	4.2	4.1	4.5	4.3	4.2	4.1	3.7	3.7	3.8
Huntsville, AL	3.8	3.9	3.6	3.2	3.5	4.6	4.2	3.8	3.6	3.6	3.1	3.1
Indianapolis, IN	3.4	3.6	3.3	3.0	3.3	3.8	3.6	3.8	3.2	3.6	3.6	3.3
Jacksonville, FL	4.1	3.7	3.7	3.4	3.4	4.0	4.2	3.8	3.0	3.0	3.0	3.2
Kansas City, MO	4.3	3.9	3.9	3.6	3.9	3.8	4.3	3.9	3.0	2.7	2.8	3.2
Lafayette, LA	4.3	3.9	4.3	4.3	4.6	5.8	5.6	5.3	4.8	4.4	4.3	4.0
Las Cruces, NM	5.7	5.3	4.8	4.2	3.9	5.5	5.4	5.3	4.9	4.8	4.7	4.8
Las Vegas, NV	5.5	5.3	5.4	5.2	4.6	4.9	4.9	5.1	4.8	4.6	4.5	4.6
Lexington, KY	3.0	3.6	3.4	3.0	3.2	4.0	3.8	3.2	3.2	3.3	2.7	2.8
Lincoln, NE	2.7	2.6	2.6	2.6	2.6	2.9	2.8	2.6	2.4	2.5	2.2	2.3
Little Rock, AR	3.8	3.8	3.7	3.4	3.3	3.6	3.4	3.2	3.2	3.1	3.1	3.4
Los Angeles, CA	4.8	4.5	4.2	4.1	4.1	4.9	5.1	5.1	4.8	4.7	4.6	4.6

Table continued on next page.

City	2018											
	Jan.	Feb.	Mar.	Apr.	May	Jun.	Jul.	Aug.	Sep.	Oct.	Nov.	Dec.
Louisville, KY	3.7	4.1	4.0	3.6	4.3	4.7	4.8	3.9	4.5	4.1	3.4	3.6
Madison, WI	2.1	2.1	2.1	1.8	2.1	2.8	2.4	2.3	2.0	2.1	2.0	1.9
Manchester, NH	3.1	3.0	3.0	2.8	2.7	2.8	2.7	2.7	2.5	2.2	2.3	2.1
McAllen, TX	5.0	4.9	5.0	4.8	4.5	5.1	4.9	4.9	4.5	4.1	4.1	4.5
Miami, FL	4.6	4.6	4.9	4.1	3.9	4.1	4.3	4.1	3.7	3.5	3.2	3.5
Midland, TX	2.4	2.5	2.4	2.1	2.2	2.4	2.3	2.2	2.2	2.1	2.1	2.1
Minneapolis, MN	3.0	2.9	2.9	2.5	2.3	2.9	2.7	2.5	2.2	2.1	1.9	2.5
Nashville, TN	2.7	2.6	2.6	2.1	2.2	3.1	3.0	3.0	2.9	2.9	2.6	2.3
New Orleans, LA	4.4	4.0	4.3	4.3	4.7	6.2	6.1	5.9	5.2	4.8	4.5	4.2
New York, NY	4.6	4.6	4.3	3.9	3.6	4.2	4.4	4.3	3.8	4.0	3.7	4.0
Oklahoma City, OK	4.0	3.8	3.6	3.5	3.7	3.7	3.4	3.3	2.9	2.9	2.7	2.9
Omaha, NE	3.4	3.3	3.3	3.2	3.1	3.4	3.5	3.1	2.9	3.0	2.8	3.0
Orlando, FL	3.5	3.2	3.1	2.8	2.9	3.2	3.3	3.1	2.5	2.5	2.5	2.7
Peoria, IL	5.5	5.0	5.3	4.6	4.9	5.7	5.6	5.6	5.0	5.6	5.6	6.3
Philadelphia, PA	6.3	6.3	5.8	5.2	5.0	5.7	6.0	6.0	5.2	5.2	5.0	4.9
Phoenix, AZ	4.5	4.4	4.1	3.9	3.5	4.2	4.3	4.5	4.2	3.9	3.9	4.5
Pittsburgh, PA	5.0	4.9	4.3	3.9	3.8	4.5	4.5	4.3	3.8	3.9	3.7	3.7
Portland, OR	3.6	3.7	3.7	3.4	3.1	3.6	3.5	3.5	3.3	3.6	3.5	3.5
Providence, RI	6.2	6.2	5.9	5.0	4.9	4.9	5.4	4.9	4.5	4.0	4.7	4.5
Provo, UT	2.4	2.8	2.7	2.4	2.4	3.4	3.0	3.0	2.6	2.3	2.2	2.4
Raleigh, NC	4.2	4.1	3.9	3.4	3.3	3.9	3.7	3.6	2.7	3.0	3.1	3.4
Reno, NV	4.5	4.1	4.1	3.8	3.3	3.4	3.5	3.7	3.4	3.3	3.2	3.4
Richmond, VA	4.3	4.0	3.9	3.4	3.4	3.8	3.5	3.7	3.3	3.3	3.2	3.2
Roanoke, VA	4.1	3.8	3.7	3.2	3.2	3.7	3.3	3.4	2.8	2.8	2.7	2.7
Rochester, MN	3.0	3.0	2.8	2.4	2.0	2.4	2.1	2.0	1.9	1.8	1.8	2.5
Salem, OR	4.5	4.5	4.6	4.1	3.8	4.3	4.4	4.4	4.0	4.4	4.3	4.4
Salt Lake City, UT	2.8	3.0	3.0	2.8	2.5	3.1	2.8	3.3	2.9	2.6	2.7	2.7
San Antonio, TX	3.4	3.4	3.4	3.1	3.2	3.7	3.5	3.4	3.3	3.1	3.0	3.1
San Diego, CA	3.6	3.4	3.2	2.8	2.8	3.5	3.4	3.3	3.1	3.2	3.1	3.1
San Francisco, CA	2.7	2.5	2.4	2.1	2.1	2.7	2.5	2.4	2.2	2.3	2.2	2.2
San Jose, CA	3.0	2.9	2.7	2.4	2.3	3.0	2.8	2.7	2.5	2.6	2.5	2.5
Santa Rosa, CA	3.3	3.2	2.9	2.7	2.5	3.2	3.0	2.8	2.5	2.5	2.5	2.6
Savannah, GA	4.9	4.7	4.2	3.8	3.7	4.5	4.2	4.1	3.5	4.0	3.7	4.0
Seattle, WA	3.8	3.4	3.1	2.7	3.0	3.4	3.2	2.9	3.1	2.9	3.2	3.0
Sioux Falls, SD	3.5	3.5	3.2	3.0	2.5	2.5	2.1	2.4	2.2	2.2	2.4	2.6
Springfield, IL	4.4	4.0	4.1	3.4	3.5	4.7	4.5	4.7	4.0	4.4	4.4	5.0
Tallahassee, FL	4.1	3.6	3.6	3.4	3.3	4.2	4.2	3.8	3.0	3.1	3.1	3.4
Tampa, FL	4.0	3.6	3.7	3.3	3.4	4.0	4.0	3.7	3.0	3.0	3.0	3.3
Topeka, KS	3.8	4.1	3.7	3.5	3.6	4.0	4.3	3.9	3.3	3.4	3.4	3.6
Tyler, TX	3.7	3.7	3.6	3.4	3.5	4.0	3.7	3.6	3.4	3.4	3.3	3.4
Virginia Beach, VA	3.5	3.1	3.1	2.7	2.8	3.1	2.8	3.0	2.7	2.8	2.7	2.6
Visalia, CA	5.3	5.1	4.7	4.1	3.9	5.6	5.6	5.2	4.7	4.8	4.7	4.8
Washington, DC	5.9	5.9	5.7	5.2	5.3	6.0	6.0	5.8	5.5	5.3	5.1	4.9
Wilmington, NC	4.5	4.4	4.2	3.6	3.6	4.1	4.0	3.7	3.5	3.9	3.8	4.0
Winston-Salem, NC	4.8	4.8	4.4	3.9	3.9	4.7	4.5	4.3	3.2	3.5	3.5	3.8
U.S.	4.5	4.4	4.1	3.7	3.6	4.2	4.1	3.9	3.6	3.5	3.5	3.7

Note: Data is not seasonally adjusted and covers workers 16 years of age and older; All figures are percentages
Source: Bureau of Labor Statistics, Local Area Unemployment Statistics

Unemployment Rate: Metro Area

Metro Area[1]	2018											
	Jan.	Feb.	Mar.	Apr.	May	Jun.	Jul.	Aug.	Sep.	Oct.	Nov.	Dec.
Albany, NY	5.0	5.2	4.7	4.2	3.6	3.9	3.8	3.7	3.4	3.1	3.1	3.3
Albuquerque, NM	5.3	5.0	4.7	4.1	3.8	4.9	4.8	4.6	4.4	4.3	4.3	4.4
Allentown, PA	5.3	5.3	4.9	4.3	3.9	4.5	4.7	4.7	4.2	4.1	3.9	4.0
Anchorage, AK	7.1	7.5	7.1	6.9	6.4	6.2	5.4	5.1	5.3	5.3	5.5	5.6
Ann Arbor, MI	3.6	3.6	3.1	2.8	3.1	3.6	4.0	3.0	2.8	2.9	2.6	2.7
Athens, GA	4.0	4.1	3.8	3.4	3.2	4.1	3.7	3.5	3.0	3.4	3.0	3.4
Atlanta, GA	4.3	4.3	4.0	3.6	3.4	4.0	3.8	3.6	3.1	3.4	3.2	3.6
Austin, TX	3.0	3.0	3.1	2.8	2.8	3.2	3.1	3.0	2.9	2.7	2.7	2.7
Baton Rouge, LA	3.9	3.5	3.8	3.8	4.2	5.4	5.3	5.0	4.5	4.2	4.0	3.9
Billings, MT	4.4	4.4	4.1	3.1	2.5	3.4	3.3	3.0	3.0	3.0	3.1	3.4
Boise City, ID	3.6	3.1	2.9	2.6	2.4	2.6	2.8	2.3	2.1	2.2	2.5	2.6
Boston, MA[4]	3.2	3.3	3.1	2.7	2.9	3.5	3.5	3.1	2.8	2.5	2.2	2.2
Boulder, CO	2.9	2.9	2.5	2.3	2.1	2.7	2.7	3.1	2.8	2.8	2.9	3.3
Cape Coral, FL	3.8	3.5	3.4	3.2	3.2	3.8	3.8	3.7	2.9	2.9	2.9	3.2
Cedar Rapids, IA	4.0	3.8	3.3	2.8	2.4	2.7	2.7	2.6	2.4	2.1	2.2	2.7
Charleston, SC	4.2	3.9	3.5	2.3	2.4	3.1	3.0	3.1	2.8	2.8	2.6	2.8
Charlotte, NC	4.4	4.3	4.0	3.4	3.4	3.9	3.8	3.7	2.9	3.2	3.2	3.4
Chicago, IL[2]	4.9	4.6	3.9	3.6	3.3	4.4	4.1	3.9	3.5	3.6	3.3	3.6
Clarksville, TN	4.3	4.3	4.1	3.5	3.7	5.1	5.1	4.6	4.5	4.4	3.8	3.5
College Station, TX	3.1	3.0	3.0	2.7	2.8	3.5	3.3	3.3	2.9	2.7	2.7	2.8
Colorado Springs, CO	3.9	3.9	3.4	3.1	2.8	3.6	3.7	4.1	3.6	3.6	3.9	4.5
Columbia, MO	2.9	2.6	2.6	2.3	2.3	2.6	2.9	2.6	1.9	1.6	1.8	2.1
Columbia, SC	4.9	4.4	3.9	2.7	2.8	3.5	3.4	3.6	3.2	3.2	3.0	3.1
Columbus, OH	3.9	3.7	3.5	3.3	3.5	4.5	4.1	3.8	3.6	3.7	3.5	4.0
Dallas, TX[2]	3.6	3.7	3.7	3.4	3.4	3.8	3.6	3.6	3.4	3.2	3.2	3.2
Denver, CO	3.2	3.2	2.8	2.5	2.3	2.9	2.9	3.3	3.0	3.0	3.3	3.7
Des Moines, IA	3.4	3.3	2.9	2.3	2.1	2.4	2.3	2.2	2.1	1.9	1.9	2.4
Durham, NC	4.0	4.0	3.8	3.3	3.3	3.8	3.6	3.5	2.7	3.0	3.0	3.3
Edison, NJ[2]	4.6	4.5	4.3	4.0	3.5	4.2	4.4	4.2	3.9	3.7	3.4	3.7
El Paso, TX	4.6	4.5	4.5	4.2	4.1	4.7	4.4	4.4	4.2	3.9	3.9	4.0
Eugene, OR	4.4	4.6	4.6	4.1	3.8	4.3	4.4	4.4	4.1	4.4	4.3	4.3
Evansville, IN	3.2	3.4	3.0	2.8	3.1	3.5	3.3	3.5	2.9	3.4	3.3	3.1
Fargo, ND	3.2	3.2	3.1	2.7	2.1	2.6	2.2	2.2	2.1	1.8	1.9	2.3
Fayetteville, NC	5.9	5.8	5.4	4.7	4.7	5.4	5.5	5.3	4.1	4.6	4.6	4.9
Fort Collins, CO	2.9	2.9	2.5	2.2	2.0	2.6	2.5	3.0	2.7	2.7	2.9	3.2
Fort Wayne, IN	3.2	3.3	2.9	2.6	3.0	3.3	3.2	3.4	2.7	3.2	3.2	3.0
Fort Worth, TX[2]	3.6	3.6	3.7	3.3	3.4	3.8	3.7	3.6	3.4	3.2	3.2	3.3
Gainesville, FL	3.9	3.4	3.4	3.1	3.0	3.7	3.6	3.4	2.7	2.8	2.8	3.0
Grand Rapids, MI	4.0	4.0	3.5	3.0	2.9	3.3	3.6	2.7	2.6	2.6	2.5	2.8
Greeley, CO	3.1	3.1	2.7	2.4	2.2	2.7	2.8	3.2	2.8	2.8	3.0	3.5
Green Bay, WI	3.0	3.3	3.0	2.6	2.5	3.2	3.0	2.9	2.4	2.4	2.4	2.4
Greensboro, NC	4.9	4.7	4.5	3.9	3.9	4.5	4.4	4.2	3.2	3.5	3.6	3.9
Honolulu, HI	2.0	1.9	1.9	1.9	1.9	2.6	2.0	2.1	2.4	2.3	2.5	2.2
Houston, TX	4.8	4.7	4.6	4.2	4.2	4.6	4.4	4.3	4.1	3.8	3.8	3.9
Huntsville, AL	3.6	3.7	3.4	3.0	3.3	4.4	3.9	3.6	3.4	3.4	2.9	3.0
Indianapolis, IN	3.2	3.4	3.0	2.8	3.0	3.4	3.3	3.5	2.9	3.3	3.4	3.1
Jacksonville, FL	3.9	3.5	3.5	3.2	3.1	3.7	3.8	3.5	2.8	2.9	2.9	3.1
Kansas City, MO	4.0	3.8	3.6	3.3	3.6	3.5	3.9	3.5	2.8	2.7	2.7	3.1
Lafayette, LA	4.6	4.3	4.6	4.5	4.9	6.1	5.9	5.5	5.0	4.7	4.5	4.3
Las Cruces, NM	6.9	6.7	6.4	5.5	4.9	6.0	5.8	5.4	5.2	5.1	5.3	5.7
Las Vegas, NV	5.4	5.2	5.1	5.0	4.4	4.7	4.7	4.9	4.7	4.4	4.4	4.5
Lexington, KY	3.2	3.7	3.5	3.1	3.3	4.1	3.9	3.3	3.3	3.4	2.7	2.9
Lincoln, NE	2.7	2.6	2.6	2.6	2.6	2.9	2.8	2.6	2.4	2.5	2.2	2.3
Little Rock, AR	3.8	3.8	3.6	3.2	3.2	3.5	3.3	3.0	3.0	3.0	3.0	3.3
Los Angeles, CA[2]	4.9	4.7	4.5	4.3	4.2	4.8	5.2	5.0	4.7	4.6	4.5	4.6

Table continued on next page.

Metro Area[1]	2018											
	Jan.	Feb.	Mar.	Apr.	May	Jun.	Jul.	Aug.	Sep.	Oct.	Nov.	Dec.
Louisville, KY	3.6	4.0	3.7	3.4	4.0	4.3	4.5	3.8	4.2	3.9	3.4	3.5
Madison, WI	2.3	2.5	2.4	1.9	2.1	2.8	2.4	2.3	2.0	2.1	2.0	1.9
Manchester, NH[3]	2.9	2.9	2.8	2.6	2.5	2.5	2.6	2.5	2.3	2.0	2.1	1.9
McAllen, TX	7.6	7.1	6.9	6.6	6.2	7.2	7.0	6.6	6.2	5.4	5.8	6.7
Miami, FL[2]	4.1	4.0	4.3	3.9	3.7	4.0	3.9	4.0	3.8	3.6	3.3	3.5
Midland, TX	2.4	2.5	2.4	2.1	2.1	2.4	2.2	2.2	2.2	2.1	2.1	2.1
Minneapolis, MN	3.4	3.4	3.3	2.7	2.3	2.8	2.6	2.5	2.2	2.1	2.0	2.8
Nashville, TN	2.8	2.7	2.7	2.2	2.3	3.2	3.2	3.1	3.0	2.9	2.6	2.3
New Orleans, LA	4.1	3.7	4.0	4.0	4.4	5.7	5.6	5.3	4.8	4.4	4.2	3.9
New York, NY[2]	4.6	4.5	4.3	4.0	3.5	4.2	4.4	4.2	3.9	3.7	3.4	3.7
Oklahoma City, OK	3.8	3.7	3.6	3.5	3.6	3.7	3.3	3.2	2.8	2.8	2.6	2.8
Omaha, NE	3.2	3.1	3.0	2.9	2.8	3.1	3.1	2.8	2.6	2.6	2.5	2.7
Orlando, FL	3.7	3.4	3.4	3.1	3.0	3.5	3.6	3.4	2.7	2.7	2.7	3.0
Peoria, IL	5.4	5.0	5.0	4.1	4.2	5.0	4.9	4.9	4.4	4.8	4.8	5.7
Philadelphia, PA[2]	5.8	5.8	5.3	4.8	4.6	5.2	5.5	5.5	4.8	4.8	4.6	4.5
Phoenix, AZ	4.5	4.4	4.1	3.8	3.4	4.2	4.3	4.5	4.2	3.9	3.9	4.5
Pittsburgh, PA	5.4	5.3	4.7	4.0	3.6	4.4	4.4	4.4	3.8	3.8	3.7	3.9
Portland, OR	3.9	4.1	4.0	3.7	3.4	3.8	3.8	3.8	3.5	3.8	3.7	3.8
Providence, RI[3]	5.3	5.3	4.8	4.1	3.9	3.8	4.2	3.9	3.5	3.1	3.6	3.7
Provo, UT	2.7	3.0	3.0	2.7	2.5	3.4	3.1	3.2	2.8	2.5	2.5	2.6
Raleigh, NC	4.0	3.9	3.8	3.3	3.2	3.7	3.5	3.4	2.6	2.9	3.0	3.3
Reno, NV	4.5	4.2	4.2	3.9	3.3	3.5	3.6	3.7	3.4	3.3	3.2	3.4
Richmond, VA	3.8	3.5	3.5	3.0	3.0	3.4	3.1	3.2	2.9	2.9	2.8	2.8
Roanoke, VA	3.7	3.4	3.4	2.8	2.9	3.4	2.9	3.1	2.7	2.7	2.6	2.5
Rochester, MN	3.6	3.6	3.4	2.8	2.1	2.6	2.3	2.2	1.9	1.9	1.9	2.8
Salem, OR	4.4	4.5	4.5	4.0	3.6	4.2	4.3	4.2	3.9	4.2	4.2	4.3
Salt Lake City, UT	3.0	3.2	3.2	3.0	2.7	3.4	3.1	3.4	3.0	2.7	2.7	2.8
San Antonio, TX	3.4	3.4	3.5	3.1	3.2	3.7	3.5	3.5	3.3	3.1	3.1	3.2
San Diego, CA	3.6	3.5	3.2	2.9	2.9	3.7	3.5	3.4	3.2	3.3	3.2	3.2
San Francisco, CA[2]	2.6	2.5	2.3	2.1	2.0	2.6	2.4	2.4	2.2	2.2	2.1	2.1
San Jose, CA	3.0	2.9	2.7	2.4	2.3	3.0	2.8	2.7	2.5	2.5	2.4	2.5
Santa Rosa, CA	3.2	3.0	2.8	2.6	2.4	3.0	2.8	2.7	2.4	2.5	2.5	2.6
Savannah, GA	4.2	4.1	3.8	3.4	3.3	4.0	3.7	3.6	3.1	3.5	3.2	3.6
Seattle, WA[2]	4.0	3.8	3.5	3.0	3.2	3.7	3.6	3.5	3.5	3.4	3.7	3.4
Sioux Falls, SD	3.4	3.4	3.1	2.9	2.4	2.4	2.1	2.3	2.2	2.2	2.3	2.5
Springfield, IL	4.4	4.0	4.1	3.2	3.4	4.2	4.0	4.2	3.7	4.1	4.2	5.0
Tallahassee, FL	4.0	3.6	3.6	3.2	3.2	3.9	4.0	3.7	2.9	2.9	3.0	3.2
Tampa, FL	3.9	3.6	3.6	3.2	3.3	3.8	3.8	3.6	2.9	2.9	3.0	3.2
Topeka, KS	3.7	3.8	3.5	3.2	3.3	3.7	4.0	3.5	3.0	3.2	3.1	3.3
Tyler, TX	3.8	3.8	3.7	3.4	3.5	3.9	3.7	3.7	3.5	3.4	3.4	3.5
Virginia Beach, VA	4.0	3.7	3.6	3.1	3.1	3.5	3.2	3.4	3.0	3.1	3.0	3.0
Visalia, CA	11.1	11.4	11.1	9.2	8.5	9.6	9.4	8.7	7.9	8.3	8.6	9.6
Washington, DC[2]	3.8	3.6	3.6	3.1	3.2	3.7	3.5	3.5	3.3	3.2	3.1	2.9
Wilmington, NC	4.6	4.4	4.1	3.5	3.4	3.9	3.8	3.7	3.4	3.8	3.6	3.8
Winston-Salem, NC	4.4	4.3	4.1	3.5	3.5	4.1	4.0	3.8	2.9	3.2	3.3	3.6
U.S.	4.5	4.4	4.1	3.7	3.6	4.2	4.1	3.9	3.6	3.5	3.5	3.7

Note: Data is not seasonally adjusted and covers workers 16 years of age and older; All figures are percentages; (1) Figures cover the Metropolitan Statistical Area (MSA) except where noted. See Appendix B for areas included; (2) Metropolitan Division; (3) New England City and Town Area; (4) New England City and Town Area Division
Source: Bureau of Labor Statistics, Local Area Unemployment Statistics

Average Hourly Wages: Occupations A – C

Metro Area[1]	Accountants/ Auditors	Automotive Mechanics	Book- keepers	Carpenters	Cashiers	Clerks, Gen. Office	Clerks, Recep./Info.
Albany, NY	36.48	20.49	20.76	25.71	11.78	17.04	15.79
Albuquerque, NM	32.84	20.24	18.58	18.88	10.67	12.57	13.79
Allentown, PA	37.60	20.04	18.94	25.45	10.35	17.25	14.36
Anchorage, AK	38.94	25.12	23.62	31.37	13.26	22.63	16.89
Ann Arbor, MI	35.96	25.64	19.83	31.07	11.11	16.50	15.02
Athens, GA	33.53	21.68	16.62	20.43	9.90	14.21	12.90
Atlanta, GA	37.70	21.20	20.44	23.94	10.21	15.42	14.01
Austin, TX	35.48	27.40	20.61	19.07	11.30	19.15	14.05
Baton Rouge, LA	31.48	19.91	18.59	22.77	9.52	12.58	12.11
Billings, MT	35.29	19.32	18.72	19.65	11.12	16.65	13.43
Boise City, ID	32.80	20.24	19.15	17.10	11.25	15.92	14.34
Boston, MA[2]	39.82	22.33	23.20	30.24	12.53	19.98	15.93
Boulder, CO	40.03	21.29	21.87	24.26	12.21	20.00	15.46
Cape Coral, FL	29.15	19.01	18.63	18.98	11.01	15.52	14.32
Cedar Rapids, IA	34.20	21.17	19.26	21.99	10.55	17.25	13.55
Charleston, SC	28.04	20.67	17.47	25.68	10.08	12.48	14.03
Charlotte, NC	39.52	21.49	19.60	18.00	9.93	16.12	13.81
Chicago, IL	40.28	23.11	21.37	33.87	11.41	18.37	14.90
Clarksville, TN	27.68	20.23	17.55	18.96	9.77	15.76	11.72
College Station, TX	27.77	23.34	16.34	15.08	10.55	17.17	13.04
Colorado Springs, CO	38.42	23.63	18.02	21.67	12.66	18.82	14.61
Columbia, MO	28.86	21.43	16.81	25.01	10.15	15.84	12.71
Columbia, SC	28.93	20.13	18.41	21.54	9.75	13.24	13.04
Columbus, OH	36.13	20.15	20.12	23.20	10.83	18.01	13.57
Dallas, TX	39.58	20.65	21.18	19.00	10.73	17.45	13.77
Denver, CO	41.25	23.78	21.42	23.30	12.44	20.51	16.12
Des Moines, IA	34.27	21.39	20.79	20.69	10.90	17.99	15.28
Durham, NC	38.99	21.83	21.07	17.79	10.45	17.27	14.16
Edison, NJ	48.03	23.26	23.10	32.57	12.16	17.29	16.84
El Paso, TX	29.97	16.17	16.59	15.15	9.82	14.71	10.85
Eugene, OR	31.37	21.08	18.49	22.28	12.33	16.82	14.70
Evansville, IN	29.84	19.72	17.02	23.67	9.93	15.35	12.79
Fargo, ND	30.82	20.93	18.67	20.10	11.47	18.47	13.65
Fayetteville, NC	32.58	16.91	18.54	17.71	9.56	14.59	12.55
Fort Collins, CO	33.71	24.37	20.22	23.12	12.56	18.81	15.33
Fort Wayne, IN	31.66	16.99	18.54	20.65	10.15	16.58	13.55
Fort Worth, TX	39.58	20.65	21.18	19.00	10.73	17.45	13.77
Gainesville, FL	29.59	18.12	19.52	19.03	10.33	15.17	13.40
Grand Rapids, MI	32.80	18.89	18.23	19.45	11.25	17.77	14.37
Greeley, CO	36.36	21.92	19.24	20.82	11.99	17.96	14.60
Green Bay, WI	31.11	20.08	18.11	24.55	10.09	16.99	14.42
Greensboro, NC	37.83	19.24	19.17	17.90	9.77	15.24	13.69
Honolulu, HI	31.69	22.45	19.98	36.28	12.21	16.48	15.59
Houston, TX	41.44	21.05	20.55	20.56	10.52	18.79	13.24
Huntsville, AL	35.87	19.59	19.12	19.44	10.59	12.30	12.60
Indianapolis, IN	36.73	21.58	20.02	24.12	10.44	16.84	14.28
Jacksonville, FL	32.39	18.58	19.81	19.11	10.35	16.36	13.56
Kansas City, MO	32.83	22.15	19.52	26.60	10.97	15.61	14.06
Lafayette, LA	31.98	18.27	17.77	19.76	9.49	12.32	11.83
Las Cruces, NM	30.48	17.75	16.74	19.59	10.47	11.15	12.10
Las Vegas, NV	31.72	21.34	19.30	25.54	11.24	17.25	13.44
Lexington, KY	32.33	20.23	18.97	24.20	9.90	13.71	13.53
Lincoln, NE	30.12	21.46	17.74	19.31	10.92	13.75	13.29
Little Rock, AR	32.34	19.31	18.29	18.23	10.53	15.20	13.76
Los Angeles, CA	40.70	22.82	22.70	28.88	12.91	17.80	15.64

Table continued on next page.

Metro Area[1]	Accountants/ Auditors	Automotive Mechanics	Book-keepers	Carpenters	Cashiers	Clerks, Gen. Office	Clerks, Recep./Info.
Louisville, KY	34.06	19.07	18.89	24.70	10.14	14.71	13.90
Madison, WI	33.08	20.58	19.50	25.80	11.01	17.81	15.11
Manchester, NH[2]	37.35	23.05	19.92	22.24	10.78	19.86	15.01
McAllen, TX	30.03	19.48	16.18	16.93	10.58	13.36	11.68
Miami, FL	37.40	20.63	20.41	19.92	10.54	16.44	14.60
Midland, TX	41.10	24.00	22.48	20.36	11.77	19.74	13.94
Minneapolis, MN	35.96	21.49	22.38	26.40	12.11	18.72	15.51
Nashville, TN	33.17	20.00	20.68	20.67	10.88	18.07	14.06
New Orleans, LA	35.02	20.04	18.46	20.35	9.78	12.20	12.04
New York, NY	48.03	23.26	23.10	32.57	12.16	17.29	16.84
Oklahoma City, OK	36.28	21.44	19.06	20.45	10.35	13.95	13.80
Omaha, NE	33.73	21.79	19.15	19.85	11.35	16.40	14.14
Orlando, FL	34.48	17.42	18.37	20.22	10.63	15.21	13.88
Peoria, IL	37.30	21.43	18.33	27.24	10.74	16.56	12.59
Philadelphia, PA	39.64	21.55	21.80	29.73	10.70	17.99	14.77
Phoenix, AZ	33.84	21.70	20.11	21.52	12.04	18.25	14.77
Pittsburgh, PA	34.91	19.83	18.87	27.76	9.92	16.63	13.23
Portland, OR	35.11	24.09	21.24	25.05	12.95	18.47	15.76
Providence, RI[2]	39.35	19.54	20.94	24.58	12.13	17.84	15.96
Provo, UT	32.30	21.11	18.16	19.59	11.04	15.86	13.22
Raleigh, NC	34.75	21.56	20.20	19.33	10.12	16.18	14.39
Reno, NV	33.13	23.56	19.74	26.09	11.04	18.68	14.61
Richmond, VA	38.32	23.68	20.26	21.60	10.27	17.39	14.51
Roanoke, VA	36.76	19.60	17.46	18.16	9.85	15.34	12.63
Rochester, MN	29.80	19.40	19.24	25.24	11.85	17.17	12.24
Salem, OR	33.76	20.07	20.26	22.58	12.51	17.05	15.46
Salt Lake City, UT	35.52	21.47	19.77	21.11	11.29	16.01	13.91
San Antonio, TX	36.22	22.10	19.42	19.18	10.71	16.90	13.09
San Diego, CA	41.86	22.81	22.28	25.92	12.84	16.91	16.21
San Francisco, CA	44.54	27.11	26.45	33.07	14.37	20.88	18.18
San Jose, CA	43.78	26.11	25.31	30.53	14.22	22.55	17.72
Santa Rosa, CA	39.15	24.02	25.06	34.67	14.25	19.96	16.97
Savannah, GA	33.80	23.40	18.44	21.51	9.71	15.17	13.17
Seattle, WA	39.99	24.80	22.83	31.41	14.60	20.40	16.88
Sioux Falls, SD	32.35	20.49	16.74	17.75	11.10	12.36	13.55
Springfield, IL	36.52	18.79	19.43	24.41	10.62	18.19	12.12
Tallahassee, FL	26.19	20.96	17.45	20.01	10.14	13.98	12.51
Tampa, FL	33.85	19.39	19.75	19.70	10.53	16.00	13.53
Topeka, KS	28.64	17.37	17.26	19.82	10.44	14.73	13.68
Tyler, TX	35.23	19.54	17.90	17.02	10.15	16.25	12.59
Virginia Beach, VA	37.01	23.17	19.55	21.08	9.81	15.92	13.33
Visalia, CA	33.07	17.50	20.86	20.19	12.41	18.24	14.47
Washington, DC	44.80	25.53	24.21	23.78	12.09	19.14	16.13
Wilmington, NC	35.63	18.12	19.02	19.32	9.97	14.73	13.75
Winston-Salem, NC	35.04	19.99	18.03	19.07	9.57	15.08	13.46

Notes: (1) Figures cover the Metropolitan Statistical Area (MSA) except where noted. See Appendix B for areas included;
(2) New England City and Town Area; n/a not available
Source: Bureau of Labor Statistics, May 2018 Metro Area Occupational Employment and Wage Estimates

Average Hourly Wages: Occupations C – E

Metro Area	Clerks, Ship./Rec.	Computer Programmers	Computer Systems Analysts	Comp. User Support Specialists	Cooks, Restaurant	Dentists	Electrical Engineers
Albany, NY	17.70	37.26	39.25	25.13	13.95	86.23	50.68
Albuquerque, NM	15.28	35.53	42.16	21.08	11.47	97.79	55.08
Allentown, PA	16.63	34.66	43.59	23.79	13.51	72.57	41.00
Anchorage, AK	21.02	40.35	36.98	27.95	13.77	119.82	57.93
Ann Arbor, MI	18.38	37.34	39.08	22.56	13.27	91.56	42.70
Athens, GA	16.88	37.19	33.86	21.47	11.93	64.66	n/a
Atlanta, GA	16.66	46.23	44.91	26.26	11.98	78.39	42.70
Austin, TX	15.58	41.04	43.89	24.54	12.97	70.37	54.42
Baton Rouge, LA	18.37	34.57	36.78	23.42	11.83	86.11	45.38
Billings, MT	16.62	34.64	37.33	24.50	12.41	105.39	46.40
Boise City, ID	16.37	35.04	38.15	24.11	11.78	84.42	43.22
Boston, MA[2]	19.10	45.28	45.99	31.23	15.72	87.00	55.06
Boulder, CO	18.18	45.13	47.70	29.92	14.89	102.68	47.54
Cape Coral, FL	15.71	33.51	35.04	21.68	13.74	77.15	44.43
Cedar Rapids, IA	18.63	39.52	40.88	22.46	11.35	n/a	44.24
Charleston, SC	19.45	36.63	38.57	24.47	11.95	56.32	44.07
Charlotte, NC	16.78	46.13	46.23	26.63	12.40	106.90	50.08
Chicago, IL	17.30	45.17	43.25	25.92	13.59	81.76	45.62
Clarksville, TN	17.43	36.65	29.95	23.31	10.78	102.27	43.55
College Station, TX	15.08	45.60	33.06	20.91	10.57	102.75	39.67
Colorado Springs, CO	16.08	43.73	49.25	26.28	13.39	65.60	54.60
Columbia, MO	15.51	32.56	28.44	20.85	11.89	112.82	38.59
Columbia, SC	14.66	39.73	35.42	22.40	11.19	88.16	44.13
Columbus, OH	15.61	39.73	46.81	26.32	13.52	101.48	38.64
Dallas, TX	16.01	47.02	45.82	24.86	12.32	91.47	50.39
Denver, CO	16.92	46.15	45.93	30.24	14.36	86.18	46.68
Des Moines, IA	18.35	39.23	41.21	24.98	13.34	113.42	40.57
Durham, NC	16.62	45.62	43.55	26.86	12.96	112.23	49.47
Edison, NJ	17.97	44.60	54.65	31.08	15.34	79.10	53.94
El Paso, TX	13.79	38.77	39.69	18.53	10.07	81.30	38.63
Eugene, OR	15.46	35.46	30.15	25.04	13.12	108.19	47.12
Evansville, IN	16.48	41.79	37.61	21.89	12.44	77.27	40.13
Fargo, ND	16.75	36.84	40.65	27.55	14.54	81.13	39.66
Fayetteville, NC	15.44	36.01	34.73	21.85	11.99	119.91	38.00
Fort Collins, CO	16.24	47.73	43.49	27.49	13.67	98.48	52.99
Fort Wayne, IN	15.06	36.35	34.47	21.25	11.54	120.25	42.32
Fort Worth, TX	16.01	47.02	45.82	24.86	12.32	91.47	50.39
Gainesville, FL	15.85	29.64	36.19	21.73	12.54	76.16	45.33
Grand Rapids, MI	15.92	33.98	37.43	23.17	12.37	97.48	36.73
Greeley, CO	16.75	39.70	49.88	21.93	13.22	95.88	49.32
Green Bay, WI	17.25	33.81	41.78	24.87	12.06	110.41	38.99
Greensboro, NC	15.69	38.93	45.37	25.02	11.31	81.32	49.16
Honolulu, HI	18.77	35.75	38.89	23.13	14.97	105.22	42.73
Houston, TX	16.51	43.75	53.05	28.97	12.65	93.08	52.12
Huntsville, AL	15.71	46.35	44.94	21.31	11.72	n/a	49.75
Indianapolis, IN	15.05	40.86	39.79	24.08	12.15	70.59	42.11
Jacksonville, FL	16.53	39.35	39.77	24.82	12.49	82.64	40.96
Kansas City, MO	16.44	36.59	38.50	23.67	12.82	87.20	44.15
Lafayette, LA	16.00	38.94	27.20	20.44	11.72	52.52	38.75
Las Cruces, NM	15.33	n/a	34.71	17.82	10.59	66.66	45.73
Las Vegas, NV	16.61	38.69	39.47	23.62	15.95	91.15	43.25
Lexington, KY	17.49	33.25	35.09	25.01	10.46	55.65	43.00
Lincoln, NE	17.02	33.09	36.24	22.15	13.59	70.31	45.44
Little Rock, AR	15.45	36.58	34.70	22.45	11.46	83.49	43.43
Los Angeles, CA	16.64	44.66	45.83	28.50	14.17	63.86	54.15

Table continued on next page.

Metro Area	Clerks, Ship./Rec.	Computer Programmers	Computer Systems Analysts	Comp. User Support Specialists	Cooks, Restaurant	Dentists	Electrical Engineers
Louisville, KY	16.28	36.38	36.92	22.80	12.41	76.09	43.37
Madison, WI	17.50	37.09	43.82	27.76	13.10	112.50	45.55
Manchester, NH[2]	17.45	38.95	45.58	25.97	13.67	104.93	50.62
McAllen, TX	11.94	36.68	n/a	19.66	11.28	100.51	53.27
Miami, FL	15.29	38.17	42.05	23.95	13.97	77.18	42.46
Midland, TX	16.69	n/a	44.29	26.28	13.14	n/a	n/a
Minneapolis, MN	18.27	42.71	45.57	27.33	14.56	111.47	48.23
Nashville, TN	15.43	41.76	38.08	24.29	12.49	90.41	42.84
New Orleans, LA	14.19	43.62	37.49	22.71	11.30	71.39	47.54
New York, NY	17.97	44.60	54.65	31.08	15.34	79.10	53.94
Oklahoma City, OK	15.71	39.65	35.85	22.98	12.12	73.73	46.46
Omaha, NE	16.28	38.49	37.83	24.89	13.25	71.98	42.22
Orlando, FL	15.69	44.30	40.65	23.52	13.33	95.92	46.75
Peoria, IL	16.17	35.97	42.90	23.59	12.43	80.38	n/a
Philadelphia, PA	17.50	44.18	49.15	27.26	14.26	79.69	50.59
Phoenix, AZ	16.62	47.54	43.26	25.25	14.11	91.86	49.73
Pittsburgh, PA	17.40	37.51	44.55	23.87	12.48	61.96	46.78
Portland, OR	18.13	41.22	43.88	26.75	14.54	81.95	44.46
Providence, RI[2]	18.98	45.82	47.63	26.94	14.67	117.26	52.31
Provo, UT	14.62	45.31	48.33	24.94	13.02	n/a	38.38
Raleigh, NC	15.31	50.62	45.37	25.74	13.71	116.99	45.17
Reno, NV	18.46	38.97	36.20	23.20	13.86	128.56	45.39
Richmond, VA	16.23	46.20	46.99	24.31	11.81	78.07	50.12
Roanoke, VA	16.06	40.73	38.05	23.34	11.56	69.18	39.48
Rochester, MN	18.04	46.26	40.74	26.05	13.35	109.74	43.43
Salem, OR	17.43	41.00	41.53	25.01	12.86	99.68	42.04
Salt Lake City, UT	15.03	39.11	37.83	23.81	13.39	71.52	47.41
San Antonio, TX	14.99	42.75	46.90	23.52	12.03	85.20	49.74
San Diego, CA	16.88	48.73	48.11	29.39	14.49	69.03	49.27
San Francisco, CA	19.70	50.90	56.89	35.39	16.93	87.25	55.14
San Jose, CA	18.93	51.05	57.88	39.88	15.97	77.31	63.82
Santa Rosa, CA	18.63	42.81	43.35	29.50	15.50	69.89	50.91
Savannah, GA	17.55	35.32	36.83	22.28	11.31	93.15	47.19
Seattle, WA	19.51	62.16	48.84	31.37	16.23	80.97	56.53
Sioux Falls, SD	15.76	27.97	35.60	19.29	12.44	99.82	37.34
Springfield, IL	15.38	40.45	43.44	22.26	12.26	70.01	44.84
Tallahassee, FL	15.97	30.18	30.42	22.07	12.45	72.04	44.40
Tampa, FL	15.63	37.45	43.56	24.47	12.62	89.66	45.64
Topeka, KS	19.42	33.84	33.80	22.16	11.19	113.83	42.67
Tyler, TX	16.76	34.48	34.75	22.66	11.87	73.99	47.74
Virginia Beach, VA	16.76	40.51	42.27	25.34	12.83	90.20	44.76
Visalia, CA	15.38	n/a	39.68	29.56	13.17	74.88	42.54
Washington, DC	18.86	47.11	50.67	30.97	14.34	98.36	59.52
Wilmington, NC	15.16	40.12	42.75	24.60	12.23	88.67	51.49
Winston-Salem, NC	15.31	38.87	43.61	22.76	11.14	91.18	47.06

Notes: (1) Figures cover the Metropolitan Statistical Area (MSA) except where noted. See Appendix B for areas included;
(2) New England City and Town Area; n/a not available
Source: Bureau of Labor Statistics, May 2018 Metro Area Occupational Employment and Wage Estimates

Average Hourly Wages: Occupations E – I

Metro Area	Electricians	Financial Managers	First-Line Supervisors/ Mgrs., Sales	Food Preparation Workers	General/ Operations Managers	Hairdressers/ Cosmetolo-gists	Internists
Albany, NY	28.64	67.20	21.20	12.65	60.53	14.27	123.51
Albuquerque, NM	21.95	52.99	19.82	10.93	52.03	11.01	125.99
Allentown, PA	29.98	79.16	21.61	11.28	59.85	14.56	n/a
Anchorage, AK	35.48	55.50	22.10	13.33	59.23	15.17	110.42
Ann Arbor, MI	33.14	64.04	22.05	13.27	64.93	12.64	n/a
Athens, GA	22.95	60.99	20.56	10.37	49.13	12.08	n/a
Atlanta, GA	25.67	74.02	22.69	10.58	59.01	13.30	49.83
Austin, TX	26.12	69.25	21.67	12.56	59.84	14.58	73.02
Baton Rouge, LA	25.43	52.39	18.49	9.11	59.27	12.32	n/a
Billings, MT	30.20	57.14	23.42	11.25	51.74	13.07	n/a
Boise City, ID	23.31	51.10	21.28	11.79	40.94	15.58	n/a
Boston, MA[2]	32.80	73.79	23.99	14.59	69.21	20.43	118.10
Boulder, CO	26.70	83.83	25.24	13.74	69.06	21.84	110.42
Cape Coral, FL	23.77	51.94	22.75	11.78	49.58	12.76	n/a
Cedar Rapids, IA	25.47	59.32	20.00	11.84	53.06	12.14	n/a
Charleston, SC	20.19	54.99	20.70	12.34	51.20	11.48	119.53
Charlotte, NC	21.46	79.00	23.48	11.45	65.40	16.46	123.22
Chicago, IL	38.35	73.01	21.23	12.31	64.39	14.16	88.21
Clarksville, TN	25.05	47.49	19.89	9.72	39.33	12.51	n/a
College Station, TX	21.15	57.15	22.84	10.23	47.44	11.91	n/a
Colorado Springs, CO	24.81	67.39	20.62	12.69	57.98	17.95	n/a
Columbia, MO	24.99	64.35	21.96	11.69	38.50	13.93	n/a
Columbia, SC	22.28	64.80	19.72	10.87	50.19	15.23	n/a
Columbus, OH	23.52	66.63	21.86	11.30	60.15	14.11	109.79
Dallas, TX	22.71	76.78	23.13	11.10	63.80	11.70	59.73
Denver, CO	26.81	83.16	25.80	13.27	69.04	16.36	103.78
Des Moines, IA	26.31	62.45	20.44	11.97	53.85	16.42	n/a
Durham, NC	21.37	78.87	22.54	11.29	70.36	17.85	n/a
Edison, NJ	38.93	100.32	25.78	13.35	81.05	16.43	101.23
El Paso, TX	18.95	52.68	20.74	9.99	49.88	10.71	n/a
Eugene, OR	29.81	53.28	22.97	12.25	46.23	12.92	n/a
Evansville, IN	27.76	53.86	19.42	10.11	43.51	14.11	n/a
Fargo, ND	25.80	65.29	21.60	12.27	53.38	15.92	n/a
Fayetteville, NC	19.37	70.54	19.61	9.77	54.79	12.33	n/a
Fort Collins, CO	27.70	62.14	24.59	13.00	49.63	16.47	n/a
Fort Wayne, IN	27.24	59.26	19.73	10.77	49.36	12.98	n/a
Fort Worth, TX	22.71	76.78	23.13	11.10	63.80	11.70	59.73
Gainesville, FL	18.22	60.58	21.41	10.91	46.87	14.69	n/a
Grand Rapids, MI	24.99	57.87	22.14	12.19	61.55	14.29	66.95
Greeley, CO	24.78	65.28	24.92	11.68	57.33	12.98	n/a
Green Bay, WI	26.33	57.70	20.01	10.80	55.91	15.23	n/a
Greensboro, NC	21.96	68.40	23.74	10.35	61.05	12.56	n/a
Honolulu, HI	36.75	59.69	21.95	13.32	57.90	16.33	103.09
Houston, TX	27.16	75.52	21.82	11.54	67.19	12.75	81.33
Huntsville, AL	22.88	62.63	20.29	10.20	66.05	11.71	n/a
Indianapolis, IN	27.17	65.93	19.97	11.04	56.08	14.97	115.47
Jacksonville, FL	21.45	67.36	21.07	11.37	55.97	18.30	n/a
Kansas City, MO	29.15	67.04	20.56	10.82	52.86	13.11	n/a
Lafayette, LA	22.48	48.83	18.15	9.02	52.47	10.12	n/a
Las Cruces, NM	18.96	43.72	20.25	10.95	43.18	n/a	n/a
Las Vegas, NV	31.23	59.44	21.45	14.15	63.96	11.07	123.31
Lexington, KY	23.60	57.96	19.04	11.63	43.18	11.87	88.01
Lincoln, NE	25.16	55.92	19.76	11.67	46.53	11.71	n/a
Little Rock, AR	20.74	49.40	20.37	12.06	43.69	11.36	n/a
Los Angeles, CA	32.39	75.90	21.60	12.78	68.01	13.92	96.18

Table continued on next page.

Metro Area	Electricians	Financial Managers	First-Line Supervisors/ Mgrs., Sales	Food Preparation Workers	General/ Operations Managers	Hairdressers/ Cosmetolo- gists	Internists
Louisville, KY	26.85	60.38	18.26	10.92	48.99	16.00	92.79
Madison, WI	28.58	64.00	22.90	11.97	61.88	15.51	n/a
Manchester, NH[2]	27.03	58.89	22.92	12.68	63.72	13.99	n/a
McAllen, TX	18.87	48.97	22.23	11.82	46.91	12.00	n/a
Miami, FL	22.30	68.03	23.57	11.89	57.38	15.44	91.81
Midland, TX	26.64	68.20	23.41	13.36	76.31	10.88	n/a
Minneapolis, MN	37.17	67.83	22.07	13.34	58.79	15.02	120.67
Nashville, TN	23.80	59.37	20.69	10.96	57.38	14.22	95.92
New Orleans, LA	25.23	51.94	19.49	9.13	58.22	9.86	113.59
New York, NY	38.93	100.32	25.78	13.35	81.05	16.43	101.23
Oklahoma City, OK	26.25	54.10	21.23	9.79	54.35	12.42	85.93
Omaha, NE	25.47	56.00	20.24	11.83	48.95	14.69	125.96
Orlando, FL	22.89	64.69	21.57	11.95	52.65	13.54	131.58
Peoria, IL	30.23	61.92	19.42	10.98	54.68	14.45	n/a
Philadelphia, PA	35.35	80.30	24.02	11.56	73.87	15.12	99.05
Phoenix, AZ	23.10	58.69	20.09	12.00	51.79	13.87	103.35
Pittsburgh, PA	33.76	76.19	22.39	11.34	63.17	13.01	n/a
Portland, OR	34.27	60.57	21.50	13.29	57.51	15.40	118.66
Providence, RI[2]	27.87	68.99	26.04	14.23	68.65	14.64	113.58
Provo, UT	26.63	54.88	18.18	11.78	40.53	10.89	n/a
Raleigh, NC	20.33	65.10	22.42	11.67	69.86	12.97	n/a
Reno, NV	25.48	64.49	20.52	12.93	56.55	11.26	n/a
Richmond, VA	23.16	77.13	21.94	10.81	66.17	17.80	129.42
Roanoke, VA	22.78	62.87	21.07	9.93	50.42	12.39	68.41
Rochester, MN	30.82	53.07	19.68	12.12	42.08	13.88	n/a
Salem, OR	29.95	48.04	22.22	12.08	47.60	12.28	n/a
Salt Lake City, UT	27.52	55.62	19.21	12.46	42.53	13.73	108.77
San Antonio, TX	23.01	69.07	21.28	12.08	58.04	12.20	49.47
San Diego, CA	29.84	68.58	22.99	13.26	64.34	16.94	113.60
San Francisco, CA	44.42	88.63	21.76	15.20	76.53	17.21	113.23
San Jose, CA	37.98	88.63	23.61	13.89	77.59	14.47	103.94
Santa Rosa, CA	32.99	68.05	23.46	14.39	59.56	13.11	n/a
Savannah, GA	22.38	47.47	19.94	10.23	49.54	11.79	n/a
Seattle, WA	35.00	71.85	26.42	15.02	65.20	20.68	99.70
Sioux Falls, SD	22.04	69.77	23.53	11.53	67.09	14.10	140.08
Springfield, IL	32.24	61.19	19.64	11.15	45.42	19.01	n/a
Tallahassee, FL	20.82	n/a	20.83	10.68	n/a	20.36	n/a
Tampa, FL	20.64	67.66	22.54	11.64	57.26	15.26	91.49
Topeka, KS	24.79	58.57	20.20	10.26	39.95	n/a	n/a
Tyler, TX	20.35	62.20	21.15	9.74	47.05	9.77	68.45
Virginia Beach, VA	23.02	64.00	20.62	10.36	59.71	14.57	110.86
Visalia, CA	30.19	57.80	22.80	13.44	50.19	13.87	n/a
Washington, DC	30.44	82.22	24.58	12.38	73.83	16.82	78.15
Wilmington, NC	20.70	70.25	20.99	11.28	52.90	11.92	n/a
Winston-Salem, NC	22.27	78.89	22.50	10.91	66.69	12.03	n/a

Notes: (1) Figures cover the Metropolitan Statistical Area (MSA) except where noted. See Appendix B for areas included;
(2) New England City and Town Area; n/a not available
Source: Bureau of Labor Statistics, May 2018 Metro Area Occupational Employment and Wage Estimates

Average Hourly Wages: Occupations J – N

Metro Area	Janitors/ Cleaners	Landscapers	Lawyers	Maids/ House-keepers	Main-tenance Repairers	Marketing Managers	Nuclear Medicine Techs
Albany, NY	14.07	16.14	55.15	12.00	19.91	70.17	40.92
Albuquerque, NM	11.83	13.60	53.06	10.30	17.93	48.26	37.10
Allentown, PA	15.06	14.32	52.49	11.47	20.13	68.18	35.47
Anchorage, AK	15.25	18.37	58.09	13.89	23.82	49.62	n/a
Ann Arbor, MI	14.93	14.16	57.31	12.33	17.77	65.79	36.28
Athens, GA	11.90	15.22	43.13	10.23	16.89	72.38	n/a
Atlanta, GA	12.01	14.31	65.81	10.26	18.71	70.27	38.05
Austin, TX	12.78	14.42	60.63	10.64	18.21	67.09	37.47
Baton Rouge, LA	10.39	13.09	49.16	9.74	18.65	54.03	30.98
Billings, MT	14.90	15.92	50.02	14.94	19.40	n/a	n/a
Boise City, ID	12.23	13.88	50.99	10.23	17.20	55.30	n/a
Boston, MA[2]	17.32	18.17	82.08	15.78	23.89	70.16	40.06
Boulder, CO	14.39	17.65	77.91	12.54	22.26	92.26	n/a
Cape Coral, FL	12.61	13.07	57.69	11.52	17.57	55.63	34.75
Cedar Rapids, IA	14.59	15.63	56.70	11.20	22.32	54.05	n/a
Charleston, SC	10.71	13.35	38.01	10.61	18.82	54.78	36.43
Charlotte, NC	12.10	13.57	67.70	10.67	19.84	71.41	33.88
Chicago, IL	14.73	15.36	76.87	13.62	22.16	63.55	42.01
Clarksville, TN	12.06	13.45	35.54	10.56	20.44	n/a	n/a
College Station, TX	12.63	13.05	43.46	11.51	16.18	73.30	n/a
Colorado Springs, CO	13.48	14.71	50.84	11.46	18.30	77.50	37.74
Columbia, MO	13.68	14.01	46.10	10.95	16.42	42.21	n/a
Columbia, SC	12.14	12.83	57.30	9.78	17.24	52.58	32.40
Columbus, OH	13.71	14.23	58.19	11.00	19.87	71.79	35.36
Dallas, TX	12.73	13.75	77.34	11.01	20.38	67.05	39.16
Denver, CO	13.90	16.21	75.00	12.50	20.51	82.07	42.19
Des Moines, IA	13.52	14.57	59.71	11.84	19.63	60.84	n/a
Durham, NC	12.08	13.86	68.19	12.20	20.05	71.51	n/a
Edison, NJ	17.24	16.83	82.70	17.35	22.94	91.16	44.79
El Paso, TX	10.94	11.13	57.35	9.44	14.56	58.28	37.30
Eugene, OR	13.83	15.51	50.98	12.70	18.00	42.92	n/a
Evansville, IN	14.31	12.22	52.74	10.83	19.34	53.89	n/a
Fargo, ND	13.36	16.89	57.63	11.47	18.89	55.95	n/a
Fayetteville, NC	11.68	12.08	57.86	10.30	18.17	n/a	30.58
Fort Collins, CO	14.34	16.30	62.54	12.48	20.13	75.44	n/a
Fort Wayne, IN	11.44	13.03	62.48	10.01	19.74	59.50	n/a
Fort Worth, TX	12.73	13.75	77.34	11.01	20.38	67.05	39.16
Gainesville, FL	12.43	12.99	50.26	11.19	17.20	63.91	n/a
Grand Rapids, MI	12.56	14.82	46.53	12.08	18.87	61.37	33.30
Greeley, CO	13.44	16.51	44.59	11.31	20.76	63.42	n/a
Green Bay, WI	13.12	14.73	51.79	11.48	20.93	54.35	n/a
Greensboro, NC	11.52	14.35	49.74	9.31	19.18	70.41	n/a
Honolulu, HI	14.95	15.28	54.27	19.18	22.72	56.40	44.22
Houston, TX	11.41	14.04	84.32	10.15	18.95	79.92	39.42
Huntsville, AL	11.87	13.14	62.11	9.50	20.55	68.60	26.03
Indianapolis, IN	12.69	14.21	53.57	10.78	19.71	54.48	35.25
Jacksonville, FL	12.89	12.88	57.84	11.13	18.29	56.19	35.02
Kansas City, MO	13.62	17.27	59.02	10.70	19.37	68.71	37.90
Lafayette, LA	10.28	11.93	44.67	9.27	17.22	43.97	33.00
Las Cruces, NM	10.82	11.78	56.19	10.13	15.49	n/a	n/a
Las Vegas, NV	15.14	14.22	66.86	15.50	22.46	70.57	39.07
Lexington, KY	13.10	13.75	55.03	10.32	18.51	51.75	31.98
Lincoln, NE	12.82	14.12	47.98	11.54	18.96	46.45	n/a
Little Rock, AR	11.44	12.68	46.40	10.11	16.06	60.79	35.58
Los Angeles, CA	16.05	16.50	84.63	13.95	21.19	73.15	52.08

Table continued on next page.

Metro Area	Janitors/ Cleaners	Landscapers	Lawyers	Maids/ House- keepers	Main- tenance Repairers	Marketing Managers	Nuclear Medicine Techs
Louisville, KY	12.99	13.69	52.74	10.97	20.25	62.47	33.34
Madison, WI	14.70	16.03	59.13	11.75	20.59	60.38	43.86
Manchester, NH[2]	13.24	15.92	60.12	11.23	20.92	70.53	n/a
McAllen, TX	11.30	11.37	n/a	9.16	13.09	56.36	n/a
Miami, FL	11.93	13.50	69.92	11.38	17.43	59.06	34.17
Midland, TX	11.72	14.39	n/a	11.47	20.89	76.71	n/a
Minneapolis, MN	15.58	18.13	59.60	14.21	22.50	68.49	41.09
Nashville, TN	12.76	12.49	61.00	11.37	19.06	61.03	37.56
New Orleans, LA	10.89	12.08	58.96	10.64	18.30	44.21	32.07
New York, NY	17.24	16.83	82.70	17.35	22.94	91.16	44.79
Oklahoma City, OK	11.71	13.46	55.00	10.10	16.80	57.18	35.68
Omaha, NE	13.23	15.31	55.37	11.61	20.34	50.88	33.77
Orlando, FL	11.53	12.73	59.59	11.18	16.58	53.94	34.93
Peoria, IL	13.95	12.18	59.86	11.81	19.95	66.07	n/a
Philadelphia, PA	14.83	15.52	73.12	12.68	21.06	76.73	38.85
Phoenix, AZ	12.65	13.81	74.14	11.93	18.85	57.26	40.91
Pittsburgh, PA	13.58	13.95	63.62	11.36	19.01	71.57	30.03
Portland, OR	14.81	17.27	61.23	13.61	20.52	57.96	42.72
Providence, RI[2]	15.09	16.51	58.77	13.45	21.67	74.31	42.53
Provo, UT	10.57	14.48	59.45	11.45	18.38	55.47	n/a
Raleigh, NC	11.38	14.87	65.24	10.54	20.11	72.69	34.09
Reno, NV	12.24	14.59	74.22	11.26	20.47	61.47	n/a
Richmond, VA	11.37	15.04	70.92	10.65	19.98	81.64	33.88
Roanoke, VA	11.65	12.20	49.70	10.30	17.39	63.78	34.14
Rochester, MN	15.10	15.71	39.45	11.93	20.18	67.68	n/a
Salem, OR	13.89	14.02	56.68	12.23	17.65	50.83	n/a
Salt Lake City, UT	11.72	14.48	56.54	11.89	19.35	55.49	n/a
San Antonio, TX	12.38	13.77	53.70	10.51	17.31	73.17	32.50
San Diego, CA	15.55	15.60	75.31	13.60	20.85	73.12	55.77
San Francisco, CA	17.60	19.19	88.01	18.04	26.44	87.78	56.12
San Jose, CA	17.16	20.85	99.98	16.03	26.19	94.77	54.99
Santa Rosa, CA	16.07	18.71	74.51	14.02	24.25	73.49	n/a
Savannah, GA	11.56	12.73	47.57	9.93	17.45	48.93	n/a
Seattle, WA	17.72	18.85	71.00	14.18	22.47	76.26	46.06
Sioux Falls, SD	12.40	14.13	67.21	11.09	17.92	64.54	30.46
Springfield, IL	15.24	14.56	56.57	11.23	18.89	56.11	n/a
Tallahassee, FL	12.24	13.33	56.74	9.76	16.14	48.85	n/a
Tampa, FL	13.95	13.34	54.56	11.30	17.32	61.10	34.72
Topeka, KS	12.04	15.57	46.02	10.08	18.31	61.37	n/a
Tyler, TX	11.28	12.22	44.28	9.16	17.22	n/a	n/a
Virginia Beach, VA	11.33	13.40	56.84	10.29	18.71	65.14	34.67
Visalia, CA	14.69	14.88	55.50	12.07	18.88	85.09	n/a
Washington, DC	14.50	15.81	86.53	14.36	23.18	82.15	39.45
Wilmington, NC	11.25	14.10	41.46	10.25	18.52	68.72	n/a
Winston-Salem, NC	10.46	13.84	66.15	9.74	18.94	65.26	35.56

Notes: (1) Figures cover the Metropolitan Statistical Area (MSA) except where noted. See Appendix B for areas included;
(2) New England City and Town Area; n/a not available
Source: Bureau of Labor Statistics, May 2018 Metro Area Occupational Employment and Wage Estimates

Average Hourly Wages: Occupations N – R

Metro Area	Nurses, Licensed Practical	Nurses, Registered	Nursing Assistants	Packers/ Packagers	Physical Therapists	Postal Mail Carriers	R.E. Brokers
Albany, NY	20.67	33.56	14.09	15.12	37.40	24.76	n/a
Albuquerque, NM	23.07	36.06	14.34	10.16	44.98	25.04	n/a
Allentown, PA	23.95	32.55	15.15	13.90	41.52	25.06	n/a
Anchorage, AK	28.12	42.39	18.52	16.45	48.25	25.26	35.75
Ann Arbor, MI	24.41	35.38	15.72	12.17	41.12	24.23	n/a
Athens, GA	21.12	32.36	12.62	10.93	43.61	24.40	n/a
Atlanta, GA	21.21	35.19	13.36	11.79	40.95	24.56	28.02
Austin, TX	22.39	33.78	13.74	12.85	43.16	24.51	n/a
Baton Rouge, LA	18.49	29.05	11.46	11.77	40.80	24.16	n/a
Billings, MT	21.18	34.26	13.53	12.76	38.68	25.21	n/a
Boise City, ID	22.48	33.17	13.73	11.86	38.21	24.36	24.49
Boston, MA[2]	29.40	45.80	16.64	13.50	44.10	25.73	58.41
Boulder, CO	25.69	36.68	15.80	12.62	40.40	24.66	32.73
Cape Coral, FL	20.76	32.26	14.13	11.01	44.26	24.26	39.52
Cedar Rapids, IA	20.37	27.91	13.87	13.98	37.23	24.73	n/a
Charleston, SC	20.79	36.43	13.79	11.06	39.17	24.76	28.58
Charlotte, NC	21.60	30.85	12.07	11.58	41.02	24.33	39.36
Chicago, IL	26.51	37.36	14.37	12.70	44.47	25.24	49.66
Clarksville, TN	19.52	29.67	13.89	11.26	38.66	24.26	n/a
College Station, TX	21.61	33.00	12.92	9.33	39.30	24.73	n/a
Colorado Springs, CO	23.74	35.34	14.76	12.38	43.14	24.53	37.91
Columbia, MO	20.23	32.79	11.60	11.91	39.66	24.86	n/a
Columbia, SC	20.79	30.51	12.59	10.61	42.97	24.67	31.88
Columbus, OH	20.63	32.49	13.11	12.36	40.70	24.59	28.78
Dallas, TX	24.41	35.65	13.36	12.47	45.99	25.23	39.92
Denver, CO	26.09	36.22	16.49	13.24	38.93	24.92	n/a
Des Moines, IA	21.52	29.92	14.61	14.54	41.28	24.64	25.06
Durham, NC	22.86	32.23	13.92	11.14	38.06	24.90	28.60
Edison, NJ	26.75	43.83	17.67	12.62	45.28	25.42	55.75
El Paso, TX	22.80	33.86	12.20	12.07	44.12	24.39	n/a
Eugene, OR	25.48	43.68	16.41	12.95	39.90	24.18	24.14
Evansville, IN	21.25	29.29	13.27	13.46	37.70	24.37	n/a
Fargo, ND	21.89	32.33	16.11	12.74	37.34	24.18	n/a
Fayetteville, NC	21.84	33.65	11.88	10.10	37.72	24.30	25.33
Fort Collins, CO	24.64	35.51	15.54	12.34	36.09	23.98	32.13
Fort Wayne, IN	21.23	27.73	12.86	13.58	41.84	24.80	n/a
Fort Worth, TX	24.41	35.65	13.36	12.47	45.99	25.23	39.92
Gainesville, FL	24.75	32.97	12.96	11.12	40.56	24.72	23.16
Grand Rapids, MI	20.92	31.70	13.83	11.59	41.17	24.63	32.44
Greeley, CO	23.51	34.48	13.75	12.61	42.09	23.52	26.23
Green Bay, WI	20.49	31.63	14.36	12.14	41.33	24.90	53.28
Greensboro, NC	20.52	32.07	12.03	10.44	43.28	24.82	32.50
Honolulu, HI	24.06	47.88	17.11	12.39	43.71	26.38	48.59
Houston, TX	23.42	38.54	13.68	11.41	44.72	24.80	49.98
Huntsville, AL	18.99	27.48	12.25	12.75	43.22	24.58	n/a
Indianapolis, IN	22.32	33.31	13.74	12.50	40.20	24.76	52.37
Jacksonville, FL	21.22	30.13	12.70	10.99	39.31	25.42	22.79
Kansas City, MO	22.07	32.37	13.14	13.12	37.80	24.52	25.42
Lafayette, LA	18.97	30.26	9.95	11.52	39.90	24.71	23.95
Las Cruces, NM	21.92	31.64	11.54	9.15	51.28	24.29	n/a
Las Vegas, NV	27.70	42.27	17.24	10.53	55.41	24.89	47.79
Lexington, KY	21.42	30.68	13.61	13.84	40.10	24.81	n/a
Lincoln, NE	20.17	30.96	13.90	11.91	38.44	24.71	26.34
Little Rock, AR	20.23	31.27	13.02	10.67	38.88	24.94	32.06
Los Angeles, CA	25.96	48.05	16.16	12.84	46.25	25.98	34.20

Table continued on next page.

Metro Area	Nurses, Licensed Practical	Nurses, Registered	Nursing Assistants	Packers/ Packagers	Physical Therapists	Postal Mail Carriers	R.E. Brokers
Louisville, KY	21.04	31.05	13.95	12.38	39.39	24.71	26.43
Madison, WI	22.90	38.37	15.78	16.84	39.97	24.81	n/a
Manchester, NH[2]	26.67	35.22	15.42	11.00	41.37	24.94	n/a
McAllen, TX	22.31	34.14	11.22	10.95	54.09	25.35	n/a
Miami, FL	22.51	33.41	12.64	11.72	42.31	25.42	38.00
Midland, TX	23.47	30.26	13.74	9.99	44.32	23.44	n/a
Minneapolis, MN	23.54	40.15	16.95	13.70	40.26	25.16	30.17
Nashville, TN	20.75	30.69	13.32	11.94	34.72	24.70	43.47
New Orleans, LA	20.44	32.08	11.71	11.21	41.46	24.51	n/a
New York, NY	26.75	43.83	17.67	12.62	45.28	25.42	55.75
Oklahoma City, OK	20.57	31.33	12.82	11.04	41.45	24.60	n/a
Omaha, NE	21.51	31.59	14.01	12.42	37.77	25.02	31.14
Orlando, FL	21.22	31.23	12.49	11.70	42.73	24.85	27.93
Peoria, IL	21.10	32.07	12.75	12.54	40.59	25.01	n/a
Philadelphia, PA	26.61	37.35	14.70	12.64	44.35	25.20	n/a
Phoenix, AZ	26.92	37.54	15.34	13.15	42.76	25.08	33.42
Pittsburgh, PA	21.58	31.85	14.57	12.03	38.84	24.54	35.72
Portland, OR	25.47	44.99	16.30	14.49	41.77	24.49	43.73
Providence, RI[2]	27.20	37.65	15.02	13.21	40.71	24.67	n/a
Provo, UT	20.27	30.34	12.67	11.81	42.66	24.38	n/a
Raleigh, NC	21.69	31.18	12.47	11.94	40.76	24.76	29.18
Reno, NV	26.84	37.59	16.39	13.25	41.08	25.21	27.57
Richmond, VA	21.17	34.24	13.39	11.03	46.92	24.35	45.51
Roanoke, VA	20.98	31.39	12.90	10.81	44.72	24.90	n/a
Rochester, MN	22.78	36.43	n/a	13.15	39.96	24.76	n/a
Salem, OR	25.70	42.53	14.32	12.93	37.79	23.72	24.27
Salt Lake City, UT	26.89	32.52	14.15	12.50	40.44	24.90	n/a
San Antonio, TX	21.74	34.74	12.95	10.17	38.66	24.90	44.18
San Diego, CA	27.32	47.33	16.68	13.10	44.50	25.67	49.22
San Francisco, CA	31.45	62.01	21.28	14.91	46.60	26.38	49.86
San Jose, CA	30.60	61.83	19.05	14.09	49.32	26.50	43.05
Santa Rosa, CA	30.04	47.76	17.35	13.45	46.85	25.14	n/a
Savannah, GA	19.69	29.78	12.08	10.26	37.82	24.27	n/a
Seattle, WA	28.14	41.27	15.97	15.35	41.92	25.21	36.27
Sioux Falls, SD	18.68	28.27	13.12	11.84	34.24	25.11	n/a
Springfield, IL	21.21	32.84	14.11	n/a	42.04	24.88	n/a
Tallahassee, FL	20.34	30.05	11.81	10.83	42.25	24.90	n/a
Tampa, FL	21.26	32.70	13.41	10.72	40.85	25.00	34.08
Topeka, KS	21.01	31.42	12.84	13.82	44.25	24.03	n/a
Tyler, TX	21.54	29.07	11.86	15.45	48.56	24.72	n/a
Virginia Beach, VA	20.17	32.27	15.24	10.74	41.83	24.42	37.56
Visalia, CA	22.33	42.83	13.59	12.47	50.77	24.64	n/a
Washington, DC	26.09	39.17	15.20	12.68	43.83	24.77	41.67
Wilmington, NC	21.27	29.62	11.65	12.01	49.75	24.73	22.96
Winston-Salem, NC	21.47	33.21	13.20	11.95	44.78	24.90	n/a

Notes: (1) Figures cover the Metropolitan Statistical Area (MSA) except where noted. See Appendix B for areas included;
(2) New England City and Town Area; n/a not available
Source: Bureau of Labor Statistics, May 2018 Metro Area Occupational Employment and Wage Estimates

Average Hourly Wages: Occupations R – T

Metro Area	Retail Salespersons	Sales Reps., Except Tech./Scien.	Sales Reps., Tech./Scien.	Secretaries, Exc. Leg./ Med./Exec.	Security Guards	Surgeons	Teacher Assistants
Albany, NY	13.64	33.03	51.87	19.97	16.62	136.40	14.69
Albuquerque, NM	12.72	28.39	49.88	17.14	13.37	131.23	9.88
Allentown, PA	12.68	37.33	41.17	17.71	13.01	111.67	13.63
Anchorage, AK	14.70	27.22	39.04	20.13	23.75	n/a	18.85
Ann Arbor, MI	13.84	37.33	41.49	20.39	13.28	n/a	14.59
Athens, GA	11.83	30.76	26.21	16.49	n/a	n/a	9.19
Atlanta, GA	12.68	31.63	37.45	17.41	13.82	126.82	11.24
Austin, TX	13.29	30.65	61.20	17.79	14.98	106.21	12.36
Baton Rouge, LA	11.69	28.83	41.10	15.69	13.75	n/a	10.35
Billings, MT	15.26	27.68	52.66	16.62	13.57	n/a	12.45
Boise City, ID	13.08	32.58	46.09	16.34	14.65	106.34	11.77
Boston, MA[2]	14.50	38.76	45.91	22.79	17.19	117.15	17.15
Boulder, CO	15.02	44.39	51.64	19.08	15.69	51.30	15.41
Cape Coral, FL	12.50	32.35	52.15	17.13	13.10	104.53	14.23
Cedar Rapids, IA	13.64	31.57	41.99	17.86	13.29	n/a	13.38
Charleston, SC	13.01	33.67	34.46	17.50	16.46	n/a	10.39
Charlotte, NC	12.54	39.95	45.05	18.31	13.78	127.59	11.85
Chicago, IL	13.63	34.15	41.62	19.11	16.13	107.91	13.78
Clarksville, TN	12.66	29.89	32.16	15.37	16.55	n/a	12.74
College Station, TX	13.38	33.45	44.72	15.82	15.45	n/a	10.02
Colorado Springs, CO	13.80	28.37	52.24	17.08	15.44	n/a	13.37
Columbia, MO	14.88	30.52	39.40	16.61	13.97	n/a	13.12
Columbia, SC	12.96	32.47	35.18	17.40	16.89	n/a	11.36
Columbus, OH	13.41	32.08	35.35	18.69	16.62	122.02	14.24
Dallas, TX	12.80	33.79	43.46	18.42	14.54	109.65	11.42
Denver, CO	14.93	38.76	46.43	19.68	17.27	118.19	14.71
Des Moines, IA	13.36	36.01	42.49	18.77	14.77	85.50	12.85
Durham, NC	12.49	37.16	50.41	19.52	17.15	n/a	12.15
Edison, NJ	14.56	36.95	50.95	20.41	16.99	124.85	15.33
El Paso, TX	12.71	21.76	54.24	14.02	12.93	n/a	12.75
Eugene, OR	15.75	30.18	54.30	17.80	15.44	n/a	15.10
Evansville, IN	12.84	32.06	36.63	14.96	14.64	136.25	11.78
Fargo, ND	14.96	31.29	30.68	18.34	16.62	n/a	15.26
Fayetteville, NC	11.50	24.67	n/a	16.81	20.38	n/a	10.51
Fort Collins, CO	13.63	33.69	51.44	17.56	12.96	135.16	13.17
Fort Wayne, IN	12.31	33.24	44.93	16.08	16.21	n/a	12.28
Fort Worth, TX	12.80	33.79	43.46	18.42	14.54	109.65	11.42
Gainesville, FL	12.15	29.63	38.20	15.72	12.58	n/a	11.27
Grand Rapids, MI	12.96	37.84	40.40	17.68	13.28	41.76	13.65
Greeley, CO	17.17	31.21	46.29	17.59	16.75	n/a	14.81
Green Bay, WI	12.87	32.30	42.11	17.92	12.94	n/a	15.61
Greensboro, NC	12.99	32.20	39.33	17.23	13.66	n/a	11.22
Honolulu, HI	14.65	25.22	42.76	19.52	15.72	n/a	14.58
Houston, TX	12.42	37.52	46.02	18.09	14.37	117.13	10.94
Huntsville, AL	13.05	27.45	43.36	18.10	14.32	129.02	11.69
Indianapolis, IN	12.52	38.07	55.58	16.96	13.89	127.77	12.18
Jacksonville, FL	12.50	31.68	36.12	17.04	12.02	n/a	12.07
Kansas City, MO	13.46	32.92	39.23	17.97	18.01	103.56	13.02
Lafayette, LA	12.72	28.33	28.58	14.22	11.58	n/a	11.21
Las Cruces, NM	12.52	25.96	n/a	15.20	13.40	n/a	13.07
Las Vegas, NV	13.29	31.90	50.14	19.44	14.46	n/a	15.28
Lexington, KY	13.18	27.28	43.69	17.29	11.44	135.80	15.83
Lincoln, NE	13.02	28.88	41.90	17.09	16.05	n/a	13.06
Little Rock, AR	12.50	28.19	31.25	16.15	14.49	n/a	10.75
Los Angeles, CA	15.38	34.61	44.48	20.95	16.09	92.22	17.53

Table continued on next page.

Metro Area	Retail Salespersons	Sales Reps., Except Tech./Scien.	Sales Reps., Tech./Scien.	Secretaries, Exc. Leg./ Med./Exec.	Security Guards	Surgeons	Teacher Assistants
Louisville, KY	12.45	34.99	48.19	16.72	11.59	133.59	14.52
Madison, WI	12.64	32.72	33.85	18.61	15.21	128.44	14.28
Manchester, NH[2]	13.29	30.98	50.71	17.78	15.92	n/a	13.02
McAllen, TX	11.08	27.23	53.28	14.14	11.64	n/a	11.66
Miami, FL	13.10	29.20	39.59	17.47	13.23	103.71	11.14
Midland, TX	15.30	41.74	44.86	18.28	17.69	n/a	10.99
Minneapolis, MN	14.13	36.31	42.02	20.51	16.65	n/a	15.81
Nashville, TN	14.60	31.02	40.92	17.59	13.26	n/a	12.50
New Orleans, LA	12.04	29.75	33.29	16.81	14.53	137.55	11.20
New York, NY	14.56	36.95	50.95	20.41	16.99	124.85	15.33
Oklahoma City, OK	14.03	29.17	40.90	15.82	15.78	129.11	9.84
Omaha, NE	13.20	28.80	33.20	17.22	16.97	137.45	12.68
Orlando, FL	12.25	28.96	43.15	16.68	12.28	110.12	11.61
Peoria, IL	14.78	28.35	42.57	16.55	16.18	n/a	11.89
Philadelphia, PA	14.07	37.49	38.94	19.35	14.26	127.01	13.28
Phoenix, AZ	13.06	31.32	40.89	17.82	14.16	n/a	12.30
Pittsburgh, PA	13.34	35.99	36.57	17.32	12.63	127.84	13.46
Portland, OR	14.66	35.16	47.27	19.86	14.56	n/a	16.35
Providence, RI[2]	14.74	35.63	43.92	20.48	14.91	124.15	15.49
Provo, UT	12.58	26.81	36.27	15.65	17.79	n/a	12.88
Raleigh, NC	13.12	35.74	50.04	17.97	16.32	n/a	11.87
Reno, NV	14.56	32.88	45.03	18.95	13.69	n/a	13.85
Richmond, VA	13.00	38.87	45.68	18.56	13.80	135.28	12.54
Roanoke, VA	13.19	32.44	35.03	16.32	14.01	103.92	10.22
Rochester, MN	13.17	31.75	41.44	16.54	14.63	n/a	15.01
Salem, OR	14.59	32.44	34.85	19.23	14.52	n/a	16.20
Salt Lake City, UT	13.77	29.91	49.89	17.12	16.01	n/a	12.10
San Antonio, TX	13.45	32.68	42.44	16.71	14.65	108.92	11.84
San Diego, CA	14.84	33.47	43.03	20.70	15.02	135.63	16.72
San Francisco, CA	16.11	39.71	46.75	23.99	17.72	98.44	18.28
San Jose, CA	15.57	38.14	48.75	22.59	18.14	138.17	19.21
Santa Rosa, CA	15.84	34.70	53.66	21.33	16.59	n/a	16.25
Savannah, GA	12.22	38.11	45.77	16.25	15.52	n/a	11.59
Seattle, WA	17.90	36.56	42.38	22.07	18.74	116.09	18.12
Sioux Falls, SD	14.87	33.13	43.65	14.25	13.86	n/a	11.80
Springfield, IL	13.41	27.20	28.81	17.39	23.33	n/a	11.77
Tallahassee, FL	12.46	28.03	41.30	17.22	13.75	n/a	12.39
Tampa, FL	12.90	29.76	41.22	16.90	14.81	n/a	13.32
Topeka, KS	12.34	30.64	36.12	15.97	13.20	n/a	12.36
Tyler, TX	13.00	27.09	48.05	15.82	15.08	n/a	11.05
Virginia Beach, VA	11.67	35.34	41.04	17.61	15.31	n/a	12.84
Visalia, CA	14.39	33.09	48.12	18.59	13.27	n/a	17.06
Washington, DC	14.25	38.12	48.14	21.99	20.86	128.45	15.82
Wilmington, NC	12.86	31.34	38.93	17.35	16.01	130.48	10.47
Winston-Salem, NC	11.87	36.42	43.74	17.60	16.40	n/a	10.56

Notes: (1) Figures cover the Metropolitan Statistical Area (MSA) except where noted. See Appendix B for areas included;
(2) New England City and Town Area; n/a not available
Source: Bureau of Labor Statistics, May 2018 Metro Area Occupational Employment and Wage Estimates

Average Hourly Wages: Occupations T – Z

Metro Area	Teachers, Elementary School	Teachers, Secondary School	Tele-marketers	Truck Driv., Heavy/ Trac. Trail.	Truck Drivers, Light	Waiters/ Waitresses
Albany, NY	31.77	34.30	13.91	21.01	17.59	14.27
Albuquerque, NM	25.61	23.18	12.71	20.24	17.74	10.32
Allentown, PA	36.19	33.59	n/a	23.52	17.56	12.37
Anchorage, AK	35.89	38.64	n/a	27.50	21.88	12.08
Ann Arbor, MI	31.19	28.87	n/a	23.07	18.55	11.43
Athens, GA	25.67	27.19	9.92	24.66	19.67	10.58
Atlanta, GA	27.51	28.29	12.13	21.15	18.38	9.82
Austin, TX	28.33	27.85	19.92	19.42	19.90	12.85
Baton Rouge, LA	23.94	25.57	n/a	20.70	15.37	8.98
Billings, MT	26.76	28.07	n/a	23.10	18.11	11.19
Boise City, ID	23.65	24.88	14.26	21.26	16.83	9.90
Boston, MA[2]	39.77	38.60	20.38	24.26	20.26	15.53
Boulder, CO	30.90	31.02	16.31	18.69	17.09	13.93
Cape Coral, FL	30.62	31.08	13.65	18.91	15.75	11.22
Cedar Rapids, IA	26.71	26.16	13.07	20.79	16.27	10.36
Charleston, SC	23.46	24.69	9.77	22.65	16.40	9.46
Charlotte, NC	23.28	24.15	16.47	21.28	16.36	11.04
Chicago, IL	31.57	37.38	14.17	24.19	19.81	11.23
Clarksville, TN	29.73	27.89	n/a	17.86	16.06	11.01
College Station, TX	23.34	23.56	n/a	20.99	15.66	9.33
Colorado Springs, CO	22.88	23.70	n/a	21.93	16.56	12.28
Columbia, MO	n/a	n/a	13.09	19.92	17.28	9.41
Columbia, SC	24.51	25.34	n/a	20.83	16.18	9.55
Columbus, OH	30.77	30.51	15.48	21.66	16.85	10.93
Dallas, TX	28.59	29.41	15.74	22.95	19.28	10.98
Denver, CO	27.48	28.36	14.62	24.70	19.51	11.99
Des Moines, IA	28.60	30.54	n/a	23.61	17.30	12.22
Durham, NC	22.60	23.95	10.91	21.10	17.56	12.08
Edison, NJ	40.25	42.53	15.21	25.40	19.12	16.38
El Paso, TX	30.75	31.41	8.85	21.80	14.69	10.07
Eugene, OR	32.15	30.41	13.22	22.64	17.46	13.76
Evansville, IN	23.09	26.20	n/a	21.02	16.09	9.77
Fargo, ND	33.01	30.59	15.56	22.24	17.72	9.62
Fayetteville, NC	20.54	21.92	n/a	18.43	15.62	9.91
Fort Collins, CO	25.32	25.89	14.70	19.49	17.42	13.91
Fort Wayne, IN	24.13	25.73	12.47	21.11	15.76	10.46
Fort Worth, TX	28.59	29.41	15.74	22.95	19.28	10.98
Gainesville, FL	20.26	21.51	12.54	16.45	17.00	11.71
Grand Rapids, MI	27.76	28.43	12.97	21.07	17.70	13.60
Greeley, CO	23.21	24.73	n/a	24.17	15.43	11.03
Green Bay, WI	25.21	26.97	22.25	21.37	15.25	9.79
Greensboro, NC	22.93	23.75	11.90	23.70	17.15	9.39
Honolulu, HI	29.59	29.13	12.22	23.70	18.22	25.23
Houston, TX	28.13	29.24	13.04	21.78	18.44	12.57
Huntsville, AL	24.39	25.59	11.37	19.31	15.68	8.89
Indianapolis, IN	27.40	26.53	15.77	22.61	17.14	11.33
Jacksonville, FL	28.55	29.05	11.74	22.55	18.65	12.18
Kansas City, MO	26.51	27.61	12.53	22.82	18.05	10.30
Lafayette, LA	23.23	24.38	n/a	18.96	13.72	8.77
Las Cruces, NM	35.62	37.67	n/a	17.55	14.95	10.86
Las Vegas, NV	26.93	27.34	14.14	23.37	18.16	12.58
Lexington, KY	27.55	28.11	n/a	22.07	19.25	8.90
Lincoln, NE	26.63	26.69	11.69	n/a	18.29	11.79
Little Rock, AR	25.34	26.08	10.92	22.42	15.98	9.96
Los Angeles, CA	40.37	38.62	14.96	22.79	18.97	13.70

Table continued on next page.

Metro Area	Teachers, Elementary School	Teachers, Secondary School	Tele-marketers	Truck Driv., Heavy/ Trac. Trail.	Truck Drivers, Light	Waiters/ Waitresses
Louisville, KY	28.19	29.56	13.01	23.60	18.81	10.05
Madison, WI	27.82	27.28	13.77	23.62	17.15	14.77
Manchester, NH[2]	27.07	28.62	n/a	22.33	19.76	11.76
McAllen, TX	26.33	27.41	10.74	17.60	13.83	9.78
Miami, FL	20.76	25.74	12.41	19.87	17.09	12.62
Midland, TX	24.99	26.80	n/a	23.09	18.93	9.22
Minneapolis, MN	33.28	32.66	16.30	25.06	20.79	12.59
Nashville, TN	25.33	25.75	15.18	22.88	17.60	9.62
New Orleans, LA	24.31	24.89	16.07	22.49	18.17	9.14
New York, NY	40.25	42.53	15.21	25.40	19.12	16.38
Oklahoma City, OK	20.49	21.20	14.28	21.00	16.22	9.98
Omaha, NE	28.10	27.82	12.82	21.27	17.06	12.74
Orlando, FL	22.82	24.15	11.66	21.10	16.92	13.05
Peoria, IL	22.96	27.28	16.73	19.88	18.10	9.96
Philadelphia, PA	33.79	32.30	15.02	23.50	17.78	12.14
Phoenix, AZ	21.87	24.46	14.55	22.19	19.21	14.87
Pittsburgh, PA	30.99	32.45	12.93	23.05	16.70	12.34
Portland, OR	33.94	37.46	15.60	24.02	18.41	13.69
Providence, RI[2]	34.56	34.55	15.68	23.38	17.19	13.28
Provo, UT	32.45	34.24	18.08	20.04	16.32	11.61
Raleigh, NC	23.10	22.97	12.65	22.81	16.73	11.90
Reno, NV	28.29	28.52	14.07	23.63	19.33	10.01
Richmond, VA	27.62	28.10	13.25	19.87	18.83	11.36
Roanoke, VA	25.23	25.26	n/a	21.58	18.50	10.20
Rochester, MN	26.21	31.37	n/a	23.12	16.57	10.62
Salem, OR	32.01	36.97	n/a	21.05	19.20	16.31
Salt Lake City, UT	27.63	26.96	15.44	21.58	17.81	11.39
San Antonio, TX	28.08	28.60	14.88	20.82	19.23	10.51
San Diego, CA	34.61	37.32	15.12	22.17	18.97	15.22
San Francisco, CA	39.20	39.94	18.53	25.31	20.79	17.54
San Jose, CA	36.72	40.93	n/a	25.31	20.94	15.18
Santa Rosa, CA	36.14	36.81	n/a	25.81	20.12	14.45
Savannah, GA	25.37	26.97	n/a	21.33	16.22	9.93
Seattle, WA	32.32	33.29	17.33	24.34	20.54	18.82
Sioux Falls, SD	21.92	22.11	n/a	20.71	16.88	10.55
Springfield, IL	25.73	26.94	n/a	22.33	15.43	10.45
Tallahassee, FL	22.07	23.64	13.77	17.42	16.32	10.29
Tampa, FL	28.12	28.70	12.12	20.02	16.80	12.46
Topeka, KS	23.00	23.90	n/a	20.69	18.27	10.05
Tyler, TX	23.67	25.47	n/a	19.90	14.92	11.25
Virginia Beach, VA	33.02	32.73	10.11	20.16	15.96	11.45
Visalia, CA	36.75	35.85	n/a	18.05	17.53	12.86
Washington, DC	37.09	37.62	15.26	21.87	18.91	14.09
Wilmington, NC	21.54	23.50	n/a	19.08	15.73	10.05
Winston-Salem, NC	22.47	23.40	15.25	20.83	16.07	9.77

Notes: (1) Figures cover the Metropolitan Statistical Area (MSA) except where noted. See Appendix B for areas included;
(2) New England City and Town Area; Hourly wages for elementary and secondary school teachers were calculated by the editors from annual wage data assuming a 40 hour work week; n/a not available
Source: Bureau of Labor Statistics, May 2018 Metro Area Occupational Employment and Wage Estimates

Means of Transportation to Work: City

City	Car/Truck/Van		Public Transportation			Bicycle	Walked	Other Means	Worked at Home
	Drove Alone	Car-pooled	Bus	Subway	Railroad				
Albany, NY	62.5	8.1	14.1	0.2	0.0	0.9	10.6	1.2	2.5
Albuquerque, NM	79.9	9.1	1.8	0.0	0.1	1.4	2.0	1.3	4.3
Allentown, PA	67.4	17.0	5.0	0.1	0.0	0.2	5.5	0.6	4.2
Anchorage, AK	75.8	11.7	1.7	0.0	0.0	1.2	3.4	2.4	3.8
Ann Arbor, MI	54.2	6.7	10.9	0.1	0.0	4.4	15.3	0.9	7.4
Athens, GA	74.5	10.3	4.5	0.1	0.0	1.3	3.9	1.2	4.2
Atlanta, GA	68.7	6.9	6.8	3.1	0.2	0.9	4.4	1.5	7.6
Austin, TX	73.8	9.5	3.7	0.1	0.1	1.3	2.3	1.3	7.9
Baton Rouge, LA	79.4	10.2	2.8	0.0	0.0	0.6	3.0	0.9	2.9
Billings, MT	82.3	8.9	0.8	0.0	0.0	0.6	2.9	0.7	3.8
Boise City, ID	80.6	7.4	0.6	0.0	0.0	2.7	2.0	1.1	5.4
Boston, MA	39.0	5.8	14.2	17.4	1.1	2.1	14.6	2.5	3.3
Boulder, CO	50.9	5.6	7.7	0.0	0.0	10.4	11.3	1.2	12.8
Cape Coral, FL	82.9	9.3	0.1	0.0	0.0	0.1	0.7	1.3	5.5
Cedar Rapids, IA	83.8	9.0	1.1	0.0	0.0	0.5	2.0	0.9	2.7
Charleston, SC	76.6	6.0	1.2	0.0	0.0	2.9	5.4	1.5	6.4
Charlotte, NC	76.6	10.2	2.9	0.3	0.2	0.2	2.0	1.3	6.3
Chicago, IL	49.2	7.9	13.7	12.5	1.8	1.7	6.7	1.9	4.6
Clarksville, TN	86.8	6.6	1.1	0.0	0.0	0.1	1.6	1.4	2.4
College Station, TX	77.7	9.0	3.4	0.0	0.0	2.4	3.2	1.0	3.2
Colorado Springs, CO	78.8	10.9	1.1	0.0	0.0	0.6	1.8	1.0	5.9
Columbia, MO	76.4	10.2	1.6	0.0	0.0	1.3	5.2	1.2	4.1
Columbia, SC	64.3	5.9	1.6	0.0	0.0	0.5	22.2	2.1	3.4
Columbus, OH	80.0	8.3	3.1	0.0	0.0	0.7	2.9	1.1	3.8
Dallas, TX	76.2	11.3	3.3	0.5	0.3	0.2	1.9	1.6	4.6
Denver, CO	69.9	8.1	5.3	0.9	0.4	2.2	4.4	1.3	7.6
Des Moines, IA	80.6	9.8	2.1	0.0	0.0	0.4	2.9	1.0	3.1
Durham, NC	75.9	10.5	4.2	0.0	0.0	0.7	2.6	1.2	5.0
Edison, NJ	68.3	9.9	0.5	0.7	12.3	0.3	2.2	0.9	5.0
El Paso, TX	80.3	11.1	1.7	0.0	0.0	0.2	1.6	1.9	3.2
Eugene, OR	65.6	9.6	4.1	0.0	0.0	6.5	7.2	1.1	5.9
Evansville, IN	82.9	9.0	2.3	0.0	0.0	0.3	2.5	1.3	1.7
Fargo, ND	82.8	8.0	1.2	0.0	0.0	0.9	3.4	0.8	2.9
Fayetteville, NC	78.0	9.0	0.7	0.0	0.0	0.1	7.6	1.0	3.5
Fort Collins, CO	72.4	7.9	1.9	0.1	0.0	6.4	3.5	1.1	6.8
Fort Wayne, IN	83.9	9.0	1.0	0.0	0.0	0.3	1.2	0.9	3.7
Fort Worth, TX	81.5	11.4	0.6	0.0	0.2	0.2	1.3	1.2	3.6
Gainesville, FL	68.0	7.0	7.3	0.0	0.0	4.8	5.8	2.7	4.2
Grand Rapids, MI	75.0	10.8	4.1	0.1	0.0	1.1	3.8	1.2	3.9
Greeley, CO	77.8	12.9	0.8	0.0	0.0	0.8	2.9	1.1	3.7
Green Bay, WI	79.2	10.3	1.3	0.0	0.0	0.6	3.1	2.2	3.2
Greensboro, NC	82.2	8.2	1.5	0.0	0.0	0.2	1.6	1.0	5.5
Honolulu, HI	56.6	13.1	12.2	0.0	0.0	1.9	8.6	4.1	3.6
Houston, TX	76.6	11.3	3.7	0.1	0.1	0.5	2.1	2.0	3.6
Huntsville, AL	86.7	6.8	0.3	0.0	0.0	0.3	1.2	1.5	3.1
Indianapolis, IN	82.2	9.3	1.9	0.0	0.0	0.5	1.8	1.1	3.2
Jacksonville, FL	80.3	9.6	2.0	0.0	0.0	0.5	1.8	1.4	4.5
Kansas City, MO	80.4	8.4	2.8	0.0	0.0	0.3	2.1	1.2	4.8
Lafayette, LA	82.1	9.4	1.0	0.0	0.0	1.1	2.3	1.0	3.2
Las Cruces, NM	78.6	11.9	0.5	0.0	0.0	1.4	2.8	1.0	3.8
Las Vegas, NV	77.7	10.4	4.1	0.0	0.0	0.4	1.6	2.3	3.5
Lexington, KY	78.7	9.3	2.0	0.0	0.0	0.7	3.8	1.2	4.4
Lincoln, NE	81.5	9.0	1.3	0.0	0.0	1.4	3.1	0.7	3.0
Little Rock, AR	82.5	9.9	1.0	0.0	0.0	0.2	1.7	1.1	3.7

Table continued on next page.

| City | Car/Truck/Van | | Public Transportation | | | Bicycle | Walked | Other Means | Worked at Home |
	Drove Alone	Car-pooled	Bus	Subway	Railroad				
Los Angeles, CA	68.9	9.0	8.7	0.9	0.2	1.1	3.5	1.8	5.9
Louisville, KY	80.4	8.9	3.0	0.0	0.0	0.4	2.1	1.6	3.8
Madison, WI	63.5	7.4	9.4	0.0	0.0	4.8	9.6	1.1	4.2
Manchester, NH	79.1	11.7	0.9	0.0	0.1	0.4	3.2	1.1	3.5
McAllen, TX	76.7	11.6	0.7	0.0	0.0	0.5	1.0	5.1	4.3
Miami, FL	70.0	8.5	9.6	0.9	0.3	1.0	4.0	1.5	4.2
Midland, TX	85.5	10.4	0.2	0.0	0.0	0.0	0.6	1.4	1.9
Minneapolis, MN	61.0	7.9	11.9	1.0	0.2	4.1	7.0	1.5	5.4
Nashville, TN	79.1	9.9	2.1	0.0	0.1	0.2	2.1	1.0	5.6
New Orleans, LA	68.5	9.2	6.8	0.0	0.0	3.2	5.0	2.3	4.9
New York, NY	22.0	4.6	10.7	43.9	1.5	1.2	10.0	2.1	4.1
Oklahoma City, OK	82.3	11.2	0.5	0.0	0.0	0.2	1.4	0.8	3.5
Omaha, NE	82.1	9.1	1.4	0.0	0.0	0.3	2.4	1.2	3.6
Orlando, FL	78.3	8.2	4.1	0.1	0.0	0.6	1.9	1.8	5.1
Peoria, IL	79.7	8.9	3.8	0.0	0.0	0.5	3.2	1.1	2.8
Philadelphia, PA	51.0	8.4	16.8	5.2	2.9	2.1	8.3	1.8	3.5
Phoenix, AZ	74.6	12.5	3.0	0.1	0.1	0.7	1.7	2.0	5.4
Pittsburgh, PA	55.8	8.5	16.3	0.5	0.0	2.0	11.1	1.3	4.6
Portland, OR	57.7	8.9	9.6	1.1	0.3	6.5	5.7	2.6	7.6
Providence, RI	62.9	11.3	5.5	0.1	1.2	1.2	10.7	1.5	5.4
Provo, UT	62.7	12.8	1.5	0.2	1.3	2.6	12.5	1.6	4.8
Raleigh, NC	78.5	8.9	1.9	0.1	0.0	0.4	1.8	1.3	7.1
Reno, NV	76.3	11.5	2.3	0.0	0.0	0.8	3.9	1.4	3.9
Richmond, VA	70.7	10.4	5.1	0.1	0.1	1.9	5.7	1.9	4.2
Roanoke, VA	78.8	9.3	3.5	0.1	0.0	0.7	3.3	1.7	2.6
Rochester, MN	71.7	11.7	6.7	0.0	0.0	1.1	4.3	0.8	3.7
Salem, OR	73.7	13.2	2.6	0.0	0.1	1.1	3.5	1.0	4.8
Salt Lake City, UT	67.7	11.4	4.8	0.3	0.6	2.6	5.4	2.4	4.7
San Antonio, TX	79.0	11.1	3.1	0.0	0.0	0.2	1.7	1.3	3.7
San Diego, CA	74.9	8.6	3.7	0.0	0.1	1.0	3.1	1.6	7.1
San Francisco, CA	34.3	6.8	22.0	8.3	1.5	3.9	11.1	5.4	6.7
San Jose, CA	75.9	11.7	2.8	0.2	1.2	0.9	1.7	1.4	4.1
Santa Rosa, CA	77.3	10.7	1.8	0.0	0.0	1.3	2.2	1.3	5.4
Savannah, GA	73.6	10.1	4.2	0.1	0.0	2.1	4.2	2.0	3.7
Seattle, WA	48.8	7.6	20.0	0.9	0.1	3.5	10.2	1.8	7.0
Sioux Falls, SD	83.9	8.8	1.0	0.0	0.0	0.5	2.0	0.9	3.0
Springfield, IL	81.9	7.9	2.2	0.1	0.0	0.5	2.5	1.2	3.6
Tallahassee, FL	79.4	8.9	2.3	0.0	0.0	0.9	3.3	1.5	3.7
Tampa, FL	78.1	8.4	2.4	0.0	0.0	1.3	2.4	1.3	6.1
Topeka, KS	81.4	10.8	1.2	0.0	0.0	0.3	2.4	1.5	2.4
Tyler, TX	82.6	9.8	0.4	0.0	0.0	0.5	1.3	2.2	3.2
Virginia Beach, VA	82.1	8.4	0.8	0.0	0.0	0.6	2.7	1.5	3.8
Visalia, CA	80.9	11.3	1.0	0.0	0.0	1.2	1.1	1.0	3.6
Washington, DC	34.0	5.4	14.2	20.7	0.3	4.6	13.2	1.9	5.7
Wilmington, NC	79.0	7.2	1.7	0.0	0.0	1.2	2.6	1.2	7.0
Winston-Salem, NC	82.9	7.5	1.5	0.0	0.0	0.2	2.3	1.0	4.6
U.S.	76.4	9.2	2.5	1.9	0.6	0.6	2.7	1.3	4.7

Note: Figures are percentages and cover workers 16 years of age and older
Source: U.S. Census Bureau, 2013-2017 American Community Survey 5-Year Estimates

Means of Transportation to Work: Metro Area

Metro Area	Car/Truck/Van		Public Transportation			Bicycle	Walked	Other Means	Worked at Home
	Drove Alone	Car-pooled	Bus	Subway	Railroad				
Albany, NY	80.1	7.7	3.3	0.1	0.1	0.3	3.5	0.9	4.1
Albuquerque, NM	80.4	9.1	1.4	0.0	0.3	1.0	1.8	1.3	4.8
Allentown, PA	81.8	8.5	1.7	0.1	0.1	0.2	2.5	1.1	4.2
Anchorage, AK	75.1	11.7	1.5	0.0	0.0	1.0	3.1	3.2	4.3
Ann Arbor, MI	72.2	7.7	5.1	0.0	0.0	1.7	6.5	0.7	5.9
Athens, GA	78.4	9.8	2.8	0.0	0.0	0.8	2.6	1.1	4.4
Atlanta, GA	77.6	9.8	2.1	0.8	0.1	0.2	1.3	1.5	6.5
Austin, TX	76.6	9.6	2.1	0.0	0.1	0.8	1.7	1.2	7.8
Baton Rouge, LA	84.7	8.9	0.9	0.0	0.0	0.3	1.4	0.9	2.8
Billings, MT	80.4	9.9	0.7	0.0	0.0	0.5	3.0	0.9	4.6
Boise City, ID	79.7	8.9	0.4	0.0	0.0	1.3	1.7	1.2	6.9
Boston, MA	67.2	7.1	4.2	6.5	2.1	1.0	5.3	1.6	5.0
Boulder, CO	64.7	7.9	4.7	0.0	0.0	4.5	5.1	1.2	11.8
Cape Coral, FL	79.9	9.7	0.8	0.0	0.0	0.6	1.0	2.3	5.6
Cedar Rapids, IA	84.4	8.3	0.6	0.0	0.0	0.3	2.1	0.7	3.6
Charleston, SC	81.1	8.3	1.1	0.0	0.0	0.8	2.5	1.1	5.2
Charlotte, NC	80.9	9.3	1.3	0.2	0.1	0.1	1.4	1.1	5.7
Chicago, IL	70.5	7.8	4.5	4.1	3.2	0.7	3.1	1.3	4.7
Clarksville, TN	84.5	7.3	0.8	0.0	0.0	0.1	3.4	1.5	2.4
College Station, TX	78.1	11.5	2.1	0.0	0.0	1.6	2.4	1.0	3.3
Colorado Springs, CO	77.5	10.5	0.8	0.0	0.0	0.5	3.3	1.1	6.4
Columbia, MO	77.7	11.0	1.1	0.0	0.0	0.9	3.9	1.2	4.2
Columbia, SC	81.0	8.3	0.6	0.0	0.0	0.1	4.5	2.1	3.4
Columbus, OH	82.7	7.6	1.6	0.0	0.0	0.4	2.1	0.9	4.6
Dallas, TX	80.7	9.8	0.9	0.2	0.3	0.2	1.3	1.4	5.2
Denver, CO	75.8	8.4	3.2	0.6	0.3	0.8	2.1	1.2	7.6
Des Moines, IA	83.9	8.0	1.1	0.0	0.0	0.2	1.9	0.7	4.2
Durham, NC	75.0	9.6	4.0	0.0	0.0	0.8	3.2	1.1	6.1
Edison, NJ	50.0	6.5	7.7	19.3	3.8	0.6	5.9	1.8	4.3
El Paso, TX	79.7	11.0	1.5	0.0	0.0	0.2	2.0	2.1	3.5
Eugene, OR	71.1	10.2	3.0	0.0	0.0	3.8	5.0	1.0	5.9
Evansville, IN	86.4	7.3	1.0	0.0	0.0	0.1	1.7	1.0	2.5
Fargo, ND	82.0	8.4	0.9	0.0	0.0	0.6	3.0	0.9	4.1
Fayetteville, NC	80.8	8.8	0.6	0.0	0.0	0.1	5.1	1.1	3.4
Fort Collins, CO	75.0	8.8	1.2	0.0	0.0	3.7	2.5	1.2	7.5
Fort Wayne, IN	84.8	8.4	0.7	0.0	0.0	0.3	1.2	0.7	3.9
Fort Worth, TX	80.7	9.8	0.9	0.2	0.3	0.2	1.3	1.4	5.2
Gainesville, FL	74.7	9.2	3.9	0.0	0.0	2.5	3.2	1.9	4.5
Grand Rapids, MI	81.9	9.0	1.5	0.0	0.0	0.5	2.2	0.9	4.1
Greeley, CO	80.0	10.6	0.6	0.0	0.0	0.3	2.1	0.9	5.5
Green Bay, WI	83.3	8.0	0.6	0.0	0.0	0.3	2.3	1.2	4.3
Greensboro, NC	83.4	8.9	0.8	0.0	0.0	0.1	1.2	0.8	4.7
Honolulu, HI	64.0	14.3	8.5	0.0	0.0	1.2	5.4	2.9	3.7
Houston, TX	80.4	10.4	2.1	0.0	0.0	0.3	1.4	1.4	3.9
Huntsville, AL	87.9	6.6	0.2	0.0	0.0	0.1	0.8	1.2	3.3
Indianapolis, IN	83.9	8.1	0.9	0.0	0.0	0.3	1.5	0.9	4.3
Jacksonville, FL	81.0	8.9	1.3	0.0	0.0	0.5	1.5	1.5	5.3
Kansas City, MO	83.5	8.2	1.0	0.0	0.0	0.2	1.3	0.9	4.9
Lafayette, LA	83.2	9.9	0.5	0.0	0.0	0.4	2.0	1.4	2.6
Las Cruces, NM	81.1	10.4	0.4	0.0	0.0	0.8	2.2	0.9	4.2
Las Vegas, NV	78.9	9.9	3.7	0.0	0.0	0.4	1.6	1.9	3.6
Lexington, KY	79.7	9.6	1.4	0.0	0.0	0.5	3.2	1.2	4.4
Lincoln, NE	81.8	8.8	1.1	0.0	0.0	1.2	3.0	0.7	3.4
Little Rock, AR	84.1	9.6	0.5	0.0	0.0	0.2	1.3	1.0	3.3

Table continued on next page.

Metro Area	Car/Truck/Van		Public Transportation			Bicycle	Walked	Other Means	Worked at Home
	Drove Alone	Car-pooled	Bus	Subway	Railroad				
Los Angeles, CA	74.9	9.6	4.5	0.4	0.3	0.9	2.5	1.5	5.4
Louisville, KY	82.5	8.7	1.8	0.0	0.0	0.2	1.6	1.2	3.9
Madison, WI	74.1	8.2	4.5	0.0	0.0	2.3	5.1	0.9	4.8
Manchester, NH	81.5	8.4	0.7	0.0	0.1	0.2	2.2	0.8	6.1
McAllen, TX	80.4	8.8	0.2	0.0	0.0	0.2	1.2	4.3	4.9
Miami, FL	78.2	9.1	3.2	0.3	0.2	0.6	1.7	1.5	5.2
Midland, TX	84.9	9.9	0.2	0.0	0.0	0.0	0.9	1.6	2.4
Minneapolis, MN	77.7	8.2	4.3	0.2	0.2	0.9	2.2	1.0	5.3
Nashville, TN	81.8	9.3	1.0	0.0	0.1	0.1	1.3	1.1	5.4
New Orleans, LA	78.6	9.9	2.5	0.0	0.0	1.2	2.4	1.7	3.6
New York, NY	50.0	6.5	7.7	19.3	3.8	0.6	5.9	1.8	4.3
Oklahoma City, OK	83.3	9.9	0.4	0.0	0.0	0.3	1.5	0.9	3.7
Omaha, NE	84.0	8.4	0.9	0.0	0.0	0.2	1.8	1.0	3.7
Orlando, FL	80.2	9.6	1.7	0.0	0.1	0.4	1.0	1.4	5.5
Peoria, IL	84.7	7.6	1.4	0.0	0.0	0.3	2.1	0.9	3.0
Philadelphia, PA	73.1	7.5	5.3	1.8	2.4	0.7	3.7	1.1	4.5
Phoenix, AZ	76.6	11.0	1.9	0.0	0.0	0.8	1.5	1.8	6.3
Pittsburgh, PA	77.4	8.2	4.9	0.2	0.0	0.4	3.4	1.1	4.4
Portland, OR	70.4	9.7	4.8	0.7	0.2	2.4	3.3	1.7	6.8
Providence, RI	80.5	8.6	1.6	0.1	0.9	0.3	3.3	0.9	3.7
Provo, UT	73.2	11.8	0.8	0.2	0.8	1.1	4.1	1.3	6.7
Raleigh, NC	80.2	8.8	0.9	0.0	0.0	0.2	1.2	1.0	7.7
Reno, NV	77.9	11.2	1.9	0.0	0.0	0.6	2.8	1.3	4.3
Richmond, VA	81.6	8.6	1.4	0.0	0.1	0.4	1.9	1.3	4.8
Roanoke, VA	82.6	8.4	1.3	0.0	0.0	0.3	2.2	1.0	4.1
Rochester, MN	74.6	11.0	4.4	0.0	0.0	0.7	3.6	0.8	4.9
Salem, OR	75.6	12.9	1.5	0.0	0.0	0.7	3.1	1.1	5.0
Salt Lake City, UT	75.1	11.8	2.3	0.4	0.6	0.8	2.2	1.5	5.5
San Antonio, TX	79.7	10.7	2.1	0.0	0.0	0.2	1.6	1.2	4.5
San Diego, CA	76.0	8.9	2.6	0.0	0.2	0.7	2.9	1.7	7.0
San Francisco, CA	58.8	9.7	7.6	7.2	1.2	1.9	4.7	2.7	6.3
San Jose, CA	75.2	10.6	2.5	0.2	1.4	1.8	2.1	1.4	4.8
Santa Rosa, CA	75.0	11.0	1.8	0.1	0.0	1.0	3.1	1.1	6.9
Savannah, GA	80.4	9.3	2.0	0.0	0.0	0.9	2.2	1.6	3.7
Seattle, WA	68.7	9.9	8.6	0.3	0.5	1.1	3.8	1.3	5.8
Sioux Falls, SD	84.3	8.1	0.7	0.0	0.0	0.3	2.0	0.8	3.8
Springfield, IL	83.3	7.8	1.4	0.1	0.0	0.4	2.0	1.1	3.9
Tallahassee, FL	81.4	9.5	1.3	0.0	0.0	0.6	2.1	1.3	3.7
Tampa, FL	80.0	8.5	1.3	0.0	0.0	0.8	1.4	1.5	6.5
Topeka, KS	83.0	9.8	0.7	0.0	0.0	0.2	1.8	1.1	3.3
Tyler, TX	83.7	9.5	0.2	0.0	0.0	0.3	1.0	1.9	3.4
Virginia Beach, VA	81.6	8.3	1.5	0.1	0.0	0.5	3.4	1.4	3.4
Visalia, CA	78.0	14.3	0.6	0.0	0.0	0.6	1.7	1.7	3.1
Washington, DC	66.0	9.5	5.1	7.9	0.8	0.9	3.3	1.2	5.4
Wilmington, NC	80.4	8.4	0.8	0.0	0.0	0.7	1.6	1.3	6.8
Winston-Salem, NC	84.3	8.4	0.7	0.0	0.0	0.1	1.4	0.9	4.3
U.S.	76.4	9.2	2.5	1.9	0.6	0.6	2.7	1.3	4.7

Note: Figures are percentages and cover workers 16 years of age and older; (1) Figures cover the Metropolitan Statistical Area—see Appendix B for areas included
Source: U.S. Census Bureau, 2013-2017 American Community Survey 5-Year Estimates

Travel Time to Work: City

City	Less Than 10 Minutes	10 to 19 Minutes	20 to 29 Minutes	30 to 44 Minutes	45 to 59 Minutes	60 to 89 Minutes	90 Minutes or More
Albany, NY	16.0	44.8	22.6	10.8	3.1	1.7	1.1
Albuquerque, NM	11.4	37.2	27.4	17.3	3.1	2.4	1.3
Allentown, PA	11.7	34.1	27.2	15.6	4.6	4.1	2.7
Anchorage, AK	16.2	45.5	22.5	10.3	2.7	1.3	1.6
Ann Arbor, MI	13.8	44.1	19.7	13.8	4.8	2.9	0.9
Athens, GA	16.1	48.8	16.9	9.3	3.9	3.2	1.9
Atlanta, GA	7.2	29.6	27.8	20.5	7.2	4.9	2.8
Austin, TX	9.6	33.0	24.2	21.4	6.6	3.7	1.5
Baton Rouge, LA	11.0	37.7	28.2	14.8	3.6	3.2	1.4
Billings, MT	17.5	53.8	20.0	4.9	1.3	1.3	1.1
Boise City, ID	14.9	45.1	24.9	11.0	1.7	1.3	1.0
Boston, MA	7.2	19.9	20.4	29.4	11.3	9.6	2.3
Boulder, CO	18.9	45.9	16.6	10.3	4.7	2.5	1.1
Cape Coral, FL	7.4	24.5	23.9	27.5	9.6	4.9	2.2
Cedar Rapids, IA	17.9	49.3	18.1	9.7	2.1	1.9	1.0
Charleston, SC	12.4	33.3	25.2	21.0	5.3	1.8	1.2
Charlotte, NC	9.1	29.2	25.7	23.8	6.9	3.4	1.8
Chicago, IL	4.8	16.4	17.9	30.1	14.7	12.6	3.6
Clarksville, TN	11.7	34.3	25.2	16.5	5.0	6.1	1.2
College Station, TX	18.5	54.6	18.2	5.8	0.7	1.3	1.0
Colorado Springs, CO	12.2	37.5	27.5	15.1	3.2	2.7	2.0
Columbia, MO	20.6	53.8	12.9	7.6	2.9	1.1	1.0
Columbia, SC	32.9	36.9	16.2	9.7	1.6	1.7	1.0
Columbus, OH	10.2	34.9	30.0	18.4	3.7	1.8	1.0
Dallas, TX	8.6	26.8	22.9	26.0	8.1	5.5	2.0
Denver, CO	8.7	29.4	24.4	24.6	7.3	4.1	1.6
Des Moines, IA	14.0	43.8	25.7	11.8	2.2	1.4	1.0
Durham, NC	10.0	38.7	25.6	16.9	3.9	3.0	1.8
Edison, NJ	7.2	24.1	17.6	17.7	10.7	13.3	9.4
El Paso, TX	9.4	35.2	27.6	20.0	4.0	2.3	1.6
Eugene, OR	17.5	49.5	19.7	7.4	1.4	3.0	1.4
Evansville, IN	17.5	46.7	17.7	11.8	3.2	2.0	1.1
Fargo, ND	20.8	55.7	16.9	3.6	0.9	1.3	0.7
Fayetteville, NC	19.1	40.6	22.8	11.0	3.2	2.1	1.2
Fort Collins, CO	16.5	45.0	19.4	10.4	4.4	3.2	1.1
Fort Wayne, IN	13.2	39.9	27.5	12.3	3.3	2.0	1.7
Fort Worth, TX	8.9	28.2	22.3	23.3	9.0	6.3	2.0
Gainesville, FL	14.8	51.3	20.2	9.4	2.0	1.4	1.0
Grand Rapids, MI	16.0	42.0	24.2	11.4	3.0	2.3	1.2
Greeley, CO	17.8	38.4	16.0	13.9	5.4	6.4	2.1
Green Bay, WI	18.1	48.4	19.0	7.5	3.8	1.8	1.4
Greensboro, NC	11.4	43.3	24.3	14.2	3.1	2.2	1.6
Honolulu, HI	8.3	35.0	23.4	22.3	5.8	4.0	1.2
Houston, TX	7.9	26.3	22.5	27.0	8.4	6.1	1.7
Huntsville, AL	13.5	42.4	26.4	14.0	1.9	0.8	1.1
Indianapolis, IN	10.5	30.0	30.4	21.0	4.2	2.5	1.4
Jacksonville, FL	8.9	28.2	28.8	23.9	5.8	2.7	1.7
Kansas City, MO	11.5	33.7	28.3	19.2	4.6	1.7	1.0
Lafayette, LA	16.4	43.2	19.9	12.0	2.1	2.9	3.5
Las Cruces, NM	20.3	47.8	15.7	8.8	3.0	3.5	0.9
Las Vegas, NV	7.2	25.5	29.6	27.5	5.6	2.6	1.9
Lexington, KY	12.7	38.8	26.7	14.5	3.5	2.5	1.3
Lincoln, NE	16.5	45.5	22.7	9.7	2.7	2.1	0.8
Little Rock, AR	13.5	43.1	28.6	10.6	1.9	1.1	1.2
Los Angeles, CA	6.4	22.8	19.7	27.6	10.3	9.6	3.5

Table continued on next page.

City	Less Than 10 Minutes	10 to 19 Minutes	20 to 29 Minutes	30 to 44 Minutes	45 to 59 Minutes	60 to 89 Minutes	90 Minutes or More
Louisville, KY	9.6	32.8	30.0	20.1	4.1	2.3	1.2
Madison, WI	15.0	41.0	23.8	14.6	3.0	2.0	0.7
Manchester, NH	15.0	38.5	19.5	13.9	5.5	4.4	3.2
McAllen, TX	15.8	42.7	23.4	12.7	2.2	1.3	1.9
Miami, FL	5.9	23.8	23.4	29.2	9.0	6.7	2.1
Midland, TX	16.8	48.6	17.6	10.7	2.6	2.0	1.7
Minneapolis, MN	8.4	33.0	30.2	20.1	4.2	3.0	1.2
Nashville, TN	8.5	29.3	27.8	23.3	6.2	3.4	1.4
New Orleans, LA	9.7	33.6	25.3	20.4	4.6	4.5	1.9
New York, NY	4.0	12.6	13.5	27.5	16.2	18.9	7.2
Oklahoma City, OK	11.5	36.1	29.3	17.1	2.8	1.5	1.6
Omaha, NE	14.5	41.3	27.7	12.3	2.1	1.3	0.8
Orlando, FL	7.9	28.5	26.8	24.9	6.3	3.5	2.2
Peoria, IL	17.6	48.3	20.8	8.1	2.2	2.1	1.0
Philadelphia, PA	6.0	19.4	20.0	28.2	12.1	10.2	4.1
Phoenix, AZ	9.2	28.0	25.0	24.7	7.2	4.1	1.8
Pittsburgh, PA	9.9	32.7	25.1	21.9	5.4	3.4	1.6
Portland, OR	8.0	27.7	27.2	23.2	7.1	5.0	1.9
Providence, RI	14.1	41.4	18.9	12.5	5.0	4.8	3.3
Provo, UT	22.8	45.6	16.4	8.6	2.6	2.6	1.5
Raleigh, NC	10.8	33.2	26.1	20.3	5.3	2.5	1.9
Reno, NV	15.3	45.0	21.9	10.7	3.5	2.4	1.3
Richmond, VA	10.9	37.6	28.1	16.1	2.7	2.4	2.2
Roanoke, VA	13.2	43.5	16.3	19.7	3.5	2.6	1.2
Rochester, MN	19.7	56.6	12.5	6.2	2.2	1.7	1.2
Salem, OR	14.0	42.5	20.6	11.4	5.3	4.6	1.7
Salt Lake City, UT	13.0	44.5	23.6	12.1	3.8	2.0	1.0
San Antonio, TX	9.1	31.4	27.3	21.6	5.7	3.0	1.9
San Diego, CA	7.9	32.6	28.4	21.3	5.0	3.0	1.8
San Francisco, CA	4.1	18.9	21.2	29.7	11.9	11.0	3.3
San Jose, CA	5.5	23.9	23.8	26.7	9.9	7.6	2.6
Santa Rosa, CA	14.4	41.6	19.2	13.4	4.0	4.5	2.9
Savannah, GA	17.7	38.1	21.8	14.4	4.1	2.6	1.3
Seattle, WA	7.1	24.3	24.6	27.6	9.9	5.1	1.5
Sioux Falls, SD	17.0	52.1	21.6	5.2	1.6	1.6	1.0
Springfield, IL	19.1	50.0	19.1	5.7	2.2	2.4	1.4
Tallahassee, FL	15.5	45.2	23.4	11.4	1.8	1.6	1.0
Tampa, FL	12.0	31.1	24.2	20.8	6.4	3.8	1.7
Topeka, KS	18.4	54.4	14.5	7.5	1.6	2.5	1.0
Tyler, TX	17.9	41.7	18.9	13.2	3.8	2.5	2.0
Virginia Beach, VA	10.7	30.3	27.7	21.5	5.7	2.6	1.5
Visalia, CA	16.8	42.9	17.2	12.4	6.0	2.9	1.8
Washington, DC	5.4	19.6	23.0	31.7	11.6	6.6	2.0
Wilmington, NC	16.1	47.9	21.6	8.4	2.6	1.7	1.6
Winston-Salem, NC	13.5	43.9	22.3	12.8	3.4	2.2	1.9
U.S.	12.7	28.9	20.9	20.5	8.1	6.2	2.7

Note: Figures are percentages and include workers 16 years old and over
Source: U.S. Census Bureau, 2013-2017 American Community Survey 5-Year Estimates

Travel Time to Work: Metro Area

Metro Area	Less Than 10 Minutes	10 to 19 Minutes	20 to 29 Minutes	30 to 44 Minutes	45 to 59 Minutes	60 to 89 Minutes	90 Minutes or More
Albany, NY	12.7	32.1	24.7	20.4	6.1	2.5	1.4
Albuquerque, NM	11.4	32.5	25.4	20.1	5.7	3.2	1.7
Allentown, PA	12.6	28.1	22.1	18.6	7.5	7.2	4.0
Anchorage, AK	15.6	41.5	21.0	10.5	4.6	4.4	2.4
Ann Arbor, MI	11.2	33.5	24.1	19.0	6.9	4.1	1.2
Athens, GA	13.4	41.4	21.2	13.5	4.8	3.5	2.1
Atlanta, GA	7.3	22.8	20.0	24.4	12.2	9.9	3.5
Austin, TX	9.8	28.0	22.2	22.7	9.6	5.8	1.9
Baton Rouge, LA	9.9	27.5	22.9	22.1	9.3	6.1	2.2
Billings, MT	16.9	46.2	22.2	8.8	2.3	2.0	1.6
Boise City, ID	12.6	34.4	25.8	19.6	4.3	2.2	1.2
Boston, MA	9.3	22.6	18.4	24.2	11.8	10.4	3.3
Boulder, CO	15.0	35.2	21.5	16.4	6.5	4.0	1.4
Cape Coral, FL	8.6	26.3	22.5	26.1	9.7	4.6	2.2
Cedar Rapids, IA	17.9	40.3	21.7	13.3	3.5	2.0	1.2
Charleston, SC	9.9	27.0	24.4	25.0	8.2	4.1	1.5
Charlotte, NC	9.8	28.0	22.7	23.8	9.1	4.7	1.9
Chicago, IL	8.5	21.9	18.5	24.9	12.3	10.6	3.3
Clarksville, TN	15.6	32.5	21.8	17.2	5.8	5.5	1.5
College Station, TX	18.4	46.5	18.9	10.3	2.4	2.0	1.4
Colorado Springs, CO	12.1	33.5	26.6	17.4	4.9	3.3	2.1
Columbia, MO	17.2	48.6	18.4	10.2	3.5	1.2	0.9
Columbia, SC	13.3	29.6	24.1	21.5	6.5	3.2	1.7
Columbus, OH	11.2	30.4	26.5	21.4	6.3	3.0	1.3
Dallas, TX	9.1	25.4	21.1	25.1	10.5	6.7	2.0
Denver, CO	8.5	25.3	23.3	25.8	9.7	5.6	1.8
Des Moines, IA	15.4	36.3	27.0	15.5	3.1	1.5	1.2
Durham, NC	10.2	33.9	24.6	20.0	6.0	3.6	1.6
Edison, NJ	7.2	19.0	16.3	23.7	12.4	14.7	6.7
El Paso, TX	10.3	33.0	26.6	21.2	4.7	2.5	1.7
Eugene, OR	16.4	41.7	22.6	12.5	2.2	2.9	1.8
Evansville, IN	15.5	37.5	23.8	15.3	4.2	2.4	1.3
Fargo, ND	19.5	50.3	18.7	7.4	1.7	1.5	0.9
Fayetteville, NC	15.5	34.4	25.2	16.6	4.4	2.4	1.5
Fort Collins, CO	14.9	36.3	21.9	14.2	5.9	5.0	1.7
Fort Wayne, IN	13.8	35.6	27.9	15.3	3.9	1.9	1.7
Fort Worth, TX	9.1	25.4	21.1	25.1	10.5	6.7	2.0
Gainesville, FL	10.6	39.0	25.3	16.4	4.8	2.5	1.4
Grand Rapids, MI	15.2	34.8	24.9	16.3	4.7	2.5	1.6
Greeley, CO	12.8	27.9	19.5	21.9	8.8	7.0	2.2
Green Bay, WI	17.9	39.4	22.0	12.9	4.3	2.1	1.5
Greensboro, NC	11.6	36.4	25.3	17.7	4.9	2.4	1.7
Honolulu, HI	9.2	24.5	19.6	25.4	9.9	8.5	3.0
Houston, TX	8.0	23.9	19.6	25.9	11.5	8.7	2.4
Huntsville, AL	10.5	32.6	28.4	21.0	5.0	1.5	1.1
Indianapolis, IN	11.9	27.7	24.8	23.4	7.1	3.6	1.5
Jacksonville, FL	9.3	25.7	25.4	24.8	8.6	4.3	1.9
Kansas City, MO	12.6	30.9	25.1	21.2	6.6	2.4	1.1
Lafayette, LA	16.1	32.8	20.0	18.2	4.8	3.5	4.5
Las Cruces, NM	16.0	40.0	21.1	13.7	4.6	3.4	1.2
Las Vegas, NV	7.8	28.3	29.8	25.0	4.9	2.5	1.8
Lexington, KY	14.5	35.1	24.5	17.8	4.5	2.3	1.3
Lincoln, NE	16.7	42.5	23.4	11.6	3.0	2.0	0.9
Little Rock, AR	12.7	32.3	24.6	19.4	6.7	3.0	1.2
Los Angeles, CA	7.4	25.1	20.0	25.1	9.9	9.2	3.4

Table continued on next page.

Metro Area	Less Than 10 Minutes	10 to 19 Minutes	20 to 29 Minutes	30 to 44 Minutes	45 to 59 Minutes	60 to 89 Minutes	90 Minutes or More
Louisville, KY	10.2	30.3	26.8	22.4	6.2	2.8	1.4
Madison, WI	16.3	32.6	24.0	18.5	5.0	2.5	1.1
Manchester, NH	12.1	28.8	20.2	19.3	8.6	7.4	3.6
McAllen, TX	13.8	38.6	25.1	15.8	2.6	2.0	2.1
Miami, FL	6.9	23.7	22.6	27.2	9.9	7.3	2.4
Midland, TX	16.6	45.1	19.0	12.3	2.8	2.5	1.7
Minneapolis, MN	10.5	27.6	24.9	23.3	8.1	4.3	1.3
Nashville, TN	9.4	26.8	22.3	23.4	10.0	6.2	1.9
New Orleans, LA	10.6	30.6	22.3	21.1	7.3	5.6	2.5
New York, NY	7.2	19.0	16.3	23.7	12.4	14.7	6.7
Oklahoma City, OK	13.0	32.5	25.6	19.9	5.2	2.3	1.6
Omaha, NE	14.3	36.7	27.0	15.9	3.5	1.6	1.0
Orlando, FL	7.2	24.2	23.5	27.7	10.2	4.9	2.2
Peoria, IL	17.1	35.8	24.8	15.4	3.6	1.8	1.5
Philadelphia, PA	9.6	24.2	20.5	23.8	10.7	8.2	3.1
Phoenix, AZ	10.0	26.9	23.7	23.7	8.8	5.1	1.6
Pittsburgh, PA	12.0	27.1	21.2	22.3	9.4	5.9	2.0
Portland, OR	10.6	27.6	22.7	22.6	8.8	5.6	2.1
Providence, RI	12.4	30.9	21.9	19.0	7.0	5.7	3.0
Provo, UT	18.9	36.1	19.6	14.8	5.4	3.5	1.6
Raleigh, NC	9.7	27.7	25.1	23.7	8.0	4.0	1.8
Reno, NV	12.3	39.5	25.4	14.9	3.8	2.5	1.6
Richmond, VA	9.2	29.5	27.3	22.5	6.1	3.2	2.2
Roanoke, VA	11.8	33.5	21.3	22.7	5.4	3.7	1.6
Rochester, MN	19.0	42.2	18.5	12.4	3.8	2.4	1.6
Salem, OR	15.6	33.4	22.2	15.4	6.4	5.1	1.9
Salt Lake City, UT	10.9	32.9	27.7	19.6	5.3	2.5	1.1
San Antonio, TX	9.5	28.8	24.6	22.6	8.1	4.3	2.2
San Diego, CA	8.8	29.8	25.0	22.7	7.1	4.5	2.2
San Francisco, CA	6.8	22.9	18.1	23.9	12.1	11.9	4.3
San Jose, CA	7.2	26.1	24.2	24.0	8.9	7.0	2.7
Santa Rosa, CA	15.7	32.5	19.6	16.8	5.7	6.0	3.6
Savannah, GA	11.9	30.7	24.0	21.3	6.7	4.0	1.4
Seattle, WA	8.0	23.3	21.3	25.1	10.9	8.4	3.1
Sioux Falls, SD	17.0	43.7	24.5	9.8	2.3	1.6	1.2
Springfield, IL	16.5	41.0	23.7	11.6	3.2	2.6	1.5
Tallahassee, FL	11.8	34.1	24.2	20.5	5.4	2.5	1.5
Tampa, FL	10.0	27.4	22.0	22.8	9.5	6.1	2.1
Topeka, KS	16.5	42.5	19.2	13.5	3.8	3.0	1.5
Tyler, TX	13.1	32.8	24.2	19.1	5.0	2.9	2.8
Virginia Beach, VA	11.3	31.1	24.4	20.9	7.0	3.7	1.7
Visalia, CA	17.8	35.1	18.6	16.1	6.2	3.9	2.2
Washington, DC	6.0	19.2	17.8	25.8	13.9	12.8	4.5
Wilmington, NC	12.6	38.8	24.0	15.6	4.8	2.4	1.9
Winston-Salem, NC	12.0	34.3	24.6	18.5	5.7	3.1	1.9
U.S.	12.7	28.9	20.9	20.5	8.1	6.2	2.7

Note: Figures are percentages and include workers 16 years old and over; Figures cover the Metropolitan Statistical Area—see Appendix B for areas included
Source: U.S. Census Bureau, 2013-2017 American Community Survey 5-Year Estimates

2016 Presidential Election Results

City	Area Covered	Clinton	Trump	Johnson	Stein	Other
Albany, NY	Albany County	59.4	34.2	3.4	1.8	1.2
Albuquerque, NM	Bernalillo County	52.2	34.5	10.8	1.3	1.2
Allentown, PA	Lehigh County	50.0	45.3	2.5	0.9	1.4
Anchorage, AK	State of Alaska	36.6	51.3	5.9	1.8	4.4
Ann Arbor, MI	Washtenaw County	67.6	26.6	3.1	1.3	1.4
Athens, GA	Clarke County	65.1	28.0	4.4	0.7	1.8
Atlanta, GA	Fulton County	67.7	26.8	3.6	0.1	1.8
Austin, TX	Travis County	65.8	27.1	4.7	1.6	0.8
Baton Rouge, LA	East Baton Rouge Parish	52.3	43.1	2.5	0.8	1.2
Billings, MT	Yellowstone County	31.5	58.1	6.1	1.3	3.1
Boise City, ID	Ada County	38.7	47.9	5.1	1.6	6.7
Boston, MA	Suffolk County	78.4	16.1	2.6	1.4	1.5
Boulder, CO	Boulder County	70.3	22.0	4.3	2.0	1.4
Cape Coral, FL	Lee County	37.9	58.1	2.1	0.6	1.2
Cedar Rapids, IA	Linn County	50.3	41.3	4.7	0.9	2.7
Charleston, SC	Charleston County	50.6	42.8	4.1	1.0	1.5
Charlotte, NC	Mecklenburg County	62.3	32.9	3.3	0.3	1.3
Chicago, IL	Cook County	73.9	20.8	2.7	1.5	1.1
Clarksville, TN	Montgomery County	37.7	56.1	4.1	0.9	1.2
College Station, TX	Brazos County	34.4	57.6	5.7	0.8	1.5
Colorado Springs, CO	El Paso County	33.9	56.2	6.2	1.3	2.4
Columbia, MO	Boone County	49.0	43.2	5.1	1.5	1.2
Columbia, SC	Richland County	64.0	31.1	2.3	0.8	1.7
Columbus, OH	Franklin County	59.8	33.9	3.4	1.0	1.9
Dallas, TX	Dallas County	60.2	34.3	3.1	0.8	1.5
Denver, CO	Denver County	73.7	18.9	4.5	1.7	1.3
Des Moines, IA	Polk County	51.7	40.4	4.3	0.8	2.8
Durham, NC	Durham County	77.7	18.2	2.6	0.3	1.3
Edison, NJ	Middlesex County	58.8	37.4	1.7	1.1	1.1
El Paso, TX	El Paso County	68.5	25.7	3.5	1.4	0.9
Eugene, OR	Lane County	53.5	35.0	4.4	3.3	3.8
Evansville, IN	Vanderburgh County	38.9	55.2	4.4	0.3	1.2
Fargo, ND	Cass County	38.8	49.3	7.5	1.5	2.9
Fayetteville, NC	Cumberland County	56.2	40.2	2.6	0.1	0.9
Fort Collins, CO	Larimer County	47.5	42.6	5.9	1.6	2.4
Fort Wayne, IN	Allen County	37.3	56.5	4.6	0.5	1.2
Fort Worth, TX	Tarrant County	43.1	51.7	3.6	0.8	0.7
Gainesville, FL	Alachua County	58.3	36.0	3.1	1.2	1.4
Grand Rapids, MI	Kent County	44.6	47.7	4.6	1.3	1.9
Greeley, CO	Weld County	34.3	56.6	5.5	1.0	2.5
Green Bay, WI	Brown County	41.4	52.1	3.9	1.1	1.6
Greensboro, NC	Guilford County	58.0	38.1	2.6	0.3	1.0
Honolulu, HI	Honolulu County	61.5	31.6	3.7	2.3	1.0
Houston, TX	Harris County	54.0	41.6	3.0	0.9	0.5
Huntsville, AL	Madison County	38.4	54.8	4.1	0.8	1.9
Indianapolis, IN	Marion County	58.0	35.5	5.0	0.2	1.3
Jacksonville, FL	Duval County	47.1	48.5	2.6	0.7	1.1
Kansas City, MO	Jackson County	55.5	38.1	3.6	1.2	1.7
Lafayette, LA	Lafayette Parish	31.0	64.6	2.7	0.8	0.9
Las Cruces, NM	Dona Ana County	53.7	35.9	7.7	1.3	1.3
Las Vegas, NV	Clark County	52.4	41.7	2.9	0.0	2.9
Lexington, KY	Fayette County	51.2	41.7	3.8	1.2	2.1
Lincoln, NE	Lancaster County	45.4	45.2	5.2	1.4	2.7
Little Rock, AR	Pulaski County	56.1	38.3	2.7	1.0	1.9
Los Angeles, CA	Los Angeles County	71.8	22.4	2.6	2.2	1.0
Louisville, KY	Jefferson County	54.0	40.7	2.9	0.9	1.4

Table continued on next page.

City	Area Covered	Clinton	Trump	Johnson	Stein	Other
Madison, WI	Dane County	70.4	23.0	3.4	1.4	1.8
Manchester, NH	Hillsborough County	46.5	46.7	4.3	0.8	1.7
McAllen, TX	Hidalgo County	68.1	27.9	2.2	1.1	0.8
Miami, FL	Miami-Dade County	63.2	33.8	1.3	0.6	1.0
Midland, TX	Midland County	20.4	75.1	3.4	0.4	0.7
Minneapolis, MN	Hennepin County	63.1	28.2	3.6	1.5	3.6
Nashville, TN	Davidson County	59.8	33.9	3.9	1.0	1.4
New Orleans, LA	Orleans Parish	80.8	14.7	2.2	1.5	0.8
New York, NY	Bronx County	88.5	9.5	0.6	1.1	0.3
New York, NY	Kings County	79.5	17.5	0.9	1.5	0.6
New York, NY	New York County	86.6	9.7	1.4	1.4	0.9
New York, NY	Queens County	75.4	21.8	1.0	1.3	0.5
New York, NY	Richmond County	41.0	56.1	1.3	1.0	0.6
Oklahoma City, OK	Oklahoma County	41.2	51.7	7.1	0.0	0.0
Omaha, NE	Douglas County	47.3	45.0	4.3	1.2	2.2
Orlando, FL	Orange County	59.8	35.4	2.6	0.9	1.4
Peoria, IL	Peoria County	48.1	45.0	4.7	1.4	0.8
Philadelphia, PA	Philadelphia County	82.3	15.3	1.0	0.9	0.4
Phoenix, AZ	Maricopa County	44.8	47.7	4.3	1.2	2.0
Pittsburgh, PA	Allegheny County	55.9	39.5	2.5	0.8	1.4
Portland, OR	Multnomah County	73.3	17.0	3.2	3.2	3.2
Providence, RI	Providence County	57.5	36.6	2.7	1.3	1.9
Provo, UT	Utah County	14.0	50.2	3.2	0.5	32.2
Raleigh, NC	Wake County	57.4	37.2	3.7	0.3	1.4
Reno, NV	Washoe County	46.4	45.1	4.4	0.0	4.0
Richmond, VA	Richmond City	78.6	15.1	3.5	1.1	1.8
Roanoke, VA	Roanoke City	56.5	37.5	3.3	1.0	1.7
Rochester, MN	Olmsted County	45.3	44.5	4.4	1.4	4.4
Salem, OR	Marion County	42.2	46.3	5.2	2.1	4.2
Salt Lake City, UT	Salt Lake County	41.5	32.6	3.8	1.2	20.9
San Antonio, TX	Bexar County	53.7	40.4	3.4	1.1	1.3
San Diego, CA	San Diego County	56.3	36.6	4.0	1.7	1.4
San Francisco, CA	San Francisco County	84.5	9.2	2.2	2.4	1.7
San Jose, CA	Santa Clara County	72.7	20.6	3.6	1.8	1.3
Santa Rosa, CA	Sonoma County	68.8	22.0	3.9	3.1	2.2
Savannah, GA	Chatham County	55.1	40.4	3.1	0.3	1.1
Seattle, WA	King County	69.8	21.0	4.0	1.7	3.4
Sioux Falls, SD	Minnehaha County	39.1	53.7	6.1	0.0	1.1
Springfield, IL	Sangamon County	41.6	50.8	4.6	1.5	1.6
Tallahassee, FL	Leon County	59.8	35.0	2.9	0.9	1.4
Tampa, FL	Hillsborough County	51.0	44.2	2.6	0.8	1.4
Topeka, KS	Shawnee County	44.2	46.8	4.4	2.3	2.3
Tyler, TX	Smith County	26.3	69.5	2.4	0.4	1.3
Virginia Beach, VA	Virginia Beach City	44.8	48.4	4.1	0.9	1.9
Visalia, CA	Tulare County	41.7	51.1	3.3	1.4	2.5
Washington, DC	District of Columbia	90.9	4.1	1.6	1.4	2.1
Wilmington, NC	New Hanover County	45.6	49.5	3.5	0.4	1.1
Winston-Salem, NC	Forsyth County	53.0	42.6	3.0	0.3	1.2
U.S.	U.S.	48.0	45.9	3.3	1.1	1.7

Note: Results are percentages and may not add to 100% due to rounding
Source: Dave Leip's Atlas of U.S. Presidential Elections

House Price Index (HPI)

Metro Area[1]	National Ranking[3]	Quarterly Change (%)	One-Year Change (%)	Five-Year Change (%)
Albany, NY	218	-0.78	2.46	11.59
Albuquerque, NM	202	0.27	3.37	17.54
Allentown, PA	178	0.25	4.58	17.09
Anchorage, AK	243	-0.82	-1.17	8.57
Ann Arbor, MI	38	-0.05	9.08	40.94
Athens, GA	150	-2.93	5.58	36.35
Atlanta, GA	35	0.03	9.25	49.09
Austin, TX	137	-0.29	5.91	49.36
Baton Rouge, LA	216	-0.30	2.56	19.32
Billings, MT	229	0.65	1.55	18.99
Boise City, ID	2	1.37	16.65	68.50
Boston, MA[2]	117	0.76	6.37	33.50
Boulder, CO	97	-0.63	6.85	60.11
Cape Coral, FL	176	-0.07	4.64	51.21
Cedar Rapids, IA	196	-0.95	3.59	13.75
Charleston, SC	165	1.03	4.98	48.51
Charlotte, NC	26	1.67	9.83	42.67
Chicago, IL[2]	194	0.05	3.62	22.76
Clarksville, TN	n/r	n/a	10.44	22.32
College Station, TX	n/r	n/a	7.27	42.28
Colorado Springs, CO	10	1.17	11.41	47.12
Columbia, MO	185	0.56	4.16	17.20
Columbia, SC	147	1.65	5.62	22.45
Columbus, OH	81	0.05	7.41	36.68
Dallas, TX[2]	106	0.13	6.58	56.33
Denver, CO	64	0.08	8.15	64.63
Des Moines, IA	160	0.68	5.16	25.14
Durham, NC	65	0.93	8.05	36.19
Edison, NJ[2]	170	0.47	4.80	26.94
El Paso, TX	240	-1.59	0.41	9.71
Eugene, OR	57	-0.49	8.37	41.87
Evansville, IN	109	3.54	6.54	21.71
Fargo, ND	230	0.01	1.38	26.29
Fayetteville, NC	32	9.25	9.49	13.78
Fort Collins, CO	59	0.18	8.29	57.61
Fort Wayne, IN	33	1.27	9.35	29.51
Fort Worth, TX[2]	41	1.15	9.03	53.26
Gainesville, FL	n/r	n/a	3.51	36.42
Grand Rapids, MI	39	1.14	9.07	48.85
Greeley, CO	16	1.53	10.68	73.05
Green Bay, WI	71	0.51	7.79	27.00
Greensboro, NC	130	0.40	6.06	20.16
Honolulu, HI	148	3.13	5.62	32.46
Houston, TX	161	-0.13	5.13	36.79
Huntsville, AL	157	0.82	5.28	16.19
Indianapolis, IN	47	1.62	8.69	32.10
Jacksonville, FL	100	0.05	6.78	47.34
Kansas City, MO	37	1.59	9.16	37.00
Lafayette, LA	241	-0.23	-0.36	9.63
Las Cruces, NM	n/r	n/a	3.26	10.08
Las Vegas, NV	1	3.20	17.63	73.68
Lexington, KY	204	-2.81	3.28	23.17
Lincoln, NE	107	-0.15	6.55	30.61
Little Rock, AR	227	2.46	1.86	12.54
Los Angeles, CA[2]	77	0.51	7.61	44.06

Table continued on next page.

Metro Area[1]	National Ranking[3]	Quarterly Change (%)	One-Year Change (%)	Five-Year Change (%)
Louisville, KY	131	0.80	6.06	27.94
Madison, WI	140	-1.20	5.82	26.68
Manchester, NH	168	-0.78	4.92	26.94
McAllen, TX	n/r	n/a	9.27	24.90
Miami, FL[2]	66	0.91	8.04	55.38
Midland, TX	n/r	n/a	11.61	29.71
Minneapolis, MN	122	-0.88	6.31	31.91
Nashville, TN	46	1.21	8.84	53.68
New Orleans, LA	214	0.41	2.71	22.67
New York, NY[2]	170	0.47	4.80	26.94
Oklahoma City, OK	191	0.26	3.87	21.60
Omaha, NE	120	-0.24	6.33	27.96
Orlando, FL	68	0.48	7.92	55.21
Peoria, IL	221	1.82	2.14	3.12
Philadelphia, PA[2]	70	1.56	7.87	28.08
Phoenix, AZ	27	1.14	9.75	47.59
Pittsburgh, PA	158	-0.29	5.23	23.09
Portland, OR	167	-0.70	4.92	54.27
Providence, RI	133	-0.17	6.04	29.27
Provo, UT	12	1.34	11.35	46.94
Raleigh, NC	92	0.57	7.08	35.91
Reno, NV	7	1.48	11.84	77.15
Richmond, VA	121	1.10	6.32	27.93
Roanoke, VA	207	0.36	3.03	14.73
Rochester, MN	91	1.02	7.08	33.87
Salem, OR	8	0.87	11.70	62.33
Salt Lake City, UT	20	0.88	10.48	46.37
San Antonio, TX	103	1.95	6.71	39.55
San Diego, CA	128	0.50	6.10	38.19
San Francisco, CA[2]	14	-1.55	11.04	61.65
San Jose, CA	11	0.76	11.39	57.33
Santa Rosa, CA	141	-1.36	5.75	48.61
Savannah, GA	132	0.68	6.05	29.50
Seattle, WA[2]	99	-1.36	6.80	63.88
Sioux Falls, SD	144	-0.10	5.68	29.97
Springfield, IL	213	0.80	2.77	9.93
Tallahassee, FL	n/r	n/a	-0.05	21.69
Tampa, FL	40	0.54	9.06	56.78
Topeka, KS	113	2.47	6.42	16.66
Tyler, TX	n/r	n/a	3.48	23.48
Virginia Beach, VA	232	-1.12	1.25	13.22
Visalia, CA	217	-2.07	2.50	35.12
Washington, DC[2]	164	0.47	5.00	24.05
Wilmington, NC	54	2.85	8.45	36.94
Winston-Salem, NC	62	1.61	8.22	23.65
U.S.[4]	–	1.12	5.73	32.81

Note: The HPI is a weighted repeat sales index. It measures average price changes in repeat sales or refinancings on the same properties. This information is obtained by reviewing repeat mortgage transactions on single-family properties whose mortgages have been purchased or securitized by Fannie Mae or Freddie Mac in January 1975; (1) figures cover the Metropolitan Statistical Area (MSA) unless noted otherwise—see Appendix B for areas included; (2) Metropolitan Division—see Appendix B for areas included; (3) Rankings are based on annual percentage change, for all MSAs containing at least 15,000 transactions over the last 10 years and ranges from 1 to 245; (4) figures based on a weighted division average; all figures are for the period ended December 31, 2018; n/a not available; n/r not ranked
Source: Federal Housing Finance Agency, House Price Index, February 26, 2019

Home Value Distribution: City

Area	Under $50,000	$50,000 -$99,999	$100,000 -$149,999	$150,000 -$199,999	$200,000 -$299,999	$300,000 -$499,999	$500,000 -$999,999	$1,000,000 or more
Albany, NY	4.4	12.4	19.4	29.7	24.7	7.6	1.5	0.3
Albuquerque, NM	5.3	5.4	19.1	25.3	27.6	14.2	2.8	0.4
Allentown, PA	5.3	26.5	32.6	22.7	8.8	3.1	0.5	0.5
Anchorage, AK	5.5	2.0	4.3	7.4	29.5	39.3	11.0	0.9
Ann Arbor, MI	3.1	4.9	7.3	12.1	30.3	29.2	11.8	1.4
Athens, GA	7.4	18.0	22.2	20.6	16.9	10.8	3.8	0.4
Atlanta, GA	7.4	13.6	10.8	11.3	15.9	16.9	16.5	7.6
Austin, TX	3.1	3.5	8.2	13.3	24.9	28.3	15.4	3.2
Baton Rouge, LA	7.0	19.1	17.9	19.1	18.9	12.0	4.7	1.3
Billings, MT	6.5	4.3	11.3	25.3	35.9	12.7	3.5	0.5
Boise City, ID	4.4	3.9	15.6	23.9	27.4	18.5	5.7	0.6
Boston, MA	2.1	0.4	1.2	2.9	12.5	39.3	32.2	9.4
Boulder, CO	5.6	1.6	2.6	4.2	5.6	18.3	47.5	14.8
Cape Coral, FL	2.3	8.4	18.8	21.8	26.6	16.6	4.8	0.9
Cedar Rapids, IA	5.3	18.1	34.8	21.2	14.6	4.6	1.2	0.2
Charleston, SC	2.1	3.3	6.0	14.6	27.5	25.5	14.7	6.3
Charlotte, NC	3.3	11.6	21.4	17.3	18.3	16.0	9.3	2.8
Chicago, IL	3.6	8.7	13.2	15.7	23.3	21.6	10.5	3.3
Clarksville, TN	5.3	18.7	29.9	25.7	15.3	4.3	0.5	0.3
College Station, TX	3.0	2.9	13.6	28.5	30.1	17.8	3.6	0.5
Colorado Springs, CO	4.3	3.2	9.8	20.5	32.1	22.6	6.4	1.1
Columbia, MO	3.7	8.7	21.7	21.8	24.4	16.1	3.3	0.3
Columbia, SC	5.3	17.1	21.2	14.9	15.4	15.1	9.8	1.3
Columbus, OH	6.8	23.8	26.7	20.1	15.5	5.5	1.4	0.2
Dallas, TX	8.7	24.8	15.6	9.0	12.4	15.6	10.2	3.7
Denver, CO	2.5	3.1	6.7	10.8	23.0	29.9	19.9	4.2
Des Moines, IA	6.9	26.1	34.0	19.1	8.6	3.9	1.4	0.1
Durham, NC	2.6	7.1	19.4	22.7	27.1	15.7	4.5	0.8
Edison, NJ	3.5	1.7	1.9	3.2	19.8	46.5	22.0	1.4
El Paso, TX	5.9	27.6	33.0	16.8	10.8	4.4	1.2	0.2
Eugene, OR	5.7	2.2	6.9	14.5	36.9	26.1	6.9	0.7
Evansville, IN	12.5	47.0	22.7	9.2	5.8	1.9	0.8	0.2
Fargo, ND	3.7	6.9	20.0	23.9	28.0	14.5	2.5	0.5
Fayetteville, NC	6.1	26.2	27.6	18.5	13.7	5.8	1.6	0.4
Fort Collins, CO	4.1	0.9	3.3	7.3	31.9	41.9	10.0	0.7
Fort Wayne, IN	12.3	33.6	28.8	13.8	7.8	2.8	0.8	0.1
Fort Worth, TX	8.1	23.0	22.7	18.8	15.4	8.3	2.9	0.8
Gainesville, FL	6.6	21.7	22.8	20.6	18.2	7.9	1.9	0.2
Grand Rapids, MI	7.7	28.0	32.6	17.6	9.6	3.3	1.1	0.1
Greeley, CO	8.5	4.7	14.0	22.1	32.0	15.8	2.5	0.3
Green Bay, WI	3.5	24.5	37.2	17.9	11.0	4.4	1.1	0.3
Greensboro, NC	3.6	20.0	25.4	18.2	17.5	10.7	3.7	0.8
Honolulu, HI	1.3	1.0	1.0	1.6	9.2	23.4	43.9	18.7
Houston, TX	7.3	24.1	18.9	11.6	12.7	14.0	8.5	2.9
Huntsville, AL	5.8	19.8	16.8	16.4	22.0	14.1	4.1	1.1
Indianapolis, IN	8.8	26.3	29.0	16.1	10.1	6.7	2.3	0.6
Jacksonville, FL	9.4	20.2	20.4	18.0	18.9	9.1	3.1	1.0
Kansas City, MO	12.6	20.9	20.5	17.8	16.7	8.2	2.7	0.6
Lafayette, LA	7.0	10.0	17.0	22.7	21.9	14.6	5.3	1.5
Las Cruces, NM	10.4	13.0	26.6	26.4	16.0	5.6	1.9	0.1
Las Vegas, NV	3.6	9.5	14.7	19.2	27.4	19.1	5.2	1.4
Lexington, KY	3.4	11.1	22.8	21.1	21.1	14.2	5.0	1.2
Lincoln, NE	4.6	11.8	30.0	23.1	20.3	8.3	1.6	0.3
Little Rock, AR	7.4	20.3	18.3	16.8	16.2	14.0	5.4	1.6
Los Angeles, CA	2.0	0.9	0.9	1.8	8.5	30.7	37.8	17.4

Table continued on next page.

Area	Under $50,000	$50,000 -$99,999	$100,000 -$149,999	$150,000 -$199,999	$200,000 -$299,999	$300,000 -$499,999	$500,000 -$999,999	$1,000,000 or more
Louisville, KY	6.7	18.2	26.7	17.1	15.7	11.4	3.5	0.6
Madison, WI	2.3	2.9	11.0	24.0	34.1	20.4	4.7	0.6
Manchester, NH	2.8	4.4	9.6	27.4	42.5	12.1	1.0	0.1
McAllen, TX	9.1	29.0	26.8	16.2	12.5	4.4	1.8	0.2
Miami, FL	3.5	8.3	9.4	13.0	23.5	24.2	12.5	5.7
Midland, TX	6.1	11.5	14.7	20.0	23.8	16.7	6.1	1.1
Minneapolis, MN	2.2	6.0	14.1	19.7	28.9	19.3	8.2	1.6
Nashville, TN	3.0	8.1	21.0	20.5	21.5	17.1	7.3	1.4
New Orleans, LA	3.8	9.5	15.9	19.7	18.5	18.9	10.6	3.0
New York, NY	3.5	1.6	2.1	2.9	7.9	28.0	38.2	15.8
Oklahoma City, OK	8.7	19.9	22.1	20.0	17.1	8.6	2.9	0.7
Omaha, NE	5.4	17.0	29.8	19.8	16.6	8.2	2.7	0.6
Orlando, FL	6.1	15.8	14.8	14.1	22.4	18.9	6.4	1.6
Peoria, IL	13.1	26.5	21.1	15.8	14.5	6.4	2.3	0.3
Philadelphia, PA	8.6	21.1	19.7	18.0	17.8	9.8	3.9	1.1
Phoenix, AZ	6.4	11.1	15.0	18.1	21.3	19.2	7.4	1.4
Pittsburgh, PA	14.8	31.8	17.1	11.3	10.7	9.1	4.5	0.8
Portland, OR	2.9	1.0	3.2	8.1	23.3	37.0	22.1	2.4
Providence, RI	2.7	8.4	21.0	24.6	18.7	14.7	8.3	1.5
Provo, UT	5.5	2.3	11.4	20.3	31.4	20.7	6.9	1.6
Raleigh, NC	2.5	3.4	15.5	21.3	25.9	20.8	9.1	1.4
Reno, NV	6.4	5.8	7.9	12.3	27.0	31.4	8.2	1.1
Richmond, VA	3.1	13.1	15.7	15.9	21.6	18.6	9.5	2.6
Roanoke, VA	5.1	23.5	31.4	18.6	11.2	7.2	2.0	1.0
Rochester, MN	4.6	7.3	22.1	26.5	23.0	13.7	2.4	0.5
Salem, OR	8.0	3.4	13.7	24.2	31.8	16.6	1.8	0.4
Salt Lake City, UT	3.3	2.3	10.5	17.5	24.0	26.7	13.3	2.3
San Antonio, TX	8.6	28.8	21.2	17.0	14.5	7.2	2.2	0.5
San Diego, CA	2.3	1.1	1.2	2.1	8.9	31.7	41.1	11.5
San Francisco, CA	1.6	0.6	0.5	0.5	1.4	6.3	46.3	42.8
San Jose, CA	2.3	2.0	1.3	1.2	2.5	13.5	56.0	21.2
Santa Rosa, CA	4.1	2.2	1.6	1.7	9.2	40.8	35.9	4.6
Savannah, GA	6.4	22.3	22.7	19.8	16.3	8.0	3.7	0.8
Seattle, WA	1.2	0.4	0.9	2.3	9.3	31.5	43.3	11.1
Sioux Falls, SD	6.7	8.9	22.3	25.9	21.3	11.2	2.8	0.8
Springfield, IL	11.8	26.0	24.1	15.1	14.4	6.2	2.1	0.2
Tallahassee, FL	4.4	12.5	17.2	21.8	24.8	15.7	2.9	0.7
Tampa, FL	6.9	17.2	14.6	13.4	16.6	17.3	10.2	3.7
Topeka, KS	14.6	35.2	23.5	14.2	8.8	2.6	0.8	0.3
Tyler, TX	8.8	21.9	21.2	18.8	14.8	10.5	3.3	0.7
Virginia Beach, VA	3.1	1.3	6.3	14.6	34.8	27.6	10.2	1.9
Visalia, CA	4.4	6.5	14.6	22.1	29.8	16.4	5.7	0.5
Washington, DC	2.1	1.2	1.5	2.9	12.1	26.8	37.6	15.8
Wilmington, NC	3.6	5.9	13.9	17.4	25.5	20.2	10.6	2.9
Winston-Salem, NC	7.4	20.2	26.6	19.9	12.2	8.3	4.5	0.9
U.S.	8.3	13.9	14.7	14.6	18.7	17.3	9.7	2.7

Note: Figures are percentages and cover owner-occupied housing units.
Source: U.S. Census Bureau, 2013-2017 American Community Survey 5-Year Estimates

Home Value Distribution: Metro Area

MSA[1]	Under $50,000	$50,000 -$99,999	$100,000 -$149,999	$150,000 -$199,999	$200,000 -$299,999	$300,000 -$499,999	$500,000 -$999,999	$1,000,000 or more
Albany, NY	5.1	8.0	14.1	21.8	28.9	17.9	3.7	0.6
Albuquerque, NM	6.7	8.6	19.0	22.6	24.2	13.9	4.2	0.8
Allentown, PA	4.9	8.3	15.3	20.6	27.9	18.9	3.5	0.6
Anchorage, AK	5.3	2.8	5.0	10.2	31.8	35.0	9.2	0.7
Ann Arbor, MI	7.2	7.7	10.5	15.9	25.1	23.7	8.6	1.4
Athens, GA	9.8	16.0	18.9	17.1	19.3	13.6	4.6	0.7
Atlanta, GA	5.6	13.7	17.6	17.7	19.8	16.9	7.3	1.5
Austin, TX	4.3	5.4	11.5	16.6	26.0	23.1	10.6	2.5
Baton Rouge, LA	10.2	13.7	16.9	20.9	21.6	12.2	3.6	0.9
Billings, MT	8.8	5.0	10.5	21.4	32.7	16.3	4.3	1.0
Boise City, ID	5.4	7.8	18.0	21.6	24.7	17.5	4.5	0.5
Boston, MA	2.4	1.2	2.2	4.7	18.0	39.3	26.3	5.9
Boulder, CO	3.7	1.0	2.3	5.8	16.5	31.7	31.4	7.6
Cape Coral, FL	8.7	13.6	14.6	15.6	20.6	16.9	7.6	2.4
Cedar Rapids, IA	6.8	15.7	27.8	20.1	19.2	7.6	2.3	0.5
Charleston, SC	7.4	9.3	14.3	17.2	21.3	17.8	9.4	3.4
Charlotte, NC	5.9	13.6	19.7	17.4	19.9	15.5	6.5	1.6
Chicago, IL	4.1	8.8	14.1	16.9	24.3	20.6	8.9	2.1
Clarksville, TN	7.6	20.3	24.9	21.7	16.6	7.0	1.5	0.4
College Station, TX	12.1	16.5	17.3	19.2	18.7	11.6	3.8	0.7
Colorado Springs, CO	4.3	3.0	9.5	19.3	30.8	24.1	7.9	1.0
Columbia, MO	5.4	10.3	21.2	20.8	22.8	15.3	3.6	0.6
Columbia, SC	10.1	17.9	23.9	18.0	16.2	9.5	3.6	0.7
Columbus, OH	5.7	15.9	20.8	19.4	20.5	13.1	3.9	0.6
Dallas, TX	5.9	15.6	18.6	17.2	19.7	15.7	5.8	1.6
Denver, CO	3.2	2.2	4.9	9.8	26.1	35.2	15.9	2.6
Des Moines, IA	5.2	13.4	21.7	21.2	22.5	12.0	3.5	0.4
Durham, NC	5.4	8.3	15.5	17.7	22.8	20.0	9.0	1.3
Edison, NJ	2.8	1.7	2.8	4.8	15.6	36.3	28.0	8.1
El Paso, TX	8.9	28.9	31.5	15.6	9.8	4.0	1.1	0.2
Eugene, OR	7.7	3.5	9.4	18.5	31.6	22.0	6.6	0.9
Evansville, IN	8.9	26.4	23.4	18.6	13.8	6.6	2.0	0.3
Fargo, ND	4.5	7.4	18.8	23.1	27.1	14.8	3.7	0.4
Fayetteville, NC	9.6	23.5	24.3	19.2	15.9	5.9	1.2	0.3
Fort Collins, CO	5.0	1.3	2.9	9.5	29.7	36.9	13.3	1.3
Fort Wayne, IN	10.1	27.6	27.0	15.6	12.1	5.9	1.5	0.3
Fort Worth, TX	5.9	15.6	18.6	17.2	19.7	15.7	5.8	1.6
Gainesville, FL	7.6	19.4	17.9	18.3	20.3	12.0	4.1	0.4
Grand Rapids, MI	8.4	15.5	23.8	20.6	18.5	9.8	2.7	0.6
Greeley, CO	6.1	4.6	9.2	15.5	29.9	26.2	7.4	1.0
Green Bay, WI	4.4	13.7	25.3	23.3	21.7	9.1	2.2	0.4
Greensboro, NC	7.7	21.2	24.1	17.4	16.2	9.8	3.0	0.6
Honolulu, HI	1.1	0.8	0.9	1.3	6.9	22.2	52.7	14.0
Houston, TX	6.5	16.7	19.9	17.2	18.3	13.6	5.9	1.9
Huntsville, AL	7.7	15.8	19.2	17.9	22.1	13.5	3.3	0.7
Indianapolis, IN	6.9	18.8	24.9	17.9	16.1	11.0	3.6	0.7
Jacksonville, FL	7.4	16.0	17.3	16.9	21.2	14.2	5.4	1.6
Kansas City, MO	7.5	15.4	19.7	19.3	20.6	12.9	3.8	0.8
Lafayette, LA	17.0	18.6	16.4	18.3	17.1	8.9	3.1	0.6
Las Cruces, NM	14.5	18.3	20.5	18.9	15.1	9.3	3.1	0.2
Las Vegas, NV	5.2	8.8	13.4	18.7	27.6	19.6	5.3	1.3
Lexington, KY	4.7	11.8	23.6	20.6	19.7	13.4	4.9	1.4
Lincoln, NE	4.4	11.2	27.7	22.1	21.0	10.7	2.6	0.4
Little Rock, AR	9.2	19.3	23.3	19.0	16.8	8.9	2.7	0.8
Los Angeles, CA	2.8	1.6	1.4	2.0	7.8	30.2	40.7	13.4

Table continued on next page.

MSA[1]	Under $50,000	$50,000 -$99,999	$100,000 -$149,999	$150,000 -$199,999	$200,000 -$299,999	$300,000 -$499,999	$500,000 -$999,999	$1,000,000 or more
Louisville, KY	6.4	16.5	24.6	18.2	18.7	11.3	3.5	0.8
Madison, WI	2.9	4.3	11.5	19.9	32.2	22.2	6.0	1.0
Manchester, NH	2.7	2.8	6.9	15.1	38.9	27.6	5.3	0.7
McAllen, TX	25.6	35.9	18.0	9.6	6.8	2.6	1.1	0.2
Miami, FL	6.0	10.4	11.7	13.6	22.0	22.6	10.0	3.8
Midland, TX	10.1	12.5	14.2	17.9	22.7	16.2	5.4	1.1
Minneapolis, MN	3.6	4.1	11.6	20.0	30.4	21.9	7.1	1.2
Nashville, TN	4.0	8.9	19.2	18.8	22.0	17.4	7.9	1.7
New Orleans, LA	5.3	10.1	18.2	21.7	23.5	14.4	5.3	1.3
New York, NY	2.8	1.7	2.8	4.8	15.6	36.3	28.0	8.1
Oklahoma City, OK	8.7	20.0	22.8	19.3	16.7	8.9	2.9	0.8
Omaha, NE	4.9	14.0	27.3	20.0	19.6	10.8	2.8	0.6
Orlando, FL	8.0	13.6	15.7	18.9	23.0	14.8	4.6	1.3
Peoria, IL	8.1	25.5	24.0	18.0	15.4	7.0	1.7	0.4
Philadelphia, PA	4.5	7.7	10.8	15.3	26.6	24.5	9.0	1.5
Phoenix, AZ	7.0	8.3	12.8	17.4	24.4	20.3	7.9	1.9
Pittsburgh, PA	10.4	22.5	20.1	17.5	15.9	10.2	3.0	0.6
Portland, OR	4.4	1.6	4.0	9.5	27.7	35.4	15.3	2.0
Providence, RI	3.0	2.5	7.7	17.0	32.6	27.5	8.1	1.6
Provo, UT	3.3	1.3	7.3	16.8	35.0	26.8	8.3	1.1
Raleigh, NC	4.5	5.7	15.1	17.7	24.8	23.1	7.8	1.2
Reno, NV	5.9	5.7	8.1	12.5	26.6	27.9	10.5	2.8
Richmond, VA	3.2	6.0	14.0	20.1	28.6	20.3	6.7	1.2
Roanoke, VA	5.4	11.6	21.8	21.5	20.7	13.6	4.4	1.0
Rochester, MN	5.9	8.8	20.0	22.9	21.7	15.7	4.1	1.0
Salem, OR	8.0	3.8	12.6	22.2	29.1	18.3	5.3	0.8
Salt Lake City, UT	4.0	1.7	8.9	16.7	30.9	27.1	9.3	1.3
San Antonio, TX	8.7	21.8	18.5	17.5	17.4	11.3	3.9	1.0
San Diego, CA	3.5	2.0	1.7	2.2	8.5	34.9	37.8	9.4
San Francisco, CA	2.0	1.2	1.2	1.6	5.0	17.7	44.8	26.5
San Jose, CA	2.1	1.6	1.2	1.1	2.2	11.3	46.1	34.4
Santa Rosa, CA	4.5	2.9	1.5	1.6	7.1	30.9	41.7	9.9
Savannah, GA	6.1	13.6	18.3	20.0	21.4	12.5	6.5	1.4
Seattle, WA	3.6	1.6	3.5	7.3	21.0	33.2	24.4	5.4
Sioux Falls, SD	6.6	10.0	20.8	24.1	22.0	12.5	3.2	0.8
Springfield, IL	9.7	23.8	22.8	17.5	17.2	6.9	1.9	0.3
Tallahassee, FL	9.3	16.8	16.6	18.7	21.1	13.3	3.5	0.7
Tampa, FL	11.1	17.5	16.4	16.7	19.2	12.7	5.0	1.3
Topeka, KS	11.1	26.0	23.5	18.1	14.1	5.8	1.3	0.2
Tyler, TX	12.7	20.0	19.4	19.0	16.1	9.2	2.8	0.8
Virginia Beach, VA	4.3	3.7	10.8	18.3	31.2	23.3	7.2	1.2
Visalia, CA	5.7	11.2	19.1	21.4	23.6	13.4	4.7	0.9
Washington, DC	2.2	1.3	2.8	6.1	18.6	34.4	28.7	5.9
Wilmington, NC	5.5	8.1	14.1	18.7	24.4	19.6	7.6	2.0
Winston-Salem, NC	8.8	18.2	25.4	19.5	15.7	8.6	3.1	0.7
U.S.	8.3	13.9	14.7	14.6	18.7	17.3	9.7	2.7

Note: (1) Figures cover the Metropolitan Statistical Area (MSA)—see Appendix B for areas included; Figures are percentages and cover owner-occupied housing units.
Source: U.S. Census Bureau, 2013-2017 American Community Survey 5-Year Estimates

Homeownership Rate

Metro Area	2009	2010	2011	2012	2013	2014	2015	2016	2017
Albany, NY	72.8	72.4	70.6	67.9	67.5	65.9	61.3	64.1	62.2
Albuquerque, NM	65.5	67.1	62.8	65.9	64.4	64.3	66.9	67.0	67.9
Allentown, PA	71.5	75.7	75.5	71.5	68.2	69.2	68.9	73.1	72.1
Anchorage, AK	n/a	n/a	n/a	n/a	n/a	n/a	n/a	n/a	n/a
Ann Arbor, MI	n/a	n/a	n/a	n/a	n/a	n/a	n/a	n/a	n/a
Athens, GA	n/a	n/a	n/a	n/a	n/a	n/a	n/a	n/a	n/a
Atlanta, GA	67.2	65.8	62.1	61.6	61.6	61.7	61.5	62.4	64.0
Austin, TX	65.8	58.4	60.1	59.6	61.1	57.5	56.5	55.6	56.1
Baton Rouge, LA	70.3	72.0	71.4	66.6	64.8	64.2	64.8	66.9	66.6
Billings, MT	n/a	n/a	n/a	n/a	n/a	n/a	n/a	n/a	n/a
Boise City, ID	n/a	n/a	n/a	n/a	n/a	n/a	n/a	n/a	n/a
Boston, MA	66.0	65.5	66.0	66.3	62.8	59.3	58.9	58.8	61.0
Boulder, CO	n/a	n/a	n/a	n/a	n/a	n/a	n/a	n/a	n/a
Cape Coral, FL	n/a	n/a	n/a	n/a	n/a	62.9	66.5	65.5	75.1
Cedar Rapids, IA	n/a	n/a	n/a	n/a	n/a	n/a	n/a	n/a	n/a
Charleston, SC	n/a	n/a	n/a	n/a	n/a	65.8	62.1	67.7	68.8
Charlotte, NC	66.1	63.6	58.3	58.9	58.1	62.3	66.2	64.6	67.9
Chicago, IL	68.2	67.7	67.1	68.2	66.3	64.3	64.5	64.1	64.6
Clarksville, TN	n/a	n/a	n/a	n/a	n/a	n/a	n/a	n/a	n/a
College Station, TX	n/a	n/a	n/a	n/a	n/a	n/a	n/a	n/a	n/a
Colorado Springs, CO	n/a	n/a	n/a	n/a	n/a	n/a	n/a	n/a	n/a
Columbia, MO	n/a	n/a	n/a	n/a	n/a	n/a	n/a	n/a	n/a
Columbia, SC	74.1	69.0	65.6	68.9	69.5	66.1	63.9	70.7	69.3
Columbus, OH	62.2	59.7	60.7	60.5	60.0	59.0	57.5	57.9	64.8
Dallas, TX	63.8	62.6	61.8	59.9	57.7	57.8	59.7	61.8	62.0
Denver, CO	65.7	63.0	61.8	61.0	61.9	61.6	61.6	59.3	60.1
Des Moines, IA	n/a	n/a	n/a	n/a	n/a	n/a	n/a	n/a	n/a
Durham, NC	n/a	n/a	n/a	n/a	n/a	n/a	n/a	n/a	n/a
Edison, NJ	51.6	50.9	51.5	50.6	50.7	49.9	50.4	49.9	49.7
El Paso, TX	n/a	n/a	n/a	n/a	n/a	n/a	n/a	n/a	n/a
Eugene, OR	n/a	n/a	n/a	n/a	n/a	n/a	n/a	n/a	n/a
Evansville, IN	n/a	n/a	n/a	n/a	n/a	n/a	n/a	n/a	n/a
Fargo, ND	n/a	n/a	n/a	n/a	n/a	n/a	n/a	n/a	n/a
Fayetteville, NC	n/a	n/a	n/a	n/a	n/a	n/a	n/a	n/a	n/a
Fort Collins, CO	n/a	n/a	n/a	n/a	n/a	n/a	n/a	n/a	n/a
Fort Wayne, IN	n/a	n/a	n/a	n/a	n/a	n/a	n/a	n/a	n/a
Fort Worth, TX	63.8	62.6	61.8	59.9	57.7	57.8	59.7	61.8	62.0
Gainesville, FL	n/a	n/a	n/a	n/a	n/a	n/a	n/a	n/a	n/a
Grand Rapids, MI	76.4	76.4	76.9	73.7	71.6	75.8	76.2	71.7	73.0
Greeley, CO	n/a	n/a	n/a	n/a	n/a	n/a	n/a	n/a	n/a
Green Bay, WI	n/a	n/a	n/a	n/a	n/a	n/a	n/a	n/a	n/a
Greensboro, NC	68.8	62.7	64.9	67.9	68.1	65.4	62.9	61.9	63.2
Honolulu, HI	54.9	54.1	56.1	57.9	58.2	59.6	57.9	53.8	57.7
Houston, TX	61.4	61.3	62.1	60.5	60.4	60.3	59.0	58.9	60.1
Huntsville, AL	n/a	n/a	n/a	n/a	n/a	n/a	n/a	n/a	n/a
Indianapolis, IN	68.8	68.3	67.1	67.5	66.9	64.6	63.9	63.9	64.3
Jacksonville, FL	70.0	68.0	66.6	69.9	65.3	62.5	61.8	65.2	61.4
Kansas City, MO	68.8	68.5	65.1	65.6	66.1	65.0	62.4	62.4	64.3
Lafayette, LA	n/a	n/a	n/a	n/a	n/a	n/a	n/a	n/a	n/a
Las Cruces, NM	n/a	n/a	n/a	n/a	n/a	n/a	n/a	n/a	n/a
Las Vegas, NV	55.7	52.9	52.6	52.8	53.2	52.1	51.3	54.4	58.1
Lexington, KY	n/a	n/a	n/a	n/a	n/a	n/a	n/a	n/a	n/a
Lincoln, NE	n/a	n/a	n/a	n/a	n/a	n/a	n/a	n/a	n/a
Little Rock, AR	n/a	n/a	n/a	n/a	n/a	65.8	64.9	61.0	62.2
Los Angeles, CA	49.7	50.1	49.9	48.7	49.0	49.1	47.1	49.1	49.5
Louisville, KY	63.4	61.7	63.3	64.5	68.9	67.7	67.6	71.7	67.9

Table continued on next page.

Metro Area	2009	2010	2011	2012	2013	2014	2015	2016	2017
Madison, WI	n/a	n/a	n/a	n/a	n/a	n/a	n/a	n/a	n/a
Manchester, NH	n/a	n/a	n/a	n/a	n/a	n/a	n/a	n/a	n/a
McAllen, TX	n/a	n/a	n/a	n/a	n/a	n/a	n/a	n/a	n/a
Miami, FL	63.8	64.2	61.8	60.1	58.8	58.6	58.4	57.9	59.9
Midland, TX	n/a	n/a	n/a	n/a	n/a	n/a	n/a	n/a	n/a
Minneapolis, MN	71.2	69.1	70.8	71.7	69.7	67.9	69.1	70.1	67.8
Nashville, TN	70.4	69.6	64.9	63.9	67.1	67.4	65.0	69.4	68.3
New Orleans, LA	66.9	63.9	62.4	61.4	60.6	62.8	59.3	61.7	62.6
New York, NY	51.6	50.9	51.5	50.6	50.7	49.9	50.4	49.9	49.7
Oklahoma City, OK	70.0	69.6	67.3	67.6	65.7	61.4	63.1	64.7	64.6
Omaha, NE	73.2	71.6	72.4	70.6	68.7	69.6	69.2	65.5	67.8
Orlando, FL	70.8	68.6	68.0	65.5	62.3	58.4	58.5	59.5	58.5
Peoria, IL	n/a	n/a	n/a	n/a	n/a	n/a	n/a	n/a	n/a
Philadelphia, PA	70.7	69.7	69.5	69.1	67.0	67.0	64.7	65.6	67.4
Phoenix, AZ	66.5	63.3	63.1	62.2	61.9	61.0	62.6	64.0	65.3
Pittsburgh, PA	70.4	70.3	67.9	68.3	69.1	71.0	72.2	72.7	71.7
Portland, OR	63.7	63.7	63.9	60.9	59.8	58.9	61.8	61.1	59.2
Providence, RI	61.0	61.3	61.7	60.1	61.6	60.0	57.5	58.6	61.3
Provo, UT	n/a	n/a	n/a	n/a	n/a	n/a	n/a	n/a	n/a
Raleigh, NC	65.9	66.7	67.7	65.5	65.5	67.4	65.9	68.2	64.9
Reno, NV	n/a	n/a	n/a	n/a	n/a	n/a	n/a	n/a	n/a
Richmond, VA	68.1	65.2	67.0	65.4	72.6	67.4	61.7	63.1	62.9
Roanoke, VA	n/a	n/a	n/a	n/a	n/a	n/a	n/a	n/a	n/a
Rochester, MN	n/a	n/a	n/a	n/a	n/a	n/a	n/a	n/a	n/a
Salem, OR	n/a	n/a	n/a	n/a	n/a	n/a	n/a	n/a	n/a
Salt Lake City, UT	65.5	66.4	66.9	66.8	68.2	69.1	69.2	68.1	69.5
San Antonio, TX	70.1	66.5	67.5	70.1	70.2	66.0	61.6	62.5	64.4
San Diego, CA	54.4	55.2	55.4	55.0	57.4	51.8	53.3	56.0	56.1
San Francisco, CA	58.0	56.1	53.2	55.2	54.6	56.3	55.8	55.7	55.6
San Jose, CA	58.9	60.4	58.6	56.4	56.4	50.7	49.9	50.4	50.4
Santa Rosa, CA	n/a	n/a	n/a	n/a	n/a	n/a	n/a	n/a	n/a
Savannah, GA	n/a	n/a	n/a	n/a	n/a	n/a	n/a	n/a	n/a
Seattle, WA	60.9	60.7	60.4	61.0	61.3	59.5	57.7	59.5	62.5
Sioux Falls, SD	n/a	n/a	n/a	n/a	n/a	n/a	n/a	n/a	n/a
Springfield, IL	n/a	n/a	n/a	n/a	n/a	n/a	n/a	n/a	n/a
Tallahassee, FL	n/a	n/a	n/a	n/a	n/a	n/a	n/a	n/a	n/a
Tampa, FL	68.3	68.3	67.0	65.3	64.9	64.9	62.9	60.4	64.9
Topeka, KS	n/a	n/a	n/a	n/a	n/a	n/a	n/a	n/a	n/a
Tyler, TX	n/a	n/a	n/a	n/a	n/a	n/a	n/a	n/a	n/a
Virginia Beach, VA	61.4	62.3	62.0	63.3	64.1	59.4	59.6	65.3	62.8
Visalia, CA	n/a	n/a	n/a	n/a	n/a	n/a	n/a	n/a	n/a
Washington, DC	67.3	67.6	66.9	66.0	65.0	64.6	63.1	63.3	62.9
Wilmington, NC	n/a	n/a	n/a	n/a	n/a	n/a	n/a	n/a	n/a
Winston-Salem, NC	n/a	n/a	n/a	n/a	n/a	n/a	n/a	n/a	n/a
U.S.	67.4	66.9	66.1	65.4	65.1	64.5	63.7	63.4	63.9

Note: Figures are percentages and cover the Metropolitan Statistical Area—see Appendix B for areas included
Source: U.S. Census Bureau, Housing Vacancies and Homeownership Annual Statistics: 2009-2017

Year Housing Structure Built: City

City	2010 or Later	2000 -2009	1990 -1999	1980 -1989	1970 -1979	1960 -1969	1950 -1959	1940 -1949	Before 1940	Median Year
Albany, NY	0.9	2.5	3.3	5.6	9.2	8.2	10.0	7.9	52.4	<1940
Albuquerque, NM	2.5	17.0	15.6	15.5	19.4	11.2	11.5	4.5	2.7	1980
Allentown, PA	1.8	5.5	3.6	5.0	11.3	11.0	16.7	8.3	36.9	1953
Anchorage, AK	2.7	12.6	11.4	26.2	28.9	10.7	5.8	1.3	0.4	1981
Ann Arbor, MI	2.2	6.7	10.4	10.4	16.8	17.7	14.0	5.8	16.0	1968
Athens, GA	2.5	17.3	19.7	16.0	18.0	12.0	6.9	2.6	4.9	1983
Atlanta, GA	4.7	23.5	10.6	7.8	8.7	13.6	11.5	6.3	13.2	1976
Austin, TX	7.5	19.6	16.4	20.4	17.3	7.9	5.3	2.7	2.9	1987
Baton Rouge, LA	3.4	10.3	9.2	13.6	21.5	18.0	12.6	6.0	5.4	1974
Billings, MT	4.8	12.8	12.2	11.9	19.1	10.4	14.6	6.5	7.7	1976
Boise City, ID	3.6	12.5	22.4	15.9	19.8	7.3	7.9	4.2	6.5	1983
Boston, MA	2.8	6.7	4.0	6.1	7.7	8.4	7.3	5.8	51.3	<1940
Boulder, CO	3.7	8.5	10.5	16.2	23.6	18.9	8.7	2.1	7.7	1975
Cape Coral, FL	2.0	39.3	17.0	23.4	12.2	5.0	0.7	0.2	0.2	1995
Cedar Rapids, IA	4.2	12.2	14.0	8.1	14.8	14.4	12.2	4.4	15.7	1972
Charleston, SC	7.1	22.3	12.5	14.1	12.3	8.6	6.5	4.6	12.0	1984
Charlotte, NC	5.1	23.9	20.4	15.5	12.2	10.1	6.9	2.9	3.0	1990
Chicago, IL	1.5	8.1	4.7	4.2	7.4	9.8	12.2	9.1	43.1	1948
Clarksville, TN	11.0	24.6	21.2	12.0	12.5	9.2	5.0	2.1	2.3	1993
College Station, TX	10.2	25.9	19.5	18.1	17.9	4.3	2.1	0.9	1.0	1993
Colorado Springs, CO	3.5	16.8	15.9	19.2	18.5	10.7	7.5	2.0	5.9	1983
Columbia, MO	6.9	23.7	17.4	14.0	12.7	11.3	5.6	2.7	5.8	1989
Columbia, SC	4.2	16.2	11.1	9.5	10.5	13.0	14.4	10.0	11.0	1971
Columbus, OH	3.5	12.3	15.1	12.8	15.8	12.1	11.1	5.2	12.1	1976
Dallas, TX	4.2	11.3	10.1	18.0	17.7	13.8	13.8	5.6	5.6	1976
Denver, CO	5.3	12.2	6.8	7.7	14.3	11.2	15.7	7.1	19.7	1967
Des Moines, IA	2.1	7.7	7.0	6.3	12.8	10.6	16.7	8.5	28.3	1958
Durham, NC	6.4	21.7	17.6	16.1	10.9	9.3	7.1	4.3	6.5	1987
Edison, NJ	1.0	4.7	9.6	24.4	14.3	19.8	17.0	4.5	4.9	1973
El Paso, TX	7.3	16.0	13.5	13.8	16.8	12.0	11.9	4.3	4.5	1980
Eugene, OR	4.5	11.6	16.8	8.3	22.7	13.2	10.5	5.0	7.3	1976
Evansville, IN	0.9	6.0	7.1	8.6	12.9	10.5	17.7	12.1	24.1	1958
Fargo, ND	10.3	15.9	18.9	13.9	15.1	6.8	6.7	2.8	9.5	1986
Fayetteville, NC	5.4	13.2	17.6	17.8	21.0	13.4	7.2	2.8	1.6	1982
Fort Collins, CO	5.9	18.4	21.3	16.1	19.5	8.1	3.6	1.6	5.6	1987
Fort Wayne, IN	0.8	6.6	14.1	11.7	16.7	15.6	12.2	6.9	15.3	1970
Fort Worth, TX	6.6	26.4	11.6	13.0	10.4	8.5	11.5	5.4	6.5	1986
Gainesville, FL	2.5	13.8	15.6	19.9	21.1	12.3	9.2	3.0	2.6	1981
Grand Rapids, MI	1.2	4.2	6.0	7.1	8.8	10.6	15.9	8.9	37.3	1952
Greeley, CO	3.6	19.5	16.4	10.6	20.1	11.3	7.4	2.6	8.6	1980
Green Bay, WI	1.3	7.4	9.7	12.8	17.0	13.7	14.3	6.6	17.3	1969
Greensboro, NC	3.0	14.5	18.3	18.3	15.8	11.2	9.8	3.6	5.5	1982
Honolulu, HI	2.6	7.2	8.0	9.8	25.4	23.2	13.0	5.6	5.1	1971
Houston, TX	4.9	14.4	9.9	14.2	22.5	14.2	10.8	4.6	4.4	1977
Huntsville, AL	7.8	14.2	11.3	14.4	15.1	20.8	10.6	2.8	2.9	1978
Indianapolis, IN	2.2	10.0	13.1	11.9	14.0	13.2	12.8	6.0	16.9	1971
Jacksonville, FL	3.9	19.7	15.1	15.8	13.1	10.7	11.3	5.1	5.3	1983
Kansas City, MO	2.8	10.6	9.2	8.5	12.3	13.6	14.7	6.8	21.4	1965
Lafayette, LA	4.4	13.9	9.5	18.4	21.7	13.8	10.6	4.6	3.2	1978
Las Cruces, NM	6.3	24.7	16.4	15.0	14.4	8.9	9.2	2.5	2.7	1988
Las Vegas, NV	3.1	24.2	31.9	17.4	10.0	7.4	4.2	1.3	0.4	1993
Lexington, KY	4.0	16.1	16.1	14.5	15.3	13.6	9.8	3.2	7.3	1980
Lincoln, NE	4.3	14.9	15.2	11.2	15.2	10.8	11.3	3.4	13.8	1977
Little Rock, AR	3.7	11.1	13.3	17.2	19.8	13.9	9.4	4.7	6.9	1978
Los Angeles, CA	1.8	5.9	5.7	10.2	13.9	13.8	17.8	10.2	20.6	1961

Table continued on next page.

City	2010 or Later	2000 -2009	1990 -1999	1980 -1989	1970 -1979	1960 -1969	1950 -1959	1940 -1949	Before 1940	Median Year
Louisville, KY	2.6	11.7	11.7	7.3	13.6	13.4	14.8	7.3	17.6	1968
Madison, WI	3.8	15.9	13.4	11.4	14.5	11.5	11.1	4.8	13.6	1976
Manchester, NH	1.5	6.6	7.5	16.0	10.5	7.7	10.7	6.1	33.3	1960
McAllen, TX	5.1	24.2	19.6	19.7	16.7	7.4	3.9	1.6	1.9	1989
Miami, FL	4.0	19.5	6.4	8.1	12.8	10.3	15.1	13.6	10.3	1971
Midland, TX	8.1	9.0	14.5	19.5	13.2	13.1	17.9	3.1	1.6	1981
Minneapolis, MN	3.3	7.4	3.3	6.2	9.2	7.5	10.0	7.3	45.8	1946
Nashville, TN	4.7	15.2	12.3	16.1	15.4	13.4	11.7	5.0	6.3	1979
New Orleans, LA	2.4	7.9	3.8	7.4	13.5	11.4	11.6	8.2	33.8	1957
New York, NY	1.7	5.9	3.6	4.7	7.1	12.7	13.3	10.4	40.5	1949
Oklahoma City, OK	6.2	13.9	10.0	15.3	15.9	13.0	10.8	6.2	8.8	1977
Omaha, NE	2.2	6.7	12.4	11.0	15.9	14.6	11.7	4.7	20.8	1969
Orlando, FL	5.2	23.1	17.0	17.3	14.0	7.8	9.3	3.2	3.1	1987
Peoria, IL	2.1	8.7	7.3	6.9	14.6	13.7	15.8	8.3	22.6	1962
Philadelphia, PA	1.5	3.2	3.2	3.9	6.7	10.7	16.1	13.6	41.1	1946
Phoenix, AZ	2.5	17.4	16.1	17.8	19.7	10.9	10.7	2.9	2.0	1982
Pittsburgh, PA	1.2	3.4	3.3	4.5	6.9	8.1	12.1	9.1	51.4	<1940
Portland, OR	3.2	10.9	8.8	6.0	11.0	9.1	12.1	8.5	30.3	1959
Providence, RI	0.6	5.5	4.5	5.2	8.2	5.9	8.4	7.3	54.3	<1940
Provo, UT	2.3	12.3	21.7	13.2	18.8	10.4	7.7	5.9	7.8	1980
Raleigh, NC	6.6	26.6	19.9	17.6	10.7	8.3	5.1	2.0	3.1	1992
Reno, NV	3.4	21.3	18.5	14.5	17.8	10.0	7.4	3.3	3.6	1985
Richmond, VA	2.5	5.6	4.8	5.9	11.2	12.6	15.5	9.5	32.4	1955
Roanoke, VA	0.9	5.5	5.9	6.6	12.0	13.2	20.9	10.3	24.7	1957
Rochester, MN	4.8	19.5	14.7	14.3	13.8	11.6	9.7	3.6	8.1	1982
Salem, OR	2.2	13.0	16.3	11.6	22.7	9.4	10.4	5.7	8.6	1977
Salt Lake City, UT	2.7	6.1	6.9	7.5	13.4	9.7	13.7	10.0	30.1	1957
San Antonio, TX	4.9	16.8	13.8	16.9	15.7	10.4	10.2	5.7	5.6	1981
San Diego, CA	2.1	10.3	11.7	18.1	21.4	12.8	12.4	4.3	6.9	1976
San Francisco, CA	1.9	6.7	4.4	5.3	7.5	8.1	8.6	9.4	48.0	1942
San Jose, CA	3.1	9.8	10.8	13.1	24.5	18.9	11.5	3.2	5.2	1975
Santa Rosa, CA	1.5	13.1	13.1	18.8	22.9	12.2	7.7	5.3	5.5	1978
Savannah, GA	4.6	10.9	7.5	10.1	13.4	13.3	14.9	8.2	16.9	1967
Seattle, WA	5.8	13.7	8.6	7.9	8.2	9.1	10.9	8.8	27.1	1964
Sioux Falls, SD	8.8	19.3	15.9	11.3	14.6	7.7	8.9	4.8	8.7	1985
Springfield, IL	1.5	9.2	12.8	9.9	15.0	13.4	11.9	7.0	19.2	1969
Tallahassee, FL	2.8	19.3	21.2	18.0	17.0	9.5	7.6	2.9	1.6	1986
Tampa, FL	5.0	19.0	12.0	11.8	11.7	10.7	15.8	5.2	8.8	1978
Topeka, KS	0.9	7.3	9.8	9.9	14.5	16.1	16.4	6.7	18.5	1965
Tyler, TX	4.5	16.0	12.1	13.6	16.9	12.4	14.7	4.8	5.0	1978
Virginia Beach, VA	2.8	11.2	13.7	28.5	22.2	12.6	6.5	1.6	1.1	1982
Visalia, CA	3.5	22.5	14.5	17.1	19.2	9.6	7.0	3.8	2.8	1984
Washington, DC	4.4	8.7	3.0	4.5	7.8	11.6	12.8	11.9	35.3	1952
Wilmington, NC	3.5	14.8	22.0	16.4	13.6	7.8	6.5	6.2	9.3	1984
Winston-Salem, NC	3.2	14.8	11.6	13.6	16.4	14.9	12.7	4.9	7.9	1976
U.S.	3.2	14.5	14.0	13.6	15.5	10.8	10.5	5.1	12.9	1977

Note: Figures are percentages except for Median Year
Source: U.S. Census Bureau, 2013-2017 American Community Survey 5-Year Estimates

Year Housing Structure Built: Metro Area

Metro Area	2010 or Later	2000 -2009	1990 -1999	1980 -1989	1970 -1979	1960 -1969	1950 -1959	1940 -1949	Before 1940	Median Year
Albany, NY	2.8	8.7	9.8	11.2	12.1	9.1	10.9	5.9	29.6	1964
Albuquerque, NM	2.6	18.4	18.2	16.8	18.0	9.6	9.3	3.8	3.2	1984
Allentown, PA	1.9	11.7	10.5	10.8	12.8	9.7	11.6	5.4	25.8	1968
Anchorage, AK	3.2	17.8	13.0	25.9	24.9	8.9	4.8	1.1	0.4	1984
Ann Arbor, MI	2.2	13.5	17.3	11.1	16.4	12.3	10.9	4.5	11.9	1976
Athens, GA	2.9	19.2	20.6	16.9	17.4	9.9	5.9	2.3	5.0	1986
Atlanta, GA	3.3	25.7	22.3	17.9	12.9	7.9	4.9	2.0	3.1	1991
Austin, TX	9.9	27.4	19.4	17.6	12.5	5.2	3.6	2.0	2.4	1993
Baton Rouge, LA	5.9	21.9	14.9	15.3	17.4	10.8	7.3	2.9	3.7	1985
Billings, MT	4.6	13.8	12.9	12.6	20.4	9.4	11.8	5.2	9.5	1977
Boise City, ID	6.0	25.9	22.3	10.9	16.9	4.9	4.8	3.3	5.1	1992
Boston, MA	2.4	7.8	7.5	10.5	11.1	10.4	10.8	5.6	33.9	1960
Boulder, CO	3.8	12.9	19.2	16.9	21.5	12.0	5.0	1.8	6.9	1982
Cape Coral, FL	3.0	32.8	17.7	21.9	15.3	5.6	2.6	0.5	0.7	1992
Cedar Rapids, IA	4.4	14.7	15.3	7.3	13.7	12.7	10.0	3.9	17.9	1974
Charleston, SC	7.0	23.7	16.5	17.4	14.5	8.9	5.4	2.8	3.8	1988
Charlotte, NC	5.4	25.3	20.2	14.1	12.0	8.7	6.7	3.3	4.3	1990
Chicago, IL	1.4	11.7	11.1	8.9	14.1	11.9	13.3	6.2	21.4	1968
Clarksville, TN	8.6	21.9	20.2	11.3	15.5	10.4	6.0	2.5	3.6	1990
College Station, TX	8.4	21.9	18.1	17.9	16.8	6.1	5.4	2.4	3.0	1989
Colorado Springs, CO	4.5	20.0	17.0	17.9	17.4	9.3	6.7	1.6	5.4	1985
Columbia, MO	5.7	21.9	18.5	14.1	16.2	10.4	5.2	2.4	5.6	1987
Columbia, SC	5.3	20.5	18.5	14.9	16.1	10.3	7.4	3.1	3.8	1986
Columbus, OH	3.5	14.8	16.6	11.9	14.7	11.3	10.5	4.3	12.4	1978
Dallas, TX	6.1	21.6	16.7	18.8	14.5	9.0	7.6	2.8	2.9	1987
Denver, CO	4.4	17.2	15.4	14.4	19.2	9.7	9.7	3.0	7.0	1981
Des Moines, IA	7.1	18.0	13.5	8.7	13.8	9.0	9.7	4.5	15.7	1978
Durham, NC	5.7	20.4	19.0	16.7	12.8	9.4	6.7	3.3	5.9	1987
Edison, NJ	1.7	7.1	6.1	8.0	10.0	13.8	16.1	9.0	28.2	1958
El Paso, TX	8.0	17.5	14.7	14.4	16.2	10.8	10.6	3.8	4.1	1983
Eugene, OR	3.1	11.6	15.5	8.9	23.4	13.9	9.7	6.4	7.5	1975
Evansville, IN	2.3	11.7	13.0	11.0	15.6	9.6	13.0	7.7	16.1	1972
Fargo, ND	9.8	18.7	15.9	11.3	16.0	7.7	8.0	2.9	9.8	1985
Fayetteville, NC	6.4	18.0	20.8	16.2	17.6	10.8	6.0	2.3	1.9	1987
Fort Collins, CO	5.6	20.2	20.8	14.1	19.9	7.6	3.9	1.8	6.2	1988
Fort Wayne, IN	2.5	11.0	15.2	11.0	15.1	13.3	10.5	5.7	15.6	1973
Fort Worth, TX	6.1	21.6	16.7	18.8	14.5	9.0	7.6	2.8	2.9	1987
Gainesville, FL	3.0	18.4	19.7	20.5	18.4	8.6	6.6	2.1	2.5	1986
Grand Rapids, MI	2.4	13.0	16.3	12.5	14.5	9.8	10.8	5.2	15.5	1976
Greeley, CO	6.2	30.9	17.0	7.8	15.5	6.6	4.8	2.3	9.0	1992
Green Bay, WI	3.2	15.8	16.1	12.1	15.9	10.0	9.3	4.5	13.1	1978
Greensboro, NC	3.0	15.9	19.1	15.6	15.3	10.9	9.4	4.5	6.2	1982
Honolulu, HI	3.5	10.6	11.9	12.3	24.2	19.0	11.0	4.1	3.3	1975
Houston, TX	7.6	23.1	14.7	15.8	18.2	8.9	6.5	2.7	2.5	1987
Huntsville, AL	7.2	20.9	19.1	15.6	12.5	13.4	6.8	2.1	2.5	1988
Indianapolis, IN	4.1	16.6	16.8	10.7	12.9	10.9	10.5	4.4	13.1	1979
Jacksonville, FL	5.2	23.5	16.7	17.3	12.8	8.6	8.2	3.6	4.1	1987
Kansas City, MO	2.7	14.3	14.5	12.4	16.0	12.1	11.8	4.6	11.6	1976
Lafayette, LA	6.6	17.7	13.1	15.6	16.9	10.5	9.5	4.5	5.7	1982
Las Cruces, NM	5.5	21.3	19.3	18.5	15.4	7.5	6.6	2.7	3.2	1988
Las Vegas, NV	4.3	32.0	29.2	15.1	10.8	5.3	2.3	0.7	0.4	1995
Lexington, KY	4.0	17.7	17.5	14.3	15.3	11.7	8.2	3.3	8.0	1982
Lincoln, NE	4.5	15.4	15.2	10.7	15.5	10.5	10.5	3.2	14.5	1977
Little Rock, AR	6.3	18.8	18.0	15.1	17.6	10.5	6.9	3.2	3.6	1985
Los Angeles, CA	1.7	6.4	7.6	12.5	16.3	15.9	18.9	8.6	12.0	1967

Table continued on next page.

Metro Area	2010 or Later	2000 -2009	1990 -1999	1980 -1989	1970 -1979	1960 -1969	1950 -1959	1940 -1949	Before 1940	Median Year
Louisville, KY	2.7	13.9	14.4	9.4	15.8	12.2	12.5	6.2	12.9	1974
Madison, WI	3.8	17.3	16.0	11.3	15.7	9.5	8.2	3.6	14.6	1979
Manchester, NH	1.9	10.3	10.4	21.2	15.3	9.6	7.3	3.7	20.3	1976
McAllen, TX	6.7	30.4	22.8	16.5	11.9	5.4	3.3	1.5	1.5	1994
Miami, FL	2.1	13.6	15.2	19.6	21.7	12.6	10.0	3.0	2.3	1980
Midland, TX	9.5	10.3	15.2	19.6	13.3	11.7	15.8	3.0	1.6	1982
Minneapolis, MN	3.0	14.9	14.5	14.7	15.0	9.9	9.9	3.8	14.4	1978
Nashville, TN	5.9	20.9	18.7	14.9	14.0	9.9	7.5	3.4	4.8	1987
New Orleans, LA	2.6	12.5	9.8	13.5	19.4	13.9	9.7	5.2	13.5	1974
New York, NY	1.7	7.1	6.1	8.0	10.0	13.8	16.1	9.0	28.2	1958
Oklahoma City, OK	6.2	15.6	11.5	15.1	17.4	12.4	9.9	5.3	6.5	1979
Omaha, NE	4.4	15.0	12.9	10.1	14.8	11.9	9.1	3.8	17.9	1975
Orlando, FL	4.9	25.3	21.2	20.7	13.5	6.2	5.4	1.3	1.6	1991
Peoria, IL	2.2	9.0	8.7	6.2	17.3	13.3	15.3	8.2	19.9	1965
Philadelphia, PA	1.9	8.1	9.6	10.1	12.2	12.1	15.8	8.3	22.0	1963
Phoenix, AZ	3.8	26.8	20.6	17.6	16.4	7.3	5.3	1.3	1.0	1991
Pittsburgh, PA	1.8	6.6	7.6	7.3	12.1	11.4	17.0	9.1	27.1	1958
Portland, OR	3.8	15.3	18.8	11.4	17.7	8.7	7.2	4.6	12.6	1980
Providence, RI	1.2	6.5	8.2	10.8	12.2	10.6	11.8	6.5	32.0	1960
Provo, UT	8.0	27.9	20.3	9.4	15.3	5.2	5.1	3.5	5.2	1993
Raleigh, NC	7.6	28.2	24.1	15.7	9.8	6.1	4.0	1.6	2.8	1994
Reno, NV	3.0	22.7	20.6	15.5	18.6	9.1	5.6	2.3	2.6	1988
Richmond, VA	3.9	15.8	15.6	15.8	15.5	9.7	9.7	4.5	9.5	1981
Roanoke, VA	1.7	12.3	12.7	12.1	16.6	12.9	13.2	5.9	12.5	1973
Rochester, MN	4.0	18.6	14.9	12.2	13.8	9.8	8.1	3.7	15.0	1980
Salem, OR	2.5	14.6	17.6	10.8	23.7	10.3	7.9	4.4	8.3	1978
Salt Lake City, UT	5.4	16.1	16.0	12.9	19.2	9.0	9.1	4.0	8.3	1980
San Antonio, TX	7.4	22.1	14.9	15.9	14.0	8.7	7.8	4.4	4.8	1986
San Diego, CA	2.2	12.2	12.5	19.6	22.8	12.0	10.8	3.5	4.4	1978
San Francisco, CA	1.9	8.0	8.3	11.3	15.0	13.3	14.0	8.0	20.3	1966
San Jose, CA	3.2	9.3	10.7	12.7	22.1	18.4	14.5	4.0	5.0	1974
Santa Rosa, CA	1.4	10.9	13.5	18.7	21.2	11.6	8.6	5.4	8.7	1977
Savannah, GA	5.6	22.6	15.9	14.3	11.8	8.3	8.4	4.7	8.4	1986
Seattle, WA	4.7	15.8	16.0	14.8	14.8	11.0	7.7	4.5	10.6	1981
Sioux Falls, SD	7.7	20.1	15.6	10.1	14.6	7.2	8.0	4.4	12.2	1983
Springfield, IL	2.2	10.3	13.4	9.4	15.8	12.5	12.2	6.9	17.3	1971
Tallahassee, FL	2.9	19.4	23.0	19.7	16.0	8.4	6.2	2.4	2.0	1988
Tampa, FL	3.4	17.0	14.1	20.4	21.6	10.1	8.6	2.0	2.8	1982
Topeka, KS	1.3	9.7	12.7	10.6	16.5	13.7	12.2	5.2	18.0	1971
Tyler, TX	4.9	17.9	16.0	16.9	16.7	9.6	10.4	3.6	4.0	1983
Virginia Beach, VA	3.7	13.3	15.2	19.4	16.0	11.9	10.1	4.7	5.7	1981
Visalia, CA	3.3	17.1	14.6	15.6	18.7	10.6	8.6	5.5	6.0	1980
Washington, DC	4.1	15.1	14.6	16.1	14.6	12.2	9.6	5.1	8.5	1980
Wilmington, NC	4.3	21.4	24.7	16.1	13.2	6.5	5.0	3.8	5.0	1990
Winston-Salem, NC	2.8	16.4	17.1	15.6	16.8	11.5	9.3	4.2	6.4	1981
U.S.	3.2	14.5	14.0	13.6	15.5	10.8	10.5	5.1	12.9	1977

Note: Figures are percentages except for Median Year; Figures cover the Metropolitan Statistical Area—see Appendix B for areas included
Source: U.S. Census Bureau, 2013-2017 American Community Survey 5-Year Estimates

Gross Monthly Rent: City

City	Under $500	$500 -$999	$1,000 -$1,499	$1,500 -$1,999	$2,000 -$2,499	$2,500 -$2,999	$3,000 and up	Median ($)
Albany, NY	11.4	49.6	32.3	4.9	1.0	0.4	0.4	924
Albuquerque, NM	9.0	56.9	27.5	5.1	0.8	0.2	0.4	833
Allentown, PA	11.0	47.3	34.1	6.4	0.9	0.1	0.1	938
Anchorage, AK	3.9	21.7	40.6	17.9	12.0	2.6	1.3	1,261
Ann Arbor, MI	5.3	30.6	38.6	14.9	6.2	2.0	2.3	1,166
Athens, GA	8.8	61.9	22.1	5.4	1.4	0.1	0.2	815
Atlanta, GA	11.9	35.1	34.0	13.6	3.4	1.1	1.0	1,037
Austin, TX	3.4	29.2	42.9	17.3	4.9	1.2	1.2	1,165
Baton Rouge, LA	10.6	59.8	21.0	5.4	2.1	0.8	0.3	827
Billings, MT	11.8	57.0	21.0	5.8	1.0	0.7	2.7	826
Boise City, ID	7.4	59.8	26.2	3.9	1.5	0.2	1.0	875
Boston, MA	18.2	13.1	21.2	23.1	12.1	6.2	6.0	1,445
Boulder, CO	3.0	16.7	36.1	23.7	10.7	4.5	5.2	1,412
Cape Coral, FL	1.2	31.5	49.7	12.5	3.5	0.8	0.8	1,136
Cedar Rapids, IA	19.6	63.9	13.8	1.4	0.8	0.2	0.4	729
Charleston, SC	7.4	31.5	37.5	16.2	4.0	1.6	1.8	1,135
Charlotte, NC	4.4	43.8	39.0	9.8	1.9	0.4	0.7	1,018
Chicago, IL	9.9	37.9	29.9	13.5	5.1	2.1	1.6	1,029
Clarksville, TN	6.2	51.2	34.3	6.5	1.7	0.1	0.1	930
College Station, TX	2.2	54.7	25.4	12.1	4.7	0.6	0.2	940
Colorado Springs, CO	5.0	44.0	33.3	13.1	2.7	1.2	0.7	1,013
Columbia, MO	8.3	60.8	22.1	4.9	2.9	0.6	0.2	825
Columbia, SC	12.0	54.5	26.3	5.6	1.3	0.00	0.3	878
Columbus, OH	7.9	56.3	29.0	4.8	1.5	0.2	0.3	889
Dallas, TX	5.4	51.6	29.7	8.5	2.7	1.1	0.8	937
Denver, CO	8.8	31.1	33.5	17.2	6.3	1.8	1.3	1,131
Des Moines, IA	11.5	64.3	20.0	3.2	0.7	0.2	0.1	797
Durham, NC	7.3	48.3	34.1	7.8	1.4	0.3	0.7	958
Edison, NJ	2.3	9.1	44.7	33.3	9.3	0.7	0.5	1,438
El Paso, TX	19.6	53.6	22.4	3.2	0.8	0.3	0.2	792
Eugene, OR	8.4	46.5	32.3	8.6	2.8	0.5	0.9	956
Evansville, IN	15.1	69.4	14.4	0.7	0.2	0.0	0.1	738
Fargo, ND	9.6	69.6	15.7	3.6	1.3	0.2	0.0	765
Fayetteville, NC	7.1	56.5	32.3	3.5	0.4	0.0	0.2	892
Fort Collins, CO	4.1	29.4	38.7	21.5	5.3	0.6	0.4	1,191
Fort Wayne, IN	16.0	70.7	10.8	1.6	0.7	0.1	0.1	708
Fort Worth, TX	5.8	48.0	31.8	10.7	2.3	0.9	0.5	967
Gainesville, FL	7.5	56.6	27.2	6.4	1.4	0.5	0.4	886
Grand Rapids, MI	11.5	56.8	24.4	5.8	1.2	0.3	0.1	854
Greeley, CO	12.0	49.1	26.0	10.5	1.5	0.4	0.5	881
Green Bay, WI	16.6	70.5	11.5	0.9	0.2	0.0	0.3	682
Greensboro, NC	8.1	68.6	19.2	2.5	0.9	0.3	0.4	813
Honolulu, HI	6.7	15.4	33.4	20.7	10.9	6.1	6.8	1,411
Houston, TX	4.7	51.9	28.5	10.1	2.7	1.1	1.1	940
Huntsville, AL	14.6	61.9	20.2	2.2	0.5	0.3	0.3	773
Indianapolis, IN	7.4	64.4	23.5	3.5	0.7	0.2	0.3	840
Jacksonville, FL	7.0	44.9	37.6	8.2	1.6	0.4	0.3	984
Kansas City, MO	10.7	55.4	27.3	4.7	1.3	0.2	0.5	862
Lafayette, LA	11.3	57.3	23.7	5.4	2.0	0.2	0.1	853
Las Cruces, NM	15.2	60.3	20.9	2.5	0.9	0.0	0.2	770
Las Vegas, NV	5.4	42.3	38.4	10.6	2.2	0.6	0.4	1,024
Lexington, KY	11.9	56.7	24.9	4.0	1.7	0.3	0.5	828
Lincoln, NE	13.8	61.4	20.1	3.0	0.6	0.4	0.8	788
Little Rock, AR	9.7	60.1	25.0	3.3	1.1	0.3	0.4	842
Los Angeles, CA	5.8	21.5	35.0	19.9	9.8	4.2	3.8	1,302

Table continued on next page.

City	Under $500	$500 -$999	$1,000 -$1,499	$1,500 -$1,999	$2,000 -$2,499	$2,500 -$2,999	$3,000 and up	Median ($)
Louisville, KY	15.9	60.6	19.1	3.3	0.6	0.3	0.1	779
Madison, WI	4.3	45.0	34.4	11.2	3.2	1.1	0.8	1,008
Manchester, NH	6.9	36.2	44.2	10.2	2.1	0.1	0.4	1,063
McAllen, TX	14.5	63.7	17.2	3.2	0.9	0.1	0.4	758
Miami, FL	11.3	34.6	28.8	14.7	5.7	2.7	2.2	1,056
Midland, TX	2.6	30.0	41.5	19.1	4.1	1.9	0.8	1,179
Minneapolis, MN	14.1	42.0	28.1	10.8	3.5	0.9	0.5	941
Nashville, TN	9.4	44.0	34.2	8.7	2.6	0.7	0.4	970
New Orleans, LA	12.7	42.5	31.4	9.6	2.5	0.7	0.6	954
New York, NY	11.1	17.2	31.6	20.4	9.0	4.5	6.3	1,340
Oklahoma City, OK	9.7	61.7	21.8	5.2	1.1	0.3	0.3	819
Omaha, NE	9.3	57.0	26.9	4.7	1.3	0.4	0.3	861
Orlando, FL	3.8	35.6	44.9	12.3	2.5	0.6	0.4	1,091
Peoria, IL	17.7	60.6	15.4	4.1	1.3	0.5	0.4	756
Philadelphia, PA	11.8	41.6	32.0	9.3	3.1	1.2	1.1	970
Phoenix, AZ	6.0	48.8	34.1	8.3	1.8	0.6	0.4	954
Pittsburgh, PA	15.3	46.3	25.2	9.3	2.7	0.8	0.4	887
Portland, OR	7.4	33.9	34.4	15.9	5.3	1.8	1.3	1,109
Providence, RI	19.6	36.7	33.7	6.7	2.0	0.7	0.6	949
Provo, UT	14.6	55.7	21.1	6.7	1.8	0.1	0.1	793
Raleigh, NC	4.1	44.9	38.8	9.1	1.9	0.4	0.8	1,010
Reno, NV	7.9	51.8	27.5	10.4	1.7	0.5	0.1	906
Richmond, VA	12.6	44.6	31.9	8.1	2.3	0.3	0.3	942
Roanoke, VA	14.7	62.8	19.5	2.0	0.3	0.4	0.2	776
Rochester, MN	10.8	47.7	28.2	9.6	2.0	0.4	1.3	891
Salem, OR	7.8	58.5	24.5	6.4	1.5	0.3	1.0	861
Salt Lake City, UT	10.3	52.2	26.7	8.5	1.6	0.5	0.2	881
San Antonio, TX	8.9	50.8	31.1	7.3	1.2	0.4	0.4	918
San Diego, CA	3.8	15.2	30.9	24.4	15.7	6.3	3.8	1,503
San Francisco, CA	10.2	14.5	17.9	17.8	13.7	10.5	15.4	1,709
San Jose, CA	4.8	8.5	20.7	24.7	18.3	12.2	10.6	1,822
Santa Rosa, CA	5.7	13.5	35.4	27.3	13.6	3.4	1.1	1,432
Savannah, GA	11.5	45.7	33.6	6.4	1.5	0.5	0.8	942
Seattle, WA	7.6	17.9	32.4	24.1	10.1	4.5	3.4	1,377
Sioux Falls, SD	11.3	68.2	16.5	2.5	0.4	0.7	0.5	771
Springfield, IL	14.8	64.8	16.7	2.4	0.7	0.5	0.1	765
Tallahassee, FL	5.9	49.7	32.6	8.1	3.0	0.5	0.3	957
Tampa, FL	9.2	38.0	34.3	12.3	3.9	1.3	0.9	1,031
Topeka, KS	16.9	61.9	15.8	3.1	1.8	0.2	0.3	751
Tyler, TX	8.4	59.3	23.4	6.5	1.7	0.2	0.5	864
Virginia Beach, VA	2.9	16.2	49.0	22.3	6.7	1.6	1.3	1,296
Visalia, CA	5.9	48.8	32.8	9.3	2.8	0.4	0.1	958
Washington, DC	11.0	16.7	25.7	19.5	12.6	7.0	7.6	1,424
Wilmington, NC	14.9	48.9	28.3	5.8	0.9	0.3	0.9	889
Winston-Salem, NC	13.8	64.8	17.4	2.5	1.1	0.0	0.4	765
U.S.	10.5	41.1	28.7	11.7	4.5	1.8	1.7	982

Note: Figures are percentages except for Median; Gross rent is the contract rent plus the estimated average monthly cost of utilities (electricity, gas, and water and sewer) and fuels (oil, coal, kerosene, wood, etc.) if these are paid by the renter (or paid for the renter by someone else).
Source: U.S. Census Bureau, 2013-2017 American Community Survey 5-Year Estimates

Gross Monthly Rent: Metro Area

MSA[1]	Under $500	$500 -$999	$1,000 -$1,499	$1,500 -$1,999	$2,000 -$2,499	$2,500 -2,999	$3,000 and up	Median ($)
Albany, NY	9.1	46.4	33.3	7.8	2.1	0.7	0.7	956
Albuquerque, NM	8.9	55.5	28.2	5.7	1.0	0.2	0.5	850
Allentown, PA	10.3	40.8	35.7	10.2	1.9	0.5	0.6	990
Anchorage, AK	4.2	23.5	39.9	17.9	11.0	2.3	1.2	1,237
Ann Arbor, MI	5.9	42.1	34.1	11.3	3.6	1.4	1.6	1,025
Athens, GA	9.2	62.3	21.5	5.1	1.3	0.3	0.2	813
Atlanta, GA	5.1	39.5	40.8	11.0	2.4	0.7	0.6	1,053
Austin, TX	3.6	30.5	41.8	17.3	4.6	1.2	1.1	1,155
Baton Rouge, LA	10.1	54.9	25.2	6.9	2.1	0.5	0.3	873
Billings, MT	12.5	56.7	21.4	5.5	1.1	0.6	2.2	822
Boise City, ID	9.9	55.4	28.3	4.5	1.1	0.2	0.5	879
Boston, MA	13.3	16.4	30.2	22.0	10.2	4.3	3.6	1,335
Boulder, CO	4.8	19.9	36.6	23.1	9.1	3.2	3.3	1,334
Cape Coral, FL	4.4	42.0	38.2	9.4	3.2	1.2	1.7	1,035
Cedar Rapids, IA	20.2	63.1	14.0	1.5	0.7	0.1	0.4	714
Charleston, SC	6.7	38.2	37.1	12.2	3.2	1.3	1.2	1,054
Charlotte, NC	7.1	50.5	32.0	7.6	1.7	0.5	0.6	935
Chicago, IL	8.0	38.1	33.0	13.4	4.6	1.6	1.3	1,048
Clarksville, TN	9.7	52.5	30.2	6.1	1.1	0.2	0.1	878
College Station, TX	5.7	57.7	22.9	9.6	3.4	0.5	0.2	885
Colorado Springs, CO	4.6	40.0	34.8	15.8	2.9	1.3	0.7	1,070
Columbia, MO	8.8	61.1	22.4	4.3	2.7	0.5	0.2	826
Columbia, SC	8.6	55.5	27.8	6.1	1.4	0.3	0.3	889
Columbus, OH	9.0	55.2	28.4	5.3	1.4	0.4	0.3	887
Dallas, TX	4.2	43.9	35.4	11.8	3.0	1.0	0.8	1,022
Denver, CO	5.4	28.1	37.4	19.8	6.3	1.6	1.3	1,203
Des Moines, IA	8.8	58.4	26.0	4.6	1.1	0.5	0.5	857
Durham, NC	7.8	48.3	32.4	8.0	1.9	0.7	0.9	953
Edison, NJ	9.5	16.9	34.1	21.1	9.1	4.2	5.1	1,341
El Paso, TX	19.6	53.2	22.5	3.5	0.8	0.2	0.2	789
Eugene, OR	8.6	50.4	31.2	6.8	2.0	0.3	0.6	921
Evansville, IN	15.9	66.6	15.4	1.1	0.2	0.2	0.5	732
Fargo, ND	10.6	66.9	16.4	4.3	1.3	0.3	0.1	770
Fayetteville, NC	7.8	56.1	30.8	4.5	0.6	0.0	0.1	883
Fort Collins, CO	4.9	33.4	36.7	18.7	4.6	1.0	0.6	1,140
Fort Wayne, IN	16.8	68.4	12.1	1.7	0.8	0.1	0.1	714
Fort Worth, TX	4.2	43.9	35.4	11.8	3.0	1.0	0.8	1,022
Gainesville, FL	7.8	52.5	29.7	7.2	1.5	0.8	0.5	912
Grand Rapids, MI	9.0	62.9	21.4	5.0	1.0	0.2	0.5	826
Greeley, CO	9.7	44.4	29.9	12.6	2.1	0.6	0.6	955
Green Bay, WI	13.2	70.0	14.8	1.3	0.4	0.0	0.3	736
Greensboro, NC	12.1	67.6	16.7	2.3	0.8	0.2	0.3	777
Honolulu, HI	5.4	11.9	26.5	20.4	14.4	9.4	12.1	1,653
Houston, TX	4.7	45.9	32.4	11.8	3.0	1.1	1.1	995
Huntsville, AL	14.1	60.8	20.8	3.0	0.8	0.3	0.2	779
Indianapolis, IN	7.5	60.4	26.0	4.5	1.0	0.3	0.3	859
Jacksonville, FL	6.1	42.2	37.7	10.5	2.4	0.6	0.5	1,019
Kansas City, MO	9.5	52.6	29.4	6.1	1.5	0.3	0.5	894
Lafayette, LA	17.9	59.0	17.8	4.0	1.1	0.1	0.1	769
Las Cruces, NM	18.8	58.2	18.7	3.1	0.6	0.0	0.5	735
Las Vegas, NV	3.3	42.2	38.4	12.1	2.7	0.7	0.5	1,048
Lexington, KY	13.1	58.8	22.9	3.4	1.3	0.2	0.4	808
Lincoln, NE	14.0	61.3	20.0	2.9	0.6	0.4	0.8	784
Little Rock, AR	10.7	63.6	21.6	3.1	0.6	0.2	0.3	805
Los Angeles, CA	4.6	17.8	34.8	23.0	11.0	4.8	3.9	1,393

Table continued on next page.

MSA[1]	Under $500	$500 -$999	$1,000 -$1,499	$1,500 -$1,999	$2,000 -$2,499	$2,500 -2,999	$3,000 and up	Median ($)
Louisville, KY	15.0	60.6	20.1	3.1	0.7	0.3	0.2	792
Madison, WI	5.8	49.6	32.2	8.9	2.3	0.7	0.5	958
Manchester, NH	6.4	29.6	43.8	16.7	2.7	0.5	0.2	1,132
McAllen, TX	22.0	62.2	12.9	1.9	0.7	0.2	0.1	699
Miami, FL	5.7	24.1	39.1	20.0	6.9	2.4	1.9	1,232
Midland, TX	2.8	29.5	41.6	19.3	4.1	1.8	0.7	1,177
Minneapolis, MN	9.8	40.1	32.7	12.7	3.1	0.9	0.7	1,001
Nashville, TN	9.4	46.0	32.3	8.4	2.5	0.8	0.6	951
New Orleans, LA	9.8	46.8	32.6	8.1	1.7	0.5	0.5	947
New York, NY	9.5	16.9	34.1	21.1	9.1	4.2	5.1	1,341
Oklahoma City, OK	9.4	61.1	22.6	5.3	1.0	0.3	0.3	827
Omaha, NE	9.5	56.3	26.6	5.3	1.4	0.3	0.6	865
Orlando, FL	3.0	35.0	44.6	13.7	2.5	0.7	0.6	1,107
Peoria, IL	16.7	63.2	14.8	2.9	1.2	0.5	0.7	739
Philadelphia, PA	8.7	34.5	36.9	13.0	4.3	1.3	1.2	1,075
Phoenix, AZ	4.6	42.4	37.5	11.0	2.8	0.9	0.9	1,032
Pittsburgh, PA	18.1	55.1	19.3	4.8	1.6	0.5	0.6	776
Portland, OR	5.5	33.5	38.8	15.5	4.4	1.2	1.2	1,118
Providence, RI	16.4	42.4	30.0	8.2	2.0	0.5	0.5	925
Provo, UT	7.8	46.6	30.0	11.6	2.8	0.8	0.5	950
Raleigh, NC	5.2	44.0	37.8	9.5	2.2	0.5	0.8	1,008
Reno, NV	6.6	48.6	30.2	11.3	2.2	0.5	0.5	946
Richmond, VA	7.8	37.7	40.3	10.4	2.4	0.7	0.7	1,044
Roanoke, VA	13.4	62.2	19.7	3.7	0.6	0.3	0.2	804
Rochester, MN	14.0	50.5	24.6	7.7	1.8	0.3	1.0	835
Salem, OR	7.8	56.3	27.3	6.2	1.5	0.3	0.7	877
Salt Lake City, UT	6.2	42.9	35.7	11.8	2.2	0.7	0.5	1,009
San Antonio, TX	8.3	47.4	32.4	8.9	1.9	0.6	0.6	949
San Diego, CA	3.9	14.8	33.5	24.1	14.0	5.7	4.0	1,467
San Francisco, CA	6.6	11.8	23.4	23.5	15.7	9.0	10.0	1,673
San Jose, CA	3.9	7.2	17.6	24.0	20.2	13.4	13.5	1,940
Santa Rosa, CA	5.5	14.4	32.9	26.4	14.1	4.3	2.3	1,456
Savannah, GA	9.2	41.2	37.0	9.2	2.0	0.7	0.6	997
Seattle, WA	6.0	22.0	35.7	22.5	8.6	3.1	2.3	1,297
Sioux Falls, SD	12.1	67.2	16.6	2.5	0.4	0.7	0.5	771
Springfield, IL	13.3	65.0	17.7	2.7	0.5	0.6	0.1	777
Tallahassee, FL	7.4	50.1	31.3	7.8	2.8	0.4	0.2	938
Tampa, FL	5.5	43.2	35.9	10.9	2.8	0.9	0.8	1,014
Topeka, KS	18.0	59.9	16.2	3.3	1.8	0.2	0.7	751
Tyler, TX	8.3	58.2	25.1	6.6	1.1	0.2	0.4	873
Virginia Beach, VA	7.3	31.1	39.8	15.5	4.3	1.2	0.8	1,124
Visalia, CA	11.4	51.8	28.0	6.5	1.9	0.3	0.1	877
Washington, DC	5.0	9.6	29.5	29.6	14.9	6.3	5.1	1,600
Wilmington, NC	11.3	48.2	31.0	6.8	1.5	0.3	0.9	929
Winston-Salem, NC	15.3	65.7	15.4	2.4	0.7	0.2	0.3	732
U.S.	10.5	41.1	28.7	11.7	4.5	1.8	1.7	982

Note: (1) Figures cover the Metropolitan Statistical Area (MSA)—see Appendix B for areas included; Figures are percentages except for Median; Gross rent is the contract rent plus the estimated average monthly cost of utilities (electricity, gas, and water and sewer) and fuels (oil, coal, kerosene, wood, etc.) if these are paid by the renter (or paid for the renter by someone else).
Source: U.S. Census Bureau, 2013-2017 American Community Survey 5-Year Estimates

Highest Level of Education: City

City	Less than H.S.	H.S. Diploma	Some College, No Deg.	Associate Degree	Bachelors Degree	Masters Degree	Profess. School Degree	Doctorate Degree
Albany, NY	10.4	25.8	17.2	8.3	19.7	13.0	2.8	2.6
Albuquerque, NM	10.5	22.8	24.2	8.3	18.9	10.6	2.4	2.4
Allentown, PA	21.7	37.2	18.2	7.9	10.0	3.4	0.9	0.6
Anchorage, AK	6.6	23.8	26.3	8.7	22.0	8.8	2.6	1.2
Ann Arbor, MI	3.2	7.4	11.3	4.0	29.5	26.8	7.2	10.7
Athens, GA	13.4	21.0	17.7	6.6	20.7	12.3	2.6	5.7
Atlanta, GA	10.1	19.4	16.8	5.0	27.3	14.1	5.1	2.2
Austin, TX	11.5	16.3	18.1	5.2	30.8	12.7	3.1	2.4
Baton Rouge, LA	12.1	27.8	22.8	5.0	19.0	8.3	2.5	2.5
Billings, MT	7.1	28.1	24.4	7.9	22.2	7.2	2.1	1.1
Boise City, ID	5.6	20.7	24.1	8.7	26.6	9.7	2.7	1.8
Boston, MA	13.9	20.9	13.1	4.6	26.1	13.7	4.4	3.1
Boulder, CO	3.5	7.1	12.0	3.6	34.8	24.6	5.7	8.7
Cape Coral, FL	9.0	35.8	22.2	10.5	15.1	5.4	1.2	0.7
Cedar Rapids, IA	6.1	26.6	23.4	12.1	22.4	6.7	1.6	1.2
Charleston, SC	5.7	17.8	17.3	7.8	32.3	12.3	4.6	2.3
Charlotte, NC	11.4	18.1	20.2	7.5	28.2	11.1	2.5	1.1
Chicago, IL	16.2	22.9	17.7	5.7	22.3	10.5	3.0	1.6
Clarksville, TN	7.9	28.2	28.8	9.6	17.7	6.3	0.7	0.7
College Station, TX	6.1	12.6	19.0	6.5	28.5	15.4	2.7	9.1
Colorado Springs, CO	6.8	19.6	24.6	10.6	23.4	11.6	2.0	1.4
Columbia, MO	5.8	16.9	17.8	6.1	28.3	15.1	4.5	5.5
Columbia, SC	11.8	19.7	19.4	6.7	23.6	12.6	3.9	2.3
Columbus, OH	10.9	25.8	21.1	7.1	22.9	8.8	1.8	1.6
Dallas, TX	24.1	21.4	18.3	4.5	19.9	7.9	2.8	1.1
Denver, CO	13.3	17.6	17.3	5.3	28.4	12.3	4.0	1.9
Des Moines, IA	13.6	30.5	21.4	9.2	17.6	5.2	1.6	0.8
Durham, NC	12.7	15.7	16.8	6.1	25.6	14.3	4.0	4.8
Edison, NJ	8.1	19.5	11.8	5.8	29.5	20.2	2.7	2.4
El Paso, TX	21.0	23.6	23.6	7.7	16.3	5.8	1.2	0.7
Eugene, OR	6.6	17.6	26.5	8.2	23.1	11.6	3.1	3.2
Evansville, IN	13.1	34.8	23.2	8.2	13.7	5.3	1.0	0.7
Fargo, ND	6.2	20.3	20.4	14.3	27.4	7.4	2.0	2.0
Fayetteville, NC	8.8	23.9	30.5	10.8	17.2	6.8	1.1	0.9
Fort Collins, CO	3.6	15.2	19.1	8.4	31.8	15.4	2.5	4.0
Fort Wayne, IN	11.4	29.0	23.0	9.8	17.6	7.0	1.5	0.7
Fort Worth, TX	18.5	24.8	21.6	6.7	19.0	7.0	1.3	1.0
Gainesville, FL	8.5	21.2	17.6	9.6	21.5	13.0	3.8	4.8
Grand Rapids, MI	14.0	22.3	21.4	7.5	22.5	8.7	1.9	1.5
Greeley, CO	16.4	25.9	23.3	8.5	16.8	6.7	1.0	1.3
Green Bay, WI	12.9	31.5	19.4	11.3	18.0	5.1	1.2	0.6
Greensboro, NC	10.1	22.2	22.7	7.6	23.5	9.7	2.4	1.9
Honolulu, HI	11.5	24.0	18.6	9.6	23.4	7.9	3.0	2.1
Houston, TX	22.1	22.8	18.3	5.1	19.3	8.3	2.5	1.6
Huntsville, AL	10.0	19.3	20.9	8.2	25.6	12.4	1.6	2.0
Indianapolis, IN	14.5	28.0	20.7	7.1	19.2	7.3	2.1	1.1
Jacksonville, FL	11.0	28.4	22.9	10.1	18.8	6.3	1.6	0.7
Kansas City, MO	10.9	26.0	22.4	7.3	20.9	9.1	2.3	1.2
Lafayette, LA	13.3	25.3	20.9	4.5	24.1	7.7	2.7	1.6
Las Cruces, NM	13.2	20.4	24.8	8.6	19.7	9.4	1.9	2.0
Las Vegas, NV	16.0	28.2	24.9	7.8	15.2	5.5	1.8	0.7
Lexington, KY	9.5	20.5	20.3	7.9	23.9	11.6	3.5	2.9
Lincoln, NE	7.1	22.2	22.0	11.0	24.2	8.9	2.2	2.5
Little Rock, AR	8.7	22.5	22.8	5.7	24.0	9.8	3.8	2.7
Los Angeles, CA	23.6	19.5	17.8	6.1	21.8	7.2	2.7	1.3

Table continued on next page.

City	Less than H.S.	H.S. Diploma	Some College, No Deg.	Associate Degree	Bachelors Degree	Masters Degree	Profess. School Degree	Doctorate Degree
Louisville, KY	11.5	28.9	23.0	7.9	16.8	8.5	2.2	1.2
Madison, WI	4.6	14.1	15.8	8.4	32.2	15.5	4.4	5.1
Manchester, NH	12.6	30.8	19.1	9.3	18.9	7.3	1.3	0.8
McAllen, TX	26.1	19.3	19.2	6.1	20.7	6.1	1.6	0.9
Miami, FL	24.4	29.8	12.5	7.0	16.3	6.0	3.1	1.0
Midland, TX	15.9	24.7	24.3	6.9	20.5	5.3	1.8	0.7
Minneapolis, MN	10.7	16.4	17.5	7.1	29.3	12.7	3.9	2.5
Nashville, TN	12.2	23.2	19.5	6.5	24.3	9.7	2.6	1.9
New Orleans, LA	14.1	23.0	21.7	4.7	20.7	9.5	4.3	2.0
New York, NY	18.9	24.1	13.9	6.4	21.5	10.7	3.1	1.5
Oklahoma City, OK	14.4	25.3	23.4	7.2	19.5	7.0	2.1	1.0
Omaha, NE	11.6	22.5	22.9	7.4	23.0	8.4	2.8	1.5
Orlando, FL	9.9	24.3	19.3	10.7	23.7	8.3	2.6	1.1
Peoria, IL	11.8	23.9	20.6	9.2	20.9	9.8	2.7	1.1
Philadelphia, PA	16.7	33.8	16.8	5.5	15.8	7.5	2.4	1.4
Phoenix, AZ	18.8	23.5	22.1	7.8	17.8	7.1	1.9	1.0
Pittsburgh, PA	7.9	26.7	15.4	8.0	22.1	12.3	3.9	3.6
Portland, OR	8.2	15.7	21.0	7.0	28.8	13.2	3.9	2.2
Providence, RI	22.2	26.9	15.6	5.1	16.2	8.2	2.8	2.9
Provo, UT	7.6	14.3	26.7	9.0	28.5	9.2	1.7	3.1
Raleigh, NC	8.5	15.6	18.2	7.7	31.9	13.2	2.6	2.2
Reno, NV	13.0	22.6	24.8	7.6	20.0	7.9	2.2	1.9
Richmond, VA	15.5	23.0	18.8	5.3	22.3	10.3	3.1	1.8
Roanoke, VA	15.0	31.8	20.9	9.2	14.3	5.5	2.4	1.0
Rochester, MN	6.0	19.4	19.1	10.8	24.7	11.1	5.1	3.9
Salem, OR	13.3	25.4	26.0	8.2	16.5	7.4	1.9	1.3
Salt Lake City, UT	11.5	17.2	19.4	6.8	25.0	12.0	4.1	3.9
San Antonio, TX	18.0	26.2	22.6	7.5	16.6	6.5	1.7	1.0
San Diego, CA	12.1	15.7	20.4	7.4	26.3	11.7	3.5	3.0
San Francisco, CA	12.1	12.3	14.5	5.3	33.4	14.7	4.9	2.7
San Jose, CA	16.5	17.4	17.5	7.3	24.7	12.6	1.8	2.1
Santa Rosa, CA	13.7	19.1	26.0	9.5	20.0	7.4	2.8	1.5
Savannah, GA	13.3	26.1	25.8	6.6	17.3	8.2	1.5	1.2
Seattle, WA	5.8	10.1	15.8	6.7	35.9	17.0	5.1	3.6
Sioux Falls, SD	8.3	25.6	21.6	10.8	23.0	7.4	2.3	1.1
Springfield, IL	8.6	26.2	22.0	7.3	21.6	9.7	3.2	1.3
Tallahassee, FL	6.7	16.3	19.2	9.8	26.3	13.8	3.8	4.1
Tampa, FL	12.9	25.9	16.8	8.2	22.1	9.1	3.4	1.5
Topeka, KS	10.3	31.4	24.2	5.9	17.4	7.5	2.0	1.3
Tyler, TX	16.5	20.5	25.8	9.6	18.3	6.0	2.2	1.1
Virginia Beach, VA	6.6	21.9	26.1	10.5	22.7	9.1	2.0	1.0
Visalia, CA	18.3	22.6	27.0	9.4	14.8	5.5	1.7	0.8
Washington, DC	9.7	17.6	13.0	3.1	23.8	20.2	8.3	4.3
Wilmington, NC	8.7	20.2	21.0	8.9	27.4	9.1	2.7	1.9
Winston-Salem, NC	13.2	23.7	21.6	7.3	20.5	9.0	2.9	1.7
U.S.	12.7	27.3	20.8	8.3	19.1	8.4	2.0	1.4

Note: Figures cover persons age 25 and over
Source: U.S. Census Bureau, 2013-2017 American Community Survey 5-Year Estimates

Highest Level of Education: Metro Area

Metro Area	Less than H.S.	H.S. Diploma	Some College, No Deg.	Associate Degree	Bachelors Degree	Masters Degree	Profess. School Degree	Doctorate Degree
Albany, NY	7.8	26.8	17.0	12.3	20.0	11.9	2.3	2.0
Albuquerque, NM	11.8	24.5	24.2	8.2	17.5	9.7	2.0	2.1
Allentown, PA	10.5	34.5	17.4	9.3	17.7	7.9	1.5	1.1
Anchorage, AK	7.0	25.9	27.2	8.9	19.9	7.9	2.3	1.1
Ann Arbor, MI	4.9	15.3	18.4	7.0	25.7	18.6	4.4	5.7
Athens, GA	13.3	25.1	18.1	7.1	18.4	10.9	2.7	4.5
Atlanta, GA	11.1	24.3	20.2	7.3	23.3	9.9	2.4	1.4
Austin, TX	10.7	19.2	20.7	6.4	27.8	11.0	2.4	1.8
Baton Rouge, LA	12.6	32.3	21.6	5.9	18.0	6.5	1.8	1.4
Billings, MT	7.0	30.3	24.1	8.4	21.0	6.5	1.8	0.9
Boise City, ID	8.7	25.9	25.5	9.0	21.0	7.0	1.7	1.2
Boston, MA	8.7	22.8	14.9	7.2	25.5	14.5	3.3	3.1
Boulder, CO	5.4	12.4	15.6	6.2	32.6	18.6	3.9	5.3
Cape Coral, FL	12.7	30.9	20.4	8.9	17.1	6.9	2.1	1.1
Cedar Rapids, IA	5.7	29.2	22.5	12.5	21.0	6.7	1.3	1.0
Charleston, SC	9.9	25.6	21.1	9.3	21.9	8.5	2.3	1.4
Charlotte, NC	11.7	24.2	21.5	8.8	22.9	8.4	1.7	0.9
Chicago, IL	12.1	24.2	19.9	7.1	22.3	10.5	2.5	1.4
Clarksville, TN	10.1	30.4	26.8	9.3	15.4	6.3	1.0	0.7
College Station, TX	14.8	23.2	20.6	6.1	19.4	9.1	2.0	4.7
Colorado Springs, CO	6.2	20.3	25.0	11.2	22.6	11.5	1.8	1.3
Columbia, MO	6.5	21.0	19.5	7.1	25.9	12.3	3.6	4.1
Columbia, SC	11.0	27.0	21.5	8.6	19.8	9.0	1.8	1.3
Columbus, OH	9.1	28.3	20.0	7.4	22.6	9.1	2.1	1.5
Dallas, TX	15.2	22.4	21.9	6.8	22.2	8.7	1.8	1.1
Denver, CO	9.5	20.2	20.7	7.6	26.8	11.2	2.6	1.5
Des Moines, IA	7.6	25.3	20.8	10.2	25.2	7.6	2.3	1.0
Durham, NC	11.3	18.6	16.9	6.8	23.7	13.5	4.0	5.1
Edison, NJ	14.1	25.2	15.2	6.8	22.5	11.6	3.1	1.5
El Paso, TX	23.3	24.1	23.1	7.5	15.1	5.2	1.1	0.6
Eugene, OR	8.5	23.9	28.9	9.1	17.7	8.0	2.0	1.9
Evansville, IN	10.0	33.4	22.3	9.4	15.7	6.9	1.5	0.8
Fargo, ND	5.6	21.6	21.4	14.4	26.4	7.4	1.5	1.7
Fayetteville, NC	10.2	26.3	29.1	10.9	15.6	6.2	0.9	0.7
Fort Collins, CO	4.2	19.5	21.4	8.9	27.6	12.8	2.1	3.4
Fort Wayne, IN	10.4	30.8	22.3	10.4	17.2	6.8	1.5	0.7
Fort Worth, TX	15.2	22.4	21.9	6.8	22.2	8.7	1.8	1.1
Gainesville, FL	8.4	23.4	18.5	10.3	20.2	10.7	4.0	4.4
Grand Rapids, MI	9.6	27.2	22.2	9.2	21.0	8.0	1.7	1.1
Greeley, CO	12.3	27.3	24.3	9.1	18.6	6.4	1.1	0.9
Green Bay, WI	8.6	32.7	19.5	12.1	19.2	5.9	1.4	0.6
Greensboro, NC	13.7	27.4	21.8	8.5	18.7	7.0	1.5	1.3
Honolulu, HI	8.6	26.2	20.8	10.5	22.4	7.6	2.5	1.5
Houston, TX	17.2	23.3	21.0	6.7	20.4	8.1	2.0	1.4
Huntsville, AL	10.7	23.1	20.8	8.2	23.4	10.9	1.4	1.5
Indianapolis, IN	10.7	28.2	20.2	7.7	21.4	8.4	2.1	1.2
Jacksonville, FL	9.6	27.8	22.7	10.0	20.0	7.2	1.8	0.9
Kansas City, MO	8.5	25.9	22.3	7.6	22.7	9.6	2.3	1.1
Lafayette, LA	17.6	35.5	19.2	5.6	15.6	4.6	1.2	0.7
Las Cruces, NM	20.8	22.2	21.8	7.8	16.2	8.0	1.5	1.7
Las Vegas, NV	14.7	28.8	25.3	7.9	15.5	5.4	1.5	0.8
Lexington, KY	10.7	24.6	20.5	8.0	21.0	10.0	2.9	2.3
Lincoln, NE	6.7	22.6	21.8	11.6	24.0	8.7	2.2	2.4
Little Rock, AR	9.8	29.4	23.7	7.3	18.8	7.4	2.0	1.5
Los Angeles, CA	20.3	19.9	19.6	7.1	21.5	7.8	2.4	1.4

Table continued on next page.

Metro Area	Less than H.S.	H.S. Diploma	Some College, No Deg.	Associate Degree	Bachelors Degree	Masters Degree	Profess. School Degree	Doctorate Degree
Louisville, KY	10.8	30.4	22.5	8.2	16.8	8.2	2.0	1.1
Madison, WI	5.0	21.4	18.5	10.4	27.2	11.5	3.0	3.1
Manchester, NH	8.2	26.8	18.4	10.1	23.4	10.4	1.6	1.2
McAllen, TX	36.3	23.2	18.1	4.6	12.8	3.8	0.9	0.4
Miami, FL	14.9	27.1	18.0	9.3	19.5	7.3	2.7	1.2
Midland, TX	16.5	25.7	24.0	7.2	19.3	5.2	1.6	0.5
Minneapolis, MN	6.6	21.9	20.6	10.3	26.5	9.8	2.5	1.6
Nashville, TN	10.9	27.5	20.5	7.1	22.1	8.4	2.0	1.4
New Orleans, LA	14.0	28.6	22.8	5.6	18.3	6.8	2.7	1.3
New York, NY	14.1	25.2	15.2	6.8	22.5	11.6	3.1	1.5
Oklahoma City, OK	11.6	27.2	24.3	7.4	19.4	7.2	1.8	1.2
Omaha, NE	8.8	24.0	23.5	8.6	23.1	8.6	2.2	1.2
Orlando, FL	10.9	26.6	20.8	11.4	20.4	7.2	1.8	0.9
Peoria, IL	8.4	30.2	23.0	10.3	18.7	7.2	1.4	0.8
Philadelphia, PA	10.0	29.8	17.1	6.9	21.5	10.3	2.6	1.8
Phoenix, AZ	13.1	23.4	24.7	8.5	19.3	8.0	1.8	1.1
Pittsburgh, PA	6.7	33.7	16.2	9.9	20.5	9.3	2.1	1.6
Portland, OR	8.5	20.4	24.3	8.8	23.7	9.9	2.5	1.7
Providence, RI	13.7	28.6	18.1	8.6	18.9	8.7	1.9	1.5
Provo, UT	6.1	16.4	27.7	10.9	26.8	8.6	1.7	1.8
Raleigh, NC	9.0	18.5	18.6	8.8	28.8	12.1	2.1	2.1
Reno, NV	12.3	23.8	25.9	8.2	18.7	7.3	2.0	1.6
Richmond, VA	10.9	25.8	20.7	7.3	22.0	9.6	2.2	1.5
Roanoke, VA	11.4	30.5	21.3	9.8	17.3	6.6	2.0	1.1
Rochester, MN	6.0	24.7	20.7	11.7	21.9	8.9	3.6	2.5
Salem, OR	14.0	26.8	26.7	8.3	15.6	6.2	1.5	0.9
Salt Lake City, UT	9.7	23.1	25.2	8.9	21.2	8.2	2.1	1.5
San Antonio, TX	15.4	26.3	23.1	7.8	17.6	7.1	1.6	1.0
San Diego, CA	13.3	18.6	22.4	8.3	23.0	9.5	2.7	2.1
San Francisco, CA	11.5	16.0	18.4	6.8	28.1	12.8	3.8	2.7
San Jose, CA	12.7	15.1	16.2	6.9	26.5	16.5	2.7	3.5
Santa Rosa, CA	12.3	19.1	25.2	9.5	21.7	7.9	2.8	1.4
Savannah, GA	10.8	26.3	24.3	7.5	19.3	8.4	2.0	1.4
Seattle, WA	7.8	19.9	21.9	9.3	25.9	10.9	2.6	1.8
Sioux Falls, SD	7.5	26.6	21.4	12.1	22.7	6.7	2.0	1.0
Springfield, IL	7.6	28.1	22.7	8.0	21.2	8.7	2.6	1.1
Tallahassee, FL	9.8	23.4	20.1	9.1	21.6	10.3	2.9	2.9
Tampa, FL	10.9	29.2	21.1	10.0	18.6	7.2	1.9	1.1
Topeka, KS	8.1	32.7	24.1	7.0	18.0	7.4	1.6	1.1
Tyler, TX	15.1	24.6	25.7	9.4	17.4	5.4	1.6	0.8
Virginia Beach, VA	9.2	25.2	25.4	9.5	19.0	8.9	1.7	1.2
Visalia, CA	31.4	25.8	21.7	7.3	9.3	3.2	0.9	0.4
Washington, DC	9.5	18.4	16.5	5.7	25.5	17.1	4.2	3.1
Wilmington, NC	8.8	23.4	22.0	9.6	23.9	8.5	2.2	1.5
Winston-Salem, NC	13.8	29.5	21.3	9.0	17.1	6.5	1.6	1.1
U.S.	12.7	27.3	20.8	8.3	19.1	8.4	2.0	1.4

Note: Figures cover persons age 25 and over; Figures cover the Metropolitan Statistical Area—see Appendix B for areas included
Source: U.S. Census Bureau, 2013-2017 American Community Survey 5-Year Estimates

School Enrollment by Grade and Control: City

City	Preschool (%)		Kindergarten (%)		Grades 1 - 4 (%)		Grades 5 - 8 (%)		Grades 9 - 12 (%)	
	Public	Private	Public	Private	Public	Private	Public	Private	Public	Private
Albany, NY	60.1	39.9	86.4	13.6	89.8	10.2	82.2	17.8	80.7	19.3
Albuquerque, NM	57.1	42.9	85.2	14.8	91.1	8.9	88.4	11.6	90.6	9.4
Allentown, PA	76.2	23.8	84.9	15.1	88.1	11.9	86.6	13.4	90.5	9.5
Anchorage, AK	51.7	48.3	90.9	9.1	92.8	7.2	93.8	6.2	93.5	6.5
Ann Arbor, MI	24.8	75.2	91.7	8.3	91.4	8.6	84.4	15.6	93.8	6.2
Athens, GA	64.7	35.3	90.6	9.4	89.7	10.3	89.9	10.1	84.5	15.5
Atlanta, GA	53.8	46.2	83.7	16.3	85.5	14.5	81.1	18.9	78.3	21.7
Austin, TX	48.6	51.4	87.5	12.5	89.5	10.5	89.5	10.5	91.6	8.4
Baton Rouge, LA	63.8	36.2	72.1	27.9	79.4	20.6	79.6	20.4	81.1	18.9
Billings, MT	43.1	56.9	86.0	14.0	88.3	11.7	87.6	12.4	91.1	8.9
Boise City, ID	39.2	60.8	91.7	8.3	88.3	11.7	91.2	8.8	90.1	9.9
Boston, MA	48.7	51.3	84.7	15.3	86.0	14.0	87.4	12.6	89.4	10.6
Boulder, CO	38.5	61.5	84.1	15.9	90.2	9.8	92.5	7.5	97.0	3.0
Cape Coral, FL	71.9	28.1	94.4	5.6	94.8	5.2	93.7	6.3	95.0	5.0
Cedar Rapids, IA	64.6	35.4	82.2	17.8	88.5	11.5	91.0	9.0	92.6	7.4
Charleston, SC	44.5	55.5	81.1	18.9	82.6	17.4	76.7	23.3	81.3	18.7
Charlotte, NC	48.0	52.0	89.9	10.1	90.1	9.9	88.6	11.4	88.9	11.1
Chicago, IL	61.9	38.1	81.5	18.5	86.2	13.8	86.7	13.3	87.0	13.0
Clarksville, TN	63.0	37.0	95.1	4.9	94.1	5.9	96.0	4.0	94.9	5.1
College Station, TX	44.2	55.8	86.9	13.1	87.0	13.0	93.4	6.6	91.9	8.1
Colorado Springs, CO	59.5	40.5	89.8	10.2	92.0	8.0	92.9	7.1	92.6	7.4
Columbia, MO	39.7	60.3	71.2	28.8	77.5	22.5	87.7	12.3	88.7	11.3
Columbia, SC	49.6	50.4	76.3	23.7	89.0	11.0	86.2	13.8	89.6	10.4
Columbus, OH	58.5	41.5	88.2	11.8	89.6	10.4	87.6	12.4	88.4	11.6
Dallas, TX	69.0	31.0	90.0	10.0	91.3	8.7	91.1	8.9	91.4	8.6
Denver, CO	63.1	36.9	88.2	11.8	90.7	9.3	90.6	9.4	93.0	7.0
Des Moines, IA	77.7	22.3	91.0	9.0	89.0	11.0	89.6	10.4	90.4	9.6
Durham, NC	42.6	57.4	84.4	15.6	89.2	10.8	87.9	12.1	91.7	8.3
Edison, NJ	33.3	66.7	66.0	34.0	89.3	10.7	89.0	11.0	89.3	10.7
El Paso, TX	79.0	21.0	92.4	7.6	95.2	4.8	94.1	5.9	96.0	4.0
Eugene, OR	35.3	64.7	82.1	17.9	91.5	8.5	91.1	8.9	90.8	9.2
Evansville, IN	60.2	39.8	83.0	17.0	87.0	13.0	82.7	17.3	90.8	9.2
Fargo, ND	57.8	42.2	92.9	7.1	90.1	9.9	90.0	10.0	89.3	10.7
Fayetteville, NC	63.8	36.2	87.6	12.4	87.0	13.0	89.6	10.4	88.3	11.7
Fort Collins, CO	45.2	54.8	91.3	8.7	94.0	6.0	94.8	5.2	95.1	4.9
Fort Wayne, IN	50.5	49.5	84.8	15.2	83.3	16.7	82.5	17.5	82.9	17.1
Fort Worth, TX	65.8	34.2	89.7	10.3	93.3	6.7	90.5	9.5	92.1	7.9
Gainesville, FL	51.5	48.5	79.0	21.0	85.7	14.3	83.2	16.8	89.6	10.4
Grand Rapids, MI	61.8	38.2	78.3	21.7	81.0	19.0	85.3	14.7	85.3	14.7
Greeley, CO	64.2	35.8	83.6	16.4	92.9	7.1	92.4	7.6	94.5	5.5
Green Bay, WI	67.7	32.3	86.1	13.9	89.8	10.2	89.4	10.6	91.1	8.9
Greensboro, NC	55.3	44.7	89.7	10.3	93.5	6.5	89.0	11.0	93.2	6.8
Honolulu, HI	37.2	62.8	85.1	14.9	85.3	14.7	76.0	24.0	72.7	27.3
Houston, TX	68.4	31.6	90.8	9.2	93.2	6.8	92.4	7.6	93.0	7.0
Huntsville, AL	51.9	48.1	82.3	17.7	83.8	16.2	83.9	16.1	87.2	12.8
Indianapolis, IN	54.5	45.5	85.2	14.8	88.7	11.3	86.6	13.4	87.7	12.3
Jacksonville, FL	58.4	41.6	83.3	16.7	83.6	16.4	81.7	18.3	83.4	16.6
Kansas City, MO	56.6	43.4	87.7	12.3	89.1	10.9	87.2	12.8	86.4	13.6
Lafayette, LA	60.0	40.0	78.9	21.1	81.2	18.8	74.7	25.3	76.4	23.6
Las Cruces, NM	75.0	25.0	94.5	5.5	93.7	6.3	94.3	5.7	92.7	7.3
Las Vegas, NV	61.1	38.9	85.5	14.5	92.0	8.0	91.8	8.2	92.6	7.4
Lexington, KY	46.0	54.0	85.8	14.2	85.5	14.5	85.6	14.4	86.7	13.3
Lincoln, NE	53.8	46.2	82.7	17.3	84.4	15.6	84.9	15.1	85.7	14.3
Little Rock, AR	49.9	50.1	76.6	23.4	83.4	16.6	78.1	21.9	79.4	20.6
Los Angeles, CA	60.7	39.3	88.0	12.0	89.3	10.7	88.7	11.3	88.7	11.3

Table continued on next page.

City	Preschool (%)		Kindergarten (%)		Grades 1 - 4 (%)		Grades 5 - 8 (%)		Grades 9 - 12 (%)	
	Public	Private	Public	Private	Public	Private	Public	Private	Public	Private
Louisville, KY	50.0	50.0	82.1	17.9	81.7	18.3	80.8	19.2	81.0	19.0
Madison, WI	51.7	48.3	85.9	14.1	89.0	11.0	84.2	15.8	92.1	7.9
Manchester, NH	39.2	60.8	81.8	18.2	90.7	9.3	90.4	9.6	90.4	9.6
McAllen, TX	73.0	27.0	85.3	14.7	92.7	7.3	97.4	2.6	97.8	2.2
Miami, FL	57.4	42.6	83.5	16.5	85.9	14.1	88.4	11.6	89.7	10.3
Midland, TX	59.2	40.8	83.8	16.2	84.1	15.9	85.2	14.8	90.6	9.4
Minneapolis, MN	57.8	42.2	85.7	14.3	87.3	12.7	86.7	13.3	87.6	12.4
Nashville, TN	52.2	47.8	86.9	13.1	85.5	14.5	82.7	17.3	83.0	17.0
New Orleans, LA	56.0	44.0	81.3	18.7	80.5	19.5	79.0	21.0	78.3	21.7
New York, NY	58.5	41.5	79.3	20.7	83.5	16.5	82.7	17.3	83.3	16.7
Oklahoma City, OK	70.8	29.2	91.6	8.4	91.4	8.6	89.6	10.4	90.6	9.4
Omaha, NE	57.9	42.1	83.0	17.0	85.9	14.1	87.0	13.0	84.8	15.2
Orlando, FL	59.7	40.3	81.5	18.5	93.0	7.0	86.6	13.4	92.0	8.0
Peoria, IL	70.0	30.0	71.8	28.2	83.2	16.8	80.0	20.0	84.1	15.9
Philadelphia, PA	52.7	47.3	79.3	20.7	80.0	20.0	79.2	20.8	81.6	18.4
Phoenix, AZ	63.0	37.0	91.9	8.1	93.6	6.4	93.2	6.8	94.0	6.0
Pittsburgh, PA	54.1	45.9	77.0	23.0	75.9	24.1	77.4	22.6	80.9	19.1
Portland, OR	38.2	61.8	81.4	18.6	87.5	12.5	88.0	12.0	85.2	14.8
Providence, RI	56.5	43.5	85.1	14.9	86.6	13.4	84.9	15.1	85.3	14.7
Provo, UT	45.4	54.6	95.5	4.5	95.4	4.6	94.8	5.2	87.7	12.3
Raleigh, NC	43.3	56.7	90.2	9.8	90.3	9.7	89.1	10.9	90.6	9.4
Reno, NV	55.8	44.2	89.4	10.6	92.7	7.3	91.9	8.1	95.3	4.7
Richmond, VA	59.2	40.8	86.5	13.5	89.1	10.9	78.3	21.7	87.2	12.8
Roanoke, VA	66.1	33.9	87.0	13.0	89.7	10.3	92.1	7.9	93.5	6.5
Rochester, MN	51.3	48.7	78.8	21.2	85.0	15.0	83.9	16.1	93.6	6.4
Salem, OR	59.7	40.3	91.2	8.8	90.7	9.3	92.7	7.3	95.5	4.5
Salt Lake City, UT	51.3	48.7	91.1	8.9	91.2	8.8	90.8	9.2	93.5	6.5
San Antonio, TX	70.6	29.4	91.8	8.2	93.4	6.6	93.0	7.0	93.9	6.1
San Diego, CA	52.9	47.1	90.8	9.2	91.3	8.7	90.3	9.7	91.0	9.0
San Francisco, CA	32.8	67.2	75.0	25.0	72.6	27.4	71.1	28.9	76.6	23.4
San Jose, CA	43.1	56.9	80.8	19.2	88.4	11.6	88.4	11.6	88.5	11.5
Santa Rosa, CA	50.9	49.1	96.3	3.7	95.2	4.8	95.4	4.6	91.5	8.5
Savannah, GA	66.7	33.3	96.0	4.0	92.0	8.0	89.3	10.7	88.9	11.1
Seattle, WA	33.8	66.2	78.4	21.6	79.6	20.4	76.8	23.2	82.2	17.8
Sioux Falls, SD	52.2	47.8	84.5	15.5	88.7	11.3	89.6	10.4	85.4	14.6
Springfield, IL	65.3	34.7	81.2	18.8	82.6	17.4	84.6	15.4	85.9	14.1
Tallahassee, FL	49.3	50.7	87.8	12.2	83.8	16.2	79.7	20.3	87.1	12.9
Tampa, FL	57.1	42.9	88.7	11.3	90.3	9.7	85.9	14.1	86.7	13.3
Topeka, KS	67.9	32.1	93.1	6.9	89.2	10.8	88.8	11.2	92.7	7.3
Tyler, TX	73.2	26.8	93.2	6.8	87.6	12.4	88.8	11.2	90.6	9.4
Virginia Beach, VA	36.9	63.1	81.9	18.1	91.8	8.2	90.8	9.2	92.9	7.1
Visalia, CA	72.3	27.7	91.9	8.1	93.6	6.4	92.4	7.6	94.6	5.4
Washington, DC	76.7	23.3	90.8	9.2	85.9	14.1	82.2	17.8	82.7	17.3
Wilmington, NC	71.7	28.3	90.7	9.3	87.8	12.2	83.2	16.8	91.1	8.9
Winston-Salem, NC	59.1	40.9	92.7	7.3	92.6	7.4	90.7	9.3	93.0	7.0
U.S.	58.8	41.2	87.7	12.3	89.7	10.3	89.6	10.4	90.3	9.7

Note: Figures shown cover persons 3 years old and over
Source: U.S. Census Bureau, 2013-2017 American Community Survey 5-Year Estimates

School Enrollment by Grade and Control: Metro Area

Metro Area	Preschool (%)		Kindergarten (%)		Grades 1 - 4 (%)		Grades 5 - 8 (%)		Grades 9 - 12 (%)	
	Public	Private	Public	Private	Public	Private	Public	Private	Public	Private
Albany, NY	47.4	52.6	89.5	10.5	91.4	8.6	90.9	9.1	90.9	9.1
Albuquerque, NM	62.5	37.5	85.9	14.1	90.5	9.5	88.5	11.5	90.4	9.6
Allentown, PA	46.4	53.6	80.9	19.1	89.5	10.5	89.5	10.5	90.0	10.0
Anchorage, AK	55.9	44.1	88.7	11.3	90.9	9.1	91.6	8.4	91.3	8.7
Ann Arbor, MI	46.3	53.7	88.5	11.5	87.7	12.3	87.3	12.7	91.3	8.7
Athens, GA	64.6	35.4	90.8	9.2	89.1	10.9	86.9	13.1	84.3	15.7
Atlanta, GA	57.3	42.7	86.3	13.7	90.7	9.3	89.8	10.2	89.8	10.2
Austin, TX	50.5	49.5	88.7	11.3	91.0	9.0	91.2	8.8	93.3	6.7
Baton Rouge, LA	56.1	43.9	73.4	26.6	81.2	18.8	80.7	19.3	81.1	18.9
Billings, MT	43.2	56.8	86.8	13.2	90.5	9.5	89.5	10.5	89.6	10.4
Boise City, ID	41.6	58.4	87.6	12.4	91.1	8.9	92.8	7.2	91.2	8.8
Boston, MA	45.2	54.8	86.6	13.4	90.9	9.1	89.6	10.4	87.2	12.8
Boulder, CO	50.1	49.9	85.5	14.5	91.5	8.5	91.8	8.2	94.7	5.3
Cape Coral, FL	67.6	32.4	92.3	7.7	93.2	6.8	91.8	8.2	92.9	7.1
Cedar Rapids, IA	68.6	31.4	85.0	15.0	89.4	10.6	91.7	8.3	93.4	6.6
Charleston, SC	51.0	49.0	85.6	14.4	90.2	9.8	88.8	11.2	89.6	10.4
Charlotte, NC	51.4	48.6	90.1	9.9	90.5	9.5	89.5	10.5	90.2	9.8
Chicago, IL	58.6	41.4	84.8	15.2	88.8	11.2	89.1	10.9	90.4	9.6
Clarksville, TN	69.0	31.0	94.3	5.7	91.3	8.7	92.1	7.9	91.6	8.4
College Station, TX	62.2	37.8	85.8	14.2	88.9	11.1	90.5	9.5	93.0	7.0
Colorado Springs, CO	62.9	37.1	88.8	11.2	92.0	8.0	92.0	8.0	92.9	7.1
Columbia, MO	45.3	54.7	76.4	23.6	82.0	18.0	90.0	10.0	90.8	9.2
Columbia, SC	54.9	45.1	86.1	13.9	91.9	8.1	92.6	7.4	92.1	7.9
Columbus, OH	52.2	47.8	87.1	12.9	89.6	10.4	88.3	11.7	89.0	11.0
Dallas, TX	58.3	41.7	89.7	10.3	92.6	7.4	92.1	7.9	92.2	7.8
Denver, CO	59.5	40.5	90.5	9.5	92.9	7.1	92.3	7.7	92.9	7.1
Des Moines, IA	64.7	35.3	89.6	10.4	90.9	9.1	90.5	9.5	91.1	8.9
Durham, NC	43.4	56.6	86.5	13.5	89.2	10.8	89.8	10.2	89.4	10.6
Edison, NJ	53.1	46.9	81.8	18.2	86.1	13.9	86.3	13.7	85.8	14.2
El Paso, TX	82.2	17.8	93.2	6.8	95.7	4.3	94.5	5.5	96.4	3.6
Eugene, OR	46.2	53.8	85.1	14.9	91.9	8.1	91.0	9.0	90.8	9.2
Evansville, IN	50.2	49.8	81.4	18.6	82.5	17.5	81.3	18.7	87.9	12.1
Fargo, ND	65.7	34.3	92.5	7.5	89.9	10.1	89.1	10.9	90.7	9.3
Fayetteville, NC	62.4	37.6	88.3	11.7	89.4	10.6	89.9	10.1	89.6	10.4
Fort Collins, CO	52.3	47.7	91.6	8.4	91.7	8.3	92.7	7.3	94.1	5.9
Fort Wayne, IN	46.6	53.4	78.1	21.9	79.9	20.1	79.5	20.5	82.9	17.1
Fort Worth, TX	58.3	41.7	89.7	10.3	92.6	7.4	92.1	7.9	92.2	7.8
Gainesville, FL	49.8	50.2	82.5	17.5	87.4	12.6	82.8	17.2	90.6	9.4
Grand Rapids, MI	63.1	36.9	83.3	16.7	84.0	16.0	85.8	14.2	86.5	13.5
Greeley, CO	69.5	30.5	88.8	11.2	92.0	8.0	93.2	6.8	91.7	8.3
Green Bay, WI	68.1	31.9	85.7	14.3	89.0	11.0	90.1	9.9	94.0	6.0
Greensboro, NC	49.7	50.3	89.2	10.8	91.2	8.8	90.5	9.5	91.6	8.4
Honolulu, HI	37.0	63.0	80.7	19.3	86.0	14.0	78.8	21.2	75.1	24.9
Houston, TX	59.8	40.2	90.0	10.0	92.8	7.2	93.1	6.9	93.4	6.6
Huntsville, AL	50.3	49.7	87.3	12.7	85.5	14.5	85.8	14.2	87.5	12.5
Indianapolis, IN	50.4	49.6	86.4	13.6	89.1	10.9	88.4	11.6	89.2	10.8
Jacksonville, FL	53.9	46.1	84.9	15.1	86.0	14.0	84.3	15.7	86.1	13.9
Kansas City, MO	54.3	45.7	88.5	11.5	89.0	11.0	89.1	10.9	90.0	10.0
Lafayette, LA	66.0	34.0	78.4	21.6	79.8	20.2	77.4	22.6	79.2	20.8
Las Cruces, NM	84.3	15.7	94.9	5.1	95.0	5.0	95.4	4.6	95.2	4.8
Las Vegas, NV	60.3	39.7	89.1	10.9	92.7	7.3	93.6	6.4	93.6	6.4
Lexington, KY	47.8	52.2	86.9	13.1	87.2	12.8	86.1	13.9	87.2	12.8
Lincoln, NE	52.6	47.4	82.6	17.4	84.6	15.4	85.3	14.7	86.8	13.2
Little Rock, AR	59.8	40.2	86.1	13.9	89.4	10.6	87.0	13.0	87.2	12.8
Los Angeles, CA	58.8	41.2	88.7	11.3	90.8	9.2	90.9	9.1	91.5	8.5

Table continued on next page.

Metro Area	Preschool (%)		Kindergarten (%)		Grades 1 - 4 (%)		Grades 5 - 8 (%)		Grades 9 - 12 (%)	
	Public	Private	Public	Private	Public	Private	Public	Private	Public	Private
Louisville, KY	47.3	52.7	82.5	17.5	83.3	16.7	82.5	17.5	83.1	16.9
Madison, WI	63.0	37.0	89.5	10.5	90.0	10.0	89.4	10.6	94.7	5.3
Manchester, NH	39.3	60.7	81.7	18.3	88.8	11.2	90.1	9.9	88.4	11.6
McAllen, TX	88.0	12.0	93.2	6.8	96.6	3.4	98.2	1.8	98.4	1.6
Miami, FL	49.4	50.6	83.6	16.4	86.6	13.4	87.0	13.0	87.5	12.5
Midland, TX	56.7	43.3	85.9	14.1	86.7	13.3	87.2	12.8	90.8	9.2
Minneapolis, MN	59.6	40.4	87.5	12.5	89.0	11.0	89.6	10.4	91.0	9.0
Nashville, TN	47.1	52.9	87.6	12.4	87.9	12.1	85.4	14.6	84.7	15.3
New Orleans, LA	53.1	46.9	75.9	24.1	76.6	23.4	76.3	23.7	75.4	24.6
New York, NY	53.1	46.9	81.8	18.2	86.1	13.9	86.3	13.7	85.8	14.2
Oklahoma City, OK	71.7	28.3	89.4	10.6	91.1	8.9	90.4	9.6	91.6	8.4
Omaha, NE	58.4	41.6	85.7	14.3	87.6	12.4	88.3	11.7	87.7	12.3
Orlando, FL	56.1	43.9	83.6	16.4	88.0	12.0	87.9	12.1	90.2	9.8
Peoria, IL	61.3	38.7	82.3	17.7	87.9	12.1	86.6	13.4	88.9	11.1
Philadelphia, PA	44.0	56.0	81.6	18.4	84.9	15.1	84.0	16.0	83.3	16.7
Phoenix, AZ	60.1	39.9	91.2	8.8	92.8	7.2	93.2	6.8	93.8	6.2
Pittsburgh, PA	48.8	51.2	84.3	15.7	88.1	11.9	88.5	11.5	89.7	10.3
Portland, OR	42.3	57.7	85.2	14.8	88.4	11.6	90.1	9.9	91.2	8.8
Providence, RI	53.7	46.3	87.9	12.1	89.8	10.2	89.4	10.6	87.2	12.8
Provo, UT	50.0	50.0	92.7	7.3	93.6	6.4	94.1	5.9	94.1	5.9
Raleigh, NC	40.7	59.3	88.1	11.9	89.4	10.6	89.4	10.6	90.0	10.0
Reno, NV	58.0	42.0	90.0	10.0	93.2	6.8	91.5	8.5	93.9	6.1
Richmond, VA	43.4	56.6	87.8	12.2	90.5	9.5	88.7	11.3	90.6	9.4
Roanoke, VA	57.9	42.1	89.8	10.2	89.9	10.1	90.7	9.3	91.3	8.7
Rochester, MN	60.8	39.2	83.3	16.7	87.0	13.0	87.3	12.7	93.3	6.7
Salem, OR	58.8	41.2	88.1	11.9	90.3	9.7	91.6	8.4	93.8	6.2
Salt Lake City, UT	55.1	44.9	91.4	8.6	93.0	7.0	93.2	6.8	93.9	6.1
San Antonio, TX	66.0	34.0	91.1	8.9	93.1	6.9	92.5	7.5	93.6	6.4
San Diego, CA	54.9	45.1	89.8	10.2	92.4	7.6	91.6	8.4	92.2	7.8
San Francisco, CA	40.8	59.2	84.7	15.3	86.1	13.9	85.9	14.1	87.8	12.2
San Jose, CA	37.6	62.4	80.8	19.2	86.3	13.7	86.7	13.3	87.5	12.5
Santa Rosa, CA	52.0	48.0	94.1	5.9	91.9	8.1	90.8	9.2	90.0	10.0
Savannah, GA	65.5	34.5	90.4	9.6	88.2	11.8	84.5	15.5	85.9	14.1
Seattle, WA	40.8	59.2	84.5	15.5	88.4	11.6	88.7	11.3	90.5	9.5
Sioux Falls, SD	54.9	45.1	86.0	14.0	89.1	10.9	90.7	9.3	87.9	12.1
Springfield, IL	65.3	34.7	85.4	14.6	87.4	12.6	87.4	12.6	90.3	9.7
Tallahassee, FL	54.2	45.8	86.3	13.7	85.7	14.3	81.3	18.7	87.5	12.5
Tampa, FL	58.5	41.5	86.5	13.5	88.2	11.8	87.4	12.6	89.4	10.6
Topeka, KS	71.3	28.7	92.1	7.9	90.1	9.9	88.6	11.4	92.2	7.8
Tyler, TX	73.0	27.0	88.6	11.4	88.6	11.4	90.4	9.6	89.0	11.0
Virginia Beach, VA	54.1	45.9	86.9	13.1	90.4	9.6	90.1	9.9	91.8	8.2
Visalia, CA	83.9	16.1	95.3	4.7	96.6	3.4	96.4	3.6	96.6	3.4
Washington, DC	44.2	55.8	86.2	13.8	88.9	11.1	87.9	12.1	88.5	11.5
Wilmington, NC	56.1	43.9	87.3	12.7	89.7	10.3	86.7	13.3	92.9	7.1
Winston-Salem, NC	56.5	43.5	91.3	8.7	92.5	7.5	90.1	9.9	92.5	7.5
U.S.	58.8	41.2	87.7	12.3	89.7	10.3	89.6	10.4	90.3	9.7

Note: Figures shown cover persons 3 years old and over; Figures cover the Metropolitan Statistical Area—see Appendix B for areas included
Source: U.S. Census Bureau, 2013-2017 American Community Survey 5-Year Estimates

Educational Attainment by Race: City

City	High School Graduate or Higher (%)					Bachelor's Degree or Higher (%)				
	Total	White	Black	Asian	Hisp.[1]	Total	White	Black	Asian	Hisp.[1]
Albany, NY	89.6	93.4	84.3	84.0	78.2	38.1	49.8	12.8	49.2	24.0
Albuquerque, NM	89.5	91.1	92.2	82.2	82.0	34.3	37.1	30.9	46.1	20.8
Allentown, PA	78.3	81.3	81.0	86.3	68.3	14.9	17.5	10.0	37.7	6.1
Anchorage, AK	93.4	96.6	90.3	78.9	87.1	34.6	41.0	20.3	26.4	19.9
Ann Arbor, MI	96.8	98.3	85.0	96.1	92.5	74.2	76.4	35.6	84.7	69.5
Athens, GA	86.6	90.3	80.0	94.0	49.6	41.3	52.1	15.6	79.3	13.4
Atlanta, GA	89.9	97.2	83.1	96.9	79.4	48.7	75.7	22.9	83.8	43.1
Austin, TX	88.5	90.0	89.1	92.9	70.2	49.0	52.0	24.7	73.5	23.8
Baton Rouge, LA	87.9	95.6	82.0	84.1	82.4	32.4	52.7	14.9	50.3	24.3
Billings, MT	92.9	93.6	82.0	85.2	79.4	32.6	33.3	20.0	45.2	10.4
Boise City, ID	94.4	95.3	75.6	86.2	83.4	40.9	41.4	20.3	51.8	21.2
Boston, MA	86.1	92.1	82.5	77.0	67.8	47.4	63.1	21.3	50.5	20.3
Boulder, CO	96.5	97.4	95.8	91.6	73.2	73.8	74.9	52.9	69.1	42.4
Cape Coral, FL	91.0	91.4	90.3	88.1	81.3	22.5	23.0	17.4	12.7	19.0
Cedar Rapids, IA	93.9	95.0	80.4	95.5	74.3	31.9	32.1	14.5	64.8	19.1
Charleston, SC	94.3	97.2	84.0	92.3	91.6	51.4	60.0	19.6	73.1	39.7
Charlotte, NC	88.6	92.1	88.9	81.8	59.5	42.9	53.5	27.9	55.4	16.8
Chicago, IL	83.8	87.5	84.1	87.8	65.0	37.5	48.9	20.2	59.4	14.9
Clarksville, TN	92.1	92.6	91.6	81.2	86.4	25.5	26.7	21.4	27.6	16.9
College Station, TX	93.9	94.9	87.0	96.3	80.3	55.8	56.5	24.8	80.5	45.9
Colorado Springs, CO	93.2	95.0	93.6	84.4	77.4	38.4	41.7	21.6	43.6	19.4
Columbia, MO	94.2	95.4	88.4	91.6	88.3	53.4	56.7	18.6	71.5	41.3
Columbia, SC	88.2	94.5	81.6	91.5	73.4	42.3	61.0	19.3	76.1	31.3
Columbus, OH	89.1	91.3	86.0	83.2	70.0	35.1	40.3	18.8	57.2	19.6
Dallas, TX	75.9	74.1	85.1	84.3	47.9	31.6	37.6	17.4	62.9	9.1
Denver, CO	86.7	88.6	87.3	80.7	61.4	46.5	51.3	23.0	49.7	13.5
Des Moines, IA	86.4	89.3	82.9	63.6	57.1	25.2	27.6	13.6	18.9	8.5
Durham, NC	87.3	90.3	86.8	91.5	45.2	48.8	60.6	33.1	74.3	13.3
Edison, NJ	91.9	91.8	93.6	93.4	82.8	54.8	37.3	30.9	75.4	29.6
El Paso, TX	79.0	79.2	94.1	91.3	74.6	24.1	24.1	27.5	49.4	20.0
Eugene, OR	93.4	94.7	92.0	91.8	68.2	41.1	41.6	35.1	62.6	20.5
Evansville, IN	86.9	87.6	83.3	94.0	53.4	20.7	21.9	11.9	40.0	10.6
Fargo, ND	93.8	95.5	79.4	74.1	78.5	38.8	40.0	18.5	50.3	19.9
Fayetteville, NC	91.2	93.1	90.2	83.0	87.4	26.0	29.8	22.3	34.3	20.5
Fort Collins, CO	96.4	96.8	96.9	97.1	82.4	53.6	54.2	37.4	73.2	29.3
Fort Wayne, IN	88.6	91.4	83.3	63.2	58.4	26.8	29.5	13.3	32.6	9.9
Fort Worth, TX	81.5	83.8	86.8	81.0	56.9	28.3	32.5	19.7	41.4	10.8
Gainesville, FL	91.5	94.3	83.7	93.0	91.5	43.1	49.9	18.1	67.6	45.0
Grand Rapids, MI	86.0	90.2	80.3	71.8	49.5	34.7	41.4	14.9	41.3	10.2
Greeley, CO	83.6	86.3	81.5	66.8	63.1	25.8	27.8	17.6	33.0	8.9
Green Bay, WI	87.1	90.3	85.9	69.5	47.8	24.9	27.3	9.6	21.6	6.2
Greensboro, NC	89.9	93.4	88.9	69.2	61.4	37.4	48.2	23.5	37.4	15.3
Honolulu, HI	88.5	97.2	97.5	84.8	90.6	36.4	52.3	24.9	35.4	25.6
Houston, TX	77.9	76.5	87.5	86.7	56.2	31.7	35.6	21.6	58.3	12.0
Huntsville, AL	90.0	93.0	83.2	91.5	58.3	41.6	48.0	24.7	58.3	16.7
Indianapolis, IN	85.5	87.7	84.4	77.7	55.4	29.7	34.8	17.0	47.5	10.8
Jacksonville, FL	89.0	90.7	86.2	84.9	82.5	27.5	30.4	17.7	46.2	24.0
Kansas City, MO	89.1	92.9	85.6	77.1	66.2	33.5	41.7	15.5	45.0	16.2
Lafayette, LA	86.7	92.2	73.6	88.8	51.9	36.0	45.0	14.1	44.2	22.6
Las Cruces, NM	86.8	86.9	96.9	93.6	78.9	33.0	32.1	52.8	56.2	18.6
Las Vegas, NV	84.0	86.8	87.4	90.0	62.5	23.2	25.2	17.3	39.8	9.1
Lexington, KY	90.5	92.8	84.9	89.5	59.8	41.8	45.7	18.8	67.8	17.4
Lincoln, NE	92.9	94.7	88.5	80.1	64.9	37.8	39.1	19.0	43.2	16.2
Little Rock, AR	91.3	94.0	88.2	94.3	60.5	40.3	52.9	20.7	74.8	10.8
Los Angeles, CA	76.4	80.1	87.5	90.0	54.3	33.0	38.2	24.7	53.7	11.2

Table continued on next page.

City	High School Graduate or Higher (%)					Bachelor's Degree or Higher (%)				
	Total	White	Black	Asian	Hisp.[1]	Total	White	Black	Asian	Hisp.[1]
Louisville, KY	88.5	89.4	86.2	81.5	76.9	28.7	31.6	16.3	47.3	24.1
Madison, WI	95.4	96.8	89.1	89.7	76.3	57.1	59.1	24.0	68.6	33.4
Manchester, NH	87.4	88.1	88.6	76.9	68.1	28.3	27.8	24.9	45.5	10.4
McAllen, TX	73.9	75.6	86.3	93.2	69.7	29.3	29.9	17.2	59.1	25.1
Miami, FL	75.6	76.8	70.3	82.5	73.2	26.3	29.0	12.1	56.3	22.8
Midland, TX	84.1	85.6	83.7	79.7	68.2	28.3	30.7	14.2	39.3	11.5
Minneapolis, MN	89.3	95.6	74.9	80.4	56.1	48.3	58.7	14.4	50.0	16.6
Nashville, TN	87.8	90.1	86.7	77.9	58.0	38.5	43.3	26.8	47.2	14.5
New Orleans, LA	85.9	95.3	80.1	73.2	78.5	36.5	62.7	18.3	38.5	33.2
New York, NY	81.1	87.7	82.4	75.3	66.9	36.7	49.1	23.6	41.2	17.4
Oklahoma City, OK	85.6	86.8	88.6	80.2	52.5	29.6	32.1	19.7	40.4	9.3
Omaha, NE	88.4	90.3	85.6	69.9	48.7	35.6	38.3	18.6	48.0	10.2
Orlando, FL	90.1	92.8	83.8	91.9	85.4	35.8	40.3	21.3	59.0	25.3
Peoria, IL	88.2	92.0	78.9	95.4	62.2	34.4	38.9	12.8	74.9	21.7
Philadelphia, PA	83.3	87.5	83.3	69.5	64.7	27.1	37.4	15.7	36.9	13.1
Phoenix, AZ	81.2	83.9	87.2	84.1	59.3	27.8	29.9	20.2	55.4	9.5
Pittsburgh, PA	92.1	93.5	88.3	90.7	87.0	41.9	47.3	17.7	78.2	47.7
Portland, OR	91.8	94.3	87.0	76.6	72.7	48.2	52.1	21.5	38.0	27.1
Providence, RI	77.8	83.7	79.8	76.1	65.1	30.1	39.2	19.8	48.4	9.5
Provo, UT	92.4	93.2	86.5	89.1	74.5	42.5	43.0	41.4	53.0	20.5
Raleigh, NC	91.5	95.2	89.8	88.2	58.2	50.0	60.3	30.6	59.7	21.0
Reno, NV	87.0	88.6	90.6	87.5	60.6	32.0	33.4	19.4	43.5	11.1
Richmond, VA	84.5	91.2	77.6	87.6	51.0	37.5	58.4	15.2	65.1	12.2
Roanoke, VA	85.0	87.2	82.9	55.4	65.8	23.2	28.6	9.1	32.7	12.3
Rochester, MN	94.0	96.0	82.2	83.3	72.8	44.7	45.4	22.5	57.8	23.8
Salem, OR	86.7	89.6	89.2	82.4	55.3	27.1	29.3	14.5	38.7	8.1
Salt Lake City, UT	88.5	94.3	79.1	85.4	59.2	45.1	49.8	25.2	63.1	15.4
San Antonio, TX	82.0	82.3	90.1	86.0	74.1	25.7	26.0	24.0	51.8	15.7
San Diego, CA	87.9	89.4	89.9	88.7	68.1	44.4	47.0	23.6	51.9	19.2
San Francisco, CA	87.9	95.8	89.2	78.6	76.6	55.8	70.9	27.3	44.4	32.3
San Jose, CA	83.5	87.9	90.7	86.0	65.1	41.3	41.8	33.9	53.7	14.1
Santa Rosa, CA	86.3	90.9	87.9	84.6	61.9	31.6	35.3	28.5	39.4	11.5
Savannah, GA	86.7	91.7	82.8	86.1	72.1	28.3	41.9	15.9	50.8	26.1
Seattle, WA	94.2	97.5	84.5	85.3	82.4	61.7	67.9	25.5	55.1	42.6
Sioux Falls, SD	91.7	93.9	74.2	70.8	62.6	33.8	35.9	14.5	34.8	11.4
Springfield, IL	91.4	92.8	84.3	91.1	85.9	35.8	38.2	19.9	67.7	30.5
Tallahassee, FL	93.3	96.8	87.0	96.8	85.2	48.0	56.0	29.1	84.0	40.5
Tampa, FL	87.1	89.3	81.8	87.3	76.3	36.2	41.5	16.8	63.6	20.8
Topeka, KS	89.7	91.1	83.9	89.1	71.6	28.2	30.2	12.4	64.9	11.2
Tyler, TX	83.5	83.4	85.0	97.0	44.7	27.6	31.8	11.6	69.8	7.3
Virginia Beach, VA	93.4	94.9	90.6	89.8	85.6	34.8	36.9	25.3	41.9	23.9
Visalia, CA	81.7	82.7	83.9	78.0	68.4	22.7	22.8	33.6	37.6	11.1
Washington, DC	90.3	97.7	85.6	93.8	71.3	56.6	88.4	25.5	79.7	46.1
Wilmington, NC	91.3	93.9	82.9	77.0	60.4	41.1	47.1	14.4	51.9	18.8
Winston-Salem, NC	86.8	88.5	87.4	87.2	51.2	34.1	41.4	21.7	61.1	10.9
U.S.	87.3	89.3	84.9	86.5	66.7	30.9	32.2	20.6	52.7	15.2

Note: Figures shown cover persons 25 years old and over; (1) People of Hispanic origin can be of any race
Source: U.S. Census Bureau, 2013-2017 American Community Survey 5-Year Estimates

Educational Attainment by Race: Metro Area

Metro Area	High School Graduate or Higher (%)					Bachelor's Degree or Higher (%)				
	Total	White	Black	Asian	Hisp.[1]	Total	White	Black	Asian	Hisp.[1]
Albany, NY	92.2	93.5	85.0	87.3	80.3	36.1	36.7	19.2	62.9	26.0
Albuquerque, NM	88.2	89.9	92.5	85.0	79.7	31.2	34.0	29.8	46.3	18.3
Allentown, PA	89.5	90.7	86.4	88.8	73.3	28.3	28.8	20.7	56.9	11.7
Anchorage, AK	93.0	95.5	90.4	79.0	87.9	31.0	35.3	19.4	26.0	19.3
Ann Arbor, MI	95.1	96.2	88.1	95.7	85.2	54.3	56.2	25.4	81.5	39.7
Athens, GA	86.7	89.5	78.4	91.6	50.3	36.4	41.3	15.1	72.5	14.4
Atlanta, GA	88.9	90.2	89.5	86.7	63.1	37.0	40.8	28.7	55.4	18.6
Austin, TX	89.3	90.5	90.1	92.2	72.0	42.9	44.6	27.9	68.9	21.3
Baton Rouge, LA	87.4	90.6	82.0	85.2	71.5	27.6	31.9	18.3	52.4	18.3
Billings, MT	93.0	93.5	83.6	81.2	77.3	30.2	30.8	21.0	41.2	11.7
Boise City, ID	91.3	92.4	83.0	86.4	65.9	30.9	31.4	24.0	47.7	12.2
Boston, MA	91.3	93.8	84.1	85.5	70.7	46.4	48.8	25.7	60.5	20.9
Boulder, CO	94.6	95.6	92.4	90.2	70.9	60.4	61.5	40.3	66.4	23.7
Cape Coral, FL	87.3	89.0	76.1	89.3	66.2	27.2	28.5	15.6	37.5	13.9
Cedar Rapids, IA	94.3	95.0	81.4	94.1	77.8	30.1	30.1	15.3	62.7	23.4
Charleston, SC	90.1	93.0	83.5	86.6	69.5	34.1	40.8	15.6	47.1	20.4
Charlotte, NC	88.3	90.1	87.2	84.9	61.8	33.9	36.3	25.3	55.7	16.4
Chicago, IL	87.9	90.7	87.0	90.9	65.2	36.7	40.1	21.8	63.9	13.9
Clarksville, TN	89.9	90.3	89.1	79.7	85.3	23.4	24.1	19.4	32.8	16.3
College Station, TX	85.2	87.8	82.0	92.1	60.1	35.3	38.2	13.2	76.6	15.8
Colorado Springs, CO	93.8	95.1	94.2	85.1	80.2	37.2	39.6	23.8	41.6	19.8
Columbia, MO	93.5	94.5	87.9	91.5	79.1	45.9	47.6	17.6	70.2	35.8
Columbia, SC	89.0	91.3	86.4	87.0	63.9	31.9	36.9	22.0	52.0	17.5
Columbus, OH	90.9	92.1	86.8	87.7	73.3	35.3	36.8	21.0	62.7	22.8
Dallas, TX	84.8	85.3	89.9	88.2	57.6	33.7	34.6	25.6	60.1	12.5
Denver, CO	90.5	92.0	89.5	84.9	68.6	42.1	44.3	25.1	50.5	14.8
Des Moines, IA	92.4	93.8	85.0	77.5	61.3	36.1	37.3	18.9	40.7	13.2
Durham, NC	88.7	91.2	86.0	91.8	49.4	46.3	52.9	29.4	72.7	15.7
Edison, NJ	85.9	90.2	84.5	83.0	69.7	38.7	43.9	24.5	53.2	18.2
El Paso, TX	76.7	77.3	94.0	91.7	72.2	22.1	22.3	27.8	48.6	18.1
Eugene, OR	91.5	92.4	92.6	89.1	69.1	29.6	29.7	31.7	54.5	16.9
Evansville, IN	90.0	90.5	84.8	93.6	61.8	24.9	25.5	12.6	53.1	18.0
Fargo, ND	94.4	95.7	80.0	77.6	77.3	37.0	37.8	21.3	46.7	20.3
Fayetteville, NC	89.8	91.7	89.4	82.5	83.6	23.4	25.6	21.6	31.7	19.4
Fort Collins, CO	95.8	96.2	92.0	94.8	81.1	45.9	46.3	34.2	69.0	23.4
Fort Wayne, IN	89.6	91.5	84.0	66.5	61.0	26.2	27.5	14.3	35.5	10.4
Fort Worth, TX	84.8	85.3	89.9	88.2	57.6	33.7	34.6	25.6	60.1	12.5
Gainesville, FL	91.6	93.3	84.3	94.1	88.3	39.4	42.0	19.0	72.2	38.0
Grand Rapids, MI	90.4	92.4	82.7	75.8	60.0	31.8	33.3	16.8	36.1	13.4
Greeley, CO	87.7	89.3	85.6	81.3	64.5	27.0	28.0	26.6	41.6	8.9
Green Bay, WI	91.4	93.0	86.7	80.5	55.4	27.1	27.9	16.2	41.2	9.0
Greensboro, NC	86.3	88.1	86.2	73.7	55.5	28.5	31.2	21.7	39.0	12.3
Honolulu, HI	91.4	97.1	96.5	88.3	92.2	34.0	47.4	27.2	34.9	22.9
Houston, TX	82.8	82.8	89.8	87.5	61.7	31.9	32.3	26.3	57.1	13.7
Huntsville, AL	89.3	90.6	85.4	92.9	64.5	37.3	39.3	27.9	57.7	22.7
Indianapolis, IN	89.3	90.8	85.3	83.2	61.0	33.1	35.1	19.7	55.5	14.6
Jacksonville, FL	90.4	91.9	86.4	86.8	84.4	29.9	32.1	18.2	48.7	26.6
Kansas City, MO	91.5	93.2	87.6	84.6	66.3	35.7	38.2	19.3	53.7	16.2
Lafayette, LA	82.4	86.1	72.4	65.7	64.5	22.1	25.4	11.2	26.2	14.7
Las Cruces, NM	79.2	79.5	95.1	93.6	69.3	27.4	27.1	47.4	59.5	15.2
Las Vegas, NV	85.3	87.5	88.5	89.6	65.0	23.3	24.5	17.2	37.5	9.3
Lexington, KY	89.3	90.7	85.4	90.0	58.6	36.2	38.1	18.6	64.6	15.7
Lincoln, NE	93.3	94.9	88.5	80.3	64.7	37.3	38.4	19.3	43.2	16.3
Little Rock, AR	90.2	91.4	87.4	88.5	67.2	29.7	31.9	20.8	58.1	11.9
Los Angeles, CA	79.7	82.3	89.2	87.8	60.2	33.1	35.2	25.6	51.6	12.2

Table continued on next page.

Metro Area	High School Graduate or Higher (%)					Bachelor's Degree or Higher (%)				
	Total	White	Black	Asian	Hisp.[1]	Total	White	Black	Asian	Hisp.[1]
Louisville, KY	89.2	89.7	86.5	85.1	72.5	28.0	29.2	17.1	53.0	21.1
Madison, WI	95.0	96.0	89.3	89.8	73.0	44.8	45.1	23.3	67.2	25.0
Manchester, NH	91.8	92.1	87.5	88.4	71.2	36.5	35.9	24.7	63.8	18.8
McAllen, TX	63.7	64.6	80.8	92.2	60.2	17.8	17.6	18.3	63.6	15.6
Miami, FL	85.1	86.5	80.4	86.6	79.5	30.6	33.4	18.5	49.8	25.8
Midland, TX	83.5	84.7	83.4	81.9	67.0	26.6	28.5	14.1	45.1	10.8
Minneapolis, MN	93.4	95.9	82.2	80.2	66.5	40.5	42.6	20.9	43.7	18.5
Nashville, TN	89.1	90.2	86.9	83.3	61.7	34.0	35.2	26.0	50.2	15.3
New Orleans, LA	86.0	90.0	80.6	74.7	74.2	29.0	35.4	16.9	39.1	19.0
New York, NY	85.9	90.2	84.5	83.0	69.7	38.7	43.9	24.5	53.2	18.2
Oklahoma City, OK	88.4	89.4	89.8	82.9	58.9	29.6	31.0	20.7	44.3	12.0
Omaha, NE	91.2	92.6	87.3	75.9	56.3	35.1	36.3	21.8	49.9	13.6
Orlando, FL	89.1	90.7	84.8	87.5	82.7	30.3	31.8	20.8	50.9	20.7
Peoria, IL	91.6	92.9	79.6	94.2	71.7	28.2	28.4	12.9	71.7	20.7
Philadelphia, PA	90.0	92.5	86.4	83.9	68.9	36.2	40.1	20.0	55.6	16.7
Phoenix, AZ	86.9	88.8	89.1	87.4	65.6	30.3	31.3	23.9	55.9	11.8
Pittsburgh, PA	93.3	93.7	89.2	88.1	87.4	33.5	33.8	19.3	71.8	35.0
Portland, OR	91.5	93.1	88.1	86.0	66.8	37.9	38.6	25.0	49.3	18.5
Providence, RI	86.3	88.0	82.3	83.9	69.3	31.0	32.3	20.8	50.8	13.1
Provo, UT	93.9	94.5	88.9	93.2	71.9	38.9	39.1	33.5	55.3	19.0
Raleigh, NC	91.0	93.3	88.2	91.8	59.5	45.2	48.6	29.9	71.3	19.3
Reno, NV	87.7	89.3	89.8	88.7	61.1	29.7	30.9	21.2	42.8	10.2
Richmond, VA	89.1	91.9	83.8	87.8	68.5	35.2	40.6	20.9	61.4	19.7
Roanoke, VA	88.6	89.7	84.3	74.8	72.5	27.0	28.9	13.0	43.4	14.6
Rochester, MN	94.0	95.1	82.7	83.5	72.4	36.9	36.6	22.6	56.6	20.9
Salem, OR	86.0	88.3	82.2	83.6	55.7	24.2	25.6	16.9	34.7	7.8
Salt Lake City, UT	90.3	93.6	84.0	85.4	66.1	33.1	35.0	26.3	49.4	12.8
San Antonio, TX	84.6	85.0	91.1	86.4	75.2	27.4	27.8	28.2	51.5	16.1
San Diego, CA	86.7	87.7	90.7	88.9	67.6	37.4	38.3	24.3	50.1	16.3
San Francisco, CA	88.5	92.6	89.8	86.6	69.8	47.4	53.2	26.0	53.2	19.7
San Jose, CA	87.3	90.0	91.5	90.1	67.2	49.2	47.5	36.2	63.5	15.7
Santa Rosa, CA	87.7	92.0	88.2	87.3	60.5	33.8	37.3	25.2	42.8	12.6
Savannah, GA	89.2	91.3	85.3	86.7	78.9	31.1	36.3	19.3	49.6	25.8
Seattle, WA	92.2	94.5	88.5	87.7	71.9	41.1	42.1	23.5	53.2	21.0
Sioux Falls, SD	92.5	94.1	74.9	72.2	64.7	32.5	33.8	15.1	35.9	13.5
Springfield, IL	92.4	93.4	84.2	91.6	86.5	33.6	34.6	19.9	65.4	31.0
Tallahassee, FL	90.2	93.5	82.6	96.2	81.3	37.7	42.7	23.2	79.5	32.7
Tampa, FL	89.1	90.2	85.7	85.9	78.7	28.8	29.3	21.2	50.5	20.6
Topeka, KS	91.9	92.9	84.0	86.6	75.0	28.1	29.3	13.0	59.4	13.4
Tyler, TX	84.9	85.0	85.7	96.0	48.4	25.2	27.2	12.7	62.8	7.5
Virginia Beach, VA	90.8	93.4	86.1	87.3	85.2	30.8	34.9	20.9	42.1	23.1
Visalia, CA	68.6	69.3	80.7	77.0	53.3	13.8	14.2	20.0	29.4	6.0
Washington, DC	90.5	93.4	90.9	90.9	66.5	49.9	57.7	33.5	64.2	24.9
Wilmington, NC	91.2	93.3	83.6	80.2	60.2	36.1	39.8	15.7	51.9	17.9
Winston-Salem, NC	86.2	87.0	86.8	86.2	52.8	26.3	27.2	21.6	49.7	10.8
U.S.	87.3	89.3	84.9	86.5	66.7	30.9	32.2	20.6	52.7	15.2

Note: Figures shown cover persons 25 years old and over; Figures cover the Metropolitan Statistical Area—see Appendix B for areas included; (1) People of Hispanic origin can be of any race
Source: U.S. Census Bureau, 2013-2017 American Community Survey 5-Year Estimates

Cost of Living Index

Urban Area	Composite	Groceries	Housing	Utilities	Transp.	Health	Misc.
Albany, NY	109.8	107.2	119.4	98.9	100.8	105.2	108.6
Albuquerque, NM	97.0	104.7	91.3	93.7	98.5	102.0	98.7
Allentown, PA	106.1	98.6	117.7	104.6	105.8	100.8	100.3
Anchorage, AK	129.1	134.0	142.9	123.0	109.3	144.0	120.5
Ann Arbor, MI	n/a	n/a	n/a	n/a	n/a	n/a	n/a
Athens, GA	n/a	n/a	n/a	n/a	n/a	n/a	n/a
Atlanta, GA	102.0	99.6	106.6	87.1	99.8	108.9	102.6
Austin, TX	98.6	88.8	101.0	96.6	90.9	104.0	102.2
Baton Rouge	100.3	106.6	92.9	87.4	103.1	110.3	105.5
Billings, MT	n/a	n/a	n/a	n/a	n/a	n/a	n/a
Boise City, ID	97.3	95.8	91.9	87.5	112.8	103.8	100.0
Boston, MA	150.2	108.5	214.4	121.8	116.2	133.9	130.5
Boulder, CO	n/a	n/a	n/a	n/a	n/a	n/a	n/a
Cape Coral, FL	95.3	105.0	86.1	100.0	114.1	102.5	92.2
Cedar Rapids, IA	93.9	95.6	84.9	109.0	97.1	95.4	95.9
Charleston, SC	100.8	95.2	94.8	127.1	90.0	106.3	103.5
Charlotte, NC	97.2	99.6	85.6	94.1	94.8	107.4	106.2
Chicago, IL	123.3	102.6	157.5	93.0	125.2	101.6	112.5
Clarksville, TN	n/a	n/a	n/a	n/a	n/a	n/a	n/a
College Station, TX	n/a	n/a	n/a	n/a	n/a	n/a	n/a
Colorado Springs, CO	98.9	96.4	100.3	89.9	104.8	100.9	99.3
Columbia, MO	93.0	96.6	81.8	99.7	91.1	101.3	98.8
Columbia, SC	97.4	109.2	77.0	124.1	91.8	91.4	105.3
Columbus, OH	90.9	95.8	77.7	87.4	92.5	92.1	100.4
Dallas, TX	105.6	107.0	106.7	105.8	98.1	105.2	106.0
Denver, CO	113.3	99.0	139.3	81.0	104.2	102.9	109.0
Des Moines, IA	90.6	95.9	82.1	89.5	102.2	98.5	92.0
Durham, NC	91.3	93.1	82.5	93.3	100.9	93.7	94.8
Edison, NJ[1]	117.5	104.1	139.7	106.7	110.9	106.4	109.7
El Paso, TX	n/a	n/a	n/a	n/a	n/a	n/a	n/a
Eugene, OR	n/a	n/a	n/a	n/a	n/a	n/a	n/a
Evansville, IN	92.3	89.4	82.2	109.3	92.8	98.4	96.8
Fargo, ND	99.3	110.4	89.2	89.9	99.8	115.4	103.9
Fayetteville, NC	n/a	n/a	n/a	n/a	n/a	n/a	n/a
Fort Collins, CO	n/a	n/a	n/a	n/a	n/a	n/a	n/a
Fort Wayne, IN	88.1	87.4	67.0	91.1	101.7	100.6	100.1
Fort Worth, TX	98.1	94.7	89.8	105.2	103.2	104.5	102.5
Gainesville, FL	n/a	n/a	n/a	n/a	n/a	n/a	n/a
Grand Rapids, MI	97.1	89.7	90.6	98.3	102.2	93.1	104.2
Greeley, CO	n/a	n/a	n/a	n/a	n/a	n/a	n/a
Green Bay, WI	89.6	87.9	81.1	93.4	93.4	102.6	93.9
Greensboro, NC[2]	92.9	95.5	67.3	94.7	103.9	117.0	107.0
Honolulu, HI	190.1	165.9	311.0	172.1	140.7	116.3	124.2
Houston, TX	96.3	85.7	97.3	109.9	98.6	93.3	95.9
Huntsville, AL	93.6	93.4	74.2	96.3	93.1	100.6	108.6
Indianapolis, IN	93.0	94.3	79.5	105.6	94.2	91.5	100.4
Jacksonville, FL	92.0	98.2	86.4	97.4	87.4	82.9	95.2
Kansas City, MO	95.1	102.7	85.1	99.0	93.7	99.9	99.5
Lafayette, LA	90.1	99.4	78.7	88.2	103.6	87.8	93.4
Las Cruces, NM	90.0	110.1	76.2	83.7	91.9	105.6	93.2
Las Vegas, NV	104.6	96.6	121.6	95.5	106.9	102.8	95.4
Lexington, KY	94.3	88.5	89.6	93.1	98.5	87.7	100.6
Lincoln, NE	94.5	97.5	81.0	91.0	96.9	103.3	103.8
Little Rock, AR	97.4	94.9	88.9	95.5	98.8	87.2	107.0
Los Angeles, CA	148.4	112.0	238.0	109.7	118.6	107.4	109.9
Louisville, KY	93.3	88.7	78.7	92.0	100.9	97.6	105.3

Table continued on next page.

Urban Area	Composite	Groceries	Housing	Utilities	Transp.	Health	Misc.
Madison, WI	106.1	105.4	109.4	99.4	103.3	118.5	104.4
Manchester, NH	109.3	103.8	106.9	115.0	97.4	117.1	114.2
McAllen, TX	77.5	83.1	62.7	101.9	89.1	71.8	79.1
Miami, FL	116.4	110.1	146.5	101.1	105.4	96.1	102.7
Midland, TX	96.3	89.7	82.3	105.3	105.8	92.3	106.2
Minneapolis, MN	106.4	105.3	104.0	97.6	107.9	105.8	110.9
Nashville, TN	99.3	95.3	93.4	96.7	94.7	83.9	109.6
New Orleans, LA	100.8	104.3	117.0	81.5	109.3	103.2	88.2
New York, NY[3]	182.0	124.2	324.8	120.7	110.1	110.1	127.5
Oklahoma City, OK	84.7	92.1	72.1	94.5	85.6	92.9	88.8
Omaha, NE	95.1	97.1	89.0	99.7	103.2	98.4	95.7
Orlando, FL	95.8	106.0	88.3	102.2	93.0	89.1	98.1
Peoria, IL	95.2	94.9	82.8	92.7	100.0	98.0	104.8
Philadelphia, PA	113.5	116.7	124.8	107.4	113.5	103.3	105.6
Phoenix, AZ	97.5	98.7	94.7	111.3	98.9	95.3	95.8
Pittsburgh, PA	99.2	107.6	95.6	107.7	108.9	92.1	95.1
Portland, OR	131.2	112.3	182.2	88.1	116.8	111.2	112.9
Providence, RI	122.5	109.4	142.1	121.2	102.3	111.0	118.1
Provo, UT	99.2	94.2	99.9	87.1	106.8	102.6	101.1
Raleigh, NC	91.6	93.4	85.1	93.0	94.0	100.5	94.2
Reno, NV	111.9	121.8	116.7	82.3	113.6	111.9	111.2
Richmond, VA	95.0	86.6	88.6	96.5	92.5	115.4	101.3
Roanoke, VA	88.7	86.6	79.0	101.6	87.4	102.5	93.1
Rochester, MN	n/a	n/a	n/a	n/a	n/a	n/a	n/a
Salem, OR	n/a	n/a	n/a	n/a	n/a	n/a	n/a
Salt Lake City, UT	102.8	109.7	102.0	89.8	104.5	99.0	104.3
San Antonio, TX	86.9	86.9	76.4	88.9	87.3	84.7	95.5
San Diego, CA	147.3	112.6	231.0	131.6	121.9	108.0	105.6
San Francisco, CA	196.7	130.6	357.1	126.7	132.2	126.2	130.6
San Jose, CA	n/a	n/a	n/a	n/a	n/a	n/a	n/a
Santa Rosa, CA	n/a	n/a	n/a	n/a	n/a	n/a	n/a
Savannah, GA	88.1	93.7	64.8	96.5	97.0	99.3	99.6
Seattle, WA	155.0	127.0	213.2	111.1	135.0	123.2	137.1
Sioux Falls, SD	97.0	98.0	85.5	92.8	95.4	112.2	105.9
Springfield, IL	n/a	n/a	n/a	n/a	n/a	n/a	n/a
Tallahassee, FL	96.7	110.3	91.7	87.0	95.9	99.0	98.2
Tampa, FL	89.2	103.7	71.8	87.7	99.6	95.4	95.2
Topeka, KS	90.9	97.1	79.4	100.4	95.4	93.4	94.3
Tyler, TX	91.0	92.6	78.0	107.4	94.7	95.3	95.5
Virginia Beach, VA[4]	96.6	96.8	92.7	96.0	91.3	96.7	101.3
Visalia, CA	n/a	n/a	n/a	n/a	n/a	n/a	n/a
Washington, DC	162.9	116.9	268.2	115.6	102.7	99.6	127.7
Wilmington, NC	96.1	99.5	81.8	95.4	101.6	117.1	103.0
Winston-Salem, NC	92.9	95.5	67.3	94.7	103.9	117.0	107.0
U.S.	100.0	100.0	100.0	100.0	100.0	100.0	100.0

Note: The Cost of Living Index measures regional differences in the cost of consumer goods and services, excluding taxes and non-consumer expenditures, for professional and managerial households in the top income quintile. It is based on more than 50,000 prices covering almost 60 different items for which prices are collected three times a year by chambers of commerce, economic development organizations or university applied economic centers in each participating urban area. The numbers shown should be read as a percentage above or below the national average of 100. For example, a value of 115.4 in the groceries column indicates that grocery prices are 15.4% higher than the national average. Small differences in the index numbers should not be interpreted as significant. In cases where data is not available for the city, data for the metro area or for a neighboring city has been provided and noted as follows: (1) Middlesex-Monmouth NJ; (2) Winston-Salem, NC; (3) Brooklyn, NY; (4) Hampton Roads-SE Virginia
Source: The Council for Community and Economic Research (formerly ACCRA), Cost of Living Index, 2018

Grocery Prices

Urban Area	T-Bone Steak ($/pound)	Frying Chicken ($/pound)	Whole Milk ($/half gal.)	Eggs ($/dozen)	Orange Juice ($/64 oz.)	Coffee ($/11.5 oz.)
Albany, NY	11.77	1.39	2.47	2.16	3.51	4.08
Albuquerque, NM	11.22	1.69	2.11	1.93	3.64	5.41
Allentown, PA	12.77	1.35	1.83	1.85	3.23	3.79
Anchorage, AK	12.90	1.67	2.61	2.31	4.24	5.60
Ann Arbor, MI	n/a	n/a	n/a	n/a	n/a	n/a
Athens, GA	n/a	n/a	n/a	n/a	n/a	n/a
Atlanta, GA	12.21	1.39	1.90	1.98	3.50	4.77
Austin, TX	9.85	1.15	1.52	1.70	3.09	3.84
Baton Rouge	12.45	1.33	2.54	2.12	3.91	4.21
Billings, MT	n/a	n/a	n/a	n/a	n/a	n/a
Boise City, ID	11.85	1.24	1.46	1.30	3.74	4.78
Boston, MA	13.18	1.76	1.97	2.02	3.51	4.52
Boulder, CO	n/a	n/a	n/a	n/a	n/a	n/a
Cape Coral, FL	11.05	1.43	2.33	2.10	3.54	3.54
Cedar Rapids, IA	10.86	1.42	1.98	1.32	3.00	4.20
Charleston, SC	9.60	1.16	1.81	1.97	3.37	3.40
Charlotte, NC	10.48	1.10	1.75	1.39	3.67	3.76
Chicago, IL	12.25	1.36	2.09	1.82	4.40	4.59
Clarksville, TN	n/a	n/a	n/a	n/a	n/a	n/a
College Station, TX	n/a	n/a	n/a	n/a	n/a	n/a
Colorado Springs, CO	12.98	1.36	1.50	1.74	3.21	4.71
Columbia, MO	11.04	1.53	1.93	1.38	3.39	4.27
Columbia, SC	12.27	1.30	1.88	2.02	3.92	4.70
Columbus, OH	11.12	1.25	1.56	1.13	3.11	7.51
Dallas, TX	10.82	1.63	2.62	1.87	3.77	5.29
Denver, CO	11.79	1.42	1.65	1.96	3.67	4.88
Des Moines, IA	10.79	1.85	1.89	2.22	3.06	4.07
Durham, NC	10.54	1.15	1.51	1.51	3.22	4.18
Edison, NJ[1]	12.29	1.39	2.28	2.13	3.24	4.07
El Paso, TX	n/a	n/a	n/a	n/a	n/a	n/a
Eugene, OR	n/a	n/a	n/a	n/a	n/a	n/a
Evansville, IN	11.68	1.25	0.96	1.21	3.36	3.27
Fargo, ND	13.91	1.70	2.79	2.00	3.80	4.43
Fayetteville, NC	n/a	n/a	n/a	n/a	n/a	n/a
Fort Collins, CO	n/a	n/a	n/a	n/a	n/a	n/a
Fort Wayne, IN	11.93	1.03	1.47	1.02	3.28	4.29
Fort Worth, TX	11.55	1.50	1.53	1.29	3.27	4.07
Gainesville, FL	n/a	n/a	n/a	n/a	n/a	n/a
Grand Rapids, MI	10.45	1.06	1.77	1.53	3.32	3.36
Greeley, CO	n/a	n/a	n/a	n/a	n/a	n/a
Green Bay, WI	13.06	1.41	1.70	1.08	3.31	4.35
Greensboro, NC[2]	10.16	1.46	1.45	1.31	3.63	3.75
Honolulu, HI	10.50	2.36	4.18	4.00	5.36	8.20
Houston, TX	10.31	1.15	1.18	1.58	3.29	3.51
Huntsville, AL	11.92	1.42	1.73	1.17	3.30	4.03
Indianapolis, IN	11.80	1.38	1.51	1.44	3.40	4.31
Jacksonville, FL	11.17	1.39	2.42	2.21	3.27	3.86
Kansas City, MO	11.76	1.44	2.10	1.79	3.35	4.19
Lafayette, LA	12.83	1.28	2.42	1.80	3.47	3.85
Las Cruces, NM	11.10	1.50	2.22	1.94	3.98	5.44
Las Vegas, NV	7.45	1.21	2.51	2.03	4.18	4.93
Lexington, KY	12.34	1.17	1.52	1.43	3.34	3.76
Lincoln, NE	10.96	1.53	2.50	1.93	3.27	3.98
Little Rock, AR	9.69	1.26	2.16	1.52	3.36	4.04
Los Angeles, CA	13.27	1.70	2.08	2.77	3.43	5.55

Table continued on next page.

Urban Area	T-Bone Steak ($/pound)	Frying Chicken ($/pound)	Whole Milk ($/half gal.)	Eggs ($/dozen)	Orange Juice ($/64 oz.)	Coffee ($/11.5 oz.)
Louisville, KY	10.78	1.29	1.05	1.50	3.35	3.73
Madison, WI	13.82	1.84	2.32	1.83	3.28	4.65
Manchester, NH	12.83	1.52	2.96	1.53	3.31	4.12
McAllen, TX	9.04	0.98	1.39	1.76	3.05	3.91
Miami, FL	11.55	1.54	2.59	2.15	3.78	3.61
Midland, TX	10.70	1.04	1.55	1.79	3.32	4.24
Minneapolis, MN	13.75	2.10	2.51	1.82	3.68	4.70
Nashville, TN	12.08	1.16	1.78	1.51	3.22	4.03
New Orleans, LA	12.05	1.00	2.99	2.38	3.74	3.87
New York, NY[3]	11.51	1.78	2.49	2.60	4.02	4.71
Oklahoma City, OK	10.29	1.27	1.90	1.50	3.28	3.96
Omaha, NE	11.65	1.61	1.67	1.64	3.32	4.03
Orlando, FL	10.51	1.39	2.46	2.05	3.59	3.91
Peoria, IL	12.16	1.78	0.80	1.53	3.86	4.17
Philadelphia, PA	11.47	1.65	2.04	2.41	4.17	4.55
Phoenix, AZ	11.54	1.72	1.42	2.14	3.86	4.84
Pittsburgh, PA	12.95	1.69	1.89	1.78	3.56	4.46
Portland, OR	12.84	1.52	1.87	1.85	4.08	5.42
Providence, RI	12.69	1.64	3.21	2.11	3.55	4.26
Provo, UT	11.08	1.49	1.52	1.31	3.71	4.38
Raleigh, NC	10.07	1.12	1.52	1.45	3.47	3.99
Reno, NV	10.93	1.71	2.75	2.50	3.95	5.38
Richmond, VA	10.43	1.04	1.42	0.97	3.11	3.57
Roanoke, VA	9.74	1.06	1.77	1.15	3.22	3.39
Rochester, MN	n/a	n/a	n/a	n/a	n/a	n/a
Salem, OR	n/a	n/a	n/a	n/a	n/a	n/a
Salt Lake City, UT	11.55	2.35	1.70	2.50	3.88	4.63
San Antonio, TX	11.23	1.03	1.51	2.01	2.99	4.12
San Diego, CA	12.21	1.59	2.08	2.77	3.43	5.55
San Francisco, CA	13.41	1.66	2.86	3.37	4.34	6.58
San Jose, CA	n/a	n/a	n/a	n/a	n/a	n/a
Santa Rosa, CA	n/a	n/a	n/a	n/a	n/a	n/a
Savannah, GA	11.11	1.32	2.00	1.76	3.18	4.08
Seattle, WA	14.53	1.91	1.97	2.04	3.91	5.65
Sioux Falls, SD	10.07	1.83	2.04	1.53	3.15	4.53
Springfield, IL	n/a	n/a	n/a	n/a	n/a	n/a
Tallahassee, FL	10.69	1.54	2.43	2.38	3.82	3.97
Tampa, FL	9.23	1.41	2.54	2.16	3.22	3.86
Topeka, KS	10.28	1.74	1.56	1.22	3.51	4.61
Tyler, TX	10.20	1.01	1.66	1.24	3.24	3.69
Virginia Beach, VA[4]	10.13	1.27	1.96	1.13	3.54	4.07
Visalia, CA	n/a	n/a	n/a	n/a	n/a	n/a
Washington, DC	14.28	1.75	2.49	1.74	3.66	4.50
Wilmington, NC	11.08	1.41	1.86	1.91	3.70	3.74
Winston-Salem, NC	10.16	1.46	1.45	1.31	3.63	3.75
Average*	11.35	1.42	1.94	1.81	3.52	4.35
Minimum*	7.45	0.92	0.80	0.75	2.72	3.06
Maximum*	15.05	2.76	4.18	4.00	5.36	8.20

*Note: **T-Bone Steak** (price per pound); **Frying Chicken** (price per pound, whole fryer); **Whole Milk** (half gallon carton); **Eggs** (price per dozen, Grade A, large); **Orange Juice** (64 oz. Tropicana or Florida Natural); **Coffee** (11.5 oz. can, vacuum-packed, Maxwell House, Hills Bros, or Folgers); (*) Values for the local area are compared with the average, minimum, and maximum values for all 291 areas in the Cost of Living Index report; n/a not available; In cases where data is not available for the city, data for the metro area or for a neighboring city has been provided and noted as follows: (1) Middlesex-Monmouth NJ; (2) Winston-Salem, NC; (3) Brooklyn, NY; (4) Hampton Roads-SE Virginia*
Source: The Council for Community and Economic Research (formerly ACCRA), Cost of Living Index, 2018

Housing and Utility Costs

Urban Area	New Home Price ($)	Apartment Rent ($/month)	All Electric ($/month)	Part Electric ($/month)	Other Energy ($/month)	Telephone ($/month)
Albany, NY	415,615	1,289	-	75.20	82.89	187.10
Albuquerque, NM	315,185	963	-	100.64	45.36	182.50
Allentown, PA	386,339	1,472	-	100.18	77.54	183.50
Anchorage, AK	569,477	1,192	-	103.73	126.81	187.00
Ann Arbor, MI	n/a	n/a	n/a	n/a	n/a	n/a
Athens, GA	n/a	n/a	n/a	n/a	n/a	n/a
Atlanta, GA	348,121	1,334	-	91.36	36.83	179.50
Austin, TX	312,376	1,377	-	106.13	50.37	179.90
Baton Rouge	314,060	1,029	133.63	-	-	173.60
Billings, MT	n/a	n/a	n/a	n/a	n/a	n/a
Boise City, ID	320,087	958	-	69.52	70.97	164.60
Boston, MA	663,942	2,962	-	85.42	151.20	174.00
Boulder, CO	n/a	n/a	n/a	n/a	n/a	n/a
Cape Coral, FL	301,867	935	165.32	-	-	181.80
Cedar Rapids, IA	326,278	731	-	138.07	59.23	175.20
Charleston, SC	288,601	1,339	246.79	-	-	181.60
Charlotte, NC	267,528	1,130	153.16	-	-	174.20
Chicago, IL	500,332	2,051	-	83.93	48.57	197.70
Clarksville, TN	n/a	n/a	n/a	n/a	n/a	n/a
College Station, TX	n/a	n/a	n/a	n/a	n/a	n/a
Colorado Springs, CO	323,230	1,273	-	88.75	50.07	176.50
Columbia, MO	301,682	756	-	95.13	66.53	185.40
Columbia, SC	254,119	938	-	122.61	116.25	180.10
Columbus, OH	250,447	1,007	-	65.88	67.05	174.20
Dallas, TX	327,946	1,440	-	126.07	58.11	179.90
Denver, CO	489,272	1,439	-	63.54	47.34	178.30
Des Moines, IA	312,876	673	-	79.68	59.16	175.10
Durham, NC	278,773	876	150.79	-	-	174.40
Edison, NJ[1]	475,549	1,545	-	121.21	69.69	174.30
El Paso, TX	n/a	n/a	n/a	n/a	n/a	n/a
Eugene, OR	n/a	n/a	n/a	n/a	n/a	n/a
Evansville, IN	287,646	861	-	121.89	73.70	178.60
Fargo, ND	323,100	909	-	76.53	57.71	182.70
Fayetteville, NC	n/a	n/a	n/a	n/a	n/a	n/a
Fort Collins, CO	n/a	n/a	n/a	n/a	n/a	n/a
Fort Wayne, IN	237,439	674	-	87.68	53.38	178.60
Fort Worth, TX	275,461	1,243	-	125.46	57.39	179.10
Gainesville, FL	n/a	n/a	n/a	n/a	n/a	n/a
Grand Rapids, MI	288,912	1,158	-	98.08	67.91	174.00
Greeley, CO	n/a	n/a	n/a	n/a	n/a	n/a
Green Bay, WI	286,068	805	-	81.59	70.58	172.90
Greensboro, NC[2]	216,667	865	154.91	-	-	174.20
Honolulu, HI	1,158,492	2,969	388.65	-	-	172.70
Houston, TX	315,436	1,249	-	157.46	40.04	178.40
Huntsville, AL	237,350	985	158.50	-	-	175.80
Indianapolis, IN	250,625	1,052	-	105.38	79.02	178.60
Jacksonville, FL	262,790	1,244	156.94	-	-	182.70
Kansas City, MO	276,197	1,092	-	91.74	68.59	184.50
Lafayette, LA	269,749	856	-	85.05	49.43	175.40
Las Cruces, NM	273,244	772	-	75.17	39.88	183.40
Las Vegas, NV	438,895	1,106	-	123.00	35.56	172.90
Lexington, KY	308,662	987	-	74.43	71.89	179.50
Lincoln, NE	288,296	827	-	66.38	65.88	190.00
Little Rock, AR	339,778	730	-	90.31	59.65	184.40
Los Angeles, CA	809,182	2,730	-	127.92	64.29	184.70

Table continued on next page.

Urban Area	New Home Price ($)	Apartment Rent ($/month)	All Electric ($/month)	Part Electric ($/month)	Other Energy ($/month)	Telephone ($/month)
Louisville, KY	264,566	924	-	74.48	71.89	175.00
Madison, WI	396,381	1,067	-	106.73	63.18	173.00
Manchester, NH	330,128	1,439	-	124.19	91.51	174.40
McAllen, TX	225,685	640	-	123.82	48.66	179.90
Miami, FL	424,876	2,245	168.06	-	-	182.60
Midland, TX	269,904	1,027	-	142.15	41.25	178.70
Minneapolis, MN	362,307	1,158	-	95.34	66.40	176.70
Nashville, TN	318,571	1,029	-	94.60	62.48	179.40
New Orleans, LA	404,584	1,297	-	75.14	39.44	175.50
New York, NY[3]	1,130,943	3,265	-	86.82	135.61	188.30
Oklahoma City, OK	244,210	828	-	87.20	63.38	179.30
Omaha, NE	294,858	1,086	-	89.69	69.18	189.30
Orlando, FL	287,772	1,120	171.56	-	-	182.30
Peoria, IL	308,294	769	-	75.05	65.31	185.70
Philadelphia, PA	414,251	1,433	-	107.90	76.26	186.50
Phoenix, AZ	319,590	1,065	203.07	-	-	176.50
Pittsburgh, PA	306,332	1,232	-	102.43	84.43	184.00
Portland, OR	549,358	2,595	-	77.40	65.93	163.10
Providence, RI	451,509	1,832	-	119.05	108.75	183.40
Provo, UT	353,314	1,078	-	68.45	59.48	179.90
Raleigh, NC	268,630	1,100	-	90.19	59.78	174.20
Reno, NV	407,087	1,256	-	80.97	38.29	172.20
Richmond, VA	300,306	1,010	-	88.14	73.54	172.40
Roanoke, VA	280,915	816	177.04	-	-	172.40
Rochester, MN	n/a	n/a	n/a	n/a	n/a	n/a
Salem, OR	n/a	n/a	n/a	n/a	n/a	n/a
Salt Lake City, UT	361,743	1,109	-	75.10	60.85	179.90
San Antonio, TX	257,175	923	-	95.94	37.37	179.90
San Diego, CA	830,914	2,355	-	209.36	58.62	171.20
San Francisco, CA	1,243,239	3,821	-	181.80	55.33	192.90
San Jose, CA	n/a	n/a	n/a	n/a	n/a	n/a
Santa Rosa, CA	n/a	n/a	n/a	n/a	n/a	n/a
Savannah, GA	206,878	850	158.73	-	-	176.60
Seattle, WA	725,929	2,508	193.68	-	-	188.60
Sioux Falls, SD	308,639	850	-	96.79	46.96	181.80
Springfield, IL	n/a	n/a	n/a	n/a	n/a	n/a
Tallahassee, FL	312,353	1,043	124.35	-	-	184.30
Tampa, FL	215,261	1,032	127.66	-	-	182.70
Topeka, KS	287,385	794	-	96.10	67.76	185.30
Tyler, TX	233,225	1,116	-	147.22	45.26	175.00
Virginia Beach, VA[4]	306,794	1,125	-	90.69	69.73	172.40
Visalia, CA	n/a	n/a	n/a	n/a	n/a	n/a
Washington, DC	933,450	2,808	-	145.55	68.80	178.90
Wilmington, NC	296,596	788	157.19	-	-	174.30
Winston-Salem, NC	216,667	865	154.91	-	-	174.20
Average*	347,000	1,087	165.93	100.16	67.73	178.70
Minimum*	200,468	500	93.58	25.64	26.78	163.10
Maximum*	1,901,222	4,888	388.65	246.86	332.81	197.70

*Note: **New Home Price** (2,400 sf living area, 8,000 sf lot, in urban area with full utilities); **Apartment Rent** (950 sf 2 bedroom/1.5 or 2 bath, unfurnished, excluding all utilities except water); **All Electric** (average monthly cost for an all-electric home); **Part Electric** (average monthly cost for a part-electric home); **Other Energy** (average monthly cost for natural gas, fuel oil, coal, wood, and any other forms of energy except electricity); **Telephone** (price includes the base monthly rate plus taxes and fees for three lines of mobile phone service); (*) Values for the local area are compared with the average, minimum, and maximum values for all 291 areas in the Cost of Living Index report; n/a not available; In cases where data is not available for the city, data for the metro area or for a neighboring city has been provided and noted as follows: (1) Middlesex-Monmouth NJ; (2) Winston-Salem, NC; (3) Brooklyn, NY; (4) Hampton Roads-SE Virginia*
Source: The Council for Community and Economic Research (formerly ACCRA), Cost of Living Index, 2018

Health Care, Transportation, and Other Costs

Urban Area	Doctor ($/visit)	Dentist ($/visit)	Optometrist ($/visit)	Gasoline ($/gallon)	Beauty Salon ($/visit)	Men's Shirt ($)
Albany, NY	108.38	102.67	127.12	2.75	41.97	36.31
Albuquerque, NM	104.83	105.24	105.98	2.42	52.05	35.66
Allentown, PA	89.68	110.19	112.61	2.91	37.06	25.53
Anchorage, AK	190.50	142.69	200.29	3.11	52.50	37.95
Ann Arbor, MI	n/a	n/a	n/a	n/a	n/a	n/a
Athens, GA	n/a	n/a	n/a	n/a	n/a	n/a
Atlanta, GA	110.08	120.36	103.60	2.64	44.77	28.68
Austin, TX	104.33	108.31	112.50	2.45	47.08	31.68
Baton Rouge	121.03	113.42	118.72	2.43	46.67	44.42
Billings, MT	n/a	n/a	n/a	n/a	n/a	n/a
Boise City, ID	124.59	91.27	117.18	2.89	34.87	31.83
Boston, MA	191.62	132.93	105.58	2.71	54.96	56.59
Boulder, CO	n/a	n/a	n/a	n/a	n/a	n/a
Cape Coral, FL	115.00	99.50	64.66	2.60	26.00	25.49
Cedar Rapids, IA	112.26	79.30	104.10	2.52	32.49	40.60
Charleston, SC	120.07	105.09	97.71	2.41	43.22	25.96
Charlotte, NC	106.56	115.25	122.56	2.57	37.13	40.97
Chicago, IL	105.00	102.00	97.00	3.34	69.90	32.00
Clarksville, TN	n/a	n/a	n/a	n/a	n/a	n/a
College Station, TX	n/a	n/a	n/a	n/a	n/a	n/a
Colorado Springs, CO	123.78	89.03	107.53	2.60	39.00	24.50
Columbia, MO	138.83	84.03	89.20	2.45	36.42	37.78
Columbia, SC	105.22	90.00	90.67	2.41	48.47	31.56
Columbus, OH	107.45	82.73	62.59	2.53	36.00	31.38
Dallas, TX	110.28	101.77	103.33	2.38	46.95	36.69
Denver, CO	120.06	95.38	100.40	2.53	41.83	34.91
Des Moines, IA	128.15	82.71	100.87	2.61	32.24	21.60
Durham, NC	91.20	95.26	103.54	2.44	40.18	18.89
Edison, NJ[1]	96.97	117.83	112.58	2.78	34.27	35.59
El Paso, TX	n/a	n/a	n/a	n/a	n/a	n/a
Eugene, OR	n/a	n/a	n/a	n/a	n/a	n/a
Evansville, IN	106.38	92.08	119.53	2.59	33.29	28.61
Fargo, ND	167.97	98.00	102.20	2.47	35.60	28.20
Fayetteville, NC	n/a	n/a	n/a	n/a	n/a	n/a
Fort Collins, CO	n/a	n/a	n/a	n/a	n/a	n/a
Fort Wayne, IN	126.33	90.67	94.17	2.64	31.50	49.31
Fort Worth, TX	118.48	97.67	97.68	2.51	54.22	47.17
Gainesville, FL	n/a	n/a	n/a	n/a	n/a	n/a
Grand Rapids, MI	96.94	87.78	91.61	2.79	37.61	35.08
Greeley, CO	n/a	n/a	n/a	n/a	n/a	n/a
Green Bay, WI	143.22	89.31	58.89	2.29	22.06	30.86
Greensboro, NC[2]	136.11	118.88	126.67	2.51	39.62	37.62
Honolulu, HI	129.38	101.17	172.56	3.54	62.33	51.71
Houston, TX	84.62	97.84	108.89	2.40	52.70	31.93
Huntsville, AL	107.26	96.19	125.87	2.43	41.42	44.35
Indianapolis, IN	93.91	92.23	60.20	2.64	39.63	39.87
Jacksonville, FL	62.89	89.40	65.58	2.51	52.72	24.03
Kansas City, MO	94.24	106.60	100.58	2.50	30.23	34.80
Lafayette, LA	87.50	81.13	69.86	2.30	36.27	23.78
Las Cruces, NM	121.50	105.24	106.29	2.58	51.95	25.00
Las Vegas, NV	110.90	101.37	114.22	2.83	45.60	31.44
Lexington, KY	99.86	77.91	75.47	2.66	43.33	34.56
Lincoln, NE	134.07	86.40	112.02	2.56	39.62	37.92
Little Rock, AR	114.28	69.92	74.89	2.46	41.43	41.64
Los Angeles, CA	102.78	107.00	119.80	3.28	63.13	36.00

Table continued on next page.

Urban Area	Doctor ($/visit)	Dentist ($/visit)	Optometrist ($/visit)	Gasoline ($/gallon)	Beauty Salon ($/visit)	Men's Shirt ($)
Louisville, KY	137.11	78.53	75.94	2.75	44.39	46.65
Madison, WI	182.00	101.33	59.00	2.51	41.78	31.99
Manchester, NH	149.21	118.08	101.83	2.31	37.37	34.64
McAllen, TX	53.95	62.55	91.11	2.42	31.67	17.49
Miami, FL	91.11	95.28	94.86	2.74	56.11	26.39
Midland, TX	81.11	94.39	102.58	2.65	34.45	38.11
Minneapolis, MN	144.82	85.76	88.91	2.57	34.88	34.24
Nashville, TN	94.52	74.93	79.10	2.49	45.67	39.40
New Orleans, LA	120.49	96.34	82.95	2.42	40.62	23.98
New York, NY[3]	115.67	116.30	100.11	2.64	71.88	50.22
Oklahoma City, OK	89.82	91.21	97.00	2.24	35.63	20.12
Omaha, NE	138.94	74.45	99.55	2.51	37.03	27.33
Orlando, FL	85.25	82.50	79.07	2.52	53.24	21.86
Peoria, IL	103.07	93.47	119.16	2.67	28.80	34.58
Philadelphia, PA	131.51	96.79	101.11	2.80	56.15	31.16
Phoenix, AZ	99.00	94.50	87.75	2.67	56.67	24.50
Pittsburgh, PA	100.97	85.45	75.79	2.94	35.42	21.70
Portland, OR	129.73	102.12	136.32	3.17	49.32	42.73
Providence, RI	154.86	92.86	128.37	2.31	54.21	34.81
Provo, UT	106.15	109.25	89.33	2.77	34.05	24.11
Raleigh, NC	104.67	100.92	104.05	2.60	45.87	23.04
Reno, NV	129.30	107.33	117.45	3.19	36.53	25.48
Richmond, VA	127.68	122.40	113.50	2.43	44.33	32.58
Roanoke, VA	98.42	112.72	91.70	2.34	30.79	17.34
Rochester, MN	n/a	n/a	n/a	n/a	n/a	n/a
Salem, OR	n/a	n/a	n/a	n/a	n/a	n/a
Salt Lake City, UT	106.87	92.92	86.99	2.73	35.60	24.03
San Antonio, TX	92.75	75.38	84.43	2.25	39.00	21.88
San Diego, CA	111.80	104.50	112.17	3.27	57.33	33.13
San Francisco, CA	148.84	131.50	133.29	3.50	71.62	44.33
San Jose, CA	n/a	n/a	n/a	n/a	n/a	n/a
Santa Rosa, CA	n/a	n/a	n/a	n/a	n/a	n/a
Savannah, GA	115.88	94.74	82.13	2.42	35.62	26.38
Seattle, WA	123.47	133.08	146.41	3.42	43.74	45.00
Sioux Falls, SD	147.74	96.51	132.58	2.61	28.07	37.09
Springfield, IL	n/a	n/a	n/a	n/a	n/a	n/a
Tallahassee, FL	98.80	97.06	90.48	2.57	36.33	27.04
Tampa, FL	108.31	90.56	87.92	2.57	34.33	23.68
Topeka, KS	88.42	88.44	121.81	2.41	32.67	33.63
Tyler, TX	91.76	91.33	118.11	2.42	42.53	31.64
Virginia Beach, VA[4]	98.13	94.43	96.66	2.42	32.20	42.49
Visalia, CA	n/a	n/a	n/a	n/a	n/a	n/a
Washington, DC	107.59	94.35	78.30	2.57	67.14	42.07
Wilmington, NC	128.89	126.74	121.02	2.54	42.92	35.35
Winston-Salem, NC	136.11	118.88	126.67	2.51	39.62	37.62
Average*	110.71	95.11	103.74	2.61	37.48	32.03
Minimum*	33.60	62.55	54.63	1.89	17.00	11.44
Maximum*	195.97	153.93	225.79	3.59	71.88	58.64

Note: **Doctor** (general practitioners routine exam of an established patient); **Dentist** (adult teeth cleaning and periodic oral examination); **Optometrist** (full vision eye exam for established adult patient); **Gasoline** (one gallon regular unleaded, national brand, including all taxes, cash price at self-service pump if available); **Beauty Salon** (woman's shampoo, trim, and blow-dry); **Men's Shirt** (cotton/polyester dress shirt, pinpoint weave, long sleeves); (*) Values for the local area are compared with the average, minimum, and maximum values for all 291 areas in the Cost of Living Index report; n/a not available; In cases where data is not available for the city, data for the metro area or for a neighboring city has been provided and noted as follows: (1) Middlesex-Monmouth NJ; (2) Winston-Salem, NC; (3) Brooklyn, NY; (4) Hampton Roads-SE Virginia
Source: The Council for Community and Economic Research (formerly ACCRA), Cost of Living Index, 2018

Number of Medical Professionals

City	Area Covered	MDs[1]	DOs[1,2]	Dentists	Podiatrists	Chiropractors	Optometrists
Albany, NY	Albany County	580.1	39.8	89.8	8.1	20.0	17.8
Albuquerque, NM	Bernalillo County	445.4	21.9	84.8	8.6	23.9	15.8
Allentown, PA	Lehigh County	340.4	84.8	87.0	13.9	30.3	19.1
Anchorage, AK	Anchorage (B) Borough	342.3	43.7	123.7	4.4	59.1	26.8
Ann Arbor, MI	Washtenaw County	1,221.9	41.1	173.5	6.8	24.8	16.9
Athens, GA	Clarke County	290.4	12.8	54.3	4.7	22.8	16.5
Atlanta, GA	Fulton County	501.0	12.0	70.8	4.9	52.8	15.9
Austin, TX	Travis County	312.0	20.4	69.0	4.5	33.1	16.1
Baton Rouge, LA	East Baton Rouge Parish	377.0	7.1	72.8	4.0	11.2	13.4
Billings, MT	Yellowstone County	351.4	24.7	96.9	5.7	34.6	25.2
Boise City, ID	Ada County	290.1	31.1	78.6	3.3	54.9	18.8
Boston, MA	Suffolk County	1,433.5	15.5	204.5	9.1	13.5	32.5
Boulder, CO	Boulder County	358.4	30.5	100.2	6.2	73.8	26.4
Cape Coral, FL	Lee County	184.9	28.9	48.7	8.0	26.8	12.7
Cedar Rapids, IA	Linn County	177.1	22.1	73.2	8.5	56.2	17.0
Charleston, SC	Charleston County	793.1	30.5	105.1	4.7	46.1	21.2
Charlotte, NC	Mecklenburg County	316.1	11.2	67.6	3.3	31.2	13.6
Chicago, IL	Cook County	434.2	22.8	89.5	12.5	27.1	19.8
Clarksville, TN	Montgomery County	102.2	18.0	45.0	2.5	15.5	13.0
College Station, TX	Brazos County	256.0	20.0	50.7	3.1	16.6	14.4
Colorado Springs, CO	El Paso County	191.6	30.7	102.3	4.3	41.6	23.5
Columbia, MO	Boone County	789.0	66.8	65.1	5.0	33.7	26.9
Columbia, SC	Richland County	356.6	16.4	87.2	6.1	24.1	19.0
Columbus, OH	Franklin County	420.6	66.0	86.8	6.7	24.4	26.6
Dallas, TX	Dallas County	326.0	20.6	82.1	4.2	35.3	13.1
Denver, CO	Denver County	590.7	33.4	73.4	7.1	34.2	15.6
Des Moines, IA	Polk County	201.2	110.6	69.7	9.1	51.1	22.0
Durham, NC	Durham County	1,101.6	15.3	73.2	4.5	18.9	14.8
Edison, NJ	Middlesex County	369.9	19.8	86.1	10.0	23.7	18.0
El Paso, TX	El Paso County	186.8	15.4	44.4	3.8	8.7	9.3
Eugene, OR	Lane County	239.2	15.5	72.0	3.7	26.7	16.5
Evansville, IN	Vanderburgh County	269.0	23.1	71.6	12.7	22.6	34.1
Fargo, ND	Cass County	388.3	16.6	78.7	3.4	64.1	29.2
Fayetteville, NC	Cumberland County	196.7	20.7	97.7	5.4	10.5	18.0
Fort Collins, CO	Larimer County	244.3	32.5	79.9	4.7	56.1	20.6
Fort Wayne, IN	Allen County	259.5	21.6	63.6	5.4	20.7	24.1
Fort Worth, TX	Tarrant County	178.0	37.4	57.7	4.1	25.2	15.2
Gainesville, FL	Alachua County	904.9	26.1	170.4	3.7	26.2	17.6
Grand Rapids, MI	Kent County	326.2	70.1	71.1	4.8	33.8	23.7
Greeley, CO	Weld County	108.1	17.0	43.3	4.3	22.7	12.1
Green Bay, WI	Brown County	241.2	22.3	75.9	3.4	43.5	18.7
Greensboro, NC	Guilford County	252.5	12.6	56.0	4.6	14.2	10.4
Honolulu, HI	Honolulu County	341.9	18.2	96.6	3.4	17.9	22.5
Houston, TX	Harris County	321.0	11.7	67.5	4.8	21.8	19.4
Huntsville, AL	Madison County	277.8	13.5	55.7	3.9	22.7	18.0
Indianapolis, IN	Marion County	437.7	21.7	87.4	5.9	14.9	18.9
Jacksonville, FL	Duval County	349.6	23.0	81.5	8.5	23.5	15.9
Kansas City, MO	Jackson County	300.2	59.9	84.6	6.3	43.6	20.2
Lafayette, LA	Lafayette Parish	356.6	7.0	65.6	3.7	30.9	13.6
Las Cruces, NM	Dona Ana County	164.1	14.5	61.2	5.1	16.2	8.3
Las Vegas, NV	Clark County	175.5	27.6	62.5	4.0	19.3	12.3
Lexington, KY	Fayette County	706.2	34.2	144.1	7.5	21.1	21.1
Lincoln, NE	Lancaster County	213.8	10.9	92.6	5.4	40.1	21.0
Little Rock, AR	Pulaski County	730.0	16.5	72.9	4.8	21.1	20.1
Los Angeles, CA	Los Angeles County	291.6	13.1	85.0	6.1	28.9	17.2
Louisville, KY	Jefferson County	473.3	11.3	104.5	8.0	28.0	14.7

Table continued on next page.

City	Area Covered	MDs[1]	DOs[1,2]	Dentists	Podiatrists	Chiropractors	Optometrists
Madison, WI	Dane County	587.3	20.7	69.0	4.8	41.9	22.4
Manchester, NH	Hillsborough County	233.7	23.5	79.6	5.4	25.9	19.8
McAllen, TX	Hidalgo County	113.5	3.1	26.0	1.2	8.1	6.2
Miami, FL	Miami-Dade County	333.7	17.2	64.8	9.8	17.7	13.2
Midland, TX	Midland County	152.9	10.4	53.9	3.0	13.3	13.3
Minneapolis, MN	Hennepin County	501.1	19.3	94.6	4.6	69.6	19.2
Nashville, TN	Davidson County	619.1	11.5	74.4	4.2	24.4	16.3
New Orleans, LA	Orleans Parish	752.6	15.0	71.7	3.8	7.6	6.1
New York, NY	New York City	472.3	16.5	85.2	13.1	15.5	15.9
Oklahoma City, OK	Oklahoma County	403.7	44.8	101.5	4.8	26.0	18.1
Omaha, NE	Douglas County	531.2	30.6	92.9	5.5	39.4	19.4
Orlando, FL	Orange County	298.5	23.4	48.3	3.5	25.4	12.8
Peoria, IL	Peoria County	544.5	47.5	82.0	8.2	49.2	19.7
Philadelphia, PA	Philadelphia County	545.4	49.8	74.5	17.5	14.9	17.1
Phoenix, AZ	Maricopa County	242.0	33.4	66.8	6.1	33.6	15.0
Pittsburgh, PA	Allegheny County	626.7	38.5	96.8	10.7	43.5	19.5
Portland, OR	Multnomah County	615.8	32.1	96.0	5.4	71.9	21.5
Providence, RI	Providence County	481.7	18.4	60.2	10.7	19.6	20.1
Provo, UT	Utah County	115.8	18.5	60.0	3.8	24.7	10.6
Raleigh, NC	Wake County	273.7	10.7	69.3	3.3	25.2	15.6
Reno, NV	Washoe County	295.5	20.6	70.1	4.1	25.6	21.1
Richmond, VA	Richmond City	726.2	24.9	131.3	10.6	6.6	13.2
Roanoke, VA	Roanoke City	570.5	71.2	75.1	14.0	17.0	23.0
Rochester, MN	Olmsted County	2,412.8	56.8	112.3	6.5	43.9	21.9
Salem, OR	Marion County	173.3	13.4	79.7	4.7	30.8	14.7
Salt Lake City, UT	Salt Lake County	361.3	15.5	75.8	6.2	26.4	13.6
San Antonio, TX	Bexar County	319.5	21.3	83.0	5.1	15.9	16.4
San Diego, CA	San Diego County	314.4	17.1	86.5	4.0	33.6	17.5
San Francisco, CA	San Francisco County	781.2	12.1	149.0	10.0	37.4	27.4
San Jose, CA	Santa Clara County	401.8	9.2	113.6	6.4	40.6	26.2
Santa Rosa, CA	Sonoma County	268.7	15.1	88.1	5.9	38.3	16.5
Savannah, GA	Chatham County	352.8	19.4	65.4	7.2	18.2	13.8
Seattle, WA	King County	473.7	15.7	106.7	6.5	45.5	21.6
Sioux Falls, SD	Minnehaha County	353.7	26.3	53.0	5.8	55.7	19.6
Springfield, IL	Sangamon County	623.0	22.8	85.0	5.6	39.2	21.9
Tallahassee, FL	Leon County	292.3	11.8	45.1	3.4	22.4	17.9
Tampa, FL	Hillsborough County	343.5	28.4	56.9	5.5	25.8	12.8
Topeka, KS	Shawnee County	200.4	25.3	61.7	5.6	25.3	24.7
Tyler, TX	Smith County	343.1	24.4	59.7	6.6	27.2	15.8
Virginia Beach, VA	Virginia Beach City	255.2	13.5	75.5	7.5	26.4	16.0
Visalia, CA	Tulare County	113.3	6.1	50.4	3.9	10.3	12.3
Washington, DC	The District	795.7	15.3	119.9	8.5	8.5	13.8
Wilmington, NC	New Hanover County	343.1	30.5	76.1	7.0	33.5	19.4
Winston-Salem, NC	Forsyth County	625.9	30.1	59.0	5.6	16.2	16.2
U.S.	U.S.	279.3	23.0	68.4	6.0	27.1	16.2

Note: All figures are rates per 100,000 population; Data as of 2017 unless noted; (1) Data as of 2016 and includes all active, non-federal physicians; (2) Doctor of Osteopathic Medicine
Source: U.S. Department of Health and Human Services, Health Resources and Services Administration, Bureau of Health Professions, Area Resource File (ARF) 2017-2018

Health Insurance Coverage: City

City	With Health Insurance	With Private Health Insurance	With Public Health Insurance	Without Health Insurance	Population Under Age 18 Without Health Insurance
Albany, NY	92.8	66.8	38.1	7.2	2.4
Albuquerque, NM	89.5	60.4	40.0	10.5	4.6
Allentown, PA	86.4	47.0	48.3	13.6	5.3
Anchorage, AK	86.8	70.4	26.6	13.2	10.0
Ann Arbor, MI	96.5	87.9	18.8	3.5	1.5
Athens, GA	85.3	67.7	26.3	14.7	8.3
Atlanta, GA	87.2	66.5	28.8	12.8	5.5
Austin, TX	84.7	70.7	20.8	15.3	9.2
Baton Rouge, LA	87.2	60.3	36.0	12.8	3.1
Billings, MT	89.3	70.8	31.5	10.7	6.8
Boise City, ID	90.3	75.6	26.2	9.7	3.5
Boston, MA	96.1	66.5	37.1	3.9	1.4
Boulder, CO	94.7	84.3	18.2	5.3	2.3
Cape Coral, FL	85.5	63.1	36.7	14.5	9.2
Cedar Rapids, IA	95.0	76.4	31.7	5.0	3.2
Charleston, SC	90.5	76.9	25.3	9.5	4.4
Charlotte, NC	85.7	67.0	26.1	14.3	6.8
Chicago, IL	87.2	57.2	36.6	12.8	3.8
Clarksville, TN	90.4	72.6	30.5	9.6	3.5
College Station, TX	90.9	83.7	13.4	9.1	5.3
Colorado Springs, CO	91.3	69.4	34.7	8.7	4.1
Columbia, MO	93.2	83.0	18.9	6.8	3.8
Columbia, SC	89.5	70.9	28.7	10.5	2.5
Columbus, OH	89.4	63.8	33.3	10.6	5.8
Dallas, TX	75.1	49.6	31.2	24.9	14.6
Denver, CO	88.5	63.7	32.7	11.5	5.8
Des Moines, IA	91.8	63.4	40.0	8.2	3.8
Durham, NC	86.4	67.9	28.2	13.6	6.9
Edison, NJ	92.5	81.3	20.3	7.5	2.2
El Paso, TX	79.3	52.7	33.5	20.7	9.7
Eugene, OR	91.3	69.5	34.6	8.7	3.8
Evansville, IN	88.3	61.1	39.9	11.7	4.9
Fargo, ND	92.4	79.6	24.1	7.6	5.2
Fayetteville, NC	88.4	65.2	38.0	11.6	4.7
Fort Collins, CO	93.1	79.6	22.8	6.9	5.1
Fort Wayne, IN	88.3	63.5	34.7	11.7	7.0
Fort Worth, TX	80.7	59.4	27.9	19.3	11.4
Gainesville, FL	89.0	74.8	22.0	11.0	3.0
Grand Rapids, MI	89.8	61.0	38.9	10.2	3.4
Greeley, CO	90.5	64.7	36.2	9.5	4.5
Green Bay, WI	91.3	64.4	37.2	8.7	4.0
Greensboro, NC	87.9	65.5	32.5	12.1	4.6
Honolulu, HI	95.2	77.2	33.4	4.8	3.2
Houston, TX	75.9	50.5	31.2	24.1	12.9
Huntsville, AL	88.9	71.7	31.7	11.1	3.9
Indianapolis, IN	87.4	60.5	35.9	12.6	6.1
Jacksonville, FL	87.0	64.0	33.6	13.0	7.0
Kansas City, MO	86.7	66.9	29.2	13.3	6.9
Lafayette, LA	87.0	66.3	30.6	13.0	4.9
Las Cruces, NM	89.6	57.2	46.8	10.4	4.6
Las Vegas, NV	84.2	60.9	32.9	15.8	10.2
Lexington, KY	91.5	71.8	30.4	8.5	4.4
Lincoln, NE	91.2	77.1	25.4	8.8	4.6
Little Rock, AR	89.0	65.1	34.8	11.0	5.7
Los Angeles, CA	84.5	52.9	37.7	15.5	5.5

Table continued on next page.

City	With Health Insurance	With Private Health Insurance	With Public Health Insurance	Without Health Insurance	Population Under Age 18 Without Health Insurance
Louisville, KY	92.5	67.7	37.6	7.5	2.8
Madison, WI	94.8	83.2	21.9	5.2	2.8
Manchester, NH	88.8	64.6	34.2	11.2	3.8
McAllen, TX	72.7	46.7	31.6	27.3	15.5
Miami, FL	76.1	41.7	37.6	23.9	9.1
Midland, TX	80.9	68.6	19.9	19.1	18.0
Minneapolis, MN	91.5	66.6	32.8	8.5	4.9
Nashville, TN	86.3	65.3	29.7	13.7	7.1
New Orleans, LA	87.6	55.4	40.0	12.4	4.3
New York, NY	90.2	56.6	42.0	9.8	3.0
Oklahoma City, OK	84.1	62.7	31.7	15.9	7.5
Omaha, NE	88.9	70.5	27.9	11.1	5.6
Orlando, FL	81.9	58.4	30.1	18.1	10.0
Peoria, IL	92.8	63.4	41.1	7.2	2.1
Philadelphia, PA	89.4	56.3	43.1	10.6	4.2
Phoenix, AZ	83.6	55.3	35.2	16.4	10.6
Pittsburgh, PA	93.1	72.7	32.5	6.9	3.5
Portland, OR	91.2	69.3	31.7	8.8	3.3
Providence, RI	88.5	51.8	43.4	11.5	4.8
Provo, UT	88.2	77.7	16.9	11.8	10.3
Raleigh, NC	88.1	73.2	23.1	11.9	5.6
Reno, NV	87.5	66.1	31.4	12.5	8.6
Richmond, VA	85.1	60.4	34.3	14.9	6.3
Roanoke, VA	86.4	59.8	37.9	13.6	6.2
Rochester, MN	95.0	78.9	29.5	5.0	2.8
Salem, OR	90.5	64.0	40.0	9.5	4.2
Salt Lake City, UT	85.4	70.3	22.6	14.6	12.2
San Antonio, TX	82.7	59.9	32.4	17.3	8.7
San Diego, CA	89.6	69.1	29.3	10.4	5.3
San Francisco, CA	94.5	73.9	29.2	5.5	2.0
San Jose, CA	92.6	70.5	29.7	7.4	2.8
Santa Rosa, CA	90.6	66.8	36.4	9.4	4.5
Savannah, GA	81.5	57.1	33.4	18.5	7.9
Seattle, WA	94.0	79.4	23.4	6.0	2.1
Sioux Falls, SD	92.1	77.1	26.1	7.9	4.1
Springfield, IL	94.2	68.1	40.8	5.8	1.8
Tallahassee, FL	90.5	75.7	23.8	9.5	4.2
Tampa, FL	87.0	61.0	33.6	13.0	5.5
Topeka, KS	89.2	69.9	35.1	10.8	6.1
Tyler, TX	82.2	60.7	32.4	17.8	8.7
Virginia Beach, VA	91.1	80.0	24.0	8.9	3.9
Visalia, CA	92.5	57.8	44.2	7.5	2.3
Washington, DC	95.3	69.3	36.1	4.7	2.3
Wilmington, NC	88.3	68.6	31.9	11.7	4.1
Winston-Salem, NC	86.6	61.8	35.5	13.4	4.3
U.S.	89.5	67.2	33.8	10.5	5.7

Note: Figures are percentages that cover the civilian noninstitutionalized population
Source: U.S. Census Bureau, 2013-2017 American Community Survey 5-Year Estimates

Health Insurance Coverage: Metro Area

Metro Area	With Health Insurance	With Private Health Insurance	With Public Health Insurance	Without Health Insurance	Population Under Age 18 Without Health Insurance
Albany, NY	95.4	77.1	33.0	4.6	2.0
Albuquerque, NM	89.2	59.2	41.6	10.8	5.0
Allentown, PA	92.8	73.5	33.5	7.2	3.4
Anchorage, AK	86.0	68.7	27.8	14.0	10.2
Ann Arbor, MI	95.3	83.3	24.4	4.7	2.2
Athens, GA	86.7	69.0	27.8	13.3	6.9
Atlanta, GA	85.7	68.0	26.3	14.3	7.8
Austin, TX	86.3	73.2	21.6	13.7	8.6
Baton Rouge, LA	89.3	67.2	31.7	10.7	3.3
Billings, MT	89.6	71.7	31.2	10.4	7.3
Boise City, ID	88.5	70.8	29.2	11.5	5.4
Boston, MA	96.7	76.5	32.1	3.3	1.5
Boulder, CO	93.8	78.8	24.3	6.2	3.1
Cape Coral, FL	84.4	60.2	42.7	15.6	10.2
Cedar Rapids, IA	95.6	77.9	31.3	4.4	2.7
Charleston, SC	88.1	69.7	30.9	11.9	5.5
Charlotte, NC	88.3	69.6	28.7	11.7	5.5
Chicago, IL	90.5	68.8	31.0	9.5	3.5
Clarksville, TN	90.1	69.3	33.8	9.9	5.6
College Station, TX	85.7	71.9	22.5	14.3	9.6
Colorado Springs, CO	92.0	71.9	33.1	8.0	4.0
Columbia, MO	92.6	80.8	21.5	7.4	4.0
Columbia, SC	89.2	69.6	32.5	10.8	4.3
Columbus, OH	92.1	71.4	30.6	7.9	4.3
Dallas, TX	82.6	64.7	25.3	17.4	11.0
Denver, CO	90.6	71.6	28.1	9.4	5.2
Des Moines, IA	94.8	77.1	29.7	5.2	2.6
Durham, NC	88.5	71.3	28.5	11.5	6.3
Edison, NJ	90.9	66.3	34.6	9.1	3.5
El Paso, TX	77.7	50.1	33.9	22.3	10.6
Eugene, OR	91.0	65.3	40.7	9.0	4.7
Evansville, IN	92.0	71.8	33.6	8.0	3.9
Fargo, ND	93.6	81.4	24.1	6.4	5.1
Fayetteville, NC	88.4	64.9	37.2	11.6	4.4
Fort Collins, CO	92.7	76.0	27.8	7.3	5.2
Fort Wayne, IN	89.6	68.6	31.6	10.4	7.4
Fort Worth, TX	82.6	64.7	25.3	17.4	11.0
Gainesville, FL	88.9	71.7	27.6	11.1	5.6
Grand Rapids, MI	93.3	74.9	30.7	6.7	3.2
Greeley, CO	91.0	70.4	30.4	9.0	5.6
Green Bay, WI	93.8	74.3	30.8	6.2	3.6
Greensboro, NC	88.2	65.3	33.9	11.8	5.5
Honolulu, HI	96.0	79.8	31.3	4.0	2.4
Houston, TX	81.1	61.4	26.4	18.9	11.0
Huntsville, AL	90.0	74.8	29.1	10.0	3.4
Indianapolis, IN	90.1	70.4	30.0	9.9	5.6
Jacksonville, FL	88.1	67.8	32.3	11.9	6.8
Kansas City, MO	90.1	74.7	26.6	9.9	5.5
Lafayette, LA	87.2	63.1	34.2	12.8	4.3
Las Cruces, NM	86.7	49.2	49.3	13.3	6.2
Las Vegas, NV	85.3	63.8	30.8	14.7	9.8
Lexington, KY	91.8	71.1	32.1	8.2	4.6
Lincoln, NE	91.8	78.5	24.7	8.2	4.2
Little Rock, AR	90.4	66.7	36.4	9.6	4.9
Los Angeles, CA	87.4	59.1	35.1	12.6	5.3

Table continued on next page.

Metro Area	With Health Insurance	With Private Health Insurance	With Public Health Insurance	Without Health Insurance	Population Under Age 18 Without Health Insurance
Louisville, KY	92.6	71.8	34.1	7.4	3.6
Madison, WI	95.0	82.8	24.2	5.0	2.7
Manchester, NH	92.7	77.0	27.1	7.3	2.5
McAllen, TX	68.4	35.6	37.3	31.6	15.5
Miami, FL	82.1	56.3	33.2	17.9	9.2
Midland, TX	80.8	68.5	19.9	19.2	17.4
Minneapolis, MN	94.7	78.0	28.1	5.3	3.5
Nashville, TN	89.4	70.8	28.5	10.6	5.2
New Orleans, LA	87.6	60.6	36.5	12.4	4.5
New York, NY	90.9	66.3	34.6	9.1	3.5
Oklahoma City, OK	86.6	67.6	30.3	13.4	6.8
Omaha, NE	91.5	75.9	26.3	8.5	4.2
Orlando, FL	85.0	63.1	31.1	15.0	9.0
Peoria, IL	94.5	73.9	35.3	5.5	2.7
Philadelphia, PA	92.9	73.0	32.2	7.1	3.4
Phoenix, AZ	87.9	64.4	33.9	12.1	8.9
Pittsburgh, PA	94.9	77.1	34.2	5.1	2.3
Portland, OR	92.0	71.9	31.8	8.0	3.4
Providence, RI	94.5	70.4	37.2	5.5	2.8
Provo, UT	90.7	80.7	16.9	9.3	6.6
Raleigh, NC	89.7	74.9	24.0	10.3	4.9
Reno, NV	88.2	68.0	31.1	11.8	8.8
Richmond, VA	90.7	74.9	28.2	9.3	4.8
Roanoke, VA	90.6	70.8	33.8	9.4	5.1
Rochester, MN	94.9	79.8	29.3	5.1	3.5
Salem, OR	90.5	63.9	40.8	9.5	5.0
Salt Lake City, UT	88.1	75.7	20.5	11.9	9.1
San Antonio, TX	84.6	64.6	30.7	15.4	8.4
San Diego, CA	89.6	67.7	31.4	10.4	5.4
San Francisco, CA	93.6	74.4	29.4	6.4	2.9
San Jose, CA	93.7	75.3	26.6	6.3	2.5
Santa Rosa, CA	91.6	70.6	34.9	8.4	3.9
Savannah, GA	85.5	67.0	28.8	14.5	6.9
Seattle, WA	92.6	75.1	28.0	7.4	3.3
Sioux Falls, SD	92.9	79.5	24.6	7.1	4.0
Springfield, IL	95.1	73.6	36.5	4.9	1.6
Tallahassee, FL	90.0	72.4	28.9	10.0	5.1
Tampa, FL	86.7	62.2	36.4	13.3	7.4
Topeka, KS	91.4	75.2	32.2	8.6	4.9
Tyler, TX	82.4	62.3	32.5	17.6	11.3
Virginia Beach, VA	90.1	74.6	28.6	9.9	4.5
Visalia, CA	87.8	43.3	51.9	12.2	3.7
Washington, DC	91.2	77.7	23.9	8.8	4.8
Wilmington, NC	88.4	69.8	32.6	11.6	5.0
Winston-Salem, NC	88.3	66.0	34.7	11.7	4.7
U.S.	89.5	67.2	33.8	10.5	5.7

Note: Figures are percentages that cover the civilian noninstitutionalized population; Figures cover the Metropolitan Statistical Area (MSA)—see Appendix B for areas included
Source: U.S. Census Bureau, 2013-2017 American Community Survey 5-Year Estimates

Crime Rate: City

City	All Crimes	Violent Crimes				Property Crimes		
		Murder	Rape	Robbery	Aggrav. Assault	Burglary	Larceny -Theft	Motor Vehicle Theft
Albany, NY	4,349.4	8.1	55.0	251.6	577.5	440.0	2,906.1	111.0
Albuquerque, NM	8,735.0	12.5	84.3	521.9	750.5	1,246.2	4,750.8	1,368.8
Allentown, PA	3,193.9	13.2	57.9	222.6	167.2	524.7	1,954.9	253.3
Anchorage, AK	6,619.1	9.1	132.0	262.7	799.5	748.2	3,619.7	1,048.0
Ann Arbor, MI	1,941.3	0.0	46.7	43.5	122.2	228.0	1,419.7	81.2
Athens, GA	3,562.0	4.8	45.6	98.5	266.6	546.8	2,415.5	184.1
Atlanta, GA	5,712.1	16.4	58.6	293.6	567.2	704.3	3,387.2	685.0
Austin, TX	3,604.4	2.6	85.8	101.5	224.9	450.6	2,525.0	213.9
Baton Rouge, LA	6,620.8	38.3	44.0	381.7	562.9	1,418.6	3,739.6	435.8
Billings, MT	5,951.5	1.8	68.3	78.2	345.0	703.4	3,998.5	756.4
Boise City, ID	2,723.8	0.9	63.8	22.6	191.9	326.1	1,965.2	153.3
Boston, MA	2,758.2	8.3	42.5	205.6	412.8	308.8	1,603.7	176.5
Boulder, CO[1]	3,235.7	0.0	47.6	27.5	161.2	512.0	2,286.9	200.6
Cape Coral, FL	1,694.1	1.6	8.7	22.2	94.9	309.2	1,165.2	92.2
Cedar Rapids, IA	4,035.5	4.5	25.8	91.8	158.5	704.4	2,791.2	259.3
Charleston, SC	2,581.0	4.4	36.5	73.1	169.5	291.6	1,784.5	221.4
Charlotte, NC	n/a	9.4	n/a	220.5	433.5	701.5	2,827.0	286.7
Chicago, IL	4,362.7	24.1	65.1	439.3	570.4	477.1	2,358.8	427.8
Clarksville, TN	3,501.1	9.1	52.2	82.8	479.5	484.7	2,235.6	157.2
College Station, TX	2,196.7	0.9	45.9	42.5	110.1	260.1	1,635.8	101.4
Colorado Springs, CO	3,740.9	6.1	103.4	101.9	312.7	530.3	2,235.1	451.4
Columbia, MO	3,431.9	7.3	93.8	95.4	301.0	412.0	2,305.3	217.0
Columbia, SC	6,020.4	7.4	48.9	202.3	475.7	706.9	3,993.1	586.1
Columbus, OH	4,458.4	16.3	105.4	225.1	166.7	815.3	2,650.9	478.8
Dallas, TX	3,959.7	12.5	62.1	327.0	373.1	737.7	1,856.3	591.2
Denver, CO	4,342.7	8.3	98.9	174.4	394.0	612.9	2,267.3	786.8
Des Moines, IA	5,083.4	12.9	33.6	167.5	456.1	1,099.1	2,734.3	579.9
Durham, NC	n/a	8.5	n/a	316.6	467.1	867.4	2,675.7	283.2
Edison, NJ	1,287.3	0.0	6.8	45.8	56.5	180.1	882.2	115.9
El Paso, TX	2,197.7	2.8	53.9	58.1	264.1	188.3	1,514.4	116.2
Eugene, OR	4,115.6	1.8	60.0	105.2	219.8	670.8	2,734.2	323.8
Evansville, IN	5,699.9	16.8	62.8	155.0	456.6	723.0	3,887.9	397.9
Fargo, ND	3,538.0	2.4	67.2	55.1	277.9	480.4	2,410.3	244.7
Fayetteville, NC	n/a	11.7	n/a	142.1	537.9	885.0	3,202.0	202.0
Fort Collins, CO	2,755.4	3.6	26.8	25.1	164.6	272.6	2,139.2	123.5
Fort Wayne, IN	3,537.2	13.9	51.1	112.3	180.3	491.3	2,488.6	199.8
Fort Worth, TX	3,775.5	8.0	65.2	147.3	339.7	586.0	2,319.4	309.9
Gainesville, FL	4,315.5	3.0	123.5	132.6	457.9	376.6	2,948.6	273.4
Grand Rapids, MI	2,784.7	6.1	71.3	177.4	456.9	385.6	1,504.0	183.5
Greeley, CO	2,986.6	4.7	70.8	53.8	294.6	404.1	1,907.4	251.2
Green Bay, WI	2,511.1	0.0	72.2	61.7	338.9	304.8	1,650.0	83.5
Greensboro, NC	n/a	15.9	n/a	228.9	480.6	710.9	2,559.5	291.7
Honolulu, HI	n/a	n/a	n/a	n/a	n/a	n/a	n/a	n/a
Houston, TX	5,223.6	11.5	58.4	418.0	607.3	731.7	2,900.8	495.9
Huntsville, AL	5,635.0	11.3	88.1	184.5	621.0	731.7	3,462.6	535.9
Indianapolis, IN	5,745.8	17.9	76.7	400.2	839.1	1,027.2	2,821.5	563.2
Jacksonville, FL	4,158.0	12.2	60.1	153.8	405.2	631.1	2,568.6	326.9
Kansas City, MO	6,268.1	30.9	91.8	383.1	1,218.5	960.5	2,670.4	912.9
Lafayette, LA	5,116.1	17.1	16.3	136.0	390.9	785.6	3,539.5	230.8
Las Cruces, NM[1]	n/a	4.9	n/a	49.8	150.5	811.0	3,612.2	255.0
Las Vegas, NV	3,562.3	12.6	79.6	211.2	315.5	805.2	1,635.2	503.1
Lexington, KY	4,133.0	9.0	62.0	169.7	110.1	647.5	2,739.7	394.9
Lincoln, NE[1]	3,463.1	3.6	79.0	67.9	207.4	448.5	2,531.5	125.2
Little Rock, AR	8,565.9	27.6	87.8	251.9	1,266.3	1,193.1	5,172.2	566.9

Table continued on next page.

City	All Crimes	Violent Crimes				Property Crimes		
		Murder	Rape	Robbery	Aggrav. Assault	Burglary	Larceny -Theft	Motor Vehicle Theft
Los Angeles, CA	3,297.2	7.0	61.3	269.9	423.2	416.0	1,641.0	479.0
Louisville, KY	4,769.3	15.9	25.6	193.8	411.8	821.6	2,736.0	564.6
Madison, WI	3,036.5	4.3	37.1	82.9	250.1	362.3	2,130.9	168.8
Manchester, NH	3,298.5	1.8	83.1	157.2	431.1	443.7	2,014.4	167.2
McAllen, TX	2,923.8	4.9	18.7	34.0	86.7	128.3	2,619.3	31.9
Miami, FL	4,735.1	11.2	22.7	211.2	475.8	527.0	3,090.9	396.3
Midland, TX	2,197.8	1.4	26.6	42.5	200.8	310.2	1,458.0	158.3
Minneapolis, MN	5,742.6	10.0	122.7	434.2	534.4	897.9	3,173.5	570.0
Nashville, TN	4,956.1	16.3	72.9	303.1	745.8	631.3	2,806.6	380.0
New Orleans, LA	5,365.2	39.5	144.7	329.1	608.1	560.8	3,046.2	636.8
New York, NY	1,987.5	3.4	27.6	162.4	345.5	128.9	1,253.2	66.6
Oklahoma City, OK	4,539.8	12.5	73.1	172.8	529.0	941.8	2,378.8	431.9
Omaha, NE	4,527.5	6.9	91.2	139.1	410.1	464.6	2,636.7	778.8
Orlando, FL	6,198.6	8.1	64.4	213.0	458.5	840.9	4,125.3	488.4
Peoria, IL	4,973.0	10.5	56.9	246.2	445.9	980.2	2,940.7	292.6
Philadelphia, PA	4,011.1	20.1	75.0	382.5	470.0	418.3	2,297.2	348.0
Phoenix, AZ	4,431.6	9.5	69.5	200.3	481.6	778.6	2,426.7	465.5
Pittsburgh, PA	3,770.8	18.0	29.4	262.1	346.8	526.3	2,365.9	222.3
Portland, OR	6,192.7	3.7	67.4	160.9	283.6	729.1	3,824.6	1,123.3
Providence, RI	3,828.1	6.7	57.8	141.8	327.5	563.2	2,408.6	322.5
Provo, UT	1,858.1	0.9	44.2	24.7	56.2	131.9	1,500.8	99.5
Raleigh, NC	n/a	n/a	n/a	n/a	n/a	n/a	n/a	n/a
Reno, NV	3,759.3	7.6	57.1	153.7	455.1	542.0	1,967.6	576.2
Richmond, VA[2]	4,432.5	19.5	27.2	221.5	247.7	726.9	2,794.8	394.9
Roanoke, VA	4,893.7	16.0	41.0	79.0	265.9	486.9	3,718.0	286.9
Rochester, MN	2,054.2	0.9	52.9	39.9	100.7	249.9	1,524.8	85.0
Salem, OR	4,621.2	3.5	25.9	98.5	250.1	529.0	3,206.4	507.8
Salt Lake City, UT	8,928.1	5.1	171.3	260.6	441.6	966.3	6,115.9	967.3
San Antonio, TX	5,552.3	8.2	83.5	151.1	464.7	770.8	3,622.6	451.4
San Diego, CA	2,209.6	2.5	39.3	99.0	225.9	268.0	1,214.4	360.6
San Francisco, CA	6,883.0	6.4	41.6	365.4	301.6	560.0	5,059.5	548.5
San Jose, CA	2,844.4	3.1	55.0	132.6	212.9	378.4	1,284.7	777.6
Santa Rosa, CA	2,249.4	2.8	61.8	71.4	273.3	297.7	1,309.2	233.0
Savannah, GA	3,893.9	14.4	41.2	156.8	250.3	549.5	2,494.8	386.9
Seattle, WA	5,891.3	3.7	36.9	210.0	382.1	1,082.0	3,673.5	503.2
Sioux Falls, SD	3,307.7	2.2	68.0	56.2	323.8	368.2	2,225.6	263.6
Springfield, IL	5,810.4	9.5	80.5	217.2	747.6	1,047.0	3,437.8	270.8
Tallahassee, FL	5,679.8	8.8	98.7	180.8	492.6	789.3	3,722.9	386.6
Tampa, FL	2,208.1	10.1	31.5	105.6	317.2	321.3	1,274.8	147.5
Topeka, KS	5,742.2	21.3	44.2	212.4	335.6	790.5	3,731.5	606.5
Tyler, TX	3,582.0	5.7	61.3	56.5	313.8	420.3	2,586.8	137.6
Virginia Beach, VA	2,072.2	3.1	22.4	59.9	52.2	166.0	1,667.6	101.0
Visalia, CA	3,672.5	6.8	61.3	109.0	168.8	634.9	2,234.7	457.1
Washington, DC	5,105.0	16.7	63.8	338.8	529.4	260.5	3,529.0	366.7
Wilmington, NC	n/a	15.1	n/a	163.3	448.0	835.7	2,544.8	235.3
Winston-Salem, NC	n/a	n/a	n/a	n/a	n/a	n/a	n/a	n/a
U.S.	2,756.1	5.3	41.7	98.0	248.9	430.4	1,694.4	237.4

Note: Figures are crimes per 100,000 population in 2017 except where noted; n/a not available; (1) 2016 data; (2) 2015 data
Source: FBI Uniform Crime Reports, 2015, 2016, 2017

Crime Rate: Suburbs

Suburbs[1]	All Crimes	Violent Crimes				Property Crimes		
		Murder	Rape	Robbery	Aggrav. Assault	Burglary	Larceny -Theft	Motor Vehicle Theft
Albany, NY	1,983.6	1.3	39.0	49.9	126.1	234.5	1,463.2	69.6
Albuquerque, NM	3,169.7	3.1	37.9	70.7	522.2	582.4	1,543.1	410.2
Allentown, PA	1,687.4	1.4	14.9	32.0	151.5	182.6	1,237.2	67.8
Anchorage, AK	6,349.5	5.8	5.8	63.7	393.6	387.8	4,479.9	1,012.9
Ann Arbor, MI	1,971.1	4.5	71.3	51.0	256.7	237.3	1,223.6	126.7
Athens, GA	1,855.9	1.2	18.1	14.5	111.2	289.0	1,349.3	72.5
Atlanta, GA	3,012.4	5.9	23.2	99.6	188.4	459.6	1,963.5	272.3
Austin, TX	1,839.9	2.4	44.7	28.9	138.1	262.4	1,263.5	100.0
Baton Rouge, LA	3,686.9	8.7	23.1	56.5	279.3	597.7	2,583.9	137.7
Billings, MT	2,017.8	3.3	33.3	8.3	173.3	279.9	1,296.3	223.3
Boise City, ID	1,658.3	1.0	40.7	11.1	161.6	310.4	998.0	135.6
Boston, MA	1,425.8	1.6	25.2	43.0	175.7	171.3	918.2	90.7
Boulder, CO[2]	2,202.7	0.5	79.1	24.2	132.6	264.8	1,571.8	129.8
Cape Coral, FL	1,869.4	7.5	41.7	89.5	230.4	308.6	1,050.9	140.7
Cedar Rapids, IA	1,273.6	1.5	27.0	12.4	115.9	313.5	720.3	83.1
Charleston, SC	n/a	9.0	39.4	88.9	302.1	n/a	2,028.9	272.8
Charlotte, NC	5,044.6	3.0	n/a	55.1	183.5	437.4	1,663.6	122.6
Chicago, IL	n/a	3.5	26.6	58.5	n/a	217.8	1,218.6	96.5
Clarksville, TN	2,159.1	0.8	31.5	36.8	112.6	490.2	1,352.8	134.4
College Station, TX	2,595.9	4.9	58.4	55.6	235.7	424.8	1,694.9	121.7
Colorado Springs, CO	1,720.0	1.6	52.9	21.0	179.8	238.7	1,061.1	164.8
Columbia, MO	2,125.9	1.8	23.0	21.3	175.4	240.9	1,500.5	163.0
Columbia, SC	n/a	7.1	44.2	77.4	396.0	560.6	n/a	380.8
Columbus, OH	2,208.5	1.8	36.1	38.2	52.4	334.7	1,650.9	94.4
Dallas, TX	n/a	3.5	44.1	74.6	157.1	n/a	1,628.0	206.1
Denver, CO	n/a	3.4	64.2	66.8	195.0	n/a	1,961.0	441.4
Des Moines, IA	n/a	n/a	n/a	n/a	n/a	n/a	n/a	n/a
Durham, NC	n/a	2.7	n/a	50.2	140.3	542.9	1,371.1	81.5
Edison, NJ	1,766.4	2.8	22.9	122.1	246.6	148.9	1,152.2	70.8
El Paso, TX	1,369.9	1.3	44.2	20.2	192.5	193.8	855.4	62.5
Eugene, OR	2,760.4	2.4	35.7	35.7	215.0	393.9	1,862.8	215.0
Evansville, IN	1,625.2	3.0	22.3	25.3	131.6	302.1	1,040.8	100.2
Fargo, ND	1,777.2	0.9	43.2	14.7	90.7	266.8	1,204.7	156.3
Fayetteville, NC	n/a	3.9	n/a	36.0	89.9	401.7	1,011.3	42.1
Fort Collins, CO	2,225.9	0.0	57.3	19.1	181.9	269.5	1,576.4	121.8
Fort Wayne, IN	n/a	1.2	30.2	28.5	106.7	201.6	n/a	91.9
Fort Worth, TX	n/a	4.8	44.9	116.9	177.1	n/a	1,582.1	271.5
Gainesville, FL	2,291.7	3.3	56.8	80.5	338.6	439.6	1,260.7	112.2
Grand Rapids, MI	1,623.8	2.1	80.0	23.8	129.2	233.1	1,080.0	75.7
Greeley, CO	1,458.2	2.0	20.0	14.3	129.0	217.1	930.9	144.9
Green Bay, WI	1,131.9	0.0	26.5	4.7	68.4	116.3	885.8	30.2
Greensboro, NC	n/a	7.8	n/a	75.3	224.3	583.0	1,766.2	138.5
Honolulu, HI	n/a	n/a	n/a	n/a	n/a	n/a	n/a	n/a
Houston, TX	n/a	3.7	34.8	96.5	201.5	n/a	1,432.2	n/a
Huntsville, AL	2,220.1	4.2	32.4	31.2	227.3	432.2	1,337.1	155.6
Indianapolis, IN	1,942.6	1.1	26.9	39.6	145.0	233.5	1,338.8	157.7
Jacksonville, FL	1,941.0	2.3	30.5	36.7	191.1	329.9	1,239.0	111.7
Kansas City, MO	n/a	n/a	n/a	n/a	n/a	n/a	n/a	n/a
Lafayette, LA	n/a	6.0	26.9	51.0	313.1	647.1	n/a	n/a
Las Cruces, NM[2]	6,167.1	5.4	n/a	13.4	192.2	408.5	853.6	140.3
Las Vegas, NV	2,892.5	5.7	42.9	147.5	380.8	589.1	1,364.3	362.1
Lexington, KY	n/a	2.6	31.5	57.2	50.4	536.7	n/a	189.6
Lincoln, NE[2]	1,218.2	0.0	49.8	2.2	54.1	190.4	852.5	69.2
Little Rock, AR	3,533.2	5.9	51.3	64.1	370.1	651.8	2,092.7	297.4

Table continued on next page.

Suburbs[1]	All Crimes	Violent Crimes				Property Crimes		
		Murder	Rape	Robbery	Aggrav. Assault	Burglary	Larceny -Theft	Motor Vehicle Theft
Los Angeles, CA	2,654.4	3.9	28.5	136.3	214.8	432.3	1,443.0	395.5
Louisville, KY	2,096.6	2.3	20.4	43.4	93.2	326.7	1,401.4	209.2
Madison, WI	1,427.7	1.0	24.5	22.2	87.9	195.9	1,023.3	72.9
Manchester, NH	1,064.9	0.7	37.4	13.7	63.7	116.1	782.3	51.0
McAllen, TX	2,783.7	4.3	54.0	44.1	220.5	427.2	1,929.7	104.0
Miami, FL	3,437.1	5.7	33.3	127.1	270.8	410.4	2,302.8	287.1
Midland, TX	2,505.9	0.0	8.8	64.6	199.8	358.4	1,559.9	314.3
Minneapolis, MN	2,286.0	1.7	32.8	46.7	94.0	281.4	1,661.8	167.7
Nashville, TN	2,209.0	3.2	32.7	35.8	271.0	297.4	1,425.7	143.3
New Orleans, LA	2,673.9	6.9	21.3	69.7	214.0	370.4	1,844.6	147.0
New York, NY	1,433.3	2.4	14.0	67.0	97.7	170.1	977.9	104.3
Oklahoma City, OK	2,391.4	3.3	45.0	43.2	152.9	481.4	1,477.0	188.6
Omaha, NE	1,870.1	0.8	30.8	24.2	84.7	259.2	1,272.1	198.3
Orlando, FL	2,836.4	4.6	44.9	78.9	277.0	472.2	1,780.3	178.4
Peoria, IL	1,755.3	0.8	52.7	19.9	163.8	350.2	1,090.4	77.5
Philadelphia, PA	1,952.1	4.0	18.6	72.7	152.5	254.8	1,350.4	99.2
Phoenix, AZ	2,676.9	3.7	39.5	65.6	207.4	378.5	1,798.3	183.9
Pittsburgh, PA	1,562.8	3.5	19.3	43.1	155.5	215.6	1,070.5	55.3
Portland, OR	n/a	2.3	54.8	35.3	107.6	n/a	1,384.2	304.8
Providence, RI	1,756.4	1.4	37.1	52.1	174.4	275.5	1,105.7	110.1
Provo, UT	1,551.3	1.2	22.2	12.6	32.9	179.5	1,220.6	82.3
Raleigh, NC	n/a	n/a	n/a	n/a	n/a	n/a	n/a	n/a
Reno, NV	2,269.1	0.9	40.5	55.3	236.3	395.6	1,277.5	263.0
Richmond, VA[3]	2,200.0	5.0	24.8	47.3	100.7	315.7	1,618.6	87.9
Roanoke, VA	1,556.9	4.7	33.6	19.6	91.5	175.6	1,133.8	98.1
Rochester, MN	782.8	0.0	24.3	4.9	62.2	131.1	506.0	54.4
Salem, OR	2,476.1	3.2	28.0	38.6	145.1	329.2	1,610.0	322.1
Salt Lake City, UT	4,043.8	3.4	65.9	65.6	173.3	519.7	2,708.2	507.7
San Antonio, TX	n/a	3.7	49.4	37.9	141.0	n/a	1,451.0	165.0
San Diego, CA	1,901.8	2.4	28.0	83.2	201.7	275.9	1,072.1	238.5
San Francisco, CA	n/a	3.7	38.5	184.2	195.7	378.3	n/a	534.0
San Jose, CA	2,303.4	1.7	26.6	57.6	120.8	316.4	1,534.9	245.4
Santa Rosa, CA	1,714.2	2.1	57.4	45.9	290.4	265.5	926.0	127.0
Savannah, GA	n/a	2.0	20.3	39.9	215.1	n/a	1,718.4	136.7
Seattle, WA	n/a	2.8	37.6	77.4	172.0	n/a	2,163.0	476.0
Sioux Falls, SD	1,146.9	2.5	32.0	2.5	110.8	224.0	710.1	65.2
Springfield, IL	1,582.4	2.1	47.6	21.2	205.3	333.4	860.6	112.2
Tallahassee, FL	2,593.3	4.2	51.0	33.7	344.7	533.6	1,504.5	121.6
Tampa, FL	2,467.0	2.7	37.6	62.9	211.2	348.8	1,639.4	164.5
Topeka, KS	1,805.3	4.7	27.4	14.1	128.3	331.1	1,144.1	155.6
Tyler, TX	2,158.7	2.5	42.0	20.6	213.2	581.9	1,097.9	200.8
Virginia Beach, VA	3,281.5	9.6	38.8	106.6	244.4	410.8	2,275.7	195.6
Visalia, CA	2,594.8	7.3	24.5	73.2	260.3	462.0	1,279.3	488.3
Washington, DC	1,630.4	3.0	24.3	64.3	96.8	143.6	1,176.8	121.6
Wilmington, NC	n/a	4.2	n/a	38.0	103.9	479.5	1,612.4	66.5
Winston-Salem, NC	n/a	n/a	n/a	n/a	n/a	n/a	n/a	n/a
U.S.	2,756.1	5.3	41.7	98.0	248.9	430.4	1,694.4	237.4

Note: Figures are crimes per 100,000 population in 2017 except where noted; n/a not available; (1) All areas within the metro area that are located outside the city limits; (2) 2016 data; (3) 2015 data
Source: FBI Uniform Crime Reports, 2015, 2016, 2017

Crime Rate: Metro Area

Metro Area[1]	All Crimes	Violent Crimes				Property Crimes		
		Murder	Rape	Robbery	Aggrav. Assault	Burglary	Larceny -Theft	Motor Vehicle Theft
Albany, NY	2,245.9	2.0	40.8	72.3	176.1	257.3	1,623.2	74.2
Albuquerque, NM	6,583.9	8.9	66.3	347.5	662.2	989.7	3,511.0	998.3
Allentown, PA	1,904.4	3.1	21.1	59.5	153.8	231.9	1,340.6	94.5
Anchorage, AK	6,604.2	8.9	125.1	251.7	777.1	728.3	3,667.1	1,046.0
Ann Arbor, MI	1,961.2	3.0	63.2	48.5	212.3	234.2	1,288.4	111.7
Athens, GA	2,882.3	3.4	34.7	65.0	204.7	444.1	1,990.8	139.7
Atlanta, GA	3,233.3	6.7	26.1	115.4	219.4	479.7	2,080.0	306.0
Austin, TX	2,650.7	2.5	63.6	62.3	178.0	348.9	1,843.2	152.3
Baton Rouge, LA	4,484.3	16.7	28.8	144.9	356.4	820.8	2,898.0	218.7
Billings, MT	4,573.5	2.3	56.0	53.7	284.8	555.1	3,051.9	569.6
Boise City, ID	1,996.9	1.0	48.0	14.8	171.2	315.4	1,305.3	141.2
Boston, MA[2]	1,613.8	2.6	27.7	65.9	209.1	190.7	1,015.0	102.8
Boulder, CO[3]	2,550.7	0.3	68.5	25.3	142.2	348.0	1,812.7	153.7
Cape Coral, FL	1,825.9	6.1	33.5	72.8	196.8	308.8	1,079.2	128.7
Cedar Rapids, IA	2,627.4	3.0	26.4	51.3	136.8	505.1	1,735.4	169.5
Charleston, SC	n/a	8.2	38.9	86.2	278.8	n/a	1,985.9	263.7
Charlotte, NC	3,216.6	5.3	21.8	115.1	274.1	533.1	2,085.2	182.1
Chicago, IL[2]	n/a	9.4	37.5	166.7	n/a	291.5	1,542.5	190.6
Clarksville, TN	2,877.1	5.2	42.6	61.4	308.9	487.3	1,825.1	146.6
College Station, TX	2,418.2	3.1	52.9	49.8	179.8	351.5	1,668.6	112.7
Colorado Springs, CO	3,046.5	4.6	86.0	74.1	267.0	430.1	1,831.7	352.9
Columbia, MO	3,020.1	5.6	71.5	72.1	261.4	358.0	2,051.6	200.0
Columbia, SC	n/a	7.1	45.0	97.8	409.0	584.4	n/a	414.4
Columbus, OH	3,156.3	7.9	65.2	116.9	100.6	537.2	2,072.1	256.3
Dallas, TX[2]	n/a	5.2	47.3	120.5	196.4	n/a	1,669.5	276.0
Denver, CO	n/a	4.6	72.7	93.1	243.6	n/a	2,035.7	525.7
Des Moines, IA	n/a	n/a	n/a	n/a	n/a	n/a	n/a	n/a
Durham, NC	n/a	5.4	n/a	176.0	294.6	696.1	1,987.1	176.7
Edison, NJ[2]	1,763.0	2.8	22.8	121.6	245.3	149.1	1,150.3	71.1
El Paso, TX	2,042.9	2.5	52.1	51.0	250.7	189.4	1,391.1	106.1
Eugene, OR	3,372.0	2.1	46.7	67.0	217.2	518.8	2,256.0	264.1
Evansville, IN	3,159.5	8.2	37.5	74.1	253.9	460.6	2,112.9	212.3
Fargo, ND	2,685.7	1.7	55.6	35.5	187.3	377.0	1,826.7	201.9
Fayetteville, NC	n/a	8.1	n/a	92.8	329.9	660.6	2,185.0	127.8
Fort Collins, CO	2,482.6	1.7	42.5	22.0	173.5	271.0	1,849.2	122.6
Fort Wayne, IN	n/a	9.0	43.0	79.8	151.8	378.9	n/a	158.0
Fort Worth, TX[2]	n/a	5.2	47.3	120.5	196.4	n/a	1,669.5	276.0
Gainesville, FL	3,236.9	3.2	87.9	104.8	394.3	410.2	2,049.0	187.5
Grand Rapids, MI	1,840.5	2.8	78.3	52.5	190.3	261.6	1,159.2	95.8
Greeley, CO	1,995.6	3.0	37.8	28.2	187.2	282.9	1,274.2	182.3
Green Bay, WI	1,585.5	0.0	41.5	23.4	157.4	178.3	1,137.1	47.8
Greensboro, NC	n/a	10.9	n/a	133.7	321.7	631.6	2,067.7	196.7
Honolulu, HI	3,020.7	3.2	28.8	91.7	122.7	336.3	2,073.9	364.1
Houston, TX	n/a	6.4	42.8	205.2	338.8	n/a	1,928.8	n/a
Huntsville, AL	3,685.7	7.3	56.3	97.0	396.3	560.7	2,249.3	318.9
Indianapolis, IN	3,576.9	8.3	48.3	194.6	443.3	574.6	1,975.9	331.9
Jacksonville, FL	3,258.4	8.2	48.1	106.3	318.3	508.9	2,029.1	239.6
Kansas City, MO	n/a	n/a	n/a	n/a	n/a	n/a	n/a	n/a
Lafayette, LA	n/a	8.9	24.1	73.2	333.4	683.2	n/a	n/a
Las Cruces, NM[3]	3,220.3	5.1	44.8	30.8	172.2	600.7	2,171.5	195.1
Las Vegas, NV	3,387.2	10.8	70.0	194.5	332.6	748.7	1,564.3	466.2
Lexington, KY	n/a	6.6	50.7	127.9	88.0	606.4	n/a	318.7
Lincoln, NE[3]	3,146.1	3.1	74.8	58.7	185.7	412.1	2,294.5	117.3
Little Rock, AR	4,886.7	11.7	61.1	114.6	611.1	797.4	2,920.9	369.9

Table continued on next page.

Metro Area[1]	All Crimes	Violent Crimes				Property Crimes		
		Murder	Rape	Robbery	Aggrav. Assault	Burglary	Larceny -Theft	Motor Vehicle Theft
Los Angeles, CA[2]	2,847.0	4.8	38.3	176.3	277.2	427.4	1,502.4	420.5
Louisville, KY	3,512.3	9.5	23.1	123.1	261.9	588.9	2,108.3	397.5
Madison, WI	2,054.7	2.3	29.4	45.8	151.1	260.8	1,455.0	110.3
Manchester, NH	1,667.1	1.0	49.7	52.4	162.8	204.4	1,114.5	82.4
McAllen, TX	2,807.2	4.4	48.1	42.4	198.1	377.2	2,045.1	92.0
Miami, FL[2]	3,534.6	6.1	32.5	133.4	286.2	419.1	2,362.0	295.3
Midland, TX	2,258.5	1.2	23.1	46.8	200.6	319.7	1,478.1	189.0
Minneapolis, MN	2,688.6	2.6	43.3	91.8	145.3	353.2	1,837.8	214.5
Nashville, TN	3,183.4	7.8	47.0	130.7	439.4	415.8	1,915.5	227.2
New Orleans, LA	3,512.1	17.1	59.7	150.5	336.7	429.7	2,218.9	299.6
New York, NY[2]	1,668.5	2.8	19.8	107.5	202.8	152.6	1,094.7	88.3
Oklahoma City, OK	3,396.3	7.6	58.2	103.8	328.8	696.7	1,898.8	302.4
Omaha, NE	3,149.4	3.7	59.9	79.5	241.4	358.1	1,929.0	477.8
Orlando, FL	3,217.8	5.0	47.1	94.1	297.6	514.1	2,046.4	213.6
Peoria, IL	2,732.2	3.7	54.0	88.6	249.5	541.5	1,652.1	142.8
Philadelphia, PA[2]	2,484.3	8.1	33.2	152.8	234.5	297.0	1,595.1	163.5
Phoenix, AZ	3,285.9	5.7	49.9	112.4	302.6	517.4	2,016.4	281.6
Pittsburgh, PA	1,851.3	5.4	20.6	71.7	180.5	256.2	1,239.8	77.1
Portland, OR	n/a	2.6	58.2	68.4	154.0	n/a	2,027.8	520.6
Providence, RI	1,986.4	2.0	39.4	62.0	191.4	307.4	1,250.4	133.7
Provo, UT	1,609.8	1.1	26.4	14.9	37.3	170.4	1,274.0	85.6
Raleigh, NC	n/a	n/a	n/a	n/a	n/a	n/a	n/a	n/a
Reno, NV	3,064.4	4.5	49.4	107.8	353.0	473.7	1,645.8	430.1
Richmond, VA[4]	2,588.3	7.5	25.2	77.6	126.3	387.2	1,823.2	141.3
Roanoke, VA	2,619.3	8.3	36.0	38.5	147.1	274.7	1,956.6	158.2
Rochester, MN	1,454.3	0.5	39.4	23.4	82.5	193.9	1,044.1	70.6
Salem, OR	3,335.6	3.3	27.2	62.6	187.1	409.2	2,249.6	396.5
Salt Lake City, UT	4,835.2	3.7	83.0	97.1	216.8	592.0	3,260.3	582.2
San Antonio, TX	n/a	6.4	70.3	107.4	339.8	n/a	2,784.4	340.8
San Diego, CA	2,032.6	2.4	32.8	89.9	212.0	272.6	1,132.5	290.4
San Francisco, CA[2]	n/a	4.2	39.1	218.0	215.4	412.1	n/a	536.7
San Jose, CA	2,584.0	2.4	41.3	96.5	168.6	348.5	1,405.1	521.5
Santa Rosa, CA	1,900.9	2.4	58.9	54.8	284.4	276.7	1,059.7	164.0
Savannah, GA	n/a	9.7	33.3	112.6	237.0	n/a	2,201.1	292.3
Seattle, WA[2]	n/a	3.0	37.5	102.1	211.1	n/a	2,444.4	481.0
Sioux Falls, SD	2,630.1	2.3	56.7	39.4	257.0	323.0	1,750.3	201.4
Springfield, IL	3,908.7	6.2	65.7	129.0	503.7	726.0	2,278.6	199.5
Tallahassee, FL	4,146.4	6.5	75.0	107.7	419.1	662.3	2,620.8	254.9
Tampa, FL	2,434.8	3.6	36.9	68.2	224.4	345.4	1,593.9	162.3
Topeka, KS	3,948.1	13.8	36.5	122.1	241.1	581.1	2,552.4	401.0
Tyler, TX	2,822.2	4.0	51.0	37.3	260.1	506.5	1,792.0	171.3
Virginia Beach, VA	2,964.4	7.9	34.5	94.3	194.0	346.6	2,116.3	170.8
Visalia, CA	2,902.5	7.1	35.0	83.4	234.2	511.4	1,552.0	479.4
Washington, DC[2]	2,018.8	4.5	28.8	95.0	145.2	156.7	1,439.7	149.0
Wilmington, NC	n/a	8.7	n/a	90.0	246.6	627.2	1,999.1	136.5
Winston-Salem, NC	n/a	n/a	n/a	n/a	n/a	n/a	n/a	n/a
U.S.	2,756.1	5.3	41.7	98.0	248.9	430.4	1,694.4	237.4

Note: Figures are crimes per 100,000 population in 2017 except where noted; n/a not available; (1) Figures cover the Metropolitan Statistical Area except where noted; (2) Metropolitan Division; (3) 2016 data; (4) 2015 data
Source: FBI Uniform Crime Reports, 2015, 2016, 2017

Temperature & Precipitation: Yearly Averages and Extremes

City	Extreme Low (°F)	Average Low (°F)	Average Temp. (°F)	Average High (°F)	Extreme High (°F)	Average Precip. (in.)	Average Snow (in.)
Albany, NY	-28	37	48	58	100	35.8	63
Albuquerque, NM	-17	43	57	70	105	8.5	11
Allentown, PA	-12	42	52	61	105	44.2	32
Anchorage, AK	-34	29	36	43	85	15.7	71
Ann Arbor, MI	-21	39	49	58	104	32.4	41
Athens, GA	-8	52	62	72	105	49.8	2
Atlanta, GA	-8	52	62	72	105	49.8	2
Austin, TX	-2	58	69	79	109	31.1	1
Baton Rouge, LA	8	57	68	78	103	58.5	Trace
Billings, MT	-32	36	47	59	105	14.6	59
Boise City, ID	-25	39	51	63	111	11.8	22
Boston, MA	-12	44	52	59	102	42.9	41
Boulder, CO	-25	37	51	64	103	15.5	63
Cape Coral, FL	26	65	75	84	103	53.9	0
Cedar Rapids, IA	-34	36	47	57	105	34.4	33
Charleston, SC	6	55	66	76	104	52.1	1
Charlotte, NC	-5	50	61	71	104	42.8	6
Chicago, IL	-27	40	49	59	104	35.4	39
Clarksville, TN	-17	49	60	70	107	47.4	11
College Station, TX	-2	58	69	79	109	31.1	1
Colorado Springs, CO	-24	36	49	62	99	17.0	48
Columbia, MO	-20	44	54	64	111	40.6	25
Columbia, SC	-1	51	64	75	107	48.3	2
Columbus, OH	-19	42	52	62	104	37.9	28
Dallas, TX	-2	56	67	77	112	33.9	3
Denver, CO	-25	37	51	64	103	15.5	63
Des Moines, IA	-24	40	50	60	108	31.8	33
Durham, NC	-9	48	60	71	105	42.0	8
Edison, NJ	-8	46	55	63	105	43.5	27
El Paso, TX	-8	50	64	78	114	8.6	6
Eugene, OR	-12	42	53	63	108	47.3	7
Evansville, IN	-23	42	53	62	104	40.2	25
Fargo, ND	-36	31	41	52	106	19.6	40
Fayetteville, NC	-9	48	60	71	105	42.0	8
Fort Collins, CO	-25	37	51	64	103	15.5	63
Fort Wayne, IN	-22	40	50	60	106	35.9	33
Fort Worth, TX	-1	55	66	76	113	32.3	3
Gainesville, FL	10	58	69	79	102	50.9	Trace
Grand Rapids, MI	-22	38	48	57	102	34.7	73
Greeley, CO	-25	37	51	64	103	15.5	63
Green Bay, WI	-31	34	44	54	99	28.3	46
Greensboro, NC	-8	47	58	69	103	42.5	10
Honolulu, HI	52	70	77	84	94	22.4	0
Houston, TX	7	58	69	79	107	46.9	Trace
Huntsville, AL	-11	50	61	71	104	56.8	4
Indianapolis, IN	-23	42	53	62	104	40.2	25
Jacksonville, FL	7	58	69	79	103	52.0	0
Kansas City, MO	-23	44	54	64	109	38.1	21
Lafayette, LA	8	57	68	78	103	58.5	Trace
Las Cruces, NM	-8	50	64	78	114	8.6	6
Las Vegas, NV	8	53	67	80	116	4.0	1
Lexington, KY	-21	45	55	65	103	45.1	17
Lincoln, NE	-33	39	51	62	108	29.1	27
Little Rock, AR	-5	51	62	73	112	50.7	5
Los Angeles, CA	27	55	63	70	110	11.3	Trace

Table continued on next page.

City	Extreme Low (°F)	Average Low (°F)	Average Temp. (°F)	Average High (°F)	Extreme High (°F)	Average Precip. (in.)	Average Snow (in.)
Louisville, KY	-20	46	57	67	105	43.9	17
Madison, WI	-37	35	46	57	104	31.1	42
Manchester, NH	-33	34	46	57	102	36.9	63
McAllen, TX	16	65	74	83	106	25.8	Trace
Miami, FL	30	69	76	83	98	57.1	0
Midland, TX	-11	50	64	77	116	14.6	4
Minneapolis, MN	-34	35	45	54	105	27.1	52
Nashville, TN	-17	49	60	70	107	47.4	11
New Orleans, LA	11	59	69	78	102	60.6	Trace
New York, NY	-2	47	55	62	104	47.0	23
Oklahoma City, OK	-8	49	60	71	110	32.8	10
Omaha, NE	-23	40	51	62	110	30.1	29
Orlando, FL	19	62	72	82	100	47.7	Trace
Peoria, IL	-26	41	51	61	113	35.4	23
Philadelphia, PA	-7	45	55	64	104	41.4	22
Phoenix, AZ	17	59	72	86	122	7.3	Trace
Pittsburgh, PA	-18	41	51	60	103	37.1	43
Portland, OR	-3	45	54	62	107	37.5	7
Providence, RI	-13	42	51	60	104	45.3	35
Provo, UT	-22	40	52	64	107	15.6	63
Raleigh, NC	-9	48	60	71	105	42.0	8
Reno, NV	-16	33	50	67	105	7.2	24
Richmond, VA	-8	48	58	69	105	43.0	13
Roanoke, VA	-11	46	57	67	105	40.8	23
Rochester, MN	-40	34	44	54	102	29.4	47
Salem, OR	-12	41	52	63	108	40.2	7
Salt Lake City, UT	-22	40	52	64	107	15.6	63
San Antonio, TX	0	58	69	80	108	29.6	1
San Diego, CA	29	57	64	71	111	9.5	Trace
San Francisco, CA	24	49	57	65	106	19.3	Trace
San Jose, CA	21	50	59	68	105	13.5	Trace
Santa Rosa, CA	23	42	57	71	109	29.0	n/a
Savannah, GA	3	56	67	77	105	50.3	Trace
Seattle, WA	0	44	52	59	99	38.4	13
Sioux Falls, SD	-36	35	46	57	110	24.6	38
Springfield, IL	-24	44	54	63	112	34.9	21
Tallahassee, FL	6	56	68	79	103	63.3	Trace
Tampa, FL	18	63	73	82	99	46.7	Trace
Topeka, KS	-26	43	55	66	110	34.4	21
Tyler, TX	-2	56	67	77	112	33.9	3
Virginia Beach, VA	-3	51	60	69	104	44.8	8
Visalia, CA	18	50	63	76	112	10.9	0
Washington, DC	-5	49	58	67	104	39.5	18
Wilmington, NC	0	53	64	74	104	55.0	2
Winston-Salem, NC	-8	47	58	69	103	42.5	10

Source: National Climatic Data Center, International Station Meteorological Climate Summary, 9/96

Weather Conditions

City	Temperature			Daytime Sky			Precipitation		
	10°F & below	32°F & below	90°F & above	Clear	Partly cloudy	Cloudy	0.01 inch or more precip.	1.0 inch or more snow/ice	Thunder-storms
Albany, NY	n/a	147	11	58	149	158	133	36	24
Albuquerque, NM	4	114	65	140	161	64	60	9	38
Allentown, PA	n/a	123	15	77	148	140	123	20	31
Anchorage, AK	n/a	194	n/a	50	115	200	113	49	2
Ann Arbor, MI	n/a	136	12	74	134	157	135	38	32
Athens, GA	1	49	38	98	147	120	116	3	48
Atlanta, GA	1	49	38	98	147	120	116	3	48
Austin, TX	< 1	20	111	105	148	112	83	1	41
Baton Rouge, LA	< 1	21	86	99	150	116	113	< 1	73
Billings, MT	n/a	149	29	75	163	127	97	41	27
Boise City, ID	n/a	124	45	106	133	126	91	22	14
Boston, MA	n/a	97	12	88	127	150	253	48	18
Boulder, CO	24	155	33	99	177	89	90	38	39
Cape Coral, FL	n/a	n/a	115	93	220	52	110	0	92
Cedar Rapids, IA	n/a	156	16	89	132	144	109	28	42
Charleston, SC	< 1	33	53	89	162	114	114	1	59
Charlotte, NC	1	65	44	98	142	125	113	3	41
Chicago, IL	n/a	132	17	83	136	146	125	31	38
Clarksville, TN	5	76	51	98	135	132	119	8	54
College Station, TX	< 1	20	111	105	148	112	83	1	41
Colorado Springs, CO	21	161	18	108	157	100	98	33	49
Columbia, MO	17	108	36	99	127	139	110	17	52
Columbia, SC	< 1	58	77	97	149	119	110	1	53
Columbus, OH	n/a	118	19	72	137	156	136	29	40
Dallas, TX	1	34	102	108	160	97	78	2	49
Denver, CO	24	155	33	99	177	89	90	38	39
Des Moines, IA	n/a	137	26	99	129	137	106	25	46
Durham, NC	n/a	n/a	39	98	143	124	110	3	42
Edison, NJ	n/a	90	24	80	146	139	122	16	46
El Paso, TX	1	59	106	147	164	54	49	3	35
Eugene, OR	n/a	n/a	15	75	115	175	136	4	3
Evansville, IN	19	119	19	83	128	154	127	24	43
Fargo, ND	n/a	180	15	81	145	139	100	38	31
Fayetteville, NC	n/a	n/a	39	98	143	124	110	3	42
Fort Collins, CO	24	155	33	99	177	89	90	38	39
Fort Wayne, IN	n/a	131	16	75	140	150	131	31	39
Fort Worth, TX	1	40	100	123	136	106	79	3	47
Gainesville, FL	n/a	n/a	77	88	196	81	119	0	78
Grand Rapids, MI	n/a	146	11	67	119	179	142	57	34
Greeley, CO	24	155	33	99	177	89	90	38	39
Green Bay, WI	n/a	163	7	86	125	154	120	40	33
Greensboro, NC	3	85	32	94	143	128	113	5	43
Honolulu, HI	n/a	n/a	23	25	286	54	98	0	7
Houston, TX	n/a	n/a	96	83	168	114	101	1	62
Huntsville, AL	2	66	49	70	118	177	116	2	54
Indianapolis, IN	19	119	19	83	128	154	127	24	43
Jacksonville, FL	< 1	16	83	86	181	98	114	1	65
Kansas City, MO	22	110	39	112	134	119	103	17	51
Lafayette, LA	< 1	21	86	99	150	116	113	< 1	73
Las Cruces, NM	1	59	106	147	164	54	49	3	35
Las Vegas, NV	< 1	37	134	185	132	48	27	2	13
Lexington, KY	11	96	22	86	136	143	129	17	44
Lincoln, NE	n/a	145	40	108	135	122	94	19	46
Little Rock, AR	1	57	73	110	142	113	104	4	57

Table continued on next page.

City	Temperature			Daytime Sky			Precipitation		
	10°F & below	32°F & below	90°F & above	Clear	Partly cloudy	Cloudy	0.01 inch or more precip.	1.0 inch or more snow/ice	Thunder-storms
Los Angeles, CA	0	< 1	5	131	125	109	34	0	1
Louisville, KY	8	90	35	82	143	140	125	15	45
Madison, WI	n/a	161	14	88	119	158	118	38	40
Manchester, NH	n/a	171	12	87	131	147	125	32	19
McAllen, TX	n/a	n/a	116	86	180	99	72	0	27
Miami, FL	n/a	n/a	55	48	263	54	128	0	74
Midland, TX	1	62	102	144	138	83	52	3	38
Minneapolis, MN	n/a	156	16	93	125	147	113	41	37
Nashville, TN	5	76	51	98	135	132	119	8	54
New Orleans, LA	0	13	70	90	169	106	114	1	69
New York, NY	n/a	n/a	18	85	166	114	120	11	20
Oklahoma City, OK	5	79	70	124	131	110	80	8	50
Omaha, NE	n/a	139	35	100	142	123	97	20	46
Orlando, FL	n/a	n/a	90	76	208	81	115	0	80
Peoria, IL	n/a	127	27	89	127	149	115	22	49
Philadelphia, PA	5	94	23	81	146	138	117	14	27
Phoenix, AZ	0	10	167	186	125	54	37	< 1	23
Pittsburgh, PA	n/a	121	8	62	137	166	154	42	35
Portland, OR	n/a	37	11	67	116	182	152	4	7
Providence, RI	n/a	117	9	85	134	146	123	21	21
Provo, UT	n/a	128	56	94	152	119	92	38	38
Raleigh, NC	n/a	n/a	39	98	143	124	110	3	42
Reno, NV	14	178	50	143	139	83	50	17	14
Richmond, VA	3	79	41	90	147	128	115	7	43
Roanoke, VA	4	89	31	90	152	123	119	11	35
Rochester, MN	n/a	165	9	87	126	152	114	40	41
Salem, OR	n/a	66	16	78	118	169	146	6	5
Salt Lake City, UT	n/a	128	56	94	152	119	92	38	38
San Antonio, TX	n/a	n/a	112	97	153	115	81	1	36
San Diego, CA	0	< 1	4	115	126	124	40	0	5
San Francisco, CA	0	6	4	136	130	99	63	< 1	5
San Jose, CA	0	5	5	106	180	79	57	< 1	6
Santa Rosa, CA	n/a	43	30	n/a	365	n/a	n/a	n/a	2
Savannah, GA	< 1	29	70	97	155	113	111	< 1	63
Seattle, WA	n/a	38	3	57	121	187	157	8	8
Sioux Falls, SD	n/a	n/a	n/a	95	136	134	n/a	n/a	n/a
Springfield, IL	19	111	34	96	126	143	111	18	49
Tallahassee, FL	< 1	31	86	93	175	97	114	1	83
Tampa, FL	n/a	n/a	85	81	204	80	107	< 1	87
Topeka, KS	20	123	45	110	128	127	96	15	54
Tyler, TX	1	34	102	108	160	97	78	2	49
Virginia Beach, VA	< 1	53	33	89	149	127	115	5	38
Visalia, CA	0	23	106	185	99	81	44	< 1	5
Washington, DC	2	71	34	84	144	137	112	9	30
Wilmington, NC	< 1	42	46	96	150	119	115	1	47
Winston-Salem, NC	3	85	32	94	143	128	113	5	43

Note: Figures are average number of days per year
Source: National Climatic Data Center, International Station Meteorological Climate Summary, 9/96

Air Quality Index

MSA[1] (Days[2])	Percent of Days when Air Quality was...					AQI Statistics	
	Good	Moderate	Unhealthy for Sensitive Groups	Unhealthy	Very Unhealthy	Maximum	Median
Albany, NY (365)	83.8	16.2	0.0	0.0	0.0	90	39
Albuquerque, NM (365)	45.2	53.7	1.1	0.0	0.0	119	52
Allentown, PA (365)	48.2	50.1	0.8	0.8	0.0	200	51
Anchorage, AK (365)	78.4	20.0	1.4	0.3	0.0	155	31
Ann Arbor, MI (365)	77.8	21.4	0.8	0.0	0.0	119	40
Athens, GA (360)	87.2	12.8	0.0	0.0	0.0	97	38
Atlanta, GA (365)	47.7	49.3	3.0	0.0	0.0	150	51
Austin, TX (365)	71.8	27.1	1.1	0.0	0.0	130	43
Baton Rouge, LA (365)	62.5	35.3	2.2	0.0	0.0	140	46
Billings, MT (365)	85.5	13.2	1.4	0.0	0.0	141	25
Boise City, ID (365)	49.9	42.5	6.3	0.8	0.5	243	51
Boston, MA (365)	48.8	49.9	1.4	0.0	0.0	147	51
Boulder, CO (357)	67.2	29.7	3.1	0.0	0.0	149	45
Cape Coral, FL (363)	89.5	10.5	0.0	0.0	0.0	90	37
Cedar Rapids, IA (365)	76.7	23.3	0.0	0.0	0.0	100	40
Charleston, SC (361)	83.7	16.1	0.3	0.0	0.0	101	40
Charlotte, NC (365)	58.6	40.0	1.4	0.0	0.0	115	48
Chicago, IL (365)	43.0	50.1	6.3	0.5	0.0	177	53
Clarksville, TN (362)	82.0	18.0	0.0	0.0	0.0	87	42
College Station, TX (365)	100.0	0.0	0.0	0.0	0.0	23	0
Colorado Springs, CO (365)	65.5	33.7	0.8	0.0	0.0	116	46
Columbia, MO (245)	89.4	10.6	0.0	0.0	0.0	77	41
Columbia, SC (365)	74.0	25.5	0.5	0.0	0.0	113	44
Columbus, OH (365)	77.3	21.9	0.8	0.0	0.0	112	42
Dallas, TX (365)	52.6	40.8	6.6	0.0	0.0	147	50
Denver, CO (365)	19.7	69.3	10.7	0.3	0.0	155	62
Des Moines, IA (365)	80.0	19.7	0.3	0.0	0.0	135	40
Durham, NC (365)	72.3	27.4	0.3	0.0	0.0	110	44
Edison, NJ (365)	42.2	52.6	4.7	0.5	0.0	159	52
El Paso, TX (365)	46.6	47.1	5.8	0.5	0.0	159	51
Eugene, OR (365)	65.2	26.6	4.4	3.0	0.5	380	39
Evansville, IN (365)	57.5	39.7	2.7	0.0	0.0	126	48
Fargo, ND (362)	84.5	15.5	0.0	0.0	0.0	77	38
Fayetteville, NC (365)	73.4	26.6	0.0	0.0	0.0	100	43
Fort Collins, CO (365)	53.7	43.0	3.0	0.3	0.0	153	49
Fort Wayne, IN (365)	70.7	29.0	0.3	0.0	0.0	105	44
Fort Worth, TX (365)	52.6	40.8	6.6	0.0	0.0	147	50
Gainesville, FL (355)	89.0	11.0	0.0	0.0	0.0	92	37
Grand Rapids, MI (365)	77.8	22.2	0.0	0.0	0.0	100	40
Greeley, CO (365)	58.4	39.5	1.9	0.3	0.0	154	47
Green Bay, WI (364)	86.3	13.2	0.5	0.0	0.0	112	37
Greensboro, NC (365)	77.8	21.9	0.3	0.0	0.0	112	42
Honolulu, HI (365)	93.7	6.3	0.0	0.0	0.0	91	31
Houston, TX (365)	50.4	42.7	6.0	0.8	0.0	177	50
Huntsville, AL (336)	89.9	10.1	0.0	0.0	0.0	100	39
Indianapolis, IN (365)	54.0	43.6	2.5	0.0	0.0	122	48
Jacksonville, FL (365)	74.2	25.5	0.3	0.0	0.0	101	42
Kansas City, MO (365)	55.3	42.7	1.9	0.0	0.0	129	48
Lafayette, LA (365)	71.8	27.9	0.3	0.0	0.0	105	42
Las Cruces, NM (365)	35.9	54.8	7.4	1.1	0.0	617	57
Las Vegas, NV (365)	37.3	54.8	7.7	0.3	0.0	154	58
Lexington, KY (365)	86.3	13.7	0.0	0.0	0.0	100	40
Lincoln, NE (344)	92.2	7.3	0.6	0.0	0.0	113	33
Little Rock, AR (365)	69.0	30.7	0.3	0.0	0.0	115	44

Table continued on next page.

MSA[1] (Days[2])	Percent of Days when Air Quality was...					AQI Statistics	
	Good	Moderate	Unhealthy for Sensitive Groups	Unhealthy	Very Unhealthy	Maximum	Median
Los Angeles, CA (365)	10.4	56.2	20.8	10.4	2.2	224	79
Louisville, KY (365)	59.5	38.9	1.6	0.0	0.0	119	47
Madison, WI (365)	80.5	19.5	0.0	0.0	0.0	93	39
Manchester, NH (365)	93.7	6.0	0.3	0.0	0.0	101	37
McAllen, TX (365)	77.0	23.0	0.0	0.0	0.0	95	38
Miami, FL (358)	59.5	38.3	2.2	0.0	0.0	143	47
Midland, TX (n/a)	n/a	n/a	n/a	n/a	n/a	n/a	n/a
Minneapolis, MN (365)	47.7	52.1	0.3	0.0	0.0	115	51
Nashville, TN (365)	63.8	35.9	0.3	0.0	0.0	133	45
New Orleans, LA (365)	69.3	30.1	0.5	0.0	0.0	129	44
New York, NY (365)	42.2	52.6	4.7	0.5	0.0	159	52
Oklahoma City, OK (365)	62.2	35.9	1.9	0.0	0.0	119	47
Omaha, NE (365)	54.2	45.2	0.5	0.0	0.0	114	48
Orlando, FL (365)	73.4	25.8	0.8	0.0	0.0	147	43
Peoria, IL (365)	70.7	28.5	0.8	0.0	0.0	115	44
Philadelphia, PA (365)	34.5	59.5	5.5	0.5	0.0	166	55
Phoenix, AZ (365)	8.8	65.2	22.5	3.0	0.3	365	84
Pittsburgh, PA (365)	25.2	66.0	8.5	0.3	0.0	164	59
Portland, OR (365)	73.2	22.5	2.7	1.4	0.3	212	40
Providence, RI (365)	71.5	26.6	1.4	0.5	0.0	151	43
Provo, UT (365)	50.1	46.0	3.0	0.8	0.0	161	50
Raleigh, NC (365)	66.3	33.7	0.0	0.0	0.0	100	45
Reno, NV (365)	55.3	43.6	1.1	0.0	0.0	126	49
Richmond, VA (365)	78.1	21.6	0.0	0.3	0.0	154	42
Roanoke, VA (365)	87.1	12.6	0.3	0.0	0.0	116	38
Rochester, MN (365)	85.5	14.5	0.0	0.0	0.0	87	37
Salem, OR (362)	83.7	13.8	2.5	0.0	0.0	150	30
Salt Lake City, UT (365)	44.7	43.0	12.1	0.3	0.0	155	53
San Antonio, TX (362)	72.4	26.0	1.1	0.6	0.0	188	43
San Diego, CA (365)	22.7	60.3	15.3	1.6	0.0	174	65
San Francisco, CA (365)	46.3	49.3	2.2	1.9	0.3	205	52
San Jose, CA (365)	61.4	35.3	2.5	0.8	0.0	182	45
Santa Rosa, CA (365)	85.2	13.4	0.5	0.8	0.0	165	38
Savannah, GA (365)	79.2	20.8	0.0	0.0	0.0	84	38
Seattle, WA (365)	60.8	32.6	3.6	2.7	0.3	202	47
Sioux Falls, SD (365)	87.1	12.9	0.0	0.0	0.0	97	35
Springfield, IL (364)	81.9	17.6	0.5	0.0	0.0	115	40
Tallahassee, FL (363)	71.1	28.9	0.0	0.0	0.0	92	41
Tampa, FL (365)	69.0	29.9	1.1	0.0	0.0	150	45
Topeka, KS (361)	82.8	17.2	0.0	0.0	0.0	93	39
Tyler, TX (364)	92.3	7.7	0.0	0.0	0.0	90	37
Virginia Beach, VA (365)	86.8	13.2	0.0	0.0	0.0	97	39
Visalia, CA (365)	25.5	39.7	26.3	8.5	0.0	168	80
Washington, DC (365)	40.3	57.5	2.2	0.0	0.0	133	53
Wilmington, NC (365)	93.2	6.8	0.0	0.0	0.0	67	33
Winston-Salem, NC (365)	70.1	29.9	0.0	0.0	0.0	100	44

Note: The Air Quality Index (AQI) is an index for reporting daily air quality. EPA calculates the AQI for five major air pollutants regulated by the Clean Air Act: ground-level ozone, particle pollution (also known as particulate matter), carbon monoxide, sulfur dioxide, and nitrogen dioxide. The AQI runs from 0 to 500. The higher the AQI value, the greater the level of air pollution and the greater the health concern. There are six AQI categories: "Good" The AQI is between 0 and 50. Air quality is considered satisfactory; "Moderate" The AQI is between 51 and 100. Air quality is acceptable; "Unhealthy for Sensitive Groups" When AQI values are between 101 and 150, members of sensitive groups may experience health effects; "Unhealthy" When AQI values are between 151 and 200 everyone may begin to experience health effects; "Very Unhealthy" AQI values between 201 and 300 trigger a health alert; "Hazardous" AQI values over 300 trigger health warnings of emergency conditions; Data covers the entire county unless noted otherwise; (1) Data covers the Metropolitan Statistical Area—see Appendix B for areas included; (2) Number of days with AQI data in 2017
Source: U.S. Environmental Protection Agency, Air Quality Index Report, 2017

Air Quality Index Pollutants

MSA[1] (Days[2])	Percent of Days when AQI Pollutant was...					
	Carbon Monoxide	Nitrogen Dioxide	Ozone	Sulfur Dioxide	Particulate Matter 2.5	Particulate Matter 10
Albany, NY (365)	0.0	0.0	70.1	0.0	29.9	0.0
Albuquerque, NM (365)	0.0	0.5	70.7	0.0	7.9	20.8
Allentown, PA (365)	0.0	0.3	35.6	1.9	62.2	0.0
Anchorage, AK (365)	0.3	0.0	45.5	0.0	36.4	17.8
Ann Arbor, MI (365)	0.0	0.0	65.8	0.0	34.2	0.0
Athens, GA (360)	0.0	0.0	52.2	0.0	47.8	0.0
Atlanta, GA (365)	0.0	4.4	44.4	0.0	51.2	0.0
Austin, TX (365)	0.0	4.9	51.0	0.0	44.1	0.0
Baton Rouge, LA (365)	0.0	0.5	38.4	2.7	58.4	0.0
Billings, MT (365)	0.0	0.0	0.0	9.0	91.0	0.0
Boise City, ID (365)	0.3	2.5	52.6	0.0	43.3	1.4
Boston, MA (365)	0.0	1.1	29.3	0.0	69.6	0.0
Boulder, CO (357)	0.0	0.0	92.2	0.0	7.8	0.0
Cape Coral, FL (363)	0.0	0.0	74.1	0.0	24.8	1.1
Cedar Rapids, IA (365)	0.0	0.0	44.7	5.2	49.6	0.5
Charleston, SC (361)	0.0	1.1	56.2	0.0	42.1	0.6
Charlotte, NC (365)	0.0	0.3	56.7	0.0	43.0	0.0
Chicago, IL (365)	0.0	5.8	41.6	3.0	44.9	4.7
Clarksville, TN (362)	0.0	0.0	63.0	0.0	37.0	0.0
College Station, TX (365)	0.0	0.0	0.0	100.0	0.0	0.0
Colorado Springs, CO (365)	0.0	0.0	89.0	0.5	10.4	0.0
Columbia, MO (245)	0.0	0.0	100.0	0.0	0.0	0.0
Columbia, SC (365)	0.0	0.0	61.4	0.0	38.4	0.3
Columbus, OH (365)	0.0	7.9	55.1	0.0	36.2	0.8
Dallas, TX (365)	0.0	4.1	57.3	0.0	38.6	0.0
Denver, CO (365)	0.0	20.0	62.5	0.0	13.2	4.4
Des Moines, IA (365)	0.0	1.1	59.2	0.0	39.7	0.0
Durham, NC (365)	0.0	0.0	50.1	0.5	49.3	0.0
Edison, NJ (365)	0.0	14.5	33.2	0.0	52.3	0.0
El Paso, TX (365)	0.0	7.4	56.7	0.0	35.3	0.5
Eugene, OR (365)	0.0	0.0	25.2	0.0	74.0	0.8
Evansville, IN (365)	0.0	0.0	37.8	15.3	46.8	0.0
Fargo, ND (362)	0.0	0.3	48.1	0.0	47.5	4.1
Fayetteville, NC (365)	0.0	0.0	44.4	0.0	55.3	0.3
Fort Collins, CO (365)	0.0	0.0	88.8	0.0	11.2	0.0
Fort Wayne, IN (365)	0.0	0.0	49.6	0.0	50.4	0.0
Fort Worth, TX (365)	0.0	4.1	57.3	0.0	38.6	0.0
Gainesville, FL (355)	0.0	0.0	61.4	0.0	38.6	0.0
Grand Rapids, MI (365)	0.0	0.0	65.5	0.3	34.2	0.0
Greeley, CO (365)	0.0	0.0	69.3	0.0	30.7	0.0
Green Bay, WI (364)	0.0	0.0	60.2	1.4	38.5	0.0
Greensboro, NC (365)	0.0	0.0	55.9	0.0	40.0	4.1
Honolulu, HI (365)	0.3	2.2	70.7	11.5	15.3	0.0
Houston, TX (365)	0.0	5.2	48.8	0.0	45.8	0.3
Huntsville, AL (336)	0.0	0.0	68.5	0.0	15.5	16.1
Indianapolis, IN (365)	0.0	0.8	37.8	2.5	58.9	0.0
Jacksonville, FL (365)	0.3	0.8	51.8	1.9	45.2	0.0
Kansas City, MO (365)	0.0	2.7	46.0	0.5	45.2	5.5
Lafayette, LA (365)	0.0	0.0	65.8	0.0	34.2	0.0
Las Cruces, NM (365)	0.0	0.3	70.4	0.0	8.2	21.1
Las Vegas, NV (365)	0.0	12.6	62.7	0.0	21.6	3.0
Lexington, KY (365)	0.0	3.0	52.6	0.3	43.8	0.3
Lincoln, NE (344)	0.0	0.0	57.0	24.4	18.6	0.0
Little Rock, AR (365)	0.0	0.5	41.6	0.0	57.8	0.0

Table continued on next page.

MSA[1] (Days[2])	Carbon Monoxide	Nitrogen Dioxide	Ozone	Sulfur Dioxide	Particulate Matter 2.5	Particulate Matter 10
	Percent of Days when AQI Pollutant was...					
Los Angeles, CA (365)	0.0	7.7	48.5	0.0	43.3	0.5
Louisville, KY (365)	0.0	4.7	41.6	0.0	53.7	0.0
Madison, WI (365)	0.0	0.0	53.4	1.9	44.7	0.0
Manchester, NH (365)	0.0	0.0	97.0	0.3	2.7	0.0
McAllen, TX (365)	0.0	0.0	39.2	0.0	60.8	0.0
Miami, FL (358)	0.0	1.7	24.6	0.0	70.4	3.4
Midland, TX (n/a)	n/a	n/a	n/a	n/a	n/a	n/a
Minneapolis, MN (365)	0.0	1.6	26.8	0.0	36.2	35.3
Nashville, TN (365)	0.0	4.9	37.3	0.5	57.3	0.0
New Orleans, LA (365)	0.0	0.8	46.0	9.0	44.1	0.0
New York, NY (365)	0.0	14.5	33.2	0.0	52.3	0.0
Oklahoma City, OK (365)	0.0	4.7	60.5	0.0	34.8	0.0
Omaha, NE (365)	0.0	0.0	33.7	6.0	48.5	11.8
Orlando, FL (365)	0.0	3.6	60.8	0.0	35.3	0.3
Peoria, IL (365)	0.0	0.0	57.0	1.1	41.9	0.0
Philadelphia, PA (365)	0.0	0.8	32.1	0.5	66.3	0.3
Phoenix, AZ (365)	0.0	3.3	37.0	0.0	15.9	43.8
Pittsburgh, PA (365)	0.0	0.0	24.4	7.7	67.7	0.3
Portland, OR (365)	0.0	4.9	52.9	0.0	42.2	0.0
Providence, RI (365)	0.0	4.7	55.6	0.0	39.7	0.0
Provo, UT (365)	0.0	8.2	69.6	0.0	20.8	1.4
Raleigh, NC (365)	0.0	1.1	44.4	0.0	54.5	0.0
Reno, NV (365)	0.0	2.2	74.8	0.0	20.0	3.0
Richmond, VA (365)	0.0	2.2	62.7	0.0	35.1	0.0
Roanoke, VA (365)	0.0	2.5	52.9	4.4	40.3	0.0
Rochester, MN (365)	0.0	0.0	56.4	0.0	43.6	0.0
Salem, OR (362)	0.0	0.0	39.0	0.0	61.0	0.0
Salt Lake City, UT (365)	0.0	3.0	69.9	0.0	26.3	0.8
San Antonio, TX (362)	0.0	1.7	58.0	0.6	39.8	0.0
San Diego, CA (365)	0.0	0.8	66.3	0.0	32.9	0.0
San Francisco, CA (365)	0.0	4.9	28.2	0.0	66.8	0.0
San Jose, CA (365)	0.0	1.9	61.6	0.0	35.9	0.5
Santa Rosa, CA (365)	0.0	0.0	68.2	0.0	31.2	0.5
Savannah, GA (365)	0.0	0.0	27.4	9.6	63.0	0.0
Seattle, WA (365)	0.0	6.6	49.0	0.0	44.4	0.0
Sioux Falls, SD (365)	0.0	1.1	72.3	0.0	24.4	2.2
Springfield, IL (364)	0.0	0.0	76.6	0.0	23.4	0.0
Tallahassee, FL (363)	0.6	0.0	36.6	0.0	62.8	0.0
Tampa, FL (365)	0.0	0.0	54.0	2.2	43.6	0.3
Topeka, KS (361)	0.0	0.0	64.5	0.0	34.9	0.6
Tyler, TX (364)	0.0	2.2	97.8	0.0	0.0	0.0
Virginia Beach, VA (365)	0.0	11.5	61.6	0.0	26.8	0.0
Visalia, CA (365)	0.0	0.3	64.7	0.0	32.6	2.5
Washington, DC (365)	0.0	6.6	44.9	0.0	48.5	0.0
Wilmington, NC (365)	0.0	0.0	48.8	3.3	47.9	0.0
Winston-Salem, NC (365)	0.0	2.5	53.2	0.0	44.4	0.0

Note: The Air Quality Index (AQI) is an index for reporting daily air quality. EPA calculates the AQI for five major air pollutants regulated by the Clean Air Act: ground-level ozone, particle pollution (also known as particulate matter), carbon monoxide, sulfur dioxide, and nitrogen dioxide. The AQI runs from 0 to 500. The higher the AQI value, the greater the level of air pollution and the greater the health concern; (1) Data covers the Metropolitan Statistical Area—see Appendix B for areas included; (2) Number of days with AQI data in 2017
Source: U.S. Environmental Protection Agency, Air Quality Index Report, 2017

Air Quality Trends: Ozone

MSA[1]	1990	1995	2000	2005	2010	2012	2014	2015	2016	2017
Albany, NY	0.086	0.079	0.070	0.082	0.072	0.071	0.061	0.062	0.068	0.061
Albuquerque, NM	0.072	0.070	0.072	0.073	0.066	0.070	0.062	0.066	0.065	0.069
Allentown, PA	0.093	0.091	0.091	0.086	0.080	0.075	0.068	0.070	0.071	0.067
Anchorage, AK	n/a	n/a	n/a	n/a	n/a	n/a	n/a	n/a	n/a	n/a
Ann Arbor, MI	n/a	n/a	n/a	n/a	n/a	n/a	n/a	n/a	n/a	n/a
Athens, GA	n/a	n/a	n/a	n/a	n/a	n/a	n/a	n/a	n/a	n/a
Atlanta, GA	0.104	0.103	0.101	0.087	0.076	0.079	0.072	0.070	0.073	0.068
Austin, TX	0.088	0.089	0.088	0.082	0.074	0.074	0.062	0.073	0.064	0.070
Baton Rouge, LA	0.105	0.091	0.090	0.090	0.075	0.074	0.071	0.069	0.066	0.069
Billings, MT	n/a	n/a	n/a	n/a	n/a	n/a	n/a	n/a	n/a	n/a
Boise City, ID	n/a	n/a	n/a	n/a	n/a	n/a	n/a	n/a	n/a	n/a
Boston, MA	n/a	n/a	n/a	n/a	n/a	n/a	n/a	n/a	n/a	n/a
Boulder, CO	n/a	n/a	n/a	n/a	n/a	n/a	n/a	n/a	n/a	n/a
Cape Coral, FL	n/a	n/a	n/a	n/a	n/a	n/a	n/a	n/a	n/a	n/a
Cedar Rapids, IA	n/a	n/a	n/a	n/a	n/a	n/a	n/a	n/a	n/a	n/a
Charleston, SC	0.068	0.071	0.078	0.073	0.067	0.063	0.060	0.054	0.058	0.062
Charlotte, NC	0.098	0.091	0.101	0.090	0.082	0.085	0.068	0.069	0.069	0.069
Chicago, IL	0.074	0.094	0.073	0.084	0.070	0.082	0.068	0.066	0.074	0.071
Clarksville, TN	n/a	n/a	n/a	n/a	n/a	n/a	n/a	n/a	n/a	n/a
College Station, TX	n/a	n/a	n/a	n/a	n/a	n/a	n/a	n/a	n/a	n/a
Colorado Springs, CO	n/a	n/a	n/a	n/a	n/a	n/a	n/a	n/a	n/a	n/a
Columbia, MO	n/a	n/a	n/a	n/a	n/a	n/a	n/a	n/a	n/a	n/a
Columbia, SC	0.093	0.079	0.096	0.082	0.070	0.065	0.056	0.056	0.065	0.059
Columbus, OH	0.090	0.091	0.085	0.084	0.073	0.077	0.067	0.066	0.069	0.065
Dallas, TX	0.095	0.105	0.096	0.097	0.080	0.080	0.076	0.077	0.070	0.073
Denver, CO	0.077	0.070	0.069	0.072	0.070	0.079	0.070	0.073	0.071	0.072
Des Moines, IA	n/a	n/a	n/a	n/a	n/a	n/a	n/a	n/a	n/a	n/a
Durham, NC	n/a	n/a	n/a	n/a	n/a	n/a	n/a	n/a	n/a	n/a
Edison, NJ	0.101	0.106	0.090	0.091	0.081	0.079	0.069	0.075	0.073	0.070
El Paso, TX	0.080	0.078	0.082	0.075	0.072	0.072	0.068	0.070	0.068	0.073
Eugene, OR	0.068	0.062	0.056	0.068	0.058	0.061	0.058	0.070	0.057	0.072
Evansville, IN	0.088	0.092	0.076	0.072	0.072	0.078	0.067	0.067	0.071	0.067
Fargo, ND	n/a	n/a	n/a	n/a	n/a	n/a	n/a	n/a	n/a	n/a
Fayetteville, NC	0.087	0.081	0.086	0.084	0.071	0.068	0.061	0.060	0.064	0.063
Fort Collins, CO	0.066	0.072	0.074	0.076	0.072	0.077	0.071	0.069	0.070	0.067
Fort Wayne, IN	0.086	0.094	0.086	0.081	0.067	0.076	0.063	0.061	0.068	0.063
Fort Worth, TX	0.095	0.105	0.096	0.097	0.080	0.080	0.076	0.077	0.070	0.073
Gainesville, FL	n/a	n/a	n/a	n/a	n/a	n/a	n/a	n/a	n/a	n/a
Grand Rapids, MI	0.102	0.089	0.073	0.085	0.071	0.083	0.069	0.066	0.075	0.065
Greeley, CO	n/a	n/a	n/a	n/a	n/a	n/a	n/a	n/a	n/a	n/a
Green Bay, WI	n/a	n/a	n/a	n/a	n/a	n/a	n/a	n/a	n/a	n/a
Greensboro, NC	n/a	n/a	n/a	n/a	n/a	n/a	n/a	n/a	n/a	n/a
Honolulu, HI	0.034	0.051	0.044	0.042	0.047	0.043	0.057	0.049	0.048	0.048
Houston, TX	0.119	0.114	0.102	0.087	0.079	0.080	0.064	0.083	0.066	0.070
Huntsville, AL	0.079	0.080	0.088	0.075	0.071	0.076	0.064	0.063	0.066	0.063
Indianapolis, IN	0.086	0.095	0.082	0.080	0.069	0.074	0.063	0.064	0.068	0.066
Jacksonville, FL	0.080	0.068	0.072	0.076	0.068	0.059	0.062	0.060	0.057	0.059
Kansas City, MO	0.075	0.098	0.088	0.084	0.072	0.085	0.066	0.063	0.066	0.069
Lafayette, LA	n/a	n/a	n/a	n/a	n/a	n/a	n/a	n/a	n/a	n/a
Las Cruces, NM	0.073	0.075	0.075	0.070	0.060	0.074	0.065	0.070	0.063	0.071
Las Vegas, NV	n/a	n/a	n/a	n/a	n/a	n/a	n/a	n/a	n/a	n/a
Lexington, KY	0.078	0.088	0.077	0.078	0.070	0.078	0.065	0.069	0.066	0.063
Lincoln, NE	0.057	0.060	0.057	0.056	0.050	0.058	0.061	0.061	0.058	0.062
Little Rock, AR	0.080	0.086	0.090	0.083	0.072	0.078	0.066	0.063	0.064	0.060
Los Angeles, CA	0.129	0.110	0.089	0.082	0.074	0.077	0.082	0.081	0.081	0.090
Louisville, KY	0.075	0.087	0.088	0.083	0.076	0.086	0.066	0.070	0.070	0.064

Table continued on next page.

MSA[1]	1990	1995	2000	2005	2010	2012	2014	2015	2016	2017
Madison, WI	0.077	0.084	0.072	0.079	0.062	0.074	0.068	0.064	0.068	0.064
Manchester, NH	n/a	n/a	n/a	n/a	n/a	n/a	n/a	n/a	n/a	n/a
McAllen, TX	n/a	n/a	n/a	n/a	n/a	n/a	n/a	n/a	n/a	n/a
Miami, FL	0.068	0.072	0.075	0.065	0.064	0.062	0.062	0.061	0.061	0.064
Midland, TX	n/a	n/a	n/a	n/a	n/a	n/a	n/a	n/a	n/a	n/a
Minneapolis, MN	0.068	0.084	0.065	0.074	0.066	0.073	0.063	0.061	0.061	0.062
Nashville, TN	0.089	0.092	0.084	0.078	0.073	0.079	0.067	0.065	0.068	0.063
New Orleans, LA	0.082	0.088	0.091	0.079	0.074	0.071	0.069	0.067	0.065	0.063
New York, NY	0.101	0.106	0.090	0.091	0.081	0.079	0.069	0.075	0.073	0.070
Oklahoma City, OK	0.078	0.086	0.082	0.077	0.071	0.080	0.068	0.067	0.066	0.069
Omaha, NE	0.054	0.075	0.063	0.069	0.058	0.066	0.059	0.055	0.063	0.061
Orlando, FL	0.081	0.075	0.080	0.083	0.069	0.071	0.062	0.060	0.063	0.067
Peoria, IL	0.071	0.082	0.072	0.075	0.064	0.072	0.064	0.062	0.067	0.066
Philadelphia, PA	0.102	0.109	0.099	0.091	0.083	0.084	0.071	0.074	0.075	0.073
Phoenix, AZ	0.080	0.087	0.082	0.077	0.076	0.080	0.075	0.072	0.071	0.075
Pittsburgh, PA	0.080	0.095	0.082	0.082	0.075	0.079	0.065	0.069	0.068	0.066
Portland, OR	0.081	0.065	0.059	0.059	0.056	0.059	0.057	0.064	0.057	0.073
Providence, RI	0.106	0.107	0.087	0.090	0.072	0.072	0.067	0.070	0.075	0.076
Provo, UT	0.070	0.068	0.083	0.078	0.070	0.077	0.068	0.073	0.072	0.073
Raleigh, NC	0.093	0.081	0.087	0.082	0.071	0.071	0.063	0.065	0.069	0.066
Reno, NV	0.074	0.070	0.067	0.069	0.068	0.072	0.069	0.071	0.070	0.068
Richmond, VA	0.083	0.089	0.080	0.082	0.079	0.076	0.063	0.062	0.065	0.063
Roanoke, VA	0.075	0.079	0.081	0.076	0.073	0.070	0.060	0.062	0.064	0.058
Rochester, MN	n/a	n/a	n/a	n/a	n/a	n/a	n/a	n/a	n/a	n/a
Salem, OR	n/a	n/a	n/a	n/a	n/a	n/a	n/a	n/a	n/a	n/a
Salt Lake City, UT	n/a	n/a	n/a	n/a	n/a	n/a	n/a	n/a	n/a	n/a
San Antonio, TX	0.090	0.095	0.078	0.084	0.072	0.081	0.069	0.079	0.071	0.073
San Diego, CA	0.108	0.088	0.080	0.073	0.072	0.069	0.073	0.068	0.070	0.072
San Francisco, CA	0.058	0.074	0.057	0.055	0.061	0.057	0.065	0.062	0.059	0.060
San Jose, CA	0.079	0.085	0.070	0.065	0.073	0.064	0.069	0.067	0.063	0.065
Santa Rosa, CA	0.063	0.071	0.061	0.050	0.053	0.058	0.062	0.059	0.055	0.062
Savannah, GA	n/a	n/a	n/a	n/a	n/a	n/a	n/a	n/a	n/a	n/a
Seattle, WA	0.082	0.062	0.056	0.053	0.053	0.059	0.052	0.059	0.054	0.076
Sioux Falls, SD	n/a	n/a	n/a	n/a	n/a	n/a	n/a	n/a	n/a	n/a
Springfield, IL	n/a	n/a	n/a	n/a	n/a	n/a	n/a	n/a	n/a	n/a
Tallahassee, FL	n/a	n/a	n/a	n/a	n/a	n/a	n/a	n/a	n/a	n/a
Tampa, FL	0.080	0.075	0.081	0.075	0.067	0.066	0.065	0.062	0.064	0.064
Topeka, KS	n/a	n/a	n/a	n/a	n/a	n/a	n/a	n/a	n/a	n/a
Tyler, TX	n/a	n/a	n/a	n/a	n/a	n/a	n/a	n/a	n/a	n/a
Virginia Beach, VA	0.085	0.084	0.083	0.078	0.074	0.069	0.061	0.061	0.062	0.059
Visalia, CA	0.099	0.100	0.095	0.096	0.087	0.088	0.082	0.085	0.082	0.086
Washington, DC	0.088	0.093	0.082	0.081	0.077	0.075	0.065	0.067	0.068	0.065
Wilmington, NC	0.082	0.079	0.080	0.075	0.062	0.064	0.063	0.057	0.060	0.057
Winston-Salem, NC	0.084	0.086	0.089	0.080	0.078	0.074	0.067	0.065	0.069	0.066
U.S.	0.088	0.089	0.082	0.080	0.073	0.075	0.067	0.068	0.069	0.068

Note: (1) Data covers the Metropolitan Statistical Area—see Appendix B for areas included; n/a not available. The values shown are the composite ozone concentration averages among trend sites based on the highest fourth daily maximum 8-hour concentration in parts per million. These trends are based on sites having an adequate record of monitoring data during the trend period. Data from exceptional events are included.
Source: U.S. Environmental Protection Agency, Air Quality Monitoring Information, "Air Quality Trends by City, 1990-2017"

Maximum Air Pollutant Concentrations: Particulate Matter, Ozone, CO and Lead

Metro Aea	PM 10 (ug/m³)	PM 2.5 Wtd AM (ug/m³)	PM 2.5 24-Hr (ug/m³)	Ozone (ppm)	Carbon Monoxide (ppm)	Lead (ug/m³)
Albany, NY	n/a	6.9	15	0.061	0	n/a
Albuquerque, NM	126	7.5	19	0.071	1	0
Allentown, PA	29	8.8	25	0.07	n/a	n/a
Anchorage, AK	119	5.7	30	0.043	4	n/a
Ann Arbor, MI	n/a	8	19	0.069	n/a	n/a
Athens, GA	n/a	7.8	16	0.063	n/a	n/a
Atlanta, GA	41	10.4	23	0.074	2	n/a
Austin, TX	39	10	25	0.07	1	n/a
Baton Rouge, LA	71	9.1	19	0.073	1	0
Billings, MT	n/a	7.5	31	n/a	n/a	n/a
Boise City, ID	138	10.3	45	0.076	4	n/a
Boston, MA	31	7.3	17	0.075	1	n/a
Boulder, CO	47	6.7	19	0.073	n/a	n/a
Cape Coral, FL	51	n/a	n/a	0.065	n/a	n/a
Cedar Rapids, IA	57	7.8	20	0.062	1	n/a
Charleston, SC	29	n/a	n/a	0.064	n/a	n/a
Charlotte, NC	40	8.7	18	0.068	1	n/a
Chicago, IL	108	10.3	24	0.079	1	0.02
Clarksville, TN	n/a	8.2	17	0.062	n/a	n/a
College Station, TX	n/a	n/a	n/a	n/a	n/a	n/a
Colorado Springs, CO	49	6	17	0.07	1	n/a
Columbia, MO	n/a	n/a	n/a	0.061	n/a	n/a
Columbia, SC	32	8.1	18	0.06	1	0
Columbus, OH	52	8.8	22	0.07	2	0.01
Dallas, TX	38	9	18	0.077	1	0.17
Denver, CO	116	9.7	27	0.076	2	n/a
Des Moines, IA	47	7.3	17	0.06	1	n/a
Durham, NC	29	8.6	17	0.061	n/a	n/a
Edison, NJ	32	9.6	23	0.079	2	0.01
El Paso, TX	104	9	24	0.075	5	0.02
Eugene, OR	226	13.6	134	0.073	n/a	n/a
Evansville, IN	26	8.9	19	0.068	1	n/a
Fargo, ND	71	n/a	n/a	0.061	n/a	n/a
Fayetteville, NC	27	8.7	18	0.063	n/a	n/a
Fort Collins, CO	50	7.4	18	0.075	1	n/a
Fort Wayne, IN	n/a	8.2	20	0.064	n/a	n/a
Fort Worth, TX	38	9	18	0.077	1	0.17
Gainesville, FL	n/a	6.7	17	0.063	n/a	n/a
Grand Rapids, MI	29	9.1	26	0.066	1	0
Greeley, CO	56	8.6	22	0.072	1	n/a
Green Bay, WI	n/a	6.1	16	0.067	n/a	n/a
Greensboro, NC	30	7.7	16	0.065	n/a	n/a
Honolulu, HI	38	4.4	14	0.049	1	0
Houston, TX	80	10.1	24	0.079	2	n/a
Huntsville, AL	27	7.5	17	0.063	n/a	n/a
Indianapolis, IN	54	10.1	21	0.069	3	0.02
Jacksonville, FL	51	n/a	n/a	0.062	1	n/a
Kansas City, MO	117	9.9	23	0.07	1	n/a
Lafayette, LA	69	8	21	0.064	n/a	n/a
Las Cruces, NM	475	8.3	37	0.077	n/a	n/a
Las Vegas, NV	119	9.1	28	0.076	3	n/a
Lexington, KY	40	7.8	18	0.064	n/a	n/a
Lincoln, NE	n/a	6.7	19	0.062	n/a	n/a
Little Rock, AR	36	9.6	21	0.062	2	n/a
Los Angeles, CA	111	13.3	53	0.111	4	0.09

Table continued on next page.

Metro Aea	PM 10 (ug/m³)	PM 2.5 Wtd AM (ug/m³)	PM 2.5 24-Hr (ug/m³)	Ozone (ppm)	Carbon Monoxide (ppm)	Lead (ug/m³)
Louisville, KY	39	9.2	21	0.074	1	n/a
Madison, WI	28	7.8	21	0.065	n/a	n/a
Manchester, NH	n/a	2.9	10	0.066	0	n/a
McAllen, TX	49	10.1	26	0.055	n/a	n/a
Miami, FL	94	9.8	22	0.068	2	n/a
Midland, TX	n/a	n/a	n/a	n/a	n/a	n/a
Minneapolis, MN	150	8.7	20	0.063	4	0.11
Nashville, TN	34	9.7	19	0.064	2	n/a
New Orleans, LA	81	8.2	23	0.066	2	0.13
New York, NY	32	9.6	23	0.079	2	0.01
Oklahoma City, OK	52	7.8	16	0.071	1	n/a
Omaha, NE	113	9.7	21	0.064	2	0.05
Orlando, FL	59	7.8	18	0.068	1	n/a
Peoria, IL	n/a	8.3	22	0.066	n/a	n/a
Philadelphia, PA	69	11.4	27	0.079	3	n/a
Phoenix, AZ	416	15.1	38	0.079	3	0.05
Pittsburgh, PA	93	13.4	37	0.072	4	0.01
Portland, OR	59	8.2	36	0.083	1	n/a
Providence, RI	30	8.3	18	0.076	2	n/a
Provo, UT	88	8.5	29	0.073	2	n/a
Raleigh, NC	31	8.5	18	0.066	1	n/a
Reno, NV	101	8	24	0.069	2	n/a
Richmond, VA	25	7.5	15	0.067	1	n/a
Roanoke, VA	n/a	7	14	0.058	1	0.02
Rochester, MN	n/a	6.9	18	0.062	n/a	n/a
Salem, OR	n/a	n/a	n/a	0.078	n/a	n/a
Salt Lake City, UT	87	9.2	39	0.081	2	n/a
San Antonio, TX	73	8.9	25	0.073	1	n/a
San Diego, CA	67	9.6	19	0.09	1	0.02
San Francisco, CA	59	12.8	43	0.079	2	n/a
San Jose, CA	74	10.8	37	0.075	2	0.07
Santa Rosa, CA	152	8.1	26	0.062	1	n/a
Savannah, GA	n/a	n/a	n/a	0.057	n/a	n/a
Seattle, WA	n/a	9.7	44	0.094	2	n/a
Sioux Falls, SD	54	5.6	14	0.066	1	n/a
Springfield, IL	n/a	8.6	21	0.069	n/a	n/a
Tallahassee, FL	n/a	8	19	0.063	0	n/a
Tampa, FL	63	8.1	22	0.068	2	0.13
Topeka, KS	49	8.8	21	0.062	n/a	n/a
Tyler, TX	n/a	n/a	n/a	0.063	n/a	n/a
Virginia Beach, VA	20	6.9	16	0.064	1	n/a
Visalia, CA	140	16.3	75	0.089	n/a	n/a
Washington, DC	44	10.2	21	0.072	2	n/a
Wilmington, NC	19	6.1	14	0.057	n/a	n/a
Winston-Salem, NC	23	8.1	18	0.066	n/a	n/a
NAAQS[1]	150	15	35	0.075	9	0.15

Note: Data from exceptional events are included; Data covers the Metropolitan Statistical Area—see Appendix B for areas included; (1) National Ambient Air Quality Standards; ppm = parts per million; ug/m³ = micrograms per cubic meter; n/a not available Concentrations: Particulate Matter 10 (coarse particulate)—highest second maximum 24-hour concentration; Particulate Matter 2.5 Wtd AM (fine particulate)—highest weighted annual mean concentration; Particulate Matter 2.5 24-Hour (fine particulate)—highest 98th percentile 24-hour concentration; Ozone—highest fourth daily maximum 8-hour concentration; Carbon Monoxide—highest second maximum non-overlapping 8-hour concentration; Lead—maximum running 3-month average Source: U.S. Environmental Protection Agency, Air Quality Monitoring Information, "Air Quality Statistics by City, 2017"

Maximum Air Pollutant Concentrations: Nitrogen Dioxide and Sulfur Dioxide

Metro Area	Nitrogen Dioxide AM (ppb)	Nitrogen Dioxide 1-Hr (ppb)	Sulfur Dioxide AM (ppb)	Sulfur Dioxide 1-Hr (ppb)	Sulfur Dioxide 24-Hr (ppb)
Albany, NY	n/a	n/a	n/a	4	n/a
Albuquerque, NM	10	45	n/a	4	n/a
Allentown, PA	10	44	n/a	105	n/a
Anchorage, AK	n/a	n/a	n/a	n/a	n/a
Ann Arbor, MI	n/a	n/a	n/a	n/a	n/a
Athens, GA	n/a	n/a	n/a	n/a	n/a
Atlanta, GA	18	53	n/a	7	n/a
Austin, TX	13	47	n/a	4	n/a
Baton Rouge, LA	10	46	n/a	29	n/a
Billings, MT	n/a	n/a	n/a	32	n/a
Boise City, ID	n/a	n/a	n/a	3	n/a
Boston, MA	14	46	n/a	11	n/a
Boulder, CO	n/a	n/a	n/a	n/a	n/a
Cape Coral, FL	n/a	n/a	n/a	n/a	n/a
Cedar Rapids, IA	n/a	n/a	n/a	53	n/a
Charleston, SC	1	n/a	n/a	5	n/a
Charlotte, NC	11	40	n/a	5	n/a
Chicago, IL	16	55	n/a	36	n/a
Clarksville, TN	n/a	n/a	n/a	n/a	n/a
College Station, TX	n/a	n/a	n/a	13	n/a
Colorado Springs, CO	n/a	n/a	n/a	22	n/a
Columbia, MO	n/a	n/a	n/a	n/a	n/a
Columbia, SC	4	37	n/a	3	n/a
Columbus, OH	11	40	n/a	3	n/a
Dallas, TX	12	45	n/a	7	n/a
Denver, CO	27	70	n/a	16	n/a
Des Moines, IA	6	38	n/a	1	n/a
Durham, NC	n/a	n/a	n/a	31	n/a
Edison, NJ	20	67	n/a	7	n/a
El Paso, TX	10	58	n/a	5	n/a
Eugene, OR	n/a	n/a	n/a	n/a	n/a
Evansville, IN	8	29	n/a	94	n/a
Fargo, ND	4	34	n/a	4	n/a
Fayetteville, NC	n/a	n/a	n/a	n/a	n/a
Fort Collins, CO	n/a	n/a	n/a	n/a	n/a
Fort Wayne, IN	n/a	n/a	n/a	n/a	n/a
Fort Worth, TX	12	45	n/a	7	n/a
Gainesville, FL	n/a	n/a	n/a	n/a	n/a
Grand Rapids, MI	n/a	n/a	n/a	21	n/a
Greeley, CO	n/a	n/a	n/a	n/a	n/a
Green Bay, WI	n/a	n/a	n/a	11	n/a
Greensboro, NC	n/a	n/a	n/a	n/a	n/a
Honolulu, HI	4	33	n/a	55	n/a
Houston, TX	14	52	n/a	19	n/a
Huntsville, AL	n/a	n/a	n/a	n/a	n/a
Indianapolis, IN	13	39	n/a	47	n/a
Jacksonville, FL	11	35	n/a	32	n/a
Kansas City, MO	12	47	n/a	18	n/a
Lafayette, LA	n/a	n/a	n/a	n/a	n/a
Las Cruces, NM	6	43	n/a	n/a	n/a
Las Vegas, NV	27	61	n/a	6	n/a
Lexington, KY	5	n/a	n/a	4	n/a
Lincoln, NE	n/a	n/a	n/a	44	n/a
Little Rock, AR	8	39	n/a	8	n/a
Los Angeles, CA	25	83	n/a	14	n/a

Table continued on next page.

Metro Area	Nitrogen Dioxide AM (ppb)	Nitrogen Dioxide 1-Hr (ppb)	Sulfur Dioxide AM (ppb)	Sulfur Dioxide 1-Hr (ppb)	Sulfur Dioxide 24-Hr (ppb)
Louisville, KY	15	47	n/a	14	n/a
Madison, WI	n/a	n/a	n/a	3	n/a
Manchester, NH	n/a	n/a	n/a	3	n/a
McAllen, TX	n/a	n/a	n/a	n/a	n/a
Miami, FL	15	44	n/a	1	n/a
Midland, TX	n/a	n/a	n/a	n/a	n/a
Minneapolis, MN	13	44	n/a	18	n/a
Nashville, TN	14	51	n/a	5	n/a
New Orleans, LA	10	45	n/a	53	n/a
New York, NY	20	67	n/a	7	n/a
Oklahoma City, OK	16	43	n/a	2	n/a
Omaha, NE	n/a	n/a	n/a	55	n/a
Orlando, FL	4	30	n/a	5	n/a
Peoria, IL	n/a	n/a	n/a	23	n/a
Philadelphia, PA	12	46	n/a	12	n/a
Phoenix, AZ	31	67	n/a	10	n/a
Pittsburgh, PA	10	37	n/a	116	n/a
Portland, OR	12	40	n/a	3	n/a
Providence, RI	18	50	n/a	11	n/a
Provo, UT	15	n/a	n/a	n/a	n/a
Raleigh, NC	9	35	n/a	2	n/a
Reno, NV	13	52	n/a	5	n/a
Richmond, VA	12	43	n/a	18	n/a
Roanoke, VA	5	32	n/a	40	n/a
Rochester, MN	n/a	n/a	n/a	n/a	n/a
Salem, OR	n/a	n/a	n/a	n/a	n/a
Salt Lake City, UT	13	43	n/a	n/a	n/a
San Antonio, TX	8	40	n/a	29	n/a
San Diego, CA	16	52	n/a	1	n/a
San Francisco, CA	17	59	n/a	16	n/a
San Jose, CA	17	52	n/a	n/a	n/a
Santa Rosa, CA	5	29	n/a	n/a	n/a
Savannah, GA	n/a	n/a	n/a	53	n/a
Seattle, WA	20	44	n/a	n/a	n/a
Sioux Falls, SD	4	30	n/a	5	n/a
Springfield, IL	n/a	n/a	n/a	n/a	n/a
Tallahassee, FL	n/a	n/a	n/a	n/a	n/a
Tampa, FL	10	29	n/a	15	n/a
Topeka, KS	n/a	n/a	n/a	n/a	n/a
Tyler, TX	2	15	n/a	n/a	n/a
Virginia Beach, VA	7	40	n/a	3	n/a
Visalia, CA	11	56	n/a	n/a	n/a
Washington, DC	15	58	n/a	4	n/a
Wilmington, NC	n/a	n/a	n/a	2	n/a
Winston-Salem, NC	7	38	n/a	4	n/a
NAAQS[1]	53	100	30	75	140

Note: Data from exceptional events are included; Data covers the Metropolitan Statistical Area—see Appendix B for areas included; (1) National Ambient Air Quality Standards; ppb = parts per billion; n/a not available
Concentrations: Nitrogen Dioxide AM—highest arithmetic mean concentration; Nitrogen Dioxide 1-Hr—highest 98th percentile 1-hour daily maximum concentration; Sulfur Dioxide AM—highest annual mean concentration; Sulfur Dioxide 1-Hr—highest 99th percentile 1-hour daily maximum concentration; Sulfur Dioxide 24-Hr—highest second maximum 24-hour concentration
Source: U.S. Environmental Protection Agency, Air Quality Monitoring Information, "Air Quality Statistics by City, 2017"

Appendix B: Metropolitan Area Definitions

Metropolitan Statistical Areas (MSA), Metropolitan Divisions (MD), New England City and Town Areas (NECTA), and New England City and Town Area Divisions (NECTAD)

Note: In September 2018, the Office of Management and Budget (OMB) announced changes to metropolitan and micropolitan statistical area definitions. Both current and historical definitions (December 2009) are shown below. If the change only affected the name of the metro area, the counties included were not repeated.

Albany-Schenectady-Troy, NY MSA
Albany, Rensselaer, Saratoga, Schenectady and Schoharie Counties

Albuquerque, NM MSA
Bernalillo, Sandoval, Torrance, and Valencia Counties

Allentown-Bethlehem-Easton, PA-NJ MSA
Carbon, Lehigh, and Northampton Counties, PA; Warren County, NJ

Anchorage, AK MSA
Anchorage Municipality and Matanuska-Susitna Borough

Ann Arbor, MI MSA
Washtenaw County

Athens-Clarke County, GA MSA
Clarke, Madison, Oconee, and Oglethorpe Counties

Atlanta-Sandy Springs-Roswell, GA MSA
Barrow, Bartow, Butts, Carroll, Cherokee, Clayton, Cobb, Coweta, Dawson, DeKalb, Douglas, Fayette, Forsyth, Fulton, Gwinnett, Haralson, Heard, Henry, Jasper, Lamar, Meriwether, Morgan, Newton, Paulding, Pickens, Pike, Rockdale, Spalding, and Walton Counties
Previously Atlanta-Sandy Springs-Marietta, GA MSA
Barrow, Bartow, Butts, Carroll, Cherokee, Clayton, Cobb, Coweta, Dawson, DeKalb, Douglas, Fayette, Forsyth, Fulton, Gwinnett, Haralson, Heard, Henry, Jasper, Lamar, Meriwether, Newton, Paulding, Pickens, Pike, Rockdale, Spalding, and Walton Counties

Austin-Round Rock, TX MSA
Previously Austin-Round Rock-San Marcos, TX MSA
Bastrop, Caldwell, Hays, Travis, and Williamson Counties

Baton Rouge, LA MSA
Ascension, East Baton Rouge, East Feliciana, Iberville, Livingston, Pointe Coupee, St. Helena, West Baton Rouge, and West Feliciana Parishes
Previously Baton Rouge, LA MSA
Ascension, East Baton Rouge, Livingston, and West Baton Rouge Parishes

Billings, MT MSA
Carbon and Yellowstone Counties

Boise City, ID MSA
Previously Boise City-Nampa, ID MSA
Ada, Boise, Canyon, Gem, and Owyhee Counties

Boston, MA

Boston-Cambridge-Newton, MA-NH MSA
Previously Boston-Cambridge-Quincy, MA-NH MSA
Essex, Middlesex, Norfolk, Plymouth, and Suffolk Counties, MA; Rockingham and Strafford Counties, NH

Boston, MA MD
Previously Boston-Quincy, MA MD
Norfolk, Plymouth, and Suffolk Counties

Boston-Cambridge-Nashua, MA-NH NECTA
Includes 157 cities and towns in Massachusetts and 34 cities and towns in New Hampshire
Previously Boston-Cambridge-Quincy, MA-NH NECTA
Includes 155 cities and towns in Massachusetts and 38 cities and towns in New Hampshire

Boston-Cambridge-Newton, MA NECTA Division
Includes 92 cities and towns in Massachusetts
Previously Boston-Cambridge-Quincy, MA NECTA Division
Includes 97 cities and towns in Massachusetts

Boulder, CO MSA
Boulder County

Cape Coral-Fort Myers, FL MSA
Lee County

Cedar Rapids, IA, MSA
Benton, Jones, and Linn Counties

Charleston-North Charleston, SC MSA
Previously Charleston-North Charleston- Summerville, SC MSA
Berkeley, Charleston, and Dorchester Counties

Charlotte-Concord-Gastonia, NC-SC MSA
Cabarrus, Gaston, Iredell, Lincoln, Mecklenburg, Rowan, and Union Counties, NC; Chester, Lancaster, and York Counties, SC
Previously Charlotte-Gastonia-Rock Hill, NC-SC MSA
Anson, Cabarrus, Gaston, Mecklenburg, and Union Counties, NC; York County, SC

Chicago, IL

Chicago-Naperville-Elgin, IL-IN-WI MSA
Previous name: Chicago-Joliet-Naperville, IL-IN-WI MSA
Cook, DeKalb, DuPage, Grundy, Kane, Kendall, Lake, McHenry, and Will Counties, IL; Jasper, Lake, Newton, and Porter Counties, IN; Kenosha County, WI

Chicago-Naperville-Arlington Heights, IL MD
Cook, DuPage, Grundy, Kendall, McHenry, and Will Counties
Previous name: Chicago-Joliet-Naperville, IL MD
Cook, DeKalb, DuPage, Grundy, Kane, Kendall, McHenry, and Will Counties

Elgin, IL MD
DeKalb and Kane Counties
Previously part of the Chicago-Joliet-Naperville, IL MD

Gary, IN MD
Jasper, Lake, Newton, and Porter Counties

Lake County-Kenosha County, IL-WI MD
Lake County, IL; Kenosha County, WI

Clarksville, TN-KY MSA
Montgomery and Stewart Counties, TN; Christian and Trigg Counties, KY

College Station-Bryan, TX MSA
Brazos, Burleson and Robertson Counties

Colorado Springs, CO MSA
El Paso and Teller Counties

Columbia, MO MSA
Boone and Howard Counties

Columbia, SC MSA
Calhoun, Fairfield, Kershaw, Lexington, Richland and Saluda Counties

Columbus, OH MSA
Delaware, Fairfield, Franklin, Licking, Madison, Morrow, Pickaway, and Union Counties

Dallas, TX

Dallas-Fort Worth-Arlington, TX MSA
Collin, Dallas, Denton, Ellis, Hunt, Johnson, Kaufman, Parker, Rockwall, Tarrant, and Wise Counties

Dallas-Plano-Irving, TX MD
Collin, Dallas, Denton, Ellis, Hunt, Kaufman, and Rockwall Counties

Denver-Aurora-Lakewood, CO MSA
Previously Denver-Aurora-Broomfield, CO MSA
Adams, Arapahoe, Broomfield, Clear Creek, Denver, Douglas, Elbert, Gilpin, Jefferson, and Park Counties

Des Moines-West Des Moines, IA MSA
Dallas, Guthrie, Madison, Polk, and Warren Counties

Durham-Chapel Hill, NC MSA
Chatham, Durham, Orange, and Person Counties

Edison, NJ
See New York, NY (New York-Jersey City-White Plains, NY-NJ MD)

El Paso, TX MSA
El Paso County

Eugene, OR MSA
Previously Eugene-Springfield, OR MSA
Lane County

Evansville, IN-KY MSA
Posey, Vanderburgh, and Warrick Counties, IN; Henderson County, KY
Previously Evansville, IN-KY MSA
Gibson, Posey, Vanderburgh, and Warrick Counties, IN; Henderson and Webster Counties, KY

Fargo, ND-MN MSA
Cass County, ND; Clay County, MN

Fayetteville, NC MSA
Cumberland, and Hoke Counties

Fort Collins, CO MSA
Previously Fort Collins-Loveland, CO MSA
Larimer County

Fort Wayne, IN MSA
Allen, Wells, and Whitley Counties

Fort Worth, TX

Dallas-Fort Worth-Arlington, TX MSA
Collin, Dallas, Denton, Ellis, Hunt, Johnson, Kaufman, Parker, Rockwall, Tarrant, and Wise Counties

Fort Worth-Arlington, TX MD
Hood, Johnson, Parker, Somervell, Tarrant, and Wise Counties

Gainesville, FL MSA
Alachua, and Gilchrist Counties

Grand Rapids-Wyoming, MI MSA
Barry, Kent, Montcalm, and Ottawa Counties
Previously Grand Rapids-Wyoming, MI MSA
Barry, Ionia, Kent, and Newaygo Counties

Greeley, CO MSA
Weld County

Green Bay, WI MSA
Brown, Kewaunee, and Oconto Counties

Greensboro-High Point, NC MSA
Guilford, Randolph, and Rockingham Counties

Honolulu, HI MSA
Honolulu County

Houston-The Woodlands-Sugar Land-Baytown, TX MSA
Austin, Brazoria, Chambers, Fort Bend, Galveston, Harris, Liberty, Montgomery, and Waller Counties
Previously Houston-Sugar Land-Baytown, TX MSA
Austin, Brazoria, Chambers, Fort Bend, Galveston, Harris, Liberty, Montgomery, San Jacinto, and Waller Counties

Huntsville, AL MSA
Limestone and Madison Counties

Indianapolis-Carmel, IN MSA
Boone, Brown, Hamilton, Hancock, Hendricks, Johnson, Marion, Morgan, Putnam, and Shelby Counties

Jacksonville, FL MSA
Baker, Clay, Duval, Nassau, and St. Johns Counties

Kansas City, MO-KS MSA
Franklin, Johnson, Leavenworth, Linn, Miami, and Wyandotte Counties, KS; Bates, Caldwell, Cass, Clay, Clinton, Jackson, Lafayette, Platte, and Ray Counties, MO

Lafayette, LA MSA
Acadia, Iberia, Lafayette, St. Martin, and Vermilion Parishes

Las Cruces, NM MSA
Doña Ana and San Miguel Counties
Previously Las Cruces, NM MSA
Doña Ana County

Las Vegas-Henderson-Paradise, NV MSA
Previously Las Vegas-Paradise, NV MSA
Clark County

Lexington-Fayette, KY MSA
Bourbon, Clark, Fayette, Jessamine, Scott, and Woodford Counties

Lincoln, NE MSA
Lancaster and Seward Counties

Little Rock-North Little Rock-Conway, AR MSA
Faulkner, Grant, Lonoke, Perry, Pulaski, and Saline Counties

Los Angeles, CA

Los Angeles-Long Beach-Anaheim, CA MSA
Previously Los Angeles-Long Beach-Santa Ana, CA MSA
Los Angeles and Orange Counties

Los Angeles-Long Beach-Glendale, CA MD
Los Angeles County

Anaheim-Santa Ana-Irvine, CA MD
Previously Santa Ana-Anaheim-Irvine, CA MD
Orange County

Louisville/Jefferson, KY-IN MSA
Clark, Floyd, Harrison, Scott, and Washington Counties, IN; Bullitt, Henry, Jefferson, Oldham, Shelby, Spencer, and Trimble Counties, KY

Madison, WI MSA
Columbia, Dane, and Iowa Counties

Manchester, NH

Manchester-Nashua, NH MSA
Hillsborough County

Manchester, NH NECTA
Includes 11 cities and towns in New Hampshire
Previously Manchester, NH NECTA
Includes 9 cities and towns in New Hampshire

McAllen-Edinburg-Mission, TX
Hidalgo County

Miami, FL

Miami-Fort Lauderdale-West Palm Beach, FL MSA
Previously Miami-Fort Lauderdale-Pompano Beach, FL MSA
Broward, Miami-Dade, and Palm Beach Counties

Miami-Miami Beach-Kendall, FL MD
Miami-Dade County

Midland, TX MSA
Martin, and Midland Counties

Minneapolis-St. Paul-Bloomington, MN-WI MSA
Anoka, Carver, Chisago, Dakota, Hennepin, Isanti, Le Sueur, Mille Lacs, Ramsey, Scott, Sherburne, Sibley, Washington, and Wright Counties, MN; Pierce and St. Croix Counties, WI

Nashville-Davidson-Murfreesboro-Franklin, TN MSA
Cannon, Cheatham, Davidson, Dickson, Hickman, Macon, Robertson, Rutherford, Smith, Sumner, Trousdale, Williamson, and Wilson Counties

New Orleans-Metarie-Kenner, LA MSA
Jefferson, Orleans, Plaquemines, St. Bernard, St. Charles, St. James, St. John the Baptist, and St. Tammany Parish
Previously New Orleans-Metarie-Kenner, LA MSA
Jefferson, Orleans, Plaquemines, St. Bernard, St. Charles, St. John the Baptist, and St. Tammany Parish

New York, NY

New York-Newark-Jersey City, NY-NJ-PA MSA
Bergen, Essex, Hudson, Hunterdon, Middlesex, Monmouth, Morris, Ocean, Passaic, Somerset, Sussex, and Union Counties, NJ; Bronx, Dutchess, Kings, Nassau, New York, Orange, Putnam, Queens, Richmond, Rockland, Suffolk, and Westchester Counties, NY; Pike County, PA
Previous name: New York-Northern New Jersey-Long Island, NY-NJ-PA MSA
Bergen, Essex, Hudson, Hunterdon, Middlesex, Monmouth, Morris, Ocean, Passaic, Somerset, Sussex, and Union Counties, NJ; Bronx, Kings, Nassau, New York, Putnam, Queens, Richmond, Rockland, Suffolk, and Westchester Counties, NY; Pike County, PA

Dutchess County-Putnam County, NY MD
Dutchess and Putnam Counties
Dutchess County was previously part of the Poughkeepsie-Newburgh-Middletown, NY MSA. Putnam County was previously part of the New York-Wayne-White Plains, NY-NJ MD

Nassau-Suffolk, NY MD
Nassau and Suffolk Counties

New York-Jersey City-White Plains, NY-NJ MD
Bergen, Hudson, Middlesex, Monmouth, Ocean, and Passaic Counties, NJ; Bronx, Kings, New York, Orange, Queens, Richmond, Rockland, and Westchester Counties, NY
Previous name: New York-Wayne-White Plains, NY-NJ MD
Bergen, Hudson, and Passaic Counties, NJ; Bronx, Kings, New York, Putnam, Queens, Richmond, Rockland, and Westchester Counties, NY

Newark, NJ-PA MD
Essex, Hunterdon, Morris, Somerset, Sussex, and Union Counties, NJ; Pike County, PA
Previous name: Newark-Union, NJ-PA MD
Essex, Hunterdon, Morris, Sussex, and Union Counties, NJ; Pike County, PA

Oklahoma City, OK MSA
Canadian, Cleveland, Grady, Lincoln, Logan, McClain, and Oklahoma Counties

Omaha-Council Bluffs, NE-IA MSA
Harrison, Mills, and Pottawattamie Counties, IA; Cass, Douglas, Sarpy, Saunders, and Washington Counties, NE

Orlando-Kissimmee-Sanford, FL MSA
Lake, Orange, Osceola, and Seminole Counties

Peoria, IL MSA
Marshall, Peoria, Stark, Tazewell, and Woodford Counties

Philadelphia, PA

Philadelphia-Camden-Wilmington, PA-NJ-DE-MD MSA
New Castle County, DE; Cecil County, MD; Burlington, Camden, Gloucester, and Salem Counties, NJ; Bucks, Chester, Delaware, Montgomery, and Philadelphia Counties, PA

Camden, NJ MD
Burlington, Camden, and Gloucester Counties

Montgomery County-Bucks County-Chester County, PA MD
Bucks, Chester, and Montgomery Counties
Previously part of the Philadelphia, PA MD

Philadelphia, PA MD
Delaware and Philadelphia Counties
Previous name: Philadelphia, PA MD
Bucks, Chester, Delaware, Montgomery, and Philadelphia Counties

Wilmington, DE-MD-NJ MD
New Castle County, DE; Cecil County, MD; Salem County, NJ

Phoenix-Mesa-Scottsdale, AZ MSA
Previously Phoenix-Mesa-Glendale, AZ MSA
Maricopa and Pinal Counties

Pittsburgh, PA MSA
Allegheny, Armstrong, Beaver, Butler, Fayette, Washington, and Westmoreland Counties

Portland-Vancouver-Hillsboro, OR-WA MSA
Clackamas, Columbia, Multnomah, Washington, and Yamhill Counties, OR; Clark and Skamania Counties, WA

Providence, RI

Providence-New Bedford-Fall River, RI-MA MSA
Previously Providence-New Bedford-Fall River, RI-MA MSA
Bristol County, MA; Bristol, Kent, Newport, Providence, and Washington Counties, RI

Providence-Warwick, RI-MA NECTA
Includes 12 cities and towns in Massachusetts and 36 cities and towns in Rhode Island
Previously Providence-Fall River-Warwick, RI-MA NECTA
Includes 12 cities and towns in Massachusetts and 37 cities and towns in Rhode Island

Provo-Orem, UT MSA
Juab and Utah Counties

Raleigh, NC MSA
Previously Raleigh-Cary, NC MSA
Franklin, Johnston, and Wake Counties

Reno, NV MSA
Previously Reno-Sparks, NV MSA
Storey and Washoe Counties

Richmond, VA MSA
Amelia, Caroline, Charles City, Chesterfield, Dinwiddie, Goochland, Hanover, Henrico, King William, New Kent, Powhatan, Prince George, and Sussex Counties; Colonial Heights, Hopewell, Petersburg, and Richmond Cities

Roanoke, VA MSA
Botetourt, Craig, Franklin and Roanoke Counties; Roanoke and Salem cities

Rochester, MN MSA
Dodge, Fillmore, Olmsted, and Wabasha Counties

Salem, OR MSA
Marion and Polk Counties

Salt Lake City, UT MSA
Salt Lake and Tooele Counties

San Antonio-New Braunfels, TX MSA
Atascosa, Bandera, Bexar, Comal, Guadalupe, Kendall, Medina, and Wilson Counties

San Diego-Carlsbad, CA MSA
Previously San Diego-Carlsbad-San Marcos, CA MSA
San Diego County

San Francisco, CA

San Francisco-Oakland-Hayward, CA MSA
Previously San Francisco-Oakland- Fremont, CA MSA
Alameda, Contra Costa, Marin, San Francisco, and San Mateo Counties

San Francisco-Redwood City-South San Francisco, CA MD
San Francisco and San Mateo Counties

Previously San Francisco-San Mateo-Redwood City, CA MD
Marin, San Francisco, and San Mateo Counties

San Jose-Sunnyvale-Santa Clara, CA MSA
San Benito and Santa Clara Counties

Santa Rosa, CA MSA
Previously Santa Rosa-Petaluma, CA MSA
Sonoma County

Savannah, GA MSA
Bryan, Chatham, and Effingham Counties

Seattle, WA

Seattle-Tacoma-Bellevue, WA MSA
King, Pierce, and Snohomish Counties

Seattle-Bellevue-Everett, WA MD
King and Snohomish Counties

Sioux Falls, SD MSA
Lincoln, McCook, Minnehaha, and Turner Counties

Springfield, IL MSA
Menard and Sangamon Counties

Tallahassee, FL MSA
Gadsden, Jefferson, Leon, and Wakulla Counties

Tampa-St. Petersburg-Clearwater, FL MSA
Hernando, Hillsborough, Pasco, and Pinellas Counties

Topeka, KS MSA
Jackson, Jefferson, Osage, Shawnee, and Wabaunsee Counties

Tyler, TX MSA
Smith County

Virginia Beach-Norfolk-Newport News, VA-NC MSA
Currituck County, NC; Chesapeake, Hampton, Newport News, Norfolk, Poquoson, Portsmouth, Suffolk, Virginia Beach and Williamsburg cities, VA; Gloucester, Isle of Wight, James City, Mathews, Surry, and York Counties, VA

Visalia, CA MSA
Previously Visalia-Porterville, CA MSA
Tulare County

Washington, DC

Washington-Arlington-Alexandria, DC-VA-MD-WV MSA
District of Columbia; Calvert, Charles, Frederick, Montgomery, and Prince George's Counties, MD; Alexandria, Fairfax, Falls Church, Fredericksburg, Manassas Park, and Manassas cities, VA; Arlington, Clarke, Culpepper, Fairfax, Fauquier, Loudoun, Prince William, Rappahannock, Spotsylvania, Stafford, and Warren Counties, VA; Jefferson County, WV
Previously Washington-Arlington-Alexandria, DC-VA-MD-WV MSA
District of Columbia; Calvert, Charles, Frederick, Montgomery, and Prince George's Counties, MD; Alexandria, Fairfax, Falls Church, Fredericksburg, Manassas Park, and Manassas cities, VA; Arlington, Clarke, Fairfax, Fauquier, Loudoun, Prince William, Spotsylvania, Stafford, and Warren Counties, VA; Jefferson County, WV

Washington-Arlington-Alexandria, DC-VA-MD-WV MD
District of Columbia; Calvert, Charles, and Prince George's Counties, MD; Alexandria, Fairfax, Falls Church, Fredericksburg, Manassas Park, and Manassas cities, VA; Arlington, Clarke, Culpepper, Fairfax, Fauquier, Loudoun, Prince William, Rappahannock, Spotsylvania, Stafford, and Warren Counties, VA; Jefferson County, WV
Previously Washington-Arlington-Alexandria, DC-VA-MD-WV MD
District of Columbia; Calvert, Charles, and Prince George's Counties, MD; Alexandria, Fairfax, Falls Church, Fredericksburg, Manassas Park, and Manassas cities, VA; Arlington, Clarke, Fairfax, Fauquier, Loudoun, Prince William, Spotsylvania, Stafford, and Warren Counties, VA; Jefferson County, WV

Wilmington, NC MSA
New Hanover and Pender Counties
Previously Wilmington, NC MSA
Brunswick, New Hanover and Pender Counties

Winston-Salem, NC MSA
Davidson, Davie, Forsyth, Stokes, and Yadkin Counties

Appendix C: Government Type and Primary County

This appendix includes the government structure of each place included in this book. It also includes the county or county equivalent in which each place is located. If a place spans more than one county, the county in which the majority of the population resides is shown.

Albuquerque, NM
Government Type: City
County: Bernalillo

Albany, NY
Government Type: City
County: Albany

Allentown, PA
Government Type: City
County: Lehigh

Anchorage, AK
Government Type: Municipality
Borough: Anchorage

Ann Arbor, MI
Government Type: City
County: Washtenaw

Athens, GA
Government Type: Consolidated
    city-county
County: Clarke

Atlanta, GA
Government Type: City
County: Fulton

Austin, TX
Government Type: City
County: Travis

Baton Rouge, LA
Government Type: Consolidated city-parish
Parish: East Baton Rouge

Billings, MT
Government Type: City
County: Yellowstone

Boise City, ID
Government Type: City
County: Ada

Boston, MA
Government Type: City
County: Suffolk

Boulder, CO
Government Type: City
County: Boulder

Cape Coral, FL
Government Type: City
County: Lee

Cedar Rapids, IA
Government Type: City
County: Linn

Charleston, SC
Government Type: City
County: Charleston

Charlotte, NC
Government Type: City
County: Mecklenburg

Chicago, IL
Government Type: City
County: Cook

Clarksville, TN
Government Type: City
County: Montgomery

College Station, TX
Government Type: City
County: Brazos

Colorado Springs, CO
Government Type: City
County: El Paso

Columbia, MO
Government Type: City
County: Boone

Columbia, SC
Government Type: City
County: Richland

Columbus, OH
Government Type: City
County: Franklin

Dallas, TX
Government Type: City
County: Dallas

Denver, CO
Government Type: City
County: Denver

Des Moines, IA
Government Type: City
County: Polk

Durham, NC
Government Type: City
County: Durham

Edison, NJ
Government Type: Township
County: Middlesex

El Paso, TX
Government Type: City
County: El Paso

Eugene, OR
Government Type: City
County: Lane

Evansville, IN
Government Type: City
County: Vanderburgh

Fargo, ND
Government Type: City
County: Cass

Fayetteville, NC
Government Type: City
County: Cumberland

Fort Collins, CO
Government Type: City
County: Larimer

Fort Wayne, IN
Government Type: City
County: Allen

Fort Worth, TX
Government Type: City
County: Tarrant

Gainesville, FL
Government Type: City
County: Alachua

Grand Rapids, MI
Government Type: City
County: Kent

Greeley, CO
Government Type: City
County: Weld

Green Bay, WI
Government Type: City
County: Brown

Greensboro, NC
Government Type: City
County: Guilford

Honolulu, HI
Government Type: Census Designated Place
    (CDP)
County: Honolulu

Houston, TX
Government Type: City
County: Harris

Huntsville, AL
Government Type: City
County: Madison

Indianapolis, IN
Government Type: City
County: Marion

Jacksonville, FL
Government Type: City
County: Duval

Kansas City, MO
Government Type: City
County: Jackson

Lafayette, LA
Government Type: City
Parish: Lafayette

Las Cruces, NM
Government Type: City
County: Doña Ana

Las Vegas, NV
Government Type: City
County: Clark

Lexington, KY
Government Type: Consolidated city-county
County: Fayette

Lincoln, NE
Government Type: City
County: Lancaster

Little Rock, AR
Government Type: City
County: Pulaski

Los Angeles, CA
Government Type: City
County: Los Angeles

Louisville, KY
Government Type: Consolidated city-county
County: Jefferson

Madison, WI
Government Type: City
County: Dane

Manchester, NH
Government Type: City
County: Hillsborough

McAllen, TX
Government Type: City
County: Hidalgo

Miami, FL
Government Type: City
County: Miami-Dade

Midland, TX
Government Type: City
County: Midland

Minneapolis, MN
Government Type: City
County: Hennepin

Nashville, TN
Government Type: Consolidated city-county
County: Davidson

New Orleans, LA
Government Type: City
Parish: Orleans

New York, NY
Government Type: City
Counties: Bronx; Kings; New York; Queens;
    Staten Island

Oklahoma City, OK
Government Type: City
County: Oklahoma

Omaha, NE
Government Type: City
County: Douglas

Orlando, FL
Government Type: City
County: Orange

Peoria, IL
Government Type: City
County: Peoria

Philadelphia, PA
Government Type: City
County: Philadelphia

Phoenix, AZ
Government Type: City
County: Maricopa

Pittsburgh, PA
Government Type: City
County: Allegheny

Portland, OR
Government Type: City
County: Multnomah

Providence, RI
Government Type: City
County: Providence

Provo, UT
Government Type: City
County: Utah

Raleigh, NC
Government Type: City
County: Wake

Reno, NV
Government Type: City
County: Washoe

Richmond, VA
Government Type: Independent city
County: Richmond city

Roanoke, VA
Government Type: Independent city
County: Roanoke city

Rochester, MN
Government Type: City
County: Olmsted

Salem, OR
Government Type: City
County: Marion

Salt Lake City, UT
Government Type: City
County: Salt Lake

San Antonio, TX
Government Type: City
County: Bexar

San Diego, CA
Government Type: City
County: San Diego

San Francisco, CA
Government Type: City
County: San Francisco

San Jose, CA
Government Type: City
County: Santa Clara

Santa Rosa, CA
Government Type: City
County: Sonoma

Savannah, GA
Government Type: City
County: Chatham

Seattle, WA
Government Type: City
County: King

Sioux Falls, SD
Government Type: City
County: Minnehaha

Springfield, IL
Government Type: City
County: Sangamon

Tallahassee, FL
Government Type: City
County: Leon

Tampa, FL
Government Type: City
County: Hillsborough

Topeka, KS
Government Type: City
County: Shawnee

Tyler, TX
Government Type: City
County: Smith

Virginia Beach, VA
Government Type: Independent city
County: Virginia Beach city

Visalia, CA
Government Type: City
County: Tulare

Washington, DC
Government Type: City
County: District of Columbia

Wilmington, NC
Government Type: City
County: New Hanover

Winston-Salem, NC
Government Type: City
County: Forsyth

Appendix D: Chambers of Commerce

Albany, NY
Capital Region Chamber
Albany Office
5 Computer Drive South
Colonie, NY 12205
Phone: (518) 431-1400
Fax: (518) 431-1402
http://capitalregionchamber.com

Albuquerque, NM
Albuquerque Chamber of Commerce
P.O. Box 25100
Albuquerque, NM 87125
Phone: (505) 764-3700
Fax: (505) 764-3714
http://www.abqchamber.com

Albuquerque Economic Development Dept
851 University Blvd SE
Suite 203
Albuquerque, NM 87106
Phone: (505) 246-6200
Fax: (505) 246-6219
http://www.cabq.gov/econdev

Allentown, PA
Greater Lehigh Valley Chamber of
Commerce
Allentown Office
840 Hamilton Street, Suite 205
Allentown, PA 18101
Phone: (610) 751-4929
Fax: (610) 437-4907
http://www.lehighvalleychamber.org

Anchorage, AK
Anchorage Chamber of Commerce
1016 W Sixth Avenue
Suite 303
Anchorage, AK 99501
Phone: (907) 272-2401
Fax: (907) 272-4117
http://www.anchoragechamber.org

Anchorage Economic Development
Department
900 W 5th Avenue
Suite 300
Anchorage, AK 99501
Phone: (907) 258-3700
Fax: (907) 258-6646
http://aedcweb.com

Ann Arbor, MI
Ann Arbor Area Chamber of Commerce
115 West Huron
3rd Floor
Ann Arbor, MI 48104
Phone: (734) 665-4433
Fax: (734) 665-4191
http://www.annarborchamber.org

Ann Arbor Economic Development
Department
201 S Division
Suite 430
Ann Arbor, MI 48104
Phone: (734) 761-9317
http://www.annarborspark.org

Athens, GA
Athens Area Chamber of Commerce
246 W Hancock Avenue
Athens, GA 30601
Phone: (706) 549-6800
Fax: (706) 549-5636
http://www.aacoc.org

Athens-Clarke County Economic
Development Department
246 W. Hancock Avenue
Athens, GA 30601
Phone: (706) 613-3233
Fax: (706) 613-3812
http://www.athensbusiness.org

Atlanta, GA
Metro Atlanta Chamber of Commerce
235 Andrew Young International Blvd NW
Atlanta, GA 30303
Phone: (404) 880-9000
Fax: (404) 586-8464
http://www.metroatlantachamber.com

Austin, TX
Greater Austin Chamber of Commerce
210 Barton Springs Road
Suite 400
Austin, TX 78704
Phone: (512) 478-9383
Fax: (512) 478-6389
http://www.austin-chamber.org

Baton Rouge, LA
Baton Rouge Area Chamber
451 Florida Street
Suite 1050
Baton Rouge, LA 70801
Phone (225) 381-7125
http://www.brac.org

Billings, MT
Billings Area Chamber of Commerce
815 S 27th St
Billings, MT 59101
Phone: (406) 245-4111
Fax: (406) 245-7333
http://www.billingschamber.com

Boise City, ID
Boise Metro Chamber of Commerce
250 S 5th Street
Suite 800
Boise City, ID 83701
Phone: (208) 472-5200
Fax: (208) 472-5201
http://www.boisechamber.org

Boston, MA
Greater Boston Chamber of Commerce
265 Franklin Street
12th Floor
Boston, MA 02110
Phone: (617) 227-4500
Fax: (617) 227-7505
http://www.bostonchamber.com

Boulder, CO
Boulder Chamber of Commerce
2440 Pearl Street
Boulder, CO 80302
Phone: (303) 442-1044
Fax: (303) 938-8837
http://www.boulderchamber.com

City of Boulder Economic Vitality Program
P.O. Box 791
Boulder, CO 80306
Phone: (303) 441-3090
http://www.bouldercolorado.gov

Cape Coral, FL
Chamber of Commerce of Cape Coral
2051 Cape Coral Parkway East
Cape Coral, FL 33904
Phone: (239) 549-6900
Fax: (239) 549-9609
http://www.capecoralchamber.com

Cedar Rapids, IA
Cedar Rapids Chamber of Commerce
424 First Avenue NE
Cedar Rapids, IA 52401
Phone: (319) 398-5317
Fax: (319) 398-5228
http://www.cedarrapids.org

Cedar Rapids Economic Development
50 Second Avenue Bridge
Sixth Floor
Cedar Rapids, IA 52401-1256
Phone: (319) 286-5041
Fax: (319) 286-5141
http://www.cedar-rapids.org

Charleston, SC
Charleston Metro Chamber of Commerce
P.O. Box 975
Charleston, SC 29402
Phone: (843) 577-2510
http://www.charlestonchamber.net

Charlotte, NC
Charlotte Chamber of Commerce
330 S Tryon Street
P.O. Box 32785
Charlotte, NC 28232
Phone: (704) 378-1300
Fax: (704) 374-1903
http://www.charlottechamber.com

Charlotte Regional Partnership
1001 Morehead Square Drive
Suite 200
Charlotte, NC 28203
Phone: (704) 347-8942
Fax: (704) 347-8981
http://www.charlotteusa.com

Chicago, IL
Chicagoland Chamber of Commerce
200 E Randolph Street
Suite 2200
Chicago, IL 60601-6436
Phone: (312) 494-6700
Fax: (312) 861-0660
http://www.chicagolandchamber.org

City of Chicago Department of Planning
and Development
City Hall, Room 1000
121 North La Salle Street
Chicago, IL 60602
Phone: (312) 744-4190
Fax: (312) 744-2271
https://www.cityofchicago.org/city/en/depts
/dcd.html

Clarksville, TN
Clarksville Area Chamber of Commerce
25 Jefferson Street
Suite 300
Clarksville, TN 37040
Phone: (931) 647-2331
http://www.clarksvillechamber.com

College Station, TX
Bryan-College Station Chamber of
Commerce
4001 East 29th St, Suite 175
Bryan, TX 77802
Phone: (979) 260-5200
http://www.bcschamber.org

Colorado Springs, CO
Colorado Springs Chamber and EDC
102 South Tejon Street
Suite 430
Colorado Springs, CO 80903
Phone: (719) 471-8183
https://coloradospringschamberedc.com

Columbia, MO
Columbia Chamber of Commerce
300 South Providence Rd.
PO Box 1016
Columbia, MO 65205-1016
Phone: (573) 874-1132
Fax: (573) 443-3986
http://www.columbiamochamber.com

Columbia, SC
The Columbia Chamber
930 Richland Street
Columbia, SC 29201
Phone: (803) 733-1110
Fax: (803) 733-1113
http://www.columbiachamber.com

Columbus, OH
Greater Columbus Chamber
37 North High Street
Columbus, OH 43215
Phone: (614) 221-1321
Fax: (614) 221-1408
http://www.columbus.org

Dallas, TX
City of Dallas Economic Development
Department
1500 Marilla Street
5C South
Dallas, TX 75201
Phone: (214) 670-1685
Fax: (214) 670-0158
http://www.dallas-edd.org

Greater Dallas Chamber of Commerce
700 North Pearl Street
Suite1200
Dallas, TX 75201
Phone: (214) 746-6600
Fax: (214) 746-6799
http://www.dallaschamber.org

Denver, CO
Denver Metro Chamber of Commerce
1445 Market Street
Denver, CO 80202
Phone: (303) 534-8500
Fax: (303) 534-3200
http://www.denverchamber.org

Downtown Denver Partnership
511 16th Street
Suite 200
Denver, CO 80202
Phone: (303) 534-6161
Fax: (303) 534-2803
http://www.downtowndenver.com

Des Moines, IA
Des Moines Downtown Chamber
301 Grand Ave
Des Moines, IA 50309
Phone: (515) 309-3229
http://desmoinesdowntownchamber.com

Greater Des Moines Partnership
700 Locust Street
Suite 100
Des Moines, IA 50309
Phone: (515) 286-4950
Fax: (515) 286-4974
http://www.desmoinesmetro.com

Durham, NC
Durham Chamber of Commerce
PO Box 3829
Durham, NC 27702
Phone: (919) 682-2133
Fax: (919) 688-8351
http://www.durhamchamber.org

North Carolina Institute of Minority
Economic Development
114 W Parish Street
Durham, NC 27701
Phone: (919) 956-8889
Fax: (919) 688-7668
http://www.ncimed.com

Edison, NJ
Edison Chamber of Commerce
939 Amboy Avenue
Edison, NJ 08837
Phone: (732) 738-9482
http://www.edisonchamber.com

El Paso, TX
City of El Paso Department of Economic
Development
2 Civic Center Plaza
El Paso, TX 79901
Phone: (915) 541-4000
Fax: (915) 541-1316
http://www.elpasotexas.gov

Greater El Paso Chamber of Commerce
10 Civic Center Plaza
El Paso, TX 79901
Phone: (915) 534-0500
Fax: (915) 534-0510
http://www.elpaso.org

Eugene, OR
Eugene Area Chamber of Commerce
1401 Williamette Street
Eugene, OR 97401
Phone: (541) 484-1314
Fax: (541) 484-4942
http://www.eugenechamber.com

Evansville, IN
Evansville Chamber of Commerce &
Tourism
8 West Main Street
Evansville, WI 53536
Phone: (608) 882-5131
http://www.evansvillechamber.org

Southwest Indiana Chamber
318 Main Street
Suite 401
Evansville, IN 47708
Phone: (812) 425-8147
Fax: (812) 421-5883
https://swinchamber.com

Fargo, ND
Chamber of Commerce of Fargo Moorhead
202 First Avenue North
Fargo, ND 56560
Phone: (218) 233-1100
Fax: (218) 233-1200
http://www.fmchamber.com

Greater Fargo-Moorhead Economic
Development Corporation
51 Broadway, Suite 500
Fargo, ND 58102
Phone: (701) 364-1900
Fax: (701) 293-7819
http://www.gfmedc.com

Fayetteville, NC
Fayetteville Regional Chamber
1019 Hay Street
Fayetteville, NC 28305
Phone: (910) 483-8133
Fax: (910) 483-0263
http://www.fayettevillencchamber.org

Fort Collins, CO
Fort Collins Chamber of Commerce
225 South Meldrum
Fort Collins, CO 80521
Phone: (970) 482-3746
Fax: (970) 482-3774
https://fortcollinschamber.com

Fort Wayne, IN
City of Fort Wayne Economic Development
1 Main St
1 Main Street
Fort Wayne, IN 46802
Phone: (260) 427-1111
Fax: (260) 427-1375
http://www.cityoffortwayne.org

Greater Fort Wayne Chamber of Commerce
826 Ewing Street
Fort Wayne, IN 46802
Phone: (260) 424-1435
Fax: (260) 426-7232
http://www.fwchamber.org

Fort Worth, TX
City of Fort Worth Economic Development
City Hall
900 Monroe Street, Suite 301
Fort Worth, TX 76102
Phone: (817) 392-6103
Fax: (817) 392-2431
http://www.fortworthgov.org

Fort Worth Chamber of Commerce
777 Taylor Street
Suite 900
Fort Worth, TX 76102-4997
Phone: (817) 336-2491
Fax: (817) 877-4034
http://www.fortworthchamber.com

Gainesville, FL
Gainesville Area Chamber of Commerce
300 East University Avenue
Suite 100
Gainesville, FL 32601
Phone: (352) 334-7100
Fax: (352) 334-7141
http://www.gainesvillechamber.com

Grand Rapids, MI
Grands Rapids Area Chamber of Commerce
111 Pearl Street N.W.
Grand Rapids, MI 49503
Phone: (616) 771-0300
Fax: (616) 771-0318
http://www.grandrapids.org

Greeley, CO
Greeley Chamber of Commerce
902 7th Avenue
Greeley, CO 80631
Phone: (970) 352-3566
https://greeleychamber.com

Green Bay, WI
Economic Development
100 N Jefferson St
Room 202
Green Bay, WI 54301
Phone: (920) 448-3397
Fax: (920) 448-3063
http://www.ci.green-bay.wi.us

Green Bay Area Chamber of Commerce
300 N. Broadway
Suite 3A
Green Bay, WI 54305-1660
Phone: (920) 437-8704
Fax: (920) 593-3468
http://www.titletown.org

Greensboro, NC
Greensboro Area Chamber of Commerce
342 N Elm St.
Greensboro, NC 27401
Phone: (336) 387-8301
Fax: (336) 275-9299
http://www.greensboro.org

Honolulu, HI
The Chamber of Commerce of Hawaii
1132 Bishop Street
Suite 402
Honolulu, HI 96813
Phone: (808) 545-4300
Fax: (808) 545-4369
http://www.cochawaii.com

Houston, TX
Greater Houston Partnership
1200 Smith Street
Suite 700
Houston, TX 77002-4400
Phone: (713) 844-3600
Fax: (713) 844-0200
http://www.houston.org

Huntsville, AL
Chamber of Commerce of
Huntsville/Madison County
225 Church Street
Huntsville, AL 35801
Phone: (256) 535-2000
Fax: (256) 535-2015
http://www.huntsvillealabamausa.com

Indianapolis, IN
Greater Indianapolis Chamber of Commerce
111 Monument Circle
Suite 1950
Indianapolis, IN 46204
Phone: (317) 464-2222
Fax: (317) 464-2217
http://www.indychamber.com

The Indy Partnership
111 Monument Circle
Suite 1800
Indianapolis, IN 46204
Phone: (317) 236-6262
Fax: (317) 236-6275
http://indypartnership.com

Jacksonville, FL
Jacksonville Chamber of Commerce
3 Independent Drive
Jacksonville, FL 32202
Phone: (904) 366-6600
Fax: (904) 632-0617
http://www.myjaxchamber.com

Kansas City, MO
Greater Kansas City Chamber of Commerce
2600 Commerce Tower
911 Main Street
Kansas City, MO 64105
Phone: (816) 221-2424
Fax: (816) 221-7440
http://www.kcchamber.com

Kansas City Area Development Council
2600 Commerce Tower
911 Main Street
Kansas City, MO 64105
Phone: (816) 221-2121
Fax: (816) 842-2865
http://www.thinkkc.com

Lafayette, LA
Greater Lafayette Chamber of Commerce
804 East Saint Mary Blvd.
Lafayette, LA 70503
Phone: (337) 233-2705
Fax: (337) 234-8671
http://www.lafchamber.org

Las Cruces, NM
Greater Las Cruces Chamber of Commerce
505 S Main Street, Suite 134
Las Cruces, NM 88001
Phone: (575) 524-1968
Fax: (575) 527-5546
http://www.lascruces.org

Las Vegas, NV
Las Vegas Chamber of Commerce
6671 Las Vegas Blvd South
Suite 300
Las Vegas, NV 89119
Phone: (702) 735-1616
Fax: (702) 735-0406
http://www.lvchamber.org

Las Vegas Office of Business Development
400 Stewart Avenue
City Hall
Las Vegas, NV 89101
Phone: (702) 229-6011
Fax: (702) 385-3128
http://www.lasvegasnevada.gov

Lexington, KY
Greater Lexington Chamber of Commerce
330 East Main Street
Suite 100
Lexington, KY 40507
Phone: (859) 254-4447
Fax: (859) 233-3304
http://www.commercelexington.com

Lexington Downtown Development
Authority
101 East Vine Street
Suite 500
Lexington, KY 40507
Phone: (859) 425-2296
Fax: (859) 425-2292
http://www.lexingtondda.com

Lincoln, NE
Lincoln Chamber of Commerce
1135 M Street
Suite 200
Lincoln, NE 68508
Phone: (402) 436-2350
Fax: (402) 436-2360
http://www.lcoc.com

Little Rock, AR
Little Rock Regional Chamber
One Chamber Plaza
Little Rock, AR 72201
Phone: (501) 374-2001
Fax: (501) 374-6018
http://www.littlerockchamber.com

Los Angeles, CA
Los Angeles Area Chamber of Commerce
350 South Bixel Street
Los Angeles, CA 90017
Phone: (213) 580-7500
Fax: (213) 580-7511
http://www.lachamber.org

Los Angeles County Economic
Development Corporation
444 South Flower Street
34th Floor
Los Angeles, CA 90071
Phone: (213) 622-4300
Fax: (213) 622-7100
http://www.laedc.org

Louisville, KY
The Greater Louisville Chamber of
Commerce
614 West Main Street
Suite 6000
Louisville, KY 40202
Phone: (502) 625-0000
Fax: (502) 625-0010
http://www.greaterlouisville.com

Madison, WI
Greater Madison Chamber of Commerce
615 East Washington Avenue
P.O. Box 71
Madison, WI 53701-0071
Phone: (608) 256-8348
Fax: (608) 256-0333
http://www.greatermadisonchamber.com

Manchester, NH
Greater Manchester Chamber of Commerce
889 Elm Street
Manchester, NH 03101
Phone: (603) 666-6600
Fax: (603) 626-0910
http://www.manchester-chamber.org

Manchester Economic Development Office
One City Hall Plaza
Manchester, NH 03101
Phone: (603) 624-6505
Fax: (603) 624-6308
http://www.yourmanchesternh.com

Miami, FL
Greater Miami Chamber of Commerce
1601 Biscayne Boulevard
Ballroom Level
Miami, FL 33132-1260
Phone: (305) 350-7700
Fax: (305) 374-6902
http://www.miamichamber.com

The Beacon Council
80 Southwest 8th Street
Suite 2400
Miami, FL 33130
Phone: (305) 579-1300
Fax: (305) 375-0271
http://www.beaconcouncil.com

Midland, TX
Midland Chamber of Commerce
109 N. Main
Midland, TX 79701
Phone: (432) 683-3381
Fax: (432) 686-3556
http://www.midlandtxchamber.com

Minneapolis, MN
Minneapolis Community Development
Agency
Crown Roller Mill
105 5th Avenue South, Suite 200
Minneapolis, MN 55401
Phone: (612) 673-5095
Fax: (612) 673-5100
http://www.ci.minneapolis.mn.us

Minneapolis Regional Chamber
81 South Ninth Street
Suite 200
Minneapolis, MN 55402
Phone: (612) 370-9100
Fax: (612) 370-9195
http://www.minneapolischamber.org

Nashville, TN
Nashville Area Chamber of Commerce
211 Commerce Street
Suite 100
Nashville, TN 37201
Phone: (615) 743-3000
Fax: (615) 256-3074
http://www.nashvillechamber.com

Tennessee Valley Authority Economic
Development
400 West Summit Hill Drive
Knoxville TN 37902
Phone: (865) 632-2101
http://www.tvaed.com

New Orleans, LA
New Orleans Chamber of Commerce
1515 Poydras St
Suite 1010
New Orleans, LA 70112
Phone: (504) 799-4260
Fax: (504) 799-4259
http://www.neworleanschamber.org

New York, NY
New York City Economic Development
Corporation
110 William Street
New York, NY 10038
Phone: (212) 619-5000
http://www.nycedc.com

The Partnership for New York City
One Battery Park Plaza
5th Floor
New York, NY 10004
Phone: (212) 493-7400
Fax: (212) 344-3344
http://www.pfnyc.org

Oklahoma City, OK
Greater Oklahoma City Chamber of
Commerce
123 Park Avenue
Oklahoma City, OK 73102
Phone: (405) 297-8900
Fax: (405) 297-8916
http://www.okcchamber.com

Omaha, NE
Omaha Chamber of Commerce
1301 Harney Street
Omaha, NE 68102
Phone: (402) 346-5000
Fax: (402) 346-7050
http://www.omahachamber.org

Orlando, FL
Metro Orlando Economic Development
Commission of Mid-Florida
301 East Pine Street
Suite 900
Orlando, FL 32801
Phone: (407) 422-7159
Fax: (407) 425.6428
http://www.orlandoedc.com

Orlando Regional Chamber of Commerce
75 South Ivanhoe Boulevard
PO Box 1234
Orlando, FL 32802
Phone: (407) 425-1234
Fax: (407) 839-5020
http://www.orlando.org

Peoria, IL
Peoria Area Chamber
100 SW Water St.
Peoria, IL 61602
Phone: (309) 495-5900
http://www.peoriachamber.org

Philadelphia, PA
Greater Philadelphia Chamber of
Commerce
200 South Broad Street
Suite 700
Philadelphia, PA 19102
Phone: (215) 545-1234
Fax: (215) 790-3600
http://www.greaterphilachamber.com

Phoenix, AZ
Greater Phoenix Chamber of Commerce
201 North Central Avenue
27th Floor
Phoenix, AZ 85073
Phone: (602) 495-2195
Fax: (602) 495-8913
http://www.phoenixchamber.com

Greater Phoenix Economic Council
2 North Central Avenue
Suite 2500
Phoenix, AZ 85004
Phone: (602) 256-7700
Fax: (602) 256-7744
http://www.gpec.org

Pittsburgh, PA
Allegheny County Industrial Development
Authority
425 6th Avenue
Suite 800
Pittsburgh, PA 15219
Phone: (412) 350-1067
Fax: (412) 642-2217
http://www.alleghenycounty.us

Greater Pittsburgh Chamber of Commerce
425 6th Avenue
12th Floor
Pittsburgh, PA 15219
Phone: (412) 392-4500
Fax: (412) 392-4520
http://www.alleghenyconference.org

Portland, OR
Portland Business Alliance
200 SW Market Street
Suite 1770
Portland, OR 97201
Phone: (503) 224-8684
Fax: (503) 323-9186
http://www.portlandalliance.com

Providence, RI
Greater Providence Chamber of Commerce
30 Exchange Terrace
Fourth Floor
Providence, RI 02903
Phone: (401) 521-5000
Fax: (401) 351-2090
http://www.provchamber.com

Rhode Island Economic Development
Corporation
Providence City Hall
25 Dorrance Street
Providence, RI 02903
Phone: (401) 421-7740
Fax: (401) 751-0203
http://www.providenceri.com

Provo, UT
Provo-Orem Chamber of Commerce
51 South University Avenue
Suite 215
Provo, UT 84601
Phone: (801) 851-2555
Fax: (801) 851-2557
http://www.thechamber.org

Raleigh, NC
Greater Raleigh Chamber of Commerce
800 South Salisbury Street
Raleigh, NC 27601-2978
Phone: (919) 664-7000
Fax: (919) 664-7099
http://www.raleighchamber.org

Reno, NV
Greater Reno-Sparks Chamber of
Commerce
1 East First Street
16th Floor
Reno, NV 89505
Phone: (775) 337-3030
Fax: (775) 337-3038
http://www.reno-sparkschamber.org

The Chamber Reno-Sparks-Northern
Nevada
449 S. Virginia St.
2nd Floor
Reno, NV 89501
Phone: (775) 636-9550
http://www.thechambernv.org

Richmond, VA
Greater Richmond Chamber
600 East Main Street
Suite 700
Richmond, VA 23219
Phone: (804) 648-1234
http://www.grcc.com

Greater Richmond Partnership
901 East Byrd Street
Suite 801
Richmond, VA 23219-4070
Phone: (804) 643-3227
Fax: (804) 343-7167
http://www.grpva.com

Roanoke, VA
Roanoke Regional Chamber of Commerce
210 S. Jefferson Street
Roanoke, VA 24011-1702
Phone: (540) 983-0700
Fax: (540) 983-0723
http://www.roanokechamber.org

Rochester, MN
Rochester Area Chamber of Commerce
220 South Broadway
Suite 100
Rochester, MN 55904
Phone: (507) 288-1122
Fax: (507) 282-8960
http://www.rochestermnchamber.com

Salem, OR
Salem Area Chamber of Commerce
1110 Commercial Street NE
Salem, OR 97301
Phone: (503) 581-1466
Fax: (503) 581-0972
http://www.salemchamber.org

Salt Lake City, UT
Department of Economic Development
451 South State Street
Room 425
Salt Lake City, UT 84111
Phone: (801) 535-7240
Fax: (801) 535-6331
http://www.slcgov.com/economic-developm
ent

Salt Lake Chamber
175 E. University Blvd. (400 S)
Suite 600
Salt Lake City, UT 84111
Phone: (801) 364-3631
http://www.slchamber.com

San Antonio, TX
The Greater San Antonio Chamber of
Commerce
602 E. Commerce Street
San Antonio, TX 78205
Phone: (210) 229-2100
Fax: (210) 229-1600
http://www.sachamber.org

San Antonio Economic Development
Department
P.O. Box 839966
San Antonio, TX 78283-3966
Phone: (210) 207-8080
Fax: (210) 207-8151
http://www.sanantonio.gov/edd

San Diego, CA
San Diego Economic Development
Corporation
401 B Street
Suite 1100
San Diego, CA 92101
Phone: (619) 234-8484
Fax: (619) 234-1935
http://www.sandiegobusiness.org

San Diego Regional Chamber of Commerce
402 West Broadway
Suite 1000
San Diego, CA 92101-3585
Phone: (619) 544-1300
Fax: (619) 744-7481
http://www.sdchamber.org

San Francisco, CA
San Francisco Chamber of Commerce
235 Montgomery Street
12th Floor
San Francisco, CA 94104
Phone: (415) 392-4520
Fax: (415) 392-0485
http://www.sfchamber.com

San Jose, CA
Office of Economic Development
60 South Market Street
Suite 470
San Jose, CA 95113
Phone: (408) 277-5880
Fax: (408) 277-3615
http://www.sba.gov

The Silicon Valley Organization
101 W Santa Clara Street
San Jose, CA 95113
Phone: (408) 291-5250
https://www.thesvo.com

Santa Rosa, CA
Santa Rosa Chamber of Commerce
1260 North Dutton Avenue
Suite 272
Santa Rosa, CA 95401
Phone: (707) 545-1414
http://www.santarosachamber.com

Savannah, GA
Economic Development Authority
131 Hutchinson Island Road
4th Floor
Savannah, GA 31421
Phone: (912) 447-8450
Fax: (912) 447-8455
http://www.seda.org

Savannah Chamber of Commerce
101 E. Bay Street
Savannah, GA 31402
Phone: (912) 644-6400
Fax: (912) 644-6499
http://www.savannahchamber.com

Seattle, WA
Greater Seattle Chamber of Commerce
1301 Fifth Avenue
Suite 2500
Seattle, WA 98101
Phone: (206) 389-7200
Fax: (206) 389-7288
http://www.seattlechamber.com

Sioux Falls, SD
Sioux Falls Area Chamber of Commerce
200 N. Phillips Avenue
Suite 102
Sioux Falls, SD 57104
Phone: (605) 336-1620
Fax: (605) 336-6499
http://www.siouxfallschamber.com

Springfield, IL
The Greater Springfield Chamber of
Commerce
1011 S. Second Street
Springfield, IL 62704
Phone: (217) 525-1173
Fax: (217) 525-8768
http://www.gscc.org

Tallahassee, FL
Greater Tallahassee Chamber of Commerce
300 E. Park Avenue
PO Box 1638
Tallahassee, FL 32301
Phone: (850) 224-8116
Fax: (850) 561-3860
http://www.talchamber.com

Tampa, FL
Greater Tampa Chamber of Commerce
P.O. Box 420
Tampa, FL 33601-0420
Phone: (813) 276-9401
Fax: (813) 229-7855
http://www.tampachamber.com

Topeka, KS
Greater Topeka Chamber of Commerce/
GO Topeka
120 SE Sixth Avenue
Suite 110
Topeka, KS 66603
Phone: (785) 234-2644
Fax: (785) 234-8656
http://www.topekachamber.org

Tyler, TX
Tyler Area Chamber of Commerce
315 N Broadway Ave
Suite 100
Tyler, TX 75702
Phone: (903) 592-1661; (800) 235-5712
Fax: (903) 593-2746
http://www.tylertexas.com

Virginia Beach, VA
Hampton Roads Chamber of Commerce
500 East Main Street
Suite 700
Virginia Beach, VA 23510
Phone: (757) 664-2531
http://www.hamptonroadschamber.com

Visalia, CA
Visalia Chamber of Commerce
222 North Garden Street
Suite 300
Visalia, CA 93291
Phone: (559) 734-5876
http://www.visaliachamber.org

Washington, DC
District of Columbia Chamber of
Commerce
1213 K Street NW
Washington, DC 20005
Phone: (202) 347-7201
Fax: (202) 638-6762
http://www.dcchamber.org

District of Columbia Office of Planning and
Economic Development
J.A. Wilson Building
1350 Pennsylvania Ave NW, Suite 317
Washington, DC 20004
Phone: (202) 727-6365
Fax: (202) 727-6703
http://www.dcbiz.dc.gov

Wilmington, NC
Wilmington Chamber of Commerce
One Estell Lee Place
Wilmington, NC 28401
Phone: (910) 762-2611
http://www.wilmingtonchamber.org

Winston-Salem, NC
Winston-Salem Chamber of Commerce
411 West Fourth Street
Suite 211
Winston-Salem, NC 27101
Phone: (336) 728-9200
http://www.winstonsalem.com

Appendix E: State Departments of Labor

Alabama
Alabama Department of Labor
P.O. Box 303500
Montgomery, AL 36130-3500
Phone: (334) 242-3072
https://www.labor.alabama.gov

Alaska
Dept of Labor and Workforce Devel.
P.O. Box 11149
Juneau, AK 99822-2249
Phone: (907) 465-2700
http://www.labor.state.ak.us

Arizona
Industrial Commission or Arizona
800 West Washington Street
Phoenix, AZ 85007
Phone: (602) 542-4411
https://www.azica.gov

Arkansas
Department of Labor
10421 West Markham
Little Rock, AR 72205
Phone: (501) 682-4500
http://www.labor.ar.gov

California
Labor and Workforce Development
445 Golden Gate Ave., 10th Floor
San Francisco, CA 94102
Phone: (916) 263-1811
http://www.labor.ca.gov

Colorado
Dept of Labor and Employment
633 17th St., 2nd Floor
Denver, CO 80202-3660
Phone: (888) 390-7936
https://www.colorado.gov/CDLE

Connecticut
Department of Labor
200 Folly Brook Blvd.
Wethersfield, CT 06109-1114
Phone: (860) 263-6000
http://www.ctdol.state.ct.us

Delaware
Department of Labor
4425 N. Market St., 4th Floor
Wilmington, DE 19802
Phone: (302) 451-3423
http://dol.delaware.gov

District of Columbia
Department of Employment Services
614 New York Ave., NE, Suite 300
Washington, DC 20002
Phone: (202) 671-1900
http://does.dc.gov

Florida
Florida Department of Economic
Opportunity
The Caldwell Building
107 East Madison St. Suite 100
Tallahassee, FL 32399-4120
Phone: (800) 342-3450
http://www.floridajobs.org

Georgia
Department of Labor
Sussex Place, Room 600
148 Andrew Young Intl Blvd., NE
Atlanta, GA 30303
Phone: (404) 656-3011
http://dol.georgia.gov

Hawaii
Dept of Labor & Industrial Relations
830 Punchbowl Street
Honolulu, HI 96813
Phone: (808) 586-8842
http://labor.hawaii.gov

Idaho
Department of Labor
317 W. Main St.
Boise, ID 83735-0001
Phone: (208) 332-3579
http://www.labor.idaho.gov

Illinois
Department of Labor
160 N. LaSalle Street, 13th Floor
Suite C-1300
Chicago, IL 60601
Phone: (312) 793-2800
https://www.illinois.gov/idol

Indiana
Indiana Department of Labor
402 West Washington Street, Room W195
Indianapolis, IN 46204
Phone: (317) 232-2655
http://www.in.gov/dol

Iowa
Iowa Workforce Development
1000 East Grand Avenue
Des Moines, IA 50319-0209
Phone: (515) 242-5870
http://www.iowadivisionoflabor.gov

Kansas
Department of Labor
401 S.W. Topeka Blvd.
Topeka, KS 66603-3182
Phone: (785) 296-5000
http://www.dol.ks.gov

Kentucky
Department of Labor
1047 U.S. Hwy 127 South, Suite 4
Frankfort, KY 40601-4381
Phone: (502) 564-3070
http://www.labor.ky.gov

Louisiana
Louisiana Workforce Commission
1001 N. 23rd Street
Baton Rouge, LA 70804-9094
Phone: (225) 342-3111
http://www.laworks.net

Maine
Department of Labor
45 Commerce Street
Augusta, ME 04330
Phone: (207) 623-7900
http://www.state.me.us/labor

Maryland
Department of Labor, Licensing &
Regulation
500 N. Calvert Street
Suite 401
Baltimore, MD 21202
Phone: (410) 767-2357
http://www.dllr.state.md.us

Massachusetts
Dept of Labor & Workforce Development
One Ashburton Place
Room 2112
Boston, MA 02108
Phone: (617) 626-7100
http://www.mass.gov/lwd

Michigan
Department of Licensing and Regulatory
Affairs
611 W. Ottawa
P.O. Box 30004
Lansing, MI 48909
Phone: (517) 373-1820
http://www.michigan.gov/lara

Minnesota
Dept of Labor and Industry
443 Lafayette Road North
Saint Paul, MN 55155
Phone: (651) 284-5070
http://www.doli.state.mn.us

Mississippi
Dept of Employment Security
P.O. Box 1699
Jackson, MS 39215-1699
Phone: (601) 321-6000
http://www.mdes.ms.gov

Missouri
Labor and Industrial Relations
P.O. Box 599
3315 W. Truman Boulevard
Jefferson City, MO 65102-0599
Phone: (573) 751-7500
https://labor.mo.gov

Montana
Dept of Labor and Industry
P.O. Box 1728
Helena, MT 59624-1728
Phone: (406) 444-9091
http://www.dli.mt.gov

Nebraska
Department of Labor
550 S 16th Street
Lincoln, NE 68508
Phone: (402) 471-9000
https://dol.nebraska.gov

Nevada
Dept of Business and Industry
3300 W. Sahara Ave
Suite 425
Las Vegas, NV 89102
Phone: (702) 486-2750
http://business.nv.gov

New Hampshire
Department of Labor
State Office Park South
95 Pleasant Street
Concord, NH 03301
Phone: (603) 271-3176
https://www.nh.gov/labor

New Jersey
Department of Labor & Workforce
Development
John Fitch Plaza, 13th Floor
Suite D
Trenton, NJ 08625-0110
Phone: (609) 777-3200
http://lwd.dol.state.nj.us/labor

New Mexico
Department of Workforce Solutions
401 Broadway, NE
Albuquerque, NM 87103-1928
Phone: (505) 841-8450
https://www.dws.state.nm.us

New York
Department of Labor
State Office Bldg. # 12
W.A. Harriman Campus
Albany, NY 12240
Phone: (518) 457-9000
https://www.labor.ny.gov

North Carolina
Department of Labor
4 West Edenton Street
Raleigh, NC 27601-1092
Phone: (919) 733-7166
https://www.labor.nc.gov

North Dakota
North Dakota Department of Labor and
Human Rights
State Capitol Building
600 East Boulevard, Dept 406
Bismark, ND 58505-0340
Phone: (701) 328-2660
http://www.nd.gov/labor

Ohio
Department of Commerce
77 South High Street, 22nd Floor
Columbus, OH 43215
Phone: (614) 644-2239
http://www.com.state.oh.us

Oklahoma
Department of Labor
4001 N. Lincoln Blvd.
Oklahoma City, OK 73105-5212
Phone: (405) 528-1500
https://www.ok.gov/odol

Oregon
Bureau of Labor and Industries
800 NE Oregon St., #32
Portland, OR 97232
Phone: (971) 673-0761
http://www.oregon.gov/boli

Pennsylvania
Dept of Labor and Industry
1700 Labor and Industry Bldg
7th and Forster Streets
Harrisburg, PA 17120
Phone: (717) 787-5279
http://www.dli.pa.gov

Rhode Island
Department of Labor and Training
1511 Pontiac Avenue
Cranston, RI 02920
Phone: (401) 462-8000
http://www.dlt.state.ri.us

South Carolina
Dept of Labor, Licensing & Regulations
P.O. Box 11329
Columbia, SC 29211-1329
Phone: (803) 896-4300
http://www.llr.state.sc.us

South Dakota
Department of Labor & Regulation
700 Governors Drive
Pierre, SD 57501-2291
Phone: (605) 773-3682
http://dlr.sd.gov

Tennessee
Dept of Labor & Workforce Development
Andrew Johnson Tower
710 James Robertson Pkwy
Nashville, TN 37243-0655
Phone: (615) 741-6642
http://www.tn.gov/workforce

Texas
Texas Workforce Commission
101 East 15th St.
Austin, TX 78778
Phone: (512) 475-2670
http://www.twc.state.tx.us

Utah
Utah Labor Commission
160 East 300 South, 3rd Floor
Salt Lake City, UT 84114-6600
Phone: (801) 530-6800
https://laborcommission.utah.gov

Vermont
Department of Labor
5 Green Mountain Drive
P.O. Box 488
Montpelier, VT 05601-0488
Phone: (802) 828-4000
http://labor.vermont.gov

Virginia
Dept of Labor and Industry
Powers-Taylor Building
13 S. 13th Street
Richmond, VA 23219
Phone: (804) 371-2327
http://www.doli.virginia.gov

Washington
Dept of Labor and Industries
P.O. Box 44001
Olympia, WA 98504-4001
Phone: (360) 902-4200
http://www.lni.wa.gov

West Virginia
Division of Labor
749 B Building 6
Capitol Complex
Charleston, WV 25305
Phone: (304) 558-7890
https://labor.wv.gov

Wisconsin
Dept of Workforce Development
201 E. Washington Ave., #A400
P.O. Box 7946
Madison, WI 53707-7946
Phone: (608) 266-6861
http://dwd.wisconsin.gov

Wyoming
Department of Workforce Services
1510 East Pershing Blvd.
Cheyenne, WY 82002
Phone: (307) 777-7261
http://www.wyomingworkforce.org

*Source: U.S. Department of Labor;
Original research*

2019 Title List
Visit www.GreyHouse.com for Product Information, Table of Contents, and Sample Pages.

General Reference
America's College Museums
American Environmental Leaders: From Colonial Times to the Present
Encyclopedia of African-American Writing
Encyclopedia of Constitutional Amendments
Encyclopedia of Human Rights and the United States
Encyclopedia of Invasions & Conquests
Encyclopedia of Prisoners of War & Internment
Encyclopedia of Religion & Law in America
Encyclopedia of Rural America
Encyclopedia of the Continental Congress
Encyclopedia of the United States Cabinet, 1789-2010
Encyclopedia of War Journalism
Encyclopedia of Warrior Peoples & Fighting Groups
The Environmental Debate: A Documentary History
The Evolution Wars: A Guide to the Debates
From Suffrage to the Senate: America's Political Women
Gun Debate: An Encyclopedia of Gun Rights & Gun Control in the U.S.
Opinions throughout History: National Security vs. Civil and Privacy Rights
Opinions throughout History: Immigration
Opinions throughout History: Drug Use & Abuse
Opinions throughout History: Gender: Roles & Rights
Opinions throughout History: The Environment
Opinions throughout History: Social Media Issues
Opinions throughout History: The Death Penalty
Opinions throughout History: Voters' Rights
Political Corruption in America
Privacy Rights in the Digital Age
The Religious Right: A Reference Handbook
Speakers of the House of Representatives, 1789-2009
This is Who We Were: 1880-1900
This is Who We Were: A Companion to the 1940 Census
This is Who We Were: In Colonial America
This is Who We Were: In the 1900s
This is Who We Were: In the 1910s
This is Who We Were: In the 1920s
This is Who We Were: In the 1940s
This is Who We Were: In the 1950s
This is Who We Were: In the 1960s
This is Who We Were: In the 1970s
This is Who We Were: In the 1980s
This is Who We Were: In the 1990s
This is Who We Were: In the 2000s
U.S. Land & Natural Resource Policy
The Value of a Dollar 1600-1865: Colonial Era to the Civil War
The Value of a Dollar: 1860-2019
Working Americans 1880-1999 Vol. I: The Working Class
Working Americans 1880-1999 Vol. II: The Middle Class
Working Americans 1880-1999 Vol. III: The Upper Class
Working Americans 1880-1999 Vol. IV: Their Children
Working Americans 1880-2015 Vol. V: Americans At War
Working Americans 1880-2005 Vol. VI: Women at Work
Working Americans 1880-2006 Vol. VII: Social Movements
Working Americans 1880-2007 Vol. VIII: Immigrants
Working Americans 1770-1869 Vol. IX: Revolutionary War to the Civil War
Working Americans 1880-2009 Vol. X: Sports & Recreation
Working Americans 1880-2010 Vol. XI: Inventors & Entrepreneurs
Working Americans 1880-2011 Vol. XII: Our History through Music
Working Americans 1880-2012 Vol. XIII: Education & Educators
Working Americans 1880-2016 Vol. XIV: Industry Through the Ages
Working Americans 1880-2017 Vol. XV: Politics & Politicians
World Cultural Leaders of the 20th & 21st Centuries

Education Information
Charter School Movement
The Comparative Guide to American Elementary & Secondary Schools
Complete Learning Disabilities Resource Guide
Educators Resource Guide
Special Education: A Reference Book for Policy and Curriculum
 Development

Health Information
Comparative Guide to American Hospitals
Complete Resource Guide for Pediatric Disorders
Complete Resource Guide for People with Chronic Illness
Complete Resource Guide for People with Disabilities
Complete Mental Health Resource Guide
Diabetes in America: Analysis of an Epidemic
Guide to Health Care Group Purchasing Organizations
Guide to U.S. HMO's & PPO's
Medical Device Market Place
Older Americans Information Resource

Business Information
Complete Television, Radio & Cable Industry Guide
Business Information Resources
Directory of Mail Order Catalogs
Guide to Venture Capital & Private Equity Firms
Environmental Resource Handbook
Financial Literacy Starter Kit
Food & Beverage Market Place
The Grey House Homeland Security Directory
The Grey House Performing Arts Industry Guide
The Grey House Safety & Security Directory
Hudson's Washington News Media Contacts Directory
New York State Directory
Sports Market Place

Statistics & Demographics
American Tally
America's Top-Rated Cities
America's Top-Rated Smaller Cities
Ancestry & Ethnicity in America
The Asian Databook
The Comparative Guide to American Suburbs
The Hispanic Databook
Nations of the World
Profiles of America
"Profiles of" Series - State Handbooks
Weather America

Financial Ratings Series
Financial Literacy Basics
TheStreet Ratings' Ultimate Guided Tour of Stock Investing
Weiss Ratings' Investment Research Guide to Bond & Money Market
 Mutual Funds
Weiss Ratings' Investment Research Guide to Stocks
Weiss Ratings' Investment Research Guide to Exchange-Traded Funds
Weiss Ratings' Investment Research Guide to Stock Mutual Funds
Weiss Ratings' Consumer Guides
Weiss Ratings' Financial Literary Basic Guides
Weiss Ratings' Guide to Banks
Weiss Ratings' Guide to Credit Unions
Weiss Ratings' Guide to Health Insurers
Weiss Ratings' Guide to Life & Annuity Insurers
Weiss Ratings' Guide to Property & Casualty Insurers

Bowker's Books In Print® Titles
American Book Publishing Record® Annual
American Book Publishing Record® Monthly
Books In Print®
Books In Print® Supplement
Books Out Loud™
Bowker's Complete Video Directory™
Children's Books In Print®
El-Hi Textbooks & Serials In Print®
Forthcoming Books®
Law Books & Serials In Print™
Medical & Health Care Books In Print™
Publishers, Distributors & Wholesalers of the US™
Subject Guide to Books In Print®
Subject Guide to Children's Books In Print®

Grey House Publishing | Salem Press | H.W. Wilson | 4919 Route, 22 PO Box 56, Amenia NY 12501-0056

2019 Title List

Visit **www.GreyHouse.com** for Product Information, Table of Contents, and Sample Pages.

Canadian General Reference

Associations Canada
Canadian Almanac & Directory
Canadian Environmental Resource Guide
Canadian Parliamentary Guide
Canadian Venture Capital & Private Equity Firms
Canadian Who's Who
Financial Post Bonds
Financial Post Directory of Directors
Financial Post Equities
Financial Post Survey
Financial Services Canada
Government Canada
Health Guide Canada
The History of Canada
Libraries Canada
Major Canadian Cities

Grey House Publishing | Salem Press | H.W. Wilson | 4919 Route, 22 PO Box 56, Amenia NY 12501-0056

2019 Title List

Visit www.SalemPress.com for Product Information, Table of Contents, and Sample Pages.

Science, Careers & Mathematics

Ancient Creatures
Applied Science
Applied Science: Engineering & Mathematics
Applied Science: Science & Medicine
Applied Science: Technology
Biomes and Ecosystems
Careers in the Arts: Fine, Performing & Visual
Careers in Building Construction
Careers in Business
Careers in Chemistry
Careers in Communications & Media
Careers in Environment & Conservation
Careers in Financial Services
Careers in Green Energy
Careers in Healthcare
Careers in Hospitality & Tourism
Careers in Human Services
Careers in Law, Criminal Justice & Emergency Services
Careers in Manufacturing
Careers in Nursing
Careers Outdoors
Careers Overseas
Careers in Physics
Careers in Protective Services
Careers in Psychology
Careers in Sales, Insurance & Real Estate
Careers in Science & Engineering
Careers in Social Media
Careers in Sports & Fitness
Careers in Sports Medicine & Training
Careers in Technology Services & Equipment Repair
Careers in Transportation
Computer Technology Innovators
Contemporary Biographies in Business
Contemporary Biographies in Chemistry
Contemporary Biographies in Communications & Media
Contemporary Biographies in Environment & Conservation
Contemporary Biographies in Healthcare
Contemporary Biographies in Hospitality & Tourism
Contemporary Biographies in Law & Criminal Justice
Contemporary Biographies in Physics
Earth Science
Earth Science: Earth Materials & Resources
Earth Science: Earth's Surface and History
Earth Science: Physics & Chemistry of the Earth
Earth Science: Weather, Water & Atmosphere
Encyclopedia of Energy
Encyclopedia of Environmental Issues
Encyclopedia of Environmental Issues: Atmosphere and Air Pollution
Encyclopedia of Environmental Issues: Ecology and Ecosystems
Encyclopedia of Environmental Issues: Energy and Energy Use
Encyclopedia of Environmental Issues: Policy and Activism
Encyclopedia of Environmental Issues: Preservation/Wilderness Issues
Encyclopedia of Environmental Issues: Water and Water Pollution
Encyclopedia of Global Resources
Encyclopedia of Global Warming
Encyclopedia of Mathematics & Society
Encyclopedia of Mathematics & Society: Engineering, Tech, Medicine
Encyclopedia of Mathematics & Society: Great Mathematicians
Encyclopedia of Mathematics & Society: Math & Social Sciences
Encyclopedia of Mathematics & Society: Math Development/Concepts
Encyclopedia of Mathematics & Society: Math in Culture & Society
Encyclopedia of Mathematics & Society: Space, Science, Environment
Encyclopedia of the Ancient World
Forensic Science
Geography Basics
Internet Innovators
Inventions and Inventors
Magill's Encyclopedia of Science: Animal Life
Magill's Encyclopedia of Science: Plant life
Notable Natural Disasters

Principles of Artificial Intelligence & Robotics
Principles of Astronomy
Principles of Biology
Principles of Biotechnology
Principles of Business: Accounting
Principles of Business: Economics
Principles of Business: Entrepreneurship
Principles of Business: Finance
Principles of Business: Globalization
Principles of Business: Leadership
Principles of Business: Management
Principles of Business: Marketing
Principles of Chemistry
Principles of Climatology
Principles of Ecology
Principles of Modern Agriculture
Principles of Pharmacology
Principles of Physical Science
Principles of Physics
Principles of Programming & Coding
Principles of Research Methods
Principles of Sociology: Group Relationships & Behavior
Principles of Sociology: Personal Relationships & Behavior
Principles of Sociology: Societal Issues & Behavior
Principles of Sustainability
Science and Scientists
Solar System
Solar System: Great Astronomers
Solar System: Study of the Universe
Solar System: The Inner Planets
Solar System: The Moon and Other Small Bodies
Solar System: The Outer Planets
Solar System: The Sun and Other Stars
USA in Space
World Geography

Literature

American Ethnic Writers
Classics of Science Fiction & Fantasy Literature
Critical Approaches to Literature
Critical Insights: Authors
Critical Insights: Film
Critical Insights: Literary Collection Bundles
Critical Insights: Themes
Critical Insights: Works
Critical Survey of Drama
Critical Survey of Graphic Novels: Heroes & Superheroes
Critical Survey of Graphic Novels: History, Theme & Technique
Critical Survey of Graphic Novels: Independents/Underground Classics
Critical Survey of Graphic Novels: Manga
Critical Survey of Long Fiction
Critical Survey of Mystery & Detective Fiction
Critical Survey of Mythology and Folklore: Gods & Goddesses
Critical Survey of Mythology and Folklore: Heroes & Heroines
Critical Survey of Mythology and Folklore: Love, Sexuality & Desire
Critical Survey of Mythology and Folklore: World Mythology
Critical Survey of Poetry
Critical Survey of Poetry: American Poets
Critical Survey of Poetry: British, Irish & Commonwealth Poets
Critical Survey of Poetry: Cumulative Index
Critical Survey of Poetry: European Poets
Critical Survey of Poetry: Topical Essays
Critical Survey of Poetry: World Poets
Critical Survey of Science Fiction & Fantasy Literature
Critical Survey of Shakespeare's Plays
Critical Survey of Shakespeare's Sonnets
Critical Survey of Short Fiction
Critical Survey of Short Fiction: American Writers
Critical Survey of Short Fiction: British, Irish, Commonwealth Writers
Critical Survey of Short Fiction: Cumulative Index
Critical Survey of Short Fiction: European Writers
Critical Survey of Short Fiction: Topical Essays

Grey House Publishing | Salem Press | H.W. Wilson | 4919 Route, 22 PO Box 56, Amenia NY 12501-0056

2019 Title List

Visit www.SalemPress.com for Product Information, Table of Contents, and Sample Pages.

Critical Survey of Short Fiction: World Writers
Critical Survey of World Literature
Critical Survey of Young Adult Literature
Cyclopedia of Literary Characters
Cyclopedia of Literary Places
Holocaust Literature
Introduction to Literary Context: American Poetry of the 20th Century
Introduction to Literary Context: American Post-Modernist Novels
Introduction to Literary Context: American Short Fiction
Introduction to Literary Context: English Literature
Introduction to Literary Context: Plays
Introduction to Literary Context: World Literature
Magill's Literary Annual
Magill's Survey of American Literature
Magill's Survey of World Literature
Masterplots
Masterplots, 2002-2018 Supplement
Masterplots II: African American Literature
Masterplots II: American Fiction Series
Masterplots II: British & Commonwealth Fiction Series
Masterplots II: Christian Literature
Masterplots II: Drama Series
Masterplots II: Juvenile & Young Adult Literature, Supplement
Masterplots II: Nonfiction Series
Masterplots II: Poetry Series
Masterplots II: Short Story Series
Masterplots II: Women's Literature Series
Notable African American Writers
Notable American Novelists
Notable Playwrights
Notable Poets
Novels into Film: Adaptations & Interpretation
Recommended Reading: 600 Classics Reviewed
Short Story Writers

History and Social Science
The 1910s in America
The 2000s in America
50 States
African American History
Agriculture in History
American First Ladies
American Heroes
American Indian Culture
American Indian History
American Indian Tribes
American Presidents
American Villains
America's Historic Sites
Ancient Greece
The Bill of Rights
The Civil Rights Movement
The Cold War
Countries: Their Wars & Conflicts: A World Survey
Countries, Peoples & Cultures
Countries, Peoples & Cultures: Central & South America
Countries, Peoples & Cultures: Central, South & Southeast Asia
Countries, Peoples & Cultures: East & South Africa
Countries, Peoples & Cultures: East Asia & the Pacific
Countries, Peoples & Cultures: Eastern Europe
Countries, Peoples & Cultures: Middle East & North Africa
Countries, Peoples & Cultures: North America & the Caribbean
Countries, Peoples & Cultures: West & Central Africa
Countries, Peoples & Cultures: Western Europe
Defining Documents: American Revolution
The Criminal Justice System
Defining Documents: American West
Defining Documents: Ancient World
Defining Documents: Asia
Defining Documents: Business Ethics
Defining Documents: Capital Punishment
Defining Documents: Civil Rights

Defining Documents: Civil War
Defining Documents: Court Cases
Defining Documents: Dissent & Protest
Defining Documents: Emergence of Modern America
Defining Documents: Exploration & Colonial America
Defining Documents: The Free Press
Defining Documents: The Gun Debate
Defining Documents: Immigration & Immigrant Communities
Defining Documents: The Legacy of 9/11
Defining Documents: LGBTQ+
Defining Documents: Manifest Destiny
Defining Documents: Middle Ages
Defining Documents: Middle East
Defining Documents: Nationalism & Populism
Defining Documents: Native Americans
Defining Documents: Political Campaigns, Candidates & Debates
Defining Documents: Postwar 1940s
Defining Documents: Prison Reform
Defining Documents: Reconstruction
Defining Documents: Renaissance & Early Modern Era
Defining Documents: Secrets, Leaks & Scandals
Defining Documents: Slavery
Defining Documents: Supreme Court Decisions
Defining Documents: 1920s
Defining Documents: 1930s
Defining Documents: 1950s
Defining Documents: 1960s
Defining Documents: 1970s
Defining Documents: The 17th Century
Defining Documents: The 18th Century
Defining Documents: The 19th Century
Defining Documents: The 20th Century: 1900-1950
Defining Documents: Vietnam War
Defining Documents: Women's Rights
Defining Documents: World War I
Defining Documents: World War II
Education Today
The Eighties in America
Encyclopedia of American Immigration
Encyclopedia of Flight
Encyclopedia of the Ancient World
Ethics: Questions & Morality of Human Actions
Fashion Innovators
The Fifties in America
The Forties in America
Great Athletes
Great Athletes: Baseball
Great Athletes: Basketball
Great Athletes: Boxing & Soccer
Great Athletes: Cumulative Index
Great Athletes: Football
Great Athletes: Golf & Tennis
Great Athletes: Olympics
Great Athletes: Racing & Individual Sports
Great Contemporary Athletes
Great Events from History: 17th Century
Great Events from History: 18th Century
Great Events from History: 19th Century
Great Events from History: 20th Century (1901-1940)
Great Events from History: 20th Century (1941-1970)
Great Events from History: 20th Century (1971-2000)
Great Events from History: 21st Century (2000-2016)
Great Events from History: African American History
Great Events from History: Cumulative Indexes
Great Events from History: Human Rights
Great Events from History: LGBTQ Events
Great Events from History: Middle Ages
Great Events from History: Modern Scandals
Great Events from History: Secrets, Leaks & Scandals
Great Events from History: Renaissance & Early Modern Era
Great Lives from History: 17th Century
Great Lives from History: 18th Century

2019 Title List

Visit www.SalemPress.com for Product Information, Table of Contents, and Sample Pages.

Great Lives from History: 19th Century
Great Lives from History: 20th Century
Great Lives from History: 21st Century (2000-2017)
Great Lives from History: American Heroes
Great Lives from History: American Women
Great Lives from History: Ancient World
Great Lives from History: Asian & Pacific Islander Americans
Great Lives from History: Cumulative Indexes
Great Lives from History: Incredibly Wealthy
Great Lives from History: Inventors & Inventions
Great Lives from History: Jewish Americans
Great Lives from History: Latinos
Great Lives from History: Renaissance & Early Modern Era
Great Lives from History: Scientists & Science
Historical Encyclopedia of American Business
Issues in U.S. Immigration
Magill's Guide to Military History
Milestone Documents in African American History
Milestone Documents in American History
Milestone Documents in World History
Milestone Documents of American Leaders
Milestone Documents of World Religions
Music Innovators
Musicians & Composers 20th Century
The Nineties in America
The Seventies in America
The Sixties in America

Sociology Today
Survey of American Industry and Careers
The Thirties in America
The Twenties in America
United States at War
U.S. Court Cases
U.S. Government Leaders
U.S. Laws, Acts, and Treaties
U.S. Legal System
U.S. Supreme Court
Weapons and Warfare
World Conflicts: Asia and the Middle East

Health

Addictions, Substance Abuse & Alcoholism
Adolescent Health & Wellness
Aging
Cancer
Complementary & Alternative Medicine
Community & Family Health Issues
Genetics & Inherited Conditions
Infectious Diseases & Conditions
Magill's Medical Guide
Nutrition
Psychology & Behavioral Health
Psychology Basics
Women's Health

Grey House Publishing | Salem Press | H.W. Wilson | 4919 Route, 22 PO Box 56, Amenia NY 12501-0056

 **WILSON**
 **WILSON**

2019 Title List
Visit **www.HWWilsonInPrint.com** for Product Information, Table of Contents and Sample Pages.

Current Biography
Current Biography Cumulative Index 1946-2013
Current Biography Monthly Magazine
Current Biography Yearbook: 2003
Current Biography Yearbook: 2004
Current Biography Yearbook: 2005
Current Biography Yearbook: 2006
Current Biography Yearbook: 2007
Current Biography Yearbook: 2008
Current Biography Yearbook: 2009
Current Biography Yearbook: 2010
Current Biography Yearbook: 2011
Current Biography Yearbook: 2012
Current Biography Yearbook: 2013
Current Biography Yearbook: 2014
Current Biography Yearbook: 2015
Current Biography Yearbook: 2016
Current Biography Yearbook: 2017
Current Biography Yearbook: 2018

Core Collections
Children's Core Collection
Fiction Core Collection
Graphic Novels Core Collection
Middle & Junior High School Core
Public Library Core Collection: Nonfiction
Senior High Core Collection
Young Adult Fiction Core Collection

The Reference Shelf
Affordable Housing
Aging in America
Alternative Facts: Post Truth & the Information War
The American Dream
American Military Presence Overseas
The Arab Spring
Artificial Intelligence
The Brain
The Business of Food
Campaign Trends & Election Law
Conspiracy Theories
Democracy Evolving
The Digital Age
Dinosaurs
Embracing New Paradigms in Education
Faith & Science
Families: Traditional and New Structures
The Future of U.S. Economic Relations: Mexico, Cuba, and Venezuela
Global Climate Change
Graphic Novels and Comic Books
Guns in America
Immigration
Immigration in the U.S.
Internet Abuses & Privacy Rights
Internet Safety
LGBTQ in the 21st Century
Marijuana Reform
New Frontiers in Space
The News and its Future
The Paranormal
Politics of the Ocean
Prescription Drug Abuse
Racial Tension in a "Postracial" Age
Reality Television
Representative American Speeches: 2008-2009
Representative American Speeches: 2009-2010
Representative American Speeches: 2010-2011
Representative American Speeches: 2011-2012
Representative American Speeches: 2012-2013
Representative American Speeches: 2013-2014

Representative American Speeches: 2014-2015
Representative American Speeches: 2015-2016
Representative American Speeches: 2016-2017
Representative American Speeches: 2017-2018
Representative American Speeches: 2018-2019
Rethinking Work
Revisiting Gender
Robotics
Russia
Social Networking
Social Services for the Poor
The South China Seas Conflict
Space Exploration & Development
Sports in America
The Supreme Court
The Transformation of American Cities
The Two Koreas
U.S. Infrastructure
U.S. National Debate Topic: Educational Reform
U.S. National Debate Topic: Surveillance
U.S. National Debate Topic: The Ocean
U.S. National Debate Topic: Transportation Infrastructure
Whistleblowers

Readers' Guide
Abridged Readers' Guide to Periodical Literature
Readers' Guide to Periodical Literature

Indexes
Index to Legal Periodicals & Books
Short Story Index
Book Review Digest

Sears List
Sears List of Subject Headings
Sears: Lista de Encabezamientos de Materia

Facts About Series
Facts About American Immigration
Facts About China
Facts About the 20th Century
Facts About the Presidents
Facts About the World's Languages

Nobel Prize Winners
Nobel Prize Winners: 1901-1986
Nobel Prize Winners: 1987-1991
Nobel Prize Winners: 1992-1996
Nobel Prize Winners: 1997-2001
Nobel Prize Winners: 2002-2018

World Authors
World Authors: 1995-2000
World Authors: 2000-2005

Famous First Facts
Famous First Facts
Famous First Facts About American Politics
Famous First Facts About Sports
Famous First Facts About the Environment
Famous First Facts: International Edition

American Book of Days
The American Book of Days
The International Book of Days

Monographs
American Game Changers
American Reformers

Grey House Publishing | Salem Press | H.W. Wilson | 4919 Route, 22 PO Box 56, Amenia NY 12501-0056

2019 Title List

Visit **www.HWWilsonInPrint.com** for Product Information, Table of Contents and Sample Pages.

The Barnhart Dictionary of Etymology
Celebrate the World
Guide to the Ancient World
Indexing from A to Z
Nobel Prize Winners
The Poetry Break
Radical Change: Books for Youth in a Digital Age
Speeches of American Presidents

Wilson Chronology

Wilson Chronology of Asia and the Pacific
Wilson Chronology of Human Rights
Wilson Chronology of Ideas
Wilson Chronology of the Arts
Wilson Chronology of the World's Religions
Wilson Chronology of Women's Achievements

Grey House Publishing | Salem Press | H.W. Wilson | 4919 Route, 22 PO Box 56, Amenia NY 12501-0056